BOOTS AND SADDLES:
Cavalry During The Maryland Campaign Of September 1862

Second Edition

By

LAURENCE H. FREIHEIT

Camp Pope Publishing

2013

Second Edition

ISBN: 978-1-929919-48-2

Library of Congress Control Number: 2013930259

Camp Pope Publishing
P.O. Box 2232
Iowa City, Iowa 52244
www.camppope.com

Cover Illustrations:
Front: Lee, McClellan, Stuart and Pleasonton courtesy of LOC;
Skirmish at Tunstall's Station from *The Soldier in Our Civil War*, 1:349.
Back: "Cavalry marching out of Harpers Ferry" sketch by Alfred Waud,
and "Antietam, a cavalry orderly " courtesy LOC;
Cavalry fight at Yellow Tavern, from *The Soldier in Our Civil War*, 2:270-271

Contents

Preface

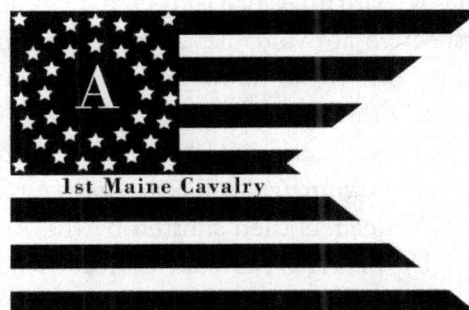

1st Maine Cavalry

MY INTEREST IN U.S. HISTORY began in earnest when I transferred to a new job in Washington, D.C., in 1986 for the then U. S. Veterans Administration. While I had visited historic sites in and around my home state of Connecticut, the Washington area sparked a renewed interest in American history. Working within a block of the White House and spending lunch hours walking around the buildings and monuments made history immediate and real, while touring the Chesapeake and Ohio Canal (C&O) towpath as well as the Washington and Old Dominion rail trail added to those experiences.

My specific interest in the Civil War came in 1993 when I moved to Ashburn, Virginia (Farmwell during the Civil War). I learned more about that area during the war including the Town of Leesburg, Battle of Ball's Bluff, and First and Second Bull Run. I attended tours and reenactments and joined many preservation organizations as I noticed the effects the encroaching suburbs were having on the once pristine areas in the region. After I retired in 2000, my wife, Terri, encouraged me to pursue a master's degree in history and fortunately I found American Public University which offered an online degree with a concentration in the U.S. Civil War.

My fundamental fascination with the Maryland Campaign was sparked by Dr. Joseph L. Harsh's book *Taken at the Flood: Robert E. Lee and Confederate Strategy in the Maryland Campaign*, which was an assigned text for a class. Harsh's critical comments on Stuart and that commander's influence on Lee's decisions were enlightening and intriguing. His well-written analysis of the campaign is the exemplar of an American Civil War campaign study—every serious student of this campaign and the Battle of Antietam must read it. I wrote this book because of the encouragement of one of my professors at American Public University, Dr. Barry J. Shollenberger, to do so, as I had written a paper for him about cavalry during the Maryland Campaign, which he believed had potential to become a book. This campaign became the most important one of the war for me as I came to agree with many historians that it was the pivotal battle of the American Civil War, in addition to the most sanguinary day in United States history. Had McClellan lost and Lee continued north into Pennsylvania, the outcome of the Civil War would likely have been different. A more mundane reason is that Antietam is close to my home and the remainder of the area of the Maryland Campaign is within easy driving distance. I also have explored Antietam, Harpers Ferry, South Mountain, etc., on foot, by bicycle and by car, for several years so I am aware of the pastoral beauty of most of these areas, some relatively untouched since the Civil War. I joined Save Historic Antietam Foundation (SHAF) specifically because it concentrates on this campaign and has done so well in preserving the Antietam battlefield and adjacent areas; it will receive a portion of each book sale. I also volunteer at the Newcomer House on the Antietam National Battlefield.

This cavalry book is not the first one should read about Antietam or the Maryland Campaign as it focuses on the cavalry. I suggest it be read by someone already familiar with the events of September 1862 garnered from such books as *Landscape Turned Red* by Stephen Sears or The *Gleam of Bayonets* by James V. Murfin. Once those are digested, two more books with more detail especially from the soldier's perspective are valuable: *Before Antietam: The Battle for South Mountain* and *Antietam: The Soldiers' Battle* both by John M. Priest. The best series of books for the Maryland Campaign dealing with primarily the Confederate perspective is by Joseph L. Harsh: *Confederate Tide Rising: Robert E. Lee and Confederate Strategy, 1861-1862*; *Taken at the Flood: Robert E. Lee and Confederate Strategy in the Maryland Campaign*; and *Sounding the Shallows: A Confederate Companion for the Maryland Campaign of 1862*. Readers then smitten by the Antietam bug should read *The Maryland Campaign of September 1862* by Ezra A. Carman, edited by Joseph Pierro or Dr. Thomas Clemens. Carman has been the foundation for virtually all books written about Antietam and the Maryland Campaign. Thomas Clemens's version of Carman's manuscript is helpful in filling in gaps in Carman's manuscript as well as giving more details about Carman's sources. He also provides useful maps. With Dr. Harsh's death in 2010, Dr. Clemens, as Harsh's student, research assistant, and friend, is now the best living authority for the Maryland Campaign, and this book would not be what it is without his help. There are helpful books about parts of the campaign which detail limited aspects such as *Sealed with Their Lives: The Battle for Crampton's Gap* by Timothy J. Reese, *The History of the Harpers Ferry Cavalry Expedition, September 14 & 15, 1862* by Alan L. Tischler, and *Artillery Hell: The Employment of Artillery at Antietam* by Curt Johnson and Richard C. Anderson, Jr.

As this book is not for beginning students of the American Civil War or the Maryland Campaign, I have chosen to include only a few biographies of mostly less well-known participants as advanced readers will know about the protagonists. I have also chosen to include some asides, usually in footnotes, on topics which I found interesting and relevant to the story—I hope the reader finds them informative too. And please enjoy the occasional polysyllabicisms and sometimes long, but I hope helpful, footnotes.

I began writing about the cavalry during this campaign having preconceptions that the cavalry was mostly useless during Lee's Maryland adventure and that the Confederate cavalry literally ran circles around Yankee cavalry not only there, but also in campaigns in the east leading up to the Maryland Campaign. I came away several years later believing neither of these notions. Union cavalry did well much of the time during the Peninsular Campaign and in many other confrontations leading to Maryland in September 1862. My discussions about cavalry actions earlier in 1862 will show that Union troopers often did well against their sometimes better organized and more competently led counterparts. Certainly there were advantages and disadvantages for the mounted troops of both sides which affected their respective performances. Confederate horsemen would have been more challenged had Union cavalry units been better organized and under the control of its own commanders vice infantry generals. Usually on a trooper-on-trooper level, both sides' horsemen did well. Union and Confederate cavalry did perform well during the Maryland Campaign given the circumstances but they certainly could have done better. The reasons for their successes and failures will be studied and I hope the reader will come away with the realization that Confederate cavalry did not always have control of the field and that both sides' mounted arm did a creditable job in September 1862.

Craig Swain, who researched and wrote the driving chapter with its valuable maps, supplied much assistance with location of cavalry sites in Maryland, Virginia, and West Virginia, did a magnificent job. Without his help, the value of this book would be much diminished.

Once my book began to take shape, it could not have been written in such detail without the help of many contributors, several from a Google Internet group chat website, "Talk Antietam." Some came forward with details about various aspects of the campaign which saved me from tedious digging in obscure files while others read all or parts of the manuscript and offered comments and suggested sources. "Jake" Pierro allowed me to see an early copy of his Ezra Carman book, and Timothy R. Snyder sent me a chapter from his manuscript on the "C&O Canal in the Civil War" covering Potomac River fords in detail. Dr. Thomas Clemens and Steve French read my draft and supplied helpful suggestions. Others concentrated on particular chapters: John Frye, Jim Rosebrock, Tom Ryan, Mark Duderow, and Ted Alexander. Some commented on specific segments in the book, supplied materials, and helped clarify issues: Steve Bockmiller, Bill Christen, Steve Cowie, Dean Essig, Terri Freiheit, Dave Gaddy, Philip Laino, Dr. Ronald Limbaugh, Gerry Mayers, Julie Maynard, J.D. Petruzzi, Dave Powell, Stephen Recker, Brian Richardson, Jim Rosebrock, Tom Shay, Teej Smith, Allan Tischler, and Eric Wittenberg. Brian Downey from "Antietam on the Web," http://antietam.aotw.org/, allowed use of maps and photographs; Robert Doyle who has a comprehensive website about Myles Keogh, http://www.myleskeogh.org/, supplied a copy of Keogh's description of the service of Brig. Gen. John Buford in the Civil War.

For my Harpers Ferry chapter, Michelle Hammer at the Harpers Ferry Research Library and Dennis Frye, Chief Historian at Harpers Ferry National Park, supplied invaluable help; without Ms. Hammer's assistance in supplying materials and other references, that chapter would not be as detailed. Thomas Clemens was very generous in allowing me access to his copies of hundreds of Carman's letters and other materials as well as patiently answering many questions. Ted Alexander, Chief Historian at Antietam National Battlefield Park, gave me access to the Antietam National Battlefield Library (ANBL). Mark Vopelak, Supervisor of the Rare Books and Manuscripts section of the Indiana State Library, promptly supplied copies of original letters from troopers of the 3rd Indiana Cavalry. Christopher Damiani of the Historical Society of Philadelphia researched John Buford holdings and supplied requested documents items from the John Gibbon papers.

Almost all maps and illustrations are from the Library of Congress (LOC). I've included maps from the LOC drawn by H.W. Mattern with troop position symbols believed to have been added by hand to the photocopy War Department base maps by Gen. Ezra A. Carman. Thomas Clemens believes that the handwriting on them is Carman's. The maps are obviously early drafts from Carman but valuable as they were part of Carman's work though incomplete. The Carman-Copes 1908 series of maps done for the Battle of Antietam are also available from LOC as is the *Atlas to Accompany the Official Records of the Union and Confederate Armies* (*Official Atlas*). Note that the direction, north, is toward the top of the map, whether in portrait or landscape, unless otherwise stated. Thanks to Dennis Frye and Morningside Books for assistance with escape from Harpers Ferry maps and use of his article from "Morningside Notes." Dr. Ronald H. Limbaugh supplied illustrations from 1862 from *Harper's Weekly*. Clark Kenyon at Camp Pope Publishing supplied expertise and patience in bringing this book to press.

No book is perfect and mine is no exception but I take full responsibility for any errors herein. Should any reader desire to inform me of any errors please do so. You may send mail to me at PO Box 613, Berkeley Springs, WV 25411. Be specific about the location of the error and its correction. Should a revised printing occur, I will fix errors and add relevant information. As astute readers will find, there is a slight bias toward the Union, perhaps inevitable, as I lived my first 40 years in Connecticut. I chose the Yankee names for battle locations, e.g., Antietam vice Sharpsburg, but I did make an effort to be as fair as possible.

Finally, without the love, support, and assistance of my wife, Terri, this book would never have been completed—my heartfelt thanks—"Go Huskies and Buckeyes." And to fellow Marines—to the memories of all Marines who served on board ships in the Pacific with PFC Laurence W. Freiheit in the 1930's, especially on the U.S.S. Houston, and in the air wings on the east coast, Japan, and Chu Lai, RVN, with Sgt. Laurence H. Freiheit in the 1960's, Semper Fidelis!

THIS SECOND EDITION CORRECTS some typographical errors and supplies updates based on new sources, primarily the excellent book by D. Scott Hartwig, *To Antietam Creek: The Maryland Campaign of September 1862*. This is his first of two books and covers the Maryland Campaign to the eve of the Battle of Antietam. Mr. Hartwig's extraordinary research and narrative has made this volume and certainly his next one must read additions to the Maryland Campaign library.

Dr. Thomas Clemens has also published his next volume of Carman's manuscript, *The Maryland Campaign of September 1862, Vol. II: Antietam*. More good news is that he plans on a third volume to cover post-Antietam events. Tom's footnotes to his volumes show the depth of his knowledge about Carman and the Maryland Campaign—they are invaluable and were used in this second edition. His three volumes along with Hartwig's two volumes, when added to Dr. Joseph Harsh's trilogy, will be required reading for all serious students of the Maryland Campaign.

I wish to thank all who have supplied helpful comments for the second edition of this book and especially to Steve French and Tim Snyder who have helped immensely with valuable marketing suggestions. And thanks again to my publisher, Clark Kenyon, at Camp Pope Publishing, who continues to help a novice author navigate the publishing labyrinth. I look forward to using his expertise again for my next book, a biography of Maj. Gen. Joseph King Fenno Mansfield.

Finally, I must thank my spouse, Terri, for her efforts in keeping track of all the accounting requirements which bookselling creates.

Larry Freiheit
January 2013

Chapter 1

Introduction

THIS BOOK WILL EXAMINE the use of Union and Confederate cavalry during Confederate Gen. Robert E. Lee's Maryland Campaign in September 1862. Areas to be discussed include the movements of the Union and Confederate forces from Virginia into Maryland before the campaign, with an overview of cavalry actions from the Peninsular Campaign through the Battle of Chantilly. To better understand the use of the cavalry, a review of its two main components, cavalry horses and cavalrymen, will precede this overview. This book will also examine and evaluate Lee's strategic and tactical movements during the campaign and Union Maj. Gen. George B. McClellan's responses to them. Evaluations of participants' actions will be done both in light of what they probably knew at the time and then reviewed with the clearer lens of hindsight. The cavalry discussion will center on cavalry with McClellan's Army of the Potomac, Maj. Gen. John Pope's Army of Virginia, Lee's Army of Northern Virginia, and its predecessor, Gen. Joseph E. Johnston's Army of the Potomac.

The book's emphasis will be an in-depth look at individual cavalry actions and skirmishes including the Union Cavalry breakout from Harpers Ferry on 14 to 15 September. Major contributions of the cavalry during the Maryland Campaign will be assessed, and the battles/skirmishes reviewed, which played a part in those contributions. Use of the horse artillery will be included. Next, the book will appraise the overall performances of the Union and Confederate cavalry commanders, Confederate Maj. Gen. James Ewell Brown (Jeb) Stuart and Union Brig. Gen. Alfred Pleasonton, in light of the respective army commanders' expectations, and the traditional roles of the cavalry during this time of the war. This will be followed by a critique of McClellan's and Lee's use of the cavalry during the campaign and the contribution cavalry made to intelligence operations.

The Maryland Campaign was noteworthy for many reasons, but arguably the two most important were that its outcome was a Union strategic victory, the first major victory in the Eastern Theater, one which allowed President Abraham Lincoln to issue his preliminary Emancipation Proclamation on 22 September 1862. The Union victory, in addition to driving the best army that the South possessed back to Virginia after its unbroken string of victories beginning on the Peninsula, also meant that European powers, most importantly England, would postpone any further assistance to the Confederacy. The issuance of the Emancipation Proclamation changed the meaning of the war for the North and South. Lincoln sensed that it was time, both politically and militarily, to take the first major step to free the slaves. Admittedly, it did so only in a limited number of areas in the South, but it was a needed, first small step giving an official imprimatur to the administration's growing anti-slavery stance. This step also made it easier to enlist African Americans in the U.S. Army and to legitimize their employment in the armed forces both as soldiers and laborers. Lincoln saw the practical need for recruiting black soldiers to help with the war effort in addition to appeasing the Radical Republican Abolitionists.

While no one battle in the Civil War determined its outcome, some argue the Battle of Antietam on 17 September 1862 was the key battle, or at least one of the key battles, of the war. James M. McPherson believes that the battle "changed the course of the war...[because it] arrested Southern military momentum, forestalled foreign recognition of the Confederacy, reversed a disastrous decline in the morale of Northern soldiers and civilians, and offered Lincoln the opportunity to issue a proclamation of emancipation."[1] Another interesting aspect of the campaign was Gen. Lee's saving his army from a crushing defeat after he divided his army into four and then five parts during the campaign. It reveals how the best general in the Confederacy and arguably the best on either side, commanding the foremost army in the South, dealt with superior numbers and the loss of his operational plan to McClellan. A surprising major contributor to Gen. Lee's near disaster was Jeb Stuart, the finest cavalry general the South produced, as he failed to do all Lee needed, and materially contributed to the near loss of Lee's army, despite leading the best cavalry division formed in the Civil War. How did this excellent general and cavalry commander almost come to grief in the verdant fields and valleys in the Old Line State? This book will supply some answers.

Lee's rival's actions are also examined. McClellan, the often-reviled Union army leader, performed uncharacteristically well in Maryland during this campaign, as he fooled Lee by moving rapidly north and west from Washington to confront him. He reorganized his troops on the move, which included the majority from his Army of the Potomac, as well as parts of Pope's recently defeated Army of Virginia, leavened with regiments of raw recruits. The best organizer of all the generals Lincoln had in the east shown brightly here in his finest campaign, but he missed an excellent chance to do even more damage to Lee after he found Lee's operational plan for the campaign, S.O. 191, the "Lost Order." McClellan's use of his cavalry forces reflect its importance to him as well as its shortcomings, some of which were born during its use on the Peninsula and were his fault.

---

[1] James M. McPherson, *Crossroads of Freedom: Antietam* (New York: Oxford University Press, 2002), 8-9; xvi. McPherson's book is the best single volume summarizing the totality of the Antietam Campaign discussing the events, political and military, leading up to the campaign as well as briefly talking about the battles themselves, and their aftermath. See also Joseph L. Harsh, *Sounding the Shallows: A Confederate Companion for the Maryland Campaign of 1862* (Kent, OH: The Kent State University Press, 2000), 73. This book is one of the companions to Harsh's *Taken at the Flood: Robert E. Lee and Confederate Strategy and the Maryland Campaign of 1862* (Kent, OH: The Kent State University Press, 1999). The former will hereafter be cited as "*Shallows*" and the latter as "*Flood.*" The proem to *Flood* is *Confederate Tide Rising: Robert E. Lee and the Making of Southern Strategy, 1861-1862* (Kent, OH: The Kent State University Press, 1998), hereafter cited as "*Rising.*" Harsh's books are the preeminent works on the Army of Northern Virginia and Lee during the campaign and before. For British government opinions see Allan Nevins, *The War for the Union*, vol. 1 (New York: Charles Scribner's Sons, 1959), 388-394, and vol. 2, 242-274 *passim*, showing that it would be difficult for Britain to intervene especially due to the South's adamant position on slavery. Compare Howard Jones, *Blue & Gray Diplomacy: A History of Union and Confederate Foreign Relations* (Chapel Hill, NC: The University of North Carolina Press, 2010), 203-251, in which he argues that there was a very good chance of British intervention in the fall of 1862 in the form of mediation especially after the Union defeat at Second Bull Run but the British waited for the outcome of Lee's excursion north of the Potomac. After Lee returned to Virginia, there was still talk of mediation between the Union and Confederacy but given the Union strategic victory, the belief in England was that the Union was unlikely to agree. The desire for mediation remained in England because the war now seemed headed for a stalemate and the Emancipation Proclamation was not generally viewed with favor: "Contrary to the traditional story, the battle of Antietam and the Emancipation Proclamation did not stop the British movement toward intervention; rather, they only slowed down a process that once again had gotten under way," 235. See also James A. Rawley, *Turning Points of the Civil War* (Lincoln, NE: University of Nebraska Press, 1966), 101-104, where Rawley believes that a Confederate victory at Antietam might have led to mediation by Britain and France. James V. Murfin agreeing with McPherson wrote that "Tactically, Antietam was a draw. Strategically, politically, diplomatically and morally, it was a Union victory of high magnitude," *The Gleam of Bayonets: The Battle of Antietam and the Maryland Campaign of 1862* (Baton Rouge: Louisiana State University Press, 1965), 26.

Most historians agree that the cavalry played only a minor role during the campaign.[2] Of the various reasons offered to show this meager level of contribution, the most obvious is the low cavalry casualty figures for both sides. While the 17 September Battle of Antietam is justifiably called the bloodiest day in American history with approximately 23,000 casualties, and for the entire Maryland Campaign with some 29,000, the total losses for the Union cavalry for the entire campaign, excluding Harpers Ferry, are 109, and Confederate, 148.[3] This total of 257 casualties for both sides' cavalry admittedly does pale in

---

[2] Stephen Z. Starr, *The Union Cavalry in the Civil War, Volume 1, From Fort Sumter to Gettysburg 1861-1863* (Baton Rouge: Louisiana State University Press, 1979), "Except for Stuart's Chambersburg Raid, cavalry played a minor role in the Maryland Campaign," 309; "The 4,320 Union cavalry present at the Antietam had only a passive role in the battle," 316. See also Allan L. Tischler, *The History of the Harpers Ferry Cavalry Expedition, September 14 & 15, 1862* (Winchester, VA: Five Cedars Press, 1993), "the cavalry operations in both armies during the First Maryland Campaign were almost mundane," 186. Patrick Brennan, "The Best Cavalry in the World," *North & South*, 2, no. 2 (January 1999): "The Maryland Campaign... provided the cavalry with few opportunities for offensive operations," 17. Ted Alexander, "Battle of Antietam: Two Great American Armies Engage in Combat," *Civil War Times*, September 2006: "Cavalry played a limited role at Antietam," Internet; Robert J. Trout, *They Followed the Plume: The Story of J.E.B. Stuart and His Staff*, Mechanicsburg, PA: Stackpole Books, 1993), hereafter cited as "*Plume*," "The Sharpsburg Campaign did not give too many of the [Confederate cavalry] staff members opportunities to distinguish themselves," 14. See also Eric J. Wittenberg, *The Union Cavalry Comes of Age: Hartwood Church to Brandy Station, 1863* (Washington, DC: Potomac Books, Inc., 2003), hereafter cited as *Hartwood Church*, "the army of the Potomac suffered nearly 13,000 casualties, but only twenty-eight of them were in the cavalry," 5. See also Benjamin W. Crowninshield, *A History of the First Regiment of Massachusetts Cavalry Volunteers* (Boston: Houghton, Mifflin and Company, 1891); reprint (Baltimore: Butternut and Blue, 1995), "During the Antietam Campaign the cavalry of McClellan's army did nothing worthy of it. It moved aimlessly about," 13-14; and "At this time the cavalry was not well organized, was used in an ineffective manner, and this month's history of this regiment affords ample proof of the statement," 77. Sadly, even McClellan admits that he little used the cavalry on 17 September: "The cavalry had little field for operations during the engagement, but was employed in supporting the horse-artillery batteries in the center, and in driving up stragglers, while awaiting opportunities for other service, U.S. War Department, *The War of the Rebellion: A Compilation of the Official Records of the Union and Confederate Armies*, 128 vols. (Washington, DC: GPO, 1880-1901; reprint, Harrisburg: Broadfoot Publishing Company, 1985), pt. 1, vol. 19, 31; hereafter cited as *OR*; the series number will not be shown unless it is other than 1. See also William F. Fox, *Regimental Losses in the American Civil War 1861-1865* (Albany, NY: Brandow Printing Company, 1898; reprint, Dayton, OH: Morningside House, Inc., 1985), where Fox, in discussing "the more important of the numerous battles in which the Cavalry of the Army of the Potomac were engaged" only begins with the organization of the cavalry into one command in April 1863, 110. See also Albert G. Brackett, *History of the United States Cavalry, from the Formation of the Federal Government to the 1st of June, 1863* (n.p., 1865, reprint, Freeport, NY: Books for Libraries Press, 1970), "At the terrible battle of Antietam...the cavalry took very little part, as it could not be advantageously used on that dreadful day, which was purely a contest between the infantry and artillery of both sides," 249.

[3] *OR*, pt. 1, vol. 19, 34-36. Ezra A. Carman, *The Maryland Campaign of September 1862: Ezra A. Carman's Definitive Study of the Union and Confederate Armies at Antietam*, ed. Joseph Pierro (New York: Routledge Taylor & Francis Group, 2008), 474, 481, hereafter cited as "Carman, Pierro;" 469, 473, 474, 481. Carman's manuscript is the "Bible" of the Maryland Campaign and has, until this publication, existed mainly in a difficult-to-read 1,800 page handwritten manuscript on microfilm at the Library of Congress in Washington, D.C. Carman was a participant in the Battle of Antietam as an infantry colonel commanding the 13th New Jersey. He also was long-term historian serving on the Antietam National Battlefield Board and toured the various battlefields with veterans and exchanged hundreds of letters with them as well as interviewing residents. Carman wrote the text for the battlefield tablets and also positioned units on the famous series of Copes Antietam maps published in 1904 and revised in 1908. The sum of the materials he collected in his decades studying the campaign including the letters and maps from veterans, oral interviews, and his physical knowledge of the battlefield gives the best single source of primary and secondary materials available. An unpublished 2002 doctoral dissertation done at George Mason University, "Ezra Ayres Carman and the Maryland Campaign of September 1862," by Dr. Thomas G. Clemens transcribed Carman's first seven chapters. His thesis is a more lightly edited version of Carman however it discusses in more depth Carman's presentation and uses modern sources. It is printed by ProQuest Company: http://wwwlib.umi.com/dxweb/gateway, UMI order number 3045272. Clemens's thesis will be hereafter cited as "Clemens, thesis." Clemens has recently published a book covering Carman's manuscript through South Mountain, *The Maryland Campaign of September 1862, Vol. 1: South Mountain*, ed. Thomas G. Clemens (New York, NY: Savas Beatie LLC), 2010. Dr. Clemens has supplied more detailed footnotes concerning Carman and his sources than in Pierro's book but does not include the biographies found in his thesis. Clemens book has many maps not found in Pierro as Carman's maps are far too large to include in any book. Additionally, Carman's maps were made only for 17 September. Clemens also evaluates Carman's efforts as an historian. Clemens's book will be cited as "Carman, Clemens."

comparison with the armies' 29,164 infantry and artillery campaign losses. While Confederate cavalry losses are higher because of its more active role in the campaign, they do not compare to losses in the other two branches.[4] However, Confederate data is notoriously inaccurate compared with Union tabulations so it is likely that Confederate cavalry casualties are higher than 148.[5] The total cavalry loss is less than three percent of the numbers of cavalry on the rolls, 8,820, while infantry casualties during the campaign give over a 24 percent casualty rate.[6]

A close reading of sources detailing cavalry activities makes it clear that while no deciding cavalry or cavalry-on-infantry actions took place, intense skirmishing occurred almost daily in several locations in Maryland such as Poolesville, Sugarloaf Mountain, Frederick, Middletown, and Boonsboro near South Mountain, and even in northern Virginia, before the cavalry crossed the Potomac River. The Union cavalry escape from Harpers Ferry during the campaign was the highpoint for Union horsemen, especially when their capture of part of Maj. Gen. James Longstreet's ammunition train is considered. Excellent screening by Stuart's troopers led to many minor, albeit sometimes frantic and deadly actions, as each side endeavored to learn about the other's troop movements.[7] During this campaign, the primary functions of the cavalry were scouting/reconnaissance, picketing and screening, and guarding the flanks.

An apt quotation is taken from a newspaper report by William N. Pickerill, of the 3rd Indiana Cavalry Regiment at the Quebec School House fight, one of the many skirmishes during the campaign: "the writer never knew our complete loss or the Confederate loss. It was one of those lively little cavalry battles whose details were probably never given, or perhaps forgotten in the larger events of the battle of South Mountain next day, or of Antietam three days later. Yet it is doubtless still well remembered by those who live to remember it."[8] The Confederate cavalry commander, the Beau Sabreur Jeb Stuart, believed, like other cavalry participants, that their efforts were noteworthy: "During the Maryland campaign my command did not suffer on any *one* day as much as their comrades of other arms, but theirs was the sleepless watch and the harassing daily '*petite guerre*' in which the aggregate of casualties for the month sums up heavily. There was not a single day from the time my command crossed the Potomac till it recrossed, that it was not engaged with the enemy...the officers and men of the cavalry division recur with pride to the Maryland campaign of '62," (emphases in original).[9]

---

[4] Carman, Pierro, 479, 481. See Appendix D below. See Appendix C for a discussion of numbers during the campaign.

[5] Harsh, *Shallows*, 202, 223. John W. Thomason, Jr., *Jeb Stuart* (Lincoln, NE: University of Nebraska Press, 1994), "every statement on Southern numbers is debatable. The staff work, especially the keeping of records, lapsed altogether in many formations, and was inadequate in all...There are no cavalry returns from Stuart," 289-90. Thomason opines that Stuart had 5,000 cavalry in ten regiments but he said that "I think that is high," 290. I agree.

[6] Total cavalry is 8,820; total casualties are 257. Comparison casualties for the infantry can only be estimated from numbers engaged, 120,015, at Antietam on 17 September. Compared with campaign casualties of 28,907 (less cavalry casualties) the infantry/artillery loss is over 24 per cent. Even though Lee may have had some 75,528 in his army including cavalry on 2 September, not all entered Maryland, *Shallows*, 139. And of those who did, heavy straggling and casualties prior to Antietam left only 32,851 on the field, Carman, 465. The overall casualty numbers for the Union do not include the almost 13,000 casualties (captured) at Harpers Ferry, which includes 274 cavalry.

[7] Carman, Pierro, 46, 82-83, 86. Note that "Sugarloaf Mountain" is the modern-day spelling of "Sugar Loaf Mountain." This book will use modern terminology unless otherwise noted; quotes from contemporary sources will generally use place name spellings as found without employing "*sic*." Similarly, misspellings in quoted period verbiage will not be noted unless needed for clarification of meaning.

[8] W.N. Pickerill, "The Battle of Quebec School House," *Valley Register*, 8 April 1898. Note that the term "trooper" will refer only to a cavalryman.

[9] James Ewell Brown Stuart, "Report of General J.E.B. Stuart of Cavalry Operations on First Maryland Campaign, from August 30th to September 18th, 1862," in *Southern Historical Society Papers*, vol. III, January to June 1877 (Richmond: Southern Historical Society, n.d.; reprint, Millwood, NJ: Kraus Reprint Co, 1977), 293.

Chapter 2

The Cavalry Organizes

CONFEDERATE CAVALRY DURING the Maryland Campaign came upon the field generally better led, organized, and trained, than its Union foes, and possibly more numerous.[10] The veteran Confederate cavalry showed during the Maryland Campaign that it was often superior even in the face of the larger Union army and in mostly unfriendly country. During the campaign, when Union cavalry was tasked to undertake important actions against Confederate cavalry such as in Pleasonton's effort to take Sugarloaf, and the push west from Frederick, Maryland, through the Catoctin Mountain passes, it was usually heavily buckramed by Union infantry units.[11]

Union cavalry, at least in the east according to many historians, was not a match for its Confederate counterpart during the first half of the Civil War in virtually any area, except perhaps arms and equipment.[12] Many reasons are given including the South's ready acceptance of cavalry units early in the

---

[10] Starr, 312. Starr states that the improvement in morale in units assigned to McClellan did not extend to the cavalry. Wittenberg, *Hartwood Church*, "'Our organization was so incomplete that the operations of the cavalry during the Antietam campaign were almost insignificant,'" 3, quotation from Marcus A. Reno, "Boots and Saddles: The Cavalry of the Army of the Potomac," *National Tribune*, April 29, 1886.

[11] Carman, Pierro, 87, 91, 95.

[12] Edward G. Longacre, *Lee's Cavalrymen: A History of the Mounted Forces of the Army of Northern Virginia, 1861-1865* (Mechanicsburg, PA: Stackpole Books, 2002), hereafter cited as *Lee's Cavalrymen,* "the Confederate horsemen entered the war with a firmer grasp of horsemanship and weaponry than their adversaries, and although their advantages in experience, leadership, and tactical expertise served them well in 1861-1862, thereafter they had to battle the kind of adversity their enemy never knew: shortages," xi. It was not until Kelly's Ford in March 1863 that the Union cavalry "came of age" and was able to match its Confederate foes, ibid., 138; Starr, 350. But compare Longacre in *Lincoln's Cavalrymen: A History of the Mounted Forces of the Army of the Potomac* (Mechanicsburg, PA: Stackpole Books, 2000), where he writes that Union cavalrymen "as early as late or even mid-1862...were clearly superior to their celebrated opponents not only in arms, equipment, and horseflesh, but also in tactics, training, and the caliber of their manpower," and that it did not succeed was due more to the quality of its commanders such as McClellan, than that it could not contribute more in battle, 333. Further, he opines that while the Union cavalry did perform well earlier in the war "more than two years passed before the ingredients of lasting victory— proper organization, tactical versatility, and effective leadership—combined to make Lincoln's cavalrymen unbeatable," 335. See also W.W. Blackford, *War Years with Jeb Stuart* (Baton Rouge: Louisiana State University Press, 1993), "Up to this time [Brandy Station, June 1863] the cavalry of the [Union] enemy had not been able to stand before us, but during the past winter great attention had been bestowed upon that branch of their service and it had become much more formidable," 213. Henry B. McClellan, *I Rode with Jeb Stuart: The Life and Campaigns of Major General J.E.B. Stuart* (Bloomington, IN: Indiana University Press, 1958; reprint, Cambridge, MA: Da Capo Press, 1994), hereafter cited as *Stuart,* "Up to that time [Brandy Station, June 1863] confessedly inferior to the Southern horsemen, they [Union cavalrymen] gained on this day that confidence in themselves and in their commanders which enabled them to contest so fiercely the subsequent battle-fields of June, July and October," 294. See also Paddy Griffith, *Battle in the Civil War* (n.p.: Field Books, 1986), hereafter cited as *"Battle,"* 42-43, where he summarizes the reasons for Confederate cavalry superiority. But see *OR,* vol. 19, pt. 2, Governor Curtin's report about the Confederate cavalry entering Hagerstown, Maryland, on 11 September 1862: "Cavalry are in better condition [than the infantry]—well equipped and armed, except that they have no carbines," 268. Likely the Confederate cavalry were fairly well

war versus the North's initial reluctance to field cavalry;[13] the South's quicker realization that grouping the cavalry into large units makes it more effective;[14] the South's receiving the lion's share of cavalry officers from the "Old" U.S. Army;[15] and the South's use of the cavalry in a more mobile, fluid type of

---

equipped thanks to battlefield gleanings after the Seven Days and Second Bull Run. As they crossed into Maryland, another observer described their uniforms as poor but their horses were "excellent" "and they were well armed with guns '"mostly captured from our own cavalry, for whom they express utter contempt,'" Mary Bandy Daughtry, *Gray Cavalier: The Life and Wars of General W.H.F. "Rooney" Lee*, Cambridge, MA: Da Capo Press, 2002, 91. Some of these horses may have been part of the 500 captured at Stuart's Raid at Catlett's Station on 22 August, as well as part of the 40,000 small arms taken after the Battle of Second Manassas, Heros von Borcke, *Memoirs of the Confederate War for Independence* (Edinburgh: W. Blackwood & Sons, 1866; reprint, Nashville, TN: J.S. Sanders & Company, 1999), page citations from reprint, 89, 112. Wittenberg, *Hartwood Church*, "The Army of the Potomac's cavalry was never used efficiently or effectively during the first two years of the war," 5. "The United States government unwillingly furnished us with at least one-third of our horses, saddles, bridles and carbines and Colts army pistols and, last, but not least, blankets and haversacks," Ulysses R. Brooks, *Butler and His Cavalry in the War of Secession 1861-1865* (N.P., n.d.; reprint, Camden, SC: Gray Fox Books, n.d), 70-77. "During the first year of the war the Confederate cavalry surpassed the Federal in nearly everything that went to make good soldiers....The North was rich in men, money, and draft-horses, but comparatively poor in riding-horses, riders, and marksmen. The Confederate cavalrymen came mostly from the best families in the South, were nearly all accomplished horsemen, and more or less accustomed to the use of firearms. It took but little drilling to convert the Confederate cavalry recruit into an efficient trooper. The Federal cavalry was recruited from offices, mines, and workshops, many of the men having never been on a horse or handled a firearm The Confederate cavalry was mounted for the greater part on well-bred horses, well broken to the saddle; the Federal on indifferent horses imperfectly broken," John Bigelow, Jr. *The Campaign of Chancellorsville: A Strategic and Tactical Study* (New Haven, CT: Yale University Press, 1910), 23. According to Roy P. Stonesifer, Jr., "Two years of field service were necessary before this body [cavalry of the Army of the Potomac] could successfully challenge its superb opponent, the cavalry corps of the Army of Northern Virginia," " The Union Cavalry Comes of Age," *Civil War History*, vol. 11, no. 3, September 1965, 274. Union Maj. Gen. Wesley Merritt commented after the war: "If the [Union] cavalry was not efficient during the first two years of the war, it was not its fault. Our want of proper organization and concentration was to blame, and until the end of the war we had the lack of experience to contend with," quoted by Jay Luvaas in "Cavalry Lessons of the Civil War," *Civil War Times Illustrated*, vol. VI, no. 9, January 1968, 25-26.

[13] Starr, 65-68, 262-64. also Thomas F. Thiele, "The Evolution of Cavalry in the American Civil War; 1861-1863," (Ph.D. dissertation, University of Michigan, 1951): "the Southern Government, with a pre-existing advantage in raw material, launched a respectable body of Cavalry into the field at once and achieved a real advantage," 37.

[14] Edward G. Longacre, *Lincoln's Cavalrymen: A History of the Mounted Forces of The Army of the Potomac, 1861-1865* (Mechanicsburg, PA: Stackpole Books, 2000), hereafter cited as "*Lincoln's*, 56. Starr, 235-37, 263-66. Wittenberg, *Hartwood Church*, 3-4. See also Thiele, showing that Confederate Gen. Joseph E. Johnston argued in September 1861 that the cavalry should be brigaded thus setting the stage for the early concentration of cavalry under Stuart in the east and making it more effective than its foes who were much more scattered, 159-162.

[15] Out of the 176 officers of the five original cavalry regiments in the prewar U.S. Army, 104 (59.1%) cast their lot with their native Southern states at the beginning of the Civil War. As a result, the Confederate cavalry had more experienced leadership which contributed to battlefield superiority during the first two years of the war, Clayton R. Newell and Charles R. Shrader, *Of Duty Well and Faithfully Done: A History of the Regular Army in the Civil War* (Lincoln, NB: University of Nebraska Press, 2011), 245-246. Newell and Shrader give an excellent summary of the six Regular Army cavalry regiments during the Civil War, 245-263. The nascent Union cavalry had many inexperienced officers in command of mostly green and untested troops. "Introduction to Civil War Cavalry by Alethea D. Sayers; http://ehistory.osu.edu/uscw/features/regimental/cavalry.cfm; Internet accessed 5 February 2008; Ethan S. Rafuse, "Culture and Cavalry, Discourse and Reality: Some Observations on the War in the East," *North & South*, hereafter cited as *Culture*, 10, no. 4, January 2008, 80. Compare Gen. Jubal A. Early's comments in "Comments on Count of Paris' Civil War in America,' in *Southern Historical Society Papers*, vol. III, showing 31 officers of the old army 1st and 2nd Cavalry Regiments who joined the Union army and 24 who joined the Confederate army, 145. See also Thiele, Appendix A, showing of 52 officers of cavalry regiments in the period 1855-1860 who became general officers in the Union or Confederate armies, 29 were Confederates and 23 Union; "Good leadership can overcome or compensate for deficiencies in equipment, strategy, and numbers as well as for other handicaps...produces good morale, intelligent discipline, and efficient fighting... [they] apply especially to the Cavalry in the Civil War," 486. With the exception of Ashby in the Shenandoah Valley, "Confederate commanders of Cavalry had achieved a high degree of ability in 1862," 501. Edward G. Longacre in *The Cavalry at Gettysburg: A Tactical Study of Mounted Operations during the Civil War's Pivotal Campaign, 9 June-14 June 1863*, hereafter cited as *Gettysburg* (Rutherford, NJ: Fairleigh Dickinson University Press, 1986, reprint, Lincoln: University of Nebraska Press, 1993), recounts Stuart's experience and prowess as a cavalry commander and in reconnaissance,

warfare.[16] Additionally, the martial spirit of the South embodied in its horsemanship and blooded animals, likely made a difference in the Confederate superiority.[17] Many opined that the major turning

---

24-25. Stuart's "First Ride Around McClellan in June 1863 brought him to the South's as well as the North's public attention. Stuart's Catlett's Station raid on 23 August again showed his abilities as a cavalry leader and raider. See also Starr, "these regiments were officered largely by southerners, many of whom placing loyalty to their states ahead of their allegiance to the national government, resigned their commissions," 58.

[16] Rafuse, *Culture*, cavalry thrive on a fluid war of flexibility and speed where maneuver would offset the Union army's advantages of superior numbers, artillery, and engineering, 76. Lee needed his cavalry in this type of warfare whereas McClellan had less of a need as he was relying more on his numbers and engineering to win the "battle of posts."

[17] Longacre, *Lee's*, 24, 30; Daughtry, 54. See Grady McWhiney and Perry D. Jamieson, *Attack and Die: Civil War Military Tactics and the Southern Heritage* (Tuscaloosa, AL: The University of Alabama Press, 1982), in which they argue that the martial spirit found in the South and lacking in the North was due to the South's Celtic heritage fighting "with the same courageous dash and reckless abandon that had characterized their Celtic ancestors for two thousand years," xv. But see Robert E. Beringer, Herman Hattaway, Archer Jones, William N. Still, Jr., *Why the South Lost the Civil War* (Athens, GA: The University of Georgia Press, 1986), which successfully disputes McWhiney and Jamieson's thesis that it was a Celtic heritage which required Southern soldiers to attack more than their foes, 465. Compare Robert L. Bonner, "Roundheaded Cavaliers? The Context and Limits of a Confederate Racial Project," *Civil War History*, vol. 48, no. 1, March 2002, pp. 34-59, which discusses the notions of racial differences between the north and south—Puritans versus the Cavaliers; Jeb Stuart is described as the "prototypical Cavalier," 58. Bonner finds that this Cavalier image was developed during the "Lost Cause" era rather than before or during the war. See also James M. McPherson, *Ordeal by Fire: The Civil War and Reconstruction* (New York: McGraw-Hill, 2001), where he discusses the Cavalier image finding that many southerners believed that they were descended from the Cavaliers in Britain, who were descended from the Norman knights, they were superior to northern Roundheads and Puritans and thus had more of a martial spirit and were superior in all ways to the vulgar northerners, 54-55. Virginia, which contributed the large majority of Stuart's cavalry, had "certainly the strongest military tradition of any Southern state [and] had a fairly well-developed militia....in the wake of the abolitionist John Brown's attack on Harpers Ferry, the Old Dominion had experienced something of a renascence of its military strength," according to historian Richard M. McMurry in his *Two Great Rebel Armies: An Essay in Confederate Military History* (Chapel Hill, NC: The University of North Carolina Press, 1989), 77. As of 15 December 1860, Virginia Militia had five regiments of cavalry; the volunteer force had 92 troops of cavalry although many were not fully armed or equipped for war, *OR*, Series 4, vol. 1, 381-383; *OR*, vol. 2, 912. While militia troops were not often known for their military prowess, McMurry opines that "Virginia was able to draw from her militia far more men with at least some military knowledge and experience than was any other Rebel state" and very likely any Union state, 97. But more importantly especially early in the war, the Army of Northern Virginia numbered Men who had received both a college education and military training in school [and] were present in far greater numbers...than in any other Civil War military force. Their presence made that army a far better military organization than any of it American contemporaries....The military schools provided hundreds of such well-qualified junior officers and noncommissioned officers to the Army of Northern Virginia. No other Civil War army was so well supplied in 1861 with men capable of stepping immediately into junior command positions, training the new troops, and exercising effective leadership at the company level," 99. Many of these men likely found their way into cavalry units and were able to leaven the raw recruits and provide much needed martial knowledge and training; some 1,796 Virginia Military Institute (VMI) cadets and alumni served in the Confederate army. "Virtually every Virginia unit included several men who had studied at VMI....Thomas T. Munford's Second Virginia Cavalry had almost two dozen, and Munford himself was a member of the Institute's Class of 1852," 102. McMurry later wrote that "An army able to draw upon military school alumni as the nucleus of its junior officer corps would have a ready-made cadre of small unit leaders and hence a greater than average strength of command. One—and only one—Civil War army found itself so endowed [the Army of Northern Virginia]," "Civil War Leaders" in *Leadership During the Civil War: The 1989 Deep Delta Civil War Symposium: Themes in Honor of T. Harry Williams*, edited by Roman J. Heleniak and Lawrence L. Hewitt (Shippensburg, PA: White Mane Publishing Company, Inc., 1992), 179. Douglas Southall Freeman also credits VMI cadets with valuable training in 1861, *R.E. Lee: A Biography*, 4 vols. (New York: Charles Scribners Sons, 1936), 1:494, hereafter cited as *Lee*. He also wrote that "within less than three months from the day Virginia seceded, one third of the field officers of the 'provisional' regiments of the State, were men who had been trained at V.M.I." Douglas Southall Freeman, *Lee's Lieutenants*, 3 vols. (New York: Charles Scribners Sons, 1942-1944), 1:718, hereafter cited as *Lee's Lieutenants*, 718. Thus it is arguable that officers and noncommissioned officers were better equipped to supply leadership at all levels early in the war which Union officers, other than the regulars who remained with the Union, could not usually match. This helps explain why even though trooper on trooper Union matched Confederate, Union cavalry units suffered under inexperienced leaders. Not all historians agreed with these ideas. Marcus Cunliffe wrote that southern military volunteer organizations "were rivaled, and outmatched in number

point for Union cavalry came under Maj. Gen. Joseph Hooker who, after taking command of the Army of the Potomac from Maj. Gen. Ambrose E. Burnside, reorganized the army's cavalry in February 1863 into one corps.[18]

Thus Confederate cavalry had advantages over its foes often outperforming and sometimes humiliating them during the first two years of the war. The Confederate cavalry superiority gave their troopers confidence in their abilities and developed an esprit de corps almost unequalled for Union cavalry. One of the best examples is the renown the Black Horse Troop won at First Bull Run. Northern soldiers grew to dread these men on their black Morgan horses holding them in awe while the Southern public hailed them as heroes.[19] Just the mention of the Black Horse was enough to frighten Union troops. Their brigade and later division commander, Jeb Stuart "[i]n many ways...epitomized not only the Southern soldier but the Southern soul."[20] While the generalization stressing the superiority of the Confederate cavalry early in the war is mostly correct and well-founded, as with all generalizations, it is at once both correct and incorrect. It is correct in that most of the time in 1861 Rebel cavalry was superior given its better leadership and experience. However, in 1862, Yankee cavalry, benefitted by time in the saddle, developed better leaders, rid itself of incompetent officers, and began to give its foes more spirited contests, saber-to-saber, beginning on the Peninsula. The development of the Union cavalry is better seen then as beginning at a lower level of competency overall than its foes in 1861 for the reasons given, but continually improving throughout the war, while its foe abilities declined after 1862. In the Maryland Campaign, the Confederate cavalry usually performed better when facing Union horsemen on an equal footing, but cavalry skirmishes in Maryland were rarely such.

The generalization about Confederate early-war cavalry superiority is also incorrect because there was a gradual improvement in Union cavalry performance reflected during 1862, which is shown by looking at individual cavalry actions from the Peninsula to the Maryland Campaign. There were impressive Union cavalry victories which would not have occurred if the Yankee horsemen were in fact incompetent. And while Confederate cavalry more often than not prevailed, this was not due to the fault of the individual cavalryman on the Union side—trooper-against-trooper action almost always found

---

and variety, by equivalent companies in the North," *Soldiers and Civilians: Martial Spirit in America, 1775-1865* (New York, NY: Free Press, 1973), 355-356, 360-369.

[18] Starr, 339. See also the positive effect this had on Union cavalry morale as it resulted in a Union cavalry victory at Kelly's Ford in March 1863, Longacre, *Lincoln's*, 138; Starr 345-50. But see also Thiele, showing that Gen. John Pope's organization of his cavalry into larger units also had a salutary effect, 89-90.

[19] Thomason, 72. John Scott, "The Black Horse Cavalry," *Annals of the War Written by Leading Participants North and South* (Philadelphia, PA: Philadelphia Weekly Times, 1879; reprint, Edison, NJ: Blue & Grey Press, 1996), 590-613. The Northern press and public grew to associate virtually all of Stuart's troopers with the Black Horse Cavalry. Historian Michael C.C. Adams argues that the Union army's lack of success after First Bull Run in the eastern theater was mainly due to its fear of the military prowess of the Army of Northern Virginia to the point that it seemed virtually invincible, and that the Confederates also believed, some almost to the end, in their overwhelming superiority. Adams wrote that the Black Horse did not even chase the Zouaves at First Bull Run. Even McClellan evidenced this fear on the Peninsula and later in Maryland, *Our Masters the Rebels: A Speculation on Union Military Failure in the East, 1861-1865* (Cambridge, MA: Harvard University Press, 1978); reprint, *Fighting for Defeat: Union Military Failure in the East, 1861-1865*, Lincoln, NE: Bison Books, University of Nebraska Press, 1992), 94-95.

[20] Brennan, 12. The Black Horse Cavalry (or Troop) was one company of Confederate cavalry that eventually became Company H of the 4th Virginia Cavalry. It was formed in Fauquier County in 1859 as an independent volunteer cavalry company and mustered into the service of Virginia in May 1861. The name "Black Horse Troop" continued to be used but was sometimes erroneously applied to Confederate cavalry as a whole by Union troops and the northern press. Members of the Black Horse included a great many young men from the oldest families of Fauquier County and were expert horsemen. It first became famous when it escorted John Brown to the gallows in December of 1859. At First Bull Run, the company was attached to Lt. Col. T.T. Munford's squadron of the 30th Virginia Cavalry. The troop often served as Gen. Thomas J. "Stonewall" Jackson's escort; information from Harry Smeltzer's blog, "Bull Runnings."

that the Union horseman matched his opponent. The newsworthy cavalry events on the Peninsula unfairly touted Rebel prowess: the failed Union cavalry charge at Gaines's Mill and Stuart's First Ride Around McClellan, while minimizing the good service given by Yankee horsemen in general. Stuart's cavalry exploits before Second Bull Run such as capturing Pope's huge supply base and his generally winning cavalry activities, were concatenated with Gen. Lee's success in battle, thus masking good Union efforts during the Second Bull Run Campaign. As will be seen, Confederate cavalry advantages during the Maryland Campaign were mitigated by Stuart's and Gen. Lee's assumptions, and by Stuart's penchant for frivolity. Stuart's maneuvers in mostly hostile country also contributed to neutralizing Rebel advantages as they were less familiar with the country and had less enthusiastic civilian assistance. Union cavalry may have been sometimes outclassed during the Maryland Campaign, but it gave a good account of itself, showing Stuart that as on the Peninsula, they could not be routinely brushed aside.

Union cavalry vidette enjoying a smoke, 12 Nov. 1863, by Edwin Forbes. Courtesy LOC.

Many of the defects under which the Union cavalry in the Army of the Potomac labored were due to McClellan's decisions early in the Peninsular Campaign. He assigned cavalry units to infantry divisions and corps as headquarters guards, couriers, and pickets, while keeping a small Cavalry Reserve composed of mainly regular units. This effectively put cavalry under infantry command in addition to reducing the ability of any sizeable units to confront Confederate cavalry or to do extensive reconnaissance, screening, or raiding. Due to this scattering, Union cavalry could not have had a major impact during McClellan's Peninsular Campaign. Because they had not operated or trained together, they were ineffective as a unified command even when they could be reassembled.[21] So even though Union cavalry did not affect McClellan's strategy or enhance his ability to win there, it did an adequate job in most of its assignments.

Based on his observation and acceptance of European tactics obtained during the Crimean War, McClellan believed that without this required seasoning, his inexperienced troopers could do little regardless of their organization.[22] He also shared the beliefs of fellow regular army officers that volunteers, especially volunteer cavalry, would be of minimal use in any event.[23] When McClellan formed his divisions into corps, he probably believed that the corps formation should resemble the structure that Napoleon used in his army: a combined arms group which was fully integrated with all three arms, and could act independently from the army. Unfortunately, given the terrain over which he had to operate, independent corps could not be well used, and resulted in each corps' cavalry and artillery being used piecemeal; McClellan was fighting a modern war with improved weaponry by using an outmoded organization. Only when cavalry and artillery were massed into large, separate groups, were they able to be much more effectively used.[24] There was a pervasive early-war belief extant that

---

[21] Thiele states that McClellan's tour abroad during the Crimean War which resulted in the invention of the McClellan saddle as well as some information in his official report of that tour recommending tactical formations and the functions of cavalry in wartime was advice which he mostly ignored as an army commander, 26. Thiele also asserts that McClellan's scattering of his cavalry units spread it too thin for it to confront Confederate cavalry and did not allow for the units to train new troopers. Additionally, the "safety in numbers" aspect was lost for these green cavalrymen, 81-82. The scattered cavalry units were used as orderlies, personal escorts and couriers, in addition to pickets and videttes, 83. Thiele additionally points out that McClellan had also scattered his cavalry units even in the fall of 1861 after taking over the defense of Washington as commander of the Army of the Potomac on 20 August 1861: "Eleven of his few [cavalry] companies were distributed among seven headquarters ranging from Washington to Harpers Ferry, Virginia, and later, one regiment was assigned to each division," 248. Amazingly, McClellan reported 10,764 cavalry present for duty on 12 November 1861, with 4,755 under Stoneman in Washington and Fairfax Court House and 6,009 under the twelve infantry division commanders; these units ranged in size from 75 in Blenker's Division to 946 in W. F. Smith's Division, *OR*, vol. 5, 650. Gen. Johnston reports Confederate cavalry in November 1861 as 3,396 aggregate present and absent and 2,293 present for duty, *OR*, vol. 5, 974. Yet with this reported large disparity in numbers, Confederate cavalry almost always held sway in these early confrontations, see *OR*, vol. 5, 437-454.

[22] Starr, 262-64; Longacre, *Lincoln's*, 65-68.

[23] Wittenberg, *Hartwood Church*, 3. See also Paddy Griffith, *Battle Tactics of the Civil War*, hereafter cited as *Tactics* (New Haven, Connecticut: Yale University Press, 2001), where he argues that the Mexican War showed many regular army officers that militia and volunteer troops were best suited for a defensive role since they were insufficiently trained to undertake more complicated maneuvers especially during the attack, 125. Similarly, Archer Jones, *Civil War Command and Strategy: The Process of Victory and Defeat* (New York: The Free Press, 1992), argues that the Mexican War taught regular officers that untrained militia and volunteers were best on the defense, 269. Clearly, Mexican War veteran officers for the most part little trusted volunteer infantry and by extension, arguably mistrusted volunteer cavalry even more. See also Edward P. Tobie, *History of the First Maine Cavalry, 1861-1865* (Boston, MA: Press of Emery & Hughes, 1887; reprint, Salem, MA: Higginson Book Company, n.d.), "Up to the spring of 1863 the cavalry of the Army of the Potomac, at least, had been of little use as a separate branch of the service. In the first place, the regular army officers had no faith in volunteer cavalry, characterizing it as a 'mounted mob,'....there was a prejudice against cavalry in general, and volunteer cavalry in particular," 122. See also George B. McClellan, *The Civil War Papers of George B. McClellan: Selected Correspondence, 1860-1865*, edited by Stephen W. Sears (New York: Ticknor & Fields, 1989. Reprint, Cambridge, MA: Da Capo Press, 1992), hereafter Sears, McClellan, *Papers*, stating on 16 September 1861: "As to the regular Cavalry—I have directed all of it to be concentrated in one mass that the numbers in each company may be increased & that I many have a reliable & efficient body on which to depend in a battle. For all present duty of Cavalry in the upper Potomac volunteers will suffice as they will have nothing to do but carry messages & act as videttes," 101. McClellan's massing apparently did not mean that it should be organized into cavalry-only units given what transpired during his Peninsular Campaign. Confederate cavalry in Virginia was greatly helped by the interest taken in it by Confederate Gen. Joseph E. Johnston, who made efforts not only to consolidate his cavalry under Jeb Stuart, but made many requests to Richmond for more cavalry, Thiele, 262.

[24] Marion V. Armstrong Jr., *Unfurl Those Colors! McClellan, Sumner, and the Second Army Corps in the Antietam Campaign* (Tuscaloosa, AL: The University of Alabama Press, 2008), hereafter cited as "*Colors*," 29; Griffith, *Tactics*, 165-166, 182. One historian pointed out that "McClellan was not alone in scattering his cavalry broadcast. In the West, Generals Frémont and Buell did the same," Starr, 237. Early in the war, Confederate Gen. "Albert Sidney Johnston had parceled out most of his

the conflict would be short with it being decided in one or two large battles, so the two-year training period thought needed to properly train new cavalry recruits would limit the need for any new cavalry—the five regular army regiments would suffice.[25] Additionally, the expense of equipping cavalry units was very high, some $500,000 to $600,000 per regiment, and the cost of maintaining the units once formed remained high primarily due to the cost of feeding and replacing mounts.[26] McClellan was aware of the early problems the Lincoln government had with finding funds to enlarge the army so it is probable given his perception that large numbers of cavalry would not be needed, it would be more cost justified to spend available monies on infantry giving more fighting men for the dollar.[27]

---

cavalry, attaching from one to seven companies of it to each of his infantry brigades, but he also organized a separate cavalry brigade, and when Braxton Bragg took over command in the West, he grouped all his cavalry into two brigades, one commanded by Forrest and the other by Joseph Wheeler," ibid., 238.

[25] Starr, 59, n. 33, shows that estimates for training ranged from one to three years. See also Thiele, stating that Maj. Gen. Winfield Scott was one who thought that cavalry was not needed since the war would be too short to train them, the expense would not be justified, and the wooded character of the country militated against its use, 31. But the Confederate administration had few qualms about accepting cavalry units. Confederate forces while not necessarily much larger than its foes were more quickly in the field learning mounted skills while Federal units were mostly preparing for the field, 126-139. See also Adams, *Fighting for Defeat*, who wrote that Scott was not alone in believing that large numbers of cavalry were not needed as "the country south of the Potomac was not suitable for mounted operations and that the number of cavalry in the service could be reduced," 77-78. Brig. Gen. Israel B. Richardson ["J.B. Richardson" incorrect in text; "I" mistaken as "J"] testified on 24 December 1861 about the Army of the Potomac's cavalry: "I consider the cavalry in this army worse than nothing at all, and it will be so for the next three years, until you get rid of two-thirds of the men. It is the poorest arm in the service unless it is well drilled and disciplined....I thought that four regiments of regular cavalry would be enough....We know that one regiment of cavalry costs about the same as two regiments of infantry to keep it up; and the horses are getting poor and in bad condition," Joint Committee on the Conduct of the War (JCCW), vol. 1, 113-115; Brig. Gen. Samuel P. Heintzelman testified on 24 December 1861 when asked about cavalry needed: "Not a very large force. The country is not adapted to cavalry, at least as far out as I have been....I think we have more cavalry than we want," 119; Brig. Gen. William B. Franklin testified on 26 December 1861 that "I have in my division now one regiment of cavalry. I would be very glad to get rid of two-thirds of that regiment, which numbers about 1,000 men." He said that he would retain the third for pickets and scouts as he "would never think of making a cavalry fight or a cavalry charge," 124. He also testified that "a cavalry soldier needs much more instruction than an infantryman does. You have got to teach him how to ride, and to teach the horse how to behave himself under fire. Then you have to feed the horses, which is an important thing....we have a great deal more cavalry than any of us need....I really think that two thousand cavalry is all that we want for the whole army, 124; Brig. Gen. Irvin McDowell testified on 26 December 1861 that he could do with one-third less cavalry than he had, one regiment in his division—"Cavalry regiments are of six squadrons each [one squadron is two companies], and there are two squadrons to a brigade. That amount might be diminished....If we were to be organized by corps of three divisions each, two regiments of cavalry would be perfectly sufficient for the three divisions," 139-140. Division commanders at the end of the first year of the war still believed that cavalry was of little use except as pickets and scouts and should be divided among infantry units; Quarter Master Gen. Montgomery C. Meigs testified on 27 December 1861 "That we have too much cavalry....I find the great difficulty is to supply them with provender, and as most of the men are raw, and some of them are not very efficient, I think it probable we could do with less cavalry than we have here. The field for cavalry, I think, is in the west," 152-153.

[26] Starr, 66. But see Crowninshield's opinion that the cost was only $300,000, 6. See also John V. Barton, "The Procurement of Horses," *Civil War Times Illustrated*, Vol. VI, no. 8, December 1967, discussing the early Union units which supplied their own horses which were "rented to the government at the rate of fifty cents per day. If his horse were killed or became unserviceable, he left his unit until he could provide himself with another" and if not, he was sent to the infantry. If the volunteer regiment could not supply its own horses, they were supplied by the Quartermaster Department, the governor of the state, mustering officers, or regimental quartermasters. "After July 1862, a new order placed the burden of providing all cavalry mounts upon the Government," 17. *O.R.*, series III, vol. 1, 153. For the fiscal year 30 June 1861 to 30 June 1862, the Federal government spent $6,202,834 for cavalry and artillery horses and $3,139,552 for forage, *OR*, ser. III, vol. 2, 788. See also Thiele, stating that the Union Ordnance Department from the beginning of the war to 30 June 1862 had spent over $3,000,000 on carbines and pistols most of which went to the cavalry, 65-66.

[27] McClellan apparently knew as did other informed government officials that the state of the Union's finances was not good in 1861. See Jane Flaherty, "'The Exhausted Condition of the Treasury' on the Eve of the Civil War," *Civil War History*, vol. 55, no. 2, June 2009, "the [U.S.] Treasury faced 'being placed before the world in the aspect of a mendicant'...'little more' than $500,000 remained in the central depository in Washington....the Union started the war with an exhausted Treasury and poor

Maj. Gen. George Brinton McClellan. Courtesy LOC.

credit, they had few resources available to deal with the setbacks of late 1861 that resulted from the contingencies of war....The 'exhausted condition of the Treasury' at the start of the war exacerbated the problems that arose as the Lincoln administration scrambled to find funds to field an army," 244-245, 276-277. The problem of how to raise funds to conduct the war was a subject of much debate in 1861 in the U.S. Congress, see for example, Allan Nevins, *War for the Union, Vol. 1, The Improvised War, 1861-1862* (New York: Konecky and Konecky, 1971), 195-198, stating that the Secretary of the Treasury, Salmon P. Chase, estimated that the government would need $320,000,000 for 1862, but like most other government officials, thought that the war would be short so he proposed raising only $80,000,000 by taxes, relying on tariffs and bonds for the remaining funds.

Some argue that an important factor driving the differences in the quality of the opposing cavalry was the overall military cultures of the opposing sides. The Union, given its more organized, industrial society and economy, tended to favor the methodical "style of war associated with the limited wars of the 18th century...[while the Confederacy] was better suited to the fluid war of maneuver and battle exemplified by the early campaigns of Napoleon."[28] This philosophy was well served by cavalry with its ability to move long distances quickly, so the Confederate government had no qualms about accepting mounted units very early in the war. McClellan believed that the advantages of large cavalry forces allowing a fluid battlefield would not be needed given his studied approach and methodical method of attack he planned for advance to Richmond. Lee knew that if McClellan on the Peninsula were allowed to continue his "battle of posts," that the Union juggernaut could not be easily stopped. Lee stated that he had to "bring McClellan out" so that the Union's superior artillery and engineering would not have to be faced head on.[29]

Because Union cavalry saw little effective use under McClellan, their skills as individual cavalrymen and as cohesive units did not quite match that of the Confederate cavalry during much of the Maryland Campaign.[30] Their lack of training and experience was obvious. The 12th Pennsylvania may have been the "greenest" of Pleasonton's regiments in Maryland. It fortunately was on detached duty as provost guard at the Battle of Antietam behind the Union First and Twelfth Corps having only been mounted since mid-July 1862 and with little training or drill.[31] The 1st Massachusetts is a good example of a "trained" Union regiment as it had been in active service about a year although most of that time was spent on the South Carolina coast battling disease, boredom, and mosquitoes. That time however, did allow for some training; drill and discipline were learned and used to advantage in Maryland.[32]

The next step up in Union cavalry experience could be called "veteran," and was exemplified by the 6th Pennsylvania Cavalry, Rush's Lancers. Most were mounted by the end of September 1861, and the new troopers as well as their more experienced officers began to become acquainted with their equine comrades. The next month, they received their full complement of weapons just in time to be ordered to Washington at the end of October. But much to most troopers' chagrin, their regimental commanding officer acceded to McClellan's suggestion that the regiment be armed with lances. Drilling commenced with these outmoded weapons until the regiment embarked on trains for Washington in December 1861. At the beginning of McClellan's Peninsular Campaign, they were brigaded with the 5th and 6th U.S. Cavalry in Brig. Gen. Philip St. George Cooke's Cavalry Reserve thus benefiting by serving with veteran, regular troopers. Unfortunately, armed with lances, they were the butt of jokes as they were initially relegated to support duty. They were described by an infantryman in an uncomplimentary fashion:

---

[28] Rafuse, *Culture*, 72-86. See also Thiele, showing that the South and in particular the Border States were better able to quickly field cavalry and that the Union which "was at a disadvantage in producing good mounted troops," 27-28.

[29] Robert E. Lee, *The Wartime Papers of R. E. Lee*, ed. by Clifford Dowdey and Louis H. Manarin (New York: Bramhall House, 1961), 184.

[30] Pope's cavalry mostly exhausted itself leading up to Second Bull Run so very few cavalry units which served under Pope served with McClellan in Maryland, however, some of these units did patrol south of the Potomac River in Northern Virginia and in the Washington area. Units from outside the Army of the Potomac did serve with McClellan in Maryland but as escorts or on detached service: the 1st Maine Cavalry had served with Pope, it was on detached duty in Frederick, Maryland; one company of the 1st Michigan Cavalry serving as escort to the Twelfth Army Corps was from the Army of Virginia; 2nd New York companies A, B, I, and K were from the Army of Virginia and served as First Army Corps escort; see note 4, page 34 below. *OR*, ser. I, vol. 12, part 3, 581-588. See also Edward G. Longacre, *Grant's Cavalryman: The Life and Wars of General James H. Wilson* (Mechanicsburg, PA: Stackpole Books, 1972), 55, where Wilson joined McClellan's staff temporarily on 8 September 1862 when he and other aides such as Custer were put to work but only as couriers.

[31] Samuel P. Bates, *History of Pennsylvania Volunteers, 1861-1865*, http://12thpacavalry.8k.com/1862.html; Internet: accessed 6 February 2008.

[32] Crowninshield, ii.

They made a circus-like appearance with their lances, at the head of which each had a small piece of red flannel cloth fastened, calculated, I suppose, to strike terror to the hearts of the Johnnies....If that was not the reason, I don't know what was, unless it was to look pretty. Or perhaps the flannel might have been intended to work on the Jonnies the same as it does on a mad bull....The boys had a way of jeering at them...with remarks and epithets as: 'The great American toad-stickers,' or "Father Abraham's sucker spearers," and other pleasing observations calculated to make the lancers feel that they were appreciated and their appearance noticed.[33]

As the Union army moved up the peninsula, the Lancers were involved in scouting and skirmishing, ending up battling Confederates, although still with lances and pistols. The Lancers' first encounter with Stuart may have not ended well as the regiment, after beginning a charge valiantly, lost heart, turned and ran, being chased three miles with their route defined by discarded lances. The routing of the Lancers is described by one of Stuart's aides; he wrote that the skirmish took place on 27 June 1862 near the left flank of Gen. Lee's army in the vicinity of Cold Harbor, against a whole regiment of lancers with "red-and-white pennon, and their fresh, well-fitting blue uniforms turned up with yellow...this...regiment turned tail and fled in disorder, strewing the whole line of their retreat with their picturesque but inconvenient arms....I do not believe that out of the whole body of 700 men more than twenty retained their lances." Note that his description is not found in a contemporary history of the Lancers so it may be embellished as many of von Borcke's tales are. Another southern description was similar: "At five hundred yards, down came the lances, and the enemy troopers started off in fine style to meet the Confederate charge. The Confederates held their fire until the distance was narrowed to twenty-five yards, then crashed a volley into the Lancer's leading files. Men and horses went down. Other enemy troopers crashed into the melee, stumbling over the fallen horses and men and as order was lost, panic swept through the Lancers' well-tailored ranks. Before the Confederates could get among them and test their deadly lances, the Federals turned and fled. Only a few stayed around to fight."[34] The Lancers later performed well during the Seven Days Campaign and joined McClellan's reforming army in Maryland, as a "veteran" cavalry unit along with its brother regiments, the 5th and 6th U.S. Cavalry; it did not totally give up its lances until May 1863.[35]

---

[33] Thomas H. Mann, *Fighting with the Eighteenth Massachusetts: The Civil War Memoir of Thomas H. Mann*, ed. by John J. Hennessy (Baton Rouge, LA: Louisiana State University Press, 2000), 81.

[34] The routing of the Lancers is described by von Borcke, 38. Note that his description is not found in Wittenberg's history of the Lancers so it may be embellished as many of von Borcke's tales are. R. Shepard Brown in *Stringfellow of the Fourth* which describes a Rebel trooper's service in the 4th Virginia Cavalry (New York: Crown Publishers, Inc., 1960), echoes von Borcke, 140-142. Eric J. Wittenberg, *Rush's Lancers: The Sixth Pennsylvania Cavalry in the Civil War* (Yardley, PA: Westholme Publishing, LLC, 2007), hereafter cited as *Lancers*, 1-48 passim. See also Alonzo Gray, *Cavalry Tactics as Illustrated by the War of the Rebellion: Together with Many Interesting Facts Important for Cavalry to Know* (Leavenworth, KS: Press of Ketcheson Printing Co, 1910; reprint, Whitefish, MT: Kessinger Publishing, n.d.), "The lance cannot be used to advantage in a close wooded country such as is found everywhere along the Atlantic coast. The greatest use of the lance is in the shock," 28. It is strange that McClellan would have asked that the Sixth be armed with lances unless it was merely for show; he apparently enjoyed their company as his escort with the red pennons from their lances contributing to McClellan's penchant for showmanship. The commander, Col. Rush, described the lances: "It is about nine feet long, with an eleven inch three-edged blade; the staff is of Norway fir, about one and a quarter inches in diameter, with ferule and counter- poise at the heel; the whole weighing four pounds thirteen ounces, with a scarlet swallow-tailed pennon. They were furnished by the Ordnance Department, under contracts which they made from patterns submitted by me," S.L. Gracey, *Annals of the Sixth Pennsylvania Cavalry* (N.p.: E. H. Butler & Co., 1868), 34. Von Borcke may be describing the failed charge by Union cavalry at Gaines's Mill on 27 June; see below Chap. 3. Members of the 6th Pennsylvania were with the cavalry there and it is likely that some did participate in the charge but there is no evidence of the mass route described by von Borcke.

[35] Strother, serving in McClellan's headquarters, commented on 10 September that "I saw Rush's lancers pass at a distance with their red pennants and long lances; they had quite a 'middle ages' appearance," David Hunter Strother, *A Virginia Yankee in the*

As all of Pleasonton's green, trained, and veteran regiments quickly learned in Maryland, their more experienced foes would often prove to be hard fighters. Virtually all of the Confederate cavalry units had been together from the beginning of the war and had fought in many battles and skirmishes. Those which had been under Stuart's command, profited from his attention to training and aggressive tactics, allowing those units to be classified as "veteran" troopers. Some had prewar existence as militia units so had a head start on most of their foes.[36] Stuart had helped train many of these units starting when he took command of them at Harpers Ferry under Col. Thomas J. Jackson on 10 May 1861. The next weeks after retreating from Harpers Ferry, and before First Bull Run, Stuart continued training. "Jeb immediately began a training program for the green troopers."[37] He led them in reconnaissance and raids against troops under Union Maj. Gen. Robert Patterson between Martinsburg and Winchester, Virginia. He took them into situations where they were surrounded and had to find a way out and taught them all aspects of skirmishing and attacking.[38] A Confederate trooper who appreciated Stuart's abilities as a cavalry commander and leader of men, wrote in glowing detail of his initial encounter with the "Chevalier of the Lost Cause," and subsequent training Stuart administered:

I saw him for the first time when he was a colonel, in command of the little squadron of horsemen known as the first regiment of Virginia cavalry. The company to which I belonged was assigned to this regiment immediately after the evacuation of Harper's Ferry by the Confederates. General Johnston's army was at Winchester, and the Federal force under General Patterson lay around Martinsburg. Stuart, with his three or four hundred men, was encamped at Bunker Hill, about midway between the two, and thirteen miles from support of any kind. He had chosen this position as a convenient one from which to observe the movements of the enemy, and the tireless activity which marked his subsequent career so strongly had already begun. As he afterwards explained, it was his purpose to train and school his men, quite as much as anything else, that prompted the greater part of his madcap expeditions at this time, and if there be virtue in practice as a means of perfection, he was certainly an excellent school-master.

My company arrived at the camp about noon, after a march of three or four days, having traveled twenty miles that morning....We were weary after our long journey, and disposed to welcome the prospect of rest which our arrival in the camp held out....We had been in camp perhaps an hour, when an order came directing that the company be divided into three parts, each under command of a lieutenant, and that these report immediately for duty. Reporting, we were directed to scout through the country around Martinsburg, going as near the town as possible, and to give battle to any cavalry force we might meet. Here was a pretty lookout, certainly! Our officers knew not one inch of the country, and might fall into all sorts of traps and ambuscades; and what if we should meet a cavalry force greatly superior to our own? This West Point colonel was rapidly forfeiting our good opinion. Our lieutenants were brave fellows, however, and they led us boldly if ignorantly, almost up to the very gates of the town occupied by the enemy. We saw some cavalry but met none, their orders not being so peremptorily belligerent, perhaps, as ours were; wherefore they gave us no chance to fight them. The next morning our unreasonable colonel again ordered us to mount, in spite of the fact that there were companies in the camp which had done nothing at all the day before. This time he led us himself, taking pains to get us as nearly as possible surrounded by infantry, and then laughingly telling us that our chance for getting out of the difficulty, except by cutting our way through, was an exceedingly small one. I think we began about this time to suspect that we were learning something, and that this reckless colonel was

Civil War: The Diaries of David Hunter Strother, ed. By Cecil D. Eby, Jr. (Chapel Hill, NC: The University of North Carolina Press, 1961), 103, hereafter Strother, *Diaries*.

[36] Robert J. Driver, Jr., *1st Virginia Cavalry* (Lynchburg, VA: H. E. Howard, Inc., 1991), hereafter cited as *1st*, 1-4: some militia units had been active for more than two years before the beginning of the Civil War. See also Thiele, 120-121. Harsh wrote that "On September 2, 1862, there was no army of either North or South to match the battle experience of the Army of Northern Virginia," Harsh, *Flood*, 39.

[37] Driver, *1st*, 3; Brennan, 12.

[38] Emory M. Thomas, *Bold Dragoon: The Life of J.E.B. Stuart* (New York: Harper & Row, 1986; reprint, New York: Random House, 1988), 71-73. Driver, *1st*, 7-8.

trying to teach us. But that he was a hare-brained fellow, lacking the caution belonging to a commander, we were unanimously agreed. He led us out of the place at a rapid gait, before the one gap in the enemy's lines could be closed, and then jauntily led us into one or two other traps, before taking us back to camp.

But it was not until General Patterson began his feint against Winchester that our colonel had full opportunity to give us his field lectures. When the advance began, and our pickets were driven in, the most natural thing to do, in our view of the situation, was to fall back upon our infantry supports at Winchester, and I remember hearing various expressions of doubt as to the colonel's sanity when, instead of falling back, he marched his handful of men right up to the advancing lines, and ordered us to dismount. The Federal skirmish line was coming toward us at a double-quick, and we were set going toward it at a like rate of speed, leaving our horses hundreds of yards to the rear. We could see that the skirmishers alone outnumbered us three or four times, and it really seemed that our colonel meant to sacrifice his command deliberately. He waited until the infantry was within about two hundred yards of us, we being in the edge of a little grove, and they on the other side of an open field. Then Stuart cried out, "Backwards — march! steady, men, — keep your faces to the enemy!" and we marched in that way through the timber, delivering our shot-gun fire slowly as we fell back toward our horses. Then mounting, with the skirmishers almost upon us, we retreated, not hurriedly, but at a slow trot, which the colonel would on no account permit us to change into a gallop. Taking us out into the main road he halted us in column, with our backs to the enemy.

"Attention!" he cried. "Now I want to talk to you, men. You are brave fellows, and patriotic ones too, but you are ignorant of this kind of work, and I am teaching you. I want you to observe that a good man on a good horse can never be caught. Another thing: cavalry can trot away from anything, and a gallop is a gait unbecoming a soldier, unless he is going toward the enemy. Remember that. We gallop toward the enemy, and trot away, always. Steady now! don't break ranks!"

And as the words left his lips a shell from a battery half a mile to the rear hissed over our heads. "There," he resumed. "I've been waiting for that, and watching those fellows. I knew they'd shoot too high, and I wanted you to learn how shells sound."

We spent the next day or two literally within the Federal lines. We were shelled, skirmished with, charged, and surrounded scores of times, until we learned to hold in high regard our colonel's masterly skill in getting into and out of perilous positions. He seemed to blunder into them in sheer recklessness, but in getting out he showed us the quality of his genius; and before we reached Manassas, we had learned, among other things, to entertain a feeling closely akin to worship for our brilliant and daring leader. We had begun to understand, too, how much force he meant to give to his favorite dictum that the cavalry is the eye of the army.[39]

Even the greenest of Stuart's troopers present during the Maryland Campaign, the 2nd South Carolina Cavalry, were as well trained and experienced as were many of Pleasonton's troopers. Overall however, Southern training was less precise and its troopers less disciplined than its Union counterparts, but the Rebel horseman made up for any deficiencies by his spirit, ability to ride well, and familiarity with firearms.[40] Confederate Lt. George Baylor of the 12th Virginia Cavalry, Baylor Light Horse, which operated in the Shenandoah Valley, wrote of his views comparing early war Rebel and Union troopers, horses, and arms:

No arms or equipments were furnished the company by the Confederate Government, the men owned their horses, and Uncle Sam very kindly and very soon provided us the very best pistols, sabers, saddles and bridles he had in stock. Everything but ourselves was branded U. S. For the carbine we had no liking and no use. Early in the conflict we recognized the fact that the Federal officer was our equal, and that our chief strength and superiority lay in our rank and file. If our opponents were fought at long range, the officers had the opportunity to bring to their aid discipline and authority over the actions and conduct of their men; when

---

[39] George Cary Eggleston, *A Rebel's Recollections* (New York: G.P. Putnam's Sons, 1897), 110-117.
[40] James A. Schaefer, "The Tactical and Strategic Evolution of Cavalry During the American Civil War," (PhD. diss., The University of Toledo, 1982), 53-54.

in close contact, they lost control, and their men, lacking individuality, became as sheep without a shepherd; while with us, every private was a general and needed no guidance or direction from his officer. In the camp and in the field the Confederate soldier was ruled by affection and example, and was treated as an equal. Especially was this the case in our company, where we bore the relation of brother, cousin, school-mate, neighbor, and friend.[41]

He also related a humorous account of his experience with his quartermaster when he needed a new pair of cavalry boots while giving insight into the perspective of the volunteer Rebel horseman:

During the spring and early summer of 1861, the men did not dream that they were to be paid anything for their services, or even that the government was to clothe them. They had bought their own uniforms, and whenever these wore out they ordered new ones to be sent, by the first opportunity, from home. I remember the very first time the thought of getting clothing from the government ever entered my own mind. I was serving in Stuart's cavalry, and the summer of 1861 was nearly over. My boots had worn out, and as there happened at the time to be a strict embargo upon all visiting on the part of non-military people, I could not get a new pair from home. The spurs of my comrades had made uncomfortable impressions upon my bare feet every day for a week, when someone suggested that I might possibly buy a pair of boots from the quartermaster, who was for the first time in possession of some government property of that description. When I returned with the boots and reported that the official had refused my proffered cash, contenting himself with charging the amount against me as a debit to be deducted from the amount of my pay and clothing allowance, there was great merriment in the camp. The idea that there was anybody back of us in this war—anybody who could, by any ingenuity of legal quibbling, be supposed to be indebted to us for our voluntary services in our own cause—was too ridiculous to be treated seriously.[42]

Combat experience under Stuart not only gave the 1st Virginia troopers valuable lessons but also showed them Stuart's abilities as a cavalry commander. Stuart made a point of drills and training when possible, even without actual combat, and instilled in his men and commanders esprit-de-corps early. He also impressed on them his bravery as he almost single handedly captured a company of Federal infantry on 2 July 1861 at Falling Waters, Virginia.[43] His performance at First Bull Run and after, was recognized, as he was made a brigadier general on 24 September 1861 in command of six cavalry regiments.[44] His veteran 1st Virginia troopers became the nucleus of some of the best cavalry fielded during the Civil War. One of its officers who would later win renown, Fitzhugh Lee, instructed new troopers in the 1st Virginia during the autumn of 1861. "Fitz's teaching experience at Carlisle Barracks and West Point served him so well that he quickly became known throughout the regiment as a master tutor."[45] His cousin, Lt. Col. William Henry Fitzhugh "Rooney" Lee of the 9th Virginia Cavalry, drilled his companies twice a day in early 1862 seeing that his new troopers were unused to drill and discipline.[46]

Also during this time, Stuart was choosing his staff and commanders who would serve him well in Maryland. Officers such as Col. Fitzhugh Lee would be one of his best commanders with Capt. John

---

[41] George Baylor, *Bull Run to Bull Run or Four Years in the Army of Northern Virginia* (Richmond, VA: B.F. Johnson Publishing Company, 1900), 38.

[42] Eggleston, 40-41.

[43] Thomas, 75.

[44] Ibid., 87-88. "Colonel Stuart drilled the regiment now regularly," Blackford, 48-49. See also Thiele, "Stuart was not averse to attending personally the minutia of training. His men were not, perhaps, good parade ground soldiers, but he saw to it that they knew their business," 141.

[45] Edward G. Longacre, *Fitz Lee: A Military Biography of Major General Fitzhugh Lee, C.S.A.* (Cambridge, MA: Da Capo Press, 2005), hereafter cited as *Fitz Lee*, 40. "Colonel Lee was a fine drill officer and drilled us all the time, and I learned more about it than I had ever done before," Blackford, 50.

[46] Daughtry, 60, 64, 86.

Pelham, the brilliant artillerist, leading the Stuart Horse Artillery. Pelham would earn the sobriquet of the "Gallant Pelham" from none other than Gen. Robert E. Lee. Stuart's staff included William Willis Blackford who would later pen an excellent memoir of service with Stuart, as would the famous Prussian, Maj. Heros von Borcke, Stuart's Chief of Staff. Stuart made an effort to include those men on his staff and as commanders those with whom he could work well, and who shared his active combat philosophy as well as a penchant for fun. The future bane of Union forces in Northern Virginia, John S. Mosby, was one of Stuart's early favorites. Mosby described his first commander in early 1861, Capt. William E. "Grumble" Jones, a West Point graduate, and his efforts to train his men: "Captain Jones had strict ideas of discipline, which he enforced, but he took good care of his horses as well as his men. There was a horse inspection every morning, and the man whose horse was not well groomed got a scolding mixed with some cursing by Captain Jones….He drilled his own company and also a company of cavalry from Marion, which had come to our camp to get the benefit of this instruction in cavalry tactics." Stuart's future nemesis, "Grumble" Jones, was an excellent veteran cavalry commander who began drilling his company in January 1861 when it was a militia company. It eventually became part of the 1ˢᵗ Virginia Cavalry under Col. Jeb Stuart.[47] Stuart continued his own training as a new brigadier by delegating supervision to his subordinates as he would do throughout his career.[48] This early combat experience he and his troopers enjoyed, combined with their constant employment as scouts, pickets and on reconnaissance, meant that they arrived on the Peninsula as veteran troopers, and their experience there added to their abilities.[49]

The horse artillery was the only part of the cavalry for which the Union roughly matched the Confederates during the Maryland Campaign. Confederate horse artillery, like its brother cavalry, was very well-trained and experienced, some having been part of militia units before the Civil War.[50] The Stuart Horse Artillery commander, Maj. John Pelham, was West Point trained, and had joined the Confederate army on 16 March 1861. While he had no prewar combat experience, he quickly began to develop his skills as he trained a regular battery near Winchester, Virginia. Based on his excellent service at First Bull Run, he was given command of a regular battery which was then assigned on 29 November 1861 to Stuart for service as horse artillery. The training he gave his battery bore fruit on the Peninsula

[47] Mosby, 12, 23, 30. Jones as well as other Confederate cavalry commanders such as Wade Hampton and Thomas Munford were not impressed with Stuart's showy manner as will be seen during Stuart's "Sabers and Roses" Ball in Urbana, Maryland, on 11 September 1862. Jones was not with Stuart during the Maryland Campaign; he may have been convalescing after being slightly wounded on 2 August 1862 at Orange Court House. He was admitted to Lynchburg General Hospital No. 1 on 30 August 1862, for an unstated reason and treated in private quarters, Armstrong, *7ᵗʰ Virginia Cavalry*, 172. Jones and Stuart clashed during Stuart's Second Ride Around McClellan in October 1862 so Gen. Lee sent Jones to command the Valley District. Jones resigned before Brandy Station but Lee convinced him to remain. Jones did well but again quarreled with Stuart in the fall after Gettysburg; Stuart had him arrested and Jones was convicted of disrespect. Lee sent him to serve in the Department of Southwest Virginia and East Tennessee where he did well. He served in other commands and was killed in combat in June 1864 near Piedmont, Virginia.

[48] Thomas, 90-91, 97; Blackford, 17.

[49] Out of the 18 individual Confederate cavalry and horse artillery units which fought in Maryland, 13 (72 percent) were from Virginia as opposed to about 25 percent of infantry units; it is therefore likely that they were more closely knit than their sister infantry units as well as being as experienced in combat. All the Virginia cavalry units had been in existence from very early in the war and had fought in most of the battles leading up to the Maryland Campaign, Harsh, *Shallows*, 87, 103. Pleasonton's division contained no fighting regiments which had fought with Pope at Second Bull Run, Edward J. Stackpole, *From Cedar Mountain to Antietam* (Harrisburg, PA: Stackpole Books, 1993), 306, but as listed above in note 30, a few cavalry units which were under Pope's command did serve under Pleasonton in Maryland but as escorts or on detached duty.

[50] Robert J. Trout, *Galloping Thunder: The Story of the Stuart Horse Artillery Battalion*, Mechanicsburg, PA: Stackpole Books, 2002), hereafter cited as *Thunder*, "[these] were the premier batteries, simply because they saw more hard service and performed more consistently high level as horse artillery than the other batteries," 7.

as it performed well garnering Stuart's praise and resulted in his appointment as the commander of Stuart's three horse artillery batteries.[51]

The Confederate "Ashby" Battery of horse artillery was the first horse artillery battery organized for the Confederates in the Civil War, having been formed on 11 November 1861, under Capt. Roger P. Chew. He was known as one of the best artillery officers in the Army of Northern Virginia. Although his battery did not join Stuart until August 1862, it had previously performed well with Turner Ashby in the Shenandoah Valley.[52] Chew, along with Ashby, inadvertently set a precedent for the horse artillery by having it accompany the cavalry in a charge, helping rout Union cavalry.[53] James F. Hart's South Carolina battery was also a veteran unit, while not as renowned or as experienced as its brother horse artillery units. It had recently converted from a mounted artillery unit in the Hampton Legion to horse artillery, bringing with it two, six pounder and four, twelve pounder howitzers.[54] Stuart always ensured that his horse artillery had the pick of captured artillery. His batteries tended to employ larger guns but when the sizes of teams decreased from six to four animals, the ability of the horse artillery to keep up with the cavalry diminished, thus the tradeoff between firepower and mobility was marked.[55] But the quality of southern-made ammunition and fuses denigrated the ability of the horse artillery even when its fire was well-aimed. Confederate-made powder was sometimes of poorer quality than that used by Union artillery, but Confederate fuses were notoriously poor. The historian of the Confederate horse artillery, Robert J. Trout, wrote that "the Confederate horse artillery was plagued with inferior ammunition....when any advantage was gained through position or number of guns, it frequently was negated by the poor quality of the Confederate-manufactured ammunition, which exploded too early, too late, or not at all. Captured ammunition helped overcome this to some extent but never enough to alter the situation significantly."[56]

---

[51] Trout, *Plume*, 205-208. While Pelham was administratively in charge of Stuart's Horse Artillery in Maryland, each battery was attached to one cavalry brigade: Pelham's eight guns served with Brig. Gen. Fitzhugh Lee's Brigade, Capt. Roger P. Chew's Battery served with Robertson's Brigade which was commanded by Col. Thomas Munford, and Capt. James F. Hart's Battery was assigned to Brig. Gen. Wade Hampton's Brigade, Harsh, *Shallows*, 88-90.

[52] Trout, *Thunder*, 79.

[53] Jennings Cropper Wise, *The Long Arm of Lee or The History of the Artillery of the Army of Northern Virginia*, vol. 1 (Lynchburg, VA: J.P. Bell Company., 1915 ; reprint, Lincoln, NE: University of Nebraska Press, 1991), 166-167.

[54] Longacre, *Lee's*, 127.

[55] At the Battle of Antietam on 17 September, only Pelham's Battery was engaged with four, three inch ordnance rifles; one, twelve pound Napoleon; and one Blakely. It had abandoned two howitzers for Ordnance rifles captured on 27 August 1862 at Manassas Junction. Hart's Battery had four, twelve pound Blakeley guns and Chew's Battery had two or three, three inch Ordnance rifles, one Blakely Rifle and one, twelve pound smoothbore howitzer, letter to Carman from Sterling Murray, 23 June 1897, copy courtesy Thomas Clemens; Curt Johnson and Richard C. Anderson, Jr., *Artillery Hell: The Employment of Artillery at Antietam* (College Station, TX: Texas A&M University Press, 1995), 100-101. Union horse artillery, 2nd U.S. Battery A, had six, twelve pound smooth bore Napoleons; 2nd U.S. Batteries B and L had four, twelve pound smooth bore Napoleons; and Battery M of the 2nd had six, three inch Ordnance rifles. Batteries C and G of the 3rd U.S. Artillery had six, three inch Ordnance rifles, Johnson and Anderson, *Artillery Hell*, 35. The heterogeneity of Chew's Battery reflects the problems with the mixed guns in Lee's batteries at Antietam: of 59 of those batteries only 5 had uniform armament, Johnson and Anderson, *Artillery Hell*, 5. Compare the Union horse artillery batteries with each having uniform types of guns. Supplying ammunition for a variety of guns in one unit was usually problematical.

[56] Trout, *Thunder*, 8. Philip Katcher, *American Civil War Artillery 1861-1865, Field and Heavy Artillery* (Oxford, UK: Osprey Publishing Ltd, 2001), 17-19, 85-86; "Southern-made ammunition was universally condemned," 85. See also Edward Porter Alexander, *Fighting for the Confederacy: The Personal Recollections of General Edward Porter Alexander*, ed. by Gary W. Gallagher (Chapel Hill, NC: The University of North Carolina Press, 1989), "The captured Federal guns, & artillery ammunition too, were much superior to most of ours," 122; "We were always liable to premature explosion of shell & Shrapnel, & our infantry knew it by sad experience, & I have known of their threatening to fire back at our guns if we opened over their heads," 248. Federal ammunition also had problems but not to the extent of its foes, L. VanLoan Naisawald, *Grape and Canister: The Story of the Army of the Potomac, 1861-1865* (n.p.: Oxford University Press, 1960; reprint, Gaithersburg, MD: Olde Soldier Books, Inc., n.d.), "The Yankee gunners blamed part of their failure on their ammunition. No less than twelve Yankee battery

Union horse artillery was also well-trained since all of the Union horse artillery existed before the Civil War as regular batteries of the 2nd and 3rd U.S. Artillery. The conversion to horse artillery involved adding additional horses so that all of the cannon crew could ride a horse or on the caissons, and using smaller-sized artillery pieces, such as the 3.1 inch Blakely gun, or small howitzers. Even though Union artillery may have been superior "in organization, drill, discipline, material, and equipment," the exceptional courage and skill of many artillery commanders among its Confederate foes made Southern artillery more than an even match on many occasions.[57]

Battery A, 2nd U.S. Artillery, was the first to reach Washington, D. C., arriving in January 1861. It was a part of the expedition for the relief of Fort Pickens, Florida, in April, but returned in time to take part in the Battle of First Bull Run. In September 1861, it was made a horse battery, the first in the United States Army in the Civil War. In the spring of 1862, it went to the Peninsula forming, with Batteries B, L, and M of the 2nd, and Battery C of the 3rd U.S. Artillery, the famous Horse Artillery Brigade. Battery B of the 2nd U.S. was earlier consolidated with Battery L, and early in 1862 was converted to a "horse battery" before going with McClellan to the Peninsula. It was in the siege of Yorktown and was involved in several other battles including Williamsburg, New Bridge, Mechanicsville, Gaines's Mill, and Malvern Hill.[58] The 2nd U. S. Artillery Battery G, reached Washington in May 1861, and was made a light battery also taking part in the Battle of First Bull Run. In the Peninsular Campaign, it was attached to the Third Corps, and was in the battles of Glendale and Malvern Hill. In the Maryland Campaign, it was not actively engaged.

Thus the Union horse artillery and its Confederate foes were composed of veteran units, well-trained, and well-led. The substantive differences between them were the higher quality of Union ammunition, especially fuses, while the Confederate artillery was arguably better in the quality of its leadership and combat experience. Union battery leadership while experienced and solid, was not a

---

commanders complained bitterly over one type of shell or another exploding prematurely, failing to take the rifling, or failing to detonate. That the complaints were not uniform as to the type for make of shell or fuze is significant," 243; Trout, *Thunder*, 8.

[57] Wise, 326. See also John Gibbon, *Artillerist's Manual*, Second Edition (n.p.: 1863: reprint, n.p., n.d.), "In horse-artillery, the cannoneers, of which there are eleven to each piece, are mounted on horses, from which they have to dismount before attending on the piece, the two extra men holding the horses of the rest....The horse-artillery was originally and is still designed for service with the cavalry, receiving the lightest guns, which enable it to move at the same rate as the cavalry, and to keep it up for a considerable time," 214.

[58] "Crossed Sabers," Blog of Donald Caughey, Battery M, 2nd US Artillery, 29 September 29, 2008; "History of the 2nd U.S. Artillery," Lt. W. A. Simpson, Adjutant 2D U.S. Artillery, The Second Regiment of Artillery, U.S. Army Center of Military History, internet: http://www.history.army.mil/books/R&H/R&H-2Art.htm. Note that during the Mexican-American War Maj. Samuel B. Ringgold devised a new use for light field artillery: "a young artillery major named Sam Ringgold created a system of direct fire support to the infantry using the light 6-pounder gun. Key to Ringgold's aggressive use of the light gun was speed which earned it the nickname 'Ringgold's Flying Artillery.' Not only could this piece move around the battlefield quickly, but the small crew needed to fire the gun and high rate of fire made it the ideal weapon to support maneuver troops. Because Ringgold's light artillery could adapt to the changing battle, it could be placed amongst the infantry and cavalry. This was a first. Major Ringgold worked hard to prove to superiors that his new artillery tactic would be successful. However, not until the "Flying Artillery" proved itself in battle did he succeed," Jameson Riley Johnson, *Modern Artilleryman*, "The Birth Of Modern Artillery In The 1846-48 War Against Mexico," Winter 1998, vol. 20, no. 1. Samuel B. Ringgold (1796 – May 11, 1846) was an artillery officer who was called the "Father of Modern Artillery." He was among the first U.S. officers to die in the Mexican-American War from wounds received at the Battle of Palo Alto. An Act of Congress, 2 March 1821, reorganized the U.S. Army. It provided "that in each regiment of artillery, one company should be designated and equipped as light artillery. In 1838 the initiatory steps were taken to carry this provision into effect. Brvt. Major Samuel Ringgold, captain 3d Artillery, was selected by Secretary Poinsett for this work. Hitherto the great objection to carrying the law into execution was the attendant expense. But now a number of horses rendered surplus, after some of the southern Indians had been removed, were available for the purpose of mounting C company as horse artillery in which rôle it served until after the Mexican War. Companies of the other artillery regiments were also soon afterwards mounted, but as field artillery," The Third Regiment of Artillery, U.S. Army Center of Military History, internet: http://www.history.army.mil/books/R&H/R&H-3Art.htm

match for the gallant and often spectacular Confederate commanders such as Pelham and Chew. Union batteries may also have had the advantage of extra horses to employ to more quickly maneuver their cannon. But as will be seen, Confederate horse artillery during the Maryland Campaign was more active than its Union foes making substantial contributions not only to Stuart's cavalry but also to sister infantry units on 17 September, at the north end of the Antietam battlefield. Pleasonton's artillery was also involved on the ridges east of the Middle Bridge but in primarily counter battery fire.[59]

The Union did have a marked advantage in cavalry weaponry, especially in carbines. The Model 1859 Sharps Breechloading Carbine, among others, gave a noticeable advantage in firepower to troopers which could not be matched by their Southern counterparts. The 5th and 6th U.S. Cavalry, the 3rd, 4th, 6th, and 8th Pennsylvania, and the 8th Illinois, had Sharps Carbines; the 3rd Indiana had Gallagher carbines; the 1st Massachusetts had Sharps and Smith carbines; the 1st New York had Gallagher and Burnside carbines; and the 8th New York had Sharps carbines after a first issue of the old Hall carbine.[60] Because of the great difficulty in loading while mounted, breech-loading carbines with their firepower and range were much preferred over pistols, shotguns, and sabers usually used by Southern troopers. The firepower of the carbines proved to be especially important when cavalry units fought dismounted. Confederates who were battling dismounted cavalry sometimes thought that because of the volume of fire, they were actually fighting Union infantry. Confederate cavalry early in the war had mainly pistols and shotguns with few carbines and rifles. As battlefield captures increased, units became better armed with carbines.[61] "Southern troops did rather well in equipping themselves with Union types of arms, ammunition, and equipment of all sorts....In fact, battlefield salvage was quite well organized and paid tremendous dividends. However, muzzle-loading carbines predominated in the Confederate cavalry units, and double-barreled shotguns were quite popular."[62] The arms of early Confederate cavalry units were decidedly mixed as reported by Col. Jubal A. Early on 8 June 1861 from Lynchburg, Virginia:

---

[59] See Harsh, *Shallows*, in which he analyzes experience of Confederate infantry showing that over 80 percent had been in two or more major battles. Harsh did not quantify cavalry experience but it is likely to be at least comparable, 102-103. Johnson in *Artillery Hell* holds that "The Federal Army of the Potomac was armed with guns that were entirely modern and equivalent to the best material in service in the in the world....By contrast, the Army of Northern Virginia fielded a large number of Mexican War-vintage M-1841 6-lb. guns, reliable and efficient pieces but sorely inferior in both hitting power and range to the more modern weapons of their opponents. Whenever possible, these antique pieces were replaced by captured or imported guns." The Rebels' capture of some 30 Union guns at Second Bull Run was a help as the Confederate artillery reorganized after that battle leaving weakened batteries and horses behind, 6.

[60] Frederick P. Todd, *American Military Equipage, 1851-1872, Volume. II, State Forces* (published privately by M.P. Todd/Damerel, 1983), hereafter cited as *State*, Pennsylvania units, 1137; Illinois, 765; Indiana, 784; Massachusetts, 906; New York, 1044. During the Maryland Campaign, all of these units had pistols, mainly Colt army revolvers and sabers in addition to long arms except for the Third Indiana which had no pistols. Note that most companies of the 6th Pennsylvania, Rush's Lancers, had lances until 1863 along with revolvers; twelve Sharps carbines were issued per company. For U.S. units, Frederick P. Todd, *American Military Equipage, 1851-1872, Part I: The United States Army* (New York: Charles Scribner's Sons, 1980), 372. The regimental historian of the 6th New York Cavalry wrote that it was issued carbines on 6 September 1862, in Washington, DC, Hillman A. Hall, Chairman, *History of the Sixth New York Cavalry (Second Ira Harris Guard)* (Worcester, MA: The Blanchard Press, 1908, reprint, Salem, MA: Higginson Book Company, n.d.), 53.

[61] Todd, *State*, Virginia, 1269-1270, 1272-1273; North Carolina, 1070; South Carolina, 1179; Georgia, 742; Mississippi, Jeff Davis Legion, 940. Cobb's Georgia Legion probably had the Maynard rifle. Confederate troopers very early in the war were generally poorly armed despite desperate efforts by the Confederate and state governments, until battlefield captures had an effect, Thiele, 146-151. See Robert J. Driver, *5th Virginia Cavalry* (Lynchburg, VA: H.E. Howard, 1997), showing in early 1862, one company of some seventy total men and officers had five pistols, fifty-two revolvers, 20 flint lock pistols, 20 sabers, and fifty-eight double barrel guns, 10.

[62] Berkeley R. Lewis, *Notes on Cavalry Weapons of the American Civil War 1861-1865* (Washington, DC: The American Ordnance Association, 1961), 15-17.

There is no company of cavalry here fully armed. Two companies have double-barreled shot-guns, bought by their counties, but no sabers, and are but beginning to drill. There are two companies tolerably well drilled, with forty or fifty sabers each. One has no guns and the other a few. There are two other companies, one of which has about forty sabers and a few guns, just commencing to drill. There are about a hundred flint-lock pistols, which have been gathered from old companies. A number of sabers, of old patterns, have also been collected. All the companies want cartridge–boxes and cap-boxes....All the companies here are well mounted, and would make fine companies if there were arms for them.[63]

As with long arms, the Union's advantage in manufacturing and supply meant that its cavalry almost always had plentiful firearms, sabers and equipment, although very early in the war the supply was sometimes lacking. This same material advantage applied to its horse artillery, which became a serious contender to its rivals on the field earlier than the rest of the cavalry. Thus the Union cavalry as well as its horse artillery profited from the immense Northern industrial and transportation capabilities to usually appear on the field better armed and equipped.[64]

Another of the reasons the Confederate cavalry was often better than its foe during the first half of the Civil War and during the Maryland Campaign, was the quality of mounts most southern troopers brought to the field. Since the most fundamental requirement for an effective cavalry trooper was a good mount, early in the war Southern troopers had the advantage. The Confederates had by far the better horses due to the expedient Confederate government policy requiring its cavalrymen to supply their own mounts. The government reimbursed troopers a set rate, 40 cents a day for most of the war, for their service. The major benefit of this policy was that horses were quickly available for the Southern cavalry. Given the enormous difficulties the Union underwent in supplying horses despite its superior transportation base and funding, the Confederacy probably had no better options because of the poor state of its railroads and paucity of readily available monies.[65] But not everyone agreed that the Southern horse supply method worked well, even early in the war. A Virginia cavalryman, Allen C. Redwood, wrote after the war that this "theory...did not work out in practice. The careful horseman, taking an interest in keeping his charge in good condition, was apt to be sometimes *too* regardful when the needs of the service demanded that he should not spare his steed, while on the other hand the temptation of a furlough—'horse details' we called them—led many to purposely neglect the proper care of their horses (emphasis in original)."[66]

---

[63] *OR*, vol. 2, 913.

[64] H.V. Redfield, "Characteristics of the Armies," *Annals of the War*, "But it was in cavalry equipment that the Federal soldier stood out pre-eminently superior...Much of the Southern cavalry was ridiculously equipped," 361. Even though the author was describing the Western Theater, Confederate cavalry in the east suffered similar problems as Confederate troopers in all theaters sought Union equipment, horses, and arms at every opportunity. The author does note that in his experience although the Union had better fed horses, equipment and arms, the "Southerners were altogether the best riders....the Southern cavalry was no doubt superior....[G]radually [Union] skill in horsemanship equaled their equipment, and then the Union cavalry became of extraordinary efficiency," 368. Interestingly, Thiele suggests that in one area, horseshoes, Confederate horses may have benefited by the Southern experience with horses: "Southern Cavalrymen were more adept at caring for and shoeing their animals than their counterparts in the Federal service. Horseshoes, while not plentiful, were not a rare item in the South, and the Government works at Augusta manufactured some 1,400 shoes with nails per day for several months," 226.

[65] Thiele: "This system [self-supply of horses by troopers] ...permitted the South to put a well mounted Cavalry in the field almost at once. Furthermore, since the horses belonged to the men, they were much more likely to get better care than the Federals gave their Government issue animals," 214.

[66] Allen C. Redwood, "The Horseman in Gray," in *Civil War Times Illustrated*, vol. IX, no. 3, June 1970, 6; from *Journal of the Military Service Institution*, vol. XLIX. He also believed that "Probably no nation ever went to war richer in its cavalry raw material; the cavalry was already a species of *corps d'elete*. Some of the best animal strains of the Virginia and Kentucky stables were used, and the riders have been aptly described as 'daredevils, born jockeys, and natural dead-shots,'" 5. Pvt. Joseph Dunbar Shields, Jr. of the Jeff Davis Legion wrote in a letter dated 2 June 1862 commenting on his company's care of its horses: "We have seen some pretty hard times since the battle of Williamsburg but I don't see that it has hurt any of us. The men seem to

Confederate horses were generally of high quality, many "blooded," and were able to perform much better than their Union counterparts.[67] Many areas in Southern or border states like Virginia and Kentucky were known for the quality of their horseflesh, so availability of above-average animals was better than in the North, either through voluntary donations, sales, impressments, or theft. Southern horses were described as a "fusion of English thoroughbreds with local stock [producing] progenitors of the Quarter Horse and Saddlebred; most horses used in the war were of heterogeneous blend."[68] One writer stated that "the best type of cavalry mount was the Saddle bred, formerly known as the Kentucky Horse, of which the Confederates had the greater proportion…[it was] 'very valuable for cavalry service because of other reasons than merely his superior powers of endurance. His smoother action and easier gaits render a march less fatiguing to the rider; he succumbs less readily to privations and exposure, and responds more cheerfully to kind and careful treatment. He acquires more promptly and perfectly the drills and habits of the camp and march, and his intelligence and courage make him more reliable on the field.'"[69]

The planter class and other well-to-do southerners prided themselves on the abilities of their equine servants "and the affection the men had for their animals was genuine. Coupled with an underlying responsibility to protect the family investment, the troopers paid special attention to the welfare of their charges, making the overall health of the Confederate horse far superior to that of their opponents."[70] Early southern cavalry volunteers usually were able to choose the best animal for their military adventures and made it a matter of personal or family pride to ride a superior mount. The quality of these horses also meant that they were healthy and fit for service for the most part although some were perhaps a bit too delicate for long, arduous duty. So even though many horses were imported into the South from Northern suppliers, Southern breeders and owners made sure that the stock they received was in prime condition.[71]

An argument can also be made that the South's tobacco growing culture encouraged the development of well-bred riding horses to help supervise the large plantations. Working horses could not be used to cultivate tobacco as the plant was delicate so had to be worked by hand, therefore saddle horses were more useful to plantation owners. One expert on the history of horses in the United States wrote that "the Cavalier character; the general intention to found great estates and live on them as superiors and supervisors; the promotion of this notion by access to a supply of labor incredibly cheap— once the initial investment was made; the nature of the crop and the soil" made the Southern saddle horses superior and more important to the southern economy than working horses.[72]

---

keep very good spirits, They make more fuss about food for their horses than anything else," Elizabeth Dunbar Murray, *My Mother Used to Say: A Natchez Belle of the Sixties* (Boston, MA: The Christopher Publishing House, 1959), 128.

[67] Wise, 331-332. But see Holmes Conrad, "The Cavalry Corps of the Army of Northern Virginia," in *Photographic History of the Civil War*, volume four, ed. by Theo. F. Rodenbough (New York, NY: The Review of Reviews Co. 1911), that some blooded horses were too nervous for military duty: "Blooded horses proved unfit for the service; they fretted and exhausted themselves on a quiet march, and proved to be unmanageable in field engagements," 84.

[68] David J. Gerleman, "War Horse! Union Cavalry Mounts, 1861-1865," *North & South*, 2, no. 2, January 1999, 48-49.

[69] J.M. Brereton, *The Horse in War* (New York: Arco Publishing Company, Inc., 1976), 104. Confederate Col. Basil Duke supplied the quotation.

[70] Brennan, 13.

[71] Gerleman, "Abundant breeding of horses in the North resulted in large herds being taken South regularly for sale in the years prior to the war," 48. E.H. Derby wrote in the *Atlantic Monthly* after Stuart's Second Ride Around McClellan that "Thus far in the contest the South has possessed one great advantage. The planter's son, reared to no profession, in a region where the pursuits of trade and the mechanic arts have little honor, has been accustomed from childhood to the use of the horse and rifle," E.H. Derby, "Resources of the South," *Atlantic Monthly*, Oct. 1862, 506.

[72] Philip D. Strong, *Horses and Americans* (Garden City, NY: Garden City Publishing Co., Inc., 1939), 22-23.

This southern usage of horses combined with the northern usage of horses more as draft animals gave the South an advantage:

> The first months of the war showed that there had been a recession of Northern horses prior to the secession of Southern men. The cotton planters and tobacco raisers had turned to mules as animals of utility, and for travel and sport they were raising many more fine horses, Thoroughbreds, than their neighbors to the north....A great part of the Northern power now lay in what had been, within a generation, the "frontier" states, and these were breeding horses for the plow and the wagon....The South...was able to assemble almost at once an excellent cavalry force of runners, trotters, hunters, all far more accustomed to the saddle than the traces. The Northerners for the most part simply took the horse most nearly resembling a saddler out of the tugs or shafts and rode off to war....These slow, heavy, comfortable and peaceful farm-horses had little chance against saddlers trained to the pressure of a knee or the drop of a rein since colthood and bred for speed and flexibility....After (the first year of the war) the replacement facilities of the North tended to equalize things.[73]

Another writer however, wrote that some of the Northern horses made worthwhile cavalry horses:

> There were good horses in the North, too, but those with the best bloodlines were trotters and other harness horses....Good riding horses were still to be found in parts of the North. In New England and New York there were Morgans, descendant of that powerful little stallion, Justin Morgan, and they would turn out to be first-rate cavalry mounts. In some northern states and in Canada, too, were herds of hardy animals, short-legged, with long manes and tails, and of great endurance.[74]

There are many exploits recorded of the fine mounts Confederates rode and the ease with which they generally outdistanced their Federal pursuers. Stuart's famous close escapes hail them as due to his superior mounts as well as his skills in handling them.[75] "He chose the best mounts he could find. Most of them were bays with black points, animals of the hunter type with distinguished bloodlines."[76] Superior mounts would not be as important if Southerners could not ride them well, utilizing the horses' abilities to their utmost. Stuart and most of his staff and officers were at least very good riders but mostly excellent, and proud of their skills so when one of their coterie was less than very good or made an error while mounted, merry comments ensued.

Since the horse was owned by the trooper, he was almost certain to supply it with correct and ample fodder whenever possible, and to groom and care for it as well as he could under the circumstances. Care and feeding proved critical when requiring a mount to perform at its best for long periods of time. Knowing the horse's quirks, abilities, and limitations, also ensured that the animal was not unconsciously pushed beyond its abilities. Because they were better cared for, they were capable of

---

[73] Ibid., 224-225.

[74] Fairfax Downey, *Famous Horses of the Civil War* (New York: Thomas Nelson & Sons, 1959), 13, 14.

[75] McClellan, *Stuart*, 230-231; "Splendidly mounted on his favorite mare Virginia, Stuart took the ditch at a running leap, and landed safely on the other side with several feet to spare," 328. See also Anon., "Generals in the Saddle" in *Southern Historical Society Papers*, vol. 19, January 1891 (Richmond: Southern Historical Society, n.d., reprint, Millwood, NJ: Kraus Reprint Co, 1977), citing Stuart as a "grand horseman.... No man could ride better or faster than Stuart. He carried a careless rein, gripping the saddle with a knee clasp, which prevented his being unseated," 173. Wade Hampton was also stated to be "a splendid figure in the saddle, which he sat while on the gallop with rare ease, scarcely a swing being noticeable, despite the rapid pace," 171. Stuart's escape from the Federal cavalry was described by Downey: "once General Stuart and several of his staff officers, resting at a farmhouse, were surprised by Yankee cavalry....The staffers mounted and escaped by a gate, but the Blue cavalrymen, yelling and shooting, cut Jeb off from it. He ran to Skylark, grazing unbridled, and vaulted into the saddle. A rider like Stuart needed no reins. He put the charger at the fence. They soared over it in a beautiful leap, and were off at a thundering gallop..." 38-40.

[76] Downey, 37.

better performance than their Union equine counterparts. Since their Confederate owners knew their horses' capabilities and idiosyncrasies, there were fewer surprises in combat. As in other areas such as weapons and equipment, captured Union horses later in the war were important for Confederate troopers as the Southern supply of horseflesh rapidly diminished. Southern troopers quickly replaced their civilian saddles and equipment for McClellan saddles helpfully supplied in ample numbers by their foes.[77]

One Confederate trooper who joined the Old Dominion Dragoons in May 1861, wrote about his preparations for his service in his memoirs: "Preparations for leaving home and severing home ties, the selection of my mount, and the body servant that my mother was to give me were topics of much discussion. My mother was desirous that I be properly equipped and had given me a fine thoroughbred mare named Corral. She was the finest of our stables and was endowed with almost human intelligence."[78]

This self-supplying of horses although an early benefit to Confederate cavalry in the first two years of the war, gradually became a severe liability for several reasons. Since troopers had to furnish their own remounts, they often returned home for the allowed 30 days to do so. Many times troopers spent much more than a month securing new mounts. Not only due to a desire for some rest, the inability to find good horses due to Union occupation of some Southern states, combined with incursions which swept up available horses, meant that it was much harder to find suitable replacements. Later in the war, scarce horses cost as much as $2,500 or more, far beyond what most Southern troopers could afford. As the war continued, Confederate troopers began to rely more on captures of Union horses. This method of resupply was also partly due to Confederate government policy only to pay troopers for loss of their horses if disabled or killed in battle, the value determined when the horse was mustered in. Thus rampant inflation eroded its value if it survived many months; since most horses did not die in battle, the Confederate owner of a non-heroic steed got nothing. Rebel cavalry units habitually operated at far less than authorized strengths because of chronic absenteeism due to men seeking remounts, or being absent purportedly seeking remounts. Since men who could not find new horses were assigned to non-cavalry units, many chose not to return, especially later in the war. Discipline in the Confederate cavalry was arguably much more lax than in its infantry, also contributing to large numbers of troopers absent.[79] Col. Munford, after the war, nicely summarized the Confederate method of horse supply:

[77] Josiah Gorgas, "Notes on the Ordnance Department of the Confederate Government," *Southern Historical Society Papers*, vol. 12, January to December 1894 (Richmond, VA: Southern Historical Society, n.d. Reprint, Millwood, NJ: Kraus Reprint Co, 1977), 78-79. He discusses the McClellan tree versus the Jenifer tree which was good until the horses became thin; southern copies of the McClellan saddle were better but the best was a Federal saddle. He also discusses the horseshoe supply which he said was problematical due to both the lack of iron and labor. But compare Thiele above.

[78] Robert S. Hudgins II, *Recollections of an Old Dominion Dragoon: The Civil War Experiences of Sgt. Robert S. Hudgins II, Company B, 3rd Virginia Cavalry*, ed. by Garland C. Hudgins and Richard B. Kleese (Orange, VA: Publisher's Press, Inc., 1993), 19.

[79] Brennan, 13. Starr, "the hallmark, of Confederate cavalry was its lack of discipline....nowhere in the Union army was it carried to such outlandish extremes as among the Confederate mounted troops," 222. See also Thiele, "If the [Confederate trooper's] horse were captured by the enemy, worn out, or disabled, the loss fell upon the owner who was then required to procure another mount or be transferred to another arm of the service," 214. Thiele also finds that Confederate cavalrymen in "Company Q" awaiting remounts sometimes were not in any hurry to return to the fray, 217. The decline in the availability of horses to its cavalry may have been the major contribution to its decline in the last half of the war: "Perhaps no single factor in the decline of Southern mounted superiority was as evident as the deterioration in the supply and quality of animals. While the Federals found a partial solution to the same problems in a Cavalry Bureau and in Governmental supervision of supply, the Confederacy was unable even to approximate a solution, and it suffered accordingly," 227. A trooper of the 12th Virginia Cavalry was a good example of a cavalryman returning home to secure another mount; he missed the action at Antietam on 17 and 18 September "as I had gotten a permit to go to the Valley of Virginia to get a fresh horse. When I rejoined my company, the battle was over," *George William Watson The Last Survivor: The Memoirs of George William Watson, A Horse Soldier in the 12th*

A soldier can cheerfully submit to personal privations and toil…but a horse loses spirit and strength, and the more spirit he has the worse it is for him as soon as his rations are cut down and double duty imposed upon him. We could get grass sometimes, when corn could not be had, and when in camp they could live; but the finest horse in the best physical condition, casting a shoe on a rough, rocky road and forced rapidly over it, will be rendered wholly unfit for service in half a day….They were expected to move promptly and quickly, the loss of a shoe was not taken as a valid excuse when dispatch was demanded….The service was too precarious to admit of wagons…so that with the best management, it often happened neither shoes, nails or smith could be had. I have seen my men many a time have the hoof of a dead horse strapped to their saddles, which they had cut off at the ankle with their pocket-knives, and would carry them until they could find a smith to take it off with his nippers….In the Valley the roads were McAdamized, and exceedingly hard on the horse's feet. One horse, however well managed, could not perform the duty required of a cavalryman. It took many horses for each man….When the war commenced it was an easy matter to secure a horse, but the demand increased so rapidly and the number decreased at a so much greater ratio that at last it would cost five year's pay in Confederate money to purchase a good cavalry horse. The Government only agreed to pay for horses killed in battle, and it would take weeks and sometimes months to get the money after all the papers had gone through the 'tape of office in Richmond.' Many a cavalryman mortgaged his property to supply himself with horses….The Government…could not send the men and horses back to their homes when necessary to exchange their *jaded ones* for fresh horses; neither would it pay the extra expense he incurred to accomplish this object.

[Men on leave to obtain fresh horses] kept an average at least one-third of a regiment on the road to and from home to remount. One-third of a regiment would generally be sick and wounded. In a fight (dismounted) it took one-fourth of the men to hold the horses of the dismounted men, and when we were far from our camps or wagons, about one-eighth of the men would be detailed to secure food for the horses and rations for the men.[80]

Trooper Hudgins described his ordeal with his horses later in the war: "During August of 1863, I had terrible luck with my horses. I lost my favorite mount, Corral, and another that same month, which placed me in the dismounted cavalry. I always hated walking and determined to get another horse as soon as possible. I secured a sixty-day furlough to go to 'Olden Place' in Dinwiddie County, where I felt confident I could get a new mount. Word had been passed to me to get there before the Yankees….Upon reaching Dinwiddie, I…succeeded in purchasing a mount, though of far inferior quality when compared to Corral and the horses I had been used to."[81]

The glamour and prestige of serving in the cavalry led to a larger percentage of southern wealthy men, and men from wealthy families, joining the mounted branch, than either the artillery or infantry. Almost 30 percent of the Confederate cavalry overall had personal and family wealth of over $10,000, the highest by far among the three branches (artillery, 18 percent, infantry, 19 percent). Similarly, almost 53% of cavalry men owned slaves, slightly higher than artillery men, 52 percent, and infantry 41

Virginia Cavalry (Confederate States Army), ed. Brian Stuart Kesterson (Washington, WV: Night Hawk Press, 1993), 19. Glatthaar found that almost one in every 11 troopers was absent without leave and about one in five deserted at least once during his enlistment, *Joseph T. Glatthaar, Soldiering in the Army of Northern Virginia: A Statistical Portrait of the Troops Who Served Under Robert E. Lee. NC: Chapel Hill, The University of North Carolina Press, 2011,* 39.

[80] Thomas T. Munford, "Reminiscences of Cavalry Operations," *SHSP*, vol. 12, 346-347. Applying Munford's arithmetic, two-thirds of an average Confederate cavalry regiment of some 800 sabers, 528, are missing before a battle starts. Of the 272 remaining, one-eighth of those are foraging leaving 238 available for battle, and only three-quarters of those, 179, are wielding sabers. For much of the war for most of the cavalry regiments, this number appears too small. If his estimation is computed using the remainders after each calculation and reversing the sequence of calculation for foragers and horse holders, then the number available holding sabers is about 230 which is more reasonable given available data for a veteran cavalry regiment. For Munford in Maryland, he had about that average number for each of his regiments. {[(800 x .66) x .66] x .88} x .75 = 230.

[81] Hudgins, 87.

percent. Not only did this mean that cavalry men likely brought better quality mounts to the service, but could more easily replace them, either by purchase, or by returning home to exchange or replace the horse from one's family or friends. As the members of the cavalry were also wealthier, this meant that it was more likely that they owned slaves thus making them more motivated toward joining and remaining in the service, but also having personal slaves to help maintain the troopers' horses. And arguably the horsemen were more motivated to fight for their new country and its slave-based society and economy, as they had more to lose. The men from upper classes in the south or who were otherwise wealthy, likely owned slaves and had more patriotic motivations than less wealthy soldiers as "members of planter families and of slaveholding professional families—voiced patriotic sentiments a almost twice the rate of nonslaveholding soldiers."[82] Wealthy and highly motivated Confederate troopers, both officers and enlisted, contributed greatly to the prestige and performance of the southern cavalry.

In Maryland, Gen. Lee, and certainly his cavalry, hoped to take advantage of the abundance of horses there to resupply their needs after months of strenuous campaigning. "The country is enormously rich. It abounds in fat cattle, cereals, horses, and mules."[83] Everyone believed that the state was rich in horses as well as food and fodder needed for Lee's cavalry and horses. Since the area into which they were marching was largely untouched by war, Lee and his men must have expected that the abundance there would be available for appropriation. Frederick County, Maryland, into which Lee was marching, had the largest number of horses, 11,287, than any other county in Maryland or Virginia according to the 1860 census.[84] Washington County, next one to the west, had 8,027 horses, ranking third in Maryland in numbers of horses. Thus Lee was rightfully hopeful to be able to purchase horses and fodder in Maryland, although payment in Confederate currency or certificates of indebtedness, undoubtedly led

---

[82] Joseph T. Glatthaar, "Everyman's War: A Rich and Poor Man's Fight in Lee's Army," *Civil War History*, vol. 54, no. 3, September 2008, 236-238. James M. McPherson, *For Cause and Comrades: Why Men Fought in the Civil War* (New York: Oxford University Press, 1997), 101. Glatthaar also learned that cavalry soldiers were most likely to have lived in rural areas and were mostly farmers but 22% were students reflecting the wealth of their families, and 68% were single or if married 28% had no children, *Soldiering*, 33-37. Age of cavalrymen was also different compared to other branches as the troopers were both older and younger. Glatthaar opined that men in their forties would have an easier time riding while the adventure of cavalry service appealed to younger worthies, Joseph T. Glatthaar, *Soldiering in the Army of Northern Virginia: A Statistical Portrait of the Troops Who Served under Robert E. Lee* (Chapel Hill, NC: The University of North Carolina Press, 2011), 34. Glatthaar also found in his sample that 55.3% were born in Virginia, 16.3% from South Carolina, 12.8% from North Carolina, and 6.4% from Georgia; 61.7% were residing in Virginia at the time of the war. He also learned that the cavalry had the largest proportion of students, 21.6%, than the other branches which emphasized that cavalrymen were wealthier than men in the artillery or infantry, 34-35. Importantly, he found that during the war, 8.7% of troopers were absent without leave and 18.7% deserted at least once during their service, with none returning to their units, 39. These statistics confirm that especially later in the war that cavalrymen left in larger numbers likely due to being mounted and when they had trouble with their mounts, they left to find replacements or if they could not, they were converted into infantrymen. He also found that wealthier men tended to remain with their units compared to poorer men probably due to the comforts that wealth could buy although he also shows that these wealthier men suffered more casualties although less disease, 40-42. Having money to help maintain one was obviously a factor in the mounted forces of the Army of Northern Virginia. Glatthaar wrote that "Compared to the infantry, service in Lee's mounted branch proved far less lethal and much less demanding. Cavalrymen rode most of the time, had mobility to scavenge food and to seek relief from the humdrum of camp life, and did not shoulder the burdens of combat that infantrymen and artillerymen regularly did," 42.

[83] Carman, Pierro, 49, quoting from "Our Army in Maryland," *Richmond Dispatch*, September 17, 1862. Thiele comments that many of the horses taken from farmers in Maryland "lacked the stamina that the rangy Kentucky and Virginia animals had. The accretions from the raids failed to equal the normal loss in horseflesh, and the unchecked losses seriously decreased the mobility of Lee's Cavalry," 219. See also Trout, *Thunder*, "the real focus of their foraging expedition [on 10 September] was something of more immediate importance—horses. The campaign had been hard on the horses of both the cavalry and the artillery. Before the day was out, many a farmer in the region saw his fine horses trotted out of their stables and led away," 92. See also John Michael Priest, *Before Antietam: The Battle for South Mountain* (New York: Oxford University Press, 1996), hereafter cited as *Before Antietam*, 80-81.

[84] *Shallows*; statistics are from the 1860 census and includes all types of horses, draft, carriage, and riding, 119.

many farmers to drive their horses north to Pennsylvania rather than accept worthless Confederate paper.[85] While there is no record of the numbers of horses bought or stolen by the Confederates, there were likely many, even though they might have been fewer than Stuart captured during his Second Ride Around McClellan on 10 October, a month after the end of the Maryland Campaign.[86]

However, not all Rebel troopers were good horse traders. One witness recalled an incident in which a Frederick youth bought a condemned Union horse for $13 hoping to nurse it back to health, but the boy had little success. Apparently he was a better horse trader than veterinarian, as he was successful at convincing a Confederate soldier that the forlorn-looking creature was worth $80 in hard money even though the horse would only stand on three legs. The youth described the horse to the soldier as "a natural racker which always stands on three legs." The same observer commented that Ashby's troopers and Hampton's men when passing through Frederick "are more neat and cleanly than the infantry that preceded them, and their horses, of good stock, are well-groomed and fed."[87] A Confederate artillery captain described how in Frederick he had bargained to buy a splendid, prize-winning, young horse belonging to a citizen's daughter. The officer left to collect the Confederate monies agreed upon, then awaited the owner's return with the horse; the officer soon realized that he would never see the owner or the horse again.[88]

Satiric cartoon showing the difference between the portrayals of Southern horsemen versus the reality. *Harper's Weekly*, 4 October 1862. Courtesy LOC.

Southern cavalry were usually better horsemen than were Union cavalrymen. The more industrialized north had more and better highways, trains, and even canals than the South, and more large population centers. While it had many farms, and rural areas, horses were used more as draught animals, not for riding: pulling carts, wagons, drays, trolley cars, etc. were their primary uses. "In the North, particularly in the East, the population of farmers and mechanics...[was] as a rule strange to any

[85] *OR*, vol. 19, pt. 2, 596. Carman, Pierro, 54.
[86] Carman, Pierro, 388. Blackford wrote that Stuart returned with "twelve or fifteen hundred horses," 180.
[87] Lewis H. Steiner, *Report of Lewis H. Steiner, M. D., Inspector of the Sanitary Commission, Containing a Diary Kept During the Rebel Occupation of Frederick, Maryland, and an Account of the Operations of the U. S. Sanitary Commission During the Campaign in Maryland, September, 1862* (New York: Anson D. F. Randolph, 1862), 18-19, 23.
[88] William Thomas Poague, *Gunner with Stonewall* (Jackson, TN: McCowat-Mercer Press, 1957; reprint, Lincoln, NB: University of Nebraska Press, 1998), 42-43.

horse but a work-horse; and not one in a hundred a good rider....Nearly all horses kept for pleasure were trotters used in harness and never mounted. In the South, every man and boy was ...used to horses, and all were good riders."[89] Frederick Whittaker wrote the following:

> At its inception the Southern cavalry were far superior to that of the North. Born in a country where roads were bad, and wheeled vehicles, except heavy wagons and old lumbering stage-coaches, almost unknown, the Southerners as a rule made all their excursions for business or pleasure on horseback. As a consequence the poor riders were the exception, good riders the rule, among high and low. In the North the rule was reversed. Buggies were and are the rule, riders the exception. Thus it will be seen that a nation of good riders started with a great advantage over those who, as a nation, considered the horse as a driving machine, to be hauled at with both hands. The consequence was as might be expected. In the first year of the war the Southern cavalry displayed a marked superiority. On horseback they felt at home, while the green levies from the North were in a strange and uncomfortable position."[90]

The more rural south, in addition to having the requirement to ride horses due to poorer roads and lack of alternatives, had a tradition of horsemanship from its earliest colonial history and plantation environment. Excellent horsemanship and the knowledge of horses were qualities almost entirely lacking in most Northern cavalry recruits.[91] One European observer recounted "that every Southern trooper who came to his notice 'rode well, in which particular they present a striking contrast to the Northern cavalry, who can scarcely sit their horses, even when trotting....Every man in the South rides from childhood.... In the North thousands keep horses,' but as a means of powering carriages and wagons."[92] One Confederate cavalryman serving in Stonewall Jackson's Shenandoah Valley Campaign in 1862 wrote that Wheat's Tigers captured some Union troopers who had difficulty dismounting as ordered by their captors: "Prisoners and spoil were promptly secured. The horse was from New England, a section in which horsemanship was an unknown art, and some of the riders were strapped to their steeds. Ordered to dismount, they explained their condition, and were given time to unbuckle. Many breastplates and other protective devices were seen here, and later at Winchester. We did not know whether the Federals had organised cuirassiers, or were recurring to the customs of Gustavus Adolphus. I saw a poor fellow lying dead on the pike, pierced through breastplate and body by a rifle-ball. Iron-clad men are of small account before modern weapons."[93]

As one Union cavalry veteran observed after the war: "it is a well-known fact that the people of the north were sadly deficient in horsemanship as compared to their southern foes, and that the northern cavalry men for the most part were obliged to learn to ride, in addition to learning the drill and other duties; and thus the work of making volunteer regiments of cavalry into good troopers was necessarily one which required much time and much actual experience."[94] One trooper of the 1st Maine Cavalry,

---

[89] Crowninshield, 4.

[90] Frederick Whittaker, *Cavalry Doctrine: the Lessons of the Decade by a Volunteer Cavalryman* (New York: Printed by Author, 1871), 22. See also Thiele, stating that Union cavalry recruits, unlike their Southern foes, had to be trained to ride a horse but the Union army was slow to set up training criteria for new troopers, 55-56.

[91] But see Thiele, showing that some few Union regiments did well in training its troopers such as the 1st and 6th Pennsylvania Cavalry, and the 6th New York Cavalry. A Union cavalry school set up at Annapolis, Maryland, in June 1862 had little effect until later in the war, 60-61.

[92] Thomason, 68-72. Longacre, *Lee's*, 30, quoting Lord Wolseley (Field Marshal Garney Jospeh Wolsely) from Fairfax Downey, *Clash of Cavalry: The Battle of Brandy Station, June 9, 1863* (New York: n.p., 1959), 17-18.

[93] Richard Taylor, *Destruction and Reconstruction: Personal Experiences of the Late War in the United States* (Edinburgh, Scotland: William Blackwood and Sons, 1879), 63. This may be one of the few true accounts of Union soldiers who early in the war wore metal protective plates under their blouses.

[94] Tobie, 122. See also Starr: "Inferior horsemanship was a major contributing factor in the poor performance of the Federal cavalry," 142. In a 6 February 1862 report by the Army of the Potomac's medical director, Charles S. Tripler, he noted that "In

who began his training before leaving his home state, described his first drill: "My horse would crowd and kick and I could not manage him at all in the ranks, and of course the boys had the laugh on me which did not add anything to my comfort. At last the captain ordered me into camp and to ride around the track awhile until I could manage him. I was glad to get out of the ranks with that horse and made up my mind to conquer him or kill him. As there was no one to watch me, I put him around the track as fast as I dared for about two hours and by the time the company came in from drill, I had him so I could do anything with him that I wanted to."[95] A Union cavalry officer commented: "All Southerners were good riders, particularly those of the better class. A good horse was a gentleman's pride, and the more important the gentleman, the better his horse. Consequently, their cavalry combined the men of the best class, mounted on the best horses."[96] Union Col. George Henry Gordon commanding the 2nd Massachusetts Infantry and acting brigade commander under Maj. Gen. Nathanial P. Banks in the Shenandoah Valley after the Battle of Kernstown, wrote in April 1862 that when he told his cavalry commander to attack some of Col. Turner Ashby's cavalry, the commander said "'I can't catch them, sir; they leap the fences and walls like deer: neither our men nor our horses are so trained.'"[97]

The Confederate equine heritage was well reflected in the many horse militia units formed south of the Mason and Dixon line before the war. While the North did have a few such units, there was no comparison to their popularity in the south.[98] There, these units flourished both as social and political organizations, but became more serious about martial affairs after the John Brown raid at Harpers Ferry in 1859, some having lapsed in enthusiasm since the Nat Turner Rebellion of 1831. Having hundreds of thousands of slaves in their midst long provided impetus to have available armed, mobile citizens to defend white families. The Brown affair certainly galvanized many to join or form mounted units and to inject more enthusiasm into training routines and mounted drill: "the militia south of the Mason-Dixon line was considerably more numerous in proportion to the total white population, and in a far more efficient state, than was the moribund militia of the northern states."[99] In Virginia, there were about 88 cavalry companies on record in 1860.[100]

The Union suffered greatly early in the war not only from having fewer experienced horsemen but from the horribly poor quality of mounts: "While the Federal government was requisitioning the cheapest mounts possible, with most animals going for $100 apiece, Virginia troopers were patrolling the

---

the cavalry regiments the sick report is swollen considerably in consequence of injuries to the men received from the horses" with two units, the 1st Pennsylvania Cavalry and 2nd New York Cavalry both reporting almost 11 per cent sick in each and the 8th Illinois Cavalry reporting almost 20 per cent on the sick list, *OR*, vol. 5, 713-720.

[95] Charles Gardner, "Three Years Experience in the First Maine Cavalry," photocopy of transcript in files of Harpers Ferry Research Library, extracted from originals in the U.S. Military History Research Collection, Carlisle, Pennsylvania, 1A.

[96] Crowninshield, 11.

[97] George Henry Gordon, *Brook Farm to Cedar Mountain in the War of the Great Rebellion*, 1861-1862 (Boston, MA: Houghton, Mifflin and Co., 1885), 136-137.

[98] Starr, "There were only a few companies of mounted militia in the North," 56.

[99] Starr, 57-58.

[100] See for example, Driver, *1st*, showing companies joining Stuart at Harpers Ferry having been organized first as militia companies from 1858-1861, 1-4, and 7-9. Todd, "John Brown's raid on Harper's Ferry....resulted in the organization of many new companies, and the revivification of some older ones throughout [Virginia], 1247. See also Thiele, 121-122. Spencer C. Tucker in *Brigadier General John D. Imboden: Confederate Commander in the Shenandoah* (Lexington, KY: The University Press of Kentucky, 2003), describes reaction to Brown's Raid in the Staunton, Virginia area: "The raid certainly heightened southerners' fears about military vulnerability and led to a renewed interest in voluntary military units. In Augusta County and the surrounding area alone, twelve volunteer military companies were organizing: nine of infantry, two troops of cavalry, and one battery of artillery," 15.

picket lines with their families' best breeds."[101] Lax rules and a corrupt system with little oversight led to disregard for standards set for Union purchases. Horses sent to some units were unfit for any purpose: many were seriously ill, blind, crippled, or far below published standards. Additionally, most of the horses were not broken to riding or trained for military use so this, combined with Union troopers having no knowledge of horses, gave predictably poor results. The Union, unlike the Confederate troopers, had very few units supply their own horses, except for a few regiments in the early months of the war. It was not until July 1863 that the Federal War Department established a Cavalry Bureau to help control all aspects of cavalry supply, most importantly horses.[102]

Another factor affecting the quality of Union cavalry versus Confederate cavalry was the care given to their mounts. As noted above, Confederate cavalry troopers usually owned their horses and had more knowledge of how to care for them. Since few Union troopers owned their horses, their mounts received generally poor care: "Horses were destroyed faster than they could be trained."[103] A trooper of the 6th New York Cavalry, Frederick Whittaker, wrote of the 3rd Indiana Cavalry:

> Our early disasters, the South's early successes arose from opposite modes of recruitment. Their cavalry owned their own horses from the first. Ours did not. A man who owns his own horse generally knows something about riding him. If he's a poor countryman he's quite certain to. So that you start with such a man with a great advantage. You don't have to teach him how to take care of a horse. All he has to learn is military riding, the combination of hand and leg. He soon learns this. The sabre he is only too eager to learn....Countrymen, too, who own a horse, have generally a gun somewhere, and are pretty fair shots—a second requisite for a modern cavalryman. The South started with these advantages in their cavalry service. Our troopers on the other hand, came from anywhere and everywhere, and so did the horses. Some knew how to ride, others did not. Many were townsmen, and had never had a gun in their hands. Prudence would have dictated drilling these men carefully before sending them into the field, and especially teaching them to ride....I remember well in 1862, when the regiment to which I belonged was still in its green stage, coming across the Third Indiana Cavalry, recruited on the Southern plan. It was already good cavalry, though no longer in the service than ourselves, and made for itself a splendid reputation even while attached to an infantry corps. Every man owned his own horse, and, as a consequence, *took care of him*. In the last four words, italicised, lies the difference between good and bad cavalry.[104]

Knowledge that mounts would be supplied when needed and lack of officer oversight, meant that horses were poorly maintained diminishing the Union cavalry's ability to perform its missions. Too, most Union troopers did not realize the amount of care horses needed since they had likely never owned or even ridden one. Union troopers never learned to care for their mounts as Southerners did but were able to make up for this by the larger supplies of horses available. This lack of care resulted from the viewpoint that they saw their mounts as fungible: merely items of equipment which could readily be

[101] Brennan, 13. But Federal prices may have actually ranged from $119 in 1861 to $185 per head in 1865, Gerleman, 50. See also Thiele stating that the average price the Union paid from 1861 to 1863 was $140 although prices were as low as $96 found at Quincy, Illinois, 188.

[102] Charles D. Rhodes, "The Mounting and Remounting of the Federal Cavalry," *The Photographic History of The Civil War: Volume 4, The Cavalry*, ed. by Francis Trevelyan Miller, vol. 4 (NY: Thomas Yoseloff, 1957), 322-336. See also Barton, "From the fall of Fort Sumter until September 1862, the Union Army purchased 150,000 horses, providing mounts for thirty-one regiments of cavalry and costing nearly $20,000,000. The average price of a cavalry horse during this time was $125, although this often dipped to $100 a head in the war-ravaged areas in the East," 17.

[103] Starr, 143. Note that the 3rd Indiana, one of the Union cavalry regiments present during the Maryland Campaign, was one of the few regiments whose troopers owned their horses upon their initial entry into service; "The quality of the horses owned by the men...was uniformly high," 130. Two other regiments which were not present, the 1st Iowa and the 9th New York, also brought their own mounts into service.

[104] Whittaker, 25-26.

exchanged. Not being familiar with animals in their civilian lives, many honestly did not know how to care for their new partners, and often, when they found out the time and effort needed for that care, decided that it was too much to give: "the men who had enlisted with an idea of riding on horseback, perhaps with the further notion that grooms would be furnished to take care of their horses when they dismounted, soon found that in addition to being a soldier, a cavalry soldier would have to be also a groom and stable keeper. The duty of taking care of sick horses under unfavorable circumstances was very irksome and trying."[105] Union cavalry officers were often cited for their lack of supervision of their men who were lax in caring for their mounts.[106] And if a cavalryman had no horse, he could not fight as cavalry, so unless rules turned him into a foot soldier, a "Company Q" trooper was left in camp and much less likely to be in danger in combat with the dreaded Rebel cavalry.

Thus most of the Confederate cavalry arrived in Maryland as well-led veterans who rode superior mounts well and had a high esprit de corps. While they may have suffered by having some inferior arms, they benefited by using cannon and small arms captured during the battles on the Peninsula and Second Bull Run. Union cavalry on the whole were somewhat greener and did not have the advantages of operating in as large units solely as cavalry as did the Southerners. Too, their leaders were generally less experienced and capable than Confederate commanders.[107] While both sides had heavily used their mounts in prior campaigning, Confederate troopers may have benefited by having shorter distances to travel into Maryland than did many Union units which were hastily thrown out of the Washington defenses to locate Lee's army. Also, McClellan's cavalry had just arrived from the Peninsula with little time for rest and refitting, suffering from the boat trips north. Many Union units joined Pleasonton's cavalry a company or squadron at a time as McClellan moved northwest probing for Lee. Had not Union infantry been close by to assist, Federal troopers would likely have fared much worse in some of the many skirmishes during the Maryland Campaign.

[105] Crowninshield, 47-48. Lack of care of mounts was the primary reason for the rapid rate at which Union cavalry horses were used up; troopers not only did not groom them but used them too harshly so that even when the cavalry was not actively campaigning in the field, losses remained high; Thiele, 200. See also Charles D. Rhodes, *History of the Cavalry of the Army of the Potomac, Including That of the Army of Virginia (Pope's), and also the History of the Operations of the Federal Cavalry in West Virginia During the War* (hereafter *History of the Cavalry*) (Kansas City, MO: Hudson-Kimberly Publishing Co., 1900), where he lists causes for the tremendous number of horse casualties: "ignorance of purchasing officers as to the proper animals for cavalry service; poor horsemanship on the part of the raw cavalry troopers, mustered in at the beginning of the war; the control of the cavalry movements by officers of other arms, ignorant of the limit of endurance of cavalry horses; the hardships inseparable from the duties of the cavalry…and ignorance and gross inefficiency on the part of many officers and men as to the condition of the horses' backs and feet, care as to food and cleanliness, and the proper treatment of the many diseases to which horses on active service are subject," 75. Data from the 16th Pennsylvania Cavalry for the year following Antietam, 18 October 1862 to 31 October 1863 detailing its use of horses may be compared to Union regiments horse usage; on hand and issued: 1,673; on hand on 31 October 1863: 425; condemned and turned in: 679; abandoned on the march: 256; killed in action: 47; died of disease: 254; captured by enemy: 12; Charles H. Miller, *History of the 16th Regiment Pennsylvania Cavalry, for the Year Ending October 31st, 1863, Commanded by Colonel John Irvin Gregg, of Centre County, Pa.* (Philadelphia, PA: King & Baird, Printers, 1864), 6.
[106] Starr, "Innumerable orders issued in 1863, 1864, and even in the spring of 1865, repeat the same admonitions, complaints, and exhortations that commanding officers had been forced to issue in 1861 and 1862." The commanding officer of the 7th Pennsylvania Cavalry noticed "'a gradual but sure neglect of horses….Less care is day after day paid to grooming and feeding….company officers are to blame,'" 164; many Federal volunteer officers had no military background and were untrained in horsemanship and leadership, and could not discipline their men, 144-165 passim.
[107] As will be seen the Regular Army Union cavalry regiments were better led and better disciplined than virtually all of the volunteer units.

Chapter 3

On the Peninsula

THE CAVALRY OF THE ARMY OF THE POTOMAC and the Army of Northern Virginia came to the Maryland Campaign with dissimilar backgrounds and reputations. Many Union cavalry units which were participants on the Peninsula with McClellan, were present in Maryland, and almost all of the Confederate units which saw action on the Peninsula with Johnston and Lee, also participated in Maryland. But most of the Confederate cavalry units also fought continuously from the Peninsula to Maryland, participating in the battles of Second Bull Run as well as Chantilly, while Union units left on the Peninsula were generally less active. Most of the Confederate units had been in existence and fighting from the earliest days of the war unlike the majority of Union cavalry units. There were many skirmishes and fights pitting Confederate and Union troopers against each other including some larger-sized battles before Second Bull Run near Brandy Station. But Confederate horsemen were seemingly busier and more successful than their Union counterparts spending more time in scouting and screening showcased by Stuart's First Ride Around McClellan 12-15 June 1862.[1] On the other hand, the Union cavalry's most newsworthy event was a spectacular charge by five squadrons of the 5th U.S. Cavalry at Gaines's Mill on 27 June which failed terribly, losing 55 men and six of seven of their officers.[2] These two events fixed in the public's eyes, both North and South, the unfair stereotype that Stuart and his horsemen were much more than a match for their Union counterparts despite the many Union cavalry successes in the fights leading up to the Maryland Campaign.

After activity on the Peninsula quieted down following the Seven Days Campaign in early July 1862, Union Maj. Gen. John Pope's cavalry units in the Army of Virginia, none of which participated on the Peninsula, remained active. Since they exhausted their horses in scouting for the Confederates in the weeks before the Battle of Second Bull Run, they were relatively ineffective compared with Stuart's men coming up from the Peninsula. Pope did, however, take a first, very valuable step, by consolidating cavalry units in August 1862, and assigning one cavalry brigade with its own chief of cavalry to each army corps. This chain of command was very convenient for Pope as he "directed cavalry operations for

---

[1] *OR*, vol. 11, pt. 2, Stuart said in his report on the Seven Days battles that the field of operations of the cavalry was extended and that during this time, his command was in contact with the enemy although "No opportunity occurred, however, for an overwhelming charge" because of the difficult nature of the country and the defensive positions taken by the enemy as well as the difficulty of seeing where the Union forces would move, 521.

[2] *OR*, vol. 11, pt. 2, 40, 42-46. Cooke's report says that the charge helped save some Union guns while Maj. Gen. Fitz John Porter said that the charge was ill-advised and added to the loss of the position: "To this [cavalry charge] alone is to be attributed our failure to hold the battle-field and to bring off our guns and wounded," 226. Cooke and others wrote reports supporting the charge but to little avail for Cooke as he never again commanded in the field. Doubtless his failure to catch Stuart, his son-in-law, during Stuart's ride two weeks before contributed to Cooke's demise as a field commander; Cooke's southern birth could also have been a factor.

his army" sometimes not going through his corps commanders to do so, with the result being that his cavalry was exhausted before the end of the campaign when they were desperately needed.[3] Perhaps this helps explain why few of Pope's horsemen in his Army of Virginia were in active use in September 1862 in Maryland as part of the Army of the Potomac's cavalry division, while McClellan's Peninsula troopers were heavily engaged in the Old Line State.[4] A trooper in the 9th New York cavalry wrote that after the Battle of Second Bull Run, "The companies of the 9th N.Y. cavalry had been reduced by the hardships of the service to an average of eighteen men and horses present for duty. Sept. 3, the regiment marched to Hall's Farm three miles above Chain Bridge where men and horses took much needed rest. While here a large number of recruits joined the regiment and fresh horses and equipments were received."[5] McClellan's cavalry while on the Peninsula did benefit by being in the field, even though often not well used by the army commander. Assigning cavalry to duties such as felling trees and destroying bridges, while an effective use of troopers on the defense, forced it too often into a static mode, especially as the Cavalry Reserve, composed of mainly regular cavalry units, the best McClellan had, was often ordered to accomplish these tasks.[6]

The journey for McClellan's Army of the Potomac to the Peninsula began by boat on 17 March 1862 at Alexandria, Virginia, but most of the cavalry was not transported until later in that month. "Of the 22,497 cavalry on 30 January 1862 listed for the Army of the Potomac, only all or parts of fifteen regiments and three unattached companies eventually sailed to the Peninsula. Interestingly, returns for the army for February 1862 show a total of 9,921 cavalry in and near Washington, D.C., while the medical director of the army, Dr. Charles Stuart Tripler, reported 14,122 horsemen on 6 February 1862. The totals were apparently "aggregate present and absent" given the large sizes of the regiments some of which show that they are newly-arrived, not having lost men to sickness, injuries, etc. Clearly, the differences in these totals for the army in early 1862 vary according to who is counting and which units are subject to the tallies. A good estimate for the cavalry in the Army of the Potomac on the Peninsula would be about 7,000 cavalry once all units had arrived.[7]

---

[3] Starr, 289-290. See also Thiele, "Pope…had the sense to concentrate all the Cavalry he could lay his hands on—a feat his predecessor never accomplished," 89-90. Cavalry units under Pope which did not join McClellan in Maryland in September did scout south of the Potomac River in September ensuring that the wily Lee did not attempt to turn McClellan's flank by attacking Washington south of the river as Maj. Gen. Henry W. Halleck and Lincoln feared. Being close to Washington supply bases ensured that Union cavalry had a supply of horses to replace some of those jaded from their efforts during Second Bull Run.

[4] See "The Opposing Forces at Cedar Mountain, VA." and "The Opposing Forces at the Second Bull Run" in *Battles and Leaders of the Civil War: Being for the Most Part Contributions by Union and Confederate Officers*, Robert U. Johnson and Clarence C. Buel, eds., 4 vols. (New York: Thomas Yoseloff, 1956), 2:495-499, hereafter *Battles and Leaders*; OR, vol. 19, pt. 1, 169-180. Some of McClellan's cavalry units assigned to him in the Maryland Campaign were not with him on the Peninsula: the 1st Maine Cavalry had served with Pope while the 1st Massachusetts Cavalry came from the Department of the South; one company of the 1st Michigan Cavalry serving as escort to the Twelfth Army Corps in Maryland was from the Army of Virginia; the 2nd New York Cavalry companies A, B, I, and K were also from the Army of Virginia; the 8th New York came from the Middle Department; and the 12th Pennsylvania Cavalry came from the Military District of Washington, Frederick H. Dyer, *A Compendium of the War of the Rebellion*, 3 vols. (Cedar Rapids, IA: 1909; reprint, New York: Thomas Yoseloff, 1959), 3:1215, 1237, 1269, 1371, 1376.

[5] Newel Cheney, *History of the Ninth Regiment, New York Volunteer Cavalry, War of 1861 to 1865* (Jamestown, NY: Martin Merz & Son, 1901), 58.

[6] OR, vol. 11, pt. 3, where Brig. Gen. Cooke on 25 June 1862 was ordered, in addition to patrolling, to fell trees and destroy bridges to be ready for retreat, 256. Thiele opined that giving it a purely defensive mission "ruined good Cavalry," 528. For McClellan's assignment of cavalry units on 24 March 1862, see OR, vol. 11, pt. 3, 36, Special Order No. 90; for the 8 July 1862 cavalry reorganization see ibid, 307-308, and the 10 August list, ibid, 367.

[7] OR, vol. 5, 711, 713-720, 732. Leon Walter Tenney, "Seven Days in 1862: Numbers in Union and Confederate Armies before Richmond," Master's thesis, George Mason University, 1992, 121; the average present for duty strength of a regular regiment was about 450 troopers and some 650 for the volunteer horsemen, 120. Totals are almost certainly aggregate present and absent, Tripler calls it "mean strength" showing it is probably an average of the daily morning reports. The medical director's

McClellan arrived at Fort Monroe on 2 April, but found that only the 3rd Pennsylvania Cavalry and the 5th U.S. Cavalry, had disembarked; the 2nd and 6th U.S. Cavalry, and part of the 1st, had arrived, but was still on board ship. Pvt. Sidney Davis of Company F, 6th U.S. Cavalry, described his arrival at Fortress Monroe:

> The debarkation of the infantry received attention in preference to the cavalry and artillery, and, as a consequence, we did not reach terra firma until the 3d of April.
>
> The mode of disembarking horses was comical. The wharves were monopolized for other purposes, and unapproachable so the horses had to be pushed overboard into the water and swim ashore. The poor frightened beasts as they were plunged into the bay, evidently thought, if an animal does think, that their last day had arrived. They would go down out of sight under the water, but rise in a moment, and strike out for the shore with the promptitude and skill of old swimmers.
>
> By waiting until the proper moment our horses were spared this unpleasant process of debarkation, as we finally secured a chance at a wharf, but here great urging was required before they would trust themselves to the mercy of the gangway. We had been on board the schooner six nights and five days.[8]

Certainly both troopers and their mounts were not very fresh for active duty upon arrival, with the horses suffering more than their companions from their confinement on the transports.

On the day Pvt. Davis disembarked, Jeb Stuart was at Rappahannock, Virginia, and reported to Longstreet accurate information that Union troops had been embarking from Alexandria for several days.[9] Facing McClellan's growing cavalry strength on the Peninsula, there were only two companies of the 3rd Virginia Cavalry at Yorktown, with the rest scattered around the Peninsula. This cavalry was under the command of Brig. Gen. John B. Magruder, Commander of the Confederate Army of the Peninsula. On 23 April 1862, Magruder reported 932 cavalry present for duty. Lt. Thomas C. Rice, commander of Company H of the 3rd Virginia, reported that during January and February 1862, "The

---

breakdown shows the following: Van Alen Cavalry (3rd New York), 860; 1st Pennsylvania Cavalry, 890; 3rd Pennsylvania Cavalry, 1,090; 8th Pennsylvania Cavalry, 1,110; 3rd Indiana Cavalry, 550; 4th New York Cavalry, 750; Cameron Cavalry (5th Pennsylvania Cavalry), 1,000; 1st U.S. Cavalry, 424; 2nd U.S. Cavalry (seven companies), and 4th U.S. Cavalry, 506; 5th U.S. Cavalry, 632; 6th U.S. Cavalry, 984; 2nd New York Cavalry, 982; 1st New Jersey Cavalry, 1,000; Lincoln Cavalry (1st New York), 1,100; 1st Michigan Cavalry 1,121; and 8th Illinois Cavalry, 1,123. These 17 units total 14,122. But see Thiele showing all or parts of 14 regiments were with McClellan starting up the Peninsula. The 9th New York Cavalry refused to serve as they were broken up into artillery and infantry units; for details of the 9th's plight, see Robert O'Neill, "'What Men We Have Got are Good Soldiers & Brave Ones Too'; Federal Cavalry Operations in the Peninsula Campaign," in *The Peninsula Campaign: Yorktown to the Seven Days*, vol. 3, ed. by William J. Miller (Campbell, CA: Savas Publishing Company, 1997), hereafter cited as *Peninsula Campaign*, explaining the ordeal of the unit which served on the Peninsula until it was shipped back to Washington where it was finally returned to its status as a cavalry regiment effective 21 June 1862, 90-96. See also note 87 below. O'Neill is the foremost authority concerning cavalry during the Peninsular Campaign and has written its definitive history. Some 15,000 horses and mules were transported to the Peninsula within thirty-seven days, George B. McClellan, *McClellan's Own Story* (New York: Charles L. Webster & Company, 1887. Reprint, Scituate, MA: Digital Scanning, Inc., 1998), hereafter cited as *Story*, quoting from a report by Assistant Secretary of War John Tucker, 238. Some horses were added in later shipments, however, perhaps up to 3,000, Thiele, 267. Compare *OR*, vol. 11, pt. 3, showing transport was needed for supplies for 20,000 horses over the twenty-eight mile long West Point and Richmond Railway, 15. This total is for all the army. Gen. Joseph E. Johnston showed 2,445 cavalry present for duty for the month of February 1862, *OR*, vol. 5, 1086. About 30 April 1862, Stuart had an "effective strength" of 1,289 troopers while on 20 July he had 4,041 "present for duty" and 6,724 "present and absent", *OR*, vol. 11, pt. 3, 484, 645. On 10 August 1862, McClellan reported 5,718 cavalry "present for duty" which included Stoneman's cavalry division of 5,176 with the rest assigned as escorts, etc. When the Union cavalry embarked between 11 August and 3 September to return to Washington, the cavalry had about 6,060 horses, so McClellan's numbers are likely accurate, O'Neill, *Peninsula Campaign*, 138. See Appendices A and B at the end of this chapter for a detailed list of probable present for duty numbers.

[8] George B. McClellan, *Report on the Organization and Campaigns of the Army of the Potomac* (New York: Sheldon & Company, 1864), 154. *OR*, vol. 11, pt. 1, 6-7; Sidney M. Davis, *Common Soldier Uncommon War: Life as a Cavalryman in the Civil War*, ed. by John H. Davis, Jr. (Baltimore, MD: Port City Press, 1993), 105, 107.

[9] Thiele, 268; *OR*, vol. 11, pt. 3, 415.

men have been engaged videtting at different points on York River and between York and James Rivers. The discipline is tolerable, arms in good order, horses very thin and rendered so by arduous vidette duty and indifferent food."[10] About 14 April 1862, Stuart arrived in Richmond with the 1st and 4th Virginia Cavalry regiments, the Jeff Davis Legion, and the Stuart Horse Artillery, totaling some 1,289 men, and headed down the Peninsula to Yorktown. Johnston, in his Yorktown withdrawal order of 2 May 1862, included this mandate: "All detached portions of cavalry serving with divisions and brigades, excepting small escorts to division commanders, will report to Brig. Gen. J.E.B. Stuart upon reaching Williamsburg." Here, Johnston, unlike McClellan, took a critical step at this time in the war when he determined that a unified cavalry command was best for his mounted arm. Johnston and then Lee continued this consolidation under Stuart later before leaving the Peninsula.[11]

Brig. Gen. George Stoneman was chief of cavalry of the Army of the Potomac, appointed by McClellan on 20 August 1861. McClellan saw this staff position as an administrative assignment, but as seen in his orders, Stoneman was not prohibited from commanding in the field should "Little Mac" so desire: "The duties of the chiefs of artillery and cavalry are exclusively administrative, and these officers will be attached to the headquarters of the Army of the Potomac....They will not exercise command of the troops of their arms unless specially ordered by the commanding general."[12] As his cavalry disembarked at Fort Monroe, McClellan found that he had to lay siege to the Confederate defenses at Yorktown, succumbing to Brig. Gen. John B. Magruder's effective theatrical display. Magruder convinced McClellan that the Army of the Potomac faced a formidable foe, estimated by McClellan to be some 100,000 men, arrayed along the flooded Warwick River, from the York to the James Rivers, so the Union commander took a month to bring up his siege guns and build fortifications to house the guns and his troops.[13]

---

[10] OR, vol. 11, pt. 3, 460; Supplement to the Official Records of the Union and Confederate Armies: Record of Events, Janet B. Hewett, et al., eds. (Wilmington, NC: Broadfoot Publishing Co., 1994), pt. II, vol. 69, 722. See also Robert T. Hubard, Jr., The Civil War Memoirs of a Virginia Cavalryman (Tuscaloosa, AL: The University of Alabama Press, 2007), 7-29, passim, describing his early tour in 1861 on the Peninsula with the 3rd Virginia Cavalry.

[11] Robert J. Trout, With Pen & Saber: The Letters and Diaries of J.E.B. Stuart's Staff Officers (Mechanicsburg, PA: Stackpole Books, 1995), 58; OR, vol. 11, pt. 3, 490. On 14 January 1862 prior to his move south to Culpeper Court House from Manassas, Gen. Johnston showed the following assignments for his cavalry units: Gen. P.G.T. Beauregard, First Division, Boykin's Rangers; near Dumfries under Brig. Gen. William Henry Chase Whiting, Shannon's cavalry and Thornton's cavalry; Leesburg under Brig. Gen. Daniel H. Hill, 2nd Virginia Cavalry (four companies); Jeb Stuart's Cavalry Brigade, 1st North Carolina Cavalry, 1st Virginia Cavalry, 2nd Virginia Cavalry, 4th Virginia Cavalry, 6th Virginia Cavalry, and the Jeff Davis Legion; Aquia District under Maj. Gen. T.H. Holmes, Caroline Light Dragoons and the Stafford Rangers; Valley District under Maj. Gen. T.J. Jackson, Col Ashby's cavalry; and not brigaded, Lewis' company of cavalry, Northern Neck, Tayloe's company of cavalry, Northern Neck, and Essex Cavalry near Tappahannock for the defense of Ft. Lowry, OR, vol. 5, 1028-1032. Gen. Johnston in Special Orders 120 28 May 1862 placed under Brig. Gen. Stuart's command the following cavalry units: the Wise Legion, the Hampton Legion Cavalry, the Cobb Legion Cavalry, and the cavalry lately serving in the Aquia District, OR, vol. 11, pt. 3, 558. Issued on 28 July by Gen. Lee, Special Orders 165 assigned to Maj. Gen. Stuart the army's two cavalry brigades: First Brigade, Brig. Gen. Wade Hampton commanding: 1st North Carolina Cavalry (Col. Lawrence S. Baker), Cobb Legion Cavalry (Lt. Col. P. M. B. Young), Jeff Davis Legion (Lt. Col. W. T. Martin), Hampton Legion Cavalry (Maj. Butler), 10th Virginia Cavalry (Lt. Col. Magruder); the Second Brigade Brig. Gen. Fitzhugh Lee commanding: 1st Virginia Cavalry (Lt. Col. Luke Tiernan Brien), 3rd Virginia Cavalry (Col. Thomas F. Goode), 4th Virginia Cavalry (Col. W. C. Wickham), 5th Virginia Cavalry (Col. Thomas L. Rosser), 9th Virginia Cavalry (Col. William Henry Fitzhugh Lee), OR, vol. 11, pt. 3, 657.

[12] OR, vol. 5, 575. OR, vol. 11, pt. 3, 40.

[13] Sears, McClellan, Papers, 232; Brian K. Burton, Extraordinary Circumstances: The Seven Days Battles (Bloomington, IN: Indiana University Press, 2001), 89, where he describes "Prince John's" activities which stopped McClellan; Magruder attacked Union pickets, shelled Union lines, and making as much commotions as possible to impress upon McClellan that the Federals were facing a substantial force. Sears, Richmond, details Magruder's theatrics, 24-39, passim. Earl C. Hastings, Jr., and David S. Hastings, A Pitiless Rain: The Battle of Williamsburg, 1862 (Shippensburg, PA: White Mane Publishing Co., Inc., 1997), described Magruder's well-placed Warwick River defense line and the vigor with which Magruder defended it, 18-20, but downplayed Magruder's theatrics.

Brig. Gen. George Stoneman, chief of cavalry for McClellan on the Peninsula, shown here as a major general. Courtesy Wikipedia.

Brig. Gen. William Hemsley Emory in command of a brigade in the Union Cavalry Reserve under Stoneman, shown here as a major general. Courtesy LOC.

In the meantime, as Union cavalry regiments arrived and organized, some volunteer units took the opportunity to drill and train their troopers, while others engaged in minor skirmishing, taking a few casualties.[14] The 3rd Pennsylvania Cavalry, assigned to the Third Corps, represented a typical regiment's actions on 4-5 April as it accompanied Brig. Gen. Fitz John Porter's first division in an advance to Big Bethel and Cockletown. The Pennsylvania cavalry, Col. William Averell commanding, was sent north to Ship Point on the York River, but found it abandoned. Thus Union cavalry regiments had some time to rest, train, and engage in reconnaissance and light skirmishing while their heavily outnumbered

---

[14] William B. Rawle, *History of the Third Pennsylvania Cavalry, Sixtieth Regiment Pennsylvania Volunteers in the American Civil War 1861-1865* (Philadelphia, PA: Franklin Printing Company, 1905, reprint, Salem, MA: Higginson Book Company, n.d.), reported two privates captured at Big Bethel because they strayed too far from the rear of their company, 44.

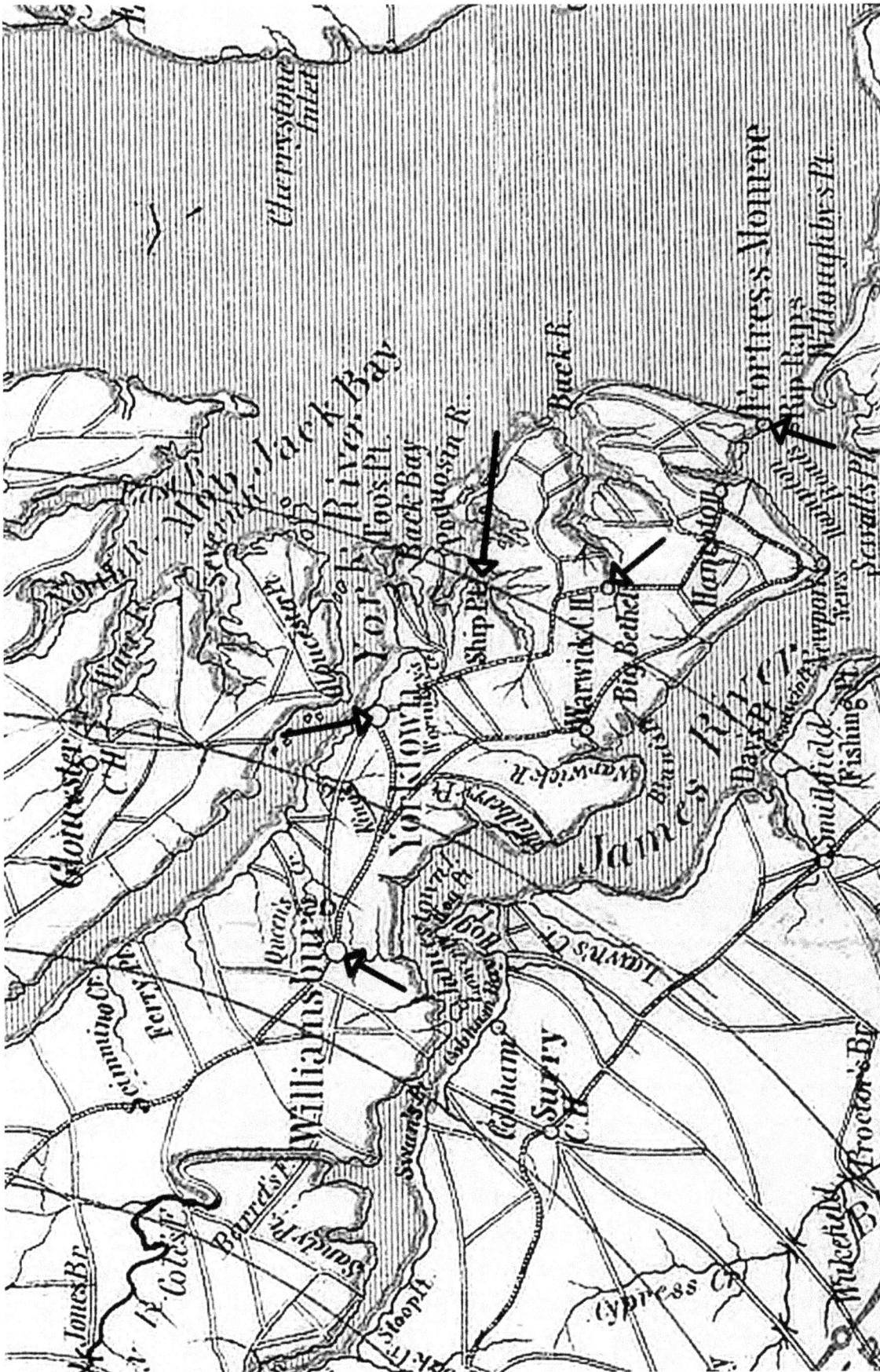

Map of area of operations at the start of the Peninsular Campaign; detail from 1863 map of Virginia by the U.S. Coast Survey Office showing Fort Monroe where the Army of the Potomac disembarked in the lower right and Yorktown to the upper center and Williamsburg to the northwest. Big Bethel and Ship Point are between Fort Monroe and Yorktown. The 6th U.S. Cavalry spent a few days at Shipping Point. Rings are showing ten-mile intervals from Richmond; Yorktown is about fifty-three air line miles from Richmond using the ring scale. Main roads are shown as two lines with cross hatching. Courtesy LOC.

Confederate counterparts were mostly used as videttes and scouts, watching the massive Union buildup. William Rawle of the 3rd Pennsylvania Cavalry wrote that the regiment had "Regimental drills morning and afternoon....Company drills morning and evening....The regiment exercised in squadron drill during the morning...The troops were exercised with carbine, sabre, and pistol....Marked improvement in character of the drill."[15] Sidney Davis wrote that after his regiment was relieved from the duty of unloading schooners at Ship Point, they began training, which other Union mounted regiments would have done well to emulate:

> [The 6th U.S. Cavalry] was now devoted to the legitimate duties of a soldier—series of drills, mounted and dismounted, by company and by regiment being instituted, and of such frequency as to take up our entire time. Each company hunted up an available field, made ditches, erected poles, put up posts to represent men, with bags stuffed with hay for their heads, at each ditch and pole, and at intervals between, and went through such a course of exercises as we had never before experienced....First, we had to ride around at a walk, avoiding the poles and ditches, and strike off the heads on the posts; then this was repeated at a trot and then at a gallop. After this we galloped around the ring, learning to jump the poles and ditches, and then to strike off the heads while our horses were in the act of leaping, and in the succeeding intervals, being obliged by the latter requirement to recover ourselves instantaneously from the shock. These performances were repeated with revolver in hand; and then, instead of striking, we had to shoot the heads....Its effect was soon visible in the soldiers, when mounted, to one of perfect freedom and ease, and an apparent 'at-homeativeness'—for want of a better expression—in the saddle.[16]

---

[15] Rawle, 42, 46.
[16] Sidney Davis, 111-112.

Westover Landing, Virginia showing Col. William W. Averell, 3rd Pennsylvania Cavalry, seated, and staff, August 1862. Left to right: Lt. W.H. Brown, 5th U.S. Cavalry; Lt. H.H. King, 3rd Pennsylvania Cavalry; Colonel Averell; Lt. Phillip Pollard, 3rd Pennsylvania Cavalry. Photograph by Alexander Gardner. Courtesy LOC.

Officers of the 4th Pennsylvania Cavalry at Westover Landing, Va., Col. James H. Childs (standing); Childs would be killed on 17 September 1862 at Antietam. August 1862 by Alexander Gardner. Courtesy LOC.

Sergeant Thomas W. Smith of the 6th Pennsylvania Cavalry, Rush's Lancers, wrote that Col. Rush was a severe disciplinarian, describing him as a tyrant, but a commander who did have his regiment train hard, including learning how to care for its horses. Many enlisted volunteer troopers, like Smith, believed they suffered under arbitrary and unkind officers and non-commissioned officers who were not qualified to lead. The Lancers, like other Union cavalry, were heavily engaged in picketing and scouting, thus gaining valuable experience operating as cavalry in the field. As the regiment moved up the Peninsula, they began to come within sight of the enemy and picketing became more serious and skirmishes with the Rebels were common. After Gaines's Mill, some of the 6th Pennsylvania was detailed as guides. Smith's descriptions of fights in which his regiment participated never revealed that lances were discarded but it would seem reasonable to assume that the first item a beleaguered Lancer would drop is the cumbersome lance. Perhaps the lances were simply not routinely carried on most scouts or reconnaissances.[17]

By 3 May, Johnston realized that there was no chance of successfully opposing McClellan's siege of Yorktown, so he wisely abandoned the works there and retreated toward Richmond. His troops slogged through muddy roads in a heavy rain which fell during the evening and continued into 5 May.[18] Confederate cavalry, with Maj. Matthew C. Butler in command of four companies of the Hampton Legion, helped cover the army's retreat. On a last sweep through Yorktown, Butler found it deserted except for two contrabands. He also learned that the retreating Confederate soldiers had planted torpedoes in several places which made his nighttime journey perilous. He encountered the 10th Virginia Cavalry (Wise Legion) destroying stores on the wharfs, but as he visited with its commanding officer, Col. J. Lucius Davis, there was an explosion and musket fire. Butler learned that there was no Yankee attack but rather some of the troopers from the 10th inadvertently set off a torpedo at an ordnance warehouse killing one and wounding another; the ammunition in the building ignited. Later on 4 May, his unit was joined by the 4th and 10th Virginia Cavalry regiments and had a relatively leisurely ride to the defenses of Fort Magruder, not being closely pursued by the Union army. There, later in the day, they would confront Union cavalry pursuing Johnston's retreat and fight some nasty affairs. Butler commented that McClellan apparently failed to have a pursuit force ready to quickly follow the retreating Confederates.[19]

McClellan was prepared to begin a siege against overwhelming odds obviously not anticipating a precipitate Confederate retreat, so he did not plan or assign units for quick pursuit. McClellan's aide, the Prince de Joinville, commented on Johnston's retreat: "The Confederates had vanished, and with them all chances of a brilliant victory....We had spent a whole month in constructing gigantic works now become useless."[20] Apparently McClellan's headquarters had some inkling of a possible withdrawal from

---

[17] Thomas W. Smith, *"We Have It Damn Hard Out Here": The Civil War Letters of Sergeant Thomas W. Smith, 6th Pennsylvania Cavalry*, ed. by Eric J. Wittenberg (Kent, OH: The Kent State University Press, 1999), 25, 29, 34-35, 48.

[18] Johnston strongly favored abandoning the Peninsula to make a stand at Richmond against the wishes of President Davis and Gen. Robert E. Lee so the retreat from Yorktown and subsequently from Williamsburg was in line with his strategic plans, Newton, 91-132 passim. Johnston had passed out retreat orders to his division commanders on 2 May, Steven H. Newton, *Joseph E. Johnston and the Defense of Richmond* (Lawrence, KS, University of Kansas Press, 1998), 134.

[19] Newton, 134. Butler's tale is from the following: Ulysses R. Brooks, *Butler and His Cavalry in the War of Secession 1861-1865*, 70-77. See also *Battles and Leaders*, 2:201, for details about the pursuit controversy.

[20] Richard Wheeler, *Sword Over Richmond: An Eyewitness History of McClellan's Peninsula Campaign* (New York: Harper and Row, 1986), 144. See Wheeler also discussing two torpedo incidents, 144. The Prince de Joinville was a former rear admiral in the French navy who sailed for the United States in August 1861 with his son and two nephews, the Comte de Paris and the Duc de Chartres. He stayed with his two nephews after they enlisted in the Union Army and joined McClellan's staff on the Peninsula as honorary captains. They left in July 1862 thus depriving McClellan of their good service. The Comte de Paris wrote an eight volume history of the Civil War in America and was a good observer of what he saw on the Peninsula as an excellent analyst of what he read of later events in the war. His writings show that he believed cavalry tactics were heavily influenced by mounted infantry and dragoon activities in the prewar Indian fighting actions and "that unfavorable terrain, inadequate

a northern newspaper reporter, Uriah H. Painter, but dismissed it out of hand. The reporter interviewed a contraband who had been a servant to a Rebel officer near Lee's Mills and had witnessed the Confederate withdrawal, but McClellan's Chief of Staff, his father-in-law, Randolph Marcy, said it was not so and dismissed the report, as they had positive intelligence that the Confederates would make a desperate fight at Yorktown.[21] An enlisted man in the 18th Massachusetts Infantry, Thomas H. Mann, lamented that "the evacuation of Yorktown took the army completely by surprise….the rebels….never did what the commanders of the Union armies anticipated….The 'skedaddle' from Yorktown and its defences was known at headquarters by daylight, but not a single cavalry-man was started in pursuit, to say nothing of the infantry, till noon or after. To say that the army was angry and chagrined at the situation is drawing it mild." Mann also commented on the Rebel torpedoes: "There was indignation over the killing of two or three of the first troops that entered the rebel works. They were murdered by the explosion of some infernal machines that had been buried…to explode at the slightest touch….Two or three hundred captured Confederates were made to unearth more than a score of these infernal machines." McClellan reported to Edwin M. Stanton on 4 May that "The rebels have been guilty of the most murderous and barbarous conduct in placing torpedoes within the abandoned works near wells and springs; near flag-staffs, Magazines, telegraph offices, in carpet-bags, barrels of flour, &c. Fortunately we have not lost many men in this manner—some 4 or 5 killed and perhaps a dozen wounded. I shall make the prisoners remove them at their own peril."[22] Col. Régis de Trobriand, commanding the 55th New

---

training, and—in the case of the Union cavalry—poor horsemanship also had discouraged the use of shock tactics," Jay Luvaas, *The Military Legacy of the Civil War: The European Inheritance* (Lawrence, KS: University Press of Kansas, 1998), 80-85.

[21] Sears, *Gates of Richmond*, 61; testimony by Painter, *JCCW*, vol. 1, 283-284. As McClellan was his own chief of intelligence, the sorting and evaluation of information was not as efficacious as it might have been had a staff officer been detailed to review raw information and assign positive collection efforts relieving the general of the army of these chores. See Appendix A for a discussion of McClellan as chief of intelligence of the Army of the Potomac during the Maryland Campaign. McClellan did have Allan Pinkerton and his staff of 11 which helped in gathering information, but they did little evaluation. He also had Professor Thaddeus Lowe and three balloons to aid his information gathering. Painter further testified that McClellan "trusts everything, so far as getting information is concerned, to a man he has there of the name of Pinkerton Allen who always questions the contrabands and deserters; and, generally, so far as I have conversed with him, throws discredit upon their statements and attaches no importance to them," Painter, *JCCW*, vol. 1, 291. Painter later testified about how he gained his information concerning the Rebel army strength: "By getting statements from prisoners, contrabands, and deserters, and learning about different divisions and brigades, and drawing conclusions from the mass of information collected. I have at different times found a great many of their muster-rolls, and learned in that way how many men they had in their regiments," ibid., 292. Thus this reporter had a better and more reliable estimate of enemy strength that did Pinkerton and McClellan who would have done well to use the same sources. For details of McClellan's use of information and Pinkerton's employment during the Peninsular Campaign see Edwin C. Fishel, *The Secret War for the Union: The Untold Story of Military Intelligence in the Civil War* (Boston: Houghton Mifflin Company, 1996), 146-164 passim. McClellan had two French aides-de-camp on his staff, Louis Philippe d'Orleans and his brother Robert, Duc de Chartes, who were assigned by McClellan in January 1862 to help summarize the plethora of information coming into army headquarters. Unfortunately for McClellan, their valuable help and reports stopped when the army moved to the Peninsula just when the army commander could have most benefitted by their assistance and when combined with Pinkerton's efforts, McClellan would likely have been able to make more reasoned decisions based on better intelligence, Edwin C. Fishel, *The Secret War for the Union: The Untold Story of Military Intelligence in the Civil War* (Boston: Houghton Mifflin Company, 1996), 123-129.

[22] Mann, 60, 61. His observations about the slow pursuit may have been aided by hindsight. Details of Union torpedo casualties are found in Russel H. Beatie, *Army of the Potomac: McClellan's First Campaign, March-May 1862* (New York: Savas Beatie, 2007), 494-495. McClellan's report, *OR*, vol. 11, pt. 3, 135. The Comte de Paris wrote that the Federals "were not early risers in the Union armies. The disappointment was so great at the sudden departure of the Confederates that at first it could not be believed; and when the evidence was conclusive, everything had to be organized for an advance, which had not been contemplated. The troops had eaten nothing; the rations had not been distributed; many regiments had sent their wagons to a distance of several leagues to obtain them. In short, the cavalry division only took up its line of march between ten and eleven o'clock….With a little more celerity the Confederate detachments which fell back upon Williamsburg from Lee's Mills would have been intercepted by the Federal cavalry before they could have reached that town," Comte de Paris, *History of the Civil War in America*, vol. 2, trans. by Louis F. Tasistro, ed. by Henry Coppee (Philadelphia, PA: Jos. H. Coates and Co., 1876), 15-16.

York Infantry, the Lafayette Guards, under McClellan, wrote that "The rain had not stopped during the night [of the 4th/5th], and it continued to pour down all day....The roads were horrible, if we could call roads the great mud-holes where the teams struggled, and the cannon and caissons, buried up to the axles, were with difficulty drawn out of one deep rut, only to fall immediately into another."[23] Even had McClellan drawn up plans for a pursuit, the rain and muddy roads would have slowed his men more than the Rebels as they had more of a chance to prepare for the retreat and travelled lighter than the Army of the Potomac.

Union cavalry start pursuit of the Confederates up the Yorktown Pike toward Williamsburg. Note telegraph lines and poles. *Harper's Weekly*, 17 May 1862, by Winslow Homer. Author's collection. Sidney Davis noted that "The telegraph line was broken down in many places....Some of the men amused themselves by catching hold of the wire...and by swinging it back and forth, knocking off the caps of those in front or rear...During one of these pleasantries...where the wire descended into the mud...a shell [torpedo] burst at that point throwing the earth around, but doing no further damage....the telegraph wire, so far as the Sixth Cavalry was concerned, remained undisturbed during the remainder of that day," 127.

One Confederate observer, Lt. Col. Edward P. Alexander, found that McClellan had done well in arranging a pursuit of the retreating Confederates, and that the movements of the Union cavalry were "well conducted, and rapid, [so] that the principal body of the Confederate cavalry under General Stuart was cut off, and with difficulty made its escape by a circuitous by-way, while the remainder was driven in upon the Confederate infantry column just as its rear was filing into the streets of Williamsburg."[24] As will be seen, Stuart did have to act quickly to avoid a difficult situation as Union troopers and infantry

---

[23] Régis de Trobriand, *Four Years with the Army of the Potomac* (Boston, MA: Ticknor and Company, 1889), 191.
[24] Edward Porter Alexander, "Sketch of Longstreet's Division—Yorktown and Williamsburg," in *Southern Historical Society Papers*, vol. X, January to December 1882 (Richmond: Southern Historical Society, n.d.; reprint, Millwood, NJ: Kraus Reprint Co, 1977), 39. Alexander wrote that a few rear guard Confederate cavalry stragglers were wounded when they set off some torpedoes and Union troops had 30 torpedo casualties including Unionist cavalry, 38-39. This pursuit Alexander described was later in the day, not early morning, however. He perhaps tried to excuse Stuart's dilemma.

closed in, and the remainder of the Confederate troopers retreating to Williamsburg also had to be on the alert once Stoneman started his pursuit up the Peninsula from Yorktown.

Other observers opined differently stating that it was almost 10 o'clock in the morning before McClellan issued orders, and another four hours before Stoneman began the pursuit. Henry B. McClellan, appointed by Stuart as Assistant Adjutant General 20 April 1863 on Stuart's staff, wrote that "The evacuation of Yorktown was a surprise to the Federal army. Nothing was in readiness for such an event, and it was midday on the 4th before an efficient pursuit could be organized....a rapid pursuit along the Telegraph Road would cut off and capture whatever portion of the Confederate rear-guard might be on the roads south of it [and] an earlier start or a more vigorous pursuit might, perhaps, have accomplished this result."[25] The Union cavalry did relatively well once it received orders to chase the Confederate retreat. The stage was set for the first cavalry clash on the Peninsula.

To cover the Confederate withdrawal from Yorktown and the Warwick River defense line, Stuart set up his line along Skiff's Creek, deploying his four regiments with himself near the center of the line at Blow's Mill, with the majority of the 3rd Virginia Cavalry under Col. Thomas F. Goode, and the South Carolina Hampton Legion led by Maj. Matthew C. Butler, near Yorktown. To his right toward the James River, he placed the Jeff Davis Legion from Mississippi, Lt. Col. Martin commanding, at a bridge over Skiff's Creek, where the Hampton Road crossed, and which Martin burned before the Yankees reached it; the 4th Virginia Cavalry was on his left along the Yorktown Road, nearer Yorktown at Burwell's Mill (Whittaker's Mill), behind Kings Creek, Lt. Col. Williams C. Wickham in command, along with a section of mountain howitzers, and part of the 3rd Virginia Cavalry. The 1st Virginia Cavalry under Col. Fitzhugh Lee, was above Stuart's line near the York River, heading for West Point above Williamsburg, anticipating a Union landing there. Virginia's Wise Legion (10th Virginia Cavalry) led by Col. J. Lucius Davis, and horse artillery, was in reserve near Williamsburg, after it left Yorktown later on 4 May; it was then joined by the 4th and 10th Virginia and part of the Hampton which had been closer to Yorktown.[26]

---

[25] Robert O'Neill, "Cavalry On the Peninsula: Fort Monroe to the Gates of Richmond, March to May, 1862," *Blue & Gray Magazine*, Vol. XIX, issue 5, 19, hereafter cited as *Fort Monroe*; McClellan, *Stuart*, 48. Beatie, 516, n. 8. wrote that "The maps and the narratives in the reports of the movement to Williamsburg are marvels of confusion." Beatie finds the Comte de Paris diary entry convincing that McClellan wasted three hours confirming that the Rebels had really fled, 513.

[26] Newton says that Johnston sent Col. Fitzhugh Lee to precede the Yorktown retreat to ride to near Eltham's Landing and West Point to watch for Union amphibious landings; he also gave operational control of Lee's regiment to Maj. Gen. Gustavus W. Smith, an infantry division commander as of 5 May, 133; John H. and David J. Eicher, Civil *War High Commands* (Stanford, CA: Stanford University Press, 2001), 495. The Hampton Road on the York River side of the Peninsula was also known as the Lee's Mill Road, Grove Road, Big Bethel Road, and the Williamsburg Road; on the James River side, the Yorktown Road was also known as the York Road and the Telegraph Road, Hastings, 30, 32; Carol K. Dubbs, *Defend This Old Town: Williamsburg During the Civil War* (Baton Rouge, LA: Louisiana State University Press, 2002), 75; compare Beatie showing some different names. During this era when there were few formal road names, local roads, outside of towns or cities, often used the names of towns between which the road ran so a longer road could have more than one name depending on where the traveler was at the time. In Yorktown, the main road to Williamsburg would be called the "Williamsburg Road" while from Williamsburg it would be named the "Yorktown Road;" in either case it could also be called the "Williamsburg-Yorktown Road." Roads also were named after landmarks or features as noticed above with "Lee's Mill Road" and the "Telegraph Road" with the idea that travelers on the road would know easily where the road leads or a stranger would be able to identify the road by obvious landmarks, natural or man-made. See "A History of Roads in Virginia" produced by the Virginia Department of Transportation Office of Public Affairs, http://www.loudounhistory.org/history/virginia-transportation.htm; see "Transportation," discussing the history of transportation in Virginia, http://xroads.virginia.edu/~HYPER/VAGuide/transp.html. Lt. Custer on loan from the 5th U.S. Cavalry to Brig. Gen. John G. Barnard, the chief engineer of the army, burned his hands while trying to put out the fire on Skiff Creek bridge, *OR*, vol. 11, pt. 1, 526. Custer, who was accompanying Brig. Gen. Winfield Scott Hancock's brigade of Smith's division, led a detachment of the 5th U.S. Cavalry from Capt. William Chambliss's two squadrons which was accompanying Hancock to put out the fire, Beatie, 516, 639-640, 651-654. See Hastings who wrote that the Custer incident was at best overblown and possibly apocryphal, 37.

Map showing where Stuart set up his strong points: lowest arrow shows the bridge over Skiff's Creek where the Hampton Road crossed defended by the Jeff Davis Legion, the arrow just above shows Stuart's headquarters at Blow's Mills, to the right the 4th Virginia was on his left along the Yorktown Road, and the 1st Virginia Cavalry under Col. Fitzhugh Lee was above Stuart's line near the York River, the river, upper right, likely defending the area between the Yorktown Road and the York River. Arrow below Ft. Magurder points to the Cheesecake Church. The Halfway House is on the Yorktown Road. Military map of south-eastern Virginia A. Lindenkohl, ca. 1862. Courtesy LOC.

Stoneman started out sometime between 11 A.M. and noon along the Yorktown Road toward Williamsburg. His force consisted of the 1st and 6th U.S. Cavalry, the 3rd Pennsylvania Cavalry, and Barker's squadron of the McClellan (Illinois) Dragoons, with Hay's Brigade of artillery of four batteries altogether about 24 cannon, under command of Lt. Col. Harp.[27] Emory's brigade was in the van with the 3rd Pennsylvania, and Maj. Barker's Dragoons with Benson's Battery M, 2nd U.S. Artillery. Next was Cooke's brigade with the 1st and 6th U.S. Cavalry, supported by Capt. Horatio Gibson's Company C, 3rd U.S. Artillery. Stoneman was ordered to "pursue and harass the rear of the retreating enemy, and if possible to cut off his rear guard, or that portion of it which had taken the Lee's Mill and Yorktown road [Hampton Road]....In harassing the enemy I was to be supported by Hooker's division, which was to follow us by a forced march along the Yorktown and Williamsburg road, and in cutting off the rear guard I was to cooperate with the division of General Smith, which was to march on the other, or Lee's Mill, road."[28] As Stoneman now took over command of the cavalry division as well as other units in pursuit of the Rebel retreat, he in effect bumped Brig. Gen. Cooke from command of the Cavalry Reserve Division. Cooke, having now no command, bumped Brig. Gen. William H. Emory, and took command of Emory's brigade, using Emory as his staff officer.[29]

A torpedo slowed the cavalry somewhat as it moved beyond the Yorktown fortifications toward Stuart's rear guard. Stoneman was to hold the road junction near Williamsburg while the troops coming up on the Hampton Road could reinforce Stoneman and Hooker. Following more slowly behind Stoneman was the Second Division of Maj. Gen. Samuel P. Heintzelman's Corps under Brig. Gen. Joseph Hooker. Brig. Gen. William F. "Baldy" Smith's Division was heading toward Williamsburg on the Hampton Road led by a squadron of 150 troopers from the 5th U.S. Cavalry commanded by Capt. William Chambliss. When Stoneman came up against Stuart's 4th Virginia Cavalry south of Fort Magruder, the Union cavalry commander "sent General Emory, with Benson's battery and the Third Pennsylvania Cavalry and Barker's squadron, across to the Lee's Mill road to cut off any force on that road and between Emory's and Smith's column, and with the remainder I pushed on...to occupy the

[27] O'Neill, *Peninsula Campaign*, 99; O'Neill, B&G, 19; Rawle, 48; Beatie, 517; George B. McClellan, *Report on the Organization and Campaigns of the Army of the Potomac* (New York: Sheldon & Company, 1864), 178. Note that Lt. Col. Harp is not mentioned other than in McClellan. Stoneman in his report, *OR*, vol. 11, pt. 1, 423-424, states that his pursuit included the 8th Illinois Cavalry but that regiment was at that time assigned to Gen. Richardson's division of Sumner's Corps and only on 10 May joined Stoneman, Abner Hard, *History of the Eighth Cavalry Regiment Illinois Volunteers, During the Great Rebellion* (Aurora, IL: n.p., 1868, reprint, Dayton, OH: Press of Morningside Bookshop, 1996), 107, 118, O'Neill, *B&G*, 41. Stoneman apparently erred in his report. Emory did not mention the 8th Illinois in his report nor did Col. Averell, *OR*, vol. 11, pt. 1, 433-436. McClellan agrees with Emory, *Report on the Organization and Campaigns*, 178-179. Unfortunately, some historians have relied on Stoneman's apparently mistaken report.

[28] Stoneman's 18 May 1862 report, *OR*, vol. 11, pt. 1, 424. Gov. William R.S. Sprague of Rhode Island accompanied Stoneman's advance toward Williamsburg on 4 May and Stoneman used him as a messenger to hurry forward the Union infantry. Sprague was under fire as his aide was seriously wounded while they were with Stoneman, Beatie, 519. Unfortunately for Stoneman, there was confusion with the infantry units so that no help arrived for hours. The day after the cavalry fight at Williamsburg, Sprague rode to Yorktown to inform McClellan of the situation at Williamsburg and to request that the army commander go to the front which he did arriving there about 5 P.M. that day, U.S. Congress, *Report of the Joint Committee on the Conduct of the War.* Washington: Government Printing Office, 1863; reprint (Wilmington, NC: Broadfoot Publishing Company, 1998), vol. 1, 430, 568-570.

[29] Beatie, 518.

junction of the road from Yorktown with that of Lee's Mill, 2 miles from Williamsburg."[30] Stoneman now had taken the intersection of the two main roads leading up the Peninsula, the one from Yorktown, and the other from Lee's Mill, the Hampton Road.

Stuart, near Blow's Mill, learned of Union cavalry cutting off his line of retreat to Williamsburg on the Lee's Mill/Hampton Road as Brig. Gen. William Emory moved his brigade to Stuart's left, so Stuart sent three companies of the 3rd Virginia, about 100 troopers under Col. Goode, to learn of the strength of the Union threat. Confederate and Union forces met each other with the McClellan Dragoons being chased by the 3rd Virginia Cavalry, routing the Yankee troopers, and capturing a Union flag. The Confederate troopers were stopped as they finally approached Col. Averell's 3rd Pennsylvania Cavalry, supported by artillery. Federal losses in the fight with Goode's men were two killed and four wounded, and the Confederates, two killed and many wounded; Stuart's report stated that the McClellan Dragoons left eight dead and many wounded in the road with Confederate troopers suffering only four wounded. The 3rd Pennsylvania Cavalry handled itself well in quickly setting up a dismounted defensive line driving off the hard-charging Confederate troopers. Stuart now knew that Union forces were, in fact, moving rapidly up the Peninsula, so the remaining Confederate troopers, covered by some of Stuart's guns, accompanied by Stuart, escaped west to the James River. They retired to Williamsburg avoiding roads and rode close to the water along the beach, hastened along when they were mistakenly fired on by the Confederate James River Squadron stationed on the river. Stuart and his troopers arrived at Williamsburg too late to participate in the success enjoyed by the 4th Virginia Cavalry, Lt. Col. Wickham commanding, the Wise Legion led by Col. Lucius Davis, and the Hampton Legion under Maj. Butler, at the first day of the Battle of Williamsburg, earlier in the day, 4 May. But Stuart crowed "that our cavalry drove the enemy from the open space near Fort Magruder, killing and capturing a number, obliging them, with the aid of the artillery, to abandon their artillery and take to the woods." Of course Union reports painted a somewhat different picture.[31]

---

[30] *OR*, vol. 11, pt. 1, 424; Beatie, 516, 518. Beatie wrote that Cooke put Emory in command sending Benson's battery, the 3rd Pennsylvania cavalry and the Dragoons to the Lee's Mill/Hampton Road to trap any Confederates coming up that way being chased by Chambliss and Smith.

[31] *OR*, vol. 11, pt. 1, 444-445; O'Neill, 99; Hastings, 31, 36. See also the report of Col. William W. Averell commanding the 3rd Pennsylvania Cavalry of the fight with Stuart near Blow's Mills, *OR*, vol. 11, pt. 1, 434-435. He reported that his regiment and Benson's battery, Emory's command, took a road to the left at a church and then found the Confederate cavalry and had the fight described above. The church may have been the Lebanon Church shown on the second map below. Note that the two maps are not congruous. The church may have been the one on the second map below at the arrow to the left of Black's Swamp.

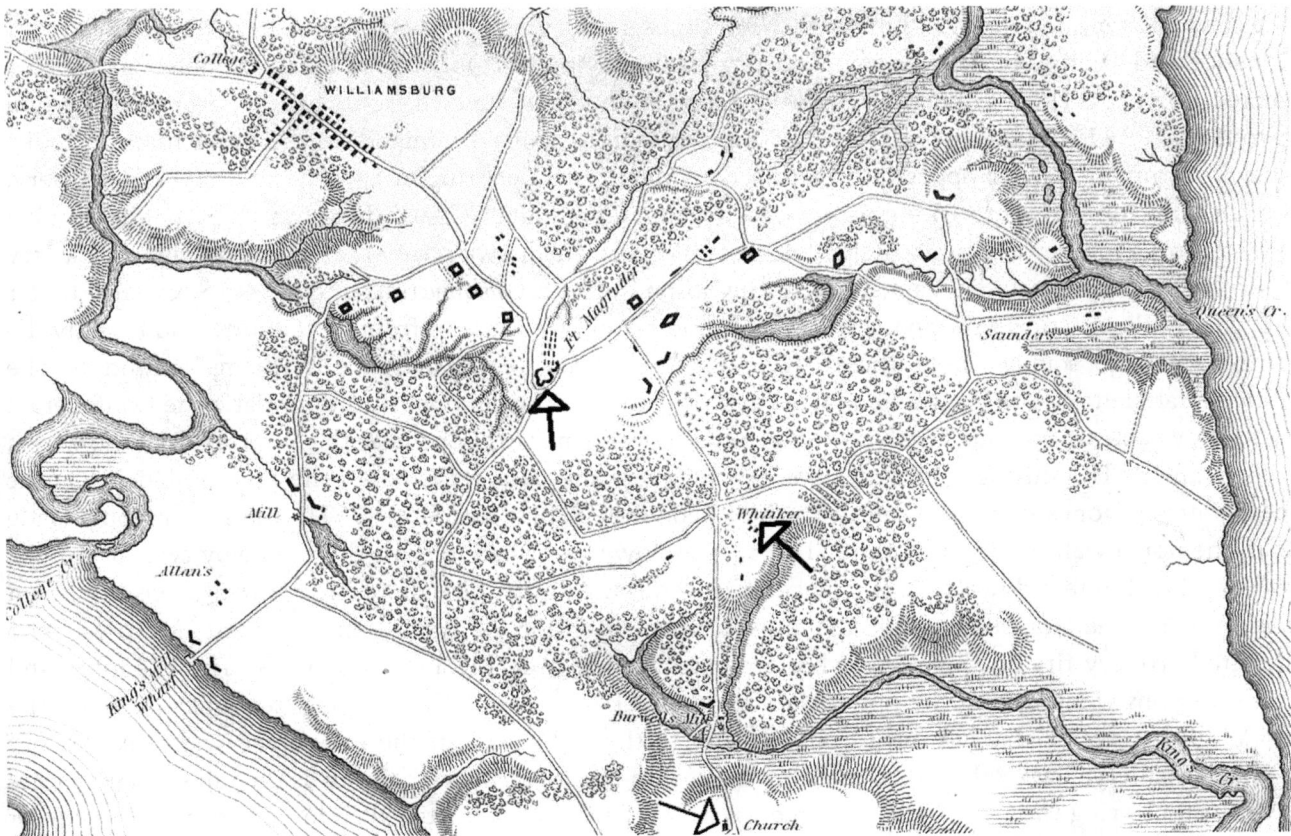

Detail from Yorktown to Williamsburg map. Lowest arrow points to Cheesecake Church not to be confused with the Lebanon Church where Union cavalry under Emory turned to confront Stuart forcing him to the northwest along the James River beach to escape; middle arrow points to Whittaker's Mill, the area which Stuart's 4th Virginia cavalry and part of the 3rd were defending on 4 May; it later became headquarters for Sumner, Keyes, and Smith after the Rebel troopers were pushed away, Beatie, 518. The arrow to the center points to Fort Magruder; Williamsburg is to the upper left. Note the Confederate camp just above Fort Magruder. Compiled by Capt. H. L. Abbot, Topographical Engineers, September 1862. Courtesy LOC.

After Stoneman had pushed Lt. Col. Wickham's forces back toward Williamsburg, Stoneman advanced in the center. He ordered Cooke to push forward and seize the junction of the two main roads below Fort Magruder. Cooke, in command of the 1st and 6th U.S. Cavalry, and Company C of the 3rd U.S. Artillery, pursuing up the Yorktown Road, came up against the Confederate main defensive line at Fort Magruder. The formidable Confederate line with Fort Magruder and 14 redoubts was anchored on both the York and James Rivers, and protected Williamsburg, as the road from Yorktown and the Hampton Road met near Fort Magruder. But as Cooke approached, the fort and surrounding redoubts were lightly manned, if at all, as Johnston decided to hurry on through Williamsburg and push on to Richmond. As the fast-closing troopers appeared before Fort Magruder though, he sent troops back to man the fort and some other positions to hold off the Federals, as the Confederates struggled north on muddy, crowded, roads.[32] Stoneman sent Emory, commanding the 3rd Pennsylvania Cavalry, the McClellan Dragoons, and the 2nd U.S. Artillery Batteries B and L, to the left to flank Rebel cavalry defenses near Fort Magruder.

About two miles from Fort Magruder, Cooke came up to another rear guard, he estimated at two companies, "at a defile of a mill and dam and a breastwork across the road. I ordered up a section of artillery, with which Lieutenant Fuller handsomely opened fire at less than 300 yards under a fire of

---

[32] Dubbs, 78-79. For a detailed discussion of the redoubts see Hastings, 131-136. Note that as of June 2011, Redoubt # 1 was part of local park with signage and trails; Redoubt # 2 adjacent appears in preparation for inclusion in the park: author visit May 2011.

musketry. After a few rounds, I ordered the advance guard, Captain Savage's squadron, Sixth Cavalry, to advance and charge, but the enemy had retreated, leaving two military wagons in flames and also a spiked howitzer. During the affair General Emory, who joined me in front, had been ordered by you [Stoneman]…with Major [Charles W.] Barker's squadron, of my command, to the other road."[33] Cooke then confronted heavier opposition around Fort Magruder consisting of cavalry, infantry and artillery, which Johnston had sent rushing back to the abandoned redoubts. Cooke thought that by boldly moving forward on a forest path on the Rebel left he could push them away. He ordered the six guns of Battery C of the 3rd Artillery under Capt. Horatio G. Gibson, with three squadrons of the 1st U.S. Cavalry under Lt. Col. William Grier, in support, to open ground about 500 yards in front of the fort. Additionally, he sent four large squadrons of the 6th U.S. Cavalry under Maj. Lawrence Williams around to the Confederate left of Fort Magruder along the forest path, seeking an opportunity to flank the Confederate fire. They came up the small path off the Yorktown-Williamsburg road near the Whittaker House which was Sumner's HQ during the battle. The 6th followed the path west, down the ravine, which has the headwaters of Jones Pond, just to the south of Redoubt # 8, past Redoubt # 7. The advanced scouts made it to the north wall of Fort Magruder. The 6th was slowed as it had to cross the ravine by twos or by file, and then had to tear down part of a fence. As it reformed on the far side of the ravine, Rebels saw them and the Yankee horsemen drew the unwelcomed attention of Brig. Gen. Lafayette McLaws, who directed artillery fire on the Yankee horsemen, as well as ordering a cavalry attack. The Hampton and Wise Legions went around the left of the fort to attack the 6th U.S. Cavalry near redoubt # 7, while the 4th Virginia Cavalry charged the 1st U.S. Cavalry to the right front of the fort which was in support of Cooke's artillery. Two Rebel companies hit the rear of the 6th Cavalry's column as the tail end companies were still clearing the ravine it had to recross as the Unionists retreated. While most of the 6th was not engaged, the remaining units of the 6th, some 200 to 300 men of the 5th Squadron composed of Companies A and M, under the command of Capt. William P. Sanders, aided by Capt. Henry B. Hays of Company M, formed and successfully attacked the Confederate cavalry. This hand-to-hand melee involved a liberal use of sabers but the Union horsemen were quickly forced back by the weight of numbers, losing twelve men wounded. Confederate losses were recorded at two killed and at least five wounded. The deep mud in the ravine added to the confusion and those 6th U.S. troopers who were unhorsed were among the first the regiment lost to capture.[34]

A member of the 6th U.S. Cavalry, Pvt. Sidney Morris Davis, kept a diary during the war, and left this riveting, first-person account of the fight:

To the left of the fort [Fort Magruder] where we see the battery at work, stretching as in a line across the plains are other earthworks but they seem to be unoccupied. We move across the marsh, and leaving the road proceed at a trot, with drawn sabres, in column of companies, across the peach orchard, and straight toward the smoking earthwork. There are no skirmishers in advance; we march as though we were going through a drill….I wonder if those men in the fort are our friends. The head of the column reaches the ditch outside of the parapet, and advances along its side until they encounter a fence at the rear, and then the regiment halts.

The movement has brought us within thirty or forty paces of the cannoneers. I…see that they are dressed in gray….They are busy with their guns and seem to take no notice of us….No other soldiers are visible.

---

[33] *OR*, vol. 11, pt. 1, 427.

[34] Hastings, 58; the regiment of the Hampton Legion was not under Stuart's command but rather under G.W. Smith; the Wise Legion and the 4th Virginia cavalry was under the overall command of Col. Lucius Davis in place of Stuart, 58. See Stoneman's, Cooke's, etc. reports on the Williamsburg fight, *OR*, vol. 11, pt. 1, 423-441; Confederate reports, 441-446. See also William H. Carter, *From Yorktown to Santiago with the Sixth U.S. Cavalry* (Baltimore, MD: The Lord Baltimore Press, The Friedenwald Company, 1900) who supplies additional details about the 6th's fight, 26-29.

A number of our troops dismount and begin to tear down the fence leading to the rear of the earthwork, and pitch the rails into the ditch. Lieutenant McClain turns in his saddle, and looking upon Company F, sternly cries out "When we enter this fort, I want every man to cut right and left!"

....At this juncture a man apparently dressed in civilian clothes is seen upon the plain toward the spot from which we have just emerged [Prince de Joinville of McClellan's staff], and beckons with his hand....Major Williams...orders the men to remount, and then....the column is in motion, I look back over my right shoulder to see what is going on in the fort....I see the artillerymen wheel their pieces around, and train them upon us. The next instant there is a roar...and a shell comes over our heads with a hissing sound...but in their excitement they have fired too high, and no one is hurt.

....Presently I see a regiment of cavalry, dressed in gray, with frock coats and low-crowned hats trot out from behind the fort we have just left, and to its right as it faces us, and come across the plain toward us. The head of our column has just reached the swamp, and we are obliged to halt and break by fours to pass down the narrow ravine leading to the crossing. The enemy have evidently divined our difficulties, for they leave the trot for the gallop. Some one by this time calls out in rear, "Cavalry coming!" and this warning is passed from company to company to the major, who, by this time, is across the marsh with the head of the command and is reforming the men into columns of companies as fast as they regain that side. The artillery of the enemy has ceased its firing, for their mounted men are between us and the fort, and in the range of their guns, closely pressing on our rear. The crackling of small arms, evidently revolvers, begins. Our men struggle hard to get across the swamp, crowding one another fearfully in their fierce efforts. The horses sink up to their breasts into the now boiling marsh, and plunge wildly forward. A great log forms an additional obstruction.

I hardly know how to get across, but I find myself riding up the slope on the safe side. Presently the men are all over, and fall into ranks, their tormentors dashing into the marsh and across it in the ardor of their pursuit. They swarm up the side of the slope like bees.

A loud, clear voice, which still rings in my ears, rises above the tumult: "Sixth Cavalry—right about wheel!"

Everybody within the reach of its sound seems to comprehend instantly its import. Two or three hundred men execute the movement, which brings them face to face with the foe, and in another moment they sweep upon them, with glittering sabres, like an irresistible avalanche, and crush them back into the marsh. Hoarse shouts of vengeance go up as the sabres flash and the strokes fall rapidly in all directions. It lasts but a moment, for our enemies retire in disorder across the plain toward their fort. Major Williams had, in the meantime, gone on with the balance of the regiment.

When the rush was made toward the swamp, my previous experience in that pool of mud warned me not to risk another submersion; so I ride to one side and begin firing upon a squad of the enemy who are huddled upon the opposite side and are shooting into our ranks....I am anxious to fire rapidly for fear that I shall be disabled before I can repeat the shots.

....By this time the confederates have retreated, and I ride slowly up the hill to rejoin the forming squadrons....The regiment regains the open fields...and there forms in column of companies...the roll is called amid profound silence, and when one does not answer to his name his comrades are asked if they know anything about him, and if any one can tell his fate he responds. We find that there are thirty-one men dead, wounded and missing....The Sixth Cavalry has received its baptism of fire, and I feel that, under the circumstances, the regiment has acted nobly.[35]

---

[35] Sidney Davis, 119-122. The Prince de Joinville was near the site of the battle as he rode with Stoneman up from Yorktown but he did not record that he directed Maj. Williams, The Prince de Joinville, *The Army of the Potomac: Its Organization, Its Commander, and Its Campaign* (New York: Anson D.F. Randolph, 1863), 48-51. The Comte de Paris and the Duc de Chartres also accompanied the cavalry advance from Yorktown and were with Stoneman, *OR*, vol. 11, pt. 1, 426. The Prince wrote that at dusk on the 4th McClellan personally congratulated Maj. Williams on his attack in front of the 6th Cavalry, 55. Davis wrote that "About four o'clock General McClellan, accompanied by his staff, arrived from the direction of Yorktown. He turned off the road when he had reached the point at which we were stationed and rode up to Major Williams, and, through the latter, tendered his thanks and compliments to the regiment for what he termed as gallant conduct the day before in front of the enemy's works....The regiment gave three hearty cheers in acknowledgement of his presence, which was instantly taken up by other troops, and soon ran along the line to the left," 124. Hastings believes that the 6th Cavalry was engaged near Redoubt # 8 to the northeast of Fort Magruder, 58.

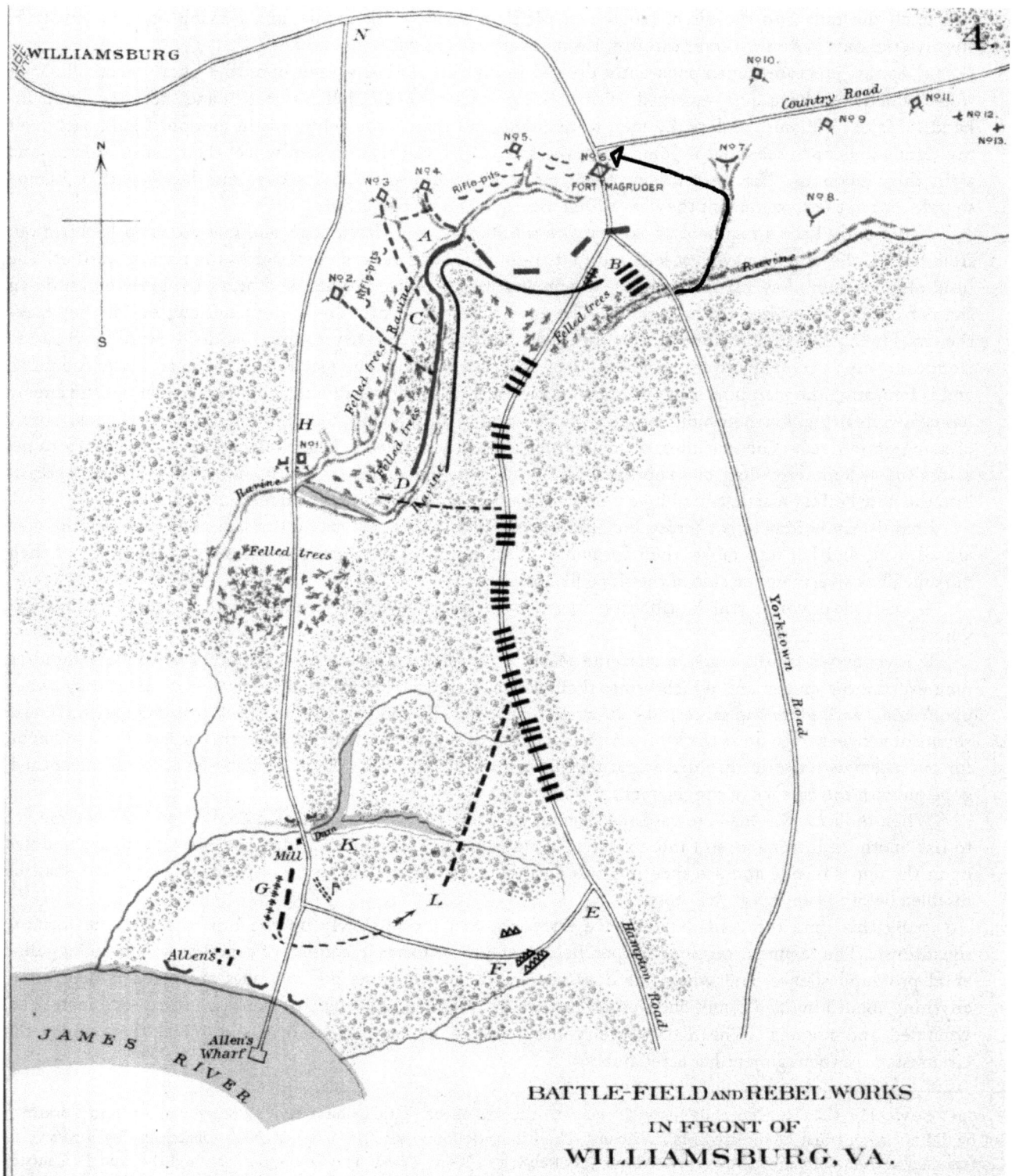

Detail of map showing Union cavalry attack at Fort Magruder on 4-5 May 1862. Fott Magruder at upper center; tail of arrow is approximate area of ravine where the 6th U.S. fought at upper right; area where 1st U.S. located at arrow near letter "B" supporting Gibson's artillery to its left. *OR*, vol. 11, pt. 1, Stoneman, 424; Cooke, 428, Williams, et al, 436-439; see also Hastings, 58, stating that the 6th U.S. "emerged into the cleared area in front of Redoubt # 8 at the head of Jones Mill Pond" which is on the left of the Confederate line. Note that few maps made then and to the present day agree on the exact locations of roads and redoubts. *Official Atlas of the Civil War*, Plate 20, no. 4. Courtesy LOC.

From the Confederate perspective, Pvt. John Taylor Chappell of Company A of the Wise Legion (10th Virginia Cavalry), wrote that as the Union and Confederate troopers engaged in the melee at the creek, "We became instantly entangled and mixed up and for about ten minutes nothing was heared but the clashing of steel." He had entered the fray "armed with two large brass-mounted 'Horse pistols,' and old sawed-off muzzle-loading musket, and a saber 'that might have been made of hoop iron.' But he emerged 'the happy owner of a brace of Colts Army revolvers, a Sharps Carbine and a handsome basket-hilted English sabre.'"[36]

Meanwhile, the 1st U.S. Cavalry was in a severe contest with the 4th Virginia Cavalry and some of the Hampton Legion in front of Fort Magruder, as the Union troopers tried to protect Gibson's cannon. The artillerymen were in a trying duel with artillery posted in the fort; Gibson fired for almost an hour expending some 250 rounds. Stoneman ordered Cooke to withdraw the guns and Gibson began limbering up and started retreating by section, but one gun became mired down blocking four caissons. Lt. Col. William Grier and some of his 1st Cavalry helped with the guns, while Confederate gunners continued firing from Fort Magruder. The Rebel cavalry charged into the struggling Union cavalrymen and artillerists, capturing one gun and three caissons, which were hopelessly bogged down. In doing so, the 4th Virginia suffered by losing Lt. Colonel Wickham to a severe saber wound inflicted by Lt. Col. Grier, its colors, and at least 15 dead and wounded. Federal troopers lost 12 killed and 32 wounded, and Grier was also wounded after slashing Wickham. Some of the 1st U.S. Cavalry charged two Confederate infantry units as the Rebel infantry began forming on the Yorktown Road, allowing the rest of Gibson's battery to escape, with the Federal units ending up at the Whittaker House, some half mile to the rear. It turned out that the Union private who captured the 4th Virginia Cavalry's flag, John Thompson, Co. G, 3rd Artillery, was accidentally sabered in the melee by a Yankee cavalryman who wrenched it away. Since the Federal cavalry had no infantry support, they were forced to give up the ground they had won. As will be seen, in the Maryland Campaign, Union cavalry always succeeded when buckrammed by infantry.[37]

In the two fights around Fort Magruder, troopers from both sides showed that they were not afraid to attack with saber, pistol and carbine, suffering casualties in their efforts, while winning the praises of Gen. McLaws on the Confederate side, and Gen. McClellan on the Union side. McClellan did criticize the over zealousness of the cavalry pursuit because it forced Johnston to return infantry units to support Fort Magruder, and many of the redoubts south of Williamsburg; McClellan had wanted the Rebels to retreat further up the Peninsula from Williamsburg to clear West Point on the York River to the east, so it could be used as a Union supply depot; he lamented as that was delayed due to his cavalry's quick pursuit, which forced the Confederates to tarry! Union regular troopers and the 3rd Pennsylvania horsemen faced veteran Confederate cavalrymen on an equal footing in these first major cavalry confrontations on the Peninsula, and did well—credit should be given both to Stoneman and Cooke.[38]

---

[36] Dubbs, quoting John Taylor Chappell, "From Yorktown to Williamsburg," manuscript in the library and manuscripts collection of the Virginia Historical Society, call no. Mss5:1 C3685:1, 81.

[37] *OR*, vol. 11, pt. 1, 424-432. Beatie, 523-527; Beatie shows that had Hooker not been blocked by another Union division he would have arrived in time to bolster the cavalry and hold the ground and road intersection it had won. See also Dubbs, 82.

[38] *OR*, vol. 11, pt. 1, 423-425; 433-434; 443-445; O'Neill, *Fort Monroe*, 20-21; O'Neill, *Peninsula Campaign*, 99-105; Hastings, 57; Rawle, 48-51; Brooks, *Butler and His Cavalry in the War of Secession 1861-1865*, 76; Sidney Davis 114-121; McClellan, *Story*, 320-322. Gibson reported that he lost a gun and caisson due to muddy ground and Rebel cavalry attacks but complements Capt. Benjamin F. Davis for his and his squadron of the 1st Cavalry efforts, 432. Note that Davis later commanded the 8th New York Cavalry at Harpers Ferry during the Maryland Campaign helping to lead the cavalry escape column out of the besieged post. Stoneman wrote in his official report on his activities for 4 and 5 May that on 5 May "my command was split up into fragments by the commanders, and I remained an idle spectator until the arrival of the general commanding," *OR*, vol. 11, pt. 1, 425. Note that on 10 July he voiced a similar complaint to McClellan, note 76 below. One assumes he meant the infantry commanders. Note that Maj. Williams commanding the 6th U.S. Cavalry reported "that on the day of the battle I was somewhat confused as to

Jeb Stuart was still on the road from the beach with the 3rd Virginia Cavalry and the Jeff Davis Legion, and would not arrive until late in the day, so the Confederate cavalry during the fights on 4 May performed well despite not having his direction. Accounts from both sides show that good platoon and company level leadership of willing troopers would result in at least adequate, if not excellent, performance. In general on the Peninsula, the side with the element of surprise, or with a markedly larger number of horsemen, often prevailed, as Yankee and Rebel horsemen met on even footing in a man-to-man contest.

Dramatic illustration of a Union cavalry charge against Rebel artillery. Note Federal cavalry using only sabers. Drawing by Winslow Homer, *Harper's Weekly*, 5 July 1862. Author's collection.

who was my immediate commander. Both Generals Cooke and Stoneman gave me orders," *OR*, vol. 11, pt. 1, 437. Hastings opined that "It has become fashionable…to denigrate the performance of the Union cavalry during the first years of the war. The performance of Stoneman's advanced guard on that Sunday afternoon [4 May], however, might give the severest critic pause. By mid-afternoon, his cavalry had cleared both of the roads to Williamsburg and caught the enemy encamped. Now, with no infantry support in sight, Stoneman and Cooke took a bold gamble. They decided to attack the line with the cavalry and artillery alone…. [but] their gamble had not paid off," 57, 59. Franklin's troops including two companies of the Lincoln Cavalry started for West Point by boat 6 May and after some skirmishing took the place and held it the next day against part of the troops under Gen. William C. Whiting which were retreating from Williamsburg, Wheeler, 166-168.

Sixth U.S. Cavalry charges Jeb Stuart's Cavalry 9 May 1862. Note that only one Rebel trooper is shown using a firearm while the rest of the combatants use sabers. Sketch by R.S. Hall from *The Soldier in Our Civil War*, pg. 341.

The next day, a rainy 5 May, brought little cavalry action during the infantry battle at Williamsburg, except for Emory. Hooker sent him, with the 3rd Pennsylvania Cavalry, four regiments of infantry, Benson's 2nd Artillery, and two batteries from Gen. Kearny's division, to his left rear, to observe Rebel movements. Emory's command skirmished in the fallen timber there near a redoubt, capturing it along with 40 prisoners, and holding it for the rest of the day.[39] Stuart on the other hand had a busy 5 May. He held his troopers ready near the two redoubts to the right of Fort Magruder, and took over the firing of cannon at those redoubts for the remainder of the day. Lt. Col. Martin, with the Jeff Davis Legion, was reconnoitering to the left of Ft. Magruder, keeping an eye on Yankee maneuvers. After the Stuart Horse Artillery arrived, having been detached for service at Bigler's Wharf, Stuart ordered Capt. John Pelham forward with some cavalry to pursue retiring Union infantry. Pelham left five guns in Williamsburg and headed south, quickly arriving on the scene at 2 P.M., with two 12 pound howitzers and one Blakely. He did well according to Stuart's report, firing on the enemy until dark, expending a total of 360 rounds despite a broken elevating screw on the Blakely. While his cavalry were not actively engaged, Stuart reported losing several casualties to Union cannon fire, including the acting commander of the 4th Virginia Cavalry, Maj. William H. Payne. Confederate cavalry covered the rear of Gen. Johnston's army as it continued its retreat up the Peninsula, leaving the Williamsburg fortifications the evening of 5 May.[40]

---

[39] James R. Burns, *Battle of Williamsburgh, with Reminiscences of the Campaign, Hospital Experiences, Debates, Etc.* (New York, n.p., 1865), 23-24. Emory could have done more damage by continuing into the rear of the redoubts but was concerned that he faced a substantial foe so he was content with his small gains.

[40] *OR*, vol. 11, pt. 1, 570-572; 574-575; O'Neill, *B&G*, 39.

The next few days found McClellan pushing cavalry units after the retreating Confederates. Stoneman pursued up the center of the Peninsula some 10 miles ahead of the army, with a mixed unit of cavalry, infantry, and artillery—the 6th U.S. Cavalry in the van—along with the newly-landed 8th Illinois Cavalry. Artillery consisted of Batteries B and L, 2nd U.S., under Capt. James Robertson, and Battery A of the 2nd, under Capt. John C. Tidball. Stoneman had most of the 8th Illinois Cavalry, despite the efforts of Brig. Gen. Erasmus D. Keyes, who was concerned because the 8th was assigned to his Fourth Corps. Keyes wrote to Stoneman on 9 May: "It is apparent from the orders which have been received from you to-day that you were not aware that the Eighth Illinois Cavalry has been assigned to my corps. It appearing evident to me, however, that you are in great need of the services of that regiment I send it to you retaining only one company to act as messengers for the corps...I trust that you will, if possible, order the regiment to rejoin me without delay. I have no other cavalry with me."[41] Stoneman sent back to Keyes Companies D and F on 9 May.

Gov. Sprague, who accompanied Stoneman from Williamsburg, later testified that "The advance were obliged to make maps for themselves from the information obtained by their own small reconnoitring parties, the maps furnished from headquarters being almost entirely inaccurate....As to what the enemy was about, that was entirely unknown. He was then asked by a Joint Committee of Congress member "What means were made use of to obtain the necessary information?" His reply showed what little information McClellan had to help fill out his intelligence of Rebel locations, movements, strength, etc., as he replied: "None whatever that I ever knew of, except the questioning of contrabands and prisoners who were brought in. They would be questioned by the provost marshal general, and what little information was obtained from that source would be communicated to headquarters." Other Union cavalry units scouted along the James and Chickahominy Rivers and the 1st New York (Lincoln's) Cavalry accompanied Franklin's expedition by boat to West Point, but the Empire State troopers did not participate in the action there. They moved northwest along the Pamunkey River arriving at White House on 15 May.[42]

Stoneman's column, still led by the 6th U.S. Cavalry, which was given the honor based on its excellent performance at Williamsburg, came up against Confederate cavalry south of Slatersville on 9 May, about two miles south of New Kent Court House. Maj. Williams's scouts reported that about 20 Rebel cavalry were in the town, so Williams sent 87 men from Capt. Lowell's squadron and Capt. Sanders's company to flank them, but the flanking column was seen by an enemy vidette, who wheeled about, followed at a gallop by the Unionists. As Capt. Lowell's men approached some buildings, they were ambushed and taken under heavy fire by dismounted Rebels inside. While this was going on, Capt. Sanders' company was diverted by a Confederate squadron on the left, which he charged, even though he was heavily outnumbered. His bold move sent the enemy into retreat, but then another Rebel squadron rapidly advanced, then also retreated as the intrepid Capt. Sanders charged them. As he saw he was over matched, he rallied his men and wisely withdrew. Meanwhile, Capt. Lowell was fighting in the town but managed to withdraw his outnumbered troopers in time to avoid severe losses. Yankee casualties in the action were four killed, eight wounded, and three missing. One Union trooper believed that two of the killed were shot after they were captured, and thought that the enemy had lost 16 killed and more wounded. Union infantry arrived as Confederate cavalry moved out from the woods to challenge them, but two Union infantry regiments, along with Robertson's horse artillery, proved to be more than a match, and the enemy cavalry prudently retired, their mission of delaying the Union

---

[41] OR, vol. 11, pt. 3, 157-158. Either Keyes was being sarcastic or more likely realized that Stoneman did, in fact, need the 8th.

[42] O'Neill, "Peninsula Campaign," 106; Hard, "our regiment [Eighth Illinois Cavalry] was sent out in detachments, to scour the country in all directions," 116, 117; O'Neill, Peninsula Campaign, 108; O'Neill, Fort Monroe, 40; O'Neill, B&G, 39; Sidney Davis, 132-133; OR, vol. 11, pt. 2, 247; JCCW, vol. 1, 570.

column accomplished. Robertson reported that "The roads were very heavy [muddy], and in places impassable for artillery. Several times during the day I was compelled to dismount my cannoneers, build causeways, and cut new roads through the woods. The roads on the 8th were much improved, and we met with no serious obstructions till about 1 p.m. on the 9th, when the enemy opened fire upon us from a concealed battery in our front....Several of our shell struck near the rebel guns, one passing entirely through a house and another killing a cavalry horse." The 6th U.S. Cavalry had done very well in this action against superior odds which included Rebel infantry. Confederate cavalry probably consisted of the 1st and 3rd Virginia Cavalry and possibly some of the 4th Virginia Cavalry.[43]

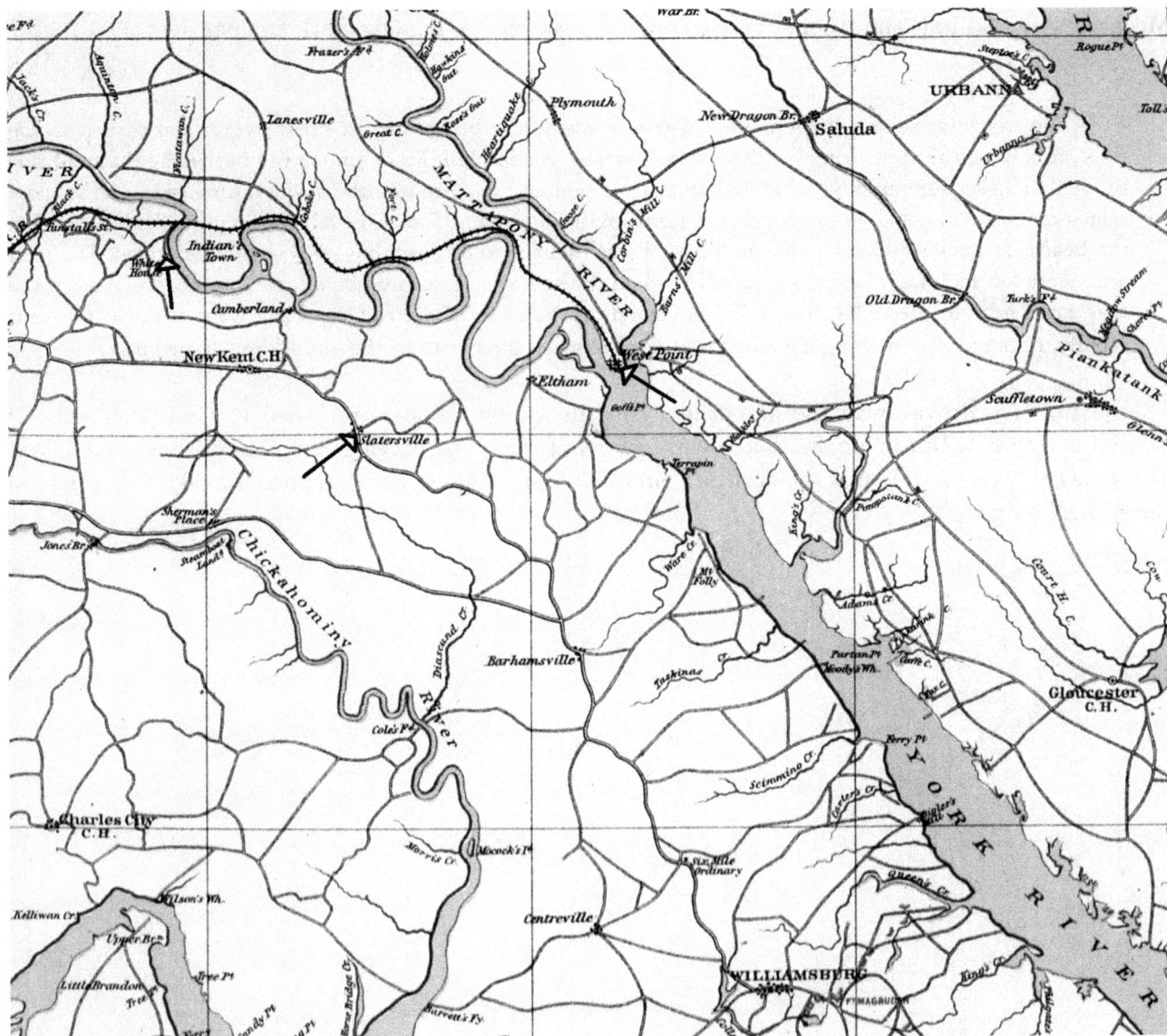

Middle left arrow points to the town of Slatersville, the scene of the cavalry fight on 9 May 1862; Williamsburg is at the lower right. Arrow in the upper left points to White House Landing, the Union main supply base. Stoneman pursued on the road from Williamsburg through Barhamsville to Slatersville. Arrow on the far right points to West Point where Franklin landed on 6 May. Note Urbanna in the upper right which was McClellan's original planned landing point. *Official Atlas of the Civil War*, Plate 16. Courtesy LOC.

43 O'Neill, *B&G*, 40; Carter, *From Yorktown to Santiago*, 30-31; Sidney Davis, 132-133.

A recently landed cavalry regiment, the 8th Pennsylvania under Col. David McMurtrie Gregg, skirmished with a mixed Rebel force of cavalry, infantry, and artillery, near Baltimore Cross Roads, but quickly retired. He also reported that on 23 May, with 8 companies of the 8th Pennsylvania Cavalry and two infantry regiments, he reconnoitered on the main road to Richmond, coming up on Rebel pickets. Following the retiring enemy, he followed through woods using infantry on his flanks, and put to flight a large body of infantry and "a force of 300 to 400 cavalry." Col. Rush with his Lancers picketed the area of New Castle Ferry, Hanovertown Ferry, and Old Church finding no enemy.[44] Confederate ambushes on May 20 and 22 caught Companies A and M of the 6th U.S. Cavalry near New Bridge, with one trooper killed and one wounded. On 22 May a detachment of the 1st New York Cavalry was ambushed near Mechanicsville, killing one trooper and wounding a second. A 1st New York trooper described the 22 May encounter:

> [The troopers] passed down a slight decline, crossed the bridge over a small stream and turned to the right, following the road along the foot of the thickly wooded hill. From among the bushes by the road side suddenly arose a large number of armed men. They poured their fire into the cavalry, broadside, and so close that some of them could almost touch the horses with their guns. Cummins fell to the ground, shot through the heart. Corporal William Anderson fell, and was thought to be dead, but he was only wounded. The men who were left mounted, turned to get away, when the enemy in great numbers came out into the road in the rear, and on both sides. The cavalry did not stand on the order of their going. They went at once and went rapidly, riding over or eluding the rebels who tried to catch the horses by the bits as they dashed past.[45]

Federal infantry drove away the ambushers and the Union troopers returned to find "the body of Cummins where he had fallen, mutilated with bayonet thrusts and his ears cut off! A prisoner taken later in the day stated that this was the acct of a South Carolina soldier who 'proposed to take the Yankee's ears to his best girl.'"[46]

---

[44] *OR.*, vol. 11, pt. 1, 649, 650.

[45] O'Neill, *B&G*, 42; O'Neill, "Peninsula Campaign," 112; Sidney Davis, 142; *OR*, vol. 11, pt. 1, 639-640; William H. Beach, *The First New York (Lincoln) Cavalry from April 19, 1861 to July 7, 1865* (New York: The Lincoln Cavalry Association, 1902; reprint, Annandale, VA: Bacon Race Books, 1988), 118-119.

[46] Beach, 119. This atrocity although possible seems unlikely; Beach does not provide enough detail to know if he saw Cummins after the mutilation or heard the Rebel prisoner's tale.

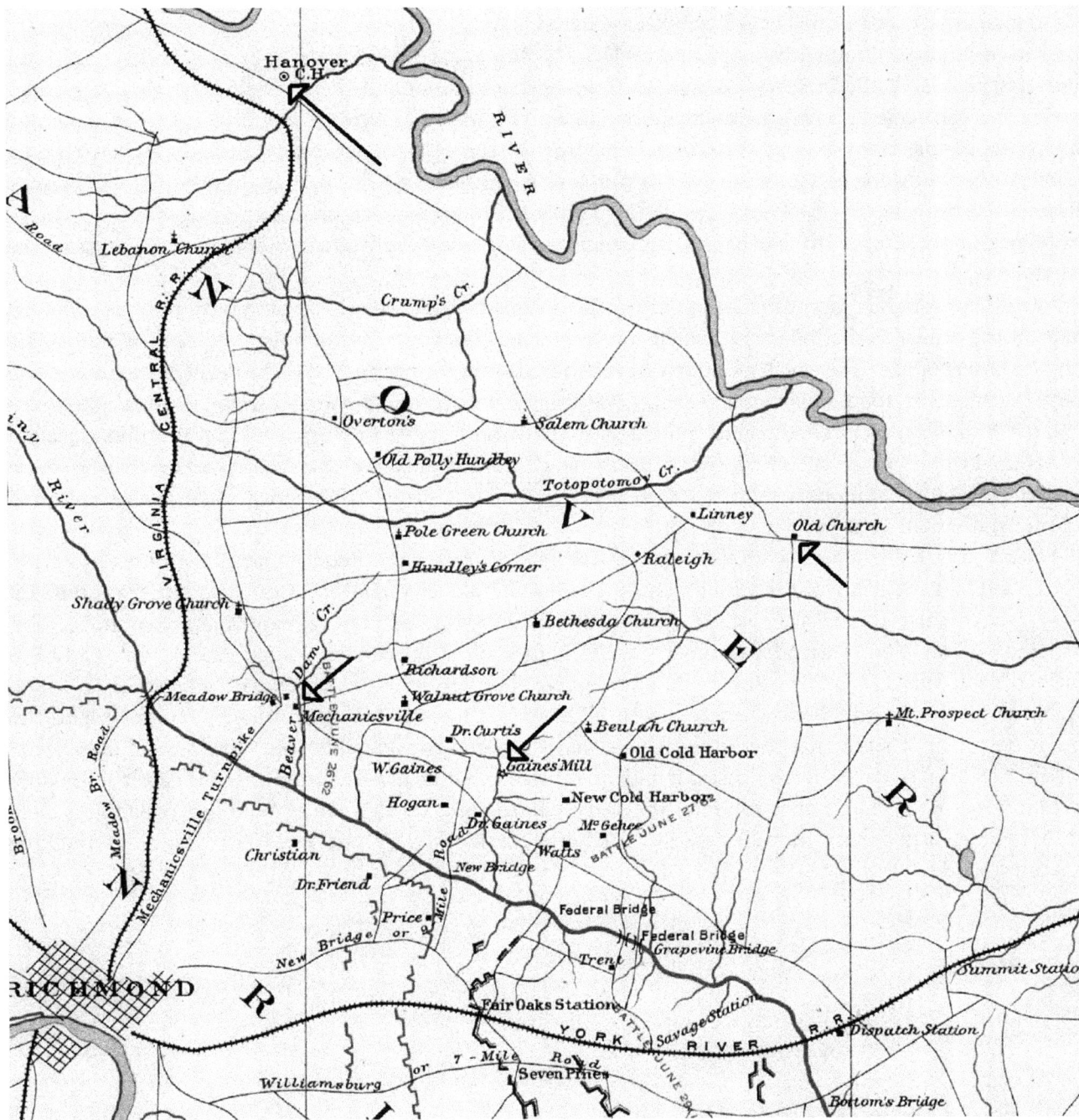

Northeast of Richmond; arrows showing Hanover Court House, Mechanicsville, Gaines's Mill, and Old Church. The Mechanicsville Turnpike leads directly to Richmond to the lower left. *Official Atlas of the Civil War*, Plate 20. Courtesy LOC.

During the remainder of May, Stoneman's force skirmished with the Confederates along the Chickahominy River east of Richmond, finally arriving within sight of the city on the 21st. Union cavalry did well during the clashes around Hanover Court House 24-29 May, burning bridges, destroying ferry landings and ferries, accompanying engineer parties, and screening for the infantry. A few miles south of Mechanicsville on the Chickahominy near New Bridge, a fight occurred involving a squadron of the 2nd U.S. Cavalry and Union infantry. Rebels burned the bridge stopping the Yankee trooper's pursuit, until Lt. George A. Custer volunteered to test the depth of the stream. Custer was commended for his actions there and McClellan sent for him to thank him. Custer modestly declined to ask for any special favors but McClellan decided to assign him to his personal staff as an aide-de-camp.

He remained on staff until Little Mac was cashiered.[47] At a battle which developed near Slash Church, Brig. Gen. Emory, along with the 5th and 6th U.S. Cavalry and horse artillery, joined Maj. Gen. Fitz-John Porter with his 12,000 infantry, to damage Confederate railroad and river crossings. After successfully acting as a screen for Porter's advance, Emory's cavalry pursued a beaten Rebel infantry force some five miles, capturing many prisoners. Also, a squadron of the 5th U.S. Cavalry detected the 4th Virginia Cavalry screening for a Confederate force moving in on Porter's left flank, giving the Union infantry time to confront it. The 6th Pennsylvania Cavalry, Rush's Lancers, captured many prisoners in a three-mile pursuit to the north, perhaps with lances, giving the Confederate infantry much impetus to surrender.

The Union cavalry's performance during this time was very successful. It served well as screeners and on the flanks of the infantry, chasing and capturing fleeing enemy infantry and destroying bridges and enemy supplies. The cavalry's efforts here differed from its role in Maryland perhaps because it had larger numbers in total, plus regular cavalry was brigaded with some volunteer units, thus its experience and discipline could be relied on and emulated by the volunteers. Emory reported that his units captured 243 infantry prisoners including five officers, while losing only six. It is noteworthy that in these instances, Emory's troopers, the 5th and 6th U.S. Cavalry, drove off enemy cavalry and captured Confederate infantry.[48]

Stuart and his troopers were also busy as rear guards screening Rebel infantry as Johnston's army continued its retreat toward the Richmond defenses. Col. Beverly H. Robertson reported that on 23-24 May, parts of the 1st and 4th Virginia cavalry, along with two infantry regiments and two guns, were ordered by Maj. Gen. Magruder to reoccupy Mechanicsville, from where Confederate cavalry had been pushed back the day before. Robertson was unable to do so as he met stiff Union resistance which Robertson reported consisted of one regiment of cavalry, three regiments of infantry, and two batteries of artillery. He thought that the Yankees must have suffered considerable loss, but knew of only seven killed; he reported seven Rebel losses. It should be noted that he also reported that his cavalry was only held in reserve.[49] While Robertson may not have been the best cavalry commander Stuart had, it is clear that he met stubborn Union resistance, including cavalry, which stymied his plans for retaking Mechanicsville.

---

[47] McClellan, *McClellan's Own Story*, 364; O'Neill, "Peninsula Campaign," 113. There are three versions of the Custer stream crossing story and his meeting with McClellan as told by Jay Monaghan, *Custer: The Life of George Armstrong Custer* (Lincoln, NE: University of Nebraska Press, 1959), 77-83.

[48] *OR*, vol. 11, pt. 1, 685-688.

[49] O'Neill, "Peninsula Campaign," 114-118; O'Neill, *Fort Monroe*, 42-46; O'Neill, *B&G*, 43-46; *OR*, vol. 11, pt. 1, 663-664; 667-668; 675-676; 677; 685-693.

Veteran officers Maj. Charles J. Whiting, Capt. James E. Harrison, and Capt. Wesley W. Owens of the 5th U.S. Cavalry, all of whom were present on the Peninsula. Whiting who led the 5th U.S. Cavalry's charge at Gaines's Mill on 27 June 1862 and was captured became part of the some 25 percent casualties. Taken November 1862, Warrenton, Va., by Alexander Gardner. Courtesy LOC.

Lt. James B. Washington, a Confederate prisoner, and classmate of Lt. George A. Custer from their West Point days. On this date, 31 May 1862, Custer was a 2ⁿᵈ Lt. in the 5ᵗʰ U.S. Cavalry on loan to the Topographical Engineers and billeted with Brig. Gen. William F. Smith's staff. Custer went aloft several times in Prof. Lowe's balloons discovering the Rebel retreat 4 May 1862 in an ascent. Custer came to the attention of McClellan and served on his staff from 5 June 1862 as an aide-de-camp. James F. Gibson, photographer. Courtesy LOC.

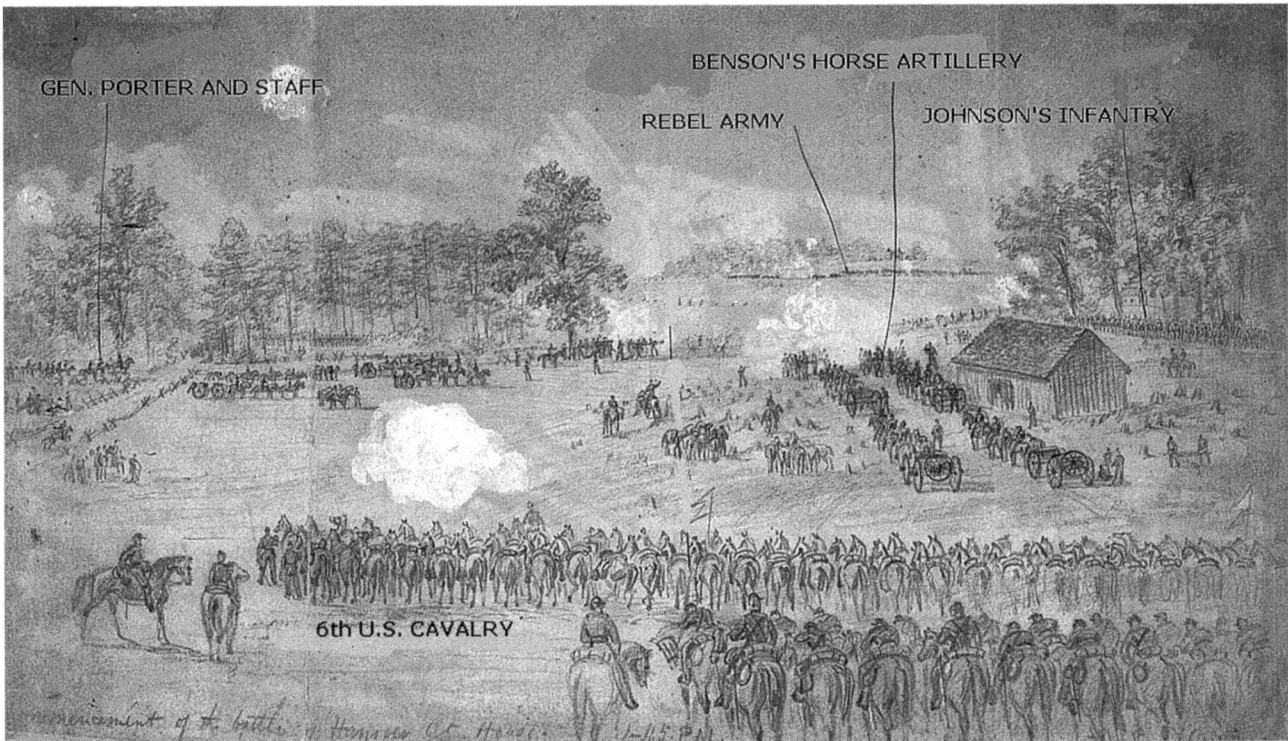

Engraving of commencement of the battle of Hanover Court House, 1:45 P.M., 27 May 1862. The dismounted 6th U.S. Cavalry is in the foreground, Rebel battle line to the right upper center at the arrow, Benson's Horse Artillery to the left of the shed at center right and Johnson's infantry at the far right. Maj. Gen. Fitz John Porter and staff are shown to the upper left at the arrow. Original drawing by Alfred Rudolph Waud. Courtesy LOC.

Lt. Custer wading in the Chickahominy River, Custer wades across the river to determine the position of the enemy, as requested by the Army Chief Engineer, Brig. Gen. John G. Barnard (on horseback), 22 May 1862. Drawn by Alfred Rudolph Waud. Courtesy LOC.

Neither the Union nor Confederate cavalry played a significant role in the Battle of Seven Pines or Fair Oaks on 31 May and 1 June, other than serving as couriers and escorts, at least in part due to the nature of the swampy, wooded terrain.[50] The cavalry horses however, suffered from the many days of activity, as the constant motion of the army toward Richmond did not allow time to care for the horses nor feed them properly.[51] This lack of care, combined with McClellan's parceling out his cavalry to infantry units, contributed to an ineffective pursuit of Stuart on 13 June as he began his First Ride Around McClellan. Confederate Gen. Robert E. Lee had taken command of the army on 1 June after Johnston was seriously wounded on 31 May at the Battle of Seven Pines or Fair Oaks. Lee's orders to Stuart to scout the enemy's right flank led to his cavalry commander's riding entirely around the Union army. Stuart picked his units but did not tell his commanders about the mission until it began at 2 A.M. on 13 June ending the next day, the 14th.[52]

Stuart picked about 1,200 troopers, which included the 1st Virginia Cavalry, commanded by Col. Fitzhugh Lee; 9th Virginia Cavalry led by Col. William H. F. "Rooney" Lee; the Jeff Davis Legion, headed by Lt. Col. William T. Martin; and two guns, a Blakely and a 12 pound howitzer, commanded by Lt. James Breathed. Eight companies of the 4th Virginia Cavalry also participated but since they did not have an available field officer, four companies were each assigned to the 1st and 9th Virginia. The Boykin Rangers from South Carolina were added to the Jeff Davis Legion. Stuart also added some troopers from the 3rd Virginia Cavalry who had lived in the area and would be of much help in this adventure. His column started out north to deceive any observers of the true direction of his scout, with the 9th Virginia Cavalry in the van, the Jeff Davis Legion bringing up the rear, and with scouts out to the front and flanks. After an uneventful day on the 13th, the column bivouacked a few miles west of Hanover Court House, while Stuart and Rooney Lee rode to Hickory Hill to spend the night. Hickory Hill was the home of the Wickham family and there Stuart found Lt. Col. Williams C. Wickham, colonel of the 4th Virginia Cavalry, convalescing after being wounded at Williamsburg. Starting at dawn on the 13th, the column reached Hanover Court House and Stuart's scouts found about 150 Union troopers, a squadron from the 6th U.S. Cavalry under Capt. J. Irvin Gregg. After sending Fitzhugh Lee with some men to the south to cut off escaping Yankees, Stuart led his column into the town, driving the Union troopers south on the Richmond Stage Road. Unfortunately, Lee had been delayed by marshy ground and only captured one Federal cavalryman. Stuart and his column moved south toward Mechanicsville, then southeast toward Enon Church. From there they headed east to Haw's Shop, where they captured videttes of the 5th U.S. Cavalry. The Rebel cavalry then came upon a stronger picket consisting of Companies F and H from the 5th U.S. Some of the 5th were placed on the defilade of a hill while the remainder was placed on the south side of a bridge over Totopotomoy Creek. The initial contact with the Union troopers at the hill slowed the 9th Virginia but a saber charge broke the Union defense, driving them back to the creek. There, expecting an ambush, the Confederates proceeded cautiously, and some dismounted to scout the banks, but they found that all their Federals foes had fled. Union troopers escaping from the bridge joined with more troopers from the 5th U.S. under Capt. William B. Royall near Old Church. Here, Stuart lost his only man in this fight with units of the 5th U.S. Cavalry. The Confederates charged two squadrons of the 5th, wounding Royall, but losing Capt. William Latane, commanding Company F of the 9th Virginia cavalry, as these two men fought each other with sabers. While Royall was seriously wounded, he survived, as the fleeing Unionists rode hard toward Cold Harbor, and some to Mechanicsville. The 9th Virginia also had five privates wounded, and the 5th U.S. had four privates killed, with Capt. Royall wounded, along with Lt. William C. Campbell, who was captured. Also captured were a Union surgeon

[50] O'Neill, *Fort Monroe*, 49.
[51] O'Neill, *Peninsula Campaign*, 119-120.
[52] See *OR*, vol. 11, pt. 3, 590-591, for Lee's order to Stuart.

and two lieutenants from the 6th Pennsylvania Cavalry. Fitzhugh Lee led the 1st Virginia Cavalry in a charge into the 5th's camp capturing "a number of horses, arms, and prisoners, as well as quantities of stores, including a keg of whiskey from an ambulance," then they burned the rest. Col. Martin, commanding the Jeff Davis Legion, reported that in the afternoon of the 14th, "25 non-commissioned officers and privates of the Fifth Regular Cavalry, U. S. Army, came in under a flag of truce, and surrendered, with horses and arms, to the rear guard, under the impression that they were surrounded."[53]

Stuart continued to Tunstall's Station on the railroad line from the York River, first coming to Garlick's Landing near Putney's Ferry, where a squadron from the 9th Virginia cavalry destroyed stores and wagons at this landing on the Pamunkey River. Two Union transports were also burned while one ship escaped, and a large number of prisoners were captured, along with some 300 horses and mules. The 1st Virginia rushed to Tunstall's, cutting telegraph wires and capturing some Union infantry, and chasing off the 11th Pennsylvania Cavalry. Stuart's men fired on a Union train with flatcars carrying Federal infantry heading for White House Landing, killing and wounding several of the infantry passengers; the train escaped under full steam heading to White House. Stuart elected not to attack White House Landing four miles away as he had information that it was well defended, and in any event, the Rebel cavalry did not have time to spend fighting there as Stuart anticipated that Union reinforcements would soon join the hunt after him. The Rebel raiders rode southeast to Talleysville where they rested, and then continued south to Providence Forge near the Chickahominy River. As the now exhausted troopers neared the Chickahominy, they found it overflowing due to recent rains. Stuart reconstructed a damaged bridge and successfully crossed his men and cannon, then burned the bridge, just as troopers from the 6th Pennsylvania approached.[54]

A BAND OF REBELS FIRING INTO THE CARS NEAR TUNSTALL'S STATION, VIRGINIA, JUNE 13, 1862.—SKETCHED BY MR. MEAD.—[SEE PAGE 426.]

Stuart's attack at Tunstall's Station on 13 June 1862. Harper's Weekly, 5 July 1862. Author's collection.

Stuart's ride, in addition to enshrining the fallen Latane as a new hero for the Confederacy, resulted in destroyed Union supplies, damaged Federal railroads and trains, two burned schooners, cut telegraph lines, chopped down telegraph poles, burned sutlers' wagons and bridges, not to mention the havoc he raised in the Union rear. They also captured 164 prisoners who were taken to Richmond, and 260 horses and mules which Stuart kept. More importantly, Stuart delivered valuable intelligence to Lee about the condition of the Union right flank, and the conditions behind enemy lines. Stuart found no evidence

---

[53] Horace Mewborn, "A Wonderful Exploit: Jeb Stuart's Ride Around the Army of the Potomac, June 12-15, 1862, *Blue & Gray*, vol. XV, issue 6, summer 1998, 10-16. Stuart's report of the raid is at *OR*, vol. 11, pt. 1, 1036-1040, followed by those of Fitz Lee, W. H. F. Lee and William T. Martin, 1042-1046.

[54] Mewborn, 46-48.

showing that McClellan was going to switch his supply base from White House Landing to the James River so a Rebel attack around the Union right flank would cut his supply line. And the boost to morale both for the Confederate army and the populace was immense, as was the chagrin with which Union soldiers and the Northern populace viewed the ride. Stuart's ride did have unintended consequences: it alerted McClellan to the vulnerability of his supply base at White House Landing and its rail line, so he decided to shift his base to Harrison's Landing on the James River; he also reinforced his lines to protect his base until the move was completed.[55]

Union pursuit was tardy and ineffective. Gen. Cooke's and the Federal cavalry's performances were criticized in reports by Col. Gouverneur K. Warren commanding the Third Brigade of Sykes's Division of the Fifth Corps, as well as Brig. Gen. Fitz John Porter, commander of the Fifth Corps, for not moving fast enough. Cooke had decided he would not chase Stuart without infantry support. In Cooke's defense, he did receive an erroneous report that Stuart was accompanied by infantry; he reported: "Lieutenant Byrnes, in the affair with Royall, reported that he had seen from three to five regiments of infantry, also artillery....I joined the advance of my cavalry at Old Hanover Court-house about 10 o'clock in advance of [our]...infantry, when I went on soon after to Old Church....The enemy was supported by infantry, no doubt. His force was, in addition, one or two brigades of cavalry, with some artillery....The heat was excessive, but the troops all bore it, together with the entire absence of baggage, very scant food, and night marching, with praiseworthy indifference and alacrity." Cooke, in retrospect, should have played down the lack of food, etc., since he utterly failed to catch his son-in-law. Cooke also reported that after he had heard of Stuart's action against Royall, and formed the 1st U.S. Cavalry and Rush's Lancers, he ordered them back to camp because they had no rations with them, and gave them two hours to prepare. He also ordered Emory to send a wagon of provisions to his brigade while Cooke retired to his tent for a cup of coffee. Obviously, Cooke was not seized with the urgency that the moment demanded. Union cavalry was unable to catch Stuart as the Rebel horsemen outdistanced their pursuers because of Cooke's poor leadership, and because whenever the Yankee cavalry confronted any of Stuart's troopers, the Unionists were heavily outnumbered. Thus Federal cavalry was undeservedly made a mockery by Stuart's daring ride in the minds of many for this well-publicized event, even though the performance of the Union cavalry was otherwise at least adequate, and in many cases meritorious, as it led McClellan's advance up the Peninsula and supported the infantry.[56]

---

[55] Edwin C. Bearss, "'Into the Very Jaws of the Enemy'; Jeb Stuart's Ride Around McClellan," in *The Peninsula Campaign: Yorktown to the Seven Days*, vol. 1, ed. by William J. Miller (Campbell, CA: Savas Publishing Company, 1995), 71-142. See also William Allan, *The Army of Northern Virginia in 1862* (Cambridge, MA: The Riverside Press, 1892; reprint, Dayton, OH: Morningside House, Inc., 1984), 62; *OR*, vol. 11, pt. I, 1006, 1008-1010, 1030.

[56] *OR*, vol. 11, pt. 1, 1005-1046; Cooke's reports at 1008-1013. See also O'Neill, *Peninsula*, "'The whole affair was a ...disgraceful failure on the part of Cooke to prevent it, Gen. Cooke is an old man & has not the vim necessary to manoever against [Stuart],'" 121. Not surprisingly, Southern responses as well as some historians were generally favorable, see, e.g., Sears, *Richmond*, 174; for an excellent summary of the ride, see John S. Mosby, "The Ride Around General McClellan," in *Southern Historical Society Papers*, vol. XXVI, January to December 1898 (Richmond: Southern Historical Society, n.d. Reprint, Millwood, NJ: Kraus Reprint Co, 1977), 254; John Esten Cooke, *Wearing of the Gray: Being Personal Portraits, Scenes, and Adventures of the War* (New York: E. B. Treat & Co., 1867, reprint, Baton Rough, LA: Louisiana University Press, 1959), agreed with Mosby giving three reasons for its value: it was the first example of a cavalry raid, gave Lee valuable information, and it was a good publicity stunt, 181; McClellan, *Stuart*, said that it resolved doubt about the location of the Union army, boosted the morale of the Confederate cavalry and army and shook the confidence of the North in General McClellan, 67. Von Borcke not surprisingly agrees with his Confederate cohorts finding the expedition "wonderfully successful" finding out the position of the enemy's army which was the mission's "chief object," 32. Freeman says that when Stuart rode up to Lee on the 15th he was "full of information" about the ground and Federal dispositions; road conditions, and Union supply lines. There was nothing Stuart could see to keep Jackson from sweeping on down toward the White House, *Lee*, 2:99-100. Lee was concerned that the raid might have alerted McClellan but found out using infantry reconnaissance that the Union had not weakened its line to extend its right flank. In short, Freeman finds that Stuart's ride was much more than a publicity stunt. Starr wrote less glowingly: "In a narrowly military sense, Stuart's ride had limited value, for it merely confirmed what General Lee already suspected, namely

Skirmish at Tunstall's Station on 13 May between Stuart's troopers and the 5th U.S. Cavalry. *The Soldier in Our Civil War*, Vol. 1, 349.

that McClellan's right wing was 'in the air,'" 272-273. Starr finds that its morale effect on the southern citizens and army perhaps had more value than its military accomplishment. And embarrassing McClellan was another plus. But Starr also finds that these splashy raids perhaps led to more such raids by Stuart, Morgan, et al., but were games not worth the candles as they rarely if ever had any significant strategic effect. Griffith, *Tactics*, agrees, viewing raids as an "abasement and corruption" of the best use of cavalry, 183-184.

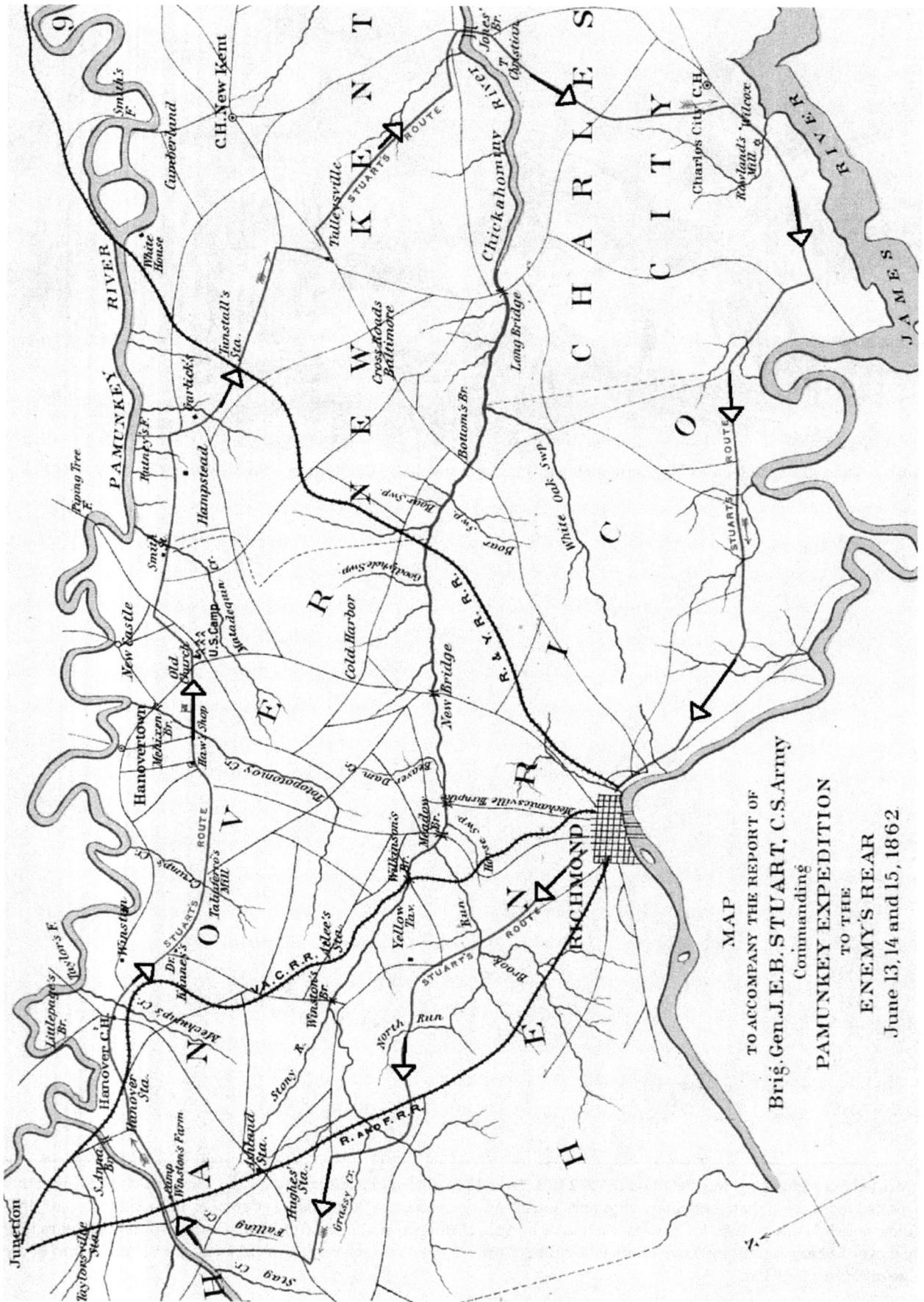

Map of Stuart's First Ride Around McClellan. *Official Atlas of the Civil War*, Plate 21. Courtesy LOC.

Etching showing Stuart's troopers raiding White House. Rebels threaten a sutler, "Hezekiah Skinflint," and run off horses and cattle. This title is in error as Stuart did not raid White House Landing during his ride but got as close as Tunstall's Station to its west which had many supplies covering 30 acres which he burned, fired on a passing train, and generally raised havoc among the panicked Yankees, Bearss, 116; Wheeler, 275-276; Cooke, *Wearing of the Gray*, 174. Stuart decided not to attack White House on this raid but when Stuart and his troopers did take White House Landing, it is unlikely that any Union sutlers were left as Union supplies were set on fire by retreating Federals. Stuart was able to salvage much needed supplies for his men, however. It certainly was not a "raid" as Union forces were retreating in haste down the Peninsula chased by Gen. Lee's army, *OR*, vol. 11, pt. 2, 516-517. Etching by Southerner Adabert John Volck, "Confederate War Etchings," *The Magazine of History with Notes and Queries*, Extra Number 60 (London, n.p., 1863-1864), reprint, Tarrytown, NY: William Abbatt, 1917).

"Several personal encounters took place during Stuart's raid. The one depicted here is described in J.S.C. Abbott's 'History of the Civil War,' and Colonel Estvan, a Prussian serving with the Confederates, is given as authority for some of the details. The Union cavalryman is described as a German. After a desperate fight with sabers, which was witnessed by the Confederate comrades, and during which both men were severely cut, the Confederate drew a revolver and shot his opponent." *Battles and Leaders*, 2:274. Fitzhugh Lee reported that Pvt. Thomas P. Clapp of Company F of the 1st Virginia Cavalry rode up to a Federal officer who was riding in advance of his men and killed him after being himself wounded, *OR*, vol. 11, pt. 1, 1043.

Federal and Confederate cavalry were mainly involved in picketing and patrolling during much of June: Union cavalry rested from their exertions in the pursuit up the Peninsula and the chase of Stuart, and Stuart's troopers also rested from their being chased up the Peninsula, and then riding around McClellan's army. McClellan's cavalry was augmented by the arrival on 24 June of the 4th Pennsylvania Cavalry, one battalion of which the army commander assigned to garrison duty at Yorktown, effectively taking it out of the conflict further north. On the 25th, he wired the Secretary of War Stanton asking for more troops, including "a couple of new regiments of cavalry." Fearing the approach of Jackson, McClellan instructed Cooke to fell trees and burn bridges to prevent enemy movement from Harris Station.[57]

On 25 June, the first of the Seven Days Battles began with the Battle of Oak Grove. There, the only Union cavalry involved was the 1st New York Cavalry serving as McClellan's escort, and spending the day observing the action.[58] The next day, the 26th, Lee planned on attacking Porter's Fifth Corps with overwhelming strength, including part of Stuart's cavalry brigade. The 4th Pennsylvania Cavalry under Col. James H. Childs, was screening the infantry when Confederate Maj. Gen. A.P. Hill attacked, beginning the Battle of Mechanicsville. Units of the 8th Illinois Cavalry under Col. John F. Farnsworth

[57] *OR,* vol. 11, pt. 3, 252, 256.
[58] Beach, 127.

also were on picket before the Confederate attack, with Emory's troopers to their right. The next day, Porter's Fifth Corps was covering bridges across the Chickahominy near Gaines's Mill.[59] Lee's attacks finally broke Porter's line on its flanks. Several batteries of Federal artillery on a hill supported Porter's lines and Porter placed Cooke, with 634 troopers, on his left, near the guns, as support.[60] Cooke's actions on that hill engendered one of the biggest controversies of the campaign for the Union cavalry, and likely led to Cooke's never commanding in the field again. Sadly, it also cast unfair aspersions on the fighting ability of Yankee cavalry.

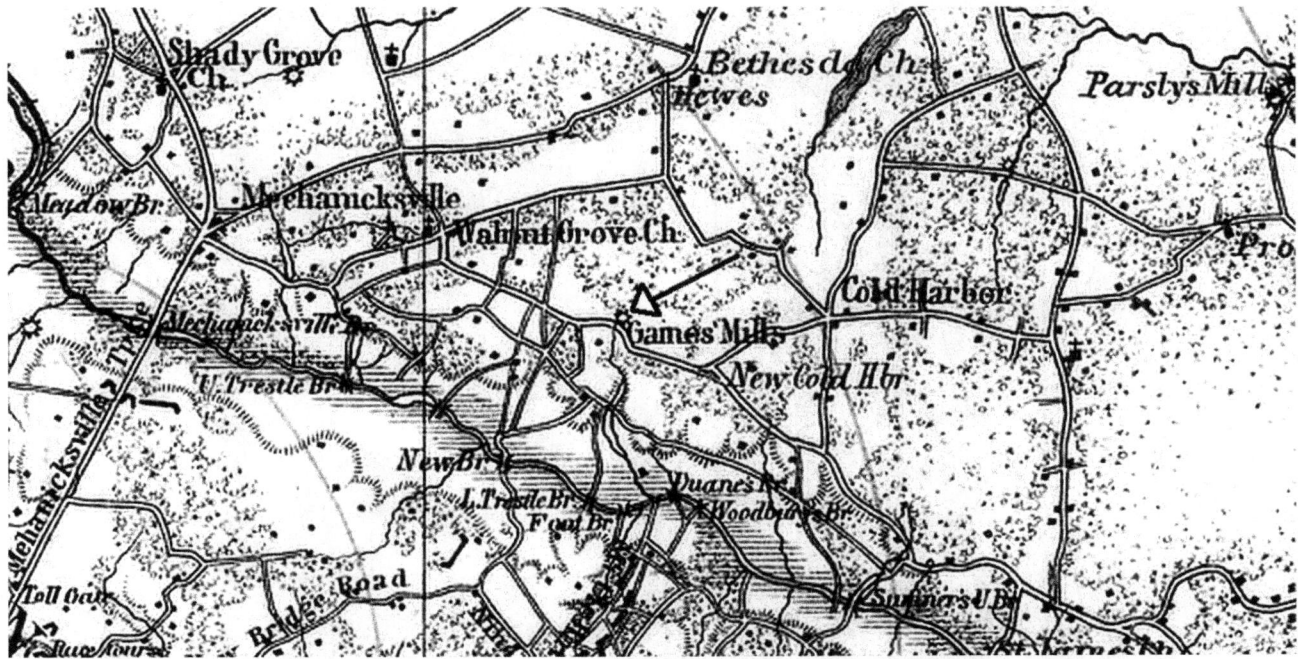

Gaines's Mills shown at center of map at arrow; Mechanicsville to upper left; outskirts of Richmond just off map at lower left corner. Military map of south-eastern Virginia A. Lindenkohl, ca. 1862. Courtesy LOC.

[59] O'Neill, *Peninsula Campaign*, 124-125.

[60] Ibid., 126, Cooke had six companies of the 5th U.S., four companies of the 1st U.S., and six companies of the 6th Pennsylvania with an additional 39 troopers from the 6th who were part of a provost guard.

Capt. Richard G. Prendergast, 1st New York Cavalry. Courtesy LOC.

What is not controversial is that during heavy fighting late in the day, as the Confederate attacks were gaining ground at the center and left of the line, Cooke ordered a cavalry charge by the 220 men present from the 5th U.S. Cavalry, to protect the reserve artillery which had begun to limber up. Cooke assured the artillerymen that his cavalry could protect them. At this time, Cooke's troopers were coming under fire as Brig. Gen. George E. Pickett's men were about 100 yards from the guns Cooke was supporting. As the 5th attacked to its left, their gallant charge was very quickly destroyed by the fire of the Confederate infantry. The 5th lost six of its seven officers killed or wounded, with 49 enlisted casualties; there were few, if any, Rebel losses.[61] The historian of the 5th Cavalry described the fight:

> The regimental headquarters, with companies A, D, F, H, and I, and small detachments of the other companies, under the command of Captain [Charles J.]Whiting, were engaged in the battle of Gaines's Mill on the 27th of June, and while making a charge against General Hood's division Lieutenant [John J.] Sweet was killed, Captain [William P.] Chambliss (severely) and Lieutenants [Abraham K.] Arnold (horse killed under him), [Louis D.] Watkins, and [Lt. Thomas E.] Maley were wounded, and Captain Whiting was captured after

---

[61] Ibid., 128-129. *OR*, vol. 11, pt. 2, the 1st U.S. Cavalry declined to join the suicidal rush due to "destructive" enemy fire, 44. See also Sears, *Richmond*, 245-246. Some of Rush's Lancers may have joined in the charge, see Wittenberg, *Lancers*, 48-49.

his horse had been killed under him. The casualties among the enlisted men aggregated forty-nine killed, wounded, and missing. Twenty-four horses were killed. Captain [Joseph H.] McArthur was the only officer who escaped unhurt.

This famous charge, concerning which there have been so many discussions and so much misrepresentation, was made by seven officers and two hundred and thirty men of the regiment under the following circumstances: Toward the end of the battle General Hood's division was seen moving from the shelter of a dense woods for the purpose of charging the National artillery, which had been severely punishing the enemy. The officer in command, having no infantry support, was retiring from the field, in order to prevent the capture of his guns, when General Cooke sent him a cavalry support, and ordered him to unlimber and go into action again. The officer cheerfully returned and opened a canister fire upon the rapidly advancing enemy. At this moment Captain Whiting understood that he was ordered to charge the enemy, which he did, but after riding over their first line he was halted by the dense woods from which they had just emerged. The audacity of the charge, together with the rapid firing of canister at a short range, impressed the enemy with the belief that fresh reserves had arrived on the field, and undoubtedly saved that part of the National army which was on the north side of the Chickahominy. General McClellan, in his telegram of the 28th of June to the Secretary of War, said: "My regulars were superb, and I count upon what are left to turn another battle in company with their gallant comrades of the volunteers.[62]

Porter blamed Cooke for the loss of the hill, writing that the battle was going in the Union's favor until Cooke's charge threw Union gunners and infantry "into confusion, and the bewildered [Union cavalry] horses, regardless of the efforts of their riders, wheeled about, and dashing through the batteries, convinced the gunners that they were charged by the enemy. To this alone is to be attributed our failure to hold the battle-field."[63] Cooke shifted any blame onto Capt. Whiting of the 5th U.S. Cavalry; Cooke said he ordered Whiting to attack only if the batteries were in danger, while Whiting and one of his men said that Cooke ordered an immediate charge.[64] Cooke maintained that the attack enabled some batteries to retire but at a cost to him of 101 troopers and 128 horses. He describes reports denigrating his performance as "false" and one of his staff called them "misrepresentations" and "arising from statements of persons who were ignorant of the facts or circulate falsehood maliciously. The cavalry did much on that day field to restore the fortunes of the day."[65] Regardless of the defense of his order to attack, he was transferred to Washington on 5 July; doubtlessly, his failure to confront Stuart on his circumferential ride combined with this action at Gaines's Mill sealed his fate.

---

[62] George F. Price, *Across the Continent with the Fifth Cavalry* (New York: D. Van Nostrand, Publisher, 1883), 108-109. Averell, in his *Battles and Leaders* article, wrote that the 5 P.M. charge included two and a half squadrons (five companies) of the 5th U.S. some 300 strong, two squadrons of the 1st U.S. Cavalry, three squadrons of Rush's Lancers, and one squadron of the 4th Pennsylvania Cavalry. Amazingly, the robust Chambliss lay on the field 10 days after being hit by seven balls, and was captured and taken to Richmond where he eventually recovered (William W. Averell, "With the Cavalry on the Peninsula," in *Battles and Leaders*, 2:430).

[63] *OR*, vol. 11, pt. 2, 226. Sears, *Richmond*, 246, Cooke may have been a convenient scapegoat for Porter.

[64] Sears, *Richmond*, 245.

[65] *OR*, vol. 11, pt. 2, 42, 43. See also Cooke's defense, Philip St. George Cooke, "The Charge of Cooke's Cavalry at Gaines's Mill," in *Battles and Leaders*, 2:344-346. Rhodes, *History of the Cavalry*, agreed with Cooke that the brave cavalry action saved the artillery as well as the "Chickahominy bridge and the capture of at least a portion of Porter's command would undoubtedly followed...The Comte de Paris, in a letter to General Cooke, February 2, 1877, has said: 'The sacrifice of some of the bravest of the cavalry certainly saved a part of the artillery....The main fact is that with your cavalry you did all that cavalry could do to stop the rout,'" 14-15. Twenty two Union guns were lost at Gaines's Mill.

THE ARMY OF THE POTOMAC—CHARGE OF THE FIFTH CAVALRY AT THE BATTLE OF FRIDAY, JUNE 27.—SKETCHED BY MR. A. R. WAUD.—[SEE PAGE 503.]

Dramatic depiction of the 5th U.S. Cavalry's doomed charge at Gaines's Mill. *Harper's Weekly* 9 August 1862, sketched by Alfred Waud. Waud incorrectly added that this charge occurred on the 28th rather than the 27th but the caption showed the correct date. Author's collection.

After the battle, the Union cavalry helped round up stragglers and screened the rear of the retreating infantry. One squadron of the 8th Illinois guarding the hospital and supplies at Dispatch Station, drove off some Confederate cavalry, chasing the Rebels three-quarters of a mile in its successful defense of its assigned area. On 28 June, Stoneman with the 2nd and 6th U.S. Cavalry and two infantry units, burned the supplies at White House, after guarding the stations on the Richmond and York Railroad, allowing many supplies to be moved. At White House, the 11th Pennsylvania Cavalry, which had had an easy time guarding the landing, joined Stoneman on the trek down the Peninsula to Yorktown and Fort Monroe, subjecting the regiment to trials to which it was not accustomed.[66]

---

[66] O'Neill, *Peninsula Campaign*, 129-130.

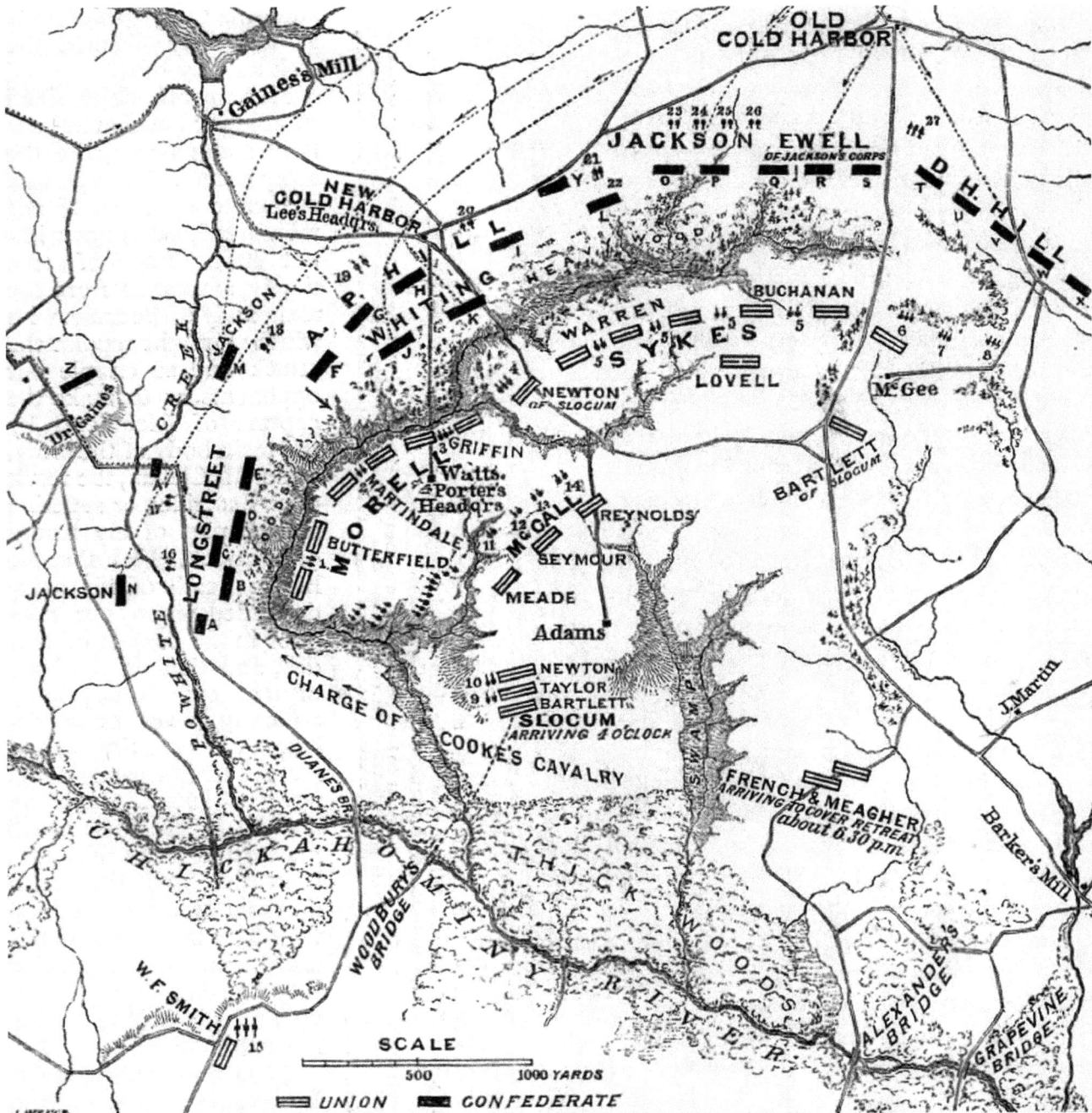

Map detail showing Cooke's failed cavalry charge by the 5th U.S. Cavalry. Map by Jacob Wells, from *Century Illustrated Monthly Magazine*, v. 30, June 1885, p. 317. Courtesy LOC.

At the end of June, a cavalry fight occurred between the 3rd Pennsylvania Cavalry, and the 1st North Carolina and 3rd Virginia Cavalry. The Confederate troopers, looking for the Union picket line near Willis Church, were drawn into an ambush, as the North Carolinians charged down a road and were met with artillery and a counter charge by the Pennsylvanians. The commander of the 1st North Carolina wrote that he was up against the main Union army consisting of a division, while the commander of the 3rd Virginia said that he was ambushed by artillery, infantry, and cavalry. The Rebel loss was some 60 men, but only six for the Union.[67] The cavalry was not much involved in the remaining battles of the

---

[67] *OR*, vol. 11, pt. 2, 525, 527; O'Neill, *Peninsula Campaign*, 132.

Seven Days—Glendale and Malvern Hill—but was used for guarding wagon trains and bridges for the retreating army. Like the infantry, the cavalrymen and their horses were worn out after a week of guarding the army's retreat, and welcomed the respite around Harrison's Landing. Even then, picket duty and scouting for the enemy added to the fatigue of the weary troopers.[68]

During Stuart's pursuit of the Federals down the Peninsula, his cavalry picked up Union stragglers and gathered in supplies and equipment. Lt. Col. Martin's report gives an example of Confederate cavalry actions during this time of the Union withdrawal, as his troopers the most active during this period. He commanded the Jeff Davis Legion and the 4th Virginia Cavalry. He recorded his adventures from 25 July to 6 August which included skirmishing north of Richmond near Ashland and Hanover Court House on 25 July with the 8th Illinois Cavalry, eventually driving them off, using the Black Horse Company of the 4th Virginia Cavalry. Martin reported killing one and wounding another suffering two wounded. On the 27th, he moved southwest toward Old Church, killing one of Rush's Lancers, wounding another, and setting to flight 1,000 to 1,500 Union horsemen, with help from Pelham's cannon. He then covered the flank of Confederates fighting at Cold Harbor (Gaines's Mill), losing one man killed and another wounded by enemy artillery fire. On the 28th he chased Union cavalry toward White House Landing, and on the 29th entered White House wondering at the destruction of the formerly beautiful plantation owned by William H.F. "Rooney" Lee, Gen. Robert E. Lee's second son. The plantation, once owned by Martha Custis who had married George Washington, was serving as the refuge for Mrs. Robert E. Lee and her daughters after leaving their Arlington House mansion. After his troops had taken the landing, McClellan made arrangements for her safe passage through the Union lines, and she relocated to Richmond. Martin continued pursuing the retreating Federals pushing them away from Forge Bridge even though the Unionists had, he reported, infantry, artillery, and cavalry. Pelham's artillerists continued their good service driving off the enemy and silencing Union counter battery fire. Skirmishing continued around Forge Bridge through 1 July. The next day in a drenching rain, a company from the Jeff Davis Legion, the Boykin Rangers, and the Black Horse Company from the 4th Virginia Cavalry, picketed a road toward Westover. The Rangers charged a squadron of Union cavalry and forced it back, killing one and wounding another. Martin then rode down the road leading to Haxall's Landing which branched off the River Road; he toted along a 12 pound howitzer from Stuart's Horse Artillery. There was an open field down to the James River so Martin's men kept out of sight of Union gunboats while gathering in Yankee stragglers in the woods, as the Confederate horsemen rode toward the river. Martin learned that the gunboat *Galena*, and the *Monitor*, were in front of a house near the shore, so he had his men carefully come up behind the home using it as cover, capturing three prisoners, one being from the *Monitor*. Yankee prisoners aided five Rebel troopers, gathering some 30 mules in the field, and then the Rebels moved off with 150 prisoners along with captured weapons and mules, back to safety. As Martin returned to his main column on the River Road, he discovered that it was in slow retreat as it had encountered Union soldiers in ambush. He brought up the howitzer and surprised the 42nd New York Infantry (Tammany) Regiment, driving it back to Berkley; Martin stopped his pursuit as he came upon a Union infantry brigade. On 4 July, Martin continued his harassment of Union troops as he skirmished with Federal cavalry and watched Union shipping on the James.[69]

Stuart arrived at Evelington Heights, a plateau commanding the Union camp at Harrison's landing. Capt. Pelham told Stuart of the advantages of holding the heights so Stuart, after forwarding Pelham's assessment to Maj. Gen. Jackson, rode with his troopers to that point. A Union cavalry squadron already there quickly retired so Pelham set up a gun and fired his last few shells at the enemy camp. Stuart reported that he was not worried about being attacked by Union infantry since he believed that

---

[68] McClellan, *Stuart*, 86. O'Neill, *Peninsula Campaign*, 133-135.
[69] *OR*, vol. 11, pt. 2, 528-531; Burton, 380-382.

Longstreet was near. Stuart was forced to give up the heights when Union infantry approached, as no Confederate troops had arrived to support him. Stuart should have known that such support was not close at hand since his intemperate action notified the Union army of its vulnerability if it did not seize Evelington Heights. Stuart erred in alerting the Federals and giving up the chance for Lee's army to occupy a point from which it could seriously annoy, if not force, the Union host onto its transports. One historian held that by Stuart's precipitous action "Lee lost the last opportunity of the campaign to inflict major damage on the Army of the Potomac."[70]

McClellan, on 8 July, reorganized his cavalry forces, removing Cooke and Emory, two of the oldest and worst performing cavalry generals on the Peninsula. Stoneman remained the cavalry division commander with Col. William W. Averell of the 3rd Pennsylvania Cavalry commanding the First Brigade, consisting of his regiment, the 3rd Pennsylvania Cavalry, and the 1st New York Cavalry along with the 4th Pennsylvania Cavalry. The Second Brigade was commanded by Col. David McM. Gregg with his 8th Pennsylvania Cavalry, the 8th Illinois Cavalry, and two squadrons of the 6th New York Cavalry. Five squadrons of cavalry were assigned to five infantry corps. The 8 July order also assigned the scouting and patrolling duties for the right wing of the army to Averell's First Brigade, and for the army's left, to Gregg's Second Brigade. Rush's Lancers were detailed to the various army corps as guides. The regular cavalry was reformed into as many squadrons as possible presumably to be ready for service when and where needed. The 6th U.S. Cavalry may have subsequently been transferred to Gregg and the 5th to Averell however, the regulars were not pleased with being brigaded with volunteers. Returns show some 4,700 Union cavalry present for duty, equipped, on 10 July.[71] The reorganized units suffered from illness both among the troopers and their horses as they performed patrols and scouting duties. The heat, humidity, and black flies, were always present. William Hyndman, a member of the 4th Pennsylvania Cavalry, Company A, wrote the following picturesque description of that time at Harrison's Landing:

> We continued to do picket and scout duty, in the vicinity of our outposts, around Harrison's Landing, during the month of July and a portion of August, encamping on the bank of James River at Westover Landing, a short distance below. The regiment was here brigaded for the first time, under command of Col. Averill, of the Third Pennsylvania Cavalry, being composed of the Third and Fourth Pennsylvania and Fifth Regular Cavalry. During the time we were encamped here, the weather being very warm, and the men not inured to the Southern climate, much sickness prevailed. The sun poured down an intense and sultry heat, steaming out of river and marsh, miasmse of the most destructive influence on health. The river was dotted with sloops and schooners loaded with hay, and the shores were covered with the dead carcasses of horses, which festered and putrified there, half on land and half in the water. On the surface of the river was a scum of refuse hay, and the oily and bilgy fragments of the decomposing animal matters on the banks. Couple with these, the still, hot, searching heats of an almost tropical sun, the cool, drenching dews of summer nights in the South, and a naturally unhealthy locality, and you have ample cause for surprise that some ghastly epidemic did not arise from this putrid sepulchre of vapors, and spread disease and death, far and wide into the country. As it was, the health of the troops suffered essentially, and many died of low fevers. Our army was well supplied during the encampment at Harrison's Landing, sutlers from the North flocking about us on all sides. Almost every luxury

---

[70] *OR*, vol. 11, pt. 2, 520; Burton, 383.

[71] *OR*, vol. 11, pt. 3, 307-308, 312. *OR* Supplement, pt. 1, vol. 2, 130. Averell writes that the 5th U.S. was assigned to his brigade; that on 5 July he was appointed acting brigadier general as Stoneman was on sick leave and Cooke had been relieved. Upon this appointment as commander of the army's cavalry, he reorganized it into a corps. After Stoneman returned that day from sick leave, Averell took command of the 1st Brigade of cavalry composed of the 5th U.S. Cavalry, the 3rd and 4th Pennsylvania Cavalry, and the 1st New York Cavalry. Averell reported cavalry losses for the Seven Days at 234 and 71 for the Confederates of which 61 were credited to the 3rd Pennsylvania Cavalry at Willis Church on 29 June, *Battles and Leaders*, 2:433. See Mann who relates that on 31 July his regiment was accompanied by 800 cavalry which aided in scouting down the Chickahominy to its junction with the James River, 81-82.

could be purchased, but unfortunately the means for buying were generally limited, if not altogether wanting. ....During the encampment here the army was in a measure re-organized. All the companies and regiments underwent this process. Vacancies having been created during the late campaign, promotions were in order, and became quite numerous. On this occasion I was promoted Corporal, a position then esteemed an honor....

On the night of July 31st, the enemy got several pieces of artillery in position, on the opposite side of the James River, and sent us their compliments in the shape of shot and shell. They continued this for some time, until our gunboats got the range of them and drove them off. Many of the shot and shell entered our camp, wounding several men and killing or injuring several horses. Joseph Snyder, a member of the company, was very severely wounded, during the night, while lying in his tent. A solid shot struck him, and from the injuries it inflicted, he was afterwards discharged. It was a notable fact that during the same firing, his horse was apparently singled out from among hundreds, and killed on the picket line. He was the first member of the company wounded by a missile from the enemy. On account of the sickness that prevailed in camp, large numbers were sent to hospitals in the North....

About this time, too, we were surrounded by an enemy whose powers of petty annoyance were greater than his skill in outright killing. Myriads of sharp-teethed, lantern-jawed, empty-mouthed and pertinacious flies came among us, to add to our discomforts. They seemed to prefer individual warfare, guerilla attacks, to assaults en masse, and darted down on the nose, and clung and stung that inoffensive member, until the tears rolled over from the peepers above. They would fight and bite the hand, nip the eye-lid, flutter and buzz in the ear, scooping up a mouthful of the flesh on their way out, and fairly revel in their dashing advances on the enemy, who all the time struck out darkly, but never quelled the foe, although his better nature was fully suppressed in the endeavor. There was no rest among these saucy and impudent fellows. They were probably rebel-flies, who left their exhausted hills and vallies on a raid among the enemy's possessions. They were especially annoying to the horses, who now had no comfort night or day. At all hours you could hear them stamping on the hard dry clay, and snapping and switching their caudal appendages— in vain efforts to repel the pestering swarms.[72]

The historian of the 3rd Pennsylvania echoed the terrible fly problems for both men and horses:

We were well placed in our camp at Westover Landing, near Harrison's Landing, on the James River, excepting that our proximity to an extensive marsh gave a rapacious breed of flies opportunity to feed upon our horses. The summer sun multiplied them into the millions, and every man who had a good horse was anxious to be sent out on picket duty, so as to get out of camp and for a time be relieved of the terrible pest, which annoyed the men as well as the animals. When the picket relief appeared, at the end of three days, the men would coax their comrades to exchange places with them so as not to have to return to camp. The horses were so worried, and wore themselves out so completely, stamping their feet and whisking their heads and tails, that many of them became unable to stand up, and actually died from exhaustion and the sting of the flies.[73]

On 3 August, Averell reported that he crossed the James River with the 5th U.S. Cavalry and the 3rd Pennsylvania Cavalry, exploring the routes toward Petersburg, when he encountered the 13th Virginia Cavalry. The 5th U.S. charged, supported by the 3rd Pennsylvania, and chased the Rebel cavalry over seven miles, destroying its camp and supplies. The Union cavalry covered McClellan's second retreat

---

[72] William Hyndman, *History of a Cavalry Company* (Philadelphia, PA: Jas. B. Rodgers Co., 1870), 60-63. McClellan reported that the 31 July-1 August shelling from Coggins Point across the James River from Harrison's Landing killed some 10 men and wounded 15. McClellan had the point occupied and fortified to prevent further demonstrations. In that same report to Halleck, McClellan wrote that "I need more cavalry; have only 3,700 for duty in cavalry division," *OR*, vol. 11, pt. 1, 76. Certainly the numbers of cavalry available in that division reflected the many which were serving other duties with army corps, etc., which McClellan himself ordered.

[73] Rawle, 98.

from Malvern Hill, gathering stragglers and maintaining picket lines.[74] The cavalry finally embarked between 11 August and 3 September with the last units arriving at Alexandria on 4 September. The 5th and 11th Pennsylvania Cavalry were left behind to garrison Williamsburg and Suffolk. Lee's cavalry was also involved in scouting and picketing and about as active as its Union counterparts during the Seven Days.[75]

Both army commanders handled their cavalry awkwardly on the Peninsula, but Lee was new to army command and McClellan was involved in his first major battle with his army. Undoubtedly, McClellan's parceling out his troopers hurt his mounted efforts but his troopers generally did well against their more experienced foes. Both mounted forces dealt with unfamiliar terrain, poor maps, bad roads, and wooded, swampy ground, unsuited for large cavalry actions, although Confederate troopers with local knowledge undoubtedly were helpful as were sympathetic residents. Union company and field grade officers with a few exceptions did well but two of its generals, Cooke and Emory, did poorly, and lost their commands.[76] One historian wrote that "Problems of vitality aside, the Federal cavalry fought harder and achieved more on the Peninsula than it has been given credit for. Were Federal troopers better than their counterparts? Absolutely not—nor did they accomplish all that they might have. But for men who only months before may not have known how to saddle or ride a horse, the Northern cavalryman's accomplishments are worthy of some admiration. Williamsburg, Hanover Court House and Willis Church are just a few reminders that the men in the short blue jackets with the yellow or orange piping did not always embarrass their country or their army. Jeb Stuart and his troopers were the standard by which these men would be judged, and embarrassing days still lay ahead, but the Northern horsemen were learning, and their defeats seldom came from lack of desire or want of valor."[77] Its green regiments were at least gaining in-saddle experience, and at best, learning how to fight like cavalry, albeit in mostly small actions.[78] Stuart likely had a slight advantage as he was fighting in friendly territory. Lee could have used his cavalry more effectively especially in chasing McClellan down the Peninsula: "Had the cavalry been divided on June 29 and half of it returned to Lee, it is not likely that the line of the enemy's retreat to the James would have been in doubt, or that the prospect of a concentration at Malvern Hill gone unreported."[79]

But at this time of the war, Stuart's cavalry were setting the standard for the cavalry while the Union troopers were still learning their trade, encumbered by poor organizational decisions by the army commander, and lackluster leadership by some of its generals. The two spectacular failures of the Union cavalry, Stuart's Ride, and Gaines's Mill, overshadowed its many positive contributions to McClellan's

[74] O'Neill, *Peninsula Campaign*, 136-138; Averell, 433.

[75] The Union Second Cavalry Brigade, for example, in its brigade orders No. 11, gave the order of embarkation on 23 August for Alexandria: 8th Pennsylvania Cavalry, 8th Illinois Cavalry, 6th U.S. Cavalry, 1st U.S. Cavalry, ambulance train after 25 August; wagons and teams will embark with squadrons and officers will remain with companies; sufficient water and forage and seven days rations will be present on embarkation, NA, RG 94, Regimental Letter, Order and Miscellaneous Book, vol. 5 of 6, 8th Illinois Cavalry.

[76] Thiele, "The campaign in general and Stuart's raid in particular clearly established the fact that Cooke lacked vigour and perception and that outside of Farnsworth, Pleasonton, and Averell, the Federal Cavalry commanders were not especially competent," 302. Infantry commanders continued their interfering with cavalry organization and operations as noted when Stoneman complained to McClellan on 10 July that "Commanding officers of scouting parties and brigade commanders complain that the men of their commands are taken away by generals, colonels, and other officers to act as orderlies, &c. I have the honor to request that the general commanding give directions that this be stopped in future," OR, vol. 11, pt. 2, 930. A few Confederate cavalry units were on familiar ground such as Company G of the 4th Virginia Cavalry, O'Neill, *B&G*, 46.

[77] O'Neill, *Peninsula Campaign*, 142.

[78] Wittenberg, *Lancers*, 53.

[79] *Lee*, 2:237-238. See also Thiele, "Stuart failed, however, to ascertain that McClellan had shifted his base, nor was his pursuit of the Federals from June 29 on adequate. Nevertheless, the unity of the Confederate Cavalry command was obviously a great advantage to them," 302.

efforts on the Peninsula, while Stuart's ride made him and his men Southern heroes in Southern eyes, and well known to Northerners. As both armies moved away from the Peninsula heading north, cavalry helped their respective army commanders in their efforts but Stuart and his men would again be in the spotlight.[80] Lee took the few weeks of respite after the end of the Seven Days to rest and refit his army, distributing the largesse that the hastily retreating Union army had left behind. While it is likely that his infantry gained the most from battlefield gleaning and captured supplies, the cavalry also gathered in supplies.[81] Newly-promoted Maj. Gen. Stuart and the bulk of his cavalry prepared to head north to face the growing threat from Union Maj. Gen. John Pope.

An evaluation of the performance of the cavalry on the Peninsula shows that Union and Confederate cavalry were overall about evenly matched in operations. The public perception of the armies respective performances were heavily colored by two incidents which were not representative of the remainder of the service for both sides' horsemen: Stuart's First Ride Around McClellan, and the Gaines's Mill failed Union cavalry attack. In the first instance, Stuart's bold and imaginative leadership combined with the inept pursuit by his father-in-law led to the broad-brush view that Confederate cavalry continued its dominance, initially shown at First Bull Run in July 1861, with the legend of the Black Horse Cavalry. Cooke's pursuit was not as vigorous as it could and should have been, but as has already been noted, his command was not large, as most of the cavalry of the Army of the Potomac was not under his command, but parceled out to other commands. Therefore, Stuart's large body of horsemen, well-handled, was able to concentrate against all opposition during his trek. Though the value of the results of his circumferential ride can be disputed, the psychological effect this ride had on the public perception in the North and South was dramatic. Later cavalry raids in the Civil War had their roots here for better or worse, but the enormously favorable effect his ride had on the morale of the South was undisputed, while the opposite effect on the Northern populace was also marked. To this point, McClellan's slow but steady progress up the Peninsula to Richmond and victory, was celebrated by most in the North. This first bump in this road followed by the Gaines's Mill defeat, then McClellan's "change of base," tainted the generally good efforts of the Union cavalry.[82]

Early in the Peninsular Campaign, many Union cavalry units which were relatively untrained and untested, perhaps with little or no field experience, did have time to learn the fundamentals of their trade. Regular army units did better as they had more experienced officers and senior enlisted men, but even volunteer units did well either by participating with or training under experienced cavalry officers. Confederate cavalry benefitted as Gen. Johnston ordered most Rebel cavalry grouped under Stuart's command, so Stuart was better able to manage his horsemen with much fewer men detailed to other tasks. While Stuart's men may have had an edge on overall experience as well as the quality of company-level leadership, his personal leadership and that of his commanders such as Fitzhugh Lee, Rooney Lee,

---

[80] Thiele, 539.

[81] *Lee*, 2:256.

[82] A Union general, Jacob D. Cox, wrote that "The use of the cavalry in 'raids,' which were the fashion, was an amusement that was very costly to both sides. Since Stuart's ride round McClellan's army in 1862, every cavalry commander, National and Confederate, burned to distinguish himself by some such excursion deep into the enemy's country, and chafed at the comparatively obscured but useful work of learning the detailed positions and movement of the opposing army by incessant outpost and patrol work in the more restricted theatre of operations of the campaign....as to the raids on both sides, the game was never worth the candle. Men and horses were used up, wholesale, without doing any permanent damage to the enemy, and never reached that training of horse and man which might have been secured by steady and systematic attention to their proper duties. Forrest...was the only cavalry officer whom Sherman though at all formidable...saying he would swap all the cavalry officers he had for Forrest," *Military Reminiscences of the Civil War*, vol. 2, 290. See also Griffith, *Battle Tactics*, where he, too, lamented this use: "the deliberate diversion of it [cavalry] into raiding during the second half" of the war was a great missed opportunity for cavalry to have helped win battles with close support of the infantry on a battlefield. He believed that the Union even more so than the Confederacy diminished the value of cavalry as so much of it was used for raiding, 183-184. See also Starr, vol. 1, 273.

William T. Martin, Matthew C. Butler, and Wade Hampton, was evident. Federal leadership under Stoneman was excellent, while less so under Cooke and Emory, both of whom would be gone by the end of the Peninsular Campaign. Lower level Union cavalry commanders would be heard from later in the war as they performed well on the Peninsula and later in 1862 and 1863: George A. Custer, David McM. Gregg, William Averell, Alfred Pleasonton, William Gamble, and Elon J. Farnsworth. Benjamin F. "Grimes" Davis would later prove to be instrumental in the escape of the Union cavalry from Harpers Ferry. Thus the spring and summer of 1862 may be viewed as the time during which the cavalry in the Army of the Potomac successfully began its transition from its fumbling beginning in 1861, to a superior mounted force in 1863. Despite public opinion and the unhelpful efforts of McClellan, it was evolving into a creditable threat to Robert E. Lee and his new Army of Northern Virginia. Union cavalry historian Stephen Z. Starr wrote that "At the beginning of September, 1862, the exhausted and nearly unhorsed Federal cavalry was back in the defenses of Washington, which it had left with high ambitions and high hopes in March and April, but it was not the same cavalry it had been. A little of the amateurishness, a little of the ineptness, had worn off, and a modest degree of professional skill was beginning to show itself."[83]

While Lee was new to his army and not familiar with his new subordinates' abilities, he utilized concentration of force and his penchant for active maneuver, not letting McClellan dictate the tempo of operations. McClellan, with his superior artillery, engineering, material, manpower, and naval support, would have succeeded, had Lee engaged in a "battle of posts," so despite some poorly coordinated attacks and lackluster performances of a few generals, Lee quickly pushed McClellan back down the Peninsula. But he desired to carve up and destroy large parts of McClellan's army, and lamented that he did not succeed in this, and also was distressed at his casualties, but had to be satisfied by removing the threat to Richmond, his primary goal. Had the capital fallen, likely the Confederacy itself would have been in jeopardy.[84]

Now Lee had to continue both on the tactical and strategic offensive, maintaining the initiative he had wrested from his foe. He knew that to have any hope of overcoming the Union juggernaut, he had to use his highly mobile army to out maneuver and out march his opponent.[85] Taking the massive Union army away from the coast and rivers would vitiate the North's superiority in ships and the ability to protect and supply McClellan. In Virginia, as later in Maryland, Lee wanted room to maneuver to catch the northern armies away from the protection of their fortifications and navy. With McClellan still on the Peninsula, Maj. Gen. Ambrose Burnside's corps north of Fredericksburg, and Pope's army heading south from Culpeper threatening the important railroad junction at Gordonsville, Lee knew he had to move. Lee could no longer wait to see which of the three Union forces he faced, McClellan, Pope or Burnside, would attack first. He decided to confront Pope's Army of Virginia before it could be reinforced. On 13 July, Lee sent some 15,000 troops to Louisa Court House: Jackson with his division, Ewell's division, and the Laurel Brigade of cavalry. Even before he was sure McClellan was withdrawing from the Peninsula, on 9 August, he then sent Longstreet to join Jackson and help ensure that Burnside and Pope did not unite. Lee now had about half of his army heading to the vicinity of Gordonsville to

---

[83] Starr, 304.

[84] Harsh, *Rising*, as a manufacturing and railroad hub, "Richmond was as vital to Virginia as Virginia was to the Confederacy," 65. Had Richmond and then Virginia fallen, it "would have led more quickly to the collapse of the Confederacy than the loss of any other area," 64. Lee likely knew that he could not continue to bleed his army at the rate he did on the Peninsula "five times faster than the North's," 96.

[85] Ibid., Lee may have known of Lincoln's call for an additional 300,000 men on 1 July 1862 fueling his desire to quickly confront Pope's army to the north and not wait for new Federal regiments to be fielded, 107; *OR*, series III, vol. 2, 187-188. A total of 421,465 were furnished the Union. See also Frederick Phisterer, *Statistical Record of the Armies of the United States* (N.p., 1883; reprint, Edison, NJ: Castle Books, 2002), showing that there was a 2 July 1862 call for 300,000 men for three years and on 4 August 1862 a call for 300,000 militia for nine months service. Under this second call 87,588 were furnished, 4-5.

confront Pope, so he decided to go there to take command, leaving on 15 August. He believed that he could not remain tied down in a strategic stalemate watching McClellan on the James River, while Burnside and Pope were at Fredericksburg and the Rapidan River. He must maintain an offensive posture so he decided to attack Pope's army. Before he departed, he left substantial numbers of infantry, artillery, and Hampton's cavalry brigade, some 40,000 men all told, to watch McClellan since Lee was not certain that he was going to soon withdraw.[86] But by 17 August, Lee was convinced that McClellan was withdrawing, and now knew he had to confront and beat Pope, before McClellan's troops could unite with him. Lee headed north.

---

[86] Harsh, *Rising*, 109, 119, 123.

Attachment 1
Cavalry Strength of McClellan's Army of the Potomac

McClellan parceled out much of his cavalry to his general headquarters, corps, and divisions to serve as headquarters and provost guards, orderlies, and messengers. McClellan's general headquarters had the 2nd U.S. Cavalry as provost guards (9 companies: 409 officers and men) commanded by Maj. Alfred Pleasonton and two companies of the 4th U.S. Cavalry (A and E) and one company of the Oneida Cavalry (total of 3 companies: 131 officers and men) as guards and orderlies. The Second Army Corps had the 8th Illinois Cavalry commanded by Col. John F. Farnsworth (12 companies: 627 officers and men), Sedgwick's Division had K Company of the 6th New York Cavalry led by Capt. R. Johnson (59 officers and men); Richardson's Division had a second company of the 6th New York Cavalry (estimated at 60 troopers). The Third Army Corps had the 3rd Pennsylvania Cavalry led by Col. William W. Averell (12 companies: 717 officers and men) and an unattached company of the 8th Pennsylvania Cavalry (estimated strength 60 troopers based on average strength of the regiment's 12 companies); and the Fourth Army Corps had two companies of the 6th New York Cavalry (estimated strength 120 officers and men). The First Division of the First Corps had the 1st New York Cavalry led by Col. Andrew T. McReynolds (12 companies: 801 officers and men). The Fifth Corps had a detachment of the 4th Pennsylvania Cavalry commanded by Capt. Samuel B.M. Young (four companies: 280 officers and men).

The cavalry reserve of the army under the command of the old regular, Brig. Gen. Philip St. George Cooke, consisted of two brigades: the first was Emory's Brigade under Brig. Gen. William H. Emory with the 5th U.S. Cavalry commanded by Capt. Joseph H. McArthur (10 companies: 228 officers and men), the 6th U.S. Cavalry led by Maj. Lawrence Williams (10 companies: 583 officers and men), and the 6th Pennsylvania Cavalry (the Lancers) under Col. Benjamin H. Rush (10 companies: 551 officers and men); the Second Brigade in Cooke's cavalry reserve was Blake's Brigade under Col. George A. H. Blake with the 1st U.S. Cavalry commanded by Lt. Col. William N. Grier (8 companies: 282 officers and men), 8th Pennsylvania Cavalry under Col. David McMurtrie Gregg (12 companies: 712 officers and men), and Barker's Squadron Illinois (McClellan) Dragoons (estimated 100 officers and men). The First Battalion (four squadrons) under Maj. William Sackett of the 9th New York Cavalry commanded by Col. John Beardsley (12 companies: 600 officers and men) was assigned to the artillery reserve; the remaining eight companies were detailed as train guards. The 11th Pennsylvania Cavalry commanded by Col. Josiah Harlan (five companies with 399 officers and men) was assigned as Quartermaster Guard under Lt. Col. Rufus Ingalls. Five troopers from the Oneida Cavalry were also assigned as part of that guard. These numbers total 6,724 shown as "present for duty" in June 1862.[87] The historian of the 6th U.S. Cavalry

---

[87] *OR*, vol. 11, pt. 1, 279-284; *OR*, vol. 5, 19-21. Stephen W. Sears, *To the Gates of Richmond: the Peninsula Campaign* (New York: Ticknor & Fields, 1992), hereafter cited as *Richmond*, 359-363. Barker's Dragoons left the Second Brigade during June 1862. Leon Walter Tenney, "Seven Days in 1862: Numbers in Union and Confederate Armies before Richmond," Master's thesis, George Mason University, 1992, 208, 209, 211, 212, 213, 219, 223, 232, 240, 249, 258, 268, 269, 271. The 6th New York Cavalry, Co. K, under Capt. Riley Johnson (59 officers and men) are shown by Tenney as escort for the Second Corps on 20 June, 219; the 8th Pennsylvania is shown as escort for the Fourth Corps. The 8th Illinois Cavalry was assigned to the Fifth Corps in early June to replace the 1st New York Cavalry which was transferred to the Sixth Corps, 240. Most of the 4th Pennsylvania Cavalry was left at Tunstall's Station in the rear, 249. Note that "present for duty" data from Tenney show numbers on 20 June 1862 unless otherwise stated. He estimated company strength at 40 or 50 each for those units without sources. Because these numbers are calculated on 20 June, those units which landed early in the campaign, in April or May, were very likely to have had more troopers available as attrition by illness and injury would have reduced the numbers tallied upon landing, therefore, those numbers probably would be about five percent higher than shown, giving 7,060. See note 7 above and note 89 below regarding the 9th New York Cavalry which never served as cavalry on the Peninsula being dismounted and often semi-mutinous. A few cavalry units shifted from one command to another, see *OR*, vol. 11, pt. 3; assignments on 24 March 1862, p. 36; as of 8 July, p. 307-308; and 10 August, p. 367. Dyer shows under the 12th Illinois Cavalry heading that "Captain Sheerer's

wrote that "The regimental return of February 28th [1862] shows that twenty-eight officers and nine hundred and fifty-three men were present for duty, and the return for May…shows twenty-four officers and six hundred and seventy men," a loss of 287, almost 30 percent, in just three months. This excellent unit was perhaps the most heavily involved of any cavalry regiment on the Peninsula.[88]

The 9th New York Cavalry in reality never served at all as cavalry on the Peninsula being dismounted and often semi-mutinous. As will be seen in Chapter 8, the 8th New York Cavalry, sister regiment to the 9th New York, was unhappy as they volunteered and expected to be cavalrymen but were forced into infantry duties. Companies C, F, K and M were detached and distributed in detachments among the batteries of the Reserve Artillery while the remaining eight companies supposedly performed duty as train-guard in the Army of the Potomac. It is not clear if Maj. William Sackett remained in command of the 1st Battalion when it was parceled out to the Artillery Reserve but clearly he could not have been in direct command as his troopers were assigned to several different batteries. The regiment was finally shipped to Washington on 22 May 1862 and was equipped and mounted then assigned to the Cavalry Brigade, First Corps, Army of Virginia; it served in Brig. Gen. Julius H. Stahel's 1st Division, Eleventh Corps, from September, 1862. Cheney, the regimental historian, wrote that the eight companies lay around camp on the Peninsula doing nothing and did not guard trains or anything else. Cheney wrote that his regiment had 500 effectives on 21 July 1862 after it returned to Washington and was mounted despite much illness which the troopers contracted on the Peninsula. Its sister regiment, the 8th New York Cavalry, also was rebellious as noted in Chapter 8 below. Both of these units were troublesome until they were mounted under good officers then both units then became competent cavalry regiments.[89]

---

and Captain Barker's Companies, McClellan Dragoons, organized at Chicago, Ill., October, 1861, were assigned as Company 'H,'" 3:1029. McClellan's Dragoons were originally Barker's Chicago Dragoons but then adopted by McClellan as his personal guard. After their enlistments expired, most reenlisted and were assigned to the 12th as Companies H and I in February 1862 but served detached until November 1863; they were referred to as Barker's Squadron or Barker's McClellan Dragoons, O'Neill, "Federal Cavalry Operations," 99, 209; Thomas M. Eddy, *The Patriotism of Illinois*, 2 vols. (Chicago: Clarke & Co., 1865), 1:566.

[88] Carter, *From Yorktown to Santiago*, 44.

[89] O'Neill, 95; Newel Cheney, *History of the Ninth Regiment, New York Volunteer Cavalry, War of 1861 to 1865* (Jamestown, NY: Martin Merz & Son, 1901), 28-29, 46, 49; Frederick Phisterer, *New York in the War of the Rebellion*, 6 vols. (Albany, NY: J.B. Lyon Company, 1912), 1:896. Estimate for the 9th as 50 officers and men per company from regimental history, 46, 49, and Tenney. See Chapter 8 below for a review of the tribulations of its sister regiment, the 8th New York Cavalry. The 9th joined Pope's Army of Virginia in late July and performed good service, Cheney, 49-58.

Attachment 2
Cavalry Strength of Lee's Army of Northern Virginia

There was a total of 4,109 cavalry under Stuart's command on 20 June 1862: 3,968 troopers plus 141 horse artillery. This number included five companies of cavalry transferred in June from Cobb's Georgia Legion. During the Seven Days, one company of Cobb's Legion cavalry (40 troopers) was detached to serve as escort to Maj. Gen. Ambrose Powell Hill. Jackson's command had 605 troopers under Munford which was part of the Valley Cavalry not under Stuart's control. Units which moved with Stuart during the Seven Days Campaign are as follows: troopers on Stuart's staff, 6; 1st Virginia led by Col. Fitzhugh Lee, 10 companies, 437 men; 4th Virginia Cavalry under Capt. Francis W. Chamberlayne, 10 companies with 393 men; 9th Virginia Cavalry led by Col. William Henry Fitzhugh Lee, 10 companies, 701 men; Cobb Georgia Legion commanded by Lt. Col. Pierce Manning Butler Young, 5 companies, 200 men; Jeff Davis Legion led by Lt. Col. William Thompson Martin, 8 companies, 250 men; Hampton Legion commanded by Maj. Matthew Calbraith Butler, 2 companies, 130 men; and the horse artillery led by Capt. John Pelham, 1 company, 141 men; total of 46 companies and 2,258 men. Troops also under Stuart's command but which remained south of the Chickahominy are as follows: 3rd Virginia Cavalry under Col. Thomas F. Goode, 10 companies, 250 men; 5th Virginia Cavalry led by Col. Thomas Lafayette Rosser, 10 companies, 400 men; 10th Virginia Cavalry commanded by Col. J. Lucius Davis, 10 companies, 400 men; 1st North Carolina Cavalry commanded by Col. Lawrence S. Baker, 8 companies, 561 men; 15th Virginia Battalion led by Maj. John Critcher, 4 companies, 244 men. Five companies of the 1st North Carolina Cavalry under Col. Baker arrived in Richmond on 27 June 1862 to join the three companies already serving with Stuart. The total number of companies is 42 with 1,851 men. Maj. Gen. Jackson had three companies as his headquarters guards: Company B, 2nd Virginia Cavalry, 42 men; Company D, 6th Virginia Cavalry, 63 men; and Elijah (Lige) White's Rebels, 50 men, along with Col. Munford's 9 companies and 450 men of the 2nd Virginia Cavalry. The majority of cavalry brigade which had served with Stonewall Jackson was left in the Shenandoah Valley to reorganize after Brig. Gen. Turner Ashby's death on 6 June 1862 and consisted of the following units: Robertson's Brigade commanded by Brig. Gen. Beverly Robertson; 6th Virginia Cavalry under Col. Thomas Stanhope Flournoy, 9 companies, 470 men; 7th Virginia Cavalry under Col. William E. Jones, 10 companies, 500 men; 11th Virginia Cavalry under Capt. W. H. Haines, 6 companies, 348 men; 12th Virginia Cavalry commanded by Col. Asher Waterman Harman, 10 companies, 500 men; Chew's Horse Battery led by Capt. Roger Preston Chew, 1 company, 75 men; total of 36 companies, 1,893 men.[90]

---

[90] Tenney, 133, 172, 173, 174. Apparently "W.H. Haines" in the 11th Virginia is William H. Harness according to the NPS Civil War Soldiers and Sailors System for the 11th Virginia Cavalry, http://www.civilwar.nps.gov/cwss/regiments.cfm

Chapter 4

From the Peninsula to the Potomac

GEN. ROBERT E. LEE WAS CONCERNED about Union Maj. Gen. John Pope to his north and was determined to confront him before major units from McClellan's army arrived to aid Pope. Pope had taken command of the newly-organized Union Army of Virginia on 26 June 1862 which had about 45,000 men and some 5,000 cavalry under staff command of chief of cavalry Brig. Gen. Benjamin S. Roberts. Pope's Special Orders No. 45 of 16 August 1862 massed the cavalry in each of his army's three corps with a corps cavalry commander allowing only an escort for the respective infantry corps commander. The corps cavalry were organized as follows: First Corps led by Maj. Gen. Franz Sigel had its cavalry commanded by Col. John Beardsley; the Second Corps commanded by Maj. Gen. Nathaniel P. Banks had Brig. Gen. John Buford as its cavalry leader; and the Third Corps led by Maj. Gen. Irvin McDowell had Brig. Gen. George Dashiell Bayard in charge of its troopers. After taking command, Pope reported that his 5,000 cavalry was "badly mounted and armed and in poor condition for service." On 17 August, Pope asked Halleck for "1,500 cavalry horses as soon as they can be sent. Our cavalry is much broken down, their horses not having been fit for anything from the beginning. Will you order them sent immediately?" As of 31 July 1862, Pope had reported the First Corps had 1,730 cavalry; Second Corps 4,104; and the Third Corps 2,904. Out of this total of 8,738, he reported 3,000 unfit for service leaving 5,738 available. Pope's Special Order No. 45 was the first notable step continuing the evolution of the Army of the Potomac's cavalry in 1862:

> Hereafter the cavalry of each army corps of this army will be massed and placed under command of the chief of cavalry of that corps.
> Commanders of army corps will be allowed to detach for duty at their own headquarters such cavalry as may be necessary for their personal escorts.
> Companies or detachments of cavalry now on duty at division or brigade headquarters will be sent at once to report to the chief of cavalry of their respective corps.
> Ten mounted men only will be allowed to each division headquarters, and five only to each brigade headquarters as orderlies. These will be obtained by requisition on the commander of the army corps to which such divisions or brigades belong.
> When divisions or brigades are temporarily detached, the cavalry required for service with them will be furnished for that temporary purpose only by the commander of the army corps.
> Whenever divisions or brigades thus detached return to their corps the cavalry with them will at once rejoin their proper command.[1]

---

[1] *OR*, vol. 12, pt. 2, 20, 53; *OR*, vol. 12, pt. 3, 581-585, 588; Starr, 289. Bayard died 14 December 1862 of wounds received at the battle of Fredericksburg, Virginia; Buford died 16 December 1863 at the Washington home of his good friend, Gen. George

Buford had replaced Brig Gen. John P. Hatch on 27 July 1862 after Hatch failed miserably in command of cavalry carrying out Pope's orders to take Gordonsville and destroy the railroad 10 or 15 miles to the east of that town, and with the remainder of his horsemen, push toward Charlottesville destroying railroad bridges. Hatch, much to Pope's dismay, left on this mission with not only his cavalry, but also infantry, artillery and wagon trains, slowing him so much that he accomplished nothing except angering his army commander. Due to Hatch's lethargic pace, advance forces from Jackson's command under Ewell had reached Gordonsville before Hatch. Pope then ordered Banks to have Hatch use only cavalry, some 1,500 to 2,000 troopers, and proceed from the west toward the railroad west of Gordonsville, destroying the tracks between there and Lynchburg. Hatch aborted his mission soon after starting, again infuriating Pope so much that Pope this time relieved Hatch. Undoubtedly Hatch's pathetic performances inspired Pope to issue General Orders No. 6 on 18 July 1862 detailing his desires for cavalry in his army: "Hereafter in any operations of the cavalry forces in this command no supply or baggage trains of any description will be used unless so stated specially in the order for the movement....Movements of cavalry must always be made with celerity, and no delay in such movements will be excused hereafter on any pretext. Whenever the order for the movement of any portion of this army emanates from these headquarters the time of marching and that to be consumed in the execution of the duty will be specifically designated, and no departure therefrom will be permitted to pass unnoticed without the gravest and most conclusive reasons."[2] Thus Pope's sacking of this veteran cavalry general very likely made an impression on his replacement, Buford, as well as Pope's other two cavalry leaders, Bayard and Beardsley. But later when cavalry under these men were exhausted before the Battle of Second Bull Run hampering Pope most just when he desperately needed these troopers, his severe handling of Hatch came back to haunt him.

Pope demonstrated his micromanagement of his cavalry in Special Orders 31 on 2 August after his experiences with Hatch, by detailed instructions to Buford and Bayard. Among other things, these veteran commanders were ordered to keep the other cavalry commander informed of "everything of importance" and to advise the infantry commanders in their rear "of all matters of interest in front....The commanders of the cavalry in their front will keep the brigade commanders constantly advised of any movement of the enemy in sufficient time to make every necessary preparation of defense. Whenever it may be necessary to concentrate these forces, or any portion of them, the senior officer present will assume command thereof, in accordance with the Regulations of the Army and irrespective of the provisions of this order."[3] Pope's order, in addition to the necessary details of location of these forces, included this last sentence which puts command of any combined forces named in the order, under the senior commander, which meant that the cavalry could be under infantry command, for better or worse, depending on the sagacity of the infantry general. Buford was appointed a brigadier general on 27 July 1862 having been a major on Pope's staff. Pope in this same order again wisely commanded that "The wagons and supplies for the commands of Generals Bayard and Buford will be kept with the respective infantry brigades in their rear."[4] Thus Hatch's poor performance as a cavalry commander had mostly positive results as Pope learned that his expectations would be better met by

---

Stoneman, the day after he was promoted to major general at Stoneman's urging. Beardsley had a less successful career and resigned from the army in April 1863 after being charged with several offenses including disloyalty, cowardice, drunkenness, and conduct unbecoming an officer and a gentleman; Roger D. Hunt, *Colonels in Blue: Union Army Colonels of the Civil War-Vol. 2: New York* (Atglen, PA: Schiffer Publishing Ltd, 2003), 42. See Attachment 1 to this chapter for a breakdown of units in Pope's three corps cavalry brigades.

[2] *OR*, vol. 12, pt. 2, 23-24, 50.

[3] *OR*, vol. 12, pt. 3, 525-526.

[4] Ibid, 526.

Maj. Gen. John Pope here shown as a brigadier general. Courtesy LOC.

Post-war picture of Brig. Gen. Benjamin S. Roberts, staff commander of Pope's cavalry. He was brevetted major general of volunteers for his actions at Second Bull Run. Courtesy LOC.

Brig. Gen. John Porter Hatch who failed Pope and was replaced by Buford. Courtesy LOC.

Brig. Gen. John Buford, Second Corps cavalry commander, one of the best Union cavalry commanders. Courtesy LOC.

Brig. Gen. George Dashiell Bayard here shown as a colonel, Third Corps cavalry leader. Courtesy Wikipedia.

being much more detailed in his orders. Unfortunately, this seeming solution to his problem ended badly by running his cavalry into the ground in its efforts to do his bidding.[5]

Pope had a sound strategic plan to trap Lee's army between himself and McClellan, but Pope did not count on McClellan's failure to maintain a sufficiently aggressive posture on the Peninsula to worry Lee. Lee now began to receive information as early as 13 August that McClellan was not going to move again on Richmond, so he could turn his attention to the growing Union threat to the north as Pope probed south. Lee moved toward Pope's army which was strung out from Fredericksburg to the Blue Ridge; he first sent Jackson in mid-July to the northwest to Gordonsville to guard against a Union incursion on that important railroad junction.

Jackson was accompanied by a cavalry unit, Robertson's Brigade, which was formerly commanded by Turner Ashby, who was with Jackson during his Shenandoah Valley Campaign; this brigade was spread from Orange to Gordonsville. The brigade's commander, Brig. Gen. Beverly H. Robertson, was not a favorite of Jackson and Jackson quickly requested Stuart's help. Jackson wrote to Gen. Lee requesting that Robertson be replaced but Lee could not immediately let Stuart leave the area east of Richmond until he was certain of McClellan's movements at Harrison's Landing. It may have been that Robertson was simply not a great field commander and that trying to discipline Ashby's former troopers was difficult even for this veteran West Point graduate. Apparently Jackson preferred Col. William E. "Grumble" Jones, but Gen. Lee was unconvinced that Jones was better qualified. Stuart arrived at Orange Court House on 16 August to consult with Lee. Jackson worked to remove Robertson but Gen. Lee

---

[5] Eicher, 153. Buford turned into one of the finest cavalry commanders in the east, Stephen Starr, 293. Starr also compared Pope's very detailed instructions with orders Gen. Lee usually gave Jeb Stuart making the implied comparison that Stuart would not need to be told how cavalry should comport itself. Sadly for Lee, Stuart unlike Jackson and Longstreet would on occasion require a tighter rein as will be seen during the first two weeks in September 1862 in Maryland and arguably during the 1863 Gettysburg Campaign.

disposed of the issue by assigning all cavalry to the command of Jeb Stuart effective 17 August 1862. On 20 August, Jackson received Lee's orders that he would lead the left wing of the Army of Northern Virginia effectively ending the existence of his Army of the Valley.[6]

William Edmonson "Grumble" Jones photographed while a colonel with the 7th Virginia Cavalry in the Army of the Valley in 1862. From *Photographic History of the Civil War: Cavalry*. Courtesy Wikipedia.

Brig. Gen. Beverly H. Robertson, not a favorite of Jackson or Stuart. Courtesy LOC.

---

[6] Robert K. Krick, *Stonewall Jackson at Cedar Mountain* (Chapel Hill, NC: The University of North Carolina Press, 1990), 8, hereafter cited as *Stonewall*; McClellan, *Stuart*, 89; *OR*, vol. 12, pt. 3, 926, 934; Robert E. Lee, *Lee's Dispatches: Unpublished Letters of General Robert E. Lee, C.S.A., to Jefferson Davis*, ed. Douglas Southall Freeman (New York: G.P. Putnam's Sons, 1915), 42-44, hereafter *Lee's Dispatches*; James I. Robertson, Jr. *Stonewall Jackson: The Man, The Soldier, The Legend* (New York: Macmillan Publishing, 1997), 543; Harsh, *Rising*, 122. See Attachment 2 to this chapter for a breakdown of Stuart's order of battle. Stuart appreciated Jones's fighting ability but did not get along with him as noted in a letter to Gen. Lee in October 1862 after recommending Munford to brigade command: "With Brigadier General Jones I feel sure of opposition, insubordination, and inefficiency to an extent that would in a short time ruin discipline and subvert authority in that brigade...I must beg the Commanding General to avert such a calamity from my division and if there are any who entertain different views in regard to General Jones, let such have the benefit of his services and his talents," Jeffry D. Wert, *Cavalryman of the Lost Cause: A Biography of J.E.B. Stuart* (New York, NY: Simon and Schuster, 2008), 225, hereafter *Cavalryman*.

Brig. Gen. Fitzhugh "Fitz" Lee. He was a nephew of Robert E. Lee and cousin of George Washington Custis Lee and W.H.F. "Rooney" Lee. An 1856 West Point graduate, he was a brigade commander for Stuart during the Maryland Campaign. From *The Photographic History of the Civil War in Ten Volumes*, 4:277.

Col. William Henry Fitzhugh "Rooney" Lee; he was colonel of the 9th Virginia Cavalry during the Maryland Campaign. He was the second son of Robert E. Lee and Mary Anna Randolph Custis, attended Harvard and was noted for his rowing prowess. He was rejected for admission to West Point due to a hand injury but was commissioned directly in the 6th U.S. Infantry in 1857; he resigned in 1859 to farm his plantation on the Virginia Peninsula. During the Maryland Campaign in the fight at Boonsboro on 15 September, he was wounded when he was unhorsed and run over but avoided capture. Effective 15 September 1862, he was promoted to brigadier general and received his own brigade, and on 23 April 1864 to major general, the youngest major general in the army. In June 1863, he was severely wounded in the thigh at Brandy Station as he was leading a charge. As he was recuperating at a relative's plantation, he was captured, not being released until March 1864. Courtesy LOC.

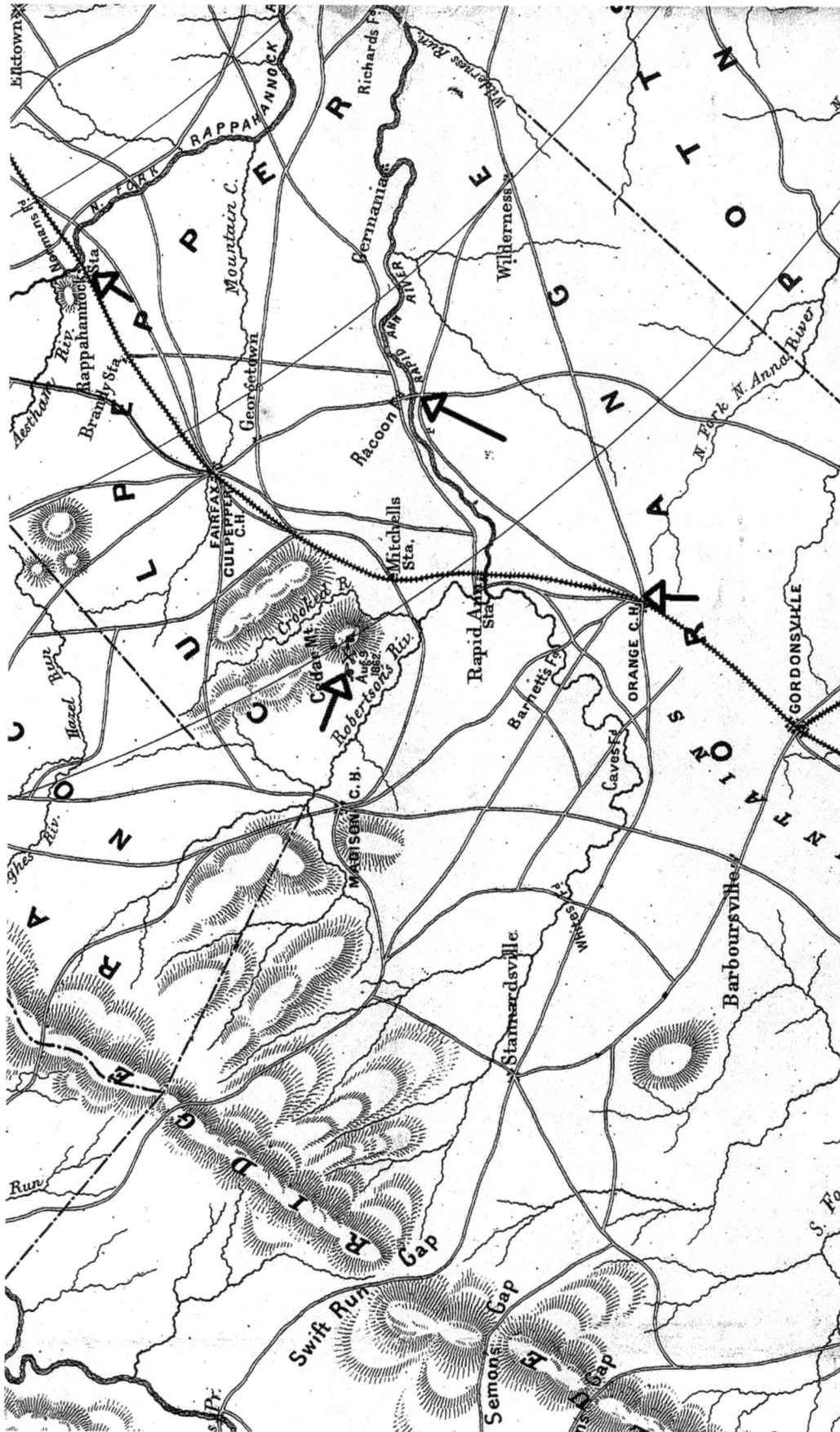

Map of area of operations of the Battle at Cedar (Run) Mountain shown at the upper center at arrow. Orange Court House is at the lower center with Gordonsville below it. Raccoon Ford is to the east of Cedar Mountain to the right of Mitchell Station; Rappahannock Station at arrow at top right. The Blue Ridge Mountains are to the west. Detail from "New map of the seat of war in Virginia and Maryland" by J. G. Bruff. 1863. Robertson River below and to the left of Cedar Mountain, and Brandy Station is at the upper right. Courtesy LOC.

Skirmishing between cavalry pickets and during reconnaissances sometimes led to bloody affairs as happened on 2 August at Orange Court House. Two Union cavalry regiments, the 1st Vermont led by Col. Charles H. Tompkins, and the 5th New York under Col. Othneil De Forest, all under command of Brig. Gen. Samuel W. Crawford, left camp near Raccoon Ford and after crossing the Rapidan River, encountered some pickets from Company F of the 11th Virginia Cavalry near the intersection of the Fredericksburg and Rapidan roads north of Orange Court House. Two Federal squadrons quickly drove in the Rebel troopers toward Orange Court House. Union troopers then came upon and pushed the rest of the Old Dominion troopers of Company F through the town to the outskirts on the Gordonsville Pike. Col. "Grumble" Jones commanding the 7th Virginia Cavalry, reported that as they arrived on the other side of the town, they found the 11th Virginia Cavalry company retreating from the attacking Unionists. Robertson believed that he had no choice but to attack so he and his regiment galloped to Orange Court House and onto the main street. Robertson fought with most of his regiment while sending a column under Maj. Thomas Marshall to attack the Union flank. Fighting continued in the town in a melee after Robertson's flank attack was outflanked; sabers were liberally used as were pistols killing and wounding men and horses. Maj. Marshall was knocked to the ground by a saber blow but Col. Robertson killed the Yankee who was about to kill Marshall. Marshall was captured and made a prisoner despite Robertson's best efforts; Robertson received a saber wound in the fight. Finally driving the Federals out of town, Confederate troopers halted, confronting obviously superior numbers. Unionists then attacked pushing the Rebel troopers back into town. Robertson gathered his troopers about a mile to the south of town and after about an hour, the Yankees began a retreat. As the Union troopers retired toward the Rapidan River, the 6th Virginia Cavalry joined the 7th Virginia Cavalry and a section of artillery to encourage a hastier Yankee retreat but the Confederates halted at Rapidan Station while the Federals continued to Raccoon Ford. The 7th Virginia cavalry had about 200 troopers in the fray while the Federals had at least twice that number. Louis N. Boudrye who wrote the regimental history of the 5th New York Cavalry was its chaplain, so likely did not personally witness this fight but opined that "This engagement clearly proved our superiority over the enemy's cavalry, which, in this instance, consisted of their best Virginia regiments lately under Col. Ashby." It is clear that the skirmish was more or less of a draw, and while the Confederate cavalry was heavily outnumbered, both it and the Yankee horsemen fought well. It had been a hard fight and afterwards, Jones reportedly said that when the Yankees had attacked his flank, "half of his men charged and half discharged." Col. Tompkins reported eight casualties in his 1st Vermont while Col. Jones wrote that the Yankees lost 11 killed, 30 wounded, and 12 missing and candidly stated that his casualties were about the same. Chaplain Boudrye wrote that "Fifty prisoners were captured, including a major, a captain, and two lieutenants.[7]

Jeb Stuart had better success fighting with Union forces near Massaponax Church south of Fredericksburg on 6 August. He reported that he attacked the Union line of march and Lee's Brigade was rounding up prisoners and booty as it carved up large pieces of the Yankee wagon train. He reported capture of about 85 prisoners, 11 wagons and teams, and 100 Enfield muskets while suffering only two mortally wounded. He continued to harass the rear of two Union infantry brigades of Gibbon and Hatch and believed that his cavalry harassment forced the Union advance to stop and eventually return to Fredericksburg.[8]

---

[7] *OR*, vol. 12, pt 2, 111-114, 181-182; Krick, *Stonewall*, 9-10; William N. McDonald, ed. by Bushrod C. Washington, *A History of the Laurel Brigade Originally the Ashby Cavalry of the Army of Northern Virginia and Chew's Battery* (Baltimore, MD: Sun Job Printing Office, 1907), 78-80; Louis N. Boudrye, *Historic Records of the Fifth New York Cavalry, First Ira Harris Guard* (Albany, NY: S. R. Gray, 1865), 37-39; David Humphreys, *Heroes and Spies of the Civil War* (New York: The Neale Publishing Company, 1903), 102-104. Crawford commanded the First Brigade in the First Division of the Second Corps.
[8] *OR*, vol. 12, pt. 2, 118-119, 120-121.

On 7 August, Jackson moved through Orange Court House with his three divisions and some 24,000 men, toward a collision with Banks's Corps near Cedar Mountain, two days hence on 9 August. Pope reported that he had about 28,500 men in his Army of Virginia assembled along the turnpike from Sperryville to Culpeper. He also reported the disposition of his cavalry as follows: Buford with five regiments was at Madison Court House with his pickets along the Rapidan River from Barnett's Ford west to the Blue Ridge Mountains; Sigel had a brigade of infantry and a battery of artillery in support. Bayard had four regiments near Rapidan Station where the Orange and Alexandria Railroad crossed the Rapidan River and had his pickets east to Raccoon Ford connecting with Buford at Barnett's Ford. From Raccoon Ford to the forks of the Rappahannock above Falmouth, Pope's cavalry pickets lined the Rapidan River. Pope established a signal station about half way between Buford and Bayard on top of Thoroughfare Mountain which overlooked the country south to Orange Court House.[9] Pope was receiving timely information about Jackson's movements from both Buford and Bayard indicating strong enemy movements and when Buford reported heavy enemy infantry in his front and rear and his cavalry was retreating to Sperryville, Pope sent Banks with two divisions from Culpepper to confront the Rebels.[10] Banks, according to Pope, was ordered to hold the enemy and fall back if they were found to be in heavy force so Pope could get Sigel's corps to reinforce Banks. Unfortunately for Banks, Sigel's corps was not ready to move forward so Banks was on his own.

Robertson's cavalry, which led Ewell's advance on 8 August, pushed back Buford's troopers but few Union casualties resulted. Bayard reported that early in the morning of 8 August, his pickets west of Robertson's River had been driven in and that the Rebels had crossed the Rapidan in force. Bayard sent the remainder of the 1st Pennsylvania Cavalry to support the pickets. Later that morning before dawn, Lt. Col. Joseph Kargé with 160 troopers from his New Jersey regiment rode to the left to turn the enemy's flank while Bayard with the remainder of the Jersey men rode to reinforce the 1st Pennsylvania and attack the enemy. Bayard made it to the Rapidan but learned that the enemy was in great force so he ordered Kargé to turn back as Bayard had done with his troopers. Confederate cavalry confronted Bayard's troopers and wounded two men but then after Kargé returned with 20 prisoners, Bayard continued his retreat. He reported that his men had to cross the Robertson River under a heavy fire of both artillery and musketry. Bayard continued retreating to Cedar Run where he posted the Pennsylvania horsemen as pickets then fell back with the New Jersey troopers.

After the battle at Cedar Mountain began in late afternoon about 5 P.M. on 9 August, the Rebel infantry advanced after initially being pushed back. Gen. Banks ordered a cavalry charge to disrupt the Rebel advance and save Union cannon—Bayard ordered Maj. Richard I. Falls commanding the First Battalion of the 1st Pennsylvania Cavalry to charge. Falls reported the following about his futile charge:

> After getting in front of the point designated, and being in column of fours, I immediately formed squadron, my command being already under fire. I moved forward at a rapid gait until within 50 yards of the enemy's lines, which I found in great force and three in number, when I gave the command, "'Charge," when, with loud and terrific cheering, my command charged through the enemy's lines, cutting and running down and scattering them in every direction, causing sad havoc and discomfiture in their ranks....After charging back and reforming, I found my command reduced from 164, rank and file, to that of 71, the remainder having been killed, wounded, or otherwise placed hors du combat by their horses falling over other killed or wounded, our little band thus proving themselves true sons of the old Keystone State.[11]

---

[9] *OR*, vol. 12, pt. 2, 24-25.
[10] Starr, 294; *OR*, vol. 12, pt. 2, 26, 130; *OR*, vol. 12, pt. 3, 541-550.
[11] *OR*, vol. 12, pt. 2, 141.

Confederates suffered few if any casualties in this encounter but rather looked on the charge as a joke and more of an entertaining interlude as well as an opportunity for target practice—not a serious attempt to halt their attack. Confederate Brig. Gen. Jubal A. Early wrote in his memoirs that

> the enemy made a desperate effort to retrieve the fortunes of the day by a charge with cavalry. We had no regular line formed at this time, and our men were much scattered in advancing, when a considerable body of cavalry came charging along the road from over the ridge, toward the position where the left of my brigade and the right of Jackson's division had rested during the action. Without being at all disconcerted or attempting to make any formation against cavalry, small regiments nearby, among which was the 13th Virginia, poured a volley into the head of the approaching cavalry, when it had got within a few yards, causing it to turn suddenly to its right up through the wheatfield, followed by the whole body, which made its escape after encountering a raking fire from our troops further to the left, by which many saddles were emptied. The attack on the enemy was thus resumed and he was driven entirely from the field.[12]

Again, as demonstrated at Gaines's Mill on the Peninsula, a mounted cavalry charge against infantry not in retreat is almost always futile.

The 1st Maine Cavalry was not heavily involved, but was concerned with chasing Rebel cavalry from the left of the Yankee line; it suffered no losses. The 1st Rhode Island Cavalry, a well-drilled unit according to Rebel observers, drew back upon the approach of Rebel infantry sustaining light casualties. Then, with other units of Bayard's cavalry, it covered well Pope's retreat from the field. Confederate cavalry otherwise were little involved during the battle itself.[13]

Col. "Grumble" Jones returned during the evening from an expedition toward Madison Court House. He had led a cavalry probing action during the night on the Rebel right with part of his 7th Virginia Cavalry going through the Confederate front line into Union lines. Jones was totally unaware of the presence of Pope, his staff, and other generals, when he charged the group of mounted men. The fleeing generals and their staffs also had to run the gauntlet of fire from a nearby Union regiment, bruising Gen. Banks in the melee when he was run over by a horse and which friendly fire also killed two enlisted men. Yankee artillery joined in sending Jones galloping away to shelter behind a nearby hill. Brig. Gen. Alpheus Williams described what he saw of this brou-ha-ha:

> I was riding toward a road in front of which I had been directed to mass my division, or what was left of it. When but a few rods off, a spirited fire of infantry was opened upon us. Just in front of me was Gen. Gordon and an escort of cavalry. Fortunately we were in a small hollow and the balls passed over us. There was, however, a general stampede of officers and dragoons. Just behind us Gens. Pope and Banks were sitting dismounted with a good many staff officers and escorts. This was a hurrying time with them and all together

---

[12] Krick, *Stonewall*, 31; *OR*, vol. 12, pt. 2, 89, 92-93, 140-141, 182; William P. Lloyd, *History of the First Regiment Pennsylvania Reserve Cavalry, from Its Organization, August, 1861, to September, 1864, with List of Names of All Officers and Enlisted Men Who Have Ever Belonged to the Regiment, and Remarks Attached to Each Name, Noting Change, etc.* (Philadelphia: King & Baird, Printers, 1864), 22-28; Starr, 294-295; Jubal Anderson Early, *Lieutenant General Jubal Anderson Early, C.S.A., Autobiographical Sketch and Narrative of the War Between the States*, ed. by R.H. Early (Philadelphia, PA: J.B. Lippincott Company, 1912), 100, hereafter cited as Early. Official casualties for the 1st Pennsylvania were 34, apparently several missing returned after the affray, *OR*, vol. 12, pt. 2, 139, 234-235.

[13] Tobie, 80; Thiele, 314; George Leonard Andrews, "The Battle of Cedar Mountain, August 9, 1862," in *Papers of the Military Historical Society of Massachusetts*, vol. II, *The Virginia Campaigns of 1862 Under General Pope* (n.p.: Military Historical Society of Massachusetts, 1895, reprint Wilmington, NC: Broadfoot Publishing Company, 1989), 420, 421, 429; *OR*, vol. 12, pt. 2, 140. Krick, *Stonewall*, 56-58, 232-237, 261-262. Paddy Griffith wrote that based on the results of cavalry charges such as at Gaines's Mill, Cedar Mountain, and at the end of the battle of Gettysburg by Gen. Kilpatrick, "the day of the cavalry charge had passed; that the rifle musket's improved firepower had given a new security to infantry, even if they had not formed squares; and that the American cavalry had really been rather wise not to charge more frequently in these battles than it did, in view of the probable outcome, *Battle Tactics of the Civil War* (New Haven, CT: Yale University Press, 2001), 180.

the skedaddle became laughable in spite of its danger. In front of the wood not over 500 yards off was an infantry regiment just come up, which opened fire with very little regard to friend or foe."[14]

David Hunter Strother one of Pope's staff also witnessed this event which occurred just after sunset on 9 August:

General Pope rode immediately to the front where he met General Banks. They and their staffs and escorts gathered on an eminence near a wood where it was supposed we had pickets....we heard some trampling in the wood and presently a body of cavalry issued from the forest and passed along until their flank entirely covered our position. Turning suddenly, they yelled and poured in upon us a rapid and continuous volley from carbines and pistols. We mounted in hot haste, as the enemy were not more than fifty paces from us. In attempting to mount, General Banks was overthrown and his hip badly hurt by the horse of a dragoon, the rider of which was killed. By the time we had started across the field, the fire in our rear became more furious. The balls struck around us so rapidly that I thought it impossible for anyone to escape....General Pope stuck his head down and, striking spur, led off at full speed. I gave my mare the reins and, as we crossed a hollow, a regiment of our own infantry seeing a dark mass of cavalry advancing opened fire....I swerved to the left to avoid the fire of the U.S. troops and with the body of the staff pushed on toward a fence....Several horses without riders galloped with us; among the missing were General Pope and Major [James F.] Meline....the batteries had been keeping up the most furious fire I ever heard It was a steady roar, and the blazing of the guns, the bursting of shells, and the vast columns of white smoke obscuring the woods and piling up like snow mountains in the moonlight was a scene so dramatic and grand that it will not be soon forgotten....Riding forward we found Generals Pope, Banks, McDowell, and Sigel sitting on a pile of fence rails under a tree....The Generals had again been doing picket duty for the army.[15]

"Grumble" Jones captured 15 prisoners including three lieutenants and a black Union Army servant. The officer's servant said that Sigel was advancing to the front confirming information Jackson had already obtained from one of Stuart's scouts, Benjamin Franklin Stringfellow, thus stalling any further movement north for his depleted troops. Jackson was likely pleased at Jones's information in what turned out to be the brightest Rebel cavalry action at Cedar Mountain, but chagrined that his cavalry commander, Robertson, was of little use on 9 August. That night, Jackson received welcome news that Jeb Stuart had arrived in answer to his request.[16]

Jackson was happy to have Stuart finally with him as "Beverley Robertson had contributed almost nothing thus far; reconnaissance seemed not to be a strong point with him. Jackson had partially anticipated his failure and had, on August 7, dispatched a note to Jeb Stuart, now a warm and trusted friend. Revealing far more than usual, Jackson wrote: 'This evening I leave for Orange C. H. en route for Culpeper C. H. I wish you could bring your command up...and make the Inspection that has been assigned to you. I desire you to make it during active operations; as I may thereby secure your services for the time being.'"[17] Jackson reported that after Stuart arrived "on a tour of inspection" he requested

[14] Alpheus S. Williams, *From the Cannon's Mouth: The Civil War Letters of General Alpheus S. Williams*, ed. Milo M. Quaife (Detroit, MI: Wayne State University Press, 1959; reprint, Lincoln, NE: University of Nebraska Press, 1995), 101.

[15] Strother, *Diaries*, 77-78. Strother was a volunteer aide-de-camp to Banks.

[16] Krick, *Stonewall*, 315-318; *OR*, vol. 12, pt. 2, 184, 239; Brown, *Stringfellow*, 155-156. During the Battle of Cedar Mountain, the Union Second Corps had Company L of the 1st Michigan Cavalry as an escort under Capt. Melvin Brewer, Company M of the 5th New York Cavalry under Lt. Eugene Dimmick, and Company H of the 1st West Virginia Cavalry led by Capt. Isaac P. Kerr. The First Division had Company M of the 1st Michigan Cavalry under Capt. R. C. Dennison as an escort. The escort loss for the Second Corps was five killed, five wounded and six missing; Bayard's cavalry brigade had a total of 61 casualties, two in the 1st Maine Cavalry; 16 in the 1st New Jersey Cavalry; 34 in the 1st Pennsylvania Cavalry; and 9 in the 1st Rhode Island Cavalry, *OR*, vol. 12, pt. 2, 136-139.

[17] Frank E. Vandiver, *Mighty Stonewall* (New York: McGraw-Hill Book Company, Inc., 1957), 343.

Jeb to take command of the cavalry and make a reconnaissance to gain information of the enemy's movements and numbers. On the morning of the 10th Stuart gathered his cavalry and rode east to the Orange and Alexandria Railroad which he followed to the Stevensburg road leading from Culpeper, in the rear of the Federal army. He had sent a detachment to Pony Mountain to capture the Union Signal Corps detachment located there. Stuart ascertained from prisoners captured as well as other information that the remaining division of McDowell's corps was expected to arrive from Fredericksburg; it became clear that the remainder of Pope's army was in supporting distance and no victory could be reasonably expected against these odds.

Lige White's Comanches, the 35th Virginia Battalion, did not accompany Stuart but rather remained in the front of Jackson's line. They were relaxing in the shade on another hot August day in the early afternoon while their horses grazed. White nonchalantly acknowledged an infantry officer's warning that the only friendly troops to his front were a few cavalrymen who were helping an ordnance officer salvage ammunition from a Union wagon. A few minutes later the somnolent Rebel cavalrymen were surprised by a Yankee squadron charging at them; White's men quickly mounted and the Federals, seeing what was in store for them if they continued their assault, turned tail and retreated. White's troopers followed up scaring Union horsemen away by a few pistol shots and rescued the Confederate ordnance officer. The noise of this action led to a minor panic among nearby Rebel troops however, and infantrymen, wagons and even two batteries headed for the rear, fearing that their lines were again flanked as happened the day before. And as happened then, Gen. Jackson had to stop the stampede by riding into its midst.[18]

On 13 August, Gen. Lee sent Longstreet to join Jackson and left Hampton's Brigade on the Peninsula to monitor McClellan's departure from Harrison's Landing.[19] Lee arrived in Gordonsville on 15 August and met with Jackson and Longstreet, his two chief commanders. Lee knew he must strike Pope quickly before the bulk of McClellan's units en route from the Peninsula could reinforce Pope's army. Lee saw that Pope was in a dangerous tactical position in the "V" of the converging Rappahannock and Rapidan Rivers. If Pope were attacked on his left and Fitzhugh Lee's cavalry could wreck the bridge at Rappahannock Station, Pope's main line of retreat would be cut and his army would be in a difficult position. Gen. Lee had to wait for the cavalry to come up so had to postpone the attack until 18 August. Stuart had ordered Fitzhugh Lee with his brigade to march to Raccoon Ford on the 17th. Gen. Lee had also placed Jackson's cavalry, Robertson's Brigade, under Stuart's command. Wade Hampton's Brigade, still on the Peninsula, would not arrive in time to participate. Unbeknownst to Stuart and Fitzhugh Lee, Gen. Lee had postponed the attack until the 19th due to logistical concerns. Stuart and his staff had ridden south to Verdiersville to await Fitzhugh Lee but were rudely awakened on the morning of the 18th to a Union cavalry scouting party. Stuart's visitors consisted of two regiments under Col. Thornton F. Brodhead, commander of the 1st Michigan Cavalry, who had gotten across an unguarded Raccoon Ford. The Federals were in hot pursuit as Stuart and his men barely escaped except for Maj. Norman R. Fitzhugh; much to his chagrin Stuart lost his famous plumed hat as well as his cloak. Fitzhugh Lee, under a misapprehension of his orders, would be another day before arriving at Raccoon Ford so Gen. Lee

---

[18] See *OR*, vol. 12, pt. 2, 89, for Bayard's report. Union cavalry losses for the battle were about 90, *OR*, vol. 12, pt. 2, 136-139. Jackson was concerned about the activities of Union cavalry as he mentioned it in his report and had Ewell post infantry pickets, *OR*, vol. 12, pt. 2, 182, 228. Krick, *Stonewall*, 327-331; Daniel A. Grimsley, *Battles in Culpeper County, Virginia, 1861-1865* (Culpeper, VA: Raleigh Travers Green, 1900), 81-82; Jedediah Hotchkiss, *Make Me a Map of the Valley: The Civil War Journal of Stonewall Jackson's Topographer*, ed. by Archie P. McDonald (Dallas, TX: Southern Methodist University Press, 1973), 67, 129; Franklin M. Myers, *The Comanches: A History of White's Battalion, Virginia Cavalry, Laurel Brig., Hampton Division., A.N.V., C.S.A.* (Baltimore, MD: Kelly, Piet & Co., Publishers, 1871; reprint, Alexandria, VA: Stonewall House, 1985), 91-93.
[19] *OR*, vol. 12, pt. 2, 184.

Portrayal of Stuart's escape on his trusty mare "Highfly" from Union cavalry after being surprised at Verdiersville on 18 August 1862 leaving his cloak and hat on the porch. Cooke, *Wearing of the Gray*, facing pg. 200.

again put off the attack until the 20th. Stuart blamed Fitzhugh Lee for this episode perhaps to divert attention from his lack of sufficient oversight which failed to impress urgency on Fitzhugh.[20]

But by then, Gen. Lee's bird had flown the coop, thanks to the satchel that Maj. Fitzhugh was carrying when captured by Brodhead's troopers. The satchel contained an order with Lee's plan to attack Pope between the two rivers. Pope added this find to information he had received on 16 August from a Union spy, Sgt. Thomas O. Harter, who brought word of Lee's movements showing his efforts to trap Pope between the Rappahannock and Rapidan Rivers—Pope beat a hasty retreat—his cavalry screened his rear, Buford to the east and Bayard to the west.[21] Lee moved his army forward in cautious pursuit with Fitzhugh Lee covering the front and right flank of Longstreet's right wing, and Stuart with Robertson in front of Jackson moving on the left of the army; a regiment of Robertson's was on Jackson's left flank. Skirmishes continued as the Rebel cavalry came up against the Union rearguard.[22]

Active Rebel cavalry actions continued under Stuart's oversight. On 20 August at about 4 A.M., Stuart reported that Fitzhugh Lee's and Robertson's brigades moved across the Rapidan at two fords, separately pursing Federal cavalry. Lee caught up with Union horsemen near Kelly's Ford and attacked,

---

[20] *Lee*, 2:279-288; Hennessy, 40-48.

[21] Fishel, 191-192. Sergeant Thomas O. Harter of the 1st Indiana Cavalry did an excellent job scouting Robert E. Lee's planned attack, which convinced Pope to withdraw. Harter disguised himself as a civilian railroad worker, and although he was imprisoned for over two weeks, he traveled to Harrisonburg, Staunton, and Richmond, observing Confederate movements. Harter was very fortunate to find Pope quickly upon returning to Union lines with his excellent intelligence of Lee's plans showing that Lee was ready to attack Pope's left. This vital piece of information allowed Pope to retreat quickly for which Harter was given $500 and a discharge from the army as his value as a spy was finished since his identity was known by the Confederates.

[22] *Lee*, 2:289-293; Hennessy, 53-54.

Union cavalry charge near Brandy Station, 20 August 1862, *Battles and Leaders*, 2:460.

capturing a stand of colors. Robertson found Yankee troopers between Stevensburg and Brandy Station. Col. Jones with the 7th Virginia cavalry led his advance but was stymied by heavy forces in some woods near Brandy Station. After resupplying his ammunition, he advanced while Robertson with the 6th, 7th, and 12th Virginia stayed to the left to flank the Union position. Jones had pushed Bayard's cavalry until they made a stand midway between Brandy Station and Rappahannock Station. While the Yankees battled Jones, Robertson's main body attacked even though apparently outnumbered and the Union horsemen retreated toward the Rappahannock River where they were protected by their batteries. Two regiments of Fitzhugh Lee's Brigade, the 1st and 5th Virginia Cavalry under Col. Rosser, arrived as reinforcement to Robertson bringing with them Pelham's battery, but the Union troopers had escaped, leaving the land south of the Rappahannock Yankee free. That night, Jackson's advance arrived as tired Rebel troopers rested, except for Munford, who had advanced to Culpeper, taking some prisoners. Stuart was proud of Jones's actions as his regiment had borne the brunt of the fight and "behaved with marked courage and determination....General Robertson had cause to be proud of the command which his superior discipline, organization, and drill had brought to the stability of veterans."[23]

Bayard's report of this incident stated that he had five regiments of his division in front of the Rebel advance, the 1st Pennsylvania Cavalry, the 1st New Jersey Cavalry, 1st Rhode Island Cavalry, the 1st New York Cavalry, and the 2nd New York. A squadron of the 1st Maine Cavalry initially found the enemy near Raccoon Ford and fell back. The 2nd New York Cavalry under Lt. Col. Hugh Judson Kilpatrick held them until the Maine men returned then Bayard fell back toward the Rappahannock following the 1st Maine and 1st Rhode Island cavalry which had been sent ahead. Bayard drew up his cavalry in line with the 1st New Jersey on the right about 600 yards in the rear of the 2nd New York and the 1st Pennsylvania

---

[23] *OR*, vol. 12, pt. 2, 726-727; 745-746. Stuart's report included the 17th Virginia, Robertson did not. Note that Robertson was not commended for his fighting skills in this rare encomium for Robertson from Stuart.

Cavalry in reserve. Kilpatrick's New Yorkers were caught in midst of a maneuver and mostly retreated when the Confederates charged followed by the fleeing New Jersey cavalry. Col. Kargé was seriously wounded when he charged virtually alone. Union cavalry was clearly bested in this confrontation with Stuart's veteran troopers in their determined attacks. Bayard's brigade casualties at Cedar Mountain and this action totaled 61. The detachment of the 1st Ohio, Companies A and C, serving as Pope's general escort lost two; Banks' escort, the detachment of the 1st Michigan, 5th New York, and 1st Virginia (Union) had a total of 18 losses.[24]

Col. Thomas Taylor Munford. Courtesy Wikipedia.

Col. Thomas Taylor Munford, a native Virginian born in Richmond, was one of Stuart's best cavalry commanders fighting for the Confederacy from First Bull Run to after Appomattox. He entered Virginia Military Institute in 1848 and by the end of his third year was appointed adjutant of the Corps of Cadets. He served as Professor Thomas J. Jackson's aide and found the professor a good man. He graduated in 1852 and returned to Lynchburg, Virginia, to farm on his family's land. Upon outbreak of hostilities with the north, he became lieutenant colonel of the 30th Virginia Mounted Infantry on 8 May 1861 finding 23 more VMI graduates in its ranks. Munford fought with this regiment at First Bull Run and was in charge

---

[24] Ibid, 89-90, 136, 139; Krick, *Stonewall*, 376; Thiele, 314.

of four companies on the right flank. Late in the day, he participated in the charge which routed the Unionists retreating across Bull Run. Relatively inactive for months after the battle, he and his four companies engaged in skirmishes and patrols in the Virginia Piedmont region earning Jeb Stuart's praise for his duties. After its first commander resigned, Munford became the regiment's colonel with his commission dating from 25 April 1862; it was redesignated the 2nd Virginia Cavalry. Munford with his regiment and the 6th Virginia Cavalry operated along the Blue Ridge Mountains in Virginia attacking Union wagon trains and troops as opportunities presented themselves. He rejoined his old professor in the Shenandoah Valley when Jackson became his commander. Brig. Gen. Turner Ashby commanded Jackson's cavalry; Munford and the two regiments were placed under Brig. Gen. George H. Steuart's temporary brigade command. Munford and his troopers did well and when Ashby was killed on 6 June, Jackson placed Munford in command of his cavalry brigade. At the end of the valley campaign, Munford did not retain command as Jefferson Davis chose Brig. Gen. Beverly Robertson to lead the brigade then consisting of the 1st, 2nd, 6th, 7th, and 12th Virginia Cavalry Regiments along with the 17th Virginia Battalion. The brigade was with Jackson during most of the Peninsular Campaign doing good service. At Second Bull Run, Munford was in the attack on Union Brig. Gen. John Buford's cavalry brigade at Lewis Ford and did well routing the Yankees; Munford suffered a saber stroke and had his horse killed under him. Robert E. Lee complimented Munford's gallant efforts. After Robertson was detached for duty in North Carolina, Munford was given command of his brigade in Maryland. After the Maryland Campaign, Munford was passed over for permanent command of the brigade with it going to Col. William E. "Grumble" Jones who had led the 7th Virginia Cavalry; Jones was made brigadier general. Unfairly criticized by Stuart for his actions during the Battle of Brandy Station on 9 June 1863, Munford redeemed himself at the skirmish at Aldie. Fighting at Gettysburg and the Wilderness Campaign, he continued his good service and took over as brigade commander in November 1864, still a colonel. He commanded Fitzhugh Lee's cavalry division in the spring of 1865 at Petersburg through Appomattox when he and his troopers, again under Fitzhugh Lee's command, escaped to Lynchburg where he disbanded his regiment, after Gen. Joseph E. Johnston's surrender on 26 April 1865. Munford became a successful cotton planter and was vice president of the Lynchburg Iron, Steel and Mining Company. He died on 27 February 1918 in Uniontown, Alabama, likely still disappointed at not being promoted to brigadier general—he and others who knew his service understood that politics often trumped ability and courage.[25]

Gen. Robert E. Lee knew he could not cross the Rappahannock River to assault Pope since Pope was well sited on higher ground, so Lee moved to his left, upstream, sending Stuart to scout ahead. As Stuart reached each ford, he met Union troopers placed by Pope on the opposite bank lively defending the ford; turning Pope's right flank was becoming more difficult than Lee had anticipated. Lee gave permission to Stuart to raid Catlett's Station well in Pope's rear hoping to break Pope's concentration. Catlett's Station is near the junction of the Warrenton Railroad, and the Orange and Alexandria Railroad, and was Pope's headquarters. On the stormy night of 22-23 August, Stuart crossed the Rappahannock with Robertson's and Lee's Brigades minus two regiments and headed to Warrenton. From there he journeyed to Catlett's Station and planned an attack. After careful scouting, he learned that the station was lightly guarded by invalids and about 160 men from the Bucktails—the 13th Pennsylvania Reserves. Stuart detailed Rosser and some of his men to capture the Yankee pickets and then had Rooney Lee and his 9th Virginia Cavalry lead the charge into the camp. Rosser would then head for the Union camp south of the railroad while the 4th Virginia Cavalry under Col. Wickham were assigned to burn the vital railroad bridge over Cedar

[25] Bruce S. Allardice, *More Generals in Gray* (Baton Rouge, LA: Louisiana State University Press, 1995), 171-172; Jeffrey Wert, "His Unhonored Service: Colonel Tom Munford—A Man of Achievement," *Civil War Times Illustrated*, vol. 24, no. 4, June 1985, 28-34.

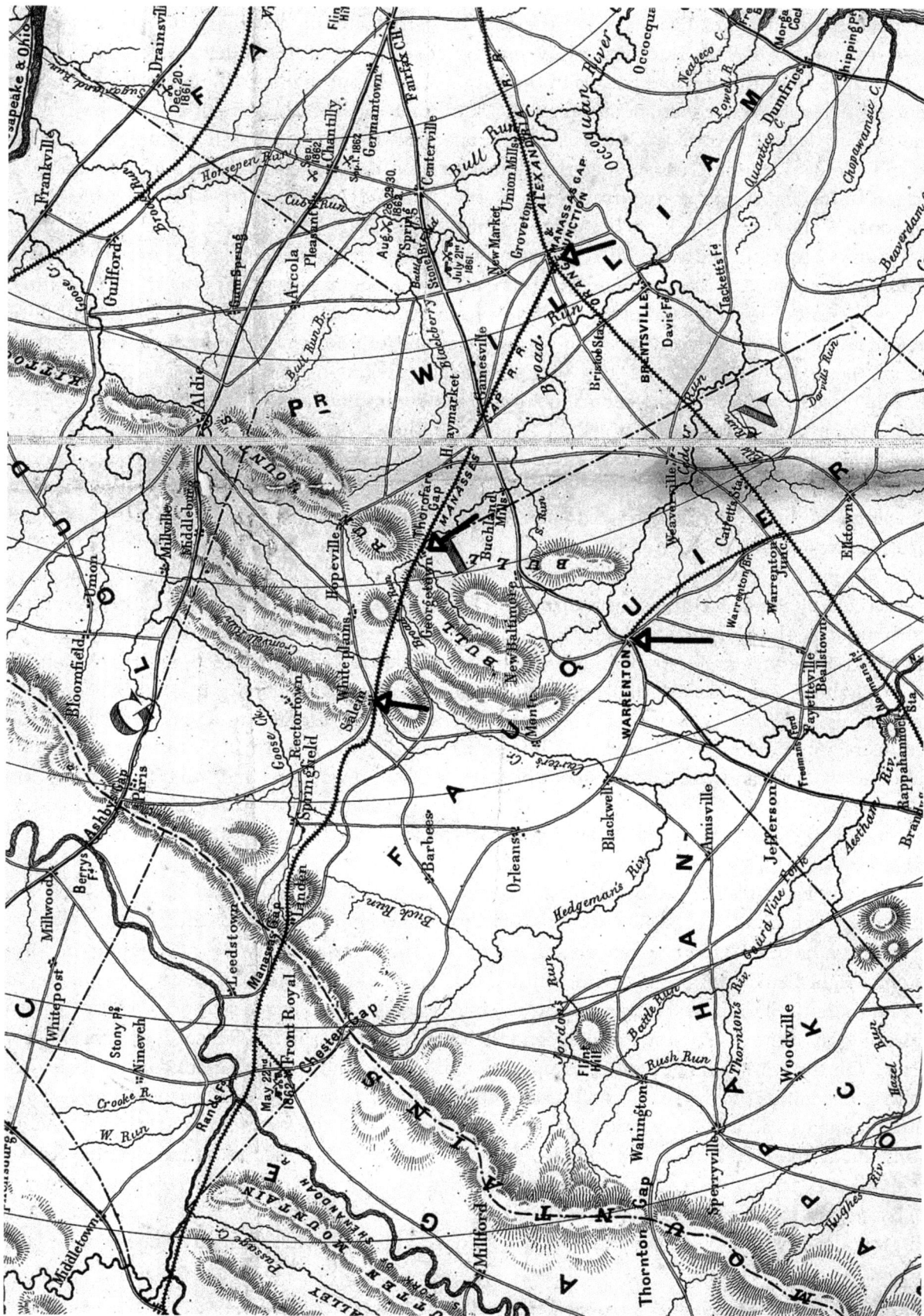

Map of area of operations for the movement of Lee up the Rappahannock River, Stuart's raid on Catlett's Station, and Jackson's approach through Thoroughfare Gap. Warrenton is in the center of the map at the arrow; Catlett's Station to its southeast. Salem is to the upper center at the arrow; Thoroughfare Gap is at the upper center arrow and Manassas Junction at the right arrow. Note that Manassas Junction is about 30 airline miles from Washington. Courtesy LOC.

Run. The Rebel attack at the station completely surprised and overwhelmed the Yankees allowing the Confederate troopers to set wagons and tents ablaze, steal horses, mules, money chests, and most importantly, find Pope's dispatch book, which was among his uniforms. This critical find contained valuable information for Gen. Lee about the numbers and disposition of Pope's army and also showed that Porter's Corps, from McClellan's Army of the Potomac, was approaching. Of additional help to Lee, was Pope's talkative field quartermaster, Maj. Charles Goulding. Stuart reported over 300 prisoners taken in the melee. The only failure in Stuart's raid, unfortunately, was a major one, as he was unable to burn the railroad bridge over Cedar Creek; Lee had wanted the Orange and Alexandria Railroad, Pope's lifeline, cut. Lee now knew he must move quickly to defeat Pope before Porter and more of McClellan's troops reached Pope's Army of Virginia.[26]

Much of Pope's cavalry was exhausted by this time with men and horses worn-out and the lack of forage compounding the animals' misery. It could not provide useful information to Pope who was not aware of what Jackson's move meant. Pope believed that the Rebels were going to move into the Shenandoah Valley and thought perhaps that the Union army could attack Lee's rear. The valuable service Buford and Bayard had rendered began to fade in the face of jaded horses and worn-out troopers just when Pope most needed fresh information about Confederate movements. Bayard and Buford both reported that "their cavalry was broken down" with Bayard stating that his troopers "would neither charge nor stand a charge" and Buford's was disorganized. In the meantime, Pope kept his focus on the Rappahannock line and was unaware of Jackson in his rear. Pope was confused not knowing where McClellan's units were let alone Lee's.[27]

Lee sent Jackson with his three divisions west with orders to cut the Orange and Alexandria Railroad, Pope's supply line. Lee assumed that Pope would retreat toward Washington when he found Jackson in his rear. Stuart would follow Jackson and Longstreet would bring up the rear; Jackson began with only the 2nd Virginia Cavalry under Col. Thomas T. Munford for cavalry support, along with a few messengers from the Black Horse Troop. On 25 August, Lee ordered Stuart to join Jackson with all his cavalry save for twenty-five members of the Black Horse Troop—Company H of Fitzhugh Lee's 4th Virginia Cavalry—which would serve as couriers for Lee. Jackson was to march through Thoroughfare Gap in the Bull Run Mountains and get in the rear of Pope's army; Longstreet was to follow thirty-six hours later and unite the army. Jackson marched some 25 miles in severely hot weather on the first day arriving in Salem.[28]

Gen. Lee on the 26th had received welcome news: a telegram from President Davis revealing that he had sent most of the troops from Richmond, including Hampton's 1,445 cavalry, to join Stuart's 3,500.[29]

---

[26] *Lee*, 2:296-300; Hennessy, 53-54; see Blackford, 99-108 for a detailed and entertaining account of the raid; *OR*, vol. 12, pt. 2, 333, 730-732; *OR*, pt. 3, 657.

[27] Hennessy, 105-111.

[28] Harsh wrote that Gen. Lee's strategy may not have been to just chase Pope toward Washington but away from Gordonsville and Richmond and then lure him into the Shenandoah Valley where Lee would have room to maneuver and hope to seriously damage Pope's army. Too, Harsh observed that "Washington was most vulnerable on its western flank on a line that menaced the upper Potomac and the Baltimore and Ohio Railroad and threatened both Pennsylvania and the capital's tenuous communications with the North through Baltimore," *Rising*, 145-146, 151.

[29] The reinforcing column numbered 25,488 including Hampton's 1,445, John O. Allen, "The Strength of the Union and Confederate Forces at Second Manassas," master's thesis, George Mason University, 1993, 202. Lee had mentioned on a few occasions to Davis his need for cavalry: "Cavalry is very much needed in this region; the service is hard, and the enemy strong in that arm. If the regiment in question [2nd North Carolina] is not needed in [North] Carolina, I respectfully request it be ordered to join General Hampton's brigade," *OR*, vol. 12, pt. 3, 944; Davis replied on 28 August that "The reinforcements asked for by you have been sent forward, and the cavalry to which you refer particularly should have joined you by this time, *OR*, vol. 12, pt. 3, 946; Lee had telegraphed Richmond on 28 August the following: "Other troops from Acquia I particularly require Hampton's Cavalry expedite the reinforcements ordered," *Lee's Dispatches*, 54.

But as Lee was riding with Longstreet's wing, he had a scare on 27 August when he and his staff were confronted by Union cavalry near Salem. Apparently, the Federal troopers had come from Warrenton on a scout and encountered Lee; the Union troopers departed believing that they were confronting a large Rebel cavalry force. This scare perhaps reminded Lee that sending away all his cavalry with Jackson leaving few to scout and screen movements for the rest of his army may have been a mistake.[30]

By the afternoon of the 26th, the hard marching Jackson was through Thoroughfare Gap finding no Union resistance and by late afternoon was in Gainesville where the Warrenton Turnpike and the Manassas Gap Railroad crossed. Stuart joined Jackson during this pause at Gainesville with Robertson's and Fitzhugh Lee's Brigades after riding for more than 12 hours. Jackson's reply to Stuart who proudly displayed Pope's coat was that he would have preferred Pope himself over his coat. Jackson decided to raid Bristoe Station south of Gainesville and about seven miles southwest of Manassas Junction, cutting the Orange and Alexandria Railroad, Pope's main line of communication. With Stuart guarding the right flank, and Munford's 2nd Virginia Cavalry in the van, the column headed for Bristoe Station. Munford surprised the small garrison and its cavalry fled while the Union infantry took cover and briefly held off Munford's troopers until Confederate infantry arrived, helping complete the takeover of the station. Although they succeeded in wrecking two incoming trains, there were few spoils found. Jackson determined to move to Manassas Junction once he learned from citizens that it was lightly protected and contained huge stores of Union supplies. After assigning Brig. Gen. Isaac Trimble the task, he then sent Stuart along to bolster Trimble's two regiments of infantry to take Manassas Junction guarded by the newly formed 12th Pennsylvania Cavalry, 115 infantry, and eight cannon.[31]

At Manassas Junction, Stuart's troopers and Trimble's two infantry regiments surprised and drove off a company of the 12th Pennsylvania Cavalry, captured over 300 men and six cannon at a cost of four casualties despite a more spirited defense than the Yankees had put up at Bristoe Station. Confederate cavalry, infantry and artillerymen, marveled at the mountains of Union supplies in warehouses and boxcars, and in an orgy of plunder likely unsurpassed before or since, took all they could, and burned the rest.[32] Now Pope on the 27th realized that a large enemy force was in his rear so he had his corps begin marching north abandoning the Rappahannock line heading for Gainesville and Manassas. That same morning, the 2nd New York Heavy Artillery which had been transformed into infantry moved from Bull Run toward Manassas Junction encountering some of Fitzhugh's videttes. As the Rebel troopers were pushed back, Jackson added A.P. Hill's brigades to bolster Rebel forces, ending with some 9,000 infantry and 28 cannon ready for all comers. As Union Col. Gustav Waagner and his 600 strong 2nd New York Heavy Artillery approached, he quickly realized that he was outnumbered and wisely retreated. But now more Federals arrived by train—Brig. Gen. George W. Taylor's New Jersey Brigade prepared to confront and brush aside what they understood to be guerillas at Manassas Junction. He unloaded his 1,200 men close to the Bull Run Bridge where the track was blocked leaving the 4th New Jersey to guard the bridge and marched along the railroad toward Manassas Junction. Taylor aligned his three remaining

---

[30] Harsh opines that Gen. Lee "still had much to learn in the effective deployment of his cavalry." First, he gave Jackson's column too few. Lee then tried to correct this mistake by assigning Stuart with both his brigades to join Jackson leaving virtually none for himself to scout Pope and to accompany Longstreet's column, Harsh, *Rising*, 139.

[31] Robertson, 551-552; Vandiver, 356-357; Hennessy, 111-113. Trimble and Stuart did not get along on this assignment even though the mission was accomplished.

[32] Larry B. Maier, *Leather & Steel: The 12th Pennsylvania Cavalry in the Civil War* (Shippensburg, PA: Burd Street Press, 2001), 39-40. Robertson, 554-558; *OR*, vol. 12, pt. 2, 722, 734; *OR*, vol. 12, pt. 3, 696. Hennessy, 113-115; see also John H. Worsham, *One of Jackson's Foot Cavalry* (New York: The Neale Publishing Company, 1912, reprint, New York: Bantam Books, 1992), for an entertaining account of the feast which followed the battle, 103-105. Maier wrote that Col. Lewis B. Pierce commanding the 12th Pennsylvania Cavalry was sick in bed during the attack but got up and rallied about 30 troopers from his command who had been left behind due to illness, 40.

New Jersey regiments and marched forward while Jackson held fire until the Yankees were less than 300 yards away and then opened fire, tearing apart the Jersey men. After seeing rebel cavalry maneuvering to cut off his retreat, Taylor fell back in good order, with Confederates in pursuit, but soon panicked when they came to a steep hill close to Bull Run Bridge. As the Unionists tried to crowd across the bridge, Robertson's and Fitzhugh Lee's troopers rode into them in a textbook case for the use of cavalry to run down a beaten and retreating enemy. Brig. Gen. Taylor was mortally wounded while many Federals jumped into Bull Run trying to escape, but many gave up and surrendered—the cavalry captured about 200 of Taylor's hapless infantry. Their loss for the day was 339 out of the original 1,200 infantry.[33]

Ewell, who remained at Bristoe Station, fought a commendable rearguard action, holding Hooker in check, and then retreated to join Jackson at Manassas. Pope rode to Bristoe Station and found Hooker's division unable to continue an immediate pursuit. Now that Jackson realized he had units of Pope's army to his west, south and east, he decided to move north to the old Bull Run battlefield to get beyond the Union left flank and battle whatever units of Pope's army came his way, while he waited for Longstreet to link up. Jackson, Lee, and Longstreet, were all well aware of the locations of each other thanks to the indefatigable Black Horse couriers shuttling between Longstreet and Jackson. Jackson then settled into a strong defensive position at the old battlefield near Groveton.[34]

Pope was now pleased that he was about to trap the Rebel army, and "bag the whole crowd," as his 50,000 men were closing in on Manassas.[35] Pope did not have much news from his cavalry as most of it was to the west just ahead of Longstreet watching his movements.[36] Buford had been operating on Longstreet's right flank sending timely and accurate information to his corps commander, Maj. Gen. McDowell.[37] Earlier that day, McDowell had received information from Buford who, at 9 A.M., had seen Longstreet's column moving through Gainesville. Strangely, McDowell did not forward this valuable information to Pope who McDowell knew believed Longstreet was not on or near the field.[38] On 28 August, Jackson gathered his forces and occupied a line flanking the Warrenton Turnpike covering the road from Haymarket to Sudley Springs. His pickets from the 1st Virginia Cavalry skirmished with some Union scouts on the Warrenton Turnpike and captured a Union courier with a copy of McDowell's marching orders for 28 August showing his army's concentration on Manassas. Jackson's desire to bring on a battle with Pope before that general could gain the strong defenses at Centerville was about to be realized as Bradley Johnson's infantry supporting the 1st Virginia Cavalry brought the lead of McDowell's column to bay a mile west of Groveton on the Warrenton Turnpike. After holding them briefly and being outflanked, Johnson withdrew. Later that day after the Federals restarted their march on the turnpike, Jackson ordered an attack on the approaching Union column consisting of four brigades from King's division, McDowell's Corps, led by the 1st Rhode Island Cavalry, beginning the battle of Second Bull Run, on the afternoon of 28 August. Jackson unwisely alerted Pope to his location while winning a

---

[33] Hennessy, 124-127; *OR*, vol. 12, pt. 2, 260, 406.

[34] Hennessy, 130-137.

[35] *OR*, vol. 12, pt. 2, 72.

[36] Ibid., 271-279. Col. William R. Lloyd commanding the 6th Ohio reported that from one to 10 horses per day dropped from exhaustion and lack of fodder; his battalion of 596 men required 448 horses for remounting. By the 29th, Col. Beardsley commanding the First Corps Cavalry Brigade reported the condition of his horses: "My horses were completely worn out and almost in a starving condition. All along our route, from White Plains and from Warrenton to Bull Run, they were dropping down with their riders and dying, so that when I reported to you [Gen. Sigel] on the morning of the 29th most of my horses were unable to carry the rider and had to be led." By having inadequate fodder and being ridden constantly, Pope ran out of cavalry when he most needed it.

[37] *OR*, vol. 12, pt. 3, 729-730; Hennessy, 141-143, 233-234.

[38] Hennessy, 234.

costly fight with Brig. Gen. John Gibbon's brigade known as the "Black Hats" at Brawner Farm.[39] Jackson drove off the Union infantry paying a heavy price then enjoyed a much-needed rest that night.

Gen. Lee, who had joined Longstreet west of the Bull Run Mountains, had to fight at Thoroughfare Gap. Sir Percy Wyndham's 1st New Jersey Cavalry brought Brig. Gen. Ricketts the first warning of Longstreet's approach to the western side of the gap. Wyndham's troopers had been busy felling trees to block the road from the gap and began the fight with Longstreet troops. In addition to warning Ricketts, he sent word to McDowell on the Warrenton Turnpike. Buford's dispatch to Brig. Gen. James Ricketts on the morning of 29 August reported the Rebel movement stating that "Seventeen regiments, one battery, and 500 cavalry passed through Gainesville three-quarters of an hour ago on the Centreville road. I think this [Buford's] division should join our forces, now engaged, at once."[40] Unfortunately, after Rickett's commander, Gen. McDowell, received this report and passed it on to Porter, McDowell did not inform Pope, to whom he gave this news only late that evening. Ricketts' division held Longstreet's infantry back until evening and then was forced back after being flanked on both ends of his line thus allowing clear passage for Longstreet's men for an early start the next morning, 29 August. On the morning of the 29th, Lee, still without Stuart's cavalry, organized a scratch cavalry force of 150 under Maj. Samuel H. Hairston to scout to Warrenton to ensure that no enemy would bother Longstreet's right flank on their march to join Jackson; Hairston found none although he reported that he picked up 46 prisoners along with 30 long arms, one deserter from the Stuart Horse Artillery, and one sutler with his wagon and driver. [41]

That morning, Jackson, believing Union forces would attack, posted Fitzhugh Lee's Brigade on his left guarding Sudley Ford over Bull Run, and adjusted his line, ensuring that he could escape north if needed. Union forces attacked Jackson piecemeal starting in the morning of the 29th after Jackson sent Stuart to locate and guide Lee and Longstreet in. Near Haymarket, Beverly Robertson and his brigade joined Gen. Lee to guide him to Jackson. Stuart shortly rode up and joined Lee and took up a flanking position on the right of Longstreet's column. Shortly after noon, Longstreet's men arrived and were substantially deployed on Jackson's right flank relieving the fears of Lee, as well as Jackson, of the army being defeated in detail. Stuart rode in the direction of Manassas down the Manassas-Gainesville road and after crossing Dawkin's Branch saw clouds of dust from Porter's approach. Knowing that without substantial infantry support which was not available from Longstreet, he had to delay the Yankees with his six regiments at hand. He had Col. Rosser's men cut down saplings and drag them on the road stirring up sufficient dust to delay Porter's Corps by presenting this bold front. Porter's delay allowed Longstreet's infantry to deploy removing the Union flanking threat.[42] Meanwhile, Jackson had an eventful day repelling several attacks. Late on 29 August, a squadron from the 2nd New York Cavalry was ordered by Lt. Col. Judson Kilpatrick to charge the Rebel right pressing down the Warrenton Turnpike but the Yankees rode into a trap. Confederate infantry in the forward line intentionally let the Union cavalry pass to be stopped by a heavy line of infantry further down the road. After this repulse, the

[39] Hennessy, 173-186. The "Black Hat" name referred to their old-style Hardee hats; they later became known as the "Iron Brigade," but was only one of a few with that sobriquet. For a discussion of the title "Iron Brigade" see Thomas Clemens, "'Black Hats' off to the Original 'Iron Brigade,'" *Columbiad*, vol. 1, no. 1, spring 1997, 46-50. Note that some historians count the battle at Groveton as distinct from Second Bull Run.

[40] *OR* vol. 12, pt. 2, 753; *OR*, vol. 12, pt. 3, 730. On 28 August, Wyndham's 1st New Jersey Cavalry had 12 companies with 533 troopers in the saddle while Ricketts' brigade had 6,886 men; they faced Longstreet's Command totaling 6,502 at the Thoroughfare Gap skirmish, John Allen, 34.

[41] *OR*, vol. 12, pt. 2, 753; *OR*, vol. 12, pt. 1, 168; *Lee*, 2:317; Hennessy, 305.

[42] Hennessy, 227; OR, vol. 12, pt. 2, 736; Harsh, *Rising*, 156.

Union horsemen beat a rapid retreat but had to run the gauntlet of even more infantry. This bloody and futile result left only 11 troopers from the squadron which was sent.[43]

Pope, on 30 August, based on erroneous reports, believed Jackson was retreating and acted on that belief, wanting to defeat him before he got away. Pope did not heed warnings of Longstreet's troops on Jackson's right which had extended the Confederate lines. Pope did little to have the left of his line reconnoitered to confirm his beliefs. His attacks were repulsed quickly on Jackson's left by the 1st Virginia Cavalry as elements of Kearney's Division crossed Bull Run to threaten Jackson's rear. Pope finally realized that the Confederates were not retreating but still there in force and full of fight. But Pope dismissed a report brought to him in person by Brig. Gen. Reynolds that the Rebels were massing for an attack on Pope's left; he did, however, deign to send Buford with some cavalry to confirm it. Pope next received a report from Sigel that the 4th New York Cavalry, which performed a reconnaissance around the Rebel right, found that the Confederates were moving against the Union left; Pope also dismissed this report.[44] Pope decided to attack Jackson's right not understanding that his men were charging into the center of the Confederate line. Longstreet, instead of sending a division to reinforce Jackson's weakened line, had several batteries of artillery enfilade the long Union lines decimating Pope's attack and he followed up with an infantry charge of some 25,000 men, sending the Federal troops reeling. Federal artillery, usually the master of the Confederate batteries, suffered one of its rare failures; it was parceled out to brigades and divisions so was unable to concentrate its fire as Rebel artillery did, since the Federal batteries worked independently.[45]

The Federal's retreat was not a rout as at First Bull Run but by nightfall, Pope was in full flight to Centerville with the Confederate pursuit stopped only by darkness.[46] Some adventurous troopers from Fitzhugh Lee's Brigade on the extreme Confederate right pursued Orlando Poe's brigade from Kearney's division as it retreated to Poplar Ford a mile above the stone bridge over Bull Run. But infantry from the 2nd Michigan shook out a firing line and as the Lee's cavalry approached the Yankees strongly discouraged eager troopers from any further pursuit emphasizing that determined infantry can handily repel a cavalry attack.[47] Fitzhugh Lee later learned that some of McClellan's units had arrived at Centerville much to Robert E. Lee's dismay. Stuart wished to launch a night attack with a brigade of infantry but the army commander wisely demurred.[48]

Bayard's cavalry helped slow the retreating blue tide as Porter ordered it to stop the fugitives from his corps. Buford, along with the 4th New York Cavalry from Beardsley's brigade, guarded the far left Union flank astride the Old Warrenton, Alexandria, and Washington Road, facing Robertson who was about a mile to the west with his troopers. Buford moved to near the Lewis and Ball's Fords on Bull Run after Longstreet had begun his attack on the Union left. Robertson followed moving toward Lewis Ford.[49]

---

[43] Hennessy, 301.

[44] Ibid., 219, 328-330.

[45] Ibid., 351.

[46] Ibid., 431.

[47] Ibid., 429.

[48] *Lee*, 2:337, 338; Hennessy, 424, 429; David A. Welker, *Tempest at Ox Hill: The Battle of Chantilly* (Cambridge, MA: Da Capo Press, 2002), 86.

[49] *OR*, vol. 12, pt. 2, 749-751.

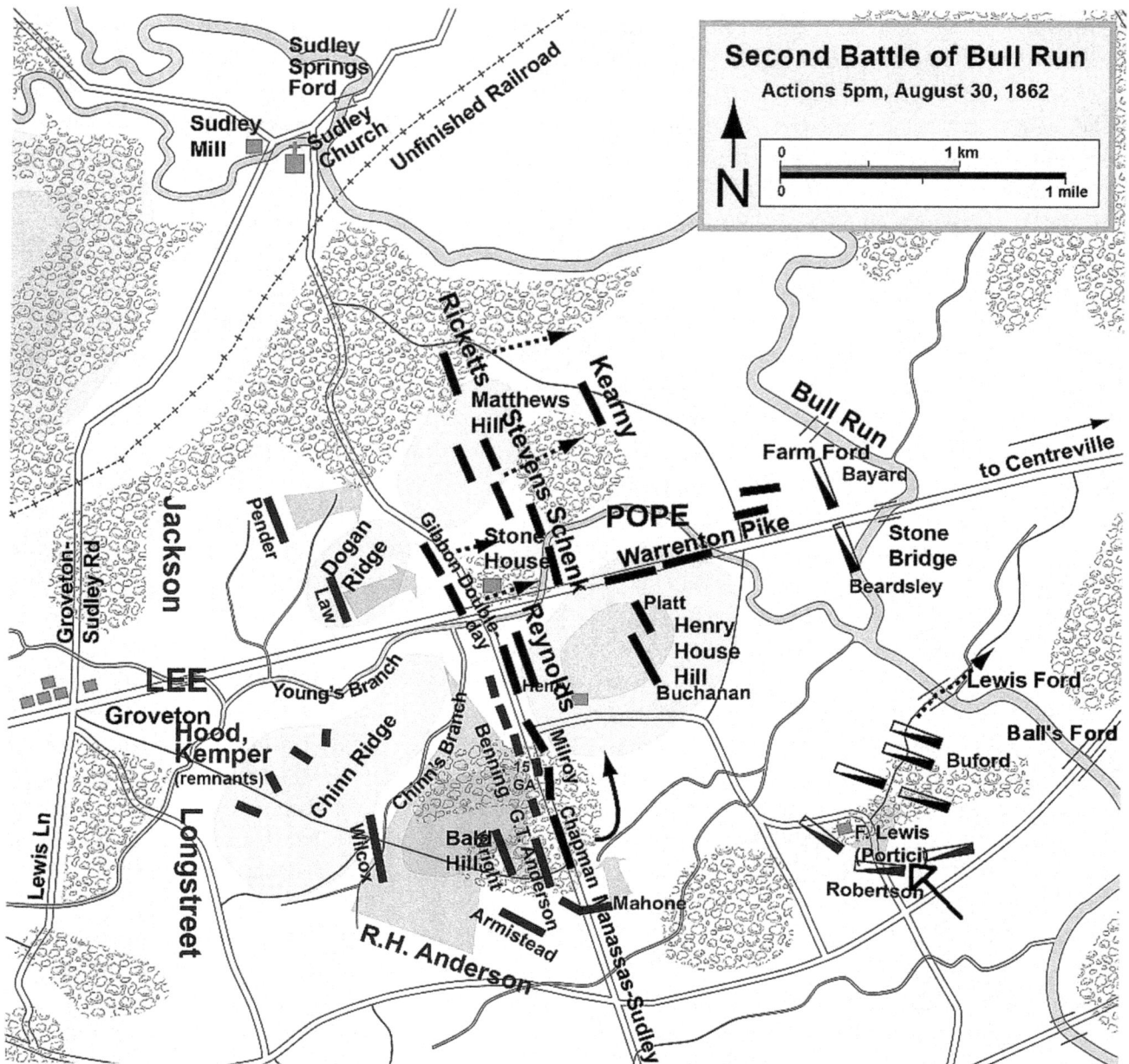

Situation 30 August at 5 P.M. Robertson confronts Buford near "Portici" owned by Francis Lewis in the lower right corner. Ball's Ford is to the southeast of Lewis Ford. Courtesy Hal Jespersen from Wikipedia.

Stuart assigned Robertson's Cavalry Brigade to watch closely the Union left flank along with Rosser's regiment. Although Robertson was apparently too slow for Stuart, Col. Rosser directed Rebel batteries holding at bay any Union efforts in that area. After posting Robertson on a ridge overlooking Bull Run, Stuart rode forward to the Groveton road when he received a report from Robertson that Union cavalry was in his front in force and asked for reinforcements. Stuart immediately dispatched the 7th and 12th Virginia Cavalry regiments along with a section of artillery but before the guns could reach the scene, Rebel troopers had won the day. Robertson had sent Munford forward—then Munford dispatched a squadron to chase off what appeared to be a company of Federal cavalry. But this squadron saw that there were many more enemy cavalry which had been hidden from view so the Rebel pursuit quickly reined in. Robertson ordered Munford to form up the rest of his 2nd Virginia in support and moved to the rear to gain a better position. The Yankees, thinking that the Confederates were retreating, charged in column of regiments according to Munford, with the 1st Michigan cavalry, the 4th New York, and the 1st West Virginia in hot pursuit. Munford's regiment suffered greatly in hand-to-hand combat as the Federal column penetrated Munford's line then surrounded the hapless Virginians. Fortunately, Robertson moved forward to support the heavily outnumbered Munford and his 2nd Virginia, with the 7th and 12th Virginia Cavalry, leaving the 6th Virginia in reserve. Apparently the 6th in its eagerness to attack the Yankee troopers tried to push by the 7th Virginia as it was forming but Capt. Samuel B. Myers leading the 7th forbade it. Robertson's fresh regiments thundered forward with the 12th Virginia Cavalry attacking Brodhead's Michiganders, and Myer's 7th Virginia taking on the 4th New York. Seeing this two-regiment frontal attack, Unionists retreated, being chased by the 2nd, 12th, and part of the 7th Virginia Cavalry regiments, through Lewis Ford where the 2nd stopped near the Centreville and Warrenton Turnpike; the 7th Virginia pursued only part of the way but Robertson did not throw in his other units, the 6th Virginia and the 17th Virginia Battalion. The 12th Virginia Cavalry dogged the Yankee cavalry to the Warrenton Pike but darkness had set in. Munford wrote that his pursuit stopped at Bull Run. The Confederate regiments had routed the remnants of the 1st Michigan and 4th New York whose retreat carried with it the 1st Vermont and 1st West Virginia Cavalry which Buford had mistakenly not formed. Col. Brodhead of the 1st Michigan was mortally wounded in the melee cut down by Adjutant Lewis Harman of the 12th Virginia cavalry. It was Brodhead's regiment which had surprised Stuart at Verdiersville 18 August. Munford was also wounded in the action. Losses amounted to some 300 Union versus 54 Confederate; 42 of these 54 were from the 2nd Virginia Cavalry. Buford, wounded in the knee with a spent ball, performed relatively well with his less experienced troopers in standing up to a massed Rebel charge even though he did not form up his entire force. Robertson's lackluster pursuit on the other hand, which stopped short of the Warrenton Turnpike down which the Union army was retreating, was poor—had he gained the road and panicked Pope's trains in the gathering dark, the Union retreat, which was more or less orderly, could have produced a major roadblock, gaining for Lee the larger destruction of Pope's army which he desperately sought.[50]

A member of Munford's cavalry, Pvt. John Gill, wrote about his part in the battle in this, his first action as a cavalryman:

> Unfortunately for me, my sabre, a poor specimen of Confederate iron, was soon bent and quite useless. I was attacked by three Yankees. I was fighting for my life, when kindly aid came from one of my comrades by the name of Nelson, who cut down two of my opponents, and at the third I made a right cut which missed him, and which nearly unhorsed me. Scarcely recovering my seat, I saw an officer coming straight at me tierce-point.

> I had only a moment to gather my thoughts, and in that moment my pistol was leveled at him, to surrender or die. He threw up his hands and surrendered—horse, foot and dragoon. He was an officer of one of the Michigan cavalry regiments. During the remainder of the war I rode in his saddle.[51]

---

[50] *OR*, vol. 12, pt. 2, 737-738, 746-748, 752; Hennessy, 430-435.

[51] John Gill, *Reminiscences of Four Years as a Private Soldier in the Confederate Army 1861-1865* (Baltimore, MD: Sun Printing Office, 1904), 73-74.

Col. Thornton Fleming Brodhead of the 1st Michigan Cavalry, a former Regular Army captain and Harvard Law School graduate, was mortally wounded at Second Bull Run, and died 2 September. He received a posthumous promotion to brigadier general effective 30 August 1862. Courtesy LOC.

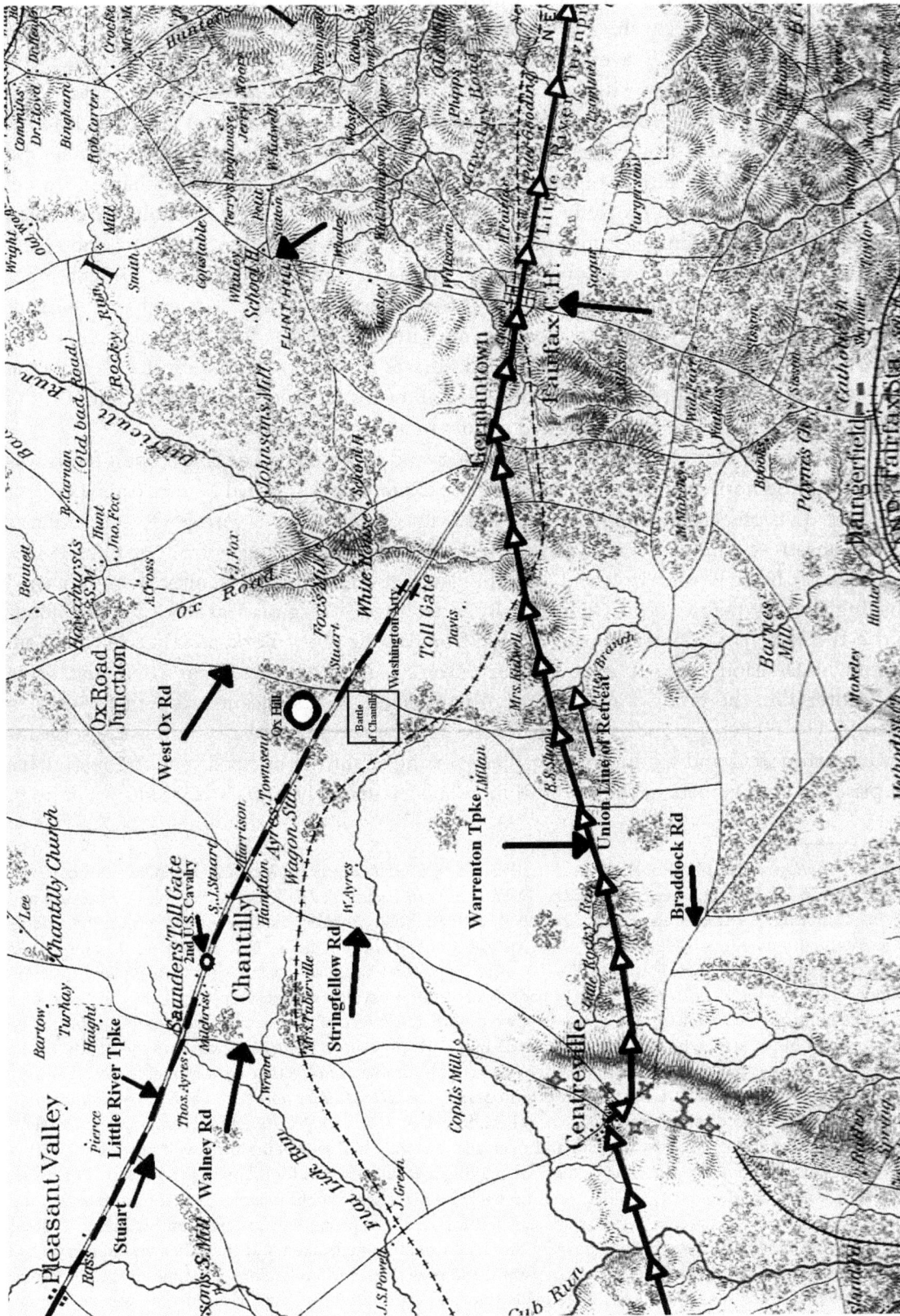

1862 map of area from Chantilly and Centerville to Fairfax Court House showing the area of the action at Chantilly on 1 September 1862. The Battle of Chantilly took place to the southwest of the intersection of the Little River Turnpike and West Ox Road. Dotted line on Little River Turnpike shows Rebel cavalry and infantry advance. Chantilly is at the upper left; the Bull Run battlefield is off the map to the lower left. Fitz Lee's fight with the 2nd U.S. Cavalry above the name "Chantilly" and the spot where Stuart fired at wagons at Germantown to the right of the square locating the Battle of Chantilly labeled "Washington Artillery." *Official Atlas*, Plate 7. Courtesy LOC.

Gen. Lee had Stuart pursue the retreating Federals early on 31 August in the middle of a heavy rainstorm. Stuart found strong Union forces near Cub Run and was halted. As Lee anxiously rode forward to gain intelligence from his cavalry, he dismounted to talk with Jackson and Longstreet. As he was holding his favorite horse's reigns, Traveller shied and Lee fell, tripping over his bulky raingear and seriously injuring his wrists. His nephew, Fitzhugh Lee, writing of Lee later at Antietam, said that "Most of the time he [Gen. Lee] was on foot....He was obliged to ride in an ambulance or let a courier lead his horse. In the tumult of battle he could ride but little along his lines on his famous war horse Traveler. So McClellan on that day had the advantage of him as he galloped about on his black charger Daniel Webster." Lee sprained both wrists and probably broke some bones in his right wrist. He likely traveled mostly by ambulance until 16 September, when on horseback, he was led by an orderly as noted by Fitzhugh. Compare the statement of his son, Robert Jr., describing the famous incident on 17 September in which Gen. Lee addressed his artilleryman son without first recognizing him: "General Lee and staff galloped up...The general reined in 'Traveller' close by my gun, not fifteen feet from me." Gen. Lee certainly did not "gallop up" since if he were not being led, he was riding slowly and carefully. Thus the army commander, who in the next three weeks would need all of his faculties and personal mobility as he fought to save his army in Maryland, was confined mainly to an ambulance.[52]

Stuart scouted Union lines near Centreville on 31 August and reported to Lee that Pope's flank was ·secure, except perhaps to the north, which was a better approach anyway, as it had better roads. Lee sent Jackson with his three divisions around Pope's right flank, east on Little River Turnpike, with Stuart's cavalry in the van. Longstreet would follow Jackson after demonstrating in Pope's front at Centreville. Lee hoped to cut Pope off from Washington and gain the destruction of the Union army which he had missed accomplishing the day before. Near Chantilly, Robertson's 12th Virginia Cavalry captured about one company of the 10th New York Cavalry. Some 30 men from the 10th New York, attached to Brig Gen. Jacob D. Cox's Kanawha Division, were on a scout from Upton's Hill. About 8 P.M. on 31 August, some three miles from Centerville, the group was challenged by a picket, so a sergeant was sent forward to answer the challenge. The picket pretended to be from the 1st Pennsylvania Cavalry but as the sergeant approached, he was surrounded and taken prisoner. Later in the night, he escaped, but the rest of his patrol was taken prisoner by members of the 12th Virginia Cavalry under Lt. Col. R.H. Burks.[53] Fitzhugh

---

[52] Harsh, *Rising*, 205-207; *Shallows*, 176, 193. Robert E. Lee, Jr., *Recollections and Letters of Robert E. Lee* (Old Saybrook, CT: Konecky & Konecky, 1998), 76-77. Fitzhugh Lee, *General Lee: A Biography of Robert E. Lee* (New York, NY: D. Appleton and Company, 1894; reprint Cambridge, MA: Da Capo Press, Inc., 1994), 210. Fitzhugh probably did not witness most of his uncle's actions on the 17th as Fitzhugh and his brigade was very busy on the Confederate left flank. Col. Armistead. L. Long, Lee's military secretary, described the general's accident: "On the day after the second battle of Manassas he was standing near the stone bridge, surrounded by a group of officers, when a squadron of Federal cavalry suddenly appeared on the brow of a neighboring hill. A movement of excitement in the group followed, with the effect of frightening the general's horse. The animal gave a quick start, and his master, who was standing beside him with his arm in the bridle, was flung violently to the ground with such force as to break some of the bones of his right hand. This disabled him so that he was unable to ride during the greater part of the campaign" Armistead. L. Long, *Memoirs of Robert E. Lee: His Military and Personal History, Embracing a Large Amount of Information Hitherto Unpublished* (New York: J. M. Stoddard & Co., 1886), 206. Sorrel wrote of the incident: "It had rained and he [Lee] was wearing a rubber poncho and over-alls, his body and legs being thus well protected. With a number of his officer he was dismounted in a thick piece of woods, making some disposition for following the enemy. His horse, a gentle, intelligent animal, was at the General's shoulder, reins on neck; he made some slight movement as if to start away, and Lee taking a step ahead for the bridle tripped in his over-alls and fell forward, not prone, but catching on his hands. He was instantly on his feet, erect, but his hands were badly damaged; one had a small bone broken and the other was nearly as bad with the twist and strain. Both were put into splints, but were painful and most uncomfortable. For some time the saddle had to be given up and the ambulance called into use. General Lee made the campaign on wheels. At Sharpsburg he was far enough cured to allow him to ride a little." G. Moxley Sorrel, *Recollections of a Confederate Staff Officer* (New York: Neale Publishing Company, 1905), 102-103.

[53] *OR*, vol. 12, pt. 2, 404-405; 749.

Lee's Brigade then took over the lead down the Little River Turnpike and found a squadron of the 2nd U.S. Cavalry under Capt. Thomas Hight resting on the turnpike. Hight with his squadron was directed by Gen. Sumner to make a reconnaissance as far as Germantown. Upon learning that they had already gone to the west of that place, they halted to rest and feed their mounts which hadn't been fed or unsaddled for 24 hours. A sentinel he had posted to the west on the pike reported seeing horsemen on the road, but Hight assumed they were just a few more stragglers which they had been encountering all day. He decided to check but before he departed, he ordered his troopers to bridle up, but his unit was immediately charged by two squadrons of Rebel cavalry followed by the rest of Stuart's troopers. A few Yankee troopers returned fire but most made for adjoining woods to escape. Hight surrendered to Fitz Lee; he reported his loss as one officer and 20 men as prisoners but after the Confederate horsemen brought in 25-30 more, his loss was about 50. He also reported that 20 Union infantry stragglers were added to the Confederate haul. His men were paroled but he and his officers were held until 2 September and paroled to Union pickets near Falls Church.[54] Von Borcke colorfully described this encounter after Fitzhugh Lee's troopers had captured the Regulars' pickets: "I joined with alacrity and pleasure the attacking detachment. There was but little fighting to be done. We rushed so suddenly and unexpectedly upon the Yankee reserves that they had not even time to mount, and two full companies with their officers fell into our hands. We captured also their horses, from among which I lost no time in exchanging a noble bay for my own worn-out animal."[55] Neither of these captured patrols were from Pope's cavalry, but rather from other commands sent to help Pope.

Stuart rode down the Little River Turnpike that evening past Ox Hill to Germantown, where he heard Union wagons. He turned to the right and from a small hill saw Union wagons crowding a road, heading east to Alexandria for replenishing. He ordered a section of his guns from the Washington Artillery to open fire on the Union wagon train on the Little River Turnpike at Germantown. Stuart reported that "The artillery was placed in position just after dark and opened upon the road. A few rounds sufficed to throw everything into confusion, and such commotion, upsetting, collisions, and smash-ups were rarely ever seen."[56] The Union report of this incident concurs with Stuart's: Union infantry under Col. Alfred T.A. Torbert first encountered stragglers from the 2nd U.S. Cavalry retreating down the pike to Germantown. Reinforcing his pickets on the pike the approaching Rebel cavalry retreated but later that evening, about 8 P.M., Tolbert wrote that the Confederates returned with three pieces of artillery and fired six shots into the train and the Union camp killing two or three horses and stampeding the train. "Drivers deserted their wagons and the greatest confusion existed....I immediately advanced a portion of my picket line opposite the artillery, which retired."[57] But by the time Union infantry responded, Stuart's troopers were long gone heading for their bivouac two miles north on Ox Road. Stuart decided to find more comfortable quarters than a tent and, along with some of his staff, left for a plantation and a family he knew some six miles north toward Herndon at Frying Pan; he did not return until after they enjoyed a hearty breakfast the next morning. Von Borcke again supplied an account of Stuart's arrival at his commander's friend's house that evening: Stuart and his staff remained talking with the family until dawn and after a "hasty but hearty breakfast" rode south to rejoin his troopers who had spent a less pleasant night.[58] Unfortunately, Stuart's cannonading the Union train

---

[54] *OR*, vol. 12, pt. 3, 809-810.

[55] Welker, 95-103.

[56] *OR*, vol. 12, pt. 2, 744. Harsh comments that Stuart made the same mistake that he made on the Peninsula at Evelington Heights as his unneeded cannon fire did little in either case except to warn the Yankees of Rebel presence, Harsh, *Rising*, 168-169.

[57] *OR*, vol. 12, pt. 2, 538.

[58] Welker, 103; von Borcke, 118-119; *OR*, vol. 12, pt. 2, 743-744, 749; Harsh, *Rising*, 167-168.

alerted Pope to the Confederate force in his rear; additionally, Stuart neglected to inform Jackson of this action until the next morning at about 8 A.M.

Pope's cavalry was of little help as it was worn-out and unable to provide all of the now much-needed scouting Pope required as he vacillated in Centerville. Pope, realizing his need for scouting, desperately asked Washington for 2,000 cavalry horses: "I need cavalry horses terribly. Send me 2,000 in lots and under strong escort. I have never yet received a single one."[59] A trooper of the 1st Pennsylvania Reserve Cavalry reported that these were "the most trying days the regiment had yet passed through, [and it] will remember the sleepless nights, after days of exhausting toil, and the commencement of another day's duty, without the preface of a breakfast or the prospect of a dinner, and as for our horses with their backs actually putrid from the constant pressure and wear of the saddles, which had not been permitted to be removed for weeks, fell down in the ranks from exhaustion and starvation, and were abandoned by the wayside." As the Keystone State horsemen retreated toward Washington and formed a picket line, it had only 100 horses and 200 men available for duty; it took six weeks for the unit to refit as it camped near Munson's Hill along the outer defenses of Washington beginning on 1 September 1862.[60]

It is interesting to note that while Stuart's troopers continued in action fully able to follow Gen. Lee's orders, Pope's cavalry was hors-de-combat. Perhaps the advantages of Confederate troopers owning their own horses and knowing how to care for them and adapt to their idiosyncrasies, allowed them to survive better the toils of constant combat and lack of forage. Operating in friendly country also likely helped, as they were probably better able to get fodder from local farmers, or perhaps even trade some horses.[61] As von Borcke wrote, Rebel cavalry took the pick of captured Union horses. Also, because Confederate cavalry were grouped in a division-sized unit, Stuart was probably able to rest some fatigued units and use those units which were fresher. Again, the advantages of having most of the cavalry under one commander in a large-sized unit helped; Pope's three brigades were used up by the end of the campaign while Stuart's division, most of which had been actively campaigning on the Peninsula and since, was still in action, doing all that Gen. Lee asked of it.[62]

On 1 September, in their 8 A.M. meeting, after Stuart informed Jackson of his capture of the two cavalry patrols and the Union defenses at Germantown, Jackson decided to wait near Sander's Toll Gate located at the intersection of the Little River Turnpike and Walney Road. Jackson had Stuart send a cavalry brigade under Fitzhugh Lee, east along the Little River Turnpike, and Robertson's Brigade south on Walney Road. Jackson had posted infantry and artillery about one mile south of the intersection of Little River Turnpike and Stringfellow Road at Chantilly, which held off an advance by some of Union Brig. Gen. Oliver O. Howard's brigade. Under orders not to bring on a general engagement, Howard withdrew, but ordered up two of Bayard's depleted cavalry regiments, the 1st New Jersey and the 1st

---

[59] *OR*, vol. 12, pt. 2, 81; Hennessy, 446-450. But Pope was energetic in setting up a defense in depth against Jackson. Welker, 93.

[60] Lloyd, 31-33.

[61] Welker, tells of a farm family which had their horses and oxen stolen, but does not relate which army took them; however, it is likely it was Union forces given the farm's location within Union lines, 118-119. Blackford relates the story of the wounding of his favorite horse, Comet, and the effort he made to help save his wounded friend, 136-138. Freeman wrote that "Stuart's troopers had taken better care of their animals and had kept their striking-power to the hour of decision," *Lee's Lieutenants*, 2:139

[62] *OR*, vol. 12, pt. 2, Pope, on 1 September at 8:50 A.M. sent a message to Halleck about his cavalry problems: "Our cavalry is completely broken down, so that there are not five horses to a company that can raise a trot. The consequence is that I am forced to keep considerable infantry along the road in my rear to make them secure and even then it is difficult to keep the enemy's cavalry off the roads....Please hurry forward cavalry horses to me under strong escort. I need them badly—worse than I can tell you," 82-83. Pope on 1 September also said to Sumner who was supplying cavalry for scouting for Pope: "We have no cavalry—not a horse that can possibly perform service," 82. But on 2 September he issued orders showing that Buford and Bayard were to escort various corps, 86.

Maine, to picket the road. These two regiments traded shots with Rebel infantry for the remainder of the afternoon; the Rebels were later reinforced by Robertson's Brigade which had returned from Walney Road.[63] Robertson may have misunderstood his assignment since he remained near Stringfellow Road, and as Jackson continued east, Stonewall's right flank became uncovered. Jackson continued marching east past the intersection at Chantilly.

Before noon, Pope received a fortuitous piece of information from two cavalrymen who had been foraging to the north, and witnessed Jackson's troops heading toward Germantown on the Little River Turnpike.[64] Pope quickly decided to send forces to strengthen his defenses at Germantown and Fairfax Court House. He also sent a blocking force under Brig. Gen. Stevens north near West Ox Road to ensure that the Confederates would not surprise Pope's men by heading south, before Union forces reached Germantown. Stevens was led by the two cavalrymen who had reported the Rebel movements to Pope. Meanwhile, Hooker on his way to Germantown to take command of the defenses there, had gathered up the 1st Rhode Island Cavalry and sent the troopers west on the Little River Turnpike searching for the Rebel column. Rosser was riding with the 5th Virginia cavalry when it came under fire from the dismounted 1st Rhode Island troopers. The Virginians retreated, but Fitzhugh Lee decided to hold the road as he formed a dismounted line on a ridge overlooking Difficult Run, along with two cannon. The Rhode Islanders retreated when supporting Union infantry, Duryee's 1st Rhode Island Brigade, came up to replace them. Fitzhugh Lee dueled with the Yankee infantry after the Rhode Island troopers departed. As Hooker's line was strengthened by troops coming from Fairfax Court House, Beardsley's cavalry brigade, including the 6th Ohio Cavalry, the 9th New York Cavalry, and a squadron from the 1st Connecticut Cavalry, kept the Warrenton Pike open to the retreating Federal units.[65] Fitz Lee brought up more troops to defend his position and employed artillery to pin down the advancing Unionists. Fitz Lee retreated late in the day as Union strength increased.[66]

Jackson, stalled at Germantown at 4 P.M., had sent two brigades south of Little River Turnpike west of West Ox Road to protect his right flank. Brig. Gen. Issac I. Stevens's and Brig. Gen. Jesse L. Reno's divisions confronted them at 4:30 P.M. just as a fierce thunderstorm broke. Stevens was killed leading his men in desperate fighting as they pushed back some Confederate units near the center of the Rebel line. Strong Confederate reinforcements quickly arrived routing the charging Unionists. Stevens' request for help finally found a commander willing to come to his aid: Maj. Gen. Philip Kearney, who rushed north from the Warrenton Pike. As he approached, Jackson adjusted his lines to meet the Union attacks he expected would continue. As Kearney was bringing up and aligning his troops in the semidarkness, he was killed. A short time later at 6:45 P.M., Longstreet appeared with his command and found Jackson, but the fighting was over. The cost to Pope to keep Gen. Lee away from the Union line of retreat was 655 Federal casualties, including the deaths of two promising Union brigadier generals, Isaac Stevens and Philip Kearny. Jackson and Longstreet placed their troops to face the expected Union morning attack. Pope's men were not seen the next day as he decided to retreat to Fairfax Court House and then into the Washington defenses. He had his fill of battling and losing to Gen. Lee on all fronts, but although he was beaten, many of his troops felt chagrined at continuing to run from the Rebels.[67]

---

[63] Welker, 118-119; *OR*, vol. 12, pt. 2, 744.

[64] Welker, 123; William Todd, *The Seventy-Ninth Highlanders, New York Volunteers in the War of Rebellion 1861-1865* (Albany, NY: Press of Brandow, Barton & Co., 1886), 215.

[65] Welker, 129-136; Frederic Denison, *Sabres and Spurs: The First Regiment Rhode Island Cavalry in the Civil War, 1861-1865* (Central Falls, RI: The First Rhode Island Cavalry Veteran Association, The Press of E. L. Freeman, and Co., 1876), 148-149. The Ocean Staters lost two men holding the pike, Denison, 148-149.

[66] Welker, 133-134.

[67] Ibid., 170, 204.

As Lee waited on 2 September for the possible Union attack, he was likely pleased to hear of the arrival of Brig. Gen. Hampton's Cavalry Brigade from Richmond to help bolster Stuart's Division. Late in the afternoon, Lee sent out Stuart's men to learn Pope's location and Stuart promptly reported to Lee the Union army's precipitate withdrawal. Stuart sent Fitzhugh Lee's Brigade to Fairfax Court House where Stuart's aide, von Borcke, planted the Rebel flag on the green, as Southern "damsels showered Stuart with kisses. Jeb even found time to visit his friend and 'spy' Antonia Ford."[68] Stuart stayed the night at her father's house. In fun, Stuart gave her an honorary commission as an officer on his staff. This reward later apparently led to her arrest and incarceration in the Old Capital Prison in March 1863, as a southern spy, after her involvement in Mosby's capture of Brig. Gen. Edwin H. Stoughton at his Fairfax Station headquarters.

Newly arrived Wade Hampton's Brigade, with the Stuart Horse Artillery, joined Fitzhugh Lee on the 2nd, and Stuart sent Hampton's fresh brigade along with Fitzhugh's troopers toward the east. Hampton reported that Stuart took him to Flint Hill, near Fairfax Court House, where Hampton's Brigade drove off Union troops using artillery and sharpshooters. Hampton followed with two pieces of horse artillery from Hart's Battery, and pursued them until dark. The Federals Hampton had pursued were part of Sedgwick's command. Capt. Pelham was in charge of the shelling of the hapless Yankee troops, until the 1st North Carolina Cavalry suffered heavy casualties in an ambush set up by the 71st Pennsylvania Infantry. Col. Wistar of the 71st described the action: "the 71st was deployed to the rear, on both sides of the road, in two battalions aligned at an obtuse angle with each other, while the column moved on. After remaining here long enough…I was about getting the regiment into the road to resume the march, when I caught sound of the tread of horses, who under cover of the thick woods and impenetrable darkness, had approached within a few yards. Not being certain the cavalry was hostile, I challenged in person: 'Halt, advance one with the countersign, quick, or you will get the fire of a brigade.' 'Fire and be d—d,' came through the darkness, as the order rang out, and the cavalry of the enemy's advanced guard gallantly made its charge. I had barely time to gallop to the rear of a battalion and give the order: 'Fire by battalion'…The two volleys crossing each other at such short distance, quickly disposed of the small cavalry force, leaving the road full of dead and struggling horses, with not a few of the riders."[69]

Some of Stuart's troopers and horse artillery caused a few casualties in Maj. Gen. Howard's corps as they probed the retreating Union line. Gen. Lee was now satisfied that Pope was beyond his reach and surely lamented that too much of the Union army survived the battles of the prior three days. Stuart and his men camped around the court house the night of 2 September. Von Borcke wrote after the charge of the Confederate horsemen into Fairfax Court House that he, "Amid all the confusion and intoxication of

[68] Von Borcke, 121-123.

[69] Harsh, *Flood*, 19; Longstreet wrote that Stuart had scouts out on 1 September to learn of Pope's rearward movements, 195; *OR*, vol. 12, pt. 2, 744; Lafayette C. Baker, *History of the United States Secret Service* (Philadelphia, PA: King & Baird Printers, 1867), 170-173; Brooks in *Stories of the Confederacy*, related how Hampton was almost shot by one of his troopers, 73-77. Col. Isaac Jones Wistar commanding the 71st Pennsylvania Infantry was in the rearguard defending against Hampton and Fitzhugh Lee's troopers. In his posthumous book *Autobiography of Isaac Jones Wistar, 1827-1905: Half a Century in War and Peace*, vol. 2 (Philadelphia, PA: The Wistar Institute of Anatomy and Physiology, 1914), 45-50, Wistar describes the trials of the skirmishes with Rebel cavalry when he was part of Sedgwick's division, Howard's brigade, and the capture of a Union cavalry unit of some 20 regular troopers. These regulars had been sent by Sedgwick to replace a poorly performing volunteer regiment: "A small and remarkably worthless regiment of volunteer cavalry had been sent early in the night to co-operate with the rearguard, but was so badly commanded that its only tendency was to disorder the infantry by clinging to its flanks, and dashing suddenly in upon it from time to time….In due time a young West Point Lieutenant with about twenty regular cavalry reported…and was promptly set to work….The Lieutenant…was a brave and capable young fellow, crossing swords with the enemy's scouting parties on our flanks whenever they gave him the opportunity, and retreating upon the infantry in perfect order, when pressed," but this squad exhausted itself and was captured by Fitzhugh Lee's troopers since pickets were not posted; the lieutenant was personally released by Lee after much needed rest and a dinner with some old West Point acquaintances, 49-50.

Brig. Gen. Wade Hampton. Courtesy LOC.

the hour…did not lose the opportunity of capturing a very good and well-equipped Yankee horse that was galloping about riderless, his master having been killed by a shell from our artillery."[70]

Late on 1 September, Gen. Lee chose Col. Munford and the 2nd Virginia Cavalry for a special task: ride to Leesburg to secure the Potomac River crossings nearby. Also, Munford was to drive off a marauding body of Unionist cavalry consisting of Capt. Samuel C. Means and his Loudoun Rangers and

---

[70] Von Borcke, 123.

some of Cole's Cavalry, bothering northern Loudoun County. The Union commander at Harpers Ferry, Col. Dixon S. Miles, had ordered Maj. Cole to harass Rebels fleeing from the battle at Manassas; Cole left his bivouac on Bolivar Heights on 1 September with three companies hoping to join Means's Rangers at Waterford. Cole's 125 troopers met with Means's depleted Rangers, perhaps 30 strong, and camped that night at Wheatland.[71] On 2 September at what became known as the Battle of Mile Hill, Munford approached Leesburg from the east from his camp near Goose Creek, split his troopers, and sent a squadron under Capt. Jesse Irvine directly through town.[72] Meanwhile, with the rest of his regiment, he turned north off the Leesburg Pike and headed for the Potomac River crossings. Irvine galloped into Leesburg finding Means and his Loudoun Rangers guarding the courthouse. A few days earlier on 26 August, Capt. Samuel C. Means, who had formed the Loudoun Rangers, a Union partisan unit which operated in and around Loudoun County, fought a losing battle in Waterford a few miles north of Leesburg with Capt. Elijah V. White and his Thirty-fifth Battalion Virginia Cavalry. The result of this internecine battle was about twenty casualties with some family members fighting each other. The Union troopers were chased seven miles, suffering 67 casualties.[73] Now, Means's Loudoun Rangers, likely remembering this recent thrashing, quickly retreated north up King Street from the court house, suffering four wounded; they fell back on Cole's Maryland Cavalry, joining north of town near Big Spring at Mile Hill on the Point of Rocks Road. Capt. Irvine was hot on their heels firing from behind shocks of wheat, driving Means back on Cole's dismounted line. Cole was holding Irvine, but then Munford surprised Cole, attacking their rear.[74]

---

[71] *OR*, vol. 51, pt. 1, 773. Miles also warned Cole to watch out for Col. B.F. Davis's 8th New York Cavalry which was operating to the west of Cole's area of operations. Taylor M. Chamberlin and John M. Souders, *Between Reb and Yank: A Civil War History of Northern Loudoun County, Virginia* (Jefferson, NC: McFarland & Company, Inc., 2011), 126-128. Wheatland is located near the Charles Town Pike about 8 1/2 airline miles south of Berlin (Brunswick), Maryland, and 8 miles northwest of Leesburg.

[72] Capt. Jesse Irvine, Jr., Driver, *2nd Virginia Cavalry*, 233; sometimes spelled "Irving." He was captain of Company G, 2nd Virginia.

[73] J. Thomas Scharf, *History of Western Maryland Being a History of Frederick, Montgomery, Carroll, Washington, Allegany, and Garrett Counties From the Earliest Period to the Present Day*, vol. I (Philadelphia, PA: Louis H. Everts, 1882; excerpt reprint *The Civil War in Western Maryland*, n.p. (A Plus Printing Company, n.d.), 227. See John Divine, et al, *Loudoun County and the Civil War* (Leesburg, VA: Willow Bend Books, 1998), 39-40. White's troopers totaled about 50 including 22 from White's company, 22 scouts from Capt. William F. Randolph's company which later became part of the 39th Battalion Virginia Cavalry, three of Stonewall Jackson's scouts, and four Louisiana Tigers. White had received permission from Gen. Richard Ewell for whom his men were serving as scouts and couriers in his cavalry division. Means's Rangers were in Waterford and totaled about 67 men with some 50 present for duty headquartered in the Waterford Baptist Church. The night of White's attack, there were about 30 Rangers in and around the church. Some 10 escaped White's initial attack, and very few of the 24 Rangers out on picket duty thought it their duty to aid of their comrades. White's troopers captured and paroled 19 men who were besieged in the church, let one free, and took two more, one of whom was later paroled and the second escaped. The Rangers lost many horses estimated at 40 to 56 as well as 200 carbines and revolvers. Means did try to get help for his men including sending a courier to Col. Miles, but Miles sent no relief, seemingly placing the blame for the Rangers' debacle on Means's poorly disciplined men. Confederate casualties were six killed and nine wounded. Means now down to 35 troopers camped at Potomac Furnace across the Potomac from the Union outpost at Point of Rocks; Chamberlin & Souders, *Between Reb and Yank*, 118-124.

[74] Scharf, 227-230, 316, 322-324. The First Regiment, Potomac Home Brigade Cavalry formed around a battalion organized during the summer of 1861 in Frederick and Washington Counties and became known as "Cole's Cavalry." The four companies which originally made up the battalion served independently until June 1862 when they were consolidated under the senior captain, Henry A. Cole, who was then promoted to major. The unit was formed under authority of Secretary of War Simon Cameron on 19 July 1861 and approved by Lincoln to protect the Chesapeake and Ohio Canal and loyal citizens on both sides of the Potomac River. While formed to protect Union interests near the Potomac, they also served in Virginia and Pennsylvania. Captain Cole was initially in command of Company A of four authorized companies which were brigaded together as the First Regiment Potomac Home Brigade Cavalry in June, 1862 becoming known as "Cole's Cavalry;" Cole was promoted to major on 1 August 1862 in command. In the spring of 1864, eight companies were added bringing it to regiment strength; Cole was promoted to colonel in command, Keith O. Gary, *Answering the Call: The Organization and Recruiting of the Potomac Home Brigade Maryland Volunteers Summer and Fall, 1861* (Bowie, MD, Heritage Books, Inc., 1996), 151-152. Initially Cole's

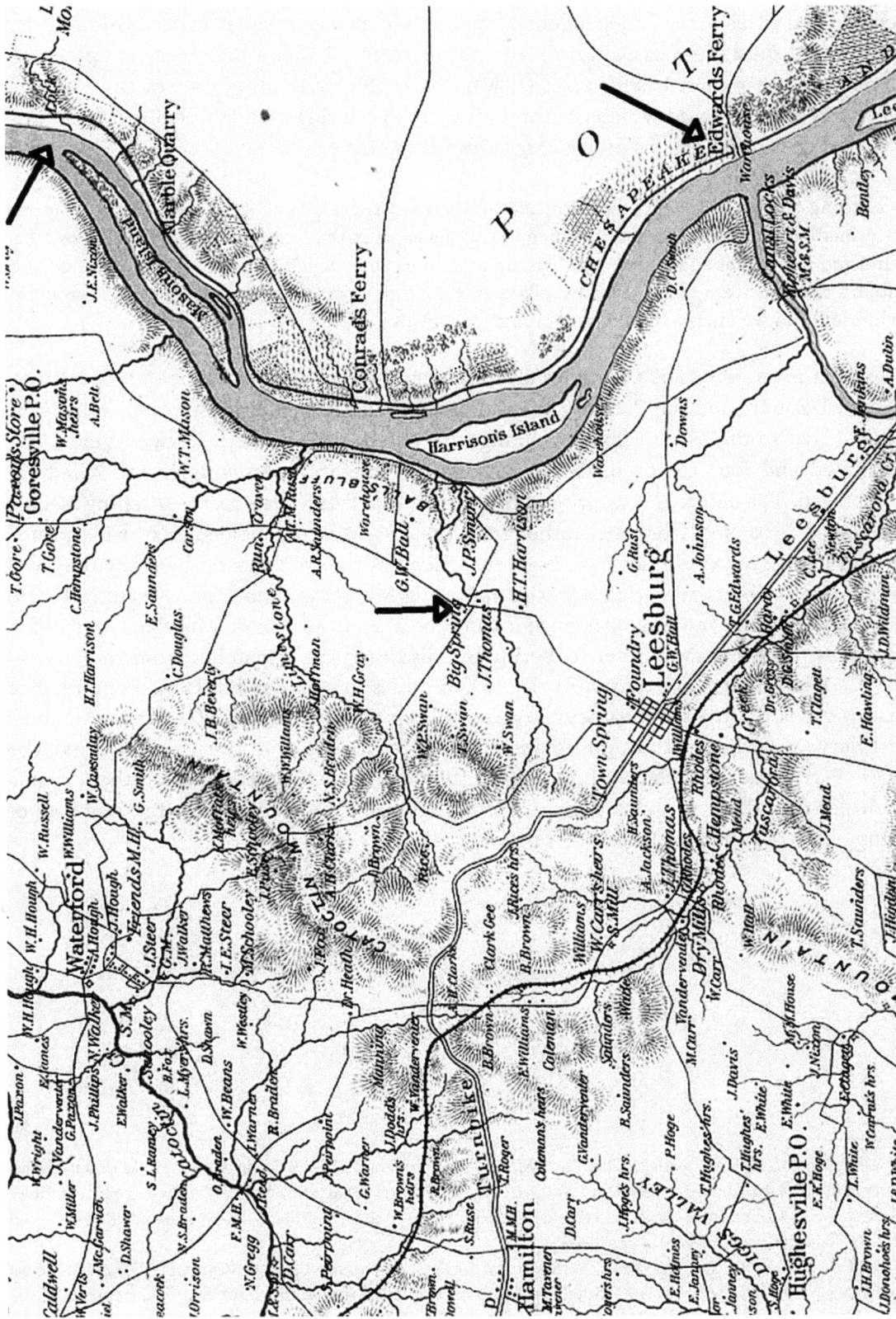

Leesburg at bottom center; Big Spring at arrow near which the battle took place. Waterford is at the upper end of Mason's Island at the arrow. Conrad's Ferry is today's Whites Ferry; it was fordable then but usually only by cavalry. The Old Waterford Road heads west from near Big Spring. Edward's Ferry is where some Rebel cavalry crossed. *Official Atlas*, Plate 7. Courtesy LOC.

company was also known as "Cole's Rangers" and consisted of 85 men, 158. After the war, Cole served as a pastor in Fulton County, West Virginia. See Chapter 8 for more about Cole's Cavalry and the Loudoun Rangers.

Before Cole could mount his three Independent Maryland Cavalry companies to face this surprise from Munford, he suffered substantial casualties. In the melee, many of Cole's men were cut down on foot. Those that were able to mount briefly engaged Munford before retreating toward the Catoctin Mountain and the Old Waterford Road which cut through a gap in the ridge. Lt. William A. McIlhenny of Cole's Cavalry Company C wrote the following about this incident:

> There was a strong post and rail fence on both sides of the road and we came to a gate and moved into a large field. We formed into line and charged the force that attacked us in the rear, but when we had done that we looked around and found that a rebel force had gotten around us and was coming at us from the other side. We suddenly found that we were surrounded by a largely superior force so Major Cole gave the command 'every man for himself' and we made a dash to get through the rebels.[75]

Munford chased Cole's troopers for some two miles driving them into Loudoun Valley before returning; he successfully cleared Leesburg and the Potomac River crossings. Of Munford's 163 troops on the field, he had two killed and five wounded; the Loudoun Rangers reported that of some 30 cavalrymen, one was killed, six wounded and four captured. Cole's Cavalry of some 150 men suffered six killed, 27 wounded, and 11 captured. The shock and surprise of Munford's attack on Cole's rear was telling as Cole reported he was attacked by a Rebel brigade, rather than the 163 Munford fielded. Had Cole posted pickets in his rear and flanks, he would not have been surprised.[76] Munford's success here augured well for his taking command of Robertson's Brigade in the upcoming Maryland Campaign. About 20 Union Loudoun Rangers were left, and they established their camp near Point of Rocks, Maryland, patrolling the Potomac fords from the Monocacy River to Berlin and also carrying dispatches from the colonel commanding the 87th Ohio Infantry at Point of Rocks, to Col. Miles in command at Harpers Ferry. The next day, Miles had Means out on a scout to Leesburg, and Means reported seeing 40 enemy regiments and 60 pieces of artillery; Miles ignored this information. Means testified later at the investigation of the surrender of Harpers Ferry that he thought Miles was drunk. Means saw Confederates on the Virginia shore and assured Miles that there was also a report from a civilian that there were large numbers of Rebels near Leesburg. On 6 September, the Rangers moved to Harpers Ferry.[77]

---

[75] Amy L. Fleagle, "A History of Cole's Cavalry: The First Maryland Potomac Home Brigade Cavalry," Masters Thesis, Shippensburg University, 2002, 27, quote from Lieutenant William A. McIlhenny, "Diary of a Soldier," (photocopy), Archives Branch, United States Army War College and Carlisle Barracks, Carlisle, Pennsylvania, 9. Miles's report showed that Cole said he was attacked by at least 800 cavalry, *OR*, vol. 12, pt. 2, 805.

[76] Divine, 41; John T. Phillips, II. Editor, *The Bulletin of the Historical Society of Loudoun County, Virginia, 1957-1976.* (Goose Creek Productions: Leesburg, Virginia, 1997), 187-190. Note that Munford may have started this fight with 203 troopers but he reported that a squadron of 40 under Capt. H. Clay Dickinson had retreated to Goose Creek and did not participate in the battle. Stuart reported that Munford had only 123 troopers in the charge, *OR*, vol. 12, pt. 2, 745.

[77] Briscoe Goodhart, *History of the Independent Loudoun Virginia Rangers, U.S. Vol. Cav. (Scouts), 1862-65* (Washington, DC: Press of McGill & Wallace, 1896), 44; *OR*, vol. 19, pt. 1, 755; pt. 2, 179. But later on 4 September, based on more information from the 8th New York Cavalry and Col. Banning at Point of Rocks, Miles began to understand that more than just Confederate cavalry scouts were in the area and alerted Halleck and Wool, ibid., 180-181.

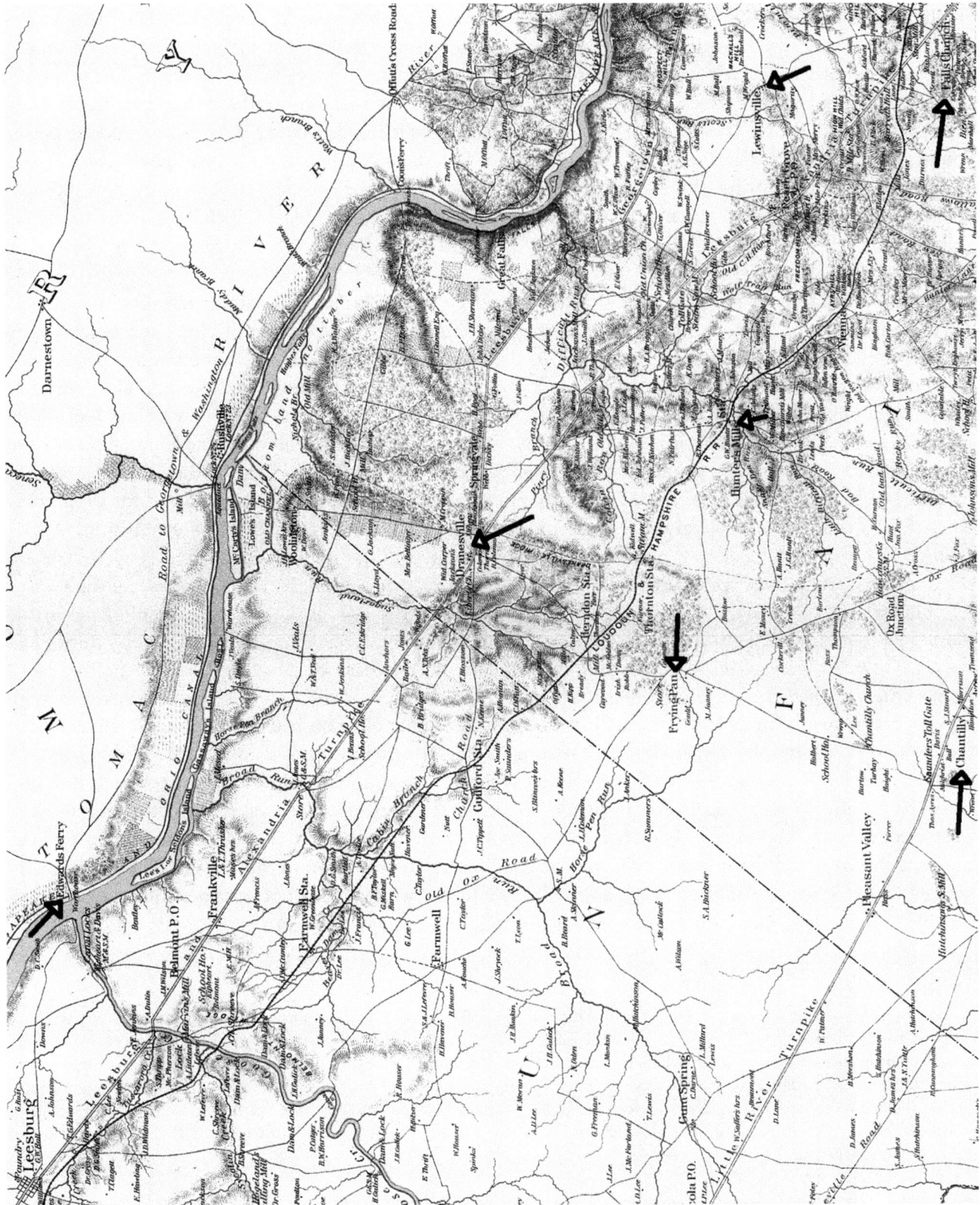

Areas of Confederate cavalry activity after Chantilly to the initial crossing of the Potomac by Lee's vanguard. Arrows point to Hunter's Mill, Dranesville, Lewinsville, Falls Church, Chantilly, Frying Pan and Edward's Ferry. Munford's clash with Cole's Cavalry took place north of Leesburg; the easternmost crossing of Confederate cavalry took place at Edward's Ferry at the upper left arrow. Frying Pan was the location of Stuart's sojourn on 31 August. *Official Atlas*, Plate 7. Courtesy LOC.

Jeb Stuart's cavalry did well at Second Bull Run but arguably less so at Chantilly.[78] His firing at the Union wagon train on 31 August alerted Pope to the Rebel movement on his left flank when he should have quietly observed that movement and reported it to Jackson. He also failed to inform Jackson until the next morning of that Union encounter, but rather spent the night comfortably some six miles away at a party at a friend's plantation. Thus, even though Confederate cavalry may have been in better condition and better organized than its Union foes, Stuart engaged in some questionable tactical and command behavior during the Battle of Chantilly. Lee however, perhaps unaware of how Stuart's actions negatively affected the chances for surprising Pope, commended his behavior and that of his troopers as "most important and valuable.... [as] It guarded the flanks of the army, protected its trains, and gave information of the enemy's movements."[79]

Pope, in his official report, commended the cavalry of his Army of Virginia, specifically Generals Bayard and Buford: "Their duties were peculiarly arduous and hazardous, and it is not too much to say that throughout the operation, from the first to the last day of the campaign, scarcely a day passed that these officers did not render service which entitles them to the gratitude of the Government."[80] Buford's action at Lewis Ford at Bull Run on 30 August was notable, as Union cavalry to that time had rarely fought so well against Stuart's best. Unfortunately for McClellan during the Maryland Campaign, most of Pope's cavalry would not participate. Its horses reflected the inability of the Union supply chain to furnish the fourteen pounds of hay and twelve pounds of corn, oats, or barley, required for each horse daily, while the Army of Virginia chased, and was chased, by the Army of Northern Virginia.[81] But while these troopers of Pope's army wore out their mounts and themselves, they gained experience and these lessons would bode well for the Union cavalry later in 1862 and in the remainder of the war.

Similarly, McClellan's Army of the Potomac cavalry on the Peninsula, gained not only time in the saddle, but benefited from training and even picket duty as they became familiar with cavalry duties and horses. Those units more heavily involved in skirmishes with Rebel horsemen, of course benefited more from actual combat duty against Rebel troopers. Volunteer units which were brigaded or served with regular army cavalry units learned much from them. A dramatic lesson learned was the failed charge at Gaines's Mill during the Seven Days Campaign: a cavalry charge against well-armed and prepared infantry will fail. Union as well as Confederate cavalry saw that a well-led and conducted mounted raid could be an effective tool against the enemy. McClellan's troopers arrived in Washington in almost as poor a condition as did Pope's. They had some benefit by their waiting at Harrison's Landing to rest but the boat trip from the Peninsula took its toll on the horses. The historian of the 1st Massachusetts Cavalry wrote that "The horses confined below decks for so long a time, at such a hot season of the year, suffered terribly. They were, many of them, entirely unshod, and the rest only in front....Maryland has stony

---

[78] Welker, 216-220.

[79] Ibid., 241-242; McClellan, *Stuart*, 109; *OR*, vol. 12, pt. 2, 558-559. Subtracting Stuart's miscue in alerting the Union with the cannon fire, Confederate cavalry performance both at Second Bull Run and Chantilly was very good. Robertson may be faulted for uncovering Jackson's right flank when he and his brigade remained near Stringfellow Road as Jackson continued east although Stonewall suffered no serious consequences. Stuart reported that "On the night of the 2d the command [Stuart's Division] bivouacked near Fairfax Court-House, except Robertson's brigade, which, by misapprehension of the order, returned to the vicinity of Chantilly before the engagement," *OR*, vol. 12, pt. 2, 745; Welker 119-120, who finds that Jackson was vulnerable on that flank.

[80] *OR*, vol. 12, pt. 2, 49.

[81] U.S. War Department, *Revised Regulations for the Army of the United States, 1861* (Philadelphia, PA: J. G. L. Brown, Publishers, 1861, reprint Harrisburg, PA: The National Historical Society, 1980), 166. The Union Quartermaster General, Montgomery G. Meigs, pointed out the difficulties of supplying forage and recommended that horses be fed on what was available in the countryside. He also criticized the care given to horses resulting in their becoming useless: "But the men are inexperienced as soldiers, and they destroy their horses by hard and unnecessary riding....In this hot season a cavalry regiment may be broken down by a few days' improper use of their horses, *OR*, vol. 12, pt. 3, 596.

roads, and without shoes the horses soon became footsore and useless."[82] Regardless, they were given no time to rest as Lee was moving north of the Potomac, so despite their condition, they were thrown out to locate the Rebel invaders. Many old cavalry foes from the Peninsula and a few from Second Bull Run were about to meet again in Maryland.

On 3 September 1862 Lee, camped near the Potomac River at Dranesville, Virginia, wrote a letter to President Davis informing his commander-in-chief why the Army of Northern Virginia was invading Maryland:

> The present seems to be the most propitious time since the commencement of the war for the Confederate Army to enter Maryland. The two grand armies of the Unites States that have been operating in Virginia, though now united, are much weakened and demoralized. Their new levies, of which I understand 60,000 men have already been posted in Washington, are not yet organized, and will take some time to prepare for the field. If it is ever desired to give material aid to Maryland and afford her an opportunity of throwing off the oppression to which she is now subject, this would seem the most favorable.[83]

And without waiting for a reply from Davis, Lee set his plan in motion the next day.[84]

---

[82] Crowninshield, 69-70. As barefooted Confederate infantry as well as unshod Union cavalry quickly learned, most of the main roads in Maryland in their theater of operations were macadamized or stony, leading to straggling and slow marching. See also Carman, Pierro, "The roads, both in the valleys and leading over the mountains by the gaps, are generally good, most of them macadamized turnpikes not excelled anywhere," 81. The crushed stone, often limestone, was not only hard on bare feet but difficult also for unshod horses and even cattle as noted for the Valley Pike running the length of the Shenandoah Valley: "To avoid cattle macerating their hooves on the turnpike surface, frequently herdsmen used the unsurfaced Middle Road, sometimes known as the 'Ox Road,' which often paralleled the pike to the west," Kenneth W. Keller, "The Best Thoroughfare in the South" in *The Great Valley Road of Virginia*, ed. by Warren R. Hofstra and Karl Raitz (Charlottesville, VA: University of Virginia Press, 2010), 161. Turnpike Companies used a new paving system invented by Scotsman John Loudon McAdam. Its use in 1823 on the National Road was the first time that true macadam was used in the United States. National Road workmen, some wearing goggles to protect their eyes, pounded stones into pieces with small hammers then inspectors passed each stone through rings assuring the correct size. It consisted of creating three layers of stones laid on a crowned sub grade with side ditches for drainage. The first two layers consisted of angular hand-broken aggregate, maximum size 3 inches, to a total depth of about 8 inches. The third layer was about 2 inches thick with a maximum aggregate size of 1 inch. Each layer would be compacted with a heavy cast-iron roller, causing the angular stones to lock together. The top layer, cemented with rainwater, became as very hard and durable. But there are numerous accounts that the limestone dust even along Maryland turnpikes was marked, although there are few complaints about mud. Note that turnpike toll keepers apparently did not attempt to collect tolls from military units or supplies sent to them although earlier in the 19th century, the costs of transportation for military units was very high; summary courtesy Wikipedia. For details of military transportation costs in the first half of the century, see Balthasar Henry Meyer, *History of Transportation in the United States before 1860* (Forge Village, MA: The Murray Printing Company, n.d.; reprint, n.p.: Peter Smith, 1948), 90-93. The part of the road from Baltimore to Cumberland, Maryland, was generally known as the "National Pike" before the entire road from Baltimore to Vandalia, Missouri, was called the "National Road." The first National Road, authorized by President Thomas Jefferson in 1806, ran from Cumberland to Wheeling, Virginia; it was begun in 1811 and completed in 1818. Banks supplied the funding the Baltimore to Cumberland section so was called the "Bank Road." It was completed to Cumberland except for a few sections by 1820. "One of the gaps was a 10-mile section between Hagerstown and Boonsboro. A turnpike company was formed to close the gap, with the banks again buying the stock in exchange for another extension of their charters (to 1845). This section of the Bank Road has the distinction of being the first use in the United States of the principles of road building conceived by John Loudon McAdam, whose name gave the pavement its name, macadam. According to historian Albert Rose: the work consisted of resurfacing a former county road. This section was in a sad state of deterioration in 1821, and in winter, stages required from 5 to 7 hours to cover the 10 mile distance. Contracts for reconstructing the road were advertised by William Lorman, the first president of the turnpike company, in September 1822. The superintendent of construction was John W. Davis of Allegany County, Maryland. The surfacing was completed in 1823," from Federal Highway Administration website: http://www.fhwa.dot.gov/infrastructure/bankroad.cfm.

[83] *OR*, vol. 19, pt. 2, 590.

[84] See Steven E. Woodworth, *Davis and Lee at War* (Lawrence, KS: The University of Kansas Press, 1995), 185. Woodworth posits that Lee and President Davis had differing views of the strategy needed to win the war. Here, Woodworth writes that Lee used Davis's silence as tacit approval for the Maryland/Pennsylvania invasion and quickly acted to move north. "This was never

In the three months since taking over command of the Confederate army near Richmond on 1 June 1862, Lee had performed miracles. First, he had driven Union forces from the Confederate capital's front door, back down the Peninsula and isolated them there. Next, he rapidly moved north to confront and defeat Pope and his Army of Virginia at the Battle of Second Bull Run. But now that units of Pope's army were firmly entrenched in and around the impregnable defenses of Washington, Lee realized that there was little hope of destroying Pope, as it was clear that he would not be able to turn Pope's flank and destroy large parts of his army. And Lee knew that the chain of forts protecting the capital would make it impossible to attack them successfully, plus investing it was similarly unrealistic. His worn-out army needed some time to rest while Lee contemplated his next move.[85] As Lee noted, "The war was thus transferred from the interior to the frontier and the supplies of rich and productive districts made accessible to our army" but now where should Lee take his victorious army?[86] Just as Lee undoubtedly knew when he took over from Johnston, neither he nor the South could be passive; the overwhelming industrial and manpower advantages the North possessed would, if given time, overwhelm the Confederacy. But the recent campaigns in which his army had fought hard resulted in major deficiencies in material, munitions, and food, needed for further campaigning. Lee had to remain aggressive, but take time to resupply, recruit, and rest his men. He resolved his dilemma by deciding to invade Maryland.

Lee's invasion plan was based not only on his desire to continue the momentum he generated in defeating McClellan during the Seven Days' Campaign, and Pope at Second Manassas, but to draw the Union hosts north of the Potomac and away from war-ravaged Virginia, permitting farmers to gather the fall harvest. Additionally, after months of hard campaigning, his troops desperately needed time to rest and recuperate so the lush, untouched farms and fields of Western Maryland, and possibly even Pennsylvania, could provide the victuals and forage his army required.[87] Lee also expressed several other

---

Davis's outlook. His confidence in Lee was now put to the test again and for even higher stakes. For the moment, his reaction was silence. Whether because of his chronic ill health or because he was simply stunned by Lee's audacity, he made no reply to Lee's September 3 letter...The president's silence was all the authorization Lee sought for this bold move, and he gave Davis no time to respond." And Lee was quick to tell Davis that the president should not visit him in Maryland. From page 198: "During the summer months [of 1862], this confidence [in Lee] had led Davis even to set aside his own basic approach to the war. Instead of surviving and striking what small blows it could with minimal risk, the Confederacy would this summer, at Lee's behest but under Davis's direction, wager heavily on long-odds gambles for an early peace....Still, his fundamental approach to the war remained unchanged. Though he might bear with Lee in grasping for the summer's opportunity, he still showed indications of believing that the Confederacy's best hope of independence lay in stubborn survival that avoided defeat and simply outlasted the northern will to preserve the Union," 198. Lee could not remain where he was due to lack of food and forage; he had to move quickly so the reinforced Union army could not come out to meet him; he could not go east and attack Washington; he could not go south and retreat to Richmond and engage in another battle of posts with the Union army; a retreat slightly southward would be possible but again return the advantage of a battle of posts to the Union army; and heading into the Shenandoah would restrict Lee's ability to maneuver and not remove the armies from Virginia. By elimination, his best maneuver would be an adventure north into Maryland allowing Virginia farmers to bring in their corps and give Marylanders the chance to rise against their Federal "oppressors." *Lee*, 2:350-351. See also Harsh, *Shallows*, 132-138. Compare William Allan, "Memoranda of Conversations with General Robert E. Lee," in *Lee the Soldier*, edited by Gary W. Gallagher (Lincoln, NB: University of Nebraska Press, 1996), where Lee in April 1868 recalls his reasons for moving north, 13.

[85] Harsh, *Rising*, 170-173.

[86] *The Wartime Papers of R. E Lee*, 312.

[87] *The Richmond Dispatch* of 17 September was very optimistic that Lee would find much in Pennsylvania let alone Maryland: "The country is enormously rich. It abounds in fat cattle, cereals, horses, and mules.....Let not a blade of grass, or a stalk of corn, or a barrel of flour, or a bushel of meal, or a sack of salt, or a horse, or a cow, or a hog, or a sheep, be left wherever they move along....Let retaliation be complete," *Rebellion Record*, vol. 5, 81. But Likely Lee was not as prepared to gather and transport food and cattle to Virginia as he was during his Gettysburg Campaign 10 months later when he ensured that he had sufficient empty wagons to transport the booty southward, see Kent Masterson Brown, *Retreat from Gettysburg: Lee, Logistics, and the Pennsylvania Campaign* (Chapel Hill, NC: The University of North Carolina Press, 2005), 33-35. Not only was Lee less able to transport foodstuffs south, he was operating in Maryland, not Pennsylvania, so he was endeavoring to keep his men under close

reasons for this campaign including luring potential recruits into his army and bringing Maryland back into the fold. Influencing the 1862 U.S. Congressional elections was likely a part of his thinking—northern public opinion was probably on Lee's mind.[88] Given Lee's views of his previous successes, and the potential for further progress toward freeing the South, Lee had very few viable strategic moves left that would give the many attainable advantages a move into Maryland could provide.

In his 3 September letter to Davis, Lee talked about aiding Maryland in throwing off her oppression, going there before the two Union armies can organize and take the field, even though Lee says his army "is not properly equipped for an invasion;" his greatest concern was for ammunition and shoes:

> What occasions me most concern is the fear of getting out of ammunition. I beg you will instruct the Ordnance Department to spare no pains in manufacturing a sufficient amount of the best kind, and to be particular, in preparing that for the artillery, to provide three times as much of the long-range ammunition as of that for smooth-bore or short-range guns. The points to which I desire the ammunition to be forwarded will be made known to the Department in time. If the Quartermaster's Department can furnish any shoes, it would be the greatest relief. We have entered upon September, and the nights are becoming cool.[89]

He further wrote that he had no intention of attacking the Federals in their Washington fortifications or investing them and then elaborated on his decision:

> After the enemy had disappeared from the vicinity of Fairfax Court House, and taken the road to Alexandria and Washington, I did not think it would be advantageous to follow him farther. I had no intention of attacking him in his fortifications, and am not prepared to invest them. If I possessed the necessary munitions, I should be unable to supply provisions for the troops. I therefore determined, while threatening the approaches to Washington, to draw the troops into Loudoun, where forage and some provisions can be obtained, menace their possession of the Shenandoah Valley, and, if found practicable, to cross into Maryland. The purpose, if discovered, will have the effect of carrying the enemy north of the Potomac, and, if prevented, will not result in much evil.[90]

---

control to avoid wholesale plundering. At this stage of the war, he was still hoping that Maryland could be brought back into the fold so sweeping it clean of food and goods would not have been in his plans.

[88] But see Harsh, *Shallows*, 138, where he says that there is no evidence Lee thought that a successful campaign would influence European governments leaning toward intervention on the South's behalf. See also Timothy J. Reese, *Sealed with Their Lives: The Battle for Crampton's Gap, Burkittsville, Maryland, September 14, 1862* (Baltimore, MD: Butternut and Blue, 1998), 3-5 (hereafter cited as *Sealed*), for a more upbeat assessment of the possibility of British intervention. Few recruits were found in Maryland: "estimates varied from fifty to 130 in Frederick, and around forty in the Middletown area. Many of these, however, quickly repented their action and returned to their homes," Richard R. Duncan, "Marylanders and the Invasion of 1862," *Civil War History*, vol. 11, no. 4, Dec. 1965, 375-376. Duncan quotes from three newspapers printed in September 1862 in notes 25 and 26 on page 376: *Frederick Examiner*, *Middletown Valley Register*, and *New York Times*.

[89] *OR*, vol. 19, pt. 2, 591.

[90] Ibid., 590.

He further believed that another military success against the Union hosts would finally discourage, demoralize, and exhaust the northern populace who had hoped for a quick, decisive victory against the Confederacy. He also knew that the large forces his government had gathered allowed him both to defend Richmond and also permit offensive action northward. Another such effort might be difficult to mount, so he had to make the most of what he hoped would be the final blow needed to end the war. He also had faith in his mostly veteran troops, who had done so well against McClellan and Pope. Lee's first invasion of the North was about to begin, which would end in less than three weeks, with the bloodiest one-day battle of the war, of which Lee said he was most proud. The next three weeks would test the mettle of his army but more importantly, of Lee himself.[91]

[91] Alexander Hunter, "A High Private's Account of the Battle of Sharpsburg" in *Southern Historical Society Papers*, vol. 10, January to June 1877 (Richmond: Southern Historical Society, n.d.; reprint, Millwood, NJ: Kraus Reprint Co, 1977), 503-504.

Attachment 1

Cavalry Strength of Pope's Army of Virginia

Pope reported the detailed organization of his army and those units from the Army of the Potomac assigned to him during the last half of August 1862 as follows: Army of Virginia headquarters escort, 1st Ohio Cavalry under Capt. Nathan D. Menken, Companies A and C, 100 men; First Army Corps, escort, 1st Indiana Cavalry under Capt. Abram Sharra, Companies I and K, 100 troopers; unattached in First Corps, 3rd West Virginia Cavalry, Company C, 49 men; Independent Brigade in the First Corps under brigade commander Brig. Gen. Robert H. Milroy, 1st West Virginia Cavalry led by Maj. Benjamin F. Chamberlain, Companies C, E, and L, 152 men; and the Cavalry Brigade for the First Corps under Col. John Beardsley, 1st Battalion Connecticut Cavalry under Capt. Louis Middlebrook, five companies, 199 men; 1st Maryland Cavalry led by Lt. Col. Charles Wetschky, 10 companies, 412 troopers; 4th New York Cavalry commanded by Lt. Col. Ferries Nazer, nine companies, 388 horsemen; 9th New York cavalry led by Maj. Charles McLean Knox, 12 companies, 445 troopers; and the 6th Ohio Cavalry led by Col. William R. Lloyd, eight companies, 439 horsemen. Total men available to Col. John Beardsley's First Corps during late August were 1,883. Compare this to the 1,730 for his troopers at the end of July, and 1,085 on 2 September as noted below.[92]

The Second Army Corps' cavalry brigade led by Brig. Gen. John Buford consisted of the 1st Michigan cavalry led by Col. Thornton F. Brodhead, 9 companies, 481 men; 5th New York cavalry commanded by Col. Othneil De Forest, 10 companies, 364 troopers; the 1st Vermont cavalry led by Col. Charles H. Tompkins, 10 companies, 504 men; and the 1st West Virginia Cavalry commanded by Lt. Col. Nathaniel P. Richmond, seven companies, 440 horsemen. Total men available to Brig. Gen. Buford during late August were 1,789 which is a dramatic reduction from the 4,104 a month earlier. This number must show the reduction due to losses in men and horses so should be viewed as troopers available for duty with mounts—present for duty, equipped.[93]

The Third Army corps cavalry brigade led by Bayard had the 1st Maine Cavalry commanded by Col. Samuel H. Allen, 11 companies, 514 horsemen; the 1st New Jersey, commanded by Col. Percy Wyndham, 12 companies, 533 troopers; the 2nd New York (Harris) cavalry led by Col. J. Mansfield Davies, eight companies, 389 troopers; the 1st Pennsylvania cavalry commanded by Col. Owen Jones, 12 companies, 702 men; and the 1st Rhode Island Cavalry led by Col. Alfred N. Duffie, 12 companies, 482 horsemen. It also had a detachment of the 3rd Indiana Cavalry under Col. Scott Carter, six companies, A through F,

---

[92] OR, vol. 12, pt. 2, 49. Troop strength compiled showing present for duty as was done with strength for the Peninsular Campaign from John Owen Allen's master's thesis. Data presented here is from 18 and 28 August 1862 with adjustments as needed from earlier dates for specific escort units. Maj. John H. Robinson was apparently in command of the squadron composed of Companies A and C of the 1st Ohio Cavalry but due to his ill health, was not in active command in the field; Capt. N. D. Menken of Company C may have been in command vice Jones as he outranked Jones but it is not clear from the record shown in the regimental history, William L. Curry, *Four Years in the Saddle: History of the First Regiment Ohio Volunteer Cavalry, War of the Rebellion, 1861-1865* (Columbus, OH: Champlin Printing Col., 1898), 233; see also appended roster of Ohio troops at the end of the book taken from vol. XI 5, 12. Note that Pope reported 1,730 for the First Corps at the end of July versus 1,883, the 153 man difference is easily attributable to gains from those who were listed as sick or on detached duty, for example.

[93] Troop strength compiled showing present for duty as was done with strength for the Peninsular Campaign from John Owen Allen's master's thesis. Data presented here is from 18 and 28 August 1862 with adjustments as needed from earlier dates for specific escort units. Col. Henry Anisansel commander of the 1st West Virginia Cavalry resigned in July 1862. Pope's report in late July for Buford of 4,104 versus 1,789 in late August reflects the fact that Buford suffered most heavily from worn-out horses as his troopers had done the lion's share of scouting for Pope leading up to Second Bull Run.

391 men. Total men available to Brig. Gen. Bayard during late August were 3,011 compared with 2,904 a month earlier.[94]

On 2 September, Beardsley's brigade had 1,085 troopers mounted and present for duty including nine in his brigade staff. His units were as follows: 1st Connecticut Battalion, Capt. Louis Middlebrook, 5 companies, 197 men; 1st Maryland Cavalry, Lt. Col. Charles Wetschky, 10 companies, 404 troopers; 4th New York Cavalry, Lt. Col. Ferries Nazer, 9 companies, 324 men; 9th New York Cavalry, Maj. Charles McLean Knox, 12 companies, 438 troopers; 6th Ohio Cavalry, 8 companies, Col. William R. Lloyd, 437 men; total men 1809. But only 60 per cent could be mounted due to lack of mounts gives 1,085 available.[95]

Buford's brigade was in better condition with 1,752 available although it is very likely that many had worn-out or unserviceable horses; he had eight in his staff and the remainder of his brigade as follows: 1st Michigan Cavalry, Maj. Charles H. Town (Col. Thornton F. Brodhead mortally wounded), 9 companies, 486 men; 5th New York Cavalry, Col. Othneil De Forest, 10 companies, 373 troopers; 1st Vermont Cavalry, Col. Charles H. Tompkins, 10 companies, 513 men; 1st West Virginia Cavalry, Lt. Col. Nathaniel P. Richmond, seven companies, 372 troopers.[96]

Bayard's brigade was the largest of the three with 5,436 total including seven on the brigade staff, with these units: 1st Maine Cavalry, Col. Samuel H. Allen, 11 companies, 511 troopers; 1st New Jersey Cavalry, Col. Percy Wyndham, 12 companies, 533 men; 2nd New York Cavalry, Col. J. Mansfield Davies, 8 companies, 306 troopers; 1st Pennsylvania Cavalry, Col. Owen Jones, 12 companies, 730 men; 1st Rhode Island Cavalry, Col. Alfred N. Duffie, 12 companies, 512 troopers. Thus the total Army of Virginia cavalry available to Pope on 2 September was 5,436.[97]

---

[94] *OR*, vol. 12, pt. 3, 581-585; John Owen Allen, 18 and 28 August 1862 with adjustments as needed from earlier dates for specific escort units. W.N. Pickerill, *History of the Third Indiana Cavalry* (Indianapolis, IN: Aetna Printing Co., 1906; reprint, Salem, MA: Higginson Book Company, n.d.), 8, 10, 182. This 3,011 is close to the 2,904 he reported one month earlier and likely reflects losses in men and unfit horses.

[95] Allen, 121.

[96] Ibid., 121-122.

[97] Ibid., 122.

Attachment 2

Cavalry Strength of Lee's Army of Northern Virginia

Maj. Gen. Jeb Stuart's cavalry division on 17 August 1862 was made up of two brigades, Lee's Brigade commanded by Brig. Gen. Fitzhugh Lee and Robertson's Brigade (Laurel Brigade) under Brig. Gen. Beverly H. Robertson. Stuart had eight troopers on his staff while Lee and Robertson each had four. Lee's Brigade had four regiments of Virginia Cavalry, the 1st, 4th, 5th, and 9th, each with 10 companies. The 1st Virginia Cavalry commanded by Lt. Col. Luke Tiernan Brien had 513 horsemen; the 4th Virginia cavalry led by Col. Williams C. Wickham had 336 troopers; the 5th Virginia Cavalry commanded by Col. Thomas L. Rosser listed 366 cavalrymen; and the 9th Virginia Cavalry had 517 troopers under Col. William H. Fitzhugh Lee; the brigade total was 1,736. Robertson's Brigade also had four Virginia cavalry regiments, the 2nd, 6th, 7th, and 12th, but in addition had the 17th Virginia Battalion and one company of White's Rebels. The 2nd Virginia consisted of nine companies totaling 450 troopers under Col. Thomas T. Munford; the 6th Virginia Cavalry had 10 companies with 410 horsemen under Col. Thomas S. Flournoy; the 7th Virginia cavalry had nine companies with 477 men led by Col. "Grumble" Jones; the 12th Virginia Cavalry had six companies 364 troopers under Col. Asher W. Harman; the 17th Virginia Battalion consisted of six companies of 383 horsemen commanded by Maj. W. Patrick; and the White's Rebels had one company of 39 troopers. Robertson's Brigade had 2,127 present for duty. The Stuart Horse Artillery had one battery under Capt. John Pelham with 125 artillerymen giving Stuart a total of 3,996 available for duty equipped.[98]

Jeb Stuart on 2 September had more troopers available in the Army of Northern Virginia than Pope could muster, 5,664 versus 5,436. Lee's Brigade had 1,959 including 4 for his staff, regiments as follows: 1st Virginia Cavalry, Lt. Col. Luke T. Brien, 10 companies, 513 men; 3rd Virginia Cavalry, Lt. Col. John Thornton, 10 companies, 223 troopers; 4th Virginia Cavalry, Col. W.C. Wickham, 10 companies, 336 troopers; 5th Virginia Cavalry, Col. Tom L. Rosser, 10 companies, 366 men; 9th Virginia Cavalry, Col. W.H.F. Lee, 10 companies, 517 troopers.[99]

Robertson's Brigade under Brig. Gen. Beverly Robertson, totaled 1,990 men including four on its staff as follows: 2nd Virginia Cavalry, Col. Thomas T. Munford, 9 companies, 408 men; 6th Virginia Cavalry, Col. T.S. Flournoy, 10 companies, 407 troopers; 7th Virginia Cavalry, Capt. Samuel B. Myers, nine companies, 474 men; 12th Virginia Cavalry, Col. A.W. Harman, 6 companies, 358 troopers; 17th Virginia Battalion, Capt. E.H. McDonald, 6 companies, 302 men; White's Rebels, Capt. Elijah White, one company, 37 troopers.[100]

The newly arrived Hampton's Brigade totaled 5,664 including its five staff, with regiments as follows: 1st North Carolina Cavalry, Col. L.S. Baker, 10 companies, 411 men; 2nd South Carolina Cavalry, Col. M.C. Butler, 4 companies, 213 troopers; 10th Virginia Cavalry, Col. James Lucius Davis, seven companies, 340 men; Cobb's Legion, Lt. Col. Pierce M.B. Young, six companies, 170 troopers; Jeff Davis Legion, Lt. Col. W.T. Martin, six companies, 306 men.[101]

The Stuart Horse Artillery totaled 262 artillery men as follows: First Battery, Capt. John Pelham, 123 men; Virginia Battery, Capt. R.P. Chew, 75 men; South Carolina Battery, Capt. J.F. Hart, 64.[102]

---

[98] Allen, 173-174; *Battles and Leaders,* 2:499-500.

[99] Allen, 201.

[100] Ibid., 201-202.

[101] Ibid., 202.

[102] Ibid.

Chapter 5

Across the Potomac

GEN. ROBERT E. LEE WAS READY to begin his adventure north of the Potomac River. He began implementing his plans but did not forget to gather in the fruits from his Second Bull Run victory. Lee's 2 September 1862 order to Maj. Gen. Daniel Harvey Hill sent him to Leesburg with his subsistence train, which was to be unloaded and immediately returned, so it could be refilled with the spoils from Lee's triumph. On the same day, Lee's order to Stuart concerned cavalry refitting and collection of battlefield gleanings. Stuart was to send troopers with horses needing rest and refitting back to the battlefield of Second Bull Run to let the horses recover along with a field forge to re-shoe them while the troopers gathered up useful items for the cavalry and the rest of the army. Brig. Gen. Robertson's 6th Virginia Cavalry, 407 troopers strong under Col. Thomas S. Flournoy, was assigned to stay near Manassas as part of Stuart's contribution to Gen. Lee's collection force to protect against inquisitive Yankees while helping to assemble loot.[1] Jackson's command moved north from Chantilly on 3 September and reached Leesburg on the 4th while Longstreet followed arriving the evening of the 4th.[2]

Gen. Lee assigned Stuart to threaten an advance on Washington to distract the Federals in an effort to ensure that Army of Northern Virginia could safely cross the Potomac east of the Blue Ridge Mountains mainly at White's Ford northeast of Leesburg. From Fairfax Court House on the morning of 3 September, Fitzhugh Lee's Brigade moved toward Alexandria while Hampton, after skirmishing with Maj. Gen. Edwin Sumner's rear guard at Flint Hill the previous day, camped near Dranesville. Robertson's Brigade, minus the 6th Virginia cavalry, arrived from Chantilly and camped near Hampton as Stuart had demonstrations continue toward Groveton near the Second Bull Run battlefield and the Chain Bridge just upstream on the Potomac from Washington. The next day, 4 September, Robertson rode toward Falls Church with the 7th and 12th Virginia Cavalry and three pieces of Chew's battery to make a demonstration, while Lee's army began crossing upriver. After encountering Pleasonton's Union cavalry pickets between Vienna and Lewinsville and driving them, he set up two guns on a hill overlooking the church there, where he posted his troopers in plain sight. He ensured that he would not be ambushed as he placed the third gun from Chew's Battery near Lewinsville. Pleasonton brought up two guns to challenge Robertson's and the cannon on both sides continued firing until evening when Robertson, concerned that Pleasonton might be flanking him, withdrew toward Leesburg to rejoin Stuart.[3] Robertson's demonstrations were to allow D.H. Hill to raid across the Potomac on the morning

[1] *OR*, vol. 19, pt. 2, 588-589.

[2] Carman, Pierro, 41-42; Allan, *Army of Northern Virginia*, 323-324; Allen, 201.

[3] Harsh, *Flood*, 67; George M. Neese, *Three Years in the Confederate Horse Artillery* (New York: The Neale Publishing Company, 1911, reprint, Clearwater, SC: Eastern Digital Resources, 2003), 133-134; *OR*, vol. 19, pt. 1, 814, 828; Harlan D.

of the 4ᵗʰ to destroy the Baltimore and Ohio (B&O) Railroad tracks and the Chesapeake and Ohio (C&O) Canal along with any telegraph lines found. But there is no evidence to show that Rebel telegraph operators routinely listened in on Union traffic during this period even though much valuable information could have been obtained from messages to and from Harpers Ferry.⁴ Two of Hill's brigades crossed above White's Ford near the mouth of the Monocacy River in the vicinity of Spinks (Hauling's) Ferry likely at Cheek's Ford or Monocacy Ford making use of the C&O Canal aqueduct at Monocacy River to get by the canal. His troops were unsuccessful in trying to destroy the well-built Monocacy Aqueduct after they easily brushed away Unionists opposing them, a detachment of 30 men of the 1ˢᵗ Regiment Potomac Home Brigade. Hill was able to have a detail of his men wreck the Little Monocacy Culvert and drain the Seven-Mile Level of the C&O Canal; the berm and towpath banks were cut down, the prism corduroyed, which allowed the artillery and trains to cross. Hill may have had some cavalry with him as Gen. Lee's order on the 5ᵗʰ instructed the cavalry squadron with Hill to return to Stuart. Another of Hill's brigades under George B. Anderson fired on trains at Berlin from the Virginia shore to help divert attention from Confederate troop crossings further down the Potomac; he successfully scared off troops Col. Miles had sent from Harpers Ferry: Col. H.B. Banning with the 87ᵗʰ Ohio, Maryland troops, and two guns; D.H. Hill's troops under Brig. Gen. Roswell S. Ripley crossed at Point of Rocks upstream from Berlin and Brig. Gen. Samuel Garland, Jr.'s at Noland's Ferry.⁵

Unrau, National Park Service, Historic Resource Study, Chesapeake & Ohio Canal National Historic Park, 1976, 735. Some of the 12ᵗʰ Virginia Cavalry may have remained in Virginia, see n. 24 below.

⁴ The telegraph in Maryland proved very useful to Union forces but was easily cut by Confederates eager to interrupt Yankee transmissions. Early in the war, recognizing the need for communication up the Potomac, Union authorities from September through December 1861 erected a telegraph line "from Washington, D.C., to Hagerstown, Maryland, via Rockville, Darnestown, Poolesville, Hyattstown, Frederick and Williamsport... [and] also a loop from Poolesville to Point of Rocks." Union Col. Dixon S. Miles, commanding at Harpers Ferry, reported on 6 September that "Our communication with Baltimore and Washington cut off." Miles's aide-de-camp, Lt. Henry M. Binney, reported on 3 September that "telegraph lines are being molested somewhere between this place [Harpers Ferry] and Baltimore while on 4 September he wrote that "telegraph communications with Baltimore are considerably interrupted." Binney reported that on 6 September, "Our telegraphic communications eastward cut off; obliged to forward via Wheeling, Pittsburg, &c. The operator receives the following dispatch: 'How are you, General Pope? General Jackson's army.'" Historian Scharf related that on 5 September, "Jackson's division crossed near the Point of Rocks, tore up the Baltimore and Ohio Railroad tracks, and cut off all telegraphic and other connection from Harper's Ferry to Washington." Wool states that he received the last telegraphic message from Harpers Ferry on the 7ᵗʰ as "The telegraph wires were cut, and the road from Monocacy to Harper's Ferry was in the hands of the rebels." Some telegraphic communications remained however, as Miles sent a telegraph to Halleck on 11 September showing that he still had telegraphic or dispatch capabilities on that date. Lincoln stated that Wheeling, Virginia, reported that the line from Harpers Ferry was cut as nothing was received from there or Martinsburg. Apparently, while direct lines eastward to Washington were cut, other lines out of Harpers Ferry were still operating as late as 11 September. Messages from Harpers Ferry went through Wheeling, Virginia, to Pittsburgh, and then to Washington, OR, vol. 19, pt. 2, 209. An historian of the telegraph during the war, William R. Plum, also implies that the line to Harpers Ferry was cut on the 7ᵗʰ when he wrote that one L.D. McCandless led a party of line repairers and builders along with operator Conway riding to Point of Rocks but found no connection to Washington. They backtracked the line toward Poolesville meeting many Rebel stragglers. They found the break on the bank of the Monocacy River where a piece of the wire had been cut and removed. This break was not repaired until after the Rebels moved west to Sharpsburg; OR, vol. 51, pt. 1, 794; OR, vol. 19, pt. 1, 533; OR, vol. 19, pt. 1, 534. See also Scharf, 228; OR, vol. 19, pt. 1, 520; OR, vol. 19, pt. 2, 266; vol. 51, pt. 1, 819; OR, vol. 19, pt. 2, 270. William R. Plum, The Military Telegraph during the Civil War in the United States, vol. 1 (Chicago, IL: Jansen, McClurg & Company, 1882), 82-84; 230, 232. On 6 September, a B&O Railroad supervisor reported that telegraph lines were cut by the Rebels on the east side of Monocacy Bridge, OR, vol. 19, pt. 2, 198. Lincoln telegraphed McClellan on 12 September that communication with Harper Ferry and Wheeling has stopped meaning that the line west of Harpers Ferry has been cut as the Rebels were recrossing the Potomac at Williamsport, OR, vol. 19, pt. 2, 270.

⁵ OR, vol. 19, pt. 2, 595, Special Order 188 also ordered the company of cavalry from Cobb's Legion to report to Stuart, and Stuart should replace that company with one from the 12ᵗʰ Virginia Cavalry. It is interesting to note that Lee's order to the cavalry with D.H. Hill said that the company should report to Stuart "upon his taking the advance." Lee obviously knew that it was Hill in advance not Stuart crossing into Maryland so is evidence to show that he did not expect Stuart's cavalry to shield the

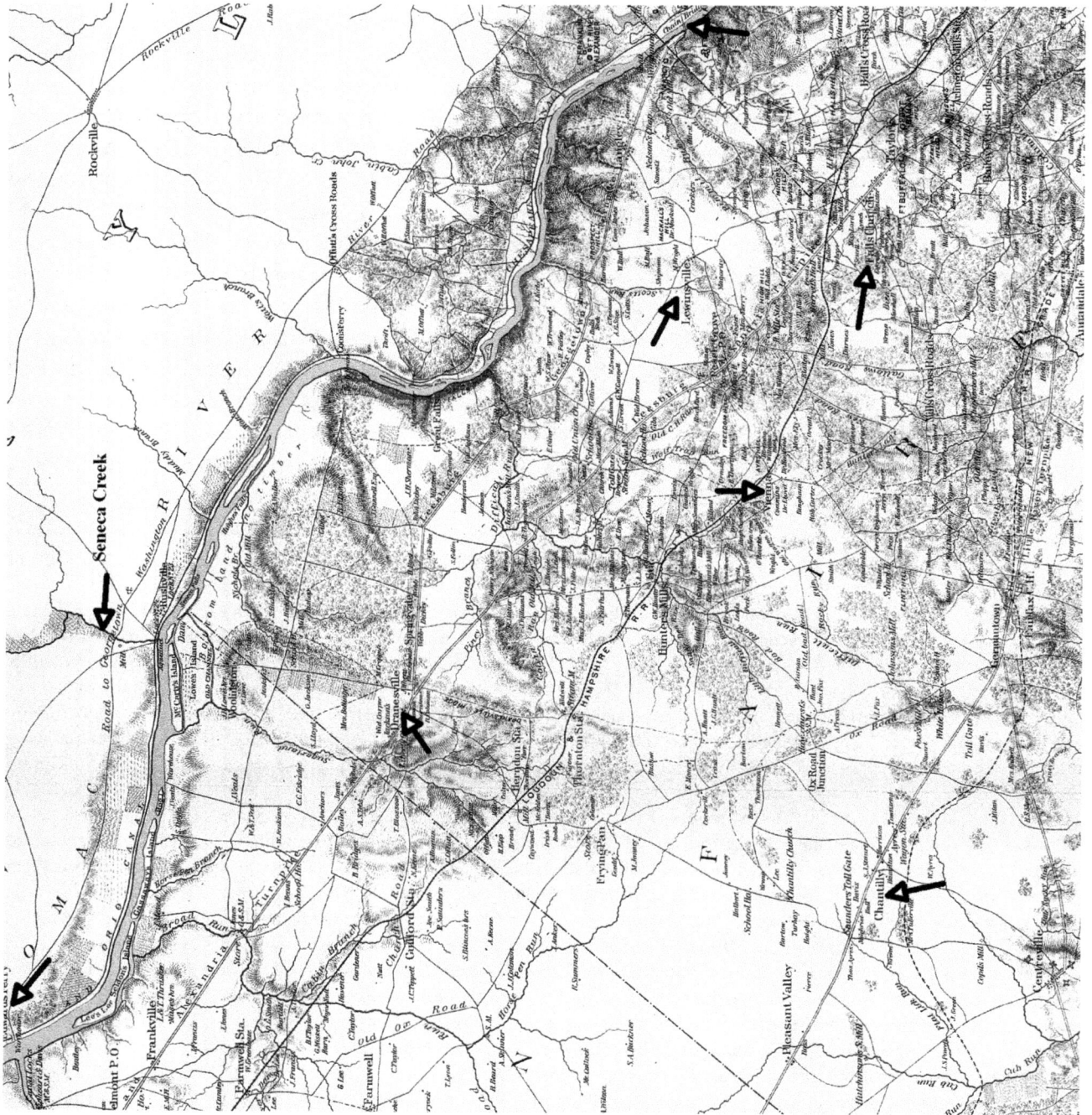

Area of operations before Stuart crossed the Potomac showing places where Stuart's cavalry was involved in skirmishes. Edward's Ferry is at the upper left arrow, Dranesville to the center left, Chantilly to the lower left, Vienna to the lower center, Falls Church at the lower right, Lewinsville above it, and Chain Bridge to the far right center. Union cavalry patrols were active from Washington which is off the map to the lower right to Seneca Creek. *Official Atlas*, Plate 7. Courtesy LOC.

infantry's movement into Maryland. Conrad's Ferry is today's White's Ferry and Berlin today is Brunswick; Carman, Pierro, 45; Harsh, *Flood*, 71; *Shallows*, 153-155; Timothy R. Snyder, "Civil War Fords of the Potomac River," Unpublished Manuscript, 11.

Stuart crossing under C&O Canal through a culvert at McCoy's Ferry 11 miles upriver from Williamsport (eight airline miles) during his Second Ride Around McClellan in October 1862. This shows one easy method for getting across the difficult barrier of the canal. The most time consuming would be to build a bridge across it but that could be expedited by adding a canal boat to the bridge's superstructure. Even if the canal is drained, a bridge is needed unless the banks are completely cut down, a difficult task for infantry especially given some of the rocky areas through which the canal passes. This drawing is similar to those by Theodore R. Davis in the 8 November 1862 *Harper's Weekly*, although this drawing was not printed there. Courtesy LOC.

Rebels destroying the C&O Canal by cutting through the towpath. *Harper's Weekly*, 30 July 1864. Author's collection.

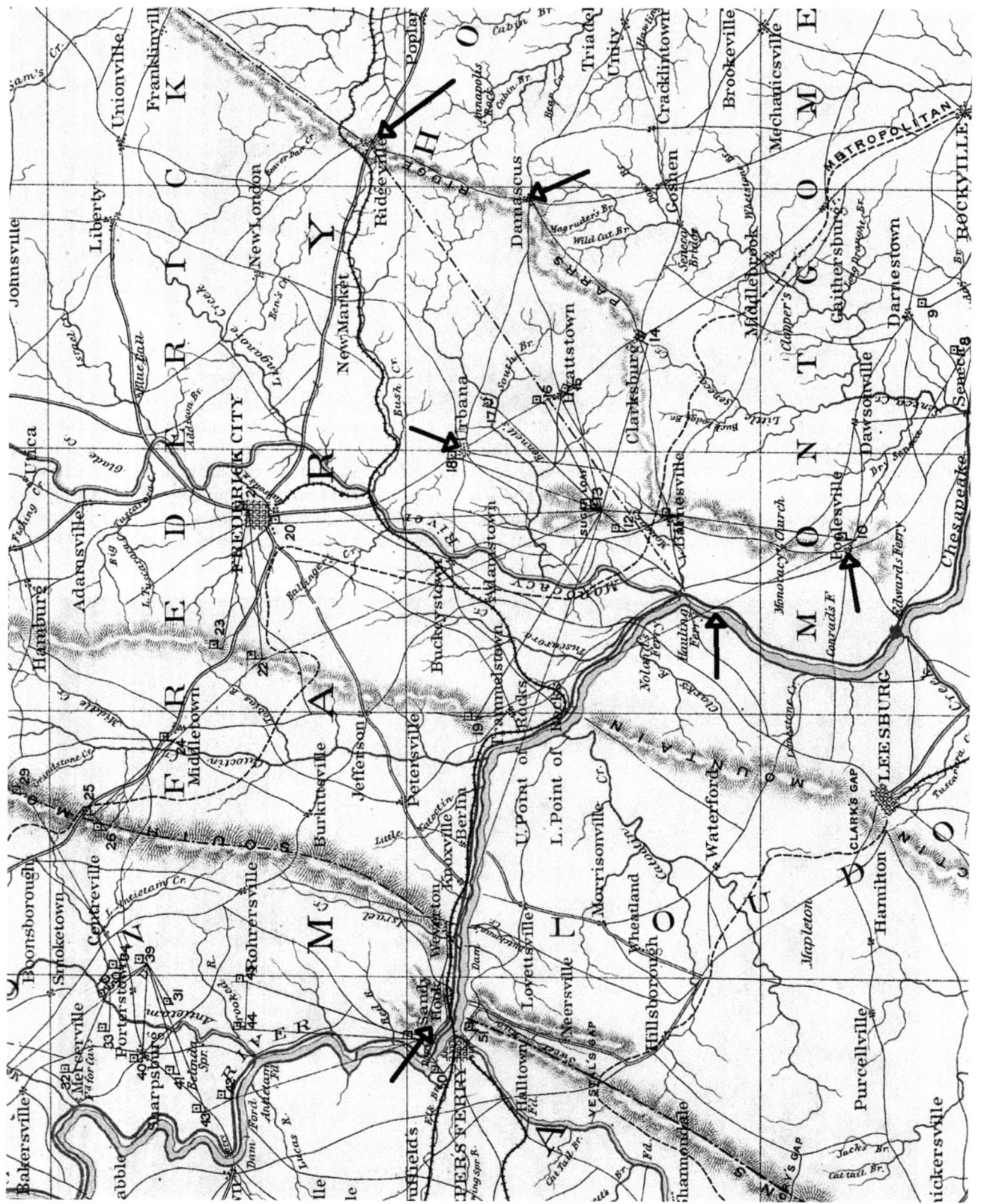

Left: view of the area of operations of the movements of the cavalry in early September 1862. Gen. Lee's goal was to form his army around Frederick, Maryland at the upper right center behind the Monocacy River barrier. Poolesville is in the lower right center of the map at the bottom arrow; Stuart's headquarters at Urbana south of Frederick (Frederick City); it was on the main road from Washington to Frederick; Frederick was on the National Pike from Baltimore. Sugarloaf Mountain is to the Northeast of Poolesville next to Barnesville; White's Ford is almost due west of Barnesville at the arrow northwest of Poolesville. Edward's Ferry is where Fitzhugh Lee crossed and had a fight with Union cavalry at Poolesville at the lower center of the map at the arrow. D.H. Hill's men crossed just upstream near the mouth of the Monocacy River at fords close to Hauling Ferry. Conrad's Ferry below White's Ford is today White's Ferry. White's Ferry is about three river miles below White's Ford. Parr's Ridge is the ridge farthest to the right which runs through Damascus, Maryland, at the arrow at the right. The valley between the Catoctin Mountains and Parr's Ridge is sometimes called Monocacy Valley. The Catoctin Mountains, the Maryland extension of the Bull Run Mountains in Virginia, are just west of Frederick and to their west is the South Mountain Range. Between them is the Middletown (or Catoctin) Valley. West of South Mountain near Harpers Ferry is Elk Mountain or Elk Ridge which terminates at Harpers Ferry and is called Maryland Heights at that point; Elk Ridge is the Maryland extension of the Virginia Blue Ridge Mountains. It is not shown here but is located at the arrow near Sandy Hook just above Harpers Ferry. Pleasant Valley lies between South Mountain and Elk Ridge. The initial line Stuart set up, the Parr's Ridge/Sugarloaf Line ran from Poolesville, through Hyattstown to New Market. Rebel pickets were initially located at Clarksburg, Hyattstown, Damascus, Ridgeville, Barnesville, Poolesville, and around Sugarloaf. Fitz Lee's men were also posted at New Market on the National Pike. Harpers Ferry is about fifty airline miles from Washington while Frederick is about forty miles. On 4 September, McClellan reported his disposition as follows: First Corps at Upton's Hill, the Ninth Corps on the 7th Street Road, the Second and Twelfth Corps at Tenallytown, the Sixth Corps at the Alexandria Seminary, and Couch's division at Tenallytown, *Report on the Organization and Campaigns of the Army of the Potomac*, 349. *Official Atlas*, Plate 27. Courtesy LOC.

Stuart and his staff spent Thursday, 4 September, in needful "strange, blessed, uninterrupted quietude" in camp near Dranesville, Virginia. He and his coterie stayed at the Drover's Inn on the Leesburg Pike, Stuart likely regaling his men about his battle at Dranesville on 20 December of the previous year. An officer in the 3rd Virginia Cavalry, William R. Carter, described this easy day on the 4th: "Moved this morning into field beyond Drainesville and spent the day resting & feeding our horses. Camped here to-night."[6]

Despite Stuart's units demonstrating toward Groveton and Chain Bridge, neither Halleck nor cavalry commander, Brig. Gen. Alfred Pleasonton, were deceived into thinking Lee was planning on attacking Washington. Pleasonton on 4 September opined correctly that the Confederate probes were for the purpose of "making a show of force to conceal his movements on the Upper Potomac."[7] Later in the campaign however, Halleck reminded McClellan not to leave Washington open to attack from south of the Potomac and Halleck remained concerned throughout the Maryland Campaign about this route, which is probably why he required that the Harpers Ferry garrison remain in place much longer than they should have given Lee's movements to its east, north, and finally to the west and south.[8] All of

[6] *OR*, vol. 19, pt. 1, 828; von Borcke, 126. William R. Carter, *Sabres, Saddles, and Spurs*, ed. by Walbrook D. Swank (Shippensburg, PA: Burd Street Press, 1998), 12; Harsh, *Flood*, 57. Stuart's cavalry certainly needed rest given its exertions the previous weeks and Gen. Lee's infantry also required rest but got little perhaps increasing the numbers of stragglers as will be seen. The Drover's Inn was one of a collection of several taverns and inns in the vicinity of Dranesville crossroads of the Leesburg and Alexandria and Leesburg and Georgetown Turnpikes; there is only one left today, the Dranesville Tavern, owned by Fairfax County, Virginia. Stuart might have had to embellish his story about Dranesville as the action there resulted in his repulse as he failed in his mission to gather forage from the vicinity. Stuart used Rowser's Ford north of Dranesville for his venture north to Gettysburg in late June 1863.

[7] *OR*, vol. 19, pt. 2, 178. See also *OR*, vol. 51, pt. 1, 785, and vol. 19, pt. 2, 179, detailing Union efforts addressing the feint. Pleasonton was in charge of cavalry at this location but his troopers were replaced by cavalry from Buford and Bayard as McClellan desired Pleasonton in Maryland, *OR*, vol. 51, pt. 1, 787.

[8] *OR*, vol. 19, pt. 2, 201, 7 September, "Until we can get better advices about the numbers of the enemy at Dranesville, I think we must be very cautious about stripping too much the forts on the Virginia side. It may be the enemy's object to draw off the

Stuart's brigades were now gathering at Leesburg to cover the rear of the Army of Northern Virginia as it crossed the Potomac.[9] Gen. Lee and Stuart probably were not very concerned about the cavalry screening the army's advance as it headed north of the Potomac as they were aware of no large, organized Union forces near the river crossings, and those there were likely only militia or small-sized units sent out by Col. Miles at Harpers Ferry. And with Fitzhugh Lee's Brigade crossing downriver from Gen. Lee's infantry at Edward's Ferry, the Army of Northern Virginia was protected from the large Union forces assembling around Washington. Lee was certain that remnants of Pope's army and McClellan's troops were inside the Washington forts licking their wounds as they reformed around the capital. Additionally, Confederate infantry units were so large that the Rebels could easily brush aside any videttes and outposts which Col. Miles or Gen. Wool may have posted along the B&O near the Potomac and toward Frederick. While Lee was correct about the lack of any serious opposition in the area, he and other Army of Northern Virginia commanders wrongly assumed that Union forces would remain huddled in the strong Washington defenses refitting and training new replacements for many weeks, allowing Lee's army untrammeled access to Maryland's bounty.

Lee was correct however, believing that the few Union units in the area picketing the Maryland side of the Potomac fords, the B&O Railroad and C&O Canal, would skedaddle as large Rebel forces moved across the river. Units such as the Maryland 1st Potomac Home Brigade attempted to engage D.H. Hill's units at Cheek's Ford at the mouth of the Monocacy River but the detachment of thirty-one infantry predictably had little success. Another detachment from the Maryland brigade, part of Company F, skirmished briefly with the Rebels at Edward's Ferry about eight river miles below White's Ford, but quickly fell back.[10] Potomac Home Brigade members at Point of Rocks were also unsuccessful in stopping the Rebel advance. A company of the brigade stationed in Frederick under command of Capt. William T. Faithful, received orders from its commander, Col. Miles at Harpers Ferry, instructing Faithful to "destroy all quartermaster and commissary stores." Faithful showed uncommon good sense and did not panic. He decided not to destroy what could be saved, so acting quickly, he sent all of the horses to Pennsylvania, and loaded the quartermaster and commissary stores on railroad cars and sent them to Baltimore. He described his actions: "[I] then proceeded to gather all Government wagons, with others that I pressed into service, and loaded them with the most costly of hospital stores, and all books and papers of the quartermaster's and commissary departments, and placed them under the command of

---

mass of our forces and then attempt to attack from the Virginia side of the Potomac." Ibid., 280, 13 September, "I am of opinion that the enemy will send a small column toward Pennsylvania, so as to draw your forces in that direction; then suddenly move on Washington." Ibid., 14 September, "I fear you are exposing your left flank, and that the enemy can cross in your rear." See also Carman, Pierro, 102-103, showing Halleck's fears that Confederates are operating in the Shenandoah Valley. Late on the 13th, McClellan had the Lost Order and telegraphed Halleck about it and that "I feel confident that there is now no rebel force immediately threatening Washington or Baltimore," *OR*, vol. 19, pt. 2, 282; but see Halleck, 16 September, "I think, however, you will find that the whole force of the enemy in your front has crossed the river. I fear now more than ever that they will recross at Harper's Ferry or below, and turn your left, thus cutting you off from Washington. This has appeared to me to be a part of their plan, and hence my anxiety on the subject," *OR*, vol. 19, pt. 1, 41. Halleck's exchanges with McClellan had their origins when Lincoln believed that McClellan left insufficient forces in the Washington defenses to protect Washington as he left for his Peninsular Campaign. Lincoln was constantly concerned about the loss of his capitol from the beginning of the war and these worries are reflected in Halleck's telegrams.

[9] Carman, Pierro, 43-44. *OR*, vol. 19, pt. 2, 176-178.

[10] Daniel Carroll Toomey, *The Civil War in Maryland* (Baltimore, MD: Toomey Press, 1983), 46. The Potomac Home Brigade was formed on 19 July 1861 under the authority of Secretary of War Simon Cameron to guard and protect the C&O Canal and the area adjacent to the Potomac River from the Monocacy to the western border of Maryland but not to serve outside of lands adjacent to the Potomac. Troops were to be recruited for three years' service from loyal citizens from both sides of the river. One company of cavalry per regiment was authorized; the four companies were consolidated into the First Regiment Potomac Home Brigade Cavalry in June 1862 commanded by Capt. Henry A. Cole who was promoted to major on 1 August. Only three regiments of infantry were finally formed; Gary, 6-10, 152.

Lieut. G.T. Castle...and sent them on toward Pennsylvania, after which I sent some 275 convalescents from the hospital to Gettysburg....Such hospital stores as could not be sent off for the want of transportation I ordered to be destroyed...then ordered the telegraph operator to detach his instruments and leave for Baltimore or Washington."[11] He left medical and other necessities for the some 600 patients in the general hospital in Frederick per Miles's orders. "Joined by Lieutenant Burke's detachment, which had fallen back from the mouth of the Monocacy, he led the party—about one hundred men—on the Harper's Ferry Road through Jefferson, Petersville, and Knoxville, joining his regiment at Sandy Hook, a short distance south of Harper's Ferry, on the afternoon of the sixth."[12]

On 6 September, Frederick diarist Jacob Engelbrecht reflecting less martial steel and more trepidation wrote: "Tremendous excitement 'Jackson is coming'....The Provost Marshal received a telegraph dispatch, that in the event of the enemy's approaching, to destroy the government stores. Accordingly about 10 o'clock they commenced burning beds & cots that were stored at 'Kemp Hall'...and burnt them in Church Street....At the Barracks they burnt some stores also at the depot they burnt tents, cots, beds, guns, (muskets)."[13] Fortunately for the Union cause, Lt. Faithful did not succumb to the panic which most of the citizens of Frederick and other towns in Maryland and southern Pennsylvania felt at the approach of Lee's army. *Harper's Weekly* reported the following:

The correspondent of the *Baltimore American* thus described the entrance of the rebels into Frederick:

> They made their appearance in the city about 10 o'clock in the morning, and marched in quietly, evidently having full knowledge that there was no opposition to be made to them. The force was halted on Market Street, and a proclamation issued to the people.
>
> The foraging parties sent out in various directions to secure cattle, returned during the evening with droves of sheep, hogs, beeves, cows, and horses. They seized everything they wanted, and are said to have tendered payment in Federal "green backs," whether counterfeit or good, is not known. These cattle were all driven toward the Potomac. The purchases made in Frederick are said to have been paid for partly in Federal money, but mostly in Virginia and South Carolina money.
>
> A rebel Provost Marshal was appointed, with a strong guard, to preserve order, and during the afternoon the streets were thronged with rebel soldiers visiting the stores —which the Provost Marshal ordered to be opened—and purchasing shoes and clothing, of which they were in great want. So far as we could learn, strict order was preserved.[14]

---

[11] *OR*, vol. 51, pt. 1, 136-137.

[12] Carman, Pierro, 47.

[13] Jacob Engelbrecht, *The Diary of Jacob Engelbrecht*, ed. by William R. Quynn (Frederick, MD: Historical Society of Frederick County, 2001), 947

[14] *Harper's Weekly*, 27 September 1862, 618.

Rebels crossing the Potomac before Antietam. Union pickets in foreground firing at what appears to be cavalry crossing in three lines. Of the three possibilities where large bodies of Confederate cavalry crossed, White's Ford, Conrad's Ferry, and Edward's Ferry, this may be White's Ford as the other two do not have large hills on the Virginia shore. Drawn by Alfred Rudolph Waud. Courtesy LOC.

Confederate cavalry crossing the Potomac River possibly at White's Ford or less likely at Conrad's Ferry as the accompanying story says that artillery and infantry crossed in addition to cavalry. Note the bare foot on the unkempt first horseman and the welcoming civilians on the left pointing the way. There is what appears to be a pontoon bridge in the background, but there were none constructed by Rebel troops during the campaign. The accompanying story elaborates: "The rebels appear to have begun their crossing on 4th, and to have thrown bodies of men steadily forward ever since. The artillery crossed on a pontoon bridge, the cavalry and infantry forded the stream, the water being knee and thigh deep. A person who watched them cross said of them: The rebels are wretchedly clad, and generally destitute of shoes. The cavalry men are mostly barefooted, and the feet of the infantry are bound up in rags and pieces of rawhide. Their uniforms are in tatters, and many are without hats or caps. They are very sanguine of success, and say that when they get to Baltimore they will get everything they need," *Harper's Weekly*, 27 September 1862, 613, 618. Courtesy LOC. There is no record of construction of a pontoon bridge by Confederates across the Potomac in September 1862, the only pontoon bridge was at Harpers Ferry constructed by the Federals which McLaws used on 15 September after Miles's surrender of the Union garrison. But note that one of Baker's operatives wrote on 5 September that a captain from the 1st Michigan Cavalry reported that Rebels were crossing at the mouth of Monocacy Creek and were building a bridge to cross artillery, *OR*, vol. 19, pt. 2, 187. There is no record of Gen. Lee having pontoon boats before or during the Maryland Campaign, so the bridge being built may be one to cross the C&O Canal or the Monocacy River.

Von Borcke painted a picturesque tableau as he described the cavalry's crossing at White's Ford:

It was, indeed, a magnificent sight as the long column of many thousand horsemen stretched across this beautiful Potomac. The evening sun slanted upon its clear placid waters, and burnished them with gold, while the arms of the soldiers glittered and blazed in its radiance. There were few moments, perhaps, from the beginning to the close of the war, of excitement more intense, of exhilaration more delightful, than when we ascended the opposite bank to the familiar but now strangely thrilling music of "Maryland, my Maryland." As I gained the dry ground, I little thought that in a short time I should recross the river into Virginia, under circumstances far different and far less inspiring.

The passage of the Potomac by the cavalry column occupied about two hours, and was attended with some difficulty to our artillery, as the water in many places rose quite up to the middle of the horses' bodies. Having safely accomplished it, we continued our march toward the little town of Poolesville.[15]

On 4 September Pleasonton, McClellan's cavalry commander in the field, received some bad news from McClellan's headquarters which was likely not too surprising based on what had recently happened at Second Bull Run: "Bayard's and Buford's cavalry are used up, and have difficulty in doing the little service now required of them. They are not available for your service."[16] Most of Pope's cavalry would remain south of the Potomac scouting for any indication of Confederate activity threatening Washington; the majority of Pleasonton's cavalry therefore would be from the Army of the Potomac from the Peninsula. Buford, however, would be selected by McClellan on 10 September to be his administrative chief of cavalry, with Pleasonton commanding in the field. Buford had little to do perhaps other than hurrying units forward to Pleasonton and getting supplies to him as Buford remained at

---

[15] Von Borcke, 130. There are roads leading to Poolesville from both White's Ford and Edward's Ferry. This is perhaps one of von Borcke's least overwrought descriptions for the campaign. Note that he does not mention a pontoon bridge for the artillery.

[16] OR, vol. 51, pt. 1, 789. Note that McClellan reported that on 3 September he had "sent such cavalry as was available to the fords near Poolesville, to watch and impede the enemy in any attempt to cross in that vicinity," OR, vol. 19, pt. 1, 38. This cavalry was the first involved in a losing action at Poolesville as will be seen. Also on 3 September Pleasonton reported from his camp near Fort Albany located south of the Potomac on Columbia Pike that the 8th Illinois reported to Gen. Cox and that he, Pleasonton, ordered the 8th Pennsylvania to him to join 10 companies of the 6th Cavalry already in camp, OR, vol. 19, pt. 2, 172. He also said that his second brigade was complete less four companies of the 1st Cavalry. The 1st Cavalry was not assigned to the Second Brigade but had four companies under Capt. Reno assigned as quartermaster guard. The Second brigade commanded by Col. John F. Farnsworth was composed of the 8th Illinois Cavalry under Maj. William H. Medill, the 3rd Indiana Cavalry led by Maj. George H. Chapman (6 companies present), the 1st Massachusetts Cavalry commanded by Col. Robert Williams (8 companies) and the 8th Pennsylvania Cavalry under Lt. Col. Amos E. Griffiths; Carman, Pierro, 413. The historian of the 1st Massachusetts Cavalry said however that his regiment was not brigaded with the Second until 12 September and up to that time, it had operated directly under Pleasonton, Crowninshield, 73. This 12 September date looks more accurate as the 8th Illinois order book shows that Second Brigade Orders No. 14, 11 September 1862 given at Barnesville assigned the 1st Massachusetts Cavalry to Col. Farnsworth's command, NA, RG 94, Regimental Letter, Order and Miscellaneous Book, vol. 5 of 6, 8th Illinois Cavalry. An earlier order promulgated at Muddy Run by Second Brigade orders No. 13 on 6 September 1862 by McClellan's order, these commands were made up for temporary field service: I. 1st and 6th U.S. Cavalry under command of Capt. William P. Sanders of the 6th U.S.; II. 8th and 12 Pennsylvania Cavalry and 1st Massachusetts commanded by senior officer present; and III. 8th Illinois and 3rd Indiana Cavalry commanded by Col. Farnsworth, ibid. On 4 September, the 8th Illinois Cavalry was ordered to report to Pleasonton, OR, vol. 51, pt. 1, 786. Later on the 4th, Pleasonton was ordered to move all his troopers across the Potomac to Tennallytown in northwest Washington to await orders, ibid, 787. Buford and Bayard were ordered to take Pleasonton's place in scouting east and south of Washington, ibid. Carman wrote that "On the morning of the fourth, Pleasonton (then in camp at Fort Albany, on the Virginia side of the Potomac) was ordered to Falls Church to ascertain, if possible, the intentions of the enemy. With the 6th U.S. Cavalry (Captain William P. Sanders) and two companies of another regiment, he reached the village, where he was joined by the 8th Illinois Cavalry and the 8th Pennsylvania Cavalry. (The two last named skirmished with Munford's cavalry brigade about a mile north of the village.) Cox, commanding the Kanawha Division at Upton Hills, reported early in the morning an accumulation of evidence that the main body of the enemy had gone in the direction of Leesburg and that the movements in his front were feints. Pleasonton came to the same conclusion and, around noon, dispatched his opinion that the Confederates were only making a show of force in his front to conceal their movements on the upper Potomac. Pleasonton was now ordered to withdraw from Falls Church and, with such forage and subsistence as could be carried on his horses, cross the Aqueduct Bridge, proceed to Tennallytown, and await orders. He moved promptly with two regiments, and on reaching Tennallytown received orders to move up the Potomac. Early on the fifth, he was in motion, marching by way of Rockville to Darnestown, reconnoitering all the fords of the river as far north as Seneca Mills....Exploration of the various fords south of Seneca Creek showed them to be unoccupied, and small parties were left to observe them. Pleasonton with his main force took position on Muddy Branch," Carman, Pierro, 81-82. Reorganization of cavalry units into brigades was in flux in these early days of the campaign as was the reorganization of the rest of McClellan's army.

McClellan's headquarters.[17] On 30 August, Buford had been hit below the knee by a spent bullet, and was likely anxious to again confront Robertson's Rebel troopers who had bested him in that cavalry battle at Lewis Ford at Second Bull Run. There is no official record of Buford commanding in the field during the Maryland Campaign, but one of Buford's staff reported that Buford was active in moving cavalry on the flanks under McClellan's direction at South Mountain on 14 September.[18] McClellan, seemingly having learned little about cavalry on the Peninsula, still had much of his cavalry on escort or provost duty with his headquarters or with corps headquarters totaling some twenty-three companies.[19] McClellan was, however, actively involved in getting cavalry units unloaded from ships and moving them around in northern Virginia and in Washington, to ensure that as many regiments of troopers as possible would be available to his headquarters. His experience on the Peninsula did teach him that scouting for the enemy was critical, so he made an effort to gather up as many good units as were available to scout west and north of Washington as the Army of Northern Virginia crossed into Maryland.[20]

---

[17] Some of McClellan's cavalry units assigned to him in the Maryland Campaign were not with him on the Peninsula: the 1st Maine Cavalry had served with Pope while the 1st Massachusetts Cavalry came from the Department of the South but with only eight companies according to Crowninshield, the regiment's historian, 68-69, 255-256, who wrote that the 3rd battalion, companies I, K, L, and M remained in South Carolina—confirmed by Dyer, 3:1237-1238. One company of the 1st Michigan Cavalry serving as escort to the Twelfth Army Corps in Maryland was from Pope's Army of Virginia; 2nd New York Cavalry companies A, B, I, and K were also from the Army of Virginia; the 8th New York came from the Middle Department under Wool and was stationed in Harpers Ferry under Miles; and the 12th Pennsylvania Cavalry came from the Military District of Washington, Dyer, 3:1215, 1237, 1269, 1371, 1376; OR, vol. 19, pt., 2, 242. Note that there is no record that any large or small bodies of Union cavalry crossed the Potomac at any fords from Virginia to Maryland during the Maryland Campaign, but Union cavalry did patrol much of the southern side of the Potomac; Harsh, *Flood*, 84. See Appendix C for cavalry units available to Pleasonton on his journey to Antietam. One trooper from the 3rd Indiana wrote to his parents on 16 September that "Our regiment and the 8th Illinois Cavalry have taken the advance day about all the way from Poolesville. We have fought the enemy more than 1 dozen times. Our regiment has lost about 40 men," Flavius J. Bellamy file, courtesy Indiana State Library.

[18] Myles Keogh, "Etat de Service [service record] of Major Genl Jno. Buford from his promotion to Brig Genl to his death," found in Special Collections, USMA Library; copy supplied to author by Robert Doyle who maintains a website about Myles Keogh. Keogh wrote that all of Buford's staff had been wounded or had their horses shot in the fight on 30 August. He also wrote that Buford performed the same activity at Antietam on the 17th. Note that on 5 September McClellan ordered Buford to report to his headquarters, OR, vol. 51, pt. 1, 797, likely to discuss the Union cavalry command.

[19] Thiele, "Evolution of Cavalry," 90.

[20] See, for example, 29 August, "Have ordered most of Twelfth Pennsylvania Cavalry to report to General Barnard for scouting duty toward Rockville, Poolesville, &c. If you apprehend a raid of cavalry on your side of river I had better send a brigade or two of Sumner's to near Tennallytown, where, with two or three old regiments in Forts Allen and Marcy, they can watch both Chain Bridge and Tennallytown," OR vol. 12, pt. 3, 722; 30 August, "The general commanding directs that you have the First Massachusetts Cavalry, Colonel Williams, landed as fast as possible when it arrives, OR, vol. 51, pt. 1, 770; 1 September, "Order Colonel Williams to send all the cavalry he has disembarked at daybreak [and direct him] to report to the general at his house.... The rest of his command to follow him as fast as they debark," 774; 2 September, "Push the embarkment of Averell's cavalry as rapidly as possible and send them to Georgetown," 777. On 4 September, he ordered Pleasonton to report to him will all available troopers and to leave picketing the Falls Church area in northern Virginia to Bayard as "the duty about to be intrusted [to Pleasonton] is of the utmost importance," 786-787. Buford was also ordered to support Bayard's left and not to move north of the Potomac; however, the 3rd Pennsylvania Cavalry was ordered to service on the Upper Potomac on its north side. It followed behind Pleasonton and did not participate in any fights under Pleasonton as it was assigned to the First Corps. Its historian described the trip through Maryland as being "very different from anything we had previously experienced. Fine farms lay all along the line of march. We passed elegant old mansions, with well-filled barns. The pleasant smiles of the citizens, the displaying of the Stars and Stripes from the houses as we passed, the waving of greetings by lovely women and pretty girls, and gifts of good things to eat, all tended to make our stay among them far different from our first year's sojourn in the enemy's country. Turkeys and chickens, with a profusion of fresh vegetables, took the place of our former scant supplies of salt meat and hard bread—but they did not come to us by way of the Commissary Department. We paid for them, of course—when we had the money. How could we when we did not? Marching as we were, over the hills and through the green fields of Maryland, was being "in God's country," as we were wont to express it," Rawle, 118.

The 6th U.S. Cavalry had arrived from the Peninsula and "was pushed rapidly to the front to retain contact with and determine the strength of the invading army. During the night of 5 September the regiment crossed the Aqueduct bridge and proceeded to Tennallytown, which was reached the next day. The day following [7 September], the march was resumed via Darnestown and Dawsonville, where the regiment halted for a rest. September 8th, the regiment reached Barnesville, and sent scouting parties toward Frederick City and Point of Rocks. Picketing roads and scouting were actively continued until the 10th, when the enemy was encountered at Sugar Loaf Mountain, where Captain William P. Sanders with the regiment, reinforced by two guns, endeavored to dislodge them, but was unsuccessful. The regiment lost one man killed and four wounded in this action.[21]

The actual numbers of troopers available for use for Stuart and Pleasonton in Maryland leading up to the Battle of Antietam are very difficult to estimate. No copies or published accounts of morning reports have been found for the period from the time the armies left Virginia to the returns made after the Battle of Antietam. Only a few official and anecdotal reports give any hint at numbers available on horseback after Stuart crossed the Potomac and after Pleasonton began the chase north of the Potomac. Records which are available usually show that very often various companies from regiments are sent off for duty other than directly confronting the enemy, or that stated numbers vary markedly. Col. Munford and Maj. Henry B. McClellan for example reported that Munford's 2nd Virginia Cavalry had less than 200 troopers on 6 September, while his 12th Virginia had seventy-five. Stuart's report that Munford had 163 men in the 2nd Virginia Cavalry in his attack on Means's and Cole's force at Leesburg on 2 September helps corroborate Maj. McClellan's statement. The 9th Virginia Cavalry had less than 200 troopers fit for duty on 20 September as reported by its historian, R.L.T. Beale.[22] Complete data are available for 2 September for units of the Confederate Army of Northern Virginia and the Union Army of Virginia before any cavalry crossed into Maryland.[23] But these numbers should be used with caution to project troopers available in Maryland, for example, these data show that the strength for the 2nd Virginia Cavalry on 2 September was 408 but four days later on 6 September it had less than 200; the 12th Virginia

---

[21] Carter, *From Yorktown to Santiago*, 57-58. The 8th Illinois Cavalry historian wrote that "September 10th, the Sixth United States Regular Cavalry attempted to take this mountain [Sugarloaf] and capture the signal station, but were unsuccessful. One or two companies of the Eighth Illinois were ordered to support them, but when the rebel artillery opened their fire, the Sixth Cavalry beat a hasty retreat, leaving our men in a very critical and dangerous position. They however extricated themselves without loss, while the Sixth Cavalry lost a number killed and wounded," Hard, 174. Carman wrote that "On the fifth, the 1st New York Cavalry, which had come up from Aquia Creek on the third, marched through Washington and bivouacked near Rockville, reporting early next day to Pleasonton. It was immediately marched to Middlebrook, and four companies were advanced to occupy Clarksburg and picket the line of the Seneca, scouting at the same time the country toward Hyattstown, near which place Hampton's cavalry brigade was encountered. On the same day, a squadron of the 1st U.S. Cavalry moved to Brookeville and scouted to Unity, Goshen, and Cracklintown in the direction of the Baltimore and Ohio Railroad, while the 8th Illinois Cavalry and the 3rd Indiana Cavalry pushed beyond Darnestown, picketing the roads in the direction of Poolesville and the fords of the Potomac," Carman, Pierro, 82. The 5th U.S. Cavalry and the 4th Pennsylvania Cavalry were still on board ship on 5 September and expected to disembark on the 6th, *OR*, vol. 19, pt. 2, 183.

[22] McClellan, *Stuart*, 109, 110; *OR*, vol. 19, pt. 1, 814, 815; 825. These reports which support each other for a regiment's strength are rare for the Maryland Campaign. Looking at the similarity of these numbers, it is likely that Stuart's staff member, McClellan, took his numbers from Stuart's official report. During the Maryland Campaign, he was adjutant for the 3rd Virginia Cavalry. See R.L.T. Beale, *History of the Ninth Virginia Cavalry in the War Between the States* (Richmond, VA: B. F. Johnson Publishing Company, 1899; reprint, Salem, MA: Higginson Book Company, 1998), 43, hereafter cited as Beale, *9th Virginia*. Carman wrote that the 2nd and 12th Virginia Cavalry had about two hundred men each and with Chew's Battery of four guns added totaled less than five hundred men, Carman, Pierro, 86. Reese, *Sealed*, chap. 1, n. 26, found that Munford's 2nd Virginia Cavalry was split up: Company A was with Walker on Loudoun Heights on 10 September; while D was scouting in Virginia until 20 September; Munford had Companies C and E and portions of Company B with him while records do not show the location of Companies G and H; data from NARA, M234, rolls 15-24.

[23] See Appendix C for a discussion of cavalry strengths during the Maryland Campaign.

Cavalry on 2 September is shown with 358 versus seventy-five on the 6th.[24] The penchant for Confederate troopers to straggle may account for some of these reductions as it is likely many decided that they did not wish to cross the Potomac, but perhaps needed a new horse or just needed a rest after months of strenuous campaigning. Others decided that this would be a good time to secure furloughs, further reducing the ranks.[25] Gen. Robert E. Lee was well aware of straggling from his army on its journey into Maryland as he wrote Davis on 13 September: "I have received as yet no official list of the casualties in the late battles, and from the number of absentees from the army, and the vice of straggling, a correct list cannot now be obtained. The army has been so constantly in motion, its attention has been so unremittingly devoted to what was necessary, that little opportunity has been afforded for attention to this subject....Our ranks are very much reduced, I fear from a third to a half of the original numbers."[26] He later wrote to Davis that "A great many men belonging to the army never entered Maryland at all; many returned after getting there, while others who crossed the river kept aloof. The stream has not lessened since crossing the Potomac, though the cavalry has been constantly employed in endeavoring to arrest it."[27] One may question in this last quote who is guarding the guardians as Confederate cavalry is well known for its casual approach to discipline, foraging, and straggling. A Confederate soldier, John N. Opie, who joined the 6th Virginia Cavalry after Antietam, echoed Lee's worries: "after the second battle of Manassas, nearly one-half of his [Lee's] army flanked out, and instead of crossing over into Maryland, this great multitude of stragglers, knowing that Lee would return south by way of the [Shenandoah] Valley, poured in a vast stream over the Blue Ridge Mountains into that beautiful, fertile, and as yet undevastated, country....they had been overmarched and overtasked, living

[24] John Owen Allen, "The Strength of the Union and Confederate Forces at Second Manassas," master's thesis, George Mason University, 1993. For the majority of Union cavalry regiments from the Army of the Potomac arriving from the Peninsula, their strengths in Maryland would not be near those shown during the Seven Days due to the losses of horses due to illness in transit as well as the refitting needed, compare Leon Tenney, "Seven Days in 1862: Numbers in Union and Confederate Armies before Richmond," Master's thesis, George Mason University, 1992. Mark R. Stricker, "Dragoon or Cavalryman, Major General John Buford in the American Civil War," Master's Thesis, U.S. Army Command and General Staff College, 1994, shows 200 for the 2nd Virginia and 125 (for six companies) for the 12th Virginia on 30 August, 139. Carman in an undated note wrote about the 1st North Carolina Cavalry: "James W. Moore (Gen.) Hampton CH. S.C says its regiment was much reduced by long and arduous service and thinks its average was not over 40 to the five squadrons, or an aggregate of about 200," copy of letter courtesy of Thomas Clemens. Carman has a note that Col. T.B. Massie said that after Jackson left the Shenandoah Valley to go east presumably for the Peninsular Campaign, he did not hear from him again until Jackson ordered him to join him west of Martinsburg as Jackson's column headed there and then to Harpers Ferry. Massie said that Jackson had no cavalry with him at the time although Jackson did have cavalry assigned—some of the Black Horse Troop as personal escort. Massie had two companies of the 12th Virginia Cavalry with him and two companies of Maryland cavalry joined him at Harpers Ferry after it fell. Massie in his 14 May 1897 letter to Carman said that he was in command of all the cavalry at Harpers Ferry. Lewis Harmon wrote to Carman that eight companies of the 12th Virginia Cavalry went into Maryland and two companies remained in Virginia (B and I) presumably those with Massie. Carman wrote that Massie apparently estimated the 12th's strength at 450 to 500 men, note from Carman courtesy of Thomas Clemens; given previous numbers by others this strength datum is optimistic. The historian of the Laurel Brigade wrote that when the 2nd Virginia crossed into Maryland, it had 200 and the 12th Virginia had 120; Company B remained behind in the Shenandoah valley when Jackson moved to the Peninsula with the rest of his cavalry, but rejoined Jackson at Harpers Ferry on 14 September and rode to Antietam the next day, William N. McDonald, *A History of the Laurel Brigade Originally the Ashby Cavalry of the Army of Northern Virginia and Chew's Battery*, ed. by Bushrod C. Washington (Baltimore, MD: Sun Job Printing Office, 1907), 90. One must be careful to make the important distinction between "present for duty" numbers versus "carried into battle." The latter number will always be lower than the former and often is much lower.

[25] But it is somewhat unlikely that cavalrymen would be able to use the excuse of not having shoes to avoid entering Maryland as Hubard pointed out, 57-58. See also Beale, *9th Virginia*: "A good many furloughs were granted, and some servants returned to their homes, 37. See Munford's excellent diatribe on Southern methods of horse supply and how that affected cavalry above in Chapter 2, page 26. Note the barefooted cavalryman in the illustration on page 141 in this chapter.

[26] *OR*, vol. 19, pt. 2, 605-606.

[27] Ibid., pt. 1, 143.

upon green corn and apples, many of them barefooted and broken down by the long-continued forced marches and many battles."[28]

Union cavalry, although likely having more troopers on average per regiment than their opponents, also suffered depleted numbers due to jaded horses and tired troopers, but it was unlike the Confederate cavalry in one respect: it had more units assigned as escorts. The Maryland Campaign was similar to the Gettysburg Campaign in that virtually all cavalry units actively engaged between 2 September and 20 September did not take morning musters, making accurate estimates problematical.[29] Given the paucity of data available, only a rough estimate can be made of the average strength of regiments of troopers in the saddle available for duty during the Maryland Campaign: a Union regiment, 350; a Confederate regiment, 250. It must also be noted that some Union regiments did not join Pleasonton until the Battle of Antietam so his reported strength of 4,320 on 17 September was not the number he had available as he left Washington in early September, scouting for Lee north of the Potomac.[30]

Similarly, the 4,500 reported for Stuart on 17 September (including horse artillery), likely includes stragglers which had rejoined from Virginia as well as those with jaded horses or without horses.[31] The

---

[28] John N. Opie, *A Rebel Cavalryman with Lee, Stuart, and Jackson* (Chicago: W. B. Conkey Company, 1899; reprint, Dayton, OH: Morningside Press, 1997), 77.

[29] Crowninshield, 76-77; Thiele, 125, 129-130; John W. Busey and David G. Martin, *Regimental Strengths and Losses at Gettysburg* (Hightstown, NJ: Longstreet House, 2005), 3-5. Dr. Martin is now completing a study of the Antietam Campaign but he estimates that it will not be completed for some years; personal conversation of author with Dr. Martin July 2007.

[30] On 15 October 1862, McClellan reported his estimate for Union cavalry present for duty on 17 September of 4,320, while his morning reports for 20 September show 4,543, *OR*, vol. 19, pt. 1, 67; pt. 2, 336. See for example, McClellan's request on 9 September that "all of Averell's cavalry [be sent forward] as rapidly as possible to these headquarters as fast as it is disembarked," *OR*, vol. 51, pt. 1, 804. Note also Pleasonton's report to McClellan showing that on 6 September he had only eight regiments at his disposal, *OR*, vol. 19, pt. 2, 194; his troopers on hand at that time at 350 per regiment could have numbered only 2,800 at best. Carman wrote that the 4,500 for the Confederate cavalry is based on no official records but adopted from Confederate writers, Carman, Pierro, 465. See Appendix C for a discussion of the actual number of troopers in the saddle available to Pleasonton during the campaign. McClellan also on 9 September reminded superior officers to be with their troops on the march to prevent straggling: "The safety of the country depends upon what this army shall now achieve; it cannot be successful if its soldiers are one-half skulking to the rear," *OR*, vol. 19, pt. 2, 225. As with the Confederate army, infantry straggling was more apparent than that of the cavalry. Appendix C shows Union cavalry total of almost 10,000 and Confederate of 5,228 as available for duty at the end of the Peninsular Campaign for the Union and at the end of the Battle of Second Bull Run for the Confederates. There is no doubt that these numbers are far from the actual number of men in the saddle available for Pleasonton or Stuart to use during the campaign. Carman wrote that "Pleasonton reported on September 6 that Lee's entire army had crossed the Potomac with the evident intention of moving on Washington—Jackson by the Frederick Road and another column by the road running through Poolesville and Darnestown. Late in the day, his information was that Jackson was to lead an advance upon Baltimore by way of Damascus, Clarksburg, and Cooksville, whereupon he extended his right as far as Mechanicsville and called for reinforcements. Pleasonton had the 3rd Indiana Cavalry and the 8th Illinois Cavalry in Darnestown, the 1st New York Cavalry at Middlebrook, and the 1st U.S. Cavalry at Brookeville and Mechanicsville, picketing and scouting the country thoroughly from the Potomac and Seneca Mills to Cooksville, on the Baltimore and Frederick Turnpike. Sumner, with his own corps and that of Williams, was but a short distance in his rear," Carman, Pierro, 82. Pleasonton wrote on 6 September: "When the regiment [1st Massachusetts] arrives at Mechanicsville, I shall have the country thoroughly picketed from the Potomac, at Seneca Mill, to Cooksville, on the Baltimore and Frederick turnpike. My stations are: Darnestown, two regiments; Middlebrook, one regiment; Brookville, one regiment; and the pickets extend to Clarksburg, Seneca Bridge, on the road to Poolesville, and near Edward's Ferry. The enemy crossed yesterday at Spinkle's [Spinks] Ferry and Conrad's Ferry....I have the Potomac, below Edward's Ferry, thoroughly picketed. The regiment to report to me at Rockville I shall post at Brookville, to scout the country and picket on our right and front. At this point I have two batteries and three regiments, doing picket and station duty," *OR*, vol. 19, pt. 2, 194. The 1st New York at Middlebrook had four companies at Clarksburg, ibid. Burnside's regiment, the 3rd Pennsylvania Cavalry, was with him on 8 September as Burnside reported that it was at Unity and would picket Tridelphia and Cooksville scout toward Franklinville and Liberty, *OR*, vol. 19, pt. 2, 213.

[31] Note that Priest shows that at Antietam, Stuart's Division had 1,600 troopers while Pleasonton had 4,320, John M. Priest, *Antietam: The Soldiers' Battle* (Shippensburg, PA: White Mane Publishing Company, 1989), 330, 343, hereafter cited as *Antietam*. The almost 3,000 disparity between Priest's 1,600 Rebel troopers and Carman's 4,500 is difficult to explain. Perhaps

relatively small numbers for each side help to understand why Union cavalry often fell back on infantry support, and why Confederate cavalry did virtually no scouting on the eastern side of Parr's Ridge or around McClellan's right flank. That the Rebel troopers were able to defend so well key road crossings and towns on the Sugarloaf Line, on and near Parr's Ridge, against Pleasonton's troopers, showed that when fighting against roughly equal odds, Stuart's horsemen often prevailed. One of Stuart's staff, William W. Blackford, had this observation about the Union cavalry: "The [Confederate] cavalry covered the rear and engaged in constant and fierce conflicts with the advanced guard of the foe. Their cavalry never, at this time, ventured within our reach without heavy infantry support, so that all we could do was to drive them back a short distance behind their reserves."[32]

Thus it was very unlikely that any Confederate cavalry regiment was even at a quarter of its authorized strength on the skirmish line and very few Union regiments at a third of their full strength on the line. As noted, often a company or squadron was detailed from a regiment temporarily for an assignment, so not all companies in a given regiment on a certain date were available to be sent into action. A full Union regiment had 1,361 officers and men as of 17 July 1862 in its official table of organization, and a Confederate regiment perhaps 800.[33] The Union cavalry, like their infantry and artillery, "always showed an absurd and oftentimes alarming discrepancy between the troopers actually in ranks and the theoretical organization provided by existing law."[34] But in the cavalry, unlike the infantry, those who might be listed "present for duty" might not have mounts available; Thomas L. Livermore, who studied the numbers and losses during the war, routinely discounted cavalry "effectives" at eighty-five percent of those listed as present for duty.[35] But even with few troopers, Confederate horsemen when properly led, performed well; this is best demonstrated by Munford who shouldered a major burden during the campaign on the right of Stuart's screen up to the Battle of Antietam, having only two or three under-strength regiments under his command.[36]

As already noted, losses suffered by the cavalry on both sides are minuscule in comparison with those of the infantry or artillery. Total losses for the Union cavalry for the entire campaign, excluding Harpers Ferry, are 109, and for the Confederate troopers, 148.[37] Overall casualties (excluding for the Union the almost 13,000 Union casualties at Harpers Ferry including 274 cavalry) show 257 casualties for both sides' cavalry which pale in comparison to infantry losses.[38] It is not a surprise that during the

---

1,600 was the actual number in the saddle and available on the field at Antietam versus the number present for duty for the cavalry and horse artillery on 17 September including all Confederate cavalry in the greater Sharpsburg/Shepherdstown area.

[32] Blackford, 142. Blackford did exaggerate or at least over generalize as Yankee cavalry did have success in skirmishes without infantry support such as when Farnsworth routed Munford near Poolesville.

[33] Starr, 464-465: a cavalry regiment "was far more likely to be a mere two or three hundred or even fewer;" OR, ser. 3, vol. 2, 281, Public Act No. 166, sec. 11, which, among other changes, added two troops (two companies) giving a regiment twelve vice ten companies. This is dated 17 July 1862 and War Department General Order no. 91 implementing this is dated 29 July 1862. When the 6th U.S. was created in July 1861 first as the 3rd U.S. Cavalry, it had 12 companies, Clayton R. Newell and Charles R. Shrader, Of Duty Well and Faithfully Done: A History of the Regular Army in the Civil War (Lincoln, NB: University of Nebraska Press, 2011), 248, 250.

[34] Rhodes, History of the Cavalry, 48.

[35] Thomas L. Livermore, Numbers and Losses in the Civil War in America 1861-65 (Boston, MA: n.p., 1900), reprint (Carlisle, PA: John Kallmann, Publishers, 1996) 68-69. As is seen in the Maryland Campaign, his 15 percent discount is far too small.

[36] Harsh, Flood, 231. When Munford's activities before 17 September are compared with those of the other two of Stuart's brigade commanders, Fitzhugh Lee and Hampton, Munford fought more often with fewer troopers and unless overwhelmed by superior forces did very well. However, one might argue that he did stumble as a new commander on 8 September near Barnesville and at Crampton's Gap on 14 September.

[37] Carman, Pierro, 469, 474; OR, vol. 19, pt. 1, 34-36.

[38] Harsh, Shallows, 202, 223. Thomason, "every statement on Southern numbers is debatable. The staff work, especially the keeping of records, lapsed altogether in many formations, and was inadequate in all...There are no cavalry returns from Stuart," 289-90. He opines that Stuart had 5,000 cavalry in ten regiments but he said that "I think that is high," 290: I agree.

Civil War cavalry losses are less severe in a given battle or campaign in which infantry plays the major role. In this campaign, there were no massed cavalry on cavalry or cavalry on infantry assaults, nor did large numbers of dismounted cavalry get involved during the severe fighting during the Battle of Antietam on 17 September. And with the reduced numbers of cavalry scattered about until Antietam, heavy casualties were less likely. Too, at this stage of the war, there were still some chivalric aspects to cavalry actions unlike later in the war when arguably more vicious "black flag" fighting occurred. Paroles were generally quickly given when cavalry were captured as the depleted units of the captors could not afford to detail men to escort prisoners so unless infantry were handy or the troopers were near a Confederate camp, they were often released on parole. The notable incidents when Maryland citizens aided Union troopers by firing at Rebel horsemen in Frederick, Middletown or Boonsboro, resulted in no reported casualties; in Poolesville when citizens obstructed Yankee cavalry, there were losses, but none reported as a result of residents shooting at the Unionists. The greatest numbers of casualties for the cavalry were from captured or missing troopers.

Stuart, on 5 September, joined Generals Lee, Longstreet and possibly Jackson at Lee's headquarters in Leesburg to get final instructions for the Potomac crossing. While Stuart met with his commander at the home of Henry T. Harrison, Harrison Hall, von Borcke and other staff officers had an early dinner across the street with an elderly gentleman, and then about 2 P.M. took to horse to begin crossing the Potomac. Stuart screened the rear of Jackson's column, the cavalry with Jackson was sufficient to brush away any militia or home guards north of the river. Stuart was unable to get through the jams at the fords to do immediate screening on Jackson's right on the northern side of the Potomac, but Stuart did well screening and demonstrating on the Virginia side, even though not fooling the Union command. Stuart crossed the Potomac after Jackson on the afternoon of the 5th with Hampton's Brigade, as Fitzhugh Lee's Brigade crossed at Edward's Ferry, about seven miles further downstream to avoid the jam at White's Ford, and to screen closer to Washington.[39]

On 5 September, much to Stuart's relief, Brig. Gen. Beverly Robertson was relieved of command of his brigade and sent to the Department of North Carolina to organize and instruct cavalry; Col. Munford was placed in command.[40] Robertson, not a friend of Stuart, Jackson, or Gen. Lee, had performed poorly under Jackson at the Battle of Cedar Mountain on 9 August 1862, and with mixed results later under Stuart. Robertson was a veteran soldier, having served in the Old Army in the 2nd Dragoons, but performed poorly in combat. He was however, seen as a good administrator, trainer and disciplinarian. The same order which reassigned Robertson, assigned Cobb's Legion to Stuart from A.P. Hill's command, to be replaced by a squadron from the 12th Virginia Cavalry, and a squadron assigned to D.H. Hill, was also returned to Stuart. Lee, as well as Johnston, saw the value of consolidating his cavalry here especially as Lee anticipated important work for the cavalry in Maryland. While nothing has been found to indicate that Stuart and Jackson met that night to discuss the cavalry's role, face-to-face discussions with Gen. Lee in Leesburg, as well as later again with Jackson, were likely.[41] Jackson did have the Black

[39] Von Borcke, 128-129. Hampton may also have had some troopers cross at Conrad's Ferry to avoid the jam at White's Ford. D. Scott Hartwig, *To Antietam Creek: The Maryland Campaign of September 1862* (Baltimore, MD: The Johns Hopkins Univ. Press, 2012), 102-103.

[40] McClellan, *Stuart*, 109; *OR*, vol. 19, pt. 2, 595. Jeb Stuart wrote to his wife on 12 September commenting on Robertson's transfer: "'Joy's mine.' My command is now okay,'" Wert, *Cavalryman of the Lost Cause*, 141. Gen. Lee's order likely resulted from the Leesburg conference attended by Stuart and Jackson, ibid., 140.

[41] Harsh, *Flood*, 71-72, 88-91. Robert K. Krick, *9th Virginia Cavalry* (Lynchburg, VA: H.E. Howard, Inc., 1982), has the 9th Virginia Cavalry crossing at 3 P.M. on 5 September at Edward's Ferry, 9; von Borcke, 128-129. Perhaps Lee and Stuart also discussed the need for cavalry screening and decided that it was not critical to dedicate large numbers of Stuart's troopers to that task given the tactical realities of little Union resistance plus Jackson's having some cavalry with him as only scouting was needed.

Horse Troop of the 4th Virginia Cavalry, along with Capt. Lige White leading a company of scouts. A company of cavalry under command of Capt. Robert Randolph moved in advance and scouted on Jackson's right, and also kept in touch with Stuart's men. White, in a 2 June 1896 letter to Carman, wrote that the night before crossing the Potomac, Jackson's headquarters was at Big Spring two miles northeast of Leesburg. Jackson asked White to lead the next day and he did so crossing at White's Ford, ahead of Jackson, and camped close to Three Springs near Frederick that night. Later that night, Jackson ordered White to join him in a ride back the way they had marched that day, almost returning to the Potomac, and then both returned to camp. During this ride, Jackson never spoke a word.[42]

As information piled up in Washington showing Gen. Lee's army moving north of the Potomac, Union cavalry was quickly sent along the Maryland side of the river to scout for Confederate penetrations. Pleasonton was cautious however, perhaps even more so after the 1st Massachusetts Cavalry's encounter with Rebel cavalry at Poolesville. Late on 2 September, McClellan ordered the 1st Massachusetts Cavalry to "watch all the fords on the Potomac between Great Falls and Harper's Ferry….Not a moment must be lost in starting off your command, and it must go fast." Given the number of fords involved versus the troopers available to the regiment, this was a difficult task unless only a few men were assigned to picket each ford. Coordination with Wool and Miles would have helped as there were already Union troops located along the B&O. Fortunately, food and forage for two days was also ordered, as 24 hours later their orders were elaborated that it must move without cooking rations, and that it is charged with watching and reporting on the enemy but not engaging him.[43] Several fords could have concerned the Union high command between Great Falls and Harpers Ferry. There are at least five fords downriver from the one at Edward's Ferry which might have been used.[44] In

---

[42] Carman, Pierro, 46; copy of White's letter courtesy Thomas Clemens. Jackson had at least one other similar ride after Cedar Mountain the month before on 19/20 August when he along with Sandie Pendleton and a cavalry squad rode all night meandering along unknown paths, ending up on Clark's Mountain, the Confederate signal station, Robertson, 543; Vandiver, 347-348. Jackson ordered Randolph's troopers to cut the telegraph at Monocacy Junction and capture the operator. They did so scaring away Co. G, 1st Maryland Home Brigade, Hartwig, *To Antietam Creek*, 102.

[43] *OR*, vol. 51, pt. 1, 781, 783. Carman wrote that "The movement of the Union army northward from Washington was initiated by the 1st Massachusetts Cavalry. This regiment had been in service in South Carolina and disembarked from steamers at Alexandria on September 2. Early that day Pope telegraphed Halleck from Fairfax Court House and said that it would be well for him to look out for his communications, as 'the enemy from the beginning has been throwing his rear toward the north, and every movement shows that he means to make trouble in Maryland,' whereupon orders were given that this Massachusetts regiment should move up the Potomac, watching all the fords between Great Falls and Harper's Ferry. Not a moment was to be lost in the execution of the order, as it was probable that the enemy might attempt to cross that night. Such was the confusion at Alexandria that the officers of the regiment could not be found on the second and the orders were repeated on the third, with the advice that it was not expected the regiment would engage the enemy but simply watch carefully his operations and give timely notice should he appear on the Potomac above Great Falls. Three times was this order repeated on the third, but not until the morning of the fourth did the regiment cross the Potomac by the Aqueduct Bridge and push out beyond Tennallytown, where it was halted for orders," Carman, Pierro, 81.

[44] "Conn's Island Ford (Conn's Ford, Coon's Ford, Great Falls Ford) passed over the head of Conn's Island just above Great Falls, short of C&O Canal mile marker 15. Because of its proximity to the defenses of Washington, the Confederates did not use it, but the Federals carefully watched and patrolled the vicinity throughout the war….Muddy Branch Ford named after Muddy Branch, a small tributary of the Potomac, enters the river at about mile marker 20 on the canal. Seneca Ford (Rowser's Ford, Rouse's Ford) was located below the mouth of Seneca Creek, just beyond Dam Number 2, at Lock 23, at about mile marker 22." This was the one used by Stuart during his crossing of the Potomac as he headed north during the Gettysburg Campaign. Young's Island Ford (Young's Ford, Lee's Island, Seldon Island) was located between mile markers 28 and 29, crossed over Young's Island, now Seldon Island, located in the river near the Virginia shore. As Maj. Gen. Joseph Hooker's army prepared to pursue Lee to the Potomac in 1863, he ordered Maj. Gen. Henry W. Slocum to examine the most practical fords. On 24 June 1863 Slocum reported, "'I have had all the fords within 10 miles of Edward's Ferry examined. Young's Island Ford, three miles below Edward's Ferry, is the best one, and can be crossed with trains.'" This ford was not used by large armies, however, and the Confederates likely ignored it because it was heavily picketed and too close to the defenses of Washington. Inadequate roads to and from the ford may also have contributed to its being relatively overlooked by all but cavalry." Timothy R. Snyder,

September 1862, the Potomac was at its usual low stage, although von Borcke wrote that at some points at White's Ford, the water was halfway up the horses' bodies.[45]

White's Ford was described by Brig. Gen. Jubal A. Early as less than ideal: "On the 5th [of September 1862] we resumed the march and crossed the Potomac at White's Ford, about seven miles above Leesburg, into Maryland. This ford was an obscure one on the road through the farm of Captain Elijah White, and the banks of the river had to be dug down so that our wagons and artillery might cross. On the Maryland side of the river the Chesapeake & Ohio Canal runs along the bank, and the canal had to be bridged over a lock to enable our wagons to pass, as they could not get through the culvert where the road ran." Crossing the canal, especially when watered, was not easy, so draining the canal in the vicinity of active operations was a help and actively done during the Maryland Campaign by the Confederates. Even when drained and the mud dried, crossing the six plus-foot deep canal prism could not be done without bridging, crossing at locks, using canal boats, or utilizing culverts under it. The canal was 50 to 60 feet wide at the towpath level and 30 to 40 feet at the bottom with a minimum depth of six feet.[46]

Confederate horse artillery during their crossing enjoyed what refreshments they could find, as one gunner noted that "'At a point of the B&O Railroad, a lot of whiskey and salt fish fell into our hands. Rubber buckets and camp kettles were filled, and hung onto the gun carriages, and the contents sloshed out as we proceeded. The men made a grotesque appearance as they munched the fish and washed it down with the beverage, and some of them imbibing too freely were in a hilarious mood, and felt able to annihilate the enemy at once.'"[47]

The 1st Massachusetts Cavalry took a few days getting ready for its scouting mission as some of its units were still on boats and its officers were not available. The journey of the 1st Massachusetts from

---

"Securing the Potomac: Colonel Charles P. Stone and the Rockville Expedition, June-July 1861," in *Catoctin History*, issue no. 11, 2009, 15; Snyder, Manuscript, 6-8, describes the five fords below the one at Edward's Ferry.

[45] Von Borcke, 130.

[46] Early, 134; George B. Davis, "The Antietam Campaign," *Papers of the Military Historical Society of Massachusetts, Campaigns in Virginia, Maryland, and Pennsylvania, 1862-1863*, vol. III, 27-28; Lee D. Barron, *The Chesapeake & Ohio Canal: "As It Is and As It Was,"* (Sharpsburg, MD: Graphics Design Press, 1973), chapter 1. White's Ford was used more by Confederates during the war than Union troops. Rebel cavalry would often cross one way by White's Ford or Conrad's Ferry and return by the other ford to confuse Union pursuers, Charles T. Jacobs, *Civil War Guide to Montgomery County, Maryland* (Rockville, MD: The Montgomery County Historical Society, 1996), 60. Historian Timothy R. Snyder wrote the following succinctly describing a desirable Civil War ford: All nineteenth century river fords were not the same. Those that served local citizens may not have been sufficient to pass an army. In addition, a ford that permitted the passage of cavalry may not have been sufficient to pass infantry…[and] a ford that allowed the passage of infantry may not have been sufficient to pass artillery and wagon trains. The conditions of fords also varied greatly during a year. During high water, typically in the spring, a ford that previously permitted infantry to cross might only allow cavalry to pass. In addition, high water might carry obstructions to a ford that was previously passable. During periods of low water the river was usually fordable in dozens of additional locations….The ideal river ford, sufficient to allow passage of all three branches of the army and wagon trains, required three primary features: Low water was the obvious feature; no more than three feet is ideal since the water would not extend to the men's waists and therefore would not require the soldiers to take special precautions to prevent their cartridge boxes from getting wet. The second important characteristic of a ford was a good river bottom over which to cross. An ideal ford had a bedrock bottom with a minimum of silt over it. This prevented wagons from getting mired in the mud and the men from getting their shoes pulled off by the thick muck….The bottom of a good ford was also free of pits and obstructions, such as sink holes, crevices, large rocks, fallen trees or sunken boats that could trip up men and horses and snag passing wagons. The third significant feature of a good ford was the approaches. An otherwise fine ford was of little value if an army could get into the river, but only with great difficulty get out of it. This condition not only slowed the passage of the army, but put it at risk of attack in a vulnerable position. A gentle grade to and from a ford was especially important for artillery and wagon trains since their weight made it difficult for mules and horses to pull them up a steep and slippery bank. Snyder, Manuscript, 4. The author has forded White's Ford as well as Boteler's Ford and agrees with Mr. Snyder adding that heavy river weed can also be a problem as it can tangle feet and hide the bottom thus concealing obstacles.

[47] Robert H. Moore, II, in *The 1st and 2nd Stuart Horse Artillery* (Lynchburg, VA: H.E. Howard, Inc., 1985), 32.

South Carolina to Maryland was eventful. Only eight companies were sent north and four of those spent 17 days on board ship in hot weather so the horses suffered immensely. The remaining four companies joined on 2 September but horses and men were not prepared, and were given no time to become so. Most horses were unshod, while a few had shoes only for the forefeet, so travelling on the macadamized Maryland roads quickly made them footsore and crippled. The men had only light clothing and no tents as their baggage was not available. They were armed with pistols and sabers with only 10 men in each company given Sharp's carbines. Upon arriving in Virginia, those without carbines were issued the poorly performing Smith carbine.[48] McClellan sent repeated requests on 2 and 3 September for the regiment to take the field so, the regiment started out with most of its horses still unshod. A detachment of 100 of these Bay State troopers rode out of Tennallytown in northwest Washington and ran into trouble with Brig. Gen. Fitzhugh Lee's Brigade of cavalry, led by the 5th Virginia Cavalry at Poolesville, Maryland, on 5 September. Earlier that day, Lee's Brigade, after breakfasting on roasted corn and apples, had crossed at Edward's Ferry "gaily singing 'My Maryland' – 'My Maryland'" while Hampton's Brigade crossed the Potomac at White's Ford.[49] Stuart left Robertson's Brigade behind as rear guard. White's Ford is about three river miles upstream from today's White's Ferry, but about six road miles from it.[50]

---

[48] Joseph G. Bilby, *Civil War Firearms: Their Historical Background, Tactical Use and Modern Collecting and Shooting* (Conshohocken, PA: Combined Books, Inc., 1996), 139.

[49] Hard, 169-171; Carter, *Sabres, Saddles, and Spurs*, 12. Trout, *Thunder*, has Hampton crossing at Conrad's Ferry, and Fitz Lee at White's Ford, but with both brigades' goal as Poolesville, 89. R. Channing Price, aid-de-camp to Jeb Stuart, wrote that he was told that some Confederate cavalry had crossed at Conrad's Ferry, copy of page from Price's Papers courtesy Harpers Ferry Research Library. Some accounts relate crossing the Potomac near the site of the Ball's Bluff battle; the ford closest to that place is Conrad's Ferry and the next closest is Edward's Ferry, Brooks, *Stories of the Confederacy*, 78. Gill, a member of the 2nd Virginia Cavalry, and a Marylander familiar with the area wrote that "We crossed the river at Edward's Ferry, marching in the direction of Frederick City," adding that he "was now well mounted and well equipped with Yankee sabre, Yankee saddle, Yankee boots and Yankee horse, ready for the Maryland campaign of 1862," 75. Harsh wrote that Stuart and Lee's Brigade crossed at White's Ford, but given the congestion there it is likely that some of Lee's troopers crossed at Edward's Ferry as well as Conrad's Ferry, which was closer to White's Ford, 89. Beale, the historian of the 9th Virginia Cavalry, wrote that his regiment brought up the rear while the 5th Virginia was in the van as they crossed at Edward's Ferry, Beale, *9th Virginia* 37. The 4th Virginia was split when some crossed near Leesburg probably at Conrad's Ferry while Co. H crossed further upriver at White's Ford with Jackson, Kenneth L. Stiles, *4th Virginia Cavalry* (Lynchburg, VA: H.E. Howard, Inc., 1985), 19. But see Lewis Marshall Helm, *Black Horse Cavalry: Defend Our Beloved Country* (Falls Church, VA: Higher Education Publications, 2004), who wrote that the Black Horse Troop, Co. H, crossed at Edward's Ferry, screening Jackson, 121. It is possible that the troop was split and crossed at both fords but if it escorted Jackson, it must have crossed at White's Ford. Thomason wrote that Stuart's division "crosses in turn, at Edward's Ferry and White's Ford" but left out Conrad's Ferry, 261. Some wrote that Hampton's Brigade crossed at Conrad's Ferry, Chris J. Hartley, *Stuart's Tarheels: James B. Gordon and His North Carolina Cavalry* (Baltimore, MD: Butternut and Blue, 1996), 124. Note that Crowninshield wrote that Fitzhugh Lee had crossed at Edward's Ferry, 71. The 1st Massachusetts had not wasted its time in South Carolina rather engaging in regular drills and learning army discipline: "The horses developed wonderfully, and the men, constantly subject to a most rigid discipline, got to know the officers, and the officers the men. Drilling every day shook the whole together. The result was a very effective body of cavalry, that would have disgraced no regular army," Crowninshield, 63. These eight companies would do excellent service for McClellan in Maryland despite their early stumble in Poolesville. Hartwig writes that Gen. Lee ordered Stuart (Hampton and Fitz Lee) to cross at Edward's Ferry, Hartwig, *To Antietam Creek*, 103.

[50] The Potomac was fordable at White's Ferry during the Civil War when it was named Conrad's Ferry but usually only by cavalry as it was a deep area even at low water. White's Ford is about seven miles from Leesburg and about three and one-half miles downstream from the Monocacy River. Edward's Ferry is about seven miles downstream of White's Ford and about four miles southwest of Poolesville, Maryland. White's Ford is named after the farmer which owned the land on the Potomac River on which the ford is located on the Virginia side. Capt. Elijah White was the owner at the time and a well-known Confederate cavalry leader and partisan ranger. When he was attached to Jackson's command after Second Bull Run, he advised that his farm ford could be used to cross the Potomac. Its high banks did need some work to allow the passage of wagons, however. The Union army rarely used the ford as it was deemed too rocky for heavy wagons. White's Ford was also used by Stuart to return after his famous Second Ride Around McClellan in October 1862 and by Jubal Early during his return from his expedition to Washington, D.C., in 1864. Fords were of concern to both Union and Confederate high commands since there were no bridges

About dusk on Friday 5 September, the Bay State horsemen rode through the streets of Poolesville toward the Potomac, looking for any signs of Confederate activity, not knowing that many in the town harbored strong southern sympathies, and had done so due to close association with Loudoun County to the south across the Potomac. After they passed through the tiny town, some Rebel sympathizers placed obstacles such as stones, furniture and other debris in the road behind the Unionists. Soon, routed by superior numbers from Fitzhugh Lee's 3rd and 5th Virginia Cavalry, some dismounted, the retreating Union troopers raced back through town with their horses falling over the obstacles. Thanks to the help of secesh townsfolk, the commander of the Union troopers, Capt. Samuel E. Chamberlain, and thirty men, were captured, with some nine wounded. The Confederates lost three killed and four wounded in this first cavalry fight of the Maryland Campaign, a clear Confederate victory, as the outnumbered Union men had no chance especially as their flight was hindered by Poolesville's residents. After this affray, Fitzhugh Lee's Brigade, followed by Hampton's, bivouacked about two miles east of Poolesville for the night.[51]

Flavius J. Bellamy, an enlisted trooper in Company A of the 3rd Indiana Cavalry, wrote that the 1st Massachusetts men were "immediately paroled....They [Confederate captors] told them that all who refused to take a parole would be instantly shot and I guess their threat was serious as they do not wish to be bothered with prisoners."[52]

---

across the Potomac River upriver from the Chain Bridge at Washington, D.C. Confederate Col. Thomas J. Jackson had the bridges burned at Shepherdstown, Point of Rocks, Berlin, and Harpers Ferry on 9 June 1861 during the Rebel retreat back into Virginia. Additionally, Brig. Gen. Joseph E. Johnston had ordered his engineers "to demolish the seventeen railroad bridges from Point of Rocks, a station ten miles south of the town (Harpers Ferry), to Martinsburg, Virginia, fifteen miles north of Harpers Ferry, Mike High, *The C&O Canal Companion* (Baltimore, MD: The Johns Hopkins University Press, 1997), 138-144. See also Beale, *9th Virginia*, 37; Priest, *Before Antietam*, 7; *OR*, vol. 2, 806; Jeffrey N. Lash, "Joseph E. Johnston and the Virginia Railways, 1861-62," *Civil War History*, vol. 35, no. 1, March 1989, 8; Harsh, *Flood*, 89.

[51] Harsh, *Flood*, 98. Crowninshield, 71-72. *OR*, vol. 19, pt. 2, 186; Pleasonton's report records Capt. Chamberlain missing and 21 men captured. William R. Carter of the 3rd Virginia Cavalry wrote that the brigade succeeded in "capturing some thirty four prisoners and several horses & killed several. Parts of the 3rd & 5th Regiments were engaged," 12. It is not clear where in Poolesville the running battle took place as roads from both Conrad's Ferry and Edward's Ferry enter the town. These unfriendly civilians were not the norm for the Union troops as the large majority of civilians in Frederick and Washington counties were pro-Union, Harsh, *Flood*, 90-91. Poolesville was in Montgomery County, east of Frederick County, and had a higher percentage of slave owners. In the 1860 presidential election, only five percent of Montgomery County voters cast their ballots for Lincoln and even in the 1864 election, only twenty five percent voted for Lincoln and seventy five percent for McClellan, Jacobs, 2, 39. In Washington County to the west of Frederick County, fewer than 100 electors cast their votes for Lincoln in 1860 and only one in the Sharpsburg District, Susan W. Trail, "Remembering Antietam: Commemoration and Preservation of a Civil War Battlefield," PhD dissertation, University of Maryland, 2005, 33. In 1864, Maryland abolished slavery with the vote for the new constitution 2,441 in favor to 985 opposed, 68. Further east and south in Maryland, Southern sentiment was most pronounced. "The six counties located below Baltimore comprised 36 percent of the state's slaveholders....slaves constituted 44 percent of the population," William A. Blaire, "Maryland, Our Maryland," in *The Antietam Campaign*. Western Maryland settled with many Germans who "had little need for slaves on their farms because agricultural production focused primarily on grain and corn....Slaves as property or as a workforce were a minor factor in western Maryland," Kevin Conley Ruffner, *Maryland's Blue and Gray: A Border State's Union and Confederate Junior Officer Corps* (Baton Rouge, LA: Louisiana State University Press, 1997), 22. A union infantry officer, Capt. Francis Adams Donaldson, in *Inside the Army of the Potomac: The Civil War Experience of Captain Francis Adams Donaldson* (Mechanicsburg, PA: Stackpole Books, 1998), wrote that in Rockville, Maryland, in Montgomery County, "There is not much Union sentiment in this county, I fear...the women in such little towns habitually stand in their doors and scowl at us as we pass by," 118. See also Beale, *9th Virginia*, 37, saying that after staying the night, a squadron of the 9th Virginia Cavalry was left at Beallsville on picket duty. Richard Henry Watkins in a 7 September 1862 letter wrote that he and his troopers received a cordial reception as the town folk "receive us kindly, many joyfully," ANBL Files, folder with Virginia Cavalry, Lee's Brigade. Beallsville was also known as Monocacy Church.

[52] Copy of Flavius J. Bellamy letter 8 September 1862 from Flavius Bellamy file, courtesy of the Indiana State Library. He also wrote that only three cavalry regiments were available and that the population thronged to see the masses of men and "to carry them loads of the choicest delicacies" but wrote that "it wouldn't be long until they want it out again."

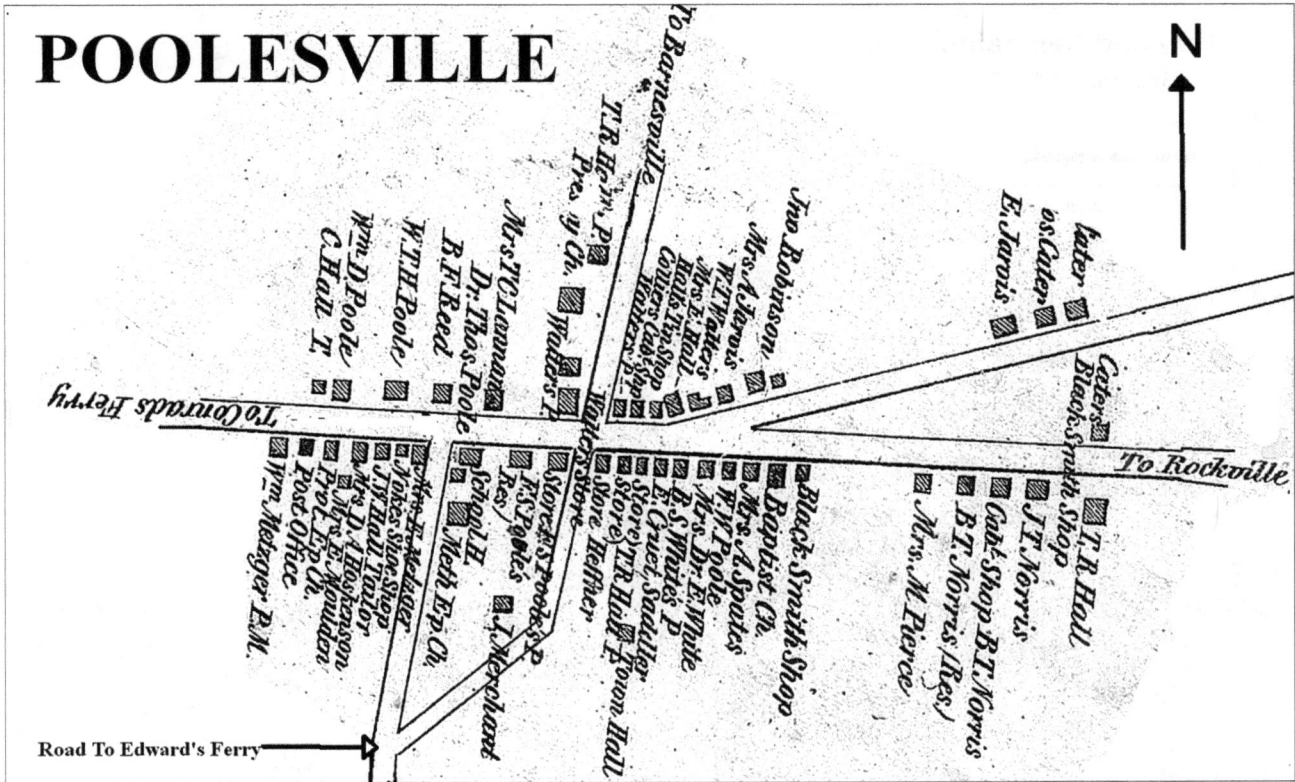

Location of first cavalry action in Maryland between the 1st Massachusetts Cavalry and elements of the 3rd and 5th Virginia Cavalry. The Unionists were probably chased from the bottom where the road leads in from Edward's Ferry. Obstacles were placed on Edward's Ferry Road or more likely on Main Street before the road splits. Edward's Ferry Road leading south from Poolesville is named West Willard Road which leads into Westerly Road then to Edward's Ferry Road. Detail from Martenet and Bond's map of Montgomery County, Maryland 1865. Courtesy LOC.

Map of Maryland Campaign to 15 September 1862 showing general troop movements. Map courtesy of Hal Jespersen from Wikipedia.

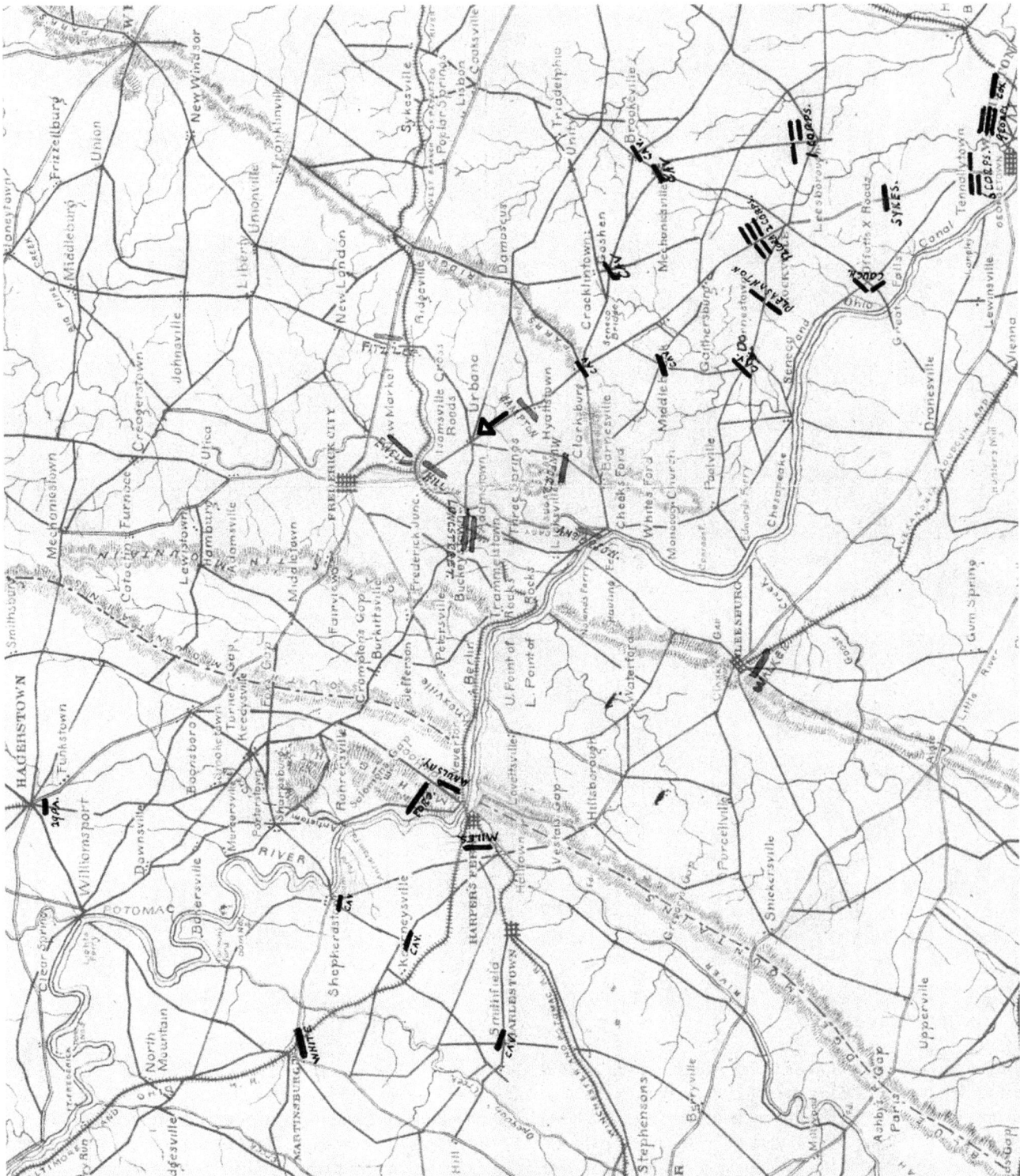

Situation map night of 6 September. Jackson and Stuart enter Maryland while Union cavalry continue probing north and west. Stuart sets up his headquarters at Urbana at the arrow which was near the center of his screening line. Union units shown in black and Confederate in gray. Remaining at Leesburg on the Virginia side is Robertson's Brigade of Stuart's Cavalry now under Col. Thomas Munford providing the rear guard for the army. On this day, McClellan reported his disposition as follows: First and Ninth Corps at Leesboro, the Second and Twelfth Corps at Rockville, the Sixth Corps at Tenallytown, Couch's division at Offut's Cross Roads, and Sykes's division at Tenallytown, *Report on the Organization and Campaigns of the Army of the Potomac*, 349. This is the first of a series of map with troop position symbols believed to have been added by hand to the photocopy War Department base maps by Gen. Ezra A. Carman. Drawn by H.W. Mattern. Courtesy LOC.

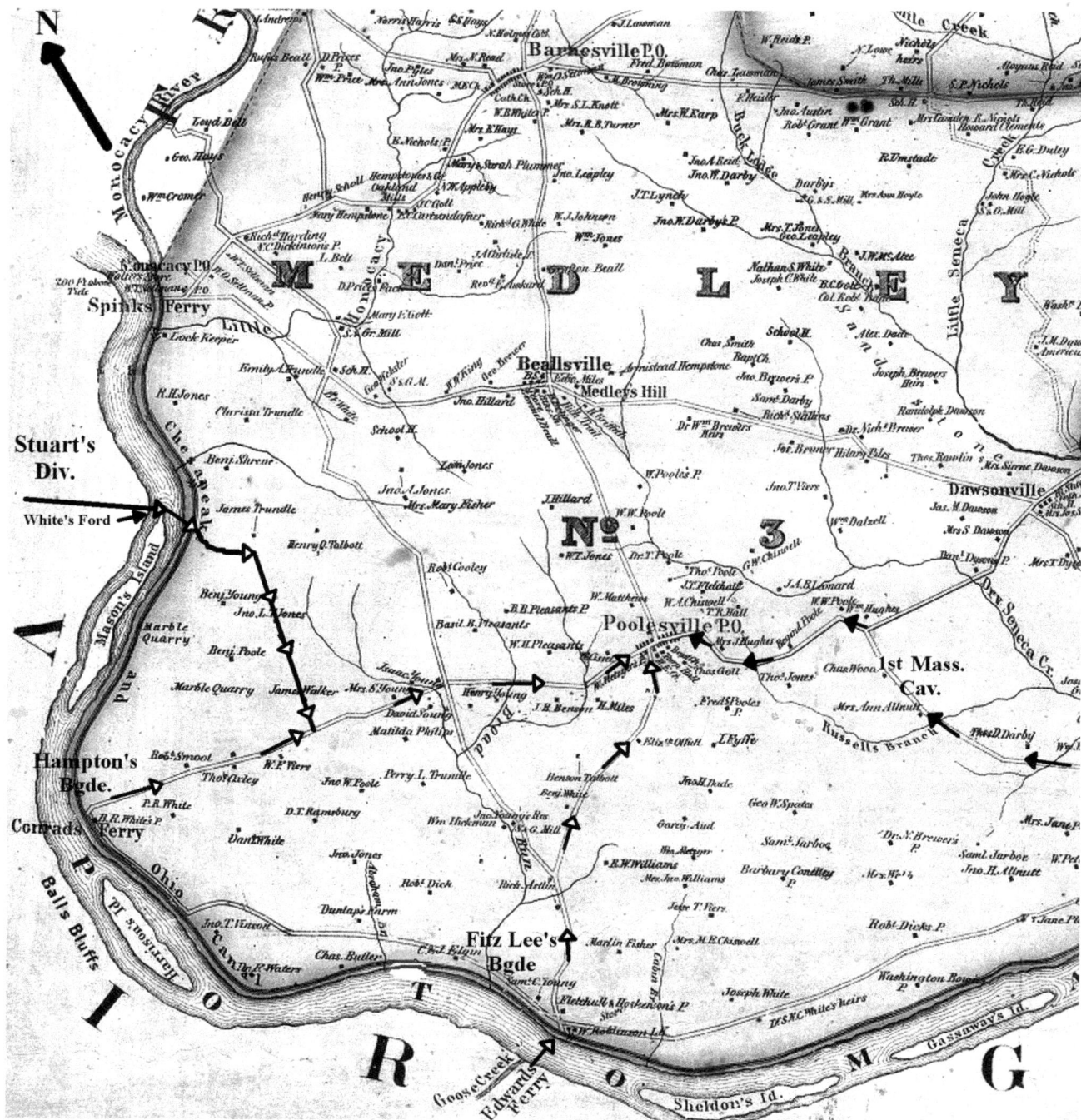

Map shows the route of Lee's Cavalry Brigade from Edward's Ferry at the center bottom to Poolesville. White's Ford is in the center left. Conrad's Ferry is modern-day White's Ferry. Stuart's aide, von Borcke, wrote that the island there "offered us a momentary resting-place half-way in our passage of the river," 130. The ford was about three miles downstream of the mouth of the Monocacy River. Fords were often found near the mouths of tributaries of rivers as they carried sediment which was deposited downstream from the mouths. See n. 49 above for more information about which fords Stuart's troopers used. Note Beallsville and Barnesville north of Poolesville which will be locations of subsequent actions. Detail from Martenet and Bond's map of Montgomery County, Maryland, 1865. Courtesy LOC.

On 6 September, Hampton took the lead heading for Frederick, Maryland, while Fitzhugh Lee's 5th Virginia Cavalry remained behind at Poolesville, paroling the troopers from the 1st Massachusetts Cavalry; some of the 5th Virginia then stayed near Poolesville but it is not stated whether they were ordered to do so acting as videttes, or merely enjoying the hospitality of the numerous southern sympathizers. A squadron of the 9th Virginia Cavalry, Companies A and I under command of Capt. Thomas C. Waller, was left at Barnesville on the 7th after buying shoes the previous day in Poolesville, the sellers willingly accepting Confederate currency. Other Confederate troopers also took advantage of the local merchants' willingness to accept Confederate script as William R. Carter of the 3rd Virginia Cavalry wrote that "The men supplied themselves here with boots, gloves, & hats at very low prices, the merchant taking confederate money without any hesitation."[53] A newspaper report said that four potential recruits for Stuart's cavalry were turned down by him because "The Rebels only sought riders who brought saddles, bridles and spurs....Stuart suggested that they join a Confederate infantry regiment or return to their homes." Union pickets arrested them on their way home.[54] Horses may also have been bought or requisitioned as Pelham requested and received 28 horses to make good his recent losses at Manassas.[55] The remainder of the 9th Virginia Cavalry was further north at New Market on the National Pike.[56] Fitzhugh Lee, after he occupied New Market on the B&O Railroad, threw out scouts toward Ridgeville on Parr's Ridge. Hampton occupied Hyattstown with his forward picket posts at Damascus and Clarksburg also on Parr's Ridge. Munford's three regiments held Stuart's right at Sugarloaf Mountain and Poolesville thus covering the front from the mouth of the Monocacy River on the right to the B&O Railroad on the left. The rest of Gen. Lee's army was behind the Monocacy River, well-shielded by Stuart's cavalry.[57] Federal cavalry was probing north and west: on the 6th, the 1st New York Cavalry moved to Middleburg, and sent four companies to occupy Clarksburg, and scout the countryside to Hyattstown. The 1st U.S. Cavalry rode to Brookville, to scout in the direction of the B&O Railroad. The 8th Illinois and 3rd Indiana Cavalry moved also on the 6th in advance of Darnestown, picketing the roads in the direction of Poolesville and the Potomac fords.[58]

Also on 6 September, Stuart showed how those who did not agree with him or perhaps disliked his showy demeanor, affected his command skills, when he and Capt. Elijah Viers White had a confrontation. White commanded a company of Virginia Cavalry, had scouted for Jackson in Virginia, served under Ashby, and could have done good service in Maryland, but for this clash. Stuart ordered White to return to Virginia with his company, but White "protested, saying that he was a Marylander by birth and had fought as hard as any man for the privilege of fighting once upon the soil of his native State." Seemingly wanting to pick a fight with White, Stuart began the quarrel by twisting White's statement that he had done as much as any man for the South. The quarrel continued, so finally Stuart directly ordered White to go back to Virginia and watch for Yankees flanking through Dranesville or Fairfax Courthouse from Washington. White refused, saying that he wanted to talk with Gen. Lee. Stuart said that he would take him to the army commander so off they went. Stuart went into Lee's tent to talk with him first alone, and White waited outside when Jackson, who had been inside with Lee,

[53] Beale, *9th Virginia*, 37. Carter, *Sabres, Saddles, and Spurs*, 12; Krick, *9th Virginia Cavalry*, 9.
[54] Paul and Rita Gordon, *Never the Like Again* (Frederick, MD: M&B Printing Inc.), 1995, 129.
[55] Robert Moore, 32. Union troopers also found horses to add to the picket rope as described by Crowninshield of the 1st Massachusetts Cavalry: "While in Maryland, a new horse would occasionally appear, and frequently the owner, not long after, in search of a lost animal. The captain would say, 'Come, look over the picket rope; see if you can find your horse here.' Somehow they never could," Crowninshield, 292. The Bay State horsemen disguised horses: "With a pair of scissors, a very nice imitation of a brand would be made to appear on the shoulder or hip. A little hair dye would remove all white marks, and the same scissors would so change mane and tail as to make the animal unrecognizable. A piece of horse hair drawn about the coronet [just above the horse's hoof] would produce an immediate and unaccountable lameness....Almost any change in appearance or gait could be produced at short notice by the cunning trooper," ibid., 291.
[56] Krick, *9th Virginia Cavalry*, 9.
[57] Carman, Pierro, 46.
[58] *OR*, vol. 19, pt. 1, 208. Col. Carter with the 3rd Indiana along with a battery reported to Pleasonton on 5 September, *OR*, vol. 19, pt. 2, 185.

came out. White was distraught and was crying with frustration as Jackson attempted to learn the source of White's discomposure. Jackson, in his usual forthright manner, told White he had just heard Stuart tell Lee that White requested to return to Loudoun County and this made White even more despondent. Jackson's advice was to obey orders and he told White a Mexican War story in which he had been ordered to the rear just before a battle. But his movement to the rear allowed him to earn distinction which would not have happened had he remained at the front. Jackson suggested that White should obey orders and trust in Providence. Stuart emerged from Lee's tent and said: "'Capt. White, did you say you was a Marylander?' 'Yes sir,' said White. 'Ah!' said the general, 'I didn't know that. Gen. Lee wants you. Go in and see him.'" White hurried in and Lee ordered him to scout toward Harpers Ferry but then said that White would report to Lee which White appreciated as he was removed from Stuart's unwelcome command. White had an eventful September as he captured 35 Yankee infantry on his farm on the Potomac, but Union cavalry with these Yankees escaped across the Potomac. White next confronted Brig. Gen. Judson Kilpatrick on 17 September in Leesburg. Kilpatrick had some 400 Union cavalry with four guns and was advancing to that town looking for Rebels. In Leesburg, Capt. White found Co. A of the 6th Virginia Cavalry under Capt. Gibson, and some 40 Mississippi infantry under Capt. Young, who was the provost marshal of the town. White was wounded by his own supporting Confederate infantry as he was organizing a charge which then fell apart. He was hors-de-combat until late October 1862.[59]

On 7 September, Capt. Charles Russell and Company I of the 1st Maryland Union Cavalry attacked Confederates fording the Potomac River at Point of Rocks, killing three and capturing 17.[60] Also on 7 September, Maj. George H. Chapman, commander of the 3rd Indiana Cavalry, lead two squadrons of the 8th Illinois Cavalry, and two squadrons of the 3rd Indiana Cavalry, on a foray into Poolesville, taking two Rebel cavalrymen prisoner along with one horse with its saddle and equipment. His brigade commander, Col. John F. Farnsworth, had apparently decided on his own to prove that there were few Rebels in Poolesville and sent his troopers to verify his belief. They suffered no casualties but set up a more serious confrontation for the following day with Munford's Confederate cavalry.[61]

---

[59] The detailed report of this confrontation is found in Myers, *The Comanches,* 107-113. Note that the company with Capt. White in Maryland is described as a Virginia company in this regimental history vice a Maryland company as found in Carman, Clemens, 227. The Maryland Company under Capt. George W. Chiswell joined White's company on 12 September, and then by Lt. Myers who joined them at Waterford, Myers, 109-110; introduction in reprint by Lee W. Wallace, Jr., unnumbered page. White convalesced until late October 1862 when his companies were mustered into service as White's Battalion and he was elected major, Myers, 121.

[60] Daniel Carroll Toomey, *The Civil War in Maryland* (Baltimore, MD: Toomey Press, 1983), 47.

[61] *OR*, vol. 19, pt. 1, 208, written 19 September; compare Pleasonton's inaccurate report written 7 September, *OR*, vol. 19, pt. 2, 201: "Have just received the report of Colonel Farnsworth, Eighth Illinois Cavalry, of his occupation of Poolesville to-day. He drove the rebels, some 60 in number, from the town, capturing 3. One was badly wounded, and this man he paroled. The two others I sent to the Provost-Marshal-General. They belong to the Fifth Virginia Cavalry, Colonel Rosser." Carman, Pierro, 82, wrote that Maj. George H. Chapman of the 3rd Indiana was in command during this action and does not mention Farnsworth; Carman gives no sources. See also Priest, *Before Antietam*, 32, 37; Pickerill, *Third Indiana*, 24, quotes Pleasonton's 19 September report. Hard, 170-171, describing Capt. Farnsworth's role in capturing two Rebels vice three; Farnsworth reportedly rode them down. Hard, in his regimental history of the 8th Illinois, said that Capt. Elon Farnsworth, who was the nephew of the brigade commander, John F. Farnsworth, was in command during the charge on the 7th. Records show, however that he was the assistant quartermaster of the Fourth Corps during this time having previously served in the 8th Illinois Cavalry. He may have remained at least informally on his uncle's staff as Couch's Fourth Corps was in the area where the 8th Illinois was active so it is highly likely that since that corps was in the general area and given the fluid situation, that Capt. Farnsworth did command the attack or at least the two squadrons of the 8th, and that Pleasonton did not mention him as Capt. Farnsworth was technically not under his command. Capt. Farnsworth was however a favorite of Pleasonton as he promoted Farnsworth from captain to brigadier general on 29 June 1863 although he was never confirmed in that rank, John H. Eicher and David J. Eicher, *Civil War High Commands* (Stanford, CA: Stanford University Press, 2001), 596. Note that Pleasonton commended E.J. Farnsworth in the Second Brigade among others for his gallant service, *OR*, vol. 19, pt. 1, 213. Col. Farnsworth was on 30 days sick leave from 5

Col. John F. Farnsworth, commander of the Second Brigade of Pleasonton's division and probably the best Union cavalry commander on the field during the Maryland Campaign. Courtesy LOC.

August, NA, RG 94, 12 July 1862, Special Orders No. 120, Regimental Letter, Order and Miscellaneous Book, vol. 5 of 6, 8th Illinois Cavalry; Hard, 169.

Arriving in Urbana the evening of the 7th, Munford's troopers ended their weary journey from their midnight Potomac crossing acting as Stuart's rear guard. After fourteen hours in the saddle, they were happy to bed down for the night but little did they know that they would be retracing their steps early the next morning, thanks to Farnsworth's foray at Poolesville; Munford had left two pickets there as he passed through and Farnsworth gobbled them up. Early the next morning on Monday, 8 September, Stuart ordered Munford to retake Poolesville from Farnsworth's cavalry. Munford took two guns from Chew's Battery, a howitzer and a Blakely, as added support, and rode south enjoying the sunny, relatively cool weather—the 12th Virginia leading his column and the 2nd Virginia Cavalry bringing up the rear. He detailed the 2nd to remain in Barnesville to secure his line of retreat, and continued south toward Monocacy Church, less than two miles due north of Poolesville. As Munford's scouts from the 12th neared Poolesville, they met Farnsworth with his 8th Illinois Cavalry, accompanied by the 3rd Indiana Cavalry. The Hoosiers quickly drove Munford's scouts north to the line he had established about a mile away with his guns on a little hill along a patch of woods. Chew's Blakeley and howitzer fire drove the Federal cavalry back toward Poolesville, but then two Union guns from Battery M, 2nd U.S. Horse Artillery under Lt. Robert H. Chapin, came up, answering well the Rebel cannoneers, driving them from their guns. A gunner in Chew's Battery, George M. Neese, complimented the Union horse artillery: "I believe that the confounded Yankees can shoot better in the United States than they can when they come to Dixieland. They did better shooting with their artillery to-day than any I have seen since I have been in service."[62] A Rebel participant, Capt. Charles T. O'Ferrall from the 12th Virginia described his eventful day:

> In the encounter with this cavalry I was disabled in my right arm by a sabre-stroke; it was broken two or three inches above the wrist joint, and but for the timely assistance of Sergeant-Major J.H.H. Figgatt, of my regiment, I would have been cut down. A stalwart Federal sergeant, into whose face I had thrust my pistol and pulled the trigger with only the result of an exploded cap, had given me the blow, and while I was dodging his other strokes and endeavoring to get away from him, Figgatt dashed up, and taking the fellow off my hands, with a well-directed blow about the head or neck knocked him from his saddle. I have always believed that Figgatt saved my life, for I had not thought of surrendering, and the fellow, apparently maddened by the narrow escape he had made from death by the failure of my pistol to fire, seemed determined to finish me.[63]

O'Ferrall's wound was severe enough to send him back home to Virginia for a few weeks. Meanwhile, the 3rd Indiana Cavalry flanked Munford's left, with part of the regiment heading north to block Munford's retreat. Surprised at now being attacked from three sides, the Confederate horseman rallied to confront the Yankee assaults; the 7th Virginia under Capt. Myers charged north, while the 12th Virginia with its eighty-three troopers tried to face the rest of the 3rd's charge from the east. The Rebel cannoneers attempted to limber their guns as troopers from both sides fought among them. The guns were saved but during the fight, the 12th Virginia lost eight men and the 7th, two; Pleasonton reported that Union troopers lost 13, 12 from the 3rd Indiana and 1 from the 8th Illinois. Neese saw Munford who was in charge of the fighting in the vicinity and described him as "unduly excited" shouting "'Cut loose from your pieces!'" but the nineteen-year-old Chew in command of the artillery remained cool and disregarded Munford's orders yelling to the cannoneers to "stick to [y]our guns" until the cannon could

---

[62] Neese, 137. See also Trout, *Thunder*, 89-90. Stuart's report is found in *OR*, vol. 19, pt. 1, 815, showing 15 casualties. Perhaps Neese had not directly faced regular U.S. artillery units.
[63] Charles T. O'Ferrall, *Forty Years of Active Service* (New York: The Neale Publishing Company, 1904), 51-52.

be limbered up and taken to the rear. Neese described this fight as "the most hazardous and eventful situation the battery was ever in." Munford reported only one killed and one wounded.[64]

Munford wrote in his official report that part of Col. Harman's 12th Virginia Cavalry, now composed of 75 men, "behaved very badly" without specifying what they did. Perhaps he was disappointed at their precipitate retreat upon their first encounter with Union troopers in Maryland. Munford rapidly retreated toward Barnesville followed by Farnsworth in pursuit with the 8th Illinois which had replaced the fought-out 3rd Indiana. Farnsworth was stopped at Monocacy Church by some 2nd Virginia Troopers, whose sharpshooters had hurried south from Barnesville to aid Munford.[65] Chew's gunner Neese commented on the Federal cavalry: "If to-day's proceedings is an average specimen of the treatment the dear Yanks intend to give us…, I think the best thing we can do is to go back to Dixie right away."[66] Pleasonton undoubtedly would have been proud of this reaction to his troopers' efforts in this fight. This confused melee would have resulted in the capture of the Rebel guns had not the 7th Virginia saved the day. Here again, the experience of the Confederate cavalry, along with good leadership, retrieved Munford's fortunes despite the reported bad behavior of some of the 12th Virginia—perhaps Munford was seeking a scapegoat for this close call? It must be noted that during the rest of the campaign however, Munford's performance was generally excellent. Perhaps being new to command of Robertson's Brigade, he was still learning the capabilities of his men (and himself) under severe battle conditions; he might also have been surprised at the aggression the Yankees showed.

A trooper from the 3rd Indiana Cavalry wrote a letter home about one trooper who charged the Rebels, trying to capture a flag: "after emptying his pistol and gun cut for their flag—4 men protected it and he would have had it in one minute more but one bullet cut his sword handle just above his thumb—another thru his cartridge box another thru holster & another thru his left hand—they cut down his sword & it dropped & wounded his bridle hand he wheeled out." The writer opined that if the rest of his regiment were ordered around the Rebels "we would have captured the whole bunch."[67]

Also on 8 September, Burnside was being helpful to McClellan and Pleasonton as he reported that there was a regiment of Union cavalry at Unity, Maryland, which he would use, the 6th New York (eight companies) under Col. Thomas C. Devin, and he would have a squadron of this cavalry cross the National Pike and B&O Railroad and move up toward Franklinville and Liberty northeast of Frederick. At this period of the campaign, the right flank of the Union army still had to cover Baltimore as that was one of the destinations suspected for the Rebel army.

---

[64] Neese, 138. See also Trout, *Thunder*, describing how Munford panicked when attacked from three sides ordering the artillery to cut loose their pieces and flee, 89-90; *OR*, vol. 19, pt. 1, 208; Pleasonton wrote that Confederate loss was 30: eight killed, 16 wounded, and six captured. One Indiana trooper wrote home on 11 September it was a confused melee into which his Companies A and B charged some 400 enemy with 80 troopers. He reported 10 wounded and one killed while the Rebels had 15 killed and 15 or 20 wounded, letter from Mildred Wright file, courtesy of Indiana State Library.

[65] Carman, Pierro, 82-83. Note the not unusual discrepancies in casualties in the various reports cited in Carman, 83, Pierro, n. 11. *OR*, vol. 19, pt. 1, 825, gives Munford's report and Stuart's at 815. McClellan, *Stuart*, says that Munford's 12th Virginia had seventy-five men and the 2nd less than two hundred. His 7th Virginia Cavalry was detached later this day to join Jackson's command. It is very likely that Munford was outnumbered as he initially employed the 7th and 12th with an estimated 300 sabers (excluding artillery) facing the 3rd Indiana with about 300 troopers and the 8th Illinois with at least 400 men. If the 3rd and the 8th still had only four squadrons (eight companies) which were involved at Poolesville the previous day, it still is likely they outnumbered their foes but by a smaller margin. As in many cavalry fights, aggression is a major factor and the Yankees here demonstrated that they were not afraid of their foes.

[66] Neese, 139. Longstreet agreed, James Longstreet, *From Manassas to Appomattox* (Philadelphia, PA: J.B. Lippincott Company, 1895; reprint, Cambridge, MA: Da Capo Press), 1992, "At this very time [8 September]…the Union cavalry was active and aggressive in work against the Confederates at Poolesville," 281.

[67] Letter from Mildred Wright file, courtesy of Indiana State Library.

Col. Thomas Casimer Devin commanding the 6th New York Cavalry; here shown as a major general. Courtesy LOC.

On the morning of the 9th, Col. Farnsworth rode toward Barnesville and spotted a squadron of Rebel cavalry near Monocacy Church. He ordered Capt. Farnsworth's squadron from the 8th Illinois Cavalry to flank the Rebels, and succeeded in capturing several prisoners from the 12th Virginia, and also its battle flag.[68] Farnsworth continued to Barnesville chasing Confederate cavalry through and beyond the village, fighting them along the way, killing four, wounding five, and capturing 27 while suffering no casualties.[69] The historian of the 8th Illinois described the encounter:

> on the morning of the 9th were again moving forward in the direction of Barnesville....Passing over the scenes of the previous fight, a short distance brought the contending forces again into close quarters. The regiment was now divided into several detachments. One of these under command of Captain Farnsworth, encountered the Ninth Virginia Cavalry, and immediately charged them. The enemy formed in line and withstood the attack for a moment, but gave way before the determined charge of our men, in doing which some of their horses were shot down, and others falling over these, both men and horses were thrown into heaps. Some escaped through fields and woods, while others were chased and overtaken by our superior horsemen. The enemy sustained a loss of one killed and several wounded, and eight prisoners together with their regimental colors all of which were brought to headquarters.
>
> On a road a few miles to the right, another detachment commanded by Captain Kelly met the rebels and engaged them in a fierce combat, driving them at full speed through Barnesville and nearly two miles beyond. In this engagement they captured thirteen prisoners and wounded five men.
>
> After passing Barnesville the enemy attempted several times to rally, but at each attempt were frustrated and broken up. A Lieutenant Williams was firing his revolver at our men when Captain Kelly came upon him. It was a desperate moment. The Captain ordered him to surrender, but he refused, at the same time pointing his pistol at his opponant, was about to fire, when Captain Kelly, being a little more expert, fired first, the ball passing through his liver and lodging in the abdomen, produced a mortal wound. He was taken to a farm house and all the care and attention bestowed upon him that the case demanded, but he did not survive the day. Before his death Captain Kelly called upon him and expressed his regret at the necessity which compelled him to fire. The Lieutenant exhonerated him from all blame, saying "I refused to surrender, and would have shot you if I could have fired first."[70]

Also on the 9th, a battalion of the 1st New York Cavalry, led by Maj. Alonzo W. Adams, charged into Hyattstown, driving out pickets of Hampton's cavalry. Hampton's troopers returned next day with artillery and after a spirited fight, the Empire State horsemen prevailed, buckramed by a squadron of the 1st U.S. Cavalry under Capt. Marcus A. Reno. Hampton's troopers retreated and the Union cavalry returned to Clarksburg.[71]

At this time, there is no indication that there were Confederate pickets south from the tiny town of Comus at the foot of Sugarloaf Mountain to the Potomac. Perhaps the presence of Confederate signalmen and lookouts on the mountain obviated that need so the four-mile-wide gap between that

[68] OR, vol. 19, pt. 1, 208. The colors are currently in the Museum of the Confederacy in Richmond, Virginia, returned by the 8th Illinois Cavalry Veterans Association in 1905 after Congress passed legislation mandating return of captured flags to their states of origin. A 3rd Indiana trooper thought that 60 enemy were captured along with the colors, letter from Mildred Wright file, courtesy of Indiana State Library. Another trooper from the 3rd, Company A, wrote that after the Rebels were dislodged, "Companies A&B were sent in pursuit A in the lead under the command of Major Chapman. We chased them about 3 miles to a place called Bunker Hill [probably Barnesville] there they made a stand and we fought them about half an hour before we drove them which we did effectively. Our loss [Company A loss] was 6 wounded and 1 [David Fallis] killed. Company B loss was 2 wounded. We lost about 1 dozen horses. Secesh loss was 6 killed 6 mortally wounded 15 wounded 10 prisoners including one officer. We took about 8 horses and killed about 1 dozen more. A part of each of our companies had been sent out on picket so that we did not have over 100 men to fight Ashby's old regiment the force that was opposed to us," letter from Pvt. Flavius J. Bellamy file, courtesy of Indiana State Library.
[69] Ibid., 208-209. It is not clear the number of troopers Col. Farnsworth commanded in this action as Pleasonton described the force as "Farnsworth with his command," ibid., 208. Given his success he probably had at least the four squadrons he employed the previous day.
[70] Hard, 171-173. As noted above, a squadron of 9th Virginia Cavalry was left at Beallsville on picket duty.
[71] Carman, Pierro, 83; Beach, 168. Note that a company of the 1st Pennsylvania Cavalry had been sent by Wool to scout west from Baltimore. It met Burnside's 3rd Pennsylvania Cavalry scouts at Cooksville, OR, vol. 19, pt. 2, 222.

point and the Potomac made little practical difference. On 9 September however, a Confederate infantry brigade from Walker's Division had to chase away some pickets, members of the Potomac Home Brigade, at the Catoctin aqueduct at the mouth of the Monocacy River, quickly doing so while sustaining only one casualty. Given the density of the foliage and the distance from Sugarloaf to the junction of the Potomac and the Monocacy, it is probable that lookouts on the mountain were not able to see small groups of soldiers near the aqueduct. Still, the absence of cavalry pickets extending to the Potomac would have worried Gen. Lee had he been aware of the gap.[72] McClellan, on 9 September, wanted to check on Confederate activity toward Baltimore, so he instructed Burnside to have his attached cavalry make a reconnaissance to Damascus, and beyond Ridgeville, as well as north of the B&O Railroad toward Westminster. Devin with the 6th New York Cavalry had earlier reported that he had confronted some cavalry near Hyattstown, driving in their pickets. This activity continued to worry McClellan and Burnside that Lee was moving toward Baltimore, around the Union right flank.[73] Union Brig. Gen. Jacob D. Cox, commander of the Kanawha Division of the Ninth Corps did not think much of the Union cavalry's scouting:

[My division] on the 9th ...reached Goshen, where it lay on the 10th, and on the 11th reached Ridgeville on the railroad. The rest of the Ninth Corps was an easy march behind us. Hooker had been ordered further to the right on the strength of rumors that Lee was making a circuit toward Baltimore, and his corps reached Cooksville and the railroad some ten miles east of my position. The extreme left of the army was at Poolesville, near the Potomac, making a spread of thirty miles across the whole front. The cavalry did not succeed in getting far in advance of the infantry, and very little valuable information was obtained. At Ridgeville, however, we got reliable evidence that Lee had evacuated Frederick the day before, and that only cavalry was east of the Catoctin Mountains.[74]

It is not of record whether McClellan received this valuable information and if so, what his reaction was.

After Stuart arrived in Frederick in the afternoon of the 7th and reported to Gen. Lee, he received orders to sow disinformation and screen the army: "Stuart with his cavalry was close up to the enemy and doing everything possible to keep him in ignorance and to deceive him by false reports which he industriously circulated." Additionally, he was to "divide his cavalry and threaten both Baltimore &

[72] Harsh, *Flood*, 122; Priest, *Before Antietam*, 56. It may be that Lee either did not know of the gap near the Potomac or knew that any large Union movements could be seen from his Sugarloaf signal station to which he could quickly respond with infantry.

[73] *OR*, vol. 19, pt. 2, 213, 221-223; Armstrong, *Colors*, 92. On 10 September McClellan ordered Burnside to "occupy Ridgeville in force as soon as possible," *OR*, vol. 19, pt. 2, 239. Clearly up to that time Stuart had the opportunity to push scouts to the east of Parr's Ridge who may have detected the large Union forces advancing from Washington. Gen. Reno then ordered Gen. Cox and his Kanawha division to Ridgeville and to "send your cavalry [1st Maine Cavalry] in front," ibid., 240. Note that later on the 10th Cox wrote Burnside's chief of staff, Maj. Gen. J.G. Parke, that due to his order Cox's movement was countermanded, *OR*, vol. 19, pt. 2, 240. McClellan wanted other movements of his army to help cover the movement to Ridgeville. The 1st Maine Cavalry which was part of Pope's Army of Virginia, reached Leesboro, Maryland, on 7 September after a dusty march. The entire regiment was assigned then to Reno's division with Company G as his body guard, and Companies A and I as bodyguard for Gen. Rodman, and Companies M and H for Fitz John Porter. Burnside appointed the regiment's commander, Col. Samuel H. Allen, as military governor for the Frederick area, six companies of the 1st Maine reached Frederick on 12 September and remained there under command of Col. Calvin S. Douty until 2 November as provost guard patrolling the area as well as scouting, reconnoitering and guarding Rebel prisoners. The regiment benefitted by receiving 250 recruits to help fill up its ranks for those who were discharged or died. Company G led by Capt. Zebulon B. Blethen, was detailed as orderlies and escort for Maj. Gen. Jesse L. Reno, commander of the Ninth Corps on 7 September. After Reno was killed at South Mountain the company has the unhappy duty of escorting his body back to Middletown. Then it was assigned to guard Burnside's headquarters train and did not arrive at Antietam until after the battle, Tobie, 92-94, 97-98.

[74] Jacob D. Cox, *Military Reminiscences of the Civil War*, vol. 1 (New York, NY: Charles Scribner's Sons, 1900), 267-268. His articulate and thoughtful reminiscences are among the best available for the Civil War in the author's opinion.

Washington on both flanks of McClellan, giving out on each flank that he (Lee) was behind with his whole force."[75] It is interesting to note that no mention is made of scouting toward Washington. And Stuart did not do much if any threatening on the Union left flank, and little on its right flank. The excellent Confederate screens which Stuart set up during the first part of the Maryland Campaign consisted of roughly three lines, the first and furthest east on 7 to 9 September can be called the "Parr's Ridge/Sugarloaf Line," the next line to the west is the Catoctin Mountain Line held on 10 September, and finally the last, the South Mountain Line, farthest to the west on 13-14 September. Stuart's first line, the Parr's Ridge/Sugarloaf Line, included the roads through Parr's Ridge and Sugarloaf Mountain, but Parr's Ridge petered out as it neared the Potomac, however it served its purpose as it screened Lee's infantry force behind the Monocacy River, an effective barrier in its own right. Sugarloaf Mountain was just in the rear of the Parr's Ridge/Sugarloaf Line which extended from the Potomac River south of Poolesville through Hyattstown with New Market on the north on the National Pike and the B&O Railroad coming from Baltimore. Given the depleted condition of the Confederate cavalry brigades, only small groups could serve as pickets or manning observation posts watching the roads leading through Parr's Ridge from Washington, in addition to guarding the area around Sugarloaf. Fortunately for Stuart, Pleasonton was wary certainly after the debacle involving the 1st Massachusetts Cavalry at Poolesville, so his initial probes were tentative, but as Union infantry came up and more of his cavalry joined him, he became increasingly aggressive as shown when Farnsworth pushed Munford away from Poolesville. McClellan noted in a telegraph to Halleck on 8 September, that "I am rather weak in cavalry on the right but am hourly expecting more of Averell's Brigade." Then on the 9th, McClellan wrote "I am anxious for the prompt arrival of the rest of my cavalry from Fort Monroe....Thus far my cavalry have gained the advantage."[76] Then again on the 9th to Fitz John Porter: "Our Cavalry have had some handsome affairs today fully maintaining the morale they gained on the Peninsula. We have regained Barnesville & Sugar Loaf Mt." His announcement of the recapture of Sugarloaf was premature as will be seen.[77]

Stuart made his headquarters in Urbana, in the center of his line, to be within an easy ride of Gen. Lee's army headquarters near the Best Farm, east of Frederick, Maryland, and to be on the main road from Washington, the Georgetown Turnpike; he settled his headquarters on the grounds of the friendly Cockey family and rode toward Frederick to consult with Gen. Lee.[78]

---

[75] Robert E. Lee, *Lee the Soldier*, ed. Gary W. Gallagher (Lincoln: University of Nebraska Press, 1996), 7-8, 25-26.

[76] McClellan, *Civil War Papers*, 439, 442. In July on the Peninsula, Col. William W. Averell of the 3rd Pennsylvania Cavalry commanded the First Brigade consisting of his regiment, the 3rd Pennsylvania Cavalry, and the 1st New York Cavalry and 4th Pennsylvania Cavalry. Averell was on sick leave suffering from a relapse of malaria and did not participate in the Maryland Campaign, Longacre, *Lincoln's Cavalrymen*, 101; *OR*, vol. 19, pt. 2, 219.

[77] McClellan, *Civil War Papers*, 443.

[78] Priest, *Before Antietam*, 23. The pike was also known as the Rockville-Frederick road, Matthew Forney Steele, *American Campaigns*, vol. 1 (Washington, DC: Byron S. Adams, 1909), 264. During the 19th century, roads and turnpikes outside of the geographical limits of cities and towns usually had no formal names being most often named for the towns they connected. McClellan, *Stuart*, 110. Munford had to cover his large right end of the Parr's Ridge/Sugarloaf Line with only three depleted regiments, the rest being off on other duties; the 2nd and 7th Virginia Cavalry likely had less than 200 troopers each, and the 12th had some 75. The estimate for the 2nd Virginia given by McClellan may be low. Stuart in *OR*, vol. 19, pt. 1, 814-816, shows the disposition of his brigades and also comments on Munford's units. Munford's other units were detached as follows: the 6th Virginia Cavalry was left in Centreville, Virginia, collecting arms and equipment after Second Bull Run and Chantilly, the 7th Virginia Cavalry was sent on 13 September to accompany Jackson on his Harpers Ferry expedition, and the 17th Battalion was detached before crossing the Potomac and sent on an expedition to western Virginia. Carman, Pierro, 46. Forage was available but food was not plentiful, Carman, Pierro, 54. Not all troopers suffered from lack of victuals as one Union trooper from the 1st Maine Cavalry wrote home that he was well fed on apples, grapes, pork, fish, coffee, bread, and milk some supplied by willing Marylanders as well as the Union commissary, William B. Baker letters, copies from ANBL Union Cavalry Files. As noted, Munford was initially near Urbana but then sent back to Poolesville on 8 September as noted above, Harsh, *Flood*, 115; see also

William R. Carter of the 3rd Virginia Cavalry wrote that after Lee's Brigade moved on the morning of the 7th crossing the B&O Railroad at Monrovia and halting just beyond New Market, they picketed the road leading toward Hyattstown, while the rest of his regiment picketed the Baltimore and Frederick Turnpike (National Pike). His regiment "Spent a very good night, the people being reasonably kind & we having on hand a good deal of forage & stores captured at Monrovia."[79] Lee must have been unconcerned about the Union army as he firmly believed that it was still in its forts and camps around Washington. But Stuart should have been more aggressive in his scouting so his commander would not have been lulled into a false sense of complacency. McClellan did not move most of his army up to Parr's Ridge from the Washington area until 10 September, so Stuart would have had a reasonable chance to penetrate beyond the ridge to investigate Union progress had he desired to do so.[80] On 8 September, "McClellan had some 66,000 men in a sixteen-mile-wide battleline, which was on average twelve miles beyond the [Washington] forts."[81] Federal cavalry was beginning to come up near the eastern side of Parr's Ridge so Stuart would have begun to have difficulty in learning about Union movements to the east starting as early as 8 September, had he deigned to send scouts out that far. At the very least, the increased Federal cavalry pressure should have warned Stuart that it was likely Union infantry was not far behind, yet his attention on 8 September turned to more joyful pursuits.

Modern-day view of the Cockey house in Urbana on the Georgetown Pike which served as Stuart's headquarters during the early days of the campaign. The Landon School is about 170 yards to the northeast (right of the house). Courtesy Gardener's General Contractor, Inc.

Richard L. Armstrong, *7th Virginia Cavalry* (Lynchburg, VA: H.E. Howard, Inc., 1992), hereafter "*7th*," 42. Munford's 12th Virginia Cavalry was at Poolesville, *OR*, vol. 19, pt. 1, 815, 825.

[79] Carter, *Sabres, Saddles, and Spurs*, 12.

[80] Armstrong, *Colors*, 94-95. McClellan quickly suspended the general movements of his army pending further reconnaissance; unfortunately for McClellan, Pleasonton had not taken Sugarloaf so McClellan was still unaware of the movements of the Rebel army away from Frederick, 95-98. Late on the 9th, Strother met with McClellan who asked him to serve on his staff. He told Strother that 100,000 Rebels lay behind the Monocacy and that the 80,000 strong Army of the Potomac would advance to Parr's Ridge occupying Ridgeville, Damascus, Clarksville [Clarksburg], and Barnesville. Strother gave him information about the ridge and the countryside down to Harpers Ferry. McClellan also said that "his cavalry had entirely the prestige of Stuart's, having cowed it in many combats so that it would not stand at all," Diaries, 103. Perhaps he was referring to the 7 and 8 September actions won by Col. John F. Farnsworth who bested Munford in and north of Poolesville; see above. In a midnight telegram to Lincoln on 10 September, McClellan said that Pleasonton is watching all the fords up to Conrad's Ferry and picketed to the mouth of the Monocacy River while Burnside sent a reconnaissance in force to Ridgeville. He also reported that he ordered the army to the line of Parr's Ridge, McClellan, *Civil War Papers*, 443, 444.

[81] Harsh, *Flood*, 114, 121; *OR*, vol. 19, pt. 2, 596-597, 600-601. Gen. Lee told Davis on both 7 and 8 September that the Union had not left Washington when in fact they had.

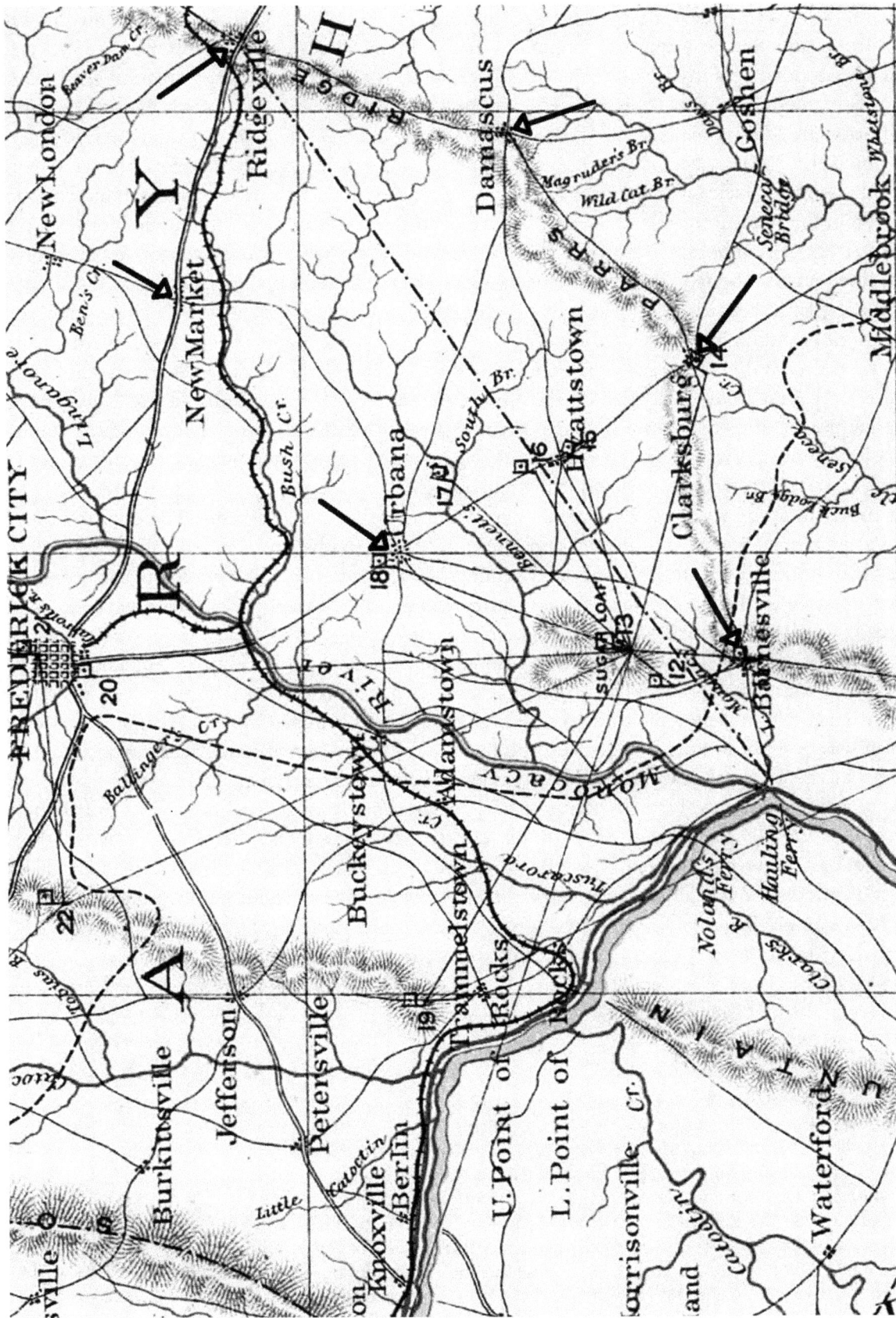

Parr's Ridge shown at the right as are the roads through the ridge on which Stuart placed his videttes. This map shows Parr's Ridge going further south than other maps. Lines radiating from Sugarloaf Mountain and other points show Union signal corps lines of communication; Sugarloaf is station 13. Urbana, Stuart's headquarters is at the arrow at the upper center, on the main road from Georgetown to Frederick. Rebel pickets were initially located at Clarksburg, Hyattstown, Damascus, Ridgeville, Barnesville, Poolesville, and around Sugarloaf. Fitz Lee's men were also posted at New Market on the National Pike. Detail from *Official Atlas*, Plate 27. Courtesy LOC.

Unfortunately for Gen. Lee, Stuart was true to form in Maryland, following his well-known penchant for frolic and female attention, beginning with dinner on the evening of the 7th with the Cockeys near his headquarters in Urbana; Stuart paid special attention to his host's attractive New York cousin, whom he named "The New York Rebel." He was "fond of show and with much personal vanity, craving admiration in the parlor as well as on the field, with a taste for music and poetry and song, desiring as much the admiration of handsome women…with full appreciation of his well-won eminence"[82] is how one of Jackson's staff, Henry Kyd Douglas, described him. During this campaign, one of his most memorable and notorious escapades occurred on the evening of 8 September, north of his Urbana headquarters, which became known as the "Sabers and Roses Ball." Stuart had noticed an empty building, inspected it and deemed it a perfect location for a dance. He and his Prussian aide, Maj. Heros von Borcke, planned the ball to be held at this closed female academy to thank the Cockeys for their hospitality, and to entertain his newly found friend, "The New York Rebel."[83] Stuart supplied music employing Brig. Gen. William Barksdale's excellent 18th Mississippi band, and decorated the large eastern room on the first floor with their Mississippi regiments' battle flags. Enlisted men and junior officers were employed in cleaning the hall and inviting guests, while von Borcke supplied the hand-written invitations and supervised the decorations, adding bouquets of roses clipped from local gardens.[84]

Ladies arrived in their carriages, wearing fancy gowns, as the full moon was rising, nibbled on light refreshments in an adjoining room, and socialized with Stuart's well-dressed officers. The dim, romantic atmosphere was enhanced by two candelabra and lanterns. While the ball progressed splendidly, a few miles east toward Hyattstown on the road to Washington, trouble was brewing for Stuart's festive occasion. Five companies of the 1st New York Cavalry under Maj. Alonzo W. Adams decided on a reconnaissance toward Hyattstown, about three miles from Urbana, pushing back some of Hampton's videttes; the New Yorkers then settled in, placing dismounted pickets on a hill. But these pickets were in for a tough night as Hampton's troopers returned, and made it hot for the New Yorkers. Soon, all of the Union pickets extracted themselves from the persistent Tarheels and galloped back to Hyattstown. News of this skirmish was brought to Stuart at the ball; the Beau Sabreur and his staff mounted and rode to the scene, finding that the 1st North Carolina Cavalry, under Col. Laurence S. Baker, had already driven off the pesky New Yorkers. Stuart formed his men and led another charge pushing remaining Union troopers further down the road. Satisfied with his efforts, Stuart and his "victorious" officers then returned to the ball between midnight and 1 A.M. and recommenced the festivities, only to be interrupted by Confederate casualties being taken upstairs above the ballroom. Stuart and his officers lost many of their comely ladies as they became surgeons and nurses treating the enlisted wounded. The ball then continued until dawn.[85] Stuart and his staff spent the next day in needful relaxation, sleeping well into the morning; later that day Stuart visited army "headquarters, where he flirted with Miss Catherine Markell and her friends." That evening was spent with the Cockeys despite "the thunder of

[82] Henry Kyd Douglas, *I Rode with Stonewall: Being Chiefly the War Experiences of the Youngest Member of Jackson's Staff from the John Brown Raid to the Hanging of Mrs. Surratt* (Chapel Hill: The University of North Carolina Press, 1940; Marietta, Ga.: Mockingbird Books, 1995), 269. Douglas was not especially fond of Stuart: see n. 89 below.
[83] Sidney Davis, 195; Priest, *Before Antietam*, 36. It has also been called the "Moonlight and Roses Ball."
[84] Priest, *Before Antietam*, 45; Wert, *Cavalryman of the Lost Cause*, 141-142.
[85] Priest, *Before Antietam*, 50. See also Beach, describing the encounter between the Rebel cavalry and five companies of the 1st New York Cavalry, 168-170. See also Edward G. Longacre, *Gentleman and Soldier: A Biography of Wade Hampton III* (Nashville, TN: Rutledge Hill Press, 2003), where he discusses Hampton's disdain for this type of activity in enemy country and did not attend, 94. After Stuart's October 1862 ride around McClellan, Hampton remarked that "Stuart will as usual give all the credit to his Virginia Brigades. He praises them on all occasions, but does not give us any credit," Hartley, *Stuart's Tarheels*, 157. Hartley also wrote that some of the North Carolina troopers were "'in a poor fix for fighting'" because they were under the influence of whiskey, ibid," 126.

distant cannon." Stuart and his staff rested again on 10 September.[86] "Stuart was ready to see and talk to every good-looking woman" during his visits to Lee's army headquarters in Best's Grove.[87] Stuart's boyish desire for fun and frivolity was noticed and engaged in by his staff one of whom glowingly described Jeb's personality:

With those about him he was as affectionate as a woman, and his little boyish ways are remembered lovingly by those of his military household whom I have met since the war came to an end. On one occasion, just after a battle, he handed his coat to a member of his staff, saying—'Try that on, captain, and see how it fits you.' The garment fitted reasonably well, and the general continued, —'pull off two of the stars, and wear the coat to the war department, and tell the people there to make you a major.' He did so and was so promoted....His critics say he was vain, and he was so, as a boy is. He liked to win the applause of his friends, and he liked still better to astonish the enemy....In all this there was some vanity...but it was an excellent sort of vanity for a cavalry chief to cultivate....His audacity was due, I think, to his love of applause....he managed to surround himself with a number of persons whose principal qualification for membership of his military household was their ability to make fun. One of these was a noted banjo-player and ex-negro minstrel. He played the banjo and sang comic songs to perfection, and therefore Stuart wanted him. I have known him to ride with his banjo, playing and singing, even on a march which might be changed at any moment into a battle....With all his other boyish traits, Stuart had an almost child-like simplicity of character, and the combination of sturdy manhood with juvenile frankness and womanly tenderness of feeling made him a study to those who know him best....Stuart's was one of those magnetic natures which always impress their own likeness upon others, and so it came to be thought a piece of good luck to be detailed for duty under his personal leadership. The men liked him and his ways, one of which was the pleasant habit he had of remembering our names and faces...This and other like things served to make the men love him personally, and there can be no doubt that his skill in winning the affection of his troopers was one of the elements of his success. Certainly no other man could have got so much hard service out of men of their sort, without breeding discontent among them.[88]

Stuart's ball during this campaign, as well as other social affairs of which he was fond, have been criticized by some of his contemporaries, as well as by later historians. Stuart's subordinates such as Munford and Hampton, thought little of their leader's showy style and desire for balls in the middle of war: Hampton, Munford, and their officers did not attend the ball. Pvt. Samuel Mays, a South Carolina cavalryman who served in Brig. Gen. Wade Hampton's Brigade, closed a letter written in June 1862 containing some recollections about the officers he served under. One concerns Jeb Stuart, likely influenced by the disdain many non-Virginian troopers held for Stuart and his pet Virginia regiments. It reflects the jealously many men in Gen. Lee's army felt for the advantages given Virginians and the way those from the Old Dominion asserted their supposed superiority over others not blessed by being born in Virginia. He wrote the following in which he supplies a non-reverential view of the Beau Sabreur:

I wish to say what I think of Stuart right now... He looks more like a clown and fool than a soldier, nor can you see him without a feeling of contempt for him; yet he is generous and brave—two qualities that redeem a multitude of faults. You seldom see him on foot but on horse-back. He wears a roundabout coat, the sleeves and collar of which are gorgeous with stars and trimmings. His hat has some sort of insignia on it, I do not know what, with two long drooping ostrich plumes in it—high top dragoon boots with brass spurs and very fine, elaborate housing for his horse completes his outfit. Red hair and long red beard make up the man that is thoroughly and firmly persuaded that J. E. B. Stuart is the great man of this war. He keeps old Mike Sweeney at his headquarters to play the banjo for him....I do not know whether that this raid around

---

[86] Priest, *Before Antietam*, 53. See also von Borcke, 138-140.
[87] Douglas, 149.
[88] Eggleston, 123-137.

McClellan originated from Stuart or not, but it sounds like him, as I don't think that Gen. Lee would have thought of such a fool thing.[89]

Some civilians thought that the contrast between the war's ugly realities and the artificial grandeur of entertainments in the middle of death and devastation, was "'heartlessness & frivolity'" as a diarist wrote in 1863. But one historian has written that such gatherings "reminded soldiers of the social context and customs that had governed their lives before the war. A ball could serve, then as a coping mechanism for the attendees, reaffirming that life still held graciousness and compassion.... A ball also reinforced the notion that people could still behave in a civilized fashion despite the bloodshed surrounding them...participation in a ball was an attempt...to promote some semblance of civilized behavior and establish moral superiority in the midst of civil war." Thus the ball viewed by this historian was not unusual, and reflected "the importance that music, dancing and 'civilized' behavior in general, played in the lives of nineteenth century Americans."[90] While this importance is manifest in other entertainments by many officers on both sides during the Civil War, here, the issue must be whether these festivities were appropriate, when the enemy was so close that officers attending the ball left to assist in a skirmish just a few miles away. Too, Stuart and his officers were exhausted the next day, not in the best condition to make decisions about what was necessary to monitor the advancing Unionists. The timing of Stuart's ball was a mistake as his energies and time and those of his officers were sorely needed by Gen. Lee. Stuart took his duties too lightly during the sojourn at his Urbana headquarters.[91]

---

[89] Samuel Mays, statement from a letter supplied by historian J.D. Petruzzi to author on 31 July 2008, used with permission. Henry Kyd Douglas, an aide to Jackson, wrote long after the war of Stuart's replacement of Jackson at Chancellorsville that "Personally I never liked or admired Stuart & still believe he was vain & pretentious & greatly overrated as a soldier. [but] Genl Stuart's reputation in the corps then was, in some respects only second to Jacksons. Jackson had great admiration for him as a soldier...[and] knew the men of his corps would have more confidence in him than any man who would take his place," Wert, *Cavalryman*, 225.

[90] James A. Davis, "A War of Manners: Jeb Stuart's 'Sabers & Roses' Ball," *Catoctin History*, Issue 10, Spring/Summer 2008, 22-29; Longacre, *Gentleman and Soldier*, "Hampton...did not consider the present occasion a suitable time, nor an invaded country the proper place, for merrymaking of this sort," 94. Munford in a letter to Carman dated 11 June 1899 wrote that "Stuart kept his staff busy while he frolicked and danced and enjoyed himself with the girls. All along the line and if they could be found he was generally there too;" copy of letter courtesy of Thomas Clemens (underlining in original). None of his staff remember Stuart as using tobacco or alcohol or doing more than flirting with his female admirers: [Stuart] never in the whole course of his life having used tobacco in any shape; nor did he ever, until he received his mortal wound, drink a drop of intoxicating liquor," although he was not averse to giving and receiving kisses from young ladies, Theodore Stanford Garnett, *Riding with Stuart: Reminiscences of and Aide-de-Camp*, ed. by Robert J. Trout (Shippensburg, PA: The White Mane Publishing Co., 1994), 24, 35. Garnett also wrote in his encomium that "Music, Song and laughter were the natural allies of our beloved Commander [Stuart], 26. Note that the Pleasonton was a fancy dresser and not averse to a convivial headquarters. "The Pleasonton image featured physical affectations such as dapper uniforms, stylish accoutrements, a carefully waxed mustache, a straw skimmer in place of the usual slouch hat, white kid gloves, and a cowhide riding-whip....[he] treated his palate, whenever possible, to champagne, oysters, and other delicacies that his headquarters mess stocked even during active campaigning, Longacre, *Gettysburg*, 48.

[91] Gen. Lee was composing S.O. 191 on 9 September based on the assumption that Union troops were not in close proximity but as Stuart knew based on his pickets' encounter with Unionist probes and skirmishes, they were close; Stuart should have told Lee in detail of these fights. Had he done so, Lee probably would have ordered Stuart to probe aggressively east to learn if Yankee infantry was moving, too. Stuart's enjoyment at his ball could be dismissed as harmless except that it materially affected his commander's actions reflected in S.O. 191.

Scene of the Sabers and Roses Ball on 8 September 1862; Landon School, Urbana, Maryland. The house constructed here in 1846 became Landon Female Academy but was closed because of the war. The Landon House was built along the Rappahannock River in Virginia as a silk mill in 1754. It was relocated by barge to Urbana, Maryland in 1840 where it became The Shirley Female Academy and then the Landon Military Academy & Institute. After the war, Lt. Col. Luke Tiernan Brien purchased the home. The ballroom was on the first floor in the room on the far right. Courtesy Craig Swain, HMdb.org July 7, 2007.

But not all of Stuart's troopers appeared to be gentlemen as was demonstrated on 8 September when a supposed captain of the 1st Virginia Cavalry, Edward S. Motter, with 14 troopers, many of whom were from the Middletown Valley, entered Middletown, Maryland, on the National Pike west of Frederick. They saw a large, U.S. flag hanging from a second-story window on West Main Street and threatened to kill a young woman, Miss Nancy Crouse, who at first refused to turn it over; she quickly relented after Motter placed a pistol to her head. After securing the flag, they rode east toward Frederick. A few minutes later, a company of the Union 1st Maryland Cavalry, led by Capt. Charles H. Russell, on patrol from Harpers Ferry, arrived in Middletown and heard of the event from Miss Crouse, and took off in pursuit of the thuggish Rebel troopers galloping east on the National Pike. They found them at the summit of the Catoctin Mountains at Hagan's Tavern and chased them to the outskirts of Frederick, capturing some fourteen, but not the churlish Capt. Motter; the Marylanders then safely returned to Harpers Ferry with their captives, who included two deserters from the 1st Maryland Cavalry, and John Hagan's son, but not before they returned the flag to Miss Crouse.[92]

Fitz Lee's troopers stationed between New Market and Liberty, on the other hand, as one of his men reported, "had a very quiet time of it....Here we had some recruits & heard pretty general expression of joy at our coming, as it suspended the operation of the Yankee Draft. I rather suppose that they will be left to do as they please & can stay at home unmolested by either party. Our boys bought some horses

[92] Priest, *Before Antietam*, 41-42, quoting from "Middletown Valley and Official Programme and Souvenir of the Boosters," Festival and Home Coming Week, September 13-19, 1914; but see Kathleen A. Ernst, *Too Afraid to Cry: Maryland Civilians in the Antietam Campaign* (Mechanicsburg, PA: Stackpole Books, 1999), 75-76, describing the same incident, but relating it to the passing of Jackson's column; *OR*, vol. 19, pt. 1, 535, 545. The entertaining Crouse story in the program was likely highly embellished.

here."[93] Rebel purchases of horses and goods in Frederick were often made using Confederate script which most citizens viewed as worthless, but one enterprising Unionist woman overcharged for her honey, and then traded half of the Confederate money for more useful currency to a secessionist neighbor.[94]

Crouse House (204 West Main Street), Middletown. When the Confederates first arrived in town on 10 September Nancy Crouse had a large U.S. flag flying from the second floor balcony; "cavalrymen entered the house to remove the flag, but found Mrs. Crouse had wrapped herself in the flag and proclaimed, 'You may shoot me, but never will I willingly give up my country's flag into the hands of traitors.' Although she would lose the flag after a fight, it was later returned to her when captured at Antietam." Courtesy Craig Swain HMdb.org.

---

[93] Carter, *Sabres, Saddles, and Spurs*, 12-13.
[94] Charles S. Wainwright, *A Diary of Battle: The Personal Journals of Colonel Charles S. Wainwright 1861 – 1865*, ed. by Allan Nevins (New York: Harcourt, 1962; reprint, New York: Da Capo Press, 1998), 100.

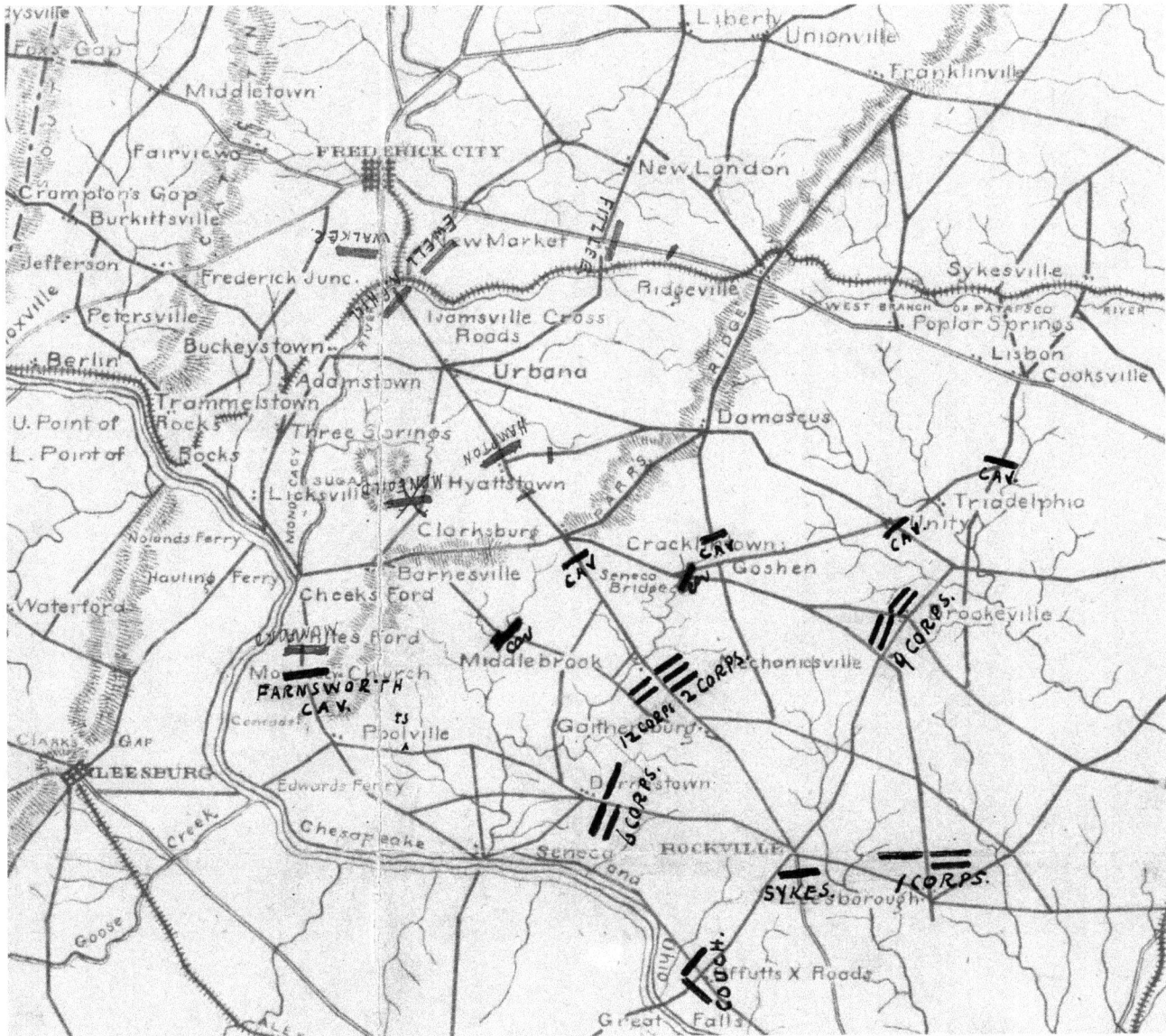

Situation map night of 8 September. Pleasonton probes Stuart's Line. Pleasonton is now probing from Poolesville to Parr's Ridge in the southwest to Damascus and Unity to the northwest. Courtesy LOC.

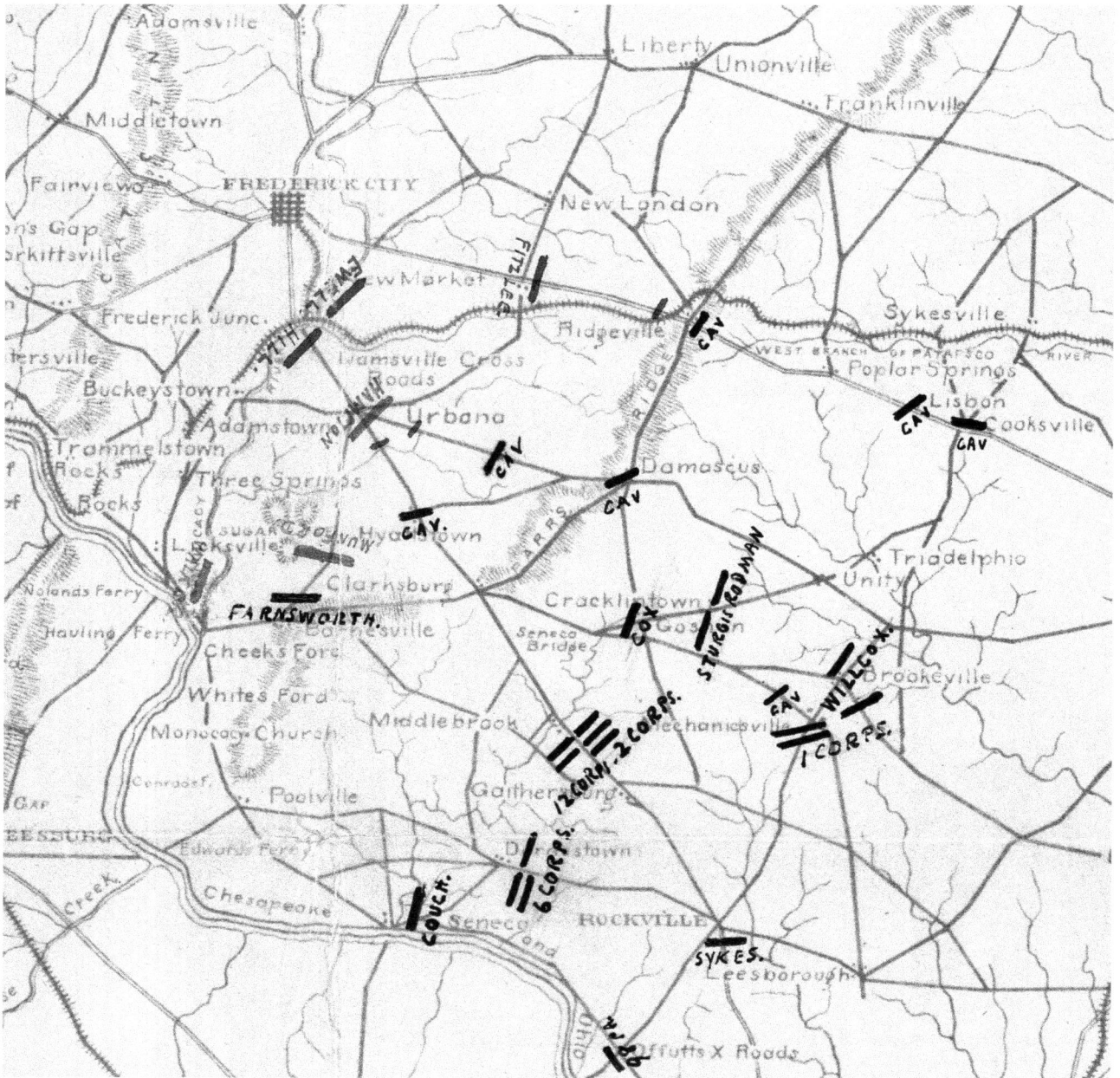

Situation map night of 9 September. Pleasonton continues pressing Stuart through Parr's Ridge as Union infantry advance. McClellan reported that on the 9th his units were located as follows: First and Ninth Corps at Brookville, Second and Twelfth Corps Middleburg, Sixth Corps at Darnestown, Couch's division at the Mouth of Seneca Creek, and Sykes's division at Rockville, *Report on the Organization and Campaigns of the Army of the Potomac*, 349. Courtesy LOC.

Union troopers were becoming more than an annoyance to Stuart's men and this should have alerted him that trouble was on the horizon for Gen. Lee and his army, as the Unionists were approaching much more quickly than either thought. In less than a week, Lee, and a third of his army, would be fighting for their lives on South Mountain.

Chapter 6

On to Frederick

THE UNION SIGNAL CORPS occupied Sugarloaf Mountain on 3 September and transmitted messages by flag to Poolesville, which were then telegraphed to Washington.[1] It was in active use spotting Confederate activity on 4 September and reported a suspected crossing into Maryland near the Monocacy River. Union flagmen on Sugarloaf are credited with sending the first official notice of the Confederate advance actually received in Washington. Union signal officers were also initially sent to Maryland Heights at Harpers Ferry, Point of Rocks, Poolesville, and Seneca. Poolesville was abandoned by Unionists as was Sugarloaf, while Seneca was only temporarily abandoned, as the Confederates advanced.[2] On September 5-6, the flagmen on Sugarloaf watched the Army of Northern Virginia cross the Potomac River to invade Maryland. The signal station on Sugarloaf had been established in the summer of 1861, one in a chain of such stations. It communicated with a signal station and the U.S. Signal Corps School, southeast of Darnestown, from which messages were relayed to Washington, and to the signal station at the Point of Rocks, railhead of the Baltimore and Ohio Railroad to the northwest, where messages would be signaled to Harpers Ferry.[3]

On his ride north to meet Gen. Lee on 6 September, Stuart rode with his cavalry to Frederick by way of Hyattstown past Sugarloaf Mountain to the west. Sugarloaf Mountain, less than three miles north-northwest of Barnesville, Maryland, was an excellent vantage point, with it being possible to see Washington some 30 miles to the southeast on a clear day, and far up the Potomac River to the Catoctin Mountains to the west.[4] Its summit is 1,282 feet above sea level and is about 800 feet higher than surrounding terrain, easily the most important key terrain feature east of the South Mountain range for both McClellan and Lee. Maj. Albert J. Myer, Chief Signal Officer of the U.S. Army, described the view from it as follows: "The range of vision from this point is unequaled by that from any other in Maryland.

---

[1] Sent on 4 September: "To Maj. Gen. Banks. [in Washington] A large wagon train—judge 50 to 75 wagons, moving out from Leesburg, easterly, in direction of Edward's Ferry. Continuous clouds of dust seen on reads leading in & out of Leesburg. A large wagon park 4 to 6 miles southeast of Leesburg, near turnpike. The enemy are now shelling the aqueduct over Monocacy river, and I judge are attempting to cross, from the reports of musketry heard," Fishel, 211.

[2] J. Willard Brown, *The Signal Corps in the War of the Rebellion* (Boston: U.S. Signal Corps Association, 1896; reprint, Baltimore: Butternut and Blue, 1996), 325-330. But see Bradley T. Johnson, "Reunion of Virginia Division A.N.V. Association," in *Southern Historical Society Papers*, vol. 12, January to December 1884 (Richmond: Southern Historical Society, n.d. Reprint, Millwood, NJ: Kraus Reprint Co, 1977), 518, concerning lack of use of potential signals from Union forces on Catoctin Mountain to Maryland Heights. He conjectures that had Burnside made use of signals on 13 September, Harpers Ferry might have been warned to hold pending relief. Harsh, *Flood*, 107-108. *OR* vol. 19, pt. 1, 815.

[3] Paul J. Scheips, "Union Signal Communications: Innovations and Conflicts, in *Civil War History*, vol. 9, no. 4, December 1993, 404-405; Willard Brown, 65.

[4] Fishel, 211; Carman, Pierro, 86.

It includes several prominent fords of the Potomac, the approaches to them in Virginia, and much of the country into which an army passing those fords would move."[5] This mountain is clearly visible from many miles away, and Stuart was close enough to notice Federal signalmen atop the mountain wig-wagging messages toward Washington. He quickly sent a detachment to capture them.

On 5 September 1862, Union 2nd Lt. Brinkerhoff N. Miner signaled that "The enemy crossed the Potomac at Noland's Ferry last evening. Pickets of Maulsby's [1st Maryland Potomac Home Brigade Regiment] regiment stationed at the aqueduct. After firing off their ammunition, passed here en route to Frederick....The [Potomac] river is easily fordable at that point. I can see about 2,000 of the enemy upon this side, scattered along from the aqueduct to Noland's Ferry; judge they are cavalry."[6] After signaling this information of the invasion of the Confederate army to Darnestown and Point of Rocks, the Federal signalmen, Miner and his flagman, Pvt. A.H. Cook, made a hasty retreat down the mountain but decided to return the next morning. They ran headfirst into the 1st North Carolina Cavalry and took advantage of mutual surprise to turn around and escape, serendipitously capturing a Confederate courier. The courier, who had unwisely ridden out ahead of the troopers unaccompanied by his cavalry guide, had messages from Richmond and President Davis. Later, the Confederates caught up with the Yankees four miles toward Urbana at the home of a young woman friend of Lt. Miner. As the hapless Union signalmen were dragged outside and searched, Stuart rode up and greeted the Federal prisoners: "Good morning, gentlemen. I am very happy to see you." Miner replied, "Good morning, General, we are sorry we cannot return the compliment...[Stuart] laughed and said, 'Oh, well, it is the fortune of war, you know,' and giving orders to his men to treat them well, he rode off."[7] The signalmen remained the guests of Stuart until after the Battle of Antietam when they and 600 others were marched to Richmond and confined in Libby Prison.[8]

An unknown Rebel trooper in Hampton's Brigade also wrote of this incident in more detail:

---

[5] Melanie Choukas-Bradley, *Sugarloaf: The Mountain's History, Geology and Natural Lore* (Charlottesville, VA: University of Virginia Press, March 2003), 11. Sugarloaf Mountain is approximately 800 feet higher than the land to the east and somewhat higher than the Frederick Valley to the west with sheer cliffs on the western side. *OR*, vol. 19, pt. 1, 118.

[6] *OR*, vol. 19, pt. 2, 184-185. Cook wrote that he had to ride to Poolesville to have this first official news sent to Washington, The U.S. Veteran Signal Corps Association book, *A Revised Roster of the Signal Corps, U.S.A., During the War of the Rebellion, with Personal Records of Service in the Corps* (n.p., 1886), 55.

[7] Willard Brown, 242. Cook wrote that as he was returning from Point of Rocks after having the Rebel sighting telegraphed to Banks, he joined Miner and rode toward the summit of the mountain but they encountered two Rebel cavalrymen. After a short chase, they captured one of them, a courier, carrying dispatches from Jefferson Davis to Gen. Lee. Cook said he advised Miner to take the courier to Washington or leave him and escape with the dispatches but doing neither, both were soon captured by a brigade led by Wade Hampton, The U.S. Veteran Signal Corps Association book, 55.

[8] The romantic version of the capture of Miner is noted in Harsh, *Flood*, 522, n. 86; Willard Brown, 242. Some of this text is from the Maryland Civil War Trails marker at the entrance to Sugarloaf Mountain. With its commanding view, the mountain was in use from early in the war and probably had a wooden tower constructed on it, see Choukas-Bradley, *Sugarloaf: The Mountain's History, Geology and Natural Lore*, 26. See also Priest, *Before Antietam*, 15-16; and Jacobs notes that a signal station was established at the Poolesville town hall communicating with Sugarloaf, Darnestown and Muddy Branch; a telegraph office was also there when Union forces were in the area used to transmit messages received by flag to Washington by telegraph, 43-44. Both Miner and Cook were on detail from Company D, 34th New York Volunteer Regiment. They were both stationed at Sugarloaf during the winter of 1861-1862 and then joined Banks' division and were in the Battle of Winchester on 23 March 1862, the Shenandoah Valley Campaign, Cedar Mountain, then with Pope and Second Bull Run; they next returned to Sugarloaf about 1 September. Cook some 23 years later quoted Stuart somewhat differently: "'Are the despatches all right? *Are the despatches all right?*' On being assured of their safety he turned to us and said, 'Good morning, gentlemen, I am very happy to see you.' We replied, 'Good morning General, we are sorry we cannot return the compliment.' He laughed and said, 'Oh well, it is the fortune of war you know,'—and giving orders to his men to treat us well, rode off," The U.S. Veteran Signal Corps Association book, 55 (emphasis in original). Note that Cook does not mention the young woman. The cheery, bantering tone of Stuart in these accounts seems plausible.

After passing through the town of Barnsville, bearing to the right of a range of mountains known as the "Sugar-Loaf Range," we were quietly pursuing our course along a by-way leading around the base of these mountains, when an alarming incident occurred, that came well-nigh affecting seriously the ensuing campaign. The Government despatches containing the matter relative to the present campaign upon which the Confederates had just entered were entrusted to a bearer, in care of our cavalry, who, with a courier, had incautiously rode on ahead of the advance guard a short distance, when they were assailed by a small party of Yankee cavalry springing suddenly upon them in the bend of the road. The bearer and all the despatches were captured; the courier succeeded in escaping back to the advance guard, who, under Captain Ruffin, were led on in instant pursuit, which was anxiously and vigorously kept up for four miles, when the objects were suddenly overtaken, being only an officer and private of the Yankee signal corps in charge of the prisoner. They, strange to say, had not examined the portmanteau conspicuously appended to the pommel of the saddle, but had leisurely called at a farm house on the roadside, not dreaming that their quiet would be so suddenly intruded upon. The officer, as the affair turned out, being a romantic youth, while on signal duty on these mountains had signalized to Cupid, who had exchanged his mischievous darts between him and the old farmer's daughter, a bouncing lass of "sweet sixteen," and had doubtless called in his course to have a tete-a-tete, to relate the adventures of the morning to his lady love. But he found his romance broken in upon as our dusty troopers dashed up to the house and led him out from the cozy embraces of his mountain Delilah, who had plowed so deeply into his affections as to have shorn him of the bright honors which would have awaited him from his sensational masters at Washington from the circumstances of such an important capture. The weeping lass mingled her sobs with his further mortification as General Stuart, who had just rode up, inflicted the right of search upon his person, extracting something more than love documents which was found to be a matter of some military importance to us. After this occurrence we pursued our march quietly on to the little village of Urbana, where Generals Stuart and Hampton established their headquarters."[9]

---

[9] Brooks, *Butler and His Cavalry in the War of Secession 1861-1865*, 78-79. Miner had been posted to Sugarloaf the previous winter so it is likely that he would have made friends in the area. It is unknown what these dispatches might be but it is certain that they did not include Davis's reply to Gen. Lee's dispatch of 4 September detailing Lee's move into Maryland. They may have involved information about Bragg's activities in the west and news of Union and Confederate movements in the Richmond area. In short, there would likely have been little of tactical use for McClellan or strategic use for Halleck and Lincoln. Note, Hampton's headquarters were actually at Hyattstown.

Sugarloaf Mountain as seen from Barnesville. Sugarloaf is to the north, northwest of this point a little over four airline miles away to the summit from Barnesville Road at West Harris Road. Courtesy Craig Swain HMdb.org.

Sugarloaf Mountain as seen from Comus on Old Hundred Road (Maryland Route 109) at Comus Road (Maryland Route 95). Sugarloaf is to the northwest of this point a little over three airline miles away to the summit. Courtesy Craig Swain HMdb.org.

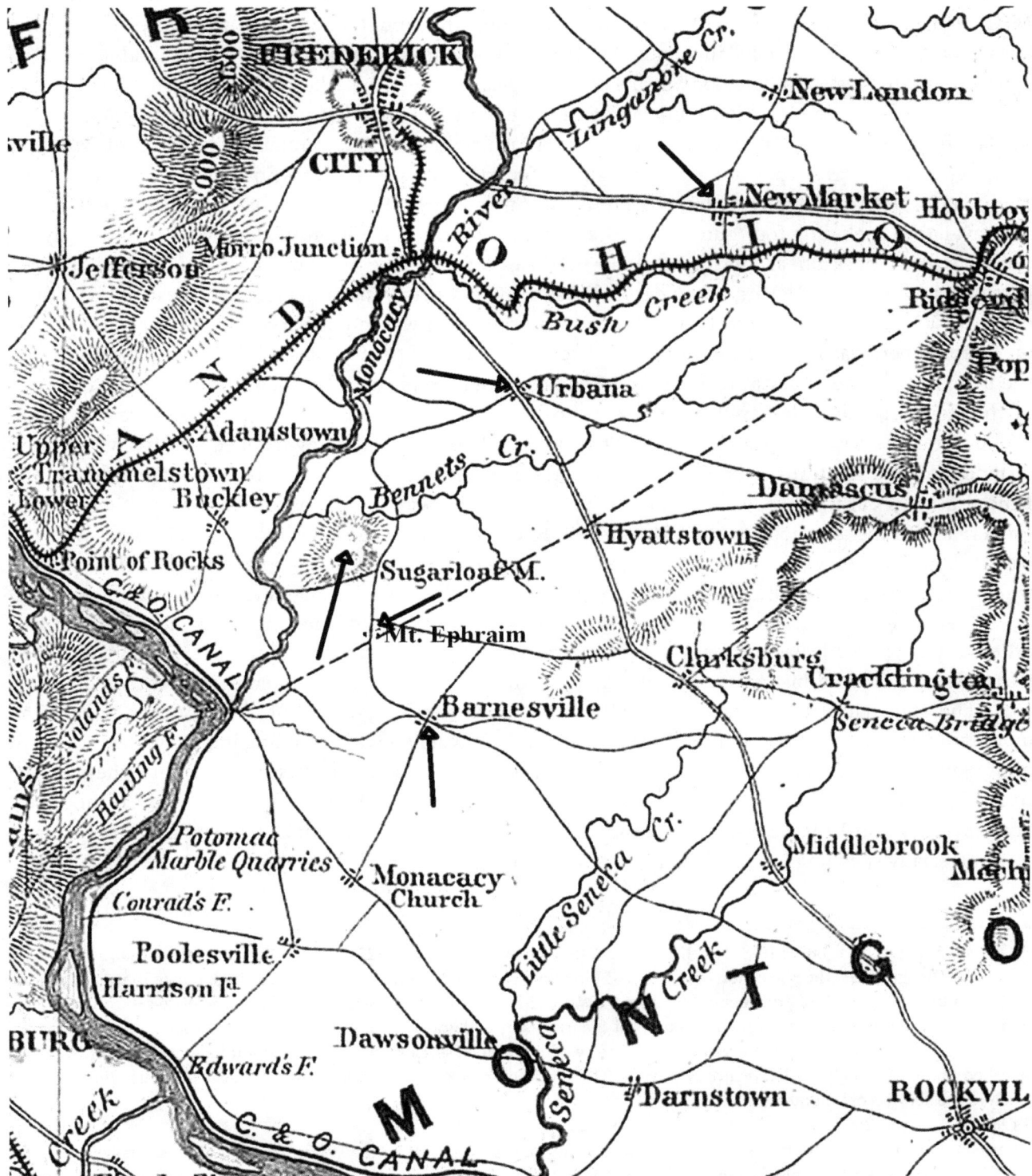

Sugarloaf Mountain, a key terrain feature coveted by McClellan, at the center left arrow. Urbana, Stuart's headquarters is in the upper center at the arrow on the Georgetown Pike. New Market at the upper right arrow is on the National Pike where Fitzhugh Lee had his headquarters while his troopers extended posts out to Ridgeville. Sugarloaf Mountain at the left center of the map was patrolled by Munford's cavalry with pickets down toward Poolesville, while between them Hampton established his headquarters at Hyattstown and had pickets at roads through Parr's Ridge at Clarksburg, Damascus, and Ridgeville; Poolesville is at the lower left. Mt. Ephraim was close to Sugarloaf on a crossroads. Thus Stuart's cavalry had Gen. Lee's eastern flank covered from the Potomac to the National Pike screening Lee's army west of the Monocacy River at this Parr's Ridge/Sugarloaf Line. Detail of map; New York, E.&G. W. Blunt 1861. Courtesy LOC.

McClellan recognized Sugarloaf's value and he assumed Pleasonton had taken it on 9 September. McClellan also told Maj. Gen. William B. Franklin to take the mountain quickly: "the earlier we gain the Sugar Loaf the better." McClellan wanted Sugarloaf because it was an "important object" and it "must be carried."[10] Halleck also understood Sugar Loaf's importance when he asked McClellan on 14 September "I fear you are exposing your left flank, and that the enemy can cross in your rear. Can you not ascertain the fact from Sugar Loaf Mountain?"[11] Confederate cavalry fought hard to retain Sugarloaf. Col. Munford on 8 September was in position on the right of Stuart's Parr's Ridge/Sugarloaf Line, but after his 7th Virginia Cavalry was detailed to Jackson on the morning of the 10th, Munford had less than five hundred men available, including four guns of Chew's Battery. Munford's 2nd Virginia, led by Lt. Col. Richard H. Burks, was in position at the cross-roads southeast of the base of the mountain, covered by rail barricades, while the 12th Virginia under Col. Asher W. Harman, was on its right and rear.[12] A squadron of the 9th Virginia Cavalry from Fitzhugh Lee's Brigade which was left at Barnesville under Capt. Waller on 6 September, was hotly pressed two days later, so the rest of the 9th moved back from New Market to the base of Sugarloaf to assist. Union cavalry had captured the picket of 10 men from the 9th and the rest of the Rebel squadron fell back on the road to New Market. The regiment met the retreating Capt. Waller near the eastern base of the mountain and checked the following Yankee cavalry which then dismounted and continued their attack. Even though outnumbered, the Rebel troopers held off the Unionists until dark and rode back through New Market by way of Urbana and Monrovia, then toward Frederick.[13] In the afternoon of the 10th, the 6th U.S. Cavalry tested the 2nd Virginia Cavalry lines near the base of Sugarloaf but failed. Pleasonton, perhaps exaggerating his efforts, reported to McClellan that he made three attempts to dislodge the Rebels and believed that the Confederates held a strong position. McClellan ordered Franklin to support Pleasonton with a brigade of infantry and at noon, Couch was ordered to support Pleasonton with a brigade, and with his whole division if necessary. Shortly, Couch was ordered to hasten his movement and told that the mountain must be taken even if it took all of his command and that of Franklin. Additionally, three more messages were sent to Pleasonton to take the mountain using Couch's and Franklin's troops—clearly McClellan was becoming impatient with the lack of progress. Then at 3 P.M., Franklin was placed in command to take the mountain. Despite these orders from McClellan's headquarters, no serious effort was made on the 10th. It is likely that had the mountain been taken on the 10th, the Confederate movements west from the Frederick area would have been seen thus materially speeding up McClellan's pursuit on the 11th.[14]

---

[10] *OR*, vol. 51, pt. 1, 801, 807, 810-811; vol. 19, pt. 2, 219, 238; Willard Brown, 327. Major Myer, the chief signal officer, on 9 September thought that "the possession of Sugar Loaf Mountain as a signal station will be of great importance to us, and that its possession by the enemy is of great benefit to them," *OR*, vol. 51, pt. 1, 802-803. While McClellan appreciated the efforts of the Signal Corps as he expressed in his general reports of the Army of the Potomac, *OR*, vol. 5, 31, he wrote that "The weak point in the signal corps as then constituted was that its officers were not trained soldiers, and therefore their judgment could not always be relied upon," McClellan, *McClellan's Own Story*, 135. McClellan, like the majority of regular army officers, did not think much of the abilities of volunteers.

[11] *OR*, vol. 19, pt. 2, 289.

[12] Carman, Pierro, 86-87. Munford may have stationed some guns on Sugarloaf by the 10th as Pleasonton's troopers were fired on "with three horse artillery pieces emplaced atop Sugar Loaf Mountain," Longacre, *Lincoln's Cavalrymen*, 103. No other reference has been found noting any guns on the top of the mountain.

[13] Beale, *9th Virginia*; Beale letter to Carman, 6 June 1897, courtesy Antietam National Battlefield Library (ANBL), 4th Virginia Cavalry Regimental File.

[14] Carman, Pierro, 87. The 6th U.S. Cavalry was busy since its arrival in Maryland on 6 September at Tennallytown but not attached directly to Pleasonton. The next day it marched through Darnestown to Dawsonville where after a day's rest, it reached Barnesville on the 8th. It sent scouting parties toward Frederick and Point of Rocks and continued scouting and picketing until the 10th when it fought the Rebels at Sugarloaf. Capt. Sanders with two guns tried to dislodge them but failed losing one killed and four wounded. On the 12th, it arrived at Middletown at 2 A.M. and then placed companies to guard the

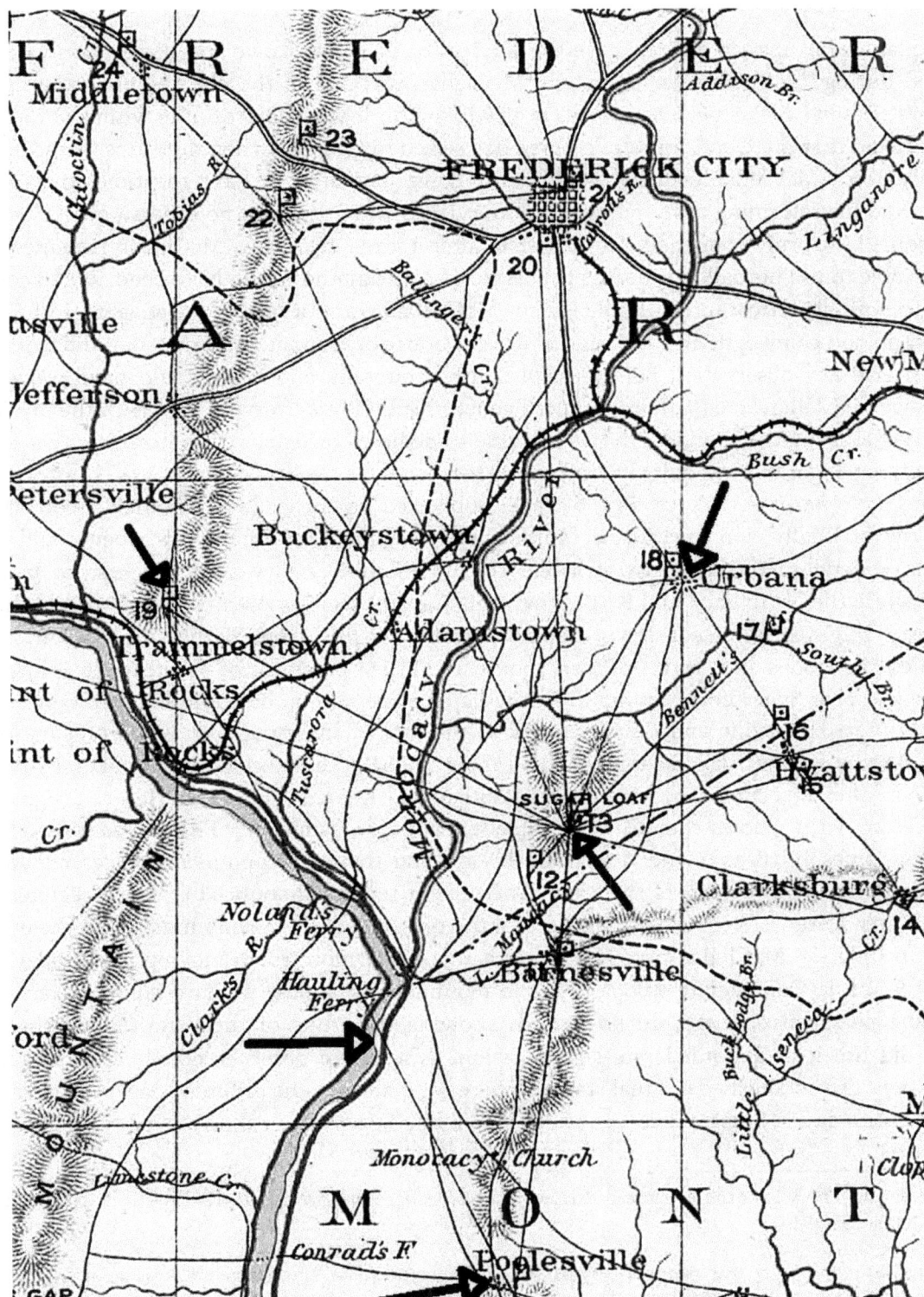

Map showing locations of Union signal stations; center arrow points to Sugarloaf, a hub for signals due to its commanding vista. Catoctin Mountain west of Frederick has numbers 22 and 23; 19 is on a hill near Point of Rocks with a view of Middletown Valley to the west. Stations east of South Mountain were back in operation on or before 14 September as Confederates moved west of South Mountain. Union signalmen followed McClellan's headquarters. Note stations at Poolesville and Urbana as well as Barnesville. Lower left arrow points to White's Ford. *Official Atlas*, Plate 27. Courtesy LOC.

fords of the Potomac from the mouth of the Monocacy upriver to Knoxville. Companies I and L scouted near Petersville and skirmished with Rebel troopers driving them off; Carter, *From Yorktown to Santiago*, 57-58.

McClellan unfortunately did not have the services of Thaddeus Lowe and his Balloon Corps which he enjoyed during his Peninsular Campaign. McClellan was one of the champions of the use of this civilian unit. Despite the value of the corps, as a civilian unit it was subject to the whims of the military, and Lowe found that the Quartermaster's Corps had seized his wagons when the corps was idle from the end of July 1862. McClellan said he would assist Lowe, but did not have the time to do so before McClellan and his reforming army moved into Maryland. Lowe received no orders until 18 September, when he joined the army commander at Antietam after a three-day delay. McClellan lamented that had Lowe been able to use his balloons during the Battle of Antietam he would have been able to completely defeat Lee before his retreat into Virginia.[15] Thus McClellan, without having the advantage of Sugarloaf's vistas early in the campaign, and lacking Lowe's balloons throughout the campaign, did not have the information the key observation point east of South Mountain, and Lowe could have provided him. Perhaps since McClellan acted as his own intelligence chief, he was overwhelmed with the myriad other duties he had as army commander, and was unable to dedicate sufficient time to ensure that Lowe was present and that Sugarloaf was quickly retaken.

On the 11th, Farnsworth's cavalry brigade, supported by Brig. Gen. Winfield Scott Hancock's infantry brigade, finally won Sugarloaf as Munford's two regiments of some 475 troopers could not stand against the Federal infantry. Farnsworth had the 8th Illinois Cavalry skirt the eastern base of the mountain while the 3rd Indiana and 8th Pennsylvania Cavalry went around the western side. Hancock's five infantry brigades followed slowly behind forming in line from Barnesville. Union signalmen accompanied the troops and "signal officers took part in the operations of the advance of the army at Poolesville and near Sugar Loaf Mountain. At the latter place, communication was maintained between Gen. Franklin at Barnesville and Gen. Hancock at the foot of the mountain, while preparations were making to occupy it. Thursday, September 11 at about 3 P.M., the mountain was retaken by our forces, and was soon after reoccupied by Lieutenants [William B.] Roe and [James S.] Hall as a signal station, communicating with Poolesville, to which place Capt. [Benjamin F.] Fisher had previously sent Lieutenants [James B.] Brooks and [Peter A.] Taylor, and thence communication was maintained by telegraph with the headquarters of the army. The earliest reports announced that two regiments of the enemy's cavalry were visible, but with no signs of the presence of the enemy in force on the east side of the Catoctin Ridge."[16] McClellan noted its use as it reported Union troops moving into Frederick on 12 September.[17] While Confederate troops held the mountain for almost six days taking advantage of its commanding perspective, there are no records showing the fruits of their use of it, although they obviously did use it as a Confederate signal station, as a Union observer noted: "On the top of the mountain they had established a signal station where we could see the different flags waved at intervals during the entire day."[18] Stuart made a good effort to retain Sugarloaf until he moved west after the army

---

[15] Charles M. Evans, *The War of the Aeronauts: A History of Ballooning During the Civil War* (Mechanicsburg, PA: Stackpole Books, Inc., 2002), 252-254.

[16] Willard Brown, 326.

[17] *OR*, vol. 19, pt. 1, 127, pt. 2, 254, 258, 271; 127; Willard Brown, 326; Harsh, *Flood*, 189. The telegraph line from Point of Rocks to Washington was apparently operating again as early as 12 September. Within a half mile of the Potomac, Point of Rocks has a vantage point almost 700 feet high giving excellent east-west views but not to the north as this point is on a ridge which runs north from the Potomac. Close to the river, the ridge is still 600 feet above sea level. Carman noted that on the 11th also "The 23d Pennsylvania, 1st New York Cavalry, and a section of artillery relieved the 55th New York at the mouth of the Monocacy," Carman, Pierro, 88.

[18] Willard Brown, 325. See also Sidney Davis, 225. Depending on how close Union observers were to the mountain, one may speculate that what they saw was only a Confederate flag vice signal flags, see for example, James H. Stevenson, *Boots and Saddles. A History of the First Volunteer Cavalry of the War, Known as the First New York (Lincoln) Cavalry and also as The Saber Regiment. Its Organization, Campaigns and Battles* (Harrisburg, PA: Patriot Publishing Company, 1879; reprint, Salem,

left Frederick, so it was obviously important to him—this might mitigate Stuart's apparently casual efforts in scouting given the commanding view from the mountain.

Heros von Borcke arrived late in the morning of the 11th with orders from Stuart to Munford to pull back, as Munford would become the army's rear guard. Not wishing to disengage in the middle of a battle, Munford rode quickly back to Urbana with von Borcke and confirmed with Stuart that his orders overrode Jackson's, who had ordered Munford to hold the mountain. As Munford withdrew to Hampton's former outpost at Hyattstown, Hampton moved toward Frederick, and Fitzhugh Lee moved through Urbana back toward New Market. Meanwhile, the 8th Illinois reached the summit of Sugarloaf and fired a volley to celebrate. The Confederates bivouacked three miles away toward Frederick, and the 9th Virginia Cavalry rejoined Fitzhugh Lee's Brigade at New Market, where Fitzhugh Lee had journeyed on the previous evening.[19] Stuart's Parr's Ridge/Sugarloaf Line was being withdrawn.

The early loss of Sugarloaf was a serious blow to the Union intelligence gathering effort during the critical early days of the campaign. That it was not captured quickly meant that Stuart's screening efforts succeeded better than they should have, leaving McClellan puzzled over Lee's intentions and movements on the 10th. Carman believes that if Sugarloaf had been carried on 10 September as it should have, except for the dilatory actions of Pleasonton, Couch, and Franklin, Lee's Army's movements out of Frederick might have been seen.[20] Thus Munford's screening efforts served Lee well during the early part of the Maryland Campaign holding Sugarloaf, while Pleasonton and Franklin must be faulted for their dilatory actions in not quickly retaking it, and also McClellan for not ensuring that his orders were more diligently followed.

MA: Higginson Book Company, n.d.), "We could see the Confederate flag plainly on Sugar Loaf Mountain," 116. While Carman writes that "one of the first acts of the Confederates upon entering Maryland was to possess themselves of the mountain and establish a signal party on it," he supplies no details or references, Carman, Pierro, 86. There is no record that Lee had a Chief Signal Officer on his staff. As required, he used a corps signal officer, of whom several are identified. During the Maryland Campaign of fall, 1862, two of the (later) corps-level signal officers were hors de combat—Capt. Wilbourn (Jackson) from a wound during Second Manassas, forcing Jackson to employ a signalman who was detailed; and Capt. Manning (Longstreet) from a painful infection, making McLaws depend on an instructed staff officer. Capt. Randolph was probably with D.H. Hill on South Mountain and Capt. Frayser (replacing Capt. J. Hardeman Stuart killed at Second Manassas) with Jeb Stuart. Generally speaking, each signal officer had a signal sergeant as a technical assistant, some of whom acted as local "officers" in charge, like warrant officers in today's military. Information from Dave Gaddy posted on "Talk Antietam" 1 March 2008. The Museum of the Confederacy has in its collection a Confederate signal flag with a white field and red square center, 41.5" x 52.5" which was "captured at the battle of Catoctin Ridge, MD, Sept. 1862 by Lt. Frank N. Wicker, U.S. Signal Corps."

[19] Carman, Pierro, 87-88; Priest, *Before Antietam*, 68-78. Curious why Munford did not trust the order von Borcke carried from Stuart and why Munford believed he was still subject to orders from Jackson which trumped Stuart's. Robertson's Brigade which Munford now led was under Jackson in the Shenandoah Valley and on the Peninsula so Munford may still have believed that Jackson's orders superseded Stuart's as Jackson was senior. Too, Munford did not think much of Stuart.

[20] Carman, Pierro, 87

View from the summit of Sugarloaf Mountain looking west across Frederick and Middletown Valleys. In the background is the Virginia side of the Catoctin Range, Furnace Mountain, where the Potomac passes Point of Rocks, Maryland, at the arrow at the right lower center. A signal station at Point of Rocks relayed messages to Harpers Ferry and by telegraph to Washington. Sugarloaf station could also communicate with a signal station and U.S. Signal Corps School southeast of Darnestown, from which messages were relayed to Washington. Airline distance from peak of Sugarloaf to Point of Rocks is a little over 8 miles. Airline distance to Frederick is about 8½ miles. South Mountain is in the distant background at the rightmost arrow. Photograph by Craig Swain from HMdb.org.

View from the summit of Sugarloaf Mountain looking east. Darnestown, Gaithersburg, and Rockville, Maryland, lay in the distance. Barnesville is about 4½ miles south of Sugarloaf, Urbana 3½, while Hyattstown is less than 4. On a clear day it is possible to see Washington, D.C. In September however, morning fog and mist likely prevented clear viewing on many mornings. Harsh shows meteorological data for Frederick for the days the Confederates were on the mountain but does not mention fog or mist for this period. This may indicate that morning conditions such as those did not prevail in Frederick although humidity readings were not included, Harsh, *Shallows*, 1-31. Photograph by Craig Swain from HMdb.org.

View from the summit of Sugarloaf Mountain looking south. The smoke stack at the upper right is a power plant one mile downstream on the Potomac from the mouth of the Monocacy River and about a mile and a half upstream from White's Ford on the Potomac which leads to Leesburg, Virginia. The mountains on the far horizon behind the smokestack are the continuation of the Catoctin Range in Loudoun County, Virginia, known as the Bull Run Mountains. It is likely that there were fewer trees between Sugarloaf and the Potomac in 1862 giving signalmen a clearer picture of Confederate and Union movements. Photograph by Craig Swain from HMdb.org.

On the afternoon of 9 September, after meeting with Longstreet and Jackson, Gen. Lee had his chief of staff, Col. Robert H. Chilton, write seven copies on single sheets, written front and back, of the order detailing the division of his army into four parts to deal with the Union garrisons remaining at Martinsburg and Harpers Ferry.[21] Here began one of the most controversial incidents of the Maryland Campaign and perhaps of the war. Copies were carried to major commanders but Jackson later made a handwritten copy for division commander Maj. Gen. Daniel H. Hill, his brother-in-law, assuming that Hill's division was still under his command. Jackson's handwritten copy was delivered to Maj. James W. Ratchford on Hill's staff by Maj. Henry Kyd Douglas, one of Jackson's staff. Chilton's copy for Hill was sent by courier and apparently lost; Chilton, in violation of normal headquarters' procedure, never questioned the missing receipt for this copy. This oversight was most likely due to the confusion of packing for the move west, and also to the relatively loose rein Lee had kept on his too small staff.[22] The various possibilities of which officer lost the order or how it was otherwise misplaced have demonstrated that it was most probably not lost by Hill or his staff but by the courier carrying the order from Chilton. One historian argues convincingly that the most likely culprit was Henry Kyd Douglas based on his

---

[21] Harsh, *Shallows*, 160-163; Harsh writes that there were at least seven and possibly eleven copies. See Attachment, Chapter 7, for the order.

[22] J. Boone Bartholomees, Jr., in *Buff Facings and Gilt Buttons: Staff and Headquarters Operations in the Army of Northern Virginia, 1861-1865* (Columbia, SC: University of South Carolina University Press, 1998), 205, wrote that "only officers, and preferably staff officers, carried verbal and important written orders. If a courier carried a message, commanders were supposed to mark it with the place and time of departure and the place and time of receipt. As in other areas, the Army of Northern Virginia did not strictly follow regulations," Confederate States of America War Department, Regulations, 1863, 51-52, 57. From the regulations which are the same for the 1862 version: "544: In the field, verbal orders and important sealed orders are carried by officers, and, if possible, by staff officers. When orders are carried by orderlies, the place and time of departure will be marked on them, and place and time of delivery on the receipt." If Douglas carried the order, then a receipt would not be required. Note that this 1862 regulation is identical to number 556 of the Union Army regulations of 1861.

personality, the opportunities he had, and that he had delivered Jackson's copy of the order earlier to Ratchford.[23] Both copies of S.O. 191 written for Hill omitted paragraph I dealing with Confederate visitation to Frederick and paragraph II pertaining to one of Lee's staff, Maj. Walter Taylor's, visit to Winchester as neither concerned Hill as a division commander.

One of Lee's commanders, Col. Bradley T. Johnson, a Maryland native, wrote about Lee's miscalculation regarding the retreat of the Federals from Martinsburg and Harpers Ferry which was the genesis for the special order: "When Lee crossed into Maryland he knew that eleven thousand Federal troops were stationed at Winchester, Martinsburg and Harpers Ferry. After he had crossed, he was informed that they had retired from Winchester. He supposed as he had a right to expect that they would evacuate the line of the Upper Potomac, and withdraw by way of Hagerstown into Pennsylvania. It is singular, but true, that whenever Lee anticipated his adversary's making a blunder he was never disappointed; whenever he relied upon his acting upon sound rules of strategy his expectations always failed. So it was, that when he relied upon the evacuation of Harpers Ferry he found that he was entirely mistaken in his calculation."[24] Lee wrote "It had been supposed that the advance upon Fredericktown would lead to the evacuation of Martinsburg and Harper's Ferry, thus opening the line of communication through the Valley. This not having occurred, it became necessary to dislodge the enemy from those positions before concentrating the army west of the mountains."[25] Since Lee planned to use the Shenandoah Valley and its extension north, the Cumberland Valley, as his own line of communication, it was critical for him that these two enemy garrisons not impede this line. Even though Lee initially expected to meet much of his food and forage needs in Maryland, ammunition was critical; Winchester was to be his major supply depot. He fell into the trap of assuming that those garrisons would follow reasonable military tactics, but he did not know that Halleck, and the veteran department commander, Maj. Gen. John Wool, had ordered the Harpers Ferry garrison, to which the Martinsburg garrison eventually retreated, to remain in place, and to fight until relieved by the Army of the Potomac. Wool intoned that "You will not abandon Harper's Ferry without defending it to the last extremity....Be energetic and active, and defend all places to the last extremity. There must be no abandoning of a post, and shoot the first man that thinks of it, whether officer or soldier." Halleck told Col. Miles commanding at Harpers Ferry that "It is important that Harper's Ferry be held to the latest moment."[26] The Confederate supply conduit of some 140 miles from Hagerstown, Maryland, to Staunton, Virginia, mostly on the well-constructed and macadamized Valley Turnpike, combined with Staunton's Virginia Central Railroad link to Richmond of some 110 miles, was critical for Lee. This line of communication had to be maintained both to supply the army and to serve as a secure line of retreat.[27] Martinsburg's Union garrison was directly on the Valley Turnpike while the much larger garrison at Harpers Ferry was close enough to menace from the east. Lee had no choice but to chase away or capture both before he could continue his march north from Hagerstown into the Cumberland Valley in Pennsylvania, to be able to continue drawing the Army of the Potomac further from its main supply base, Washington, D.C.

Thus Lee divided his army into four parts, Jackson to capture Martinsburg and gather up any escapees from Harpers Ferry, and two other parts to capture Harpers Ferry, McLaws on the Maryland

---

[23] Wilbur D. Jones, "Who Lost the Lost Order?," *Civil War Regiments: A Journal of the American Civil War*, vol. 5, no. 3 (1997). For another excellent analysis of all the mysteries surrounding the Lost Order, see Stephen W. Sears, "The Twisted Tale of the Lost Order," *North & South*, Vol. 5, No. 7 (Oct., 2002), pp. 54-65. Harsh found Jones's analysis less than persuasive, Harsh, *Shallows*, 167.

[24] Johnson, "Reunion of Virginia Division A.N.V. Association,"513.

[25] *OR*, vol. 19, pt. 2, 145.

[26] *OR*, vol. 19, pt. 1, 520, 523, 787.

[27] Carl von Clausewitz, *On War*, edited and translated by Michael Howard and Peter Paret (Princeton, N.J.: Princeton University Press, 1989), 345.

side, and Walker on the Virginia shore, while the fourth under Longstreet marched to Boonsboro with his command and the army's trains. Lee expected to reassemble his army after they eliminated the Harpers Ferry and Martinsburg garrisons and be ready to continue his Maryland adventure north into Pennsylvania.[28] Lee's wildly optimistic three-day timetable for the capture of the Union garrisons, was based on two reasonable expectations, first, that the garrisons would quickly surrender or retreat, and second, that the Union pursuit from Washington would continue to be slow, so there should be no reason to fear that his divided army would be dangerously vulnerable. Stuart materially contributed to the failure of Lee's second expectation because the usually able cavalry commander did not know how close large Union infantry forces were, behind their cavalry screen, so there was little Lee saw to fear in dividing his army in the face of an enemy advance while in hostile country. Lee's confidence in what Stuart reported to him, as well as what he perceived from his experience with Union armies under McClellan and Pope during the last three months, must have been more than adequate to not trouble him enough to allow for a more flexible timetable than the one in S.O. 191. But most dangerously, Jackson and Stuart were affected by the belief in the slowness of the Union approach—Jackson by not making more of an effort to move his "foot cavalry" more quickly after leaving Frederick, and Stuart by adhering to the timetable in S.O. 191, even when it fell seriously behind.[29] Could it have been that operating in the enemy's country with inadequate maps and intelligence made these two of Lee's commanders less sure of themselves and more cautious, or perhaps the easy days in camp around Frederick were still affecting their normally aggressive spirits?

---

[28] See *Lee's Lieutenants*, 2:162, "The actual capture of the Ferry was to be the task of Lafayette McLaws, who was to seize the Maryland Heights." Lee only specifically delegated McLaws to take Harpers Ferry with Walker and Jackson to gather up the escapees. Lee was certain that the Union garrison at Harpers Ferry would flee once it saw the approach of the Rebel host but very probably gave his generals more detailed instructions in person before they left on their various missions. Even today, many writers mistakenly state that the three parts of Lee's army were sent to besiege Harpers Ferry with Jackson in command despite the lack of documentation for either of these positions.

[29] Harsh, *Flood*, 166-167. Harsh opines that Lee's mistake was basing his decision to divide his army on faulty premises because Stuart did not provide accurate information about Union movements. The normal rule defined by Jomini held that separating parts of an army which cannot be mutually supporting can lead to disaster, Baron de Jomini, *The Art of War*, translated by G.H. Mendell and W.P. Craighill (Philadelphia, PA: J.B. Lippincott & Co., 1862, reprint, Westport, CT: Westport Press, n.d., 187-188.

10 September 1862, Lee departs Frederick. Before dawn on the 10th most of the Army of Northern Virginia, Maj. Gen. Jackson in the lead left their camps around Frederick heading northwest along the National Pike. They formed detachments called for in Gen. Lee's S.O. No. 191 to dislodge the Federal garrisons at Martinsburg and Harpers Ferry, Virginia. Jackson's Command reached near Boonsboro, Longstreet's to just beyond Middletown, and McLaws' Division to near Burkittsville. Walker's Division, on the march since about 9 P.M. on the 9th, was to destroy the Monocacy Aqueduct at the mouth of the Monocacy River, but gets new orders from Gen. Lee in S.O. 191 and backtracked to cross the Potomac into Virginia upstream at Point of Rocks. Pleasonton has pushed Stuart west of Parr's Ridge. Jackson's march was less than speedy this day. Courtesy LOC.

In paragraph VIII of S.O. 191, Gen. Lee ordered that "General Stuart will detach a squadron of cavalry to accompany the commands of Generals Longstreet, Jackson and McLaws, and with the main body of the cavalry, will cover the route of the army, bringing up all stragglers that may have been left behind." The order did not spell out details of Stuart's missions, likely because he, like Jackson and Longstreet, met and talked with Lee before Lee moved west, as all of their headquarters were within an easy ride of each other. Protecting the route of the army at least meant that Stuart must cover the rear of the infantry column as it moved west on the National Pike from the vicinity of Frederick through the Catoctin Mountains, then through the South Mountain range. It also could have meant that in view of the Confederate belief in the deliberate, measured pursuit of Union forces, Stuart would remain east of the Catoctin and South Mountain ranges, harassing and slowing even more the dilatory Federal divisions, by holding passes through those ranges. The small cavalry forces assigned to Jackson, Longstreet and McLaws, one squadron (two companies) each, would probably only give one hundred cavalry at most for each of them for scouting and serving as messengers. Clearly, with these small numbers, Lee did not believe that they would confront formidable Union cavalry during their assignments. The day after he had S.O. 191 written, 10 September, Lee evidently modified the cavalry assignments, perhaps due to entreaties from Jackson and Longstreet, directing Munford to send his entire 7th Virginia Cavalry from his brigade to Jackson, and all of Fitzhugh Lee's 1st Virginia Cavalry to Longstreet. Records do not show that Walker, McLaws, or D.H. Hill, received any of Stuart's remaining cavalry. Munford had done the lion's share of the fighting for Stuart to this time, but was left with only two depleted regiments, the 2nd and 12th Virginia Cavalry, perhaps 400 sabers; Chew's Battery added another 100 men to the colonel's stalwart band.[30] The cavalry disbursements Lee made showed that he still did not realize that Stuart would have a great deal of difficulty in retarding the advance of the Union forces, believing that Stuart would encounter mainly Union cavalry. Lee would have recalled the relative ease with which the "Beau Sabreur" had usually handled his Union foes on the Peninsula and at Second Bull Run. But Stuart should have warned Lee by at least the 11th that Union infantry had been used in support of its cavalry, and when it had done so, Stuart's troopers were forced to retreat as happened at Sugarloaf Mountain.[31] Since Stuart could not penetrate the Union cavalry screen after making only feeble attempts to do so, he was unaware that Union infantry was advancing in force and was not mostly in its Washington camps, so both Stuart and Lee believed that the Confederate cavalry could successfully retard the Union advance. Gen. Lee's primary intelligence source, Stuart, was not giving him the information he needed about the Union infantry, and obviously the Washington, D.C. based spies were not able to get information to Lee.

But as Jackson marched west on the National Pike on the 10th, even he with his personal escort of a squadron of the Black Horse in the van, was not immune from harassment from Federal cavalry, as Stuart was not actively scouting to the north and west. Jackson had ordered the 7th Virginia Cavalry to bring up the rear of his column, likely to catch stragglers, so with only his personal escort, he did not have sufficient troopers to adequately scout his advance, which would soon result in his near capture by Union cavalry.[32] On the afternoon of the 10th, after he had crossed South Mountain at Turner's Gap on the National Pike, he had his headquarters tents pitched a mile east of Boonsboro in a field across from the house of John Murdock.

Modern photograph of the John Murdock House on the National Pike; South Mountain Range is in the background. Courtesy of Craig Swain HMdb.org.

---

[30] Carman, Pierro, 86; Harsh, *Flood*, opines that Lee overnight on the 9th/10th decided to augment cavalry already with Jackson and Longstreet by assigning the 7th to Jackson and the 1st to Longstreet as Stuart would not have done so on his own, 175, n. 13. Harsh also wrote the on this critical day, the 10th, "there is no indication that Stuart undertook any special measures to gain information or to increase security as the army headed westward. The 10th was 'one day more of rest at headquarters' for the cavalry chief," *Flood*, 180. But Stuart's screen was effective as there are no Union reports that showed knowledge of Gen. Lee's movement west, "Ironically, Stuart's complaisance on the 10th indicates that he was as ignorant of McClellan's movements behind the screen of opposing cavalry, as was Pleasonton of Lee," ibid., 181. Stuart and Lee were ignorant of Franklin's 10-mile march to Barnesville, 12 miles southeast of Frederick, and Sumner's move to Damascus, 14 miles from Frederick and five miles from Stuart's headquarters at Urbana, ibid.

[31] Carman, Pierro, 87.

[32] Harsh, *Flood*, 175.

Some of his escort, about 10 of the Black Horse, with Lt. Alexander Dixon Payne in command, continued on a scouting foray on the National Pike toward Hagerstown. Col. S. Basset French, a volunteer aide-de-camp to Jackson, on loan from Virginia Governor Letcher's staff, followed the squad into town, along with a companion. Seeking a good meal, Col. French stopped in the United States Hotel on the corner of Main Street and the Boonsboro-Sharpsburg Pike to enjoy his repast of an apple pie preceded by a shot of whiskey. Another member of Jackson's staff, Lt. Henry Kyd Douglas, against Jackson's advice, followed French into town, along with a courier, "to get some information about the fords of the Potomac and incidentally to see some friends."[33] Douglas, who had lived in Ferry Hill Place, about eight miles southwest of Boonsboro near the Potomac River across from Shepherdstown, knew the area, and was likely eager to meet with some young ladies with whom he was acquainted, in addition to learning about the current state of Potomac fords and the locations of Union troops.[34]

Douglas, the youngest of Jackson's staff and the son of a clergyman, was born in Shepherdstown, Virginia, on 29 September 1840. Growing up at Ferry Hill Place, his father's farm on a bluff in Maryland overlooking the Potomac River and Shepherdstown, he became very familiar with the area. John Blackford built Ferry Hill Place just after the war of 1812 and named it after the ferry that ran at the foot of the bluff before a covered bridge was built there in 1850. Reverend Robert Douglas, son-in-law of John Blackford, bought it in 1848. Graduating from Franklin and Marshall College in Lancaster, Pennsylvania, Henry Kyd Douglas studied law under Judge John Brockenbrough, in Lexington, Virginia. After practicing law in St. Louis, Missouri, he returned to his Ferry Hill home shortly after Virginia passed the Ordinance of Secession on 17 April 1861. He began his military service when he enlisted as a private in the Shepherdstown Company, Company B, of the 2nd Virginia Infantry, and found himself a sentinel at Harpers Ferry. Ironically, in June 1861, following Col. Thomas J. Jackson's orders, he was among those men sent to burn the bridge over the Potomac at Shepherdstown near his father's farm; his father was a stockholder in the Virginia & Maryland Bridge Company which owned the bridge. After the Battle of First Bull Run, he was promoted in August to junior lieutenant in his company, and first met then Brig. Gen. Stonewall Jackson. This encounter, and likely Douglas's friendship with Alexander S. "Sandy" ("Sandie") Pendleton, already on Jackson's staff, led to Jackson's assigning Douglas in April 1862 to temporary duty as one of his staff. After an epic ride in which Douglas delivered an important message to Brig. Gen. Richard S. Ewell, Jackson rewarded him by appointing him Assistant Inspector General. He continued to perform good service on Jackson's staff with the exception of his probable losing of a copy of the Lost Order already discussed. Effective 11 November 1862, Capt. Douglas was transferred to command of his old company, Co. B of the 2nd Virginia Infantry, and on 29 December, he received the added duty of Inspector General of the Stonewall Brigade. He later served on other generals' staffs, was wounded at least twice, and commanded a brigade at Petersburg and Appomattox, before Lee's surrender, but his rank as brigadier general was never confirmed. After the war, he practiced law in Winchester, Virginia, and Hagerstown, Maryland, was a judge, and was active in

---

[33] Douglas, 153. Lewis Marshall Helm, an historian of the Black Horse, estimates their average strength as 80, 261. Helm's roster shows three casualties during the Maryland Campaign for the Black Horse, Alexander Hunter captured at Sharpsburg on 17 September, John Johnson wounded, and James Vass wounded, 276, 277, 290. Jackson's order of march was reported to Gov. Curtin from a Union parolee; Curtin also reported to Halleck that Hagerstown was threatened and Capt. William J. Palmer and his troopers were needed for scouting but lacked horses, OR, vol. 19, pt. 2, 247. Palmer promoted colonel effective 8 September, 1862. Boonsboro-Shepherdstown Pike is also called Boonsboro-Sharpsburg Pike.
[34] Lee's Lieutenants, 2:163; Clemens, thesis, 426. The commander of the 7th Virginia Cavalry, Capt. Samuel B. Myers, detached from Munford, was apparently in the rear of Jackson's column but after Jackson crossed the Potomac, he and his troopers saw action as a detachment of his command scouted ahead of Jackson on the 11th and on the morning of the twelfth, entered the town, followed during the day by the rest of Jackson's command, Carman, Pierro, 110.

veterans' organizations and politics, as well as a writer of his wartime experiences. He died in Hagerstown in 1903.[35]

Unbeknownst to Jackson, as he apparently had no scouts or pickets south on the Boonsboro-Sharpsburg Pike, contrary to prudent marching doctrine, a Union patrol of 19 men from the 1st Maryland Cavalry was riding north. It was commanded by Capt. Francis Shamburg of Company A, who was accompanied by the commander of the 3rd Maryland Infantry at Kearneysville, Virginia, Lt. Col. Stephen W. Downey.[36] The 20 men were stationed at Kearneysville, near Martinsburg, some 18 miles southwest of Boonsboro, and were on a long scout seeking information about Lee's army. Seeing only Douglas and his companion who had not yet dismounted to follow French into the hotel, the Unionists charged the pair. The first Douglas knew of Downey's approach was the pounding of hooves, but then saw the Union cavalry as it rounded the corner in a column of fours, firing their pistols. The first casualty was Col. French's horse, thus stymieing his escape, so French followed a black servant into the basement to avoid capture by hiding in a coal cellar. Pvt. Bernard P. Green who had been in the general store in the lobby of the restaurant at the beginning of the attack, mounted his horse after the Union troopers took off in pursuit of Douglas. Green galloped after Lt. Payne and the Black Horse troopers to warn them but was forced to run the gauntlet of unfriendly fire from townsfolk shooting at him as he rode by.

---

[35] Douglas, 13-54 passim, 198, 338-340; Robertson, 359-360; Eicher and Eicher, 595; Eicher shows alternate birth years of 1838 or 1844; 1840 is taken from *I Rode with Stonewall.* Some historians view Douglas's accounts as highly embellished but given his service on several generals' staffs and acquaintance with Confederate higher society, his tales supply details not found elsewhere. See Dennis E. Frye, "Henry Kyd Douglas Challenged by His Peers," in *Civil War, The Magazine of the Civil War Society,* vol. IX, no. V, Sept.-Oct. 1991, 40. Frye details a possible alternative to the Boonsboro action. Frye includes a letter by Dr. Hunter McGuire to Jedediah Hotchkiss dated 22 January 1897: "I had, only a few weeks ago, a long talk with Col. Bassett French about the little affair at Boonsboro, and his recollection and mine perfectly accord. You remember in all of this campaign about Manassas and Maryland we had as couriers and guard for our headquarters the famous company of Black Horse cavalry. Jackson with his staff and this company, were in front of the column, and all stopped on top of a little hill overlooking Boonsboro. We got off our horses and laid down under the shade trees, and Col. French, Maj. Douglas, and one or two cavalrymen rode down into Boonsboro to buy or pillage anything they may have wanted. Jackson never left the staff and the company of cavalry; indeed the head of the column of infantry was directly behind us. While these four or five men were in the village a company of Yankee cavalry came suddenly into the town and Douglas and the rest came back at a full run toward us. We, seeing some commotion going on in the streets, sent the Black Horse cavalry in a gallop down into the town. One regiment of infantry was also gotten ready to follow the cavalry and see what was the matter. All of the party returned to us except French. He had tied his horse when the Yankee cavalry came. The people in [Boonsboro] hid him in a meal box only partly filled with meal. The Yankees, as soon as they saw our men coming, retreated and as they passed French's horse they did not have time to unfasten him and carry him away but one of them shot the horse through the leg, breaking the bone. French was a very ridiculous object when he came out of the house covered with meal. The horse was one that Jackson had ordered the quartermaster to lend to Col. French. I remember the first thing Jackson said to French when he met him: 'Col. French, you must pay Maj. Harman for that horse,' and eventually he did make him pay for it," 42. Gary M. Petrichick, "The C&O Canal in the Civil War," in *Along the Towpath,* vol. XLI, no. 2, June 2009, 15. Eicher shows that Douglas was twice wounded while other sources such as Petrichick and Fletcher M. Green in comments in *I Rode with Stonewall* show six wounds. As of May 2011, no comprehensive biography of Douglas has been written; it is needed.

[36] Frederick Whittaker, *Cavalry Doctrine: the Lessons of the Decade by a Volunteer Cavalryman* (New York: Printed by Author, 1871), 89-90. Whittaker, while listing the order in which a cavalry column should march, does show common-sense precautions on the march such as seeing the enemy first and preventing him from learning anything of the friendly force and picketing side roads. Here obviously Jackson's cavalry escort failed.

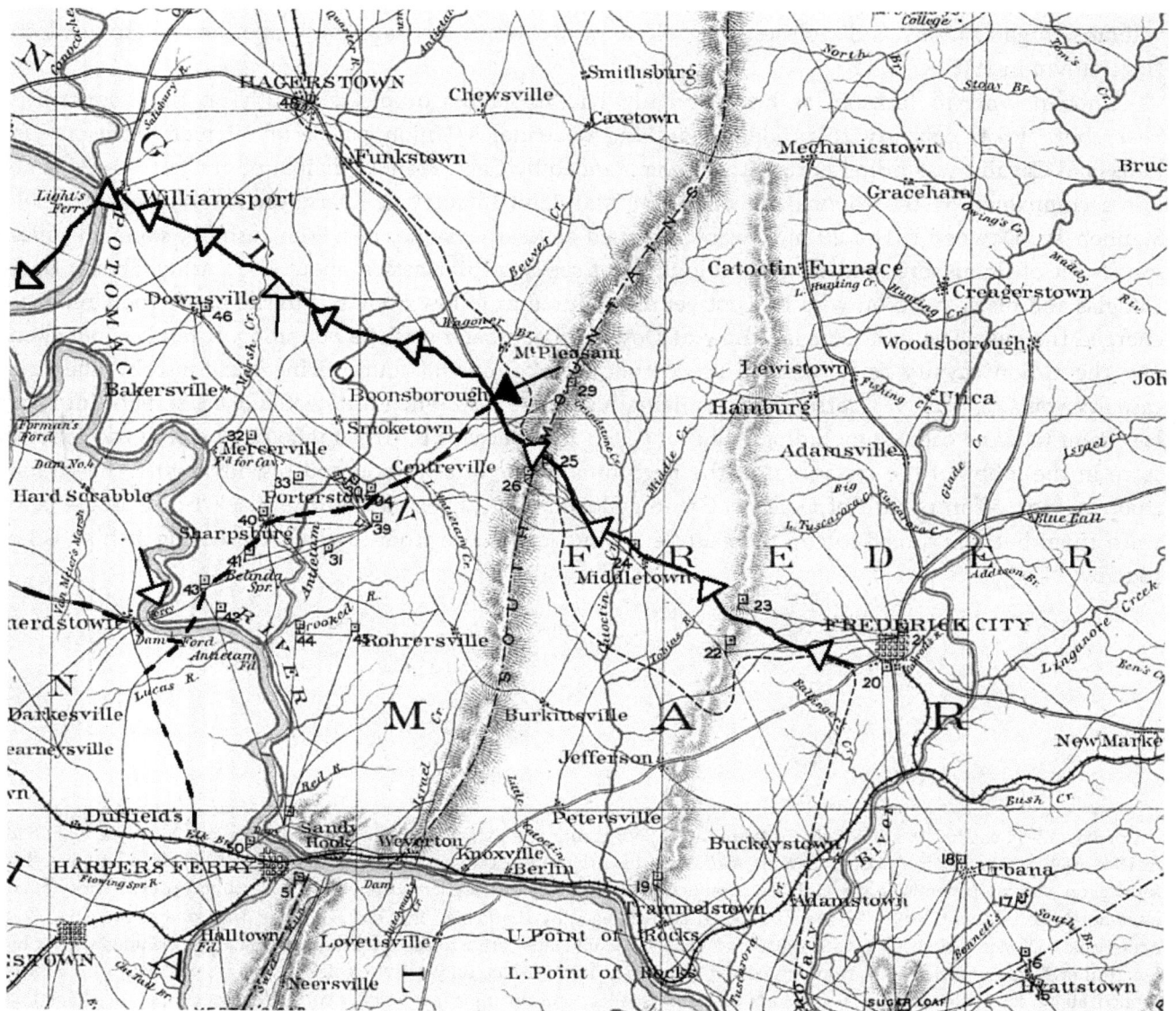

Map of the Douglas Action at Boonsboro on 11 September. Boonsboro is in the upper left center at the arrow. The road from which Downey approached enters Boonsboro from the southwest from Sharpsburg and Keedysville shown by the dotted line. Rather than taking this route to Martinsburg and Harpers Ferry, Jackson instead continued on to Williamsport taking the road to the northwest, the Boonsboro-Williamsport Pike at the arrow to cross the Potomac taking extra time which Lee did not calculate in his S.O. 191. Dotted routes show those Jackson might have taken. Douglas's home, Ferry Hill, is located on the east side of the Potomac River just to the east of Shepherdstown to the southwest of Sharpsburg at the arrow. Once Jackson reached Boteler's Ford across the Potomac, he would have gone east to Martinsburg but likely also sent some troops south to Harpers Ferry to scout the Union defenses. *Official Atlas*, Plate 27. Courtesy LOC.

Douglas and his courier returned Shamburg's fire and galloped back toward Jackson's camp as bullets whistled by them: one pierced Douglas's hat knocking the cherished, ostrich-plumed beauty into the dust. As Douglas crested a hill, he saw Jackson on the other side walking his horse toward the town. Seeing Douglas and after hearing the shots, now understanding the situation, Jackson rapidly mounted and retreated toward the Confederate camp. As Jackson rode away, Pvt. Thomas W. Latimer of the 1st Virginia Cavalry passed Jackson going in the opposite direction, and joined Douglas and his courier. Douglas, knowing that the Union cavalry could not see over the hill, saw their hesitation and decided to fool them into thinking Confederate cavalry was coming to the rescue—the group of three charged the 20 Unionists who turned and retreated. From the west end of town, Payne and his squad of Black Horse joined the fray upon hearing the firing and being warned by Pvt. Green. The Union cavalry now saw that it was they who were the prey and turned south down the Boonsboro-Sharpsburg Pike and galloped away, with the Black Horse and Douglas in pursuit.[37] In this exchange of fire, Col. Downey was slightly wounded in the head and his horse was killed, while his escort lost one killed and three wounded. Despite a Union claim that Rebel losses were nine or ten, those numbers are not confirmed. For his efforts, Downey was criticized by the commander at Harpers Ferry, Col. Dixon Miles: "Your dash upon the enemy with nineteen cavalry at Boonsborough was hazardous and not called for. The reconnaissance was proper, but with your small force [you should] have kept at a distance and not encountered a larger force than your own."[38] When put in context of Miles's later dreadful performance at Harpers Ferry, his criticism of Lt. Col. Downey should perhaps be interpreted as praise. Brig. Gen. Julius White in command at Martinsburg sent a message to Maj. Gen. Wool in Baltimore, reporting Downey's encounter and then quite accurately stated that "He [Downey] does not state whether [the enemy is moving] in this direction [southerly toward Martinsburg] or toward Hagerstown; probably cannot tell. The enemy in considerable force."[39] At the very least, Downey gave accurate information to his superiors regarding numbers which was properly passed up the chain of command.

For Douglas and the Black Horse, this fight was viewed as an adventure, but should have reminded Jackson, Douglas, and Payne, that in the enemy's country, pickets were needed to cover main roads even if friendly cavalry and infantry were close by. It also likely this chance encounter influenced Jackson to not use the Boonsboro-Sharpsburg Pike through Sharpsburg to cross the Potomac to Martinsburg, but rather to take the longer journey through Williamsport on the Boonsboro-Williamsport Road. The time this detour added seriously affected Lee's timetable, so Downey's impetuous attack may not have been in vain after all.[40] Douglas happily reported that he recovered his plumed hat along with capturing the cap belonging to his enemy, Capt. Shamburg, but Douglas was most pleased with finding and returning Jackson's gloves to the general, as he did not have to listen to any lecture from Jackson about not following his advice against entering the town.[41]

---

[37] Harsh, *Flood*, 176-177, *Shallows*, 164. Douglas, 152-154; Priest, *Before Antietam*, 69-70; *Lee's Lieutenants*, 2:163-164. But see Clemens, thesis, who says that even though Carman accepted Douglas's story Carman did not add Jackson to the tale, 496.

[38] *OR*, vol. 19, pt. 1, 535-536; Ibid., pt. 2, 249; *Ibid.*, vol. 51, pt. 1, 820.

[39] *OR*, vol. 19, pt. 2, 249.

[40] Harsh, *Flood*, 177. Hartwig writes that Jackson crossed at Williamsport because he had learned White still held Martinsburg, *To Antietam Creek*, 225.

[41] Douglas, 154. As noted above, some historians believe that Douglas may have embellished some of the events he described in his memoirs as von Borcke likely did in his own memoirs. Cox called some of von Borcke's tales as "those who have a fancy for learning how Munchausen could have told" the stories, *Reminiscences*, 157. Dennis E. Frye, in his article cited above about Douglas, described a letter from Jedediah Hotchkiss who wrote that "I recollect very well the dash of cavalry near Boonsborough when French, Douglas and others had straggled to the front. I do not recall that Jackson was to the front or that he and his staff were stampeded," 42. Compare Ernst, 78-79, whose sources agree with much of Douglas; her primary source is S. Basset French, *Centennial Tales: Memoirs of Colonel "Chester" S. Bassett French, Extra Aide-de-Camp to Generals Lee and Jackson, The Army of Northern Virginia, 1861-1865*, comp. Glen Oldaker (New York: A Reflection Book, 1962), 62-66. French wrote that he thanked the landlady who saved him by telling the Yankee cavalrymen that the Rebel had run out the back door by giving her a purse and even by hugging the servant or vice-versa as he was unsure in his excitement, but his apple pie had disappeared.

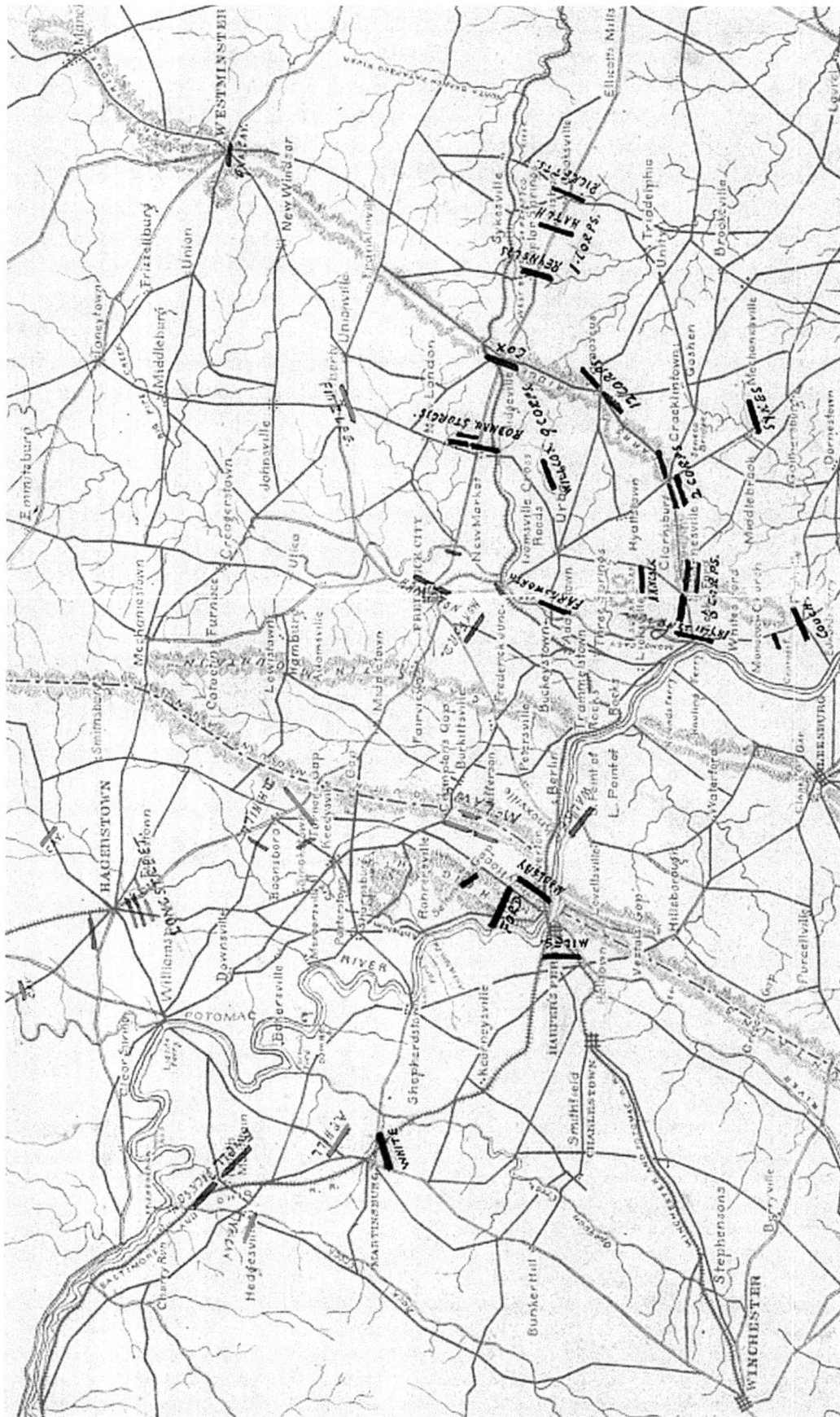

Situation map night of 11 September. McClellan begins the chase in earnest. Jackson, McLaws and Walker move toward Martinsburg or Harpers Ferry. Stuart maintains his protection of Lee's rear as he slowly pulls back behind the Monocacy River. Munford south of Frederick, Hampton in Frederick, and Fitzhugh Lee, after riding to Liberty, ends just west of the Monocacy River north of Frederick. Union cavalry and infantry took Sugarloaf Mountain. Courtesy LOC.

On 11 September, Stuart now had to defend against Union cavalry and infantry which began to move more quickly once McClellan realized that Gen. Robert E. Lee had left Frederick, with what McClellan believed was 120,000 men; in reality, Lee had less than half that number. In a report to Lincoln on 10 September, McClellan said that "statements I get regarding the enemy's forces that have crossed to this side [of the Potomac] range from 80,000 to 150,000." He seems to have settled on the estimate of 120,000 as realistic based on the reports he saw.[42] Shortly after noon McClellan, received information from Generals Cox at Ridgeville, and Hooker at Cooksville, that Lee had abandoned Frederick, and was moving northward, reports later confirmed by dispatches from Governor Curtin of Pennsylvania, who feared Lee intended to move into Pennsylvania.[43] McClellan gave orders for a rapid movement on Frederick with the Ninth Corps, under Virginia-born Brig. Gen. Jesse L. Reno, directly from New Market on the National Pike, "the First Corps by way of Ridgeville and New Market (following Reno), and a corresponding movement of all the troops in the center and on the left in the direction of Urbana. McClellan reported that, up to this time, his movements were for the purpose of feeling the enemy—'to compel him to develop his intentions—at the same time that the troops were in position readily to cover Baltimore or Washington, to attack him should he hold the line of the Monocacy, or to follow him into Pennsylvania if necessary.' Cautious and deliberate as was McClellan's advance, there were reasons for it beyond Halleck's warnings: the condition of the transportation and artillery, the vigilance and superb handling of the Confederate cavalry, and the consequent ignorance of Confederate movements."[44]

[42] Harsh, *Flood*, 171, 201, 202. *OR*, vol. 19, pt. 2, 233. Harsh shows that the Confederate fit for duty on 2 September 1862 before crossing the Potomac was 75,528, *Shallows*, 139, while Lee's strength for those actually fighting on 17 September at Antietam was 37,351 with 10,316 becoming casualties. Harsh's data is taken from Carman, Pierro, 465, 474. Carman's numbers show "men in action" vice "present for duty;" Union numbers at Antietam show 55,956, and with 12,401 as casualties on 17 September, 469. These numbers include all three branches, infantry, artillery, and cavalry. See also Clemens for a view on McClellan's estimates showing that he received estimates ranging from 75,000 to 200,000, and that overestimating enemy numbers was not a flaw confined to only McClellan as most Civil War commanders did so at one time or another, Clemens, thesis, 381. Governor Curtin telegraphed McClellan on the 10th that 200,000 Rebels massed in and around Frederick, *OR*, vol. 19, pt. 2, 248. Thomas J. Rowland, "George B. McClellan Revisited," *Civil War History*, vol. 40, no. 3, September 1994, 202-225, agrees with Clemens: McClellan "was not the only Federal commander to doodle with arithmetic when it came to gauging enemy numbers. Nor was he alone in proceeding with studied caution in assuming the tactical offensive," 220. Historian Michael Adams wrote that McClellan although an intelligent and patriotic man bought into the stereotypes of the time which made the South into a more martial and more disciplined society than the North. Therefore, McClellan like most other Union generals believed in overwhelming Southern strength and its "vast machine" was a formidable foe which much be confronted with caution. McClellan again like other senior Union officers distrusted civilian leadership, volunteer soldiers, and disbelieved that cavalry was of much use. "McClellan saw in the South what he would have liked the North to be: it was an image of the ideal. In so stereotyping the two sides he gave his opponents the psychological advantage. They used this against him," 92-97. Even the best cavalry scout McClellan had during this campaign, Capt. William J. Palmer, passed on information on 14 September stating that the combined number Lee had in Maryland was 100,000. Palmer, the careful scout, showed who his sources were and therefore why the numbers may have been worth noting, Charles H. Kirk, *History of the Fifteenth Pennsylvania Cavalry, Which Was Recruited and Known as the Anderson Cavalry in the Rebellion of 1861-1865* (Philadelphia, PA: Historical Committee of the Society of the Fifteenth Pennsylvania Cavalry, 1906), 646. Palmer was actually reporting to Pennsylvania governor Curtin at this time not to McClellan. On 9 September Curtin asked that the regular cavalry and their officers at Carlisle Barracks as well as the Anderson Troop be put at his disposal under command of Capt. Palmer to be used as scouts south of the Pennsylvania state line and repeated his request as it was apparently misunderstood by Halleck when Halleck seemed to deny it, *OR*, vol. 19, pt. 2, 228-229. On 10 September, Curtin renewed his request to Halleck who instructed him to communicate with Wool who was in charge of organizing military forces north of the Susquehanna, ibid, 247.
[43] *OR*, vol. 19, pt. 2, 267; *OR*, vol. 19, pt. 2, 268; *OR*, vol. 19, pt. 2, 268.
[44] Carman, Pierro, 88. Note that Reno was posthumously promoted to major general effective 18 July 1862, Eicher, *High Commands*, 704.

Stuart on 11 September apparently sent a note to Gen. Lee informing him of his pending retreat from Frederick, telling him it would probably take place on 13 September. Lee replied telling Stuart not to retire too quickly or to scatter his cavalry. This instruction shows that both Stuart and Lee believed only Federal cavalry was in pursuit since Stuart would not have been able in any event to stop, or seriously impede, Union infantry. Lee also in a curious phrase, told Stuart to "Keep me advised of the movements of the enemy, and do not let him discover, if possible, our movements." It is strange that here the army commander is emphasizing the two most important requirements of cavalry at this time during the war: reconnaissance and screening. One might speculate that Lee's emphasis was designed to draw Stuart's attentions to shortcomings in his performance, or perhaps simply that Stuart should send more frequent messages to Lee. Possibly Lee was just reminding Stuart of the vulnerable condition of the army due to its widely scattered parts.[45] Stuart to this point had done well in Carman's opinion: "The Confederate cavalry completely masked Lee's movements. It occupied every avenue of approach and resisted every attempt to drive it. From the Potomac on its right to the Baltimore and Ohio Railroad on the left, it covered Lee's entire front and no scout could penetrate it. Consequently there was a want of reliable information, and McClellan knew neither the strength, position, nor purpose of his adversary. Rumors of the most conflicting character came to him hourly, upon which he and his lieutenants built theories of the most plausible and irreconcilable kind."[46] It would not be until 13 September when McClellan had Lee's S.O. 191 in his hands, that the scales fell from his eyes. It is interesting to see that Carman did not address scouting potential of cavalry units Miles had available, which did in fact scout in Maryland, as well as northern Virginia, as will be seen below in the Harpers Ferry chapter. It may be since Miles was not under McClellan's command, and had great difficulty in communicating with him, that realistically the Harpers Ferry cavalry was of no practical use to McClellan, even if he had wanted to use them.

Stuart may have not moved with his accustomed speed and care early in this initial withdrawal from his Parr's Ridge/Sugarloaf Line in the heavy rain on the 11th; he combined most of two of his brigades, Hampton's and Munford's, in the area of the Urbana Pike southeast of Frederick instead of the National Pike to the north on which McClellan was also advancing in strength. He also sent his third brigade, Fitzhugh's, north to Liberty on a fruitless mission to scout behind the enemy's rear later that day. Stuart wanted to know if the approach of Union forces was merely a reconnaissance or the advance of large parts of McClellan's army. Fitzhugh Lee never was able to learn anything useful as Union cavalry successfully blocked his attempts. Fitzhugh Lee along with his 3rd, 4th, and 5th Virginia Cavalry, accompanied by Lt. James Breathed's section of horse artillery, marched through Urbana on their journey north to New Market. He was followed by Hampton's Brigade, which headed for Frederick, and was composed of the 1st North Carolina, 2nd South Carolina, 10th Virginia, Cobb's Legion, and the Jeff Davis Legion.[47] Stuart now had no effective contact with either flank of McClellan's army and he left the National Pike open. He also left no pickets close to the Potomac, thus exposing the rear of McLaws and Walker near Harpers Ferry. Stuart was still operating under the assumption that Federal forces were moving slowly and that in any event, by the time any Union forces approached Harpers Ferry, it would have already fallen. Too, the roads close to the Potomac River which Couch and Franklin would use as they ventured further from Washington were poor, so their movements, had they stayed close to the river, would have been retarded even further.

---

[45] Harsh, *Flood*, 196-197.
[46] Carman, Pierro, 88.
[47] Priest, *Before Antietam*, 78; letter to Carman from G.W. Beale dated 3 June 1897, ANBL 9th Virginia Cavalry Regimental File.

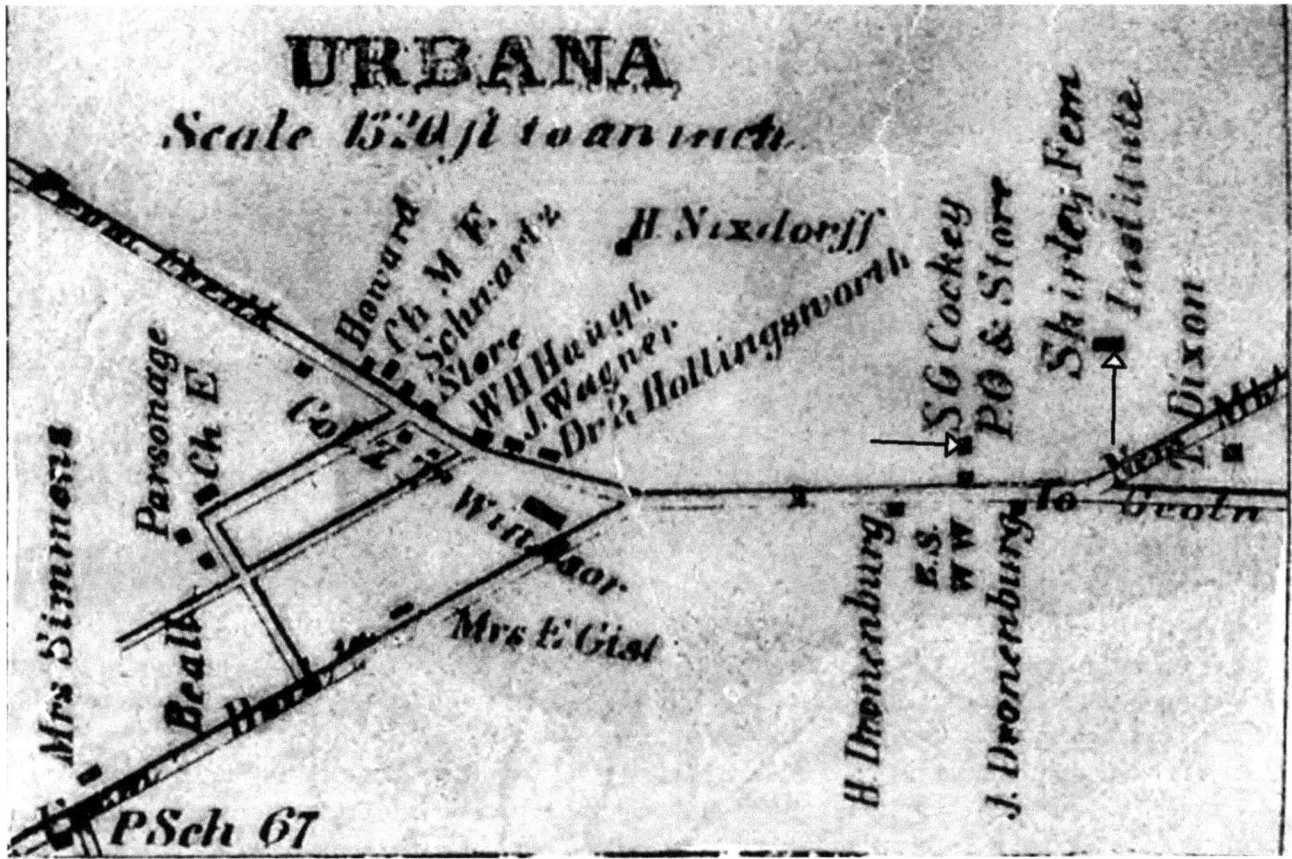

Detail from Bond map showing the town of Urbana. The Cockey house where Stuart spent some delightful time with the Cockey's is at the right center at the arrow on the main road from Frederick to Georgetown. The Landon House where Stuart had his ball is to the upper right arrow. Courtesy LOC.

Stuart, meanwhile, spent this time out of the rain, with the ladies of the Cockey family on their verandah in Urbana, but left later in the day, likely after Hampton rode through.[48] Stuart retired closer to the east side of the Monocacy River to a farm near Frederick. Before Stuart withdrew from Frederick, he related that on the 11th Fitzhugh Lee fell back from his post at New Market, seven miles to Liberty, and then six miles west to cross the Monocacy on the morning of the 12th. On the 12th Stuart directed Fitzhugh to retrace his steps and head back east reconnoitering toward New Market, and to gain the enemy's right flank and rear to the north, to help Stuart understand whether the Union movements were merely a reconnaissance in force, or a general movement of the Union army.[49] Fitzhugh Lee's northern trip, which did little to help Stuart or Gen. Lee other than adding to the Union information gatherers' confusion about the destination of Lee's army, meant that Lee's troopers were unavailable to Stuart for three days. William R. Carter of the 3rd Virginia Cavalry wrote his recollection of Fitzhugh Lee's Brigade activities during this period: on the 9th the brigade moved toward Hyattstown and picketed the line near Barnesville exchanging shots with some Union cavalry. On the 10th, the brigade moved north again and camped near Frederick after crossing the Monocacy River and the next day changed camp to near a mill; on the 12th, they left camp early and established a new camp near the Catoctin Mountains. The following day the peripatetic troopers crossed Catoctin Mountain and stopped at

[48] Priest, *Before Antietam*, 346, n. 33. Priest's cogent analysis of evidence showing that von Borcke's breathless tale about artillery shells chasing Stuart away followed closely by Union infantry is a fantasy as there was no Union artillery in the vicinity and there is no record of Munford holding the town against any Union force.
[49] *OR*, vol. 19, pt. 1, 815-816.

Highland just off the western slope of the mountain west of Hamburg and drew two days rations. While there, they sent back sick horses and some troopers went scouting capturing nine prisoners, an ambulance and several horses. They then returned and camped near Myersville northwest of Middletown on the Old Hagerstown Pike.[50] But there was some benefit to this activity for about 500 Rebel troopers, who, at 7:30 P.M. on the 12th, according to a Baltimore newspaper, rode into Westminster, twenty-five miles northeast of Frederick. The troopers, under command of Col. Thomas L. Rosser, took possession of the town and placed pickets around the place to prevent escape of Union sympathizers. Men were "firing their pistols, capturing the local provost marshal, burning the conscription enrollment books, and damaging a small bridge of the B&O." One man named Crothers was reported killed by the Rebels as he tried to escape through the pickets. The Rebel troopers also "seized the post-office and train depot; ascertaining that there was a locomotive and two passenger and four freight-cars a short distance from the town, they also dispatched a force and brought them in. Upon being established in the town, the rebels proceeded to lay hands upon all the boots, shoes, and clothing that they could find in the stores, for which they tendered in payment confederate money." They made little distinction between Southern sympathizers and Union men "stating that they had been deceived relative to the secession feeling in Maryland."[51] While some of Fitzhugh Lee's troopers might have left Westminster better shod, Stuart had not gained any information about Federal troop movements. The 3rd Virginia, after having spent that day "resting & feeding our horses" after passing through Myersville and Smoketown, camped in Boonsboro that night of the 14th but was ordered to horse at midnight to cover the retreat of the Confederates from South Mountain.[52]

Stuart later admitted that he was unable to judge the enemy's movements as they did not display any force except for Burnside's corps and did not build campfires around Frederick. Clearly, Stuart was not aware that McClellan's troops were now moving in force all along his front toward the west and northwest. Stuart implied that he hoped Fitzhugh Lee would have been able to supply more details about Federal movements, but got nothing: "I confidently hoped by this time to have received the information which was expected from Brig. Gen. Fitz. Lee."[53] Additionally, Stuart did not know and made no recorded effort to learn if the three-day timetable in S.O. 191 for the taking of Harpers Ferry was seriously behind schedule; he believed that the three days he held the Unionists away from South Mountain was sufficient to allow his retirement, since the Harpers Ferry capture was to be finished on the 12th according to Gen. Lee's order. On 11 September, he had left the Parr's Ridge/Sugarloaf Line and pulled back an average of some eight miles to the northwest behind the Monocacy River. The Union cavalry was also in motion, with Farnsworth's brigade riding toward Frederick through Urbana, while the 6th New York Cavalry, which would be among the first Union cavalry entering Frederick, was followed by Col. Andrew T. McReynolds's Fourth Cavalry Brigade, as they chased Fitzhugh Lee to

[50] Carter, *Sabres, Saddles, and Spurs*, 13. In a letter to Carman, R.B. Lewis of Company C of the 9th Virginia Cavalry wrote that on its retreat from Sugarloaf Confederate signalmen joined the regiment as it headed northwest to Hamburg. The 9th Virginia was followed by the 4th Virginia Cavalry and they camped on the top of the Blue Ridge [Catoctin Mountain] on the 14th; the next morning [15th] they camped on the west slope of the mountain overlooking Boonsboro [South Mountain]. Shortly after sunrise on the 15th, they rode down to Boonsboro arriving about 10 A.M., ANBL Files, 9th Virginia Cavalry.

[51] Harsh, *Flood*, 205; *Rebellion Record*, vol. V, 78. See also Frank Moore, ed., *The Rebellion Record: A Diary of American Events, with Documents, Narratives, Illustrative Incidents, Poetry, Etc*, vol. 5 (New York: G. P. Putnam, 1863; reprint, New York: Arno Press, 1977), 78. Rosser's 5th Virginia Cavalry apparently did not accompany Fitz Lee after Westminster as Rosser turned up at Turner's Gap on the 13th with two guns of Pelham's Battery; Stuart posted them to Fox's Gap that evening, Carman, Pierro, 94. It is not clear why Rosser left New Market on the morning of the 11th and did not accompany Fitz Lee who arrived at Boonsboro late on the 14th, unless Rosser remained separated from Fitzhugh Lee's Brigade after Rosser made his Westminster visit; Carman, Pierro, 175; Driver, *5th Virginia Cavalry*, 39.

[52] Carter, *Sabres, Saddles, and Spurs*, 13-15.

[53] *OR*, vol. 19, pt. 1, 817.

Westminster.[54] Carman wrote that "Colonel Andrew T. McReynolds of the 1st New York Cavalry was put in charge of a brigade (consisting of his own regiment, the 8th Pennsylvania Cavalry, and a section of Hains's Battery M, 2d U.S. Artillery) and ordered to Gettysburg, for which place a body of Stuart's cavalry was reported moving."[55] Cpl. William Hyndman of the 4th Pennsylvania Cavalry, told of his experiences on 11 September: "Gen. Burnside's command was organized to meet the rebel army immediately, and at once it marched forth from the Capital, our regiment acting as escort to the commanding general and staff. We first met the enemy on the night of Sept. 11th, when our battalion, commanded by Capt. Young, entered Rockville, Maryland, in advance of Burnside's column, on a reconnoissance, drove their advance back, and returning reported to headquarters. The next day we entered Frederick City, Maryland, capturing 450 rebels, most of whom were sick, and routing and driving out the force who were occupying the city."[56]

Overleaf: Situation map night of 12 September. McClellan continued the chase; Stuart's cavalry withdraws from Frederick; Fitzhugh Lee is off on a reconnaissance to the northeast to Westminster being followed by the 6th New York Cavalry while Munford moves back to Jefferson; Hampton rides up the National Pike toward Middletown after his clash in Frederick. Lee further divides his army into five parts as D.H. Hill moves to Boonsboro, Longstreet to Hagerstown, Walker to Hillsborough, McLaws on Elk Ridge, and Jackson south of Martinsburg. Courtesy LOC.

---

[54] *Ibid.*, 815; Harsh, *Flood*, 188. See also Driver, *1st Virginia*, "[Fitz] Lee and his regiments operated around Frederick but could find no openings to exploit," 46. Hall, 59. On the 11th Pleasonton reported that his cavalry had covered all the ferries and fords downriver from the mouth of the Monocacy River; he also sent two regiments and artillery to the mouth of that river and one and a half regiments to Greenfield Mills on the Monocacy, *OR*, vol. 19, pt. 2, 258. If he is accurate the Potomac from the Monocacy to Washington was adequately covered.

[55] Carman, Pierro, 92.

[56] Hyndman, 65-66.

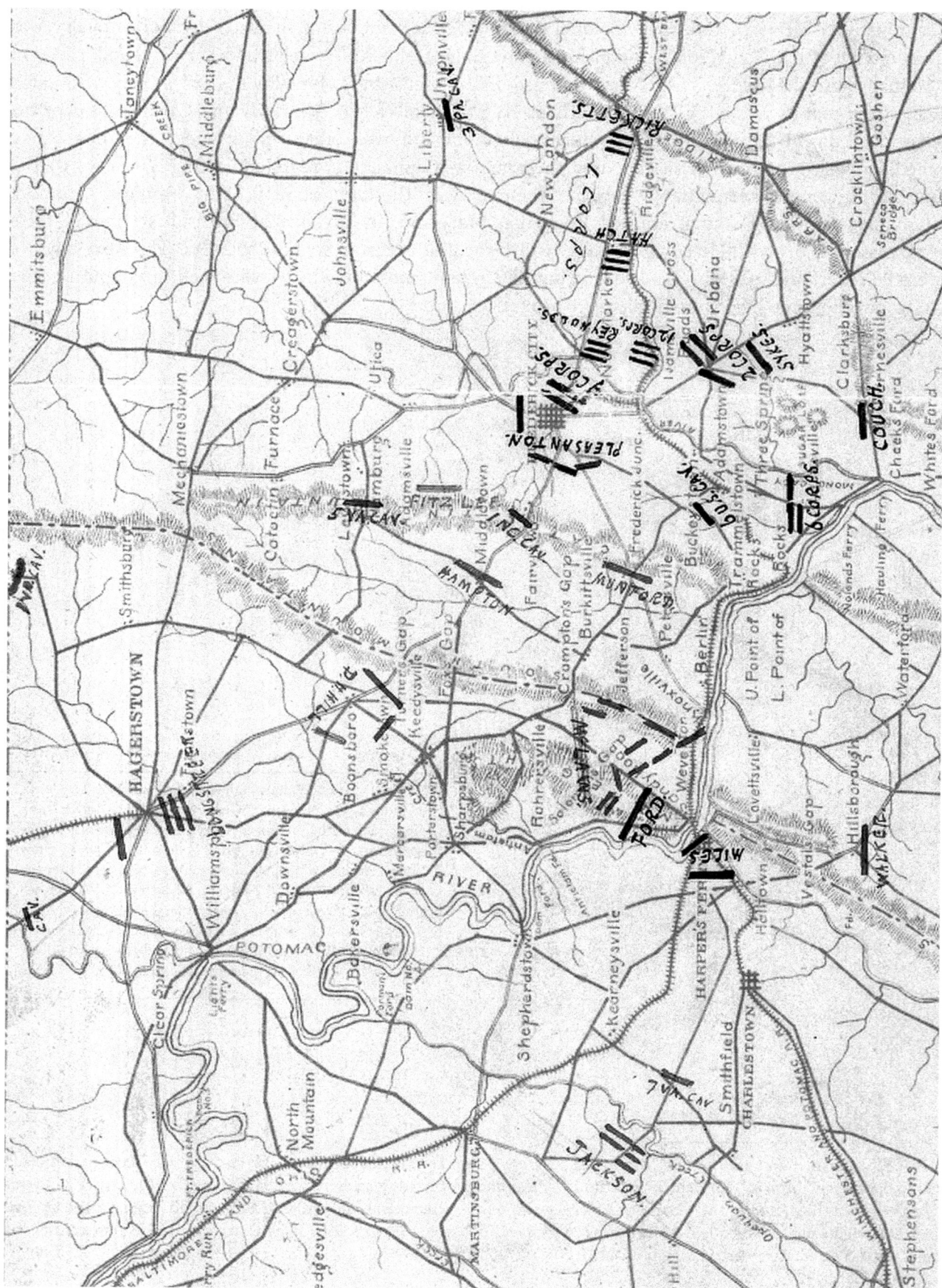

Union Brig. Gen. Cox, commanding the Kanawha Division in Reno's Ninth Corps, was in pursuit along with the other divisions in the Ninth Corps on the right of McClellan's line. He outlined his movements as follows:

"At Ridgeville [on Parr's Ridge east of New Market on the National Pike], however, we got reliable evidence that Lee had evacuated Frederick the day before, and that only cavalry was east of the Catoctin Mountains. Hooker got similar information at about the same time. It was now determined to move more rapidly, and early in the morning of the 12th I was ordered to march to New Market and thence to Frederick.... It had been thought that we were likely to be attacked at Ridgeville, and on reaching the village I disposed the division so as to cover the place and to be ready for an engagement. I ordered the brigades to bivouac in line of battle, covering the front with outposts and with cavalry vedettes from the Sixth New York Cavalry (Colonel Devin), which had been attached to the division during the advance."[57]

On 12 September, in the early afternoon, Stuart, Fitzhugh Lee and Hampton, along with their aides, were having a delightful lunch in Frederick, dining with Mrs. Catherine S. Markell, her family, and "all the girls" at the Markell residence on East Market Street. Her husband had left earlier in the day on his way to Hagerstown. The ladies played "Southern Yankee Doodle" and Stuart responded by summoning his banjo player, Sweeny, who played "Old Gray Hoss" and several other favorite songs. The ever gallant Stuart gave Mrs. Markell a piece from the plume on his hat, and signed her autograph album. He excused himself to write out a parole to a terrified prisoner and then returned to the festivities. Around 4 P.M., the fun came to a sudden halt when a courier arrived and informed Stuart that enemy drums were heard, and McClellan's columns were within view. Hampton had already left to help form the rear guard, so Stuart was the only commander left. During the subsequent skirmish with the advancing Unionists, Mrs. Markell reported that part of her front door was shot away.[58]

Union Brig. Gen. Reno was the one about to spoil Stuart's fun as he moved toward Frederick on the National Pike, with a company of the 1st West Virginia Cavalry, under Lt. James Abraham, in the van. Hampton and his troopers had the assignment to hold the center of Stuart's line around Frederick. Hampton had two squadrons and a battery protecting the road at the Monocacy Bridge leading from Frederick to Urbana on the Urbana Pike, and was concerned that they would be cut off as the Federals approached on the National Pike to the north. To help slow the Federal advance on the Urbana Pike, Hampton added a rifled cannon to the two guns from Hart's Battery, and he sent a squadron from Butler's 2nd South Carolina Cavalry, led by Lt. John Meighan, in their first action since arriving from South Carolina. Reno's men opened fire on the Rebels on the National Pike who, once the two squadrons guarding the Monocacy Bridge joined them, pulled back to the city. Meighan lost two troopers in this action. Hampton sent his horse artillery west of Frederick to protect his line of retreat where they occupied a position between the Catoctin Mountains and Frederick, awaiting further orders.[59]

---

[57] Cox, *Reminiscences*, 155.

[58] Priest, *Before Antietam*, 90. Note that Priest wrote that this dinner was at the home of prominent secessionist lawyer, Mr. William J. Ross but the diary of Mrs. Catherine S. Markell says the officers dined at her and her husband's home, Catherine S. Markell, *Frederick Maryland in Peace and War, 1856-1864: The Diary of Catherine Susannah Thomas Markell*, edited by David H. Wallace (Frederick, MD: Signature Book Printing, Inc., 2006), 108. Blackford wrote that he only paid a final visit to the Ross family who were friends since his father studied law with Mr. Ross. As he was leaving in the midst of Hampton's defense of Frederick, one of the Ross ladies handed him a plum cake which he strapped to his saddle and enjoyed with Stuart and the rest of the staff that night. Compare von Borcke's dramatic account, n. 73 below, which said that the plum pudding was hurled as a bomb to Blackford; perhaps the lady just had an excellent throwing arm.

[59] Priest, *Before Antietam*, 90-91.

The Union approach was related by Brig. Gen. Cox who described the advance from New Market with his division. He first sent the 6th New York Cavalry off to the right to cover the flank and "to investigate reports that heavy bodies of the enemy's cavalry were north of us," which were Fitzhugh Lee's troopers. As his infantry moved rapidly toward Frederick, there was little opposition until they reached the Monocacy River about half a mile from the town, where they met some of Hampton's cavalry. The highway crossed the river by the substantial Monocacy stone bridge, but the ground on the Union east side was markedly higher than on the opposite bank. Union artillery exchanged fire with Hampton's guns but the Federal guns enjoyed the advantage of higher ground. Union infantry took the bridge and also forded the Monocacy a quarter of a mile to the north. As soon as Col. Augustus Moor's second infantry brigade of Cox's Division was over, it was deployed on the right and left of the turnpike, which was bordered on either side by a high, strong post-and-rail fence. Scammon's brigade went over the bridge next and deployed as a second line; the 11th Ohio Infantry remained in column in the road.[60]

Map of Frederick County, Md. by Isaac Bond, 1858. The Monocacy Bridge on the National Pike is to the lower right at the arrow. New Market is about 7½ airline miles east. The center right arrow points to the bridge over Carroll Creek in Frederick and the bend to the left described in the cavalry action. The Georgetown (also Urbana) Pike at the lower center leads south from Frederick goes through Urbana; Urbana is about 7 airline miles southeast; it is named Market Street in Frederick and the National or Baltimore Pike is Patrick Street inside the city. The Harpers Ferry Road, today Rt. 180, is at the lower left arrow, and Harpers Ferry is about 18 straight line miles southwest; the Hagerstown Road—National Pike is at the center left arrow, and Hagerstown is about 23 airline mines away and 14½ to Boonsboro; the Hamburg Road is at the upper left arrow. Courtesy LOC.

---

[60] Cox did not mention the attempted Rebel destruction of the bridge which von Borcke related, 142-143.

Col. Moor, the portly, German-born former commander of the 28th Ohio Infantry, one of Reno's regiments, and now commander of the Second Brigade of the Kanawha Division, was in immediate command of the Union pursuers. Moor was in the front line with a troop of Chicago Dragoons under the command of Capt. Frederick Schambeck, a company of the 1st Regiment of (West) Virginia Cavalry Volunteers led by Lt. James Abraham, and an artillery piece from Capt. Seth J. Simmonds's Kentucky battery. Gen. Cox rode behind Moor and witnessed what transpired culminating in Moor's impetuous dash into town. Hampton's troopers were not in sight, however, as the road turned sharply to the left just as it entered the town obscuring the view of the approaching troops. A young staff officer from corps headquarters rode up to Cox who related the encounter and the following actions which led to Moor's unwise attack:

> [The staff officer] exclaimed in a boisterous way, "Why don't they go in faster? There's nothing there!" [Cox] said to the young man, "Did General Reno send you with any order to me?" "No," he replied. "Then," said I, "when I want your advice I will ask it." He moved off abashed, and I did not notice what had become of him, but, in fact, he rode up to Colonel Moor, and repeated a similar speech. Moor was stung by the impertinence which he assumed to be a criticism upon him from corps headquarters, and, to my amazement, I saw him suddenly dash ahead at a gallop with his escort and the gun. He soon came to the turn of the road where it loses itself among the houses; there was a quick, sharp rattling of carbines, and Hampton's cavalry was atop of the little party. There was one discharge of the cannon, and some of the brigade staff and escort came back in disorder. I ordered up at "double quick" the Eleventh Ohio, which, as I have said, was in column in the road, and these, with bayonets fixed, dashed into the town. The enemy had not waited for them, but retreated out of the place by the Hagerstown road. Moor had been ridden down, unhorsed, and captured. The artillery-men had unlimbered the gun, pointed it, and the gunner stood with the lanyard in his hand, when he was struck by a charging horse; the gun was fired by the concussion, but at the same moment it was capsized into the ditch by the impact of the cavalry column. The enemy had no time to right the gun or carry it off, nor to stop for prisoners. They forced Moor on another horse, and turned tail as the charging lines of infantry came up on right and left as well as the column in the road, for there had not been a moment's pause in the advance. It had all happened, and the gun with a few dead and wounded of both sides were in our hands, in less time than it has taken to describe it.[61]

Sources from the Rebel perspective also provided details of Moor's capture and this action in town. Hampton reported that "the enemy now pressed forward, and, planting a gun in the suburbs of the city, supported by a body of cavalry and a regiment and a half of infantry, opened fire upon the crowded thoroughfares of the place."[62] Hampton watched some 800 yards away in front of the City Hotel with his staff while a local physician, Dr. Lewis H. Steiner, observed and commented on Hampton's and Ashby's troopers: "The men are more neat and cleanly than the infantry that preceded them, and their horses, of good stock, are well-groomed and fed. Bragging is the order of the day with the cavalry. They boast that they never met more than one Federal regiment that dared cross sabers with them, and that was the First Michigan Cavalry".[63] Capt. David Waldhauer of the Georgia Hussars, Jeff Davis Legion, of

[61] Cox, *Reminiscences*, 156-157.

[62] *OR*, vol. 19, pt. 1, 816.

[63] Johnson, "Reunion of Virginia Division A.N.V. Association," 517; Steiner, 23. Only Company L of the 1st Michigan Cavalry was with McClellan during the Maryland Campaign serving as escort to the Twelfth Corps; the 1st Michigan Cavalry had been in the Shenandoah Valley and then in the battles at Cedar Mountain and Second Bull Run, Dyer, 3:1269. The 1st Michigan was heavily involved on 30 August at Second Bull Run with Robertson's Brigade during which the 1st's colonel was mortally wounded and 300 of its troopers were casualties. It is not clear which of Hampton's units had confronted the 1st Michigan in combat unless Steiner heard this from some of Ashby Turner's troopers who faced the Michigan troopers in the Shenandoah Valley, *OR*, vol. 12, pt. 2, 737. One Frederick citizen apparently saw different troopers as he reported that "The horses of the

Hampton's Brigade, provided these details of the action in the streets of Frederick. The adjutant general of Hampton's Brigade, Maj. Barker, ordered Waldhauer to "picket the byways, prevent straggling, and push the men through. When General Hampton came along after the brigade had passed, he, in person, ordered me to gather my men and take the rear." Waldhauer gathered about 20 troopers from mixed commands in the brigade excepting the absent 2nd South Carolina. After a squadron of the 2nd South Carolina galloped through, he faced his group of now 24 troopers, four Hussars in the front of his column of fours, to face the Union cavalry he saw approaching on the National Pike. Waldhauer, with his attention focused on affairs in his front, assumed that Hampton assigned the 2nd South Carolina Cavalry as a reserve behind his troopers, as he received orders thorough his lieutenant, William W. Gordon, from Col. Butler, who commanded the Second, to charge. Even though Waldhauer believed that he was under Hampton's orders rather than Butler's, he decided to charge when the Unionists reached the brow of a long hill as they would be "spent and disordered, and an easy prey."[64]

When the Union column led by Moor saw the charging Rebel cavalry, it panicked and in its haste to deploy its cannon and troopers, fired wildly, causing casualties among their own men, and upsetting the cannon as it fired. Then, as the Union troopers fled before the Confederates got within easy pistol range, Lt. Gordon of Waldhauer's band captured Col. Moor and his "coal-black steed." According to Waldhauer, 2nd South Carolina troopers were only incidentally involved, despite what other Confederates reported. Waldhauer stated that the Union killed, wounded and captured, numbered more than 24. Also contrary to other reports, he said the horses pulling the Union cannon were not killed but merely knocked down. He also said that Lt. Meighan who had been credited with Moor's capture in other reports did not capture him.[65]

Lt. Gordon reported as follows:

"We killed and wounded badly fifteen or twenty and carried off the Colonel...besides eleven more prisoners, some eight or ten horses and as many rifles and pistols as our men chose to pick up. We had to leave the cannon as the horses had fallen into a ditch by the side of the street and were all tangled up and on top of each other. We lost two men killed and one left behind with a broken thigh, and 2 slightly wounded. We had scarcely 20 men in our rear guard but were followed by a squadron of Colonel Butler's Regiment, 2nd SC Cavalry."[66]

Other less plausible accounts give different versions. These stories credit two 2nd South Carolina Cavalry squadrons and Meighan's troopers, aided by forty men gathered from the Rebel provost guard, led by Capt. J. Frederick Waring of the Jeff Davis Legion, all directed by Col. Calbraith Butler. In these versions, Moor was captured after a hand-to-hand combat with Lt. Meighan, during which Moor wrested Meighan's saber from his hand; Meighan dodged Moor's blow and grabbed the colonel by the collar and unhorsed him. After the colonel surrendered, his fine black charger became part of Hampton's

---

Rebel cavalry appeared to be 'in poor appearance. They bore the evidence of hard usage and scarcity of provender,'" Gordon, *Never the Like Again*, 150.

[64] David Waldhauer, "The Affair at Frederick City," in *Southern Historical Society Papers*, vol. 13, January to December 1885 (Richmond: Southern Historical Society, n.d. Reprint, Millwood, NJ: Kraus Reprint Co, 1977), 417-418.

[65] Ibid., 418-419. Waldhauer's account is more plausible with its detail and sequence of events; both he and Gordon were eyewitnesses and participants adding credulity to their reports. Other versions such as von Borcke's, credit Butler and his South Carolinians with Moor's capture and the routing of the Federals, 142-143. There is no evidence that von Borcke witnessed the fight. Stuart was near Middletown at this time. Waldhauer while writing that the horses drawing the cannon were not "killed" but "knocked down" might also have meant that they were wounded and had not just fallen.

[66] Donald A. Hopkins in *The Little Jeff: The Jeff Davis Legion, Cavalry Army of Northern Virginia* (Shippensburg, PA: White Mane Books, 1999), relied on Waldhauer's account bolstered Lt. Gordon's which corroborates Waldhauer's account, 92-93, n. 14.

livery.[67] Seven other Unionists were captured, with Union casualties totaling some thirty men while the Confederates lost seven.[68] The Union gun the Confederates captured was retaken, as five of its horses were killed, according to Stuart's report.[69] Waldhauer's and Gordon's first-person accounts are more plausible than those of Stuart, in Brooks, et al., given the detail they supplied, as well as the realistic description of the scene written by these two active participants. Brooks also wrote that as the last of the Confederate troopers left Frederick, "some cowardly miscreant fired upon General Hampton from a window as he passed."[70]

Civilian observers' reports of this confused melee also differed. Dr. Steiner stated that the Rebels captured seven men while leaving several wounded on the ground. Additionally, he wrote that "The accidental discharge of a cannon caused the death of seven horses and the wounding of a few men."[71] A Unionist resident of Frederick, Jacob Engelbrecht, witnessed the affair and said that the Rebels stopped their slow retreat, "halted, turned right about & drew their swords & went down street in full speed. They met the advancing Union advance in the Square...where a skirmish took place. No one was killed & several slightly wounded. The Rebels took Colonel Moore 28 Ohio prisoner...& also 4 or 5 soldiers....the Union artillery discharged by which 8 horses of ours, were killed & also 6 horses had been killed between that place & Monocacy bridge."[72] While civilian and military accounts differ in details such as who captured Col. Moor, and whether the Union artillery horses were killed or merely entangled, the Union foray into Frederick was poorly handled, showing that the Confederate cavalry with its élan and good company level leadership, could handle equal or greater numbers of Union horsemen when led by unskilled (and unlucky) officers such as Moor.

This skirmish effectively slowed the Federal infantry pursuit and allowed time for Hampton to post the Jeff Davis Legion with two of Hart's guns at Hagan's Gap in the Catoctin Mountains, west of Frederick, on the National Pike. This was Stuart's second line, the Catoctin Mountain Line. Hampton joined Stuart and continued west to Middletown, with the rest of his brigade, where the generals and their staffs found comfortable quarters in a farmhouse, in which they shared a plum cake, which Capt. Blackford had earlier been given in Frederick.[73] Later in the afternoon, the 1st New York Cavalry and the 12th Pennsylvania Cavalry, Col. McReynolds' brigade, arrived in Frederick from the Urbana Pike, finding that they were not needed as the city was already celebrating its liberation by the Union infantry.[74]

---

[67] Ulysses R. Brooks, ed., "Sketches of Hampton's Cavalry" in *Stories of the Confederacy* (Columbia, SC: State Co., 1912; Reprint, Camden, SC: J. J. Fox, 1991), which credits South Carolina units, 81-82. See also Longacre, *Gentleman and Soldier*, who mirrors Brooks, 95-96; and Rod Andrew, Jr., *Wade Hampton: Confederate Warrior to Southern Redeemer* (Chapel Hill, NC: University of North Carolina Press, 2008), 116-117. See also McClellan, *I Rode with Jeb Stuart*, who repeats the South Carolina story, 114; he does not state that he was an eyewitness, however, and was likely with Stuart near Middletown.

[68] After being captured by Hampton's troopers, Moor apparently was taken to Boonsboro where he was paroled. As he returned to Union lines on the 14th, he passed Union Gen. Jacob Cox west of Middletown near Catoctin Creek. Moor asked "Where are you going?" and when Cox said that his men were reconnoitering Turner's Gap Moor expostulated "Be Careful!" but then quickly walked away remembering he was still under parole and had not been exchanged, Harsh, *Flood*, 261; Carman, Pierro, 91, 144; Jacob D. Cox, "Forcing Fox's Gap and Turner's Gap," in *Battles and Leaders*, 2:584-586.

[69] *OR*, vol. 19, pt. 1, 816. Stuart probably received his information second hand from Hampton.

[70] Brooks, *Stories of the Confederacy*, 82.

[71] Steiner, 24.

[72] Engelbrecht, 949.

[73] In his report, Stuart admitted that the captured gun could not be carried off since most of its horses were shot. Von Borcke characteristically says that the "plum-pudding...had been hurled as a beneficent bomb at Captain Blackford by a philanthropic young lady of Frederick during our retreat" 143. Compare the account of the recipient of the Plum cake, Blackford, above, n. 58, who reported the gift.

[74] Priest, *Before Antietam*, 90-100. The 12th Pennsylvania led by Maj. Congdon was busy. McClellan wrote on 30 August that "Colonel Congdon, with about 300 of his command, has been sent up the Potomac with instructions to watch carefully the river as far as Edward's Ferry. I am not kept posted as to the situation, but I know the fords above are practicable, and the appearance

On the night of the 12th, based on reports from Washington and Gov. Curtin, McClellan knew that Harpers Ferry was in great danger, and that Jackson, for some purpose not understood, had crossed the Potomac into Virginia near Williamsport. McClellan sent out what scouts he had available; Capt. Sanders commanding the 6th U.S. Cavalry was sent to Jefferson, and "From this point you will throw out scouts as far as possible toward Harper's Ferry. You will also open communications with General Pleasonton, who will be found on the National road between Middletown and the South Mountain or Blue Ridge." The 1st Rhode Island Cavalry, which had been sent from Arlington on the eleventh, and arrived at Frederick on the twelfth, was sent to Seneca Mills and Poolesville early on the thirteenth, to "watch all the fords from Seneca to the mouth of the Monocacy."[75] Late on the 12th, McClellan sent two messages to Pleasonton, the first asking him to confirm that Jackson was marching on Harpers Ferry, and the second asking Pleasonton the "state of affairs at Harper's Ferry" ordering him to send out a force at daylight to Lewistown and Mechanicstown to "ascertain if any force of the enemy has moved in that direction with a view of getting in our rear." Finally, Pleasonton was ordered to cooperate with Gen. Burnside after Burnside had secured the pass through the Catoctin Mountains, which would allow the cavalry to operate in the Catoctin Valley between the South Mountain range and the Catoctin Mountains.[76] Given the number of available troopers, Pleasonton would have been hard pressed to do all these tasks as well as McClellan needed.

Further to the northwest, some twenty-five miles away across South Mountain, the 1st Virginia Cavalry was leading Longstreet's column into Hagerstown from Boonsboro, and picketing roads to Pennsylvania. As some of the 1st Virginia Cavalry charged into Hagerstown, they captured a Union lieutenant, A. Nesbitt, and a few enlisted men.[77] One account has several troopers from the 1st Virginia Cavalry visiting close to southern Pennsylvania and, if true, then this is the farthest penetration

---

of the enemy on this side would not be extraordinary," *OR*, vol. 12, pt. 3, 753. One squadron of the 12th was still near Fort Lyon on 1 September, ibid., 790. The 12th had only received its horses in late July 1862 so was still learning how to be cavalrymen as it patrolled the Orange and Alexandria Railroad near Manassas Junction. Maier, 27, 31. The historian of the regiment quoting its commander, Maj. Congdon, writes that on 2 September it went on a long, 52-mile trek to a stream west of Hancock, Maryland, Sir John's Run, where there was a stop on the B&O, Maier, 45. By some unknown route it reappeared near Frederick, Maryland, on 12 September, Maier, 47. The regiment apparently missed elements of Lee's army which a few days earlier began crossing the Potomac. As part of Pleasonton's Fourth Brigade, it and the 1st New York Cavalry rode toward Gettysburg scouting to see if the Rebels were heading into Pennsylvania. Their first stop was at Emmitsburg where the column was at first mistaken for Confederates in this secessionist town. They reached the outskirts of Gettysburg on the 14th where more welcoming citizens fed them while some troopers had their horses shod. On the 15th, the column headed back to Emmitsburg and the 1st New York arrived in Frederick on 16 September, Maier 49, Beach, 172.

[75] *OR*, vol. 51, pt. 1, 830. The 1st Rhode Island Cavalry under Col. Alfred N. Duffie was apparently operating under McClellan's orders even though until September 1862, it was part of Bayard's cavalry brigade in the Army of Virginia. See Carman showing that the 1st Rhode Island Cavalry examined the fords below Point of Rocks, Carman, Pierro, 133. The Ocean State troopers had been sent from Arlington on 11 September and arrived at Frederick on the 12th then sent to picket Potomac fords "from Seneca to the mouth of the Monocacy," *OR*, vol. 51, pt. 1, 830, Carman, Pierro, 93. Brig. Gen. George D. Bayard reported the regiment's strength at 450 troopers on 5 September 1862, *OR*, vol. 19, pt. 2, 184. Frederic Denison wrote that on 12 September, 30 recruits were added to the ranks but they were without horses, *Sabres and Spurs*, 156. He does not show whether they received mounts before the regiment moved to the vicinity of Poolesville; if so, the regiment numbered about 480 sabers during its reconnaissance duties in Maryland before illness and casualties took their toll: five were captured on the 15th, while seven were in hospital on the 22nd, 157, 160. On 11 September, Maj. Gen. Porter reported to Brig. Gen. Williams that the 1st Rhode Island Cavalry were marching to join him at Brookville, *OR*, vol. 19, pt. 2, 258. Pleasonton received orders from McClellan to "send out scouts to-night [12 September] to endeavor to get information regarding this [Jackson moving to Harpers Ferry]. Did Captain Sanders receive his order to push his scouts in the direction of Harper's Ferry from Licksville? If not, please communicate them to him," *OR*, vol. 51, pt. 1, 824.

[76] Ibid., 824-825. "Catoctin Valley" is also known as "Middletown Valley;" the Monocacy Valley is usually applied to the valley between the Catoctin Mountains and Parr's Ridge through which the Monocacy River flows although it has also been called the "Frederick Valley."

[77] Daniel Carroll Toomey, *The Civil War in Maryland* (Baltimore, MD: Toomey Press, 1983), 50.

accomplished by the Rebels during the Maryland Campaign. Lt. Col. Luke Tiernan Brien, whose family owned a farm south of Chambersburg in Washington County, Maryland, stayed there for a night visiting his family, returning the next day after this welcome respite from the war.[78] An artist, Alfred Waud, who sketched the 1st Virginia Cavalry for *Harper's Weekly*, wrote about his encounter with these Rebel horsemen:

> Being detained within the enemy's lines, an opportunity occurred to make a sketch of one of the two crack regiments of the Confederate service. They seemed to be of considerable social standing, that is, most of them—F. F. V.'s [Founding Families of Virginia], so to speak, and not irreverently; for they were not only as a body handsome, athletic men, but generally polite and agreeable in manner. With the exception of the officers, there was little else but homespun among them, light drab-gray or butternut color, the drab predominating; although there were so many varieties of dress, half-citizen, half-military, that they could scarcely be said to have a uniform. Light jackets and trowsers with black facings, and slouched hats, appeared to be (in those cases where the wearer could obtain it) the court costume of the regiment. Their horses were good; in many cases, they told me, they provided their own. Their arms were the United States cavalry sabre, Sharp's carbine, and pistols. Some few of them had old swords of the Revolution, curved, and in broad, heavy scabbards.
>
> Their carbines, they said, were mostly captured from our own cavalry, for whom they expressed utter contempt—a feeling unfortunately shared by our own army. Finally, they bragged of having their own horses, and, in many cases, of having drawn no pay from the Government, not needing the paltry remuneration of a private. The flag represented in the picture is the battle-flag. White border, red ground, blue cross, and white stars.[79]

---

[78] Driver, *1st Virginia Cavalry*, 154; Kirk shows this telegram to Curtin's office from Greencastle: "From all that we can learn from various sources, it appears that the advance guard of the enemy has moved during the past twenty-four hours from a point about three miles southward of Hagerstown to a point on the road to this place [Greencastle] about four miles northward of Hagerstown. The main body of men, however, appears to be yet somewhere in the meridian of Hagerstown. Several parties have declared that a large force is at Williamsport, but how they reached that place is not stated. The rebel Lieutenant-Colonel Brinn [Brien] is said to have been making exceeding merry at his house about one-half mile south from the State Line, and that he is guarded by some 500 cavalry. The rebels upon entering Hagerstown placed guards at all the roads, with orders to shoot anyone who attempts to leave. Many rumors have been afloat regarding the advance of squads in various directions, but these have lacked confirmation," Kirk, 642. A local newspaper reported that on "Thursday, the 11th inst....the advance guard, a squad of the 1st Va. Cavalry, came dashing into our midst. These were followed by the whole regiment, under L. T. BRIEN, of our county, which numbered about 350. During the afternoon TOOMB's Brigade of Georgians passed through, and encamped on the Rail Road. The advance guard captured Lieut. A. Nesbitt, and four of his men, all of RUSSELL's Cavalry. During the day a few others were made prisoners, all of whom were paroled....On Friday morning about 11 o'clock, Longstreet's Division, headed by General R. Lee, made its appearance and for three hours continued in one uninterrupted stream. But about 2 P. M., it became evident, from the movements, that there was some change of programme, the march having ceased and ammunition trains were started for the rear with artillery following. Thus, having camped in two localities on the south-west and south-east of town, they remained until early on Sunday morning [14 September], when the line of march was again formed, but with a retrograde movement. Jackson, Taliaferro and Hill's forces had crossed from Boonsboro to Williamsport over the Manor road, thence to Virginia. As subsequent events prove the two last named returned by the same route, their trains joining that of Longstreet. By noon of Sunday all had passed, and seeming quiet again prevailed until midnight, when Toombs' Brigade moved down the Sharpsburg pike to Jones' Cross Roads, thence on the Manor Road to Williamsport, and about two o'clock Brien's Cavalry left for the same place....The condition and morale of the [Rebel] army is beyond description. They came among us not only badly clothed and unclean in person, but in a half-starving condition. For days, indeed, since the fights at Centreville, they have subsisted on rations of bread, irregularly issued, and green corn and fruits. Hundreds are weakened by diarrhea, and worn out by their long march, but they fight desperately because forced by hunger and want....Certain it is, that, during their sojourn here they have learned to know aright, not only the true condition of Maryland, but also the feeling at the North. Their conduct while among us, was generally correct and considerate, but threats of violence to Pennsylvania were loud and frequent. That they designed carrying Maryland, per force, into the Confederacy, was evident from their actions and conversation, and it was as plainly evidenced that they were greatly deceived at the condition of affairs; and the tendency of public sentiment in Maryland," *Herald of Freedom and Torch Light*, Sept 10-24, 1862.

[79] *Harper's Weekly*, 27 September 1862, pg. 618.

Munford, with his two depleted regiments, the 2nd and 12th Virginia, had slowly retreated with Chew's Battery southwest on the Jefferson Pike to Jefferson. There, with only his understrength regiments, he would hold the gap in the Catoctin Mountains east of the village of Jefferson, through which the turnpike from Frederick passed. From there, the pike wended its way to the southwest to Knoxville, Maryland, just to the west of Berlin near the Potomac, the main road to Harpers Ferry.[80] Munford's troopers were likely grateful for their short respite after several trying days of activity starting near Leesburg on 2 September, where it fought Capt. S.C. Means and his independent cavalry company, ending now at the gap in the Catoctin Mountains, where he would soon face overwhelming Union cavalry and infantry forces. Munford and Hampton would now defend Stuart's Catoctin Mountain Line for a day, successful in the attempt to delay Federal pursuit.

The 1st Virginia Cavalry at a halt presents a handsome picture. *Harper's Weekly*, September 27, 1862, p. 612. Author's collection.

---

[80] *OR*, vol. 19, pt. 1, 816.

Col. Andrew Thomas McReynolds, Fourth Brigade and 1st New York Cavalry commander. Courtesy LOC.

THE ARMY OF THE POTOMAC—GENERAL PLEASANTON'S CAVALRY DEPLOYED AS SKIRMISHERS. [SKETCHED BY MR. A. R. WAUD.]

Pleasonton's Cavalry deployed as skirmishers. Alfred R. Waud 1828-1891, *Harpers' Weekly*, 22 November 1862, p. 742. Author's collection.

Maj. George H. Chapman, 3rd Indiana Cavalry, at his headquarters. Courtesy LOC.

Maj. George H. Chapman, 3rd Indiana Cavalry, and staff at his headquarters. Courtesy LOC.

Maj. Heros von Borcke, photograph by E.O. Wiggins. He was a very large man who wielded a heavy saber and performed excellent service for Jeb Stuart and was devoted to him despite being sometimes the butt of his jokes. Courtesy LOC.

Chapter 7

From Frederick to South Mountain

THE MOST FAMOUS INTELLIGENCE BLUNDER in the Civil War happened during the second week of Lee's Maryland Campaign. Lee's Special Order 191, soon to become known as the "Lost Order," was about to meet avid readers as the Union Twelfth Corps advanced to Frederick on Saturday 13 September. The 27th Indiana Infantry Regiment, known as "The Giants," was in the van.[1] In the morning, the regiment rested outside Frederick in a clover field alongside the road near Myers Farm, enjoying the pleasant, late summer weather. There, at about 9 A.M., Sgt. John M. Bloss of Company F noticed something unusual lying in the grass near Cpl. Barton W. Mitchell, adjacent to the fence along the road. It was a bulky, unsealed envelope from which, as Mitchell picked it up and passed it to Bloss, two cigars and two pieces of paper fell out. As Bloss and Mitchell prepared to enjoy the cigars, Bloss began reading the paper. Seeing the names of Rebel generals and the details of what their commands would do, he quickly reasoned that it could be a valuable find; Bloss repackaged the cigars and papers and relinquishing command of his unit, went to the company commander, Capt. Peter Kop. After reading the order, Bloss and Kop went on foot to the regiment's commander, Col. Silas Colgrove, less than a half mile away. Colgrove also read it as did Brig. Gen. Nathan Kimball who was visiting from his Second Corps brigade close by perhaps to see his nephew by marriage, Bloss.[2]

Kimball advised that Colgrove skip brigade headquarters and go directly to the Twelfth Corps headquarters where Colgrove journeyed, and handed the document to Lt. Samuel E. Pittman, acting adjutant general of the corps. Upon his return to his headquarters at 10:30 A.M., the acting corps

---

[1] This regiment was perhaps the tallest in the army having an average height of 5 feet 9 inches, and having the tallest man in the army, Capt. David Van Buskirk, who was six feet 10 ½ inches in his stocking feet. See Roger S. Durham, "'The Biggest Yankee in the World'" in *Civil War Times Illustrated*, May 1974, Vol. XIII, no. 2; and Wilbur D. Jones, *Giants in the Cornfield: The 27th Indiana Infantry* (Shippensburg, PA: White Mane Publishing Co., 1997), 250-251. Both Bloss and Mitchell would be seriously wounded at Antietam in the famous Cornfield. Buskirk was not, however, the tallest man in the Civil War. That distinction belonged to seven foot 7 ½ inch tall Pvt. Henry C. Thruston in the Morgan County (Texas) Rangers and later in the 4th Missouri Cavalry, "The Tallest Confederate," *Civil War Times Illustrated*, November 1974, Vol. XIII, no. 7, 42.

[2] Priest, *Before Antietam*, 109. Carman wrote that since Cox's division arrived in the area about noon, the order could not have been found before then, Carman, Pierro, 129-130. Sgt. John McKnight Bloss (1839-1905), the most successful alumnus of the 27th, served as President of Oregon Agricultural College from 1892 until 1896. He entered Hanover College (Indiana) in 1854 and received an A.B. degree with honors in 1860; in 1864-1865 he studied medicine at Ohio Medical College in Cincinnati. Bloss fought and was wounded in several battles, including Antietam, before he resigned in 1864. His career in education included serving as a teacher; principal; superintendent of city schools in Indiana and Kansas; and the State Superintendent for Public Instruction for Indiana. In April 1892 he was selected as the third president of Oregon Agricultural College. He resigned from the College in 1896 due to failing health and returned to his farm north of Muncie, Indiana where he died in 1905. During his retirement, he established the first consolidated school (Royerton) west of the Allegheny Mountains in his home township of Hamilton, Ohio, Jones, *Giants*, 233; Oregon State University website.

commander, Brig. Gen. Alpheus Williams, and Pittman examined the paper and Pittman said he recognized Chilton's signature as genuine, having seen it in the old army. Pittman had been a civilian teller in the Michigan State Bank in Detroit and had seen Chilton's signature many times since Chilton, as paymaster, kept his accounts in that bank. Gen. Williams, without delay, sent it to McClellan's headquarters by a fast courier, accompanied by a note from Pittman vouching the authenticity of Chilton's signature. "I enclose a Special Order of General Lee, commanding rebel forces, which was found on the field where my corps is encamped. It is a document of interest and is also thought to be genuine."[3] The disposition of the cigars however, was never revealed. McClellan, the scales lifted from his eyes concerning Lee's movements, wired Lincoln at about noon on the 13th: "I think Lee has made a gross mistake, and that he will be severely punished for it....The army is in motion as rapidly as possible. I hope for a great success if the plans of the Rebels remain unchanged....I have all the plans of the rebels, and will catch them in their own trap if my men are equal to the emergency....Will send you trophies."[4]

---

[3] Jones, *Giants in the Cornfield: The 27th Indiana Infantry*, 229-242. His account has some minor differences from Carman such as three cigars vice two, who was present when it was found and the actions following that discovery. Jones's account is valuable as it includes many accounts of the finding of the Lost Order. The instant quote is from Jones who quotes an article by Samuel E. Pittman in the *National Tribune*, June 25, 1925. See also the 1886 account by Silas Colgrove which also differs on some minor details. This version is incorrect in describing Pittman's pre-war service with Chilton as is his statement that McClellan's whole army was on the move "within an hour," "The Finding of Lee's Lost Order," *Battles and Leaders*, 2:603. Carman, Pierro, 129-130, who states that the order was more likely found around noon as the Twelfth Corps arrived at about that time. But Jones's account seems more likely given the time that McClellan wired Lincoln. See Attachment to this chapter for the *OR* copy of S.O. 191. Carman incorrectly shows Pittman as a captain; Williams calls him a lieutenant, *OR*, vol. 19, pt. 1, 478.

[4] *OR*, vol. 19, pt. 2, 281. Sears, *Landscape*, 112-113. Note that there is a copy of the received telegram on United States Military Telegraph War Department letterhead in cursive writing in the Lincoln Papers, Library of Congress, The Abraham Lincoln Papers at the Library of Congress, Series 1, General Correspondence, 1833-1916, George B. McClellan to Abraham Lincoln, Saturday, September 13, 1862 showing that it was written on September 13th at "12 Midnight" from headquarters at Frederick, Maryland and received at 2:35 A.M. While it is possible that this message could have travelled so quickly, given the difficulty of sending signals to and from McClellan's headquarters near Frederick to Point of Rocks for telegraphing to Washington it seems unlikely. There was no direct telegraphic link from McClellan's HQ to Point of Rocks so the message had to go from McClellan headquarters by courier to the nearest signal station at or in Frederick and then relayed either to the Sugarloaf Mountain station or sent directly to Point of Rocks where it was then sent to Washington by telegraph. *OR*, vol. 19, pt. 1, 119; Willard Brown, 327-328. That this could be done in 2 ½ hours in the dead of night appears unlikely especially since Brown did not mention the use of lamps or use of other lights by the signal stations. Note that McClellan's telegram to Halleck sent at 11 P.M. on 13 Sept. was received by the War Department 14 hours later at 1 P.M. on 14 Sept. See Sears, *The Civil War Papers of George B. McClellan*, 453-454: "1. Telegraphic communication was not yet re-established between Frederick and Washington, and this dispatch, written at noon (12 M, or meridian) on Sept. 13, was relayed by courier or flag signal to an intermediate telegraph station and received in Washington at 2:25 A.M. on Sept. 14." Also, historians since that time such as Ezra Carman, Joseph Harsh, Stephen Sears, John Priest, and Dennis Frye, believe that it was 12 noon. James Murfin wrote that it was 12 midnight. Sears's comprehensive article covers the possibilities: "The Twisted Tale of the Lost Order," *North & South*, Vol. 5, No. 7 (Oct., 2002), 54-65. Thomas Clemens firmly believes that it was sent at midnight, see Carman, Clemens, 280, n. 7. Dr. Clemens believes the following which points toward midnight vice noon: "it makes no sense that McClellan was so ebullient at noon, he just got it, and engineers in general and McClellan in particular, are not that excitable; that he sent it to Pleasonton to validate demonstrates that he had his doubts, so why lift the President's hopes so rashly? McClellan would have followed the chain of command as he was already on thin ice with Stanton and Halleck, and Lincoln's support is tenuous. So why would he tell Lincoln such valuable information and not tell Halleck? He'd be in hot water for violating the chain of command by reporting directly to Lincoln first, and he is too much a soldier for that. Finally, I find no real evidence why anyone would "fake" the "Midnight" written on the order. Thus it is logical that after he wrote to Halleck he wrote to Lincoln," e-mail 9 December 2011. Perhaps McClellan may have wished to quickly respond to President Lincoln's 4 A.M. 12 Sept. telegram asking "How does it look now?" *OR*, vol. 19, pt. 2, 270. The explanation for the 12 midnight may just be that the transcriber in the telegraph office may have been a little groggy at 2 A.M. and mistakenly wrote "12 midnight" vice "12 noon" or "12 meridian." One might give a more nefarious bent to the probable incorrect time to make McClellan appear dilatory in notifying Washington. Signal Corps men were with McClellan as the army commander headed west from Frederick so could have relatively quickly signaled the

Pleasonton, on 13 September, continued his cavalry reconnaissance, sending the 12th Pennsylvania Cavalry, accompanied by the 1st New York Infantry, north on the Emmitsburg Road to probe the Rebel rearguard's left flank. Along with a section of artillery, Company M, 2nd U.S. Artillery, under command of Lt. Peter C. Hains, they were investigating the Confederate's left to ensure that Rebel units were not heading for Pennsylvania. Meanwhile, Rush's Lancers, the 6th Pennsylvania Cavalry, moved in Munford's wake southwest toward Jefferson, about seven miles from Frederick. They were supported by Col. Harrison S. Fairchild's brigade of Brig. Gen. Isaac P. Rodman's division of the Ninth Corps, to reinforce Franklin's column, with which the 6th U.S. Cavalry, and a battery of horse artillery, were then acting.[5] Munford had left on his ride to Jefferson early on the 12th and arrived there late in the day. The main effort of Pleasonton's cavalry however, was along the line of movement of Lee's army, the National Pike. The 3rd Indiana Cavalry, the 8th Illinois Cavalry, and the 1st Massachusetts Cavalry, rode west along the Pike, reaching the base of the Catoctin Mountain range about 9 A.M. There, some five miles from Frederick, they came under fire from two guns of Hart's Washington South Carolina Artillery, from near the crest at Hagan's Gap (also known as Braddock Pass or Fairview Gap), defended by Col. William T. Martin and a detachment from the Jeff Davis Legion. Accompanying Federal artillery, a section from Company M of the 2nd U.S. Artillery, and a section from combined battery B and L, unlimbered and opened fire, but could not reach the elevation of the Rebel guns, while the Confederate artillery initially overshot its targets. Hearing the firing early that morning, Stuart and von Borcke rode east from their Middletown headquarters, leaving Hampton's Brigade there as a reserve, until Stuart realized that the Federals were threatening in force, so Stuart quickly called Hampton and his troopers forward to help Martin hold Hagan's Gap. Stuart also sent two dispatches, one to Gen. Lee informing him of the advancing Union forces, and the second to D.H. Hill, urging him to send a brigade to Turner's Gap. Hampton placed two more pieces of artillery at Hagan's Gap to assist the two guns already there. Stuart spread out skirmishers of the 1st North Carolina fanning out to the south of the National Pike and sent von Borcke to the north of the road with a mountain howitzer. Artillery on both sides continued their mostly ineffectual duel caused by the steep gradient of the mountain, while the incline allowed Stuart and Hampton an excellent view of the action.[6]

Lost Order news directly to the Sugar Loaf or Point of Rocks station more easily during daylight than during the night when signal lamps must be used, *OR*, vol. 19, pt. 1, 119-121. Carman agrees with McClellan's telegram time of 12 noon, Carman, Pierro, 130. The editors of the *Official Records* placed the "12m." dispatch above the one to Halleck which was sent on 13 September at 11 P.M., implying that it was sent before the one to Halleck, *OR*, vol. 19, pt. 2, 281.

[5] Carman, Pierro, 94; Priest, *Before Antietam*, 109.

[6] Priest, *Before Antietam*, 105-107; von Borcke, 143-146; Brooks, *Stories of the Confederacy*, 83-84; Harsh, *Flood*, 232; *OR*, vol. 51, pt. 1, 137-138.

Modern photograph of Hagan's Tavern at Hagan's, Braddock's, or Fairview Gap on the Old National Pike formerly Braddock's Road on the eastern side of Catoctin Mountain. In this area likely nearer the crest, Hampton's rearguard stopped Pleasonton's pursuit from Frederick. The front porch is a 1914 addition to the original building which was built in the late 1700's. Hagan operated the tavern in 1830. Note that Fox's Gap in South Mountain is also sometimes called Braddock's Gap so Hagan's will be used to prevent confusion. Courtesy Craig Swain HMdb.org.

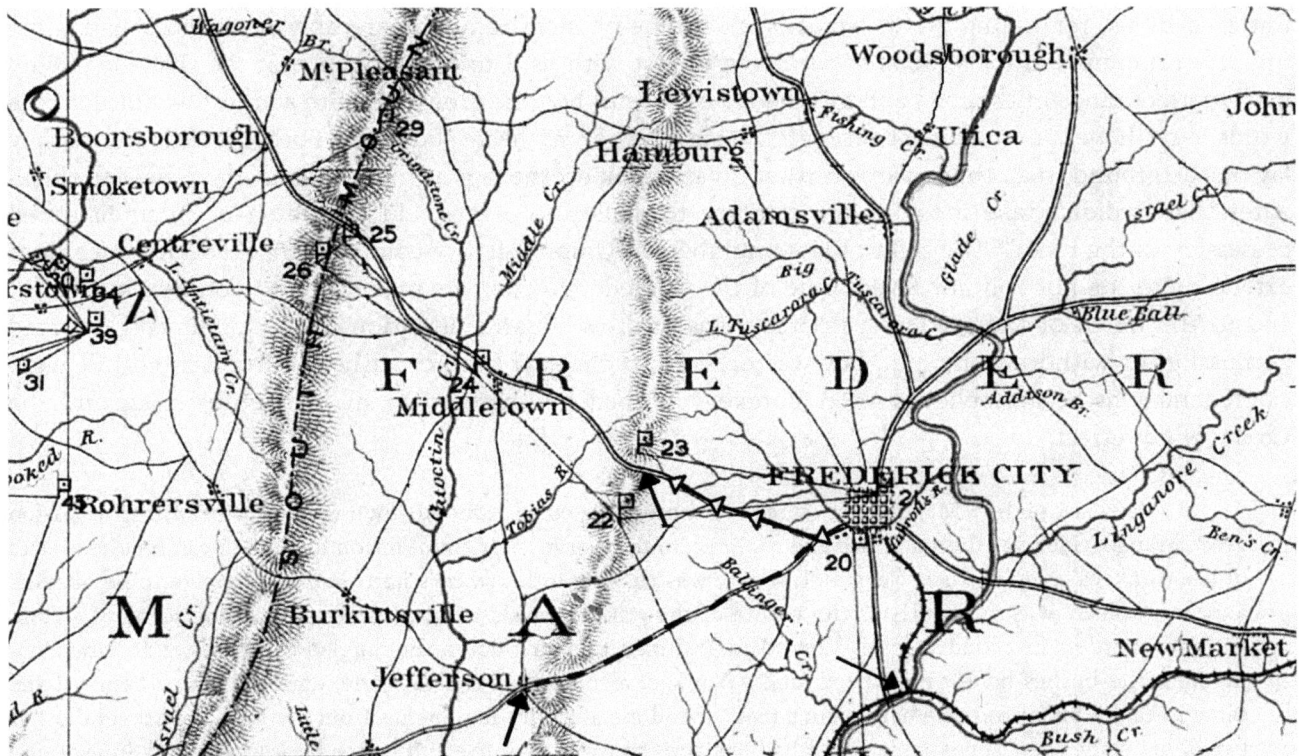

Map showing location of Pleasonton's Union cavalry pursuit west of Frederick on the National Pike and the 6th Pennsylvania Cavalry toward Jefferson at the lower left arrow on the Harpers Ferry Road shown by the dotted line. Hagan's Tavern is at the arrow in the upper center at Hagan's Gap on the National Pike. Arrow at lower right center shows location where the 27th Indiana found Gen. Lee's S.O. 191 near Monocacy Junction on 13 September. Note "Centreville" in the upper left is another name for Keedysville which is just north of Sharpsburg. The road leading west from Hamburg joins another heading north from Middletown and then goes through South Mountain to Hagerstown. The road north from Middletown was the Old Hagerstown Road while the road from Hamburg although shown here as a generally straight road west was more tortuous but still a well-used route. Hamburg Gap or Pass was more commonly the name for the passage at Hamburg on Catoctin Mountain. The gap through which the joined roads traversed South Mountain was sometimes mistakenly called "Hamburg Pass" simply because it came from Hamburg. It was known to residents as Orr's Gap. See n. 36 below for a discussion. Detail from the *Official Atlas*, Plate 27. Courtesy LOC.

McClellan received reports of the fight on the mountain and sent infantry forward to assist. Col. Edward Harland's brigade marched to bolster Pleasonton at the foot of the gap. As the Union infantry marched to aid its sister cavalry on the National Pike, Pleasonton's dismounted troopers had formed into skirmish lines on both sides of the National Pike and began moving up toward the Rebels near the crest on the east side of the mountain—the 3rd Indiana to the north and the 8th Illinois to the south of the pike, with the Bay State cavalrymen in reserve on the pike. The historian of the 3rd Indiana wrote that the troopers "counted off by fours and the dismounted men crawled up the mountainside through brush and over stone fences, and soon made it too hot for that battery to operate."[7] As they disappeared into the trees hidden from von Borcke's nervous view, he urgently requested that Stuart allow him and his cannon to retreat. As the lead Union infantry arrived and rested in the road among the cavalrymen, a Confederate cannonball announced to the green infantry in Harland's brigade that the Rebel cannon had the range, wounding three men by taking off their legs; the infantry brigade quickly deployed away from the road. A trooper from the 1st Massachusetts witnessed this incident: "Here we stood three hours resting by the side of the road and waiting for it to be opened for us. Now and then the shot and shell

---

[7] Pickerill, 24; Crowninshield, 73-74. The 1st Massachusetts Cavalry was in action on James Island near Charleston in June 1862; drilling was part of the duties at Hilton Head and Beaufort, South Carolina camps, Crowninshield, 64-65.

fluttered by us, reminding me of James Island. Some of them came disagreeably near and at last some infantry came up and for a moment sat down to rest with us. I told a Captain near me that the enemy had a perfect range of the road and he'd better be careful how he drew their fire and just as I uttered the words, r-r-r-h went a round shot through the bushes over my head, slid across Forbes and Caspar as they lay on the ground some thirty yards further on and took off the legs of three infantry men next to them. After that it didn't take long for the infantry to deploy into the field and leave us in undisturbed possession of the road."[8] The sight of large numbers of Union infantry coming from Frederick with lines extending to the horizon unnerved some of the Confederate troopers in addition to von Borcke. Above and to the north of the road, the Prussian finally drew Stuart's attention to his plight and received permission to withdraw the gun, but was ordered to check if the skirmishers lower on the hill were Confederates as Stuart believed. Von Borcke described his memory of his dangerous scout and the Confederate retreat:

> Stuart at last said— "Major, I am quite sure those shots come from our own men, who are firing at far too great a range; ride over there at once and order them to reserve their ammunition until they can see the whites of the Yankees' eyes." I knew very well that it was rushing into a wasp's nest, but orders were to be obeyed, and, making my way as quickly as the nature of the ground would admit, I proceeded to the scene of action, giving my orders in a loud voice as I heard several men breaking down the tangled thicket near at hand. In a moment the bushes before me parted, and a Yankee, as blue as ever I saw one, emerged from them. At the same instant a bullet tore the bark from a tree behind me at a very few inches from my head, and several other tirailleurs made their appearance; and I had just time to turn my horse and gallop back to General Stuart, who now fully credited my report, and made off with me as fast as our chargers could carry us over the rocky surface of the mountain. The Yankees, knowing very well that there was a noble game afoot, now advanced their whole line at a run, and with loud cries of encouragement, toward an open space over which we must ride, and where a shower of bullets fell around us, fortunately without touching a rider or a horse. The order for our general retreat was now given, and executed at a quick trot. I expected every moment to hear the roar of the Yankee artillery, which from the heights behind us must have inflicted very serious loss upon our column; but General Hampton, with admirable foresight, had so well barricaded the roads that we were out of range before they had gained our former position.[9]

After ordering the retreat of his men from the mountain at about 2 P.M., von Borcke crowed that Stuart's horsemen and the guns had held up the entire Union column for almost eight hours with two regiments and one battery against three cavalry regiments, almost 2,000 infantry, and a Union battery, sustaining no casualties against seven for the Union. However, eight hours was not enough given that Gen. Lee's Harpers Ferry expedition was at least a day behind schedule unbeknownst to both Lee and Stuart.[10]

[8] Charles Francis Adams, Jr., *A Cycle of Adams Letters 1861-1865*, vol. 1, ed. by Worthington Chauncey Ford (Houghton Mifflin Co., Boston, MA, 1920), 185-186.
[9] Von Borcke, 145-146.
[10] Priest, *Before Antietam*, 108-112. For a detailed discussion of Stuart's and Lee's assumptions and information available to them see Harsh, *Flood*, 242-252.

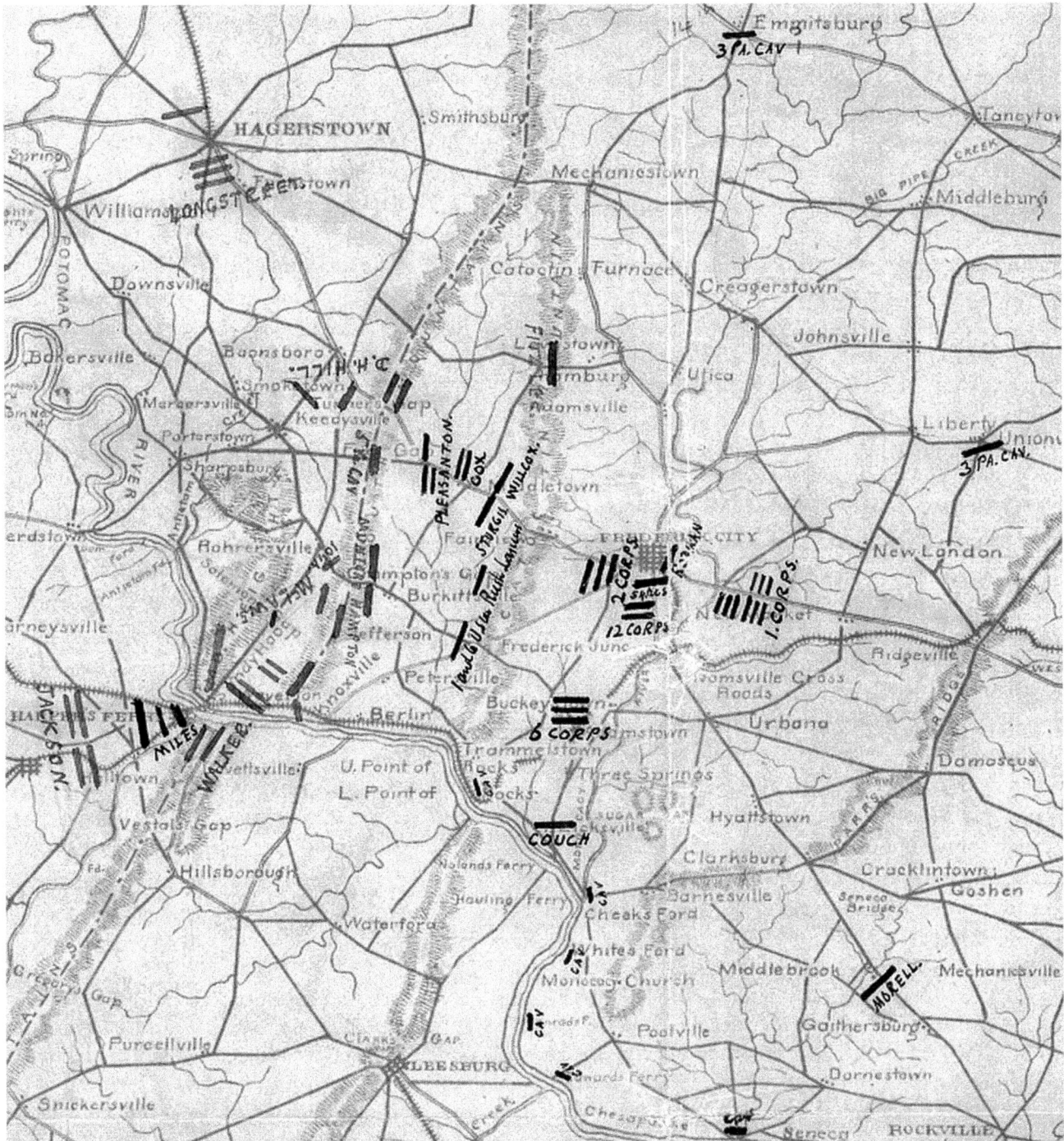

13 September 1862, McClellan closes in; Jackson invests Harpers Ferry from the west. Early on the 13th Stuart pulls the brigades of Hampton and Munford west to the line of Catoctin Mountain at Hagan's Gap (also known as Braddock's or Fairview Pass) on the National Pike and at Jefferson, respectively. He plans to delay the approaching Federal Cavalry, but by the end of the day he is pushed back by brigade-strength Federal infantry to the South Mountain gaps. The Federal cavalry supported by Ninth Corps infantry push up the National Pike and by the end of the day have driven the Confederate cavalry through Middletown to the base of Turner's Gap in South Mountain. Other of Pleasonton's brigades approach Crampton's Gap pursuing Munford and skirmish with Munford near Burkittsville. The 3rd Pennsylvania Cavalry is checking for Confederate cavalry to the north. McClellan also finds Lee's S.O. 191 after Federal cavalry movements begun. "The 3rd Pennsylvania Cavalry, which had advanced to Unionville on the twelfth in pursuit of Fitzhugh Lee's cavalry, marched on the thirteenth to Woodsborough, Creagerstown, and Emmitsburg, returning to Frederick on the fourteenth," Carman, Pierro, 95. Courtesy LOC.

Pleasonton received a copy of S.O. 191 about 3 P.M. on the 13th along with an order from McClellan to "ascertain whether this order of march has thus far been followed by the enemy. As the pass through the Blue Ridge [South Mountain] may be disputed by two columns, he desires you to approach it with great caution." Another order at 9 P.M. that night ordered Pleasonton to "fire occasionally a few artillery shots…so as to let Colonel Miles at Harper's Ferry know that our troops are near him."[11] Unfortunately for McClellan, Pleasonton was able to do little to confirm all of the movements described in Lee's order as McClellan probably surmised. His cavalry commander replied in the evening that "'As near as I can judge the order of march of the enemy that you sent me has been followed as closely as circumstances would permit.'"[12] There is no record of the number or times when Pleasonton's artillery fired signal guns for Miles, if any. McClellan probably placed minimal value in this report since he obviously knew that Pleasonton had no troopers in place to view anything west of South Mountain and south of the Potomac, but McClellan did everything he thought he could do to try to be confident in the information contained in Lee's order. He likely was aware that Harpers Ferry had not fallen since cannonading could be heard from that direction. Additionally, he received reports that large Confederate forces were near Hagerstown, but McClellan by the end of the day on the 13th believed that his copy of S.O. 191 was genuine, and he acted on it, spurring his army with orders to take the passes in South Mountain on the 14th. McClellan may have begun moving with alacrity by his own lights but as he did not put any major part of his army in motion until the morning of the 14th, he has been roundly criticized by many historians for not getting any troops, especially Franklin's corps, marching late on the thirteenth.[13]

North Carolina cavalry under Col. Lawrence S. Baker, with a section of Hart's Battery, were waiting east of Middletown on the National Pike, to slow the approaching Union host, while the rest of Hampton's troopers were west of the village and Catoctin Creek with artillery set. Capt. Thaddeus P. Siler of the North Carolina Cavalry, wounded in the thigh, tried to hold the Union cavalry, both mounted and on foot, in check, but the pressure was too much. Hampton's men were setting charges to blow up the bridge which carried the National Pike over Catoctin Creek on the western edge of the town as Stuart watched from west of Middletown. After allowing his artillery to retreat, Stuart waited too long to withdraw his dismounted North Carolinians, creating a rout as they raced down Middletown's main street trying to escape Federal shells and rifle fire. The horsemen's misery was compounded as they had to run a gauntlet of civilians firing shotguns from houses along the road while Union cavalry had no trouble fording the shallow creek at several places.[14] Von Borcke criticized his chief and described the exciting action around Middletown:

> In my judgment our admirable General here betrayed a fault which was one of the few he had as a cavalry leader; and the repetition of the error on several occasions, at later periods of the war, did us material damage. His own personal gallantry would not permit him to abandon the field and retreat, even when sound military prudence made this clearly advisable. There was no necessity whatever, here, for the safety of the main body, to sacrifice a smaller command, for we might have withdrawn with honour long before the enemy's fire had so cruelly thinned our ranks.

---

[11] *OR*, vol. 51, pt. 1, 829.

[12] Sears, *McClellan*, 284.

[13] Carman, Pierro, 130, 132. Signal Corps men had moved west with Pleasonton and McClellan from Frederick establishing a station on Catoctin Mountain and on a prominent tower on the church in Middletown. After signalmen arrived at Pleasonton's headquarters west of Middletown, a line was opened to McClellan's headquarters and one on South Mountain near Reno's position. All of these were in contact with each other as well as the stations on South Mountain and Point of Rocks so McClellan's headquarters was receiving messages about Union troop movements, Willard Brown, 330. See Harsh's analyses of McClellan, *Flood*, 238-241, wherein he assesses the Little Napoleon's actions justified and finds his plan good.

[14] Von Borcke, 147; Brooks, *Stories of the Confederacy*, 85.

I was one of the last horsemen that galloped through the town, and had a painfully accurate sight of the confusion and destruction that attended the retreat. The Yankee artillery threw a withering hail of shells along the main street of Middletown, from every by-street whistled the bullets of the sharpshooters, in our rear thundered the attack of the pursuing cavalry, while from the houses the Unionists fired at us with buck-shot and small-shot, and many fallen horses and riders impeded the road. The panic reached its height when we arrived at the bridge and found it blazing, through the premature execution of his orders by the officer in charge. Many of our horsemen Leaped into the rapid stream and gained the opposite bank by swimming. For myself, with many of my companions-in arms, I forced my horse through fire and smoke across the burning bridge, which, very soon after we had passed over it, fell with a loud crash into the water.

The hotly-pursuing enemy were now received upon the opposite bank with a deadly fire from our well-posted sharpshooters, and showers of canister from our artillery, which brought them to a stop; and after a heavy cannonade that lasted for more than an hour, we continued our retreat quietly toward the South Mountain, in the direction of Boonsboro. The Federal cavalry managed the crossing of the Kittochtan [Catoctin Creek] with commendable expedition, and were soon again on our tracks, but the two pieces detached to our rear-guard kept them at a respectful distance by occasional discharges of grape and canister.[15]

Col. Lawrence S. Baker commanding the 1st North Carolina Cavalry. Courtesy LOC.

---

[15] Von Borcke, 147-148.

Union troopers then charged into Middletown finding only grateful citizens and while taking three prisoners. Union artillerists moved quickly to the first ridge west of town and exchanged fire with Rebel horse artillery under Hart, and with some dismounted Carolina cavalry on the next ridge to the west. The Confederates only left after all of Stuart's trains had passed suffering thirteen casualties for their successful delaying efforts. Stuart had earlier sent the Jeff Davis Legion up the National Pike to the ridge top of South Mountain at Turner's Gap to hold the road at the Mountain House, located at the crest on the Pike's southern side. Turner's Gap on the National Pike was the most important pass in South Mountain. The crest of the mountain is some 600 feet higher than the floor of Middletown Valley to the east and Cumberland Valley to the west. Fox's Gap is about one mile south of Turner's Gap through which passes the Old Sharpsburg Road. It branches off to the northwest from the National Pike just west of Middletown; Crampton's Gap is six miles south of Fox's Gap through which passed a road which joined the Arnoldstown Road and the extension of Burkittsville's main street. The Burkittsville Road was a main road running south from Middletown to Burkittsville.

But Union horsemen were not done yet. As Col. Farnsworth chased Stuart toward the foot of South Mountain, Maj. William H. Medill of the 8th Illinois and other troopers were informed by excited townspeople that Stuart's wagons had gone down a side road leading southwest in the direction of Burkittsville.[16] Stuart had sent Hampton's Brigade (less the Jeff Davis Legion which was busy holding the road to Turner's Gap) with all of the cavalry trains to join Munford at Crampton's Gap. A competent veteran commander, Medill was careful, having witnessed the ability of the grey horsemen in ambushing and employing delaying tactics and, by this time, his troopers' horses needed some rest.[17]

---

[16] W. N. Pickerill, "The Battle of Quebec School House," *Valley Register*, 8 April 1898.

[17] Medill was a brave and experienced commander having first enlisted as a private in the Chicago Dragoons on 18 April 1861. McClellan was so impressed with the Dragoons, he selected them for his personal bodyguard and they joined him at Clarksburg, Virginia, in early June. Private Medill, in a personal fight with a Georgia lieutenant, distinguished himself by capturing him. After the Dragoons were mustered out in August 1861, Medill, an ardent Unionist, decided to rejoin the Union army. He raised a company and he was unanimously elected captain, refusing a majorship saying that he wanted to be in direct command of his troopers. Although Medill had little military experience he was a natural leader. And while the captain was a strict disciplinarian, he was always fair and kind to his men who recognized his martial abilities and presented him with a sword and a brace of Colt's pistols on New Year's Day 1862. It was said that "he always had the largest, best drilled and most efficient company in the regiment," and as senior captain in the regiment, was often placed in its command when senior officers were absent. The 8th Illinois performed well during the Peninsular Campaign where he commanded the regiment on its arrival at Yorktown, but Medill lamented over McClellan's inability to defeat the Rebels and the many Union generals who had a proslavery policy. After disembarking in Alexandria on 4 September 1862, the regiment led McClellan's advance into Maryland now commanded by Medill who gave Stuart's troopers all they could handle. Medill was promoted to major on 10 September. After Antietam on 10/11 October 1862, he and his regiment rode 88 miles in 32 hours in a futile pursuit of Stuart and his raiders during Stuart's Second Ride Around McClellan also known as Stuart's Chambersburg Raid. He was mortally wounded leading his battalion in an attack at Williamsport, Maryland, on 6 July 1863, dying on 16 July in Frederick, Maryland at the age of 27, James Barnet, *The Martyrs and Heroes of Illinois in the Great Rebellion* (Chicago, IL: Press of J. Barnet, 1865), 57-76; Joseph Kirkland, The Story of Chicago (Chicago, IL: The Dibble Publishing Co., 1892), 268.

Maj. William H. Medill from *The Story of Chicago* p. 268.

Medill cautiously pursued the Rebel train with a mixed column of some 230 troopers from Companies A and G of his 8th Illinois, and Companies E and F of the 3rd Indiana. Hampton was not aware that he was being pursued by one of the most competent of the volunteer Union regimental commanders in the Army of the Potomac along with veteran troopers. Unfamiliar with the roads, Medill was not able to follow in Hampton's track which was on a road further to the west, but the road he took joined with the one Hampton was on near the Quebec Schoolhouse, Primary School 83. This schoolhouse was some two and a half miles southwest of Middletown and about three miles northeast of Burkittsville at the intersection of today's Quebec School Road and the Burkittsville-Middletown Road. The stage was set for a surprise for Medill as well as the refugees in the school house on this Saturday.[18]

---

[18] Compare Carman's telling of this fight which has the Union cavalrymen on a reconnaissance toward Harpers Ferry rather than chasing Stuart's trains: "While Pleasonton, with the main body of his cavalry, was advancing to the foot of Turner's Gap, a detachment of Farnsworth's brigade consisting of one squadron of the 8th Illinois Cavalry and a part of the 3rd Indiana Cavalry (all under the command of Major William H. Medill of the 8th) left Middletown to reconnoiter in the direction of Harper's Ferry. The detachment took the road leading through Burkittsville. At the same time, Hampton, with his cavalry brigade, was moving from Turner's Gap to Crampton's Gap by the road running near the foot of the mountain—unaware of the pressure under which Munford was laboring and of the presence of an enemy near his own line of march. When near Crampton's Gap,

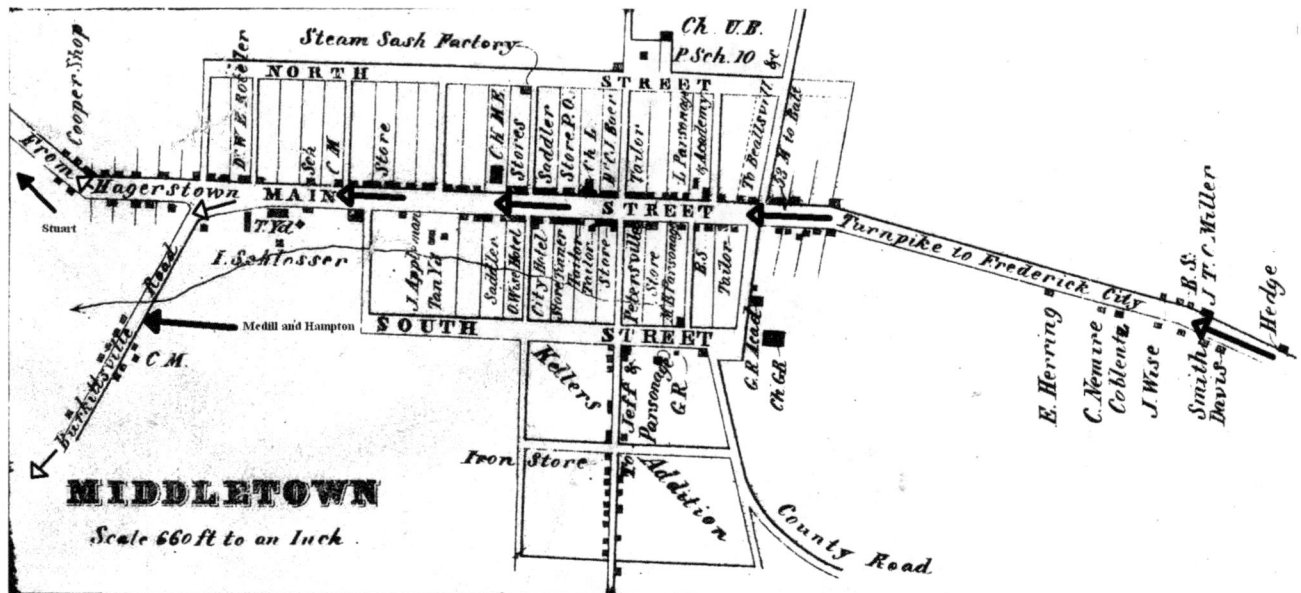

Detail of the town of Middletown, Maryland, from Bond Map 1858 LOC American Memory Map. Medill and his troopers went down the Burkittsville Road at the left arrow chasing Hampton's column. The National Pike runs east to west here labeled as "Main Street." The rest of the Confederate troopers with Union horsemen not far behind rode west toward South Mountain. Note that the unnamed road leading south at the center of the map eventually joins with the Burkittsville Road north of Burkittsville. Courtesy LOC.

Hampton saw Medill on a nearby road to the east and set up an ambush using Cobb's Georgia Legion of some 100 sabers hiding in woods north of the road. Medill, although sighting Hampton's retreating column, had ended the pursuit as he saw that the Rebels heavily outnumbered his troopers, plus there were cannon in evidence at the tail end of the Confederate wagon column. As Medill's unsuspecting troopers began their return to Middletown after a short rest, they passed near the schoolhouse, when Lt. Col. Pierce M.B. Young's cavalry opened fire from behind a fence, and then attacked the rear of the Union column with sabers. The Union troopers, although surprised, gave little ground and the Rebels broke off contact, leaving their casualties on the field, but felt assured that their foes would not be following. Confederate loss was placed at thirteen, Union at twenty to thirty. Needless to say, the refugees in the school house including several children had a much more exciting day than they could have imagined. Fortunately, no children or adults were injured.[19]

---

he saw the Union cavalry on a road parallel to the one on which he was moving. Hampton ordered Lieutenant Colonel Pierce M.B. Young to charge it with the cavalry battalion of Cobb's Legion. The order was carried out in gallant style, Young dispersing the body and capturing prisoners from both the 3rd and the 8th. Hampton's loss was four killed and nine wounded; the Union loss was about the same," Carman, Pierro, 95. Carman picked up the purpose from McClellan's Chief of Staff, Brig. Gen. Marcy, who, on 12 September, ordered Pleasonton to ascertain if "Jackson is marching on Harper's Ferry," *OR*, vol. 51, pt. 1, 824. Carman may be in error since the pursuit of the Rebel wagon train under the circumstances cited by Union cavalrymen eyewitnesses seems more plausible. The chief source for this event, Cpl. Pickerill of the 3rd Indiana, is quoted below.

[19] Reese, *Sealed*, 26-30; Reese supplies estimates of 236 for the Union cavalry: 8th Illinois Cavalry Co. A: 42, Co. G: 73; 3rd Indiana Cavalry Co. E: 61, Co. F: 60; and for the Cobb Legion: 100; *Sealed*, 26, n. 43. Reese, Timothy J. "The Cavalry Clash at Quebec Schoolhouse," *Blue & Gray Magazine*, Vol. X, issue 3, 24-29, hereafter "Quebec." Compare Priest, *Before Antietam*, who says that the Rebels drove off the Union troopers and left with their casualties and prisoners, 122-123. He also substitutes "Quaker Schoolhouse" for "Quebec Schoolhouse," 121. Compare Clemens, thesis, 386-387. Harriet Bey Mesic in *Cobb's Legion Cavalry: A History and Roster of the Ninth Georgia Volunteers in the Civil War* (Jefferson, NC: McFarland & Company, Inc., 2009), essentially follows Pickerill but misses the corrections by the editor of the paper which published Pickerill's account, Pickerill, 24-25. See an account of the skirmish in Pickerill, 25-26, in which he states that that after the fierce melee, the Rebel troopers retreated leaving the Union cavalry in possession of the field along with Confederate dead and wounded, 25-26. Pickerill also wrote an article in a local newspaper, the *Valley Register*, "The Battle of Quebec School-House," published on 8 April 1898

A participant in this action, Cpl. William N. Pickerill, Company F, 3rd Indiana Cavalry, in somewhat florid prose, described the area and the subsequent fight; he is quoted in detail as his was the only complete and comprehensive account of this fight and indeed any other Union cavalry battle during the Maryland Campaign:

> As we entered the village of Middletown four companies of cavalry, two from the Eighth Illinois, and two from the Third Indiana, were detached to go in pursuit of a Confederate wagon train which the citizens informed us was escaping by a road heading southward through the valley. The writer's company formed part of that detachment. Our pursuit of that wagon train was enthusiastic for a couple of miles, and until we came in sight of it slowly winding its way up a mountain road leading out from Burkittsville, the next hamlet below Middletown. In the rear of the train were six brass guns and cavalry enough to eat us up. We halted and formed in a meadow by the wayside and calmly viewed our retreating booty, and wisely decided to let it escape.

Pickerill then waxed poetic about the lovely, bucolic view of the valley, which at this time in September was in full bloom, with crops ready to harvest. Even today, much of this area remains just as it was then:

> From that meadow we again had a glorious vision of the beautiful Middletown valley. We were in the midst of its most fertile farms. Fields of ripening, waving corn were on every hand. Orchards were the background of many a cottage with its shrubbery bedecked lawn. Here and there herds of cattle grazed peacefully on the rich pastures or reposed under friendly shade trees sheltered from the noonday sun. In the distance were the mountain crests wreathed in the blue haze of a perfect autumn day's loveliest sunshine. And two hundred yards away from where our column had halted, on the summit of a little ridge overlooking a rough country road leading to Middletown by a shorter route than we had come, stood an old-fashioned country frame school house. It had one door opening in our direction and three windows on a side, and door and windows were all open. Half a dozen forest trees partially sheltered it from the sun and made a delightful play ground for the children. The dear old school house seemed as well adapted for playing "anty over" as for school. And school was in session. The noon day recess was over and pupils and teacher were apparently trying to give the attention to the things that pupils and teachers go to school for. But it did not seem to be a success. The teacher from the open door cast many a wistful look our way, and generally two or three of the "little tads" would follow him to the door and look out under his coat tail.[20]

Pickerill, a former schoolmaster, then likely reminisced about the scene some 36 years later perhaps embellishing somewhat for a newspaper article:

> What a scene of peace was this sacred spot in the midst of war and what memories did it bring to at least one half of the writer's company, including himself, who had been country school teachers and whose last work before entering the army had been to teach the district country schools in just that same kind of an old fashioned country school-house. Although we were equipped for war, it seemed for the moment like old times, old friends and the old school house of our far off western homes again. For the moment we were on a

---

describing the action in more detail. The article prompted a correction noted below in the same issue from a Mr. John W. Castle who was a teacher at the schoolhouse at the time who said that school was not in session as it did not start until October.

[20] Pickerill, *Valley Register*. "Anty over" is likely "Antony over" which was a "boy's popular ballgame. Two groups stand on either side of a house, or their school-house, and throw a ball back and forth over the roof," John D. Wright, *The Language of the Civil War* (Westport, CT: Oryx Press, 2001), 11. Julie Maynard, a local historian opines that the "Quebec" "name has long been a puzzle. It dates way back, having been in use in the 1840's if not before....[there is] another 'Q' name in our area: 'Quirauk,' up in the very northern end of the Middletown Valley. (There was also a Quirauk schoolhouse.).... [perhaps] both names are an attempt to make sense of an even older Native American name that settlers heard used in the valley," e-mail from Ms. Maynard 11 October 2011.

furlough from the turmoil and anxieties of war, back in the old home school house with its play grounds, and romping with the boys and girls who had been the playmates of our childhood and our boyhood.

But Pickerill and his comrades had little time to enjoy the scenery or their rest as the reality of war intruded, when Maj. Medill had the column move out:

> The major commanding gave the command to about face and we filed off down the rocky ravine road, hemmed in on either side by a very crooked worm fence, on our return to Middletown and our regiments. The rear of our column had just entered this rocky, narrow way, when a shot that seemed to come from over behind the school house whizzed over our heads and left a white spot on the body of a little hickory tree we were leaving to our right. We could not believe that innocent looking old school house concealed our enemies, but two men from the forward end of the column filed out and passing through a pair of bars started up the winding road leading to the school house door. But they never reached their destination. When half way up the hill, they as well as we, heard a yell, and over the little ridge and down upon us leaped a body of Confederate cavalry apparently twice our numbers with drawn sabers, wild-eyed, cursing us furiously and demanding our surrender. This we did not do, but instead, at the sharp command of our officers, two hundred carbines cracked together and a good many men and horses of that wild rushing mob went down, yet on they came and for the next ten minutes in that rocky ravine road there was a tussle for existence difficult to describe. The Confederate cavalry, which proved to be the Cobb Legion, dashed through the bars our men had laid down for them and slashed into our rear with their sabers, while a portion of their force fired into us from inside the fence less than twenty feet away. It was an uneven fight until the advance of our column managed to tear down the fence on the side of the road that separated us from the children's playground surrounding the old school house, when our men wheeled through the gap and went back at the enemy firing into our men from inside the fence. This unexpected move saved the day, and the Cobb Legion, with a parting shot, filed back over the ridge, leaving us in possession of the battle field....Nor was it a bloodless victory. Corporal Harvey Williamson of Company F, Third Indiana Cavalry, had his head split open by a Confederate saber and died that night in a brick church which we appropriated for a hospital in the eastern edge of Middletown. Sergeant Joseph Lewis, of Company E, same regiment, and a Confederate cavalryman lay across each other just inside of the gap where the fence had been torn down, both shot through the heart. Samuel Cross, of the same company, was shot through the lungs, and four men of Company F, Third Indiana, were captured, but returned to us next day paroled. The Eighth Illinois suffered equally with the Third Indiana.[21]

A trooper from the 8th Illinois Cavalry, F.B. Wakefield of Co. G, was reported to have had a trying time after the battle as recorded by the regimental historian:

> [Wakefield] was taken prisoner by the rebels, who after taking him a short distance attempted to kill him. They gave him several cuts over the head with sabres, and leaving him for dead fled for fear of pursuit. He, however, rallied and made his way into our lines. For this brutal treatment he swore vengeance on his would-be murderers, and it is said that he well redeemed his pledge and satisfied his wrath. Such inhuman conduct toward prisoners is now denied by rebel historians, but the Eighth Illinois Cavalry can attest to the truth of the statements.

---

[21] Pickerill, *Valley Register*. It is impossible to determine based on current evidence which roads Hampton and Medill took south from Middletown. But if Pickerill's account is correct stating that he saw the Confederate column "slowly winding its way up a mountain road leading out from Burkittsville, Union horsemen could have been on the parallel road north of Burkittsville, east of Hampton, after having taken the left at the first fork out of Middletown. From Middletown, both groups would have taken Walnut Street but Medill then bore left at the next intersection taking Picnic Woods Road while Hampton continued on toward South Mountain on Bidle Road then Mountain Church Road. Hampton, with the advantage of elevation of about 750 feet, could have seen his pursuers who were at 450 feet elevation near the schoolhouse and been able to send back the Cobb Legion on the Quebec School Road to ambush the Federals.

The wounded of this battle were placed in a church at Middletown, and the ladies turned out by scores to attend to their wants, and furnished refreshments and all necessary comforts.[22]

The Confederate charge must have seemed overwhelming as Pickerill says that they were twice the Union numbers, but were more likely about half the Federal numbers. The Union troopers returned to Middletown arriving that night and savored the victory over the Rebel cavalry, but mourned their losses, knowing that more adventures lay ahead.

The following was written by the editor of the paper which published Pickerill's recollection and clarified some errors in Pickerill's remembrance:

Mr. John W. Castle, who was teacher of the Quebec school at that time, and whose residence then as now, was close to the school-house, detects only two slight errors. Mr. Castle says that Harvey Williamson, the Union soldier so cut with a saber, was carried into the school house provided with a comfortable bed and given every attention during the night, and was removed to the church hospital in Middletown the next morning, where he died. The only other error noted by Mr. Castle is the statement that school was in session. At that time our public schools did not open after the summer vacation until in October, but he says the old school-house was filled with men, women and children who had collected there probably from a feeling of greater safety than if alone in their own homes.

According to Mr. Castle, the name of the Confederate soldier whose dead body lay across that of Joseph H. Lewis, the Union soldier, a few yards below his house, was named Barkdoll, of Georgia, that being the name found inside the case of his watch.

Mr. Castle also states that another Confederate soldier, Lieut. Cobb, was shot and fatally wounded a short distance beyond the school house and that he was carried into what is now K. T. Castle's barn, where he died.[23]

A different newspaper article had a slightly different version of the fight, very likely embellished, as it was printed in 1897 in tribute to Young after his death:

We [the Cobb Legion] had to charge down a steep, rocky lane by twos between stone fences, from whose shelter their dismounted men were firing on us, over a narrow plateau where we deployed into a company front at the run. The Dougherty Hussars of Albany (who were cut to pieces), leading the Fulton Dragoons, of Atlanta, next, then the Richmond Hussars, his [Young's] favorites always, and as we passed Colonel Young, he was lying, surrounded by dead and wounded men and horses, in front of a little country church [the schoolhouse], his dead horse pinning him to the ground. As we came by at full speed, his clarion voice rang out clear and distinct above our yells, "Give 'em hell! Boys, give 'em hell!" waving his plumed hat over that handsome face illumined by the fierce excitement of the charge.[24]

Another apparent Rebel participant in this fight, Pvt. David B. Rea, Co. C, 1st North Carolina Cavalry, provided details which not surprisingly differed from Pickerill's:

As we retired from this position [east of Middletown] it was growing late in the evening. The command was briskly moved off, turned to the left from the turnpike, and moved down the Burkittsville road to join, in

___

[22] Hard, 176-177.
[23] This is taken from the *Valley Register* 8 April 1898 article which was a correction from a Mr. John W. Castle who was a teacher at the schoolhouse at the time who said that school was not in session as it did not start until October; *Valley Register*, "The Battle of Quebec School-House" by William N. Pickerill and in the same issue, "Interesting War History," including statements by Mr. John W. Castle. Brooks in *Stories of the Confederacy* wrote that it was the Union who ambushed the Cobb Legion but the legion drove the Union troopers away in confusion, 85-86. Brooks here agrees with D.B. Rea of the 1st North Carolina Cavalry who recounted the fight. The identification of Castle as living near the schoolhouse at the time of the battle is critical for pinning down the location of the schoolhouse.
[24] "The Beau Sabreur of Georgia," from *Southern Historical Society Papers*, vol. XXV, 148.

all dispatch, the other cavalry to assist in guarding the lower passes of the Boonsboro Mountains. Wearied and worn out in the extreme by the continual watchings, marching, and fighting of the past two days, we hoped our day's work was over and a restful bivouac was ahead of us. But our active, enterprising foe was not disposed to let the sun go down upon us without another tilt at arms; and as its last lengthening shadows were being cast over our weary way, he suddenly appeared on our left as we were passing through a body of woods near Horsey's farm, and made a bold dash upon our rear guard, the Cobb's legion, commanded by Colonel P.M.B. Young, who quickly wheeled his squadrons and gallantly met the advance, driving it back through the woods down upon the main body, which he found drawn up in open ground at the mouth of a lane in mounted squadrons, with dismounted sharpshooters on each flank. Here by a quick movement he threw his two front companies into platoons, placed himself at their head and ordered a sabre charge, and dashed with all impetuosity for their centre. When at close range he was met by a most murderous fire from the front and flank files, unhorsing the greater part of those two advance companies. The brave leader and only a few of his men reached the enemy's lines, and were either cut or shot down and trampled beneath their horses' hoofs. The remainder of the legion unshrinkingly pressed forward and were met in a fierce hand to hand conflict which wavered furiously back and forth over the disputed ground in doubtful struggle for the mastery. General Hampton who, on ordering Colonel Young to make the attack, had taken the rest of the command and had borne round to the left under the cover of the thick timber unawares to the enemy, now gained his left flank and rear, opportunely swept down upon his struggling columns in a determined charge, and decided the wavering conflict. The enemy's ranks were broken on all sides and gave way, closely followed for some distance, gallantly rallying and fighting at every turn, when we were called off from further pursuit. The loss on both sides in this fiercely contested affair was unusually heavy for the short duration and the numbers engaged.

The two front companies of the legion that led the charge were literally decimated under the withering fire of the enemy's carbines that first met them. The enemy's loss was forty, killed and wounded, left on the ground, an officer and several privates captured, and quite a number of horses and equipments also fell into our hands.

Colonel Young was found among the wounded, still fastened under his horse that had been killed under him, with a serious gun-shot wound in the leg, and several sabre cuts on and about the face, one of which knocked out several of his front teeth.[25]

The fierce Confederate ambush was led by Lt. Col. Pierce Manning Butler Young, commanding Cobb's Legion, who was wounded in the leg and lost several teeth when he was thrown from his horse. Capt. Gilbert J. Wright of Company D, who had helped organize its progenitor, the Dougherty Hussars, would later command Hampton's Legion from 9 October 1863 until the Confederate surrender by Gen. Joseph E. Johnston on 26 April 1865, was also seriously wounded in the foot during the charge. As he lay on his back with his foot in the air to help stem the heavy bleeding, he reportedly shouted to his troopers: "'Give 'em hell boys! They've got me down!'"[26]

[25] D.B. Rea "Cavalry Incidents of the Maryland Campaign" in *The Maine Bugle*, January 1895, 121-122.
[26] Mesic, 25, 177-178, quoting Pvt. Wiley C. Howard, "Sketch of Cobb Legion Cavalry and Some Incidents and Scenes Remembered," (Prepared and read under appointment of Atlanta Camp 159, U.C.V., August 19, 1901), 3. D.B. Rea of the 1st North Carolina Cavalry said that Young's front teeth were knocked out by one of several sabre cuts Young received, 122. It may be both Young and Wright shouted encouragement to their troopers but most accounts favor Young. Mesic records that an 80-year-old Confederate trooper named Barksdale, was killed in this action along with his grandson, Green B. Barksdale, 190-191. Lt. Col. Pierce Manning Butler Young entered the Georgia Military Institute in Marietta, Georgia, at 13 and graduated in 1856 and briefly studied law. In 1857, he was appointed to the United States Military Academy in the class of 1861 where a close friend was George Armstrong Custer. Young resigned two months before graduation after Georgia seceded and reported for duty to Charleston, South Carolina apparently taking part in the firing on Fort Sumter. He was then appointed a second lieutenant in the 1st Georgia Infantry regiment but requested that he be assigned instead to the artillery. In July, he was promoted to first lieutenant and was attached to Gen. Braxton Bragg's staff at Pensacola, Florida, but visited Richmond to request more adventurous duty. He was appointed adjutant of Cobb's Legion, and was promoted to major in September 1861 in command of the cavalry portion of the Legion and lieutenant colonel in November. His cavalry was attached to Wade

Gen. Hampton's participation in the battle involved more than urging on his troopers as Rea noted above, but also involved a confrontation with his son, Lt. William Preston Hampton, who was serving as the general's aide-de-camp. As Hampton prepared to lead the remainder of his troopers around the Yankee left flank, he threw his overcoat to his son yelling: "Take care of my overcoat, Preston" but his gallant son "had come to Maryland to fight Yankees, and not to carry his father's overcoat." Father and son sat next to each other after the affray "next to the dropped overcoat and stared at each other. Preston turned away and looked around defiantly at the gathering circle of officers. 'I came to Maryland to fight Yankees,' he announced, 'not to carry father's overcoat.'"[27] The outspoken son was killed at Burgess's Mill on 27 October 1864 where his brother, Wade, IV, was badly wounded rescuing Preston. The martial spirit of the Hampton family was evident at the school house and on many other battlefields but at a grievous cost to Gen. Hampton.

Hampton's Brigade of Jeb Stuart's cavalry division in the Army of Northern Virginia in 1862 performing good service against McClellan on the Peninsula. He continued his distinguished career being promoted to major general in December 1864. Post war, he was a U.S. Congressman and minister to Guatemala and Honduras. He died on 6 July 1896. An active and sometimes daring commander, he was well suited for the ambush Hampton planned for Medill's column, *New York Times*, 12 July 1896; Reese, "Quebec," 26, *Appletons' Cyclopaedia of American Biography*, vol. VI, 1889, s.v. "Pierce Manning Butler Young." See also "The Beau Sabreur of Georgia," from *Southern Historical Society Papers*, vol. XXV, 146-147, describing him as a "born soldier." Col. Young also suffered the loss of his hat which was given to him by his sister who needle-worked his name and title in the lining under the sweatband. This treasured chapeau was found by a Hoosier trooper who had lost his when his horse was killed under him. Finding Young's hat, he secured it as his own. Eventually seeing Young's name, he sent it home as a souvenir but years later returned it to his former adversary in a spirit of reconciliation after seeing Young's name in a newspaper when the former Rebel was appointed minister to Guatemala and Honduras, Rea, 122-123.

[27] *Southern Historical Society Papers*, vol. 25, 148; Andrew, 117. Edward Laight Wells in his book, *Hampton and His Cavalry in '64* (Richmond, VA: B.F. Johnson Publishing Co., 1899), wrote of an incident at Brandy Station which mirrors this one, "As the General dashed to the head of his command to lead them on this occasion, his eyes 'snapping fire,' as the men used to say, he threw off his overcoat to leave his sword-arm free, and flung it to his son Preston, acting Orderly, a mere boy, who was afterwards killed at Burgess' Mill. 'Press' held the coat for a second or two, and then cast it on the ground, exclaiming in soliloquy, 'I came here to fight, not carry coats!' and galloping after his father was soon by his side in the charge. The old soldiers who noticed the incident smiled and said, 'A chip off the old block,'" 71-72. Apparently Wells mixed up the location of this incident as it is extremely unlikely that two such incidents took place. But it is probable that Wells heard tales of this incident from Hampton's troopers and merely mixed up the location. Wells wrote of this incident in a paragraph describing the killing of Gen. Hampton's younger brother, Lt. Col. Frank Hampton of the 2nd South Carolina Cavalry, at Brandy Station. Evidence shows that the overcoat incident was at the skirmish at Quebec School House not Brandy Station.

Lt. Col. Pierce Manning Butler Young. Courtesy Wikipedia.

As this fight was arguably a Union victory, it is surprising that Pleasonton did not report this fight nor did any other official Union source. Hampton reported the action as a Confederate victory:

> After withdrawing the brigade from Middletown, I proceeded toward Burkittsville, where I expected to form a junction with Colonel Munford. On a road parallel to the one on which we were, a regiment of Yankee cavalry. Taking the Cobb Legion with me, I directed Lieutenant-Colonel Young to charge this regiment. This order was carried out in gallant style, the legion crossing sabers with the Yankees and chasing them some distance. Five prisoners were taken, which a published account of the Yankees now before me admits a loss of 30 killed and wounded....Young, who led the charge, received a painful wound in the leg, and Captain Wright, whose company was in the advance, was wounded in the arm. Our loss was 4 killed and 9 wounded....Colonel Young led with great gallantry, and, after his fall, Major Delony.[28]

But Hampton failed to report a near disaster as his column continued south to Burkittsville and Crampton's Gap. Munford, who was already there after being pushed west from Jefferson Gap, had placed his guns awaiting further advance of the enemy, reported the incident: "Not knowing that General Hampton was to come up on that road, and seeing a supposed enemy, I waited until they were in easy range before ordering the artillery to fire. General Hampton perceiving intention, when the lanyard had been applied and nothing was required but the word 'fire' to be given, a white flag appeared, and I found they were our friends."[29] Neese, a gunner in Chew's Battery who was manning a gun pointing down the Middletown road, said that they were about to fire when "a courier, with a Southern

---

[28] *OR*, vol. 19, pt. 1, 824.
[29] Ibid., 826.

flag, came up the mountain and announced that it was Hampton's Legion that was coming up the Middletown road."[30] This late-day close call ended the eventful day for Hampton's Brigade as it bedded down for the night around Crampton's Gap.

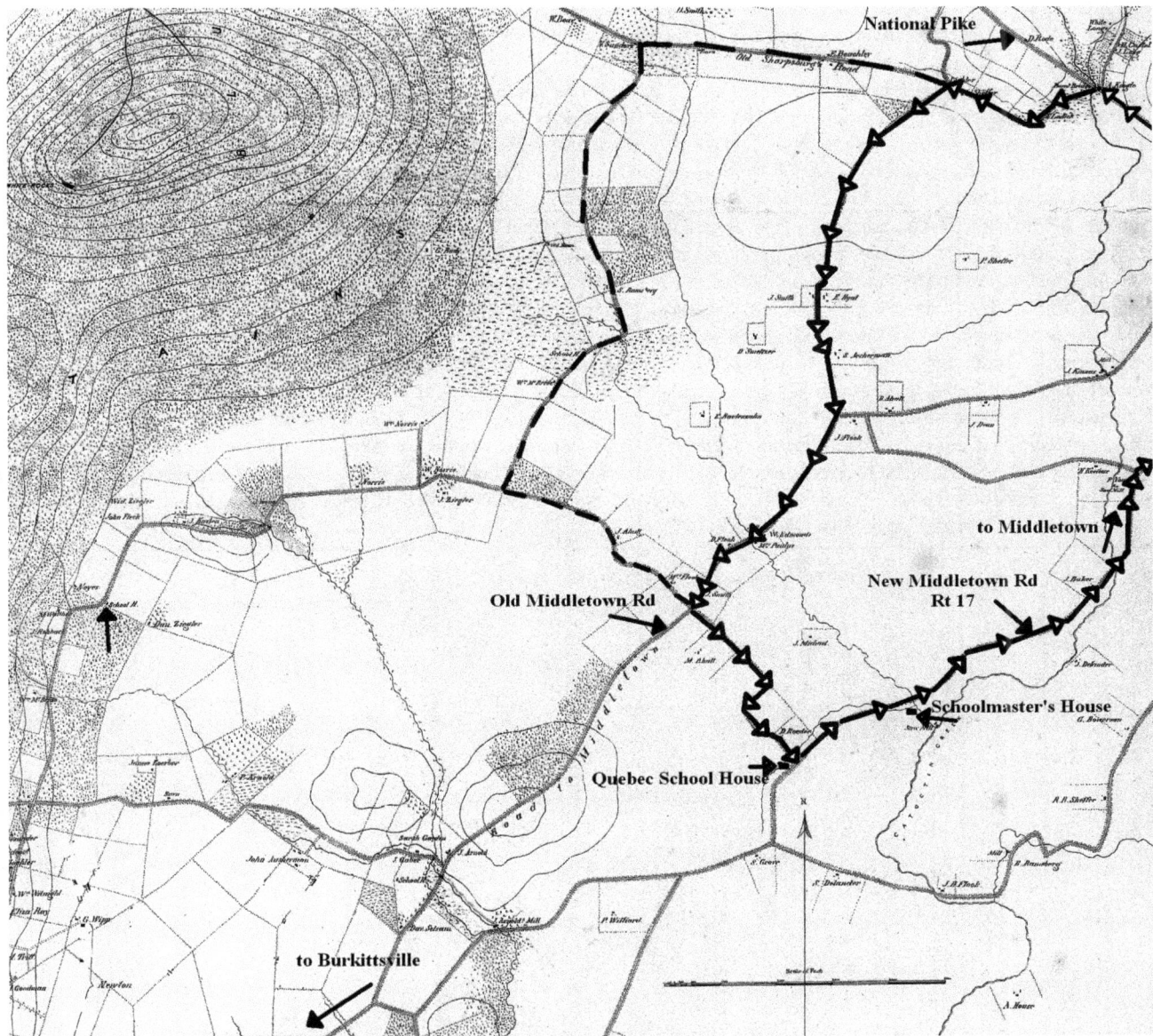

This map shows the general area of the fight at the Quebec School House on 13 September 1862, Primary School (PS) 83 on the 1858 Bond map. Quebec School House is shown at the arrow in the right lower center and was in fact the schoolhouse at which the fight took place according to a local historian who has studied the battle extensively, Julie Maynard; the road on which it was located is now officially named "Quebec School Road." Evidence reviewed by Ms. Maynard gives overwhelming evidence that PS 83 is the one which she detailed in two articles in the *Middletown Valley Citizen*, 13 and 20 January 1994: "A battle 'lost'—and found again," and "The tale of a country school." The dashed line is the route Hampton likely took while Medill's route is shown by the arrows. Hampton's and Medill's routes diverged just southwest of the National Pike at the top left of the map after they both took the same route out of Middletown. Note that the Atlas names the road to the west as "Road to Middletown" and that the two roads which lead to Middletown join at the bottom left. The parallel road next to the schoolhouse also leads to Middletown and is the approximate route of the "New" Middletown Road, Rt. 17. The arrow at the upper left shows a schoolhouse sometimes mistaken for the site of the fight. Ms. Maynard's research has found that the schoolmaster, John Castle, lived across the "New" Middletown Road (Rt. 17) and that the Castle Barn where Rebel Lt. Cobb was taken after he was mortally wounded was further up this road toward Middletown as shown on the next map. Detail from 1872 Bureau of Topographical Engineers Map of South Mountain. Courtesy LOC.

---

[30] Neese, 143. In May 1862, Neese was appointed as first corporal, the "first gunner" in the battery under Chew, 67.

Right: map shows likely routes for Hampton's and Medill's columns. Medill's column is depicted by white arrows; Hampton followed a route roughly parallel and to the west of Medill on today's Bidle and Marker Roads. The dotted route along South Mountain to the west shows Hampton's route. Modern roads comprising the old Burkittsville-Middletown Road starting from Burkittsville are the new Burkittsville Middletown Road then the Picnic Woods Road, Bidle Road, lastly Walnut Street leading to the Old National Pike, Main Street, on the west end of Middletown. The distance between the two roads range from ¾ of a mile to 1¾ mile over a relatively open valley while the distance from the road adjacent to the mountain (today Mountain Church Road) Hampton travelled to the New Middletown Road is at least ¾ mile to 1+ miles away. Pickerill wrote that "two hundred yards away from where our column had halted, on the summit of a little ridge overlooking a rough country road leading to Middletown by a shorter route than we had come, stood an old-fashioned country frame school house." Today's Quebec School Road is about ¾ road-miles long. Given the participants' lack of clarity on routes taken from Middletown to the schoolhouse fight, the roads travelled and the location of the schoolhouse remains open to discussion. Ms. Maynard believes that the Union column left the Quebec School Road just north of the schoolhouse using a farm lane and was then attacked by the Rebels who had come up northward from the Old Burkittsville Road. The exact route of the two columns is unclear but Ms. Maynard's analysis is one which follows participants' accounts based on period topography. One possibility is that part of his column which attacked Medill then went east on Quebec School Road shown by the dashes and somehow got into an ambush position without being detected. Or Hampton's entire column turned west (dashes and circles) continuing on Marker Road then southwest on Mountain Church Road; at the next intersection on Mountain Church Road with Arnoldstown Road, some of his troopers rode east, south on Picnic Woods, and then north on the New Middletown-Burkittsville Road to set up an ambush near the Quebec School House. This roundabout ride today is about four miles, at a trot it would have taken about a half hour to cover that distance or 20 minutes at a gallop, the more likely speed. The remainder of Hampton's wagon train then rode west from that intersection and the attack party could have followed behind or taken the road to Burkittsville then up to Crampton's Gap. Ms. Maynard believes that Medill's column left today's Quebec School House Road before reaching the school and was ambushed north of the school similar to the solid arrows just above the school house. Detail from 1872 Bureau of Topographical Engineers Map of South Mountain. Courtesy LOC.

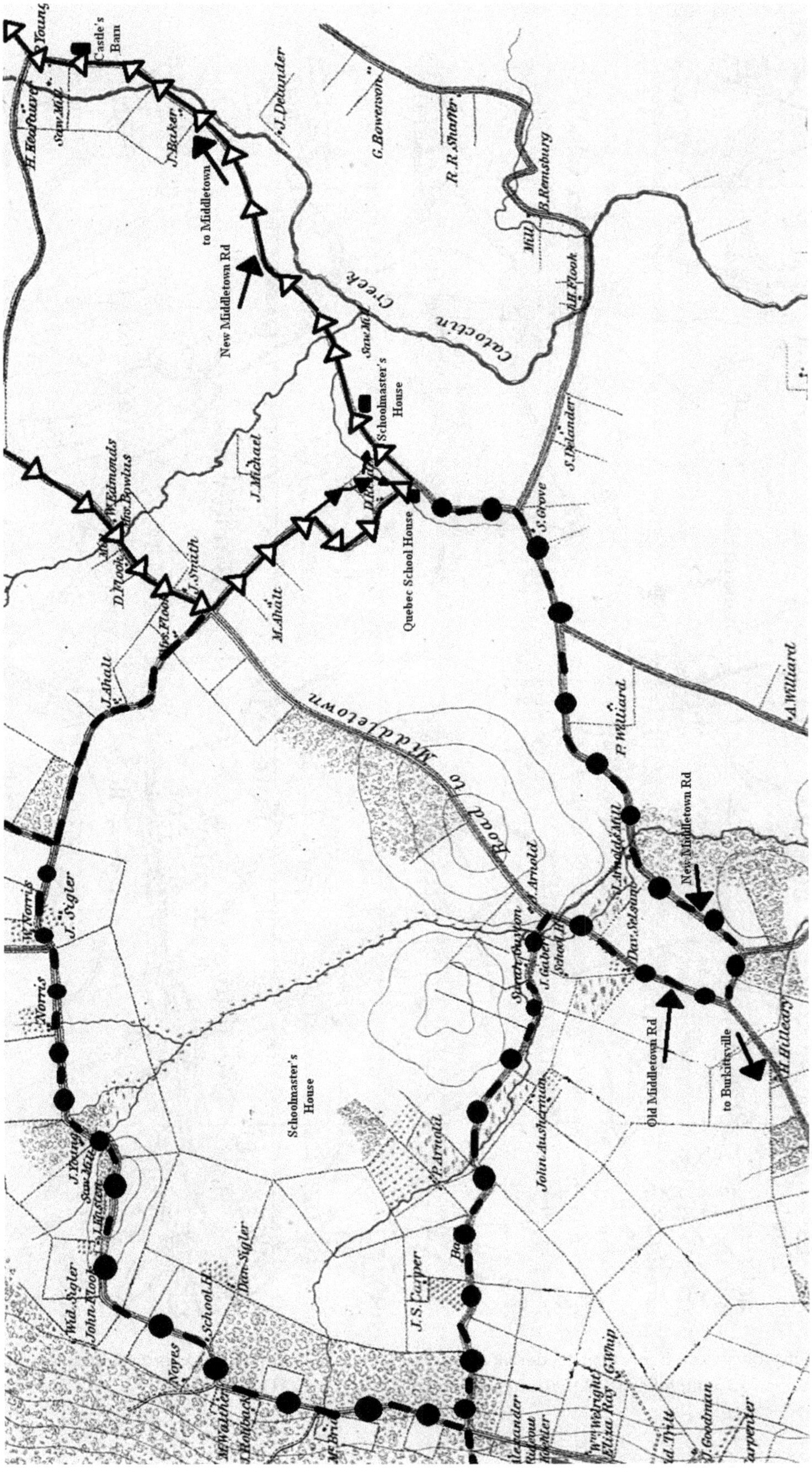
Castle's Barn
to Middletown
New Middletown Rd
Catoctin Creek
Schoolmaster's House
Quebec School House
Road to Middletown
Schoolmaster's House
New Middletown Rd
Old Middletown Rd
to Burkittsville

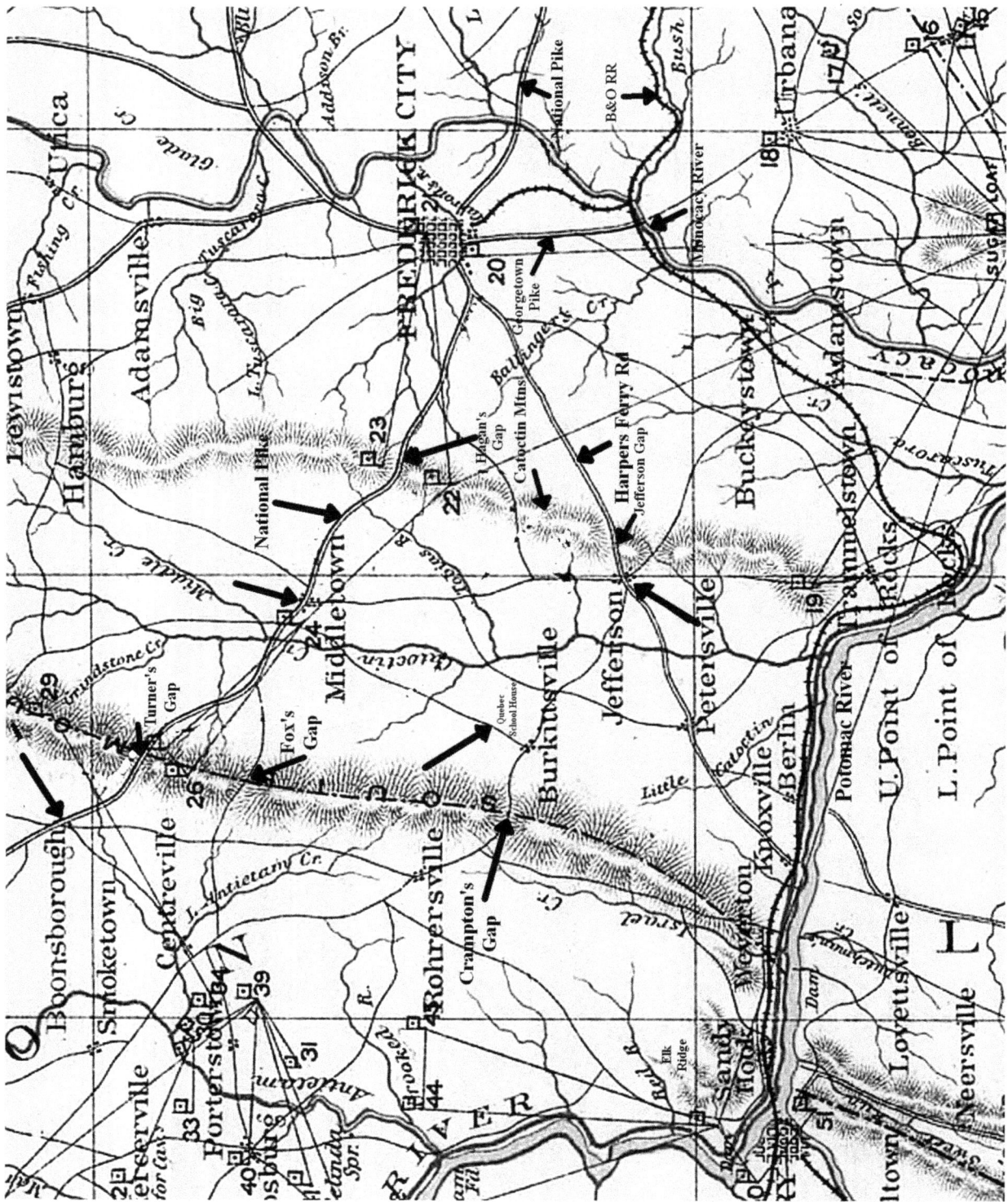

View of area of operations for cavalry fights near Frederick at Hagan's Gap, Jefferson Gap, Middletown, and near Burkittsville at the Quebec School House on 13 September 1862. *Official Atlas*, Plate 27. Courtesy LOC.

Pleasonton dispatched Rush's Lancers early on the 13th to Jefferson Gap in the Catoctins some six miles southwest of Frederick, where Col. Munford and his two small regiments waited. Led by Col. Rush, they headed south on the Jefferson Road with seven companies to search for Rebels at Jefferson Gap and the surrounding area.[31] The Lancers arrived in the early afternoon and stopped, seeing Confederate cannon in the road ahead. Not knowing what they faced, they sent back to Frederick for support—the 9th New York Infantry soon arrived, followed by the rest of Col. Harrison Fairchild's Ninth Corps brigade. As the Lancers moved out, they tangled with some of the 12th Virginia Cavalry which scattered the Pennsylvanians, who perhaps found that lances did not counter carbines and pistols. The 9th New York Infantry advanced up the mountain going about half a mile to a ravine where advance infantrymen were shot at from hidden Rebels. As more Union infantry came up from Fairchild's brigade and deployed on both sides of the road, dismounted Confederate skirmishers mounted up and joined the rest of the Rebel horsemen following their brethren in the 2nd Virginia toward South Mountain. The advance of the Union horsemen and infantry fragmented Munford's command, encouraging Chew to limber up his artillery and hasten north to Middletown to join Stuart, while being pressed by a body of Lancers led by Capt. James Haseltine. The remainder of Munford's troopers along with his wagons was pursued by the rest of the Lancers, crossing Catoctin Creek and Broad Run. When Munford approached Burkittsville, he had to send back some of the 2nd Virginia Cavalry, under Capt. Thomas B. Holland, to fend off the threatening Lancers. By the end of the day, all of the Lancers had returned to Jefferson, except for Company F, which remained at the bridge crossing Catoctin Creek; Munford guarded the road into Burkittsville as his trains safely crested South Mountain at Crampton's Gap, just to the west of the tiny village. Meanwhile, Yankee infantry enjoyed the hospitality of people in Jefferson who showed their appreciation by sharing milk, butter, and fruits, before the infantry marched back to Frederick. Perhaps sated by the victuals, the regiment accidentally left two companies of the 9th New York in Jefferson, which finally realized their regiment had gone, and belatedly marched back to Frederick. While resting in Jefferson, troops heard the cannon fire in the direction of Harpers Ferry, and also witnessed Franklin's disheveled troops marching west in a leisurely fashion. "General Franklin's command arrived and passed through the village in the direction of the firing. They were a most dilapidated looking lot, ragged and weather-beaten, and had evidently seen some pretty hard marching recently. From the leisurely way in which they marched it was plain that like the Ninth they were not under orders for Harper's Ferry, where the battle was still raging. An officer—said to be General Franklin—and his staff, dismounted, procured some refreshments, and seating themselves on the porch of a house, ate with great deliberation."[32]

Munford's adventures for 13 September were not quite done. He had listened to the firing to the north toward Middletown and then the small arms fire much closer from the fight at Quebec School House. Near dusk, Hampton approached from that direction with Stuart's wagon train and Munford was ready to confront this unknown column with his artillery. As already noted, Hampton almost became the victim of friendly fire. As night fell, Munford's troopers went to the top of the gap while Chew went

---

[31] Only seven of ten companies were available as Companies B and G were detached on 8 September to serve as headquarters escort for Franklin and the next day Company I was added to its two sister companies, Reese, *Sealed*, 19, n. 22. Modern Maryland Rt. 180, the Jefferson Pike, is the route taken.

[32] Reese, *Sealed*, 21-25, 44; *Priest, Before Antietam*, 119-121, Charles F. Johnson, *The Long Roll* (East Aurora, NY: The Roycrofters, 1911), 182-183; J.H.E. Whitney, *The Hawkins Zouaves: Their Battles and Marches* (New York: Published by Author, 1866), 128-129; Matthew J. Graham, *The Ninth Regiment New York Volunteers (Hawkins' Zouaves) Being a History of the Regiment and Veteran Association from 1860 to 1900* (New York: Coby and Co., Printers, 1900), 263-266; Carman, Pierro, 95. Note that most historians place Franklin and his troops some three miles east of Jefferson on the 13th and not crossing through the pass until the 14th.

to the western base, and Hampton remained on the east side, all bedded down after an arduous day.[33] A gunner in Chew's Battery commented on its inability to join Stuart at Middletown after the battery was push through Jefferson Gap: "when we arrived within one mile of Middletown we learned that the Yankee cavalry, which is getting bold, adventurous, mighty, and numerous in these latter days, had forced our cavalry on the National Road back a little faster than common, and had possession of Middletown."[34] It was clear to this Confederate artilleryman that the Union cavalry was as pesky now as it was when he first encountered them near Poolesville.

Earlier in the day as Medill pursued Hampton's column south from Middletown to the schoolhouse encounter, the rest of the Union troopers of Farnsworth's brigade rode west on the National Pike toward Turner's Gap following Stuart. But on the crest of a hill one mile east of the base of South Mountain, they stopped when they saw Confederate videttes at the intersection of the Bolivar Road and the National Pike; on the road leading to the top they also saw Rebel artillery. The commanders decided that the evening was too far advanced to continue pursuing the Rebels so they bivouacked for the night. But then after Pleasonton arrived and desired more information about the Rebel dispositions, the cavalry commander sent several squadrons from the 8th Illinois and 3rd Indiana Cavalry north to confront the pickets of the Jeff Davis Legion. After taking several casualties, the troopers returned with two prisoners. Fighting east of Turner's Gap on South Mountain was now over for the day.[35]

As already noted, Fitzhugh Lee's troopers were not left out of the action on 13 September. That morning, Stuart had sent a courier to Fitz Lee telling him to test McClellan's right flank. Lee was near Hamburg, a village about two and a half miles northeast of Harmony, on top of Catoctin Mountain about six miles north of Hagan's Gap. He scouted toward Frederick where his troopers ran into the rear of the 1st New York Cavalry, along with the 12th Pennsylvania Cavalry, and a section of horse artillery, who happened to be looking for Fitzhugh Lee. The confrontation resulted in a few casualties and prisoners captured on both sides, but Lee withdrew in view of superior numbers. The Federal troopers continued on to Emmitsburg thinking that Gen. Robert E. Lee was heading for Pennsylvania, but only found a good place to bivouac. Fitzhugh Lee spent much of the night near the base of the Catoctins east of Hamburg waiting for the Unionists to approach. The Federals apparently had the better rest for the night as several southern-sympathizing hosts in Emmitsburg had initially mistaken them for Confederates, and donated food and drink, before discovering the true identity of their dust-covered Yankee guests. Fitz Lee crossed the Catoctins at Hamburg the night of the 13th/14th, arriving at Boonsboro in time to be in the fight there with Union cavalry on the 15th; he had crossed South Mountain at a pass on the old Frederick stagecoach road, some three miles north of Turner's Gap thus avoiding the unpleasantness on the National Pike.[36]

---

[33] Reese, *Sealed*, 31; *Priest, Before Antietam*, 123; Neese, 143.

[34] Neese, 142.

[35] Carman, Pierro, 95.

[36] Priest, *Before Antietam*, 116-119; Beach 171. The 1st New York Cavalry never made it to Antietam for the battle on the 17th after its journeys from Emmitsburg to Frederick then to Boonsboro where it arrived at dusk on the 17th. Data about Hamburg from Louis B. O'Donoghue, *Gazetteer of Old, Odd & Obscure Place Names of Frederick County, Maryland* (Frederick, MD: The Historical Society of Frederick County, 2008), 101-102. One officer in the 9th Virginia Cavalry commented that "Hamburg was a rude and scattering village on the crest of the mountain, where the manufacture of brandy seemed to be the chief employment of the villagers, and at the early hour of our passage through the place, both the men and women gave proof that they were free imbibers of the product of their stills. It was not easy to find a sober inhabitant of either sex," George William Beale, *A Lieutenant of Cavalry in Lee's Army* (Boston, MA: The Gorham Press, 1918), 44. Hamburg Pass discussed in Harsh, *Flood*, 248, 257. Note that Harsh (or Carman) may have confused the Hamburg Pass in the Catoctin Mountains for a pass in South Mountain, see Carman, Pierro, 175, who states that the pass is through the Catoctins. See also Brig. Gen. Ripley's report using "Hamburg Pass" for the pass north of Boonsboro in South Mountain, *OR*, vol. 19, pt. 1, 1031. It is possible that they both existed with the same name but that seems unlikely. The "Hamburg Pass" so called by Confederates is properly called Orr's Gap

Thus Pleasonton had provided McClellan with valuable service in pushing Stuart west through the Catoctins, albeit with the assistance of Union infantry. Rush's Lancers were still near Jefferson while Pleasonton's main body was west of Middletown near the foot of Turner's Gap. Union troopers, even though thinly spread, were sufficient to allow little scouting opportunities for Stuart's men as Fitzhugh Lee learned north of Frederick. On the other hand, Stuart had done well without the assistance of any Confederate infantry in his fighting retreat to South Mountain, delaying strong Union forces fighting along the National Pike from Frederick to the foot of South Mountain, where his pickets stopped all Union reconnaissance efforts. Munford, with some 250 troopers, had delayed Union cavalry and infantry at Jefferson Gap, and now held Crampton's Gap and Burkittsville. Stuart and his cavalry rode through Turner's Gap and Col. Alfred Colquitt's men were ordered to the side to let it pass, while Col. Colquitt had a conference on the side of the road with Stuart. Stuart reportedly told Colquitt that only cavalry were following him and Colquitt would have no difficulty holding the pass with his brigade. Stuart must have been pleased to see that his earlier request to Maj. Gen. D.H. Hill for a brigade of infantry was answered by Colquitt's arrival at Turner's Gap. Stuart denied Colquitt's request for two cavalry companies to help picket the Rebel lines on the eastern side of the mountain.[37] Stuart's critical mistake was in not comprehending that he was not pursued by just two Yankee brigades and some cavalry but by much of the Federal army.

As Stuart descended to Boonsboro, he met the 5th Virginia Cavalry, commanded by Col. Thomas Rosser, accompanied by Pelham and a section of his battery. Rosser that morning was gathering horses north of Frederick so was unable to rejoin Stuart as Stuart retreated west chased by Union forces. Rosser finally worked his way north and west, meeting Stuart in Boonsboro in the evening. Stuart assigned him and Pelham in support, to Fox's Gap, one mile south of Turner's Gap, but forgot to tell Hill. Stuart also did not mention to Colquitt or Hill that the Old Sharpsburg Road ran southwest and then west from the National Road to Fox's Gap, thus forcing Hill to learn to his distress that Union forces the next day would also attack his flank there in strength, as well as at Turner's Gap. Stuart also sent word to Gen. Lee of the approach of the Union forces. Once Lee learned of the approach of Union forces to South Mountain and that his detached commands had not yet taken Harpers Ferry, he quickly realized that he had to prevent McLaws from being overwhelmed from the rear on Maryland Heights and Elk Ridge, as well as the lower end of Pleasant Valley: Lee now knew he had to defend the South Mountain gaps. Added concern for Lee was that his army was then fragmented into five parts since he had sent Longstreet with the army trains to Hagerstown and returning Longstreet to aid Hill would take several hours.

through which the Old Hagerstown Road passed. That road and the Old Sharpsburg Road which passed through Fox's Gap were the only main routes through South Mountain until the road through Turner's Gap was built in the mid-1700's. That road was built to lead from Frederick to Ft. Frederick and took over from the Old Sharpsburg Road as the main road in that area to the west; see Curtis L. Older, *The Braddock Expedition and Fox's Gap in Maryland* (Westminster, MD: Willow Bend Books, 2000), 172-175, and Curtis L. Older, *The Land Tracts of the Battlefield of South Mountain* (Westminster, MD: Heritage Books, 2008), 41-55 passim. By 1861, there was a more or less road west from Hamburg as shown on a Frederick County, Maryland, map prepared in 1861 under the direction of Lieut. Col. J.N. Macomb, Chief Topographical Engineer for the Maj. Gen. G.B. McClellan, from the LOC. While based on Bond's 1858 map, it shows a connecting road west of Hamburg and northeast of Myersville heading west allowing movement to the northwest toward Hagerstown not shown on Bond's map. A map in *Confederate Military History*, vol. II, following p. 184 shows even a more direct road west from Hamburg but this is not as accurate as the 1861 Macomb map. There was also a road leading from Frederick to Hamburg in the Catoctin Mountains named Hamburg Road.
[37] George D. Grattan, "The Battle of Boonsboro Gap or South Mountain," *SHSP*, vol. 39, 34.

Rush's Lancers. *The Century Illustrated Monthly Magazine*, New York: The Century Company, Volume 32, Issue: 1, June 1886, pg. 136.

Lee's instructions to Stuart on 13 September after learning more about the Union advance were to keep Maj. Gen. Lafayette McLaws on Maryland Heights "informed of the movements of the enemy."[38] Lee's dispatch the day before told McLaws that Stuart's cavalry occupied the Middletown Valley.[39] Lee also on 13 September in the early afternoon sent a reply to Stuart's note that Stuart was confronting a mixed force in Middletown Valley: "If you find that the enemy intends more than a reconnaissance, and is too strong for your cavalry, Gen. Hill can reinforce you with a brigade of infantry, and some artillery." Here again at this late hour, Lee was still not aware that Stuart was being pursued by a large part of McClellan's army, believing that a brigade of Hill's infantry sent from Boonsboro would be sufficient to stall the Unionists. Stuart obviously was not able to detect the strength of the Federal forces chasing him.[40] Lee's last dispatch to Stuart late on the 13th after Lee learned that the Harpers Ferry expedition was behind schedule, told Stuart that "The gap must be held at all hazards until the operations at Harper's Ferry are finished." It is most likely that the gap to which he referred was Turner's Gap but apparently Stuart received this dispatch on the 14th after he had left for Crampton's Gap, thus D.H. Hill at Turner's Gap had no cavalry support, and had only one regiment, Rosser's 5th Virginia Cavalry, at Fox's Gap.[41]

Stuart now must help McLaws by protecting his flanks and rear while providing him intelligence. Stuart apparently took what was to Lee just a part of Stuart's mission, as the most important aspect, as he decided to leave the defense of Turner's Gap to Hill without telling either Hill or Lee.[42] Rosser, posted to the smaller Fox's Gap, did not receive adequate instructions from Stuart, who appeared unconcerned,

---

[38] *OR*, Vol. 19, pt. 2, 607.
[39] Ibid., 606.
[40] Harsh, *Flood*, 222-223.
[41] Ibid., 249-250.
[42] Ibid., 244.

leading to Rosser's post-war comment that "Stuart did not expect the enemy would advance on Boonsboro, and was careless in guarding the roads leading that way."[43]

Likely Lee was suffering from not being more specific in his requirements to Stuart, because he believed that a substantial part of Stuart's division was holding Turner's Gap in South Mountain, with Hill's support, as part of Lee's desire that Stuart cover the army's rear. Lee learned that "the enemy was advancing more rapidly than was convenient from Fredericktown, [so Lee]...determined to return with Longstreet's command to South Mountain, to strengthen Hill's and Stuart's divisions, engaged in holding the passes of the mountains, lest the enemy should fall upon McLaw's rear, drive him from the Maryland Heights, and thus relieve the garrison at Harper's Ferry."[44] While Stuart's performance on 13 September delaying Union troops from Frederick to South Mountain was very good thanks to his skill and that of his veteran troopers, his 14 September actions were to prove less successful.

Thus 13 September ended with Gen. Lee in a position in which he could lose a large part of his army. With McLaws near Harpers Ferry, Lee must buy time by delaying the Union juggernaut at the South Mountain passes. At the close of daylight on the 13th, Stuart is resting near Boonsboro, Munford and Hampton's Brigades are at Crampton's Gap, and Fitzhugh Lee is resting at the western base of the Catoctin Mountains north of Frederick, unaware of his army commander's plight, and the more rapid movements of the Union corps west. Pleasonton has most of his cavalry in Middletown Valley, with scattered squadrons in locations such as the 1st Rhode Island Cavalry guarding fords downriver of Point of Rocks, and parts of the 6th U.S. Cavalry west of Jefferson in the lower Middletown Valley, near the Potomac.[45] Rush's Lancers were back near Jefferson after an eventful day.

On the morrow, Confederate cavalry would be more involved in the battle for South Mountain than their Union counterparts. Before Lee's army bowed to superior Union power and retreated from South Mountain, Rosser's 5th Virginia Cavalry at Fox's Gap and Munford's troopers at Crampton's Gap, through heroic efforts although vastly outnumbered, helped hold those passes. Unfortunately for Gen. Lee, Stuart believed that McClellan would make his main effort to directly relieve Harpers Ferry, so the cavalry commander sent Hampton south leaving Munford's small brigade of two depleted regiments of less than 300 troopers with Chew's horse artillery at Crampton's Gap, and Rosser at Fox's Gap, with some 200 troopers, and two guns of Pelham's horse artillery. Stuart's efforts on his South Mountain Line were his weakest and failed his commander's wishes. That evening, the Jeff Davis Legion, with two guns of Hart's Battery, remained with Stuart near Boonsboro, west of Turner's Gap, journeying south the next day.[46] On 14 September would begin Gen. Lee's battle to save his army from annihilation.

---

[43] Ibid., 234. *Lee's Lieutenants* 2:170, "Guard of the pass was regarded by Stuart as a precaution—and no more—because he thought that Harpers Ferry already had surrendered. He reasoned that Jackson, Walker, McLaws and Anderson soon would be on their way to rejoin Lee."

[44] *OR*, vol. 19, pt. 1, 140.

[45] Two regular cavalry units, the 1st and 6th were at Jefferson on 14 September according to Pleasonton and were scouting toward Harpers Ferry, *OR*, vol. 19, pt. 2, 290.

[46] Carman, Pierro, 94. Stuart was first concerned that McClellan would push quickly through Crampton's Gap but when Stuart arrived there, he saw little to concern him so he moved further south to McLaws. Note that Brig. Gen. Stoneman on 14 September was ordered with six regiments from his division to guard Potomac crossings from Great Falls upriver to Point of Rocks thus bolstering Union cavalry units watching the fords and roads near the river, *OR*, vol. 19, pt. 2, 291, 298-301. This movement was perhaps not as speedy as it could have been as this order was repeated mentioning Birney's brigade of Stoneman's division totaling 4,000 infantry, six guns, and a cavalry squadron, *OR*, vol. 19, pt. 2, 309. On 15 September Halleck recommended this movement with Stoneman in charge, perhaps to hurry Banks along. There was some discussion about Stoneman's assignment and the troops he would have for this mission. Stoneman's headquarters was to be at Poolesville by the night of 16 September and was further ordered to cooperate with Union movements on the Virginia side. Thus McClellan should have been less concerned with Rebel movements along the Maryland and Virginia sides of the Potomac behind his lines. Union cavalry had been scouting on the Virginia side up to Leesburg finding only sick Confederates, *OR*, vol. 19, pt. 2, 292.

Both Lee and Stuart were operating on the belief that McClellan would immediately move to relieve Harpers Ferry by moving directly south from Frederick, on the road through Jefferson to Knoxville on the Potomac River. But McClellan dismissed that approach believing that that route was unsuitable for his large army:

> I had received information that the enemy were anticipating our approach in that direction, and had established batteries on the south side of the Potomac which commanded all the approaches to Knoxville. Moreover the road from that point winds directly along the river bank at the foot of a precipitous mountain, where there was no opportunity of forming in line of battle, and where the enemy could have placed batteries on both sides of the river to enfilade our narrow approaching columns. Moreover the road from that point winds directly along the river bank at the foot of a precipitous mountain, where there was no opportunity of forming in line of battle, and where the enemy could have placed batteries on both sides of the river to enfilade our narrow approaching columns. The approach through Crampton's Pass, which debouches into Pleasant Valley in rear of Maryland Heights, was the only one which afforded any reasonable prospect of carrying that formidable position. At the same time the troops upon that road were in better relation to the main body of our forces.[47]

McClellan was correct in stating that the Confederates anticipated that he would march directly to relieve Harpers Ferry, but wrong about Confederate batteries commanding the approaches to Knoxville. Rebel artillery on Loudoun Heights in Virginia, Maryland Heights in Maryland, and Bolivar Heights in Virginia, did not command those approaches. Instead, McClellan decided to have Franklin's Corps take Crampton's Gap as the only reasonable alternative, and turn south through Pleasant Valley and take McLaws from the rear, while the Harpers Ferry garrison entertained the Rebels from the front. McClellan also said that Franklin's forces staying on the road to and through Crampton's Gap were in a better position to cooperate with the remainder of McClellan's forces, which would have broken through Turner's Gap, some seven miles to the north. McClellan's troops would fight their way through Turner's Gap and confront Longstreet and Lee's main body. Once Franklin and Miles crushed McLaws, they could turn north to help, if needed, in demolishing Longstreet.[48] Both Gen. Lee and Gen. McClellan were correct in seeing on the evening of the 13th, that if McClellan broke through South Mountain to Pleasant Valley, McLaws at Harpers Ferry would be in jeopardy of being crushed. Fortunately for Lee, Franklin's slow approach to and through Crampton's Gap, and halt in Pleasant Valley, sealed the fate of

---

Certainly both Halleck and McClellan were both relieved that there was no sneak attack building threatening Washington south of the Potomac.

[47] *OR*, vol. 19, pt. 1, 44-45. McClellan had visited that area from Harpers Ferry to Charles Town at least once by train on 26 February 1862 along with his staff and his body guard of the Sturgis Rifles. He was surveying the area as he was contemplating transporting a sizable force to the Harpers Ferry area perhaps with an eye to going down the Shenandoah Valley. Among other things, the B&O Railroad could not transport the numbers McClellan contemplated, William Prescott Smith, *B&O in the Civil War: From the Papers of Wm. Prescott Smith*, ed. by William E. Bain (Denver, CO: Sage Books, 1966), 154-155. "The Frederick and Harpers Ferry Turnpike, organized in 1830, was completed from Frederick, Maryland, to the Maryland abutment of the Wager [bridge from Harpers Ferry across the Potomac to Maryland] Potomac bridge by 1832. The existing road along the base of Maryland Heights west of Sandy Hook, …presumably follows the alignment of the western end of this turnpike," U.S. Dept. of the Interior, NPS, National Register of Historic Places Inventory, Harpers Ferry National Historic Park, 1966, Internet accessed 1 March 2010, item 7, pg. 3.

[48] *OR*, vol. 19, pt. 1, 44-45; Carman states that McClellan was incorrect in his belief that Confederate batteries were established on the south bank of the Potomac and that the difficulties McClellan imagined in approaching Harpers Ferry along the river were not present. But since McClellan honestly believed them it is understandable that he chose a different route, Carman, Pierro, 132. See also Ethan S. Rafuse, *McClellan's War: The Failure of Moderation in the Struggle for the Union* (Bloomington and Indianapolis: Indiana University Press, 2005), 294-295. Rafuse believes that given what he knew and believed, McClellan's plan was good, 395.

Miles, and saved McLaws. While McClellan had all the plans of the Rebels in his hands, his army did not have the legs, or the leadership, to destroy Lee.

Two controversies spawned by McClellan's finding of the Lost Order still echo today: did Lee know of McClellan's find during the Maryland Campaign, and what would have been the likely outcome had McClellan not found the Lost Order? Historians differ on the issue of Lee's knowledge of McClellan's find. Many historians such as Douglas Southall Freeman hold that Lee knew based on Stuart's report to Lee. Stuart wrote Lee that a Maryland Citizen, who was a Confederate sympathizer, was present at McClellan's headquarters on the 13th when the Union commander received the copy.[49] The sympathizer did not know it was Lee's S.O. 191, but it was clear from the reactions of McClellan and his staff that it was a document of great importance. The Marylander quickly headed west and found Stuart at Turner's Gap and told the Confederate cavalry commander of the incident. Stuart believed him and sent a courier speeding north to Lee at Hagerstown with the news, and included information of increased Federal cavalry activity at Burkittsville and Jefferson, as well as Pleasonton's push against his cavalry on the National Pike.[50] A modern historian and expert on the Maryland Campaign, D. Scott Hartwig, cogently argues that despite what Lee said after the war, his actions during the campaign show that he did not know that McClellan had found S.O. 191:

> First, Lee's correspondence to President Davis during the campaign never mentions a lost order. Second, in an 1867 letter to D. H. Hill, Charles Marshall, Lee's military secretary, wrote that until Lee read McClellan's report, which was published in August 1863, the general "frequently expressed his inability to understand the sudden change in McClellan's tactics which took place after we left Frederick." Third, Ezra A. Carman...wrote...that the civilian may have been present when McClellan received the order but did not know its contents...Lee's actions on the night of 13 September...were not those of a general who had learned the enemy possessed the operation plan of this entire army. Most likely, Lee learned nothing...beyond that the Army of the Potomac was advancing from Frederick—news that merely confirmed the picture already in place based on Stuart's and Hill's earlier reports.[51]

Thus credible evidence shows that Lee very likely did not know that McClellan had his army's operational order, but he did know that McClellan was moving faster than Lee found convenient, and that his widely scattered army was now in jeopardy of being defeated in detail. Harsh finds that Lee may have found this news more disturbing than Hartwig wrote as Lee was aware that the Harpers Ferry expedition was seriously behind schedule, and that the Army of Northern Virginia now must hold the passes in South Mountain to ensure not only the safety of McLaw's rear but also ensure that his Maryland Campaign could continue without his being forced back across the Potomac.[52] Harsh discusses Stuart's later, undocumented, message to Lee which apparently more fully described the information found by the Maryland sympathizer. Stuart may have written that McClellan could have actually been in possession of S.O. 191, perhaps due to McClellan's exuberant response, "Now I know what to do," and also that there was no other document that could have elicited such a response. Regardless, Lee was holding to his plan on the night of 13/14 September 1862, despite ominous clouds on the eastern horizon.[53]

[49] D. Scott Hartwig, "Robert E. Lee and the Maryland Campaign," in *Lee the Soldier*, edited by Gary W. Gallagher (Lincoln, NB: University of Nebraska press, 1996), 341-342. *Lee's Lieutenants*, 2:173. *OR*, vol. 19, pt. 1, 146.

[50] Carman, Pierro, 134-135.

[51] Hartwig, 342. Thomas Clemens has letters from Col. Charles Marshall, Lee's secretary, to Carman in which Marshall makes clear that Gen. Lee did not know that S.O. 191 was found until McClellan's report. Marshall also wrote that Lee intended to "threaten the Pennsylvania line" but not necessarily invade it.

[52] Harsh, *Flood*, 242-245; *Shallows*, 168.

[53] Harsh, *Flood*, 248-249.

McClellan's finding of the Lost Order also fostered speculation about the real difference it made on the campaign's outcome. Lee purportedly said that "'I went into Maryland to give battle, and could I have kept Gen. McClellan in ignorance of my position and plans a day or two longer, I would have fought and crushed him....the losing of it with the fact that it fell into Gen. McClellan's hands enabled him to discover my whereabouts: revealed to him in part my plans, and caused him so to act as to force a battle on me before I was ready for it.'"[54] Further, Lee said that "'Had the Lost Dispatch not been lost, and had McClellan continued his cautious policy for two or three days longer, I [Lee] would have had all my troops reconcentrated on Md. Side, stragglers up, men rested and *intended then to attack McClellan*, hoping the best results from state of my troops and those of enemy. Tho' it is impossible to say that victory would have certainly resulted, it is probable that the loss of the dispatch changed the character of the campaign (emphasis in original).'"[55]

One historian, Matthew Forney Steele, was less optimistic for the Confederate outlook and opined the following:

> It is idle to speculate upon what might have been the outcome of this campaign, if Lee had not detached the expedition against Harper's Ferry, and if his "lost order" had not fallen into McClellan's hands. Even with the garrison of Harper's Ferry out of the way, and his line of communications established through the Shenandoah Valley, it cannot be seen how Lee could have penetrated far into Pennsylvania. Staunton, 150 miles in rear, was the nearest railway point upon his line of communications; he could not have kept his army supplied over so great a distance by wagon-trains.
>
> He had, moreover, only 55,000 men, with little hope of reinforcements; while McClellan had nearly 90,000, with strong reinforcements on the way to join him. McClellan's army was marching, but marching very slowly, straight against Lee's line of retreat. If Lee's army had remained at Hagerstown or had gone farther northward McClellan could easily have thrown his army across its rear and cut off its retreat. Lee would then have had to fight faced to the rear against almost double his numbers. At best it could only have been the Gettysburg campaign set forward ten months; but Gettysburg might have been otherwise with Stonewall Jackson alive, and McClellan, not Meade, in command of the Union army.[56]

Steele does not address the questions of what if Lee had defeated McClellan in a pitched battle in the Cumberland Valley, or at least substantial parts of it, or that McClellan's larger force would have been perhaps one-third green. Allan, in his "Strategy of the Campaign of Sharpsburg or Antietam," opined that the one or two days McClellan gained by finding the Lost Order made Lee's stand at South Mountain necessary, and that had this not happened, "the Confederate army, loaded with the spoils of Harper's Ferry, would have reunited at Hagerstown without difficulty. No one can read the history of that campaign, no one can study McClellan's career, no one can see the doubt, the anxiety, of the Federal administration as shown by Halleck's dispatches, without feeling that these two days and more would have been Lee's had the course of events not been affected by the accident of the lost dispatch."[57]

Carman indulged in speculation about McClellan's lost opportunity after finding the order. In Carman's opinion, McClellan missed a wonderful opportunity:

---

[54] *Lee's Lieutenants*, 2:717.

[55] Ibid., 721.

[56] Matthew Forney Steele, *American Campaigns*, vol. 1, (Washington, DC: Byron S. Adams, 1909), 280. Lee on the other hand would have gathered to him the large number of stragglers in Winchester augmenting his force. Also, the Union army was unable to cut Lee's supply line during the Gettysburg Campaign despite having a larger army and with more veteran troops.

[57] William Allan, "Strategy of the Campaign of Sharpsburg or Antietam," in *Papers of the Military Historical Society of Massachusetts.*, vol. III, *Campaigns in Virginia, Maryland and Pennsylvania 1862-1863* (Boston, MA: Griffith-Stillings Press, 1903, reprint Wilmington, NC: Broadfoot Publishing Company, 1989), 86.

Had the Ninth, Second, and Twelfth Corps marched that night and reached the foot of Turner's Gap by midnight and rested until morning, they would have found to oppose them one of Stuart's cavalry regiments, the small infantry brigades of Colquitt and Brigadier General Samuel Garland Jr., and eight pieces of artillery. The gap could have been forced before D.H. Hill could have brought up his support from beyond Boonsboro, five miles away. Or, had Franklin marched at the same time, he could have taken Crampton's Gap next morning with but little opposition and descended into Pleasant Valley early in the forenoon, with the consequent result of relieving Miles at Harper's Ferry, interposing between Lee and McLaws, and, moving on the flank and rear of the Confederate forces, engaging the main body at Turner's Gap—providing always that he took advantage of opportunity. McLaws might have rejoined Lee by descending the west side of Maryland Heights and marching north by Antietam Furnace and Sharpsburg, which would have permitted Miles to reoccupy the heights and join Franklin; he might have recrossed into Virginia by Knott's Ford at the mouth of the Antietam and joined Jackson; or he might have descended the southeastern extremity of the height and, uniting his command at Weverton, marched by Knoxville and recrossed the Potomac by some of the fords below (which would have been hazardous). In fact, all three movements would have been attended with great risk and entailed the loss of many stragglers and much material. In any event, the abandonment of Maryland Heights would have been imperative.

But McClellan did not rise to the occasion. He did not take full advantage of the long afternoon [of the 13th], he did not order the night march—and thereby missed the opportunity of his life.[58]

Hartwig also wrote that McClellan would likely have continued his slow approach to South Mountain had he not found S.O. 191, and that Lee's army would have reunited after Harpers Ferry fell, but speculating about the result of the following battle between that reunited army and McClellan's forces would be just that—pure speculation.[59] Fishel opined that "The finding of Special Orders no. 191 did yield for the Federals a definitely better outcome of the Maryland campaign than they otherwise would have achieved [because otherwise] it would have gone on for weeks. By that time Lee would have had a fully assembled army fattened on Northern food, with most of its numerous stragglers recovered. In any battle he succeeded in bringing about, he doubtless would have outgeneraled McClellan as he did on the Antietam and with a result this time in the Southerners' favor."[60] It is clear that Lee wanted to meet the Army of the Potomac in the field to annihilate it once his army was reunited, resupplied, and rested. Historian Stephen Sears writes that Lee said the loss of the order was a "great calamity" and if it had not been lost, "sometime during the later half of September 1862 a great battle would have been fought in the Cumberland Valley of Pennsylvania—the Battle of Greencastle, perhaps, or the Battle of Chambersburg, or even the Battle of Gettysburg…[but] it was 'impossible to say that victory would have certainly resulted,' Lee admitted, but on one point he was clear: 'the loss of the dispatch changed the character of the campaign.'"[61] But the results of that contest which might have taken place somewhere north of Hagerstown must remain the province of alternate historians and historical fiction.

---

[58] Carman, Pierro, 134. See Clemens's note to Carman's speculation noting that two chapters earlier Carman described how disorganized the Union troops appeared but now Carman finds them in good condition to march even at night if needed to be in position to attack early on the 14th , Carman, Clemens, 288, n. 16; 290, n. 17.

[59] Hartwig, 352.

[60] Fishel, 240.

[61] Stephen W. Sears, *Controversies and Commanders: Dispatches from the Army of the Potomac* (Boston: Houghton Mifflin Company, 1999), 128.

Attachment

SPECIAL ORDERS, ⎫   HDQRS. ARMY OF NORTHERN VIRGINIA,
No. 191.   ⎬   *September* 9, 1862.

I. The citizens of Fredericktown being unwilling, while overrun by members of this army, to open their stores, in order to give them confidence, and to secure to officers and men purchasing supplies for benefit of this command, all officers and men of this army are strictly prohibited from visiting Fredericktown except on business, in which case they will bear evidence of this in writing from division commanders. The provost-marshal in Fredericktown will see that his guard rigidly enforces this order.

II. Major Taylor will proceed to Leesburg, Va., and arrange for transportation of the sick and those unable to walk to Winchester, securing the transportation of the country for this purpose. The route between this and Culpeper Court-House east of the mountains being unsafe will no longer be traveled. Those on the way to this army already across the river will move up promptly; all others will proceed to Winchester collectively and under command of officers, at which point, being the general depot of this army, its movements will be known and instructions given by commanding officer regulating further movements.

III. The army will resume its march to-morrow, taking the Hagerstown road. General Jackson's command will form the advance, and, after passing Middletown, with such portion as he may select, take the route toward Sharpsburg, cross the Potomac at the most convenient point, and by Friday morning take possession of the Baltimore and Ohio Railroad, capture such of them as may be at Martinsburg, and intercept such as may attempt to escape from Harper's Ferry.

IV. General Longstreet's command will pursue the main road as far as Boonsborough, where it will halt, with reserve, supply, and baggage trains of the army.

V. General McLaws, with his own division and that of General R. H. Anderson, will follow General Longstreet. On reaching Middletown will take the route to Harper's Ferry, and by Friday morning possess himself of the Maryland Heights and endeavor to capture the enemy at Harper's Ferry and vicinity.

VI. General Walker, with his division, after accomplishing the object in which he is now engaged, will cross the Potomac at Cheek's Ford, ascend its right bank to Lovettsville, take possession of Loudoun Heights, if practicable, by Friday morning, Keys' Ford on his left, and the road between the end of the mountain and the Potomac on his right. He will, as far as practicable, co-operate with Generals McLaws and Jackson, and intercept retreat of the enemy.

VII. General D. H. Hill's division will form the rear guard of the army, pursuing the road taken by the main body. The reserve artillery, ordnance, and supply trains, &c., will precede General Hill.

VIII. General Stuart will detach a squadron of cavalry to accompany the commands of Generals Longstreet, Jackson, and McLaws, and, with the main body of the cavalry, will cover the route of the army, bringing up all stragglers that may have been left behind.

IX. The commands of Generals Jackson, McLaws, and Walker, after accomplishing the objects for which they have been detached, will join the main body of the army at Boonsborough or Hagerstown.

X. Each regiment on the march will habitually carry its axes in the regimental ordnance wagons, for use of the men at their encampments, to procure wood, &c.

By command of General R. E. Lee:

R. H. CHILTON,
Assistant Adjutant-General.

OR, vol. 19, pt. 2, 603-604. Both copies sent to D. H. Hill, from Chilton, the Lost Order, and Jackson's copy, omitted paragraphs I and II. Images courtesy of Cornell University Library, Making of America Digital Collection.

Chapter 8

Breakout from Harpers Ferry

O F ALL THE ACTIVITIES of the cavalry during the Maryland Campaign, the most spectacular and unlikely happened at Harpers Ferry, Virginia. It involved the largest number of Union cavalry in action during the campaign in the successful breakout of 1,594 troopers from Harpers Ferry on the evening of Sunday, 14 September 1862. What added to this feat was the capture of some 97 wagons from Longstreet's ammunition train as the Union cavalry escapees made their way through Maryland to Pennsylvania. And that this adventure resulted in little reported loss to the column of Union troopers, and allowed most of the units to aid McClellan starting on the 16th, should have crowned their place in the forefront of the story of the Union effort which culminated in stopping Lee at Antietam on 17 September. Unfortunately for these stalwart riders, the sanguinary events at Antietam overshadowed their accomplishment as did the fact that these units were not under McClellan's command until they escaped from the Harpers Ferry trap. This chapter will explore how they accomplished their escape, the history of the units and their leaders, and the controversies surrounding their surprising ride.[1]

Gen. Robert E. Lee, a well-trained and experienced engineer, knew about the topography and importance of Harpers Ferry. He certainly remembered his experience there on 18 October 1859 when, in command of a company of U.S. Marines, some Virginia militia, and aided by Lt. Jeb Stuart, he captured the fanatic abolitionist John Brown and his party. Lee recognized that the town of Harpers Ferry by itself is not defensible without garrisoning the heights around it, most importantly Maryland

---

[1] Halleck told McClellan on 11 September in response to McClellan's request that Miles's command join his, that Miles's "only chance is to defend his works till you can open communication with him. When you do so he will be subject to your orders," *OR*, vol. 19, pt. 1, 758. Halleck ordered Miles on 12 September to "obey such orders as General McClellan may give you," ibid." McClellan was not able to open communications with Miles before Miles surrendered as the telegraph lines had been cut and couriers were unable to get to Harpers Ferry from McClellan's headquarters. McClellan sent three couriers from Pinkerton's men with a message for Miles dated 14 September telling Miles that the Army of the Potomac was attacking the three gaps in South Mountain and to reoccupy Maryland Heights if possible. McClellan also wrote him that the Union army held Catoctin Valley (Middletown Valley) and that Miles could cross at Berlin, *OR*, vol. 19, pt. 1, 45; Sears, McClellan *Papers*, 459. None of these three messages or the two Halleck sent reached Miles, Fishel, 215. On 12 September 1862, Wool acquiesced in giving McClellan command of his troops including those at Harpers Ferry: "You can put any of my troops under McClellan's command....you can give him authority to use them as you or he may deem proper," *OR*, vol. 19, pt. 2, 275. Carman wrote that had McClellan been put in command of Miles's troops, they would have been ordered out of Harpers Ferry and been saved, Carman, Pierro, 91, 104. Some historians may quibble over whether or not events at Harpers Ferry were really part of the Maryland Campaign as Harpers Ferry was not under McClellan's command and that Army of the Potomac units were not there. Clearly Gen. Lee's Army of Northern Virginia was heavily involved there and the outcome of the Harpers Ferry action affected the main battle at Sharpsburg on 17 September. Also, cavalry units from Harpers Ferry were at least tangentially involved in activities at and near Sharpsburg which did have an impact on events there as will be seen.

Heights just across the Potomac River. Maj. Gen. Kenton Harper, in charge of 2,000 Virginia militia, commanded the first Confederate attack at Harpers Ferry in late April 1861 and posted sentinels on Maryland Heights. Col. Thomas J. Jackson soon arrived after he was placed in command of the Virginia Provisional Army forces in and around Harpers Ferry by Gen. Lee on 27 April, and placed 500 men on Maryland Heights. Jackson wrote Lee on 6 May 1861 that "I have occupied the Virginia and Maryland Heights, and I am about fortifying the former with block-houses of sufficient strength to resist an attempt to carry them by storm....I shall construct similar works on the Maryland Heights. Thus far I have been deterred from doing so by a desire to avoid giving offense to the latter State." Then on 7 May, he wrote that "I have finished reconnoitering the Maryland Heights, and have determined to fortify them at once, and hold them, as well as the Virginia [Loudoun] Heights and the town, be the cost what it may." Jackson suggested that all the heights surrounding Harpers Ferry be fortified and armed with cannon and wrote that "this place should be defended with the spirit which actuated the defenders of Thermopylae, and, if left to myself, such is my determination." Lee replied two days later that "it is considered advisable not to intrude upon the soil of Maryland, unless compelled by the necessities of war" and then on the 10th, giving tactical advice, that "you may have been premature in occupying the heights of Maryland with so strong a force near you. If not too late, you might withdraw until the proper time." W.H.C. Whiting, a Confederate major of engineers, wrote on 28 May 1861 that a force of twelve to fifteen thousand troops would be needed to hold Harpers Ferry with most of these troops as a movable force located on the Opequon Creek in northern Virginia to allow freedom of maneuver and not be "shut up in a *cul-de-sac.*" When Confederate Gen. Joseph E. Johnston arrived in mid May 1861 to take overall command, he agreed with Jackson that unless the three heights surrounding the place were heavily garrisoned, Harpers Ferry could not be held.[2] As will be seen, this fact seems to have escaped veteran Union Col. Dixon Miles in 1862 when he was in charge of the garrison at Harpers Ferry, even though any military engineer or officer studying the topography surrounding the town must immediately recognize that the heights, unless held, make the town vulnerable.

Harpers Ferry lies at the confluence of the Shenandoah and Potomac Rivers—the Shenandoah, the Potomac's largest tributary, joining from the west, and the Potomac from the northwest. Harpers Ferry, which is on the point of land at this junction, was in Virginia (now West Virginia, admitted to the Union on 20 June 1863) with the Potomac River the border between the two states. Maryland, then, as now, owned the Potomac to the Virginia shore (low-water boundary) of the adjoining states.[3] Sitting

---

[2] *OR*, vol. 2, 785, 787, 793-4, 806, 809, 814, 822, 824-7, 890; Chester G. Hearn, *Six Years of Hell: Harpers Ferry during the Civil War* (Baton Rouge, LA: Louisiana State University Press, 1996), 61, 69, 71-72. Jackson was ordered to relieve Gen. Harper by order dated 28 April, to recruit volunteers from surrounding Virginia counties, and to expedite shipping of arms and machinery as quickly as possible out of Harpers Ferry. Gen. Lee even authorized him to pay $5 each for muskets returned by citizens in and around Harpers Ferry. Jackson wrote on 10 May that he had occupied Maryland Heights with Kentucky troops and one company of Virginia troops—grand total of 500 men. Gen. Lee on 10 May placed Jackson in command of all troops in Harpers Ferry as Lee was placed in command of all Confederate States troops in Virginia also on 10 May. Kentucky and Maryland troops replaced Virginia troops on the critical Maryland Heights, or as Lee said "the appearance of its being done by the people of that State, and not to take possession himself till necessary; but the time has been left to his discretion," *OR*, vol. 2, 860. Jackson wrote Lee on 9 May that "I have occupied the Maryland Heights with the Kentuckians and one company of infantry from Augusta County [Virginia], making about 500 in all," ibid., 824. Area residents also complained that Confederate troops had burned timber on Maryland Heights but officials assured worried Marylanders that the woods had caught fire accidentally, Timothy R. Snyder, *Trembling in the Balance: The Chesapeake and Ohio Canal During the Civil War* (Boston, MA: Blue Mustang Press, 2011), 33. According to Inspector general Lt. Col. George Deas's report dated 23 May, Jeb Stuart's cavalry "is in very good condition, and quite effective. Their arms are a small-sized revolver and a saber; no carbines. The horses are good, and all the men ride well. They are made exceedingly useful in the duties of scouts and videttes, covering a considerable extent of country to the front," *OR*, vol. 2, 869.

[3] For an in depth review of Maryland's Potomac boundaries, see Carl N. Everstine, "The Potomac River and Maryland's Boundaries," *Maryland Historical Magazine*, vol. 80, no. 4, Winter 1985, 355-370.

where it is, the town of Harpers Ferry is surrounded by hills chiseled out of the mountains around it with the most dominating being Maryland Heights at 1,381 feet tall, looming 1,100 feet above the town, across the Potomac River to the northeast; Maryland Heights is near the southern end of Elk Ridge which is parallel to the South Mountain range to its east. The verdant Pleasant Valley lies between Elk Ridge and South Mountain and is about two and one-half miles to three miles across peak to peak widening as it extends north to Keedysville. The main road to Harpers Ferry from the east in Maryland was along the foot of South Mountain, but another along the base of Elk Ridge to Sharpsburg was in poor repair.[4] Elk Ridge extends to the north for about 10 miles to Antietam Creek and then fades into surrounding countryside in the area to the west of Rohrersville. Harpers Ferry is also overlooked by the mountain to the south, Loudoun Heights, about 1,200 feet above the town, the northern terminus of the Blue Ridge in Virginia. Bolivar Heights, about 700 feet high to the west, is not as tall as these heights but still overlooks Harpers Ferry. This point of land on which Harpers Ferry sits was for many years known as "The Hole," as its low-lying location made it prone to flooding and was recognized by its first settlers as a vulnerable location. Carman provides a complete picture of the area:

> South Mountain is a continuous ridge from eight hundred to one thousand feet high and abuts the Potomac in a lofty, almost perpendicular mass of rocks overhanging the small hamlet of Weverton, the canal to Washington, the Baltimore and Ohio Railroad, and the turnpike from Harper's Ferry to Frederick, there being just enough space for them between the mountains and the river. Four miles north of Weverton Pass is Brownsville Gap, by which the road through Burkittsville debouches into Pleasant Valley, and one mile north of this is another pass known as Crampton's Gap. Six miles north of Crampton's Gap is Turner's Gap, through which the National Road pursues its way from Frederick to Hagerstown; the turnpike from Frederick to Harper's Ferry passes through Weverton, as already stated. About halfway between Weverton and Harper's Ferry is Sandy Hook. A road from Sandy Hook runs about the middle of Pleasant Valley and joins the main road along the foot of South Mountain about two miles from the Potomac. Passing from the valley going west were two roads: one along the south end of Maryland Heights and another through Solomon's Gap—a slight depression in Elk Ridge—about five miles north of the first.
>
> Elk Ridge bounds Pleasant Valley on the west; its southern extremity is more specially designated and generally known as Maryland Heights, dominating both Harper's Ferry and Loudoun Heights. Its northern extremity dips down into and is lost in the rolling country about a mile southwest of Keedysville. Where the railroad, canal, and turnpike (after passing Weverton) go under the south end of Maryland Heights, the crowded space made for them was gained by blasting the almost-perpendicular rocks for a considerable distance. The railroad bridge crosses the Potomac (here about four hundred yards wide) just under the frowning precipice of Maryland Heights, and about fifty yards above the bridge was a pontoon bridge for wagons and infantry by which communication was kept up between Harper's Ferry and the Maryland shore. The railroad bridge was defended by cannon placed on the farther end; the narrow causeway along the river under Maryland Heights by guns placed under the precipice and on the road. The Potomac thus runs along the south ends of both South Mountain and Elk Ridge, and between it and these high ridges run the Baltimore and Ohio Railroad, the Chesapeake and Ohio Canal, and the Frederick Turnpike—all centering on Harper's Ferry, on the Virginia side of the river.[5]

Thomas Jefferson in his oft-quoted description of the beauty of the location wrote in 1785:

---

[4] Carman, Pierro, 111. This road to the east ran along the Potomac and then headed northeast as a turnpike to Frederick through Jefferson, Rt. 180 today; the Harpers Ferry-Sharpsburg Road followed the canal westward then turned north to roughly follow the Potomac to Antietam Furnace and Sharpsburg. The road through Solomon's Gap was widely used as it headed east across Pleasant Valley to Brownsville Gap in South Mountain and then to Frederick or to points south to the B&O Railroad at Berlin.
[5] Ibid., 111-112. The road distance from Harpers Ferry to Weverton was just under three miles; from the middle of Sandy Hook to Weverton about two miles and from Harpers Ferry to Knoxville about 3.3 miles.

The passage of the Patowmac through the Blue Ridge is perhaps one of the most stupendous scenes in Nature. You stand on a very high point of land. On your right comes up the Shenandoah, having ranged along the foot of the mountain an hundred miles to seek a vent. On your left approaches the Patowmac, in quest of a passage also. In the moment of their junction they rush together against the mountain, rend it asunder and pass off to the sea….For the mountain being cloven asunder, she presents to your eye, through the cleft, a small catch of smooth blue horizon, at an infinite distance in the plain country, inviting you, as it were, from the riot and tumult roaring around, to pass through the breach and participate of the calm below. Here the eye ultimately composes itself; and that way too the road happens actually to lead. You cross the Patowmac above the junction, pass along its side through the base of the mountain for three miles, its terrible precipices hanging in fragments over you, and within about 20 miles reach Frederic Town, and the fine country round that. This scene is worth a voyage across the Atlantic.[6]

View east down the Potomac River shows the Baltimore and Ohio Railroad Bridge crossing the Potomac finished in 1839, which was burned by Jackson under Johnston's orders on 14 June 1861. When the B&O Bridge was completed the company destroyed the Wager Bridge just upstream from the B&O. The Wager family began their wooden bridge in 1824 then sold it to the B&O in 1839. The bridge carried the railroad and had space for wagons and pedestrians. The Potomac River enters from the left and the Shenandoah from the right with the combined river, the Potomac in the center, flowing downstream to Washington. The Federal armory is along the near side of the Potomac River behind the houses in the foreground while the Chesapeake and Ohio Canal is at the base of Maryland Heights at the center; Loudoun Heights is to the right. Drawing was done after 1839 and before 1842 as a "Y" was added at the Harpers Ferry shore which carried the B&O along the Virginia shore north to Martinsburg. Courtesy LOC.

---

[6] Thomas Jefferson, *Notes on the State of Virginia* (Np., 1787; reprint, Richmond, VA: J. W. Randolph, 1853), 17-18.

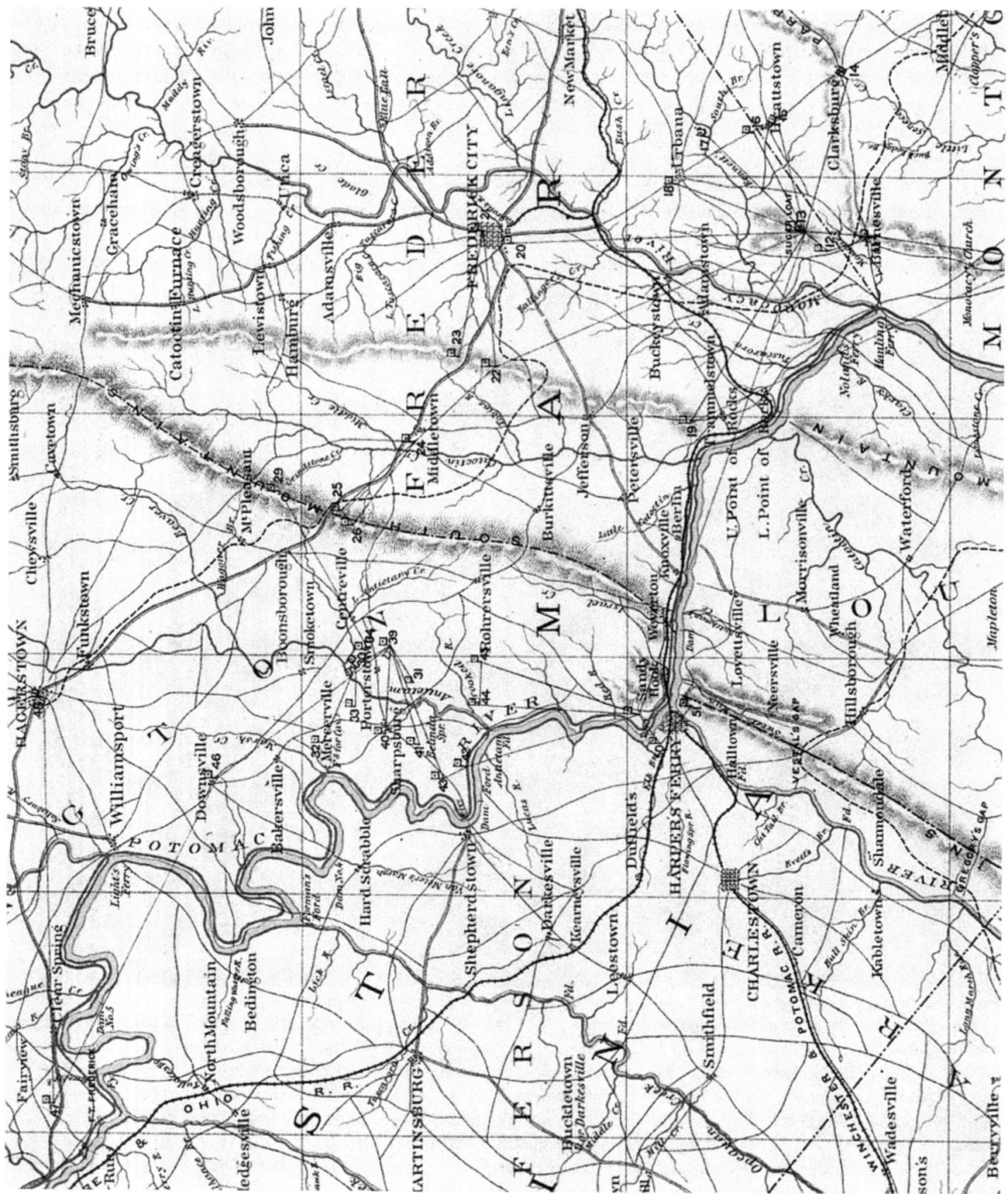

Harpers Ferry area of operations; Harpers Ferry is at the right center. *Official Atlas*, Plate 27. Courtesy LOC.

Harpers Ferry's location on these rivers and the borders of two states made it an ideal location to construct water-powered mills including the U.S. Armory and Arsenal begun in 1799. It was also an important transportation corridor through which the Baltimore and Ohio (B&O) Railroad passed as did the Chesapeake and Ohio (C&O) Canal.[7] It was also on a direct route between Frederick, Maryland, and Charles Town and Winchester, Virginia. When the Winchester and Potomac (W&P) Railroad is considered, there is no other location where it, the B&O Railroad, the C&O Canal, and the two rivers are in such close proximity. The canal was the only direct link between Washington and Harpers Ferry as well as to Cumberland, Maryland, the end of the canal, 184½ miles from Washington and 123 miles from Harpers Ferry. The 32-mile-long W&P Railroad ran from Harpers Ferry to Winchester, Virginia. Although its gauge was the same as the B&O, four feet, eight and one-half inches, its construction of a track of steel straps on wood and poor roadbed was not robust enough to allow safe passage for the heavy engines of 32 tons used on the B&O—engineers for the W&P only allowed engines weighing up to 22 tons.[8] The W&P began regular operations on 31 March 1836 and in January 1837 made a connection to the B&O at Harpers Ferry when the B&O built a bridge across the Potomac River tying the lines together.

View of Harpers Ferry, Virginia, before June 1861 from Maryland Heights, showing the covered B&O Railroad and wagon bridge in the foreground crossing the Potomac, and the covered wagon bridge across the Shenandoah in the far middle left, both of which Col. Thomas J. Jackson burned under Johnston's orders on 14 June 1861. The C&O Canal is in the right front; the Potomac River flows in from the right and the Shenandoah River from the center left. The smokestack in the center is part of the Federal armory complex along the Potomac River. Loudoun Heights is to the left and Bolivar Heights is above the town in the center. Note the low water in both rivers exposing rocks and small islands. The Harpers Ferry Road on which the cavalry escape column rode is at the bottom right on the near side of the canal. There is a bridge at the arrow allowing foot traffic to cross from the canal towpath to the road. Arrow in the center points to the boat landing ramp. Courtesy LOC.

Upon his arrival in April 1861, Col. Thomas J. Jackson took over command at Harpers Ferry and began using the W&P Railroad to transport armory machinery, tools, and other salvaged items, south to Winchester, and then via the Valley Pike up the Shenandoah Valley to the railhead of the Virginia

[7] George Washington visited Harpers Ferry in 1785; Robert Harper had set up and operated a ferry there in 1747; Harper owned 125 acres he bought from Lord Fairfax in 1751. In 1795, Washington, as president, named Harpers Ferry as the site for a new armory. For a good, short history of Robert Harper, see David T. Gilbert, *A Walker's Guide to Harpers Ferry West Virginia* (Harpers Ferry, VA: Harpers Ferry Historical Association, 2001), 46, 68.
[8] Jeffrey N. Lash, "Joseph E. Johnston and the Virginia Railways, 1861-62," *Civil War History*, vol. 35, no. 1, March 1989, 9. On 11 October 1862 Brig. Gen. Herman Haupt, chief of military railroad construction, reported that "The Winchester Railroad is perhaps the worst in the Union—thin slab rail for more than 30 miles [of its 32-mile length]. Only one siding on road holding more than 12 cars. Utmost capacity about 52 cars per day," *OR*, vol. 19, pt. 2, 412.

Central Railroad at Staunton, ending at Richmond.[9] Destruction of railroad and other bridges along with B&O and W&P rolling stock and the C&O Canal by the rebels during their retreat from Harpers Ferry in June and July 1861, dealt a serious blow to Union transportation resources in and around Harpers Ferry, Martinsburg, and Winchester. The cost of the Rebel depredations to the B&O alone was estimated at one million dollars.[10] And as Washington depended mainly on the C&O and B&O for its coal, the interruption of the railroad and canal worked a hardship on its citizens. A newspaper in the Cumberland area on 11 January 1862 reported that "Since July last. No Coal has been transported over the Baltimore and Ohio Railroad, and also by the obstructions placed in the Canal." Then, when Lee moved north in September 1862, the destruction by his army of the B&O Railroad and C&O Canal again stopped coal shipments, first interrupted the previous year.[11] Union telegraph communications were damaged as the Confederates destroyed 90 miles of telegraph line and poles from the Monocacy Bridge to Hancock, Maryland.[12]

After 1861, whenever Confederate armies or guerilla troops were in the area, the B&O Railroad was a favorite target.[13] The 379-mile-long B&O Railroad was called the "most important commercial highway in western Virginia. It furnished a convenient inlet and outlet both to the lower [Shenandoah] Valley and to the greater part of the Trans-Allegheny. It 'is the great artery that feeds our country.... We cannot do without it.'"[14] By 1861, the B&O had 236 locomotives, 128 passenger cars, and 3,451 freight

---

[9] Kirk Reynolds and Dave Oroszi, *Baltimore & Ohio Railroad* (St. Paul, MN: MBI Publishing Company, 2000), 17; Gilbert, 73, 75.

[10] Reynolds and Oroszi, 12; Festus P. Summers, *The Baltimore and Ohio in the Civil War* (New York: G. P. Putnam's Sons, 1939; reprint, Gettysburg, PA: Stan Clark Military Books, 1993), details the destruction as well as the salvaging of rolling stock, engines, machinery, etc., 96-97, 100-101, 109, 120. The Shenandoah Bridge Company's covered wagon bridge, built in 1833-1834, which crossed the river into Virginia at the foot of Bridge Street in Harpers Ferry and was destroyed by Jackson in June 1861, was not rebuilt until 1882 some 300 yards downstream, Gilbert, 27-28. Abutments for that last bridge are still plainly visible today while there is little remaining of the 1833 bridge's abutments.

[11] In 1860, the Cumberland, Maryland, coal trade marketed almost 789,000 tons but because of Rebel damage to the canal and B&O in 1861, only 270,000 tons were shipped; 318,000 in 1862, and 748,000 in 1863, and 658,000 in 1864 Ibid., 108; Katherine A. Harvey, "The Civil War and the Maryland Coal Trade," *Maryland Historical Magazine*, vol. 62, no. 4, December 1967, 364-366, 369-371, 376. Rebel action in 1864 again reduced tonnage shipped. The flour trade was also seriously affected by the interruptions caused by the war. Damage to the C&O Canal stopped traffic for 25 miles causing a loss of $50,000 to the canal company. In addition, canal receipts plunged from a high of $13,411.15 in August 1862 to $5,282.48 in September and only $538.78 in October. The canal company's income dropped from $191,890.20 in 1860 to $75,741.90 in 1861 while its operating expenses remained constant at about $100,000 per year. "Through traffic on the canal was essentially halted for the months of September and October 1862. All told, the year 1862 was even more disastrous financially for the canal company than 1861. The aggregate tonnage on the canal declined more than 12 percent from 144,814 tons in 1861 to 126,793 tons in 1862. Toll revenues plummeted nearly 10 percent from $70,566.99 in 1861 to $63,985.85 in 1862. Receipts from all sources for 1862 amounted to $72,624.95 while total expenditures were $231,711.68. As a result of the seizure of canal boats by the Federals in March, the Confederate invasion of Maryland in September, several major freshets, and the inefficiency of some division superintendents, the canal company reached its lowest ebb during the war in 1862." In addition to Rebel depredations, floods and routine maintenance interrupted canal traffic. There were heavy rains in early June 1862 which seriously damaged the canal near the Antietam Ironworks which was not repaired until the end of June stopping canal boats for almost the entire month. Work on Dam No. 5 near Williamsport also delayed canal traffic but by 24 July 1862, boats were able to make the journey from Cumberland to Georgetown. A drought in late July and early August also worried canal officials that low water would again suspend operations. Suspected disloyalty among canal employees and workers also may have slowed repairs and maintenance retarding passage on the waterway; Walter S. Sanderlin, *The Great National Project: A History of the Chesapeake and Ohio Canal* (Baltimore, MD: The Johns Hopkins Press, 1946; reprint, Ft. Washington, PA: Eastern National, 2005), 213, 217, 218. See Harlan D. Unrau's comprehensive history of the Canal especially Chap. 11, "The C&O Canal during the Civil War: 1861-1865," 733-734, 742. Courtesy National Park Service.

[12] Summers, 120.

[13] Ibid., 122 ff, 142-143.

[14] Ibid., 187.

cars.[15] The value of the railroad was confirmed as the Lincoln administration ensured through political machinations that all of the counties in western Virginia through which the vital railroad passed became part of the new State of West Virginia in 1863.[16]

The Federal arsenal at Harpers Ferry produced more arms than any other south of the Mason-Dixon Line, but in 1861 was protected by only 45-50 regular army troops and 15 volunteers commanded by Lt. Roger Jones of the Mounted Rifles, U.S. Army. His call for the assistance of local militia was ignored as most of those men favored secession, so with his few men he was only able to post guards at the entrances to town and prepare to burn the armory. Lt. Jones testified to Congress on 15 November 1861 about the events:

At 9 or 10 o'clock on the morning of the 18th of April, 1861, I received a telegraphic despatch from General Scott, telling me that three trains of troops had passed from Manassas Junction up the Manassas railroad for the supposed destruction of Harper's Ferry, and saying "Be on your guard." I immediately acknowledged the receipt of his despatch, and at about 5 in the evening of that day informed the general by telegraph that I had received intelligence confirmatory of his morning despatch. Just after the information contained in General Scott's despatch was confirmed, I learned that a force estimated at from three to four hundred men, had assembled at Halltown, on the turnpike to Charlestown, and three or four miles from the Ferry. Not satisfied that this intelligence was correct, I sent a man on horseback to ascertain in regard to it, and in about three-quarters of an hour he returned confirming the report. In the meantime, having become satisfied that an attempt would be made to seize the arsenal and workshops during the night, I made preparations for the destruction of the place, to be carried out only in the event of my being unable to defend it. I detailed twelve men of my company, and ordered six of them to get their bed-sacks, which were filled with straw, and put a keg of powder in each one of them. I proceeded in person with this party from the armory to the arsenal buildings. The arsenal buildings were detached from the main armory workshop, not in the same enclosure, but on the other side of the street, and in no way connected with it. I distributed these sacks, with powder in them, in the two arsenal buildings, which contained the arms, and with the aid of shavings and bituminous coal, which I had previously carried in there thinking that I might have to take post there to defend the place, and with a quantity of lumber lying in the buildings, I prepared things so that a fire could be kindled in an instant. These preparations were completed before 6 o'clock in the evening of the 18th of April. At about 6 o'clock a number of the workmen in the armory, perhaps in all from thirty to forty, under some of the officers of a company into which they had organized themselves at the time of the John Brown raid, offered their services to Captain Kingsbury and myself for the defence of the place. I posted a part of them along the railroad which leads to Winchester through Charlestown, and another picket on the turnpike leading to Halltown, with instructions to keep me advised of the advance of any troops, and, if possible, to hold them in check if any should attempt to come. Affairs remained in this state, everything being quiet until about 9 o'clock in the evening, when I commenced to report the condition of things there to General Scott, by letter....Up to the present time no assault or attempt to seize the government property here has been made, but there is decided evidence that the subject is in contemplation, and has been all day, by a large number of people lying in the direction of Charlestown; and at sundown this evening, several companies of troops had assembled at Halltown, about three or four miles from here, on the road to Charlestown, with the intention of seizing the government property, and the last report is that the attack will be made to-night.[17]

Jones reported to Washington that his plans to destroy the arsenal and its 15,000 stand of arms were complete. After he received a message on 18 April 1861 that 2,500 to 3,000 Rebel troops were sighted approaching town from the direction of Halltown with the intent to seize the armory, he set fire to it at 10 P.M. and then escaped north, crossing the Potomac first marching 27 miles to Hagerstown then to

[15] Hearn, 5.
[16] Summers, 182-202, tells the tale of the creation of West Virginia's "Eastern Panhandle."
[17] Extracts from Senate Rep. Com. No. 37, 37th Cong., 2d Sess. http://www.wvculture.org/history/civilwar/hfarmory02.html

Chambersburg, Pennsylvania, suffering four casualties, with two more deserting during his final march to Carlisle Barracks, Pennsylvania.[18] The Virginia troops hastening to Harpers Ferry saw the fire and rushed to the town, but by the time they reached the armory, "a carpenters shop, the main arsenal, and some 15,000 arms were lost, though citizens, fearful that the entire town would be destroyed, had acted quickly to extinguish the fires in all the other armory buildings. At midnight the main Rebel contingent under Colonel Turner Ashby marched unmolested into Harpers Ferry. The town had been taken without firing a shot." A Unionist observer, the famous "Porte Crayon," David Hunter Strother, described the scene as he approached:

> The Old Arsenal buildings on Shenandoah Street and several of the shops in the Armory inclosure on Potomac Street were in full blaze. The road was alive with men, women, and children hurrying to and fro, laden with spoils from the work-shops and soldiers' barracks. There were women with their arms full of muskets, little girls loaded with sheaves of bayonets, boys dragging cartridge-boxes and cross-belts enough to equip a platoon, men with barrels of pork or flour, kegs of molasses and boxes of hard bread on their shoulders or trundling in wheel-barrows.
>
> Taking advantage of the first opportunity that had offered during their lives perhaps, these people seem to have entered upon the work of sacking and plundering as promptly and skillfully as veteran soldiers could have done, where from I conclude that this propensity is inherent in the human character, and only awaits opportunity for development. The ground around the burning buildings was glittering with splinters of glass which had been blown out by the explosion of gunpowder used to ignite the fires.[19]

The Virginia militia was able to salvage machinery including two almost complete sets of machinery and materials including "4,287 finished firearms and enough components to assemble between 7,000 and 10,000 weapons of the latest design. For a short time after the raid, the Rifle Works on lower Hall Island continued in operation while workmen at the larger Musket Factory disassembled and packed over 300 machines, thousands of feet of belting and shafting, and 57,000 assorted tools for shipment to the Richmond armory." Shipping the machines and materials to Richmond was complicated as the W&P Railroad was unable to handle the quantities of materials quickly let alone the need to resort to wagoning them down the Valley Pike from Winchester to the Manassas Gap Railroad railhead at Strasburg. By June 13th, all the salvaged machines and spare parts had been sent to Richmond, then the

---

[18] *OR*, vol. 2, 3-5. Jones next reported that three of the missing four rejoined his command and stated that some 5,000 Rebel troops marched into Harpers Ferry and that the fire in the workshops was put out, but that the arsenal buildings with the arms were completely demolished. Apparently the townsfolk, employees, and Rebel soldiers salvaged arms as noted (*Battles and Leaders*, 1:125). Jones was a dedicated Union soldier, an 1851 graduate of West Point, a former instructor there, and a veteran of Indian Wars in the west. His cousin was Robert E. Lee. Jones testified that "When I went there [Harpers Ferry] in January [1861], the command consisted of sixty-two non-commissioned officers and men. By the 18th of April this force by deaths, desertions and discharged, had become reduced to forty-nine men," Extracts from Senate Rep. Com. No. 37, 37th Cong., 2d Sess. He also testified that he did not try to destroy the rifle works and other buildings on the Shenandoah River because "The rifle works were situated half a mile up the Shenandoah from the main works, where the troops were, and were left undestroyed; no attempt to destroy them being made for the reason that it would probably have led to the defeat of the plan which had been formed, as I was surrounded by spies and persons in the interest of the rebel cause, who watched every movement and everything that was done. I feared that by attempting too much I should fail in everything, and therefore confined myself to what I was certain could be accomplished," ibid. The army showed its appreciation for his efforts as he received a congratulatory letter two days after he arrived at Carlisle Barracks and was promoted to captain on 23 April 1861 and major on 12 November 1861. He remained in the army and died in 1889 as a brigadier general, Inspector General of the Army. See Eugene Wilkins, "'To Destroy What I Cannot Defend," *The Harpers Ferry Anthology: Civil War-era Stories by Park Rangers and Volunteers*, ed. by Catherine Baldau (Virginia Beach, VA: The Donning Company Publishers, 2011), 31-37.

[19] David Hunter Strother, "Personal Recollections of the War. By A Virginian, [First Paper]," *Harper's New Monthly Magazine*, vol. 33, June 1866, 12, hereafter Strother, "Recollections." For his complete tale of the incident see pp. 7-15. He writes that there were only a few hundred Southern troops which entered Harpers Ferry but more arrived that night and the next morning, 11-12, 14.

next day, Gen. Joseph Johnston burned the remaining armory buildings and blew up the B&O Bridge then retreated to Winchester the morning of the 15th. "On June 28, 1861, Confederates returned briefly to burn the wooden toll bridge across the Shenandoah and the nine buildings of the U.S. Rifle Factory on the Lower Hall Island."[20] "When Union troops removed a large supply of wheat from A.H. Herr's mill on Virginius Island on 17 October 1861, a Confederate force raided the town and burned the mill, thereby completing the destruction of all public and private industry in Harpers Ferry. In February 1862 a southern sniper firing from a building in the town killed a Union soldier on the Maryland side of the Potomac, in retaliation for which Union soldiers burned the entire 'point' or Ferry Lot district of hotels and stores. Despite all this destruction, because of the town's strategic importance as a railroad, highway, and canal transportation link, the Union Army reoccupied Harpers Ferry on February 25."[21]

Harper's Weekly reported the following about the Rebel destruction in June 1861:

A special agent of the press visited Harper's Ferry on 13th, and gave this account:

The Confederate army has left the place. The route of the main body was by turnpikes leading to Charlestown and Shepardstown. At five o'clock this morning the great bridge of the Baltimore and Ohio Railroad over the Potomac was fired, and soon after a tremendous report was heard, caused by an explosion of a mine under the centre span. In one hour the entire structure was in ruins and fell into the water. This was a noble piece of work, it being one thousand feet long, and was built by Engineer Latrobe but ten years since in the most scientific manner. It has six spans, and cost considerable. The damage to property is not ended here, but the Railroad Company and the United States have suffered further loses of valuable works. The body of the trestling on which the road was supported from the bridge to the end of the Government property, about half a mile in extent, is nearly all destroyed, as well as the upper bridge, of one hundred and twenty feet in length, over the Government canal. The telegraph station buildings and the other railroad works are also demolished. The long range of substantial buildings formerly occupied as the Government armory is burned to the ground,

---

[20] Merritt Roe Smith, *Harpers Ferry Armory and the New Technology: The Challenge of Change* (Ithaca, NY: Cornell University Press, 1977), 318-320, See also Hearn, 54-57, and also Claud E. Fuller and Richard D. Steuart, *Firearms of the Confederacy* (Fairfax, VA: Odysseus Editions, Inc., 1966), 25-27, 51, 54-57, and for a complete history of Harpers Ferry arsenal and its firearms see pages 58-80. For a detailed list of the destruction of the buildings, bridges, etc., see Charles W. Snell, "The Fortifications at Harpers Ferry, VA., in 1861 and Jackson's Attack, May 1862," U.S. Dept. of the Interior, National Park Service, Research Project No. HF-98A, courtesy of Harpers Ferry Research Library, 21-26. Railroad bridges at Shepherdstown, Berlin, and Point of Rocks were also burned on 9 June 1861. Capt. Turner Ashby was one of several men who met with former Virginia governor Henry A. Wise in Richmond on 16 April 1861, at the Exchange Hotel. They agreed to take over Harpers Ferry and the arms manufacturing there for Virginia. In addition to Ashby at the meeting was the ex-superintendent of the Armory, Alfred M. Barbour, John A. Barbour, Capt. Richard Ashby, Capt. John D. Imboden, and John H. Harman. They agreed on securing the arsenal and left on their respective missions even before their plan was approved by Virginia Governor Letcher or the Virginia Secession Convention, Barton H. Wise, *The Life of Henry A. Wise of Virginia, 1806-1876* (New York: The Macmillan Company, 1899), 274-278. Alfred Barbour returned to the armory and urged workers to join him in remaining loyal to Virginia, John D. Imboden, "Jackson at Harper's Ferry," *Battles and Leaders*, 1:111-118; Stephen Douglas Engle, *Thunder in the Hills: Military Operations in Jefferson County, West Virginia, During the American Civil War* (Charleston, WV: Mountain State Press, 1989), 4. Note that a few troopers from the Black Horse Cavalry from Fauquier were also present commanded by Capt. Richard Ashby and Lt. Robert Randolph. They then were sent to guard the bridge at Berlin, John Scott, "The Black Horse Cavalry," *Annals of the War*, 592. Members of the Black Horse were with Stonewall Jackson when he returned to Harpers Ferry in September 1862 serving as his escort, and acted as aides and couriers during the battle on the 17th, 601-602.

[21] U.S. Dept. of the Interior, National Park Service, National Register of Historic Places Inventory, Harpers Ferry National Historic Park, 1966, item 8, pg. 5-6, http://www.dhr.virginia.gov/registers/Counties/Loudoun/053-1094_Harpers_Ferry_National_Historical_Park_1966_Final_Nomination.pdf From the time the Confederates left Harpers Ferry, they would only occupy it for 34 days until the end of the war: "From August 18, 1861, to February 24, 1862, neither side made any effort to hold the town of Harpers Ferry. In 1862, Stonewall Jackson held the town from September 15, to 18, four days. In 1863, Federal forces evacuated the town from the evening of June 17 to the afternoon of July 14, 27 days. In 1864, Confederate forces held the town from about 9 p.m., July 4 to late evening of July 7, 1864, three days. From February 25, 1862, to July 30, 1865, the town was constantly in Union hands with the noted exception, amounting to 34 days," Snell 25.

with the exception of two at the west end, near the Shenandoah. Fire has been raging all day, and when we left it was just breaking out in the rear quarters. The rifle-works on the Shenandoah were fired in the afternoon.[22]

The burning of the Arsenal, 10 P.M. 18 April 1861. Citizens and militia shown carrying rifles and other goods saved from the fire, *Harper's Weekly* 11 May 1861, sketched by D.H. Strother. Courtesy LOC.

Burning of the Arsenal 18 April 1861, from *The Soldier in Our Civil War*. Note armed men probably the Union guard given their uniforms and that they are not carrying materials from the buildings. The view is within the Arsenal looking south toward the main entrance from the town at the Ferry Lot which was from the right past the flagpole. The flagpole in the center of the drawing which was located near the main entrance gate to the arsenal complex near the Engine House, the last building on the right facing the street. The buildings on the other side of the fence in the distance were burned by Union troopers in February 1862.

[22] *Harper's Weekly*, 6 July 1861.

Destruction of the B&O Railroad Bridge over the Potomac by the Rebels 14 June 1861. The Baltimore & Ohio Bridge was rebuilt and destroyed nine times during the war and the town changed hands 11 times. After the June 1861 destruction, it was not until 18 March 1862 that the Baltimore & Ohio Railroad completed a new bridge, Snell, 22. Courtesy LOC.

As 1861 drew to a close, Harpers Ferry had changed from a prosperous manufacturing center to a ruined, deserted town with fewer than 100 mostly elderly citizens. A few of the skilled employees of the works went to work in Northern factories, but most went south to work in the Richmond Armory or the Fayetteville, North Carolina, arsenal. These armorers and the machines and equipment from Harpers Ferry "formed the backbone of Confederate ordnance manufacture during the Civil War. Neither factory could have played this role without the rich human and technical resources of the Harpers Ferry armory."[23] There was little reason for inhabitants to return. "With the railroad gone, the bridges destroyed, the armory gutted, the rifle works demolished, and Herr's Mill torched, nothing of value remained for either side to want."[24] If it were not for its strategic geographic location as the chokepoint for the B&O Railroad and C&O Canal, Harpers Ferry would have been a ghost town for the duration of the war.

Union Maj. Gen. Nathanial P. Banks's division protected the ground from Washington to western Maryland from Rebel marauders and had troops at Harpers Ferry with Union troops occupying the area soon after the Rebels departed. On 29 March 1862, Regular U.S. Army Col. Dixon S. Miles took

---

[23] Merritt Roe Smith, 321-322. 1861 personnel records of the Confederate States Armory in Richmond reveals that the superintendent, all four of the shop foremen, and nearly one-sixth of the two hundred-member workforce were former Harpers Ferry armorers, Allison A. Crosbie and Andrew S. Lee, *Cultural Landscape Report for the United States Armory at Harpers Ferry and Potomac Riverfront, Harpers Ferry National Historical Park* (Boston, MA: Olmsted Center for Landscape Preservation Boston National Historical Park Charlestown Navy Yard, n.d.) 67.

[24] Hearn, 90.

command of the territory from Baltimore to the west border of the Department of the Potomac in charge of a Railroad Brigade; he located his headquarters in Harpers Ferry on the eastern end of Shenandoah Street in the Master Armorer quarters. His command included the troops defending the B&O from Cumberland, Maryland, east to Baltimore, as well as the W&P Railroad from Harpers Ferry to Winchester. Maj. Gen. John E. Wool was placed in command of the Middle Department on 9 June 1862, becoming commander of the succeeding Eighth Corps, with his headquarters in Baltimore. He relieved Miles of caring for the B&O from Baltimore to Point of Rocks reducing his area of responsibility for the railroad to Point of Rocks west through Harpers Ferry and just to the west of Harpers Ferry.[25]

While Harpers Ferry is difficult to defend due to its location, Gen. Robert E. Lee found in September 1862, that he still had to eliminate the Union garrison there. Lee had incorrectly assumed that the Union force would quickly flee once his army moved between it and its line of communications to Washington and points south but he did not know that Halleck and the garrison's department commander, the elderly Wool, veteran of the War of 1812, had ordered the Harpers Ferry garrison to remain in place and to fight until relieved by the Army of the Potomac.[26] Certainly Miles's options were limited if he did decide to retreat before being surrounded once the three parts of Lee's army began their moves toward him. Jackson was to his west, Walker to his south, and McLaws to his east and north—with each passing day, the Rebel noose tightened. Fighting his way out through any of these three forces would probably have led to disaster given Miles's demonstrated lack of combat leadership and also the fact that most of his troops were green. In hindsight, his best escape route would have been the same as the cavalry's on 14-15 September—across the pontoon bridge and up the Harpers Ferry-Sharpsburg Road. The other alternative, east along the Potomac following the C&O Canal past the foot of South Mountain and then up the Jefferson Pike in Middletown Valley toward Frederick would have involved considerable fighting with McLaws's troops as the pass on the Potomac at Weverton and along the road toward Jefferson was

---

[25] Hearn, 111; Samuel M. Blackwell, Jr., *In the First Line of Battle: The 12th Illinois Cavalry in the Civil War* (DeKalb, IL: Northern Illinois University Press, 2002), 27; Carman, Pierro, 101, Frank J. Welcher, *The Union Army 1861-1865, Organization and Operations, Volume I: The Eastern Theater* (Bloomington, IN: Indiana University Press, 1989), 17; OR, vol. 12, pt. 1, 663. Miles's headquarters was in Armory Dwelling No. 1 which was erected in 1858-59 as quarters for the Master Armorer; it contained 14 rooms, ample for his staff and officers. Next door was the older Armory Dwelling No. 2 which was the residence of the Master Armorer from 1818 to 1838 and was vacant at the time of the John Brown raid. U.S. Dept. of the Interior, NPS, National Register of Historic Places Inventory, Harpers Ferry National Historic Park, 1966, Internet, item 7, pg. 11. Dennis E. Frye, *Antietam Revealed* (Collingswood, NJ: C.W. Historicals, LLC, 2004), writes that Miles's headquarters was in the Master Armorer's House, 40. The Master Armorer's New Quarters is also known as Monument Building No. 36, Snell 97. Miles was previously described by Brig. Gen. Rufus Saxton's as his chief of staff while Saxton was in Harpers Ferry commanding units during Jackson's march down the Valley to Winchester and then while he chased McDowell to Williamsport, OR, vol. 12, pt. 1, 636. Saxton was assigned to command 24 May 1862. See his report, OR, vol. 12, pt. 1, 639-641. Miles was in charge of the Railroad Brigade but was superseded in command when Saxton arrived. On 1 June 1862, Stanton assigned the Harpers Ferry forces to Gen. Banks's corps and Maj. Gen. Sigel was placed in command reporting to Banks, 638. Miles was ordered by McClellan on 17 March 1862 to report his Railway Brigade command to Maj. Gen. John A. Dix in command at Baltimore "but may receive his instructions with regard to that portion of the railway lying within the geographical limits of the District of Columbia from Brig. Gen. James S. Wadsworth, military governor of that district," OR, vol. 12, pt. 3, 5. On 16 June 1862 Wool reported to Stanton that he had examined Harpers Ferry "and found it in a very indefensive condition....four regiments ought to be sent at once to Harpers Ferry....At present, Colonel Miles has not more than 300 or 400 that he can rely upon....I have assumed command of Harpers Ferry, as you desired," OR, vol. 12, pt. 3, 397-398. The Middle Department was created 22 March 1862 but its geographical limits did not include Harpers Ferry until 17 June 1862 under Wool but the geographical limits did not change only adding the troops defending the B&O and W&P. But then on 22 July 1862 the Eighth Corps was formed and included all the troops in the Middle Department, Welcher, 17.

[26] Wool was miffed that he was not considered for command of the Army of the Potomac in the field: "When elderly John E. Wool learned that he had been passed over yet again, he bitterly complained that Lincoln was 'a joker' lacking 'the first qualification to govern a great people,' a man who 'delights in relating smutty stories' and whose pets, most notably McClellan, 'have all failed.'" From Wool to Harriette Hart, Baltimore, 24 September 1862, Wool Papers, New York State Library, Albany, from Michael Burlingame, *Abraham Lincoln: A Life*, Unedited Manuscript from Knox College website, chap. 28.

well patrolled by Hampton's troopers. Crossing into Virginia then marching to Washington would have been impossible as there were no good fords across the Shenandoah River at Harpers Ferry. In short, once the three Rebel forces came within easy marching distance of Harpers Ferry, the garrison was doomed as its green troops, under an incompetent commander, had little hope of winning any battle in the field against veteran Confederate troops under excellent, experienced, commanders.

Maj. Gen. John Ellis Wool shown in dress uniform as brigadier general probably taken in 1861. Courtesy LOC.

Since Lee planned to use the Shenandoah Valley as his line of communication, it was critical that the Union garrison in Harpers Ferry, and those located in Martinsburg and Winchester, not impede his line. Even though Lee expected to meet most of his initial food and forage needs in Maryland, ammunition was critical, as were reinforcements. He designated Winchester as his major supply depot since he decided that this line in the Shenandoah Valley would be more secure than one to the east of the Blue Ridge Mountains. Lee knew that Winchester had fallen on 3 September and on 7 September he reported that he would make it his depot.[27] Thus Lee directed in Special Order No. 191 that about two-thirds of his army would march to chase off or reduce the Union garrisons which threatened his line of communication. Fortunately for Lee, Union Brig. Gen. Julius White, a political appointee, was in command at Winchester. On orders from Halleck on 2 September, who did not consult with or advise either Wool or Miles, White abandoned that city and with his 3,600-man brigade and fifteen pieces of artillery, headed north to Harpers Ferry, where he arrived late on the 3rd; his units included Companies H and I of the 1st Maryland Cavalry and the 7th Squadron Rhode Island Cavalry. A lieutenant of the Rebel cavalry unit of some 100 troopers harassing White at Winchester found much humor in White's hasty evacuation:

> Poor White! He magnified one company into three brigades, and in his great haste to get away, his imagination created intentions and embodied forms of things unknown to him. The guns were very lightly injured, and a large amount of property, consisting of guns, ammunition, clothing, forage, 175 to 200 barrels of bacon, and other valuable stores, fell into our hands. The good people of Winchester laid in their winter supply of meat and groceries. Colonel Mallory, in his testimony before the court-martial ordered to try General White for so hastily evacuating Winchester, says: "There were abandoned about 120,000 rations and about 190 to 200 barrels of bacon."[28]

In fact, there were so few Confederates around White at that time he could have easily held them at bay. But had White held out, Jackson would have shortly appeared on his doorstep and gobbled up his command. Wool was surprised at White's retreat order as Winchester was the key to the lower Shenandoah Valley and he believed it had been abandoned "without the approach or presence of an enemy."[29]

Wool wanted a regular army officer in command at Harpers Ferry, so on September 4th, he shunted White aside by ordering him to take command of the smaller Martinsburg garrison. White was incensed as he had to leave his brigade behind in Harpers Ferry and felt demeaned by Wool's action. White complained to Halleck on 6 September about this assignment by Wool and asked to have his command returned. Halleck replied that it was not he who had ordered him to Martinsburg, but on the 8th, supplemented his previous reply by wiring White that his arrival at Harpers Ferry put him under Wool's orders, ending the debate. Also at this time, McClellan was becoming more concerned with the fate of the Harpers Ferry garrison, so wisely sought to have Miles leave Harpers Ferry with his command and join the Army of the Potomac, but Halleck refused, thus sealing the fate of Miles and his Railroad Brigade.[30] McClellan had control of the Army of the Potomac in the field but did not have jurisdiction over Miles who remained under Wool, the Middle Department commander.

---

[27] *OR*, vol. 19, pt. 1, 139-140.

[28] Baylor, 68. White reported that he abandoned four, spiked 32-pound cannons, and destroyed 70,000 pounds of forage and 60,000 rations, *OR*, vol. 12, pt. 2, 766. A court of inquiry absolved White of any wrongdoing in his abandonment of Winchester and destruction of guns and supplies, *OR*, vol. 12, pt. 2, 803, 805.

[29] *OR*, vol. 19, pt. 2, 182.

[30] Harsh, *Flood*, 315; Sears, *Landscape*, 89; *OR*, vol. 19, pt. 2, 181, 198, 199, 218; *OR*, vol. 19, pt. 1, 43-44; *OR*, vol. 12, pt. 3, 800; L. Allison Wilmer, J.H. Jarrett, Geo. W.F. Vernon, *History and Roster of Maryland Volunteers, War of 1861-5*, vol. I (Baltimore, MD: Press of Guggenheimer, Weil & Co., 1989), reprint (Salem, MA: Higginson Book Company, n.d.), 702. White's arrival and

On 8 September, Brig. Gen. White, now at Martinsburg, apparently reported to Wool that Rebel infantry were advancing on him in heavy force, and requested instructions. White's garrison of some 2,500 men had no chance against a large force, so Wool allowed him to evacuate if necessary. Unfortunately, he was again instructed to move to Harpers Ferry to join Col. Dixon S. Miles's 12,500 men rather than to try to join McClellan, or fight his way east to Washington, or head west and then north to Pennsylvania. White departed by train on 11 September, arriving at Harpers Ferry, eighteen miles southeast of Martinsburg, on the 12th. Perhaps White, a political general, was not the best choice for Union command in the lower valley but events will show that Miles, a Regular Army career officer and Wool's pick, did little better at Harpers Ferry. By the time White arrived on the 12th, McLaws's troops had already exchanged fire with Union pickets on Maryland Heights. Although White, a brigadier general, outranked Miles who commanded at Harpers Ferry, White graciously deferred to the regular army officer based on Miles's longer experience at Harpers Ferry, as he had already planned its defenses, positioning guns and troops, and in any event, skirmishing had already begun, so it was not the time to quibble over rank.[31]

---

departure also given at 533, both one day later—4th and 5th. See Augustus W. Corliss, *History of the Seventh Squadron Rhode Island Cavalry* (Yarmouth, ME: "Old Times" Office, 1879), the commander of the Seventh Rhode Island Cavaliers, who writes that his unit arrived at 9 A.M. on 5 September, 2. His unit formed the rear guard of the retreat marching some 65 miles having been in the saddle for 30 hours, 10.

[31] *OR*, vol. 19, pt. 1, 520, 525, 566. Wool did testify that "I did not think he [Miles] had the capacity to embrace so large a command as he had there; but he appeared to be very zealous … Indeed, he was the only one I could place there, the only regular officer," *OR*, vol. 19, pt. 1, 792. Wool's hindsight was working well. It is curious that White so readily gave up command when he returned from Martinsburg given his earlier severe protests. Perhaps also aided by hindsight he realized that the Harpers Ferry garrison was in an untenable spot so did not wish to assume command in an impossible situation leading to a massacre or a surrender. Brig. Gen. Julius White was born at Cazenovia, New York, in 1816, and was apparently well-educated. He became a lawyer and in 1836 moved to Chicago then to Wisconsin where he served in the state legislature. He returned to Illinois where he was well established but when the war broke out, he was determined to help the Union. When Lincoln visited Evanston, Illinois, before the war, he was a guest in Julius White's house, who was then harbor master of Chicago and a friend of Lincoln. When Lincoln was elected president, he appointed White collector of the port of Chicago in the spring of 1861. But White soon resigned this office to raise a regiment, the 37th Illinois Volunteer Infantry Regiment, the "Frémont Rifles," and was mustered into service as its colonel on 18 July 1861. He was sent to Missouri where he led the regiment in the southwest Missouri campaign of John C. Frémont in late 1861 and in December he was placed in command of the 2nd Brigade, 3rd Division, Army of the Southwest, commanded by Maj. Gen. Samuel R. Curtis. He took an active part in the Battle of Pea Ridge on 7 March 1862 where his brigade of two Illinois regiments blunted the attack of the Confederates. He was wounded in the leg and on 8 March his troops participated in the final attack that defeated the Southern army. On 9 June 1862, he was promoted brigadier general of volunteers and ordered east. Maj. Gen. John Pope in his report wrote this: "Brig. Gen. Julius White, with one Brigade, was in the beginning of the campaign [Second Bull Run] placed in command at Winchester. He was selected for that position because I felt entire confidence in his courage and ability, and during the whole of his service there, he performed his duty with the utmost efficiency, and relieved me entirely from any apprehension concerning that region of country. He was withdrawn from his position by orders direct from Washington, and passed from under my command." In September 1862, White retreated to Harpers Ferry and then was sent to Martinsburg but again retreated when Jackson approached. He was taken prisoner on 15 September in Harpers Ferry. After being investigated by a court of inquiry, he was cleared of any wrongdoing and commended for his actions. After his exchange in January 1863, he was assigned to the Army of the Ohio, under Burnside. He took part in the East Tennessee campaign and returned east with the Ninth Corps serving with it until he resigned on 19 November 1864. On 13 March 1865, he was brevetted major general and after the war, was U.S. Minister to Argentina then returned to Evanston, Illinois, where he died in 1890; *Society of the Army of the Cumberland, Twenty-First Reunion, 1890* (Cincinnati, OH: Robert Clarke & Co. 1891), 271-272; Eicher, 565-566. White was apparently assigned to the Army of Virginia by Stanton but ordered to Harpers Ferry by Halleck. Wool then ordered White to Martinsburg and to turn over his troops to Miles. White complained to Halleck and was told that upon moving to Harpers Ferry he came under Wool's orders, *OR*, vol. 19, pt. 2, 198, 199, 218; John Pope, *The Campaign in Virginia, July and August 1862* (Milwaukee, WI: Jermain & Brightman, Book and Job Printers, 1863), 34-35. The Mountain Department and the Departments of the Rappahannock and of the Shenandoah merged into the Army of Virginia under Maj. Gen. John Pope on 26 June 1862, *OR*, vol. 12, pt. 1, 3.

Union Brig. Gen. Julius White. Courtesy LOC.

Close up of below photo showing boat ramp and buildings on the Point burned by Union troops in February 1862.

Harpers Ferry from the base of Maryland Heights showing the destroyed railroad and wagon bridge. Jackson destroyed the bridge in June 1861, so the armory buildings also have been burned although they appear unharmed from this distance. Since the pontoon bridge has not yet been built, the photograph was likely made by the early fall of 1861 as Ferry Lot district of hotels and stores burned in February 1862 are still standing. The B&O RR Company attempted to rebuild the bridge in August 1861; a flood the next month carried away most of the trestling. Early in March 1862, the B&O again attempted to repair the bridge, but another flood destroyed it on 22 April 1862. It was repaired and in service on 4 May, but on 4-7 June, another flood washed it away and it was not repaired again until 15 June. A temporary bridge was completed on 8 October 1862, D.E. Stinson, "The First Railroad Bridge at Harpers Ferry," Harpers Ferry National Historic Park, 10 March 1970, courtesy Western Maryland Room, Washington County Free Library. The pontoon bridge was destroyed by the retreating Rebels on 18 September 1862 and not rebuilt until about 25 September, *OR*, vol. 19, pt. 2, 333, 358. Note the C&O Canal in the lower part of the photograph appears to be dry and filled with debris. The pontoon bridge was anchored at the square-shaped break in the Potomac River wall seen in the upper right center at the arrow which was used as the boat landing for the armory. The river wall was built by the Baltimore & Ohio Railroad in 1840-1843, and extends 1,380 feet from the abutment of the site of the Armory boat landing, to the waste way above the Rolling Mill. It is about 15 feet tall above the low water level, four and one-half feet thick, with eight culverts for the tail races from the old workshops of the arsenal. "The wall was built 20 feet out from a similar river wall built by the Armory in 1837-39, which had also been constructed some 20 feet out from the previously existing shoreline and filled in behind. Portions of the second wall are still present. The railroad originally ran on an iron trestle above and behind this wall; it was moved inland to its present alignment in 1892-93," U.S. Dept. of the Interior, NPS, National Register of Historic Places Inventory, Harpers Ferry Historic District, 22 Jan. 1979, item 7, pg. 21. Photograph Courtesy LOC.

Looking at Harpers Ferry from the base of Maryland Heights probably from late 1861 as repairs to the burned B&O Railroad Bridge appear to be underway. The buildings on the Point to the left of the boat landing including the Wager House Hotel and the Potomac Restaurant are shown but were burned by Union troops in February 1862; the boat landing opening is clearly seen to the right center. Courtesy USAMHI.

Drawing from Maryland shore showing pontoon bridge in use as well as the railroad bridge; probably done after late 1862 as the railroad bridge and the armory buildings appear repaired and the buildings on the left of the boat ramp are missing. Note the bridge piers from the destroyed Shenandoah Bridge in the upper left and the temporary construction on the B&O Bridge. Courtesy USAMHI.

Union Col. Dixon Stansbury Miles, a veteran regular officer with much prewar combat experience, suffered from a tarnished reputation as he had been accused of drunkenness at First Bull Run, where he was in command of Brig Gen. Irvin McDowell's 5th Division. He was known as a heavy drinker, but due to illness before the battle, his doctor had prescribed brandy. He apparently felt the need of this medicine during the day of the battle, quarreling with his subordinates, who complained to Col. Israel B. Richardson. After McDowell ordered Richardson to relieve Miles, Miles argued with Richardson about the command change. Richardson charged him with drunkenness and a court of inquiry on 6 November 1861 found that Miles had been drunk, but that his illness was an extenuating circumstance, and did not believe that it would be in the best interest of the service to convene a court martial for him. In March 1862, he was ordered to the command of the Railroad Brigade to keep this senior, Regular Army officer, away from an important command. Unfortunately for the Union, the Army of Northern Virginia was about to seek out Miles, so the fate of some 13,000 men and the destiny of Lee's Maryland Campaign were now in the hands of an officer with a less than admirable early-war track record.[32] When Brig. Gen. White arrived at Harpers Ferry, he asked Miles "what his plans were. He [Miles] did not give me any very definite plan of operations. I think he said he had not any specific plan beyond the defense of Bolivar Heights and the bridges; that these positions being defended, Harper's Ferry was secure, and that his orders were to hold Harper's Ferry....I then suggested to him whether, in case we were attacked by a greatly superior force, he did not think it would be better to hold Maryland Heights at all hazards, even if we had to withdraw the entire force there....He also said that there was no water on Maryland Heights; that the objection to taking the entire force over there was that and the difficulty of getting up subsistence and artillery."[33]

---

[32] *OR*, vol. 2, 438-439; see Miles's report for his side of the events, 423-426, and for Richardson's 375-376. See Thomas P. Lowry, *Tarnished Eagles, The Courts-Martial of Fifty Colonels and Lieutenant Colonels* (Mechanicsburg, PA: Stackpole Books, 1997), 52-56, for a detailed account of Miles's hearing after First Bull Run; Hearn, 109-111; Dennis E. Frye, "Stonewall Attacks!—The Siege of Harpers Ferry," *Blue & Gray Magazine*, vol. V, issue 1, 12-13, hereafter "Stonewall Attacks;" Carman, Pierro, 101-102; Tischler, 20; Donald Caughey, "Crossed Sabers," http://crossedsabers.blogspot.com/search?updated-max=2007-09-17T19%3A14%3A00-07%3A00&max-results=7; Internet, accessed 12 December 2007; *OR*, vol. 19, pt. 1, 525. Tischler's book is the most comprehensive and detailed work done on the Harpers Ferry cavalry breakout and was relied upon heavily for this chapter. One officer who served under Miles in the west before the Civil War, Capt. Sigmund Elble, gave his opinion: "'Colonel Miles was a drunkard, a coward and a traitor, and if I had had the power I would have had the United States buttons taken from his coat,'" *National Tribune*, 3 March 1892, from Jack C. Mason, *Until Antietam: The Life and Letters of Major General Israel B. Richardson, U.S. Army* (Carbondale, IL: Southern Illinois University Press, 2009), 109, n. 74. Mason gives a good account of the interactions between Miles and Richardson at Second Bull Run ending up in Miles's Court of Inquiry, 96-109, which shows that Miles was clearly unable to exercise control of his command. Historian Mason opines that "the court of inquiry was deeply humbling to the old soldier, and from this point until his death, he would never drink another drop of liquor again," 109.

[33] *OR*, vol. 19, pt. 1, 716. Note that White in his *Battles and Leaders* article discusses an opposing view that had Miles retreated to Maryland Heights, the Rebels then could have crossed the Potomac into Maryland allowing them to rejoin Lee and concentrate against McClellan having bottled up Miles's troops on Maryland Heights, rather than requiring the Confederates to spend additional days taking Bolivar Heights, Julius White, "The Capitulation of Harper's Ferry," *Battles and Leaders*, 2:612-613. Certainly if Jackson were free to march up Pleasant Valley to Boonsboro on the 13th or 14th while leaving Walker and most of McLaws's men to hold Miles on the Heights, the battles at the South Mountain gaps might have had different outcomes. Or if Jackson had marched up the eastern side of South Mountain and confronted McClellan in Middletown Valley, allowing Lee to attack McClellan on his flank by returning from Hagerstown and across South Mountain, the outcome may have not resulted in a Union victory. But it is likely that Jackson would not have attacked McClellan as Lee wanted to reconcentrate his army at Hagerstown, so Jackson would probably held Pleasant Valley and Boonsboro, joining D.H. Hill until Lee decided what to do with Miles on Maryland Heights. Gen. Alpheus Williams who marched his corps to Maryland Heights and climbed it on 19 September found that there was no water but wrote on 23 September 1862 that "Two thousand men ought to have kept 20,000 at bay," Williams, 131-132. Miles was born in Maryland in 1804 and graduated from West Point in 1824 being posted to the 4th U.S. Infantry and then to the 7th U.S. Infantry serving there until 1847. He was promoted to captain in the 7th on 8 June 1836. He served in the Seminole War from 1839 to 1842 and throughout the Mexican War, in which he was brevetted major 9 May 1846 for gallant and distinguished conduct in the defense of Ft. Brown, Battle of Monterey, Texas, and lieutenant colonel 23

Col. Dixon Stansbury Miles at Harpers Ferry on steps of the Barbour House. Courtesy LOC

September 1846, for his actions at Monterrey and Veracruz; he was made major in the regular army in the 5th Infantry on 16 February 1847 and lieutenant colonel in the 3rd Infantry on 15 April 1851. He then served on the western frontier fighting Indians for several years in locations including Ft. Gibson and Ft. Washita, Indian Territory, Ft. Thorn and Ft. Fillmore, New Mexico, and was in command of the Southern column of the Gila Expedition 1 May to 26 July 1857, in combat 27 June 1857 on the Gila River north of Mount Turnbull, New Mexico. On 19 January 1859 he was appointed colonel commanding the 2nd Infantry at Ft. Kearny, Nebraska, and Ft. Leavenworth, Kansas, and although from Maryland, stayed with the Union after the war began in April 1861; Francis B. Heitman, *Historical Register and Dictionary of the United States Army, from Its Organization, September 29, 1789, to March 2, 1902,* 2 vols. (Washington, D.C.: Government Printing Office 1903, reprint, Urbana, IL: University of Illinois Press, 1965), 1:708; George T. Ness, Jr., *The Regular Army on the Eve of the Civil War,* Baltimore, MD: Toomey Press, 1990), 42.

Cavalry now in Harpers Ferry under Miles, in addition to the 575 troopers of the 12th Illinois Cavalry under Col. Arno Voss which had arrived with White from Martinsburg, were the 8th New York Cavalry, 614 troopers strong, under Col. Benjamin F. "Grimes" Davis; a squadron of the 1st Maryland Cavalry, Companies H and I, 123 troopers, commanded by Capt. Charles H. Russell of Company I; the 7th Squadron of Rhode Island Cavalry (a three-month unit), 146 troopers, under Maj. Augustus W. Corliss; a squadron of the 1st Maryland Potomac Home Brigade Cavalry (also known as "Cole's Cavalry"), 124 troopers, led by Maj. Henry A. Cole; and some 12 officers and men from the Loudoun Virginia Rangers commanded by Capt. Samuel C. Means. Miles thus had 1,594 troopers under his command to use for picketing, scouting, and, after the noose tightened, as dismounted riflemen.[34]

Capt. Samuel C. Means, in charge of the Loudoun Virginia Rangers, had a more personal interest in not being captured should Harpers Ferry be taken: there was a bounty of $5,000 placed on his dead body by Confederate authorities and he was going to attempt an escape with or without Miles's permission.[35] Means was a member of the pacifist Quaker sect but despite these beliefs, he, like some others of this church, took up arms for either the Union or Confederate side. His home town of Waterford, Virginia, a few miles northwest of Leesburg, had voted 220 to 31 against secession, in fact the northeastern part of Loudoun County with its many Quakers and other pacifist sects had voted in large majorities not to secede from the Union, thus this part of the county was in much turmoil throughout the war.[36] He was one of the Rangers' founders and the owner of the largest grist mill in Loudoun County at Waterford, and also owned a mercantile business in Point of Rocks, Maryland, just across the Potomac River on the main road leading north from Leesburg. He was employed as a station agent there for the B&O Railroad. Rebels failed to coerce him into their service so they confiscated his property after he fled to Maryland. "Forced by vigorous Confederate persecution to take refuge in Maryland, Means was summoned to Washington and offered a commission to raise a cavalry company of disaffected refugee Virginians."[37]

Samuel C. Means, from Briscoe Goodhart in his *History of the Independent Loudoun Virginia Rangers.*

---

[34] Harry Pfanz 1976 "Special History Report: Troop Movement Maps, September 12-14, 1862." Before the arrival of the cavalry units from Winchester and Martinsburg, Miles had the 8th New York Cavalry, Cole's Cavalry and Means's Loudoun Rangers employed as pickets under his command.

[35] Abraham Joseph Warner, *The Private Journal of Abraham Joseph Warner*, extracted by Herbert B. Enderton (San Diego, CA: n.p., 1973), 213; Stevan F. Meserve, *The Civil War in Loudoun County Virginia: A History of Hard Times* (Charleston, SC: The History Press, 2008), 52; Goodhart, 26, 55. See also Hearn, 113; Tischler, 77.

[36] Meserve, 20.

[37] Richard E. Crouch, "The Loudoun Rangers," The History of Loudoun County, Virginia,website. See also Meserve, 51-54.

The Rangers were a volunteer organization.

> [It] consisted of two companies of disaffected Virginians, all of whom were recruited in the German settlements northwest of Leesburg. Company A, at the outset, was commanded by Captain Daniel M. Keyes, of Lovettsville, who later resigned on account of wounds received in action. He was succeeded by Captain Samuel C. Means, of Waterford. Company B's commander was Captain James W. Grubb. The total enlistment of each company was 120 and 67, respectively. All the officers and privates were of either German, Quaker, or Scotch-Irish lineage, the first-named class predominating.
>
> The command was mustered into the Federal service at Lovettsville, the 20th day of June, 1862. Its historian, Briscoe Goodhart, a member of Company A, in his *History of the Loudoun* (Virginia) *Rangers*, has said that it "was an independent command, organized in obedience to a special order of the Honorable Edwin M. Stanton, Secretary of War, and was at first subject to his orders only, but subsequently merged into the Eighth Corps, commanded at that time by the venerable Major General John Ellis Wool. . . ."
>
> The "Rangers," as the name implies, were scouts and, in this highly useful capacity, served the enemies of their State with shameless ardor. But, as a body, they fought few engagements and none of a decisive nature.[38]

Means was sworn in as captain by Col. Miles at Harpers Ferry on 20 June 1862, with the Ranger's first headquarters at Waterford. Because most of the rest of Loudoun County was strongly Confederate, the best the Rangers could do was make periodic harassing raids and interdict Rebel supplies coming across the Potomac from Baltimore. The Rangers established semi-permanent camps on the Maryland side of the Potomac River from which they made constant forays into neighboring Virginia counties of Loudoun, Clarke, and Jefferson. Means maintained that his charter from the Secretary of War confined his area of operations to the sections of Maryland and Virginia bordering the Potomac between Harpers Ferry, and downriver to Great Falls, Virginia.

Means, while a brave leader and a staunch Union man, was always suspect. "He had no military background and had originally not wanted to take a stand. Means avoided joining the Union forces at first, he explained, because he had a brother serving in the Confederate Army and did not want to make trouble." More importantly, Means was always in trouble with his Union superiors. Much of this friction arose from the Rangers' attempts to preserve their status as an independent unit and serve only in their home territory. This was a fight the Rangers ultimately lost. Due to Army orders to consolidate his command with the 3rd West Virginia Cavalry, Means resigned his commission and left the service as of 13 April 1864. Means could not return home to Waterford while Mosby and other Rebel partisans were still active in the area, so he moved in with his daughter in Washington, D.C., and died a broken man in 1891, likely aided by his tippling. Means's drinking may have also affected his leadership during the war. A soldier from another unit described the commander of the Loudoun Rangers as a notorious drunk. Despite their Quaker upbringing, other Rangers had a rather "pronounced drinking problem," which did not help their martial abilities. Certainly many soldiers on both sides "liked to get into people's liquor when they could, but the Rangers had special opportunities. Operating on their own home ground, they tended to know exactly where alcohol could be found. They would pay visits to various local distilleries and cider mills in Loudoun County. More than once this inebriation compromised the Rangers' fighting ability and got them into trouble. And as a final reason for the Rangers' lack of success, Federal Army commanders never really trusted the loyal Virginians. They were not true to their own state, and many Union military men tended to regard a turncoat as beneath contempt. A man once turned might easily turn again. The fact that the Rangers were specially recruited under the direct command of the secretary

[38] James W. Head, *History and Comprehensive Description of Loudoun County Virginia* (n.p.: Park View Press, 1908), 151-152.

of war also rankled many Federal commanders." Thus the Rangers contributed only marginally to the overall Union war effort in and around Loudoun County, Virginia, but materially helped in the Harpers Ferry breakout, given their knowledge of the topography and homes around Washington County, and Frederick County, Maryland, and Virginia counties of Loudoun, Clarke and Jefferson.[39]

Like the Rangers, the 1st Maryland Cavalry, Companies H and I, were extremely helpful during the breakout. Company I was from Washington County, Maryland, the county in Maryland across the Potomac River north of Harpers Ferry which contained the entire route of the breakout before the column crossed into Pennsylvania. Company H was raised in Allegany County, the county to the west of Washington County. The two companies were raised in August 1861 to serve three years, and along with sister companies G and K, were attached to the 1st Virginia Union Cavalry from August 1861 to January 1862, when assigned to the 1st Maryland Cavalry. The commanding officer of the two companies, Capt. Charles H. Russell, was born in Stafford, Connecticut, and educated in Richmond, Virginia, at the Union Theological Seminary. He became pastor at the Williamsport, Maryland, Presbyterian Church until the outbreak of war when the synod split. He then left his pastorate and raised a company. He was formally enrolled on 5 August 1861 in the 1st Virginia Union Cavalry becoming the captain of his company which later became I Company of the 1st Maryland Cavalry in March 1862. His company of about 90 troopers was initially armed with carbines, pistols, and sabers, while they rode their personal horses. Both companies gave good service in late 1861 and early 1862 in the lower Shenandoah Valley, notably at Alpine Station, just across the Potomac River in Virginia near Hancock, Maryland, and Bath (now Berkeley Springs), Virginia, a few miles to the south. Company H pursued Jackson up the valley while Company I was at Harpers Ferry. Both companies remained in the valley while their regiment fought Lee's army at engagements to the east at Cedar Mountain, Second Bull Run, and Chantilly. The two companies then were involved in the evacuation of Union forces from Winchester on 2 September 1862, and skirmishes near Frederick, Maryland, on 6 September, and Boonsboro on 7 and 10 September.[40]

The College Cavaliers, 7th Squadron Rhode Island Cavalry, unlike their Maryland and Virginia comrades, were in unfamiliar territory. The unit was made up of two companies, Company A under Capt. Christopher Vaughn, which was composed of men mainly from Providence, Rhode Island, from the working classes which included many foreigners. Company B, organized by Sanford S. Burr of Dartmouth College who became its captain, was composed primarily of some 40 students of Dartmouth in New Hampshire, and 20 cadets from Norwich University in Vermont. They became known as the "College Cavaliers" due to the predominance of college students, but despite the disparity in social class, they got along well with the working-class men in Company A. The formation of the Cavaliers was not easy. The ardor of Burr's entreaties to form a student company was considerably dampened by the president and faculty of Dartmouth, and by many students' parents, so Burr appealed for assistance to the rival college across the river, Norwich University. The president and faculty of that military school were only too happy to encourage their cadets to go to war, so a command compromise was reached giving the captaincy of the company to Dartmouth, and the first and second lieutenants and first sergeant to Norwich. The students, along with some graduates, friends from other colleges like Bowdoin and Amherst, and acquaintances, volunteered their services to Rhode Island Gov. William Sprague for three months service, after being turned down by the governors of New Hampshire, Massachusetts, and Maine. The more martial Gov. Sprague was noted for his enthusiastic support of Lincoln's call for volunteers and had actually accompanied his Rhode Island units to the Battle of First Bull Run where, as

---

[39] Crouch.
[40] Tischler, 16; Wilmer, 701-702; Dyer, 3:1228.

he was riding his white horse into battle, had it shot out from under him as was the next horse he mounted.[41]

The students' company arrived in Providence on 19 June 1862, was fed a generous lunch of cheese, crackers and coffee, and then was sworn into state service, followed by uniform outfitting. Augustus Whittemore Corliss initially became their de facto commander. Originally from Maine, he had pre-war militia service as a Dragoon, so provided needed martial experience for his young charges. After moving to Waltham, Massachusetts, he was a lieutenant in the 1st Massachusetts Cavalry in 1861, and served in Burnside's North Carolina Expedition. In early 1862, as Adjutant of the 1st Rhode Island Cavalry, he helped form and train the 7th Squadron Rhode Island Cavalry. He drilled the company, being promoted to first lieutenant of Company A, and after the 7th Squadron was mustered into Federal service, the twenty-six-year old was put in command of both companies as major, effective 24 June 1862; he was mustered in on 3 July 1862.[42]

Augustus Whittemore Corliss, courtesy Nicholas Picerno.

[41] Thomas M. Aldrich, *The History of Battery A, First Regiment Rhode Island Light Artillery, In the War to Preserve the Union 1861-1865* (Providence, RI: Snow & Farnham, Printers, 1904), 20-21. William A. Ellis, ed., *Norwich University 1819-1911: Her History, Her Graduates, Her Roll of Honor* (Montpelier, VT: The Capital City Press, 1911), 410. Norwich men, all in Company B, are listed by Robert G. Poirier, *"By the Blood of Our Alumni," Norwich University Citizen Soldiers in the Army of the Potomac* (Mason City, IA: Savas Publishing Company, 1999), George A. Alvord, 1st Sgt. Co. B; Charles E. Bush, Sgt. Major; Theodore H. Kellogg 1st Lt. Co. B; Charles F. Tillinghast 2nd Lt. and adjutant; Pvt. Arthur W. Coombs died of disease on active service, Cpl. Douglas Lee died of disease, 290-322 inter alia. The remainder is as follows: George A. Bailey; Albert F. Bayard; William S. Dewey; William S. Goodwin; Charles M. Gragg; Addison T. Hastings; Walter S. Hazelton; Wallace A. King; Arthur P. Morey; Edward H. Noyes; Alfred L. Papanti; James V. Parker; Henry M. Phillips; Charles W. Smith; Ellis P. Walcott; Francis H. Walcott; and Arthur W. White. In the squadron, Norwich cadets were assigned as adjutant and sergeant major, Poirier, 158. He also shows 85 students in the company 23 from Norwich.
[42] Corliss, 1, 8-9; S. B. Pettengill, *The College Cavaliers: A Sketch of the Service of A Company of College Students in the Union Army in 1862* (Chicago: H. McAllaster & Co., 1883; reprint, Salem, MA: Higginson Book Company, n.d.), 15, 22-23. Colleges represented in Company B: Dartmouth College, 35; Norwich University: 23; Bowdoin College, 4; Union College, 4; Williams College, 1; Amherst College, 1; unknown or no college: 17; total 85; Augustus D. Ayling, *Revised Register of the Soldiers and Sailors of New Hampshire in the War of the Rebellion 1981-1865* (Concord, NH: Ira C. Evans, Public Printer, 1895), 1089-1091, 1095. In addition, William S. Dewey and George A. Bailey of Norwich University along with John S. Eaton joined and recruited 10 men from Woodstock, Vermont. Finally, two men from other Vermont towns along with one from Massachusetts and four from New Hampshire were added, Ellis, 411.

On 28 June, the 7th Squadron left for Washington, D.C., arriving two days later, pitching their tents about a mile north of the Capitol. After drawing their horses which accompanied them on their journey from Rhode Island, their training began in earnest. The aspiring troopers and their equine comrades began their acquaintanceships with mutual trepidation as most of the horses were unbroken, and the troopers unfamiliar with riding. The squadron was mustered into Federal service on 3 July with the muster rolls dated 24 June. An unexpected but welcomed event was a bounty of $15 paid to each enlisted trooper. During the next two weeks, they were able to learn the fundamentals of cavalry drill while becoming better acquainted with their mounts. The Burnside carbines they had been issued in Providence were exchanged for Colt army pistols, perhaps the carbines being sent to more experienced volunteer units, or regular cavalry. They broke camp on 19 July and marched to Alexandria, Virginia, where they joined the command of Brig. Gen. Samuel D. Sturgis in the Military District of Washington. Drilling continued until 27 July when they were moved back to Washington and loaded onto freight cars, arriving in Winchester two days later, courtesy of the B&O and the rickety W& P. White, a friend of Lincoln, was placed in command of Winchester on 26 July 1862 by Pope and had accompanied the Cavaliers on their train journey to Winchester from Washington. There, they joined White's brigade which, on 31 July numbered 3,600 men, and consisted of the 32nd Ohio Infantry under Col. Thomas H. Ford; the 60th Ohio Infantry under Col. William H. Trimble; the 39th New York Infantry under Col. Frederick G. d'Utassy; the 9th Vermont Infantry under Col. George J. Stannard, and 15 guns under Capt. Silas F. Rigby, commanding both the 1st Independent Indiana Battery, and Capt. Benjamin F. Potts's Ohio Battery. On 20 August, Capt. Charles H. Russell joined, adding his two companies of cavalry from the 1st Maryland.

The brigade's assignment was to watch the Blue Ridge passes and the valley roads, while controlling guerilla activity. The tired Ocean State troopers and equally fatigued mounts began patrolling the next day after their arrival, scouting south toward Front Royal. When not scouting or escorting wagon trains, the squadron was on picket duty during August, continuing to learn the ways of cavalrymen and occasionally engaging the enemy; on one scout they took two prisoners, five horses and thirty-two cattle. Two troopers out on a personal foraging mission were captured and not recovered despite a diligent pursuit. They were freed from Libby Prison in Richmond in late September 1862, after being exchanged. One notable Rebel capture was the famed spy, Belle Boyd, on 26 August. She was initially caught by a Federal scout, Thomas Noakes, from Martinsburg, Boyd's hometown; he would later prove extremely helpful during the escape from Harpers Ferry. Then on 2 September after returning from a scouting mission on which they captured four prisoners, the 7th Squadron troopers found their camp deserted and all their stores and tents burned by White's order, as the Winchester garrison had been ordered to Harpers Ferry. The 7th Squadron served as the column's rear guard on the march north to supposed safety.

The troopers arrived at Harpers Ferry the next day, 3 September, having been in the saddle 30 hours, marching 65 miles. They camped on Bolivar Heights, spending a dreary evening as most of their stores were lost in Winchester. They had their horses shod and tried to rest. On 5 September, White left for Martinsburg, but without the 7th Squadron and the 1st Maryland Cavalry. These units rode across the pontoon bridge to Maryland Heights and reported to Col. Thomas H. Ford, who commanded the 3rd Brigade of Miles's troops, to serve him as pickets and scouts. They were able to see Lee's columns crossing the Potomac into Maryland downriver, and two intrepid college troopers even went on a private scout up Middletown Valley, and from Catoctin heights viewed Gen. Lee's camps around Frederick. On the 13th, while heavy skirmishing was beginning on Maryland Heights, the 7th Squadron was ordered to return to Bolivar Heights, and witnessed the abandonment of Maryland Heights. On the 14th, they endured shelling primarily from Loudoun Heights, and that evening, joined the rest of the escape column in its flight from Harpers Ferry.[43]

Only two of the cavalry officer commanders at Harpers Ferry had combat experience: Maj. Henry A. Cole, commanding the 1st Maryland Potomac Home Brigade Cavalry, and Col. Benjamin F. "Grimes" Davis, commanding the 8th New York Cavalry. Cole had practical experience battling partisan ranger units and Confederate cavalry for several months as a company, then battalion commander. He was a native of Frederick, Maryland, in command of the four-company battalion, the 1st Maryland Potomac Home Brigade Cavalry, known as "Cole's Cavalry." He had been first commissioned Captain of Company A on 10 August 1861, after his election by his men. The four companies, A, B, C, and D, operated independently for the first year. The unit was formed under authority of Secretary of War Simon Cameron on 19 July 1861 and approved by Lincoln to protect the C&O Canal and loyal citizens on both sides of the Potomac River. While formed to protect Union interests near the Potomac, they also served in Pennsylvania. Cole was promoted major on 1 August 1862 when Companies A, C, and D first began operating together along the upper Potomac, while Company B, originally formed in Cumberland, Maryland, was on detached service in the mountains of western Virginia and western Maryland, not rejoining the battalion until the winter of 1862 at Harpers Ferry. The battalion became popularly known as "Cole's Cavalry" from the time he took command. As the companies were made up of local men, mainly farmers, most of whom brought their own horses, they were well aware of the topography of the area and the loyalty of its citizens. They were well-armed with Sharps carbines along with Savage and Colt pistols. In 1864 when the command was reorganized into a regiment, Cole became its colonel.

The companies were refitted and began service by patrolling the area from Frederick to Cumberland. Companies A, C and D were involved in the action with Maj. Gen. Stonewall Jackson's forces at Hancock, Maryland, in January 1862. In March 1862, Capt. Cole with Company A went on a reconnaissance to Bunker Hill, Virginia, seeking enemy troops. They came upon Ashby's Cavalry and charged them although Cole was outnumbered. With help from Union infantry, Cole pushed Ashby back, but Cole lost three casualties and had his horse shot out from under him. Later in March, Cole's company led an advance of Brig. Gen. Alpheus S. Williams' troops upon Stephenson's Station, about five miles north of Winchester. Ashby again fell back and Cole's troopers rode into Winchester being the first Union troops to occupy that staunchly Confederate town. Cole also was instrumental in scouting for Gen. Banks who had assumed command at Winchester. Cole was skirmishing with Ashby in late March at Kernstown before Jackson was defeated there on 23 March 1862, and then followed Jackson's retreat up the valley.[44] When Jackson returned and routed Banks from Winchester on 25 May 1862, Cole formed Banks's rear guard; Companies A and C went to Harpers Ferry later reuniting with Company D, joining Col. Miles's Railroad Brigade. Cole's troopers again led the advance following Jackson as he retreated up the valley. The three companies spent June and July 1862 scouting in northern Virginia around the Blue Ridge Mountains. Their picket line linked Key's Ferry on the Shenandoah River just south of Harpers Ferry, to Smithfield (Middleway) on the east side of Opequon Creek, southwest of Charles Town, Virginia, where there was a bridge. Middleway was located at the intersection of the Shepherdstown-Berryville Road and the Charles Town Turnpike about 15 miles from Harpers Ferry and six miles west of Charles Town. Cole and his three-company command kept busy with Confederate partisans such as Harry W. Gilmor and Elijah White always presenting a threat to Unionists in the area. In fact, 17 of Coles's troopers were captured at Smithfield on 23 August, after a successful ruse in which the commanding officer of Coles's detachment at Smithfield, Lt. Robert H. Milling, along with a sergeant and several men, were lured away

[43] Ayling, 1090-1092; Corliss, 8-11; Tischler, 13; Carman, Pierro, 102; *OR*, vol. 51, pt. 1, 728. Miles's brigade structure was formed on 5 September 1862; Ford was the commander of the 32nd Ohio, *OR*, vol. 19, pt. 1, 533.
[44] Christopher A. Newcomer, *Cole's Cavalry or Three Years in the Saddle in the Shenandoah Valley* (Baltimore, MD: Cushing & Company, 1895), 11-21, 33, 46; Tischler, 2-3; Wilmer, 655-656; Engelbrecht, 912; Gary, 151-152.

by a winsome Confederate damsel, and the remainder of the troopers were taken while in their camp and sent to Richmond's Belle Isle prison camp. One of their Rebel captors, Lt. George Baylor, later defended the Union lieutenant in charge who was dismissed from the service for his supposed negligence, stating that it was not his fault.[45]

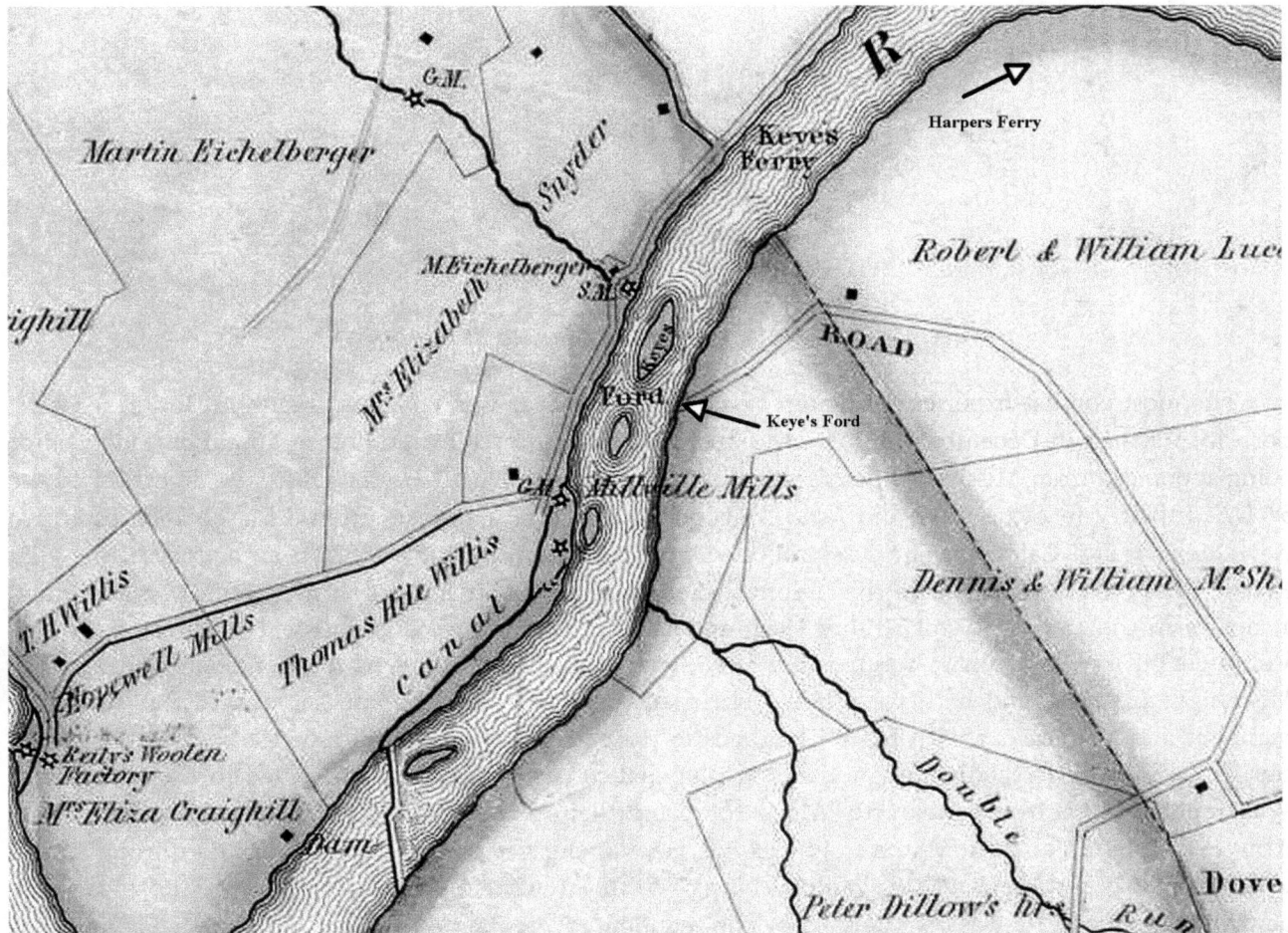

Map showing the Shenandoah River with Key's Ford and Ferry upstream from Harpers Ferry--Harpers Ferry is downstream to the right. Key's Ford was widely used by both sides during the war. The ford was less than six river miles from Harpers Ferry. 1852 Map of Jefferson County, Virginia by S. Howell Brown from actual survey with the farm limits. Oriented with north at upper right about 45 degrees. Courtesy LOC.

[45] *OR*, vol.19, pt. 2, 532; Tischler, 4; Newcomer, 25-29; George Baylor, *Bull Run to Bull Run or Four Years in the Army of Northern Virginia* (Richmond, VA: B.F. Johnson Publishing Company, 1900), 60-61, 66. Smithfield is now known as Middleway, West Virginia, with several period buildings still standing. An 1847 map of Berkeley County by John Kearfott shows a bridge across the Opequon just south of Mill Creek near Smithfield as does an 1852 map by S. Howell Brown so there was likely a bridge there in September 1862 as there is no record of its destruction. Col. Miles recommended Milling's dismissal which was accepted, *OR*, vol. 12, pt. 2, 764-765. Key's also known as Keys', Keyes, Keye's, and Keyes'.

Henry A. Cole shown here as a colonel; Newcomer facing page 116.

The most combat-experienced Union cavalry officer by far was Benjamin Franklin "Grimes" Davis. Born in Alabama in December 1831, he was an 1854 graduate of West Point, as Captain of Cadets, after being appointed from Mississippi; Jeb Stuart was one of his classmates. He served first as an officer in the 5th U.S. Infantry in Texas, then in the 1st Dragoons as a second lieutenant from 3 March 1855 in Texas, New Mexico, and California; he was wounded by Apaches on 27 June 1857 in an action on the Gila River. He elected to remain with the Union despite his southern birth and upbringing and was appointed a captain in the 1st Cavalry on 30 July 1861, and then a lieutenant colonel in the 1st California Cavalry Volunteers from 19 August to 1 November 1861. Two of his brothers served the Confederacy in the 11th Mississippi Infantry, and both were killed during the war. He chose not to serve with the California regiment and shipped out with his 1st Dragoons to the east coast, and on 30 July 1861 was promoted to captain, when the Dragoons designation was changed to the 1st Cavalry. He served in the defenses of Washington, D. C., from January to March 1862, and then in the Virginia Peninsular Campaign in the Army of the Potomac from March to June, 1862. He was engaged in the Siege of Yorktown from 5 April to 4 May 1862, and the Battle of Williamsburg, 4-5 May 1862. He and his company of the 1st Cavalry performed well and he was commended by the regimental commander, Lt. Col. William N. Grier. Davis was in command of a squadron made up of his company and Company I, and was assigned to cover the retreat of part of the 3rd Artillery, during which he engaged enemy cavalry. Grier wrote that "Captain Davis …charged the enemy, repulsing them handsomely and driving them back in confusion, protecting the battery and the wounded. In this charge a regimental standard, with the coat of arms of Virginia, was captured and a captain taken prisoner. The squadron was again charged by the enemy, who were again repulsed, and retired to the other side of the woods, where they remained."[46] Brig. Gen. Cooke echoed Grier describing the fight: "Colonel Grier then retired with his last squadron at a walk, which also assisted off the wounded, and so it was charged in the narrow road by a superior force of the enemy's cavalry. Captain Davis, its commander, wheeling about by fours, met and with the greatest gallantry repulsed them. The charge was repeated, and this brave squadron, Baker its second captain, again drove them, capturing a regimental standard and taking a captain prisoner."[47] Brig. Gen. George Stoneman, Chief of Cavalry, also wrote of the good conduct of Davis, Grier, Sanders, Cooke, and Capt. Gibson in this

---

[46] *OR*, vol. 11, pt. 1, 429-430; biography of Davis from Buford Boys website now on Internet Archive, photocopy obtained courtesy Harpers Ferry Research Library. "Grimes" or "Old Grimes" was likely a sobriquet given him at West Point as he may have been from near a locale in Mississippi called "Grimes;" no source has been found for this nickname. The historic area of Grimes was east of Tupelo, Mississippi. There is also a town in Alabama named Grimes.
[47] *OR*, vol. 11, pt. 1, 428.

fight.[48] The captain of Company C of the 3rd Artillery wrote that "I am much indebted to Capt. B.F. Davis and his squadron of the First Cavalry for their support and assistance under a severe fire concentrated upon them, and only regret that it was unavailing."[49] Based on his good service, he was appointed colonel of the 8th N.Y. Cavalry Volunteers on 11 July to take effect from 25 June 1862. He rode to Relay House, Maryland, to take command on 14 July, beginning his personal attention to their readiness for combat. Recommended by McClellan, he was appointed brevet major in the Regular Army to date from 15 September 1862 for "meritorious services in the withdrawal of the cavalry force from Harper's Ferry, Va., at the surrender of that place."[50] Later in September, he was in command of the 5th Brigade of cavalry which consisted of the 8th New York Cavalry and the 3rd Pennsylvania. He was in the Rappahannock Campaign at Belle Plain, Virginia, and vicinity in December 1862 to January 1863, and guarding the Rappahannock in June. He was engaged in several skirmishes and in combat at Beverly Ford 9 June 1863 where he was killed at age 31, in command of the 1st Brigade of cavalry under Brig Gen. John Buford. The 31-year-old Davis was buried at West Point, where Buford would join him in repose the following December.[51]

He was known in his regiment for his discipline, perhaps not surprising as he was a veteran regular army officer, and had seen combat on the frontier as well as in Virginia. The regimental historian wrote that "He was a military man clear through, the right man in the right place. He was a strict disciplinarian, and brought the regiment down under the regular army regulations. Some of the boys thought he was too severe with them. They said that no man could bring a volunteer regiment under regular army style with success."[52] But without Davis, the unruly 8th New York Cavalry would not have become one of the best mounted units in the Army of the Potomac.

Benjamin Franklin "Grimes" Davis. Courtesy USAMHI.

---

[48] *OR*, vol. 11, pt. 1, 425.
[49] Ibid., 432.
[50] Tischler, 77; Caughey. None of the units had been in existence for more than ten months. McClellan's recommendation is found in *OR*, vol. 51, pt. 1, 861. See also Murfin, 147-154. His brevet to major was for the regular army.
[51] Tischler 26-28; George W. Cullum, *Biographical Register of the Officers and Graduates of the U.S. Military Academy at West Point, N.Y. from Its Establishment, in 1802, to 1890* (Boston and New York: Houghton, Mifflin and Company, 1891), 595; Buford Boys biography. Col. Gamble, the commander of the 1st Brigade was on medical leave due to a Malvern Hill wound.
[52] Henry Norton, *Deeds of Daring or History of the Eighth N. Y. Volunteer Cavalry* (Norwich, NY: Chenango Telegraph Printing House, 1889, reprint Salem, MA: Higginson Book Company, 1998), 24.

The 8th New York Cavalry which he commanded was organized at Rochester, New York, on 28 November 1861. It had 10 companies of 886 men mustered into United States service for three years. Under the command of Col. Samuel J. Crooks, it was known as the Rochester Regiment, serving first in the defenses of Washington at Camp Seldon, but it had not been issued horses. Col. Crooks resigned under pressure and his second in command, Lt. Col. Charles R. Babbitt, took over. Unfortunately, Babbitt was a poor disciplinarian; morale suffered as they and their sister regiment, the 9th New York Cavalry had not received horses and the 9th was even requested to supply men for an artillery unit. The 8th was split from the 9th perhaps to separate the disaffected units; the 8th joined with the 1st Vermont Cavalry until 5 April when the Vermonters left to serve with Banks. The 8th then served at various points in Maryland starting at Edward's Ferry doing picket duty of the C&O Canal from Washington to Harpers Ferry; the regiment then moved to Muddy Branch, Poolesville, Harpers Ferry and Charles Town, Virginia, then Cameron's Station on the W&P Railroad until 24 May, when the regiment went to Winchester. During May, the regiment was divided into two battalions, one under Lt. Col. Babbitt, and the second under Maj. William Markell. Markell's battalion participated in the Battle of Winchester on 25 May 1862, still dismounted, and using their old, unreliable, and dangerous, Hall's carbines, suffering 31 casualties, most captured by Stonewall Jackson's troops. As they retreated, some southern sympathizers in Winchester fired at them from doors and windows. The regiment then fell back to Williamsport, Maryland, remaining there until 3 June, when it left for Harpers Ferry, arriving there the next day.[53]

After working on fortifications on Maryland Heights and guarding the Naval Battery of six guns commanded by Capt. Ulric Dahlgren, the regiment on 23 June 1862 was sent to Relay House in Maryland, to draw horses and equipment. While at Harpers Ferry, Col. Miles wanted to issue the regiment Springfield rifles to replace the virtually unserviceable Hall's carbines with the "promise" that if the regiment complied, they would be eventually be mounted and equipped as cavalrymen. While they agreed to act temporarily as infantrymen, they refused to submit to infantry drill. Miles reported on 8 June that "this regiment is in a disorganized and mutinous condition and cannot be relied on, being dissatisfied at not being mounted and being armed as infantry (at present)" and then again on 22 June that "The Eighth New York Cavalry ordered to be mounted is mutinous and disorganized. The regiment refuses to go anywhere until mounted as cavalry. General Wool ordered me to send it to Baltimore. It is no use here or elsewhere until disciplined."[54] Wool visited Harpers Ferry and reported on 15 June that Col. Miles "has 600 cavalry—New York Volunteers—without arms or horses. These men will do no work, nor, as the colonel says, anything else, not having horses nor arms." But on 17 June, Wool asked Secretary of War Stanton: "Can you not furnish me with horses for some 600 of the Eighth New York Cavalry at Harper's Ferry?"[55] Stanton may have been concerned about the mounting of the 8th as well as the 9th New York Cavalry as he had been visited by a delegation of important New Yorkers. A new commanding officer for the "undisciplined" 8th was also needed. Three officers from the 8th, Maj. Markell and Captains Edmund M. Pope and George H. Barry, visited Brig. Gen. George Stoneman in Washington. They asked his advice for regimental commander as he was recently returned from the Peninsula where he was a cavalry commander. He suggested Capt. Benjamin F. Davis who was fortuitously then at Willard's Hotel recovering from illness. Davis was appointed colonel of the 8th on 11 July 1862 to take rank from 25 June. The regiment received their new commanding officer at Relay House on 14 July and

[53] *OR*, vol. 12, pt. 1, 584-585.

[54] *OR*, vol. 51, pt. 1, 665, 690. Note that the 15th Pennsylvania Cavalry had some units refuse muskets as muskets were hallmarks of infantry which cavalrymen were loath to accept, "As we enlisted as cavalry, the men were much opposed to taking muskets and one company refused altogether. This made a very heavy and cumbersome load as we had besides to carry a heavy sabre and navy revolvers;" at this time this trooper was without a mount, *Column South with the 15th Pennsylvania Cavalry from Antietam to the Capture of Jefferson Davis*, compiled by Suzanne Colton Wilson (Flagstaff, AZ: J. F. Colton & Co., 1960), 17.

[55] *OR*, vol. 12, pt. 3, 394, 403.

their lives as true cavalry troopers began. The regiment finally received all of its horses by 20 July and began serious training under Col. Davis, drilling every day until 29 August, becoming well-trained, especially in saber drill. One trooper, Capt. Thomas Bell of Company F, wrote that Davis wanted his men to be "equal in every respect to the U.S. Cavalry, which was his frequent boast." Officers and men were both subject to drill four hours a day and the officers had two more hours at night in the adjutant's tent, studying cavalry tactics. While the regiment was training at Relay House, some 300 new recruits were added bringing the total on hand to over 1,000 troopers. After Davis took command, two captains resigned and another was dismissed. Officers as well as men learned their trade under his firm, regular army discipline. All this effort stood them well as Gen. Wool on 28 August ordered the regiment to Harpers Ferry. They returned to their old post there courtesy of the B&O Railroad arriving the next day.[56]

Col. Miles welcomed the now fully-equipped and better-trained 8th New York Cavalry with a lengthy, detailed, order to Col. Davis dated 31 August. He ordered Davis and his regiment to Summit Point, Virginia, on the W&P Railroad, which allowed Miles to supply Davis's regiment from Harpers Ferry. From Summit Point, Davis could protect Berryville, Winchester, Snicker's Ferry, and the other ferries and fords on the Shenandoah River. Miles provided information about the Rebel cavalry opposing Davis, the 12th Virginia Cavalry, giving the location of its units and its probable objectives. Davis was advised that the 12th Virginia had seven companies of about 60 men each, was headquartered at Middletown, Virginia, about seven miles south of Winchester, and had the advantage of the Union cavalry because the Rebels had "fleeter horses, light equipments, and knowledge of the by-roads of the country." Davis was to break up the 12th Virginia as well as protect the W&P Railroad even though only one train was running on it; the railroad must be allowed to continue supplying the Union command at Winchester. He was also to observe happenings at Winchester and keep Miles informed. If attacked by superior forces, Davis would "operate in its front or flank, preserving your communication with this place [Harpers Ferry], on which you will fall back, if not cut off; in that case you will retreat on Martinsburg, cross at Shepherdstown, and join my forces down the left bank [Maryland side] of the Potomac. I shall order four companies of the Twelfth Illinois Cavalry now at Martinsburg to take post at Smithfield [on the Shenandoah where a ford was located] six miles north of you with orders to communicate with you, and Captain Cole's with Means's cavalry (four companies) to operate in Loudoun County from Hillsborough, Leesburg, to Snicker's Ferry." On the same day, Miles sent an order to Capt. Cole apprising him of Davis and telling him to drive the small force of cavalry from Leesburg and to fall back on Point of Rocks or Berlin if pressed. Coles Cavalry, along with Means, were defeated in a battle near Leesburg on 2 September by Col. Munford and his 2nd Virginia Cavalry, not the small force as described by Miles.[57]

The leader of the escape column, Col. Arno Voss, commanding the 12th Illinois Cavalry, was a politician, with no combat experience, and his executive officer, Lt. Col. Hasbrouck Davis, was a lawyer before the war, and first saw combat two weeks prior to the escape from Harpers Ferry. Voss was born in Prussia in 1821 and arrived in Chicago from Ohio in 1848, joining the largest ethnic group in that city. He became the editor of the Illinois *Staats-Zeitung*, a German-language newspaper, a leading Democrat,

[56] Norton, 11-13, 17-20, 23-25; Tischler, 24-28; Phisterer, *New York in the War of the Rebellion*, 1:872-873; Dyer, 3:1376; *OR*, vol. 51, pt. 1, 768; Thomas Bell, *At Harper's Ferry, VA., September 14, 1862. How the Cavalry Escaped Out of the Toils* (n.p., n.d.), 6-15. It is impossible to square Bell's total of over 1,000 troopers with reliable research showing that the 8th New York Cavalry had 614 men during the siege of Harpers Ferry.

[57] *OR*, vol. 51, pt. 1, 772-773. Miles reported on 2 September the Leesburg battle: "Captain Cole has just arrived [at Harpers Ferry]. Reports he was attacked by at least 800 cavalry on the road to Point of Rocks." After being attacked front and rear, he reported that Capt. Means and his company ran and probably escaped to the mountains. Cole said 60 escaped and returned while others were still straggling in at Point of Rocks, *OR*, vol. 12, pt. 2, 805. See Chapter 4 for discussion of this fight.

and participated in the Joliet Convention in 1850 as a delegate from Cook County. He began practicing law in 1852 and in 1853 acted as the city's attorney. Not a loyal Republican, "Lincoln referred to him as 'a damned irreconcilable democrat' during one of his famous debates with Stephen Douglas." Voss enrolled for military service on 18 November 1861 for three years at age 42, was mustered in on 1 February 1862, and was commissioned as a colonel commanding a cavalry regiment. He was not extremely popular perhaps due to his political beliefs. Before leaving for the front, he was in charge of Camp Douglas in Chicago, Illinois, preparing it for receiving prisoners.[58] Voss was apparently not a good cavalry commander as both Brig. Gen. John Buford and Maj. Gen. Alfred Pleasonton, on 8 August 1863, observed that he was incompetent as either a regimental or brigade-level commander. The letter from the assistant adjutant general of the Army of the Potomac dated 9 August 1863 to Pleasonton on behalf of the commanding general, approved Buford's relief of Voss, and that Voss remain unassigned. The letter also directed Pleasonton to convene a board to inquire into the capacity and qualifications of Colonel Voss under the 10th dictum of the Act of July 22 1861. Voss resigned from the service on 11 August 1863 apparently to avoid being dismissed.[59]

The 12th Illinois Cavalry Voss commanded was mustered into service on 24 February 1862, 760 strong, as a two-battalion regiment of eight companies, one of which, Company I, was the former McClellan Dragoons, organized at Chicago in October 1861. They began training at Camp Douglas near Chicago with the added duty of guarding several thousand prisoners there which allowed little time for drill. They were soon transferred to Camp Butler near Springfield, Illinois, a poorly-prepared post, next to a prisoner-of-war camp. Because they had not received weapons or horses when they first arrived, they drilled as infantry usually four hours a day aided by the Mexican War veteran, Maj. John Fonda. As spring approached, they began receiving horses, equipment, and arms, including sabers, carbines, and revolvers. The new troopers met their mounts with the usual trepidation as the horses seemed mostly unbroken, but fortunately no one was killed during training. The boring routine of training and guarding prisoners sapped the troopers' morale, so they were happy to be ordered on 24 June 1862 to the town of Martinsburg, Virginia, in the Northern Shenandoah Valley. The seven companies now totaled some 700 sabers.[60] They finally arrived at Camp Wool, near Martinsburg, close to the Valley Pike, on 7 July, and

---

[58] Tischler, 20; Abraham Lincoln, *Political Debates Between Lincoln and Douglas* (Cleveland: Burrows Bros. Co., 1897), 229; Blackwell, 13.

[59] Tischler, 158-159; photocopy of letter courtesy of Harpers Ferry Research Library Voss folder; original in National Archives in Voss's military service record. In his third debate with Stephen Douglas in Jonesboro, Illinois, September 15, 1858, Lincoln mentioned that Douglas's fellow Democrats had said that the policy of the framers of the Constitution was to prevent the expansion of slavery beginning with the Northwest Ordinance of 1787. Lincoln used the following to prove the point: "So again, in that same race of 1850, there was a Congressional Convention assembled at Joliet, and it nominated R.S. Molony for Congress, and unanimously adopted the following resolution: 'Resolved, That we are uncompromisingly opposed to the extension of slavery; and while we would not make such opposition a ground of interference with the interests of the States where it exists, yet we moderately but firmly insist that it is the duty of Congress to oppose its extension into Territory now free, by all means compatible with the obligations of the Constitution, and with good faith to our sister States; that these principles were recognized by the Ordinance of 1787, which received the sanction of Thomas Jefferson, who is acknowledged by all to be the great oracle and expounder of our faith,'" Wikipedia, "Lincoln–Douglas debates of 1858." Abraham Lincoln, *The Collected Works of Abraham Lincoln*, ed. by Roy P. Basler, 9 vols. (New Brunswick, NJ: Rutgers University Press, 1953), 3:124-125.

[60] Dyer, 3:1029, Blackwell, 9-12; Tischler, 20-21. Note that Blackwell and Dyer disagree on the number of companies in Virginia: Dyer's total is seven, A through G, while Blackwell's is eleven, eight companies leaving Illinois added to three in Virginia. The Illinois Adjutant reports that while at Sharpsburg, the 12th was reinforced by two companies, the McClellan Dragoons, which had been assigned to McClellan's headquarters increasing the regiment's size apparently to nine companies. Based on a close reading of these sources, it seems that companies A through G arrived at Martinsburg and Cos. H and I did not join until after Antietam. Barker's Dragoon members were apparently absorbed into the McClellan Dragoons as Barker's was mustered out in September 1861 after having served as McClellan's escort in Western Virginia. The 700 sabers in seven

received the welcome news that their new Burnside carbines had arrived. They began patrolling the lower Shenandoah Valley fending off partisans and guerillas. As part of Brig. Gen. Julius White's brigade, they helped defend Martinsburg and the area around Winchester as enemy pressure increased in early September when Lee began his move north to Maryland.[61]

They were part of a detachment of about 2,200 men under the command of White at Winchester. It was composed of the 65th Illinois Infantry under Col. Daniel Cameron, the 125th New York Infantry commanded by Col. George L. Willard, and Battery M of the 2nd Illinois Artillery under Capt. John C. Phillips. One of the more notable actions occurred beginning on 3 September according to a report by Col. Voss. An outpost of 95 troopers of the 12th Illinois cavalry under Lt. Col. Hasbrouck Davis was posted about three miles south of Martinsburg on the Valley Pike. The next day, 10 men under Lt. Charles Roden ventured out from there on a reconnaissance toward Bunker Hill, about six miles south of the outpost. There, after surprising 12 Rebel cavalry, the Unionists chased them some three miles beyond Bunker Hill, wounding one. On the morning of 5 September, Lt. Col. Davis with Company A responded to this area, and found about 40 Confederates half a mile north of Bunker Hill, and drove them back into town. While he had only about equal numbers in this confrontation, Davis charged the dismounted Rebels, resulting in the capture of six, as he chased them for six miles. But on 7 September responding to Union pressure, Confederate cavalry made an appearance at daybreak closer to Martinsburg driving in Union pickets near the Valley Pike. Lt. Col. Davis sent Lt. Logan of Company G with 18 men to learn the enemy's location, strength, and intentions, but Logan was wounded, and he and his troopers had to cut their way out after being surrounded. One of Logan's men reported to Davis that a battalion of cavalry was confronting them, so Lt. Col. Davis requested reinforcements from Col. Voss. Voss ordered Company A under Capt. Thomas W. Grosvenor to report to Davis, followed by two other companies of the 12th, four companies of the 65th Illinois Infantry under Maj. Wood, and a section of Phillips's battery, accompanied by a third company of the 12th, although none except for Company A reached the scene in time to aid Davis.

When Company A reported to Col. Davis, he added them to his troopers at his post, and found himself in immediate command of fifty-eight men, including officers, ready for action. He then charged the Rebel cavalry on the Valley Pike, chasing them south to Darkesville, some seven miles south of Martinsburg, and about three miles north of Bunker Hill. There, he drove in their pickets and found the main body in a line in Darkesville about a mile distant. Davis formed his men into line, but while doing so, received heavy fire from the Rebels, many of whom were dismounted. Davis, seeing that his outnumbered troopers would soon be cut to pieces, decided to charge as his best option and did so, surprising the graybacks and forcing them to retreat; Davis followed their fighting retreat through Bunker Hill and then toward Winchester, capturing Rebels along the way. Col. Voss put the enemy losses at 41 prisoners and 25 killed, with none killed on the Union side, and only 13 wounded, two mortally, and one prisoner. Voss wrote that Confederate prisoners said their forces consisted of the 17th Battalion Virginia Cavalry, part of the 12th Virginia Cavalry, and Maryland Line Cavalry.[62]

---

companies seem high and may be the aggregate number on the roster for pay purposes not those present for duty let alone sabers available on the firing line. Pfanz's 1976 report shows a more realistic number of 575 troopers in the 12th.

[61] Blackwell, 17.

[62] *OR*, vol. 19, pt. 1, 516-518; Carman, Pierro, 102; Julius White, "The First Saber Charge of the War," in *Military Essays and Recollections, Papers Read Before the Commandery of the State of Illinois, Military Order of the Loyal Legion of the United States*, vol. III (Chicago, IL: The Dial Press, 1899), 26-29; Blackwell, 20-23. White's gripping account in a paper read on 12 January 1888 generally follows Voss's report but supplies interesting details not found in Voss's report. For what appears to be a wildly embellished report, see Eddy, *The Patriotism of Illinois*, 1:561-562, writing that Davis fought 800 Rebel troopers. For a detailed account with drawings of these actions see Warner, 179-193.

While the exact number of Confederate participants cannot be ascertained, it is likely given the credible accounts that the forces were roughly evenly matched, with the Rebel horsemen probably slightly outnumbering their foes. But clearly the 12th Illinois Cavalry and Lt. Col. Davis did excellent work for a green unit confronting relatively experienced Confederate horsemen. Lt. George Baylor of Company B, 12th Virginia Cavalry, provides the Confederate perspective on these actions and events leading up to it, admitting that he was broken albeit by superior numbers in his estimation:

> On September 4th Lieutenant-Colonel Massie, with Company I, of our regiment, and a squadron of the Eleventh Virginia Cavalry, joined us at Bunker Hill, and on the 5th moved down near Darkesville. On the 6th, our company drove in the enemy's pickets on the Martinsburg turnpike, a short distance from the town, capturing eight prisoners. Ascertaining that the force at Martinsburg was too strong for us, we began retiring, and had reached Darkesville, when suddenly the enemy charged our rear. Company B, covering the retreat, soon faced about, met the enemy's charge and repulsed it, taking some dozen prisoners, killing the lieutenant-colonel and 12 men of the Twelfth Illinois Cavalry. The Colonel's saddle and bridle graced my horse the remainder of the war, and was allowed me at the surrender. But the enemy, greatly outnumbering us, charged a second time, broke our column, and after a severe struggle, routed our force and pursued it nearly to Bunker Hill.[63]

Another Union unit had also seen action in the weeks leading up to the Harpers Ferry escape. Cole's Cavalry along with Means were involved in a Battle near Leesburg on 2 September, in which they were bested by Col. Munford and his 2nd Virginia Cavalry. At this battle known as the Battle of Mile Hill, Cole and his three companies were surprised and of some 150 men engaged, he suffered six killed, 27 wounded, and 11 captured. The survivors made their way back to Harpers Ferry to rest and refit in their old camp. For the next few days Cole joined with some of Means's troopers scouting the approach of Lee's army in northern Virginia and the Maryland border, skirmishing with Rebels near Edward's Ferry and other locations along the Potomac, as the noose drew tighter around Harpers Ferry. After the war, Cole claimed a pension for severe hemorrhoids incurred during September 1862. Needless to say, his efforts during the early war years took a toll on this good cavalry officer.[64]

On 1 September, activity picked up in the vicinity of Harpers Ferry as pickets from Capt. Cole's 1st Maryland Home Brigade Cavalry were gobbled up by 25 Rebel cavalry at Keyes' Ferry. Company B of the 12th Virginia Cavalry, the same one which took the Union detachment at Smithfield, raided this closer end of Coles' picket line at Keyes' Ford, less than six river miles upstream on the Shenandoah from Harpers Ferry, taking eight prisoners.[65] There was both a ford and ferry across the Shenandoah there and the closest and best ford on this river near Harpers Ferry, so Union cavalry posted pickets in the area watching for Confederate activity. The Rebels surprised the outer picket who was posted about a quarter mile from his party which was resting dismounted in a corn shed. The picket was forced into revealing this location so the Confederate troopers under command of Lt. Baylor, surprised the bluecoats, capturing them without resistance.[66]

[63] Baylor, 71-72, 408. Company B of the 12th Virginia Cavalry was commanded by George Baylor's father, Capt. Robert W. Baylor, until Robert was wounded and taken prisoner on 27 April 1862, not being released until late 1864; Lt. Milton Rouse took over command. George's two brothers were killed during their service in the company. Note that there was no Union lieutenant colonel killed in the 12th Illinois although Lt. Col. Davis's horse was felled, Tischler, 22.
[64] Photocopy of Cole's pension records at Harpers Ferry Research Library in Cole's folder. Courtesy Harpers Ferry NHP Library.
[65] Baylor, 70. For an apparently embellished account lauding Cole's actions at Mile Hill, see Newcomer, 33-36. Note that Newcomer was not present at this engagement.
[66] OR, vol. 19, pt. 1, 532. Note that the reporter of this incident, Lt. Henry M. Binney of the 10th Maine Infantry, an aide-de-camp to Miles, was sent by Miles to verify this action. To view the location of Keye's Ford, see OR Atlas, Plate 29, shown below at pg. 292; for both the ford and ferry, see W.E. Trout, III, *Rediscovering the History of the Shenandoah and its Branches*, Front Royal, VA: Virginia Canals & Navigations Society, 1997, 66.

In the meantime, cavalry units from Harpers Ferry were sent out on scouting missions both up and down the Potomac River, helping guard approaches to Harpers Ferry. Some troopers from Cole's Cavalry under Lt. Green, rode through Petersville and Middletown to within 2½ miles of Frederick, driving in enemy vedettes and causing much alarm. He suffered no losses and returned with several prisoners. On 7 September, Capt. Charles H. Russell and 50 troopers of the 1st Maryland Cavalry under his command attacked Rebel forces crossing at Point of Rocks, downriver from Harpers Ferry, capturing 17, and killing three. On 8 September, two members of Maj. Corliss's Rhode Island Cavalry, Sgt. Pettengill and Cpl. Heysinger, penetrated to within five miles of Frederick on Catoctin Mountain, close to Confederate pickets, and captured a Rebel. They climbed to the gable of a barn and watched Lee's army. Gen. Walker's march to Point of Rocks cut off their return route and while pursued for a few miles making their escape, they had to release their Rebel prisoner at Petersville.[67] On 8 September, Russell and his troopers were on the move as they reconnoitered toward Frederick again through Solomon's Gap, across Pleasant Valley, through Brownsville Gap in South Mountain, capturing a Confederate trooper at Petersville, and a Rebel sergeant major at Jefferson. Russell then rode north to a position three miles west of Frederick on the Old National Pike, where he encountered enemy pickets, pursuing them to within 1½ miles of Frederick; he captured 13, along with nine horses, including two deserters from the 1st Maryland Cavalry. Russell observed a few wagons and tents, with soldiers sleeping on sidewalks and cellar doors on the western outskirts of Frederick. South of the Potomac in Virginia on 8 September, the 8th New York Cavalry scouted to Bunker Hill, Smithfield, and Summit Point, and captured a few pickets.[68]

Ruins of the covered wagon bridge over the Shenandoah River at the foot of Bridge Street in Harpers Ferry. The bridge was destroyed by Jackson in June 1861. Loudoun Heights is to the right. Note the telegraph wires on the piers. Drawing by Alfred R. Waud, 1864. The covered wagon bridge was finished in 1844 and replaced the Shenandoah Rope Ferry. A new bridge was constructed some 300 yards downstream in 1882 but washed away in the 1936 flood. Courtesy LOC.

---

[67] Heysinger wrote that Pettengill was mistaken in describing their route through Pleasant Valley as they did not leave the Potomac until they reached Knoxville where they took the Frederick Pike; Heysinger letter to Carman 23 August 1905 NY Public Library Carman Papers courtesy Thomas Clemens.

[68] *OR*, vol. 19, pt. 1, 534, 544-545. Tischler, 2-31; Carman, Pierro, 107-108; *OR*, vol. 19, pt. 1, 516-518. The successes of the Harpers Ferry troopers were at least in part due to Jeb Stuart's occupation with the Army of the Potomac approaching from Washington, DC, as virtually all of Stuart's attention was, by Gen. Lee's order, focused there. Had McClellan been in command of the Harpers Ferry garrison, more coordinated scouting would have benefited the Army of the Potomac if McClellan had received those scouting reports.

The Loudoun Rangers, the 1st Potomac Home Brigade Cavalry, and the 1st Maryland Cavalry were bivouacked on or in the vicinity of Lower Hall Island in the Shenandoah River, next to the Shenandoah Canal, which formerly held the Hall Rifle Works; the 8th New York Cavalry was camped near the Potomac in the burned out arsenal, and the 12th Illinois and the Rhode Island troopers were probably in a ravine between Bolivar Heights and Camp Hill.[69] When the troopers were not scouting or helping defend Maryland or Bolivar Heights, these camps provided needed shelter for the troopers and their horses from the sun, and some concealment from the enemy on the surrounding heights, while being within a short walk to water.

The obvious key to holding Harpers Ferry was control of Maryland Heights. In August 1862, Wool had instructed Miles to construct a blockhouse on Maryland Heights and entrenchments and abatis on Bolivar Heights, all of which Miles failed to do.[70] Among the Union units assigned to the key Maryland Height's defense were the 7th Squadron, Rhode Island Cavalry, commanded by Maj. Corliss, two companies of the 1st Maryland Cavalry under Capt. Russell, and about 12 men of the Loudoun Rangers, totaling some 400 troopers. On 12 September, Russell, including some men from the 7th Squadron, added 50 dismounted troopers to the skirmish line occupied by the 32nd Ohio Infantry near Solomon's Gap. While Russell and some Ocean State troopers skirmished with Rebels under Kershaw near Solomon's Gap, most of the rest of the 7th Squadron scouted toward Sharpsburg. They rode through Solomon's Gap and then Harpers Ferry Road. As they rode past the mouth of Antietam Creek, they saw the 8th New York cavalry near Knott's Ford across the river in Virginia. Riding nearly to Sharpsburg, the 7th Squadron found its return by the road it had taken cut off by the brigades of Brig. Generals Joseph B. Kershaw and William Barksdale, now occupying Solomon's Gap, so it returned to camp by way of the canal towpath.[71] They had seen the detachment of the 8th New York Cavalry which was scouting toward Shepherdstown in the area, but the Empire State troopers hastily retreated to Harpers Ferry, as a Rebel column of Stonewall Jackson's men approached from Martinsburg.[72] The next day, Saturday the 13th, Capt. Russell on Maryland Heights, with his two companies and Company A from the 7th, fought dismounted, again supporting the 32nd Ohio. The cavalry was involved in the defense of the Heights as

---

[69] Goodhart, 51, 54; Hearn, 18; Tischler, 36-37. But see Bell who said that the 8th New York Cavalry was "on the old arsenal grounds, on the banks of the Shenandoah River (at the historic spot where John Brown immortalized himself)" so he felt safe from the Rebel guns on Loudoun Heights until to his horror the Union battery on Maryland Heights was thrown off the mountain, 10-11. It is more likely that the 8th was in the old Arsenal area on the Potomac since that is where "John Brown's Fort" was. The Hall works were on the Shenandoah; mistaking that river for the Potomac should not happen. On the other hand, the troopers would have been more subject to Walker's artillery fire from the closer Loudoun Heights on the Shenandoah side rather than on the Potomac River.

[70] OR, vol. 19, pt. 1, 519, 791. Halleck sagely suggested to Wool on 5 September that all Union forces in the vicinity be withdrawn to Maryland Heights, OR, vol. 19, pt. 2, 189.

[71] Carman, Pierro, 107; Tischler, 34. Heysinger wrote Carman that on this earlier scout up the Potomac that the 7th did not make it all the way to the bridge over the Antietam at the Iron Works but to a ford below it where some officer forded the Potomac to talk with Union cavalry on the Virginia shore, letter from Heysinger to Carman 23 August 1905 from the N.Y. Public Library Carman Papers, copy courtesy Thomas Clemens; compare Pettengill, 65, who also described this scout but did not mention the crossing of the river to talk with the members of the 8th New York Cavalry. Knott's Ford may have been near the mouth of Antietam Creek as Knott's Island there does not extend up to Boteler's Ford.

[72] Snyder writes of the fords near Antietam Creek which likely includes Knott's Ford: "[The] Antietam Ford…was located just below the mouth of Antietam Creek, at about mile marker 69. On 4 June 1861 a Confederate captain informed Brig. Gen. Joseph E. Johnston: 'Allow me to call your attention to a ford across the river at (just below) the mouth of Antietam Creek. . . . It is a good ford, and is now passable, and the approaches on either side very good.' During Early's 1864 invasion of Maryland, a portion of his command crossed here in addition to at Boteler's Ford and Williamsport. Antietam Ford may actually have been a series of fords in the same vicinity. On 10 June 1861 a correspondent of the Baltimore *American and Commercial Advertiser* wrote, 'Five fords have recently been discovered near the mouth of the Antietam, seven miles above Harper's Ferry. They are not more than three feet deep anywhere in low water. There is a perfect rock bed the whole way,'" Snyder, Manuscript, 14-16.

Russell reported retreating through enemy fire on his left flank. Col. Miles appeared on the Heights and ordered Corliss to take his cavalrymen back down to Bolivar Heights; perhaps Miles believed the relatively inexperienced, dismounted, Rhode Islanders would be of little additional help at this point, or possibly that they could be of more use at what he viewed as the potential point of main attack at Bolivar Heights. As Kershaw's Rebel infantry forced Unionists back toward the Naval Battery on Maryland Heights, Russell lost three men from his 1st Maryland Cavalry, including Lt. Daniel C. Hiteshew, who was mortally wounded. By 3:30 P.M. on 13 September, Russell joined in the general retreat off Maryland Heights, accompanied by the 12 Loudoun Rangers, and returned to Harpers Ferry. But before the "Rangers retired from Maryland Heights, Capt. Means marched his men into a thicket of woods, and with pick and shovel began digging a hole about two by four feet....When completed, Zack Robinson and Webb Miner lifted a box from the wagon containing the company books and papers, together with Capt. Means's papers, that he did not want to fall into the hands of the enemy, and buried them, spreading dry leaves and brush over the spot to prevent detection." McLaws now advanced his troops forward blocking all routes of escape from Harpers Ferry on the Maryland side of the Potomac.[73] The prospects for a successful defense of Harpers Ferry were extinguished.

On Sunday, 14 September, it was clear to the cavalry troopers that the Rebels would take Harpers Ferry. Confederate artillery placed on Loudoun and Maryland Heights fired at will on the troopers below. Walker noted that his artillery fire "produced great consternation and commotion among the enemy's troops, especially the cavalry" as he fired at points along the Shenandoah especially on the island where part of the 12th Illinois Cavalry, the 7th Squadron, Loudoun Rangers, 1st Maryland Potomac Home Brigade Cavalry, and the 1st Maryland Cavalry were located. White ordered Col. Voss to have a company of the 12th attack an apparently unsupported Rebel battery on the left of the Bolivar line, but after the dismounted troopers ventured about a mile toward the guns, they quickly found out that the Rebel artillery was sufficiently supported. On the other end of the Bolivar Line, Rebel infantry pushed back dismounted skirmishers of the 8th New York Cavalry, allowing Confederate cannon under Poague and Carpenter to be pushed forward. Now Jackson had the 12th Virginia Cavalry on his left flank placed to prevent any escape along the Virginia side of the Potomac, and across the Shenandoah River, Walker had his men blocking any Union retreat up the Shenandoah, or down the Potomac; the Stonewall Brigade blocked the Shenandoah on the north side. To help bolster any attempted breakout by the Yankees upriver along the southern side of the Shenandoah, Crutchfield, Jackson's chief of artillery, had 10 guns of Ewell's Division cross to the southern bank of the Shenandoah to enfilade the Union's Bolivar line. The bottle was now fully corked at least on that end of the battlefield. Jackson had also worried about an "attempt to escape across the Potomac, by means of signals I called the attention of Major-General McLaws, commanding on Maryland Heights, to the propriety of guarding against such an attempt. But McLaws, even though warned by Stuart and Jackson, quickly became preoccupied with Franklin's strong attack through Crampton's Gap leaving a thin picket line on the Maryland side of the Potomac, as he strongly reinforced his line to the north across Pleasant Valley.[74]

As the noose tightened around Harpers Ferry, the garrison was doomed unless relieved by the Army of the Potomac. On the evening of Saturday, 13 September, with Maryland Heights lost, Miles knew he had to communicate the plight of his garrison to Washington. He asked Capt. Russell of the 1st Maryland Cavalry if he could do the following:

> go with two or three men, and pass the enemy's lines, and try to reach somebody that had ever heard of the United States Army, or any general of the United States Army, and report the condition of Harper's

[73] Tischler, 34-36; Carman, Pierro, 113-115; Goodhart, 53-54; *OR*, vol. 19, pt. 1, 537.

[74] *OR*, vol. 19, pt. 1, 913, 954; Tischler, 36-37. Interesting to note that the 10 guns could apparently cross safely during the night while prior to the Confederates closing in no Union forces found any good fords across the Shenandoah up to Keys' Ferry.

Ferry….and he told me that if I could get to any general of the United States Army, or to any telegraph station, or, if possible, get to General McClellan, whom he supposed was at Frederick…to report, he thought he could hold out forty-eight hours…but if he was not relieved in that time, he would have to surrender the place.[75]

Russell chose nine of his troopers and followed the Virginia side of the Potomac northwestward through Confederate lines, then crossed to the north side of the Potomac upriver, near the mouth of Antietam Creek, probably at Knott's or Antietam Ford, again evading Confederate pickets. Crossing South Mountain on farm roads he rode to Middletown where he informed Gen. Reno of his mission. Reno gave him a fresh horse and directed him to report to McClellan who was near Frederick; he arrived at McClellan's headquarters before 9 A.M. on 14 September, and reported to the army commander directly. After reciting Miles's message, he replied negatively to McClellan's query if he could return to Miles at Harpers Ferry. McClellan then asked Russell to carry a message to Franklin who was fighting at Crampton's Gap. Russell complied and rode to Franklin staying with Franklin's troops until the next day, 15 September, when Franklin formed his corps across Pleasant Valley, facing McLaws's troops to the south after pushing through Crampton's Gap. Russell then rode to Williamsport joining some of his troopers who had escaped from Harpers Ferry the night of the 14th-15th.[76]

During the afternoon of Saturday, 13 September, commanding officers of the cavalry units met on Bolivar Heights to discuss the possibility of escaping from the Harpers Ferry trap. It is likely there were three or more informal and formal meetings, perhaps the first impromptu meeting was a conversation between Lt. Col. Hasbrouck Davis of the 12th Illinois Cavalry, and Col. "Grimes" Davis of the 8th New York Cavalry, who then had another meeting with other cavalry commanders. These two experienced commanders agreed that staying in Harpers Ferry would be useless since they could only fight dismounted as they could no longer scout—probably the other cavalry officers agreed. The two Davises then met with White who agreed with them and arranged a meeting with Miles and most other cavalry commanders late on the 13th. Perhaps given White's role as being in informal charge of cavalry at Harpers Ferry, and a general officer who was in command of some of the cavalry regiments when they were at Winchester or Martinsburg, cavalry officers felt comfortable speaking with him before Miles.[77] While White agreed to set up the meeting that evening at Miles's headquarters he decided that it would

---

[75] *OR*, vol. 19, pt. 1, 720-723. During this conversation, Miles asked if Russell could lead out the cavalry from Harpers Ferry; the conversation may have taken place after the other cavalry commanders had met with Miles and Miles was questioning if Russell privately thought it feasible. Russell testified however that both Col. Ford and Col. Davis (probably Benjamin F. Davis) and possibly Gen. White were present during this meeting. Russell also testified that he had more than one meeting with Miles. It is not proven when his first meeting took place—before or after the meeting with the other cavalry commanders.

[76] Ibid., 721. Miles sent a second messenger two hours after Russell departed, Capt. Henry Cole; he reached McClellan about three hours after Russell. Cole agreed to take a message back to Miles and arrived in time to join his troopers in the breakout, Chester G. Hearn, *Six Years of Hell: Harpers Ferry During the Civil War* (Baton Rouge, LA: Louisiana State University Press, 1996), 167-168; Newcomer, 44-45. Tischler does not find Cole's mission credible, 227, n. 5. McClellan does not mention a second messenger. Binney's testimony was that both Cole and Russell approached Miles to open up communication with McClellan and that on Sunday the 14th they left but never returned, *OR*, vol. 19, pt. 1, 586. Perhaps his recollection of the day was incorrect.

[77] Pettengill, 81; *OR*, vol. 19, pt. 1, 774-776. Carman mentions that White wanted to go with the column as most of the cavalry had been under his command but believed that it was his duty to remain at Harpers Ferry; there is no written order placing White in command of the cavalry at Harpers Ferry, but Carman wrote that White was "in temporary command of all the cavalry," Carman, Pierro, 122, based upon White's statement to that effect in his *Battles and Leaders* article. White wrote that only Col. B.F. Davis and Lt. Col. Hasbrouck Davis met with him, *Battles and Leaders*, 2:613. Voss (in Pettengill) describes this series of meetings differently as noted below. Note that Binney reports that the meeting with Miles took place on the 14th, *OR*, vol. 19, pt. 1, 538. Other participants disagree saying that it occurred on the 13th. Note that Binney later testified that he and Col. Miles rode around the left side of the Federal line late on Sunday evening, 14 September, before dark thus making that a busy evening for Miles if the main meeting between Miles and the cavalry officers was during that evening, *OR*, vol. 19, pt. 1, 586.

not be proper to lead them out under the circumstances should Miles agree to the breakout.[78] Col. Davis explained at the meeting with Miles what a boon the capture by the Rebels of the Federal cavalry would be with all its arms, equipment, and horses; that cavalry had little to do now that the garrison was surrounded; and that forage was in short supply.[79] Miles, after first denouncing the idea as "wild and impracticable, periling the lives of the whole command" finally consented to listen to a plan for the cavalry escape, but would not allow any consideration of allowing the infantry and artillery to do so, as it could not keep up with the cavalry over poor roads. Additionally, he had been ordered to hold the post which he narrowly interpreted to be only Harpers Ferry, and not the surrounding heights, so he had no intention of letting any other units escape, further weakening his forces—he obviously still thought he could hold out for a time even after losing Maryland Heights. There is some evidence that the 12th Illinois Cavalry was planning on breaking out on its own Saturday night, the 13th, but did not. The 12th Illinois Cavalry chaplain, Abraham J. Warner, wrote that on the 13th Lt. Col. Davis convinced Col. Benjamin F. Davis of the 8th New York Cavalry to also breakout that night and Lt. Col. Davis received verbal permission from Miles to do so. But Col. Voss as commander of the 12th Illinois, refused,

---

[78] *OR*, vol. 19, pt. 1, 630. Other accounts dispute both the day and time when the main meeting with Miles took place, with some showing Saturday the 13th and others the next day. Carman, adopting White's *Battles and Leaders* story, wrote that it took place on the evening of the 13th, while historian Dennis Frye wrote that it occurred about 7 P.M. on the 14th, Frye, *Blue & Gray*, Sept. 1987, 27. Most agree that there was a preliminary meeting during the afternoon of the 13th or 14th between Col. Benjamin F. Davis of the 8th New York Cavalry and Lt. Col. Hasbrouck Davis of the 12th Illinois Cavalry and Brig. Gen. White at which White agreed that he would ask for a meeting with the cavalry commanders at Miles's headquarters. Carman perhaps believed that Miles's general order for the cavalry escape "sent late in the afternoon to each cavalry commander" proved that the evening meeting discussing and approving the breakout could not have happened the same day, the 14th. Discussion of the 12th Illinois Cavalry breaking out on its own Saturday night, the 13th, is in Tischler, 130, 133-134, 136; Warner, 213-214. Norton of the 8th N.Y. wrote that Col. Davis planned on breaking out the night before, the 13th, but waited until the 14th, 27-28. Another participant, Pettengill, wrote that Corliss informed his troopers of the escape "about four o'clock in the evening" on the 14th, 77-78. Col. Voss wrote that he attended two meetings which apparently took place on the 13th, the first with Col. Benjamin F. Davis, Maj. Corliss, Lt. Green, 1st Potomac Home Brigade Cavalry, and Lt. Col. Hasbrouck Davis. Apparently then the officers decided to seek Miles's approval which they did at the second meeting later that same day, the 13th, Voss in Pettengill, 81. While Voss did not mention specifically the dates of the meetings, given the circumstances he relates they most likely took place on the 13th. Luff's account has two meetings on the 14th, the first with Col. Benjamin F. Davis and Lt. Col. Hasbrouck Davis who decided to meet with White who approved the escape plan and then arranged a meeting later at Miles's headquarters, William M. Luff, "March of the Cavalry from Harper's Ferry, September 14, 1862," *Military Essays and Recollections: Papers read before the Commandery of the State of Illinois, Military Order of the Loyal Legion of the United States*, vol. 2 (Chicago, IL: A.C. McClurg and Co., 1894), 38. Tischler writes that the two Davis's were emissaries from an earlier meeting of cavalry commanders, 157-158. Note that Warner did not accompany the 12th Illinois Cavalry on its breakout and also received the information about the meetings only second hand from Voss and Lt. Col. Davis, 213. Warner writes of a meeting on the 13th between Lt. Col. Hasbrouck Davis of the 12th Illinois Cavalry and Col. Benjamin Davis of the 8th N.Y. Cavalry who both agreed to escape; Hasbrouck then went to Voss who said he would not do so without a written order. Lt. Col. Davis went to Miles on Sunday the 14th and obtained the order, Warner, 213-214. This meeting on the 14th only between Lt. Col. Davis and Miles is unlikely given the other accounts. Although it is not impossible the meeting with Miles took place late on the 14th, it is difficult to believe that all preparations for the escape could have happened within three hours; participant accounts relate that other than ensuring that they did not carry excess baggage and carrying what food and forage they could, they saddled up and got in line. Participants did not write of the haste and chaos which would have resulted in such a short time span had the escape orders been given late on the 14th.

[79] Carman, Pierro, 122; *OR*, vol. 19, pt. 1, 583. William P. Craighill, *The 1862 Army Officer's Pocket Companion* (New York: D Van Nostrand, 1862, reprint Mechanicsburg, PA: Stackpole Books, 2002), "But little cavalry is necessary in a besieged place. During the early periods of the siege it assists in sorties, is employed in patrolling, and in completing the provisioning of the place, 205. Perhaps the cavalry commanders had read this part of the book or just employed common sense in realizing that mounted horse soldiers were of no use once they could not be used other than dismounted infantry. Or it may have been as simple as the cavalry commanders decided to escape because they could regardless of what Miles's decision might be as they understood that surrender was inevitable.

because he required written orders. Warner wrote that then Lt. Col. Davis went to Miles on the 14th and received the written order allowing the escape.

Lt. Col. Hasbrouck Davis Executive Officer of the 12th Illinois at Harpers Ferry from *In Memoriam: Hasbrouck Davis*, n.p., 1871.

There ensued much discussion and some heated argument at the 7 P.M. meeting with Miles about the route the cavalry would take: Benjamin F. Davis favored going upriver on the south (Virginia) side of the Potomac and crossing at Boteler's Ford south of Shepherdstown, while Capt. Means wanted to cross the Shenandoah River downstream of Keys' Ferry, then ride through Lovettsville and Leesburg, skirting Walker on Loudoun Heights, then down the Leesburg Pike to Washington at the Chain Bridge. Other officers suggested a third route up the Maryland side of the Potomac toward Sharpsburg. It was this last route upon which Miles seized likely believing that this route would give the cavalry the best chance to unite with McClellan's forces. The route in Maryland would start by first going over the pontoon bridge crossing the Potomac and then up the Harpers Ferry-Sharpsburg (Antietam Furnace) road. Col. Miles issued Special Order No. 120 dated 14 September detailing his decision:

The cavalry force at this post, except detached orderlies, will make immediate preparations to leave here at eight o'clock to-night, without baggage-wagons, ambulances or led horses, crossing the Potomac over the pontoon bridge, and taking the Sharpsburg Road. The senior officer, Colonel Voss, will assume the command of the whole, which will form the right at the quartermaster's office, the left up Shenandoah street, without noise or loud command, in the following order: Cole's Cavalry, Twelfth Illinois Cavalry, Eighth New York Cavalry, Seventh Squadron Rhode Island Cavalry, and the First Maryland Cavalry. No other instructions can be given to the Commander than to force his way through the enemy's lines and join our own army.[80]

Miles also told the cavalry commanders that his infantry should not know of the escape attempt as it might cause a stampede. Fortunately for the escaping troopers, an experienced guide formerly used by Gen. Nathanial P. Banks and Gen. White, Thomas Noakes, knew the area well and helped guide the escape column.[81] He may have been assisted by "a loyal citizen of Bolivar, by the name of Burkett" according to a member of the Loudoun Rangers, who also believed that the success of the escape was owed in large part to Cole's Cavalry.[82] A member of Cole's Cavalry wrote that one of Cole's officers, Lt.

[80] Carman, Pierro, 121-122; Luff, 39; Pettengill, 81. This order is not found in the Official Records. Note that the few troopers of the Loudoun Rangers were not mentioned; they were probably just in front of the 1st Maryland Cavalry at the rear according to Dennis Frye, *Blue & Gray*, Sept. 1987, 47. They numbered less than 20 men along with Means and another officer plus a sergeant, Tischler, 11. The heated argument between the two regular officers, Benjamin F. Davis and Miles, stemmed not only from the disagreement over the escape route but to a prior incident in which Miles paroled a captured Rebel cavalryman, Lt. Milton J. Rouse, a member of the 12th Virginia Cavalry, who subsequently led his troopers into Harpers Ferry after the surrender in violation of his parole, Warner, 225; Tischler, 78; Goodhart, 55; *OR*, vol. 19, pt. 1, 748, 797, 800. There is nothing of record to show why escaping up the C&O Canal towpath and canal prism was not considered. Perhaps the unspoken consensus of the officers was that the towpath could be easily blocked by Confederate pickets even though the towpath was used by the Rhode Islanders on 10 September who reported nothing of Rebel pickets, Tischler, 31. Part of the escape route, however, was close to the Potomac and the towpath on what is today known as Limekiln Road. The Rhode Islanders were also on the towpath as late as the 12th, Carman, Pierro, 107; Tischler, 34. The route crossing the Shenandoah downstream of Key's Ferry close to Harpers Ferry was not suitable as "the river was full of holes, and it was impossible to cross, *OR*, vol. 19, pt. 1, 630. Gen. White testified the following about the ford across the Shenandoah near Harpers Ferry (not Keyes Ford) after the surrender: "I went with him [Confederate Gen. A.P. Hill] to examine the ford, taking along with us a person who was familiar with it. A mounted man was sent in, and he rode some 30 or 40 yards into the water. It was found to be so deep that it would be impossible for a man to stand in the water. The water was so deep and the current so swift that it was almost impossible to stand there, and, upon going a few yards farther, the horse fell into a hole in the river and almost drowned the man," *OR*, vol. 19, pt. 1, 718. Snyder notes the following about the ford near Harpers Ferry on p. 14: "On 3 August 1861 a Confederate cavalryman informed General Joseph E. Johnston, 'There is about one [Federal] regiment at Harpers Ferry, and they have made an excellent ford at that place, so that they can cross at any time, the water not being more than three feet deep.' On the other hand, in June 1863 a Federal engineer noted that the Potomac River from Harpers Ferry to Berlin was full of rocks that inhibited fording. The river at Harpers Ferry was indeed fordable, but the rocks and difficult approaches made crossing troublesome and dangerous so that crossing on a dark night would be impossible. Because of the difficulty crossing at this point, the Union army built a number of pontoon bridges at the Ferry throughout the war, although Federal soldiers were forced to cross the ford occasionally after the bridges had been destroyed," Snyder, Manuscript, 13-14. Note that Heysinger wrote to Carman and stated emphatically that the towpath was not used during the escape, Heysinger to Carman, 17 August 1905, from N.Y. Public Library Carman Papers, copy courtesy Thomas Clemens. A ford which might be marginally useable for cavalry during the day certainly would be much less so on a dark night, however.

[81] *OR*, vol. 19, pt. 1, 558-559, for Noakes's testimony to the Harper's Ferry Military Commission. On 10 September, Col. Palmer and William B. Wilson who were working with Gov. Curtin of Pennsylvania, sent Noakes to Gen. White at Martinsburg, Noakes's employer, warning of Jackson's approach, Fishel, 219. Noakes was likely the "reliable spy" mentioned by White on 10 September who reported Rebel troop movement through Boonsboro, *OR*, vol. 19, pt. 2, 249. This was Jackson's force as Longstreet on the 10th was on the east side of South Mountain, Carman, Pierro, 129.

[82] Tischler, 74-75. See also Henry Norton, who was in the escape column as a member of the 8th New York. He reported that the "pilot knew every foot of ground through Maryland, and the scout knew how Longstreet's corps was situated, having come from there about an hour before we started from the Ferry," 29. See also Hearn, stating that Noakes was aided by Michael Burkett and scouts from the First Maryland Potomac Home Brigade and the First Maryland Cavalry, many of whom were from the area, 178. Too, members of the Loudoun County Rangers were familiar with the territory as Loudoun County borders the area in

Hanson Green, may have been in the lead with three of his men as they were very familiar with this area. Officers of Cole's Cavalry ensured that their troopers were prepared "for the worst, and every man was supplied with an extra amount of ammunition. The officers of the various companies personally superintended seeing that no man carried any extra luggage."[83]

While it is not certain that all Union troopers participated in the escape, no records have been found showing that any refused to go or were left behind unintentionally. Likely most Union soldiers in the beleaguered town wished they could escape like the cavalrymen had not Miles forbidden it.[84] Maj.

Virginia south of Harpers Ferry. Goodhart relates the Burkett conjecture as well as his opinion of the value of Cole's Cavalry, Goodhart, 58. Goodhart also tells here a story that after the Rangers arrived in Greencastle, Pennsylvania, on 15 September, they "marched" to Baltimore led by Capt. Means, obtained horses for dismounted men, and the next day, 16 September, marched from Ellicott's Mills to Boonsboro and on to Sharpsburg where they served on the right of McClellan's line carrying dispatches and gathering in Confederate stragglers, Goodhart, 58. Tischler writes that they rode to Baltimore by train with their equipments, reported to Wool, obtained horses and went to Ellicott's Mills, Tischler, 64. Chamberlin and Souders wrote that after reporting to Wool, Wool ordered Means to report directly to McClellan and Means apparently did so after gathering up the remainder of his command at Ellicott's Mills. Means's Rangers remained with McClellan for over a month in Maryland serving as messengers and gathering in stragglers, Chamberlin and Souders, *Between Reb and Yank*, 133.

[83] Newcomer, 42. Clemens agrees that Green was in the lead, Clemens, thesis, 513.

[84] John W. Mies, "Breakout at Harper's Ferry," *Civil War History*, vol. II, no. 1, March 1956, 17-19. In the Harper's Ferry Military Commission hearings, Capt. W. Angelo Powell of the engineers testified that he was told 13 mounted men had returned over the pontoon bridge after the column escaped with one wounded and one killed. He also thought that there were about 39 cavalry horses left after the escape including the 13 returned and that there might have been about 100 or more battery horses. The remaining cavalry horses were those that belonged to orderlies, men sick in hospital and to wagon teams. While the actual number of cavalry horses remaining cannot be determined, a reasonable estimate is less than 100 and it is likely that other than the 13 which may have returned, many were not fit to join the escape column, *OR*, vol. 19, pt. 1, 765-766. A Confederate infantry private walked around after the surrender looking for a horse but after having to return a fine looking one to a Union colonel he could not find another, Worsham, 85-86. The 13 men who returned were apparently deserters from the 125th New York Infantry led by Capt. Ephriam Wood who stole horses and mingled with the troopers about to cross the pontoon bridge. After crossing, they turned right followed by some 12th Illinois troopers who rode into the Rebel pickets at Sandy Hook, *OR*, vol. 19, pt. 1, 794; Tischler, 84-85. The issue of how many in the escape column returned to Harpers Ferry after taking a wrong turn is based on the number of cavalry shown captured: *OR*, vol. 19, pt. 1, 549, lists 274 for cavalry, with none killed, five wounded, and 269 missing or captured. While it is unlikely all of these returned from Sandy Hook, there is evidence that many did; Tischler quotes the 12th Illinois Cavalry chaplain, Warner, who wrote that many of Company D returned, Tischler, 137. Another 12th Illinois trooper listed 25 troopers captured and paroled from that company, Tischler, 126. Warner wrote that first Company G of the 12th Illinois took the wrong turn and were fired on by pickets from across the Potomac near Loudoun Heights, Warner, 215; some of their mounts were shot and troopers were left behind. Warner describes Company D which came in late as it was picketing on the left but then turned right over the pontoon bridge and were eventually fired on and returned reentering Harpers Ferry, 216; Warner may have witnessed the return of troopers from Company G and D although his daily diary for 14 and 15 September does not show this because he spent time conducting a funeral on the 14th and searching for his horse on the 15th, Warner, 202. Tischler lists 207 total driven back into Harpers Ferry, 97 from the 12th Illinois Cavalry (20 from Company C and 25 from Company D), 79 from the 8th New York Cavalry, and 31 from the 1st Maryland Cavalry, 134, 139. Tischler also points to a report of the Commissary General of Prisoners date 26 January 1863 asking for reimbursement of damages caused by paroled troops at Camp Douglas near Chicago. The report lists the following numbers from units which surrendered at Harpers Ferry: 8th New York Cavalry, 79; 12th Illinois Cavalry, 97; and 1st Maryland Cavalry 31, *OR*, series 2, vol. 5, 214-215. These 207 troopers were likely captured when the Confederates took Harpers Ferry, so if the 269 shown as missing or captured is accurate, then some 62 troopers returned to their units on or after 15 September 1862. Note that the Commissary General's report stated that the 8th New York Cavalry troopers in the detention camp were among the most active in destroying property, so apparently without the firm hand of Col. Benjamin Davis, they reverted to their old ways. Bell wrote that a trooper from the 8th "who managed to be left behind…was detailed on the morning following our escape by Colonel Miles as his orderly." In addition, the 8th's chaplain, J.H. Van Ingen, remained behind and helped remove Miles's body to Frederick, Bell, 14-15. The historian of the 3rd Pennsylvania Cavalry wrote the following about his regiment's finding two cavalry escapees on the 15th: "On the same day Company C of the regiment was ordered out on a scout toward Harper's Ferry. Marching for some miles along the ridge of the mountain, the party descended into the [Pleasant] valley. When the bottom had almost been reached, the advance guard saw two men jump down behind the trees. Galloping up to them, it was found that they were two of our own men from a Maryland regiment, who had escaped from Harper's Ferry by swimming the river. When taken back to Captain Jones, who commanded the party, they informed him that Harper's Ferry, with its garrison,

Augustus W. Corliss, the commander of the College Cavaliers from Rhode Island, "In characteristic language...assured them that by the 'next morning they would either be in Pennsylvania, or in hell, or on their way to Richmond.' He gave directions for a thorough grooming of the horses and inspection of saddle girths and for such other slight preparations as it was practicable to make for the perilous ride." They left everything they had except their overcoats in making their preparations but they had little left with which to concern themselves as their baggage and stores were destroyed when White left Winchester.[85]

At about 8:30 P.M. when night had fully fallen, the commands formed up along the macadamized Shenandoah Street. Some units which were bivouacked in the burned armory buildings perhaps lined up on Potomac Street; forage was distributed, and the 1,500 troopers slowly rode down to the pontoon bridge, past Miles and White standing near Miles's headquarters.[86] They were led by Cole's Cavalry with Lt. Hanson T.C. Green in the lead, despite his wounding at Leesburg on 2 September, who knew the area well, accompanied by Noakes. A treat awaited the troopers courtesy of some sutlers who realized that their goods would shortly be taken by the Rebels: "As [the troopers] moved forward toward the bridge through the gap in the Potomac River wall, men on each side of the column were seen handing up something which looked in the distance like a little piece of paper, and the students began to wonder if those 'Christian Commissioners' were giving them tracts....they reached down their hands and grasped a paper of fine cut tobacco" being given away to 'the heroes of the evening.'"[87] The troopers passed the burnt out remains of "the hotels, stores, taverns, warehouses, the B&O depot, office and restaurant as well as the bridge tollhouse located on the Ferry Lot. Fourteen buildings in all, from the armory gate to the railroad, [which had been] ...destroyed. With this conflagration and the previous destruction of the

---

had that morning surrendered to the Confederates. The party at once returned to our lines and sent the two men to General McClellan's headquarters. This, it is believed, was the first intelligence which the commanding general received of the disastrous occurrence," Rawle 119. *The New York Times* reported on 16 September from Frederick that about 2,300 cavalry were at Harpers Ferry and all escaped except about 40. Norton in his history of the 8th New York Cavalry wrote that several of the regiment were left in Harpers Ferry due to illness, 31.

[85] Pettengill, 78. Corliss, 2, 10.

[86] Isaac W. Heysinger, "The Cavalry Column from Harper's Ferry in the Antietam Campaign" in *The Journal of the U.S. Cavalry Association*, January 1914.(Reprint, Leavenworth, KS: Press of Ketcheson Printing Co., n.d), 44. Note that Heysinger is the only one who wrote that some of the column's units were waiting on Potomac Street but this is possible given the number of troopers and that they did not all appear at once to line up in the proper order so some likely waited on Potomac Street until they could insert themselves in their proper place in the column as it passed by; alternatively, they may have waited on the Armory grounds on the street between the buildings. It is noteworthy that Carman repeated almost nothing he learned from Heysinger about the escape. Obviously these horsemen on Potomac Street or the Armory street could not have passed Miles's headquarters. This may be how the sutlers managed to slip in as did the infantrymen on their borrowed horses. The sutlers may also have been on the old Ferry Lot to the right of the boat ramp. Heysinger also included more information about these sutlers. Two sutlers at Harpers Ferry which handed out packets of tobacco to the column as it headed for the pontoon bridge he reports as inserting two of their wagons into the column ahead of Heysinger's squadron. These interlopers came to grief in the pitch black night early in the escape up the Harpers Ferry road at a sharp climb about a mile from the bridge. There was a sharp curve with a steep drop off hundreds of feet deep which Heysinger remembered from his ride two days earlier trip on the road on his scout to Antietam Creek. The sutlers speeding along the road likely not knowing of the curve and drop off went over the edge and Heysinger "heard a great noise and crashing, shouts, and groans, and indescribable sounds, down the gorge, and pulled up to listen....I could distinguish the groans of horses and men, and the cries of the latter for help....Those sutlers and their outfit went no farther with us, and I have never heard of them since," 46. Note that Heysinger also wrote that he did not personally observe the wagons entering the column nor see them go over the cliff but was told of their entry by others. He did say he heard the noises as he described, letter from Heysinger to Carman 23 August 1905 N.Y. Public Library Carman Papers, copy courtesy Thomas Clemens. Even today as the Harpers Ferry Road turns north away from the Potomac there are steep drop offs on the left side as the road climbs sharply upward.

[87] Pettengill, 78-79, 82. Shenandoah Street which was macadamized in 1833 was the Harpers Ferry terminus of the Harpers Ferry-Charles Town-Smithfield Turnpike organized in 1830, U.S. Dept. of the Interior, NPS, National Register of Historic Places Inventory, Harpers Ferry National Historic Park, 1966, item 7, pg. 2.

arsenal yard, the "point" of land created by the confluence of the Potomac and the Shenandoah was left vacant, exposed, and desolate" after having been set ablaze by Union troops on 7 February 1862.[88] Sod or dirt placed on the boards helped deaden the sound of the hundreds of horses plodding across the pontoon bridge as did the noise of the water rushing over rocks in the riverbed.[89] The column crossed the towpath and canal then quietly turned left and picked up speed as best it could in the inky darkness as it rode along the base of Maryland Heights. As the column formed from a single line into twos after Maryland Heights, less than a mile into their escape, the head of the column was challenged by Rebel pickets who were answered by Lt. Green of Cole's Cavalry, responding "The advance of Stuart's Cavalry!" And before the confused Rebels could react, the column rushed past, with only a few shots fired, while the pickets scattered. It took at least two hours for the entire column to cross the pontoon bridge as the commander of the rear guard, Capt. William H. Grafflin of the 1st Maryland Cavalry, Companies H and I, testified that he started crossing about 10:30 P.M.[90]

---

[88] U.S. Department of the Interior, National Park Service, "Cultural Landscape Report: Lower Town, Harpers Ferry National Historical Park," 1993, 3-53; Joseph Barry, *The Strange Story of Harper's Ferry With Legends of the Surrounding Country* (Martinsburg, WV: Thompson Brothers, 1903), 119, gives the detailed cause of the February 1862 arson: Rebels from Capt. Baylor's company shot and killed a Union soldier, Rohr, as he and his companion were crossing the Potomac. In retaliation to try to destroy the buildings from which the Union commander, Col. John W. Geary, thought the fatal shot had originated, he ordered the buildings burned under the immediate command of Maj. Hector Tyndale. But Barry wrote that the piers of the burned bridge and even the ruins of the buildings still could have provided cover for Rebel snipers, 120.

[89] Hearn, 178; Tischler, 74. Other participants do not mention this dirt perhaps because they could not see it. Placing dirt would have taken some time and planning, thus supporting the timeline with the main meeting on the 13th, the day before the escape. Tischler said that sod was routinely placed on pontoon bridges to help prevent wear from horses' shoes and troops cleats, Tischler letter to author 12 January 2012. Dirt or hay not only would help protect the boards but would also help muffle the very loud noises from horses' hooves and soldier's boots.

[90] *OR*, vol. 19, pt. 1, 771. Under ideal conditions, at three yards per horse and one yard between horses, the 1,500 horsemen in a column of twos would be almost 1¾ miles long, while in column of fours, almost one mile, Mark Adkin, *The Gettysburg Companion: The Complete Guide to America's Most Famous Battle* (Mechanicsburg, PA: Stackpole Books, 2008), 199. It is very unlikely given the darkness early on the escape that the troopers were able to keep well closed up, however. On 14 September, sunset was at 6:21 P.M. and twilight ended at 6:48 P.M. The moon rose at 9:50 P.M. that evening and was waning gibbous with 64% illuminated; data from the U.S. Naval Observatory website; Tischler, 134. Harsh, *Shallows*, 16-18, shows that in Frederick, it was overcast in the afternoon of the 14th then clear at night with light wind, daytime temperature in the 70's night around 60. These data support statements of participants that it was very dark early in the ride but brightened later apparently as the moon rose and the clouds dissipated. Col. Voss wrote that the stars helped later in the night particularly after leaving Sharpsburg, Pettengill, 84. One participant of the 8th New York Cavalry found the night very dark and thought that the column was stretched out for 10 miles, Norton, *Deeds of Daring*, 28. Col. George L. Willard commanding the 125th New York Volunteers testified at the Harper's Ferry Military Commission that the night of the 14th was slightly hazy with moonlight, *OR*, vol. 19, pt. 1, 563. See also Bell who wrote that on nearing Sharpsburg "The night had now become starlit," 12. Heysinger wrote Carman that he was in a single file race in the rear after crossing the pontoon bridge and he rode for about a mile before he caught up with anyone and about three miles before the escapees began gathering, letter from Heysinger to Carman 23 August 1905, N.Y. Public Library Carman Papers, copy courtesy Thomas Clemens. About one mile from the Maryland side of the pontoon bridge is the point at which the Harpers Ferry Road turns sharply away from the river and starts climbing north up the heights and is a likely spot where the Rebel pickets were encountered as pickets there would have been able to cover the towpath as well as the road and the ground is more level than that further north as the road climbs sharply. Since it took at least two hours for the column to pass this point it is curious that the scattered Rebel pickets did not return with reinforcements—perhaps this testifies to the fact that McLaws had sent most of his troops up Pleasant Valley toward Franklin.

Shenandoah Street looking west on which most of the escape column formed facing to the left toward the Potomac River; Shenandoah River is to the left behind the buildings to the left rear; Loudoun Heights in the background. The sentry is standing at the entrance of Potomac Street. Col. Miles's headquarters is the building in the center at the arrow and is the point from which he and White watched the column depart. *Harper's Weekly*, 11 March 1865, sketch by A.R. Waud. Courtesy LOC.

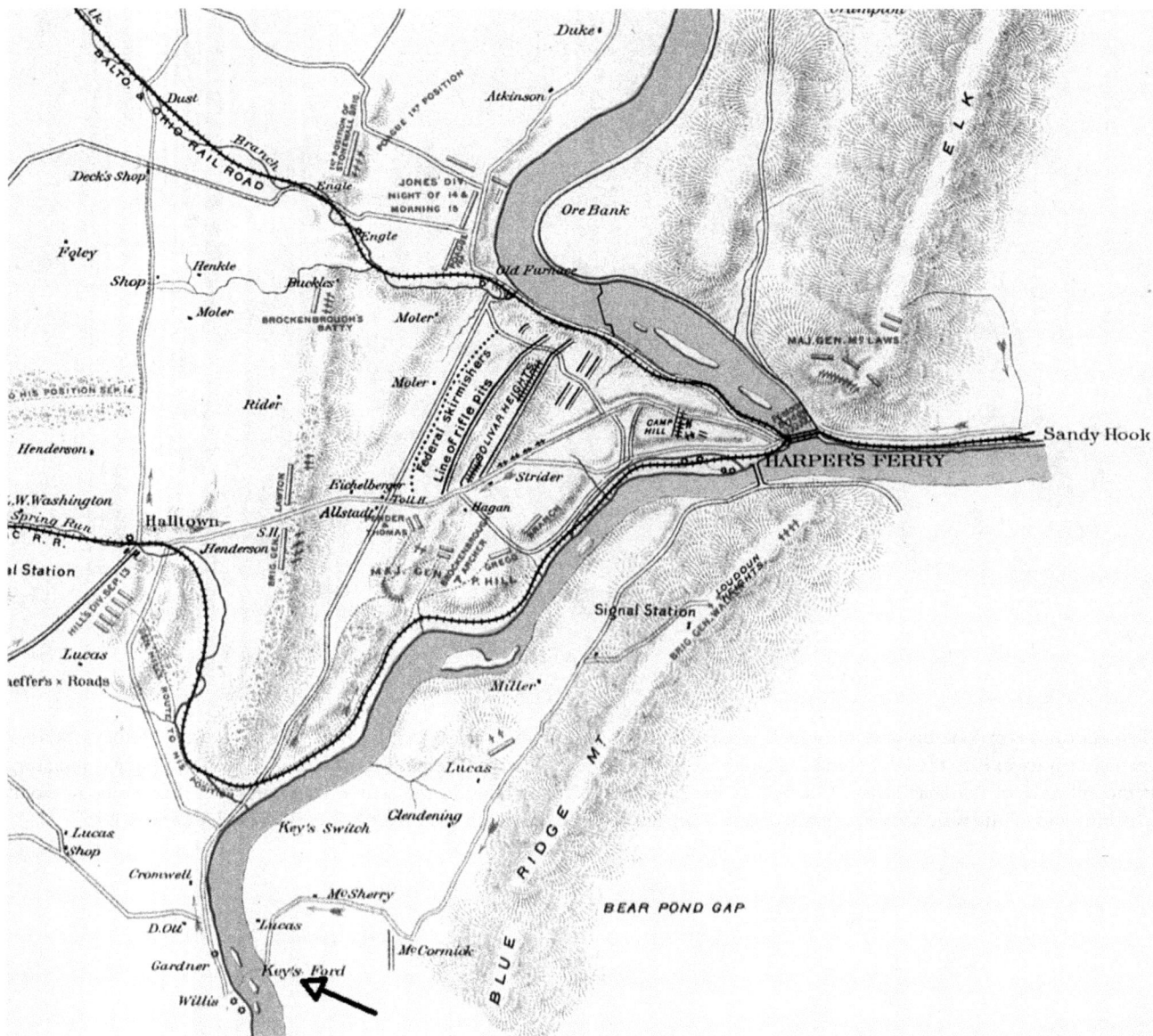

Detail of Harpers Ferry Map showing troop positions mostly on the 14th-15th. Key's Ford at the bottom left, is the closest ford across the Shenandoah River to Harpers Ferry and was heavily used by both sides during the war It is less than six river miles from the junction of the Potomac and Shenandoah Rivers. *Official Atlas*, Plate 29. Courtesy LOC.

Modern view down boat ramp to Potomac River where the Virginia end of the pontoon bridge was anchored. This modern Baltimore and Ohio bridge was not completed until 1931. Maryland Heights in background. Photo by Terri Freiheit.

Author standing in boat landing. Photo by Terri Freiheit

One of the hooks in the boat ramp wall to which a pontoon bridge cable was attached. Photo by Terri Freiheit.

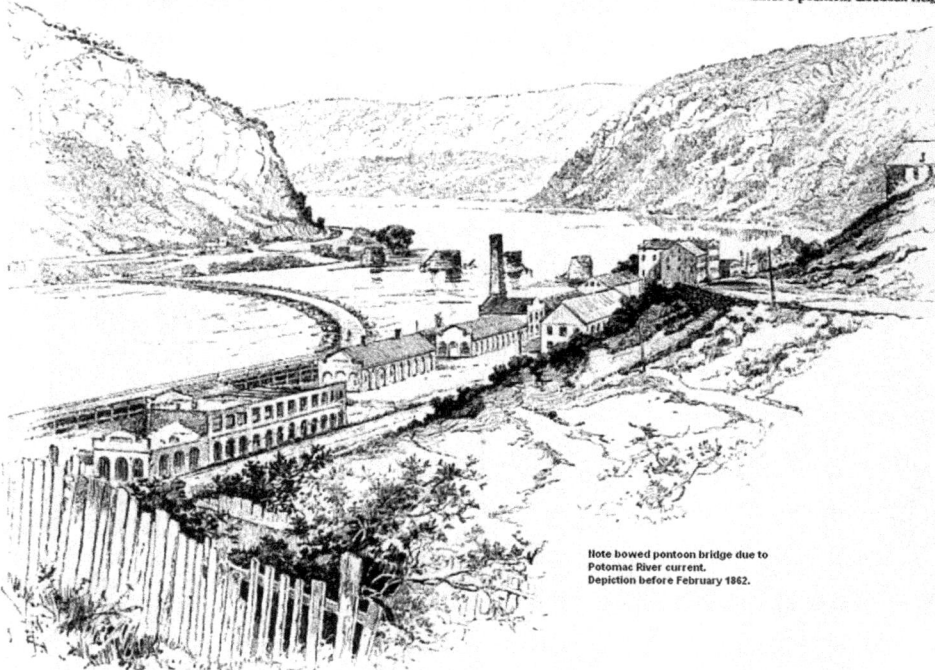

View facing south with the Potomac River in the center and the 860 foot-long pontoon bridge to the left of the burned railroad bridge. Curvature of the bridge likely due to flow of the Potomac from left to right however it seems exaggerated. *The Century Illustrated Monthly Magazine*, New York: The Century Company, Volume 32, Issue: 2, June 1886, pg. 286.

But within the first minutes of the escape, there was a fright, as Capt. George H. Shears of Company D, 12th Illinois, turned right on the towpath, rather than left, after crossing the pontoon bridge, and ran into

Confederate pickets less than a half mile east of the end of the pontoon bridge, just outside Sandy Hook. The company quickly returned as the Rebels opened fire; the Illinoisans suffered no losses.[91] As the column headed up the Harpers Ferry-Sharpsburg Road, they alternated whenever possible between trotting and galloping. Being a very dark night however, it was difficult to maintain an even pace with the only light being from sparks from the horses' shoes as they struck stones in the road. Despite an occasional picket shot, the column reached Sharpsburg near midnight, crossing Antietam Creek on the bridge at Antietam Furnace.[92] One Yankee with apparently keen eyes or sense of smell reported surprising some pickets near Antietam Creek at the Furnace who were cooking supper: "we rode pell-mell over them, scattering their fires, roasting ears, and rye coffee in every direction, pouring a volley into the darkness as we passed....The column would occasionally halt where Cole's Cavalry was acquainted and endeavor to obtain information concerning the enemy, as to location and numbers."[93] The column was fortunate that McLaws had moved most of his men north and east to defend against Franklin's invasion of Pleasant Valley after the Union general had taken Crampton's Gap on the evening of the 14th. Confederate campfires helped the column avoid Rebel camps as the Union troopers were now aware that the enemy was more plentiful in the area as they approached Sharpsburg near which some of Longstreet's men had journeyed from the battle at South Mountain as stragglers and pickets.[94]

At the edge of Sharpsburg on Harpers Ferry-Sharpsburg Road, John Shay, who lived there, recalled that the troopers asked for water "and he carried many buckets full to them. Finally the bucket was let fall and the next morning he found it at the Public Square where the horses had kicked it."[95] The saddle-weary troopers halted in Sharpsburg about midnight to allow the column to close up and to rest the horses after a harrowing ride of some 17 miles in inky darkness. Citizens warned that Rebel forces were in the area with some even in town, as the Confederate army was then retreating from South Mountain, so officers sent scouts out to the north on the Boonsboro-Sharpsburg Pike to investigate. They quickly found Rebel pickets after being fired on from a hill just outside of town near the old Lutheran Church. A participant, Lt. William M. Luff, who commanded a company in the 12th Illinois Cavalry, described the column's encounter but wrote that it took place on the Hagerstown Pike:

> A charge was ordered and promptly executed, driving the pickets and their reserve into and through the principal street of Sharpsburg on the road toward Hagerstown. Here the command was moving slowly northward, when the darkness was suddenly illumined by a sheet of flame, and the stillness broken by a rattling volley of musketry. The discharge was harmless, but it was evident that the enemy was present in considerable force, as the commotion in their camp, the commands of their officers, and the rumbling of artillery wheels could be distinctly heard. A citizen also informed an officer of the Eighth New York that the column was "going right into Lee s army."

---

[91] Luff, 41; Blackwell, 33. See also n. 84 above—it is very likely that some troopers or infantry on horses did recross the pontoon bridge and did not escape.

[92] Goodhart wrote that the time was about 3 A.M., 56; Tischler opines that the head of the column arrived in Sharpsburg about 11 P.M., 146. Tischler quoting William H. Nichols in the *National Tribune*, 12 April 1894, who wrote that he arrived in Sharpsburg about midnight, 169. D.H. Hill arrived in Sharpsburg about 2:30 A.M. finding no Yankee cavalry: "he was ordered to proceed to Sharpsburg with the two brigades under his command to drive out a Union cavalry force reported there. He was soon on the road and quickly overtaken by Colonel Robert H. Chilton of Lee's staff with contrary orders, which required him to send only a part of his force. (He selected the 5th and 6th Alabama under Colonel Gordon.) In a few minutes, however, he received an order from Longstreet to go ahead and did so with the two brigades, but found no cavalry at Sharpsburg; it had passed through the town," Carman, Pierro, 171. Clearly the escape column was through Sharpsburg before 3 A.M.

[93] Goodhart, 56. Tischler wrote that the Rebel pickets along the road were from the 13th Mississippi Infantry, 115-116.

[94] Carman noted that the brigade of "[Brig. Gen. Cadmus Marcellus] Wilcox was brought back from near the mouth of the [Pleasant] valley" but [Brig. Gen. Lewis A.] Armistead and [Brig. Gen. Winfield S.] Featherston were still picketing the Sandy Hook Road on the Maryland side of the Potomac, Carman, Pierro, 189.

[95] O.T. Reilly, "Stories of Antietam" in *The Battlefield of Antietam* (Hagerstown, MD: Hagerstown Bookbinding & Printing Co., c. 1921).

A hurried consultation was held between the officers and guides, and it was decided to turn back and try another road. The movement was quickly executed, the Twelfth Illinois, guided by Noakes, taking the advance, and leaving Sharpsburg by a road running to the left, or westward, toward Falling Waters on the Potomac.

We were not going anywhere in particular, and it was hoped the country in this direction would prove more open and unobstructed, and better "adapted to manoeuvring cavalry," than that toward Hagerstown.

The enemy had now gotten their artillery in position, and sent a few shells after us as we moved out of the village. It was necessary to avoid the main roads, which were in possession of the enemy; but Noakes, who was familiar with every foot of ground in the neighborhood, found a circuitous path through lanes and by-roads, woods and fields. So the column marched steadily and silently, threading its way between the camps of the sleeping foe, until it emerged at a point on the Hagerstown and Williamsport turnpike about two miles from Williamsport.[96]

---

[96] Luff, 42. It is possible that Rebel pickets were at the intersection of the Boonsboro Pike and Hagerstown Pike explaining why there were pickets on both roads, which makes military sense enabling coverage of the two main roads but see Heysinger below. Heysinger is certain that the church mentioned in other accounts near which the Rebel pickets were located was not the Dunker Church, letter from Heysinger to Carman 23 August 1905, N.Y. Public Library Carman Papers, copy courtesy of Thomas Clemens. Heysinger is certain that the column went up the Hagerstown Pike from Sharpsburg so the Rebel picket he asserts was not at the Dunker Church otherwise his version fails; he favors the Lutheran Church on the Sharpsburg-Boonsboro Pike as the location of the fight. The location would be the Dunker Church if the column did go up the Hagerstown Pike as that church is also uphill about 1.2 road miles from Sharpsburg. The Lutheran Church is about 150 yards from the intersection of the Hagerstown Pike and the Boonsboro Pike according to the Carman-Cope's maps. As will be discussed, participant accounts differ in the escape route primarily from Sharpsburg north to near Williamsport. It is difficult to believe that if the Confederate pickets were near the Lutheran church, they let the escape column ride north on the Hagerstown Pike for two or more hours after they fired on them. See note 98 below for a discussion regarding the Ground Squirrel Church 1.75 miles north of the Dunker Church.

Harpers Ferry map showing beginning of ride for the escape column. Adapted from 1859 map, courtesy Harpers Ferry NBP.

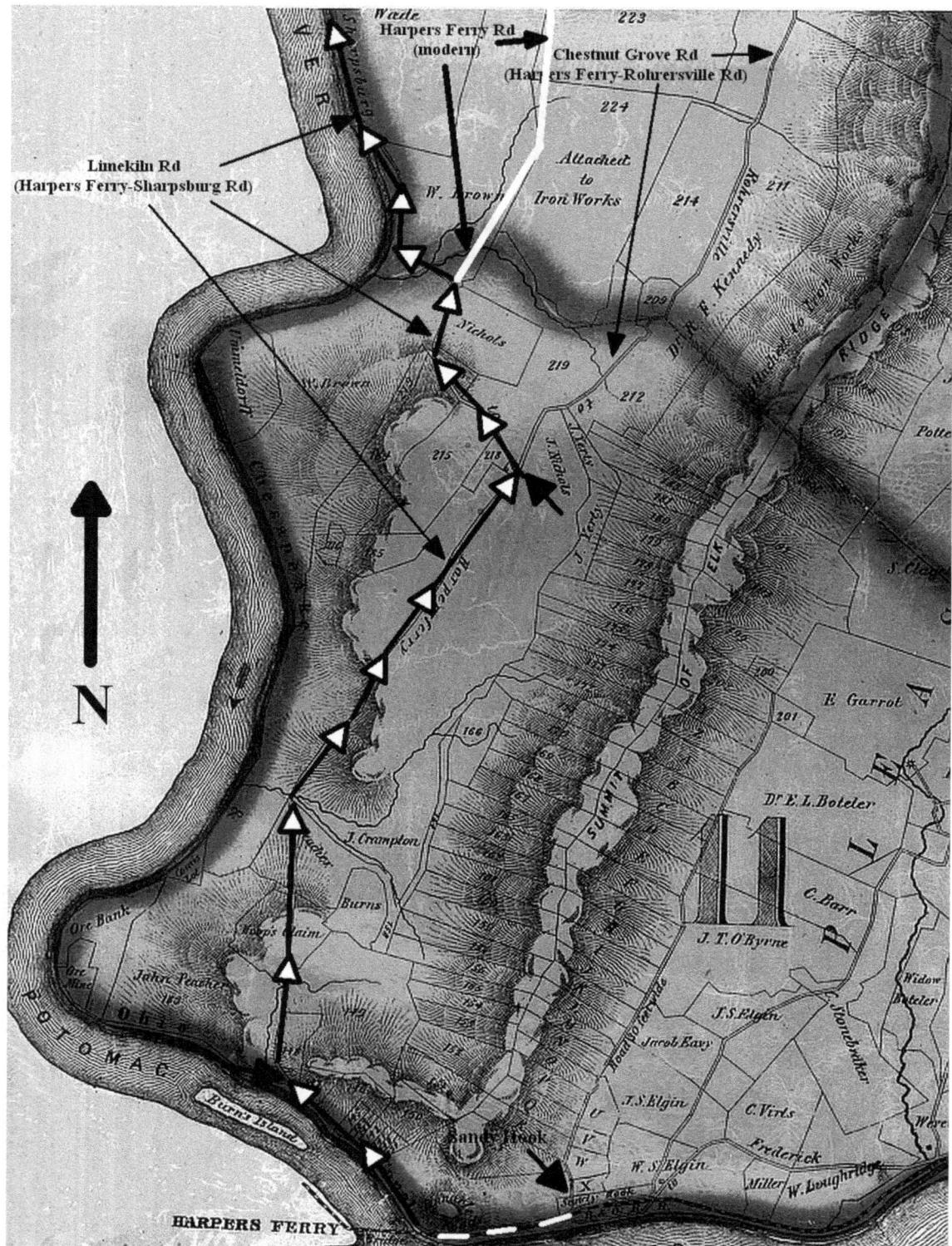

After crossing the pontoon bridge, the column rode along the C&O Canal on the Harpers Ferry-Sharpsburg Road which is on the opposite side of the towpath shown by the white arrows. Some mistakenly rode downstream after crossing the pontoon bridge toward Sandy Hook at the black arrow; white broken lines lead from the pontoon bridge; Confederate pickets fired at them. There may have been Confederate pickets also at the first sharp turn away from the canal as the column rode due north at the black arrow above Burns Island. The column then turned left toward the river at the top large black arrow. The "Rohrersville to Harpersferry" road as shown on the map is the modern Chestnut Grove Road. The modern Harpers Ferry Road leads off to the north at the modern intersection of Limekiln Road shown by the solid white line. See Appendix D: Driving Tour, Part 2, number 6. Detail of 1859 map of Washington County, Maryland, from a survey by Thomas Taggart. Courtesy LOC.

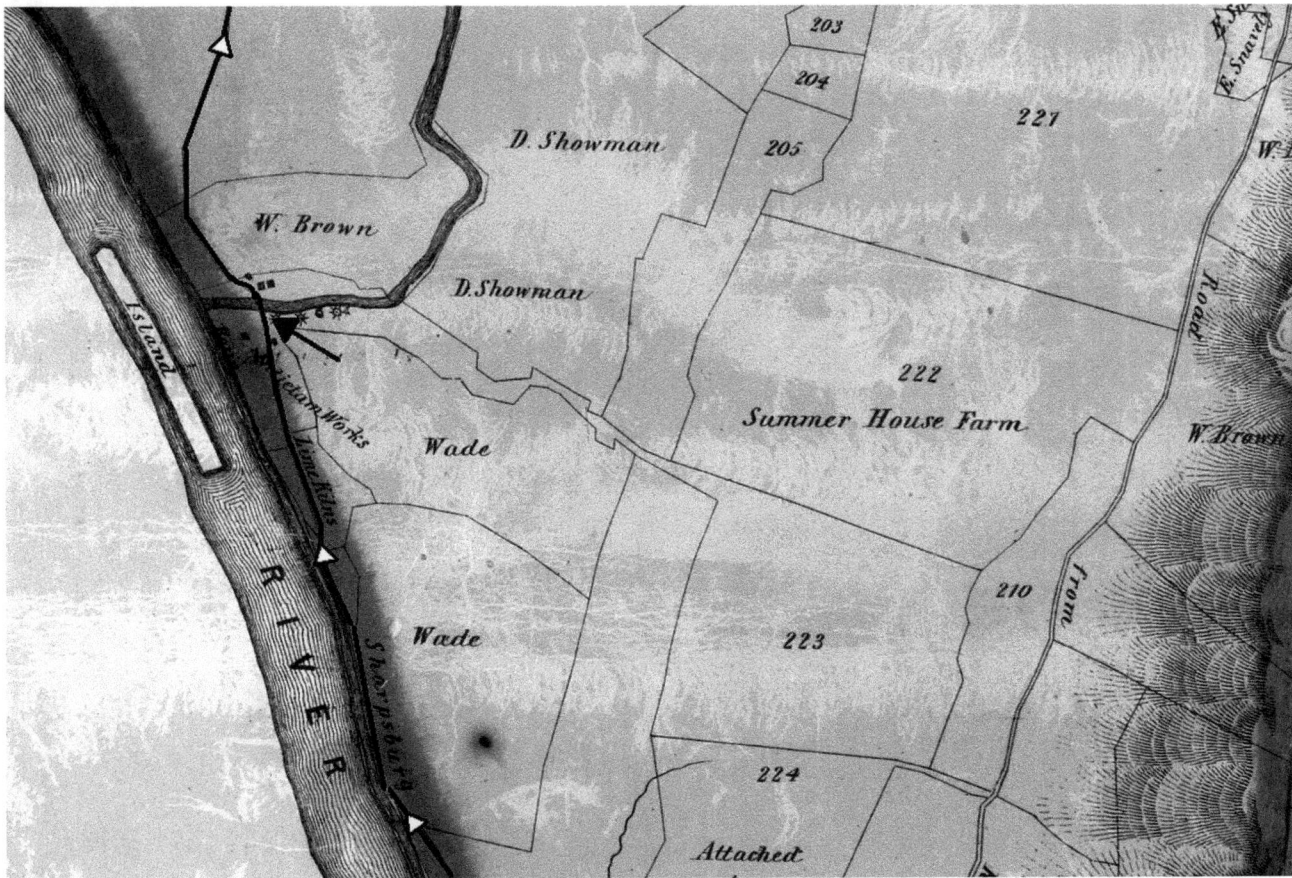

Detail of Taggart map of Washington County showing where the skirmish with Rebel pickets took place near Antietam Furnace. Courtesy LOC.

Lutheran Church on Boonsboro Pike, photograph taken facing south toward Sharpsburg after the Battle of Antietam. It was from this vicinity Rebel pickets fired at the escape column which was at the bottom of the hill to the right in the picture. The church is not extant but its cemetery is. Note battle damage to stuccoed walls, soldiers sitting on front steps and the single telegraph wire running down the street in front of the church. It appears that the Hagerstown Pike is at the lower right center of the photograph and if so, shows how close the Confederate pickets were to the head of escape column. Courtesy LOC.

Other versions of the encounter in Sharpsburg differ in some respects but most agree that there was a sharp skirmish in town. It seems clear that this confrontation must have taken place in Sharpsburg even though exactly where may be in dispute. Sharpsburg is the only town the column was in from Harpers Ferry to Greencastle. No one mentioned seeing other towns such as Williamsport or Hagerstown during the ride.

Another participant, Cpl. Isaac W. Heysinger with Co. B of the 7th Rhode Island Cavalry, also described this incident. He wrote that the column having reformed in Sharpsburg, its leaders decided to take the Hagerstown Turnpike north but had to veer off to the west beyond Sharpsburg but before Jones's Cross Roads. There, the column used farm lanes and fields closer to the Potomac away from the retreating Confederates who were reported to be in Hagerstown. Modern historians such as Dennis E. Frye, Chief Historian at Harpers Ferry National Park, and Dr. Thomas Clemens, accept Heysinger's account as likely correct for several reasons, including that Heysinger's final version was the latest full account of the escape by a participant, thus giving him the advantage of having all of the prior accounts available as references. This is important since his Rhode Island squadron was near the rear of the column and obviously he could not be aware of what was happening at the front except by hearsay and reading other accounts. Also, Heysinger was the most highly educated of all the writers as he completed his undergraduate degree, obtained a master's degree, and then a medical degree. Finally, he exchanged letters with Ezra Carman about Antietam, giving Heysinger the advantage of communicating with the foremost historian of the era for Antietam, but it is surprising that Carman chose to use Luff's version, especially concerning the route from Sharpsburg to the Hagerstown-Williamsport Turnpike.[97] Carman accepted the Luff version which was buttressed by the report of Col. Voss. Voss, the leader of the column, wrote that his scouts were sent out heading north on Sharpsburg's main street

> when suddenly a sheet of flame illumined the darkness for an instant, followed by the report of at least a hundred rifles sending their leaden messengers about our ears. This came from a strong outpost placed at the entrance of the Hagerstown road into the city of Sharpsburg, not more than one hundred and fifty paces ahead of us, furnishing the most conclusive proof that the rebels were in strong force in that direction. Before allowing the alarm to spread, the head of the column was turned in another direction, toward Falling Waters, on the Potomac, to find, if possible, a weaker point to pierce their lines. On the road thither only a few pickets were encountered. Here I ascertained from a friendly chat which my guides had with some mill-hands at work in a large flouring mill, the exact strength and location of the rebels thereabouts, and determined to make the break there. By this time a bright starlight had succeeded the impenetrable gloom of the early night, enabling us to discern surrounding object more distinctly. We were also guided in choosing our path by the faint glimmer of their bivouac fires. The column was gathered close in hand, the order to charge given, and my brave fellows, fully comprehending the importance of the movement, dashed gallantly through the bivouac of the astonished grey-coats, riding and cutting down all opposition. But few of the enemy recovered from their surprise in time to send a shot or a volley into this strange apparition, which seemed dropped from the clouds,

---

[97] Isaac W. Heysinger, *Antietam and the Maryland and Virginia Campaigns of 1862* (New York: The Neale Publishing Company, 1912), 163. Carman accepts Luff's version, Carman, Clemens, 257-258; Tischler, 162, 169. Compare Frye, "Stonewall Attacks!," who writes that the column did take the Hagerstown Pike and did not turn off until after Tilghmantown which is closer to Sharpsburg than Jones's Cross Roads, 47-48; Frye details Heysinger's version in his article, *The Morningside Notes*, no. 22, 1987, "The Cavalry Column from Harper's Ferry in the Antietam Campaign." Carman wrote that after the column rested and allowed stragglers to close up, "the march was resumed on the Mercerville [also Mercersville] Road, west of the Hagerstown Pike. Once on the road, they broke into a brisk trot and went through New Industry and Mercerville (on the Potomac)," Carman, Clemens, 257-258. Tischler disputes Heysinger's version. Bell mistook the stone bridge on the Harpers Ferry Road over the Antietam at Antietam Furnace for (Rohrbach's) Burnside Bridge but wrote that the column turned back after confronting several Rebel cavalry videttes and took a road leading westward toward Falling Waters, 12. See Frye's biography of Heysinger in his Notes article as well as Heysinger's statement why his account is the most accurate, *Journal of the U.S. Cavalry Association*, "The Cavalry Column from Harper's Ferry in the Antietam Campaign." Frye's Heysinger is an edited and endnoted version of Heysinger's article. Heysinger points out that he was born nearby [in Fayetteville, Pennsylvania about five miles east of Chambersburg and today some 45 road miles from Sharpsburg] "my relatives lived all round our route, and I was familiar from boyhood with every road, path, plain and mountain, as anyone could be who had grown up, hunted, fished, visited, went swimming, and did all the things that boys do... [I] knew every mile we traversed, and all the mills, creeks, villages, and even farms, woods, fields and dwellings, for many miles around, by night or day, for in both I was equally at home," 4-5. He added: "this narrative of mine, with its details, seems to me to be justified, because it is based on both Union and Confederate documents and reports. Also because it is written by one born and raised on the borders of Pennsylvania nearby, whose brothers, uncles and other relatives were residents of Boonsborough, Clearspring, Williamsport, and other places in the same area, and who was well acquainted with all the roads, mountains, creeks, rivers, and topography from his childhood up, and who was a roamer during his vacations (and often at other times), over all this region, up to the time when the events herein described had occurred; and often since. So that all this makes it desirable that one so familiar by night and day with these scenes, in which he was an actor, should correlate the various data into a comprehensible and authentic narrative," 8-9. One may question why he went to such great lengths to establish his bona fides but clearly his qualifications and his participation make his account among the best. His account jibes with most or helps explain differences in other accounts such as when the column turned off the Hagerstown Pike on its ride to the Greencastle Pike but it remains very disquieting that Carman chose not to believe Heysinger despite a long exchange of letters with him. I believe Carman over Heysinger but will present both alternatives on following maps.

and so we escaped comparatively harmless. We came out near St. James' College, and after drawing reins a while to blow our horses, the column entered the woods skirting the turnpike between Williamsport and Hagerstown, taking up our line of march toward the border of Pennsylvania.[98]

Right: Detail from Carman-Cope's map, Daybreak 17 September. The Lutheran Church is in the right center from which position the Rebel pickets fired; the Harpers Ferry Road leads in from the bottom center at the arrow. The Hagerstown Pike leads out of town to the north at the top right arrow, the Heysinger route. The road to Mercerville is to the top left, Carman's choice. Heysinger wrote that the column did not pass him in his position at the column's rear but it could have gone up the Hagerstown Pike for two blocks and then have taken a side road to the Mondell Road at the center black arrow to avoid the pickets. The Burnside Bridge Road leads in from the lower right corner which Bell said the column rode. Bell in his report describes incidents during the escape with which other sources disagree. Courtesy LOC.

---

[98] Pettengill, 83-84. The mill was likely Dovenberger's Mill in Mercersville, Tischler, 146, 184. In Heysinger's version the mill was likely Cross's Mill northwest of Fairplay. Heysinger wrote that the main reason the column would not have taken the Mercersville road from Sharpsburg was that route would have taken the horsemen further away from McClellan but he earlier said that no one knew where McClellan was so it seems reasonable that at the time the column was fired on in Sharpsburg, its leaders primary concern would have been to avoid running into Lee's army and move around its western flank. Heysinger gives a better reason for avoiding going near the Potomac as he said that Confederates could be just on the other side as Jackson had recently marched there the day before and could have intercepted them. A more remote possibility is that the column took the Hagerstown Pike north after being fired on by pickets near the Lutheran Church. The column then could have been again fired on by more Rebel pickets near the Ground Squirrel Church less than three miles north of Sharpsburg on the left of the pike (1 ¾ road miles north of Dunker Church), then turned around and took a right turn in about 3/10 mile onto Mondell Road to the west to Dovenberger's Mill.

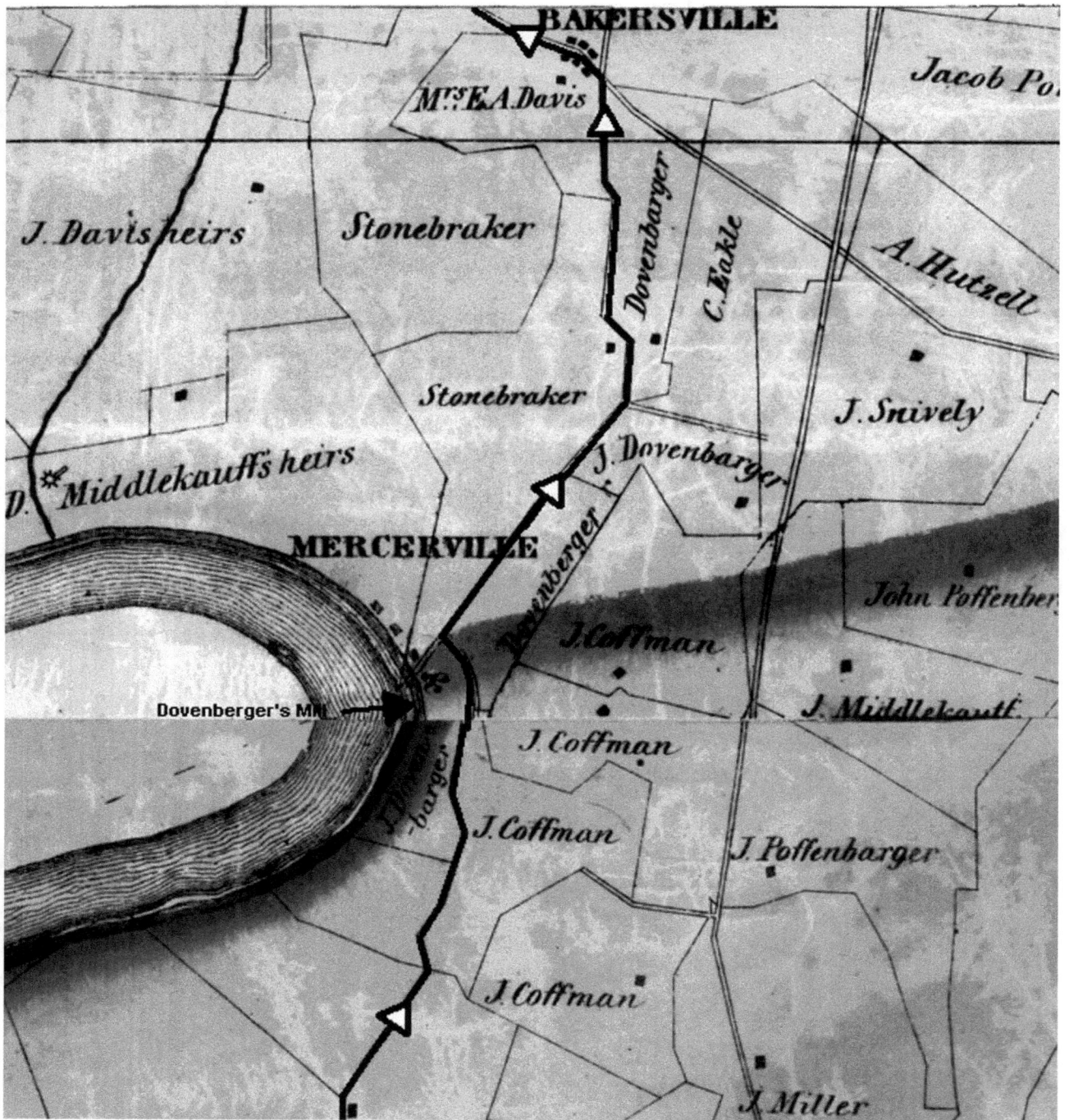

The Carman version of the escape route from Sharpsburg on Mondell Road to the road north from Mercersville to Bakersville showing Dovenberger's Mill location at black arrow. Detail of 1859 map of Washington County, Maryland, by Thomas Taggart. Courtesy LOC.

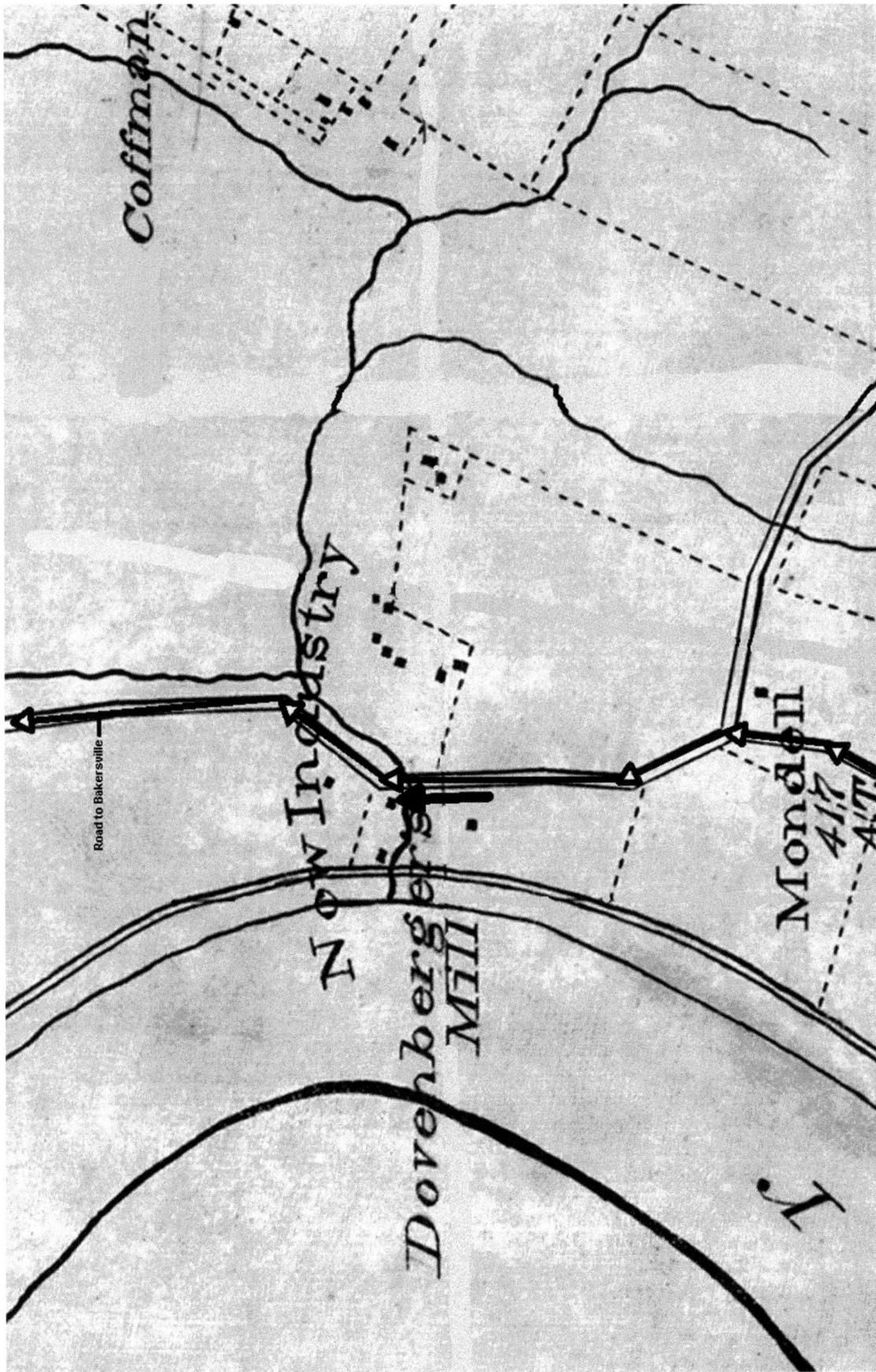

Dovenberger's Mill is likely one of the two the rectangles just below the "w" in "New" as it had to be fairly close to a stream for its waterpower and close to the canal there where it was widened would be good for loading the flour, etc. Arrow shows Mondell Road the escape column travelled under scenario two, the Carman/Luff version; it would have ridden north toward the top of the map to Bakersville. Detail from no. 1 sheet of preliminary map of Antietam by Jedediah Hotchkiss; enlarged from the "Michler" map of the War records atlas, with corrections and additions, Nov. 1894. Courtesy LOC.

Detail from 14 September Mattern Map showing that Carman believed that the cavalry took Mondell Road northwest from Sharpsburg to Mercersville. He does not show the route from Bakersville to Downsville as the roads in that area are not shown. Note he draws in "RESERVE ARTY" on the Williamsport Road through Jones's Cross Roads toward Williamsport yet shows another unnamed rectangle heading southeast from Hagerstown on the Hagerstown-Williamsport Pike. Obviously the Mattern Maps are early drafts. Courtesy LOC.

Overleaf: two variations of the escape route, the solid line with arrows shows the Carman version and the dotted line from Heysinger, et al. Arrow at bottom right shows road from Mercersville. The column then rode northwest to Downsville and then north on the Downsville Pike to the intersection of the Williamsport Road at the top arrow. Cross's Mill and Fairplay Mill mentioned by Heysinger shown here as well as Marsh Creek. Cross's Mill was on Marsh Creek (today Marsh Run south of Route 63 and St. James Run north of Route 63). The location of the capture may be near the intersection of the Downsville Pike and the Williamsport Road at arrow no. 1, *if* Longstreet's train was on the *Williamsport Road* traveling from near Boonsboro. The Rebel wagons could have been diverted onto the Downsville Pike to the north and then south on the Williamsport Turnpike. If the train was not captured on the Williamsport Road, the escape column may have proceeded up the Downsville Pike and then northwest perhaps on a road near today's Bower Avenue to the Williamsport Pike. There it turned southwest on the pike where the wagon train was captured shortly after the turn. The wagon train continued southwest on the Williamsport Pike until it was diverted on a smaller road on the Van Lear estate which was a shortcut to the Greencastle Pike. Heysinger and most other writers agree that once on the Williamsport Road, the escape column rode west then north on an unnamed connector to the Williamsport Pike (dashed line) at arrow no. 2 where it then captured the wagon train at the Williamsport Pike, then crossed the Van Lear property onto the Greencastle Pike. Most versions of the escape written by participants agree that the Rebel train was taken on the *Williamsport Pike* (also called by some the Williamsport-Hagerstown Turnpike), after the train came down from Hagerstown or across from Funkstown. Arrow 3 shows where the train would have been captured if the escape column had not captured the train on the Williamsport Road but continued up the Downsville Pike then to the Williamsport Pike. It is unlikely that the escape column in any event continued north on the Downsville Pike to intercept the road heading west from Funkstown as that would have been too close to Hagerstown. Detail from *Official Atlas*, Plate 42. The map on page 309 shows more detail from the previous map of the first part of the journey north from Bakersville.

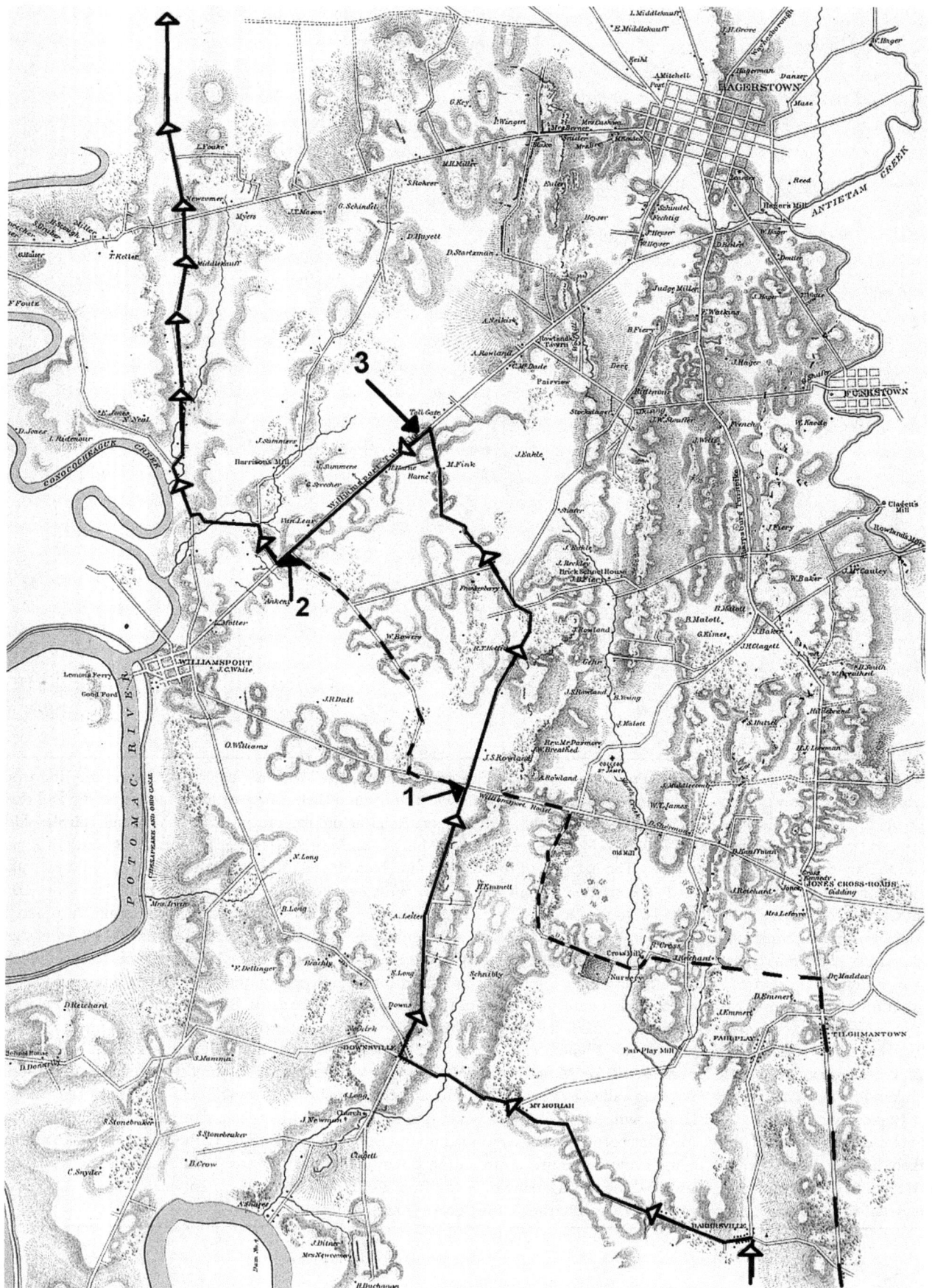

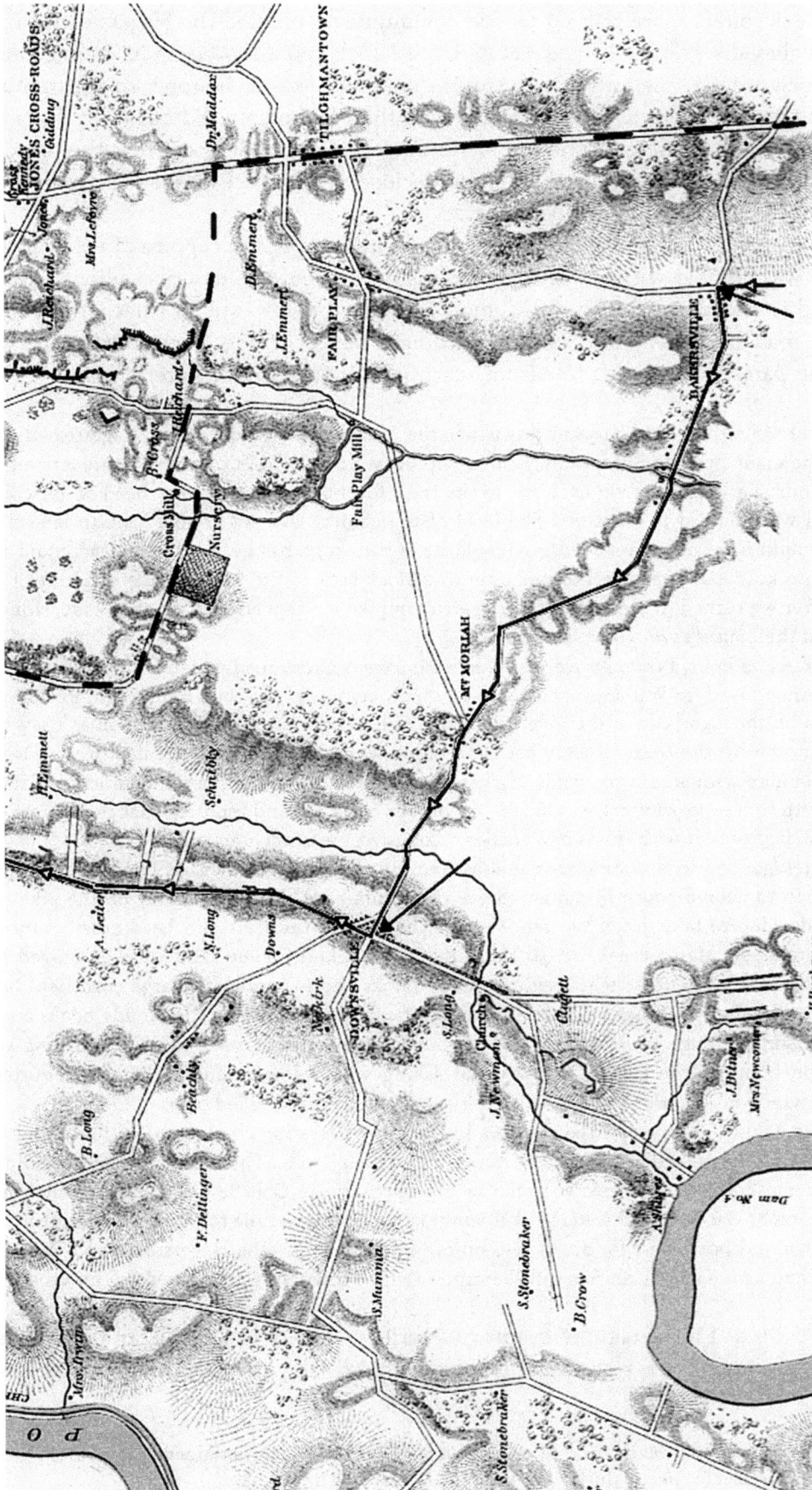

Most of the accounts agree that either the column never entered the Hagerstown Pike, or if it did enter the pike, they disagree at the point at which it left the pike and began its cross country ride. Voss wrote that Rebels were at the entrance to the Hagerstown Pike in the town so apparently the column did not get on the pike there. Other accounts relate that the column did begin on the pike but had to divert from it as pickets were encountered as Heysinger relates. Bell wrote that the principal streets of Sharpsburg had enemy troops on them so "it was decided to turn back and take another road, which led westward toward Falling Waters, on the Potomac."[99]

Heysinger's detailed account of the route from Sharpsburg to the capture of the wagon train is also plausible as he was familiar with the area. Additionally, the route he describes which is partially on the Hagerstown Pike, and also through fields and farm lanes, helps explain some other accounts which record the off-road excursions, but differ regarding when or if the Hagerstown Pike was used. His chronicle of this part of the escape route from Sharpsburg is paraphrased here:

The road we took from Sharpsburg was not the Mercersville road but the Hagerstown pike. When we halted on the main street in Sharpsburg in a bunch for two blocks back from the Confederate pickets near the Lutheran Church as they fired on us, I was in the rear. After a few minutes, the head of our column turned to the left and we followed in our turn. The head of the column did not double back to take the Mercersville Road as I would have noticed since they would have had to go by me. Also, the head could have taken the Hagerstown pike initially but then turned after one block back to the Mercersville Road. But I know they did not since after we turned to the left on the Hagerstown pike we kept straight on that wide, stone turnpike, and I recognized the houses as we headed north.

After about an hour, I thought we would be near Jones's Cross-road which led from Boonsborough, where my two brothers lived, to Williamsport and near which my uncle was then living. Just above Tilghmantown a doctor lived on the right side of the pike, Dr. Maddox; I recognized his house as soon as I saw it. The column halted and I went to the front to see what the trouble was. I was told that the doctor who lived there was a strong Union man with whom the guide was acquainted so he and the officer in command of the column went in to talk with him to learn what was ahead. An officer came out and reported that there were three divisions of Rebels in Hagerstown with trains and artillery; Longstreet was in command.

This intelligence was accurate but dated as Gen. Lee had ordered most of Longstreet's command back to Boonsborough to defend South Mountain. Since the column could no longer stay on the pike to Hagerstown, the guides decided to take down the fence across the pike to the west and head cross country. There were several old mills on Marsh creek, across those fields and I knew some who were employed in one [Cross's Mill]. Marsh creek had cut its way leaving muddy banks and it bordered a large corn field beyond through which we passed after crossing the creek. It was a difficult crossing due to the muddy banks and the hundreds of horses slogging through and drew out the column as it struggled across. I saw fires burning among the corn and someone lying on the ground drawled out asking who we were and I claimed: "Fourteenth Alabama Cavalry" to which my interlocutor replied, "Ye'r a damned liar" and rolled over.

I lost the column but recognized the area so I had my horse knock over an old fence and rode through a field when I then heard the noise of our column into which I rode. The road on which I rejoined the column enters the Boonsborough-Williamsport pike nearly opposite the College of St. James, which is about a half-mile to the north. We then followed the Williamsport road about a mile to the west, and turned off into a road running north and northwest for about two miles, where it enters the Hagerstown and Williamsport pike, a little more than a mile and a half from Williamsport, which town we thus cleared by this cross-road.[100]

Heysinger defended his version of events in a series of letters to Carman. In those letters, one topic on which he spent much time, was the route from Harpers Ferry to Sharpsburg, e.g., he assures Carman

---

[99] Bell, 12. This statement could be interpreted to mean that the column took the Mondell Road from Sharpsburg toward Mercersville or another road further up the Hagerstown Pike.

[100] Heysinger, "The Cavalry Column from Harper's Ferry in the Antietam Campaign," 23-26.

that the towpath was not taken but rather the road to Sharpsburg which he also called the "John Brown" road which went up three steep eminences. Heysinger also asserted that the column did not take any river road because the road down from the Antietam Iron Works along the Potomac did not connect with Harpers Ferry as it only led to an old lime kiln probably for the Iron Works. While Carman's questions and responses to Heysinger's letters are not available, clearly Carman was dubious of some of Heysinger's details, so much so that for the route from Sharpsburg north he used Luff's version vice Heysinger in his history of the campaign. Carman may have questioned Heysinger about whether the column from Harpers Ferry took the road toward Rohrersville then crossed the Rohrbach (Lower or Burnside) Bridge as some participants related replacing the crossing of the bridge over Antietam Creek at the Antietam Ironworks with the Rohrbach Bridge. Or as appears from Heysinger's reply, Carman asked about the road along the Potomac now known as Limekiln Road, but then as the Harpers Ferry-Sharpsburg Road. The scouts of the column would not have headed north on the Rohrersville Road, today's Chestnut Grove Road, as it would have brought it nearer to Gen. Lee's army and McLaws's troops.[101] Carman apparently responded to Heysinger's letters by stating that residents of Sharpsburg said that the cavalry column, after being fired on by Rebels at the entrance of the Hagerstown Pike, took the Mercersville Road toward the Potomac. Heysinger said this route that the townspeople reported, if taken, from the Mercersville Road to the Bakersville Road, then the Bakersville and Williamsport Road to the point on the Hagerstown-Williamsport Pike where Longstreet's wagon train was encountered,

---

[101] Pierro, Carman, 123-124. From one of Heysinger's apparent replies to Carman he asserts that those inhabitants of Sharpsburg to whom Carman spoke were not aware of the column's true route. Given that the large majority of the escapees believed that they went by the Iron Works near the mouth of the Antietam Creek, it is unlikely that the more northerly route passing Rohrersville on the right, taking the Rohrbach Bridge and entering the eastern part of town was taken. Note Strother in his *Harper's Magazine* article shows for 16 September that a local citizen apparently from the Sharpsburg/Keedysville area told Strother that the escape column had come up the towpath, Strother, "Recollections," 280. Strother did not include this report in his diary, however in *Harper's* he wrote that the column captured 110 wagons and destroyed 60, while in his diary he showed 112 captured, 62 destroyed, and 50 wagons of flour sent to Pennsylvania. His *Diaries* and *Harper's* reports apparently rely on camp rumors and hearsay since he did not relate that he spoke to any participants or eyewitnesses, *Diaries*, 109. Today, the road-mile distance measured on the Harpers Ferry Road from the pontoon bridge on the Maryland shore to the intersection of Limekiln Road is 4.8 miles, and 7.3 total miles to Antietam Furnace at the intersection of the modern Harpers Ferry Road; total distance to Sharpsburg at the Sharpsburg-Boonsboro Pike (also Boonsboro-Sharpsburg Pike) is 10.3 miles. The escape column would not have ridden by the Kennedy Farmhouse where John Brown spent three and one half months in 1859 preparing for his Harpers Ferry raid; it is about one road mile along the Mt. Lock Hill Road from the intersection of today's Limekiln Road and the Harpers Ferry Road and .7 mile road-mile distance from the intersection of today's Harpers Ferry road and Chestnut Grove Road. From the intersection of today's Limekiln Road along the old Harpers Ferry Road to Mt. Lock Hill Road is slightly less than one mile. The modern Harpers Ferry Road from Harpers Ferry to Sharpsburg branches off to the northeast and then bends northwest to meet Limekiln Road at Antietam Furnace. But note that the *Official Atlas*, Plate 42, shows a structure labeled "John Brown" a short distance before a road which leads west toward the Potomac, today's Mt. Lock Hill Road. The configuration of this road in the *Official Atlas* and current maps is similar. It is also noteworthy that this plate does not show that the Harpers Ferry road cuts over below the Brown House. Mt. Lock Hill Road today strikes Limekiln Road crossing today's Harpers Ferry Road. The Plate 29 map arguably also shows the Mt. Lock Hill Road as the one taken by the column as its shape more closely resembles that one versus the Harpers Ferry Road shape. However the Taggart map shape for the Harpers Ferry Road in this location more closely resembles today's Harpers Ferry Road-Limekiln Road configuration and does not show Mt. Lock Hill Road or any road in its vicinity. If the Plate 42 map is correct showing the Kennedy Farmhouse as "John Brown," then the road taken by the column would have been the Mt. Lock Hill Road. One might speculate that the guides would certainly know the location of the Kennedy Farmhouse and then know to take the first left after that house but the discrepancy in the two plates showing the road shapes leads to this speculation. The 1867 Weyss map is similar to Plate 42 (This map is titled "Surveyed from August 3d to Sept. 20th 1863, under the direction of Capt. N. Michler, Corps of Engrs., U.S. Army, by Major John E. Weyss" and is available from LOC. Local historian John Frye who has studied the road net in Washington County extensively said that Mt. Lock Hill Road was not a designated road in 1862 but became a public road much later so it is unlikely that this road could have been used by the escape column; the road is not shown on 1859 Taggart map or the 1877 Lake map; interview with Mr. Frye 16 July 2011. He also questions why local guides would have taken this route versus Limekiln Road as Mt. Lock Hill is more out of the way of the Sharpsburg destination.

would not have necessitated riding across fields. Most participants recalled riding through fields after leaving Sharpsburg which Heysinger says proves his assertion that the column went up the Hagerstown Pike, then cut across fields to avoid Rebel infantry.[102] Regardless, the exact route will likely never be known given the darkness and the many farm lanes and paths between Sharpsburg and Williamsport. Heysinger's account is plausible given his research and his background so despite a few exaggerations and possible factual issues it will be accepted as one of the two possible routes from Sharpsburg even though Carman did not believe Heysinger.[103]

---

[102] Letter from Heysinger to Carman 4 September 1905 N.Y. Public Library Carman Collection courtesy Thomas Clemens. It is probable that the roads from Mercersville to the Williamsport Road were not of turnpike quality so participants may have thought that the roads were farm roads or lanes.

[103] Bell, 12; Tischler opines that "leaving Sharpsburg, it was apparent the main route up toward Hagerstown was avoided, with the next stop being for the watering of the horses...at the spring at the College of St. James," 134. Tischler writes that Heysinger's detailed account of the ride up the Hagerstown Pike from Sharpsburg is incorrect and that "the Hagerstown Pike was not used," 183-4. The author's opinion is that the column, after crossing the pontoon bridge, entered Sharpsburg after riding up the Harpers Ferry Road; it then diverted to New Industry and Mercersville, took the road from Mercersville to Bakersville, next the road from Bakersville to Downsville, and followed the Downsville Pike to Williamsport Road. The column then rode west on the Williamsport Road then turned north on a road running north-northwest to Williamsport Pike where they encountered the wagon train. The Yankees diverted the wagon train on a shortcut to Greencastle Pike on the Van Lear estate.

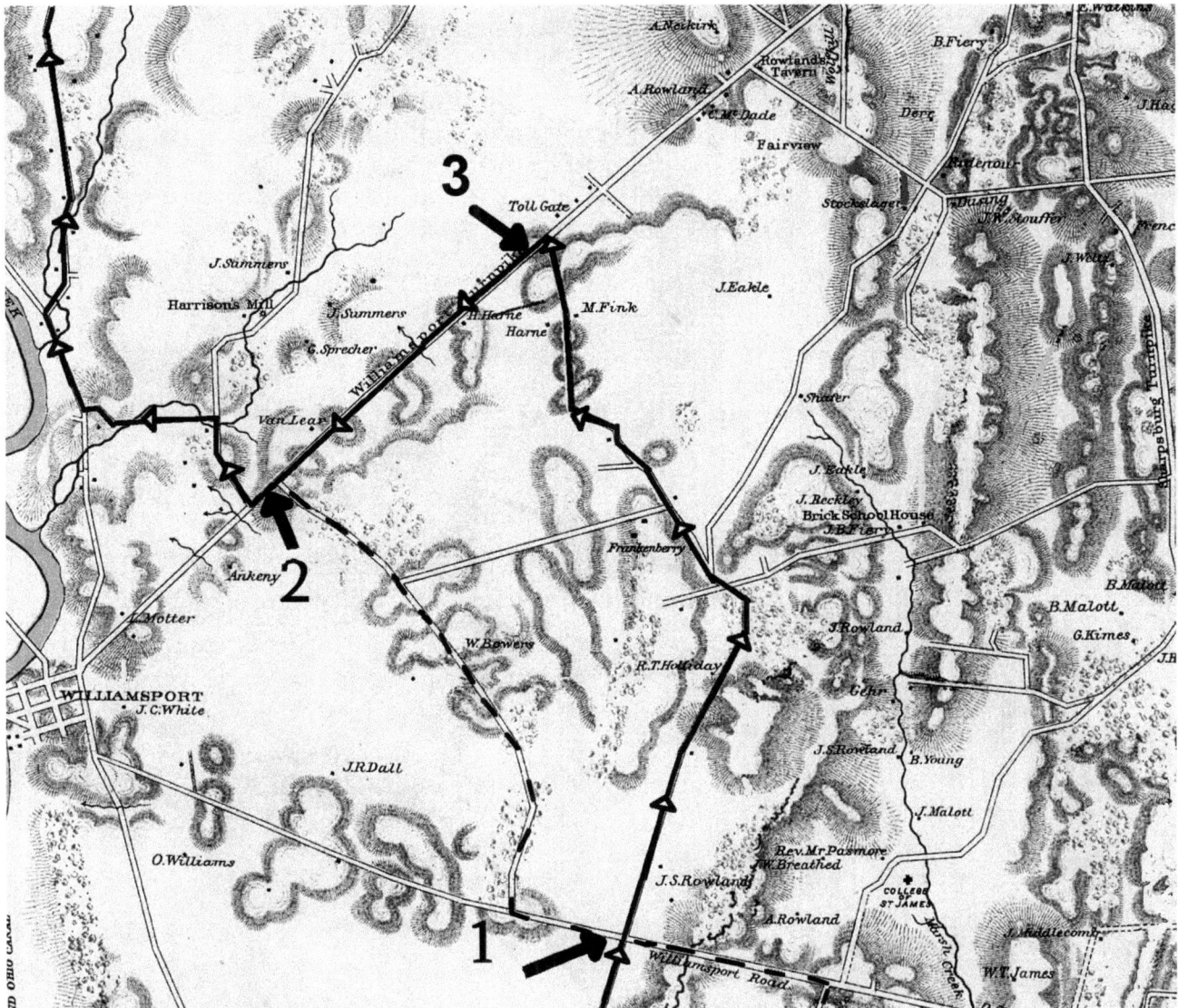

Lower black arrow at "1" shows where the train was captured if it were on the Williamsport Road from near Boonsboro. Then the column with the train could have continued north on the Downsville Pike, then to the northwest to the Williamsport Pike, then left toward Williamsport. The shortcut from the Williamsport Pike to the Greencastle Pike across the Van Lear estate is shown above the arrow labeled "2." The Greencastle Pike then continues north. Accounts differ sometimes confusing the Williamsport "Road" with the Williamsport "Pike" thus making it difficult to follow the various escape routes written by participants. Today's Williamsport Road is Lappans Road, while the Williamsport Pike is still called that, as well as Virginia Avenue and Rt. 11. Note that the Official Alas map above correctly labels these two roads. The Williamsport Road is the most direct route to Williamsport from Boonsboro but not from Funkstown or Hagerstown. Today's wayside marking the capture site is just north of the point where the solid line route meets the Williamsport Turnpike at "3." Detail from *Official Atlas*, Plate 42. Courtesy LOC.

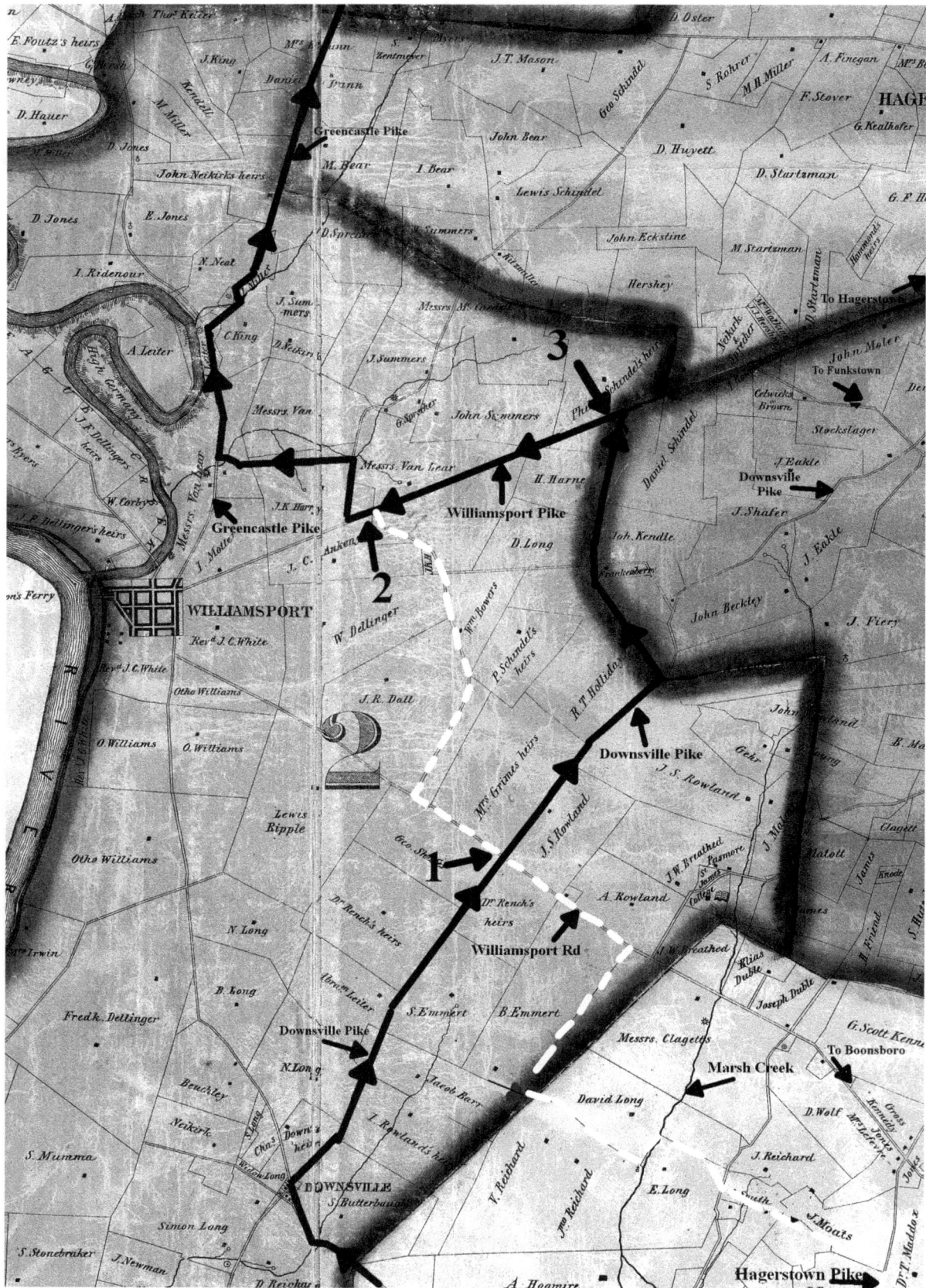

Taggart 1858 map overlaid with two possible routes; black arrows show the route with number "1" the location if the wagon train was captured on the Williamsport Road; white dashed lines show the likely Heysinger route with the number "2" at the capture site on the pike. Number "3" shows capture site if taken after a more northerly journey on the Downsville Pike. Courtesy LOC.

As dawn was nearing, the column halted to rest the horses and tired troopers who had been in their saddles now for more than eight hours; they chose a point near the Williamsport Road and Downsville Pike, about two and a half miles from Williamsport to reform. They had no way of knowing that most of the Rebel Army of Northern Virginia's wagons had been on or were on the move from Funkstown to Williamsport, and from Hagerstown to Williamsport on the Williamsport Pike, and therefore the Union troopers were inadvertently in position to interdict Lee's supplies once they reached the pike.[104] The column rode west after striking the Williamsport Road from the Downsville Pike and then rode northwest finally reaching the Williamsport Pike. At dawn, they heard the sound of many wagons approaching southeast on their right. Scouts reported a large wagon train approaching and the commanders decided to seize the opportunity to capture it. The train is described by Carman:

> The train consisted of Longstreet's reserve ammunition train which started from near Hagerstown and headed for the Potomac at midnight. Near Funkstown was a train of supplies collected in Maryland and other commissariat and quartermaster stores. There were also many wagons belonging to D.H. Hill's Division that had been pushed forward from near Boonsboro to Funkstown late in the evening, and with these were cooking details from the several brigades. Longstreet's ordnance train moved directly from Hagerstown toward the Potomac; the general supply train—about fifty wagons guarded by the 11th Georgia (Major Francis H. Little)—moved west from Funkstown by the Williamsport Road and, intercepting Longstreet's train at the intersection of the Hagerstown and Williamsport roads, fell in behind it. The men were scattered along behind what they supposed to be the regimental or brigade wagons and in the confusion of haltings and startings became weary, sleepy, and listless. Apprehending no danger, they paid no attention to the wagons and overlapped Longstreet's train as they neared Williamsport, when Colonel Benjamin F. Davis with his cavalry was upon them....[105]

Heysinger describes the scene as the now excited troopers in the column prepared to ambush the wagon train: "One regiment of cavalry [8th New York] was deployed along and back from the south side of the turnpike, concealed, as yet, by the trees and bushes....In rear of this regiment with its line of battle facing the turnpike...the 12th Illinois, was formed in column of fours, facing the left, and the Maryland and Rhode Island cavalry behind this formation, and principally to the right."[106] With most of the Union troopers hidden from view, Col. B.F. Davis, no doubt aided by his exaggerated, Mississippian drawl, with a small contingent of the 8th, captured the first wagon and sent it quickly over a dirt road, a shortcut to

---

[104] Tischler, 93-94.

[105] Carman, Pierro, 170. See Tischler, 97. Edward P. Alexander wrote that "Gen. Lee ordered me to take my ordnance train by [the] nearest country roads to ford the Potomac at Williamsport....I & the whole train ran a very narrow escape of being captured by a brigade of cavalry," means that Alexander must have been on the Williamsport Road, Alexander, *Fighting for the Confederacy,* 144. He was mistaken. As Carman correctly noted, part of the train originated in Hagerstown so the captured train was an amalgamation of several commands' wagons. Brig. Gen. William N. Pendleton, Gen. Lee's chief of artillery, wrote that on midnight of the 14th Lee ordered him to take his command which was near Boonsboro, less Col. S.D. Lee's battalion, "by the shortest route to Williamsport ....By sunrise Monday 15th, we had reached the intersection of the Hagerstown, Sharpsburg, Boonsborough, and Williamsport roads, [Jones's Cross Roads] and there received reliable intelligence of a large cavalry force of the enemy not far ahead of us." He then set up a defense and sent for infantry support to protect his train as well as a large train coming down the Hagerstown-Williamsport Turnpike heading for Williamsport, but because the Union cavalry had already passed that point heading north, Pendleton and his artillery train "narrowly missed a rather strange encounter," *OR,* vol. 19, pt. 1, 830. Carman's statement that the location of the trains' meeting "at the intersection of the Hagerstown and Williamsport roads" is difficult to square with the *Official Atlas* and the 1858 Bond map. The best interpretation of Carman is that the two trains met on the Williamsport Pike where the road west from Funkstown reaches the Williamsport Pike. The consolidated train then headed southeast on the Williamsport Pike where it was taken by the escape column. A train leaving Funkstown heading directly as possible to Williamsport would not be on the Williamsport Road but a train leaving from Boonsboro to Williamsport would be on the Williamsport Road. The route south on the Hagerstown Pike then west at Jones's Cross Roads would have been much longer. Tischler's research leads him to believe that the escape column took the train on the Williamsport Pike.

[106] Heysinger, "The Cavalry Column from Harper's Ferry in the Antietam Campaign," 37.

the Greencastle Turnpike, running from Williamsport to Greencastle, to the west and sent it speeding north.[107] One wagon at a time suffered this fate until all were sent north or destroyed. Heysinger noted that "As they turned up the Greencastle road, passing the opposite side of the triangle, they were in full view, and it was a sight to see…all hands yelling and banging the brutes, the darky drivers scared green, and urging their teams along with a pistol pointed at each side."[108] He reported that 16 of the wagons broke down and were blown up with the powder they carried; he found no food in the wagons which reached Greencastle.[109] The outnumbered 1st Virginia Cavalry escort harassed the rear of the retreating train but were not able to inflict any damage despite bringing up two guns due to the efficient screen the Union troopers provided. An articulate British-born Confederate artillery lieutenant, Lt. Francis Dawson, in charge of Longstreet's artillery wagon train, described its capture beginning after he was ordered by Longstreet to take the train to Williamsport:

At about ten o'clock at night I started. It was intensely dark and the roads were rough. Toward morning I entered the Hagerstown and Williamsport Turnpike, where I found a cavalry picket. The officer in charge asked me to move the column as quickly as I could, and to keep the trains well closed up. I asked him if the enemy were on the road, and he told me that it was entirely clear, and that he had pickets out in every direction. It was only a few miles now to Williamsport, and I could see the camp-fires of our troops across the river…I was forty or fifty yards ahead of the column, when a voice from the roadside called out "halt!"…In a moment it was repeated. I quickly rode to the side of the road in the direction of the voice, and found myself at the entrance of a narrow lane, and there down it were horses and men in a line that stretched out far beyond my vision…I said indignantly: "How dare you halt an officer in this manner." The reply was to the point: "Surrender, and dismount! You are my prisoner!"…I was placed under guard on the roadside, and as the trains came up they were halted, and the men who were with them were quietly captured. In a short time the column moved off in the direction of the Pennsylvania line. I was allowed to ride my own horse. By the side of each team a Federal soldier rode, and, by dint of cursing the negro drivers and beating the mules with their swords, the cavalrymen contrived to get the jaded animals along at a gallop…I had a cavalryman on each side of me, and tried vainly to get an opportunity to slip off into the woods. Soon after daylight we reached the little village of Greencastle, Pennsylvania, where the citizens came out to look at the "Rebel" prisoners. They hurrahed for their own men and cursed at us. Even the women joined in the game. Several of them brought their children to the roadside and told them to shake their fists at the "d—d Rebels." Still there were some kind people in Greencastle. Three or four ladies came to us, and, without pretending to have any liking for Confederates, showed their chartable disposition by giving us some bread and a cup of cold water. My horse was taken from me at Greencastle and ridden off by a dirty-looking cavalryman. Then the Confederates, numbering a hundred or more, were packed into the cars, and sent by the railway to Chambersburg.[110]

---

[107] That shortcut is today called Tammany Lane and was the entrance to John Van Lear's estate which was first built in the mid 1780's by Matthew Van Lear. Due to the large size of the estate, some 1,200 acres in 1862, a wagon road was used to shorten the distance from the Williamsport Pike to the Greencastle Pike. The continuation of Tammany Lane across Interstate 81 is Wright Road, Tischler, 101, 102. Tischler wrote that the escort for Alexander's train was a detachment from Company B from the 9th Virginia Cavalry, and the immediate command of this train was Lt. George Duffy, 97. Today's Greencastle Pike has been extensively realigned and straightened. The old Pike is today's Honeyfield Road from Williamsport, then Castle Drive, Kemps Mill Road then Rock Hill Road to the modern Greencastle Pike. Van Lear's home was named Tammany or Tammany Manor and the estate sometimes called Mount Tammany. The home still exists at 16544 Tammany Lane along with some outbuildings. There is a depression near one of the barns which was the old wagon road described by Patricia Schooley, *Architectural & Historic Treasures of Washington County, Maryland* (Keedysville, MD: Washington County Historical Trust, 2002), 297-298; File in Western Maryland Room, Washington County Free Library, "WA-I-023 ED 26 Map 48 pg. 329 Mt. Tammany Vincent Groh."
[108] Heysinger, "The Cavalry Column from Harper's Ferry in the Antietam Campaign," 38.
[109] Ibid., 39. As noted some wagons likely carried foodstuffs as they were from other commands and carried commissariat and quartermaster stores. Heysinger could not have examined the contents of all captured wagons.
[110] Francis W. Dawson, *Reminiscences of Confederate Service, 1861-1865* (Charleston, SC: The News and Courier Book Presses, 1882; reprint: Baton Rouge, LA: Louisiana State University Press, 1980), ed. By Bell I. Wiley, 64-66. Dawson's account written

Included with the Rebel prisoners were six men from Company B of the 9th Virginia Cavalry who had been detached from Fitzhugh Lee's Brigade at Highland, Maryland, on the 13th and, after missing the Brigade wagons, had fallen in with Longstreet's wagons.[111] A guide for Longstreet's train, Clagget Fitzhugh, a slave catcher from Franklin County, Pennsylvania, was also captured. As he entered Greencastle with the other Rebel captives, citizens shouted "Hang him!" and "Down with the Traitor!" He survived under protection of his Union guards.[112]

Robert E. Lee's 21 September 1862 report to President Davis was succinct and after describing the successful repulse of the Union attack at Shepherdstown on 19 September in which he lost four cannon he added:

> I regret also to report that on the night of the 14th instant, when I determined to withdraw from the gap in front of Boonsborough to Sharpsburg, a portion of General Longstreet's wagon-train was lost. When his division was ordered back from Hagerstown to the support of D.H. Hill, his train was directed to proceed toward Williamsport, with a view to its safety, and, if necessary, to its crossing the river. Unfortunately, that night the enemy's cavalry at Harper's Ferry evaded our forces, crossed the Potomac into Maryland, passed up through Sharpsburg, where they encountered our pickets, and intercepted on their line of retreat to Pennsylvania General Longstreet's train on the Hagerstown road. The guard was in the extreme rear of the train, that being the only direction from which an attack was apprehended. The enemy captured and destroyed 45 wagons, loaded chiefly with ammunition and subsistence.[113]

The 11th Georgia Volunteers under command of Maj. Francis H. Little and the 1st Virginia Cavalry were assigned to provide a guard for the train. The historian of the Georgia regiment wrote of the capture as follows:

> [My regiment] accordingly moved back [from Hagerstown] to Funkstown, in order to meet a portion of the returning wagons, and take the Williamsport road from that place. The train extended for several miles, and our small force was of necessity wholly inadequate to cover the line of its movements. But Major Little made the best possible disposition of his men. He divided the regiment, placing Captain [William H.] Mitchel[l] in command of the right wing toward the front, and moving himself with the left, in rear of the wagons. Before day next morning the right wing was in motion. About the time of their starting, two brigades (so reported) of fugitive Yankee cavalry from Harper's Ferry crossed the track of the train at the junction of the Functown [Funkstown] [Greencastle—Carman] and Hagerstown roads, and began to conduct the wagons in the direction of the former place. At first the wagoners thought they were Confederate soldiers and obeyed instructions with their usual cheerfulness. But as daylight was dawning the secret soon leaked out, and a messenger was hurried off to communicate the intelligence to Captain Mitchell. Knowing it was impossible, with his handful of men, to contend against such a force, the Captain (after consultation with his officers,) wisely resolved to fall back and connect with the left wing. But the Federals meditated nothing more than a passing notice, they were too thoroughly panic-stricken to tarry, and he had not, consequently, retreated a great way before

20 years after this event contains errors about dates and locations so it is difficult to know if he led Longstreet's train from Boonsboro or Funkstown, but given the circumstances of Longstreet's quick march to Boonsboro, it is unlikely that he would have taken all his trains with him so leaving most at Funkstown seems reasonable. Dawson may have had to ride to Funkstown to round up the trains.

[111] William R. Carter, 15.

[112] William P. Conrad and Ted Alexander, *When War Passed This Way* (Shippensburg, PA: White Mane Publishing Co., 1987), 80-81.

[113] *OR*, vol. 19, pt. 1, 142. Interesting that Lee wrote that the train was taken on the Hagerstown Road not the Williamsport Road or Pike. He may have been poorly informed about the location or just confused over road names as many in his army had not lived in that area. Virtually all participants state that the train was taken on the Williamsport Pike.

information came that the road was again clear, and he resumed his march, and reached Williamsport without further interruption. We had lost a number of wagons, and some valuable stores by this raid.[114]

The escape column led by the experienced Benjamin F. Davis and Cole, had a major effect on Longstreet's ammunition supply during the Battle of Antietam on the 17th. Lt. Col. Edward Porter Alexander, Chief of Ordnance for the Army of Northern Virginia, wrote that "when I arrived at Shepherdstown, about noon on the 16th, with my ordnance train, and rode across the river and reported to Lee, I was ordered to collect all empty wagons and go to Harper's Ferry and take charge of the surrendered ammunition; bringing back to Sharpsburg all suiting our calibres, and sending to Winchester whatever we could not use in the field. The prospect of this addition to our supply was grateful, for the expenditures had been something, at Boonsboro, Crampton's Gap, and Harper's Ferry; and the loss of the 45 loads, burned by the [enemy] cavalry, had been a severe blow at such a distance from our base at Culpeper. I was soon on my way back, and encamped that night with many wagons not far from Harper's Ferry."[115] Heysinger wrote that "General John G. Walker, who commanded alongside of Longstreet during the battle, and with whom I became well acquainted after the war, told me that we had captured in that train two-thirds of all Longstreet's small arm and artillery ammunition. That all he had left was that carried by his men, and in the caissons, except a short resupply, distributed among his troops. It was not only 'one of Longstreet's ammunition trains,' but his whole and only train."[116]

Before 10 A.M., the wagon train reached Greencastle, Pennsylvania, with ninety-seven wagons (having burned about 45 wagons), 600 prisoners, and many beef cattle. One Union trooper reported a spectacular result of burning one wagon which cost the driver his life: the driver "ran his team into the fence, completely wrecking it. As no time was to be lost getting it out, some of the boys jumped over the fence, gathered a few armsful of straw from a stack near by, placed it under the wagon, set fire to it and left it to the mercy of the flames. As the column moved forward, perhaps 200 yards, there was heard a terrific explosion….As the smoke cleared away the ground was strewn with fragments of shell and splinters of a wagon…[it] was loaded with shell."[117] Apparently many of the wagons were U.S. captures from Pope at Second Bull Run as they showed U.S. Army markings.[118] The Union troopers missed by less than an hour an encounter with Lee's reserve artillery train under Brig. Gen. William N. Pendleton. Pendleton's train was on its way to Williamsport to guard the fords there but due to reports Pendleton received about Union cavalry in the area, he slowed his movement missing the encounter.[119]

---

[114] Kittrell J. Warren, *History of the Eleventh Georgia Vols., Embracing the Muster Rolls, together with a Special and Succinct Account of the Marches, Engagement, Casualties, etc.* (Richmond: Smith, Bailey & Co., 1863), 50, from Carman Pierro, 170; corrections/additions in brackets by Carman.

[115] Edward Porter Alexander, *Military Memoirs of a Confederate: A Critical Narrative* (New York: Charles Scribner's Sons, 1907), 242; compare his *Fighting for the Confederacy*, 148.

[116] Heysinger, "The Cavalry Column from Harper's Ferry in the Antietam Campaign," 51. *The New York Times* reported from Greencastle on Monday, September 15th, that the escape column arrived at 1 P.M. and numbered about 1,600 troopers with 75 dirty and ragged prisoners and 50 wagons.

[117] Goodhart, 57. The Unionists probably burned those wagons which broke down or otherwise could not keep up otherwise they would have been taken.

[118] Ibid.

[119] Carman, Pierro, 123-124. Compare the numbers of wagons and prisoners with the account of Pvt. Matthias B. Colton of the 15th Pennsylvania Cavalry who wrote in October 1862 from Carlisle, Pennsylvania, that the wagon train "consisted of 75 wagons loaded with ammunition and 100 prisoners. They all belong to the rebel Gen. Longstreet's division. The prisoners were a sorry looking set, ragged and dirty, without uniforms and some without shoes. One I saw on horseback with a spur buckled to his barefoot," *Column South*, 18. C. B. Newton of the 15th Pennsylvania Cavalry who was serving as an orderly and actually guarded the Rebel train estimated the number at some 70 wagons, Charles H. Kirk, *History of the Fifteenth Pennsylvania Volunteer Cavalry Which Was Recruited and Known as the Anderson Cavalry in the Rebellion of 1861-1865* (Philadelphia, PA: Historical Committee of the Society of the Fifteenth Pennsylvania Cavalry, 1906), 18-19, Alexander, *Military Memoirs of a Confederate*, 232, 242. Tischler wrote that the Rebels who skirmished with the breakout column in Sharpsburg could have been

The Union column missed a possibly more dangerous encounter this time with Rebel cavalry that morning. When Hampton's Brigade rode south from Burkittsville near Crampton's Gap on the morning of 14 September, some of it went along the eastern foot of South Mountain in Middletown Valley to near Knoxville on the Potomac, to picket roads leading from Frederick and Berlin, while two regiments crossed into Pleasant Valley through Brownsville Gap, to the western side of Elk Ridge. One of these regiments, the Jeff Davis Legion, Lt. Col. Martin in command, with six guns of Hart's Battery, took up a position at Solomon's Gap in Elk Ridge to the north of Harpers Ferry; Martin sent pickets in a line down to the Potomac. Some of his pickets were those encountered by the Union escape column at the mouth of Antietam Creek near the Potomac at about 10 P.M. on 14 September. Martin did not know the result of the fighting at South Mountain, so when his scouts reported a large Union force to his south and west (the escape column), he was surprised and feared that he was being surrounded. He determined to fall back toward Hagerstown where he thought Lee and his army was located, and sent out scouts out in that direction. His scouts along the cross-roads on his left reported the large Union cavalry column moving parallel to him northerly along the Potomac River. Hart forwarded some of his six guns from his battery to cover all cross-roads and kept the remainder of his guns at the rear of Martin's column. First travelling along the east foot of Elk Ridge on the west side of Pleasant Valley, Martin's column rode south of Keedysville and crossed Antietam Creek at the Upper Bridge above Pry's Mill on the Keedysville-Williamsport Road. It travelled through Smoketown and Bakersville then Downsville to the west of the Hagerstown Pike, where just before sunrise Martin was told that the Union cavalry had already passed. Martin then quickly pursued the Unionists but soon after sunrise saw the explosions from the burning wagons of Longstreet's ordnance train. He understood that he was too late to help the wagon train, but chased the Union column with its captured wagons to near the Pennsylvania border before retreating to Williamsport. It was perhaps fortunate that Martin and his 400 to 500 troopers did not catch the Union column as the Jeff Davis Legion and Hart's Battery may not have been much of a match for the Union column of 1,600 horsemen. At Williamsport, Martin crossed the Potomac at Light's Ford into Virginia and returned to the Maryland side at Boteler's Ford the afternoon of the sixteenth, rejoining his brigade the next day.[120]

---

stragglers or some of Munford's troopers who were picketing near Rohrersville as Munford had been on the far right flank of Lee protecting his line of communications to Harpers Ferry and the bridge on Antietam Creek near the iron works, 113.

[120] Carman, Pierro, 124-125; letter to Carman 7 April 1900 from James R. Hart in N.Y. Public Library, copy courtesy of Thomas Clemens. Dr. Clemens opines that Martin's troopers likely used "Nick Road, which today exists only in two unconnected pieces, ran more or less from Solomon's Gap to Antietam Irons Works bridge, and thus served as the picket line for The Jeff Davis Legion and Hart's Battery," e-mail exchanges with Dr. Clemens, 13-15 February 2011. Unfortunately, there is no road similar to Nick Road shown on the Taggart map done in 1859 but note that the 1863 Michler map does show a road leading to the east side of Solomon's Gap across Pleasant Valley from northwest of Brownsville. But the location of Solomon's Gap on the Michler map shows its location roughly to the east of the intersection of the Harpers Ferry and Limekiln Roads as on modern maps. Thus there was a path leading over Elk Ridge at Solomon's Gap then to the west probably today's Nick Road going through a gap on another, smaller ridge to the north west of Solomon's Gap on Elk Ridge; Hawks Hill is the northern hill at that unnamed ridge pass. The distance from Solomon's Gap to the Rohrersville Road (today's Chestnut Grove Road) is about 7/8 of a mile and from that point north on Rohrersville Road to Nick Road is slightly over a mile. Note that today's Rohrersville Road (Maryland Rt. 67) is on the east side of Elk Ridge while the Taggart map shows two roads with the name of "Rohrersville" one on each side of Elk Ridge. From the intersection of that point to Antietam Furnace/Harpers Ferry Road (today's Limekiln Road) is about 10 miles (air line distances). Thus the distance the Legion pickets had to cover was about 12 miles. Another possibility was a similar route except that the gap in the "Hawks Hill Ridge" was more to the south through another unnamed gap which today has a road named Hawk's Hill Lane. Like Nick Road, today there is no direct connection between this road and extensions to today's Harpers Ferry Road. Even though today's Harpers Ferry Road north from the intersection of Limekiln Road was not show on Taggart's or Michler's maps, it is likely that there was a farm lane roughly on today's Harpers Ferry Road north from that intersection. If Hawks Hill Lane is presumed to travel directly from Rohrersville Road to today's Harpers Ferry road then to Antietam Furnace, the distance is also about 10 miles.

Another historian's description supplied some added detail about the Legion's disjointed chase of the escape column:

> The Jeff Davis Legion camped the night of September 13, near Boonsboro on the west side of South Mountain....The Jeff Davis Legion rode south [on the 14th] toward Harper's Ferry along the turnpike leading from Boonsboro toward Shepherdstown, halting at a little village named Cedarville. They remained here for most of the day, watching the battle on South Mountain, and awaiting orders. After waiting all day to move to the assistance of the infantry returning from Harper's Ferry, at about 10 P.M. the men of the Jeff Davis finally unsaddled their horses. Hardly had this been completed when they were ordered to remount and move out to defend Longstreet's wagons—except for a squadron from Company F which was sent to guard a bridge at Cadesville [Keedysville] as Confederate infantry passed that point moving toward Sharpsburg. After dispersing the remaining Yankee cavalry from around the ordnance train, the Little Jeff, still detached from the rest of Hampton's Brigade, escorted the undamaged portion of the train southwestward toward Williamsport. It accompanied the train across the upper Potomac River at about 7 A.M. the next morning. From here the sleepy troopers continued their march, now southeastward to Shepherdstown, at which place they stopped and fed their horses...That afternoon the Jeff Davis Legion moved out about nine miles from town where they bivouacked for the night. The next day, September 16, Sparkman and his comrades moved back toward Maryland at a slow trot crossing over the Potomac River near Sharpsburg about 4 P.M."[121]

The Union column with its newly-found wagons reached Greencastle about 10 A.M. There, they were enthusiastically greeted by townspeople who supplied the exhausted horsemen with comestibles, inviting them for breakfast in the town after they learned that the slouching, dust-covered troopers were not Confederates. A trooper of the 15th Pennsylvania Cavalry was on the scene and penned this reminiscence:

> One of my stirring memories of that journey down the Cumberland Valley is of a scene worth remembering. When General Miles surrendered to the rebels at Harper's Ferry, a gallant band of Union cavalry refused to yield, and cut their way out. Journeying northward, they came across a long wagon train loaded with supplies for Longstreet's corps of Lee's army. The train—consisting, so far as I recollect, of some seventy wagons—they captured together with its escort, and brought them along. I saw the dusty procession marching into Greencastle, and had the honor of being placed, loaded revolver in hand, on the hind step of an omnibus, to stand guard over the rebel prisoners of that escort, whom I conducted to the town jail. I felt almost as proud as if I had captured that wagon train myself.[122]

The escape of some 1,600 troopers from a location which was surrounded, and from which there was only one small bridge, was a remarkable event.[123] That they captured a wagon train was an added bonus. Marching over fifty miles in about thirteen hours much of it in total darkness was for these mostly green

---

[121] Donald A. Hopkins, *The Little Jeff: The Jeff Davis Legion, Cavalry Army of Northern Virginia* (Shippensburg, PA: White Mane Books, 1999), 94, 97-98. Note that Carman's account does not have the Legion riding south on the Boonsboro Pike; Carman's description is probably more accurate and is preferred. The Legion was not able to do much to save the train. It is likely that the road south from Boonsboro was the one leading not to Sharpsburg but down Pleasant Valley toward Harpers Ferry, the Rohrersville Road, today's State Rt. 67. The name "Cedarville" is not shown on period maps.

[122] Kirk, 18.

[123] Murfin, 196; Tischler, 77. The actual number of wagons and Rebels captured is not known. Numbers of Union cavalry escapees likely is 1,594 as carefully researched by Harry Pfanz "Special History Report; Troop Movement Maps, September 12-14, 1862, Harpers Ferry, NHP," Denver: NPS Center, 1976, 42. Tischler, 281-282, also shows estimates of wagons captured ranged from 40 to 175, with the probable number from 50 to 75. Tischler, 283-284, has the number of prisoners taken from 40 to 675, with the probable number from 100 to 150. Note that Carman shows 97 wagons, 600 prisoners, "and a good supply of beef cattle," Carman, Clemens, 259. Unfortunately for the Union, much of Longstreet's ordnance was destroyed during Jeb Stuart's Second Ride Around McClellan at it was burned in Chambersburg, Pennsylvania, when Stuart's troopers set ablaze railroad buildings and warehouses, *Rebellion Record*, vol. 6, Doc. 1; 3, 5.

troopers an event they would not forget. Of the 178 missing men, most would return within the next few days, meaning that the entire adventure resulted in few losses.[124] The 12th Illinois Cavalry, the 8th New York Cavalry and the Maryland troopers were claimed by McClellan and used to protect his right flank, during and after the Battle of Antietam, although apparently McClellan was unsure if they were still under the command of Wool. Halleck quickly assured McClellan that they were indeed part of his army and would remain in it.[125] The 7th Squadron, after arriving at Greencastle, Pennsylvania, rested there until the 18th when the squadron was sent to Jones's Cross Roads under McClellan's command. On picket duty for one day, they returned to Greencastle, and then on the 23rd they rode to Chambersburg, where the squadron turned in their horses and equipments and boarded a train for Providence. There, at the state capital, they were mustered out of service on 1 October 1862, having proudly done their duty, losing only one man to disease and two captured but returned.[126]

But not all events during the escape were momentous. A private in Company I of the 8th New York Cavalry, while one of the unluckiest men in the escape, did survive despite many trials. His company commander, Capt. Willard H. Healy, described Private Abraham Louck's adventure during the escape, perhaps with tongue firmly planted in cheek, providing a humorous footnote to a perilous journey:

Private Abraham Louck was a soldier who was always in trouble, but always came out somewhere. When about half way up Maryland Heights Louck lost his horse over the bank. Louck got up almost killed, as he said, and wanted to know what to do. He was told to go to some farm house and stay until morning, and then give himself up to the rebels. There we left him. About one hour after that, as the whole regiment floundered through a mud hole, who should come up but Louck, the worst looking being you ever saw; covered all over with mud and water. "Hello, Louck, where did you come from?" "Can't lose me, Captain I took one of the Pennsylvania Cavalry horses, and here I am." We came once more to a creek. Down goes Louck again, losing his horse once more, and washing the fellow quite clean, and nearly drowning him. We left him standing by the creek. On we went, and we gave him up as lost this time, but when we burned the wagons, who was blown out of the rear end of the wagon but Louck, his hair, whiskers and eyebrows burned off. We picked him up nearly dead, and as the Johnnies now came in sight, we had to get. We carried Louck to a farm house, and laid him on a bed, and as we supposed dead. Then we lit out. When we arrived at Green Castle and began to receive our rations from the farmer, who turned up again but poor Louck. He said: "Captain, I was killed once to-night by being thrown over the mountain, drowned twice, blown up and killed, but here I am, ready for all the rations I can get."[127]

Thus mostly green Union cavalrymen, fortunately with two experienced leaders, accomplished a feat that few would have thought could succeed. Certainly luck was a major factor as McLaws had reduced the numbers of pickets on the Maryland shore as he had to face overwhelming numbers of Union

[124] But see Murfin, stating that there was one killed and one wounded at the initial skirmish at Sandy Hook, 153. These were probably the interlopers from the 125th New York Infantry. The return of casualties in the *OR*, vol. 19, pt. 1, 549, lists 274 for cavalry, with none killed, five wounded, and 269 missing or captured. It is unlikely that many were captured by Jackson's command other than those who were too sick to ride or did not have healthy horses. Maj. John A. Harman, Jackson's chief quartermaster reported only 12 saddles captured and turned in during the second and third quarters of 1862, *OR*, vol. 19, pt. 1, 960. No captures are reported in the regimental histories for any of the cavalry which escaped other than Norton in the 8th New York history in which he writes "George W. Brooks and Edward Beasley, of Company H, and several others from the regiment, were left back there on account of sickness, when we went out of the Ferry," 31. The 12th Illinois Cavalry morning reports, Co. E for 14 September 1862 show that Pvt. Daniel Snyder was killed and his horse and equipments lost, then on 15 September, a captain, one sergeant, and one private were wounded with one private missing along with four horses and equipments lost, NA, RG 94, Morning Reports of 12th Illinois, Co. E, September 1862.
[125] *OR*, vol. 19, pt. 2, 384, 387.
[126] Ayling, 1090-1092; Corliss, 8-11; Tischler, 13; Carman, Pierro, 102; *OR*, vol. 51, pt. 1, 728.
[127] Norton, 142-143. Note that he mentioned he obtained another horse from the Pennsylvania cavalry so maybe the admonition to the cavalrymen before the escape began to not take led horses was not followed by all troopers.

infantry in Pleasant Valley after Franklin forced Crampton's Gap. Luck was also present when Martin's Jeff Davis Legion missed the Union column avoiding a major fight. Arguably the most important factor making the breakout a success was the number of troopers who were familiar with the area, mostly from Cole's Cavalry, along with the guides employed. And some local knowledge was present even with other troopers who had spent previous weeks patrolling and picketing the Harpers Ferry vicinity on the Maryland side. Stuart and Jackson probably both lamented the failure to capture the Union horsemen, Stuart looking to capture firearms, equipment and horses, and Jackson because he knew how dangerous enemy cavalry could be in unfriendly country, as his experience in Boonsboro demonstrated a few days earlier. And there is Jackson's usual desire to bag them, all of which must have been frustrating, knowing how close he came to so doing. Heysinger wrote that Brig. Gen. John G. Walker after the war told him that upon learning that the cavalrymen and horses were gone, Jackson had this reaction: "'Why,' he cried, 'impossible! I would rather have had them then everything else in the place.' Some of our [Heysinger's] own company, left prisoners there, heard also how he was suddenly warped out of usual equipoise, to their great amusement."[128] One of Stuart's staff, Blackford, wrote about the Yankee's escape: "To think of all the fine horses they carried off, the saddles, revolvers, and carbines of the best kind, and the spurs, all of which would have fallen to our share, and the very things we so much needed, was enough to vex a saint."[129] Stuart was doubly frustrated as he had briefed McLaws about the area around Harpers Ferry, so he could not understand how this large body of horsemen could escape literally under the noses of the Confederate infantry. Munford, however, faulted Stuart "arguing that by scattering his cavalry units he could not seal off the roads from Harper's Ferry."[130] Up to this point in the war, this Harpers Ferry escape was the highpoint of large-scale Union cavalry actions in the east, outshining Pleasonton's division activities during the prelude to Antietam, and certainly at the Battle of Antietam. Longstreet wrote in a 6 April 1880 letter to Pettengill that "'The service you refer to was very creditable, and gave us much inconvenience. The command being in retreat, and in more or less apprehension for its own safety, seems to have exercised more than usual discretion and courage.'"[131] The spectacular nature of the feat however, was overshadowed by the unprecedented number of troops captured at Harpers Ferry, as well as the horrifically sanguinary battle two days later at Antietam.

One might speculate about what might have happened to the cavalry had Miles followed Wool's orders and fortified Maryland Heights. Had the Harpers Ferry commander done so, or had he more heavily reinforced his troops on Maryland Heights and held off McLaws's troops for another day or two, the Union cavalry at Harpers Ferry could have helped hold McLaws in place in and around Elk Ridge, and prevented his early morning arrival at Sharpsburg on the 17th with his division.[132] The Union cavalry at Harpers Ferry would have been of much use if McLaws were trapped between Franklin to the north in

---

[128] Heysinger letter to Carman 17 August 1905 from New York Public Library Carman Papers copy courtesy Thomas Clemens. Walker may not be the most reliable historian, but Heysinger's statement does confirm that not all Union cavalrymen participated in the escape.

[129] Blackford, 146.

[130] Wert, *Cavalryman*, 151.

[131] Pettengill, 88.

[132] Carman wrote that McLaws's division "was composed of four brigades—Kershaw's, Cobb's (commanded by Lieutenant Colonel Christopher C. Sanders), Semmes's, and Barksdale's—and the batteries of Captains Basil C. Manly (North Carolina), John P. W. Read (Georgia), Miles C. Macon (Virginia), Edward S. McCarthy (Virginia), and Henry H. Carlton (Georgia). It was a veteran division and a good one, and had seen much hard service. Kershaw had 936 officers and men; Cobb, 398; Semmes, 709; and Barksdale, 891—an aggregate in the division of 2,934 officers and men, including the three batteries that became engaged. McLaws accounts for the small number carried into action by "the straggling of men wearied beyond ... endurance and of those without shoes. Notwithstanding that he lost over 1,100 men on the seventeenth, his absentees—who joined before the morning of the eighteenth—made his force nearly as large as it was on the morning of the seventeenth." Lafayette McLaws, "The Capture of Harper's Ferry," Philadelphia Weekly Press, September 19, 1888, from Carman, Pierro, 258. Note that Cobb was absent ill after Crampton's Gap and missed the Battle of Antietam.

Pleasant Valley and Miles to the south, by scouting the movements of the cornered Rebels both to the east of Elk Ridge in Pleasant Valley then down past Weverton, and Knoxville on the Potomac, as well as to the west up the Harpers Ferry-Sharpsburg Road, as McLaws would have likely tried to move east to cross the Potomac at the Berlin, Maryland, ford, or even further downstream at Point of Rocks. Hampton's troopers would have been outnumbered but would have given the Yankee horsemen a fierce battle around Weverton. Lee's suggestion that McLaws could try to come up to Sharpsburg along the roads on the Maryland side of the Potomac proved impractical given reports by Rebel scouts of Union troops approaching from the north. Additionally, given the poor conditions of any such roads like the Harpers Ferry-Sharpsburg Road, McLaws would have had to leave most of his wagons behind.[133] Regarding his operations in Pleasant Valley, McLaws made this report to Lee's adjutant general:

> The enemy having forced Crampton's Gap, thereby completely cutting off my route up the valley to join the forces with General Lee, as Solomon's Gap, the only road over Elk Ridge, was just in front of the one over the Blue Ridge [South Mountain—EAC] occupied by the enemy, I had nothing to do but to defend my position. I could not retire under the bluffs along the river [Maryland Heights-Elk Ridge], with the enemy pressing my rear and the forces at Harper's Ferry operating in conjunction, unless under a combination of circumstances I could not rely on to happen at the exact time needed; could not pass over the mountain except in a scattered and disorganized condition, nor could have gone through the Weverton Pass into the open country [in Middletown Valley] beyond to cross a doubtful ford when the enemy was in force on the other side of the Blue Ridge and coming down in my rear. There was no outlet in any direction for anything but the troops, and that very doubtful. In no contingency could I have saved the trains and artillery. I therefore determined to defend myself in the valley, holding the two heights [Maryland and Weverton Heights] and the two lower passes [at the bases of the two heights] in order to force a direct advance down the valley, to prevent co-operation from Harper's Ferry, and at the same time to carry out my orders in relation to the capture of that place. I received several communications from your [Gen. Lee's] headquarters in relation to my position, which were obeyed so far as circumstances permitted, and I acted, in departing from them, as I believed the commanding general would have ordered had he known the circumstances....The early surrender of Harper's Ferry relieved me from the situation, and my command joined the main army at Sharpsburg on the morning of the 17th.[134]

Union troopers could have scouted approaches to the west toward Keedysville and Sharpsburg along the Potomac on the Maryland side while Federal cavalry would have also been able to search south of the Potomac to ascertain that Jackson and Walker were mostly gone as they would have followed Gen. Lee's orders to march to Shepherdstown should Harpers Ferry have held out. Had Miles held out, Jackson and Walker would not have been available to join Lee at Sharpsburg, so Lee would have had to recross the Potomac back into Virginia, as he would be unable to hold back McClellan without Jackson, Walker, and McLaws. Then Miles and the Union cavalry in Harpers Ferry would have fallen under McClellan's command, as the Union commander would have pondered his next move which, given his cautious nature, probably would have been to ensure that the Maryland side of the Potomac was heavily defended from Hancock, Maryland, to the Chain Bridge near Washington, against a reinvasion by Lee. Lee would have then sought to continue his Maryland adventure by crossing at Williamsport should he have been able to force a crossing and beat McClellan there.

---

[133] *OR*, vol. 19, pt. 2, 609. Lee asked Munford to "discover or hear of a practicable road below Crampton's Gap by which McLaws, at Weverton at present, can pass over the mountains to Sharpsburg, send him a messenger to guide him over immediately." Munford could not do so.

[134] *OR*, vol. 19, pt. 1, 856. See Carman, Pierro, 189-194 for a thorough discussion of McLaws's options and Franklin's actions and lack of actions including "what if" Jackson joined with McLaws after Miles's surrender to attack Franklin or if Lee had joined Jackson, McLaws and Walker. Note that McLaws was unaware that little of McClellan's army was in the southern Middletown Valley to oppose his move down the Potomac.

But given that Maryland Heights did fall, and the scouting and patrolling uses of Miles's cavalry were of no benefit any longer, their escape was the best option available for the troopers, but perhaps it was unfortunate that Miles forbade any other troops the opportunity to also make any attempt with the intrepid horsemen. In hindsight, at least some of the infantry could have escaped by the same route as the escape column, and also by marching up the C&O towpath and even the canal prism.[135] The canal from Harpers Ferry to Williamsport was dewatered although some portions may still have had residual water or been muddy but useable by infantry. A Union Signal Corps observation post at Point of Rocks reported on 12 September "announcing the presence of the enemy in Pleasant Valley, and also giving the information that they had cut the canal to afford an easy passage back to Virginia in the event of disaster.[136] The *Harper's Weekly* 11 October 1862 drawing of Union pickets of the 5th New York Infantry at Blackford's (Boteler's) Ford shows them firing across the river into Virginia from a dry canal bed. Also in the immediate area of Sharpsburg, Jacob Miller, who owned a sawmill less than a mile below Boteler's Ford but above Antietam Creek, reported that "Soldiers had taken his mill on January 19, 1862, and had prevented his sawing until May 14. After that, the water was out of the canal from July 1 to 12, for nearly two weeks in August, and again from September 14 on. Following the Battle of Antietam, soldiers used the mill as a hospital and then as a pickets' rendezvous."[137] The *Washington Evening Star* reported on 12 September: "Canal navigation is suspended beyond a point twenty miles from here—that is, at Seneca Dam. From that point up, for from thirty to forty miles, there is no water in the canal, the Confederate forces having drawn it off a week ago, by blowing up a culvert, when they first crossed into Maryland—hence supplies for the army cannot be sent up by canal further than Seneca."[138] Maj. Albert J. Myer reported that his signalmen at Point of Rocks stated that the Rebels cut the canal at Knoxville to be able to cross the Potomac there back to Virginia.[139] Maj. Gen. D.H. Hill had started the dewatering on 4 September near the Monocacy Aqueduct after he drove off the 1st Maryland Potomac Home Brigade and the 87th Ohio Infantry guarding the area. By nightfall, he had his troops stop traffic on the canal and wreck the Little Monocacy Culvert and drain the canal. "The berm and towpath banks were cut down,

---

[135] Means testified that the infantry could have escaped on the same road as the cavalry used, *OR*, vol. 19, pt. 1, 752-753; see also 670, 685, 770-771.

[136] Willard Brown, 328.

[137] Unrau, 735-738, 747. See Chapter 10, page 407 for this image of troops firing from the dry canal bed. One Union infantryman reported that he and his unit slept in the canal bed the nights after the Shepherdstown battle, Robert G. Carter, *Four Brothers in Blue* (Austin, TX: University of Texas Press, 1978), 121.

[138] *Washington Evening Star*, September 12, 1862. Forty miles up the canal from Seneca is almost to Harpers Ferry. Given this report and that about Miller's mill, it appears that the canal was mostly dewatered from at least Sharpsburg to Seneca. There was apparently water still in the canal prism at Williamsport as McClellan had boats there destroyed: "Shortly after the fighting began [on 17 September], General McClellan dispatched Captain Charles H. Russell with his company of the 1st Maryland Cavalry to Williamsport to burn the pivot bridge across the canal at Lock No. 44 and to destroy the Conococheague Aqueduct in an effort to cut one of Lee's avenues of retreat. With the aid of some Pennsylvania militiamen who were holding the town, Russell's men destroyed the pivot bridge, organized demolition teams, and burned eleven boats, nine of which were loaded with coal, that had been forced to tie up at Williamsport," Unrau, 737. There was no damage to the canal above Williamsport, but the Rebels had burned the gates to guard locks three and four which supplied water to the canal, Unrau, 739. These were just above dams numbers three and four respectively, and were also known as "feeder locks" according to Lee D. Barron, *The Chesapeake & Ohio Canal: "As It Is and As It Was"* (Sharpsburg, MD: Graphics Design Press, 1973); guard lock three was at mile 62.3 just above Harpers Ferry and four at mile 85.8, about half way between Sharpsburg and Williamsport. The Canal Company filed a claim for four cargoes of coal and two boats, A.C. Greene to W.S. Ringgold, 2 December 1862, Letters Received by the Office of the President and Directors, Records of the Chesapeake and Ohio Canal Company, RG 79, Dept. of the Interior, National Archives, College Park, MD, Timothy R. Snyder, "'I Hope They Will Get Away Soon': The Chesapeake and Ohio Canal and the Federal Authorities during the U.S. Civil War," Master's thesis, Shippensburg University, 1999, 85. Snyder discusses the favored treatment the B&O Railroad received versus the shabby treatment the Federal government gave the C&O.

[139] *OR*, vol. 19, pt. 1, 120; Willard Brown wrote that "About noon [13 September] a report was received from this station [at Point of Rocks] announcing the presence of the enemy in Pleasant Valley, and also giving the information that they had cut the canal to afford an easy passage back to Virginia in the event of disaster," 328.

the prism corduroyed, and the artillery and trains started" across the canal. After arguing with Thomas Walter, the tender at Lock No. 27, Hill agreed that the Monocacy Aqueduct could not be destroyed (Hill's engineers said they hadn't enough powder) so he had his men damage Lock No. 27 and burn several canal boats, and then marched to Frederick to Join Jackson.[140]

The historian of the Army of the Potomac also offered his opinion showing how McClellan might have saved Harpers Ferry:

> But Weverton Pass, near the Potomac, afforded another approach to Maryland Heights that McClellan might advance through and at once relieve Harper's Ferry, as it was on the river but a few miles below, and if that point was attacked and carried, McLaws would be compelled to abandon his siege on Maryland Heights. Then again, if a heavy force of the Union Army had appeared at Weverton Pass [at the foot of South Mountain] the battle could have been distinctly heard at the ferry above and greatly delayed the surrender.
>
> Gen. George J. Stannard, of Vermont, whose record on the field of battle shines with a golden luster, was a colonel then, under the command of General Miles. His statement to the writer, just before he died, was that the sound of battle seemed to die away, instead of growing nearer, which would not have been the case if Weverton Pass had been attacked. Stannard advised Miles to follow the cavalry out and abandon the ferry, leaving only the stores for the enemy to capture. If this advice had been followed McLaws would have been in a still worse condition, for Miles's force would then have constituted the right wing of the attack on the morning of the 15th.
>
> Weverton Pass was occupied by two brigades of Anderson's division—Wright's and Pryor's. If the Twelfth Corps, under Mansfield, had been left as a reserve to Reno and Hooker, and the Second Corps sent to Weverton Pass on the afternoon of the 14th and attacked Wright and Pryor, those two brigades must have yielded to the superior force of the veterans of that corps. Then Fitz-John Porter's corps, assisting Franklin's at Crampton and Brownsville Gaps, would have swept the enemy from those two points, and placed McLaws, on the morning of the 15th, at the mercy of three corps and Couch's division. That would have left two corps, the Ninth and Twelfth, within easy reach if needed. The effective force of the Second, Fifth, and Sixth Corps and Couch's division was too overwhelming for McLaws to have successfully resisted.[141]

A determined effort by Miles either by fortifying Maryland Heights or breaking out along the Potomac in Maryland toward Shepherdstown, while causing more casualties to his command, would not have resulted in a surrender of his entire force, but as an Old Army veteran, he viewed as his mission to obey to the letter his direct orders to defend Harpers Ferry, and did so until his death there on the morning of Monday, 15 September 1862. Most importantly, a more determined effort by Franklin, or a

---

[140] Unrau, 565, 735. McLaws helped empty the canal: "Seeing that the canal was full of water about Weverton, I directed General Pryor…to cut the canal just above a culvert near the place, which he did, and thinks the canal was materially damaged. He also broke the canal lock," OR, vol. 19, pt. 1, 856. It appears that most of the Monocacy Division and the Antietam Division of the six C&O Canal divisions were mostly dry. The Monocacy Division during this period extended from Lock No. 23, mile 22.1 above Georgetown, to Guard Lock No. 3, mile 62.3, about one mile above Harpers Ferry. Next upriver, the Antietam Division extended from Guard Lock No. 3 to Guard Lock No. 4, mile 85.8, about one-half mile above Dam No. 4, about 12 river miles above Shepherdstown. On 12 February 1862, the six-division system was restored and lasted from that time through the end of the Civil War. John Cameron was the Superintendent of the Monocacy Division and Levin Benton of the Antietam Division. Note that the prism might not have been bone dry as one infantryman from the 118th Pennsylvania remembered that he had to wade "a canal knee-deep in water," The Survivors' Association, History of the 118th Pennsylvania Volunteers Corn Exchange Regiment (Philadelphia, PA: J.L. Smith, 1905), 80. Local historian John Frye believes that the canal bed was emptied from Williamsport to at least Weverton. Carman, when writing about McLaws's escape from Pleasant Valley, said that "It is true that he might have passed his infantry under the precipice at the foot of Maryland Heights by going up the bed of the canal (the water having been let out), but his wagons and artillery could not have gone that way," Pierro, 189. There is nothing of record to show that the escape column considered using the canal bed and tow path to Shepherdstown.

[141] James Henry Stine, A History of the Army of the Potomac (Washington, D.C.: Gibson Brothers, 1893), 178-179. Fighting a battle using hindsight almost always leads to better results. McClellan had a good case that he should attack the main body of Gen. Lee's army at Boonsboro and he also believed Miles could hold out long enough to then be relieved by Franklin.

326 BOOTS AND SADDLES

more aggressive battle plan by McClellan, giving Franklin more troops and having them start toward Crampton's Gap late on the 13th, would also have saved Miles. Miles could not rise to the occasion; retaining him in command even after he refused to follow Wool's orders to fortify Maryland Heights, showed that Wool and his superiors in Washington erred in believing this Old Army officer could succeed. Halleck's and Wool's orders to hold Harpers Ferry rather than joining McClellan's army or at least retreating north to Pennsylvania, sealed the fate of Miles's command when, at the last, he decided to follow his orders to the letter, and hold only Harpers Ferry itself. As some speculated, despite his good service before the Civil War, many years of heavy alcohol use may have ossified his thought processes. The largest surrender of U.S. forces until World War II at Corregidor, Philippine Islands, and the then the bloody Battle of Antietam, overshadowed the outstanding effort of the Union cavalry's escape, and dimmed the efforts of the brave officers and men who accomplished it.[142]

---

[142] *OR*, vol. 19, pt. 1, 600, 622-623, 631, 755, 756; compare testimony at 761, 762.

Chapter 9

From the South Mountain Passes to Antietam Creek

On SUNDAY, 14 SEPTEMBER, Stuart rose early and rode the seven miles from his camp on the western side of South Mountain near Boonsboro, down to Crampton's Gap. He probably had with him the Jeff Davis Legion and the two guns of Hart's Battery, but he left no cavalry at Turner's Gap. He apparently did not stop to confer with Rosser at Fox's Gap just under one mile south of Turner's Gap, not even replying to a message from Rosser telling Stuart of the Union Ninth Corps approaching the gap. When he arrived at Crampton's Gap, Stuart saw no Union activity and apparently did not send out scouts to investigate Union intentions. Seeing nothing of concern, he decided that Hampton, who was there waiting for orders, would be of better use with McLaws, so he sent him, with most of his brigade, south.[1] Stuart, like Gen. Lee, believed that McClellan was heading in McLaws's direction with heavy force, down Middletown Valley on the Jefferson Pike, to relieve Harpers Ferry. Seeing no evidence that any of McClellan's army was marching toward Crampton's Gap or Brownsville Gap, Stuart also rode south. He left Munford at Crampton's Gap in command, as he was senior, along with his small cavalry force, the 2nd and 12th Virginia Cavalry, totaling some 200 troopers, and part of Brig. Gen. William Mahone's Infantry.

Hampton arrived at the end of South Mountain near Weverton on the Potomac, and picketed roads from Knoxville leading to Point of Rocks and Frederick. After Stuart joined McLaws on Maryland Heights, he said he explained the topography of the area and the road net to McLaws. Stuart was stationed at Harpers Ferry the previous year as well as being involved in the John Brown raid in 1859, and was well aware of its geography. Stuart reported that he "went with him [McLaws] to the Maryland Heights, overlooking Harper's Ferry, which had not yet fallen. I explained to him the location of the roads in that vicinity, familiar to myself from my connection with the John Brown raid, and repeatedly urged the importance of his holding with an infantry picket the road leading from the Ferry by the Kennedy farm [John Brown's headquarters] toward Sharpsburg."[2]

[1] Harsh, *Flood*, 275-276. See also Hartwig, *To Antietam Creek*, 266-268.
[2] Harsh, *Flood*, 162-163; *OR*, vol. 19, pt. 1, 818. In this report, Stuart says that 500 Union cavalry escaped. Interesting to note Stuart's reference to the Kennedy farm as the escape column probably did not ride by it during its escape as noted in Chapter 8.

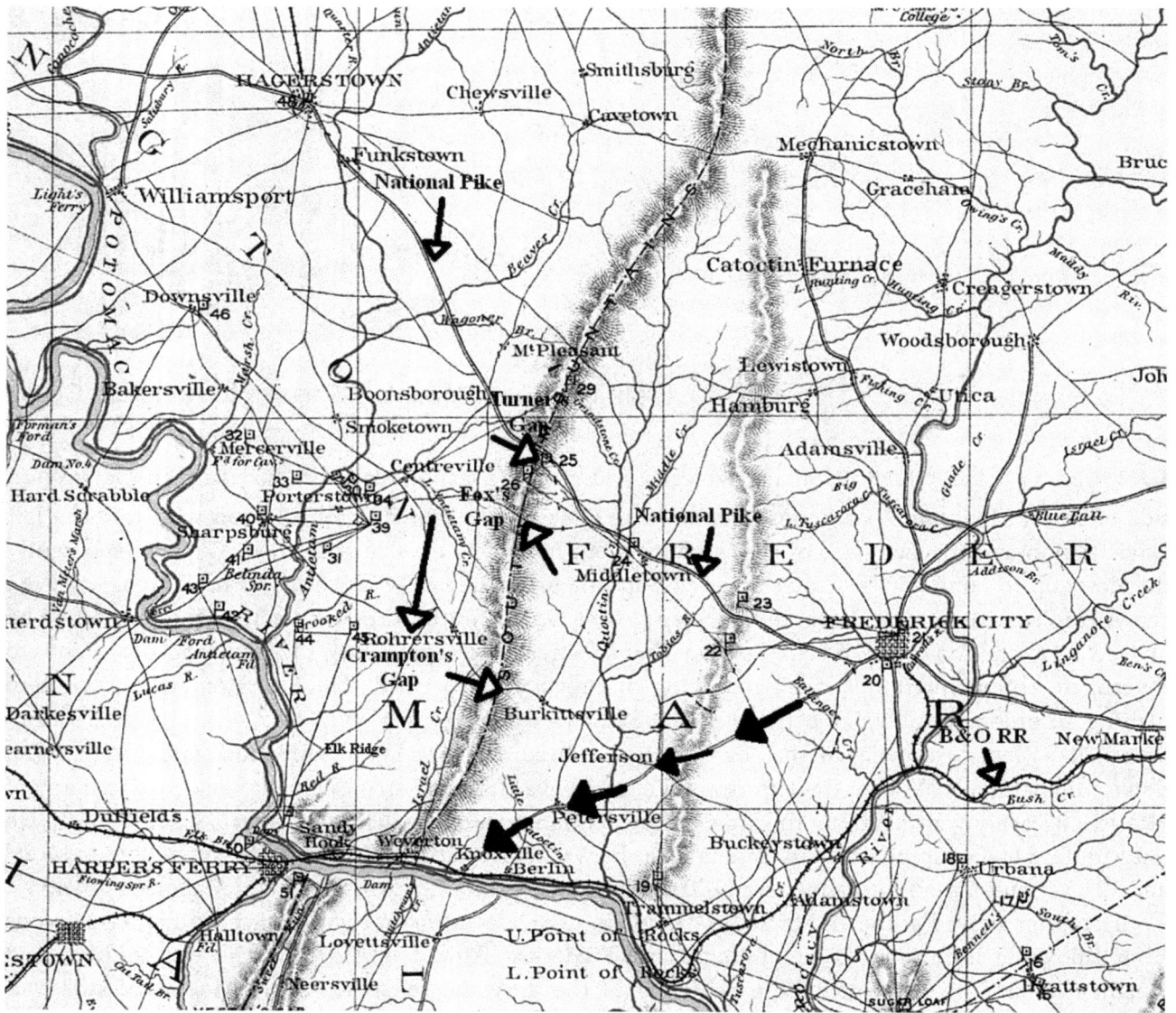

View of area of operations for Battle of South Mountain, Harpers Ferry, and Antietam showing the gaps in South Mountain fought over on 14 September 1862; Crampton's Gap is west of Burkittsville, Fox's Gap west of Middletown, and Turner's Gap just north of Fox's Gap. McLaws's infantry and Stuart's troopers are on Maryland Heights and Elk Ridge as well as in Knoxville and Jefferson. The arrows in the lower center show the direct road from Frederick through Jefferson on which Stuart and Lee thought McClellan would descend on McLaws. Gen. Lee also worried that McClellan would send part of his army south in Pleasant Valley to pin McLaws from the rear as Miles held him in the front; the large arrow at Rohrersville shows this path. McLaws had troops scattered from upriver of Maryland Heights down to Point of Rocks with Stuart's troopers under Hampton at Knoxville, Berlin and Point of Rocks. As noted in Chapter 8, the Jeff Davis Legion was on its own journeying from Pleasant Valley, and then to the west, chasing the Harpers Ferry escape column. Detail from *Official Atlas*, Plate 27. Courtesy LOC.

Stuart would blame McLaws for not properly picketing the road leading from Harpers Ferry to Sharpsburg which permitted a Union cavalry breakout of 1,500 troopers the night of the 14th/15th.[3]

---

[3] Carman, Pierro, 138; Priest, *Before Antietam*, 273; Stuart's report is in *OR*, vol. 19, pt. 1, 817-818. See also Reese, *Sealed*, stating that Munford was given a choice by Stuart of staying at Crampton's Gap or going with Stuart to join McLaws; Munford chose to stay put, a choice he must have regretted later that day. Reese also estimates that Munford had 275 troopers versus Priest's estimate of 200, 39-40. See also Daniel H. Hill, "The Battle of South Mountain, or Boonsboro," *Battles and Leaders*, 2: 558, 561. See also Thomason, "Stuart...took Hampton on to supplement McLaws, and placed him on the river at Knoxville, covering the Harper's Ferry-Frederick road....This was a mistake. Hampton would have been of more use with Munford....Or he would have been of service covering the Keedysville road that runs due north from Harper's Ferry" stopping the Union

McLaws, before Stuart had joined him, had reacted to reports of Yankees approaching Crampton's and Brownsville Gaps by sending more troops to those locations, including Brig. Gen. Howell Cobb's Brigade sent from Sandy Hook. This would have been the unit he assigned to picket the Sharpsburg Road.[4] Certainly McLaws would have appreciated having some of Stuart's troopers as scouts and pickets to help picket roads leading north and west from Harpers Ferry, toward Rohrersville and Sharpsburg. It could be that if Stuart were in communication with Jackson, he would have picketed those roads as Jackson would have been more familiar with them than McLaws, and also likely more concerned with bagging the whole lot of those people caught in the hole of Harpers Ferry.

At Fox's Gap, 5.5 miles north of Crampton's Gap, Col. Rosser and his 200 troopers of the 5th Virginia Cavalry faced overwhelming odds as would Munford later on the 14th albeit with larger Rebel infantry support from D.H. Hill and then Longstreet. Rosser and his horse artillery under Pelham was only a tiny part of the battles at Fox's and Turner's Gaps which raged all of Sunday the 14th. Rosser was the only regiment from Fitzhugh Lee's brigade which had returned from Lee's Westminster raid and wound up being the only troopers on the line at either Fox's or Turner's Gaps during the battles at those locations. Stuart failed to give Rosser any instructions and neglected to tell D.H. Hill of the presence of the regiment. Also, Rosser's warning to Stuart about Burnside's Ninth Corps approach went unheeded. Rosser's postwar statement that "Stuart did not expect the enemy would advance on Boonsboro, and was careless in guarding the roads leading that way" is a good analysis of Stuart's beliefs on which he acted, disregarding any evidence to the contrary. Rosser well used his troopers and Pelham's two guns as Union Maj. Gen. Jacob D. Cox, whose troops fought them, mistakenly said that "Stuart had the principal part of the Confederate cavalry on this line, and they were not idle spectators. Part of Lee's and Hampton's brigades were certainly there, and probably the whole of Lee's." The only Rebel cavalry near the two gaps were Rosser's small regiment and two of Pelham's guns, but they obviously performed very well, fooling Cox by making a good show.[5]

cavalry breakout, 276. Thomason must have been referring to the Harpers Ferry-Sharpsburg Road although a branch of this road continues northwest to Keedysville. Refer to the detailed maps in Chapter 8 dealing with the Union cavalry escape from Harpers Ferry. Stuart writing in hindsight may have been defending his role notifying McLaws in light of the Union cavalry breakout from Harpers Ferry later that day. Stuart likely realized that he should have been supplementing the infantry pickets on Maryland roads.

[4] Harsh, *Flood*, 276-277. McLaws was forced to weaken his pickets as he sent troops north to counter Franklin's attack.

[5] Harsh, *Flood*, 234, 275; Carman, Pierro, 138; Jacob D. Cox, "Forcing Fox's Gap and Turner's Gap," in *Battles and Leaders*, 2:587, 589. Rosser had journeyed from Westminster west through Union, Middleburg then southwest through Utica, Hamburg Pass, then turning northwest at Middletown crossed South Mountain north of Turner's Gap to Boonsboro, Letter and marked map from Rosser to Carman 10 July 1897, courtesy Thomas Clemens. Note that Cox did face other Rebel guns on the mountain in addition to Rosser's; Hill wrote that Bondurant's Battery was with Garland, *Battles and Leaders*, 2:562.

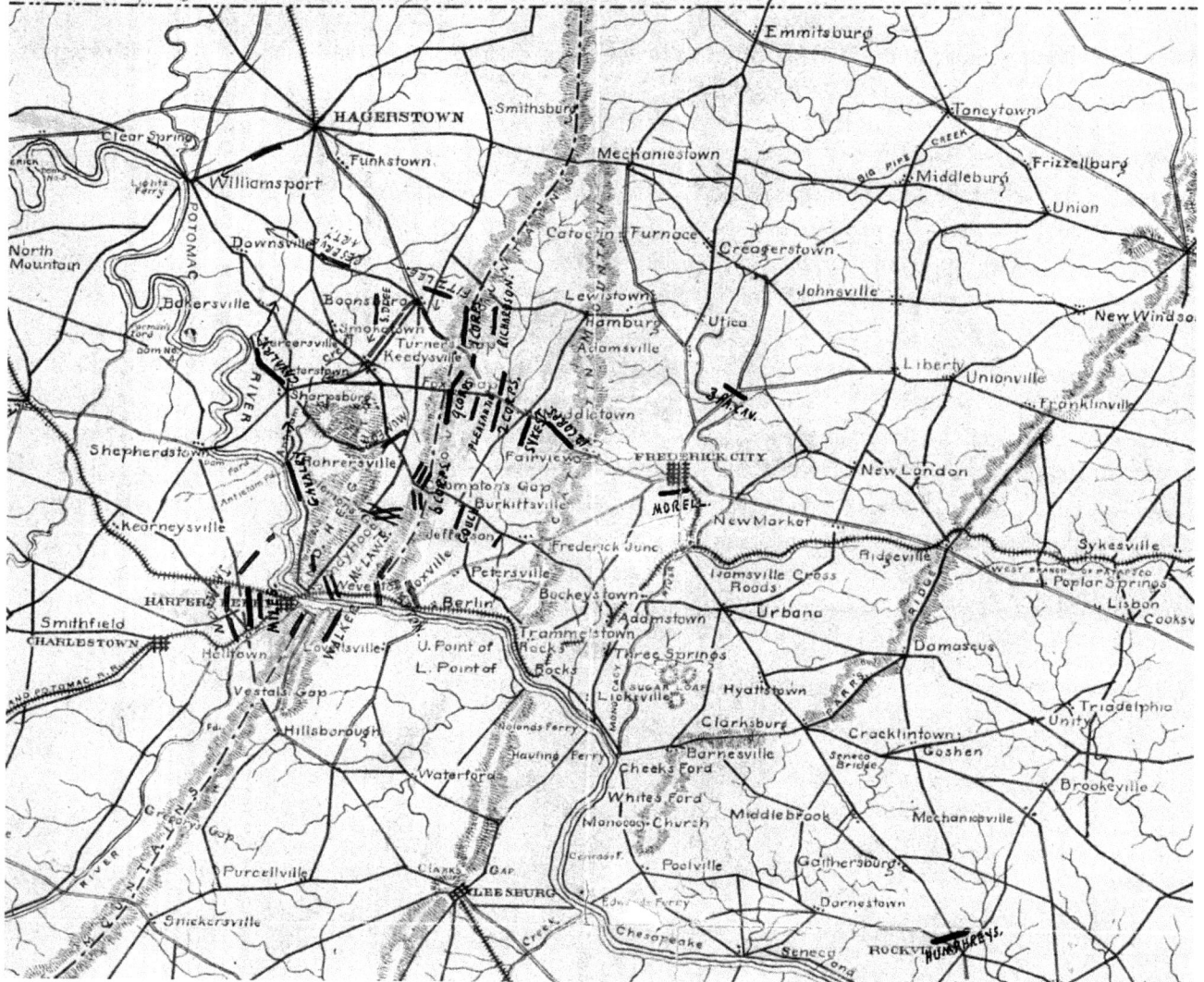

Situation map night of 14 September. Note McReynold's cavalry just to the south of Gettysburg, Pennsylvania. Courtesy LOC.

John Pelham in his 1858 West Point uniform. Courtesy Wikipedia.

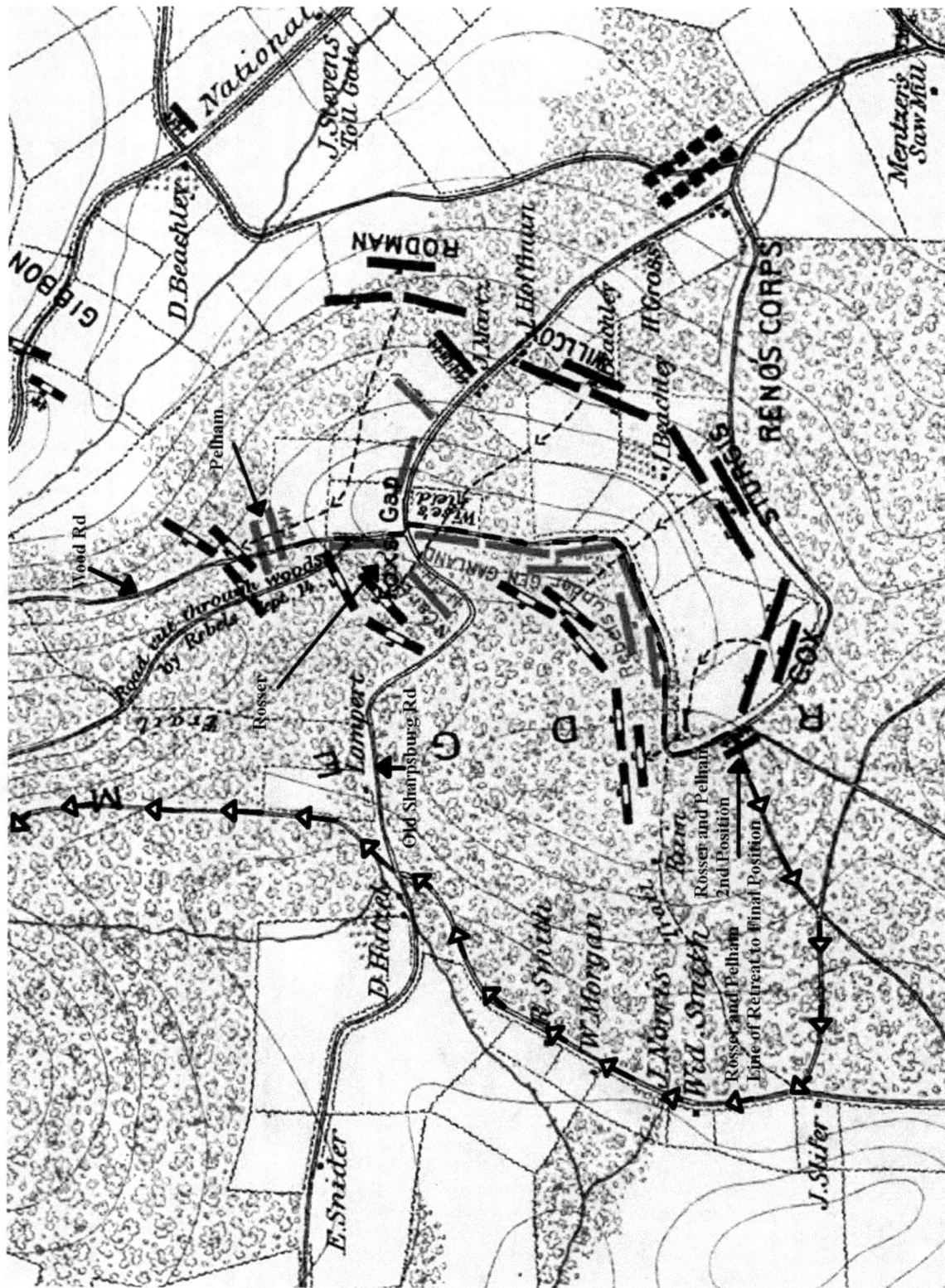

Rosser and Pelham fight at Fox's Gap, north is to the left. Pelham was first located in the area north of the gap with the cavalry closer to the road intersection. Later, to stay on the right (southern) flank of the arriving Rebel infantry, they moved to the south at the lowest arrow. The route they took is not known but it may have been on or to the west of the mountain road running along the crest as shown by the dashed line. Then later in the afternoon, then retreated down the mountain as shown along a road then to the north to set up in their final position as show on the next map. It is possible that some of Rosser's troopers may have taken the trail shown just north of the route marked but it would have been difficult for the cannon to do so. *Official Atlas*, Plate 27. Courtesy LOC.

Rosser's troopers were the first Confederates to arrive at Fox's Gap. They dismounted and served as pickets near the crest on the Old Sharpsburg Road where a farm lane, along the ridge leading from the Mountain House at Turner's Gap crossed, but the primary help he gave to preventing a Confederate rout was his use of the "Gallant" Pelham's guns the morning of the 14th. Pelham's two guns were instrumental in stopping four Federal regiments from taking the road and getting in the Confederate rear. D.H. Hill rode along the ridge road from the Mountain House at Turner's Gap during the morning and found much to his surprise the noise of men and wagon wheels coming from the direction of Fox's Gap. Hill did not realize that it was Rosser positioning his 200 troopers and Pelham's guns so he returned to the Mountain House and sent Brig. Gen. Samuel Garland, Jr., with his brigade, to the south.[6] Rosser initially deployed his two guns on the Old Sharpsburg Road but then had to move south along the farm lane on the top of South Mountain during the mid-morning by 10 A.M., to stay on the left or southern flank of Confederate regiments, which were moving south along the ridge from Turner's Gap. Rosser was deployed on the right of Garland's Brigade next to the 5th North Carolina Infantry while Bondurant's battery which was with Garland was deployed to the left of the 5th North Carolina.

Rosser was unable to return north along the ridge road after Confederate infantry were pushed back and had to retreat down a mountain road toward Rohrersville to the southwest then to the northwest finally again striking the Old Sharpsburg Road. They had faced Ninth Corps units under Brig. Gen. Jesse Reno, but after Garland was killed, North Carolina units retreated and were forced away from Fox's Gap toward Turner's Gap to the north, as Longstreet's troops began arriving in force. Rosser held onto the Old Sharpsburg Road until 10 P.M. that night and then moved to a knoll southwest of the Mountain House. Rosser's losses for this desperate struggle were some twenty-five men including Pelham's artillery.[7] At dawn, he moved back down the Old Sharpsburg Road, down the mountain, and then north

Overleaf: Rosser's location later on 14/15 September. Rosser's first position was just north of the intersection of the woods road and the Old Sharpsburg Road at the black arrow to the lower center. His second position is south along the woods road. Left black arrow shows location of last position that evening guarding the Old Sharpsburg Road to discourage Yankee pursuit. Rosser likely used the road leading down toward the Rohrersville Road and then moving north intersecting with the Old Sharpsburg Road to get to his last location. Hill wrote that "Rosser retired in better order, not, however, without having some of his men captured, and took up a position from which he could still fire upon the old road, and which he held until 10 o clock that night," *Battles and Leaders*, 2:566. Cox wrote that "The dismounted cavalry was forced to retreat with their battery across the ravine in which the Sharpsburg road descends on the west of the mountain, and took a new position on a separate hill in rear of the heights at the Mountain House. There was considerable open ground at this new position, from which their battery had full play at a range of about twelve hundred yards upon the ridge held by us," Cox, *Reminiscences*, 283. *Official Atlas*. Plate 27. Courtesv LOC.

[6] Carman wrote that Hill not only heard the noise but also found and conferred with Rosser, Pierro, 145. No record of this meeting has been found. See also Priest, *Before Antietam*, 131; Harsh, *Flood*, who writes that Rosser met with Garland that morning after Hill had sent Garland and his brigade south along the mountain road to the sound of firing, 258. In his official report, Hill said that Rosser had reported to him but nothing else about that meeting, *OR*, vol. 19, pt. 1, 1020. Hill in his *Battles and Leaders* article wrote that he sent Garland but did not mention meeting with Rosser before he sent Garland, 2:562. Hal Bridges, *Lee's Maverick General: Daniel Harvey Hill* (Lincoln, NE: University of Nebraska Press, 1991) finds nothing to refute Hill's article, 108. Clemens, Carman, 322, n. 11, finds Carman in error here since Hill never said he knew Rosser was at Fox's Gap until later that day.

[7] *OR*, vol. 19, pt. 1, 1021, 1032; Priest, *Before Antietam*, 206-208, 326; Carman, Pierro, 148-149, 449. Priest estimated 27 casualties for Rosser and Pelham, 326. Note that the Old Sharpsburg Road was also known as Braddock's Road and Fox's Gap is also known as Braddock's Gap. See also Hill, 566. Cox describes the action of Rosser in "Forcing Fox's Gap and Turner's Gap" in *Battles and Leaders*, 2:587. Pleasonton's horse artillery was among Union guns firing on Confederate positions on the 14th, Priest, *Before Antietam*, 134. Pleasonton's cavalry had also scouted to the north and south of Turner's Gap and had discovered Fox's Gap; at that early hour on the 14th, only Rosser was there and had Pleasonton attacked with force, he would have taken the gap and then gotten into Hill's rear playing havoc if Union infantry had quickly followed, Harsh, *Flood*, 260-262. West Virginia Cavalry helped as dismounted skirmishers for Lt. Col. Rutherford B. Hayes and Col. Scammon. Scammon sent a number along both sides of the Old Sharpsburg Road to flush out the enemy and when they had done so, Lt. James Abraham had them retire and take cover awaiting the infantry, Priest, *Before Antietam*, 138-139.

to Boonsboro, and finally south on the Boonsboro-Shepherdstown Pike to Keedysville, crossing the Antietam about noon of the 15th. As he saw no other cavalry in the area, he sent out videttes south beyond the Rohrbach (Burnside) Bridge and north of the Dunker Church as well as down the Smoketown Road.[8]

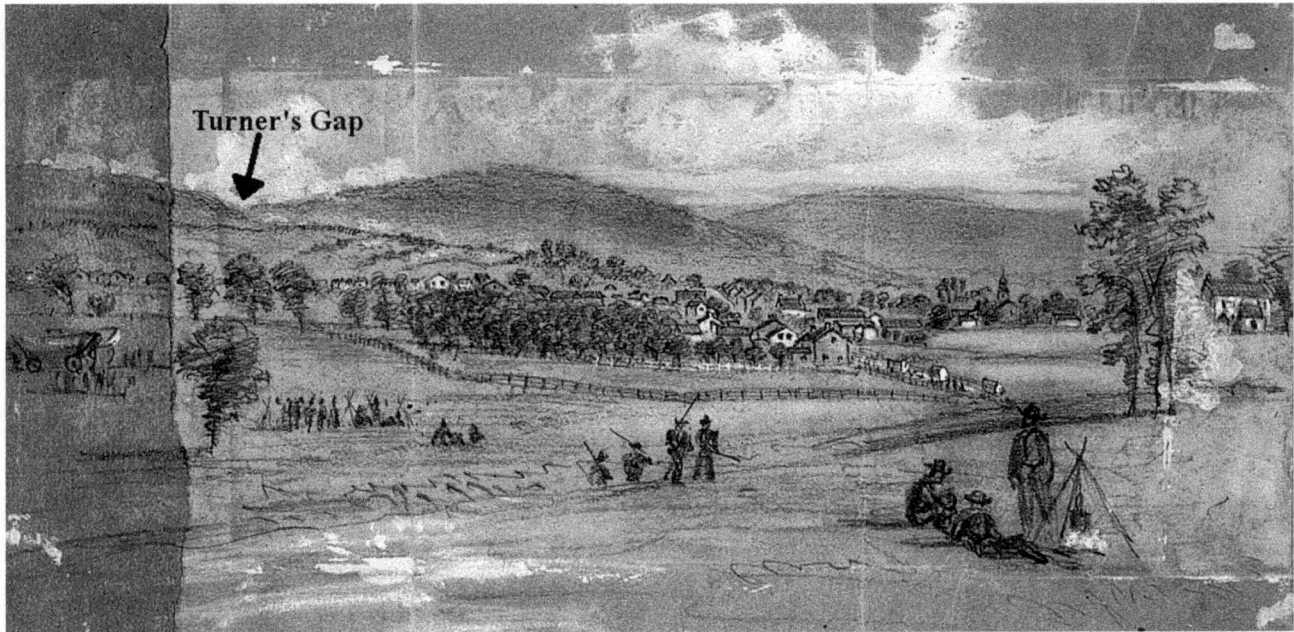

Boonsboro, MD; South Mountain is in the distance looking southeast, Turner's Gap to the left upper center through which the National Pike passes. Alfred R. Waud, Drawing done for Harpers Weekly, October 25, 1862, p. 677. Courtesy LOC.

While Stuart conferred with McLaws farther south on South Mountain near Weverton, and Rosser fought for his life at Fox's Gap, Munford, at Crampton's Gap, began to see that his tiny force was facing much more than he could handle. One of his horse artillerymen described the view east from his mountainside perch of Middletown Valley with the Union column approaching slowly "with their vast superior numbers, approached the mountain, it put one very much in mind of a lion…making exceeding careful preparations to spring on a plucky little mouse" and "so numerous that it looked as if they were creeping up out of the ground."[9] Franklin's leisurely approach with his Lancer escort's pennons flying allowed Munford to position his troops using the natural terrain features as well as stoutly-built stone walls lining roads leading up to the gap. His cavalry was in dismounted skirmish order, with the 2nd Virginia Cavalry along the right (south) side of his line on the east side of the mountain crest, with their extreme right connected with Confederate infantry skirmishers from the 32nd Virginia spreading north from Brownsville Gap, about one mile to the south. Munford's stalwart 75 troopers of the 12th Virginia Cavalry were on the left (north) and above of the Confederate infantry consisting of the 6th, 12th, and 16th Infantry of Mahone's Brigade. The troopers of the 12th Virginia Cavalry spent their time picketing the Arnoldstown Road guarding against any Union approach from the north, and thus were the most northern men on Munford's line even though they did not connect with Maj. Willis Holt's 10th Georgia Infantry from Semmes's Brigade at the base of the mountain; Col. William MacRae's 15th North Carolina Infantry from Cobb's Brigade was to their right, to the west up the mountain on the Arnoldstown Road,

[8] Carman, Clemens, 394-395, and n. 30.
[9] Neese, 146. See also Reese who points out that Company G of the 7th Virginia Cavalry which was not with Munford at this time would have been of great use as at least a quarter of its troopers were from Frederick and Washington Counties with a dozen from the lower Middletown Valley, 21; McDonald, 405-408.

and they likely had them in sight. The 10th Georgia Infantry had a busy day marching to and fro under Semmes's and Munford's orders. They moved from the Rohrersville Road to the west side of South Mountain, then down the east side, finally settling along the Mountain Church Road to the left of the 6th Virginia Infantry. The 15th North Carolina Infantry was part of the reinforcements Cobb supplied after the battle for the gap had begun. Munford told Cobb to place them and the 24th Georgia Infantry to his left. The 15th took position behind the stone wall on the east side of Arnoldstown Road. Munford placed Chew's Battery of three guns and a section of Capt. Cary F. Grimes's Portsmouth Artillery of navy howitzers under Lt. J.H. Thompson, partway up the mountain, at a location which gave them a good field of fire. Confederate artillery at Brownsville Gap also helped Munford's defense. Around noon, Munford could count on some 1,200 men to face Franklin's 12,000.[10]

The Union advance to the gap began from Jefferson with the 96th Pennsylvania in the lead along with a squadron, Companies B and G, from the 6th Pennsylvania Cavalry. Near Burkittsville, the 96th received fire from the Rebel artillery and halted. After preliminary fighting during which Confederate artillery did good work on approaching Unionists, the Federals finally shook themselves out into a mile-long line and moved forward late in the day in a spirited uphill battle, taking heavy casualties from Rebel troopers behind stone fences. The heavily outnumbered Confederates could do little to stem the blue tide and raced up the mountain despite helpful artillery fire from the Confederate guns.[11] The 2nd Virginia Cavalry on the southern flank, and the 12th Virginia Cavalry on the northern flank, fell back in disorder, as did the rest of the Confederate troops running, for the top of the mountain.[12] Brig. Gen. Howell Cobb arrived with four Confederate regiments as reinforcements: Cobb asked Munford to place the Cobb Legion and the 24th Georgia in position—he did so, on the road just to his rear behind the summit on the Burkittsville Road. Munford then placed the 15th North Carolina and the 16th Georgia on the road running to the left after crossing the gap, but Munford later reported that "they behaved badly and did not get in position before the wildest confusion commenced, the wounded coming to the rear in numbers and more well men coming with them."[13] As the Union infantry swarmed over the crest, Munford and his two regiments held the Rohrersville Road to the northwest of Crampton's Gap, losing a total of eight troopers for the day.[14] Stuart with his staff arrived on the Weverton to Rohrersville Road to witness the disorderly Confederate retreat. He met the distraught Gen. Cobb on the road described by Stuart's aide, von Borcke:

> The poor General was in a state of the saddest excitement and disgust at the conduct of his men. As soon as he recognised us in the dusk of the evening, he cried out in heartbroken accents of alarm and despair, "Dismount, gentlemen, dismount, if your lives are dear to you! the enemy is within fifty yards of us; I am expecting their attack every moment; oh! my dear Stuart, that I should live to experience such a disaster! what

[10] Harsh, *Flood*, 279-280; Reese, *Sealed*, 51, 85, 127; Carman, Pierro, 138. Grimes was mortally wounded as he directed his battery on Piper Farm on 17 September. Carman said that Munford had 13 pieces of artillery in addition to having a strong position, but as Dr. Clemens noted that number is in question, Carman, Clemens, 302, n. 32. Reese found that the 6th Pennsylvania cavalry went into camp about noon with Companies A, C, F and K near Broad Run and Company E scouted closer to the Potomac probably coordinating with the 6th U.S. Cavalry; Companies B, G, and I were detailed to Franklin's headquarters at Shafer farm, Reese, *Sealed*, 336, n. 47; Gracey, 97.

[11] Priest, *Before Antietam*, 288; George B. Sanford, *Fighting Rebels and Redskins: Experiences in Army Life of Colonel George B. Sanford 1861-1892*, ed. by E.R. Hageman (Norman, OK: University of Oklahoma Press, 1969), 173-174. Franklin apparently retained Company I of the Lancers at his headquarters, Reese, *Sealed*, 19. Note that Reese wrote that Company F of the Lancers was ahead of the 96th Pennsylvania, Reese, 51.

[12] Priest, *Before Antietam*, 292.

[13] *OR*, vol. 19, pt. 1, 827.

[14] Priest, *Before Antietam*, 301, 326; von Borcke, 151-152. Carman totaled one killed and two wounded for the 2nd Virginia and two killed and three wounded for the 12th Virginia cavalry, Carman, Pierro, 445.

can be done? what can save us?" General Stuart did his best to comfort and encourage his disconsolate friend, assisted him in rallying his scattered troops, and quickly placed in position all the artillery.[15]

Stuart did not believe that the enemy was so close, so as at Hagan's Gap the day before, he decided to send von Borcke to investigate:

> Then turning to me, he said, "Major, I don't believe the Yankees are so near at hand, but we must be certain about it; take two couriers with you, and find out at once where the enemy is." My General was very fond of sending me on these ticklish expeditions, and much as I appreciated the honour thus paid me, I did not feel greatly obliged to him on this particular occasion, as I rode forward into the darkness, feeling that I should run a narrow chance of being shot by our men on my return, if, indeed, I escaped the bullets of the Yankees. Cautiously I proceeded, fifty yards, a hundred, two hundred yards, —everything quiet; not a trace of the enemy: at last, after a ride of more than a mile, I discovered the long lines of the Federal camp-fires, where Messieurs the Yankees had halted, and were busily employed in cooking supper; and at sixty yards' distance I could see in the road a cavalry picket, clearly defined against the glare of the fires, horse and trooper, who seemed to have no idea of our approach. Leaving the hostile sentry undisturbed, we rode quietly back to our lines, where the Generals awaited my return with the greatest interest and anxiety.[16]

Stuart moved with the cavalry to the extreme left and instructed von Borcke to remain with couriers and relate any enemy movements back to Stuart. At about 10 A.M. on 15 September, the Federals began to move but after a few shots were exchanged, "a cry of joy, louder than the roar of cannon, commenced by our reserves and answered from one end of our lines to the other, brought delight to our hearts and carried despair to the foe," as word was brought from Harpers Ferry that it had surrendered.

> Stuart now came back to us, and was so delighted that he threw his arms round my neck and said, "My dear Von, is not this glorious? you must immediately gallop over with me to congratulate old Stonewall on his splendid success." Captain Farley, Captain Blackford, and Lieutenant Dabney joined us, and after a short and rapid ride we reached the magnificent scene of our magnificent victory, just in time to witness the formal ceremony of the surrender of the garrison, a sight which was certainly one of the grandest I ever saw in my life.[17]

---

[15] Von Borcke, 152.

[16] Ibid., 152-153. The cavalry picket was likely from the 6th Pennsylvania Cavalry although Franklin did have men from the 6th U.S. Cavalry at his service.

[17] Ibid., 153-154.

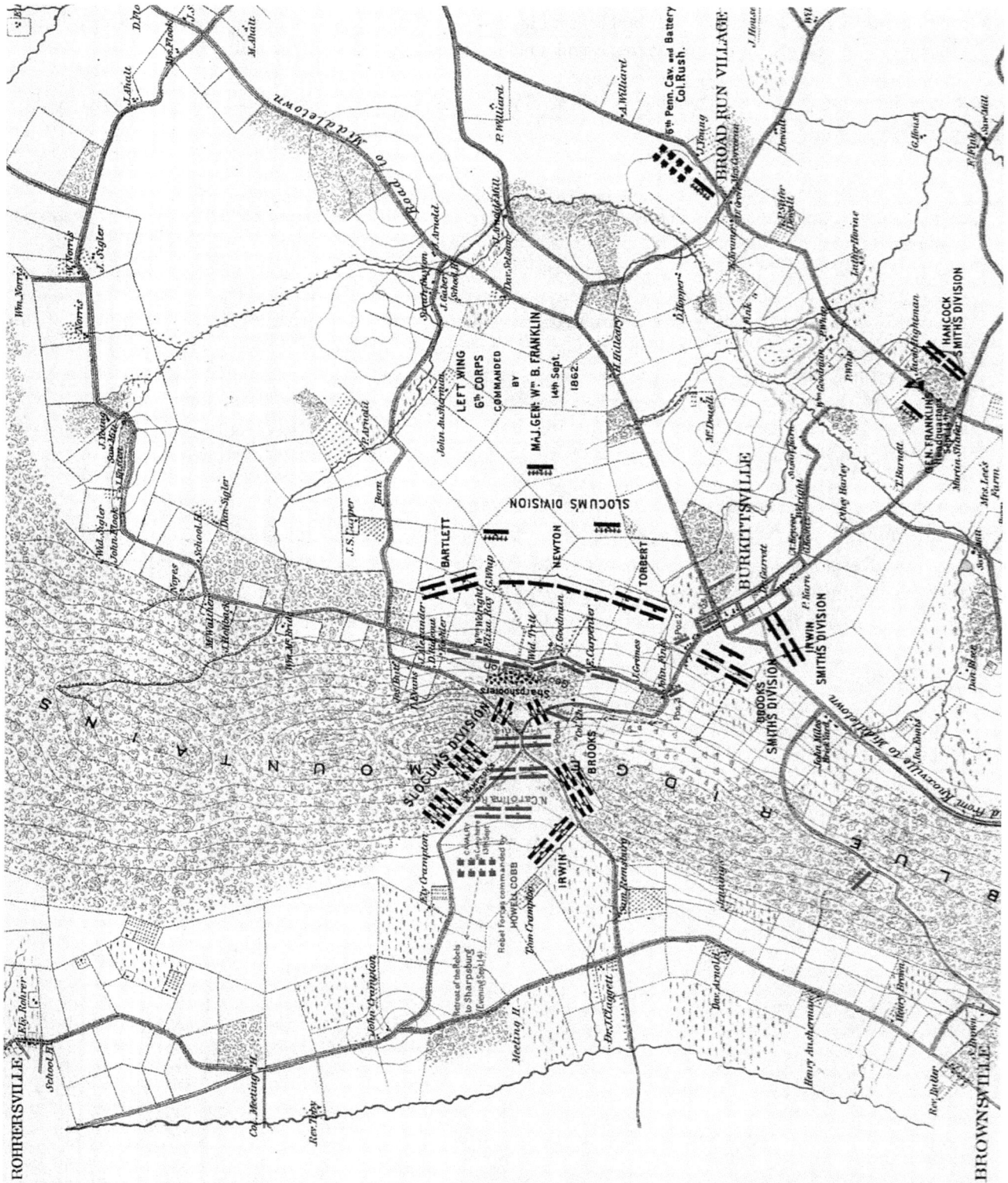

Battle of Crampton's Gap in South Mountain 14 September 1862, showing various positions as Union forces push Confederate troops off the crest despite reinforcements being brought up from Brownsville Pass. Munford's two regiments are picketing the Rohrersville Road after retreating from the gap. Detail from Official Atlas, Plate 27. Courtesy LOC.

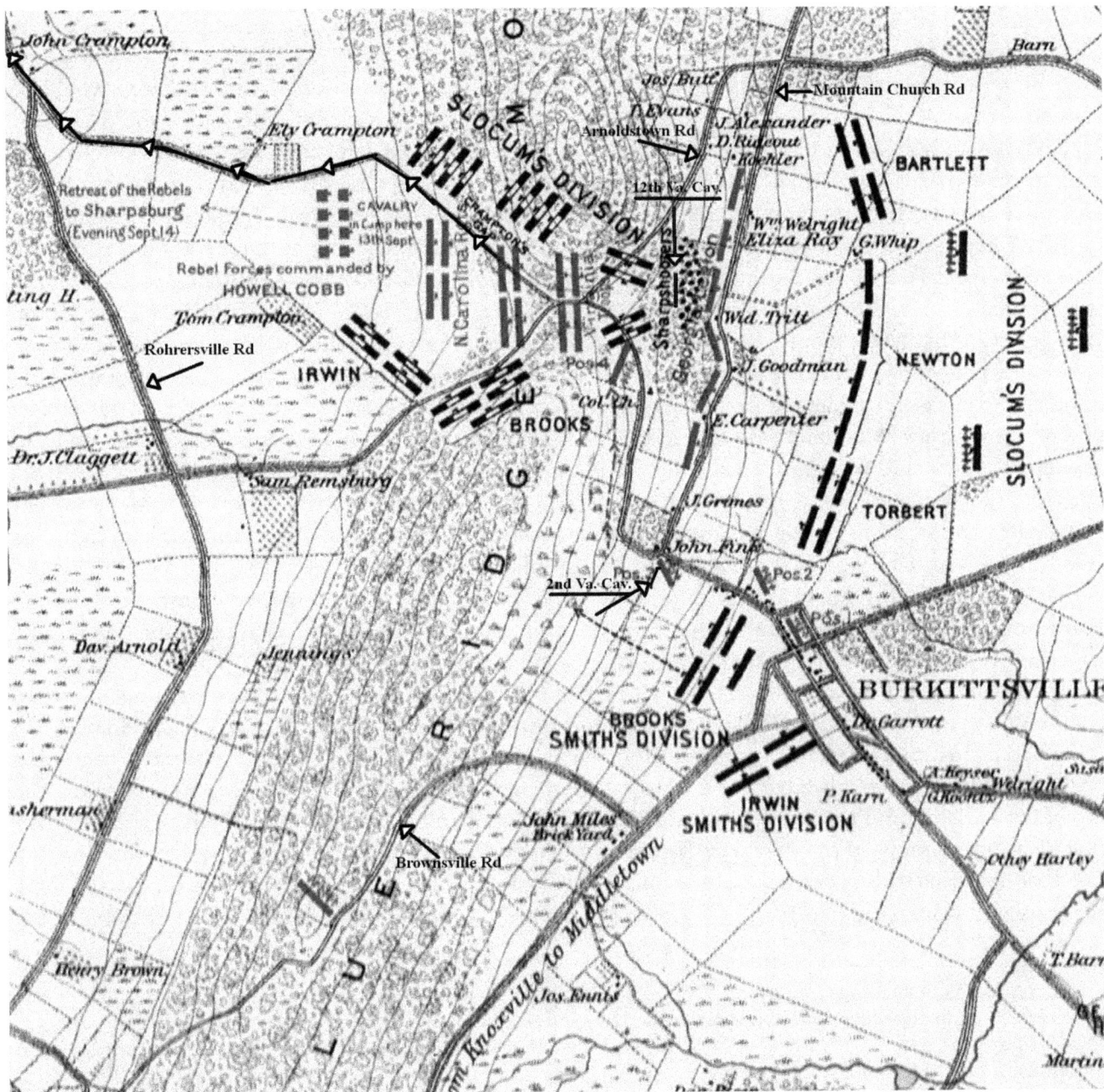

Detail from above map showing locations of Munford's cavalry. The 2nd was on his right flank acting as skirmishers to the right of the 16th Virginia Infantry and the 12th was to the left rear as skirmishers behind the 6th Virginia Infantry on Arnoldstown Road. Munford retreated as Franklin's troops closed at daylight riding north to Rohrersville and then west through Porterstown on Old Sharpsburg Road and over the Middle Bridge. Note that he may have taken a more direct route west to Sharpsburg from Rohrersville on what today is the Burnside Bridge Road over Rohrbach Bridge according to Thomas Clemens, Carman, Clemens, 395, n. 31. Official Atlas, Plate 27. Courtesy LOC.

Von Borcke then joined other staff members, Capt. Blackford and Lt. Dabney, about 5 P.M., and along with some couriers, rode to Sharpsburg. Stuart's couriers told von Borcke "that General Stuart had gone off some hours before with Hampton's and Robertson's brigades, proceeding along the tow-path of the canal on the Maryland side of the river to Sharpsburg, leaving orders for us to join him there during the night." Stuart's staff, unlike their commander, rode north on the Virginia shore to Shepherdstown where they joined Stuart at Dr. Grove's house in downtown Sharpsburg. There, after an eventful day, they bedded down for the night on the floor in the home's entrance hall.[18]

Late on the night of 14-15 September, Gen. Lee feared that McLaws on South Mountain would be trapped as Franklin assembled his force in Pleasant Valley. Lee ordered Munford, who was near Rohrersville, to help McLaws find an escape route on the Maryland side of the river, to allow McLaws to take his troops to Sharpsburg where Lee planned on concentrating his forces. Lee believed that McClellan would likely reinforce Franklin to crush McLaws in a vice between Franklin's corps and the Harpers Ferry garrison, and McLaws would have no easy way out of the trap as there was not a good ford close to Harpers Ferry or at Berlin; the closest useable ford would be at Point of Rocks, some 12 miles downstream, and farther away from Lee's rallying point at Sharpsburg. Gen. Lee and McLaws would have believed that Miles would destroy the pontoon bridge across the Potomac if Miles decided to fight to hold Harpers Ferry, while Franklin pushed south. Keyes Ford on the Shenandoah River upstream from Harpers Ferry was not suitable for rapid movement of a large body of troops. Munford was unable to find a good route on the Maryland side and so told Lee and McLaws.[19] Most of Hampton's cavalry was still guarding the strategic Weverton Pass along the Potomac, upon which Union forces could approach from the east into McLaws's rear, had McClellan decided upon that route from Jefferson.[20] McLaws, not knowing of the status of Union troops to the north toward Sharpsburg, did not contemplate marching there on the Maryland side of the river, so could not follow Lee's orders on the 15th that the army would retire through Sharpsburg back into Virginia.[21] And Jackson's orders to him to rejoin the army at Sharpsburg, would have squashed any thoughts of heading north in Maryland should he be able somehow to go around Franklin's left flank and up Middletown Valley.[22]

Fitzhugh Lee's Brigade on Monday, 15 September, was having a much more exciting day than Hampton's or even Munford's. He and his brigade, minus Rosser's 5th Virginia Cavalry and Pelham's two guns, had a long march from his journeys to the north of Frederick scouting the Federal right, beginning on 11 September. After his adventures on the Union right already discussed, he rode west crossing the Catoctins at Hamburg Pass, and finally crossing South Mountain on 14 September, arriving at Boonsboro that evening—he missed the drama at Turner's and Fox's Gaps entirely. He did not find Stuart who had left that morning riding south but was likely welcomed by Gen. Lee, as his brigade was the only substantial cavalry available for use.[23] He was quickly informed by Gen. Lee that his cavalry would

[18] Von Borcke, 156. Interesting to note that Stuart reportedly rode the towpath from Harpers Ferry to Sharpsburg, but there is no record that taking that route was considered by the Union cavalry escapees. It is very unlikely that many of Hampton's and Munford's troopers were with Stuart as we will see below that Munford wrote that his two regiments crossed the Rohrbach (Burnside) Bridge, and Hampton reported that he rode to Sharpsburg and crossed the Potomac at Knott's Ford. The couriers were reporting hearsay. Some of Hampton's troopers were the rearguard and some were almost left behind due to McLaws's neglect, said Hampton, Hartwig, *To Antietam Creek*, 578.

[19] Carman, Pierro, 169. Carman wrote that "Lee heard from Munford that McLaws could not come up the valley and that the difficulties in getting over Elk Ridge and Maryland Heights were very great. Upon the receipt of this communication, Lee determined not to make a stand at Keedysville," Carman, Pierro, 173. The ford at Berlin about 5.75 river miles below Harpers Ferry was a poor ford.

[20] Reese, *Sealed*, 171, 172.

[21] *OR*, 51, pt. 2, 618-619.

[22] *OR*, 19, pt. 1, 855-856. McLaws explained his situation on the 15th in detail in his 18 October 1862 report noting that the "early surrender of Harper's Ferry relieved me from the situation" of being trapped between the Harpers Ferry garrison and Franklin. He stated that his best option was to defend Pleasant Valley and remain on the two heights at Harpers Ferry, 856.

[23] Note that there is also a Hamburg Gap in South Mountain three miles north of Turner's Gap, Harsh, *Flood*, 248, 257. But see Paula M. Strain, *The Blue Hills of Maryland: History Along the Appalachian Trail on South Mountain and the Catoctins* (Vienna, VA: Potomac Appalachian Trail Club, 1993), who states that the name of the pass at that time was Orr's Gap and the name of Hamburg Pass was given in error by Confederate Brig. Gen. R.S. Ripley during the Battle of South Mountain, with subsequent historians repeating that error, 202. See also Chapter 7, note 36. The name may have been given as there are roads

relieve infantry pickets on the western side of South Mountain along the National Pike near Turner's Gap as the Army of Northern Virginia was retreating from the mountain. His cavalry brigade moved at 1 A.M. on the 15th riding east to the gap.[24] The ground where Fitzhugh Lee posted his brigade was uneven and narrow not inviting for extended cavalry action but he sent dismounted skirmishers well forward and posted two guns from Pelham's Battery on a knoll. Lee placed the 3rd Virginia Cavalry to the front and flanks, the 9th Virginia Cavalry in column in the road behind the guns, and the 4th Virginia Cavalry to the west in the rear, closest to Boonsboro.

Early in the morning of the 15th, about sunrise, Union Maj. Gen. Israel B. Richardson's division of the Second Corps began marching down the National Pike from Turner's Gap, Brig. Gen. Thomas Meagher's Brigade in the van. He was stopped by Lee's skirmishers at 10 A.M., so formed battle lines on both sides of the road and advanced, pushing Lee's skirmishers in. Pelham unmasked his guns and opened fire, abruptly halting the Union advance. Col. Edward W. Cross's 5th New Hampshire then came to the front as skirmishers. When the Union lines extended beyond Lee's flanks, Pelham was forced to retire, followed by the 4th and the 9th Virginia Cavalry, with the 3rd Virginia Cavalry as rear guard. Pelham limbered up and he with Rosser passed through Boonsboro and took the Boonsboro-Shepherdstown Pike toward Sharpsburg. Pelham initially reset his guns near Keedysville to discourage the Union pursuit after the Boonsboro fight which he had missed.[25]

Activity had picked up in Boonsboro before Pelham arrived in Keedysville, however. The 4th and 9th Virginia Cavalry had gone into town. While the 3rd Virginia was retreating through Boonsboro, six companies of the 8th Illinois Cavalry unexpectedly charged through Richardson's troops on the National Pike, led by its commander, Col. John. F. Farnsworth. The 3rd Virginia, led by Lt. Col. John T. Thornton, met this charge, and sent it reeling back to its infantry supports, suffering 16 casualties, with Thornton's horse being killed. The Yankee horsemen reformed and returned pushing the 3rd Virginia into Boonsboro, where it rode into dismounted troopers of Col. William Henry Fitzhugh "Rooney" Lee's 9th Virginia Cavalry, who were resting dismounted in the streets, with some of the 4th Virginia Cavalry. These cavalrymen were unaware of the seriousness of their comrades' fight to the east. Part of the 9th under Lt. Col. Richard L.T. Beale escaped on the National Pike with the 4th Virginia Cavalry following in their dust. Col. Rooney Lee had the difficult task of holding back the charging Union troopers with his remaining command, because due to the noise and confusion, only a squadron near him heard his order to face about and confront the surging Yankees. Some Rebel casualties were caused by horses falling over piles of stone in the road stacked for road repair on the National Pike. The stone piles were masked by the heavy dust thrown up from the macadamized limestone road surface which blinded men and horses; some even rode into telegraph poles. Into this confused mass of three Rebel regiments rode the Illinois horsemen, peppering the hapless throng with carbine and pistol fire, while town residents took this wonderful opportunity to fire at the struggling Confederate troopers with shotguns and pistols from

---

from the South Mountain "Hamburg Gap" which lead east to the "real" Hamburg Gap on the Catoctin Mountain range. Some contemporary maps show almost a direct road link between the two but more accurately surveyed maps show that the road is more meandering.

[24] William R. Carter, 15.

[25] Carman, Pierro, 166, 174; letter 10 July 1897 from Rosser to Carman, courtesy of Thomas Clemens. See also Armstrong, *Colors,* where he says that Confederate cavalry pickets were encountered on the morning of the 15th on the way to the Mountain House which is at the crest of Turner's Gap, therefore, it is likely that mounted pickets were more widely posted than just on the western slope of the gap, 130-131. Trout, *Thunder,* 101. Rosser then crossed Antietam Creek becoming the first Confederate cavalry unit on the field so he placed pickets east of the creek, beyond Rohrbach (Burnside) Bridge, above the Dunker Church on the Hagerstown Pike, and on the Smoketown Road facing the upper crossings of Antietam Creek. When Stuart arrived late in the afternoon of the 15th, he called in Rosser's pickets from the right. Pelham bivouacked that night near Nicodemus Heights. Rosser held back the Union pursuit led by Col. Cross and his 5th New Hampshire men but the Rebel troopers were finally forced across the Antietam where they held the Yankees on the east bank, Carman, Clemens, 402.

upper story windows. Much of the 3rd, 4th, and 9th Virginia rode toward Funkstown on the National Pike fending off pursuing Illinoisans. A squadron from the 9th Virginia formed on both sides of the pike and allowed another squadron to attack the pursuing Federals in a column of fours slowing their pursuit. These Rebel squadrons continued leapfrogging south, allowing their comrades to retreat. Col. Rooney Lee tried to reorganize his 9th Virginia, but in doing so, his horse was killed, injuring Lee when it fell. When he eventually regained consciousness, he crawled off the road and hid in a cornfield. Finally, a counter charge begun by Lt. Col. Richard L.T. Beale with the 9th Virginia, and continued by Capt. Thomas Haynes after Beale's horse was killed, pushed back the pursuing Illinois cavalry, capturing three or four Unionists. This action gave Brig. Gen. Fitzhugh Lee time to reform his three regiments. Fitzhugh Lee then continued on a road leading west from the National Pike past Keedysville to the south and crossed Antietam Creek finding the end of Gen. Robert E. Lee's left flank. Fitzhugh Lee's Brigade lost an estimated forty troopers in this melee, perhaps the largest cavalry-on-cavalry fight of the Maryland Campaign, while the 8th Illinois probably lost about twenty.[26]

Pleasonton's troopers with their blood up chased after the remnants of Fitz Lee's Brigade on the Williamsport Road branching off the National Pike leaving few Yankee horsemen to provide support to infantry pursing down the Boonsboro-Shepherdstown Pike. Col. Edward W. Cross leading his 5th New Hampshire complained that "The main body of the Army followed on consisting solely of Richardson's Division without cavalry or artillery. This was a great oversight, as the rear of the enemy might have been greatly annoyed. Union horse artillerist Tidball and Union troopers pursued Lee "resulting in a chase of several miles towards Hagerstown and thence around to the front of Lee's position behind the Antietam."[27]

---

[26] Carman, Clemens, 400; Hartwig, *To Antietam Creek*, 501-503. Apparently only a few of the Confederate troopers rode west on the Boonsboro-Shepherdstown Pike. The main body of Lee's Brigade made their way northwest from Boonsboro on the National Pike, then likely took the Williamsport Road (today's Lappans Road) to the west. It is unlikely many rode all the way to Funkstown however. On the 1859 Taggart Map there is a road shown leading southwest from Williamsport Road, today's Mill Point Road, and continues today as Wheeler Road. Comparing the Taggart map, the 1877 Washington County district map, the 1893 Antietam Board Map 1, and modern maps, the 1862 road would have continued southwest to the modern Girl Scout Road, across a gap found today to Coffman Farm Road, which continues south, then southeast, to the Boonsboro-Shepherdstown Pike to Keedysville. Had any troopers remained riding west on the Williamsport Road from the National Pike, they would have found themselves at Jones's Cross Roads where they could have ridden south on the Hagerstown Pike to the north end of Gen. Lee's forming line along the Antietam. Thomas Clemens opines that some could have continued west on the road from the Williamsport Road and then taken a road just west of Antietam Creek which would have led to Smoketown on Gen. Lee's left—the Smoketown Road.

[27] Edward E. Cross, *Stand Firm and Fire Low: The Civil War Writings of Colonel Edward E. Cross* (Lebanon, NH: University Press of New England, 2003), 44; Tidball, 62.

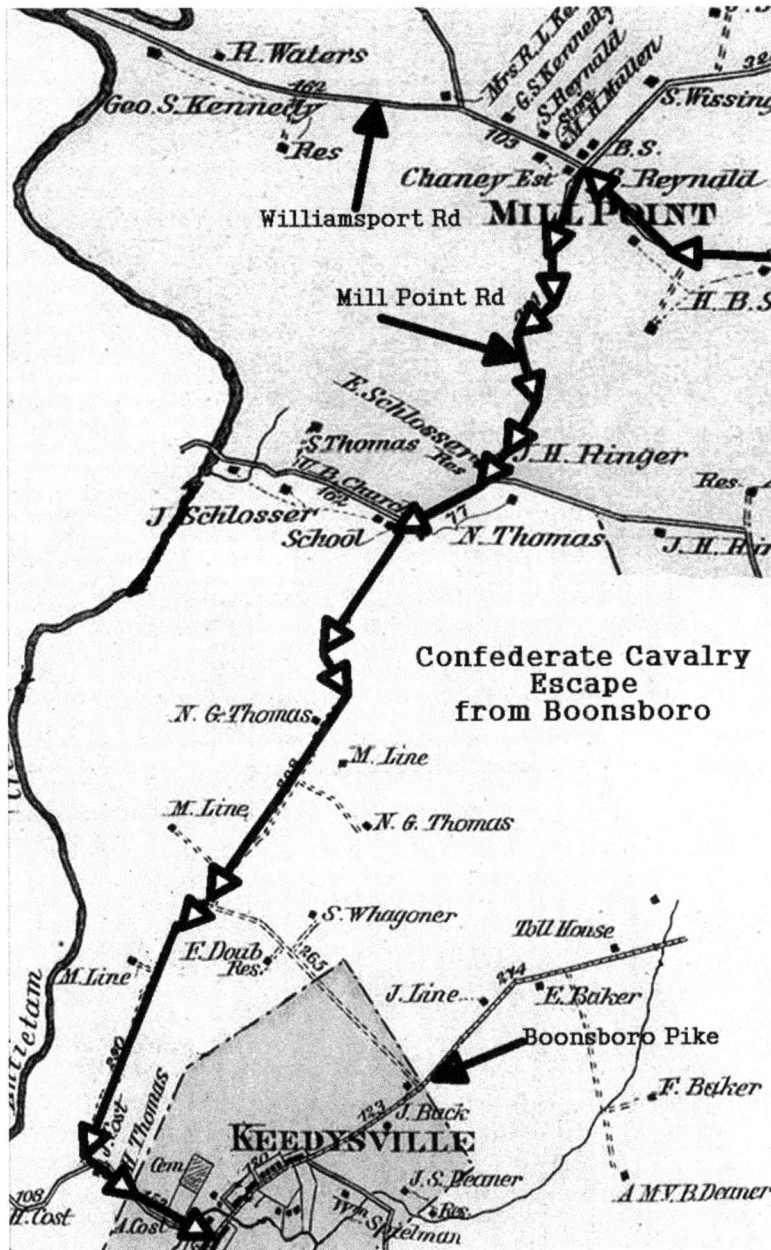

Confederate escape route from Boonsboro to Keedysville. The road from the National Pike from Boonsboro leads in from the upper right. Courtesy Western Maryland Historical Library, Washington County 1877 Atlas.

Troopers from the 9th Virginia picketed the Confederate left flank on the 15th, while some officers crossed the Potomac to find fresh horses to replace those worn out or injured at the Boonsboro fight. Part of the 4th Virginia Cavalry escaped up the road to Hagerstown during the melee in Boonsboro and did not arrive at Antietam until after dark on the evening of the 15th. They were not able to locate the rest of the 4th until the morning of the 16th and the regiment remained in position behind the infantry on the right of Fitz Lee's Brigade, out of sight of the battle line, but still exposed to shelling.[28] On the 16th

---

[28] Letter from Pitfield George to Carman 4 March 1895 courtesy of Thomas Clemens. Henry Kyd Douglas wrote that he saw his mother and sister at their house, Ferry Hill, on 16 September, caring for Rooney Lee; Douglas, *Stonewall*, 168. The six 8th Illinois companies lead by Col. Farnsworth did not have the benefit of the help of its other four companies as they were sent over South Mountain to the south and apparently did not join in the fight, Hard, 178. Hard reported 23 Federals killed and one wounded, and eight Rebels killed and many wounded; he also reported four captured cannon, 179. Hard also wrote that 500

the 9th Virginia remained on the army's left flank, but then moved more in the rear center of the line during the morning, bivouacking on the Hagerstown Pike that night. On the day of battle, Wednesday the 17th, the 9th was collecting stragglers, and that night replaced infantry pickets as they were withdrawn. By the time the regiment reformed on the Virginia shore on the 19th near Leetown, it had fewer than 200 men present for duty.[29]

Pleasonton later said of the Boonsboro fight that it was his only personal encounter during the war. He was at the head of his troopers and saw his advance troopers returning at a gallop so he "turned to the main body and said, 'Draw sabers, charge!' And I saw them try to draw their sabers, but hardly any of them could get them out; they were rusted in their scabbards....And we went in; I led them....I had no sword—only a riding whip. And we were nearly choked with dust...you could hardly see....I thought I had better have a sword." Pleasonton then rode down a panicked Rebel trooper and demanded his sword which the frightened trooper handed over.[30]

While Pleasonton and his men were busy with Fitzhugh Lee's troopers, Yankee troopers east of South Mountain had an easier day. Rush's Lancers on the 15th were consolidated near Middletown except for three companies at Franklin's headquarters; Company E picketed the road from Jefferson to South Mountain, while the 6th U.S. Cavalry continued its picketing of the southern Middletown (Catoctin) Valley.[31] Lee's and McClellan's forces were moving south for a showdown at Sharpsburg. Carman wrote that "Near midnight of the fifteenth, two companies each of the 61st and 64th New York, under command of Lieutenant Colonel Nelson A. Miles, passed along the rear of Sedgwick's division and some distance along the bluff below the Middle Bridge, then turned back and reached the bridge just as a party of Union cavalry came riding sharply over it from the south bank. They informed Miles that the enemy had fallen back [likely the 5th Virginia Cavalry pickets] and that there were none in the immediate front of the bridge. Miles then crossed the bridge and marched west on the pike about 600 yards as day broke in a heavy fog until he came upon a Rebel infantryman. His captive told Miles that the Confederate line was very near so Miles quickly about faced and recrossed the bridge."[32] The Union troopers Miles encountered were units from the 6th New York Cavalry which was attached to the Ninth Corps. They

Confederate prisoners were taken but obviously for this to be true most would not be enemy cavalry but mostly infantry and wounded men at that, 182. He did write that "Pleasonton was with us in person," 182. Col. Farnsworth told a newspaper reporter that he and his adjutant had both killed two foes with shots through their bodies, "The Press," 23 September 1862.

[29] Carman, Pierro, 175-177; Priest, *Before Antietam*, 315-318; McClellan, *Stuart*, 124-126; Hard, 178-179. But see Pleasonton's embellished report showing 80 Confederate casualties and two captured guns, *OR*, vol. 19, pt. 1, 210. G.W. Beale in a letter to Carman 6 June 1897 wrote that his father, Lt. Col. Beale, commanding the 9th Virginia Cavalry, reported the 9th's losses at two lieutenants and 16 privates killed, with 10 more privates captured, photocopy of letter from NYPL, courtesy of Thomas Clemens. See also Beale, *9th Virginia*, 39-43. Crowninshield, 75; Beale states that the 9th lost two officers and 16 privates killed and 10 privates captured. William R. Carter wrote that the 9th Virginia Cavalry received the Federal charge while the 3rd and 4th Virginia Cavalry was retreating through Boonsboro. Carter reported 16 casualties in the 9th and that though the 9th "charged him twice; but owing to the immense clouds of dust, the advantage the enemy had gained by our too long delay in the town, and their introduction of sharpshooters, we were repulsed & fell back with considerable loss to our Brigade," 15.

[30] James E. Kelly, *Generals in Bronze: Interviewing the Commanders of the Civil War*, edited by William B. Styple (Kearney, NJ: Belle Grove Publishing Company, 2005), 127-128.

[31] Reese, *Sealed*, 182, chap. 6, endnote 20, in which Reese wrote that Rush and his staff with at least four companies of the 6th Pennsylvania Cavalry halted for the day on the 15th two miles west of Middletown presumably near McClellan's headquarters at Bolivar. Company E was picketing the roads between Jefferson and South Mountain likely in concert or bolstering the 6th U.S. Cavalry which had troopers in the lower Middletown Valley and near the Potomac.

[32] Carman, Pierro, 202. Hartwig has found that the Union troopers were from the 6th New York Cavalry, and started about 2 A.M., Hartwig, *To Antietam Creek*, 583. Also on the 15th, the 28th Massachusetts and the 50th Pennsylvania, both under the command of Maj. Edward Overton, were sent to Elk Ridge (where the Rohrersville Road crosses it) to support some of Pleasonton's cavalry, which was keeping open the communication with Franklin in Pleasant Valley, Carman, Pierro, 205.

were fired on when they refused to stop at Miles's order as the Yankee horsemen crossed the Middle Bridge; three horsemen were wounded and a horse killed.[33]

ANTIETAM

Lee, with his engineering eye, chose his ground well at Sharpsburg. He formed his line, anchored at both ends on the Potomac River, just west of Antietam Creek. Antietam Creek, like the Potomac a few miles further west, runs generally north to south but with fewer large and more small perturbations than the meandering Potomac. He established his units conforming to the mostly gentle hills and ridges which also run north to south. The rolling hills composed of farmland with a few woodlots, did provide cover and concealment in many areas which became of great importance during parts of the battle. While the Antietam Creek was not deep, it had few fords due to its steep banks. These fords were poorly scouted by McClellan's cavalry and engineers leading to major flaws in the execution of Union attacks especially for Burnside on the Union left flank. The Upper Bridge (also known as the Hooker Bridge after the battle) was about .8 mile in a straight line above McClellan's headquarters at the Pry House and about .3 mile above Pry's Ford. The other important ford across the Antietam was Snavely's Ford, downstream some 1.5 miles from the Lower Bridge (also known as the Rohrbach Bridge and after the battle as Burnside Bridge). It was less than two straight-line miles from Snavely's Ford to the mouth of the Antietam at the Potomac, and about 3.5 miles along the creek. McClellan's headquarters at the Pry House was about one airline mile from the Middle Bridge. The Antietam can be crossed at other smaller fords such as cattle fords but none were suitable for large-scale, quick crossings of cavalry or infantry. Lee did not contest Pry Ford, and at Snavely's Ford Confederate forces were withdrawn after Rodman's men finally pushed the Confederates away from the area west of the ford. Of the three bridges crossing the creek on the battlefield, Lee decided to defend only one, the Lower Bridge on the Union left flank; McClellan assigned Burnside's Ninth Corps to that flank. While the Middle Bridge was in defilade from the Confederate cannon on Cemetery Hill, ridges to the west were visible. The Middle Bridge was about one straight-line mile from the Confederate cannon on Cemetery Hill. Safely enclosed within one of the Potomac's meanderings, Lee's army had one major geographical problem: there was only one good ford available across the Potomac which was about 1.3 river miles below the burned bridge which had connected Sharpsburg with Shepherdstown, Virginia. Boteler's Ford, heavily used by the Confederates, was not taken by Union forces until 19 September, when Lee's army had already retreated across it and was never seriously threatened until then.[34]

---

[33] Carman, Pierro, 193. The 6th New York Regimental History stated that "on the morning of Sept. 16th crossed the Antietam Creek and advanced on Sharpsburg with orders to develop the enemy's position. The reconnaissance was successful in unmasking the enemy's batteries, and the command was withdrawn with slight loss," Hall, 418. This was a second reconnaissance at about 8 A.M. and after Miles's scout, Hartwig, *To Antietam Creek*, 584-585. Hall does not mention the first one, however.

[34] Snyder, Manuscript, 12. He describes the various fords used during the Civil War giving some supplementary information on each. See also A.D. Kenamond, "Potomac Crossings," in *Magazine of the Jefferson County Historical Society*, vol. XXIV, December 1958; in Shepherdstown, this ford was generally best known as Pack Horse Ford; in Virginia, it was called Boteler's Ford after Boteler's cement mill close to the ford; in Maryland, it was known as Blackford's Ford as the Maryland side was owned by the Blackford family; 38. It was sometimes called the Shepherdstown Ford. Antietam Ford was near the mouth of Antietam Creek and was of good low water use according to a 10 June 1861 correspondent of the Baltimore *American and Commercial Advertiser*. "Five fords have recently been discovered near the mouth of the Antietam, seven miles above Harper's Ferry. They are not more than three feet deep anywhere in low water. There is a perfect rock bed the whole way.'"

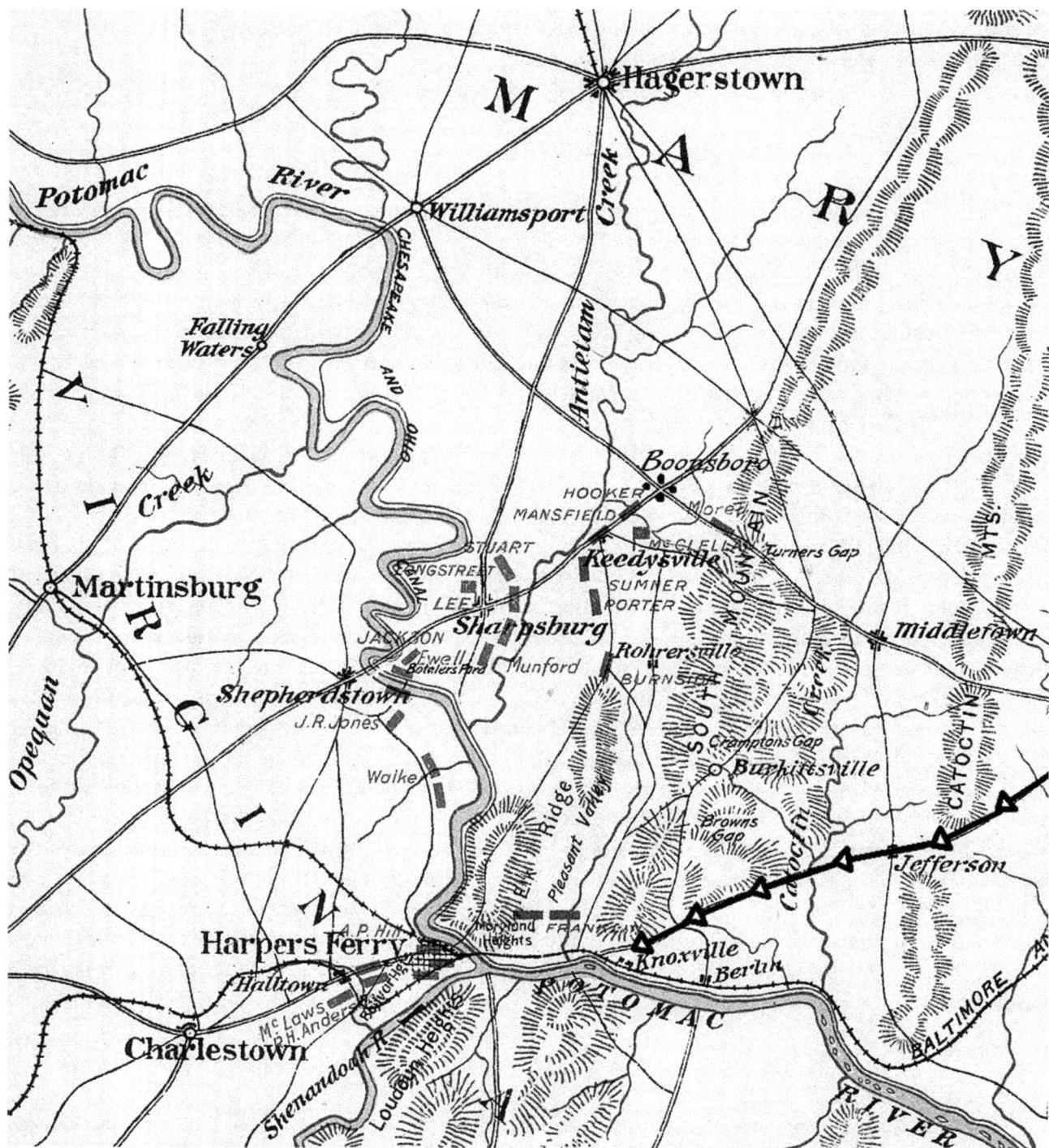

Detail of map showing the positions of the armies at 6 A.M. 16 September 1862. Arrows in lower right show direct road from Frederick to Harpers Ferry. Geo. W. Stadly & Co. Courtesy LOC.

On 15 September after sunrise, Munford started to withdraw as Franklin's troops closed on his position in Pleasant Valley. He had defended the Rohrersville Road, which ran north and south roughly paralleling South Mountain, then he rode toward Sharpsburg on the Old Sharpsburg Road (today's Millbrook Road, Mt. Briar Road, Porterstown Road, Burnside Bridge Road) over the Middle Bridge. Munford wrote that west of Rohrersville, he connected with some of the Jeff Davis Cavalry under Lt. Duncan of Savannah, near the intersection of the Rohrersville and Old Sharpsburg roads, where he had been ordered by Gen. Lee to hold his position until daylight on Monday the 16th. Munford wrote that

"[He] marched the next day [16th] over the Burnside Bridge to Sharpsburg following the Old Sharpsburg Road over Elk Ridge, through Porterstown to the Rohrbach Bridge, and journeyed to near the mouth of Antietam Creek…and reported to Gen. R.E. Lee in person. He directed me to move to the right of his army and to guard the fords south of the Burnside Bridge command by Gen. Toombs's troops. The 2nd Va. Cavalry I am sure had a squadron on the [C&O] Canal near the [Antietam] furnace on Antietam Creek and my Brigade was strengthened by 1st South Carolina Regt. of Cavalry Col. M.C. Butler commanding who I at that time ranked." Munford wrote that Butler was sent to him by Gen. Lee apparently on the 17th as Unionists sent some troops to challenge Munford. Butler was ordered to retreat, leaving the night of the 18th, before Munford's Brigade crossed the Potomac. Munford positioned his troopers on Brig. Gen. Robert A. Toombs Brigade's right covering "all the approaches to Sharpsburg from the east and south, his right being at Antietam Furnace, beyond the stone bridge at the mouth of the Antietam." Munford wrote Carman on 19 December 1894 that he had two or three videttes covering the Burnside Bridge who were peppered by sniper fire from Union sharpshooters. Munford remained at the far right (southern) flank of Lee from 16 September to 18 September protecting the bridge on Harpers Ferry Road over Antietam Creek near Antietam Furnace, and also Myer's Ford across the Antietam, and Boteler's Ford (Blackford's Ford) across the Potomac.[35] He also had troopers near Snavely's Ford as a detachment of the 48th Pennsylvania Infantry on 15 September saw them on the west bank of the stream.[36] His brigade did well watching for Union movements from Pleasant Valley and Harpers Ferry to the south and screening curious Yankees sent by Burnside to investigate that flank.

Munford's line eventually extended about 1.8 airline miles from Snavely's Ford on Antietam Creek, to Boteler's Ford on the Potomac. Munford established his headquarters at the Blackford House on Millers Sawmill Road. Munford's 7th Virginia Cavalry joined him on the evening of the 17th having spent the evening of the 16th on the Hagerstown Pike. When Walker's Division moved north from Gen. Lee's right flank during the morning of the 17th, Munford was left on his own, watching Snavely's Ford. Munford's skirmishers fired on Federal units on the afternoon of 17 September as they approached the Harpers Ferry Road and held them off. These Yankees were apparently five companies from the 6th New York Cavalry, serving under Burnside, which were ordered down Antietam Creek. The 6th New York reported capturing a major and one private along with their horses: "The regiment was again thrown out on the left, and the next day, during the battle of the 17th, five companies, under Major [John] Carwardine, were ordered to the mouth of Antietam Creek, where they succeeded in holding in check 1,000 rebel cavalry then threatening our flank, capturing a major and one private of Stuart's cavalry with their horses." It is remarkable that Burnside did not ensure that this cavalry picketed the Harpers Ferry Road more closely, although given the hilly topography, they would probably not have seen A.P. Hill's men coming up Millers Saw Mill Road to hit Burnside's right flank. Even if they were near Harpers Ferry Road, Munford's troopers would have fought hard to keep the Yankees from approaching Antietam Furnace near Antietam Creek.[37]

[35] Letters from Munford to Carman 19 December 1894 and 29 June 1897, copies courtesy Thomas Clemens. Note that the South Carolina regiment would have been the 2nd as the 1st was not in Maryland. Clemens also notes that Munford probably took the Burnside Bridge Road not the Old Sharpsburg Road, Carman, Clemens, 395, n. 32.
[36] Carman, Pierro, 204-205.
[37] Carman, Pierro, 339; Hillman A. Hall, et al, *History of the Sixth New York Cavalry (Second Ira Harris Guard)* (Worcester, MA: The Blanchard Press, 1908; reprint, Salem, MA: Higginson Book Company, n.d.), 54. Hall also wrote that "In the afternoon [17th] four companies of the Sixth New York were sent on a reconnoitering expedition, in which they captured some of Ashby's cavalry," regiments from Munford's brigade served with Ashby in the Shenandoah Valley, 62. Munford wrote to Carman on 19 December 1894 that after he retired from Crampton's Gap to Rohrersville, he reported directly to Lee then at Keedysville and then again at Sharpsburg where Lee ordered him to his right flank; copy of letter courtesy of Thomas Clemens. Also in letters dated 19 December 1894 and 7 July 1896 he wrote that Stuart was jealous of his prerogatives and wanted to insure that Munford reported to him; copies of letters courtesy of Thomas Clemens. Carwardine did not realize that Munford was not there to attack

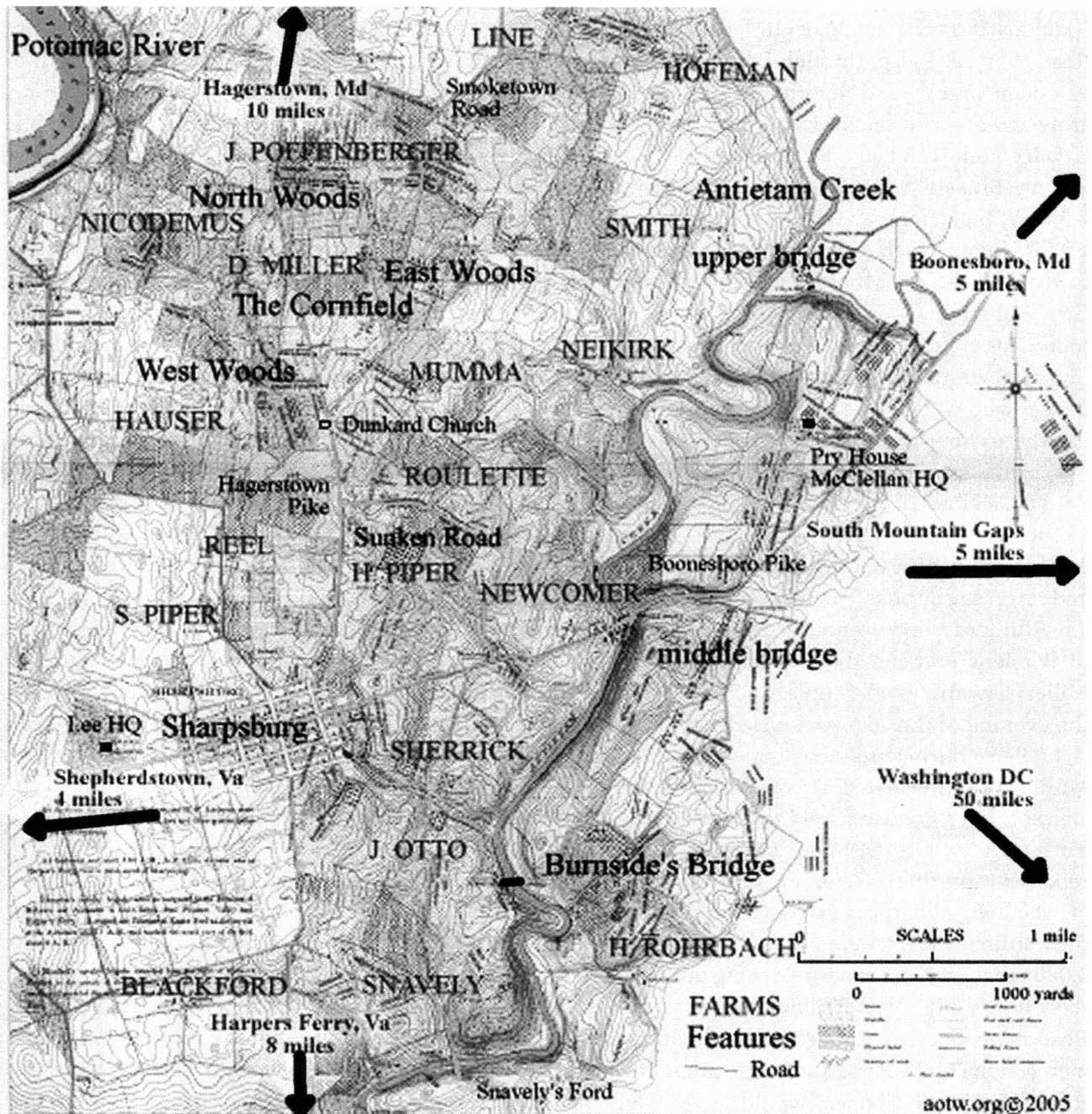

Map showing main features on the Antietam battlefield. It shows places mentioned in reports and descriptions of the battle superimposed on a Carman-Cope map. Pleasonton spent most of the 17th at the Pry House then around noon moved to the Middle Bridge. Stuart with most of his cavalry was at the far northern end southwest of the Joseph Poffenberger Farm with Munford at the far southern end near the Blackford Farm. Map courtesy Brian Downey "Antietam on the Web."

the Union left flank but protect Gen. Lee's right flank and Boteler's Ford. It is also hard to understand how Major John Carwardine leading the 6th New York Cavalry could hold off Munford's seasoned troopers should Munford have decided to push the issue. Carman commented that "It does seem probable that had one or two regiments of Pleasonton's cavalry been used on this flank some good results would have followed, not only in finding and crossing the ford but in protecting Rodman's flank from its surprise and disaster later in the day," Carman, Pierro, 339. Munford also spoke with Hill the afternoon of the 17th as he and his troops marched up from Boteler's Ford: "To the right and rear of the [Confederate] line was Munford's cavalry brigade (Munford having his headquarters at the Blackford house, where at this hour [1 P.M.] he greeted A.P. Hill, whose advance was coming upon the field.)" Carman, Pierro, 341.

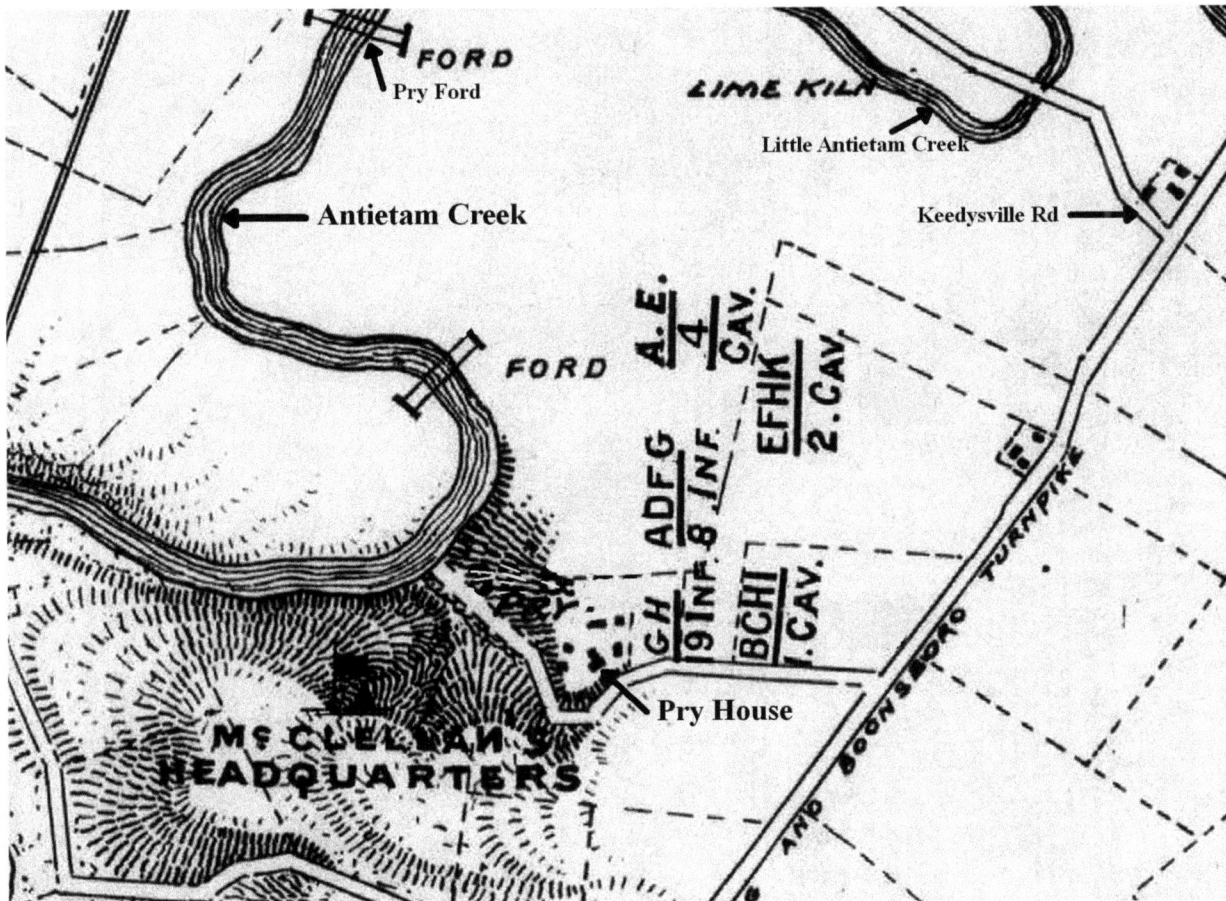

Position of regular army units at the Battle of Antietam—does not show the Oneida Company near the Pry House: Escort: Capt. James B. McIntyre commanding the 4th U.S. Cavalry squadron plus the Independent Co. Oneida, New York under Capt. Daniel P. Mann (45 officers and men); 4th U.S. Cavalry, Co. A Lt. Thomas H. McCormick (50 officers and men); 4th U.S. Cavalry, Co. E, Capt. James B. McIntyre (52 officers and men); Provost Guard Maj. William H. Wood with 2nd U.S. Cavalry, Cos. E, F, H, K Capt. George A. Gordon (121 officers and men); Quartermaster's Guard, 1st U.S. Cavalry, Cos. B, C, H, I, Capt. Marcus A. Reno (141 officers and men). Note that the Carman-Cope maps do not show the ford shown on this map closer to the Pry House and this map shows McClellan's headquarters located in front of the Pry House not in it obviously denoting the army commander's staff, etc., as McClellan stayed in the Pry House. Detail from 1893 map drawn under the direction of Antietam Board, Col. John C. Stearns, Gen. H. Heth, Theo. Friebus, Jr. Courtesy LOC.

Overleaf: Munford's Cavalry Brigade position from late on 16 September to 17 September; this detail shows it early on 17 September. Munford's troopers are in the lower center of the map. His videttes are shown near Myer's Ford and Snavely's Ford. They skirmished with some of Burnside's units in the middle afternoon of 17 September before Hill came up. Munford made his headquarters at the Blackford Farm in the left center at the arrow. Millers Sawmill Road runs left to right just above the Blackford Farm and intersects Harpers Ferry Road. Millers Sawmill Road is the road on which A.P. Hill's forces arrived late on 17 September to turn Burnside's left flank and save Lee's collapsing right. The road distance from the Maryland side of the Potomac at Boteler's Ford to the Harpers Ferry Road is about 2½ miles using Millers Sawmill Road. Snavely's Ford on the Antietam is seen in the lower right while a cattle ford is at the right arrow. The airline distance measured perpendicularly from Harpers Ferry Road to the cattle ford is about 1 mile and about ½ mile to Snavely's Ford. Some of Burnside's forces, a division commanded by Brig. Gen. Isaac P. Rodman, crossed Snavely's and the cattle ford in late morning on the 17th, and were heading north to Sharpsburg until Hill came up along Millers Sawmill Road. No records show where the 6th New York Cavalry confronted Munford's troopers, although it is unlikely that the Unionists crossed the Harpers Ferry Road. As seen on this map, the Union troopers would have seen little if they were near the Antietam Creek since they would be in a valley. They may have crossed at Snavely's Ford or Myer's Ford at the lower center. Detail from the Atlas of the battlefield of Antietam, known as the Carman-Cope maps, 1908 version. This collection has supplied several maps in this chapter. All are oriented to the north; contour intervals are ten feet. This is the most valuable and complete set of maps extant for 17 September. There is also a 1904 version but the 1908 version is preferred as it updated the earlier one. Courtesy LOC.

BURNSIDE BRIDGE
TOOMBS
2 GA.
EUBANK
ESHLEMAN
SNAVELY'S FORD
WALKER'S DIVISION
RANSOM
BRANCH
FRENCH
MANNING
MUNFORD'S CAVALRY
Harpers Ferry
Millers Sawmill Rd
Munford's HQ
MYER'S FORD

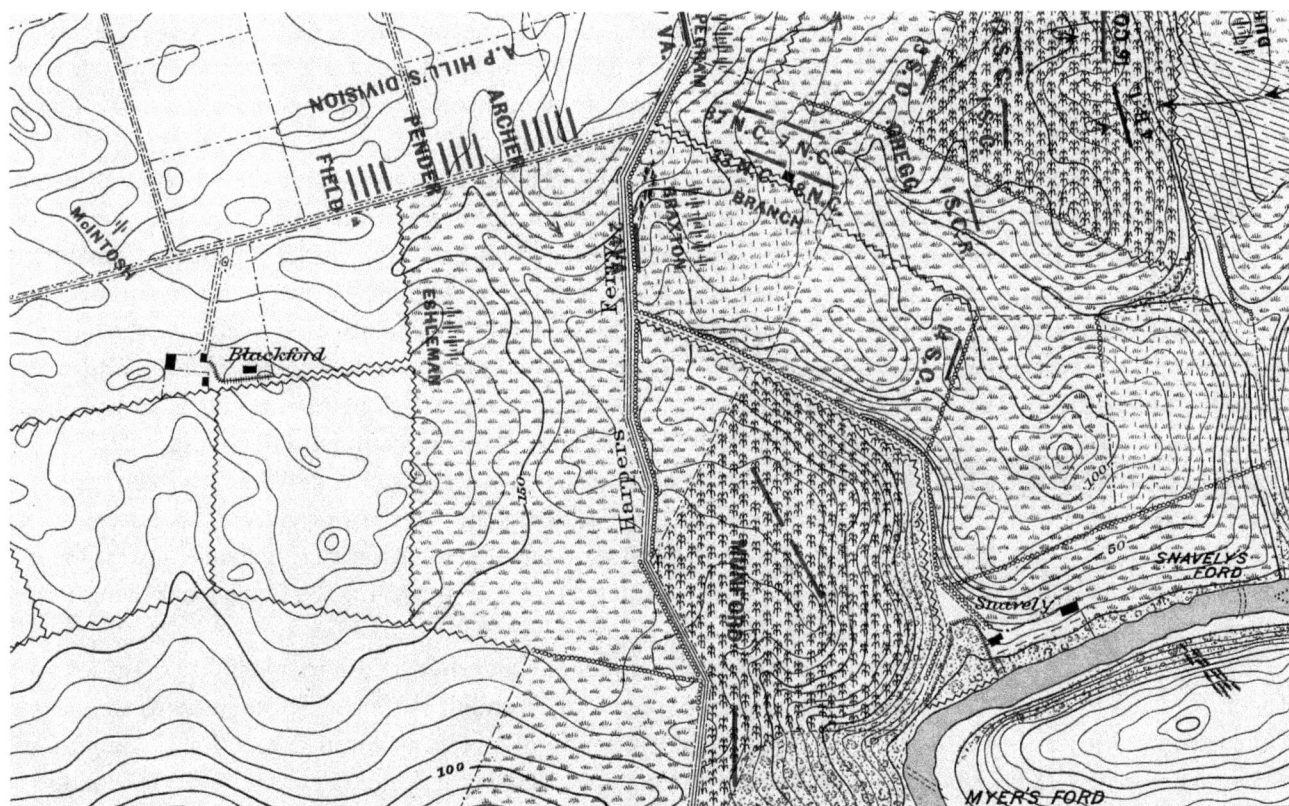

Munford's Cavalry Brigade position late on 17 September showing A.P. Hill's men approaching and well as Munford's advance. Courtesy LOC.

Stuart placed his remaining two brigades on Gen. Lee's extreme left flank, picketing from the Potomac to the left flank of Confederate infantry units. Part of Fitzhugh Lee's brigade, the 3rd, 4th, and 9th Virginia Cavalries, had arrived on the battlefield late on the 15th and journeyed to the far left flank. The 5th Virginia Cavalry which was detached on 11 September, formed on the extreme right of the army on the evening of the 15th, then on the morning of the 16th, joined the rest of the brigade on the left. The 1st Virginia Cavalry detached on the 10th to accompany Longstreet, rejoined Fitzhugh Lee's Brigade the morning of the 17th also on the left.[38] As will be seen, however, Stuart's chief contribution on the 17th would be his horse artillery and the effect it had during the Union attacks on the morning of Wednesday, 17 September. Hampton's Brigade only came up at about 9 A.M. on 17 September, as it had acted as rearguard for McLaws and Walker on their marches from Harpers Ferry, leaving there about 4

---

[38] ANBL Files, Virginia Cavalry, "Lee's Brigade." In an undated letter to Carman, G.M. Weeden wrote that the 4th Virginia Cavalry had about 400 in the regiment as it was in position on Hood's left, ANBL, Virginia Cavalry, "Lee's Brigade." He wrote that on the 11th a member of his unit took a farmer's horse as his was broken down. The farmer complained to Fitzhugh Lee who had the trooper arrested and the horse returned to the irate Maryland farmer. Fitzhugh published an order forbidding such appropriations and said if this is done, the miscreant would march on foot carrying his saddle and bridle and must keep up with the regiment. When this order was read, the men exclaimed "good." One might wonder if this exclamation was perhaps somewhat sarcastic as Rebel troopers were not loath to confiscate horses when needed but in this case it may be that the Maryland farmer was a Southern sympathizer. See Carman re the date the 1st rejoined Fitz Lee: "The 1st Virginia Cavalry, which had been detached from its brigade at New Market on the tenth to accompany Jackson and protect his flank and rear from a possible movement from Pennsylvania, remained in the vicinity of Hagerstown, scouting and picketing up to the Pennsylvania line until the fourteenth, when its scouts and pickets were withdrawn. The regiment concentrated at Hagerstown and followed the trains across the river after daybreak of the fifteenth, encamping that night at Hainesville. On the sixteenth it marched through Martinsburg to Shepherdstown Ford, where it recrossed the river and rejoined Fitzhugh Lee's Brigade on the left of the Confederate line," Carman, Pierro, 171.

A.M. It crossed the Potomac at Knott's Ford, in deep water, at the mouth of Antietam Creek, about 7 A.M. near the Antietam Iron Works, arriving on the south end of the field, Lee's extreme right flank. It rested, but after beginning to feed, it was shelled out of its position and moved nearer the river and recommenced feeding, but this time without fires which had attracted the notice of Union artillerymen.[39] About 10 A.M. it moved to the rear of Lee's headquarters just south of Sharpsburg on the Boonsboro-Shepherdstown Pike where it remained until about noon when it was hastened to the left of the line to join Fitzhugh Lee to bolster the Confederate left which had been pushed back that morning. His troopers helped serve as skirmishers while others gathered up stragglers.[40] There is no record of Gen. Lee advising Stuart of the disposition of his cavalry division but it is likely that securing the army's flanks, scouting, and ensuring that Boteler's Ford was protected, were obvious tasks for cavalry, and were accomplished without Gen. Lee's written direction. And since Lee was available and close to the lines during the 16th and 17th, it is very likely that Stuart as well as Lee's other commanders talked with him as needed. Lee did assign Maj. Gen. William N. Pendleton with the reserve artillery to help protect Boteler's Ford from the Virginia shore aiding with Munford's cavalry on the Maryland side; however, as will be seen on the 19th, this was a poor choice as Pendleton gave a lackluster performance almost losing several guns until returning infantry under A.P. Hill pushed the intruding Federals back across the Potomac.[41]

There is evidence from Stuart's aid, Maj. von Borcke, and another of Stuart's staff, an engineering officer, Capt. William W. Blackford, that Stuart and some of Fitzhugh Lee's cavalry scouted to the north at the army commander's behest on 16 September. Undoubtedly, Gen. Lee still entertained thoughts of continuing his Maryland adventure, so knowing the disposition of the enemy on the Maryland side of the Potomac from Sharpsburg north was vital. Blackford wrote that Stuart said that he was to attack with his entire cavalry force if necessary to learn the enemy's dispositions. Lee needed to know the disposition of McClellan's forces in that direction to learn if he were firmly surrounded to the north, as Lee had his army's back to the Potomac. So while other units of Fitzhugh Lee's Brigade watched the Landing Road to the west along the Potomac, and the upper crossings of the Antietam, and picketed roads to the east and north such as the Smoketown Road and the Hagerstown Pike, Stuart and Blackford ventured north. Blackford wrote that Stuart did not want to make a reconnaissance in force unless he had to do so as the ground was unfavorable for a cavalry attack, so he asked Blackford to take a half-hour's gallop north with several couriers, and to report his progress back to Stuart. Blackford began his expedition by choosing three well-mounted couriers, leaving the rest in reserve, and along with his favorite high-powered binoculars, headed for the Union right flank. Although Blackford, the only source for this story, did not state where he rode to record his observations of Union infantry pickets, the general area may be determined by the clues he presents and by examining the Carman-Cope map for early morning on the 17th. It is possible but unlikely that he used the Hagerstown Pike as it was not completely under cover, and from the Dunker Church north was somewhat open as it passed through rolling farmlands. Blackford said that he crawled to a rising point of land near enemy lines to get a good view. Also, he reported that Stuart kept his troopers under cover so they were not probably in column along the pike and as the ground was difficult for cavalry, one may infer that there were fences or other obstacles in the area. It is also unlikely that he rode north on the Landing Road closer to the Potomac and C&O Canal as Union infantry was not in that area on the 16th. Thus he probably was on a rise viewing some of Hooker's troops

---

[39] Union artillerists must have been firing at the smoke at it would have been difficult to have a direct view of the area in which Hampton was resting. Perhaps Union signalmen on Red Hill might have spotted them.

[40] Carman, Pierro, 311; Carman notes from ANBL 1st North Carolina File; Howard, 3. Knott's Island Ford is much closer to Harpers Ferry Road from the Maryland side of the Potomac, about .2 of a mile compared to over two miles at Boteler's Ford using Millers Sawmill Road but then it is about 1.2 mile up Harpers Ferry Road to the intersection of Miller's.

[41] As already noted, Gen. Lee personally talked to Munford about placement of his brigade.

who had crossed the Antietam at Pry's Ford during the afternoon somewhere to the east of the Hagerstown Pike. Blackford wrote that he could see the enemy some 150 yards ahead "crouching down behind the stumps, bushes and grassy covering of the field," so based on this description, that area may not have been in cultivation but perhaps being made ready to be totally cleared and planted. But clearly it was not in corn or part of a woodlot. Blackford identified the Union troops as infantry by blue trimmings and bayonet scabbards so those men were not dismounted 3rd Pennsylvania Cavalry which were on the field in the area skirmishing with Confederate troops. Blackford reported that the troops he saw were being fired on by Stuart's Horse Artillery, therefore, if he is correct, he saw pickets of Doubleday's division about a mile north of the Dunker Church near the Hagerstown Pike, in the area of the North Woods. Carman writes of the possible confrontation with Blackford: "Doubleday's division crossed at Pry's Ford, below the bridge, and drove some Confederate cavalrymen from a cornfield and strip of woods on the left, who hastened to inform Stuart at the Dunker Church that the Union army was crossing the upper Antietam. (Stuart, in turn, sent the information to Lee at Sharpsburg.)"[42]

Von Borcke reported that Stuart started out on the morning of the 16th and he did not see his commander until late that evening at Gen. Lee's headquarters. As von Borcke stayed in Sharpsburg for the day, any couriers from Stuart would have used the Hagerstown Pike as the most direct route to both von Borcke and Lee. The Landing Road further west may also have been used as it parallels the Hagerstown Pike closer to Sharpsburg and was more under cover from Union long-range guns across the Antietam. Gen. Lee's headquarters was just to the west of Sharpsburg a few feet north off the Boonsboro-Shepherdstown Pike. Lee also used the Grove House on the Sharpsburg Square about .6 mile east but that location was well in range of Yankee artillery. That evening, Stuart said he would meet von Borcke and Blackford in half an hour at the Dunker Church, but Stuart never arrived, so his Prussian aide appropriated part of a haystack in which to make his bed, likely to the west of Dunker Church, behind Nicodemus Heights.[43] R. Channing Price wrote in an 18 September 1862 letter that Stuart was back at his headquarters at the Grove House after dark as he was busy posting batteries all day, but soon left, while Jackson slept on the sofa most of the night.[44]

McClellan and Pleasonton hardly used the Union cavalry division at Antietam: it was not used to guard the army's flanks, and not well used for scouting. Carman takes the Union army commander severely to task for his use of his cavalry on the 16th:

From the time of McClellan's arrival on the field until Hooker's advance in the afternoon of the sixteenth, nothing seems to have been done with a view to an accurate determination of the Confederate position. From the heights east of the Antietam, the eye could trace the right and center, but the extreme left could not be definitely located, nor was the character of the country on that flank known. It was upon this flank that McClellan decided to make his attack, and one would suppose that his first efforts would be directed to ascertain how that flank could be approached and what it looked like. This was proper work for cavalry, of

[42] Carman, Pierro, 205.

[43] Von Borcke, 158-160. The distance from the Dunkard Church to Sharpsburg Square using the Hagerstown Pike is about 1¼ mile.

[44] R. Channing Price papers, University of North Carolina, copy at ANBL, Hampton's Brigade. W.H.F. Lee said however that Jackson slept near him on a side of a hill the night of the 16th, ANBL Files, Virginia Cavalry; Carman wrote that Lee told him that "I remember going up on the side of this steep ascent in my front, tying my horse during the night to a small tree, and going to sleep there. The next morning about light I was awakened by the firing of a Federal battery which seemed to have been run up during the night to a point above us, and about the first shell thrown from it exploded in one of my regiments (below us) doing much damage and killing one of my most promising Lieut. Cols. [Thornton]. I think it was the opening gun of the battle. I remember Stonewall Jackson came up on the right side of the hill where I was, tied his horse and went to sleep near me. He was without staff or courier, as I was, and was awakened by the same shot and hastened to his command, as I did to mine." Fitzhugh Lee to Carman, February 18, 1896; Carman, Pierro, 220, n. 7. Jackson slept in more than one spot that night.

which he had a good body available for the purpose. Pleasonton's cavalry division was in good shape, sated with its successful achievements (culminating in the discomfiture of Fitzhugh Lee's Brigade at Boonsboro the day before) and confident of its capacity for further good work. But it was not used. As far as we know, not a single Union cavalryman crossed the Antietam until Hooker went over in the afternoon of the sixteenth, when the 3d Pennsylvania Cavalry accompanied him. Nor can we discover that the cavalry did any productive work elsewhere. It did not ascertain that there were good fords below the Rohrbach Bridge leading directly to the right rear of the Confederate line, and we know of no orders given for its use, save a suggestion to Franklin to have his cavalry feel toward Frederick. The part taken by the cavalry this day is very briefly told by Pleasonton in his report: "On the 16ᵗʰ...my cavalry was engaged in reconnaissances, escorts, and supports to batteries." If any part of his command, except the 3d Pennsylvania Cavalry, was engaged in reconnaissance and supporting batteries, we do not know it.[45]

McClellan had not totally forgotten about Pleasonton as he told him during the midafternoon of 16 September to "collect all your cavalry, excepting such only as may be detached on important service, so as to have your command ready at a moment's notice, should it be required to make pursuit of the enemy."[46] McClellan apparently held to the Napoleonic belief for his cavalry division that a primary use of cavalry was the pursuit of a broken and fleeing enemy.

On 17 September, most of Pleasonton's cavalry sat massed in only two locations, first north of the Pry House, McClellan's headquarters near the Boonsboro-SharpsburgPike, and the second, later in the day, near the Middle Bridge, also on the Boonsboro-SharpsburgPike, apparently to be used to attack and break through a weakened Confederate line. But later, McClellan issued a circular which again showed his views on the scattering of his cavalry as he asked his corps commanders to report how much cavalry they had on duty with them and how much they needed for orderlies. They were also to tell him if they needed more horsemen for other purposes and, if so, those troopers would be furnished as a special detail from the cavalry division. There is no record which shows that he ordered any excess troopers back to Pleasonton nor that infantry commanders reported unneeded cavalry on hand.[47]

[45] Carman, Pierro, 203. Historian Matthew Forney Steele wrote simply that "If the Union cavalry had been guarding the flanks of the attack, instead of standing idle at the center, the approach of A.P. Hill's division would have been discovered in time for dispositions to be made to meet it," 283. Stuart's aide, Blackford, wrote a succinct prescription for the function of cavalry perhaps aided by hindsight: "The duty of cavalry after battle is joined is to cover the flanks to prevent the enemy from turning them. If victorious, it improves the victory by rapid pursuit. If defeated, it covers the rear and makes vigorous charges to delay the advance of the enemy—or in the supreme moment, in the crisis of the battle, when victory is hovering over the field, uncertain upon which standard to alight—when the reserves are brought into action and the death struggle has come, then the cavalry comes down like an avalanche, upon the flanks of troops already engaged, with splendid effect," 26. At Antietam Stuart covered well the flanks but had no opportunity for descending on routed Yankees; McClellan, however, should have had more cavalry on his flanks and attacked Gen. Lee down the Boonsboro Pike in conjunction with Burnside's afternoon attack using Pleasonton and Porter's troops. McClellan's view to the left of Lee's line was poor from the west of the Hagerstown Pike to the Potomac as was much of his vision to the south of Burnside's but McClellan had signal stations to his south one of which in fact did see Hill's approach on the afternoon of the 17ᵗʰ.

[46] *OR*, vol. 51, pt. 1, 840.

[47] Armstrong, *Colors*, 155.

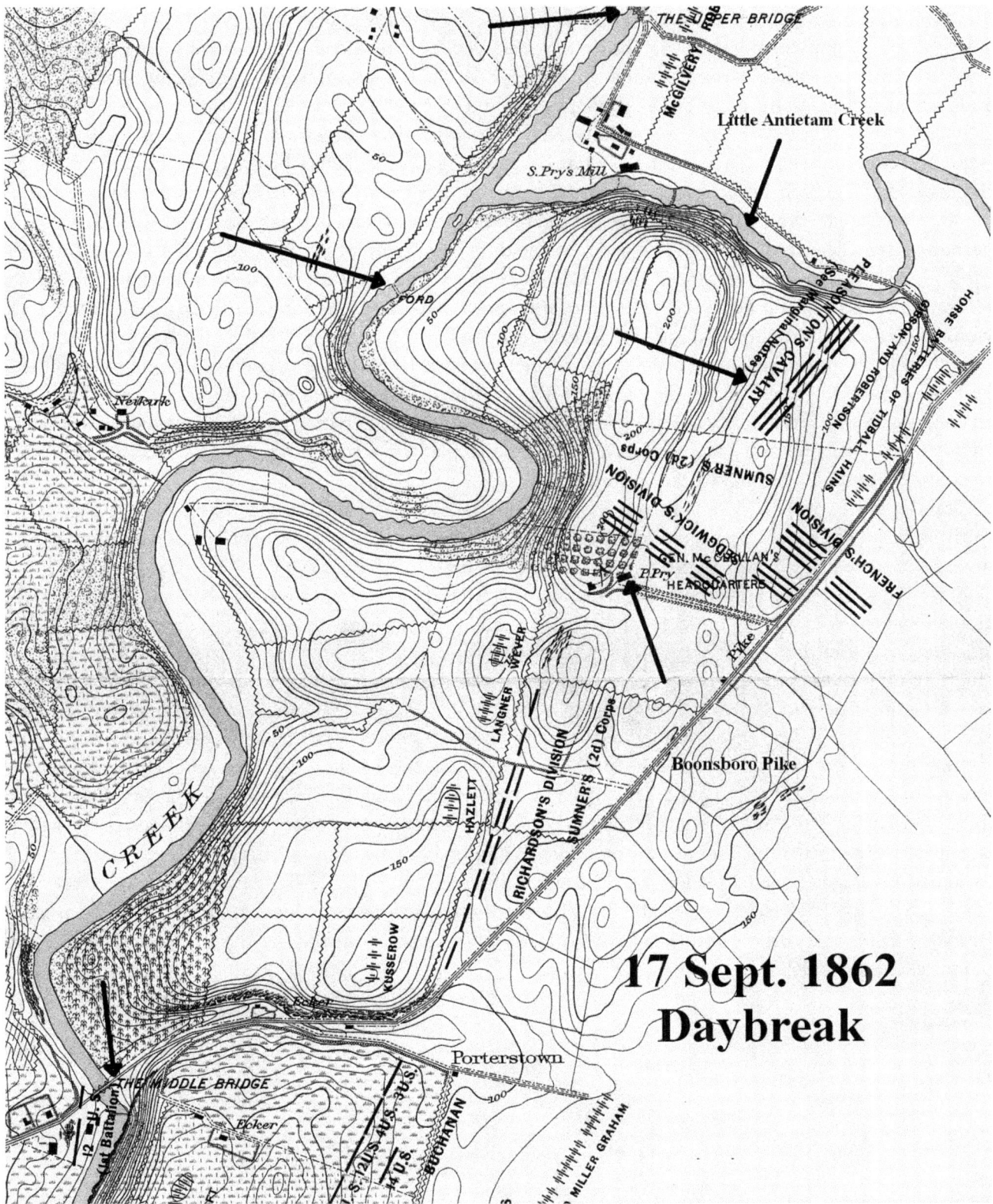

Pleasonton's cavalry division's approximate position at the center right; his division was here from late on 16 September to noon 17 September and from nightfall 17 September to 18 September. The road from the upper right running to the lower left is the Boonsboro-SharpsburgTurnpike which travels over the Middle Bridge which is at the lower left arrow. McClellan's headquarters at the Pry House is at the center arrow. Pry's Ford is at the upper left arrow; Upper [Hooker's Bridge] at the top arrow. Detail from the Carman-Cope map at daybreak on 17 September. Courtesy LOC.

McClellan finally decided to attack Lee at Sharpsburg and his plan on the evening of 16 September was not a bad one considering that he firmly believed he still faced a numerically superior enemy, entrenched behind the hills surrounding the town. If McClellan knew that he greatly outnumbered Lee, and that in fact virtually none of Lee's troops were entrenched, he very likely would have had a more aggressive battle plan. As it was, he initially desired to attack the enemy's left flank to see if Lee would stand and fight, as well as to learn if Lee's flank was in the air. McClellan planned a follow-up attack on the other flank which he believed Lee would probably have weakened to support the opposite flank. Finally, McClellan would throw his best reserves at the now much weakened center of Lee's line, perhaps using Pleasonton's cavalry division as shock troops, completing the rout of the enemy through the streets of Sharpsburg, cutting Lee off from Boteler's Ford. The Federal commander knew he could not surprise Lee, nor did he initially plan on using more than one corps for each flank attack. The attack would begin on the Rebel left early on the morning of 17 September. McClellan expected that even though neither attack would be able to get in Lee's rear since both Lee's flanks were anchored on the Potomac, the first attack on the left early in the morning could advance far enough to enfilade Lee's entire line to the south toward Sharpsburg, making it untenable. Had Union troops taken Nicodemus Heights and the northern part of Hauser's Ridge, and planted artillery on those points, the Army of Northern Virginia would have been in serious trouble.

McClellan chose Maj. Gen. Joseph Hooker for the early morning attack, knowing the aggressive spirit he possessed would be necessary. Then, believing that Hooker's First Corps might need support, he ordered Mansfield's smaller Twelfth Corps to march north to be available should Hooker request help. "Fighting Joe" Hooker did—the next morning in less than two hours after commencing his attack, Hooker's corps was wrecked and Hooker was wounded. Mansfield's corps, tardily coming to Hooker's aid, met the same fate, and Mansfield was mortally wounded. Based on erroneous early reports that Hooker's attack was meeting some success, McClellan sent Sumner's Second Corps to add weight to the attack of the First and Twelfth Corps to gain a victory perhaps without attacking the opposite flank or even the center. Sedgwick's division in Sumner's corps was soon torn to pieces, while the second of Sumner's other two divisions followed Sumner's orders, and ran head on into massed Confederate troops in the Sunken Road (Bloody Lane). This division was soon heading for the rear, also shattered. Sumner's third division under Maj. Gen. Israel Richardson, had more success at the Sunken Road, despite heavy casualties; "Fighting Dick" Richardson paid for his aggression later that morning when he was mortally wounded by a Rebel shell after his men had taken the road. Buford, McClellan's staff cavalry chief, saw Hooker wounded and rode back to the Pry House to report the news to his commander. Buford related Hooker's wish that Brig. Gen. George G. Meade take over command of the corps and McClellan promulgated the order.[48]

---

[48] Eric J. Wittenberg, "An Analysis of the Buford Manuscripts" in *Gettysburg Magazine*, No. 15, 13. John Gibbon papers in the Historical Society of Pennsylvania, typewritten manuscript, 17-18: "[Buford] was present on the right of our line when after heavy fighting at the end of which everything seemed to be going to pieces, Hooker...was wounded. Whilst lying on the ground he groaned out, 'I would give anything in the world if Meade was in command of this corps.' Meade was not entitled to command by seniority. Buford heard Hooker's remark, jumped upon his horse, rode rapidly to McClellan's Headquarters, reported what Hooker had said and as quickly as the order could be sent Meade was assigned to command in Hooker's place irrespective of rank." For French's and Sumner's actions see Armstrong, 171, 204-205.

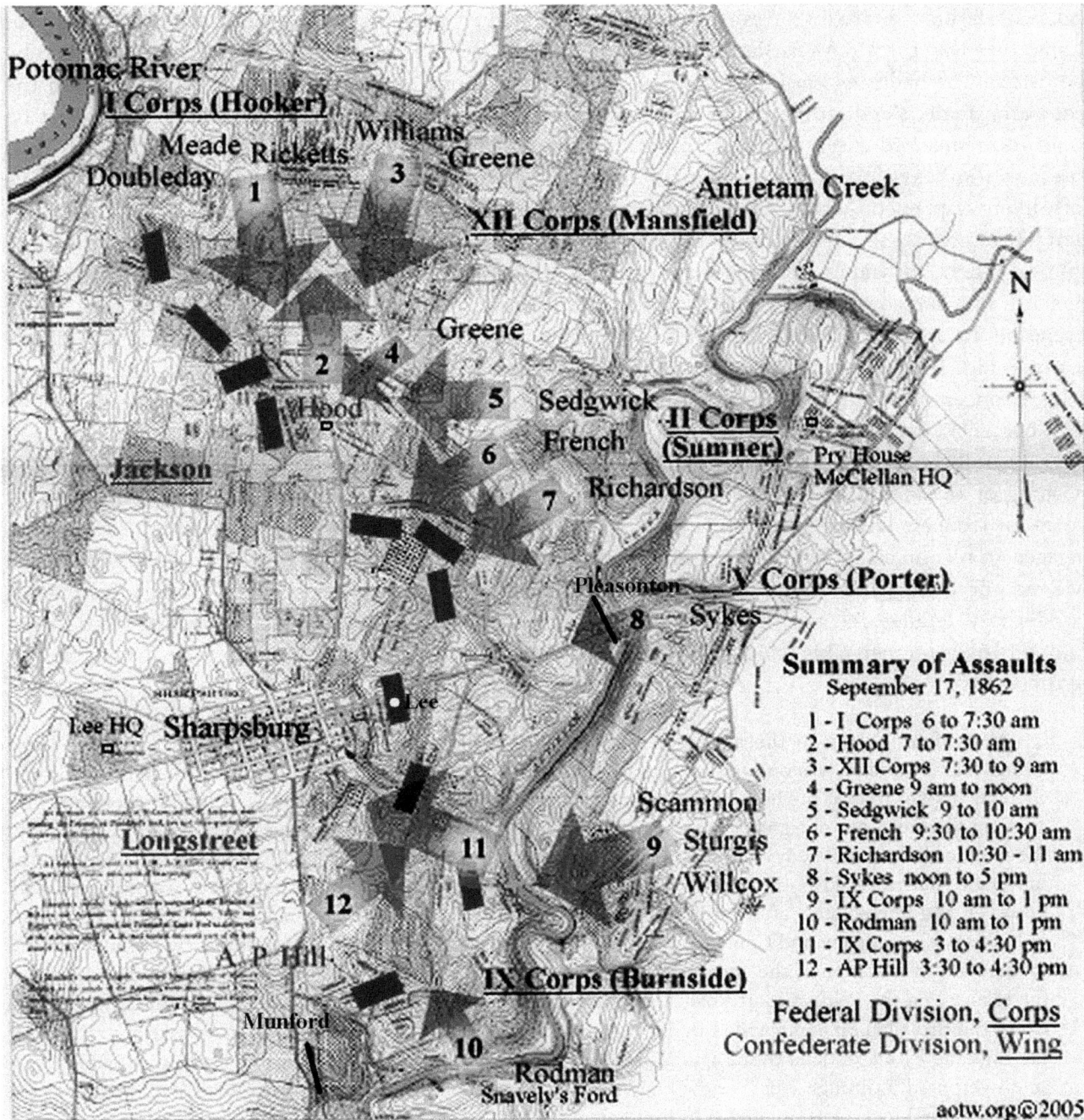

Overview of troop locations and summary of assaults on 17 September 1862. Pleasonton's cavalry near the Middle Bridge with Sykes and Munford holds Lee's right flank. The rest of Stuart's cavalry was on Lee's left flank. Lee spent much time on Sharpsburg Ridge just east of town at white dot where the National Cemetery is now located. Courtesy Brian Downey "Antietam on the Web."

Now that McClellan saw that most of the three corps he sent to his right flank were decimated, he ordered Maj. Gen. Burnside to immediately open his attack on his left flank. Burnside's inept attacks took three hours to cross the Lower Bridge over the Antietam, but by early afternoon, he had a foothold on the opposite bank. Burnside then paused to resupply and rest his troops, a pause which allowed Gen. Lee to scrape up troops to bolster his right flank and later that afternoon just enough time for Maj. Gen. A.P. Hill's men to arrive from their 14-mile forced march from Harpers Ferry. McClellan now had his last chance to win the battle with Burnside poised to attack Lee's right flank and Lee's center almost broken and his left hurt. Franklin's fresh Sixth Corps had arrived from its successful attack and capture of Crampton's Gap three days earlier, and was ready to attack, but Sumner forbade it, obviously shaken by the carnage he had seen earlier in the day, which had decimated his corps. McClellan arrived on the scene and finally sided with Sumner, much to Franklin's dismay and disgust. Franklin believed that he could have smashed the remaining Confederate troops and rolled up the rest of Lee's shattered line; based on the heavy losses Lee's forces suffered, unknown to the Union commanders, this would have very likely happened. McClellan still believed that Lee outnumbered him and therefore had sufficient men left to give these, his last fresh troops on the field, a hard fight.[49] The end finally came to the day's fighting when Burnside's restarted attack on the Union left began driving the Confederates into the outskirts of Sharpsburg. The Ninth Corps, unfortunately, ran into Maj. Gen. A.P. Hill's men. Hill's serendipitous attack on Burnside's left flank quickly pushed the Unionists back to the vicinity of the Lower Bridge finally drawing the curtain on a day of horror: "For both sides, Sharpsburg was a compact field of concentrated fury. In twelve hours, 82,000 men fought over less than 1,000 acres. Nearly 23,000 (27.1 percent) fell casualty" by sunset, a day none of the participants would ever forget.[50]

Pleasonton's division's activities on the 16th and 17th were far less active than Stuart's division. The morning of 16 September found Pleasonton's cavalry camped to the west of Keedysville while Stuart's worn-out troopers were behind Antietam Creek. Pleasonton reports that on that day, "my cavalry was engaged in reconnaissances, escorts, and supports to batteries" although as Carman noted, there is little evidence of worthwhile cavalry activity.[51] The historian of the 3rd Pennsylvania Cavalry provides a wonderfully detailed account of his regiment's advance along with Union infantry on McClellan's right flank on 16 September. This regiment saw more action on the 16th and 17th than any other Union cavalry on those days:

About four o'clock in the afternoon [on the 16th] Hooker's Corps was put in motion, and the Third Pennsylvania Cavalry was ordered by him to cross the Antietam by ...[Pry's Ford] and to take the advance. General Hooker rode at the head of the regiment until after it had all gotten across. The infantry column, after crossing the creek out of sight of the enemy's gunners, moved out to the northwestward by and alongside of the road leading from Keedysville to Williamsport, and, circling around, formed line facing by the left to the south and southwest, so as to conform to the line of the enemy's left. Before this movement was accomplished, however, and immediately after fording the creek, Captain Edward S. Jones' squadron of the Third, composed of his own (C) company and Company I under Captain Walsh, was ordered to move directly to the westward to ascertain the location of the enemy's line of battle in that direction, while Company H took the advance of the infantry on the Williamsport Road. Guided by an old farmer, Captain Jones' squadron, with Company C in front, the first platoon commanded by Lieutenant E. Willard Warren having the advance guard, moved over the hills and by a farm lane running to M. Miller's house, then turning to the left into a side road (which runs southwestwardly through what is now known as the East Woods to the Smoketown Road, and then on to the Dunker Church, which is situated at its junction with the Hagerstown Pike)....

Captain Jones' squadron, with Lieutenant Warren and the first platoon of Company C deployed as skirmishers in advance, moved forward over the hills and across the fields, the supports following by the lane running to M. Miller's house. Some vedettes were seen in the distance, and on approaching nearer to them they fell back on their reserve. In order to give time to the head of the column under Lieutenant Miller to gain ground to the right, so that the movement against the enemy should be in concert, Captain Jones halted the skirmishers, as well as the second platoon under Sergeant Thompson Miller, the latter at the proper distance in

[49] Mark A. Snell, *From First to Last: The Life of Major General William B. Franklin* (New York: Fordham University Press, 2002), 194-195.

[50] Battle summary from Laurence Freiheit, "Nutmeggers on Antietam Creek: Major Generals Joseph K. F. Mansfield, John Sedgwick, and Connecticut Regiments in the Maryland Campaign 2 September through 20 September 1862," Military History Online website; Harsh, *Flood*, 423.

[51] Carman, Pierro, 203; *OR*, vol. 11, pt. 1, 211.

rear, the second company (I, under Captain Walsh) doing the same. The two platoons numbered from twelve to sixteen men each. The men of the second platoon being in the open, some sharpshooters in a woods to the left front began taking shots at them. Captain Walsh rode on to the front where Lieutenant Warren was, to see what was going on, and in his absence Sergeant Miller ordered Private John McCoubrie, who was a crack shot, to dismount and try to pick off one or more of the troublesome sharpshooters. Four men, however, dismounted, and taking careful aim over a rail fence fired in a volley at one of the rebels as he stepped from behind a tree to take another shot. Hearing the firing, Captain Walsh came back at a gallop, and called out to Sergeant Miller: "Who ordered those men to dismount? This is no place for them to be off their horses!" The Sergeant replied that he did not want to sit there quietly and be made a target of, and that it didn't take long to mount, and at once ordered them to do so.

General Hooker, accompanied by his staff, came up to where the squadron was halted, and, when the proper moment had arrived, gave the word to advance. Accordingly, Sergeant Miller was ordered to move forward with his platoon and drive in the enemy's picket reserve. Lieutenant Warren joined him, and side by side at the head of the attacking party they advanced at the gallop, driving the rebels into the East Woods, and followed them until they suddenly came within thirty feet of a battery of artillery, which let fly at them with canister. Marvelous to relate, not a single man was hit, and but one horse slightly wounded. The party, finding the place thick with rebels, fell back upon one of the regiments of Pennsylvania Reserves [Bucktails] which was advancing toward the woods....

Meanwhile...Lieutenant Miller and his company (H) in advance turned to the left from the Williamsport Road down the Smoketown Road. "As I turned into the road," as Captain Miller relates the incident, "I met Colonel McNeil at the head of the Bucktail Regiment, which had turned in from the Williamsport Road higher up and moved to the left oblique across the fields, thus gaining ground on the advance. The Colonel asked me where I was going. Upon my telling him that my instructions were to find the enemy, he asked me if I would not like company. Upon my replying that I would, Colonel McNeil deployed one company on each side of the Smoketown Road a short distance behind the supports of the cavalry advance guard, the Colonel, afoot, walking inside the fence alongside of me, I being mounted. Everything remained perfectly quiet until the lane running eastwardly to George Lyon's [Line] farmhouse was reached, when it seemed as if the whole Confederate line opened upon us with artillery and musketry from the skirt of woods to the east of the Smoketown Road a short distance south of Lyon's house. The advance guard of Company H fell rapidly back upon the infantry supports who were following in the rear." "The Bucktails," wrote Bates, "rushed forward with a shout through a terrific fire of artillery and musketry and gained the woods—but at a fearful cost. Colonel McNeil, Lieutenant William Allison, and twenty-eight men were killed and sixty-five officers and men wounded in this single charge."

At dark our infantry formed line of battle in close proximity to the enemy. While this was in progress the main body of the Third took position in close column of squadrons on the Joseph Poffenberger farm, on the east side of the Hagerstown Pike, a short distance north of what is now known as the North Woods. Later in the night the regiment was moved forward a short distance to the southward in such close proximity to the rebels that we could distinctly hear them talking. Here we were compelled to remain until daylight, standing "to horse"—tired, hungry, and uncomfortable, in everybody's way, and of no earthly use, all because we were attached to an infantryman's command.[52]

---

[52] Rawle, 119-123; Carman, Pierro, 202; *OR*, vol. 19, pt. 1, 211; 217. Note that Carman states that infantry skirmishers preceded the cavalry, 205; Priest, *Antietam*, 11-13, 16, 17.

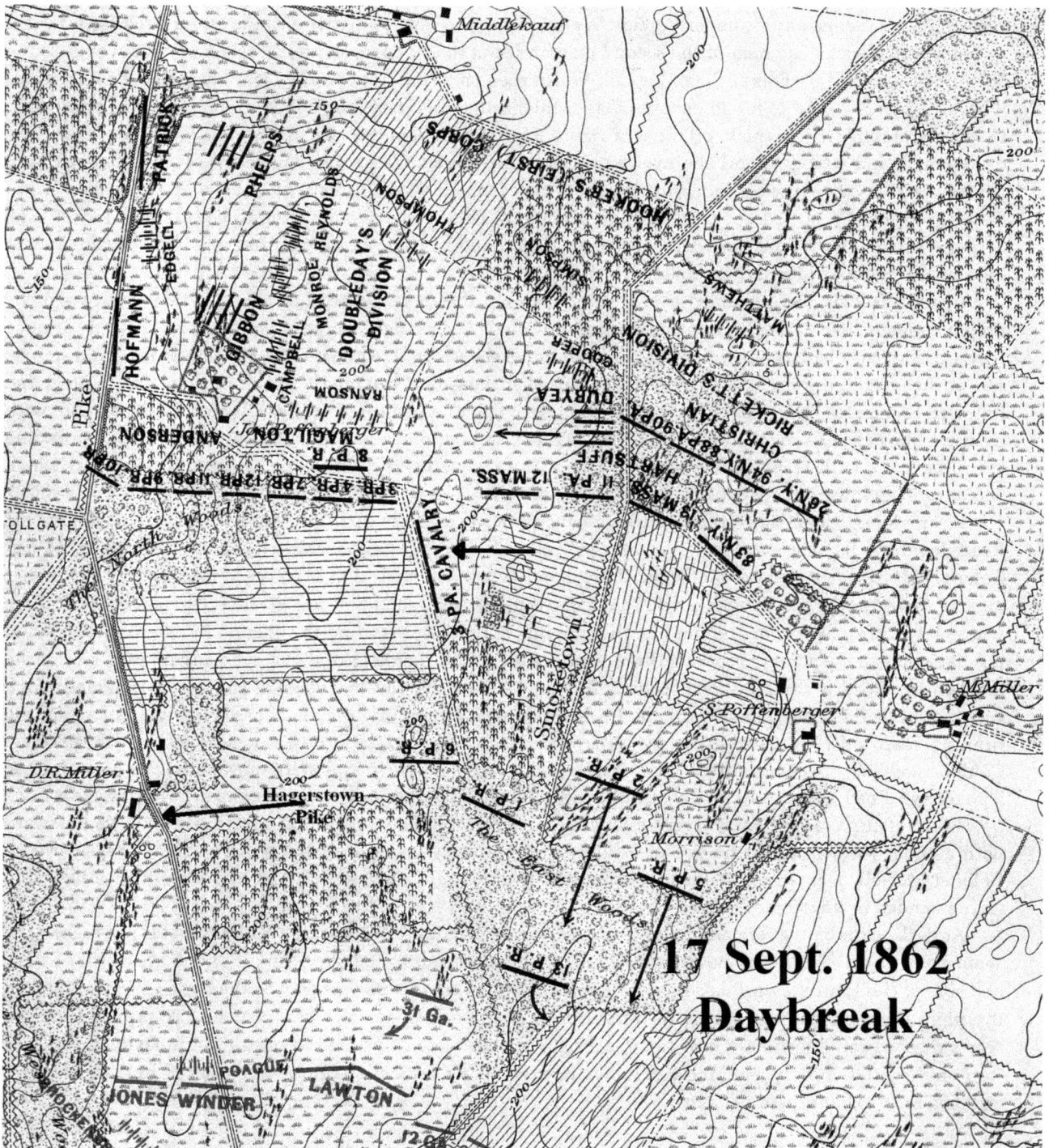

This map shows the location of the 3rd Pennsylvania Cavalry at the upper center; Hagerstown Pike at the arrow on the left; detail from Carman-Cope map, daybreak on 17 September. Courtesy LOC.

Now both Lee and McClellan knew where the battle would start the next day; Lee immediately sent reinforcements to his left. Earlier on the 16th, most of Fitzhugh Lee's Brigade was near the Dunker Church with detachments on the Hagerstown Pike and the Smoketown Road, where it could observe crossings over Antietam Creek. Lee's 9th Virginia Cavalry rode up the Smoketown Road and stopped near two of Pelham's guns which had a good field of fire down the Smoketown Road and to the Antietam. After pickets reported the Union crossings, Stuart got the rest of Lee's cavalry ready should the 9th need support. As Union pressure grew, the 9th Virginia and Pelham's guns retired behind the Dunker Church when Hood's infantry moved forward. As evening fell on the 16th, Jackson moved up with his old division on Hood's left, and Stuart fell to the rear of Hood's Division, which was resting near the church. Soon after dark, the 3rd Pennsylvania Cavalry was reformed; one squadron under "Captain Walsh with his company (I) was sent out on the 17th to support a battery, and afterwards to picket the extreme right beyond the infantry line, near and covering the junction of the Williamsport Road and Hagerstown Pike. There they remained during through the 18th" picketing roads to the west.[53]

The historian of the 3rd Pennsylvania Cavalry described what happened the next morning:

> Just as day dawned on the 17th, the artillery of both armies opened upon everything in sight, filling the air with shrieking and exploding shells. Our frightened horses soon caused our ranks to be badly broken. The wicked fire, particularly of two batteries at point blank range, soon caused us to fall back behind a hill, to re-form our ranks which had become tangled out of shape. Some of our horses were killed and many men were dismounted, as their horses had stampeded, and it took some time to get into line again and count off.
>
> It was not long before the several companies of the regiment were sent to different parts of the field of battle, some to support batteries, some to picket and cover roads on the flanks, some to prevent straggling from the infantry line of battle, and some to act as orderlies and escorts, Company M being detailed to report to General Hooker personally for the latter purpose. Captain Frank W. Hess, of Company M, and Lieutenant Edward M. Heyl, of Company I, particularly distinguished themselves by rallying and leading back to their guns some of our artillerymen whose batteries were in imminent danger of being captured.[54]

The 7th Virginia Cavalry which Stuart detached from Munford to accompany Jackson on 10 September, returned the night of the 16th, and after crossing at Boteler's Ford that afternoon, made its way along the Potomac and then dismounted at the Coffman Farm and walked to a point on the Hagerstown Pike, just north of the Ground Squirrel Church, and set up their line. Neither they, nor the 3rd Pennsylvania Cavalry, knew that they were 6/10 mile apart on the turnpike and Doubleday did not know that these Rebel troopers were less than a quarter-mile from his division. The 7th Virginia remained there until early morning, and after discovering its vulnerable position, retreated southwest to New Industry on the Potomac until late morning, when it joined Munford a mile south of Sharpsburg at the Blackford House.[55] The 17th Battalion of Munford's Brigade had rejoined Munford after its detached duty south of Harpers Ferry, where it had participated in Jackson's siege of that place, and patrolled Jackson's flanks. Munford placed them near the Potomac.[56]

Stuart's aide, Maj. von Borcke, said that he and Stuart rode about four miles early that Tuesday morning checking the lines. Stuart and Jackson seemed to have been reconnoitering the northern flank most of the night of the 16th. One of Pelham's cavalrymen that night, Robert M. Mackall, was almost

---

[53] Rawle says that a Capt. Walsh was sent out to picket the extreme right of Hooker's line covering the intersection of the Williamsport Road and Hagerstown Pike with Company I; they remained there during the 18th, 123-124. It is very unlikely that it was the Williamsport Road as that is slightly more than five airline miles north of the Dunker Church at Jones's Cross Roads. It was probably the intersection of the Hagerstown Pike and the Bakersville-Keedysville Roads; the Bakersville Road after passing through Bakersville does go to Williamsport, Carman, Pierro, 206.

[54] Rawle, 123.

[55] Carman, Pierro, 247. See the Carman-Cope map for Noon to 12:15 P.M. and 1 P.M. Note that the latter map still shows a small contingent of cavalry in that area picketing the river road but it is not the 7th Virginia.

[56] Carman, Pierro, 210; William N. McDonald, *A History of the Laurel Brigade Originally The Ashby Cavalry of the Army of Northern Virginia and Chew's Battery*, edited by Bushrod C. Washington (Baltimore, MD: Sun Job Printing Office, 1907), 94-95. McDonald wrote that the brigade was posted on the right of Gen. Lee's line near the river, however, Holmes Conrad in a letter to Carman 1 June 1897 said that the battalion crossed early on 17 September and "took position of the right of Jackson's [undecipherable] with the rest of the brigade," copy of letter courtesy Thomas Clemens. Since the rest of Munford's Brigade was clearly not on Jackson's right, Conrad's statement is in error.

stepped on by Stuart's horse as Stuart was seeking Pelham about 2 A.M. Mackall, recognizing Stuart's voice, directed him to Pelham, sleeping along a post and rail fence on the south slope of the hill. Finding him, Stuart awakened him and pointed out that he should move his guns before morning as Yankees were in the cornfield at the foot of the hill near the Nicodemus farmhouse. Stuart said that Pelham might want to have his guns moved now because waiting until daylight would find the hill swarming with Yankees. Pelham did so without delay, moving the guns by hand to the top of the hill, perhaps saving his battery from a rude surprise when Hooker's men attacked at first light at about 4 A.M.[57] Nicodemus Heights to the west of the Nicodemus farmhouse, was the most significant location for Rebel artillery on the northern end of the battlefield. The ridge of which it was part, ran south, then after a ravine interrupted it, continued as Hauser's Ridge, only 10 feet lower than Nicodemus Heights. High points on both ridges provided excellent artillery locations and as they were not subject to fire of the Union line of artillery on Porterstown ridge two and on-half miles to the west, they were crucial to the defense of Lee's northern flank the morning of the 17th.[58] Stuart bedded down in a haystack for a few minutes sleep after an exhausting day and evening examining the army's left flank, rather than returning to his Grove house headquarters. As the firing died down, weary men from both sides slept in a misty rain knowing that the next day would be eventful.[59]

View northeast from Nicodemus Heights. Joseph Poffenberger farms in the center of the photo below South Mountain. Courtesy James Rosebrock.

---

[57] Robert E. L. Krick, "Defending Lee's Flank: J. E. B. Stuart, John Pelham, and Confederate Artillery on Nicodemus Heights," in *The Antietam Campaign*, ed. Gary W. Gallagher (Chapel Hill, NC: The University of North Carolina Press, 1999), 198-200, hereafter Krick, "Defending Lee's Flank"; letter from Robert Mackall to Carman 15 March 1900, copy courtesy of Thomas Clemens.

[58] Krick, "Defending Lee's Flank,"196.

[59] Carman, Pierro, 205-206. Stuart and von Borcke slept in adjacent haystacks, von Borcke 160-161; Priest, *Antietam*, 23. The Dr. Jacob A. Grove house is at the southwest corner of the Sharpsburg town square.

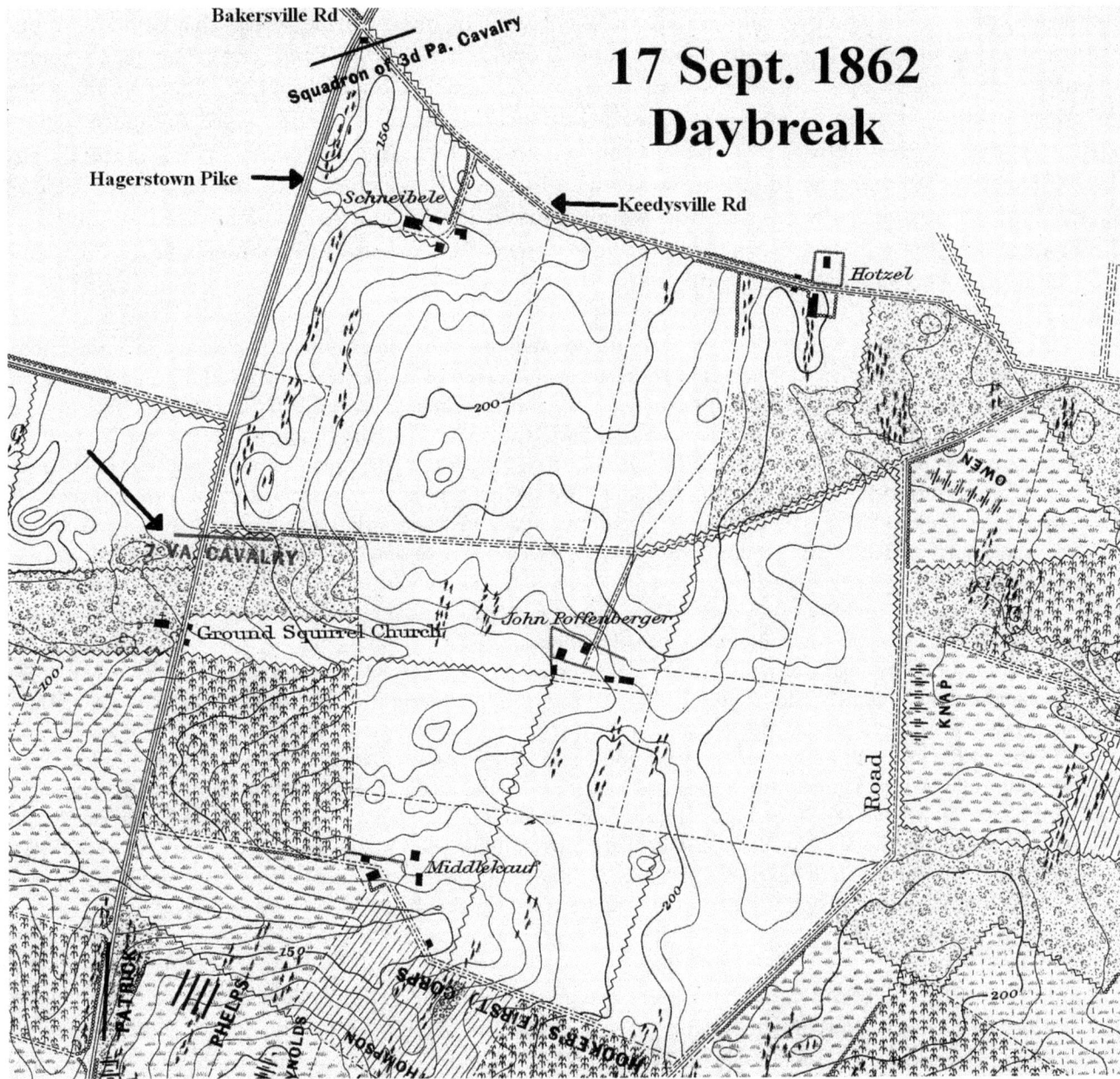

Positions of the 3rd Pennsylvania Cavalry and 7th Virginia Cavalry at the left arrow late on 16 September to early 17 September; about 6/10 mile apart. The 7th Virginia Cavalry had left its horses and walked to the pike and was almost caught between Hooker's infantry to the south and the 3rd Pennsylvania Cavalry to the north at the intersection of the Hagerstown Pike and the Keedysville-Williamsport Road. Note that the many small vertical black marks here seen to the right of the Hagerstown Turnpike between the 3rd Pennsylvania and 7th Virginia represent rock outcroppings similarly depicted on all Carman-Cope maps. Courtesy LOC.

But before Stuart could finally settle down for a few hours rest, he was possibly involved in helping to corral a stampede of some of the Jeff Davis Legion horses from three of its companies. It is difficult to locate the bivouac of the Jeff Davis Legion from the accounts given by three members of the Legion and a historian describing the events of that night. G. Moxley Sorrel of Longstreet's staff wrote a description based on what he learned from Lt. Alexander "Sandy" Duncan of the Georgia Hussars, which was part of the Jeff Davis Legion. Sorrel, along with the rest of Longstreet's staff, was camped on the Piper Farm south of the Sunken Road, when he was nearly trampled in a stampede of Legion horses. Despite the horses being well-picketed, "something seemed to pass through the animals like a quiver of motion, a faint sound as of a sign, and then the wildest scene ensued. The horses for no reason that could be found had become stampeded, in the greatest panic and excitement. They broke away from their picket ropes, and droves of different sizes, some few, some many, were thundering along over the country and about the army in wild confusion. Fortunately, they drew to our rear, and the troopers were all night and part of the next day recovering them."[60] Stuart was not mentioned by Sorrel. If Duncan's tale is correct, then the Jeff Davis Legion was near the Piper Farm which is on the Hagerstown Pike, not on the Boonsboro-SharpsburgPike. Sorrel also wrote that they were bivouacked in "thick trees" which were only found in the Piper orchard on the Piper Farm.[61] Another eyewitness, Pvt. Joseph Dunbar Shields, Jr. of Company A of the Legion wrote about the incident:

When the shelling was all over we were dismounted and most of us lying down asleep in front of our horses when all of a sudden our horses were stampeded. I was sound asleep and the first thing I knew, about a dozen horses were running over me. I tried to rise but was knocked down and Farar Conner who was next to me fell upon me and I think saved (not scared) us both. I was knocked senseless for about five sec. Farar and I lying upon one another were too high for the horses to step upon and consequently were knocked about. Farar has the print of two horses feet upon his legs and I had my left arm hurt so badly that it was two or three days before I could use it but it is all right now. None of the men were seriously hurt. Most of them were knocked down and not bruised at all. All are fit for duty. It was all over in about a second. Only two horses in our company were left. They rushed down the Pike and Gen'l Stuart with all of his couriers and aides formed across the road but could not stop them. They rushed on thorough our lines into the enemy's and were fired upon by their pickets and one gun which turned them back.

That night all but eight or ten of our horses were caught and now we have all but four or five. My horse was caught and fortunately I lost nothing. Some of the men lost everything they had. B. lost all of his clothes. There was a great many pistols lost.

I never did see such a sight. When I got up I could hardly stand....There are different rumors afloat as to the cause but no one knows. Our horses had not got over the effects of the shelling and being half asleep I suppose the least noise frightened them into a panic and the men being asleep could not rise soon enough to check them. Some thought the Yankees had charged us and had their pistols and sabres drawn. It would have been dangerous for a man to have been mounted for he would have been unsaddled in a few minutes.

The next morning [17th] we were mounted and formed a picket line to drive back the stragglers which was anything but pleasant.[62]

Stuart was definitely out much the night but mostly on the northern (left) flank of Gen. Lee. A description of the location of the Legion stated that "On his [Stuart's] immediate right Stonewall Jackson's men occupied the woods [West Woods]. The Jeff Davis Legion was in a field just to Jackson's right, separated from the rest of Stuart's cavalry....During the attack on the Confederate left the Jeff Davis Legion was formed in line along a range of hills behind Sharpsburg to stop refugees from the battlefield."[63] Given these descriptions, it is probable that if Stuart indeed did try to stop the stampede, the location was on the Hagerstown Pike and the horses were heading north toward Hooker's pickets. A Lt. William W. Gordon of the Legion's Company F wrote that the Legion bivouacked on the night of the 16th near the Sharpsburg-Shepardstown Pike but given the other accounts, it appears that this is in

[60] Sorrel, 110.

[61] The orchard was about 48,000 square feet (slightly more than one acre), 230 feet east to west, and 320 feet north to south and was enclosed by fences and walls; it probably had both apple and peach trees, ANBL, Piper Farm File. The Carman-Cope maps show no woods along the Boonsboro-Sharpsburg Pike from Sharpsburg east to the Middle Bridge nor from the Dunker Church south to Sharpsburg other than the Piper orchard and the West Woods near the church.

[62] Elizabeth Dunbar Murray, *My Mother Used to Say: A Natchez Belle of the Sixties* (Boston, MA: The Christopher Publishing House, 1959), 157-158; Hopkins, 99-100.

[63] Hopkins, 100.

error.[64] Interestingly, a biographer of Longstreet describing that night wrote that "At Longstreet's bivouac site on the Piper Farm, horses from an artillery battery stampeded through the trees, scrambling the officers from their blankets."[65] If there was only one stampede, and that one by the Legion horses and not artillery horses as Wert says, the Legion had to be camped near the Hagerstown Pike. On the other hand, there could have been two stampedes that night, and Sorrel concatenated them. Shields wrote that after Stuart couldn't stop the horses, enemy pickets fired on the horses and the horses turned back. This could easily have happened if the horses headed north on the Hagerstown Pike rather than east (or west) on the pike from Sharpsburg to Boonsboro as Union pickets were at the Middle Bridge on Antietam Creek. Carman does not show any Confederate cavalry near the Boonsboro-Sharpsburg Pike on his 17 September daybreak map and also none around the Dunker Church. The best guess for the location of the Legion's bivouac the night of the 16th -17th is near the Hagerstown Pike to the south and west of the Dunker Church behind hills located there.

View east to Miller Farm from Nicodemus Heights; the Miller Cornfield is behind and to the right. East Woods is behind the farm in center right of photo. The South Mountain gaps are directly behind. Courtesy James Rosebrock.

[64] Hopkins 98. Note that Pvt. James K. Munnerlyn, Company F of the Georgia Hussars wrote to his sister the following concerning his activities on the 15th: "A part of the army were ordered to retreat by way of Williamsport and our Regt sent as guard to them. We had not gone far before it was ascertained that a body of Yankee Cavalry was on the road ahead of us. Our company was sent ahead as advance guard, and I was sent out in advance of the company as vidette. My mare being a very fast-walker, I soon got a long way in advance before I was aware of it. I entered a village just about dawn. As I rode along the street two men turned a corner within a few yards of me I had my pistol drawn and halted them, asking them what Regt they belonged to. They said 1st Maryland Cavalry. I knew we did not have any Regt. of Maryland Cavalry, so I covered them with my pistol and told them they were my prisoners. They asked me who I was, I told them that I was a 'Rebel,' they said 'don't shoot, we surrender'. Just then one of our men rode up. I made the prisoners give up their arms and sent them to the rear. We found out from them that they belonged to a column of 16 hundred Cavalry who had escaped from Harpers Ferry and who had just passed about five [A.M.?]," "Antietam on the Web," from a letter 9 October 1862 from Pvt. James Keen Munnerlyn, Co. F, Georgia Hussars, Jeff Davis Legion Cavalry, to his sister, Mrs. D. S. Stocking of Charleston, S.C., in the James Keen Munnerlyn Papers #2790-z, Southern Historical Collection, Wilson Library, University of North Carolina at Chapel Hill.

[65] Jeffry D. Wert, *General James Longstreet: The South's Most Controversial Soldier—A Biography* (New York: Simon and Schuster, 1993), 195.

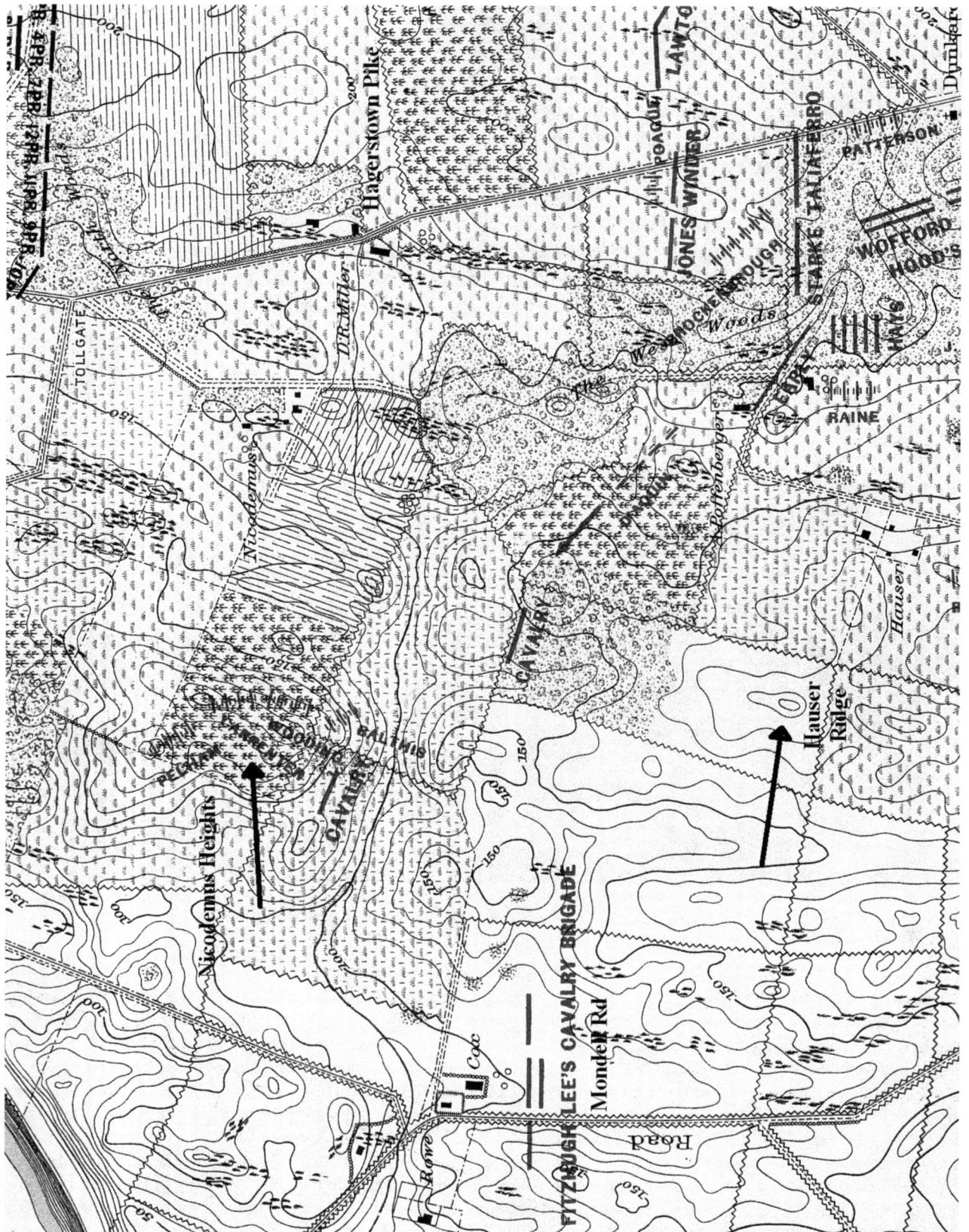

Fitzhugh Lee's Cavalry Brigade and Pelham's Guns on Nicodemus Heights late 16 September to early 17 September. Nicodemus Farm is to the right of the higher Nicodemus Heights in the upper right center of the map at the arrow. Nicodemus Heights is about 200 feet at the crest. Later in the morning, Stuart moved his cannon to Hauser's Ridge. The Dunker Church is at the bottom right corner of the map in landscape view. Courtesy LOC.

After a restless night with random rifle shots punctuating the blackness and with a light rain adding to the misery, early dawn on 17 September was heralded by gunfire continuing where it left off the day before. Stuart's guns and those corralled from Jackson did good work starting at dawn by firing at Hooker's unsuspecting batteries.[66] These Rebel guns on Nicodemus Heights joined in an artillery duel with Union batteries and also did much damage to Federal infantry to the east. Pelham's guns were part of other Confederate batteries of Carpenter, Wooding, and Balthis, totaling fifteen guns, which used the commanding vista to good effect especially during the morning attacks of the Union First and Twelfth Corps.[67] Nicodemus Heights had good fields of fire and was the vital piece of terrain on Jackson's and Stuart's line; the distance from the top of Nicodemus Heights due east to the Hagerstown Pike was less than .5 mile. The morning was particularly bad for Lt. Col. John T. Thornton of the 3rd Virginia Cavalry as it formed up and moved toward the army's left flank. He and one of his men, Cpl. T.J. Handy, in the rear of Nicodemus Heights, were hit by wood fragments thrown up by a Union shell when it exploded in a pile of cordwood. Thornton, standing with a group of officers, was hit in his left arm, fracturing it in three places, and the trooper was seriously wounded in a leg and had his horse killed.[68] Thornton died that evening after his arm was amputated, and Capt. Thomas H. Owens, as senior captain, took command. The 3rd Virginia Cavalry suffered no further losses on the 17th other than one trooper slightly wounded as the brigade supported the artillery.[69]

Mid-morning on the 17th, Pelham moved some guns and, covered by infantry, drove two Union regiments out of the West Woods and through the Nicodemus Farm, clearing the West Woods of Union troops.[70] Later in the morning probably after an hour or ninety minutes, Stuart moved some of the guns from Nicodemus Heights further south to Hauser's Ridge, to be able to fire without shooting over Confederate infantry who were being driven south. Additionally, they were less vulnerable to capture by the surging Union infantry and vicious Union counter battery fire as Jackson's lines sagged. Guns were added as they were brought up from the artillery reserve.[71] Hauser's Ridge "commanded the whole country west of the turnpike from Nicodemus's to the Dunker Church, and was thus the key to the whole of Jackson's position. Its retention was vital to the Confederates."[72] Pelham's guns remained near the northwest corner of the North Woods, supported by the 13th Virginia Infantry and some cavalry, including the 1st Virginia Cavalry.[73]

---

[66] Krick, "Defending Lee's Flank," 200.

[67] Johnson and Anderson, *Artillery Hell*, 93, 94, 100. They believe that Pelham's battery had eight guns, but only three may be identified, two 3-in. rifled guns and one Napoleon, 100, 101, 128. Note that the Carman-Cope maps show fifteen guns on Nicodemus Heights which is the total shown in Johnson and Anderson for these four batteries. Krick details the havoc Pelham and the other Rebel guns wreaked on Hooker's troops, 202. Robert Moore wrote that 19 guns were under Pelham including the Virginia batteries of the Bedford Artillery, Hampden, Alleghany, Danville, and Rockbridge Artillery and also the Louisiana Guard Artillery, 34. Carman's total of 15 guns is accepted, however. "In the absence of [Stonewall] Jackson's usual artillery subordinates, the twenty-four-year-old Major Pelham assumed Crutchfield's responsibilities and tactical control of Jackson's cannon....Command of Pelham's horse artillery thus fell to Jim Breathed, destined to become one of the army's hardest-fighting young officers," Krick, "Defending Lee's Flank," 195.

[68] William R. Carter, 16.

[69] Krick, "Defending Lee's Flank," 201; William R. Carter, 17.

[70] Priest, *Antietam*, 132-133.

[71] Krick, "Defending Lee's Flank," 204-206; Pierro, Carman, 246. The distance from Nicodemus Heights to the Hagerstown Pike was about 800 yards and less than one mile to the Dunker Church; Hauser's Ridge to the Hagerstown Pike and the Dunker church was a little over 5/10 mile, and from the northernmost part of Hauser's Ridge to the northernmost point of Nicodemus heights was about a little over 6/10 mile.

[72] Allan, 393. See also Wise, expounding on Pelham's exploits even while the Union out-gunned him, 304-305.

[73] *OR*, vol. 19, pt. 1, 820, 856; Trout, *Thunder*, 103; Robert Moore, 34. Moore writes that the 13th Virginia Cavalry also helped but it was not present, perhaps it should have been the 3rd Virginia Cavalry.

Stuart remained very active all morning supervising the guns and infantry on the left, and helped wreck Sedgwick's Division in the West Woods. Stuart directed all artillery he could find to prepare for Sedgwick's attack, including three guns from McLaws's Division, and a howitzer from the Louisiana Guard Artillery. As he was assembling the guns from McLaws, his "horse was shot, one of his couriers was killed, and eighteen of the battery's horses were destroyed. Union artillery soon knocked out all three guns after they had combined to fire only 109 rounds."[74] As Sedgwick's troops retreated under intense artillery fire and McLaws's attack, Stuart pursued them with artillery and soldiers he commandeered from John G. Walker's Division, ending up with his reestablished Rebel artillery back on Nicodemus Heights, retaking the key terrain feature. Had the Union captured it and placed artillery there, they would have wreaked havoc with enfilading fire down the Rebel lines to Sharpsburg. Pelham's cannon had the wonderful opportunity of firing into Hooker's flank as he attacked Jackson's troops. Union commanders thought that there were a line of Confederate guns all the way to the Potomac given the fierce fire they endured. The Jeff Davis Legion helped as part of the line catching stragglers and after dark, returned to Hampton's Brigade.[75] "The performance of the Confederate artillery on the northern end of the battlefield had been truly remarkable....Stuart snared guns from many sources, coordinated their activities at several key phases of the battle, displayed an excellent eye for terrain, showed his customary initiative, and repeatedly led by personal example. John Pelham demonstrated many of the same attributes on a slightly less conspicuous plane."[76] Brig. Gen. Jubal A. Early said in his official report

---

[74] Krick, "Defending Lee's Flank," 207. In a letter James McClure Scott wrote that he was with Stuart on the 16th as part of the general's bodyguard and with him as well on the 17th as Stuart rode the battlefield. McClure said that his horse (Beelzebub) was mortally wounded under him on the 17th. On the evening of the 17th, he dined with Stuart at a doctor's house in Sharpsburg (likely at Stuart's headquarters, the Grove house) listening to Yankee shells falling, ANBL Files, 10th Virginia Cavalry. One participant, Channing Price, quoted by Hartley, wrote that bullets which struck Stuart's horse were mistakenly fired by southern troops, Hartley, 138. Carman used Stuart's report: "Stuart says the enemy broke in confusion and were pursued for half a mile along the road. Evidently he did not see Early, but 'recognized in this pursuit part of Barksdale's and part of Semmes' brigades; and I also got hold of one regiment of [Brigadier General Robert] Ransom [Jr.]'s brigade, which I posted in an advantageous position on the extreme left flank after the pursuit had been checked by the enemy's reserve artillery coming into action. Having informed General Jackson of what had transpired, I was directed by him to hold this advance position, and that he would send all the infantry he could get in order to follow up the success. I executed this order, keeping the cavalry well out to the left, and awaiting the arrival of re-enforcements,'" Carman, Pierro, 272; OR, vol. 19, pt. 1, 820.

[75] Hopkins, 100-101.

[76] Krick, "Defending Lee's Flank," 211, 214. Two books relate a tale of Pelham's guns being attacked by a company of Union cavalry on 17 September. MacIver, a British lieutenant, later a brigadier general, was involved with Pelham but not recorded by Carman. Apparently before Pelham shifted his guns south to Hauser's Ridge: Lt. "MacIver....had conveyed an order from General Stuart to Captain Pelham for the latter to open fire from his guns from a certain position. Pelham, who had just received the message from the Aide, was moving his battery into action, when a heavy force of Federal cavalry appeared on his left flank. The gallant young artillery officer, who was supported by a squadron of Confederate cavalry, wheeled rapidly round, unlimbered his guns, and opened fire on the Federal troopers. By the time this manoeuvre was carried out, the enemy's cavalry were so close to Pelham's battery that they opened a revolver fire upon the gunners. At this moment MacIver, who although he could not use a sabre, had drawn his revolver with his left hand in self defence, was hit by a pistol shot. The bullet knocked out four of his upper front teeth, passing through the mouth, ripping the roof of the tongue, and finding its exit at the back of the neck, close to the jugular vein. For a few seconds the wounded man kept his seat in the saddle. Then he fell back into the outstretched arms of one of the troopers, the blood gushing from his mouth. Unfortunately the man missed his grasp, and MacIver rolled on to the ground....Lieutenant MacIver after his desperate wound was carried from the field of battle in a senseless condition, and taken to a plantation not far from the spot where had been fought the late action. The wounded man was left under the charge of a gentleman, a planter, the ladies of whose family kindly undertook to nurse him. His wound, however, was considered so dangerous that the surgeons had but little hope for his recovery, but they lost no time in commencing operations. It was necessary that a silver tube should be placed in the throat to enable him to take the necessary sustenance, and this had to be procured from the nearest city," W.D. L'Estrange, *Under Fourteen Flags Being the Life and Adventures of Brigadier-General MacIver A Soldier of Fortune*, vol. 1 (London: Tinsley Brothers, 1884), 186-189. Another author wrote that "One company of blue cavalry did penetrate to the cannon, leaving, besides its killed and wounded after it had been driven off, one of the officers who had been swept from his horse by a sponge-staff dexterously handled by one of the

that "Major-General Stuart, with the pieces of artillery under his charge, contributed largely to the repulse of the enemy, and pursued them for some distance with his artillery."[77] Jackson may have put Stuart in charge of the entire defense of the left of Jackson's line from roughly Nicodemus Heights to the Potomac but there is nothing in official records to support this assumption. Von Borcke in his memoir writes "the indefatigable Stuart, always eager to be at the place of most imminent danger, had obtained from Jackson, who had unbounded confidence in him, the charge of the left wing of his corps."[78] Moore, an artilleryman in the Rockbridge Artillery, said that on the left side of Lee's line he "passed beyond that portion held by regular infantry commands into what was defended by a mere show of force when scarcely any existed. In charge of it was Gen. J.E.B. Stuart, who demonstrated on this occasion his ability to accomplish what it would seem impossible for one man to do. With a few skeleton regiments supplied with numerous flags which he posted to show over the crests of the ridges in our rear, as if there were men in proportion, he himself took command of a line of sharpshooters in our front. This skirmish-line was composed of stragglers he had gathered up, and whom he had transformed from a lot of shirkers into a band of heroes. With black plume floating, cheering and singing, back and forth along the line he swept."[79] Brig. Gen. Early wrote that he followed Stuart's suggestion that Early place some of his troops in support of Stuart's horse artillery on Nicodemus Heights early on the 17th; Stuart also relayed to him Stonewall Jackson's request that Early take command of the Stonewall Division as Brig. Gen. Lawton had been wounded, so Early left with his brigade, minus the 13th Virginia Infantry of some 100 men he left with Stuart.[80] Thus while Stuart was not officially put in command of the left flank, as senior major general on that part of the line, it is fair to conclude that he was in actual command of not only his horse artillery and his troopers protecting it, but also the batteries augmenting it and the infantry supporting these batteries.[81] The historian Robert E.L. Krick summed up well Stuart's contribution on 17 September:

cannoneers," Charles G. Milham, *Gallant Pelham: American Extraordinary* (Washington, DC: Public Affairs Press, 1959), 162. William Woods Hassler, *Colonel John Pelham: Lee's Boy Artillerist* (Chapel Hill, NC: The University of North Carolina Press, 1960), did not mention the Union cavalry attack but did write that Hooker dispatched troopers under Abner Doubleday to quiet Pelham's guns but "Pelham managed to pepper and disperse this force with canister in a free-for-all in which Jean, the begrimed Creole sponger, deftly toppled a Federal officer on horseback who charged into the Napoleon Detachment," 91. Robert E.L. Krick who wrote the definitive study of Lee's left flank on 17 September found only Union infantry, the 23rd New York and 10th Pennsylvania Reserves assigned by Hooker and Doubleday to address the pesky Rebel guns, Krick, "Defending Lee's Flank," 203-204. L'Estrange and Milham may have embellished the event especially as no Union cavalry regiment histories relate this attack, the closest being the 3rd Pennsylvania and the 6th New York. In any event, the Union infantry never got among Pelham's guns but rather picked off the gunners by rifle fire. Carman mentions the Pennsylvania Reserves on the extreme right of Hooker's line, Carman, Pierro, 234. The Keystone State soldiers were checked by the 13th Virginia Infantry. The closest Union cavalry regiment, the 3rd Pennsylvania in its thorough regimental history which would have mentioned this event, did not do so. The Carman-Cope maps do not show any of Pelham's guns being attacked by Union cavalry on the 17th so it appears that the MacIver story cannot be corroborated leaving unexplained his severe wound. It may be that in the melee when Confederate cannon were under severe counterbattery fire as well as Union rifle fire, MacIver was wounded.

[77] Priest, *Antietam*, 114; Carman, Pierro, 269-271, 272, 275-276; Krick, 208, 211, 213-214; *OR*, vol. 19, pt. 1, 971.

[78] Krick, "Defending Lee's Flank," 201, n. 11; von Borcke, 162.

[79] Edward A. Moore, The *Story of a Cannoneer Under Stonewall Jackson* (Lynchburg, VA: J.P. Bell Company, Inc., 1910), 153-154.

[80] Early, 141-142.

[81] Carman, Pierro, 269. See Stuart's report showing that he was put in command of some of Jackson's artillery and infantry during the battle on the 17th, *OR*, vol. 19, pt. 1, 819-820, but tellingly, did not write that he was specifically put in command in that part of the line by Jackson. Von Borcke says that Jackson put Stuart in charge of the "left wing" of his corps. It should be noted that technically, Gen. Lee had not yet formed corps or named commanders; properly, Jackson and Longstreet each had a "command" not a "corps," see Carman, Pierro, 415. There is no written evidence that Jackson put Stuart in command of anything other than perhaps the guns added to Pelham on Nicodemus Heights. Borcke also said that about midday he was talking with Thurston, the commander of the 3rd Virginia Cavalry, when his arm was torn off. Priest says that that arm was later amputated, von Borcke, 162. Von Borcke while presenting some colorful details about his adventures with Stuart must be read carefully since he is sometimes loose with details; here, he characteristically misspelled Thornton's name as "Thurston." Jackson

"As Jackson's de facto chief of artillery, Stuart snared guns from many sources, coordinated their activities at several key phases of the battle, displayed an excellent eye for terrain, showed his customary initiative, and repeatedly led by personal example."[82]

The future, famous partisan leader, John Singleton Mosby, was serving on Stuart's staff during the Maryland Campaign and left this account of some of his activities on 17 September:

> I rode on and overtook Stuart, but the [Yankee] killed and wounded were strewn on the ground "like leaves of the forest when autumn hath blown," and I had to be careful not to ride over them. Whole ranks seemed to have been struck down by a volley. Although hundreds were lying all around me, my attention was in some way attracted to a wounded officer who was lying in an uncomfortable position and seemed to be suffering great agony. I dismounted, fixed him more comfortably, and rolled up a blanket on which he rested his head, and then got a canteen of water for him from the body of a dead soldier lying near him. As I passed a wounded soldier, I held the canteen toward him so that he could drink. He said, "No, take it to my Colonel, he is the best man in the world."[83]

After the war, Mosby and the colonel met; the colonel was Isaac J. Wistar, commander of the 71st Pennsylvania Volunteer Infantry. In his autobiography, he wrote of this incident in which he was wounded and his regiment decimated, and well illustrates the fury of the action in this quarter:

> As the head of column was wheeling to the left about myself as pivot, its killed and wounded falling at every step, I was myself knocked over by a bullet through the left shoulder. Rogers, the left flank sergeant of G Company was instantly at my side, and as the blood was spouting from under the sleeve at the wrist, hastily clapped on a tourniquet constructed of my pocket handkerchief and his bayonet. He offered to remain with me, and was inclined to insist, till I appealed to him to save my sword. Recognizing that obligation, he quickly took it from me, and rushed after the retiring column, and was scarcely gone till the enemy's line marched over me....the disordered Confederates...again retired over me leaving me lying between two fires. Twice again the enemy advanced over me....As this splendid line moved over me, a young lieutenant seized the occasion to leave his place to demand my sword. When he learned that it was beyond his reach, he wanted my parole, which I refused to give. The little dispute was suddenly terminated by the arrival of several General Officers whom I took to be McLaws, Walker and Stuart. These with their staffs were following and closely watching their line now heavily engaged with our troops, whose balls were striking all around us. Having lost much blood notwithstanding the tourniquet, suffering intense pain and barely able to whisper, I nevertheless managed to attract the attention of one of their couriers, who dismounted, ascertained and reported the subject of discussion to Stuart, who inquired of the lieutenant his name and regiment. "Hill, of the 12th Georgia." Join it immediately sir." The courier then rearranged the tourniquet, which, though hitherto but partially effective, had become excessively painful, handed me a drink from one of the 71st's wounded near-by, who kindly offered his canteen, and leaving me in a much more comfortable condition rode away after his General. It was not till several years after the war that a mutual friend—accidentally hearing the celebrated Confederate guerilla, John S. Mosby, relate the same circumstance in connection with my name, which he still

---

may have placed Stuart in informal charge of the far left but Jackson did not mention this assignment in his report of the battle. That Jackson and Stuart were close friends and trusted each other makes this assignment very likely. But see Krick, "Defending Lee's Flank," asserting that the events of the 17th stating that Jackson and Stuart must have worked out some arrangements for the defense of the far left flank since Jackson never visited Nicodemus Heights, 201, 207-208, 217, n. 11. Compare Priest, *Antietam*, stating that Stuart had field-promoted Early to division command to replace the wounded Lawton and placed the division behind Jackson, 98.

[82] Krick, "Defending Lee's Flank," 214.

[83] John S. Mosby, *The Memoirs of Colonel John S. Mosby* (np.: Little, Brown and Company, 1917; reprint, Nashville, TN: J.S. Sanders & Company, 1995), 144-145.

remembered—brought us together, when I learned for the first time that the friendly courier had been no other than the renowned Mosby, at that time not even a commissioned officer.[84]

Other batteries of Stuart's Horse Artillery had a much less exciting day on the 17th. Chew's Battery spent its time on the far southern end of Lee's line near the Antietam Iron Works holding the bridge with Munford's Brigade, and did not even accompany Munford when some of his troopers moved toward Sharpsburg later in the day as Burnside's Corps advanced toward the town. Hart's Battery took position on 16 September on the Boonsboro-SharpsburgTurnpike to the west of town and fired all its ammunition on the 17th save for canister. It then pulled back to the Potomac River guarding the crossings.[85]

During the midmorning on the 17th, the 12th Pennsylvania Cavalry was part of the Union provost guard rounding up stragglers and holding prisoners near Poffenberger's lane even though they lacked the capacity to gather all in. The 3rd Pennsylvania Cavalry was broken up into smaller units and used during the day also gathering stragglers, supporting batteries, and picketing and covering roads on the flanks. One company, Company M, reported to Hooker for escort duty before Hooker was wounded. One of these troopers helped Hooker off the field after the general was shot in the foot. Most of the 3rd Pennsylvania was used in open order gathering stragglers behind the infantry line.[86]

The 9th Virginia Cavalry on Gen. Lee's left flank performed duties similar to many Confederate and Union cavalry units on 17 September: "[It] was detached early in the day and reported to Jackson near the Reel house, southwest of the church. He ordered it to stop the infantry stragglers who, singly and in groups, were going to the rear. Men without ammunition—and many with it—were leisurely retiring toward Sharpsburg, and some of the Confederate batteries, having shot their last round, were leaving the field at a gallop. All these Jackson ordered stopped and supplied with ammunition from the ordnance train near the Reel house, and then marched back to the line of battle, or conducted to their proper commands. Jackson, motioning to a captain of the 9th to give him his ear, directed him in a whisper not to halt any of Hood's men, as they had liberty to retire. The regiment was on this duty the greater part of the day."[87] Late in the day, von Borcke acting under Stuart's orders, took some cavalry and infantry to the left flank to post a strong picket near the Potomac until relieved by an infantry brigade. Von Borcke then returned to Sharpsburg to rest. "When Hooker's artillery opened fire upon the Confederate batteries on Nicodemus Hill, these were supported by Fitzhugh Lee's cavalry, which had bivouacked in the valley in their rear near the Cox house, some of it in an orchard and some in open ground adjoining.

---

[84] Isaac J. Wistar, *Autobiography of Isaac Jones Wistar 1827-1905: Half a Century in War and Peace* (Philadelphia, PA: The Wistar Institute of Anatomy and Biology, 1937), 407-409. Wistar notes that Mosby was not yet a commissioned officer but Mosby states that he was a first lieutenant as an adjutant as of 17 February 1862 even though his status was in limbo for a year after his regiment was reorganized in April 1862—he resigned his commission since apparently he was not first choice of its new commander Fitzhugh Lee, Mosby, 102, 109. Note that Lee called him a "Private" when he commended his service in General Orders 74 dated 23 June 1862, *The Wartime Papers of R.E. Lee*, 198. Compare Jeffrey D. Wert, *Mosby's Rangers* (New York: Simon and Schuster, 1990), stating that since Mosby detested Lee, when Lee took over command of the First Virginia Cavalry from "Grumble" Jones, Mosby resigned his commission when he resigned as adjutant on 23 April, and while attached to Stuart's staff, he was an enlisted man although Stuart addressed him as lieutenant, 29.

[85] Trout, *Thunder*, 104.

[86] Rawle, 123, 124, 127. Earlier, on the 16th, two squadrons of the 12th Pennsylvania Cavalry apparently sent out detachments to scout the area looking for Rebel activity. The two squadrons rode toward Hagerstown where late on the 16th they had a brush with Confederate cavalry some two miles west of Boonsboro where they took a few prisoners. The squadrons then rejoined the rest of the regiment late on the 16th which was camped to the rear of McClellan's army at Keedysville, Maier, 48-49. The 12th performed provost duty on McClellan's right flank on the 17th and on the 18th was sent to scout Harpers Ferry then returning that day reporting evidence that the Confederates were retreating. The regiment performed picket duty along the Potomac until 22 September when it and the 1st New York cavalry were sent to Cumberland, Maryland, to guard the B&O there, Maier, 52-53.

[87] Carman, Pierro, 247. Beale *9th Virginia*, the 9th Virginia also sent several officers to Shepherdstown to find fresh horses to replace those killed or disabled at Boonsboro, 40-41.

Fitzhugh Lee remained in support of the guns until relieved by Early's Brigade, when he moved further to the left out of range of the artillery fire and massed his regiments near the river, picketing well to the left and guarding that flank, but was not actively engaged during the morning."[88]

Around noon on the 17th, Pleasonton moved his cavalry division from their bivouac west of Keedysville and east of McClellan's headquarters at the Pry House, a little over a mile to the Middle Bridge. With his six regiments plus a squadron, followed by the batteries of Gibson, Tidball, Hains, and Robertson, he was to support Sumner's left.[89] Pleasonton came under fire approaching the bridge which continued from Rebel skirmishers and artillery on a ridge to the west; he sent out dismounted cavalry consisting of a squadron of the 4th Pennsylvania Cavalry under Capt. Samuel B.M. Young as skirmishers to the right of the Boonsboro-Sharpsburg Pike. They were followed by a section of Tidball's battery under Lt. William N. Dennison. Coming under cannon fire from Cemetery Hill as they approached the bridge, Young raced to the top of a long hill on the other side of the bridge about 550 yards from the Middle Bridge. There, four of his men were mortally wounded or killed by a shell as they deployed on both sides of the road firing at Rebel infantry who were shooting at them from behind stone fences on the west side of the ridge. Young, now supported by Dennison's guns, attacked the Rebel infantry but the heavy Confederate fire drove the Union cannoneers back. Rebel artillery from Cemetery Hill also joined in at this time adding their firepower after seeing Dennison's guns.

Right: Pleasonton arrives just after noon and pushes Rebel skirmishers west away from the bridge and establishes his horse artillery to fire on skirmishers and return cannon fire from Cemetery Hill about one mile from the Middle Bridge and 7/10 mile from Tidball's guns. Carman-Cope map, Noon to 12:15 P.M. Courtesy LOC.

[88] Priest, *Antietam*, 30, 33, 59, 89; Blackford, 149-150; von Borcke, 160-161, 164. Murfin, 235, Carman, Pierro, 220, 221, 247, 303.

[89] Tidball's and Robertson's batteries each had six 12-lb brass Napoleons while Gibson's and Hains's each had six 3-in. Ordnance guns, Johnson and Anderson, *Artillery Hell*, 35.

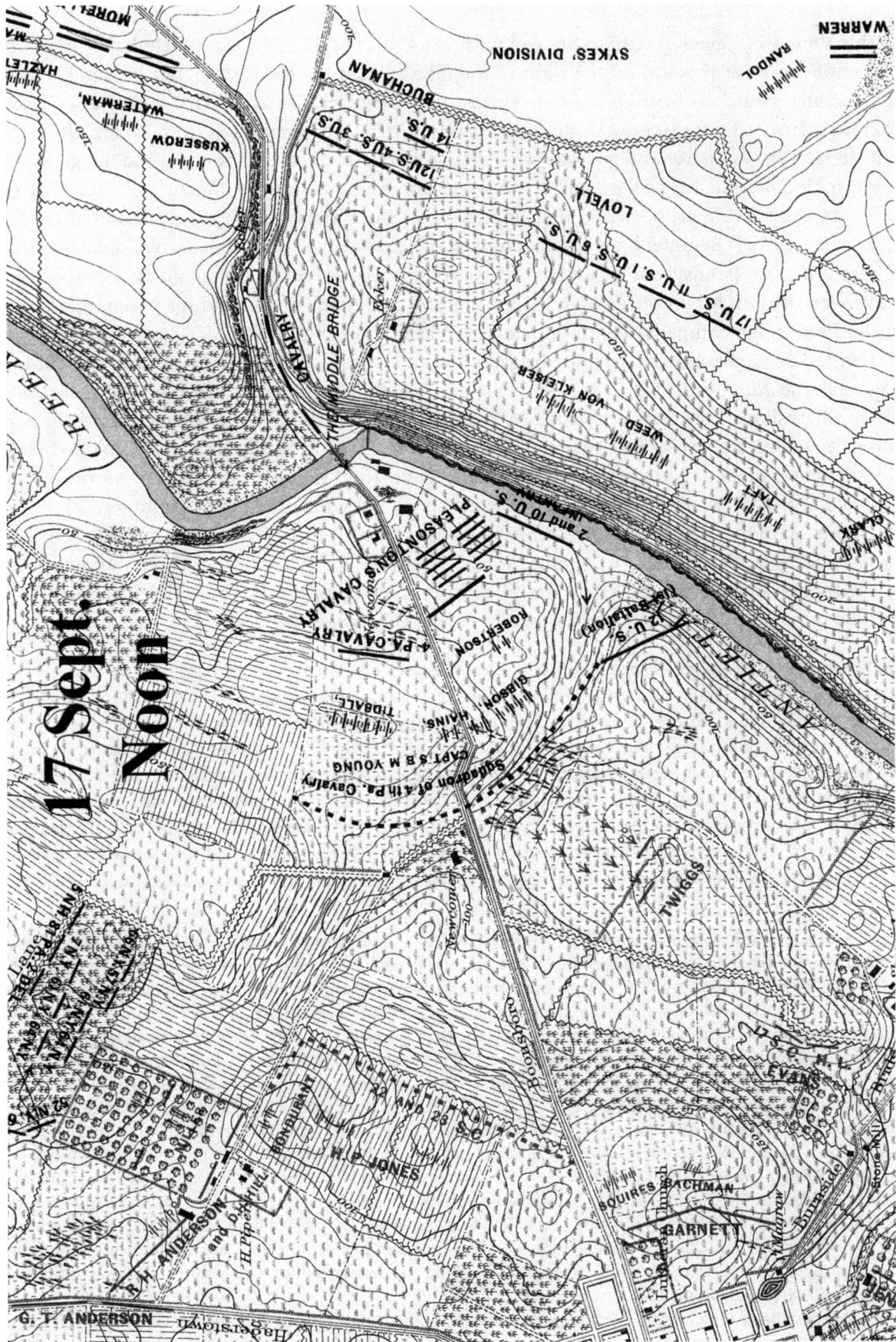

At this time, Col. James H. Childs arrived with his 4th Pennsylvania Cavalry. He halted them below the crest while he went forward on the right of the pike to examine the terrain, but he quickly saw that mounted cavalry could do little in face of the cannon fire from Cemetery Hill and the well-covered Confederate infantry. James Harvey Childs was born in Pittsburgh, graduating from Miami University in Ohio in 1852. He was a relatively large man being some six feet tall, robust, and in good health. Returning to Pittsburgh, he was a civil engineer, a dry goods merchant and manufacturer of cotton goods. Before the Civil War, he was a first lieutenant in the Pittsburgh City Guards and after the war began, joined the 12th Regiment as first lieutenant of Company K. After this enlistment expired, he helped recruit the 4th Pennsylvania Cavalry and was commissioned as lieutenant colonel of the regiment on 18 October 1861 and then on 12 March 1862 colonel commanding. He and his regiment were active during the Peninsular Campaign before moving to Washington to join the Maryland Campaign. Childs was in temporary command of Averell's brigade due to its leader's illness. As he was returning from scouting near the Middle Bridge to report to Pleasonton, he was talking with his staff on or near the Boonsboro-Sharpsburg Pike but was struck by a cannon ball on the left hip which passed through his body disemboweling him as he was thrown from his horse's back.[90] While his mind remained clear but knowing he was mortally wounded, he sent an aide, Capt. Hughes, to Pleasonton to inform him of the situation and sent another to Lt. Col. James K. Kerr, second in command of his regiment, asking him to assume command of the brigade. Then, after sending for a doctor, he called his assistant adjutant general, Capt. Henry King, a close friend, to whom he gave messages for his wife and three children. He died within a half hour and the next day Kerr was placed in command of the 4th Pennsylvania Cavalry.[91]

A trooper from the 3rd Indiana Cavalry wrote of that time under fire:

"Yesterday [17 September] our forces had to cross a large creek (called Antietam) on a narrow stone bridge to get at the secesh. The infantry would not venture across and our regiment and the 8th Illinois crossed it on a charge and planted a battery of flying artillery on the opposite hills and held it there in the very teeth of 2 batteries that were pouring a perfect storm of shot and shell (to say nothing of grape and canister) into us all the time. It was the most daring and brilliant achievement of the day. Their infantry made 2 charges on the battery but the skill of our gunners with some well directed carbine shots sent them back in confusion. (We got our carbines when we were at Fredericksburg). We were under artillery fire for about 4 hours before we were relieved by the infantry from supporting the batteries. Our company had 4 wounded, one lieutenant (Lee) 2 corporals and one private, none dangerous though. Our regiment had about 15 wounded and 2 killed.[92]

[90] Carman, Pierro, 318-320; Crowninshield, 78-79, Gracey, 100. Another account has him hit with a solid shot dying quickly after "he had requested that his organization should remember his fall, and avenge his death on the enemy," Hyndman, 39. This typical 19th century romanticized view of a death was counterbalanced by Crowninshield who, obviously not an eye-witness, and not possessing all the facts, wrote that "On the bridge lay the body of Colonel Carr, of the 4th Pennsylvania cavalry, in a pool of blood, together with the body of his horse. A solid shot had passed through the horse's forehead, lengthwise thorough his neck, and had disemboweled the colonel," 78. Cemetery Hill is the name given for the hill and ridge as there was a Lutheran cemetery next to the Lutheran Church on the west side of the ridge. Gen. Lee spent time using that vantage point to view action to the north and west as well as having artillery placed there. It was a key terrain feature on the southern part of Lee's line. Note that Pleasonton was "wounded" in his right ear due to the explosion of an artillery shell, Eicher, 431.

[91] Samuel P. Bates, *Martial Deeds of Pennsylvania* (Philadelphia, PA. T.H. Davis & Co., 1875), 435-437; Roger D. Hunt, *Colonels in Blue: Union Army Colonels of the Civil War: The Mid-Atlantic States: Pennsylvania, New Jersey, Maryland, Delaware, and the District of Columbia* (Mechanicsburg, PA: Stackpole Books, 2007), 46. Another interpretation of Bates's history is that the horse was disemboweled not Childs but in either case, Childs died quickly as presumably did his horse. One of Carman's War Department tablets states that Childs was killed by a rifle shot, Antietam Battlefield Board, marker number 91, courtesy Craig Swain HMdb.org. His actions after he was hit seem unlikely given the gravity of his wound and may be due to the Victorian custom of embellishing the last moments of one's death.

[92] Flavius J. Bellamy file, letter 18 September 1862 to his brother, courtesy Indiana State Library. He also recounted that on South Mountain he was in a dismounted group of four in the advance and was the only one not wounded at the first volley.

Col. James Harvey Childs, 4th Pennsylvania Cavalry commander, killed 17 September near the Boonsboro Pike. (Detail from Gardner photo, August 1862). Courtesy LOC.

Position of Pleasonton's cavalry division at 1 P.M. as Brig. Gen. George Sykes' 1,640 Regulars begin advance on Sharpsburg. Sykes was ordered only to support the horse artillery but could have pushed the Confederates back likely even from Cemetery Hill had he been given some support. The distance from Tidball's Battery to Cemetery Hill is about 6/10 mile. Arrow at Pleasonton's Division shows approximate location of Childs's mortal wounding. Courtesy Brian Downey "Antietam on the Web."

More Federal artillery came up to challenge the guns on the next ridge and Cemetery Hill: the two remaining sections of Tidball's battery arrived and were placed on the right of the road as Dennison's battered section followed; Hains's battery came up and also turned to the right placing its guns on Tidball's left; Robertson's battery followed forming on his left and rear; Gibson's battery then placed its guns between Robertson and Hains.[93] Confederate infantry finally retreated as they came under additional cannon fire from other guns just behind the Antietam to the east on a commanding ridge. Once all the guns were in place, Pleasonton's cavalry followed to their support. The 4th Pennsylvania remained on the right side of the road where their fallen commander placed them, and the 5th U.S. Cavalry formed on its left. The rest of the cavalry formed on the left side of the road some in the swale next to the Newcomer Barn which provided protection from Rebel artillery fire, and others to the south away from the barn, but still under cover. Carman wrote that the units in the area near and to the south of the barn were the 6th U.S. Cavalry, a squadron of the 8th Pennsylvania Cavalry, the 3rd Indiana Cavalry, the 8th Illinois Cavalry, and the 1st Massachusetts.[94]

[93] Paul Chiles, "Artillery Hell!—The Guns of Antietam," *Blue & Gray Magazine*, Vol. XVI, issue 2, it was the cannon fire during this artillery duel with Rebel guns on Cemetery Hill which caused the majority of damage in the town of Sharpsburg in which many buildings were hit and some set on fire, 50. Some buildings today show damage from shells with a few still having the shells showing. Tidball's after action report criticized the way his horse artillery were used: "the use of horse batteries being a new thing in our service, does not appear to be very well comprehended by those [indistinct] whose command they most frequently [indistinct]. The duties assigned to these batteries at the battle of Antietam could have been performed as well by any other batteries, several of which were close by unemployed. This would have left the horse batteries free for rapid movement to any part of that extended field where a concentration of artillery fire was hastily required." He also did not believe cavalry could support artillery well unless they served as dismounted infantry and because their carbines did not have enough range, Johnson and Anderson, *Artillery Hell*, 113. A War Department marker near the Middle Bridge states the following "First Brigade, Cavalry Division. Major Charles J. Whiting, 2nd U.S. Cavalry, Commanding. Organization. 5th and 6th United States Cavalry. (September 17, 1862.) The 5th United States Cavalry, Captain Joseph H. McArthur commanding, crossed the middle bridge over the Antietam shortly before noon and took position on the right of the road, its left resting at this point, in support to the Artillery in its front. It was withdrawn across the creek late in the day. The 6th United States Cavalry, Captain William P. Sanders commanding, was detached and deployed in skirmishing order, as a Provost Guard, in rear of the right wing of the Army of the Potomac," Antietam Battlefield Board, marker number 89, courtesy Craig Swain HMdb.org. Apparently not all of the 6th U.S. was with Pleasonton as some were acting as Provost Guard.
[94] Carman, Pierro, 319.

Union artillery officers participating at Antietam on 17 September. Taken near Fair Oaks, VA, June 1862. Lt. Robert Clarke, Capt. John C. Tidball, Lt. William Neil Dennison, and Lt. Alexander Cummings McWhorter Pennington, Jr. Photograph by James F. Gibson Courtesy LOC.

Fair Oaks, Virginia: brigade officers of the Horse Artillery commanded by Lt. Col. William Hays, August 1862, most of whom were present during the Maryland Campaign. Standing, left to right: Lt. Edmund Pendleton, Lt. Alexander Cummings McWhorter Pennington, Jr., Capt. Henry Benson, Capt. H.M. Gibson (?), Lt. James E. Wilson, Capt. John C. Tidball, Lt. William Neil Dennison. Seated, left to right: Capt. Horatio Gates Gibson, Lt. Peter C. Hains, Lt. Col. William Hays, Capt. James M. Robertson, and Lt. John W. Barlow. Seated on the ground, left to right: Lt. Robert H. Chapin, Lt. Robert Clarke, Lt. Albert Vincent. Courtesy LOC.

The cavalry remained under Confederate artillery fire and spent an uncomfortable afternoon on the 17th dodging shells. The nature of the country was so difficult for cavalry action that it could not be used effectively to protect the guns in any event had it been mounted. Regular U.S. infantry came up to relieve the cavalry skirmishers about 1 P.M. Also at that time, a squadron from the 8th Pennsylvania and the 12th Pennsylvania moved to the west side of the Antietam and spent the rest of the afternoon gathering stragglers until nightfall. At 3 P.M., the 1st Massachusetts Cavalry moved across to the right of the road and rode about 600 yards to the north of the Newcomer House to shelter behind a ridge. The 5th U.S. and the 5th and 6th Pennsylvania remained in support of the batteries until the guns were withdrawn, and then followed them to their old bivouac near Keedysville, east of the Pry House. The 3rd Indiana and the 8th Illinois were sent to support Meade to the north per McClellan's orders, and bivouacked on the west bank of the Antietam in the right rear of the infantry.[95] Tidball wrote that "The fire from the 24 pieces of these horse batteries was so spirited as not only to prevent the establishment of other batteries in their front, but to drive away those already there. In the course of a couple of hours these batteries expended all their ammunition and while absent for a short time replenishing their chests, the position was held by other batteries sent there from the Reserve temporarily for that purpose. The horse batteries continued to hold the position until withdrawn at dark. In addition to attending to their immediate front they, as occasion offered, directed their fire to the right upon Jackson's masses and to the left upon the troops confronting Burnside."[96]

Overleaf: Middle Bridge crossing Antietam Creek on the Boonsboro-Shepherdstown Pike looking west taken on 22 September 1862. The Sharpsburg Ridge is not visible due to the intervening ridge seen here behind the Newcomer houses. Union horse artillery was placed on this ridge and exchanged fire with Rebel artillery on Sharpsburg Ridge. The Newcomer Barn is to the middle left on the opposite bank at the arrow; the wooden lock to the lower left at the arrow is the entrance to the mill stream which powered the Newcomer grist and saw mills at the middle left. The Antietam flows right to left. The two Newcomer houses are shown in the center and the center right. Of the seven Newcomer buildings present during the battle, only the Newcomer Barn and the house on the right above are extant. The house to the middle right above the bridge was in disrepair at the time of the battle but it was likely used as a hospital as were the remainder of the Newcomer farm buildings. Note the two telegraph poles and wire on the bridge. This bridge which was built for $1,800 by Silas Harry in 1824 was destroyed in the 1889 Johnstown, Pennsylvania, flood. It was the first of the "Antietam Bridges" and was constructed at Major Christian Orndorff's mill. Next came the upper bridge built near Samuel Hitt's mill by John Weaver in 1829 for $1,413.66. In 1832, the four arch bridge was built near the mouth of the Antietam where it empties into the Potomac connecting Sharpsburg with Harpers Ferry. It was also built by Samuel Weaver. Finally in 1833, the County Commissioners appointed a committee for "viewing the site of a bridge over the Antietam on the Sharpsburg and Maple Swamp road". The contract for building this Antietam bridge again went to John Weaver at a cost of $2300. It is the most well known of the Antietam bridges. Known at various times as the Rohrbach, or Lower Bridge, history now accords it the name Burnside Bridge. Photograph Courtesy LOC. Location of Newcomer buildings described in *Antietam Farmsteads*, Keven M. Walker, narrative by K.C. Kirkman, (Sharpsburg, MD: Western Maryland Interpretive Association, 2010), 109-115; Helen Ashe Hays, *The Antietam and Its Bridges: The Annals of an Historic Stream*, (New York: G.P. Putnam's Sons, 1910), 26, 40, 43; William A. Frassanito, *Antietam: The Photographic Legacy of the America's Bloodiest Day*, (New York: Charles Scribner's Sons, 1978), 87. Bridge information courtesy James Rosebrock, blog "South from the North Woods."

---

[95] Carman, Pierro, 320. The 5th U.S. Cavalry had little combat in the campaign up to Antietam as it had been in reserve after joining the army on 8 September; Price, 110-111. Maj. Charles J. Whiting was killed along with two enlisted men mortally wounded, Pvt. John Domiers and Sgt. Thomas Barritt while one enlisted trooper was wounded, Sgt. Robert L. Jones; Price, 653, 668. Whiting apparently was assigned to the 2nd U.S. Cavalry from 17 July 1862; Heitman, 1: 67, 71, 1029.

[96] John C. Tidball, *The Artillery Service in the War of the Rebellion 1861-1865*, ed. By Lawrence M. Kaplan (Yardley, PA: Westholme Publishing, LLC., 2011), 72.

Another view of the Middle Bridge taken just after the battle from the east side showing the Newcomer Barn, workshop, saw mill, and grist mill. The older Newcomer farmhouse is at the upper right. The building at the lower left is believed to be a toll house; it still stands while the stone house across the Boonsboro Pike is gone. On 16 September, Confederate skirmishers were behind these building firing at Union troops advancing to take the Middle Bridge which they did early in the day. The bridge was never seriously contested by Gen. Lee and hills on the east bank of the Antietam would have made it untenable. Federal cavalry on the 17th crossed here, and while horse artillery took to the crest of the ridge, remaining troopers sheltered behind these buildings and the defilade areas to the left. Note that even though this photograph was taken a few days after the battle there are no wounded men in view. Note the parked army wagons at the center of the photograph. Courtesy LOC.

Three times during the afternoon Pleasonton's troopers were ordered to mount and draw sabers, but no attack resulted, much to the troopers' dismay. Despite the noise of Union cannon firing and the explosions of incoming shells, some groups of men were so exhausted that they fell asleep. Fortunately, the incoming fire was not very accurate so there were few casualties. Some believed that on that day, the cavalry was poorly used: it should have covered the Union army's flanks, done more scouting, and even broken through Lee's lines on the Boonsboro-SharpsburgPike along with Porter's troops, part of which was idle nearby. But apparently McClellan viewed the cavalry as part of his reserve force to help stem any possible Confederate foray which he feared as he remained convinced that Lee heavily outnumbered him. McClellan reported that "The cavalry had little field for operations during the engagement, but was employed in supporting the horse-artillery batteries in the center, and in driving up stragglers, while awaiting opportunity for other service."[97] Perhaps something simple as helping McClellan's engineers to scout good fords through Antietam Creek would have greatly helped Burnside in his hours' long struggle to cross it, although as it turned out, the only two useable ones were Snavely's and Myer's. And had Union troopers been on his left flank, they might have warned him of the flanking march of Maj. Gen. A.P. Hill in the afternoon, as well as pushing Munford's troopers back toward the Potomac.[98] Pleasonton even saw that Sykes regulars were having some success in pushing toward Cemetery Hill and at 4 P.M. asked Porter for a division to advance up the Boonsboro-SharpsburgPike. Unfortunately, Porter had no division to spare and even if he did, he had no orders from McClellan for such an advance—Pleasonton was not in a position to influence Porter's judgment. Had Sykes been more aggressive in his effort to

---

[97] *OR*, vol. 19, pt. 1, 31.

[98] Crowninshield, 79; George B. Davis, "The Antietam Campaign," in *Campaigns in Virginia, Maryland, and Pennsylvania, 1862-1863*, vol. 3 of *Papers of the Military Historical Society of Massachusetts* (Boston, MA: Griffith-Stilling Press, 1903, reprint, Wilmington, NC: Broadfoot Publishing Company, 1989), 55. Carman, Pierro, 338, 339. See also Thomason, "The cavalry of Pleasonton was, by some strange concept of McClellan's, stationed behind the Federal centre, with the reserve, and had no part in the battle other than provost activity. Pleasonton's horse artillery, however, under Pennington, was engaged in long range shelling," 284. Burnside should have better employed some of the cavalry he had with him, the 6th New York.

convince McClellan to attack as Burnside was advancing to Sharpsburg, it is very likely that the town could have been taken before Hill came up.[99]

Capt. Palmer who had supplied Gov. Curtin and Alexander McClure as well as McClellan with excellent information about Rebel movements especially around Hagerstown, was not finished with his services and those of his 15th Pennsylvania Cavalry recruits. One of Palmer's troopers, Pvt. Frederic J. Anspach of Co. D, wrote that early on 17 September at Jones's Cross Roads, as well as in Hagerstown, Palmer rounded up all of his troopers he could find, and headed for the sound of the guns at Sharpsburg. As they got closer riding down the Hagerstown Pike, they began to hear the "rattle of Musketry and the shriek of shells" so they took down the fence along the pike and headed east, breaking down from column of fours to twos as they entered the field heading for the Union firing line. As the column began to file right paralleling the line of battle, Pvt. Thomas H. Stockton was shot through the heart and killed. The troopers were directed to form behind the infantry and allow no one to go to the rear unless wounded, while some were detailed to assist caring for the wounded. A squad was also detailed to help Brown's New York Battery which was under heavy fire by Confederate batteries in its front near the Dunker Church: "We were in close proximity to the famous Dunkard Church, around which was the most terrible fighting of the day. Sergeant Mershon and his squad were sent in with Brown's New York Battery, and remained with it until a heavy artillery fire was poured into it from a couple of batteries in front, and then the Sergeant moved his men to a depression on the left where several of our officers were, including Major Ward and Captain Vezin." Capt. Brown and several of his men were casualties. Later in the afternoon, McClellan ordered Palmer to head up the Potomac toward Williamsport "and destroy the pontoon there, which Lee's army might otherwise use to recross into Virginia. One of the 15th's troopers described this outing: "It was a long, hard ride, most of it over the towpath between the canal and river, and at one place it was necessary to go under the canal through a tunnel and in single file. About the only orders received after we started were to 'close up,' and these were given in low tones, which, to us, indicated danger; but before dark the work was accomplished, and we marched back and closed in on the right of our army and bivouacked around a farmhouse, making a liberal use of the farmer's hay for our beds."[100] The next day they picketed Jones's Cross Roads. It was fortunate that the 15th Pennsylvania Cavalry, known as the Anderson Cavalry, had its recruits in the right place. A trooper described the end of participation of the 15th: "Our work in this field was now done. The rebel army had successfully retreated across the Potomac. Our Colonel [Palmer] was a prisoner in the hands of General Pendleton (Lee's Chief of Artillery) whose men had captured him in citizen's clothes while obtaining information, which meant death as a spy; but he escaped later and joined us at a time when he was badly needed. At Greencastle we returned the horses and accouterments we had impressed from the citizens, were then loaded on a train and in a few hours landed at our old camp at Carlisle."[101]

---

[99] Carman, Pierro, 326. Rafuse, *McClellan's*, states that "Had McClellan committed [Sykes and Pleasonton] to a determined assault against Lee's center, they undoubtedly would have been able to break the Confederate line at Antietam once and for all," 326. Allan in "Strategy of the Campaign of Sharpsburg or Antietam" commented that "The disposition of his cavalry was the weakest point in McClellan's plan of battle. It might have been of far more use on either flank," 94.

[100] Kirk, 36-39.

[101] Kirk, 40. Palmer reported to McClellan on 16 September at Keedysville and the general "at first thought he would send a large force of Pleasonton's cavalry, with artillery, to this point—which is Jones' Cross-Roads, on Sharpsburg pike [Hagerstown Pike]—but finally concluded not to send them so far off; but he ordered down the Harper's Ferry cavalry, 1,300 in number, to support my 300 [cavalry], *OR*, vol. 19, pt. 2, 311. McClellan was likely happy to have the Harpers Ferry escapees at his disposal even though he was not sure at that time that they were technically under his command. Curtin reported to Lincoln on 17 September that McClellan ordered Palmer to destroy the bridges at Williamsport and that Capt. Russell of the 1st Maryland Cavalry had just returned after burning a bridge and aqueduct [presumably at Williamsport] and who then left immediately for the [Antietam] battlefield, *OR*, vol. 19, pt. 2, 320.

Late in the day, between 3 and 4 P.M., Gen. Lee had Jackson send Stuart to the north to probe the Union extreme right flank with a design to turn it, and perhaps have the army escape to Hagerstown. Stuart called in Hampton's Brigade from near Lee's headquarters west of Sharpsburg. It had camped there after returning from Harpers Ferry earlier in the day on the 17th, crossing at Knott's Ford, with some of his troopers crossing at Boteler's. Added to Fitzhugh Lee's Brigade and the 7th Virginia Cavalry from Munford, Stuart had seven regiments of cavalry, to which he added nine guns from various batteries, one from Poague's, two from Raine's, and three from Brockenbrough's, under Capt. John Pelham, and in addition, the batteries of French and Branch, and for good measure the 48th North Carolina Infantry. Starting at about 3 P.M., the column marched to New Industry on the Potomac north from Cox's farm with the 4th Virginia Cavalry in the van. Pelham turned right on the road leading to the Hagerstown Pike where the toll gate (today's Mondell Road) was located, then turned left and took position on the higher ground some ¾ mile directly west of Doubleday's guns located on Poffenberger Hill. Pelham quickly found after firing a few rounds that Federal artillery was numerous and well placed, so withdrew within twenty minutes, perhaps regretting his laughter and his statement that "we must stir them up a little and then slip away;" Confederate guns under Branch and French placed on Nicodemus Heights were also quickly silenced. Stuart reported that because of the meander of the Potomac at this point, the Union guns were only 800 yards away leaving a much too narrow gap through which to pass. In the evening, Stuart suggested to Jackson that a knoll which had been abandoned, be reoccupied, as it was a commanding height on the northern end of the field. Jackson agreed sending some fifty men to that point to deny it to the Union.[102]

Overleaf: map shows position of Pleasonton's Cavalry Division at 5 P.M. as Brig. Gen. George Sykes's Regulars consolidate its lines near Sharpsburg showing how close Union troops came to Cemetery Hill at the arrow at left center. Cemetery Ridge was also known as Sharpsburg Ridge and the head of the arrow shows where the area where Gen. Lee spent much of his time watching the Union advance. There was a small cemetery next to the Lutheran Church but after the war, a national cemetery was established on the south side of the Boonsboro Pike uphill from the Lutheran Church Cemetery and later a county cemetery across the Boonsboro Pike was plotted. Note that Carman used the name "Cemetery Hill" for the part of the ridge to the south of the Boonsboro Pike and "Cemetery Ridge" for the ridge north of the pike, Carman, Pierro, 173. The right center arrow points to the Newcomer houses north of Boonsboro Pike and barn and mills south of the Pike. Note the mill dam just downstream of the Middle Bridge. Map courtesy Brian Downey "Antietam on the Web."

[102] Douglas, 172-173; Carman, Pierro, 309-312; OR, vol. 19, pt. 1, 957, 1010. Note Carman's remarks about Stuart's apparent surprise upon learning that the bend of the Potomac narrows so much the avenue for escape around the Union right flank. Carman apparently put his remark here even though Stuart made it the day before according to editor Pierro, Carman, Pierro, 311, n. 52. Carman opines that a single horseman could have discovered the topography of that area very easily before this time, 312. See also Krick, "Defending Lee's Flank," 212-213 writing that Pelham rounded up eight guns. Compare Poague, 47-48, who wrote that Pelham was criticized for this improvident action but then opined that it was up to Stuart and Gen. Lee, so Pelham was just following instructions. He wrote that his only remaining piece, which he contributed to Stuart's attempt, along with six or eight other guns, "failed completely, being silenced in fifteen or twenty minutes by a most terrific fire from a number of the enemy's batteries, OR, vol. 19, pt. 1, 1010. The distance from the Potomac "meander" to Doubleday's guns was about one airline mile.

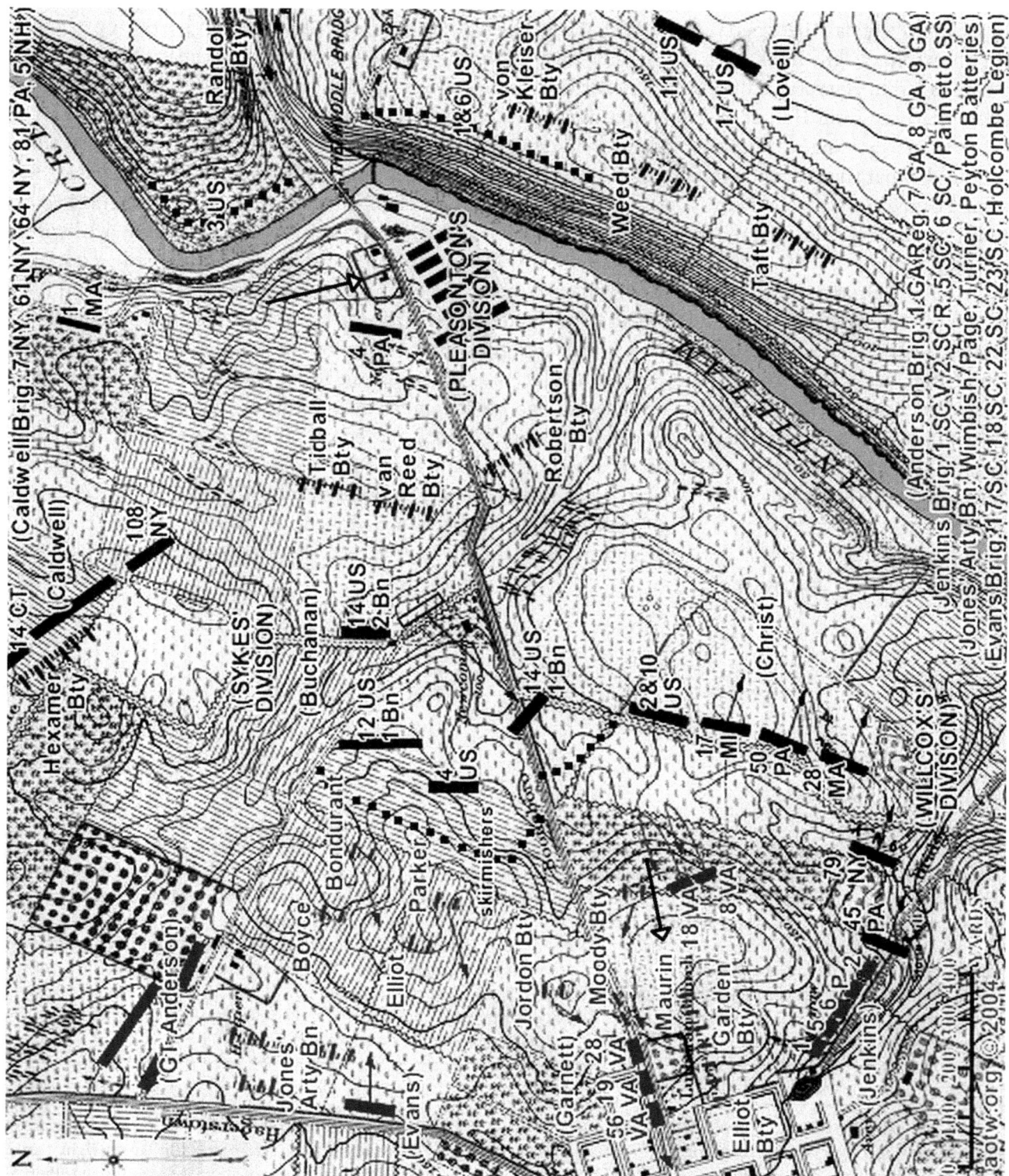

CREEK

Randol Bty

MIDDLE BRIDGE

3 US

1&6 US

von Kleiser Bty

Weed Bty

11 US

17 US (Lovell)

Taft Bty

ANTIETAM

(Caldwell Brig) 7 NY, 61 NY, 64 NY, 81 PA, 5 (NH)

1 MA

4 PA

PLEASONTON'S DIVISION

Tidball Bty

van Reed Bty

Robertson Bty

(Caldwell)

Hexamer Bty

108 NY

(SYKES DIVISION)

(Buchanan)

14 US 2 Bn

14 US 1 Bn

2&10 US

(Christ)

1/7 MI

50 PA

28 MA

(WILLCOX'S DIVISION)

14 CT

12 US 1 Bn

4 US

Bondurant

skirmishers

Parker

79 NY

45 PA

(GT Anderson)

Jones Arty Bn

Boyce

Elliot

Jordon Bty

Moody Bty

Maurin

Campbell 18 VA

8 VA

Garden Bty

6 P 2 (NJ)

(Jenkins)

Hagerstown

(Evans)

(Garnett)

56 VA

19 VA

28 VA

Elliot Bty

N

(Anderson Brig) 1 GA Reg, 7 GA, 8 GA, 9 GA

(Jenkins Brig) 1 SCV, 2 SCR, 5 SC, 6 SC, Palmetto SS

(Jones Arty Bn) Wimbish, Page, Turner, Peyton Batteries

(Evans Brig) 17 SC, 18 SC, 22 SC, 23 SC, Holcombe Legion

aotw.org © 2004

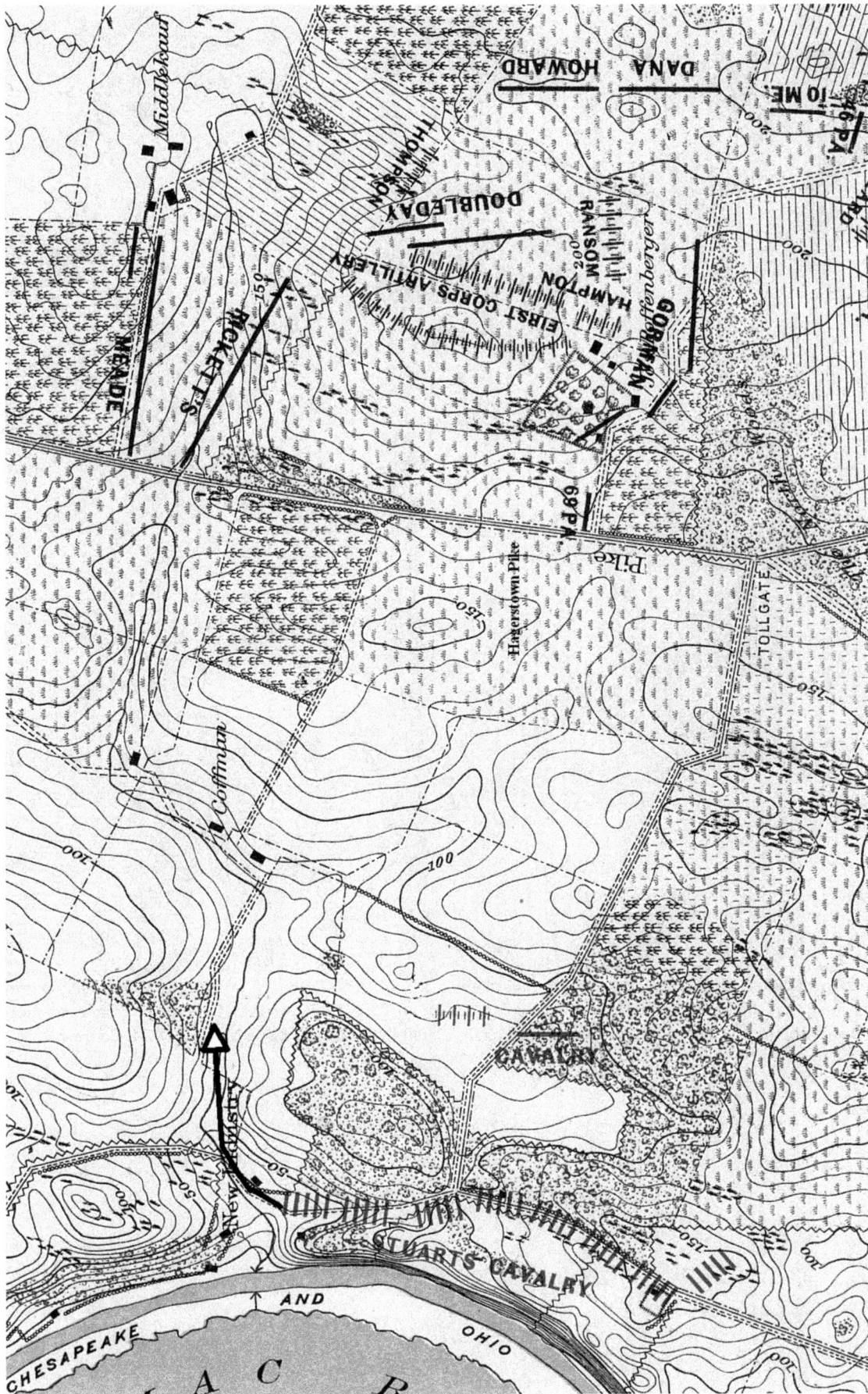

Stuart begins his Scout on Lee's left flank heading for the farm road at the Coffman Farm which connects with the Hagerstown Pike north of the Joseph Poffenberger Farm; 3:30-3:45 P.M. Hagerstown Pike to the right. Detail from Carman-Cope's map. Courtesy LOC.

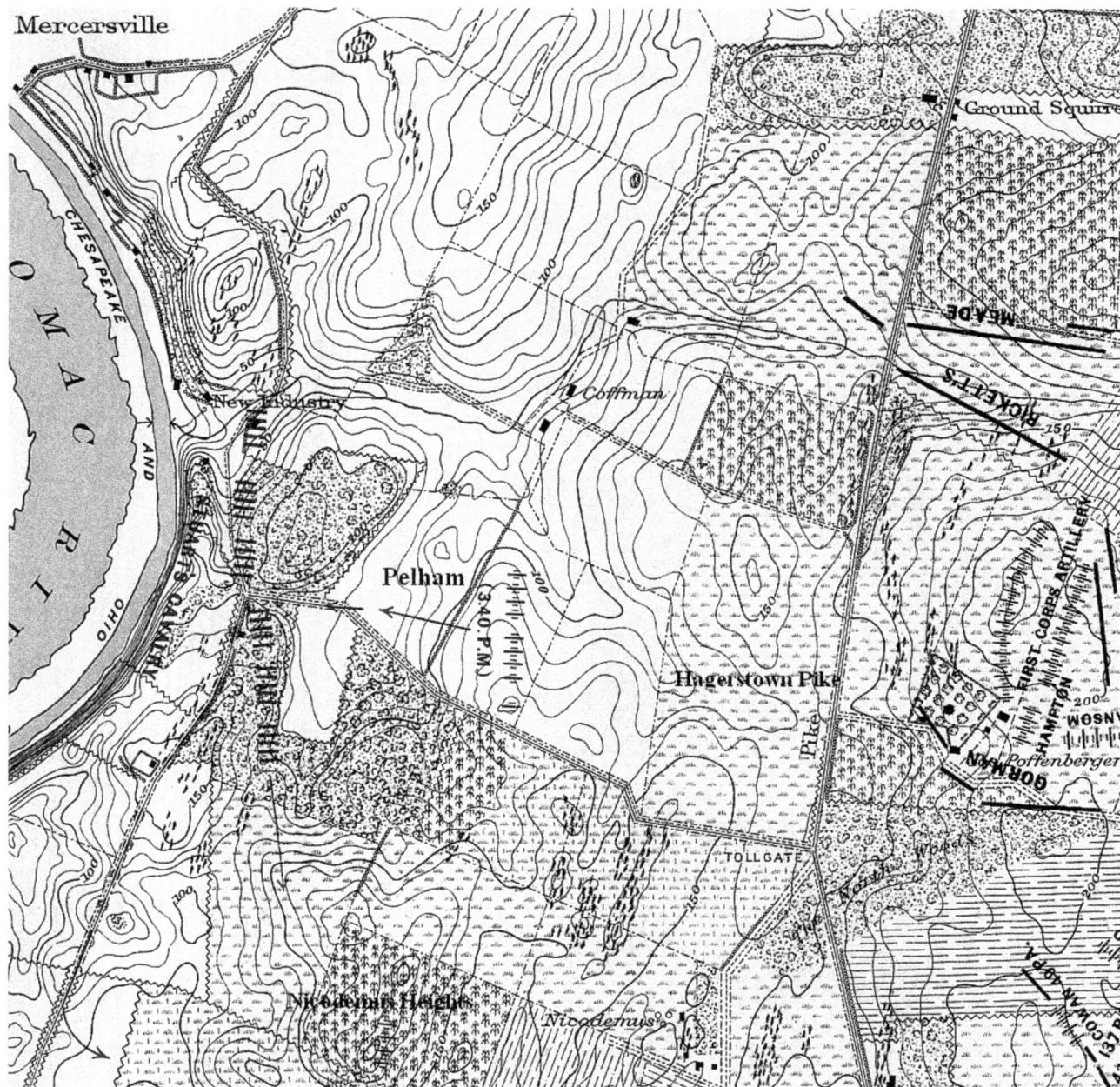

Stuart's withdrawal after failed scout on Lee's left flank; Pelham's guns came within ½ mile of the Union First Corps artillery. Nicodemus Heights at the lower center. Massed Union First Corps artillery, 44 guns total. The distance from the Union gun line to Pelham's artillery on Nicodemus Heights was about ¾ mile. Detail from Carman-Cope Map 4:20 P.M. Courtesy LOC.

Position of Stuart's Cavalry Division at 5:30 P.M. covering the left flank. Note that Stuart has twelve guns on Nicodemus Heights placed after he returned from his failed scout to the north. Courtesy LOC.

The 17th ended with the majority of Pleasonton's cavalry bivouacked where it was first located on 16 September near McClellan's headquarters toward Keedysville. Stuart was back on Nicodemus Heights with his artillery and his cavalry on a line connecting Cobb's troops to the Potomac; Munford, now with four regiments, was still guarding Gen. Lee's extreme right flank. All were awaiting McClellan's expected attack the next day, Thursday, 18 September.[103]

---

[103] Carman says that on the evening of the 17th the Union cavalry "returned to the bivouac near Keedysville," Carman, Pierro, 320. Earlier he wrote that they were located "just west of Keedysville," 202; then "his "cavalry division bivouacked on the night of the sixteenth in the west suburbs of Keedysville," 317. Interestingly, the Carman-Cope maps show the annotation that the cavalry's location is "approximate only." Crowninshield of the 1st Massachusetts Cavalry wrote that "The regiment bivouacked in a little piece of woods close on the main road, at a place called Keedysville," 76; later he recalled that "About dark (of the 17th) the cavalry was withdrawn, recrossing the Antietam Creek further to the westward, and it went into bivouac after dark in the old place at Keedysville," 80. Abner Hard of the 8th Illinois Cavalry wrote that on "September 16th, we remained in the woods a mile or two in advance of Keedysville, and not more than that distance from the enemy's line," 184. He then wrote that that evening his "regiment was marched back half a mile and rested for the night," 186, implying that they did not return to camp the night of the 17th. Likely most Pleasonton's cavalry stayed in and around the same bivouac between Keedysville and

A drawing by Alfred Rudolph Waud showing a skirmish between the Brooklyn 14th and 300 Rebel cavalry drawn 17 September 1862. The 14th Brooklyn was also known as 84th New York Infantry Regiment. There is nothing in the New Yorker's regimental history about being attacked by cavalry anytime during the Maryland Campaign or even Second Bull Run. The only possible source found in this history is an incident during which they were attacked by 500 Rebel cavalry under Fitz Lee on 18 Nov 1861 while the regiment was on picket duty near Falls Church, Virginia, losing two killed, three wounded, and 10 prisoners.[104] Waud apparently made it up as a composite or an exaggeration of what he saw and it is possible that he heard about the 1861 incident and mixed up the fact. Late on 16 September 1862 four companies of the 13th Pennsylvania Reserves fought with some Confederate Cavalry from the 9th Virginia on the Smoketown Road but the Rebel horsemen were quickly driven back. The regiment's commander, Col. Hugh W. McNeil, was killed not long after. The 13th was in the Third Division of the First Corps while the 14th was in the First Division of that corps. Carman, Pierro, 207. Courtesy LOC.

McClellan's headquarters at the Pry House from their arrival on the field on the 15th to the 19th when cavalry regiments bivouacked in Sharpsburg, 189; Crowninshield, 81. Perhaps McClellan wanted them to be close to his headquarters but also with quick access to the Keedysville-Williamsport Road and Boonsboro- Sharpsburg Pike.

[104] D.R. Marquis, C.V. Tevis, *The History of the Fighting Fourteenth, Published in Commemoration of the Fiftieth Anniversary of the Muster of the Regiment into the United States Service, May 23, 1881* (Brooklyn, NY: Brooklyn Eagle Press, 1911), 28-29.

Dramatic depiction of the use of much Confederate and Union cavalry during the battle on 17 September. Sketch by F.H. Schell from *The Soldier in Our Civil War*, Vol. 1, pg. 398.

Chapter 10

Cavalry after the Battle—Shepherdstown and Williamsport

THE DAY AFTER THE HORROR of Wednesday 17 September around Antietam Creek, was met with apprehension from soldiers in both armies. Most men on the battlefield that Thursday woke at dawn to overcast skies confident that the battle would be renewed, while more than a few Union men hoped that Lee would have retreated over the Potomac. Only a handful knew that the action on the Antietam battlefield was done, and would shift over the next few days to two locations, one in Virginia near and just downriver from Shepherdstown at Boteler's Ford, and in Maryland at Williamsport, upriver some 12 airline miles. The evening of 17 September, Lee ordered his commanders to hold their lines and bring up their stragglers so that if McClellan wanted to fight the next morning, they would be ready. Lee, hunkered down in his contracted lines, was clearly not ready to give up his Maryland adventure. McClellan pondered whether to attack but decided against it since he was not certain of a victory and he reckoned that, as his army was the last organized field army available in the east, its defeat would have meant that Lee would have free rein to attack major northern cities at will. Additionally, his troops were fatigued and somewhat demoralized and lacked food to confront Lee's numbers which McClellan still believed surpassed his own. Therefore, the 18th was not propitious for a Union attack; McClellan wanted to be resupplied, have ammunition replenished, and bring up reinforcements. He still believed Lee was dangerous and that the Federals were outnumbered—it was not a time for rash action when facing such a dangerous foe as the sanguinary battle on the 17th demonstrated all too clearly.[1]

On the 18th after pondering his option, Lee decided to cross the Potomac back to Virginia. That night, his army crossed successfully at Boteler's Ford without hindrance from McClellan. After talking with Gen. Lee that day, Jackson sent his topographical engineer, Hotchkiss, to look for other fords. Gen. Lee met with Stuart several times on the 18th and then decided to send Stuart to Williamsport to create a diversion for his army's retreat, and to secure fords there, so that Lee's army would be able to cross back

---

[1] Carman, Pierro, 365-367. Around midnight on the 18th, apparently some of Burnside's cavalry skirmished with Rebel sharpshooters at the Sherrick house northwest of Burnside Bridge. A squadron of cavalry galloped up the road from the bridge and attacked the house which was just outside of the Union line. A nearby Union infantryman wrote that "We could hear the crackling of carbines, the intermingled cheers and yells, and soon they [Union cavalry] came back, reporting that the 'Johnnies' had gone out of the house like 'rats,'" Carter, *Four Brothers in Blue*, 116. But see Priest, *Antietam*, 315, who places this encounter on the Lower Bridge Road at the same house about 8:30 P.M. when the Union cavalry rode into part of Robert Toombs's Brigade. In the affray, in which the Yankee horsemen quickly realized that the infantry there was not friendly, Toombs was wounded in the hand. He apparently was with his staff during the melee; William Y. Thompson, "Robert Toombs, Confederate General," *Civil War History*, vol. 7, no. 4, Dec. 1961, 419. Toombs was "on his way to the headquarters of Colonel Benning…when a troop of cavalry rode up. He challenged them, and they answered 'We are friends.' Captain Troup of this staff, however, detected the ruse and fired into them. The squad returned the fire. General Toombs was shot through the hand with which he was holding the reins," Pleasant A. Stovall, *Robert Toombs: Statesman, Speaker, Soldier, Sage* (New York: Cassell Publishing Company, 1892), 268. Longstreet's report perhaps with exaggeration described it as severe, *OR*, vol. 19, pt. 1, 841.

into Maryland and continue its trek to Hagerstown, and perhaps along the Cumberland Valley in Pennsylvania; even at this late date after horrendous casualties at Antietam, Lee believed his Maryland Campaign still had life and everything he did showed that he acted on that belief.[2]

Fitzhugh's Lee's Brigade spent the 18th gathering an "immense" number of Confederate stragglers and many Union wounded and that night, took position in the northern suburbs of Sharpsburg, staying awake all night into the morning of the 19th, covering the army's retreat. The brigade then crossed at Boteler's Ford and another ford nearer Shepherdstown reining in one and a half miles from the Potomac River in Virginia, resting and feeding their horses.[3] Pleasonton's men also gathered stragglers and picketed roads in addition to having two squadrons of cavalry scouting on both sides of Elk Ridge to the south near Harpers Ferry, following McClellan's somewhat vague orders to "continue to scout up and down the country as specified until further orders.[4] The main body of Pleasonton's regiments remained in bivouac in their old Keedysville campground. On the morning of the 18th, McClellan ordered Franklin to send the 1st and 6th Regiments U.S. Cavalry, and their horse artillery, to Pleasonton, certainly welcome news to the cavalry division commander. The 1st had been assigned to Quartermaster's Guard and some to McClellan's headquarters' guard; the 6th was picketing in both Middletown and Pleasant Valleys, while some remained with Franklin's Corps then north of Sharpsburg as provost guards on the army's right, also gathering in stragglers. Pleasonton was ordered to "push small cavalry reconnaissances to the right, left, and front of the position now occupied by this army, and to communicate …information…in relation to the strength, position, and movements of the enemy." Also later that morning, Burnside was ordered to send some of his cavalry to scout south toward Harpers Ferry and down to the mouth of the Antietam, likely to catch Rebel stragglers and to scout enemy movements on the left flank of the Union line. Some of Burnside's troopers later skirmished with Munford's videttes near Antietam Creek on the 18th.[5] At 4 A.M. on the 19th, McClellan ordered Pleasonton to ascertain, as had been reported by Sumner, if the Rebels were in fact felling trees behind them as they retired. And if the enemy were retreating, Pleasonton should mass his troopers and hold them ready to move in any direction. Finally, the cavalry commander was ordered "to send out small cavalry detachments on the various roads leading from our position in the direction of the enemy's retreat, to ascertain the nature and degree of the obstructions therein."[6]

---

[2] Hotchkiss, 83; Harsh, *Flood*, 444-445. On 20 September, some of Fitzhugh Lee's troopers from the 9th Virginia Cavalry accompanied A.P. Hill's Confederate infantry as it pushed intruding Yankee infantry back across the Potomac at Boteler's Ford, Beale, *9th Virginia*, 43. The troopers then picketed the ford until the next day when it followed the infantry away from Shepherdstown. See also Stonewall Jacksons report, *OR*, vol. 19, pt. 1, 957, which mentions Fitzhugh Lee's troopers.

[3] William R. Carter, 17. On the morning of the 18th the 4th Virginia Cavalry was employed on Provost Guard duty between Boteler's Ford and Sharpsburg collecting straggling infantry. About midnight on the 18th they moved to the left of the infantry line and then down that line withdrawing all the infantry pickets reaching Sharpsburg about sunrise on the morning of the 19th. There the regiment halted to rest for at least an hour while the rear guard of the retreating infantry pickets withdrew and then the 4th retreated before the advancing Union cavalry to Boteler's Ford; letter from Pitfield George to Carman 4 March 1895 courtesy of Thomas Clemens.

[4] *OR*, vol. 19, pt. 1, 212; vol. 51, pt. 1, 849, 850.

[5] *OR*, vol. 51, pt. 1, 848-849.

[6] Ibid., 852.

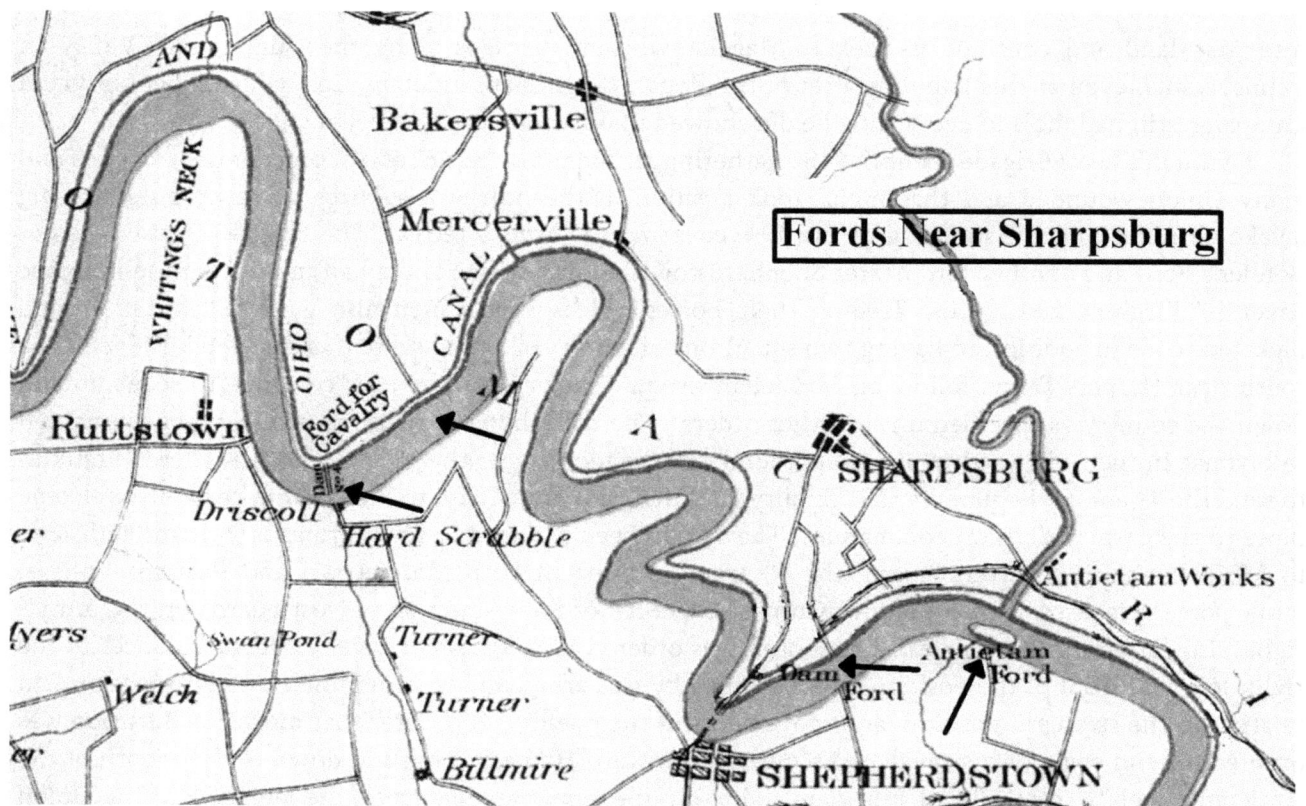

Fords are shown at arrows. "Dam Ford" is also known as Boteler's/Blackford's/Packhorse/ Shepherdstown Ford; "Antietam Ford" is also known as Knott's Ford, the island there is Knott's Island. The ford at Dam 4 was just below the dam, but distinct from Shepherd's Island Ford just below, shown here by the arrow just below Dam 4. "Shepherd's Ford (Shepherd's Island Ford, Sheppard's Ford) – Located above Mercersville (Taylor's Landing) at Shepherd's Island, at about mile marker 83 [on the C&O Canal towpath], this ford was noted as being good for cavalry in the *Official Records Atlas*," Snyder, Manuscript, 17. *Official Atlas*, Plate 69. Courtesy LOC.

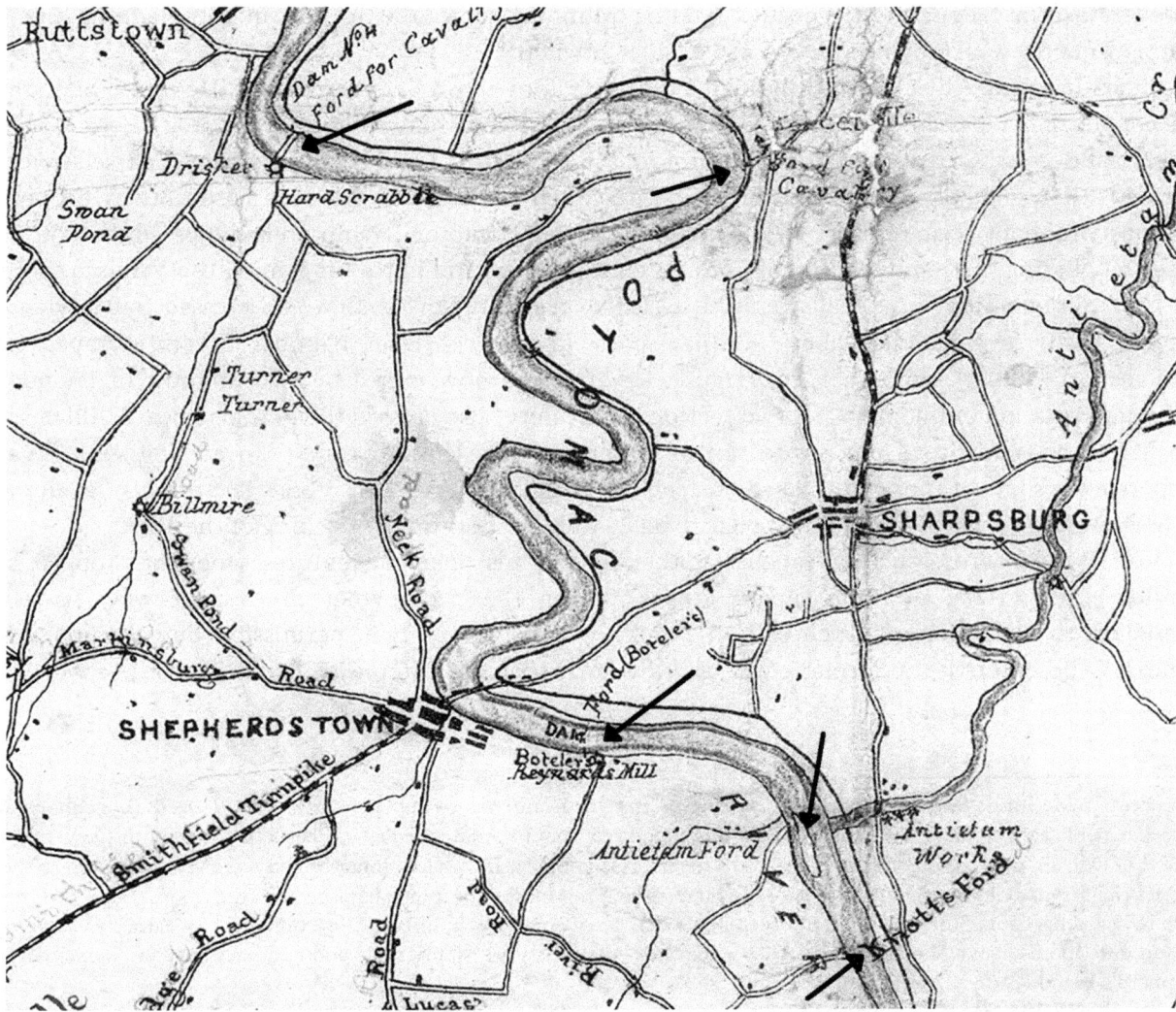

Detail from map showing five fords, from the top, a ford at Dam No. 4, upper center at arrow; just downstream of this ford is Shepherd's Island, shown here by the arrow just below Dam 4; Boteler's Ford, Antietam Ford and Knott's Ford at lower center, may be the same one, if not, then the mapmakers believed that Knott's Ford was just south of Antietam Ford. This map shows two cavalry fords above Shepherdstown one of which Hampton likely used, the one located near Mercersville at the upper center arrow. Detail from map of Upper Potomac from McCoy's Ferry to Conrad's Ferry and adjacent portions of Maryland and Virginia Col. J. N. Macomb, A.D.C. Lt. Col. Engrs with additions and corrections by Lt. Col. D.H. Strother, A.D.C. Engineer Department, 1863. Courtesy LOC.

Munford was still picketing near the mouth of Antietam Creek with the 2nd, 7th and 12th Virginia Cavalry along with the 17th Battalion of Munford's Brigade, which had rejoined Munford after its detached duty south of Harpers Ferry. He was busy that day skirmishing with some Union cavalry, the 6th New York, and never received the retreat order. Finally on the morning of the 19th, he rode to Sharpsburg and learned from Fitzhugh Lee of the retreat. He quickly returned to his troopers, formed them up, and crossed later on the 19th, ending up guarding the right of the Confederate line at Boteler's Ford on the Virginia side of the Potomac. Later in the day, Munford requested help from Pendleton, who was in command of Gen. Lee's rearguard, asking for infantry support, as he saw Union troops moving downriver on the Maryland side looking, he thought, for a place to cross and worry the retreating

Confederate army. Pendleton reported sending Munford some 100 to 200 infantry adding the 9th Virginia Infantry which by now was down to some 60 men.[7]

Stuart instructed Blackford to find a good cavalry ford above Shepherdstown. He found one which was not ideal but passable without swimming, so Stuart told him to guide Hampton there with his troopers and cross. Stuart, with part of Munford's 12th Virginia Cavalry and Pelham's Horse Artillery, vied with thousands of infantry and crossed with much difficulty at Boteler's Ford.[8] Stuart arrived in Williamsport about noon on Friday 19 September beating Hampton. Hampton had crossed the Potomac, Blackford guiding, with much difficulty, losing some troopers and horses in gaining the Virginia shore at this very difficult ford.[9] He finally arrived with five regiments of cavalry, and crossed to Maryland at Mason's Ford, several miles above Williamsport, just below Dam Number 5, and camped near Williamsport.[10] Stuart, with the 12th Virginia Cavalry, and now joined by two infantry regiments, an additional battalion of infantry, and two sections of artillery, also crossed the Potomac near Williamsport into Maryland, and drove off a squadron of Union cavalry. Union cavalry skirmishing with Stuart's troopers were some of those which had escaped from Harpers Ferry: Col. Voss's 12th Illinois Cavalry and the 8th New York Cavalry, both of which arrived at Williamsport on the evening of the 18th.

Von Borcke wrote this day about another one of his many adventures when he stopped at a farmhouse to partake of some superb grapes. Seeing the homeowner in the doorway, he asked permission to pluck some branches. Von Borcke was not only given permission but also invited to dinner. As he entered, the farmer's wife saw his torn coat and offered to mend it on the spot. As he

---

[7] Thomas A. McGrath, *Shepherdstown: Last Clash of the Antietam Campaign, September 19-20, 1862* (Lynchburg, VA: Schroeder publications, 2007), 69-70. McGrath's thorough book about the Shepherdstown battle is the only one covering this battle. *OR*, vol. 19, pt. 1, 832, contains Pendleton's report. It is not clear how many infantrymen were sent to Munford; the 9th Virginia Infantry may have been only some of the infantry sent to Munford or it may have been all the troops sent.

[8] Due to the congestion, Stuart or some of his troopers may have crossed at a different ford upriver, McGrath, 21. There were two identified fords above Shepherdstown before the Dam 4 Ford, one at Mercersville and another above at Shepherd's Ford (Shepherd's Island Ford).

[9] Blackford, 152-154. See also Snyder: "Reynold's Ford – A period newspaper identifies the location of Reynold's Ford as opposite Shepherdstown (but distinct from Botelor's Ford). While seeking additional routes of egress from Maryland after Antietam, Jeb Stuart reported that his horsemen crossed at another nearby ford that was 'obscure and rough.' Other accounts described the cavalry crossing over a fish dam....Wade Hampton's brigade became lost in the darkness and had to swim many of their horses across," Snyder, Manuscript, 16. Brooks wrote that after Antietam because they were cut off from the Shepherdstown ford they had to go up river and "on Friday night, by a circuitous route...winding down steep and dangerous cliffs, that seemed impassable for man and beast...we plunged into the channel of the river—a fording that an Indian pony would snort at and turn away from—our horses, after blundering over rocks, then plunging through eddying whirlpools, dripping and chilled, we reached the Virginia side," *Stories of the Confederacy*, 95. Howard said that "The night after the last day's fight, General Hampton led us across the Potomac between Falling Waters and Sharpsburg, at an old blind ford, and such an experience rarely comes to horse and rider. Standing on rocks half leg deep in water, the next step would plunge horse and rider into it up to the neck," 3-4. The 1st North Carolina Cavalry started fording about 11 P.M. and found the night dark and the ford difficult as it was rocky and had high bluffs so troopers crossed single file, one at a time. As the lead troopers halted some fell asleep so men in the rear stopped for about an hour not knowing the reason for the delay; guides were posted to prevent a recurrence, Carman note, ANBL, 1st North Carolina Regimental File. Hampton wrote Carman on 23 May 1897 that the ford "was a blind, rocky, and deep one, several miles above the battlefield," copy courtesy of Thomas Clemens.

[10] Hampton's crossing and ride to Williamsport was eventful in the dark with one unit getting lost, Hopkins, 101. It is not clear why he did not cross at the Williamsport Ford unless he was concerned that Yankees were possibly present. The location of Mason's Ford below Dam 5 is not clear with some sources believing that they were two fords, Mason's and one just below Dam 5; it is possible that the Dam 5 Ford and Mason's Ford are the same, Snyder, Manuscript, 19-20. Light's Ford at Williamsport was described by a South Carolina infantryman as "knee-deep, and clear enough for us to see and avoid the rocks," James Caldwell, *The History of a Brigade of South Carolinians* (Philadelphia, PA: King & Baird, Printers, 1866), 41. Neese described the ford as "about two feet deep, with a gentle current and smooth gravelly bottom," 149.

waited for the repairs in his shirtsleeves, he heard hoof beats and saw a squadron of Yankees approaching at a gallop.

> With one bound I cleared the drawing-room, leaving coat and dinner behind, and ran to my horse, which, participating in his master's alarm, was jumping and plunging so furiously that it was quite an acrobatic feat to mount him. Meanwhile the hostile dragoons had arrived within twenty steps of me, brandishing their sabres and yelling like demons….At this critical moment, a couple of shells from two of our guns, which had been put in position on an acclivity commanding the turnpike, a mile off, whizzed close over my head, and with admirable aim exploded in the very midst of the advancing foe, emptying several saddles. At the same instant was heard the war-cry of a squadron of our Virginia horsemen sent by General Stuart to my relief. Their onset and the terrible effect of our artillery made the Yankees wheel and run much faster than they had come; and thus was saved my life and liberty, coat and dinner. Joining our men in the pursuit, I had the satisfaction of overtaking and capturing several of the recent disturbers of my peace…. One of our guns on this occasion had been fired off by a fair young lady of Williamsport, re-enacting the part of the Maid of Saragossa. She had solicited the honour from General Stuart, and the cannon was ever afterwards called by our artillerymen "The Girl of Williamsport." During the afternoon we drove the enemy back for a considerable distance, and our line of pickets was established about four miles from the Potomac, on the roads leading through Maryland into Pennsylvania. Late in the evening I received orders from General Stuart to make a reconnaissance with two squadrons of the Georgia regiment of Hampton's brigade, along the turnpike leading to Hagerstown, and ran against a strong body of the Federal cavalry, whom we at once attacked and chased into the suburbs of the town. Here large reinforcements received us with so galling a fire that we were obliged to give up the pursuit.[11]

That evening, typical for Stuart and his staff, especially when away from the watchful eyes of superior generals, an enjoyable supper and entertainment was had: "At night General Stuart was invited with his Staff to a little party in Williamsburg [Williamsport], where we had a capital supper, and where, with music and the dance, in the society of some very charming young ladies, the time went merrily by, till we joined our troops, at a late hour, in their bivouac."[12] Apparently Stuart was back to form after less than ideal conditions for frivolity at Sharpsburg the previous few days.

On 20 September, von Borcke continues to write about the Confederate adventure near Williamsport, and another one of his close encounters with the Yankees thanks to Stuart:

> Our regiments moved early to the front the following day, as our scouts had reported the enemy, largely reinforced, to be advancing slowly upon our outposts. At General Stuart's request, I accompanied him on one of those little reconnoitring expeditions outside our lines, of which he was so fond, and which were always likely to terminate disastrously, as in this instance was so near being the case. We observed the precaution in the start of keeping as much as possible concealed by the dense undergrowth of the forest, but we had nevertheless been observed by some of the Yankee pickets, and a body of about twenty-five horsemen had been quietly sent to our rear, cutting us off completely from our command. We were riding along at our ease,

---

[11] Von Borcke, 171-172. The Maid of Saragossa was a heroine of Spain's war against Napoleon. On June 15, 1808, the French army stormed the Portillo, an ancient gateway into Saragossa "defended by a hodgepodge battery of old cannons and a heavily outnumbered volunteer unit. Agustina [the Maid], arriving on the ramparts with a basket of apples to feed the gunners, watched the nearby defenders fall to French bayonets. The Spanish troops broke ranks, having suffered heavy casualties, and abandoned their posts. With the French troops a few yards away, Agustina herself ran forward, loaded a cannon, and lit the fuse, shredding a wave of attackers at point blank range. The sight of a lone woman bravely manning the cannons inspired the fleeing Spanish troops and other volunteers to return and assist her. After a bloody struggle, the French gave up the assault… and abandoned their siege for a few short weeks before returning to fight their way into the city, house-by-house….[the city] was forced to surrender the city to the French. Despite the eventual defeat, Agustina's action became an inspiration to those opposing the French. Courtesy Wikipedia, "Agustina de Aragón."

[12] Von Borcke, 172.

when my sharp ear detected the little clinking sound which a sabre-scabbard often makes in striking against a tree in a ride through the woods; and, believing that one of our couriers was approaching, I turned leisurely round, and saw the long line of the hostile cavalrymen, each man riding at about twenty steps interval from his neighbour, a short distance behind us. A few quietly uttered words informed General Stuart of the impending danger, when, putting spurs to our horses, we galloped off, feeling confident that a hot pursuit would follow, in the confusion of which we might make good our escape. Accordingly, we had a regular fox-chase. The whole body of the Yankees broke forward in a run, calling out to each other, and firing their revolvers in every direction. But we were too well mounted, and too much accustomed to riding through the tangled thickets of the forest, to be overtaken; so in a short time, when the Federal troopers had been a good deal scattered by their rough and rapid motion, we slipped through them and got over to our lines again before the astonished blue-jackets had recovered from their amazement and chagrin.[13]

Von Borcke details his actions after Stuart put him in command of the left wing as Stuart and his Staff rode off to the extreme right.

My principal care was to guard a broad turnpike road leading from Williamsport into the interior of Maryland, along which an advance of a considerable body of the enemy was expected, and where small parties of their cavalry had already appeared I had two pieces of artillery very favourably posted, and two companies of infantry, which, to prevent a sudden dash of the Yankee horsemen, I employed in making a barricade across the road, flanked by small intrenchments stretching out about fifty yards on either side. From time to time I had to check the impudent advance of the Federal cavalry by a shot from my two guns, but altogether there was comparative quiet for several hours.

One of the Yankee officers, who, as I was later informed, was the colonel of the regiment that had effected its escape from Harper's Ferry, had attracted my attention the previous day by his gallantry and the excellent dispositions he made of his troops. Here I saw him again, galloping very near us on a handsome grey horse, quickly discovering our weak points, and posting and instructing his men accordingly. After having left him undisturbed for some time, I thought it necessary to put a stop to his proceedings, and, selecting a couple of my infantrymen who had been pointed out to me as the best shots, I made across the open space in front of our lines directly toward him. Having arrived within reasonable distance, I ordered my sharpshooters to fire at the daring colonel, who was moving along at an easy gallop, without paying me the slightest attention. After several bullets had whistled quite close to him, he suddenly halted, and, turning round, advanced a few steps and made me a military salute in the most graceful manner possible. Then calling out to one of his men to hand him a carbine, he raised the weapon, took a deliberate aim at me, and sent his ball so close to my head that I thought it had carried away a lock of my hair. I saluted him now on my part, and, wheeling round quietly, both of us rode back to our respective lines. So are courtesies sometimes exchanged in the midst of hostile conflict.[14]

---

[13] Ibid., 173. Von Borcke seems to have more exciting escapes from the Yankees than any other member of Stuart's staff.

[14] Ibid., 174-175. If von Borcke is correct about the Union cavalry colonel being one who had escaped from Harpers Ferry, it may have been Col. Voss leading his 12th Illinois Cavalry. Late on 19 September, Voss was at Jones's Cross Roads where he joined a detachment from Maj. Gen. Couch's division and marched to Williamsport. McClellan also informed Franklin that he would be joined by a brigade of infantry from Hagerstown under command of Brig. Gen. John R. Kenly, *OR*, vol. 51, pt. 1, 855. Kenly (also incorrectly Kenley) had cavalry available from the 15th Pennsylvania but it is not clear if these troopers were involved in action on the 20th nor is it clear if he was in command of them or any other cavalry unit. Kenly was in command of the Maryland Brigade which consisted of the 1st, 4th, 6th, 7th, and 8th Maryland Infantry and Capt. Frederick W. Alexander's Battery which operated along the upper Potomac and ventured into neighboring Virginia, Harold R. Manakee, *Maryland in the Civil War* (Baltimore, MD: Garamond/Pridemark Press, 1969), 109. When Lee invaded in September 1862, Kenly was put in command of the Maryland Brigade after having been in command of all the infantry in Baltimore and then hastened west to assist McClellan on 17 September; *OR*, vol. 19, pt. 2, 280, 312. On 24 September, Kenly reported to McClellan that he arrived in Hagerstown the night of the 19th and was ordered by Brig. Gen. Reynolds who was in command of the Pennsylvania militia, to move out on the Williamsport Pike with the Maryland Brigade and report to McClellan. Kenly did so and reported to McClellan's headquarters which then ordered him to join Gen. Couch's division at Williamsport. On 20 September, as Stuart was still there, Kenly reported that Reynolds directed him to remain in line of battle between Hagerstown and Williamsport.

As the day wore on, von Borcke and Pelham had a more pleasant encounter with some delicious fruit but their snack led to a fortuitous view of Union cavalry:

> During the afternoon, Pelham, who for the present had but little occupation with his artillery, and had been reconnoitring the enemy, rode up to me and told me that he had discovered, at five hundred yards' distance, an orchard of very fine peaches, a spot which was well worth visiting, because, while enjoying the fruit, we could obtain there a near view of the movements of the Federal cavalry, which were in considerable strength hard by, and thus combine the utile with the dulce. As all was quiet in my front, I readily consented to accompany him…and we were soon seated amid the branches of a large peach-tree, eating and looking out to our great satisfaction. The Federal cavalry, only a few hundred yards from us, was already four regiments strong, and farther off the rising clouds of dust indicated the approach of yet larger columns, so that it was evident our demonstration into Maryland had not failed of its desired effect, and that we occupied the attention of a considerable portion of M'Clellan's army.[15]

The Prussian major returned to the left flank where he received new orders from Stuart:

> I now returned to my former position, and sent an orderly with my report to General Stuart, from whom I received orders to transfer my present command to Major Pelham, and join him without delay on the   right. Here also the enemy's forces were heavily massed in front of us, and our scouts reported large columns of infantry, with cavalry and artillery, advancing upon all the roads leading toward Williamsport. In my opinion the time for our retreat had now arrived, but Stuart believed he could still hold his ground, and seemed determined not to give up until he had shown fight. As usual, he was exceedingly desirous of closely observing the enemy's movements himself, and forming his own judgment concerning them; and as he and I were riding very close upon their lines, we were several times chased by small bodies of Yankee horse, whom we only escaped by jumping the fences, which crossed the country on every hand, and which were rather too high for Northern horsemanship.
>
> In front of our centre, occupied by Hampton's brigade, no signs of the Yankees were to be observed, which led Stuart to the opinion that it would be practicable for his command to move forward under cover of the darkness of the night, make a circuit round Hagerstown, operate in the enemy's rear, and recross some ten miles higher up the Potomac. General Hampton, whose patrols had made prisoners of men belonging to several different divisions of the Federal army, believing that a very large portion, if not the whole, of M'Clellan's force was stretched out in a semicircle before him, regarded this operation as impossible, and remonstrated against it. But Stuart resolutely insisted on the execution of his daring design, and sent me back to Hampton with peremptory orders to march at once. This intrepid General instantly gave the command to move forward to what he so justly considered certain destruction, saying to me, "Good-bye, my dear friend; I don't think you will ever see me or a man of my brave brigade again." Agreeing with him perfectly as to the

---

The next day, Kenly reported to Franklin and received orders to march to Williamsport to relieve Col. Rush's command and hold the town to defend the ford over the Potomac. On the 21st, he reported that his force consisted of several battalions of his own brigade, about 1,600 men, eight guns of the Maryland battery under Capt. Wolcott, 120 cannoneers, seven companies of the 12th Illinois Cavalry, under Col. Voss, about 350 troopers, and two independent companies of Maryland cavalry under Capts. Russell and Grafflin, 100 troopers; *OR*, vol. 19, pt. 2, 356-357. Kenly also commented that the 6th Maryland Infantry and four guns, Capt. Alexander's battery, were not with him having been detained at Monocacy Junction by order of Gen. Wool even though Wool told Halleck that Wool had ordered the 6th and the artillery to Hagerstown along with Kenly's 1,700 infantry, ibid, 327. He also noted that he had sent a squadron of cavalry to Dam No. 5 five miles up the Potomac, another squadron to Hancock to watch fords from there down to Dam No. 5, and the rest of the cavalry to guard fords near Williamsport. It appears that as of 24 September, Col. Voss and seven companies of the 12th Illinois and perhaps the Maryland cavalry were still with Kenly; it is interesting that he does not mention the 15th Pennsylvania Cavalry perhaps as that was under direct command of Gen. Reynolds. On 1 October, McClellan reported that Kenly had 58 cavalry present, *OR*, vol. 19, pt. 1, 98. Apparently the 12th Illinois and a detachment of Maryland cavalry remained with Kenly as they were reported with him on 14 November, *OR*, vol. 19, pt. 2, 582.

[15] Von Borcke, 175.

impossibility of the undertaking, I felt sad and oppressed as, galloping back, I saw the last of the gallant horsemen disappearing in the darkness behind the hills.[16]

That night, Union troops continued to mass, completely surrounding Stuart's men at Williamsport, where Stuart had his back to the Potomac. He had wisely placed guns on the Virginia side to cover his retreat, which even the ever optimistic general had to realized was not too far off. Von Borcke wrote of another of his famous close calls: "Night had set in fairly when I returned to him [Stuart], and the enemy commencing to press upon us with cavalry, infantry, and artillery, a deafening cannonade ensued, filling the air with solid shot and shell, one of which latter missiles burst so near my head that for several minutes I was completely stunned."[17]

As the Unionists pressed ever closer with obvious strength, even Stuart finally realized that his Williamsport adventure was over so he sent von Borcke off to recall Hampton. Stuart told him to "'ride to him as quickly as your horse can carry you, and order him to return at once and recross the Potomac.' ....The night was pitch dark, the enemy's troops were spread out over the whole country, the ground was broken and difficult, and but partially known to me; but, more discouraging than all, my horse had been so worn down by the continued fatigues of the last few days, that I could scarcely spur him into a gallop.... After half an hour I heard the sound of hoofs in front of me, and had just put myself in readiness for the probable rencontre, when, to my surprise and delight, my challenge of 'Halt! Who are you?' was answered, 'It is I, Major—Captain Hamilton, of Hampton's Staff. Where can I find General Stuart?'"[18] Hamilton told von Borcke of Hampton's dire situation as Hampton had tried to break through the enemy's lines but had no success as his troopers met overwhelming numbers and decided to retreat against Stuart's orders. The Prussian sent Hamilton to report the situation to Stuart while he continued on to join Hampton who was by this time nearby with his column on the Williamsport-Hagerstown Pike. He piloted Hampton to and across the Potomac and then returned to Stuart who was approaching the river being hard pressed. He provides a picturesque description of Stuart's crossing: "This passage of the Potomac by night was one of those magnificent spectacles which are seen only in war. The whole landscape was lighted up with a lurid glare from the burning houses of Williamsport, which had been ignited by the enemy's shells. High over the heads of the crossing column and the dark waters of the river, the blazing bombs passed each other in parabolas of flame through the air, and the spectral trees showed their every limb and leaf against the red sky." Stuart's command marched some six miles toward Martinsburg happy that the Federals did not pursue them across the river and were also happy that they bivouacked at a large farm with abundant quantities of corn and hay sufficient for the whole command.[19] Once Gen. Lee learned of this retreat and Union strength, he knew that his plans for a return to Maryland were finished.[20]

---

[16] Ibid., 176. If von Borcke is correct, Stuart is hoping for another ride around McClellan to duplicate his Peninsula feat.

[17] Ibid., 177.

[18] Ibid., 177-178.

[19] Ibid.

[20] Carman, Pierro, 375-376; *OR*, vol. 19, pt. 1, 820-821; Trout, *Thunder*, 105; McClellan, *Stuart*, 133-134; Harsh, *Flood*, 448-452.

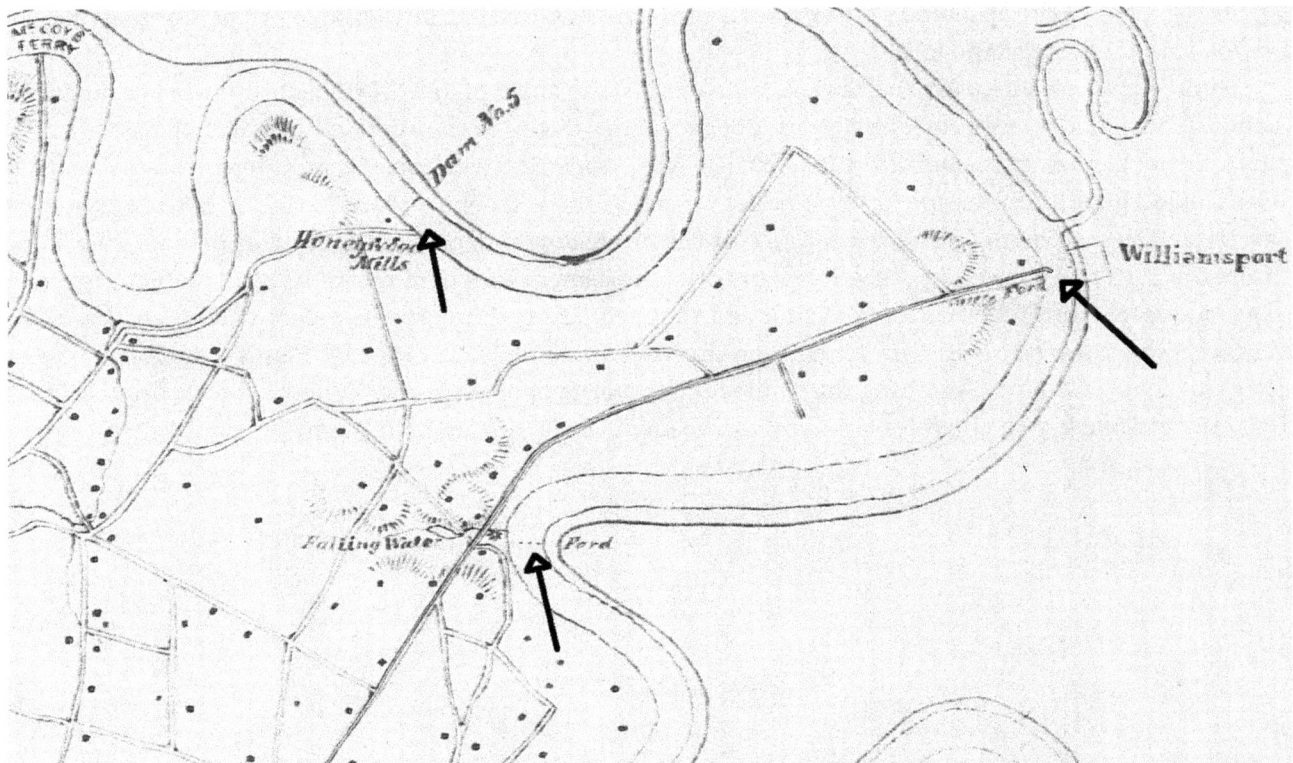

Detail of map showing fords at Williamsport at arrow, Light's Ford, and at Falling Waters below. Another ford apparently existed below Dam 5. Note McCoy's Ferry at upper left corner. There was also a ford there which Jeb Stuart used to begin his Second Ride Around McClellan in October 1862. The large road culvert under the canal helped in his ride up toward Chambersburg. Detail from Berkeley County, Virginia, by Col. J.N. Macomb for the use of Maj. Gen. Geo. B. McClellan, improved & extended by D.H. Strother, Lt. Col. 3d. Va. Cavalry, 1861. Courtesy LOC.

When McClellan heard of Stuart's incursion on the 19th, he sent Couch's division, accompanied by 2,000 cavalry and six batteries, to drive Stuart away. McClellan had ordered Pleasonton to send half of his entire cavalry force and two batteries to Porter at Shepherdstown, and the remainder to join Couch. Pleasonton received this order which was sent to him late in the evening of the 19th after he returned to his bivouac near Keedysville after his activities at Ferry Hill Place on the Potomac.[21]

While Stuart was stirring up McClellan at Williamsport, McClellan's troops were worrying Gen. Lee greatly at Boteler's Ford and further upriver at Shepherdstown. On Friday 19 September at about 8 A.M., Pleasonton rode into Sharpsburg at the head of a column of his cavalry sent by McClellan to learn if Lee had really gone. Accompanied by signalmen who would maintain a link to McClellan's headquarters, Pleasonton found much destruction; the battle had not been kind to the town as artillery damage was evident on almost every house and the fetid remains of dead horses added to the unpleasant ambiance.[22] Stopping on ridges it encountered, the horse artillery fired ahead to chase any enemy laying in ambush but found none. Pleasonton rode on, staying on the Boonsboro-Shepherdstown Pike passing the large Grove Farm on the left side of the road, then split into two groups, one of which continued down the road next to the Grove Farm to Boteler's Ford, while the other, with Pleasonton in the lead, stayed on

---

[21] *OR*, vol. 51, pt. 1, 853. Harsh opines that Stuart made too good a diversion drawing large numbers of Yankees too quickly to Williamsport as Lee was not able to get his tired army there quickly as he had to send Jackson back to defend against a Union attack at Shepherdstown, Harsh, *Flood*, 452.

[22] Hard, 187; McGrath, 34, 56; Rawle, 128. Obviously all of Pleasonton's cavalry at Shepherdstown would not leave 2,000 from his division available to send to Williamsport. Some of the cavalry from the Harpers Ferry escape were at and near Williamsport, and after Pleasonton was done at Shepherdstown, he sent troopers to Williamsport as will be seen.

the Boonsboro-Shepherdstown Pike. This road through the Grove Farm was built by the Confederates to provide a direct route to the ford.

The troopers heading for the ford ran into two companies of the 14th South Carolina Infantry at about 9 A.M. which were protecting the last of Gen. Lee's troops as they crossed the river. This rearguard fired on the Yankee horsemen from a skirmish line in a corn field about a mile from the ford as the Rebels made good their escape across Boteler's Ford.[23] These troopers were from the 3rd Pennsylvania Cavalry and the regimental historian wrote that they rode down on other dismounted troopers who were on the towpath and chased the Rebel troopers over the cement mill dam which crossed the Potomac just above the ford. The Rebel troopers abandoned their horses to run across the dam and escaped as they were well covered by Confederate artillery on the Virginia bluffs. Part of the 3rd Pennsylvania was posted along the river as videttes watching the Confederates on the opposite bank.[24] Pleasonton reported that he took "167 prisoners, one gun left behind by the enemy in his haste, and one color."[25]

Right: Pleasonton fails to catch Rebels on 19 September. Pleasonton set up guns on the hill overlooking the Potomac to amuse Confederate guns near and to the south of Shepherdstown. *Official Atlas* Plate 28. Courtesy LOC.

---

[23] Caldwell, 49; *OR*, vol. 19, pt. 1, 988-989; McGrath, 35.

[24] Rawle, 127-128.

[25] *OR*, vol. 19, pt. 1, 212. It is likely the gun was disabled and was immobile. Most of the stragglers he captured were probably wounded.

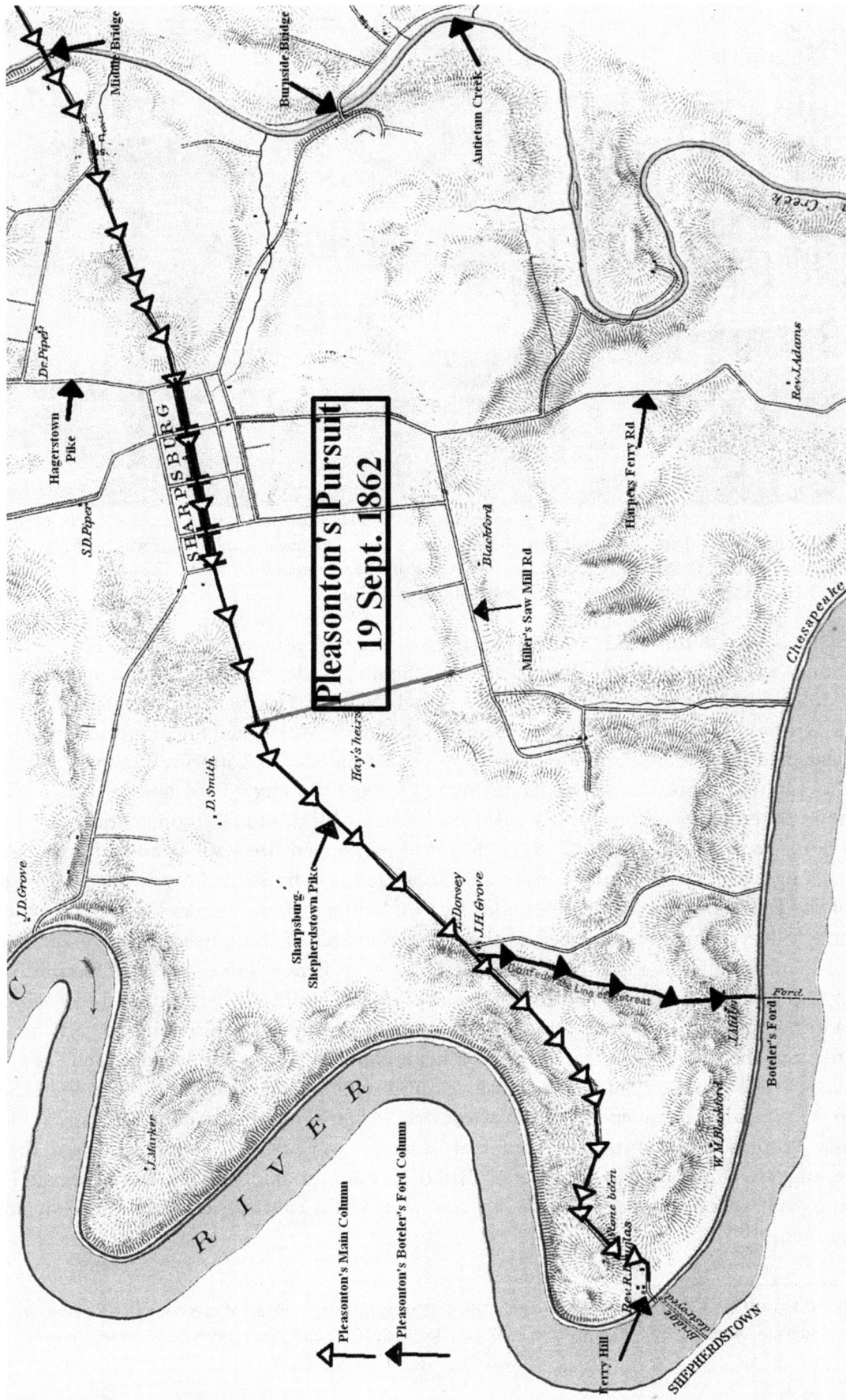

Pleasonton's Pursuit 19 Sept. 1862

Wood engraving c. 1850 from Ferry Hill looking down toward Shepherdstown, Virginia, across the Potomac River. The collection of buildings in the right foreground was known as Bridgeport. The covered toll bridge was built about 1850 by the Virginia & Maryland Bridge Company. Note also the C&O Canal in the foreground shown by the arrow. The covered bridge was burned by Jackson in June 1861. Courtesy C&O National Historical Park.

Meanwhile, Pleasonton had arrived with the rest of his division at a bluff overlooking Shepherdstown, across the Potomac River. There, on the north side of the road, was a mansion owned by the father of Stonewall Jackson's aide, Maj. Henry Kyd Douglas. The mansion was named Ferry Hill as there was a ferry at the base of the bluff at one time; the home overlooked Shepherdstown and the river giving a clear field of view. As Union troopers appeared, Confederate batteries totaling some forty-four guns on the Virginia shore below Shepherdstown, 13 above Boteler's Ford and 18 below, came into action. They opened a heavy, but mostly inaccurate fire, as Pleasonton's troopers took cover behind a ridge. His horse artillery rode to the front and Tidball exchanged fire with Pendleton's guns for about two hours, along with batteries from Gibson and Robertson; the horse artillery was soon joined by two batteries of the Federal Artillery Reserve under Lt. Col. William Hays, Batteries C and D of the 1st New York Light Artillery, which were placed to the left, downriver of the horse artillery. Confederate fire was seen to diminish after the first hour at about 11:30 A.M. Union horse artillery fire continued until Pleasonton was relieved by part of Porter's corps artillery; Pleasonton then returned to camp near the Pry House although with some misgivings. Pleasonton had ordered up his trains to feed his men but Porter's orders to the cavalry commander caused his regiments to miss the wagons, and they were not fed for a second day. It is likely also that Pleasonton had hoped for more of an active role in the pursuit of Lee, so the cavalry commander did not receive Porter's orders happily.[26] Perhaps Pleasonton remembered Porter's decision not to volunteer infantry support to Pleasonton when the cavalry commander suggested a foray against Cemetery Hill on the afternoon of the 17th, but he repaid Porter for that slight as well as for this wagon fiasco, by not sending his cavalry promptly the next morning as Porter requested.

---

[26] Hard, 187; *OR*, vol. 19, pt. 1, 212, 831, 838. Note that Tidball reports that the duel lasted one hour vice Pleasonton's two, Johnson and Anderson, *Artillery Hell*, 112. See also McGrath, 36, 52-53, 61. Pendleton reports 34 of his 44 guns were used in this duel.

"This photograph was taken looking across the Potomac River at Shepherdstown, West Virginia from Ferry Hill plantation on the Maryland side. At various times before and after the Battle of Antietam both Confederate and Union troops had camped at Ferry Hill, which is situated three miles southwest of the town of Sharpsburg, Maryland. At the bottom of the hill is a group of buildings known as Bridgeport and Lock 38 of the Chesapeake and Ohio Canal. Across the river Shepherdstown. Extending across the river are the abutments of the bridge that once connected the two states. Burned in 1861, the bridge was not replaced for 10 years, during which time once again a ferry served the crossing. The gentleman standing on the hillside (foreground) is not identified, but may be the Reverend Robert Douglas, owner of Ferry Hill plantation at the time of the Civil War." Courtesy Western Maryland Regional Library - www.whilbr.org

"Ferry Hill, across the river from Shepherdstown, on the top of the hill at the arrow, was built by John Blackford c. 1813 and was a working farm until the 20th century. Lock 38 was a busy area with traffic from the canal and travelers from West Virginia. The large white house was used as a hotel while down at the lock there was a feed store that was later converted into a bath house." Photograph from C&O National Historic Park, courtesy Western Maryland Regional Library - www.whilbr.org

A trooper from the 3rd Indiana Cavalry, Flavius J. Bellamy, wrote of the pursuit to the Potomac in a letter begun on 18 September, giving a personal and somewhat dramatic version of his experiences on the 19th:

It was our day to take the lead. Gen. Pleasonton ordered 5 regiments to cross the river. We went over the hill and down the bank (while their forces were all drawn up in line of battle on the other side) planted 2 little rifled guns we had with us to cover our crossing when the Rebs opened several batteries on us in carbine range dismounting one of our guns at the first fire. It was too hot for our Artillerists and they hitched up and went over the hill on double quick. Gen. P. after (fool like) getting us into the snap ran off and left us to our fate dismounting behind a large tree to protect himself. Our Regimental officers took us behind a low hill for shelter as soon as possible but it did very little good. While there a shell burst close to me and as I watched the curling smoke and the flying fragments a six pound shot passed over my head (grazing my hat) and went into the ground....After that I made my obeisance to every one that passed very near for fear one might pass a few inches lower than that one. They finally removed us behind a piece of woods and a hill that protected us after a number were killed and sounded. None in our Company however.[27]

McClellan, late on the 19th, ordered Pleasonton to have his cavalry and artillery at the river by daylight to cooperate with Porter's intended crossing, as well as to send half his force to Couch to confront Stuart at Williamsport. Early in the morning of the 20th, Pleasonton replied to McClellan that he was sending the required troopers to Williamsport and also would be starting for Shepherdstown. He complained about Porter's sending him back to camp late on the 19th forcing his men to miss their trains and more daringly, given that Porter was a close friend of McClellan: "I trust, after the past experience of yesterday, the general commanding will not permit corps commanders to interfere with the cavalry under my command, for it breaks up all my systems and plans. I shall do everything in my power to make up for the time we have lost." Pleasonton unnecessarily pointed out that if he had to pursue the Rebels into Virginia, "that neither provisions nor forage can be obtained...that country having been eaten out." When Porter complained the next morning that no cavalry were on the scene, McClellan's headquarters chastised him for sending the cavalry back to camp apparently against the wishes of the commanding general. Porter would not count Pleasonton as one of his friends.[28] Flavius J. Bellamy wrote that on the 20th, "they [Union infantry] attempted a crossing this morning not seeing any secesh batteries in view. The head of our column had begun to cross when they unmasked their batteries on us once more and we were withdrawn."[29]

While Porter lamented that there were no cavalry available, Rebel John N. Opie, a future member of the 6th Virginia Cavalry, reported that while on horseback on Shepherdstown's Main Street late on the 19th or early in the morning on the 20th, he saw a Union cavalry column on a parallel street. Upon seeing the Rebel trooper, the Union cavalry gave chase but could not catch him. If Opie is correct about the date, it is not clear which Union cavalry were there although there is some evidence that it might have been a few troopers of the 3rd Indiana Cavalry. Another possibility is that it was Rebel cavalry from Fitz Lee's Brigade on patrol, and did not recognize Opie in the dark.[30]

[27] Flavius J. Bellamy file, letter 18 September 1862, courtesy Indiana State Library.
[28] OR, vol. 19, pt. 1, 331, 334; vol. 51, pt. 1, 854. It is not clear why McClellan chose Pleasonton's side in this dustup.
[29] Flavius J. Bellamy file, letter 18 September 1862, courtesy Indiana State Library.
[30] Opie, 88-89; Pickerill, 30; McGrath, 101. The 3rd Pennsylvania Cavalry regimental history shows that on 20 September "The Third was ordered [by Porter] to follow the infantry. In crossing, the horses were watered, and while this was going on the unfortunate disaster occurred to the Corn Exchange Regiment...on the bluff on the opposite side....Before the men of the Third had gotten through watering their horses a bugler with General Porter sounded the 'recall' and we returned. While we were doing so the enemy's artillery on the heights got our range and several shells burst in our ranks," Rawle, 130.

Union infantry crossed into Virginia the morning of Saturday 20 September without sufficient cavalry to scout for it or provide a screen. When Pleasonton's troopers did arrive, it was too late as the incursion into Virginia was already suspended. Some horse artillery and a few troopers from the 3rd Indiana Cavalry had gotten across but accomplished nothing before they were ordered to return. A Union soldier crossing to the Virginia shore recalled that one grumbler from his unit engaged the returning horsemen in some jesting as the horses were throwing up spray onto the men: "'Are there any dead cavalrymen ahead? What guerrillas do you belong to' …to which the answer came back promptly, 'Yes, you bummers, we do the fighting and leave the dead cavalrymen for the 'dough boys' to pick up.'"[31] Perhaps as a result of the lack of help the cavalry should have given for scouting and reconnaissance, Union infantry came to grief as it incurred heavy casualties when it encountered unexpected fierce resistance on the Virginia shore. As the Union infantry tried to escape across the Potomac at the ford and on the dam under heavy enemy fire, dead and wounded multiplied, despite support from artillery and riflemen on the Maryland shore. On the 20th, the 9th Virginia Cavalry had returned to Boteler's Ford and was placed on the far right of Maj. Gen. A.P. Hill's troops whose infantry had pushed the Union troops back into Maryland.[32] Thus the day ended ignominiously for Pleasonton as well as for Porter, and his infantry. This poor performance was matched on the Confederate side by Pendleton's feeble efforts as commander of the rear guard on behalf of Robert E. Lee, in trying to defend the Virginia shore.

McClellan wisely heavily reinforced Williamsport upriver to protect the ford and ensure that no Rebel forces could reenter Maryland by that route and appear on his right flank or rear. Late on 19 September, Col. Voss with his 12th Illinois Cavalry was at Jones's Cross Roads where he joined a detachment from Maj. Gen. Couch's division, and marched to Williamsport. Later that night, McClellan ordered Couch to Williamsport with the rest of his division and ordered Pleasonton there also with half of his cavalry and two batteries, meeting Couch at Jones's Cross Roads. During the evening of 20 September, McClellan added Franklin's corps to the troops marching to Williamsport to join Couch's division, and the three brigades of cavalry now with three batteries of horse artillery; Franklin as senior would be in command. McClellan also informed Franklin that he would be joined by a brigade of infantry from Hagerstown under command of Brig. Gen. John R. Kenly. McClellan concluded his Maryland Campaign by acting with dispatch to prevent Lee from reentering Maryland while spreading his army from Harpers Ferry to Hancock.[33] The Union commander seemed determined to keep Lee's army out of Maryland but less willing to follow it into Virginia, perhaps believing that pushing the foe back into "his" country was more than enough of a victory for the present.[34] And Certainly Gen. Lee's fierce resistance at Botelor's Ford showed that the Army of Northern Virginia was still a dangerous foe.

Thus the cavalry actions ended for this episode of the Maryland Campaign but their toils were not done as they next skirmished and patrolled in Northern Virginia, and then Union troopers vainly chased Stuart's 1,800 troopers as they raided into Pennsylvania three weeks later on 10-11 October. Without doubt, McClellan's failure to actively pursue Gen. Lee further into Virginia, and then the Stuart raid into

31 Carter, *Four Brothers*, 119. The few returning Union troopers were from the 8th Illinois Cavalry, Hard, 188.

32 McGrath, 101; Beale, *9th Virginia*, 43.

33 *OR*, vol. 51, pt. 1, 854-857 passim. Kenly was a Baltimore lawyer who served as a captain in the Mexican War in the First Battalion of Baltimore and Washington Volunteers, then as a major in the District of Columbia and Maryland Regiment of Volunteers. When the war came, he raised a regiment of Union troops in April 1861 and was commissioned colonel of the First Regiment, Infantry, Maryland Volunteers, 11 June 1861. On 23 May 1862, he led troops fighting at Front Royal, Virginia, and was wounded, captured, and exchanged, then promoted to brigadier general 22 August 1862, commanding the Maryland Brigade. See Manakee, 145-146. Kenly's brigade was part of the Army of the Potomac from 12 December to 20 December 1862, Eicher, 330.

34 *OR*, vol. 51, pt. 1, 851, 853, 855; Harsh, *Flood*, 453.

Pennsylvania, sealed Little Mac's fate, while Pleasonton and his troopers continued their efforts deeper into Virginia battling fatigue and sick mounts.

The best army commander the Confederates had, combined with their best cavalry leader, saved their army from defeat at Antietam. But it is also true that they both failed earlier in the campaign to ensure that the Federals had not begun their pursuit from Washington more quickly than Gen. Lee expected. Stuart's poor scouting influenced by Gen. Lee's assumptions about the Union movements put the Confederates in a tough spot, saved in large part by the Army of Northern Virginia's experienced leaders and veteran troops. These veteran troops, although outnumbered throughout the campaign, along with Lee's inspired leadership at Antietam, his best-fought battle, allowed the Army of Northern Virginia to survive to fight another day, and to prolong the war for another two and one half years.

Ironically, McClellan also fought the best campaign of his army career, but his best was only good enough to fight Lee to a tactical draw at Antietam. Pleasonton served McClellan adequately in what may have been one of his personally best performances of his career, but the Federal army commander would have likely been better served had he chosen Buford for his cavalry field commander. After McClellan found the Lost Order, he had an opportunity to hurt Lee's army even more than he did at South Mountain, but despite a reasonably good effort, the slow-moving Army of the Potomac, combined with some notably timid leadership and tardy actions especially by Franklin and Couch, ensured Miles's surrender at Harpers Ferry, and that McLaws would get away unhurt. Although both army commanders were hampered by ineffective intelligence-gathering efforts, Lee's fewer sources made little difference to this aggressive leader, as he believed that he was the best judge of his opponent's intentions. McClellan had more numerous and more accurate sources, but this very busy army commander chose to rely on those which most closely fit his ideas; he fought to ensure that he did not lose, while Lee fought to win at all costs. Unfortunately for the Army of the Potomac and the Union, Little Mac's analyses of his opponent were no match for Bobby Lee's.[35]

---

[35] Historians have argued since the Battle of Antietam whether it was a "draw" or a victory for McClellan. For the general public at the time, a key factor to decide the victor was which army held the field after the battle. Here, Lee held the field for only a day before his retreat. McClellan had pushed the Army of Northern Virginia back on all points of the battlefield on 17 September so many would argue that since Lee retreated across the Potomac on the 18th/19th, McClellan was the victor as he not only did not retreat, but rather was contemplating an attack on the 18th postponed to the 19th to bring up ammunition, fresh troops, etc. Modern interpretations of who was the "victor" sometimes address numbers of casualties on either side either as absolute numbers or as percentages of numbers engaged. Another measure is how the result contributed to national or military strategy. Often the Battle of Antietam is not viewed alone but in combination with the Union debacle at Harpers Ferry. The Confederacy at the time preferred to view the campaign as a whole to support its appraisal that it was not a failure but an overall success. The author's opinion is that the Battle of Antietam was a Union victory as was McClellan's Maryland Campaign.

Cavalry videttes guarding the roads to the Potomac River after the battle; these must be troopers from Rush's Lancers, McClellan's escort as they were the only cavalrymen armed with lances. From *Frank Leslie's Illustrated History of the Civil War* (1895).

Boteler's Ford near Shepherdstown; pickets in the dry C&O Canal bed firing across the river into Virginia toward Boteler's Cement factory. Alfred R. Waud published in *Harper's Weekly*, 11 October 1862. Author's collection.

"Boteler's Mill, also known as Potomac Mill, is seen on the West Virginia shore of the Potomac, at left downriver from Shepherdstown. Boteler's Mill dam was made of wooden cribs filled with rubble stones and covered with planks, and provided water to the mill shown at right. The mill produced the cement that was used extensively in the early construction of the canal. According to Thomas Hahn & Emory L. Kemp's Cement Mills Along the Potomac River, Boteler's Mill was build prior to 1828 and was originally supposed to be a "Local Merchant Mill" (grist mill) built by Dr. Henry Boteler and George Reynolds. In 1828 they discovered limestone on their property and contacted the C&O Canal about contracting them to create cement for the construction of locks. They were used extensively until the Round Top Cement Mill was constructed in 1837. The barrels of cement would be transported across the river to the river inlet lock on the C&O Canal downstream of Bridgeport. The Mill was burned by Federal troops on 19 August 1861. The operation had intermittently milled both cement and flour prior to the Civil War and would switch exclusively to cement after it was rebuilt in 1867. The mill would be in operation until 1900 and then officially closed by 1916....Packhorse Ford was located half a mile below the mill." Courtesy Western Maryland Regional Library - www.whilbr.org

Cavalry Contributions to Intelligence during the Maryland Campaign

T HE CAVALRY IN THE MARYLAND CAMPAIGN was the most important supplier of information to Gen. Robert E. Lee and Maj. Gen. George B. McClellan. This appendix will examine how each side's cavalry performed its information-gathering function, as well as briefly look at other sources Lee and McClellan used to help determine the location, size, and intent of the enemy forces they faced.[1] As a discussion of the Lost Order was accomplished above in Chapter 7, it will not be repeated here in detail, but it must be remembered that McClellan fumbled the reception of the most important intelligence find during the Civil War. The Lost Order, of which McClellan said "Here is a paper with which, if I cannot whip Bobbie Lee, I will be willing to go home," cannot be left out of the evaluation of his use of intelligence during the campaign, as its finding could have led to serious damage to the widely separated parts of Lee's divided army.[2]

---

[1] Note that the terms "information" and "intelligence" were used interchangeably during the Civil War so quotations from participants do not make the modern distinction that "information" is primarily the initial gathering of facts. Even today, the terms are often used without distinction. See Bartholomees, 249. The current D.O.D. definition of "information" is this: "Facts, data, or instructions in any medium or form;" and its definition of "intelligence:" "The product resulting from the collection, processing, integration, evaluation, analysis, and interpretation of available information concerning foreign nations, hostile or potentially hostile forces or elements, or areas of actual or potential operations. The term is also applied to the activity which results in the product and to the organizations engaged in such activity," *Department of Defense Dictionary of Military and Associated Terms*, Joint Pub 1-02, 2010, 228, 234; DOD website.

[2] Murfin, 133; statement from John Gibbon's, *Personal Recollections of the Civil War* (New York: G. P. Putnam's Sons, 1928), 73. Fishel called finding the Lost Order the "greatest intelligence find of the war," 222. Sears in *Landscape Turned Red* is one among many who find McClellan seriously lacking in his efforts to bring Lee to an annihilating battle after discovering the Lost Order. Harsh is the leader among those historians who believe that given what McClellan knew or believed about Lee's dispositions and strength, he did well, or as well as a Union general commanding the Army of the Potomac could do. He is joined by others such as Ethan S. Rafuse in *McClellan's War: The Failure of Moderation in the Struggle for the Union* (Bloomington and Indianapolis: Indiana University Press, 2005). Rafuse's sympathetic perspective argues that given McClellan's political views and his philosophy, he did well accomplishing his mission during the campaign. See also Rafuse, "McClellan, von Clausewitz, and the Politics of War," in *The Ongoing Civil War: New Versions of Old Stories*, ed. by Herman Hattaway and Ethan Rafuse (Columbia, MO: University of Missouri Press, 2004), 55-57: "Indeed, it is difficult to imagine any other man available to the Lincoln administration who could have done a much better job as general in chief given the circumstances of 1861-1862." Compare Rowland commenting on McClellan's performance during the Maryland Campaign: "During these two weeks, McClellan not only had to assume command and organize the shattered remnants of Pope's army, but he had to

Lee, like McClellan, suffered from being his own "chief of intelligence" and never had a staff officer assigned specifically to intelligence work.[3] But while Lee may sometimes have lagged behind his opponents in collecting or analyzing information, he excelled at the most difficult component of intelligence—applying it.[4] Stuart came closest to being Lee's information gatherer as he was the one who brought more good quality information to Lee than anyone else. Lee affirmed this when he was notified of Stuart's death at Yellow Tavern: "He never brought me a piece of false information."[5] Lee trusted Stuart and needed him to coordinate and supervise his troopers which requirement was even more clearly shown during the Gettysburg Campaign in 1863. Lee, in that campaign, although having several brigades of cavalry at his disposal after Stuart moved to the east of Lee's army, used them poorly as Stuart was unavailable until July 2nd; Lee was stultified in his knowledge of the enemy in the Beau Sabreur's absence.[6] During the Maryland Campaign, Lee also would have profited by having Stuart stay in closer communication, especially after Lee with Longstreet marched west from Frederick on 10 September.

Neither Lee nor McClellan departed from standard operating procedures the Old Army utilized for military intelligence. Neither government during the war adopted standardized procedures for gathering or analyzing intelligence, but rather left those functions to field commanders. "Intelligence was the responsibility of the command's provost marshal in many cases, but sometimes it was assigned to the adjutant, the signal officer, or the chief of staff, and sometimes the commander himself took a major hand in the matter." Many generals from the old army viewed spies with some distaste believing that such covert action was ungentlemanly.[7]

---

integrate it with his own forces just arrived from the Peninsula and the newly mustered volunteers, hastily summoned to Washington. Moreover, he had to divine Lee's intentions and precise whereabouts, shift his army into Maryland, maneuver it through contested mountainous terrain, and bring it to the battlefield. All things considered, he acted with uncharacteristic alacrity," 222. Later commenting on McClellan's approach to war, he states: McClellan's strategy, though reflective of the unrealistic war aims of the years 1861-62, was cogent, reasoned, and consistent with conventional military wisdom and his personal views of the nature of the conflict. They were not hallucinatory or deranged but mirrored those of a sizeable, if not shrinking, majority viewpoint," 225.

[3] Fishel, 6; Bartholomees, "[Lee's] staff's role in the intelligence system—other than as direct information collectors—was one of administration rather than substance. That trend emerged early in the war....[Lee] was remarkably good (or lucky) at divining enemy intentions from the fragments of available information, and he certainly outshone his opponents in using the intelligence he gleaned." This system worked well and only failed when "the normal sources of intelligence dried up, not because of poor analysis or lack of system," 254-256. As will be discussed below, McClellan did have Allan Pinkerton to help gather information. Also, McClellan had two French aides-de-camp on his staff, Louis Philippe d'Orleans and his brother Robert who were assigned by McClellan in January 1862 to help summarize the plethora of information coming into army headquarters. Unfortunately for McClellan, their valuable help and reports stopped when the army moved to the Peninsula just when the army commander could have most benefitted by their assistance and when combined with Pinkerton's efforts, McClellan would likely have been able to make more reasoned decisions based on better intelligence, Fishel, 123-129.

[4] Fishel, 238, 571. See also William A. Tidwell, James O. Hall, and David Winfred Gaddy, *Come Retribution: The Confederate Secret Service and the Assassination of Lincoln* (Jackson: University Press of Mississippi, 1988), 112.

[5] Robert E. Lee, Jr. *Recollections and Letters of Robert E. Lee* (Old Saybrook, CT: Konecky & Konecky, 1998), 125.

[6] See Eric J. Wittenberg and J. David Petruzzi, *Plenty of Blame to Go Around: Jeb Stuart's Controversial Ride to Gettysburg* (New York: Savas Beatie, 2006), hereafter "*Blame*," 281-292, for a discussion of the cavalry brigades which were left available for Lee but were not well used.

[7] George J.A. O'Toole, *Honorable Treachery: A History of U.S Intelligence, Espionage, and Covert Action from the American Revolution to the CIA* (New York: The Atlantic Monthly Press, 1991), 127. "Amateur's game" referred to the state of the art of military intelligence during the Civil War. Fought during the Victorian Era, and without having formal organizations on either side, much of the spying and intelligence gathering was ad hoc and informal. Spies could be anyone and both sides accepted "walk-ins" who presented compelling cases to use their services and who were not otherwise obviously unsuited. On-the-job training was the norm except for the very few who were professional detectives before the war. Local unit commanders often decided on their own how to employ scouts or spies and how to react to those from the other side who were caught. Especially during the early "soft war" those caught, especially women, were not harshly treated often released after interrogation and brief jailing. As the war progressed, however, spies were more likely to be executed sometimes without trial at the lower levels of unit commands. Local unit commanders were often gathering good intelligence information but because higher levels of

Though the idea of centralized intelligence gathering was decades away, the age-old resistance to the idea was present during [the Civil War]. Neither side saw the need to create such intelligence organizations, but each side approached the idea of effectively acquiring intelligence in its own way. The Confederacy's Signal Corps, devoted primarily to communications and intercepts, included a covert agency, the Secret Service Bureau. This unit ran espionage and counter-espionage operations in the North. Late in the war, the bureau set up a secret headquarters in Canada and sent out operatives on covert missions in Northern states. The Union's Bureau of Military Information [formed in 1863], unlike the Confederacy's Secret Service Bureau, operated for specific generals rather than for the Union Army itself. But here was born the idea of what would eventually become a centralized military intelligence division.[8]

The renowned professor at West Point, Dennis Hart Mahan, who taught both Robert E. Lee and George B. McClellan, recognized the importance of ensuring that a commanding general has information on which to base the daily operations of a campaign. In his treatise, however, he spent more time on the mechanics of collecting information rather than its analysis, implementation, or how a general's staff should organize and coordinate collection activities. "There are no more important duties, which an officer may be called upon to perform, than those of collecting and arranging the information upon which either the general, or daily operations of a campaign must be based." Later in this "Reconnaissances" chapter, he perfectly describes much of the basic information a commander needs: "The main duties of a patrol are to find the enemy if in the neighborhood; gain a good idea of his position and strength; to make out his movements, and to bring in an accurate account of his distance from the out-posts of their own force; and the character of the ground between the position occupied by the respective forces."[9] His treatise reflects the generally accepted approach that the general who needs this

---

command and the national governments were not well organized to avail themselves of it or gather and analyze it that information was wasted. For the distinction between "spy" and "scout" regarding treatment reflecting the views of officers, see below the Lieber Code in which the severity of the punishment for either depends upon the wearing of a uniform. Punishment for a spy can be death but not for a scout unless in uniform of the enemy or in civilian clothes.

[8] U.S. Central Intelligence Agency website, https://www.cia.gov/library/publications/additional-publications/civil-war/introduction.html, accessed 30 May 2010. The Army of the Potomac under Hooker established the first intelligence group in 1863 led by Col. George Sharpe. George Henry Sharpe was born in 1828 in Kingston, New York and died in 1900. He was well educated, having graduated from Rutgers and studied law at Yale. He traveled, practiced law and served as a diplomat until May 1861 when he was commissioned a captain in the 20th New York State Militia; commissioned colonel 120th New York Infantry in August 1862 after he raised the regiment, then brevet brigadier general in December 1864, leaving service in June 1865 as a major general. He assumed the position of head of General Hooker's secret service in February 1863 as deputy provost marshal general under Provost Marshal General of the Army of the Potomac Marsena R. Patrick. He reported directly to Hooker. His unit, soon called the Bureau of Military Information, employed espionage, interrogation, and scouting of enemy units. He was the first to use "all source" intelligence to give full reports to Hooker: cavalry reconnaissance, balloons, Signal Corps observation stations, signal flag interceptions, review of southern newspapers, and telegraphed reports from adjacent commands. He did an excellent job as was shown by his accurate estimates of enemy strength compared to Pinkerton's fantastic numbers, Fishel, 287-294. One of Pinkerton's agents, John Babcock, also worked for Sharpe. John C. Babcock began his intelligence career as a twenty-five year old private who was hired as a mapmaker for Allan Pinkerton's group during Major General George B. McClellan's Peninsular Campaign. His architect's eye led him to produce excellent maps helped by his scouting the terrain himself sometimes on horseback, on foot or by balloon. After Pinkerton left when President Lincoln removed McClellan, Babcock was mustered out of the service with his company but was hired as a civilian intelligence agent by Burnside who had known him before the war. But he had little to do under Burnside compared to his duties under McClellan. When Hooker took over after Burnside's removal, Babcock became the informal second in command of the Bureau of Military Information under Colonel Sharpe. Babcock became Sharpe's principal interrogator and an expert on Lee's Army of Northern Virginia and also wrote many of Sharpe's reports. He continued with Sharpe until the end of the war becoming his most important operative, Fishel, 257-259.

[9] Dennis Hart Mahan, *An Elementary Treatise on Advanced-Guard, Out-Post, and Detachment Service of Troops, and the Manner of Posting and Handling Them in Presence of an Enemy* (New York, John Wiley, 1862), 105, 114. His treatises were reprinted in both the North and South during the war.

information is responsible for the methods of collection and analysis and therefore there are no prescriptions or constraints on how to accomplish those tasks.

Prior to the Maryland Campaign, Confederate spies in the Washington area were able to supply good information to the Confederates. One, Capt. Thomas N. Conrad, a chaplain of the 3rd Virginia Cavalry, operated a spy network, but during September 1862 was only able to get information to Richmond, and not directly to Stuart or Lee, due to heavy Union troop movements in Northern Virginia.[10] But one of Conrad's spies may have helped Lee by passing on information regarding McClellan's troop strength: Charles T. Cockey operated a way station on the Confederate Secret Line at Reisterstown, Maryland, northwest of Baltimore. Cockey said that he went to Frederick, Maryland, and reported information directly to Lee.[11] Another spy who worked with Stuart was Benjamin F. Stringfellow of the 4th Virginia Cavalry. He may have spied on Union activities closer to Union lines but there are no reports available of his activities, other than he was reported in Poolesville and then in Frederick on 7 September; he was also detailed as a courier during the Battle of Antietam and participated in Stuart's Second Ride Around McClellan, having also been in the first ride during the Peninsular Campaign. It is likely that his successes in scouting in the Northern Virginia area down to Richmond were due to his knowledge of that area, its topography, and its residents. In Maryland, Stringfellow did not have the luxury of being in familiar territory and it likely affected his abilities to

---

[10] Thomas Nelson Conrad, one of the Confederacy's best spies, was active in the Washington, D.C. area since he was very familiar with that territory having been a schoolmaster of a boys' school there. He was initially arrested and sent South in June 1861 after apparently sending messages by having his students in the Washington school raise and lower shades in their rooms and for giving an inflammatory speech on his school's graduation day. He then joined Jeb Stuart as chaplain of the 3rd Virginia. As such he became a cavalry scout, one of a group of young, intelligent men who worked for General Robert E. Lee and Stuart; his movements were facilitated by his appearance as a clergyman. He easily traveled within Union lines as a clergyman gathering information in addition to saving souls. He then returned to Washington and disguised his appearance becoming a resident Confederate spy. He used "secession clerks" in the War Department to which he had unfettered access to collect information which he passed south. He even placed an operative in Union spymaster Lafayette Baker's group. One of his more ambitious plans, the assassination of Winfield Scott, was turned down by the Richmond administration, but an exploratory operation to determine the feasibility of kidnapping Lincoln he did undertake. He may have been involved in a Secret Service plan in conjunction with George Bowie to capture Lincoln, and Bowie may have been assigned to capture the Maryland governor in Annapolis. Later in the war, he helped capture a Union spy, Isaac Silver, near Aquia disrupting Colonel George Sharpe's spy network in that area. His excellent use of disguises and other self-taught spying skills made him a very able spy. John Bakeless, *Spies of the Confederacy* (Philadelphia: J. B. Lippincott Company, 1970; reprint Mineola, NY: Dover Publications, Inc., 1970), 66-87. For more on Conrad, see Alan Axelrod, *The War Between the Spies: A History of Espionage During the Civil War* (New York: The Atlantic Monthly Press, 1992), 86-95; and Donald E. Markle, *Spies and Spymasters of the Civil War* (New York: Hippocrene Books, 2004), 111-114. For a discussion of "secession clerks" see Fishel, 11 and 57-58. He discusses John F. Callan who served as a clerk in both the adjutant general's office and on the Military Committee of the Senate who was originally appointed by then senator Jefferson Davis, Fishel, 57; *OR*, vol. 2, 27. John B. Jones mentions the large numbers of Federal clerks who journeyed to Richmond to work for the Confederate government and that some of them may have been spying for the Union, *A Rebel War Clerk's Diary at the Confederate States Capital*, vol. 1 (Philadelphia, PA: J.B. Lippincott & Co., 1866), 70. Even clerks who did not harbor southern sympathies were not careful with official documents as related by a reporter, Murat Halstead who wrote that some New York newspaper correspondents visited offices of the War and Navy Departments and published reports including documents clerks had given them to read even before the department heads had seen them, Bernard A. Weisberger, *Reporters for the Union* (Boston, MA: Little, Brown and Company, 1953), 83.

[11] Bakeless, 78-80. The "Secret Line" was "a network of couriers, agents, safe houses, and Southern sympathizers linking Richmond with secret Confederate assets in enemy territory....[It] transported agents, scouts, and others on official business to and from the North; carried letters and dispatches to and from the Confederate capital; procured books, newspapers, and other items from the North for the Confederate leaders; and observed and reported on Federal military movements on the Potomac River," O'Toole, 129. The line crossed the lower Potomac River and even had tendrils north into Baltimore, New York City, and Canada.

help Stuart. Not knowing who to trust certainly limited his and Stuart's other scouts' opportunities to obtain reliable information.[12]

When Lee's army was in Frederick and then further west, it was in two mostly Union-leaning areas of the state, Frederick County and Washington County, so the quantity of Confederate sympathizers available for garnering information was diminished. And Lee's fears that here in Maryland, as in Virginia, "The country is full of spies and our plans are immediately carried to the enemy" were much more likely to be true, but Lee clearly recognized the value of scouts and urged their use. Thus Stuart's reconnaissance duties were critical during this time of relatively little other incoming information for Lee.

Benjamin Franklin Stringfellow, one of Stuart's best spies, from *Stringfellow of the Fourth*.

---

[12] Benjamin Franklin Stringfellow, called one of the Confederacy's best scouts along with John S. Mosby, was born at The Retreat in Culpeper County, Virginia, and in May 1861 joined the Powhatan Troop which became Co. E of the 4th Virginia Cavalry. After seeing action at First Bull Run, his excellent scouting was brought to Jeb Stuart's notice and in September 1861 Stuart asked Stringfellow to join his headquarters staff as a scout, technically as an "aide." He was in the company of noted troopers such as John S. Mosby and Capt. Redmond Burke; Burke and another scout, Capt. William D. Farley, taught Stringfellow scouting skills. After the Battle of Fredericksburg, Stuart ordered Stringfellow to set up a spy network in Fairfax County and Alexandria with spies also located in Washington—some serving as clerks in the War Department. He was also instrumental in discovering that Hooker's right flank was in the air before the Battle at Chancellorsville. For a time, Stringfellow posed as a dentist's assistant in Union-occupied Alexandria, Virginia, while regularly sending reports of Union troop movements. Later, he used the same cover while an agent in Washington, where he even got a dental license. Stuart said of him, "In determining the enemy's real design, I rely upon you, as well as the quick transmission of the information." Stringfellow's information, Stuart said, "may be worth all the Yankee trains" that Stuart attacked. Stuart in his report of Second Bull Run wrote that "Private Stringfellow displayed great daring and enterprise as a scout," *OR*, vol. 12, pt. 2, 738. One of his most famous exploits was dressing up as a woman and attending a dance within Union lines gathering information then escaping holding a Federal lieutenant as hostage. Captured for the last time while spying in Washington, D.C., in April 1865, while on a mission from President Davis to deliver a message to a foreign embassy, he escaped then journeyed to Hamilton, Ontario, Canada, only returning to Virginia in 1867 where he tried farming then was ordained as minister. He volunteered as a chaplain in the Spanish-American war in 1898 and served in the 4th Infantry Regiment, Virginia Volunteers, along with his son for the duration of the war. He died on 8 June 1913; Bakeless, 77, 88-128 passim; R. Shepard Brown's romanticized but entertaining book, *Stringfellow of the Fourth* (New York, NY: Crown Publishers, Inc., 1960), 3-4, 13-15, 60-63, 168, 170, 172-186, 189-190, 267-293. For more on Stringfellow, see Axelrod, 145-157, and Markle, 111-114. See also Wittenberg, *Blame*, 217, 296; Tidwell, 411; Longacre, *Lee's Cavalrymen*, 31. CIA website, "The Flamboyant Spy: Jeb Stuart," CIA Website. See also Garnett, "Occasionally the monotony of camp-life would be varied by the arrival of Burke, or Stringfellow, or Toler, or Curtis, scouts who spent most of their time inside the enemy's lines....It was this tried and trusty body of scouts to which Gen. Stuart owed much of his successes in war. ...No movement of troops, not a reinforcement was ever received, nor an encampment changed in Gen. Meade's army that was not speedily reported at our Headquarters, and the information at once forwarded to Gen. Lee," 38. For Stringfellow's activities before Second Bull Run, see Krick, *Stonewall Jackson*, 16.

Lee's other sources such as newspapers were not as plentiful north of the Potomac. He lost his source of newspapers which might have been delivered to him through the Confederate Secret Line were he in Virginia, as well as those Stuart's scouts may have been able to pick up on their peregrinations. The Secret Line was one of the best sources of northern newspapers and periodicals Lee depended on. Maj. William Norris, head of the Confederate Signal Corps, related that "From the first of April [1862] to the last of September…we placed files of Baltimore papers, published one morning, in the hands of the President [Davis] next evening. New York papers, of course, a day later."[13] But Lee did find some newspapers to read such as the *Baltimore Sun*, however there is no record of useful operational information gained from them.[14] Lee was well aware of the use of newspapers as intelligence sources as well as opportunities for spreading disinformation: "I am particularly anxious that our newspapers may not give the enemy notice of our intentions" while "an enigmatical paragraph in the *Dispatch* [about D.H. Hill's movements]…may be advisable."[15] If Stuart had found newspapers in his travels containing valuable information he would have passed them on to Lee, but there is no record of his having done so. A story which appeared in the *New York Herald* newspaper on Monday 15 September could have provided Lee with invaluable information. The report, probably written due to the loose talk of some Union officers who learned about Lee's Lost Order and told it to the paper's Washington correspondent, was not read by Lee nor any Southern operatives reading northern newspapers for information during

---

13 Maj. William Norris, "The Signal Corps in the Confederate States Army," in *Southern Historical Society Papers*, vol. 16, January to December 1888 (Richmond, VA: Southern Historical Society, n.d., reprint, Millwood, NJ: Kraus Reprint Co, 1977), 100. Tidwell, 87-96. Arrangements had southern operatives, possibly 10 to 20, buying newspapers in major northern cities and sending them quickly south via the Secret Line, 37-38. Not operating within friendly lines took its toll on information sources for Lee. Rebel spies in the eastern part of Maryland especially in and around Baltimore likely had information which would have been valuable for Lee but getting it to him through Union lines was difficult. So the spies both Union and Confederate in Baltimore added little of value for Lee and for McClellan as the Union commander had more than enough information coming from official and semi-official sources; Bradley T. Johnson, *Confederate Military History*, vol. II (Atlanta, GA: Confederate Publishing Company, 1899; reprint, Harrisburg, PA: The Archive Society, 1994), 45. One of the Confederate Secret Service Bureau's "most important tasks was the obtaining of open-source material, especially newspapers, from the North, primarily through sympathizers in Maryland, including postmasters. The newspapers provided information—and, occasionally, agents' messages hidden in personal columns. The delivery system—sometimes called "our Government route"—boldly relied on the U.S. mail along part of the way. One 'mail agent,' a Marylander who lived near Washington, regularly drove his cart there, collected South-bound documents from network members, then hid the mail in manure that he picked up for his garden….Confederate mail supervisors established several accommodation addresses (as they would be called today) so that a suspiciously large amount of mail did not get delivered to one recipient,." CIA Website, "The Confederate 'Secret Line,'" CIA Website.

14 Harsh, *Flood*, 9, 79. Early in the campaign, Lee in a 4 September dispatch to President Jefferson Davis, said that he had read in the *Baltimore Sun* of the evacuation of Winchester. See also Harsh, *Flood*, 522, n. 84. See also David Mindich, "Edwin M. Stanton, the Inverted Pyramid, and Information Control," in *The Civil War and the Press*, David B, Sachsman, S. Kittrell Rushing, and Debra Reddin van Tuyll, eds. (New Brunswick, NJ: Transaction Publishers, 2000), 199-200, showing Lee's interest and two instances when he obtained specific important information about movements of McClellan on the Peninsula, Burnside moving to Grant, and Sherman moving to Goldsboro, North Carolina. Gen. Lee commented that reports from civilians that Union forces had evacuated Winchester were "confirmed by the Baltimore Sun of this morning [4 September], containing extracts from the Washington Star of yesterday," *OR*, vol. 19, pt. 2, 592. Newspapers north of the Potomac were less available to him once he crossed on the 6th.

15 Dowdy, Clifford, and Manarin, Louis H., Robert E. Lee, *The Wartime Papers of R.E. Lee* (New York: Bramhall House, 1961), 241. Lee later in the war commented on newspapers as sources of information sending copies to President Davis or summarizing stories, *Lee's Dispatches*, 241, 265-267, 272, 279, 283, 284, 362, 363. Douglas Southall Freeman's note to Lee's dispatch on pg. 241 is illuminating: "The frequent references in General Lee's dispatches to the intelligences procured from the New York and Philadelphia papers will show how valuable to either side were the newspapers of the other. The Richmond press was as diligently sought after by the Federals as were the Northern papers by the Confederates. The Richmond press, at this time, was conservative with the exception of the *Examiner*, edited by the radical John M. Daniel, an earnest opponent of the administration. The Federals appear, however, to have used the *Dispatch* most frequently to study Confederate movements."

the campaign.[16] However, intelligence in areas mostly hostile to the Southern cause was not as readily obtained or as reliable as in Virginia, thus Lee was forced to use what was at hand. Stuart and his

---

[16] Fishel, 223. Newspapers contained both strategic and tactical information as reporters discussed international, national, regional, and local news. As topics ranged widely depending upon the reporter and the newspaper, Confederate efforts at information gathering always included newspapers or clippings to be given to commanders. Observant generals carefully noted that when reports of their military movements were lacking then the enemy very likely did not know of them, Bartholomees, 249. Northern newspapers were more likely to report information valuable to the Confederacy than southern newspapers did, David S. and Jeanne T. Heidler, eds., *Encyclopedia of the American Civil War: A Political, Social, and Military History* (New York: W.W. Norton, 2000), "Newspapers," 1421, and "War Correspondents, " 2058, hereafter Heidler; Fishel, 55, 324-325. Censorship by Northern authorities was sporadic and difficult, often done by restricting reporters' access to the military telegraph, but some enterprising reporters and editors resorted to other methods of transmitting the news such as couriers; for early war efforts see Louis M. Starr, *Bohemian Brigade: Civil War Newsmen in Action* (Madison, WI: The University of Wisconsin Press, 1987), 37-42, 136. See also Margaret Leech, *Reveille in Washington 1860-1865* (New York: Harper & Row Publishers, Inc., 1941; reprint, Alexandria, VA: Time-Life Books, Inc., 1980), 199-202, describing the role newspapers and of the military censor in Washington which censored telegraph messages but sometimes after the stories had already been printed in Washington newspapers, 199-201. Halleck banned reporters from Pope's army in August 1862, *OR*, vol. 12, pt. 3, 602, but only made them use covert means to cover army news, Louis Starr, 131. Correspondents wormed their way back in to the Army of the Potomac as it entered Maryland chasing Lee and Halleck's order died of neglect, 138. One reporter, George W. Smalley, on the scene during the Battle of Antietam, carried messages for Hooker and the next day travelled by horse, train, ferry, and omnibus to get the story to his newspaper in New York, the *New York Tribune*, George W. Smalley, *Anglo-American Memories* (New York: G.P. Putnam's Sons, 1911), 146-152. "In an assessment shared by many historians, James Randall found that 'newspapers of the North, though in many ways deserving of admiration, undoubtedly did the national cause serious injury' by revealing military information, reporting official mistakes, puffing up generals, and focusing on sensational aspects of war," James G. Randall, "The Newspaper Problem in Its Bearing upon Military Secrecy During the Civil War," *The American Historical Review*, 23, no. 2 (January 1918): 303 from "Commanders, Correspondents, and the Constitution: The Birth of Conflict between the Military and the Free Press during the Civil War" by Rob Dean from MilitaryHistoryOnline.com website. A second newspaper historian gave his view: "[T]here is no doubt that many newsmen – especially in the North – revealed secrets best left unwritten, and many editors passed along material best left unpublished. Some were in tune with the 1862 lament of the Cincinnati *Commercial* that 'The people want news more than they want victories'; some were so vehemently opposed to the war that they wanted to interfere." Brayton Harris, *Blue & Gray in Black & White: Newspapers in the Civil War* (Dulles, VA: Batsford Brassey, Inc., 1999), 2. Lincoln used reporters also as another source of information which he could not obtain from formal channels, 152-162. Censorship in the South was more easily implemented and more readily accepted as the Virginia *Sentinel* printed: "The plans of our Government are, of course, not suitable matter of public proclamation. Our military boards must keep their own counsels, as it is obviously proper they should do so," Harris, 49. "The Charleston Courier suggested that Southern newspapers voluntarily adopt some reasonable guidelines: do not discuss the number or position, or announce the arrival or departure, of Confederate forces; do not describe likely enemy objectives or rebel plans; when describing a battle, do not reveal too many details and write only about completed actions. The Confederate congress authorized telegraphic censorship in May, with little opposition," 50. Harris also points out that some Southern states already had censorship such as forbidding material advocating the abolition of slavery, and Southern newspapers and the populace in general were more largely unified behind the Confederate movement. See Harris pp. 62-63 for examples of both Northern and Southern newspapers printing numbers and movements of troops in 1861 and a Confederate government's request for voluntary restraint from printing important information which could injure Southern military efforts. The Union government also made efforts to restrain Northern newspapers from printing similar information by reaching an understanding with the press by, among other things, not sending news by telegraph about movements before they take place. Interestingly, the censorship applied only to the telegraph, so creative reporters employed other methods, Harris, 64-65. After First Bull Run, the Lincoln administration published an order on 26 August 1861, under the 57th article of war from 10 April 1806 "'holding correspondence with or giving intelligence to the enemy, either directly or indirectly,' is made punishable by death, or such other punishment as shall be ordered by the sentence of a court-martial....It is therefore ordered that all correspondence and communication, verbally or by writing, printing, or telegraphing, respecting operations of the army, or military movement on land or water, respecting the troops, camps, arsenal, intrenchments, or military affairs, within the several military districts, by which intelligence shall be, directly or indirectly, given to the enemy, without the authority and sanction of the General in command, be, and the same are, absolutely prohibited, and from and after the date of this order person violating the same will be proceeded against under the fifty-seventh Article of War," *Rebellion Record*, vol. 3, Documents, 29. Rebel war clerk John B. Jones related the consternation caused by one Northern paper: "A tremendous excitement! The New York *Herald* has been received, containing a pretty accurate list of our military forces in the different camps of the Confederate States, with names and grades of the general

scouting abilities were even more important here in Maryland than previously in Virginia. While Stuart's cavalry was successful at screening near Leesburg on 4 September driving an independent company of cavalry from the town, their successful skirmishes and demonstrations by Hampton and Fitzhugh Lee at Alexandria and Groveton did not fool Pleasonton or Halleck who correctly believed that this show of force was to cover a crossing of the Upper Potomac.[17] But up until the Battle of Antietam, Halleck always remained concerned about Confederates crossing the Potomac and attacking Washington.[18]

North of the Potomac, Stuart, like Lee, was probably lulled into a sense of complacency as the Army of Northern Virginia bivouacked around Frederick, Maryland, on Sunday 7 September 1862.[19] Stuart set up his headquarters at Urbana to be close to Lee as well as to be on the main road from Washington on his Parr's Ridge/Sugarloaf Line. Lee, Stuart, as well as most of Lee's commanders believed that the Union response from the troops in and around Washington, D.C., would not be swift. And based on what they knew of McClellan and his snail-like crawl up the Peninsula three months ago, and the drubbing they gave to Pope at Second Bull Run, they were certain that it would likely take weeks for him to reorganize the defeated and demoralized army around Washington and assimilate newly arrived levies.[20] Then, many more days would pass before the rejuvenated Yankee army would leave the Washington defenses adopting its usual methodical pace. This would give Lee and his army sorely needed rest and allow it to feast on the bounty of Maryland's late summer harvest after months of arduous campaigning. Once the Federals did make an appearance, Lee's army would have regained its strength, brought up its stragglers, and then be able maneuver further away from the Union army's base and lengthen the Federal line of operation. Then, Lee would finally pounce, perhaps in Pennsylvania's Cumberland Valley, and hope to isolate parts of the Union army and destroy it as he failed to do on the Peninsula and at Second Bull Run.

But these lazy, late summer days in Maryland lulled both Lee and Stuart into a more complacent attitude than they should have adopted. Undoubtedly the lush, untouched fields and orchards along with the undamaged houses were a welcome respite from the ravaged fields and farms through which the army had fought for the last few months. Even though it is understandable based on Lee's and Stuart's experience with the Federals for the prior year, Stuart as the cavalry division commander reporting directly to Lee, should not have let the relaxed control of his army commander lower his guard. And Lee knew or should have known that Stuart, the "Gay Cavalier," needed tighter control and guidance than any of Lee's other commanders. Lee recognized that Stuart was an excellent cavalry leader and personally brave, but by now Lee should have seen that he was also prone to showy, flamboyant, and sometimes impulsive behavior, seeking and enjoying public acclaim and adoration.[21]

Unfortunately during the beginning of this campaign as has been seen, Stuart was true to form with his penchant for frolic and female attention during his famous "Sabers and Roses Ball" on the evening of

---

officers. The Secretary told me that if he had required such a list, a more correct one could not have been furnished him. Who is the traitor?" 70. A correspondent from the *Times* of London wrote on 7 July 1861 that "A swarm of newspaper correspondents has settled down upon Washington...but the Government experience the inconvenience of the smallest movements being chronicled for the use of the enemy, who, by putting one thing and another together, are no doubt enabled to collect much valuable information," Charles Howard Russell, *My Diary North and South* (Boston, MA: T. O. H. P. Burnham, 1863), 397. For a detailed look about reporters and their dealing with the Federal government and army news see Weisberger, 74-124.

[17] Carman, Pierro, 43-44.

[18] Carman, Pierro, 65, 83, 84, 193.

[19] Harsh, *Flood*, 111-113.

[20] Note that Lee was not aware of the identity of the Union army's commander until after 9 September, but Lee was still apparently confident that the demoralized armies of McClellan and Pope would need time to recover and absorb the thousands of new recruits flooding in from Lincoln's latest calls for troops, Harsh, *Flood*, 130.

[21] Burke Davis, *Jeb Stuart, The Last Cavalier* (New York: Rinehart, 1957; New York: Wings Books, 1992), 211, hereafter *Stuart*. Thomas, 128.

8 September near his headquarters at Urbana, Maryland. While Stuart's actions in camp in Maryland were similar to those in Virginia, he showed poor judgment by continuing to pursue such merriment in unfriendly country, with the real threat of the Army of the Potomac advancing toward him. One of his headquarters staff called the sojourn at the Urbana headquarters "delightful" since "[t]here was nothing to do but await the advance of the great army preparing around Washington" and enjoy "the society of the charming girls around us to the utmost" in their "oasis in the war-worn desert of our lives....General Stuart like a good soldier knew how to improve the passing hours in the enjoyment of the charming society the country round afforded."[22] Clearly, Stuart's mood of jollity in this "Merry War" and lack of serious concern about the enemy prevailed and worse, infected his staff. But complacency in the Confederate camps and even with Lee should not have prejudiced Stuart since he, as Lee's eyes and ears, ought to have watched the enemy closely, to ensure that Lee was not surprised. Waiting the advance of the great army was exactly what he should not have been doing; rather, he should have been aggressively scouting for any sign of that advance well in front of Lee's line on the Monocacy; Stuart should have gone through Parr's Ridge and gotten much closer to Washington. His poor scouting was his most egregious failure in this campaign, but Lee must indirectly share much of that blame by the relatively complacent ambiance permeating his headquarters, and directly by not ensuring that Stuart was scouting closer to Washington, and perhaps by keeping him busier to prevent him from needless frivolities.[23]

Stuart's capture of the Union lookout station on Sugarloaf Mountain on 6 September should have been of major importance to Lee as an observation point and signal station. Although Confederate troopers and signalmen held it until Pleasonton's troopers recaptured it on 11 September, nothing is reported of what use they made of this commanding vista, even after they established a signal station there.[24] Rebel signal officers had time to make use of the mountain, and with the Union equipment captured by Stuart's troopers on the 6th, they certainly had no excuse not to be able to provide information to Lee. But it may be that what they saw of Union army movements was not helpful to Lee, or their reports never reached his headquarters. One may conjecture that unless such reports were of immediate tactical importance, Lee viewed them as inconsequential, as he firmly believed that the Federal pursuit would not be imminent. Similarly, while Stuart's cavalry and the army's infantry cut telegraph wires, interrupted train service, and breached the C&O Canal, no evidence is found showing that any telegraph messages or Union correspondence were intercepted in Maryland. There is a record of some use of a Confederate "secret service fund of several hundred dollars in greenbacks... [available] through Col. Porter Alexander" to pay spies or guides—some guides were compensated for their services. Alexander wrote "I saw my first green-backs while on this very march from Richmond to the Potomac [prior to the Maryland Campaign]. I still had something to do with the secret service & a few hundred

---

[22] Blackford, 140. Perhaps fearing that he overemphasized the fun they had, he added "Our horses stood saddled day and night, and Stuart and his staff slept in the open air in the shady yard of the residence of Mr. Cocky, with clothes, boots, spurs and arms on, ready for instant action," ibid.

[23] Gen. Lee wrote Davis on 8 September that "As far as I can learn, the enemy are not moving in this direction, but continue to concentrate about Washington," OR, vol. 19, pt. 2, 600-601. Here he shows that he does not know McClellan is in command and that by this date Union movements were underway but clearly not reported by Stuart or other sources Lee had. But in his next dispatch to his president, he wrote that "From reports that have reached me, I believe that the enemy are pushing a strong column up the Potomac River by Rockville and Darnestown, and by Poolesville toward Seneca Mills. I hear that the commands of Sumner, Sigel, Burnside, and Hooker are advancing in the direction above mentioned," ibid., 602. Unfortunately, he does not reveal the sources of his "reports" but large troop movements out of Washington were likely seen by Confederate sympathizers and eventually reached Gen. Lee perhaps through some of Stuart's videttes. McClellan reported on the morning of 8 September that "Sykes, Sumner, and Banks near here [Rockville]. Burnside and Hooker move to-day to Brookville. Pleasonton will advance his cavalry to Barnesville, Hyattstown, Damascus, Unity, etc.," OR, vol. 19, pt. 2, 209.

[24] Fishel, 212; OR, vol. 19, pt. 2, 201.

dollars of green backs was committed to me by the order of Gen. Lee for use as occasion required, & I disbursed it all by giving it to trusty scouts whom Gen. Stuart selected & handled."[25]

McClellan clearly recognized the value of Sugarloaf Mountain as a key terrain feature when he directed Maj. Gen. William B. Franklin on 10 September to take the mountain quickly: "the earlier we gain the Sugar Loaf the better."[26] Taking Sugarloaf was also ordered because it was an "important object" and it "must be carried."[27] McClellan ordered Couch to assist Pleasonton in taking Sugar Loaf with his main force if necessary and then he ordered Couch to "hurry forward a brigade to the support of General Pleasonton as rapidly as possible....The mountain must be carried if it takes all your command....General Franklin has been ordered to afford you any assistance that may be necessary to accomplish the object".[28] Unfortunately for McClellan, Confederates held it until Pleasonton's troopers recaptured it on 11 September; Union signal operators had it in full operation quickly late in the afternoon of 11 September, communicating with Poolesville, and the next day a station was reopened at Point of Rocks.[29] McClellan noted its use when it reported Union troops moving into Frederick on 12 September.[30] The early loss of this post was a serious blow to the Union intelligence gathering effort during the critical first days of the campaign and Pleasonton's failure to quickly recapture it has to be seen as one of the cavalry commander's major failures. It may be argued that McClellan should have been much more emphatic about his wish that it be quickly captured as the actions of Pleasonton, Couch, and Franklin, clearly showed that they did not think its capture very urgent. In fairness to McClellan, he did urge its capture, but those to whom he assigned the task failed to appreciate the urgency as Union infantry could have easily pushed aside Confederate cavalry on the mountain had they been aggressively led. Perhaps McClellan could have expressed the critical nature of the mountain by ensuring that his orders were closely followed, and by sending staff officers to monitor its capture. This failure again demonstrates that he was unable to adequately manage all aspects of the intelligence gathering and analyzing tasks with which he burdened himself.[31] McClellan likely placed a high priority

---

[25] Harsh, *Flood*, 108; Alexander, 140. Capt. Frederick M. Colston who was later on Lee's staff wrote that "There was a fund in United States current funds kept at the headquarters to pay scouts, etc., who had to go into the enemy's lines," "Last Months in the Army of Northern Virginia, *SHSP*, vol. 38, 14. It may be that most of the routes the Union army were taking from Washington were not easily visible as they were behind Parr's Ridge. McClellan reported on 8 September that My scouts have been to-day within 3 miles of Barnesville, and met a small force of the enemy, but encountered no large bodies of troops. They have also been to near Ridgeville, on the Baltimore and Ohio Railroad, where they saw nothing of the enemy. I shall, to-morrow, send them across the railroad toward Liberty and New London...to discover whether they are advancing from Frederick toward Baltimore," ibid., 212.

[26] *OR*, vol. 19, pt. 2, 238. Carman believes that if Sugarloaf had been carried on 10 September as it should have except for the dilatory actions of Pleasonton, Couch and Franklin, Lee's movements out of Frederick might have been seen, Carman, Pierro, 87. Interestingly, McClellan reported on 9 September to Curtin that Union troop had retaken Sugarloaf, perhaps due to a misunderstood communication from Pleasonton or other source. On 9 September, Pleasonton received a message from McClellan's chief of staff, Marcy, that "Major Myer, Chief Signal Officer, thinks the possession of Sugar Loaf Mountain as a signal station will be of great importance to us, and that its possession by the enemy is of great benefit to them," *OR*, vol. 51, pt. 1, 802-803. See above Chapter 6 for more details about Sugarloaf and Signal Corps operations.

[27] *OR*, vol. 51, pt. 1, 807; Brown 327.

[28] *OR*, vol. 51 pt. 1, 808-809.

[29] *OR*, vol. 19, pt. 2, 254, 271; *OR*, vol. 19, pt. 1, 127; Brown, 326. The telegraph line from Point of Rocks to Washington was apparently operating as early as 12 September. Within a half mile of the Potomac, Point of Rocks gives a vantage point almost 700 feet high with excellent east-west views but not to the north as this point is on a ridge. Close to the river, the ridge is still 600 feet above sea level.

[30] *OR*, vol. 19, pt. 2, 258; Harsh, *Flood*, 189.

[31] Carman goes on at length about the excellent use Union signalmen could have made had it been recaptured on the 9th or 10th giving McClellan the information of the Confederate withdrawal from Frederick, Carman, Pierro, 86-88. Couch and Franklin who were the ranking Federal officers tasked with securing the height were not the most aggressive generals under McClellan's command but were the closest to the mountain.

on the recapture of Sugarloaf as the Balloon Corps, which McClellan had used with benefit on the Peninsula, was not available. Thus, Stuart's effective screening, the lack of good observation from Sugarloaf, and absence of Lowe's balloons, materially hindered McClellan's information gathering at this stage of the campaign.

While Stuart's inability to accurately gauge Union movements and numbers reflect poorly on Stuart's scouting, they also show the effectiveness of Union efforts to thwart such attempts.[32] Also, operating in a hostile country in the face of larger Union forces had to negatively affect Stuart's reconnaissance. Stuart's tardy official report dated 13 February 1864 about his Maryland Campaign typically underplays his inability to accurately understand Union deployments and movements. For example, he reported that on 12 September "The enemy studiously avoided displaying any force, except a part of Burnside's corps, and built no camp-fires in their halt at Frederick that night" so Stuart, despite taking "[e]very means…to ascertain what the nature of the enemy's movement was", was unsuccessful.[33] The normally resourceful Stuart was here frustrated by lack of campfires and was unable to use any of his ingenious schemes to surmount Union screening efforts. In a statement in a dispatch to Stuart on 12 September Lee, perhaps shows his concern with Stuart's performance, when he told him to "Keep me advised of the movements of the enemy, and do not let him discover, if possible, our movements." It is remarkable that the army commander had to remind his cavalry commander of the two most important missions of the cavalry: reconnaissance and screening during the campaign.[34] It may have been that Lee had only been in command of the army since 1 June 1862 and was still learning the abilities and limits of his generals, or perhaps due to the dearth of information from Stuart, he was concerned about his cavalry leader's performance.

Stuart's inability to give Lee accurate information of Federal movements before Lee wrote the Lost Order on 9 September, resulted in his commander not worrying about dividing his army into four parts to take Harpers Ferry and Martinsburg. Once it was found, Stuart's inaccurate reports of the ensuing Union pursuit put Lee's divided army at risk of being defeated in detail, because Stuart, and therefore Lee, believed that McClellan was marching the bulk of his forces directly to relieve Harpers Ferry. That this made good military sense for McClellan in Lee's eyes cannot be disputed. Another major factor contributing to Lee's near disaster at South Mountain was Stuart's and Lee's lack of knowledge that Jackson had not quickly taken the Martinsburg and Harpers Ferry garrisons according to plan. Once Lee learned of this delay, he quickly realized that he had to prevent McLaws from being overwhelmed from the rear, so Lee now had to defend the South Mountain gaps. Added concern for Lee was that his army was then fragmented into five parts since he had sent Longstreet with the army trains to Hagerstown, based on an inaccurate report of a Union advance from Pennsylvania. Here again, accurate information would have allowed Longstreet's forces to remain closer to Boonsboro to have given quicker support to Hill at the South Mountain passes, and not chase after phantom Union cavalry hoards descending from Pennsylvania. One could easily argue that Stuart should have been charged with helping to ensure that Lee's scattered units would remain in better contact with the army commander, but evidence shows that Lee's three forces contending at Harpers Ferry, and even Stuart himself, maintained inadequate and tardy contact with army headquarters. Poor contact among his widely-spread forces contributed to Lee's problems coordinating his army; poor communication occurred despite having cavalry detachments assigned to the far flung commands. McClellan's heavy attacks on Turner's, Fox's, and Crampton's Gaps

---

[32] Harsh, *Flood*, 205.
[33] *OR*, vol. 19, pt. 1, 816.
[34] Harsh, *Flood*, 198.

surprised Lee and Stuart, as they expected McClellan would quickly move down Middletown Valley directly from Frederick to relieve Harpers Ferry.[35]

Stuart, on 12 September, perhaps in a clumsy effort to do some effective scouting on the Union right flank as he thought Lee was planning on heading for Pennsylvania from Hagerstown, sent about a third of his cavalry off on what turned out to be a fruitless mission to the north. Fitzhugh Lee with his brigade was ordered to learn of Union movements but after terrorizing the town of Westminster, Maryland, and destroying a B&O Railroad bridge, nothing was heard from him again until he returned to Boonsboro late on Sunday the 14th. In general, Stuart's troopers could tell him little of McClellan's more rapid movements west: "The eyes and ears of the Confederate army, while neither blind nor deaf, saw and heard very little on September 12."[36]

One aspect that did work well for the Confederates was their spreading of disinformation to gullible civilians. Washington officials and McClellan's headquarters received many reports showing Lee heading for Washington, Baltimore, Harrisburg, or Philadelphia. The result was that Lincoln, Halleck, and McClellan had to ensure that both Washington and Baltimore were covered, and fend off frantic requests for assistance by Governor Andrew Curtin and other Pennsylvania officials. Confederate cavalry always seemed to do well at planting misleading information and perhaps excelled. Pleasonton reported on 7 September that Baltimore was listed as the object of the Confederate movement based on information he received from civilians. In one report, the Confederate troopers told a group of female admirers they were going to Frederick and then to Baltimore.[37] Lee certainly appreciated and encouraged this activity: "Stuart with his cavalry was close up to the enemy and doing everything possible to keep him in ignorance and to deceive him by false reports, which he industriously circulated."[38]

Lee did not suffer from reports about greatly exaggerated estimates of his opponent's troop strengths, as did McClellan. Lee would have been unconcerned as he knew that he would be outnumbered in any event, but he knew that many of the Union troops would have been untrained. McClellan firmly believed that he was outnumbered and so proceeded cautiously, even after finding the Lost Order on 13 September. McClellan's overestimates of Lee's available forces began even before Lee ventured north of the Potomac River. On 28 August 1862 McClellan informed Halleck that "Reports numerous, from

[35] Ibid., 299.

[36] Ibid., 205.

[37] *OR*, vol. 19, pt. 2, 200-201.

[38] Lee, *Lee the Soldier*, 25; The method of using disinformation could take several forms such as planting erroneous stories in newspapers, coaching soldiers with certain stories and have them "desert" to the enemy giving false information to interrogators, and using double agents by having them report some truthful information blended with false or misleading data, Tidwell 44. Pleasonton also was not averse to passing on rumors such as that on 10 September Jackson was on the National Road east of Frederick near Parr's Ridge when in fact he was twenty miles away from that point heading in the opposite direction, Stephen W. Sears, *George B. McClellan: The Young Napoleon* (New York: Da Capo Press, 1999), 278. McClellan's delay in issuing orders to his corps after finding S.O. 191 was a serious mistake which led to the surrender of the Harpers Ferry garrison, 282-286. David Strother briefly mentioned McClellan's and his 50-strong-staff's conservatism shortly after joining: "As far as I have observed, the tone of those surrounding General McClellan's person is eminently conservative. Personal grievances have perhaps biased my judgment, but my natural character leads me to prefer strong and active measures in war," *Diaries*, 104. On 14 November of 1862 just before he was to journey with Banks to Louisiana, he wrote more about his opinion of McClellan and his staff: "My opinion of McClellan is that he is the most capable man we have in military affairs. His head is clear and his knowledge complete. He wants force of character and is swayed by those around him. Fitz-John Porter...has been the evil genius, and has ruined him as he did Patterson. The people about McClellan, without taking into consideration their social and characteristic merits, were the most ungallant, good-for-nothing set of martinets that I have yet met with. I do not mean that they were inefficient in their special duties, but not a man among them was worth a damn as a military adviser—or had any show of fire or boldness. A self-indulgent and timorous policy seemed to pervade the whole surrounding and the General. His very mildness of manner, voice, and deportment show him unfitted by character to wield successfully a great power," *Diaries*, 129.

various sources, that Lee and Stuart, with large forces, are at Manassas; that the enemy, with 120,000 men, intend advancing on the forts near Arlington and Chain Bridge, with a view to attacking Washington and Baltimore."[39] McClellan's estimates of Lee's army during the campaign were based on wildly varying reports from civilian and official sources, but there is no evidence that McClellan saw any of the more realistic figures available. In a report to Lincoln on 10 September, he said that "statements I get regarding the enemy's forces that have crossed to this side range from 80,000 to 150,000."[40] He seems to have settled on the estimate of 120,000 as realistic as this number fit in with his thinking.[41]

Allan Pinkerton had contributed greatly to McClellan's intelligence gathering during the Peninsular Campaign, but did less for Union efforts during the Maryland Campaign, as his staff with McClellan was cut in half: he was operating with seven agents in Maryland, and also with a reduced staff in Washington.[42] Neither McClellan nor Pinkerton were much involved in sending out individual scouts but rather more often relied on passive intelligence such as interrogation of human sources entering or being brought into army lines, including contrabands, and free blacks, Confederate officers' servants, local civilians, refugees, prisoners of war, and deserters.[43] However, there is evidence that Pinkerton paid for information from local citizens, while some were enlisted as guides. George W. Dawson was a tax collector for the district around Poolesville and brought information to Pleasonton on 6 September. After he was put on Pinkerton's payroll, he received $50 for his efforts behind enemy lines during the next few days. As the Union army advanced, nine more were added to Pinkerton's list and others were paid small

---

[39] *OR*, vol. 12, pt. 3, 710.

[40] *OR*, vol. 19, pt. 2, 233. Harsh shows that the Confederate fit for duty on 2 September 1862 was 75,528, *Shallows*, 139; while Lee's strength for those actually fighting on 17 September at Antietam was 37,351 with 10,316 becoming casualties; *Shallows*, 201-202. McClellan estimated that Lee had 97,445 present and fit for duty on 17 September, while he had 87,164, *OR*, vol. 19, pt. 1, 67. McClellan's total casualties from 3-20 September were 15,220 *OR*, vol. 19, pt. 1, 36.

[41] Fishel, 217; *OR*, pt. 2, 254. It is interesting to note however, that he did not adopt Pennsylvania Governor Andrew Curtin's estimate of 200,000 reported from a clergyman conversing with Confederate troops before they left Frederick on 10 September. Stephen W. Sears, *Landscape Turned Red: The Battle of Antietam* (Boston: Houghton Mifflin Company, 1983), 103. Curtin, however, did report a reasonable estimate once on 8 September that the Rebel army was estimated at 30,000 to 50,000 men but in the same telegram, he included a second estimate of 75,000, *OR*, vol. 19, pt. 2, 214-215. "Unique arithmetic" refers to the data used by Pinkerton to make estimates of numbers of enemy troops for McClellan. Pinkerton and his men were not military spies and unused to military statistics and formations as well as precise writing. One main error on the Peninsula was due to his estimates that the average Confederate regiment contained 700 men perhaps twice the effectives of the average regiment. His estimates also had careless arithmetic estimating Confederate troops at 9% more than his information showed. That these numbers were "made large" was due to McClellan's desire to support his early non-Pinkerton six-figure numbers and Pinkerton's efforts to please his superior. Pinkerton clearly took extreme liberties with the data he obtained to present to McClellan what he believed the general wanted. Pinkerton was able to tinker with the numbers by claiming that he was adding enemy troop numbers to ensure a safety margin for those which were overlooked by his spies and informants, but he applied this method inconsistently. His interrogators also had a "safety first" perspective in interviewing prisoners, deserters, refugees, contrabands, etc., which made the large numbers they gave, often only rumors, more acceptable. He abandoned his estimation method of counting military units even though that would have produced more accurate numbers because he said it was too difficult to ensure the true composition of enemy forces. In August 1862 on the Peninsula he produced very accurate identification of enemy units, but his reports did not use these in his estimation of 200,000 men under Robert E. Lee. Thus Pinkerton inflated the numbers ad lib. McClellan also helped contribute to overestimates by comparing the Confederate's total force to his maneuverable force; numbers on the rolls are always higher, and sometimes much higher, than those present, equipped, and available for duty on the firing line. McClellan used enemy strength estimates as tools to explain his sluggish movements and support requests for reinforcements but he apparently truly believed in them. And Pinkerton should not be faulted for his estimates since McClellan had other sources to which Pinkerton did not have access from which the army commander should have made comparisons, Fishel, 581-587.

[42] Pinkerton had George Bangs, John Babcock, Seth Paine, Augustus Littlefield, G.H. Thiel, Alfred Cridge, and one listed only as O.F.A., Fishel, 215, 634.

[43] Fishel, 215; Sears, *Landscape*, 103.

sums for information or employment as guides.[44] Pinkerton wrote that on 16 September 1862 he "accompanied a party of cavalry sent out to reconnoitre across the Antietam. Here it was discovered that the enemy had changed the position of some of their batteries, while their left and center were upon and in front of the Sharpsburg and Hagerstown turnpike, and their extreme left rested upon the wooded

Pinkerton at left as his horse is fatally wounded on 16 September at Antietam Creek, from *Allan Pinkerton's Spy of the Rebellion*, *(New York: G.W. Dillingham Co., 1900)*, pg. 569. If Pinkerton is correct, the Union cavalry would be from the 3rd Pennsylvania as they were the cavalry regiment in that area that day accompanying Hooker's troops.

Allan Pinkerton and McClellan at a conference in 1862 at McClellan's home in Cincinnati, from Allan Pinkerton's *Spy of the Rebellion*, (New York: G.W. Dillingham Co., 1900), frontispiece. Note that Pinkerton had the artist make McClellan a lieutenant general but did not show clearly the correct arrangement of buttons on his coat—three groups of three.

[44] Fishel, 215. A guide was also used in the Union cavalry breakout from Harpers Ferry, Carman, Pierro, 135. Confederates also used guides as McLaws states in a report, Carman, Pierro, 142. The nine were Samuel Martin, Charles W. Johnson, Reuben Johnson, John Sullivan, James W. Greenwood, David W. Fowler, John Mix, J.A. Blake, and "Sam, Negro of Middletown," Fishel 634, n. 10.

heights near the cross-roads to the north. While returning from this reconnoitering expedition, fire was opened upon us from a masked battery upon the hill, and my horse, a beautiful sorrel, that had carried me for months, and to which I was much attached, was shot from under me while I was crossing the stream. Several of the men who accompanied me were seriously wounded, and I narrowly escaped with my life."[45]

McClellan described his use of what he called his "Secret Service" in the months leading up to the Maryland Campaign:

> Immediately after being assigned to the command of the troops around Washington, I organized a secret service force under Mr. E. J. Allen [Pinkerton], a very experienced and efficient person. This force, up to the time I was relieved from command, was continually occupied in procuring, from all possible sources, information regarding the strength, positions and movements of the enemy. All spies, "contrabands," deserters, refugees, and many prisoners of war, coming into our lines from the front, were carefully examined—first, by the outpost and division commanders, and then by my chief-of-staff and the provost-marshal-general. Their statements, taken in writing, and in many cases under oath, from day to day, for a long period previous to the evacuation of Manassas, comprised a mass of evidence which, by careful digests and collations, enabled me to estimate with considerable accuracy the strength of the enemy before us. Summaries, showing the character and results of the labors of the secret service force, accompany this report, and I refer to them for the facts they contain, and as a measure of the ignorance which led some journals at that time, and persons in high office, unwittingly to trifle with the reputation of an army, and to delude the country with Quaker-gun stories of the defenses, and gross understatements of the numbers, of the enemy.[46]

---

[45] Pinkerton, 569. He probably was with the 3rd Pennsylvania Cavalry. His account seems overly dramatic; no 3rd Pennsylvania troopers were reported as wounded crossing Antietam Creek, see above, Chapter 9.

[46] George B. McClellan, *Report on the Organization and Campaigns of the Army of the Potomac* (New York: Sheldon & Company, 1864), 119-120. McClellan was obviously trying to justify his overestimates of enemy strength. Allan Pinkerton was born on 25 August 1819 in Glasgow, Scotland, and died on 1 July 1884. He was one of the best known Union agents in the Civil War. He was a barrel maker in Scotland and in Illinois but quickly began his detective career after organizing a citizen's group to capture a gang of counterfeiters. Becoming sheriff of Kane County, Illinois, then Cook County, he relocated to Chicago and formed his own detective agency in 1850, the Pinkerton National Detective Agency. He guarded President-elect Lincoln from Philadelphia on his way to Washington, D.C., after one of his detectives had accidentally discovered a plot against Lincoln. He then did spying for McClellan and was next put in charge of McClellan's Department of the Ohio secret service activities. When McClellan was called to Washington, Pinkerton moved his operations with him working as a private contractor for the Union government. His operations were limited to counter-intelligence, which responsibility he shared with Lafayette Baker's group, espionage and interrogations. He concentrated too much on sending spies to Richmond using few for less strategic purposes; his men were not trained well for military spying. He worked solely for McClellan and transmitted his reports only to him. His most famous exploit was his pursuit and jailing of Confederate spy Rose O'Neal Greenhow, while more notorious were his wildly overestimated numbers of Confederate troops during the Peninsular Campaign and the Seven Days, followed by similar problems during the Antietam Campaign. He has been excused for making the "numbers large" because that is what he perceived as McClellan's desires. He left government service with McClellan's departure. Fishel, 54-76 passim, 251-255 passim, 581-587; Heidler, "Pinkerton, Allan," by Andrew Paul Bielakowski, 1525-1527. Lafayette Curry Baker was born in Stafford, N.Y., on 13 October 1826 and died on 3 July 1868 in Philadelphia. He traveled around the country as a handyman and may have taken part in vigilante activities in San Francisco before the Civil War. He was first employed as a detective in Washington, D.C., and then was employed by Brevet Lt. Gen. Winfield Scott in the summer of 1861. He was sent to Richmond but was captured near Manassas and interrogated by General P.G.T. Beauregard. In Richmond, he said he was interviewed three times by President Jefferson Davis. He next organized what he called his "National Detective Police" and he later named himself as "Chief of the United States Secret Service" which also had no foundation in law. He primarily had police authority in the general Washington, D.C., area but did send agents to Canada as well as to field armies. He seemed to have almost unlimited authority and investigated virtually all areas in addition to chasing spies and saboteurs almost leading a reign of terror. He started as a civilian employee and then received a colonelcy. He did most of his work under the aegis of Secretary of War Stanton but was directly under Stanton's former legal associate, Levi C. Turner. His group was successful in arresting spies and disloyal citizens but he was apparently not above accepting bribes to let accused persons go free. He was in charge of the party

He elaborated his desires in the following circular dated 16 December 1861 for the examination of persons coming from the enemy's direction:

The Major-General commanding directs, That all deserters, prisoners, spies, "contrabands," and all other persons whatever, coming or brought within our lines from Virginia, shall be taken immediately to the quarters of the commander of the division within whose lines they may come or be brought, without previous examination by any one, except so far as may be necessary for the officer commanding the advanced guard, to elicit information regarding his particular post: That the division commander examine all such persons himself, or delegate such duty to a proper officer of his staff, and allow no other persons to hold any communication with them: That he then immediately send them, with a sufficient guard, to the provost marshal in this city for further examination and safe keeping; and that stringent orders be given to all guards having such persons in charge not to hold any communication with them whatever; and further, that the information elicited from such persons shall be immediately communicated to the major-general commanding, or to the chief-of-staff, and to no other person whatever.

The major-general commanding further directs that a sufficient guard be placed around every telegraph station pertaining to this army, and that such guards be instructed not to allow any person, except the regular telegraph corps, general officers, and such staff officers as may be authorized by their chief, to enter or loiter around said stations within hearing of the sound of the telegraphic instruments.[47]

Then on 26 February 1862, he followed up with additional instructions in General Orders, No. 27:

All deserters from the enemy, prisoners, and other persons coming within our lines will be taken at once to the provost marshal of the nearest division, who will examine them in presence of the division commander, or an officer of his staff designated for the purpose. This examination will only refer to such information as may affect the division and those near it; especially those remote from general head-quarters.

As soon as this examination is completed, and it must be made as rapidly as possible, the person will be sent under proper guard to the provost-marshal-general, with a statement of his replies to the questions asked. Upon receiving him the provost-marshal-general will at once send him with this statement to the chief-of-staff of the Army of the Potomac, who will cause the necessary examination to be made. The provost-marshal-general will have the custody of all such persons. Division commanders will at once communicate to other division commanders all information thus obtained which affects them.[48]

McClellan goes on to explain that "In addition to the foregoing orders, the division commanders were instructed whenever they desired to send out scouts toward the enemy, to make known the object at head-quarters, in order that I might determine whether we had the information it was proposed to obtain, and that I might give the necessary orders to other commanders so that the scouts should not be molested by the guards."[49] He next attempts to show how well his orders were carried out and how accurate the information they produced was, but the numbers they produced as shown here by McClellan were wildly overblown, based on later reports by the Rebel commander, Joseph E. Johnston: "It will be seen from the report of the chief of the secret service corps, dated March 8th, that the forces of the rebel army of the Potomac at that date were as follows: At Manassas, Centreville, Bull Run, Upper Occoquan, and vicinity...80,000 men...At Brooks's Station, Dumfries, Lower Occuquan, and vicinity 18,000...At Leesburg and vicinity. 4,500...In the Shenandoah Valley...13,000...Total Number...115,500

---

which captured John Wilkes Booth on 26 April 1865, for which he was promoted to brigadier general and given a reduced reward. But his reputation was fatally tarnished after the war due to his spying on President Andrew Johnson and his lying at Johnson's impeachment trial. His memoirs published in 1867 have been found to be in many areas full of creative fiction and selective memory thus his exploits described therein are mostly untrustworthy unless corroborated by other evidence. Heidler, "Baker, La Fayette Curry," 162-163; Fishel, 24-28.

[47] McClellan, *Report on the Organization and Campaigns of the Army of the Potomac*, 120-121.

[48] Ibid., 121.

[49] Ibid., 122.

men...About three hundred field-guns, and from twenty-six to thirty siege-guns were with the rebel army in front of Washington."[50] He defends his estimates as follows: "The report made on the 17th of March, after the evacuation of Manassas and Centreville corroborates the statements contained in the report of the 8th, and is fortified by the affidavits of several railroad engineers, conductors, baggage-masters, &c., whose opportunities for forming correct estimates were unusually good. These affidavits will be found in the accompanying reports of the chief of the secret service corps."[51]

During his movement to the Peninsula, he added to his 22 March 1862 order to the commander of the Third Corps, Brig. Gen. Heintzelman, that the commanding general expected good information: "Please report to me frequently and fully the condition of things on the new field of operations, and whatever intelligence you gain as to the enemy. Engage guides in sufficient numbers at once, and endeavor to send out spies."[52]

Evidence of the use of Union spies during the Maryland Campaign is sparse but there is a statement that "a [Union] spy acting as a Confederate courier was discovered near Harpers Ferry and was at once hung to a limb of a tree on the road-side" and a report by Sumner that a spy had reported on Confederate strength.[53] Pleasonton, too, was limited to questioning civilians who may have picked up information from the Confederates passing by and from deserters and prisoners gathered in or captured by the efforts of his five brigades. Often however, prisoners purposefully gave inaccurate information or simply did not know much other than what happened to them personally or they heard through camp rumors. Stuart's cavalry screen to the east was very effective remaining virtually unbroken for most of the campaign, thus depriving Pleasonton and McClellan with first-hand knowledge of Lee's movements.[54] Carman wrote

---

[50] Ibid. In March 1862, Johnston's strength was similar to what it was during First Bull Run eight months earlier, about 36,000 near Centreville, 6,000 at Aquia Creek, and 5,000 with Stonewall Jackson in the Valley, Craig L. Symonds, *Joseph E. Johnston: A Civil War Biography* (W.W. Norton & Company: New York, NY, 1992), 141. Gen. Johnston reported for February a grand total of 47,306 aggregate present for duty and 84,222 aggregate present and absent, *OR*, vol. 5, 1086. On about 30 April 1862 Johnston reported a total effective strength of 55,633 which included troops on the Peninsula, *OR*, vol. 11, pt. 3, 479-484.

[51] McClellan, *Report on the Organization and Campaigns of the Army of the Potomac*, 122.

[52] Ibid., 153-154. As noted above in Chapter 3, Uriah H. Painter, a newspaper reporter, interviewed a contraband who had been a servant to a Rebel officer near Lee's Mills and had witnessed the Confederate withdrawal, but McClellan's Chief of Staff, his father-in-law, Randolph Marcy, said it was not so and dismissed the report as they had positive intelligence that the Confederates would make a desperate fight at Yorktown, testimony by Painter, *JCCW*, vol. 1, 283-284. As McClellan was his own chief of intelligence, the sorting and evaluation of information was not as efficacious as it might have been had a staff officer been detailed to review raw information and assign positive collection efforts relieving the general of the army of these chores. McClellan did have Pinkerton and his staff of 11 which helped McClellan in gathering information on the Peninsula but they did little evaluation. He also had Professor Thaddeus Lowe and three balloons to aid his information gathering. Painter further testified that McClellan "trusts everything, so far as getting information is concerned, to a man he has there of the name of Pinkerton Allen who always questions the contrabands and deserters; and, generally, so far as I have conversed with him, throws discredit upon their statements and attaches no importance to them," Painter, *JCCW*, vol. 1, 291. Painter later testified about how he gained his information concerning the Rebel army strength: "By getting statements from prisoners, contrabands, and deserters, and learning about different divisions and brigades, and drawing conclusions from the mass of information collected. I have at different times found a great many of their muster-rolls, and learned in that way how many men they had in their regiments," ibid., 292. Thus this reporter had a better and more reliable estimate of enemy strength that did Pinkerton and McClellan who would have done well to use the same sources. For details of McClellan's use of information and Pinkerton's employment during the Peninsular Campaign see Fishel, 146-164 passim.

[53] Bridges, *Lee's Maverick General*, 98; a quotation from Major James W. Ratchford's manuscript, 35-36. Ratchford was Hill's chief of staff. See also Armstrong, stating that Sumner reported that a reliable spy had come in from Poolesville reporting the strength of the Rebels in Maryland to be fifty thousand, 28. This number was remarkably accurate.

[54] Sears, *Landscape*, 103; Sears, McClellan, *Papers*, 442; *OR*, vol. 19, pt. 2, 194-195. Early in the campaign before Stuart's men crossed the Potomac, his troopers captured a newspaper reporter for the Philadelphia *Inquirer*, Uriah H. Painter who overheard his captors discussing the planned invasion. After escaping, he rode to Washington and warned the War Department which promptly ignored his disclosures as the revelations were not confirmed, Weisberger, 289. Had there been an agency within the War Department which was responsible for analyzing incoming information, it might have found Painter's first-hand report a

that "Cautious and deliberate as was McClellan's advance, there were reasons for it beyond Halleck's warnings: the condition of the transportation and artillery, the vigilance and superb handling of the Confederate cavalry, and the consequent ignorance of the Confederate movements....The Confederate cavalry completely masked Lee's movements. It occupied every avenue of approach and resisted every attempt to drive it. From the Potomac on its right to the Baltimore and Ohio Railroad on the left, it covered Lee's entire front and no scout could penetrate it. Consequently there was a want of reliable information, and McClellan knew neither the strength, position, nor purpose of his adversary."[55] But as effective as Stuart was in screening to the east, he could not with the relatively small forces he commanded, also screen effectively in other directions. He apparently did not view his inability to do this more extensive screening as a problem, as neither he nor Lee feared that any large Union forces would be bothering them from those directions, although as described above in the Harpers Ferry chapter, Union cavalry from Harpers Ferry did harass Rebel troops to the west and south of Frederick, Maryland. Screening worked well for both Pleasonton and Stuart, but this effective screening concomitantly inhibited good scouting for both.

Photograph taken after Antietam, likely October 1862. Men identified on accompanying list to photo as follows, not in order: William Pinkerton; George Washington (Cook); Harry Thomas; A.E. Keneaster; Lt. Col. Calhoun, A.D.C.; Capt. McLellan, A.D.C.; Sidney Denning; Chas. Hazzlett, Postmaster; Allan Pinkerton; George H. Bangs; Col. Howard, A.D.C.; Mr. Kennedy of the War Dept.; Charles Gerald; A.K. Littlefield. Arrow right center points to Pinkerton, arrow at left points to a man who appears to be John C. Babcock although this name does not appear on the list of 14 names; note there are 15 men shown in the photograph. Courtesy LOC.

---

valuable addition to other information from Northern Virginia and Southern Maryland, giving a clearer picture of Rebel intentions. Painter even sent another reporter to Point of Rocks who saw Rebel troops crossing the Potomac, but again the War Department was skeptical, Harris, 173. Perhaps Stuart's troopers should have been more careful in handling prisoners but given the Washington officials credulity Painter's efforts were for naught, Harris, 173.

[55] Carman, Pierro, 88.

Antietam, Maryland. Seated: R. William Moore and Allan Pinkerton on the right. Standing: George H. Bangs, John C. Babcock, and Augustus K. Littlefield. October 1862 by Alexander Gardner. Courtesy LOC.

As already discussed, Confederate troopers cut all telegraph lines through their areas of operations.[56] The telegraph line and the Baltimore and Ohio Railroad were cut on 6 September isolating Harpers Ferry; the telegraph line was cut beyond Harpers Ferry by 2 September.[57] But given the number of telegrams sent among Union military and civilian officials in Washington, Maryland, and Pennsylvania, rerouting on remaining lines was sufficient. Certainly the early loss of the lines to Harpers Ferry, although predictable, helped doom that garrison. There is no record of any intercepts or false information sent by telegraph other than the message received at Harpers Ferry sent by a Confederate operator but some of the best information that was obtained and transmitted for McClellan was done by telegraph by William Bender Wilson.

The services of Wilson were indirectly provided to McClellan courtesy of Governor Andrew Curtin of Pennsylvania. As rumors had Lee heading for Pennsylvania, its citizens and political representatives were almost hysterical, and Curtin was desperately concerned trying to obtain Federal troops as well as better information on Lee's movements. Curtin, at McClellan's urging, had set up an intelligence group led by Union cavalry Capt. William J. Palmer. Palmer, a very competent officer who was on leave recruiting for his unit in Kentucky, and with help from Wilson, was able to use his troopers as scouts to keep track of Confederate movements, as well as interrogate refugees and deserters. Palmer was scouting

---

[56] *OR*, vol. 19, pt. 2, 198. See also Carman, Pierro, 45, showing infantry attempting to destroy C&O Canal locks and berms and B&O Railroad facilities including presumably any Union telegraph lines in the vicinity.

[57] Carman, Pierro, 103.

in the Hagerstown area from the Pennsylvania border with Maryland to the Potomac River. With his impromptu scouts, made up of some of the recruits he enlisted and other volunteers, allowed him, with Wilson's ability to tap into telegraph wires, to send very accurate, prompt reports to Curtin.[58] A trooper of the 15th Pennsylvania Cavalry described meeting Wilson: "Another Comrade whose name I have forgotten, and myself, one morning at Greencastle were ordered to report to Colonel McClure's telegraph operator, Mr. Wilson, for scouting duty. We found him with his telegraphic apparatus on a hand car on the railroad at the State line sending dispatches to Harrisburg, and were ordered by him to take a road leading to Hagerstown paralleling the main road or pike, and to get as near that place as we could safely and procure information for him."[59] Unfortunately, Palmer's and Wilson's mostly timely and correct reporting was partially negated by Curtin's well-meaning editing before relaying the information to Washington and McClellan. As amateurs, Curtin and his assistant, Alexander McClure, a journalist and political friend, did not recognize the full value of the intelligence they received from Palmer and Wilson, and failed to summarize it well, so their condensations and interpretations distorted or left out important details. And even worse, they did not pass on some of Palmer's reports at all, and for those they did send, they did not identify Palmer as the source. McClellan knew Palmer and had recommended him to Curtin, so likely would have given the reports more weight. McClure praised Palmer's efforts:

> I was then Assistant Adjutant-General of the United States, assigned to duty at Harrisburg to make a draft under the State laws of Pennsylvania. There was no military force on the border, and not even an officer of the army who had exercised any command of troops. I was compelled, therefore, to exercise what little military authority could be enforced under the circumstances, and Governor Curtin ordered a half-organized company of cavalry, that Captain W.J. Palmer was recruiting at Carlisle, to report to me at Chambersburg for duty as scouts. I thus became commander of an army of nearly one hundred men, or about one man to each mile of border I had to guard, but Captain Palmer proved to be a host within himself, as he entered the Confederate lines every night for nearly a week under various disguises, obtained all information possible as to the movements of Lee's command, and with the aid of William W. Wilson, an expert telegrapher, who was cooperating with him, attached his instrument to the first telegraph-wire he struck and communicated to me all movements of the enemy, present and prospective, as far as he had been able to ascertain them. As rapidly as these telegrams reached me they were sent to Governor Curtin, who promptly forwarded them to the War

---

[58] Time-Life Books, *The Civil War: Spies, Scouts and Raider, Irregular Operations* (Alexandria, VA: Time-Life Books, 1985), 68-69. Pictured there is a photograph of a signalman preparing to tap into wires; a picture of a pocket key is also shown. Wilson helped Palmer by "interrogating refugees and returned scouts, writing reports of the findings of their joint effort, and serving as a clearinghouse of information...This arrangement, set up by a state government and a railroad, proved more effective than any intelligence-gathering system the Federal government had yet devised," Fishel, 219. Wilson learned how to use the telegraph when he had been a telegrapher for the Pennsylvania Central Railroad and also as a military telegrapher in Harrisburg, Pennsylvania. Curtin asked Secretary Stanton for 700 carbines with accouterments for cavalry now scouting in the Cumberland Valley. Stanton replied that the cavalry at Carlisle had already received sabers and pistols but not carbines as the rifles were not needed for scouting, *OR*, vol. 19, pt. 2, 215-216. On 9 September Curtin asked Stanton to "give me authority to use the regular cavalry and their officers at Carlisle Barracks, amid such of the Anderson Troop as I may need, for immediate service in the valley....I want to send the force under charge of Captain Palmer....I want to use them as scouts south of the State line as desired by General McClellan." Stanton referred his request to Halleck but there is no record of Curtin receiving a direct answer. He apparently either got one by other means or proceeded without a response. He followed up Halleck's unhelpful answer with this: "I have just received your message. You evidently do not understand my wishes on the subject. I want the regular cavalry, now at Carlisle garrison, and a portion of the Anderson Troop, in camp at that place, placed under my orders, to perform patrol duty at or near Hagerstown, to ascertain movements of the enemy, if any are made, and to quiet the alarm now existing among the people of the valley and along the border of the State. All the military organizations ready for the field have been sent forward to Washington. The force at Carlisle, which I want placed under my direction, is not performing any service. Can I have them? I know they can be made serviceable." *OR*, vol. 19, pt. 2, 228-229.

[59] Kirk, 41.

Department, whence they were hastened to General McClellan's headquarters, who was then moving through Maryland against Lee; and all the important information that McClellan received from the front of Lee's army until their lines faced each other at Antietam came from Captain Palmer's nightly visits within the enemy's lines and his prompt reports to me in the morning….Thus one bold, heroic, and adventurous young captain, aided by an unusually heroic young telegrapher, furnished McClellan all the reliable information he received about Lee's movements from the time McClellan left Rockville in the Antietam campaign until the shock of battle came ten days later. I met Captain Palmer at Antietam when the battle was in progress, and, after complimenting him as he so well deserved for the great work he had done, I earnestly cautioned him against attempting to repeat his experiments if Lee should be driven into Virginia. He was a young man of very few words, and made no response to my admonition beyond thanking me for my kind expressions of confidence. When Lee retreated across the Potomac, Captain Palmer followed him the next night, entered his lines again [and was captured].[60]

Pvt. Frederick J. Anspach, one of Palmer's recruits for the 15th Pennsylvania Cavalry, wrote that Wilson, "was expert telegrapher, who took the information we secured and sent it off to Harrisburg. There was no delay in this, as Wilson was generally found up near our advance pickets with his instrument connected with the wire to Harrisburg. On the night of September 11th Wilson, with J.N. Lewis and Peter Wallace, of our Regiment, took a hand car at Greencastle and started toward Hagerstown and got near the State line. Here the wire was connected, and soon the instrument was ticking away, via Greencastle to Harrisburg, what the picket posts had learned."[61]

Pennsylvania Governor Andrew Gregg Curtin. Courtesy LOC.

Capt. William Jackson Palmer Shown as a Brig. Gen. from *History of the Fifteenth Pennsylvania*, facing pg. 32.

This was the best field intelligence gathering organization formed up to this time for the Union in the east, but was ineffectively used, so materially contributed to McClellan's failure to decimate Lee.

---

[60] Alexander Kelly McClure, *Abraham Lincoln and Men of War-Times: Some Personal Recollections of War and Politics During the Lincoln Administration* (Philadelphia, PA: The Times Publishing Company, 1892), 366-368.
[61] Kirk, 33.

McClure and Curtin, in their apparently sincere but amateurish efforts to help keep McClellan and Lincoln informed of Rebel movements, did well in utilizing Palmer and Wilson, but by not transmitting Palmer's complete text and not showing who collected the information and how it was collected, its value was diminished. Therefore, when Palmer personally visited McClellan passing on more information, the army commander was not aware of how valuable Palmer's reports had been due to McClure's and Curtin's "helpful" filtering, so McClellan did not give sufficient weight to Palmer's valuable, in-person information.[62]

Palmer unknowingly helped the Harpers Ferry escape column as he had sent a local spy, Thomas Noakes, to Martinsburg on 10 September to warn them of Jackson's approaching column. Noakes helped lead the Harpers Ferry escape column to Pennsylvania on 14-15 September as he apparently remained with Union forces when they evacuated to Harpers Ferry. Palmer's group also inadvertently benefited McClellan at South Mountain on 14 September by drawing off Longstreet to Hagerstown. Some of Palmer's men were moving toward Hagerstown from Pennsylvania on 10 September, and reports reached Lee of this group, portraying it as a possible Union advance. Lee had to defend against this "threat" to not allow Union forces to menace the army's trains near Hagerstown so he sent Longstreet with troops away from Boonsboro. Thus the unintentional scare Palmer's men provided, meant that McClellan's attack at Turner's Gap initially encountered a much smaller force, as most of Longstreet's forces were near Hagerstown, and had difficulty returning to Turner's Gap when Union forces attacked unexpectedly.[63] Pvt. Frederick J. Anspach of Company D of the 15th Pennsylvania wrote the following showing how the 15th's troopers helped McClellan:

> It is hard to give in detail what these 200 men did in the next four days. They were continually on duty, either picketing or scouting, and by the activity of their movements covered such a large territory as to give the rebels in Hagerstown the impression that the force in front of them amounted to thousands. The enemy's scouts sent out returned with the message that the "Yankees were as thick as grasshoppers on the State line," and threats were made that "they would hang any of the Anderson guerrillas they caught." It seems incredible what a small force, ignorant of the methods of war, accomplished; and later, when we had learned the full duties of a soldier, it would hardly have been possible to have carried on such a campaign. The approach of two hostile forces toward each other is governed by well-known rules of warfare, and the Commander of each can fairly judge of the intentions of the other by the character of the approach. First comes the advance or a skirmish line, followed at regulation distance by the reserve, and this by the line of battle. We did nothing of the kind. Very frequently all we had were our advanced pickets, and no reserve nearer than Chambersburg—twenty miles away. What added to the confusion in the rebels' minds as to our numbers was the curiosity of our boys to see what the rebels looked like and to have their advance pickets fire a long but not dangerous shot at us. During the day some of these small scouting parties were sure to be approaching the rebel lines, not from any orders received to do so, but led by curiosity and the absence of orders. As viewed from the rebel position in Hagerstown, each one of these parties was only the advance of a much greater force behind, and the estimate they made of "ten thousand Andersons" did not seem to them to be amiss. A bold advance on their part would have dispelled this illusion, and they did make a few dashes at our pickets and nearly captured one of our posts. With only sabers and revolvers, and mounted on such farmers' horses as could be pressed into service, with civilian saddles and bridles and no spurs we were in no condition for a serious fight; but carbines were issued to us in a few days, and inspired the desire to put them to use against the enemy should the Army of Virginia cross the border.[64]

---

[62] Fishel, 218-240, *passim*.

[63] Suzanne Colton Wilson, 13-14. Some 200 of Palmer's recruits were sent by train from Carlisle to Greencastle arriving early on 10 September and after a good breakfast offered by townspeople found great excitement as fears of Rebel invasion abounded. Capt. Palmer and 20 men scouted toward Hagerstown that evening.

[64] Kirk, 32-33.

The brave William Jackson Palmer was a Quaker and an abolitionist, born in Delaware, and raised in Philadelphia, who made his name as a railroad executive prior to the Civil War, beginning as a worker on a railroad in 1853 at the age of 17. Two years later, he went to England and spent some time in France studying mines and railways, writing articles for the *Miners' Journal*. He became very familiar with railroads and did well in the railroad industry. In 1861, he determined to raise a cavalry troop "composed of young men of respectability, chosen for intelligence and patriotic spirit, and pledged not to touch intoxicating liquor during their service" to serve as a bodyguard for Maj. Gen. Robert Anderson, who was then commander of the Army of the Ohio.[65] In June 1862, Capt. Palmer was commanding the Anderson Troop, the cavalry escort for Maj. Gen. Don Carlos Buell at Huntsville, Alabama. Buell was pleased with the quality of Palmer's troopers and gave his permission through the War Department to fill a battalion of 400 men for "special service" as Buell's headquarters guard. He sent Palmer, along with a detail of troopers, to Philadelphia, Pittsburgh, and other cities in the commonwealth, where they quickly recruited their 400. Palmer soon saw that he could easily fill a regiment and received permission to do so adding 1,200 men to the rolls by the end of August. He and his cadre selected excellent candidates by requiring references. Also, his recruiters were stationed in their home towns so were acquainted with the men who applied for service, thus they could choose men knowing about their backgrounds and families.

The recruits were then sent for training to the U.S. Cavalry barracks at Carlisle, Pennsylvania, where the regiment was mustered into service on 22 August 1862 for three years or the duration of the war. Training began posthaste by regular army troopers stationed there but their schooling was soon to be interrupted by the appearance of Lee's army in Maryland. Pennsylvania Governor Curtin requested Palmer, and those of his recruits ready for service, to protect the state. Members of Palmer's recruiting party were pressed into service as temporary officers and non-commissioned officers as none had been assigned. After quickly impressing horses and accoutrements from Pennsylvania farmers and being issued pistols and sabers, some 200 of the green troopers headed south after hastily being issued uniforms. They served in various-sized detachments as scouts, pickets, messengers, etc., as well as in larger bodies used on the 17th at Antietam and on the 18th at Williamsport.[66] In the afternoon of 19 September, Palmer forded the Potomac downstream of Dam No. 4 just above Shepherdstown to learn the following:

> find out what General Lee's plans were from personal observation in his rear. He [Palmer] had been ordered by General McClellan to scout to the right of our line and strike the Potomac River at Dam No. 4 and to endeavor to ascertain what the next move of the enemy would be. Colonel Palmer was not ordered to cross the Potomac to the Virginia side, nor was it at first his intention to do so; neither did he volunteer to cross. His expedition was without the previous knowledge of headquarters, although he sent them word when he crossed. He had with him two civilians: one a cool, courageous blacksmith, and the other a patriotic parson. These he had intended to send across the ford and within the enemy's lines, but at the last moment he decided to ride across with them, see and question for himself on the Virginia side and return. It seemed to the young Colonel [then captain] that, with such a wide river as the Potomac at the back of the enemy, his retreat might become a fatal rout if the right moment could be known and promptly availed of for a vigorous attack; and although the hazardous nature of the undertaking appealed strongly to him, he would not have taken such an extra-military step had it not been for his belief that the situation for Lee's army was so critical that "perhaps," to use the Colonel's words, "the war might be ended then and there." The Colonel crossed the river toward evening, spent the night within the rebel lines and after midnight got the information he sought, to wit, that Lee's

---

[65] Donald Caughey, "Crossed Sabers: Fiddler's Green: William J. Palmer."
[66] Kirk, 13-22; 30-40.

retreat was about to begin across the Potomac, when Stuart's entire cavalry force, preparing for a raid into Pennsylvania around McClellan's rear, came up and guarded the bank forward and back, preventing the Colonel's return. He, with the blacksmith, was taken prisoner by a battery. The parson brought the information back to General McClellan, but too late.[67]

Palmer told his own story of this expedition ending with his capture. He said that he received permission from McClellan to cross the Potomac and learn if Lee's army was retreating, but McClellan ordered him to take two men with him, an army scout, Jake, and a Methodist parson, Stine. Palmer was not pleased with them but agreed and set out. They moved down to the Potomac and took a ferry over to the Virginia side making their way to the cabin of a Unionist miller named Roberts. Roberts and Jake moved into Shepherdstown while Roberts's family, Palmer, and the parson remained in the cabin. After a Rebel cavalry patrol passed the cabin, Jake returned without the miller and Palmer ordered the scout to report to McClellan. Shortly, the miller returned greatly excited and reported that many enemy troops were coming. They appeared shortly setting up some guns and going into camp. That morning, they searched the miller's house and found Palmer who had changed from his uniform into civilian clothes. He took on the role of a mine owner from Maryland and was eventually sent to Richmond and was incarcerated in Castle Thunder. After several adventures there, he was finally exchanged in January 1863, his true identity as a Union cavalry captain undiscovered.[68]

After his release, Colonel Palmer recuperated, then moved west to rejoin his regiment which had suffered during his absence by a lack of good officers. Palmer reorganized the regiment and it performed well in the Tullahoma campaign and the battle of Chickamauga, covering the army's retreat. They were detached from the army during the siege of Chattanooga, then after the siege, they led the column under Sherman, which was sent to relieve Burnside's forces at Knoxville. On 13 January 1864, Col. Palmer learned that Confederate Brig. Gen. Robert B. Vance, with a force of 300 cavalry and dismounted Indians, had advanced from North Carolina and captured a small wagon train and a number of prisoners near Sevierville. Palmer's force netted them including the entire wagon train. His gallant actions brought him a recommendation for promotion. On 6 November 1864, he was brevetted brigadier general of volunteers. On 14 January 1865, at Red Hill, Alabama, Palmer and his men attacked and defeated a larger force, capturing 200 Confederate soldiers and one fieldpiece without casualties. For this action, Palmer was awarded the Medal of Honor, February 24, 1894, because "with less than 200 men, attacked and defeated a superior force of the enemy, capturing their fieldpiece and about 100 prisoners without losing a man." Before the spring campaign of 1865 was started, Brig. Gen. Palmer was assigned a cavalry brigade command under Maj. Gen. Stoneman, and succeeded to command of a division. At the end of April 1865, Palmer's division was ordered south to help in the capture of Jefferson Davis, and then he and his regiment were mustered out of service on 21 June 1865.

After the war, Palmer resumed his railroad career and also assisted in the establishment of Hampton University in Virginia. In 1871, he acquired 10,000 acres of land east of the former territorial capital, Colorado City, and laid out and created the new city of Colorado Springs, building its first home, and founded a college there. Palmer retired in 1901 and dedicated himself and his fortune to charity, funding libraries, a tuberculosis sanatorium, and a school for the deaf in Colorado Springs. In 1906, Palmer suffered a fall from a horse while on a ride with his daughters which broke his spine. He was paralyzed and confined to a wheelchair. He never missed reunions of his 15th Pennsylvania Cavalry, so unable to travel in 1907, he paid for all the expenses of the 208 surviving veterans to come to his Colorado home for a three-day reunion and celebration. William Jackson Palmer died at his home on March 13, 1909 at

[67] Kirk, 43-44.
[68] Fishel, 241-249.

the age of 72, a celebrated, genuine war hero, railroad pioneer, and philanthropist.[69] Had Curtin and McClellan better recognized the valuable information he and his men were supplying during the Maryland campaign, it is very likely that Lee would have suffered even more, before retreating across the Potomac.

The cavalry during the Maryland Campaign for both Gen. Robert E. Lee and Maj. Gen. George B. McClellan made good contributions to both army commanders. And they both failed and succeeded equally in the two areas in which cavalry was primarily employed by this stage of the war: scouting and screening.[70] Both cavalry commanders did well in screening but poorly in scouting, obviously due to the excellent screening of the other side.[71] However, even at this time early in the war, Stuart was renowned for his abilities at scouting and giving his army commander excellent information, so his failures in Maryland should be viewed as more egregious than those of Pleasonton.[72] Pleasonton's failures in scouting matched Stuart's but McClellan personally failed to understand and utilize excellent information given him from Palmer, who was not under Pleasonton's control. Pleasonton suffered more than Stuart from numbers of troopers available as some of his regiments only joined him on the march to Antietam, or after. At the beginning of September 1862 in Maryland, Stuart likely outnumbered Pleasonton counting troopers in the saddle available for use in action by the cavalry commander. Stuart did much better in deception; he spread more and better disinformation than did Pleasonton primarily because the southern horsemen were apparently much better at this during this stage of the war; Pleasonton had little need to try to deceive the Rebels for which he was searching as he was the pursuer. Both sides used guides or civilians familiar with the area to show alternate routes of travel but the Union army had the advantage of more ardent support. Local civilians also were able to help both sides in describing activities of soldiers they had seen. But initially, when Confederate units entered Montgomery County, the easternmost county in Maryland during the campaign, they had more sympathizers than when they moved west, into Frederick County, then finally into Washington County.[73]

---

[69] John Stirling Fisher and Chase Mellen, *A Builder of the West: The Life of General William Jackson Palmer* (Caldwell, ID: The Caxton Printers, Ltd., 1939), 88-103. Donald Caughey, "Crossed Sabers: Fiddler's Green: William J. Palmer." Thomas P. Lowry, "William J. Palmer: Forgotten Union General of America's Civil War," *Civil War Times*, September 2007. Eicher, 415.

[70] "Scouting" and "reconnaissance" will be used interchangeably; note that "picketing" and "screening" are used to mean the same even though some would make the case that cavalry screening is more involved with guarding the flanks of an army on the move. Mark N. Boatner, III, *The Civil War Dictionary*, New York: David McKay Company, Inc., 1987, defines "reconnaissance" as "Efforts undertaken by an armed force to gather information of the enemy's location, strength, activities, etc. It does not include espionage. Spelled 'reconnoisance' during the Civil War," 683. Some make a distinction between "scouting" and "reconnoitering" by defining scouting as done by a single person or a small group perhaps done by soldiers wearing civilian clothes or uniforms of the opposing side, which reconnoitering implies scouting done by regular cavalry or uniformed partisans in larger groups, Jeffrey D. Wert, "reconnaissance" and "scout." In *Historical Times Illustrated Encyclopedia of the Civil War*, Patricia L. Faust, ed. (New York: Harper & Row, 1986), 618, 663. Soldiers caught in civilian clothes or in the other army's uniform were subject to sentence of death often done summarily without benefit of a trial or, at best, with a "drum-head" court. Civilian spies caught in either uniform were similarly dealt with as were spies caught in civilian clothes. Methods of dealing with spies and scouts varied from on-the-spot executions to immediate release with or without parole if the person claimed to be a soldier. Often the local commander simply sent the prisoner up the chain of command to make a determination. Fishel defines reconnaissance as the cavalry's first duty vice more publicity-producing activities such as raiding, 5.

[71] Fishel, 213. See also Carman, Pierro, 88, who says that no scout could penetrate Stuart's screen.

[72] Fishel also states that "Stuart's...cavalry reconnaissance was an area of unquestioned Confederate superiority," 568. Unfortunately for Lee, Stuart did not demonstrate this superiority during the Maryland Campaign. As noted above, Pleasonton did well as a cavalry commander on the Peninsula.

[73] The percentage of slaveholders was much higher in Montgomery County as was the number of Confederate sympathizers. As has already been seen, residents of Poolesville in this county actively took part to help capture Union cavalry in the first skirmish of the Maryland Campaign. In contrast, civilians fired on Confederate cavalry in Middletown and Boonsboro as they

Historian Stephen Sears evaluated Pleasonton's efforts and found them wanting—Pleasonton provided less information than did Stuart:

> Pleasonton was unable to furnish any firsthand intelligence, for he never succeeded in breaking through Stuart's cavalry screen for a look at the Confederate army. He did collect and evaluate dozens of secondhand accounts, however. He interrogated captives taken in skirmishes and numerous deserters and stragglers, and any number of civilians eager to tell what they knew of the invaders. In his questioning Pleasonton might have exercised the wisdom of the Frederick civilian who, after trying to find out what he could from the Rebels occupying the town, noted in his diary, "Bragging is a favorite game with them, and they do it well." Instead, he credited every tale from citizens professing loyalty to the Union. Like Pinkerton, Alfred Pleasonton combined great industry with small judgment.[74]

---

retreated through those towns and warned the Harpers Ferry escape column of Rebel presence in Sharpsburg. In April 1863, some seven months after Antietam, the Union army promulgated rules detailing, among other things, how captured partisans, scouts, spies, etc., should be handled likely codifying much of what was already in practice. Articles of interest include the following to show the viewpoints Union and most Confederate commanders might have taken before these rules were adapted. Art. 63: Troops who fight in the uniform of their enemies, without any plain, striking, and uniform mark of distinction of their own, can expect no quarter.

Art. 81: Partisans are soldiers armed and wearing the uniform of their army, but belonging to a corps which acts detached from the main body for the purpose of making inroads into the territory occupied by the enemy. If captured, they are entitled to all the privileges of the prisoner of war.

Art. 82: Men, or squads of men, who commit hostilities, whether by fighting, or inroads for destruction or plunder, or by raids of any kind, without commission, without being part and portion of the organized hostile army, and without sharing continuously in the war, but who do so with intermitting returns to their homes and avocations, or with the occasional assumption of the semblance of peaceful pursuits, divesting themselves of the character or appearance of soldiers - such men, or squads of men, are not public enemies, and, therefore, if captured, are not entitled to the privileges of prisoners of war, but shall be treated summarily as highway robbers or pirates.

Art. 83: Scouts, or single soldiers, if disguised in the dress of the country or in the uniform of the army hostile to their own, employed in obtaining information, if found within or lurking about the lines of the captor, are treated as spies, and suffer death.

Art. 88: A spy is a person who secretly, in disguise or under false pretense, seeks information with the intention of communicating it to the enemy. The spy is punishable with death by hanging by the neck, whether or not he succeed in obtaining the information or in conveying it to the enemy.

Art. 93: All armies in the field stand in need of guides, and impress them if they cannot obtain them otherwise.

Art. 94: No person having been forced by the enemy to serve as guide is punishable for having done so.

Art. 95: If a citizen of a hostile and invaded district voluntarily serves as a guide to the enemy, or offers to do so, he is deemed a war-traitor, and shall suffer death.

Art. 96: A citizen serving voluntarily as a guide against his own country commits treason, and will be dealt with according to the law of his country.

Art. 97: Guides, when it is clearly proved that they have misled intentionally, may be put to death. U.S. Adjutant General's Office, prepared by Francis Lieber, *Instructions for the Government of the United States in the Field, Originally Issued as General Order no. 100, Adjutant General's Office, 1863* (Washington, DC: Government Printing Office, 1898), 21, 26-27, 28, 29-30.

[74] Stephen W. Sears, *George B. McClellan: The Young Napoleon* (New York: Da Capo Press, 1999), 274. As already noted, providing information to his commander, as long as the source of the information is shown, along with an estimate of its veracity based on the circumstances of how the information was obtained, allows the evaluator to make his own judgment. Pleasonton sent to army headquarters information which was at best questionable, and at worst wrong, such as his report on 4 September that "From what I see of this country, I do not think they will cross the Potomac in large force below Harpers Ferry," but most of Gen. Lee's army did exactly that, *OR*, vol. 19, pt. 2, 185. He also told McClellan on 6 September that Lee planned on attacking Washington, *OR*, vol. 19, pt. 2, 192. Then on 7 September, he changed his opinion and reported to McClellan that "All reports agree that Baltimore is their destination," ibid., 200. Later that day he sent two more reports repeating that destination, ibid., 200-201. Pleasonton received an unwelcome nickname by some newspaper editors and post-war Confederate writers: "The Knight of Romance" describing his reputation as a truth teller. One historian wrote that in his efforts "to achieve public renown" Pleasonton endeavored to garner military success but "He lacked integrity and humility." In his attempts to ensure a lasting legacy, he "attempted to create a legacy by deception," Andie Custer, "The Knight of Romance: General Alfred Pleasonton in the Gettysburg Campaign," *Blue & Gray Magazine*, vol. 22, issue 2, spring 2005, 6-7; Edward G. Longacre, "Alfred

While McClellan and his forces were operating in a relatively friendly area, the information he received was so plentiful with much of it inaccurate that its analysis was difficult. Since Pleasonton's scouting efforts were nullified by Stuart's excellent screening, McClellan had to rely on other sources for information, even employing members of his staff as opportunistic scouts. Lt. James Harrison Wilson, a volunteer temporarily attached to McClellan's staff, and a future successful cavalry general in the west, wrote the following:

> With [Capt. George A.] Custer, [Capt. Wesley] Merritt, [Lt. Nicolas] Bowen, [Lt. Josiah H.] Kellogg, and Jack [Lt. John M.] Wilson, all young West Pointers, we formed a mess and soon became known as a hard-working, hard-riding gang ready for any service that might come our way....[McClellan] directed Ingalls, the chief quartermaster, to keep us supplied with fresh mounts so that we might go whenever called upon. By the end of the week we had a string of twenty-five horses, all about the best that the country could supply....Those of us who were engineers were kept going night and day, reconnoitering and scouting. Bowen and I, assisted by the French Count de Vilarceau, while operating on the left toward Crampton's Gap and Catoctin Mountain, passed through Damascus, Hyattsville, Goshen, Urbanna, Middletown, Frederick, and Keedysville, scouring the country in all directions for the enemy....Camping when night overtook us where we could find forage, we sent our information and sketches by courier to the acting chief engineer, Major Duane, without relaxing our advance in search of the enemy"[75]

Unfortunately, many of those sources other than Wilson and this "gang," while well meaning, were unhelpful, even those from officials such as Halleck and Curtin, who sometimes repeated wild and unsubstantiated rumors. And once McClellan found S.O. 191, he followed it despite numerous reports showing that Lee's army was deviating from it.[76] If there was one intelligence coup of this campaign, it was McClellan's finding Lee's S.O. 191 on 13 September. After finding this order and adding it to the information he already had, McClellan arguably had all the intelligence he needed to annihilate Lee. His fatal problem was that he was unable to discern which information was accurate and reliable, even

---

Pleasonton: 'The Knight of Romance,'" *Civil War Times Illustrated*, vol. 13, no., 8, Dec. 1974, 10-15. Custer's article details Pleasonton's shortcomings especially during and after Gettysburg. Col. Charles Russell Lowell of the 2nd Massachusetts Cavalry wrote on 23 July 1863 the following about Pleasonton in a letter: "I don't call any cavalry officer good who can't see the truth and tell the truth. With an infantry officer, this is not [so] essential, but cavalry are the eyes and ears of the army and ought to see and hear and tell truly; — and yet it is the universal opinion that P—'s own reputation, and P—'s late promotions are bolstered up by systematic lying, Edward W. Emerson, *Life and Letters of Charles Russell Lowell* (Boston, MA: Houghton Mifflin Company, 1907), 279. Capt. Charles Francis Adams, Jr., 1st Massachusetts, Cavalry, wrote on 12 May 1863 after learning that Hooker would replace Stoneman with Pleasonton: "Now Pleasonton is the *bête noire* of all cavalry officers. Stoneman we believe in. We believe in his judgment, his courage and determination. We know he is ready to shoulder responsibility, that he will take good care of us and won't get us into places from which he can't get us out. Pleasonton also we have served under. He is pure and simple a newspaper humbug. You always see his name in the papers, but to us who have served under him and seen him under fire he is notorious as a bully and toady. He does nothing save with a view to a newspaper paragraph. At Antietam he sent his cavalry into a hell of artillery fire and himself got behind a bank and read a newspaper, and there, when we came back, we all saw him and laughed among ourselves. Yet mean and contemptible as Pleasonton is, he is always *in* at Head Quarters and now they do say that Hooker wishes to depose Stoneman and hand the command over to Pleasonton. You may imagine our sensations in prospect of the change," Charles Francis Adams, *A Cycle of Adams Letters, 1861-1865*, ed. Worthington Chauncey Ford, vol. 2 (Boston, MA: Houghton Mifflin Company, 1920), 8. Pleasonton's performance during the Maryland Campaign was better than in his later Civil War career. In Maryland, he could be fairly criticized for being too credulous and by being not aggressive enough in his scouting efforts, but later in his career, he performed poorly such as his scouting and battling with Jeb Stuart as Gen. Lee's army headed north at the beginning of the Gettysburg Campaign, Fishel, 433-440, in which the author describes Pleasonton's storytelling regarding the Rebel army's movements.

[75] James Harrison Wilson, *Under the Old Flag: Recollections of Military Operations in the War for the Union, the Spanish American War, the Boxer Rebellion, Etc.*, vol. 1 (New York: D. Appleton and Company, 1920), 102-104.

[76] Fishel, 225-226.

though he was convinced that S.O. 191 was genuine, and he characteristically failed to move quickly enough even after finding the Lost Order.[77] Following his usual practice, McClellan served as his own chief of intelligence so had to review all the reports that Pinkerton generated, as well as the many telegrams and other reports sent to his headquarters. Pinkerton never came close to filling a chief of intelligence role as he was kept busy sending spies to Richmond, conducting the army's interrogation service, and turning out estimates of enemy numbers; the work of assimilating and evaluating the information from his and all of the army's other sources was left to McClellan. The modern concept of an intelligence staff assembling information from all sources and integrating it into reports to the commanding general would be one of the innovations introduced by a later commander of the Army of the Potomac, Joseph Hooker.[78] McClellan did not have the time to effectively sort out and analyze the flood of information thus once he had the Lost Order in his hands, he slavishly followed it, in fact more closely than did Lee and his generals. Clearly, he would have done much worse against Lee without this find, but he could have accomplished more, at least by ensuring that Franklin moved with at least some semblance of celerity. Stuart and Pleasonton maintained fairly effective cavalry screens thwarting both Union and Confederate efforts to gauge the other's movements. That Stuart's screening and patrolling were usually effective is shown by the fact that none of the several messengers sent to Harpers Ferry by Halleck or McClellan made it through to their destination, although as has been seen above, two couriers from Harpers Ferry did get through to McClellan.[79] Both Lee and McClellan were seriously hampered by inadequate scouting but Lee suffered more as he almost lost his army because of it. While Pleasonton's cavalry did not make a major contribution to McClellan's efforts, it did the best it could with diminished numbers and fatigued men and horses. And unlike Stuart, Pleasonton's failures did not materially contribute to his army commander's near debacle during the Maryland Campaign.

---

[77] Fishel, 238. It is questionable that his army would have had the "legs" to chase down Lee's divided army in any event.

[78] His loss of his two French aides-de-camp, Louis Philippe d'Orleans and his brother Robert Duc de Chartres, who helped summarize the information coming into army headquarters, was a blow to his ability to address the flow of data.

[79] Halleck sent two couriers to Harpers Ferry, Atkins S. Lawrence and Edward Meagher, but both failed to reach their destination. McClellan sent three couriers but none reached Harpers Ferry, *OR*, vol. 19, pt. 1, 26; Fishel, 215, chap. 9, n. 11; McClellan, *Papers*, 459. One courier sent by McClellan on 15 September to Miles, O'Sullivan, never reached Miles but returned with information that Miles surrendered at 8 A.M. that morning, *OR*, vol. 51, pt. 1, 839. Harsh summarized Lee's and McClellan's knowledge of the enemy during the Maryland Campaign: "Lee and McClellan seldom knew much that was useful about the location, strength, or organization of the opposing army. Usually, what they thought they knew was highly distorted, and sometimes it was flatly false. Spies were conspicuous only by their absence in the Maryland campaign, and the commanders knew only what they were told by excited civilians and cavalry scouts. When it is recalled that the troopers on both sides were recent volunteers and had received virtually no training in gathering intelligence, it is not surprising that the information they provided was not substantially better than that of their civilian counterparts," Harsh, *Flood*, 9-10. As this chapter has noted, the two army commanders did have more information than Harsh details but did not have the time and resources to sort out the good from the bad. There were troopers on both sides which were combat veterans such as the 6th Pennsylvania and the 5th and 6th U.S. Cavalry. Other units had training and combat experience mostly in Virginia with McClellan on the Peninsula. On the Confederate side, there were several units which had served starting early in the war such as the 1st Virginia Cavalry. As noted above in Chapter 2, all the Virginia cavalry units had been in existence from very early in the war and had fought in most of the battles leading up to the Maryland Campaign, Harsh, *Shallows*, 87, 103.

Attachment

Samples of Capt. William J. Palmer's Telegrams to Gov. Curtin's Aide, McClure from *History of the Fifteenth Pennsylvania Volunteer Cavalry Which Was Recruited and Known as the Anderson Cavalry in the Rebellion of 1861-1865.*

GREENCASTLE, PA., September 12, 1862.

MAJ. A. K. MCCLURE,
    Assistant Adjutant General, Chambersburg, Pa.

4 A.M. I have just returned from the enemy's cavalry camp, where I have been all day. I left there at 8 P.M., and was obliged to walk through the fields to avoid the pickets. Only about 250 rebel cavalry had reached Hagerstown by the Boonsboro road, but at 3 P.M. two regiments, say 1500 infantry, 2 cannon and 25 wagons, came in by the same road and camped in town. Owing to the rebel cavalry having selected the farm at which I was lodging for their camp and placed guards around the house, I was unable to ascertain what force entered by the other roads, if any, but my impression is that another infantry and cavalry force, etc. (people say Longstreet's Division), came in by Carlton road. I could not possibly ascertain the truth of this personally. The rebel sentinels told me the main body of Jackson's army, with Jackson himself, turned off at Boonsboro and went to Williamsport, probably to flank our men at Harper's Ferry. This was confirmed by the statement of another rebel cavalryman to my landlord, whom he knew, and called upon on first reaching Hagerstown. A sentinel told me, and an officer informed my landlord, that their cavalry was ordered out to go into Pennsylvania, at between 12 M. and 2 A.M. this morning, and that their infantry would follow this morning. On learning this, I left immediately for Greencastle, having no one that I could send with a message. In accordance with your instructions, and as my men would make a poor show as yet in a fight with untrained horses and miserable saddles and bridles and without spurs, I have instructed my pickets to fall back slowly, and shall have to do the same with the small mounted force here, say eighty men, in case the enemy approaches. The dismounted men will be sent to me on Greencastle road, as fast as mounted. Lieutenant Spencer's command should do the same or not come on to Chambersburg. If they had been here, we could have held the rebel cavalry at the State Line. All of Jackson's soldiers say they do not intend to injure a single Marylander, but threaten to do all sorts of bad things when they get into Pennsylvania. This movement may be a feint, but the rebel soldiers do not so understand it, and the fact of their bringing wagons and infantry shows it is no mere raid. From the conciliatory manner in which the rebels behaved yesterday toward the citizens (they even went without grain for their horses, when plenty could

640

have been seized), I think they imagine they will hold Maryland. One of their objects in invading Pennsylvania is to let the North know how invasion feels, and their policy may be to treat the non-combatants roughly, but I hardly think they will except in the matter of property. The enemy's cavalry was under command of Colonel Brinn, who resides near the State line and knows all the byroads. The infantry were under the command of Lieutenant-Colonel Drake, and number 1300 men, a number of recruits having been received since entering Maryland. They were armed with pistol, saber and carbine, and well clothed and shod, and were soldierly looking men. Some Mississippi soldiers were reported by this cavalry as being on the Covetown road, and the soldiers say more infantry would be in this morning. I tried to obtain a pass to Leitersburg from Lieutenant-Colonel Drake, of the cavalry, but he advised me to wait till morning. 4.30 A.M. A messenger from my pickets on the State Line has just reported that they heard the reveille blow in the rebel camp. The telegraph operator will put up his instruments at Marion—five miles from here. I will communicate to you further from there. The train will go on to Chambersburg. Is there a clear track? Has Lieutenant Spencer's party reached you? I shall endeavor to leave three men in citizen's clothing in Greencastle.

W. J. PALMER,
Captain Commanding Anderson Cavalry.

GREENCASTLE, PA., September 14, 1862, 9 P.M.
MAJ. A. K. McCLURE,
Assistant Adjutant General.

My scout reached Hagerstown at 3 P.M. to-day, at which time he says Longstreet's Corps, excepting Tombs' brigade, was leaving Hagerstown. They commenced leaving at about 11 A.M., and he saw rear of Longstreet's army go over the hill near Funkstown, say two miles from Hagerstown, on Boonsboro road, at 3.30 P.M. The impression of the spectators was that they were going into camp then and there; but it may have been only their wagons which stopped—these he saw in five rows, parked in a field on both sides of the road at point named. The citizens said there had been fighting at or near Middletown this morning; that McClellan had been driven back two miles, and that the final issue was so critical as to make it necessary to order back Longstreet's Corps to reinforce the rebels. He could not see any troops but Colonel Brinn's Cavalry and a few infantry sentinels anywhere in or about Hagerstown, but was informed that Tombs' brigade was still there, encamped two miles this side of town, on Greencastle road. They also thought there was fighting to-day at Harper's Ferry, from the direction of the cannonading. My scout also reports that the division of the rebel army which was encamped one and a half miles east of Hagerstown, on Boonsboro road, and which he thinks was Loring's, commenced leaving for Boonsboro this morning. This would give Loring seventeen and Longstreet nineteen miles to march to Middletown—the latter having been encamped one mile south of town on the Williamsport road.

Two more deserters have come in this evening from whom I learn the following, which is somewhat confirmed by the scout's statements. One says the rebel Virginia army consists now of the following divisions: Jackson's, Ewell's and A. P. Hill's, forming Jackson's Corps and numbering 30,000. All these turned off at Boonsboro and crossed the river into Virginia at Williamsport on Thursday, September 11th. Longstreet's Corps—the best fighting corps, and with the best artillery in their army—consists of Anderson's, Jones', Whiting's and old Longstreet's divisions, with several battalions of artillery, including the Washington and Donaldson artillery, etc., in all 30,000—this turned off at Boonsboro and marched to Hagerstown. The wagons of A. P. Hill's division, after crossing the river at Williamsport, were returned again and sent up by Williamsport pike to Hagerstown, where they went into camp with Longstreet. The next is Loring's division, a weak one, say 6000 to 8000 men, which followed Longstreet and encamped one mile east of Hagerstown, on Boonsboro pike. This may possibly have been Wilcox's division, however; if not, the remaining divisions in Maryland are Walker's, Wilcox's, Loring's and D. H. Hill's—the last containing about 10,000 men, who entered Boonsboro on Friday and were still there (when the deserter left at 9 A.M. yesterday, Saturday), encamped on a hill a quarter of a mile east of Boonsboro. He belongs to Second North Carolina regiment, of Geo. B. Anderson's brigade, D. H. Hill's division. At that time he heard that Walker's division was five miles back. An officer told him it only contained three brigades, and that two regiments had been detached before they reached Frederick. The strength of these four divisions, which with Jackson's and Longstreet's Corps includes everything they have in Maryland, our intelligent deserter (the New Yorker whom I referred to last evening) estimates at 40,000, making 100,000 in all in Maryland. The only divisions he knows of are Gustavus Smith's and Jos. E. Johnston's, both now probably under the former, as he does not believe Johnston is well yet, and numbering 40,000. These he thinks are near Centreville. This man is a gentlemanly fellow from New Orleans and seems to be acquainted with every man in Washington artillery. If the above facts be correct, neither Jackson's, Longstreet's or Loring's (perhaps Wilcox's, instead of Loring's) men could have been in the battle this morning—and they will be in the fight if it is renewed, if they can get there in time. Our cavalry reserves are at State Line, pickets in Maryland. Infantry here.

WM. J. PALMER,
Captain Commanding Anderson Cavalry.

Appraisal of the Cavalry's Performance: Robert E. Lee and Jeb Stuart versus George B. McClellan and Alfred Pleasonton

LINCOLN REMARKED ON 26 October 1862, "Stuart's cavalry outmarched ours, having certainly done more marked service on the Peninsula and everywhere since." This comment to McClellan followed another dispatch by Lincoln two days earlier: "I have just read your dispatch about sore-tongued and fatigued horses. Will you pardon me for asking what the horses of your army have done since the battle of Antietam that fatigues anything?"[1] Because Gen. Lee was forced out of Maryland, and McClellan won a strategic and arguably a tactical victory at Antietam, Stuart's performance must receive harsher

---

[1] *OR*, vol. 19, pt. 2, 485, 490. Clearly Lincoln was angry and frustrated by Stuart's Second Ride Around McClellan on 10-11 October as well as the many requests McClellan was making for more horses. In his defense, many horses were ill as well as fatigued. McClellan's response to Lincoln included this: "If any instance can be found where overworked cavalry has performed more labor than mine since the battle of Antietam, I am not conscious of it," ibid., 485. Compare Matthew Forney Steele's overall evaluation of the cavalry in *American Campaigns*, vol. 1 (Washington, D.C., United States Infantry Association, 1922): "The strategical employment of the cavalry on both sides in the campaign was excellent. The hostile cavalry forces were in contact with each other from the moment the Confederates crossed the Potomac, until the two armies confronted each other across the Antietam, each covering the columns of its own army and gathering all possible information of its enemy. Pleasonton's advanced cavalry was in touch with Stuart's squadrons at the eastern foot of Turner's Gap on the evening of September 13, and opened the battle the next morning. If it had been promptly supported by infantry in sufficient force, as it should have been, the pass would, have been in possession of the Federals within three hours," 279-280; Steele thought well of Stuart's troopers performance on the 17th: On account of the walls and fences and ledges of rock the ground was not suitable for the charge of cavalry; but the squadrons of Stuart and Munford effectually guarded the flanks of the position," 281. But this major in the Second United States Cavalry's view of Federal cavalry use was not as favorable: "If the Union cavalry had been guarding the flanks of the attack, instead of standing idle at the center, the approach of A.P. Hill's division would have been discovered in time for dispositions to be made to meet it," 283. Stackpole was carried away in his glowing evaluation of Stuart in Maryland: "the effectiveness of Stuart and his cavalrymen in reporting vital information to Lee's headquarters was nothing short of amazing" but Stackpole admitted that "[Stuart's] score was not perfect, and he occasionally failed to pinpoint the strength and dispositions of Federal troops" but "it always seemed to be Jeb Stuart who stepped into the breach, made a whirlwind reconnaissance to ascertain the true facts, and gave Lee the answers that he needed to plan his next move," 345. Stackpole further wrote that "when Lee found it necessary to hold the [South Mountain] passes for an extended period because the timetable upset in capturing Harpers Ferry, it was the cavalry that was called on to meet the emergency," 346. As has been seen, Stuart's performance holding any passes on South Mountain was poor and in fact he almost caused Gen. Lee to suffer even heavier losses at the gaps. Stackpole's analysis of Stuart's actions misses the mark.

criticism than Pleasonton's. While Stuart's performances on the Peninsula and subsequent battles leading up to the Maryland Campaign materially helped Gen. Lee, Stuart did not do as well in Maryland. Lee's casual command style influenced Stuart, and Lee failed to rein in Stuart's well-known desire for entertainment and self-aggrandizement. Lee's written communications to Stuart seem to show some of Lee's concern with the information Stuart was bringing him and perhaps can be used to evaluate Stuart's ability to comply with his commander's desires. Stuart's most controversial actions, his Urbana, Maryland, ball and his failures at South Mountain, have already been discussed. His screening efforts prior to and including the Frederick sojourn were very good; rearguard actions from Frederick to South Mountain could be described as good, his defensive actions in Sharpsburg especially at Nicodemus Hill with his artillery are excellent; his mistakes at the South Mountain gaps and Harpers Ferry are recognized as failures, as were his scouting efforts early in the campaign.[2]

Pleasanton's cavalry performance, compared to Stuart's, shows that Pleasonton, for the most part gave McClellan poorer quality intelligence than Stuart gave Lee. The spreading of disinformation by Stuart's troopers worked well. Pleasonton's screening did about as well as Stuart's, and his scouting efforts were equally as poor. Perhaps his screening efforts worked well because Stuart was not aggressively trying to penetrate the Union lines to the east, but rather was satisfied by sitting behind his own screen, not believing that the Union troops would be stirring soon from their Washington forts. Pleasonton suffered more than did Stuart both for lack of sufficient cavalry from the beginning of the campaign, but more so from the exhaustion of his horses. Here, Stuart's troopers had the advantages of buying or taking horses from Maryland farmers as well as from Union troopers.[3] Of course, the overall

---

[2] See, for example, Harsh, *Flood*, commenting that on the 8th through the 13th of September Stuart was unaware of Federal movements, "Stuart either did not discern, or detected but failed to alert Lee of, the considerable increase in the activity of the Federal cavalry on the 8th," 121; "[Lee] either failed to grasp, or else Stuart failed to provide him with the information that would allow him to grasp, the fact that the Federal advance had become serious within the last two days," 129; "Nothing indicates Stuart on the 9th perceived the Army of the Potomac to be pressing in a menacing way," 166; "On this day [10 September] critical to the success of Lee's campaign in Maryland, there is no indication that Stuart undertook any special measures to gain information or to increase security as the army headed westward," 180; "Stuart's complaisance on the 10th indicates that he was as ignorant of McClellan's movement behind the screen of opposing cavalry as was Pleasonton of Lee's. Stuart missed a significant advance by the left and center of the Federal battlefront," 181; "nothing [Lee] was hearing from Stuart [on 11 September] about the Federal's advance from Washington caused him to hesitate about further dividing the Army....[into] five rather than four independent columns," 185; "Stuart [on the 11th] moved too early and his execution too casual....his operations not only exposed the rears of Walker and McLaws to the south, but they also left uncovered in the center the National Turnpike, one of the two avenues along which the vanguard of the Federal infantry was now advancing," 188; "The eyes and ears of the Confederate army, while neither blind nor deaf, saw and heard very little on September 12," 205; "Lee's lack of alarm, at least on September 13, was ignorance due to faulty intelligence," 212; "Jeb Stuart did not at first recognize the threat imminent in the advance of the Army of the Potomac. Laboring under the mistaken notion that the expedition to the Valley had completed its mission and that the fragments of Lee's army were already reuniting, he did not grasp that time was running against the Confederates....he failed to perceive that in close order behind the enemy cavalry screen marched the long, snaking columns of infantry and artillery of the main body of the Federal army," 230.

[3] Wittenberg, *Blame*, cogently describes the care of horses: "For all their size and strength, horses are fragile beasts. They require a tremendous amount of rest, fodder, fresh water, and personal care and attention to keep them in decent physical condition," 273. As has been mentioned horseshoes are also critical: "Horseshoes of all types...were constantly in demand and worth their weight in gold....It was not uncommon to see entire hooves cut off dead horses on a battlefield," 277. Note that McClellan mentioned in a letter to his wife on 9 September that his "people....will do well now—a few days will compose them still further, increase my cavalry force & and put me in better condition generally," Sears, McClellan, *Papers*, 442. Not all Confederate horsemen rode healthy-appearing animals. Sorrel relates a story of a cavalry friend he met on 15 September in the retreat from South Mountain: "During the day I came up with my old friend and schoolmate, 'Sandy' Duncan, of the Hussars [Lt. Alexander "Sandy" Duncan of the Georgia Hussars which was part of the Jeff Davis Legion under Hampton]. He was a comical object, but doing good service mounted on a little beast, almost skin and bones, with scarcely any hair. The animal looked badly scalded. He bore Duncan and his arms however," 108. The key element to notice here is that despite the poor appearance of the horse, it was still performing.

quality of Stuart's troopers, horses, and experience, meant that Stuart and his troopers almost always had the edge over Pleasonton's men, who often used infantry support when facing the Southern horsemen. Thus both cavalry leaders were constrained in their activities, Stuart by his personality and relationship with Lee, and Pleasonton by lack of experience and aggressiveness, but more so by the quantity of his cavalry and the shortsightedness of his army commander, first in assigning much of it to infantry commanders, and finally to its marked lack of use during the Battle of Antietam. When operating with reduced numbers of cavalry as both army commanders were, it was much more important to ensure that those scarce assets were being well-used.

Stuart did well for Lee from the Peninsula to the Potomac, except for his absence from Jackson for several critical hours at Chantilly as Stuart decided to pay a visit to a friend's house, and his alerting Pope to his presence by artillery fire. His pleasant sojourn at Dranesville on 4 September could be defended as a need for rest for his horses or attacked as another example of his sometimes careless approach to his duties. His performance on the Peninsula earned him a promotion and command of the combined cavalry formed into his own division. His First Ride Around McClellan—the Chickahominy Raid—set the bar not only for his future rides (and attempted rides) around the Union army such as in October 1862 for his Second Ride Around McClellan—the Chambersburg Raid—but also for Confederate cavalry in the west, and the Union cavalry in both the eastern and western theaters. Although Lee did not use his troopers well during the Seven Days, they were still available for whatever Lee required. Aside from a bungled performance by Fitzhugh Lee who arrived too late to bag Pope who was hemmed in by two rivers before Second Bull Run, Stuart did well leading up to Cedar Mountain and Second Bull Run. His taking of the supplies at Manassas Junction was a coup, as was finding a copy of Pope's orders detailing his campaign plans; Union cavalry under Pope's command initially did well in scouting but due to lack of coordination and exhaustion, they failed just as they were most needed when Jackson and Stuart swung around his right flank. Stuart's scouting and screening after Lee assigned him to Jackson before Second Bull Run was superb. His rearguard actions leading to the crossing of the Potomac at the start of the Maryland Campaign were good although they did not fool Halleck or Pleasonton.[4]

Two major factors militated against a similar excellent performance by the Beau Sabreur during the Maryland Campaign: first was that his normal penchant for fun, frivolity and female (and male) adoration was not curbed, but probably enhanced, by Lee's estimation that the first several weeks of his expedition in Maryland would be mainly rest, relaxation, and refitting. Despite only being in command of the Army of Northern Virginia since 1 June 1862, Lee knew that Jeb was "fond of show and with much personal vanity, craving admiration in the parlor as well as on the field, with a taste for music and poetry and song, desiring as much the admiration of handsome women...with full appreciation of his well-won eminence" having known him in the Old Army.[5] Stuart's casual approach early in the campaign was probably influenced by Lee's relatively relaxed sojourn in Frederick and his light touch in

---

[4] Harsh viewed Stuart's poor scouting among the chief reasons for Lee's failure in Maryland, "Stuart's performance in the Maryland campaign has perhaps been overrated," *Flood*, 114. See also Priest, *Before Antietam*; he was not impressed with Stuart's performance and showed his less attractive sides which also infected his staff with his need to "satisfy personal needs" and who "did not overexert himself," 2-3; "in Urbana, Jeb Stuart and the division's staff...spent the day resting," 60; "As was their custom, Stuart and his staff officers had decided to spend their leisure hours in comfort," 90; and "Stuart and his close knit staff quartered themselves in a comfortable farmhouse...and generally enjoyed themselves," 102. Harsh did not find Stuart's performance universally poor, e.g., "On this occasion, Jeb Stuart justified his reputation for alert reconnaissance," 19. Not a few others also have found Stuart's actions valuable to Lee. Fishel finds that Stuart did well, "Stuart maintained a tight cavalry screen, meanwhile scouting and threatening both of the Federal's flanks and spreading reports that had the invaders marching in several directions," 213; "[Pleasonton] would have to cope with Jeb Stuart's expert screening operations," 224. Chiles, "Jeb Stuart did an excellent job of this [screening] in the Maryland Campaign," 7.

[5] Henry Kyd Douglas, *I Rode with Stonewall*, 269.

overseeing his general officers.[6] Stuart's contemporary critics such as Rosser and D.H. Hill were not his friends, so their statements must be viewed carefully.[7] Even Stuart's most active leader in Maryland, Munford, thought little of Stuart and was not careful about hiding it.[8] Second, Stuart failed to adequately perceive that his normal scouting activity would be significantly curbed by operating among a generally unfriendly populace and in a mostly unfamiliar territory. Once into Maryland, his screening against an initial tentative and weak cavalry effort led by Pleasonton kept the Federals at bay for several days, while Stuart indulged himself and his staff by attending a ball and dinners with southern sympathizers. Here, he gives the impression of lack of concern again due to Lee's comparable and well-founded belief that Union pursuit would not come for some weeks: the mauling he had just given them at Second Bull Run, and the time that would be needed to reorganize the Army of the Potomac and the Army of Virginia both now located in and near Washington, would give ample time for rest. Thus Lee may have overly trusted Stuart to do what Lee expected of him—good scouting in addition to screening. Stuart, however, entrusted much to his two relatively new brigade commanders, Hampton and Munford. Munford, who had just replaced Robertson, eventually was charged with holding the southern end of Stuart's Sugarloaf/Parr's Ridge and Catoctin Mountain Lines, and did more fighting than did Stuart's other two brigades combined. Unfortunately, he had the smallest brigade with which to hold these important sectors. Even his three small regiments were reduced to two when Stuart detached the 7th Virginia Cavalry to serve as Jackson's escort on the move to take Martinsburg and Harpers Ferry on 10 September. That detachment, combined with the increasing pressure from both Union cavalry and infantry, meant that Munford and his two regiments had to call upon help from Hampton and Fitzhugh Lee on occasion and then eventually had to retreat losing Sugarloaf, an important key terrain feature, although this was at Stuart's order as Stuart was moving back to the Catoctin Mountains. Overall, early in the campaign, Stuart's screening was effective as Carman wrote: "The Confederate cavalry completely masked Lee's movements. It occupied every avenue of approach and resisted every attempt to drive it. From the Potomac on its right to the Baltimore and Ohio Railroad on the left, it covered Lee's entire front and no scout could penetrate it. Consequently there was a want of reliable information, and McClellan knew neither the strength, position, nor purpose of his adversary."[9]

Stuart has also been faulted for his relatively casual retreat from Frederick to the Catoctin Mountains, then to South Mountain, after Gen. Lee and the army had left on its various missions as detailed in S.O. 191. With Fitzhugh Lee gone to the north, and Munford's two regiments failing to hold the gap at Jefferson in the Catoctins, Stuart had only Hampton's Brigade to hold back most of Pleasonton's cavalry and large Union infantry units pursuing on the National Pike. In Stuart's defense, he

---

[6] Ibid., 3, 4, 60; Murfin states that "Stuart had rather free license with his maneuvering" implying that Lee did not keep a tight rein on Stuart, 169.

[7] Thomas, 261. Stuart's failure to gain Rosser's promotion earlier in the war had to influence Rosser's anti-Stuart feelings noted in 1863; Bridges, 30.

[8] Priest, *Before Antietam*, "The colonel described Stuart as a self-centered, self-indulging fop, who jealously guarded his command and who did not want to share any of the plaudits concerning it with anyone else," 7. But see a somewhat contrary opinion by L. Van Loan Naisawald, "Stuart as a Cavalryman's Cavalryman," in *Civil War Times Illustrated*, vol. 1, no. 10, February 1963, "Stuart, stripped of all color, still emerges as an outstanding cavalry commander. He was imaginative, he had the necessary daring without foolhardiness, and he was a leader who quickly earned the total support and respect of all who served with him. The few off-color pages of his record can be traced with reasonable assurance to his personal vanity," 6-8, 42-46. In Maryland, Naisawald might agree that Stuart's vanity aided the poor performance he supplied Lee.

[9] Carman, Pierro, 88. On 9 September Gen. Lee was composing S.O. 191 based on the assumption that Union troops were not in close proximity, but as Stuart knew based on his pickets' encounter with Unionist probes and skirmishes, they were close. Stuart should have told Lee in detail of contact with the Yankees. Had he done so, Lee probably would have ordered Stuart to probe aggressively east to learn if Yankee infantry was moving, too. Stuart's enjoyment at his ball materially affected his commander's actions reflected in S.O. 191. Arguably, Stuart's error here was the worst of his mistakes during the campaign.

obviously believed that his delaying movement west was adequate since Jackson, McLaws, and Walker, should have already taken Martinsburg and Harpers Ferry, so all he had to do was slightly delay McClellan, then rejoin Lee in Hagerstown, where the rest of the army would be assembled. The three days he delayed McClellan he thought were sufficient. Here, his failure to adequately scout the Union advance almost resulted in his cavalry being seriously hurt, but more importantly, putting Lee's divided army in danger of being defeated in detail. Given the importance of his screening Lee's divided army, he should have done more to ensure that his assumptions were correct about Harpers Ferry and the Union advance.

Once Lee and Stuart realized that the Harpers Ferry expedition was seriously behind schedule, they acted upon the reasonable military belief that McClellan would quickly move to Harpers Ferry to relieve the garrison, attacking McLaws at his positions on Maryland Heights and in Pleasant Valley. Again, they were mistaken, as McClellan moved the bulk of his forces to the vicinity of Turner's and Fox's Gaps, just east of Boonsboro, with only one corps to Crampton's Gap. Stuart operated on that belief longer than Lee who realized that the passes in South Mountain had to be defended to prevent McClellan from gaining the passes and marching down Pleasant Valley directly on McLaw's rear and, along with Federal units Lee believed would be marching down Middletown Valley, catching McLaws between the Army of the Potomac and the Harpers Ferry garrison. Lee thought that Stuart was at Turner's and Fox's Gaps helping defend them allowing Lee time to bring up Longstreet's command to bolster Hill's division near Boonsboro. But Stuart had quickly ridden south to help defend against McClellan's expected attack on McLaws, leaving only the 5th Virginia Cavalry and two guns at Fox's Gap, with no instructions, and not even telling Hill he had done so; Stuart left no cavalry at Turner's Gap and only Munford with his two small regiments and some horse artillery at Crampton's Gap. Stuart joined McLaws with the bulk of his cavalry to help stop McClellan's expected Harpers Ferry relief mission.

One of the key complaints against Stuart has been that he seriously underestimated the forces that were pursuing him to South Mountain. Stuart asked Hill to send a brigade to South Mountain to help hold it because two Federal infantry brigades and some cavalry were chasing him. Hill sent Col. Alfred Colquitt first, and after the Union troops stopped at the base of the mountain, Colquitt talked with Stuart suggesting that the infantry could hold the turnpike, with Stuart's troopers guarding the roads around the gap. However, Stuart told Colquitt that "he could not remain—that he should move with his cavalry toward Harpers Ferry—that I would have no difficulty holding my position—that the enemy's forces, he thought, consisted of cavalry and one or two brigades of infantry."[10] After Stuart reported this inaccurate news, and believing that Turner's Gap was no place for cavalry, he moved south heading for McLaws's position, after spending the night in Boonsboro, leaving Hill to face overwhelming odds. Stuart's comments regarding use of his cavalry in and near the gap clearly show that his preferred method for fighting his cavalry was mounted, but shortly events showed dismounted Confederate cavalry at Fox's and Crampton's Gaps were also effective.[11] Perhaps Stuart was just seeking an excuse not to leave cavalry at Turner's Gap. Stuart's official report also states that he gave full information to Hill, an obvious effort to deny Hill's claims that Stuart told him little of value of the Union approach.[12] Stuart could have left more of his troopers with Hill to picket the several roads and gaps to the north of Turner's Gap, south of Fox's Gap, and to the east on the National Pike, but he clearly believed the main Union thrust would be further south as Hill did also. Stuart was correct to observe that cavalry operations on the mountain

---

[10] Bridges, 101.

[11] *OR*, vol. 19, pt. 1, "This was obviously no place for cavalry operations, a single horseman passing from point to point on the mountain with difficulty," 817.

[12] *OR*, vol. 19, pt. 1, 817; Bridges, 101, 102.

would have been difficult as it was mostly heavily wooded and steep, but picketing roads and other access points would have been much help to Hill and later, Longstreet.

Even McLaws later complained that Stuart gave him poor intelligence about the Union strength near Crampton's Gap: "[Stuart] told me he did not believe there was more than a brigade of the enemy."[13] Thus within two days, Stuart had given wildly inaccurate estimates of Union numbers to Hill at Turner's Gap, and McLaws about Crampton's Gap. In both instances, Stuart rode away from these critical areas leaving inadequate forces for their defense. Subsequently, both gaps were quickly forced by overwhelming strength. "The usually reliable Stuart was either off his form or suffering a patch of bad luck."[14] Stuart again defends his actions by noting that Fitzhugh Lee's Brigade successfully defended the rear of the Confederate retreat from Turner's Gap and Hampton's Brigade McLaw's rear from Pleasant Valley to Harpers Ferry. In fact, Lee's Brigade was only involved after the Confederates were pushed off South Mountain, and Hampton's Brigade was of little help in Pleasant Valley. He glosses over his failure to accurately gauge the Union numbers before each gap, and Lee's desires that Stuart defend the gaps. Stuart's ride from Harpers Ferry to Sharpsburg to personally bring the good news about its fall to Lee (about which Lee had already received news)[15] can be viewed as another of his unnecessary grandstanding exploits despite his statement that Jackson asked him to do so.[16] Here, as later at Gettysburg, Lee had no time to coddle Stuart and met his report with a brusque reply.[17]

Pleasonton and his troopers initially suffered from a lack of reliable horseflesh as most of his regiments had just come from the Peninsula, and were not rested or refitted, with some horses even arriving without horseshoes. And has already been noted, he did not have all of his cavalry with him until Antietam on 17 September. His cavalry's first foray was met with a resounding defeat at Poolesville, so this likely also contributed to his hesitation. With less combat experience than Stuart, he nevertheless did not personally back down and even said that at the affair at Boonsboro on 15 September, he participated in the rout of Fitzhugh Lee with the 8th Illinois Cavalry, participating in a charge with only a riding whip.[18] While both Pleasonton and Stuart suffered from depleted numbers in the ranks due to jaded horses and tired troopers, Pleasonton likely had the disadvantage of not being able to live off the country as did the less inhibited Rebel horsemen, as well as having his troopers sometimes under the de facto command of infantry major generals, as Pleasonton was only a brigadier. He also had the disadvantage of not having his trains with him since McClellan's wagons and his entire supply organization still had not reorganized itself well since disembarking from the Peninsula. Too, the renown of Stuart's troopers, and the awe many Union troopers felt, also contributed to the Union troopers' hesitancy to confront the Rebels. But in general, Pleasonton's cavalry did well when fighting mounted or dismounted against Stuart's horsemen perhaps aided by the fact that they usually were assisted by infantry. Given what men and horses he had, and limited by the Army of the Potomac's command structure, he performed as well as was possible.

Stuart's performance during the Battle of Antietam was exceptional. He was employed on Lee's far left flank covering the Confederate line from the Potomac to Jackson's left. There Stuart had, in addition

---

[13] *OR*, vol. 19, pt. 1, 854.

[14] Sears, *Landscape*, 145.

[15] Harsh, *Flood*, 307.

[16] *OR*, vol. 19, pt. 1, 819.

[17] Harsh, *Flood*, 322; Longacre, *Gettysburg*, 202; Davis, *Stuart*, 334.

[18] James E. Kelly, *Generals in Bronze: Interviewing the Commanders of the Civil War*, ed. by William B. Styple (Kearney, NJ: Belle Grove Publishing Company, 2005), 127-128. Note that this is the only source found of Pleasonton's active participation in the battle. Pleasonton may have embellished his role as he did when he told Kelly that he had been offered the command of the Army of the Potomac but turned it down; Gen. Porter strongly disagreed with that report, 194. But Pleasonton was described as "cool" and "ready" although not having a desire to enter into a melee such as Custer did, 257-258.

to his cavalry, his horse artillery under Pelham, as well as other artillery units.[19] Munford was busy protecting Gen. Lee's right flank. Lee's report stated that "General Stuart, with the cavalry and horse artillery, performed the duty intrusted to him of guarding our left wing with great energy and courage, and rendered valuable assistance in defeating the attack on that part of our line."[20] Apparently Jackson gave him de facto command of the far left flank down to the river although this is not of record. With the crisis at hand, Stuart had little time for festivities being under the watchful eyes of the army commander and senior generals. Stuart finally was able to fulfill Lee's expectations. Stuart's noteworthy actions during the battle do not mask his previous poor performances which demonstrably contributed to Lee's being forced to stand and fight on the Antietam and nearly losing much of his army.

Pleasonton at Antietam, on the other hand, did little. Most of the day of the battle he spent in bivouac or guarding the Middle Bridge, as McClellan likely waited for an opportunity for his massed cavalry and the reserve infantry to attack a weak point in Lee's line. Probably not coincidentally, McClellan kept these reserves near his headquarters at the Pry House. While concentrating cavalry for a breakthrough of a weak point or the pursuit of retreating infantry were valid tactics for Napoleonic heavy cavalry as at Marengo and Austerlitz, they reflected more outmoded Napoleonic Era uses of cavalry which the first years of the Civil War showed would usually not be effective. *The Military Hand-Book and Soldier's Manual of Information* spelled out McClellan's disposition at Antietam except that he did not use his horse on the wings: "The reserve is formed of the best troops of foot and horse to complete a victory or make good a retreat. It is placed in the rear of the center, or chief point of attack or defense. The cavalry should be distributed in echelon on the wings, and at the center on favorable ground."[21]

McClellan had contemplated a turning movement using all of Pleasonton's cavalry on Lee's left, but decided that that would place the cavalry too far from the main body of the army.[22] After the battle, Pleasonton was the first organized Federal unit entering Sharpsburg on the 19th and chased stragglers from the town and participated in an artillery duel with Confederate guns across the Potomac at Shepherdstown, but then was sent back to camp by Porter. The next morning, his troopers arrived late due to an apparent misunderstanding with Porter and most likely contributed to the defeat of the Union force sent over the river to capture Confederate artillery; Union cavalry scouting and screening would have served those Union troops well had Pleasonton not been upset at Porter's actions the day before.

The affair at Williamsport did little other than prove to Stuart that he could not hold the Maryland bridgehead against large Union cavalry and infantry forces, and to Lee after Shepherdstown on the 20th, that his Maryland adventure was finally over. While Lee made good use of his cavalry at Antietam, McClellan did not. McClellan would have been better served if he used some of his cavalry to protect his flanks as Lee did with his troopers. Had he done so, the cavalry pickets may have picked up the movement of Maj. Gen. A.P. Hill's approach toward Burnside's vulnerable left flank on the afternoon of the 17th. The failure to picket the Maryland approaches from Harpers Ferry has to be considered a major defect in McClellan's planning on 16 and 17 September as Rebel infantry could have taken that route. Confederate artillery officer Edward Porter Alexander commented after the war:

> One other feature of this battle is worthy of special note as unique. McClellan concentrated his powerful cavalry and horse-artillery force, not upon either flank, and especially not upon his left flank where were

[19] Sears, *Landscape*, 145.
[20] *OR*, vol. 19, pt. 1, 152.
[21] Louis Le Grand, *The Military Hand-Book and Soldier's Manual of Information* (New York, NY: Beadle and Company, 1862), 50-51. In McClellan's defense, his Pry House headquarters was close to the center of the Union line and gave him a good view of it except for sites to the Federal left at Burnside Bridge.
[22] Harsh, *Flood*, 314.

great opportunities for it, but at his centre, where it would have been in the way of his infantry, and where the ground was much cut up with fences and cultivation. On his right it might have been able to drive Stuart from his commanding hill. On his left, from which direction he should have expected Jackson's troops, it might have crossed the bridge over the Antietam near its mouth. Where it was, it was superfluous.[23]

Another Confederate officer put it succinctly: "[McClellan's] cavalry were to occupy the attention of the Confederate centre, and were, if necessary, to have the support of Porter who was held in reserve near the centre of the Federal army. The disposition of his cavalry was the weakest point in McClellan's plan of battle. It might have been of far more use on either flank."[24]

Criticism also came from Union Maj. Gen. Jacob D. Cox who questioned McClellan's lack of attention to his left flank as Rebel forces came up from Harpers Ferry:

Couch's division had been left north-east of Maryland Heights to observe Jackson's command, supposed still to be in Harper's Ferry. Why could it not have come up on our left as well as A. P. Hill's division, which was the last of the Confederate troops to leave the Ferry, there being nothing to observe after it was gone? Couch's division, coming with equal pace with Hill's on the other side of the [Potomac] river, would have answered our needs as well as one from Porter's corps. Hill came, but Couch did not. Yet even then, a regiment of horse watching that flank and scouring the country as we swung it forward would have developed Hill's presence and enabled the commanding general either to stop our movement or to take the available means to support it; but the cavalry was put to no such use; it occupied the center of the whole line, only its artillery being engaged during the day. It would have been invaluable to Hooker in the morning as it would have been to us in the afternoon.[25]

Another Union critic was George B. Davis who, while otherwise finding McClellan's actions during the Maryland Campaign commendable, found his cavalry poorly used during the Battle of Antietam:

Pleasonton's division was not only in perfect order but, elated with its successful achievements and confident of its capacity to obtain results, stood ready to ascertain the situation of affairs in the territory beyond the Antietam....But this was not to be, and it is one of the surprising features of this surprising battle that the Federal cavalry, instead of being posted, according to the practice of the centuries, on the flanks of the infantry, was used throughout the day in support of its own horse batteries, in rear of the Federal centre, and in a position from which it would have been impossible for it to have been used as cavalry, or even to have emerged mounted.[26]

---

[23] Edward Porter Alexander, *Military Memoirs of a Confederate*, 270-271.

[24] William Allan, "Strategy of the Campaign of Sharpsburg or Antietam," in *Papers of the Military Historical Society of Massachusetts*, vol. III, *Campaigns in Virginia, Maryland and Pennsylvania 1862-1863* (Boston: Griffith-Stillings Press, 1903; reprint Wilmington, NC: Broadfoot Publishing Company, 1989), 94. From the earliest history of the employment of cavalry with infantry dating back thousands of years, the position of cavalry at each end of the infantry line was standard operating procedure for most armies, see, for example, Victor Hanson, *A War Like No Other: How the Athenians and Spartans Fought the Peloponnesian War* (New York: Random House, 2006), 142; see also John Keegan, *A History of Warfare* (New York: Vintage Books, 1994), 271, in which he describes the Roman deployment of cavalry on each flank as the "standard classical deployment." Later he also describes another common use of cavalry: "charging against infantry disorganized by artillery fire or harrying fugitives driven to flight," 345.

[25] Jacob D. Cox, "The Battle of Antietam" in *Battles and Leaders*, 2:657-658.

[26] George B. Davis, "The Antietam Campaign," in *Campaigns in Virginia, Maryland, and Pennsylvania, 1862-1863*, vol. 3 of *Papers of the Military Historical Society of Massachusetts*, (Boston, MA: Griffith-Stilling Press, 1903. Reprint, Wilmington, NC: Broadfoot Publishing Company, 1989), 54-55; 94. Burnside did have cavalry which he used sporadically on his left flank but those troopers apparently were not instructed to watch for movement from Harpers Ferry on the Maryland or Virginia shores. McClellan also had some of the Harpers Ferry escape column regiments at Jones's Cross Roads and near Hagerstown. Davis's opinion that Pleasonton's cavalry was "in perfect order" is an exaggeration.

In the same article, Davis wrote that with the exception "of the fortnight that ended at Appomattox, no commander of the Army of the Potomac ever did so much in two weeks as did McClellan in the Sharpsburg campaign."[27] McClellan in his 15 October 1862 report of operations during the campaign complains that he had insufficient cavalry to be efficient but then seemingly admits that it should have been used otherwise: "Cavalry may be said to constitute the antennae of the army. It scouts all the roads in front, on the flanks, and in the rear of the advancing columns, and constantly feels the enemy. The amount of labor falling on this arm during the Maryland campaign was excessive."[28] It seems that no one has commended McClellan's use of the cavalry on 16 and 17 September at Sharpsburg and it deserves the condemnation it has received both at that time and since.[29]

In his defense, it may be argued that McClellan's posting of Burnside's corps on the extreme left flank provided all the blocking needed should Rebel troops ascend the Maryland side from Harpers Ferry. The corps did have some cavalry assigned as an escort, Company G of the 1st Maine, but not enough to supply adequate pickets on the hilly approaches. While most of the 6th New York Cavalry was temporarily attached to Burnside, he did not use it to scout his left flank on the 16th or 17th although five companies did confront some of Munford's troopers on the 17th near the mouth of Antietam Creek.[30] Given the terrain on Burnside's left especially the view from Botelor's Ford almost to the intersection of Millers Saw Mill Road with the Harpers Ferry Road, Union cavalry would have had to fight with Munford to get within sight of Hill's arriving troops. Munford's task was not only to hold the ford, but to ensure that Yankee horsemen would not be able to observe troop movements near the ford. Thus

---

[27] Ibid., 101.

[28] *OR*, vol. 19, pt. 1, 80.

[29] See also William P. Craighill, *The 1862 Army Officer's Pocket Companion* (New York: D Van Nostrand, 1862, reprint Mechanicsburg, PA: Stackpole Books, 2002), "Cavalry is usually best placed at the extremities of the line, because it has there a greater scope for maneuvering than at the centre, being particularly enabled to extend outwardly in order to fall on the rear of the enemy or outflank him....Offensive Battle....The cavalry hastens to the wings," 172, 175. Apparently McClellan took to heart the instruction "in the primitive order of battle, the cavalry is usually deployed a little to the rear of the wings of the infantry, especially toward that one which is least protected, or else in columns of squadrons behind the centre of the second line, that it may readily give succor in every direction," 181. See also Alonzo Gray, *Cavalry Tactics as Illustrated by the War of the Rebellion: Together with Many Interesting Facts Important for Cavalry to Know* (Leavenworth, KS: Press of Ketcheson Printing Co, 1910, reprint, Whitefish, MT: Kessinger Publishing, n.d.), "In battle, cavalry will frequently be found on the flank of infantry either as a support or as a part of the firing line....The great advantages in having cavalry on the flanks is here further illustrated. Its great mobility enables it to accomplish the results reported...while its presence on the flanks will check a turning movement of the hostile cavalry," 107, 110. A contemporary historian, Edward Hagerman, commented as follows: "At Antietam, McClellan....concentrated his entire cavalry force behind the center of his line to serve as follow-up support for an infantry breakthrough. It is surprising that a commander so sensitive to the effect of rifled fire on infantry tactics would ignore the lesson to be learned from the success of the Confederate infantry at Gaines Mill against the Union's mounted counterattack....McClellan's conservative use of cavalry...must be viewed against his stature as an expert on the subject....As the cavalry expert on the Delafield Commission to Europe, McClellan['s] report on cavalry was very technical in nature, without the sense of change to parallel his radical observations on infantry tactics....One can hardly fail to speculate on whether the otherwise forward-looking McClellan was not the victim of his vested interests in the one area where he was an established expert." *The American Civil War and the Origins of Modern Warfare: Ideas, Organization, and Field Command* (Bloomington, IN: Indiana University Press, 1992), 57. Dennis Hart Mahan in his book, *An Elementary Treatise on Advanced-Guard, Out-Post, and Detachment Service of Troops, and the Manner of Posting and Handling Them in Presence of an Enemy*, wrote that "The object being to secure the front and flanks of the position, occupied by the main-body, from any attempt either to reconnoitre, or attack it, the detachments which form the advance-posts must be so distributed as to embrace all the avenues by which the enemy can approach the position. The system adopted, in most services, to effect this object, consists of two, or three concentric lines of posts, disposed in a fan-shaped order. The exterior line, which forms the Out-Posts, embraces a wide circumference; and by means of a chain of Sentinels, posted in advance, prevents any one from penetrating to the rear between the posts, without being seen," Mahan, 87.

[30] An estimate of the size of a company would be about 50-60 troopers based on previously reported strengths for the 6th New York over recent months.

Pleasonton's troopers would have had a fight on their hands unless they would have been content to go further downstream on the Potomac past the Antietam Ironworks near the mouth of Antietam Creek, and establish a post on the Harpers Ferry Road. Had they done so, they would not have seen Hill crossing upstream at Botelor's Ford or even fords near the mouth of the Antietam. Regardless, McClellan should have taken greater efforts to use his cavalry to ensure his left flank was at least as secure as his right was at Jones's Cross Roads.[31] The 6th New York Cavalry, by itself, was not going to rout Munford. McClellan had sufficient cavalry on the right of his army with the 3rd Pennsylvania as well as many of the units from the Harpers Ferry escape column.

Both Lee's and McClellan's failures in this campaign resulted from them adhering to their beliefs without ensuring that those beliefs were in fact surviving in the face of the reality of each day's changing events. Lee was not aggressive enough in his efforts to gauge the speed of the Federal army's pursuit; he also failed to realize that the Union garrisons at Harpers Ferry and Martinsburg did not flee once he gained their rear, as normal military procedure would dictate, and as the Union garrison at Winchester had done. He also reasonably believed that McClellan would march directly to relieve Harpers Ferry but failed to ensure that that was so. He had only been in command of what he named the Army of Northern Virginia for just over three months after Gen. Joseph E. Johnston's severe wounding at Seven Pines, and was still learning the capabilities of his men and their leaders. His leadership style for this army was still one of keeping loose reins despite a few noteworthy failures during the Seven Days' Campaign, when some of his complex, but well-planned attacks, failed due to his subordinate generals' poor coordination and execution. Lee's optimistic belief in his commanding generals during the Maryland Campaign led him to divide his army into four, then five parts, without detailed written orders to any of those commanders, except perhaps Stuart, although it is fairly certain that, as in any campaign, he spoke with them, personally conveying his wishes, supplying details, and discussing alternatives.[32] There was no reason for Lee to believe that the slow-moving Federal army was going to be such a threat that unusual expediency or detailed instructions on his part were needed.

In 1889, William Allan addressed criticism aimed at Lee for dividing his army in a hostile country facing the enemy:

Lee has been severely criticized for dividing his army at this time, and in one sense he is fairly exposed to it. But at bottom, the criticism in this case is but the common one to which a bold leader is always exposed, who attempts by superior energy and skill to make up for inferiority of men and resources. General Lee's whole course during the summer of 1862, and indeed during the war, is open to this kind of criticism. There were no aggressive movements possible to an army so inferior in strength as was the Confederate that may not be condemned as rash, while on the other hand a strictly defensive war against the resources and facilities of attack possessed by the North, pointed to certain and not distant collapse. Lee's expectation in regard to the reduction of Harper's Ferry was a reasonable one, and the risk he assumed in dividing his army to effect it was less than the risk he incurred in the operations against Pope three weeks before.[33]

Carman expressed his views about McClellan's actions after receiving the Lost Order:

The find was a valuable one. The possibilities it opened to McClellan were great, possibilities that come to a commander but seldom, and not to one man more than once in a lifetime. How did he approach them? Did he even meet them halfway? He had three courses presented to him: he could move to the relief of Harper's Ferry by the road leading through Jefferson and Knoxville and thence up the east bank of the Potomac; he

---

[31] Some of the Harpers Ferry cavalry troopers were there, *OR*, vol. 19, pt. 2, 311.

[32] Harsh, *Flood*, shows a few verbal exchanges Lee had such as with Jackson and Stuart, 107-8; the infamous Brigadier John G. Walker interview which Harsh finds mostly took place in Walker's mind, 133-145; and with Jackson and Longstreet, 145-152.

[33] Allan, 85-86.

could force his left under Franklin by way of Burkittsville through Crampton's Gap, then come directly upon the rear of McLaws on Maryland Heights and interpose between him and Lee; or he could press his right, under Burnside, and his center, under Sumner, by way of Middletown through Turner's Gap, thus interposing between Lee, Longstreet, D.H. Hill, and all the reserve trains and artillery on one side and the troops beyond the Potomac on the other—and the chances were that these fifty-five thousand Union soldiers would utterly crush the fifteen thousand men that the Confederates had to oppose them. All depended, however, on celerity of movement and vigor of attack....The plan was a good one, and in the hands of an able general and enterprising subordinates it should have produced great results. McLaws had ten brigades, and these were not concentrated, nor were they in close supporting distance, and there remained to Lee beyond South Mountain but fourteen brigades aggregating, according to D.H. Hill, about fifteen thousand men. Five brigades, under Hill, were at Boonsboro; nine brigades, under Longstreet, were twelve miles in the rear near Hagerstown. (This division of command was an advantage to McClellan had he known it, but he did not, as the lost order indicated that Lee, Longstreet, Hill, and all the reserve artillery and trains were at Boonsboro.)[34]

McClellan's pursuit, while not initially speedy, was faster than Lee expected, but a key failure was his over estimation of Lee's strength. In both cases, the army commanders did not receive accurate information since effective screening thwarted these efforts. Pleasonton was also unable to give McClellan good information even after S.O. 191 was found, again due to Stuart's effective screening, and the fatigue of Union horses. And McClellan's order to Pleasonton to learn if Lee's army was still following the order of march Lee laid out in S.O. 191, was almost ludicrous, as Pleasonton had neither the time nor the men to learn much of any value.[35] McClellan followed Lee's S.O. 191 much too long, disregarding accurate information showing that the Rebel army was deviating from it. As the Union line was in danger in McClellan's eyes on the 17th, he, perhaps in desperation, asked Pleasonton: "Can you do any good by a cavalry charge?"[36] This may show why he did not split up Pleasonton's cavalry since he still thought that these fresh troopers could be used as shock troops, to either buy time for reinforcements to come up, or to occupy Lee's attention to allow the decimated Union Corps to reorganize, and for Burnside to push toward Sharpsburg. McClellan's efforts to use signal stations to cover his flanks was commendable, but given that not all parts of the field especially on his left were viewable, Union cavalry watching that flank was required.[37] Before the Battle of Antietam, moving to Frederick, McClellan was insufficiently diligent in ensuring that Sugarloaf Mountain was taken quickly. This key terrain feature would have been extremely valuable giving him the ability to see more quickly that Lee's army had moved west allowing McClellan to push Burnside's wing more quickly to Frederick. The failures of Union commanders to make more of an effort to secure the mountain lost McClellan at least one day in his pursuit and the ultimate blame for this failure must be laid at the army commander's door. His less than aggressive generals needed a much stronger push to retake the height.[38] Similarly,

---

[34] Carman, Pierro, 131-132.

[35] Ibid., 239-240.

[36] Sears, McClellan, *Papers*, 467.

[37] Willard Brown, 331-333.

[38] Carman felt strongly that failing to quickly secure Sugarloaf was a serious mistake: "Notwithstanding these urgent orders to Pleasonton, Couch, and Franklin, no serious effort was made to carry Sugar Loaf Mountain on the tenth. Had Pleasonton put more force and persistence into his attack and carried the mountain, his lookout could have seen from its summit on that clear, bright morning of September 10 the long columns of Jackson, Longstreet, D.H. Hill, and McLaws as they marched out of Frederick and over Catoctin Mountain; Walker's Division would have been seen marching down from the mouth of the Monocacy northward to Point of Rocks; and the mystery of Lee's whereabouts would have been solved. Or had one of the nine brigades of available infantry supported Pleasonton on the afternoon of the tenth, the less than eight hundred cavalry at Munford's disposal could have been driven away before night. McClellan would have known the movements of his enemy and could have made dispositions for a rapid advance on the morrow. At 11:15 p.m. Franklin was ordered to put himself in communication with Sumner at Clarksburg and to carry Sugar Loaf Mountain if possible, but if the enemy appeared too strong he was authorized to await the result of Sumner's advance on Hyattstown. (Franklin was also told that "the earlier we gain the

McClellan knew that Franklin was not an aggressive commander so he should have been more careful to keep Franklin moving.

In his preparations for his Maryland adventure, Lee took measures to ready his army including Stuart's cavalry division. In Special Orders No. 187 issued on 2 September, he directed Stuart to send men from his command who had unserviceable horses due to overwork or lack of shoes, to return to Second Manassas. There, in addition to resting and reshoeing, the men were to collect arms and other materials to be shipped to Richmond for repair and redistribution.[39] Clearly he wanted Stuart's cavalry in good condition for its upcoming exertions but one could question that Lee might have relied more on Stuart's abilities as a commander to organize his own troopers. However, as seen in some of his other communications, Lee was probably more concerned with scouring the battlefield, collecting arms and equipment, than with resting and reshoeing horses. At this stage of the war, the South still was relying on the Union as a key supplier of armaments. In hindsight, Lee might have done better if he had left fewer cavalry and more unready infantry, especially as many foot soldiers would not enter Maryland as they had no shoes. Man for man, Lee should have known that in enemy country, he would need the cavalry's ability more than infantry, and in any event, the many thousands of stragglers from Lee's infantry units could have supplied needed manpower on the Second Bull Run battlefield, collecting booty, and defending against inquisitive Yankees.

Lee's instructions to Stuart during the campaign are brief but provide some insight regarding Lee's requirements. On 5 September Lee ordered Stuart to screen for Jackson's troops as they entered Maryland, but Stuart failed to accomplish much on Jackson's behalf, leading Jackson to use part of his infantry as a screen to the east.[40] Also on 5 September, Stuart was reminded to "keep careful watch for a Federal movement from Washington and to report the slightest sign of an advance."[41] Stuart's early mission of demonstrating toward Washington and Baltimore on both flanks of the Union advances to deceive and confuse them[42] was later augmented by requirements to screen the army, scout and delay the Union advance.[43] As has been noted, Stuart's demonstrations did not fool Halleck or Pleasonton. In Special Orders No. 191, Stuart's role was described in paragraph VIII: "General Stuart will detach a squadron of cavalry to accompany the commands of Generals Longstreet, Jackson, and McLaws, and, with the main body of the cavalry, will cover the route of the army, bringing up all stragglers that may have been left behind." These assignments were poorly done since the troopers' numbers were too small to be of much use for each command as screeners or scouts and apparently were not well used as couriers given the problems Lee had communicating with McLaws and Jackson while they were at Harpers Ferry. Part of Stuart's mission was amended by Lee on 13 September, after learning more about the Union advance: Stuart was to keep McLaws on Maryland Heights "informed of the movements of the enemy."[44] Lee's dispatch the day before told McLaws that Stuart's cavalry occupied the Middletown Valley when in fact they were only at a few locations such as at Jefferson, Crampton's Gap and Middletown. Given the men he had, he could not realistically hold all the roads in the valley especially in the face of Pleasonton's troopers backed by infantry.[45] Then as before, when Stuart was defending the

---

Sugar Loaf the better.") After midnight the order was repeated, and Franklin was advised that Sumner had been directed to cooperate with him. Partly if not wholly owing to the failure to carry Sugar Loaf Mountain on the tenth, McClellan's movements on September 11 were extremely cautious," Carman, Pierro, 87.

[39] *OR*, vol. 19, pt. 2, 589.

[40] Harsh, *Flood*, 88-91.

[41] Ibid., 108.

[42] *OR.*, vol. 19, pt. 1, 145.

[43] Ibid.

[44] *OR.*, vol. 19, pt. 2, 607.

[45] Ibid., 606.

Parr's Ridge/Sugarloaf Line, he could only picket important roads and mountain passes. Stuart now must help McLaws by protecting his flanks and rear while providing him intelligence. Stuart apparently took this additional mission to help McLaws to heart as he decided to leave the defense of Turner's Gap exclusively to Hill, without telling either Hill or Lee.[46]

Taken as a whole, Lee's orders to Stuart seem to be clear enough to give sufficient detail to his cavalry commander, sometimes with more detail than would seem necessary, but Lee's failure to ensure that his orders were followed allowed Stuart too much discretion and did not impress him with the critical need for reconnaissance in addition to screening. McClellan's orders to Pleasonton were unrealistic in that Pleasonton did not have sufficient cavalry to undertake what McClellan required; even if Pleasonton had wanted to be more aggressive in his search for Lee's army, it could not be done with the horses and troopers he had ready for duty in the face of Stuart's good screening efforts.

---

[46] Ibid., 234.

Appendix C

Order of Battle and Strength*
Army of the Potomac
Brig. Gen. Alfred J. Pleasonton's Cavalry Division**

Unit	Commander	No. of Companies	Present for Duty*** Officers/Men	
Division Staff			5-10 (total)	
1st Brigade Maj. Charles J. Whiting				
5th U. S. Cavalry Capt. Joseph H. McArthur		10	21	517
6th U. S. Cavalry Capt. William P. Sanders		10	22	561 (Attachment 3 below)
2nd Brigade Col. John F. Farnsworth				
8th Illinois Cavalry Maj. William H. Medill		12	39	588
3rd Indiana Cavalry Maj. George H. Chapman		6 (A-F)	-	374 (Attachment 1 below)
1st Massachusetts Cavalry Col. Robert Williams****		8 (A-H)	-	300*****
8th Pennsylvania Cavalry Lt. Col. Amos E. Griffiths ******		12	28	684
3d Brigade Col. Richard H. Rush				
4th Pennsylvania Cavalry Col. James H. Childs-killed 17 Sept. Lt. Col. James K. Kerr		12	38	735
6th Pennsylvania Cavalry Lt. Col. C. Ross Smith		9	20	478
4th Brigade Col. Andrew T. McReynolds				
1st New York Cavalry Maj. Alonzo W. Adams		12	40	761
12th Pennsylvania Cavalry Maj. James A. Congdon		12	-	600 (est. at 50/co.)
5th Brigade Col. Benjamin F. Davis				
8th New York Cavalry Col. Benjamin F. Davis		10	-	614
3rd Pennsylvania Cavalry Lt. Col. Samuel W. Owen		12	28	689

*Order of Battle taken from *OR*, vol. 19, pt. 1, 169-180, and Carman, Pierro, Appendices A and B. Strength from many sources as noted in the text and below but mostly from Leon Walter Tenney, "Seven Days in 1862: Numbers in Union and Confederate Armies Before Richmond," and John Owen Allen, "The Strength of the Union and Confederate Forces at Second Manassas." See discussion below about strength estimates; those here must not be taken as troopers in the saddle available for combat throughout the campaign.

**Pleasonton had field command while Brig. Gen. John Buford was in administrative command as chief of cavalry, on 10 September, *OR*, vol. 19, pt. 2, 242

***When the number of officers is known it is shown separately from enlisted; when not known, "present for duty" includes officers and men.

****Carman shows Col. Robert Williams vice Crowninshield in *OR*, Carman, Pierro, 413, n. 56. Williams is correct.

*****Crowninshield, 77, 86.

******Carman shows Lt. Col. Amos E. Griffiths vice Capt. Peter Keenan in *OR*, Carman, Pierro, 413. Griffith is correct.

Unit	Commander	No. of Companies		Present for Duty Officers/Men

Unassigned/detached

Unit	Commander	No. of Companies		Present for Duty Officers/Men
1st Maine Cavalry. Col. Samuel H. Allen		6	-	276
15th Pennsylvania Cavalry Col. William J. Palmer		4	-	100-200

Cavalry Division Horse Artillery

Unit	Commander	No. of Guns		Present for Duty Officers/Men
2nd U. S. Artillery				
Battery A Capt. John C. Tidball		6	4	128
2nd U. S. Artillery				
Batteries B and L Capt. James M. Robertson		4	3	129
2nd U. S. Artillery				
Battery M Lt. Peter C. Hains		6	4	130
3rd U. S. Artillery				
Batteries C and G Capt. Horatio G. Gibson		6	3	135

Total officers and men Present for Duty   **8,212**

Other cavalry units attached to major commands as escorts, couriers, guards, etc.:

Unit	Commander	No. of Companies		Present for Duty Officers/Men

General Headquarters

Escort Capt. James B. McIntyre

Unit	Commander	No. of Companies		Present for Duty Officers/Men
Independent Co. Oneida NY Capt. Daniel P. Mann		1	2	43
4th U. S. Cavalry, Co. A Lt. Thomas H. McCormick		1	2	48*
4th U. S. Cavalry, Co. E Capt. James B. McIntyre		1	2	50*

Provost Guard Maj. William H. Wood

2nd U. S. Cavalry, Cos. E, F, H, K Capt. George A. Gordon		4	4	117 (Attachment 2 below)

Quartermaster's Guard

1st U. S. Cavalry, Cos. B, C, H, I Capt. Marcus A. Reno**		4	6	135

*Co. A Lt. Thomas H. McCormick (Army headquarters escort); Co. E Capt. James B. McIntyre (Army (McClellan's) headquarters escort) McIntyre commanding squadron; NA, RG 391, Regimental Returns. Aug. 62: Co. A; PFD 48, aggregate 68; serviceable horses 55. Co. E; 50 PFD, aggregate 75, 58 serviceable horses. Oct. 62 stationed at Berlin, MD: Co. A; PFD 58, agg. 80, 50 serviceable horses. Co. E; 45 PFD, 86 agg., 55 serviceable horses.

**From about 10 September to 17 September the 1st U.S. was assigned to Franklin's corps; Sanford, 173. The 1st then became McClellan's quartermaster's guard at his general headquarters at the Pry House on the 17th being detached from Franklin, Sanford, 177. On the 19th, the 1st was in Pleasonton's advance to the Potomac; the 1st came under heavy Rebel artillery fire from across the river but suffered no casualties, 182. Some of 1st U.S. Cavalry at Carlisle as instructors along with 3rd, 150 troopers; OR vol. 19, pt. 2, 247; Kirk, 640-1, 643-4; 646. Capt. D.H. Hastings, 1st Cavalry commanding detachment operating between Chambersburg and the Maryland state line; OR, vol. 19, pt. 2, 278.

Unit Commander	No. of Companies	Present for Duty Officers/Men	

Army Corps Escorts

First Corps

| **2nd N.Y. Cavalry, Cos. A, B, I, K** Capt. John E. Naylor | 4 | - | 200 (est.) |

Second Corps

| **6th N. Y. Cavalry, Co. D** Capt. Henry W. Lyon | 1 | - | 50 |
| **6th N. Y. Cavalry, Company K** Capt. Riley Johnson | 1 | 3 | 56 |

Fifth Corps

| **1st Maine Cavalry, detachment** Capt. George J. Summat | 2 | - | 92 |

Cos. M and H Gen. Porter, Tobie, 92.

Sixth Corps

| **6th Penn. Cavalry, Cos. B, G, I** Capt. Henry P. Muirheid | 3 | - | 150 (est. at 50/co.) |

Ninth Corps

| **1st Maine Cavalry, Company G** Capt. Zebulon B. Blethen | 1 | - | 46 |

Gen. Reno's guard, Cos. A and I Gen. Rodman's guard Tobie, 92.

Twelfth Corps

| **1st Michigan Cavalry, Company L** Capt. Melvin Brewer | 1 | - | 54 |

Unattached

| **6th N. Y. Cavalry** Col. Thomas C. Devin temporarily attached to Burnside | 6 | - | 300 (est. at 50/co.)* |
| **Ohio Cavalry, Third Independent Co.** Lt. Jonas Seamen | 1 | - | 50 (est.) |

| **Total officers and men, as escorts, couriers, guards, etc.** | **34** | | **1,466** |

West Virginia Volunteers, 1st Regiment Cavalry, two companies, attached to the Kanawha Division, First Brigade: **Gilmore's Company**, West Virginia Cavalry Lt. James Abraham and **Harrison's Company**, West Virginia Cavalry Lt. Dennis Delaney. Dyer, 3:1655; Carman, Pierro, 410; Priest, *Before Antietam*, 81, 85-86, 90-92, 95, 137, 139. Priest shows only one company commanded by Capt. James Abraham.

1st Rhode Island Cavalry under Col. Alfred N. Duffie was apparently operating under McClellan's orders even though until September 1862, it was part of Bayard's cavalry brigade in the Army of Virginia. Brig. Gen. George D. Bayard reported the regiment's strength at 450 troopers on 5 September 1862, *OR*, vol. 19, pt. 2, 184. Frederic Denison wrote that on 12 September, 30 recruits were added to the ranks but they were without horses, *Sabres and Spurs*, 156. He does not show whether they received mounts before the regiment moved to the vicinity of Poolesville; if so, the regiment numbered about 480 sabers during its reconnaissance duties in Maryland before illness and casualties took their toll: five were captured on the 15th, while seven were in hospital on the 22nd, 157, 160.

*The historian of the 6th New York wrote that "the regiment, being at that time attached to General Burnside's corps, as escort and advance guard, and being broken up in squadrons, companies and squads on special duty, was seldom anywhere as a regiment, but in that detached shape was practically all over the field," Hall, 63. His statement could be applied to most other cavalry regiments in McClellan's army.

Harpers Ferry Cavalry Units*	No. of Companies	Present for Duty
1st Potomac Home Brigade Cavalry Maj. Henry A. Cole	2	124
1st Maryland Cavalry Capt. Charles Russell	2	123
7th Squadron Rhode Island Cavalry Maj. Augustus W. Corliss	2	146
8th New York Cavalry Col. Benjamin F. Davis	10	614
12th Illinois Cavalry Col. Arno Voss	7	575**
Loudoun Rangers Capt. Samuel C. Means		12
Total	**23**	**1,594**

*Harry Pfanz "Special History Report; Troop Movement Maps, September 12-14, 1862, Harpers Ferry, NHP," Denver: NPS Center, 1976, 42.

**See note 60 in Chapter 8, Breakout From Harpers Ferry, showing the discussion of the number of companies and troopers in the 12th Illinois at Harpers Ferry. The seven companies in the field at Williamsport on 21 September numbered 350 troopers and the two companies of Maryland cavalry 100, *OR*, vol. 19, pt. 2, 357.

Army of Northern Virginia*
Numbers of Maj. Gen. James E. B. Stuart's Cavalry Division
During the Maryland Campaign

Unit	Commander	No. of Companies	Present for Duty Officers/Men
Division Staff			8
Hampton's Brigade Brig. Gen. Wade Hampton (staff 5)			
1st North Carolina Cavalry Col. Laurence S. Baker		10	411
2nd South Carolina Cavalry Col. Matthew C. Butler		4	213
10th Virginia Cavalry Col. James Lucius Davis**		7	340
Cobb's (Georgia) Legion, Lt. Col. Pierce M. B. Young, Maj. William G. Delony		6	170
Jeff. Davis Legion, Lt. Col. William T. Martin		6	306
Lee's Brigade Brig. Gen. Fitzhugh Lee (staff 4)			
1st Virginia Cavalry Lt. Col. Luke Tiernan Brien***		10	513
3rd Virginia Cavalry Lt. Col. John T. Thornton (killed 17 September)			
Capt. Thomas H. Owens		10	223
4th Virginia Cavalry Col. Williams C. Wickham		10	336
5th Virginia Cavalry Col. Thomas L. Rosser		10	366
9th Virginia Cavalry Col. William H. Fitzhugh Lee		10	517
Robertson's Brigade (Laurel Brigade) Brig. Gen. Beverly H. Robertson Col. Thomas T. Munford (staff 4)****			
2nd Virginia Cavalry Col. T.T. Munford, Lt. Col. Richard H. Burks		9	408
7th Virginia Cavalry Capt. Samuel B. Myers		9	474
12th Virginia Cavalry Col. Asher W. Harman		6	358
17th Virginia Battalion, 7 companies Maj. Thomas B. Massie*****		6	302
Horse Artillery Capt. John Pelham			
Chew's or "Ashby" Artillery (Virginia) Battery Capt. Roger P. Chew	1		75
Hart's or "Washington" (South Carolina) Battery Capt. James F. Hart	1		64
Pelham's or "First Stuart" (Virginia) Battery Capt. James Breathed	1		123

Total officers and men Present for Duty   **5,207**

Note that Pelham's Battalion existed only on paper as each battery served with only its brigade during the campaign, Chew with Munford, Hart with Hampton, and Pelham with Fitzhugh Lee.

There were other cavalry units attached to major commands as headquarter escorts, couriers, scouts, etc.:

Jackson's Command

White's Virginia Cavalry, 35th Battalion of Virginia Cavalry, (three companies) the "Comanches" Capt. E. V. White		1	37 (173)******
4th Virginia Cavalry, Co. H, "Black Horse" Capt. Robert Randolph			40 (est.)

Longstreet's Command

Independent Company, South Carolina Cavalry Capt. James Doby			40 (est.)

*OR, vol. 19, pt. 1, 810; Carman, Pierro, Appendices A and B; Harsh, *Shallows*, 33-50. Leon Walter Tenney, "Seven Days in 1862: Numbers in Union and Confederate Armies Before Richmond," and John Owen Allen, "The Strength of the Union and Confederate Forces at Second Manassas."

**The 10th Virginia Cavalry only crossed north of the Potomac after the battle at Sharpsburg. Robert. J. Driver, Jr. *10th Virginia Cavalry* (Lynchburg, VA: H.E. Howard, 1992), 23-24.

***See Driver, *1st Virginia Cavalry*, 46-47. Also see Carman who reports that the regiment accompanied Longstreet to Hagerstown having been detached from its brigade on 10 September to accompany Jackson protecting his northern flank and rear, Carman, Pierro, 129, 171.

****The 6th Virginia Cavalry remained at Centerville, Virginia, to help collect arms and equipment left after the battles at Second Bull Run and Chantilly. Carman, Pierro, 434. See also Lee's S.O. 187 directing this activity, *OR*, vol. 19, pt. 2, 589; Harsh, *Shallows*, 88; commander, Col. Thomas S. Flournoy, 10 companies, 407.

*****The 17th Virginia Battalion was sent on an expedition to Berkeley, Virginia, and never journeyed into Maryland, *Shallows*, 88, 101. This may be incorrect: William N. McDonald, *A History of the Laurel Brigade Originally The Ashby Cavalry of the Army of Northern Virginia and Chew's Battery*, edited by Bushrod C. Washington (Baltimore, MD: Sun Job Printing Office, 1907), 94-95. McDonald wrote that the brigade was posted on the right of Gen. Lee's line near the river on 17 September in Maryland, however, Holmes Conrad in a letter to Carman 1 June 1897 said that the battalion crossed early on 17 September and "took position of the right of Jackson's [undecipherable] with the rest of the brigade," copy of letter courtesy Thomas Clemens. Since the rest of Munford's Brigade was clearly not on Jackson's right, Conrad's statement is in error. It was with Jackson at Harpers Ferry and operated on his flanks. During the Battle of Antietam, it remained on the Virginia side of the Potomac on the right of Lee's position and did only minor skirmishing, McDonald, *Laurel Brigade*, 95; Harsh, *Shallows*, 89-90.

******White had an eventful September after he left Stuart as noted in Chapter 5. He captured 35 Yankee infantry on his farm on the Potomac; Union cavalry with these Yankees escaped across the Potomac however. White next confronted some 400 Union cavalry with four guns under the command of Brig. Gen. Judson Kilpatrick on 17 September in Leesburg after he received information that a Union force was advancing to that town. There he found Co. A of the 6th Virginia Cavalry under Capt. Gibson and some 40 Mississippi infantry under Capt. Young who was the provost marshal of the town. White was wounded by his own supporting Confederate infantry as he was organizing a charge which then fell apart. He was hors-de-combat until late October 1862. Note that the company with Capt. White in Maryland is described as a Virginia company in the regimental history vice a Maryland company as found in Carman, Clemens, 227. The Maryland Company under Capt. George W. Chiswell joined White's company on 12 September, and then by another company led by Lt. Myers who joined them at Waterford, Myers, 109-110.

Historian Frank J. Welcher analyzed the strength of Pleasonton's five-brigade division and concluded that it was not a strong force "and it played only a minor role in the Maryland Campaign. Farnsworth's [Second Brigade] consisted of four regiments, but the other brigade[s] had only two regiments each, thus making a total of only twelve regiments in the division. This number, too, is misleading, because part of every regiment was serving on escort or provost duty with the various corps and division of the army. Twenty-five companies, about one-sixth of the total number, were absent from their regiments."[1] The 5th Brigade was not available to Pleasonton until Antietam. The 1st Brigade was used for scouting near the Potomac in Frederick and Middletown Valleys; the 3rd Brigade, 4th Pennsylvania (12 companies) stayed with its sister 6th Pennsylvania Cavalry (Rush's Lancers) (nine companies), moved in Munford's wake southwest toward Jefferson about seven miles from Frederick and then served as Franklin's cavalry with some help from the 6th U.S.; the 4th Brigade, the 1st New York and the 12th Pennsylvania, both with 12 companies, chased Fitz Lee north and reached the outskirts of Gettysburg on the 14 September. On the 15th, the column headed back to Emmitsburg and the 1st New York arrived in Frederick on 16 September. Thus the 12th Pennsylvania was not of other use to Pleasonton until the 16th, and the 1st New York did not arrive on the battlefield until late on the 17th.[2] Pleasonton during the second week of the campaign had insufficient troopers to do all the scouting and screening McClellan needed. Once cavalry units assigned other duties are subtracted from the five brigades with 12 regiments listed for the Union cavalry during the campaign, Pleasonton used primarily the Second Brigade under Col. John F. Farnsworth: the 8th Illinois (12 companies), 3rd Indiana (six companies), 1st Massachusetts (8 companies), and the 8th Pennsylvania (12 companies). Pleasonton's strength for these four regiments for troopers on the firing line was probably between 1,200 and 1,600 troopers.[3]

The standard for measurement for the units is "present for duty." Present for duty is the number of men physically present when the return was prepared minus those "sick in camp," "detailed," or having "extra duty." This present for duty number is the maximum number of men who could be on the firing line. The present for duty number is rarely the actual number of men on the firing line, "carried into battle," for many reasons such as those who dropped out of the march to the battlefield due to illness or injury or who got lost, or decided that the time was not right for a battle—a "slacker" or those detailed by the unit commander to stay behind as camp guards, etc. But short of solid evidence of the true number present when the shooting began such as credible after action battle reports, present for duty is used as a basic starting point given no other data. Leon Walter Tenney opined that "In battle analyses the author or military analyst should use the 'carried into action' strengths. However, in campaign analyses the author or analyst should use the 'present for duty' strengths that are complete with all

---

[1] Welcher, 513.

[2] The 4th Pennsylvania Cavalry's location with its companion regiment, Rush's Lancers, at Jefferson then presumably with Franklin is taken from Harsh, *Flood*, 230. Supporting documentation detailing the 4th's activities until it appeared at the Middle Bridge on 17 September is not found. A participant from Company A, Cpl. William Hyndman, wrote of this period: "Gen. Burnside's command was organized to meet the rebel army immediately, and at once it marched forth from the Capital, our regiment acting as escort to the commanding general and staff. We first met the enemy on the night of Sept. 11th, when our battalion, commanded by Capt. Young, entered Rockville, Maryland, in advance of Burnside's column, on a reconnoissance, drove their advance back, and returning reported to headquarters. The next day we entered Frederick City, Maryland, capturing 450 rebels, most of whom were sick, and routing and driving out the force who were occupying the city. On the 14th, the successful action at South Mountain took place, in which, however, we did not participate any more than as escorts to staff officers. We had, though, opportunities of viewing the action from all the different points—from Franklin on the extreme left, to Reno on the right," 65-66. The inference is that the 6th was with or near Franklin at Crampton's Gap.

[3] Total present for duty before the start of the Maryland Campaign is 1,946. These estimates use Carman's calculation—"20 to 40 percent fewer show up on the firing line."

organizations represented."[4] During the Maryland Campaign, it is difficult to obtain counts of troopers either in a given skirmish or even present for duty on the morning of a given day.

The data above listing unit numbers for the Union and Confederates show present for duty taken from primarily from two masters theses done for Dr. Joseph L. Harsh by Leon Walter Tenney, "Seven Days in 1862: Numbers in Union and Confederate Armies Before Richmond," and John Owen Allen, "The Strength of the Union and Confederate Forces at Second Manassas." The theses provide the basis for the campaign study comparing the opposing cavalry but not of course "carried into battle" numbers. Fortunately, most of the cavalry units in the Army of the Potomac and the Army of Northern Virginia in Maryland were either in the Peninsula Campaign (both Union and Confederate cavalry units) or at Second Bull Run (Confederate cavalry units but almost no Union units). The Peninsula numbers are calculated as of 20 June 1862 while the Second Bull Run data is as of 2 September. Thus the Second Bull Run data is fresher for the Confederate cavalry than is the Union data some two and a half months older. Confederate numbers in Maryland are probably lower than the 2 September tally as more than a few troopers found other pursuits in Virginia more urgent. Perhaps it was time to go home on leave to get a fresh horse after months of hard campaigning or to take leave, authorized or not, to rest at home. Union numbers present on the Peninsula in late June are higher than numbers present in Maryland as there was considerable illness in the camps near Harrison's Landing plus the fodder was not ample for many units. Finally, the sea voyage from Hampton to Northern Virginia put some horses out of action. Also for Union units, the rushed unloading and hurrying to the front left some troopers and horses who were unfit in the dust along with many units' supply wagons. But these carefully researched numbers from Allen and Tenney even with these caveats must be given considerable weight and are used as campaign numbers corrected and supplemented by other data as available. But it is safe to conjecture that in all of the skirmishes and fights during the campaign, the numbers of troopers in the saddle in a given unit were fewer, and sometimes dramatically fewer, than those "present for duty" on the unit's morning report.[5]

The second concern with analyzing numbers of troopers present during the Maryland Campaign is the campaign's long time frame. The approximate two weeks of the campaign affects numbers present for duty at a given date as cavalry regiment and companies from regiments joined and left Pleasonton and Stuart from 4 September to 20 September. Data will be shown for dates as found to help understand the numbers of troopers available on certain dates to better understand how the cavalry commanders employed their resources. Some companies in regiments were on given days parceled out for various duties and then returned but these intramural movements are not always shown in the records thus making it more difficult to estimate those "carried into action." For Army of the Potomac cavalry units, it is safe to say that their numbers increased day-by-day right up to the Battle of Antietam.

---

[4] Tenney, 51. Gen. Lee was concerned about the numbers of stragglers and revealed that strength reports were not available; he wrote President Davis on 13 September that "I have received as yet no official list of the casualties in the late battles, and, from the number of absentees from the army and the vice of straggling, a correct list cannot now be obtained. The army has been so constantly in motion, its attention has been so unremittingly devoted to what was necessary, that little opportunity has been afforded for attention to this subject....Our ranks are very much diminished—I fear from a third to one-half of the original numbers—though I have reason to hope that our casualties in battles will not exceed 5,000 men," OR, vol. 19, pt. 2, 605-606. On 22 September in an order to Longstreet and Jackson, he reminded them that strength reports were important: "It is feared that roll-calls are neglected, and officers of companies and regiments are ignorant of the true condition of their commands, and are unable to account properly for absentees. To correct this, the general commanding wishes the prescribed roll-calls to be made at *reveille*, each man appearing under arms...," ibid., 618. Note that the cavalry submitted no returns for its commands on both the 22 and 30 September army returns, ibid., 621, 639.

[5] Allen, 17; Tenney, 51, 90-91. For a detailed discussion of terms used in the Union and Confederate armies for tallying soldiers, see Tenney, 62-75.

The third concern is the large geographical area the campaign covered especially after Gen. Lee split his army into four, then five parts detailed in Special Order 191. Sometimes regiments were segmented to accomplish more than one mission or simply because they got lost. Tracking which units were available to Pleasonton and Stuart as they maneuvered around the Maryland and Virginia countryside and the composition of amalgamated, ad hoc units is attempted.[6]

The final issue of great importance is that due to the movements of the armies while marching and fighting, most units did not make daily morning reports. Thus many strength reports for this period were made during quiet times in the fall of 1862 and therefore are likely less accurate than if they were made daily.[7]

A search for available regimental books, morning reports, etc., for units involved, finds few. Even when books are available, there are no entries for relevant time periods. Only one fairly complete morning report for a cavalry company has been found in the National Archives, for Company B of the 3rd Indiana Cavalry, and is attached below as Attachment 1, due to its rarity. It is presented showing only present for duty numbers as those are the most relevant as "carried into battle" are not part of the morning report form. This example shows that near the beginning of the campaign, 50 troopers are available while near the end during Antietam, only 41 are present for duty. The normal complement for a full company is 100 men. Attachments for the 2nd and 6th U.S. Cavalry are included for the detail found for these regiments.

Carman determined that the Union had 3,828 (4,320 with horse artillery) cavalry present for duty at Antietam while the Confederates had 4,500. He wrote that Civil War veterans know "the difference between the number of those who answered roll-call in camp or were accounted for as present and the number of those who went onto the fighting line: "present for duty" and those available for action or "in action" are usually different—20 to 40 percent fewer show up on the firing line.[8] If we apply his percentages to the 8,212 total for Union cavalry found above we obtain 6,570 or 4,927; the 60% number, 4,927, is close to Carman's estimate of 4,320 at Antietam. Using 5,111 for the Confederates and his percentages gives 4,081 or 3,066, with the 80% closer to his estimate. The 4,500 number given in the OR is obviously the best estimate Stuart could give.

Total Cavalry Strength at Antietam and After

Union

4,320 on 17 September 1862 (*OR*, vol. 19, pt. 1, 67); 4,320 (3,828 cavalry and horse 492 artillery; Carman, Pierro, 459)

4,543 present for duty on 20 and 30 September 1862; aggregate including absent: 7,686 (*OR*, vol. 19, pt. 2, 336, 374)

7,000 plus 600 horse artillery on 1 October 1862 (estimated) (*OR*, vol. 19, pt. 1, 97)

5,058 present for duty including horse artillery on 10 October 1862; aggregate including absent: 7,686 (*OR*, vol. 19, pt. 2, 410)

---

[6] Some cavalry units such as the 1st New York, 12th Pennsylvania and 15th Pennsylvania as well as the Harpers Ferry escape column spent time in Pennsylvania.

[7] Tenney, 72, noting that many company reports for the Army of the Potomac for August and September 1862 were made in October, November or December 1862.

[8] Carman, Pierro, 213, 453, 465. Using the 20 percent reduction the Union would have 3,062 while the Confederates would have 3,600; 40 percent gives 2,297 for the Union and 2,700 for the Confederates.

Confederate

4,155 on 2 September 1862 (Harsh, *Shallows*, 139)

4,500 on 17 September 1862 (Carman, Pierro, 465, Harsh, *Shallows,* 201). Carman's 60% equals 2,700(.6 x 4500); 80% is 3,600 (.8 x 4500). (See also Priest, *Antietam*, 330, showing 1,600 present on 17 September.)

5,761 present for duty 10 Oct., aggregate present and absent 10,298, *OR*, vol. 19, pt. 2, 660.

Cavalry Casualties during the Maryland Campaign*

Army of the Potomac Cavalry

Killed		Wounded		Captured or Missing		Aggregate	Remarks
Officers	Enlisted	Officers	Enlisted	Officers	Enlisted		
0	12	0	55	0	13	80	Advance Guard
0	0	0	1	0	0	1	So. Mtn. /Crampton's Gap
1	4	0	23	0	0	28	Antietam**
Total **1**	**16**	**0**	**79**	**0**	**13**	**109**	

*OR, vol. 19, pt. 1, 34-36.
**Carman shows total of 7 killed, 30 aggregate; Carman, Pierro, 469. See also Priest, *Antietam*, 343.

The data clearly show the fights the Union cavalry had with Confederate cavalry during the advance of Union forces from Washington, D. C., to Antietam giving the largest number of casualties. The remarkably low casualties for Union Cavalry during the Battle of South Mountain on 14 September reflect that the cavalry was only marginally involved. During the Battle of Antietam on 17 September, the few casualties prove that McClellan did not employ his cavalry effectively in any role other than guarding the Middle Bridge and his horse artillery there.

Union Cavalry Losses at Maryland Heights and Harpers Ferry 12-15 September 1862*

	Killed		Wounded		Captured or Missing		Aggregate	Remarks
	Officers	Enlisted	Officers	Enlisted	Officers	Enlisted		
12th IL	0	0	0	2	4	153	159	
1st MD	0	0	1	2	1	19	23	Detachment
MD	0	0	0	0	0	0	0	Cole's Battalion
8th NY	0	0	0	0	5	87	92	
RI Cav.	0	0	0	0	0	0	0	7th Squadron
Totals	**0**	**0**	**1**	**4**	**10**	**259**	**274**	

*OR, vol. 19, pt. 1, 549; Carman, Pierro, 437. Units not part of Army of Potomac but see Chapter 8, "Breakout from Harpers Ferry."

Army of Northern Virginia Cavalry

Killed	Wounded	Captured or Missing	Aggregate	Remarks
12	23	29	64	Before South Mountain*
--	--	--	27	Turner's and Fox's Gaps**
3	5	0	8	Crampton's Gap***
10	28	11	49	Antietam****
Total 25	56	40	148	

*Carman, Pierro, 46, 82, 83, 91, 95. Note Carman describes in addition Pleasonton "taking a number of prisoners," 94.

**Carman, Pierro, 449; estimate including horse artillery.

*** Carman, Pierro, 445; 2nd and 12th Virginia Cavalry.

****Harsh, *Shallows*, 201; Carman, Pierro, 474. See also Priest, *Antietam*, 331, showing 61 total casualties including horse artillery: 10 killed, 45 wounded, 6 missing.

Attachment 1

3rd Indiana Cavalry Company B[9]
Present for Duty

Date Sept. 1862	Company Location	Officers/enlisted (included are buglers, farriers, and artificers)
3	Hampton, VA	2/48
4	On ship*	2/48
5	On ship	2/48
6	On ship	2/48
7	Washington, DC	2/45
8	"On the march"	2/43
9	"On the march"	2/43
10	"On the march"	2/42
11	Barnesville, MD	2/42
12	Barnesville, MD	2/43
13	Near Buckeystown	2/43
14	Jefferson	2/41
15	Burkittsville	2/41
16	Pleasant Valley	2/41
17	Pleasant Valley	2/39
18	Battlefield**	2/39
19	Battlefield	2/38
20	Battlefield	2/36
21	"On the march"	2/36
22	Near Williamsport MD	2/37

* Assumed
**Presumed to be Antietam

---

[9] NA, RG 94, 3rd Indiana Cavalry, Company B, morning reports. The decreasing number of enlisted available are reported as being sick. Interestingly, the reports for these dates show very few "unserviceable" horses for the company. 3rd Indiana Cavalry six companies called 3rd Battalion in its record books, Regimental Descriptive and Consolidated Morning report Book; no reports for 2 September to 10 October 1862. Reports for 1 September 1862 show present for duty Co. A, 2 officers and 65 privates; Co. B, 0 officers and 57 privates; Co. C, 2 officers and 64 privates; Co. D, 1 officer, 53 privates; Co. E, 2 officers and 59 privates; Co. F, 1 officer and 59 privates; field, staff and band, 10. Present and absent totals are as follows for the companies: A = 91; B = 92; C = 94, D = 84, E = 90, F = 88. One Indiana trooper wrote home on 11 September it was a confused melee into which Companies A and B charged 400 enemy with 80 troopers, letter from Mildred Wright file, courtesy of Indiana State Library dated 11 September 1862.

Attachment 2

2nd U.S. Cavalry*

Cos. E, F, H, K Capt. George A. Gordon, Co. K, in command; Army Provost Guard; RG 391, Monthly Reports, September 1862; Gordon also in command of Anderson Cavalry, Cos. A and B of the Illinois Cavalry. Left camp near Alexandria 1 September and arrived at Sharpsburg camp 28 September. Charles E. Norris, commanding Co. E; John Green, Co. F; Charles J. Walker, Co. H; George A. Gordon, Co. K.

Company	Officers	Enlisted	Aggregate	Serviceable Horses
Co. E	1	22	70	not shown
Co. F	2	36	78	56
Co. H	1	24	67	36
Co. K	2	30	73	51
Band?	3	18	27	18

Anderson Illinois Cavalry

Co. A	1	18	89	54
Co. B	2	23	88	56

Possible stations for other 2nd U.S. Cavalry companies: Co. A, New York; Co. B, Ohio; Co. C, Mississippi; Co. D, Iowa?

July 1862: Co.'s A, B, and D are broken up, privates sent to other companies (E, F, H, K). Officers, NCOs and buglers sent off to recruiting duty. A: New York City, B: Carlisle Barracks, D: Morristown, PA. Regimental end strength present for duty at end of month: 9 officers, 240 enlisted men. (Sources: regt. returns; Lambert, p. 65. E, F, H, K, rear guard on Peninsula with a squadron of the 4th; 1 Sept. 62 marched north as provost guard to AOP, Lambert, 66.

The regiment, four companies strong, arrived from the Peninsula in Alexandria on 25 August, and went into camp at Centerville. On 1 September it was assigned as the Provost Guard for General HQ, Army of the Potomac.

Also present for duty were the regimental adjutant, 2nd Lt. James McQuesten, the regimental sergeant major, Robert Lennox, and regimental quartermaster Sgt. Edward J. Spaulding. Officer numbers are not certain as several people were promoted on 17 July 1862 but the news didn't reach the regiment until 24 September.

E: 1st Lt. William H. Harrison (news of promotion to 1st Lt arrives 25 September)
F: Capt. John Green
   2nd Lt. Paul Quirk (1st Sgt of Co. F until news arrives 24 September, date of rank 17 July)
   2nd Lt. of Co. L on detached duty with Co. F (Regt. SGM until news arrives 24 September)
H: 2nd Lt. Michael Lawless (1st Sgt of Co. H until news arrives 24 September)
K: Capt. George A. Gordon
   Peter Rinner (1st Sgt. of Co. K until news arrives 24 September)

So the more accurate strength for the battle is (officers/men):

Co. E   1/22

Co. F   1/37

Co. H   0/25

Co. K   1/31

plus Regt HQ   1/2 (McQuesten/ Lennox and Spaulding); (Spaulding also promoted to Regt QM officer 17 July and assigned 24 September)

*Courtesy Donald Caughey and from National Archives. Note that "aggregate" is the total number on the books for the company, not the number available for action, which are the numbers for officers and enlisted on each line.

Attachment 3

6th U.S. Cavalry

Capt. William P. Sanders
10 companies; Pleasonton, *OR*, vol. 19, pt. 2, 172, 3 Sept 1862

Donald Caughey's extensive research shows that all companies of the 6th U.S. were serving in Maryland during the Maryland Campaign. Historian Timothy Reese traces reports for the 6th U.S. Cavalry showing that companies (troops), **A and C**, were serving in Arizona at this time, however. Caughey has found that no units from the 6th were in Arizona until long after the war. Reese finds no rolls from Companies **H, K, L, or M**. Companies **B, D, E, G and I** were serving with Franklin on 14 September and scouted below Franklin's left also maintaining contact with Couch. **Co. F** roll made at Purcellville. Muster Roll box 1030, 1031, 1033, 1035, 1037, 1040, 1042, 1044, 1048; *Sealed*, 336, n. 48.

National Archives also records the regiment's activities as noted by the author paraphrased as follows: RG 391, Regimental Records, Company Histories. Co. D landed at Alexandria from Yorktown 2 September 1862, camped near Ft. Albany; 4 September recon to Falls Church; 5 September crossed to Maryland and part of advance under Gen. Pleasonton as far as Jeffersonville, Maryland; 17 September, marched to Sharpsburg; 22 September, marched to Harpers Ferry.

Co. I, 31 August 1862 embarked at Yorktown for Alexandria; 1 September, landed and marched to Ft. Albany near Alexandria; 2 September, detached and reported to Gen. Sigel scouting and outpost duty near Dranesville; 5 September, marched to Tenallytown, Maryland; 6 September, marched to Darnestown, ditto 7th; 8 September, marched to Barnesville; 9 September, skirmish at Sugarloaf Mountain; 10 September, scout and picketed the Monocacy; skirmish at Buckystown, marched to Licksville; 14th, detached at Jefferson; skirmish at and occupation of Petersville; 17th, bivouacked at Knoxville on picket toward Harpers Ferry; 17th, joined regiment at Burkittsville and marched to Antietam; 23rd, marched to Harpers Ferry. PFD 40, 62? agg.

Co. M, May 1862 8 WIA; 4 May, left Yorktown to pursue enemy; engagement at Williamsburg, 10 missing, 8 wounded; left 7 May in advance of pursuit-Slatersville 9 May; 10 May, New Bridge—a detachment was engaged; company up Chickahominy to Mechanicsville, left 27 May engaged enemy on 27th at Hanover Court House; left Yorktown 1 September arrived Alexandria 2 September to Ft Albany to Falls Church, Georgetown, Darnestown, Poolesville, Jefferson, Petersville, Knoxville, Burkittsville, Sharpsburg, Harpers Ferry.

(Copied from a memorandum book of Co. B found at headquarters of 6th Cavalry) Co. B, 4 May, left Camp Winfield Scott at Yorktown in pursuit; 5th, skirmish at Brick Church near Williamsburg and in battle of Williamsburg; 6th, camped in Williamsburg; 7th, pursuit with Cos. B and H "forming the 1st squadron and the only ones armed with Sharps Carbines"...acting as skirmishers met a flag of truce about 3 miles from Williamsburg. We overtook their rear Guard and a lively skirmish ensued we soon dispersed them." 9th, "Engaged the enemy at Stales? Mills charged a Brigade of Cavalry and drove them our loss in the Regiment was 5 killed 8 missing and 30 wounded." 16th, "Caught Maj. Williams in the act of communicating with the Enemy." 24th, led advance severe skirmish at Mechanicsville; 27th, led advance of Fitz John Porter drove in pickets which brought on general engagement at Hanover Court House; 25 June 1862, left camp at midnight to Hanover Court House and back to camp without rest, about 70 miles; 27th, protected right flank of Fitz John Porter retreat to Yorktown by way of White House Landing –burned supplies, 107 hours in saddle; 31 August, embarked at Yorktown for Alexandria; 3 September, disembarked and to Upton's Hill; 4th, skirmish at Falls Church; marched across Aqueduct Bridge at Georgetown to Tenallytown; 5th, marched to Darnestown and camped; 9th, marched to Poolesville; 10th, reconnaissance to Sugarloaf Mountain, severe skirmish, 1 wounded, several horses shot; 11th, marched to Greenfield, Maryland; 12th, marched to Licksville and Point of Rocks; 13th, marched to Jefferson, Maryland; 17th, marched to Burkittsville; 19th, marched through Rohrersville and camped beyond Sharpsburg; 20th, marched through Antietam from [iron] works to Harpers Ferry next day [21st] at noon.

(Report by Bvt. Capt. A.R. Chaffee, Adj. 6th Cavalry, 4 June 1866) Co. B; 31 August 1862, embarked; 3 September, arrived; 4th, marched to Upton Mills and made a reconnaissance; 5th, marched to Tenallytown then Darnestown and picketed the Frederick Road on 6th through 9th, then marched to Poolesville; 10th, reconnaissance to Sugarloaf Mountain, one private wounded; 12th, marched to Greenfield Mills; 13th, marched to Licksville and Point of Rocks; 14th through 17th, marched to Jefferson and picketed the road to Point of Rocks and canal; 19th, marched to Burkittsville; 20th, 21st, marched through Rohrersville and Sharpsburg and camped near Sharpsburg; 23rd, to Harpers Ferry.

Attachment 4

List of Killed, Wounded and Missing in the different Brigades and Batteries of the Cavalry Division commanded by Brigadier-general Pleasonton, September, 1862.

Commander.	Brigade.	Company.	Regiment.	Date.	Killed.	Wounded.	Missing.	Battle-ground.
Capt. Whiting.	1		5th U. S. Cavalry.	17		1		Antietam.
"	"		"	19		1		Sharpsburg.
"	"		6th "	10		1		Sugar Loaf Mountain.
"	"		"	4	1			Falls Church.
"	"		"	10	1			Sugar Loaf Mountain.
"	"		"	4	1			Falls Church.
Col. J. F. Farnsworth.	2		8th Ill. Cavalry.	3		1		" "
"	"		"	8		1		Poolsville.
"	"		"	13		1		Frederick.
"	"		"	"	1	8		Middletown.
"	"		"	14	1			South Mountain.
"	"		"	15	1	15	3	Boonsboro'.
"	"		"	18		1		Antietam.
"	"		8th Penn. Cavalry.	10		1	5	Frederick.
"	"		3d Ind. Cavalry.	8	1	11		Poolsville.
"	"		"	13	1	2		Cotoctin Mountain.
"	"		"	13	3	8	5	Middletown and Harper's-ferry road.
"	"		"	13		2		South Mountain.
"	"		"	17		5		Antietam.
Col. R. H. Rush.	3		6th Penn. Cavalry.	13		1		Jefferson.
"	"		"	17		3		Antietam.
"	"		4th Penn. Cavalry.	"	3	7		"
Capt. Gibson.		"C" and "G"	Horse Battery.	19	1			Sheppardstown.
" Tidball.		"A"	"	17	1	3		Antietam.
" Robertson.		"B" and "L"	"					
Lieut. Hains.		"M"	"	17	1	4		Sharpsburg.
"		"	"	19		1		Williamsport.
			Total............		17	78	13	

Pleasonton supplied a detailed list of casualties for the Maryland Campaign showing the largest loss at Boonsboro 15 September 19. Note that Pleasonton does not include the Fourth and Fifth Cavalry Brigades, indicating that they were not under his direct command during the campaign. *The Historical Magazine*, "General Pleasonton's Cavalry Division in the Maryland Campaign, September 1862," May 1863, 290.

Appendix D
By Craig Swain

Part 1

Prelude to Antietam Driving Tour Itinerary

Drive the roads and highways on this tour with care. Many are busy while others are narrow, country roads with sharp turns and drop-offs. Deer are always a concern. Do not wade in the rivers. In general when driving near larger towns or cities such as Leesburg, Virginia, and Frederick and Hagerstown, Maryland, try to avoid peak commuting hours, especially if visiting the area for the first time. Longitude and latitude are taken using various devices but cannot be guaranteed. Directions as shown are correct when the routes were driven, November 2011. Always check your odometer between stops. Mileage may vary between vehicles, however. When pulling off the road use care if not in a designated parking area and do not do so on a curve on a country road. Safety is the first concern when following these routes. You may wish to consult software programs such as Google Earth (earth.google.com) particularly "Street View," which allows you to "drive" on some roads at eye level on your computer. Research places to eat and visit on the internet before you begin to maximize your enjoyment of these tours. Text in italics is paraphrased from the body of the book for some locations.

1. Leesburg: Harrison Hall (39° 7' 3" N, 77° 33' 48" W)

Start the tour at the Glenfiddich House (known during the war as Harrison Hall) located at 205 North King Street, Leesburg, Virginia. A Civil War Trails marker stands in front of the house. Street-side parking is limited, so visitors may wish to park at the city lot, two blocks east between North and Cornwall Streets.

The starting point for the Maryland Campaign tour is Leesburg, Virginia, both geographically and historically. On 4 September 1862, Gen. Robert E. Lee arrived in Leesburg, fresh off victories at Second Manassas and Chantilly. He spent the night in the house of his relative, Henry Tazewell Harrison. Dr. Samuel Jackson, a local physician, examined Lee's injured wrists. That evening, Lee visited John Janney, former Governor and President of the Virginia secession convention. Although Janney had opposed secession, he had presented Lee the command of Virginia forces when the convention voted to secede.

But Lee's stay in Leesburg was not strictly social. The next day Lee held a council of war in the dining room of Harrison Hall. In addition to Lee, attendees included Generals Thomas J. "Stonewall" Jackson, J.E.B. (Jeb) Stuart, James Longstreet, and Lewis A. Armistead – some of the most notable leaders in the Army of Northern Virginia. In the meeting, the generals planned the invasion of Maryland.

The Glenfiddich House is a bed and breakfast (http://www.mileslehane.com/about/glenfiddichhouse/). Other sites in Leesburg include the Janney House (private property at 10 Cornwall Street) and the Balls Bluff Battlefield. On the day of the Battle of Antietam, 17 September, the 2nd New York Cavalry under Lt. Col. Judson Kilpatrick, fought a brief skirmish in town with the 35th Battalion Virginia Cavalry under Capt. Elijah V. White. See the town's website for other Civil War related sites. (http://www.leesburgva.gov/index.aspx?page=579).

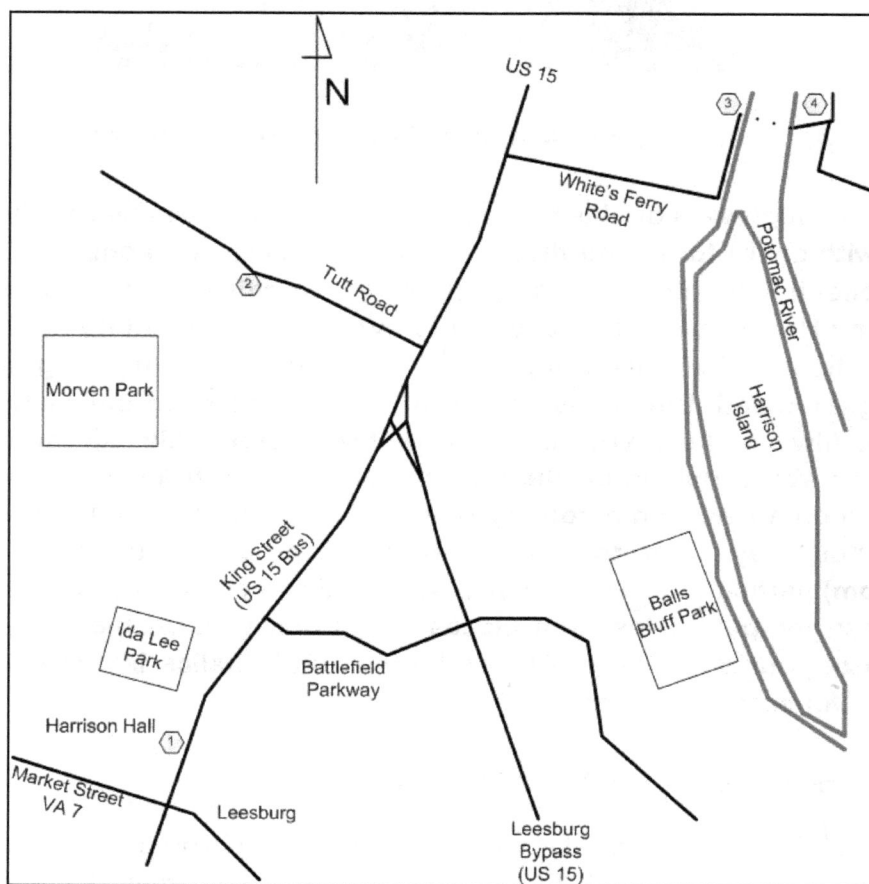

Map 1: Leesburg to White's Ferry

2. Battle of Mile Hill (39° 8' 36" N, 77° 33' 0" W)

From Harrison Hall, continue north on King Street (US Highway 15 Business). After 1.5 miles, carefully merge into James Madison Highway (US Highway 15 North). Proceed 0.3 mile north and make a left onto Tutt Road (CR 740). Drive 0.3 mile west on Tutt Road to the event (back) entrance to Morven Park. Park next to the Civil War Trails markers along the fenceline.

On 2 September, at what became known as the Battle of Mile Hill, Confederate Col. Thomas T. Munford approached Leesburg from the east from his camp near Goose Creek, split his troopers and sent a squadron, under Capt. Jesse Irvine, directly through town. Meanwhile, with the rest of his 2ⁿᵈ Virginia Cavalry regiment, he turned north off the Leesburg Pike and headed for the Potomac River crossings. Irvine galloped into Leesburg finding Samuel Means and his Loudoun Rangers guarding the courthouse. The Rangers quickly retreated north up King Street from the court house suffering four wounded; they subsequently fell back on Henry A. Cole's Maryland Cavalry, north of town, near Big Spring at Mile Hill, on the Point of Rocks Road. Capt. Irvine was hot on their heels, firing from behind shocks of wheat, driving Means back on Cole's dismounted line. Cole was holding Irvine, but then Munford surprised Cole, attacking their rear. Before Cole could mount his three companies to face this surprise from Munford, he suffered substantial casualties. In the melee, many of Cole's men were cut down on foot. Those that were able to mount briefly engaged Munford before retreating toward the Catoctin Mountain and the Old Waterford Road. Munford chased Cole's troopers for some two miles, driving them into Loudoun Valley, successfully clearing Leesburg and the Potomac River crossings for Gen. Lee's Army of Northern Virginia's advance.

3. White's (Conrad's) Ferry, VA (39° 9′ 18″ N, 77° 31′ 24″ W)

From Mile Hill, return to James Madison Highway (US Highway Rt. 15) and continue north (left) for 0.8 mile. Just before the stoplight, on the southbound side of the highway, is a Virginia state marker indicating the bivouac site of Jackson's Corps on 4 September. At the stoplight, turn right onto White's Ferry Road (CR 655). Follow the road 1.3 miles as it turns to parallel the Potomac River. Line up for the ferry ride across the river. The ferry runs daily 5 am - 11 pm and charges $5 for a one way trip, $8 for a two-way trip.

White's Ferry takes its name from colorful Confederate cavalryman and local businessman, Elijah V. White. Originally known as Conrad's Ferry, White purchased the ferry after the war. Today the ferryboat, "General Jubal Early," moves traffic across the river. This is the last active ferry on the Potomac and a good place to cross the river for Civil War tourists.

4. White's Ferry, MD (39° 9′ 19″ N, 77° 31′ 6″ W)

After crossing the Potomac, proceed off the loading ramp and turn left after the store into the parking area on the Maryland side of the ferry. Stop near the Civil War Trails markers on the northern side of the parking area. Note the river heights for floods marked on the store's front wall as well as nearby structures related to the C&O Canal.

The Potomac was fordable at White's Ferry during the Civil War but usually only by cavalry as it was a deep area even at low water. Some of Stuart's Cavalry division crossed here—possibly Hampton's Brigade—on 5 September. Mosby, later in the war, often crossed here, combining river transits with White's Ford, to confound Union pursuers. During the Antietam Campaign, most of the Army of Northern Virginia crossed the Potomac about three and a half river miles upstream at White's Ford (also named for Elijah White). Although the Northern Virginia Regional Park Authority is developing the site, along with White's residence there, access to the site is currently restricted. Access is better on the Maryland side (see stop 5 below).

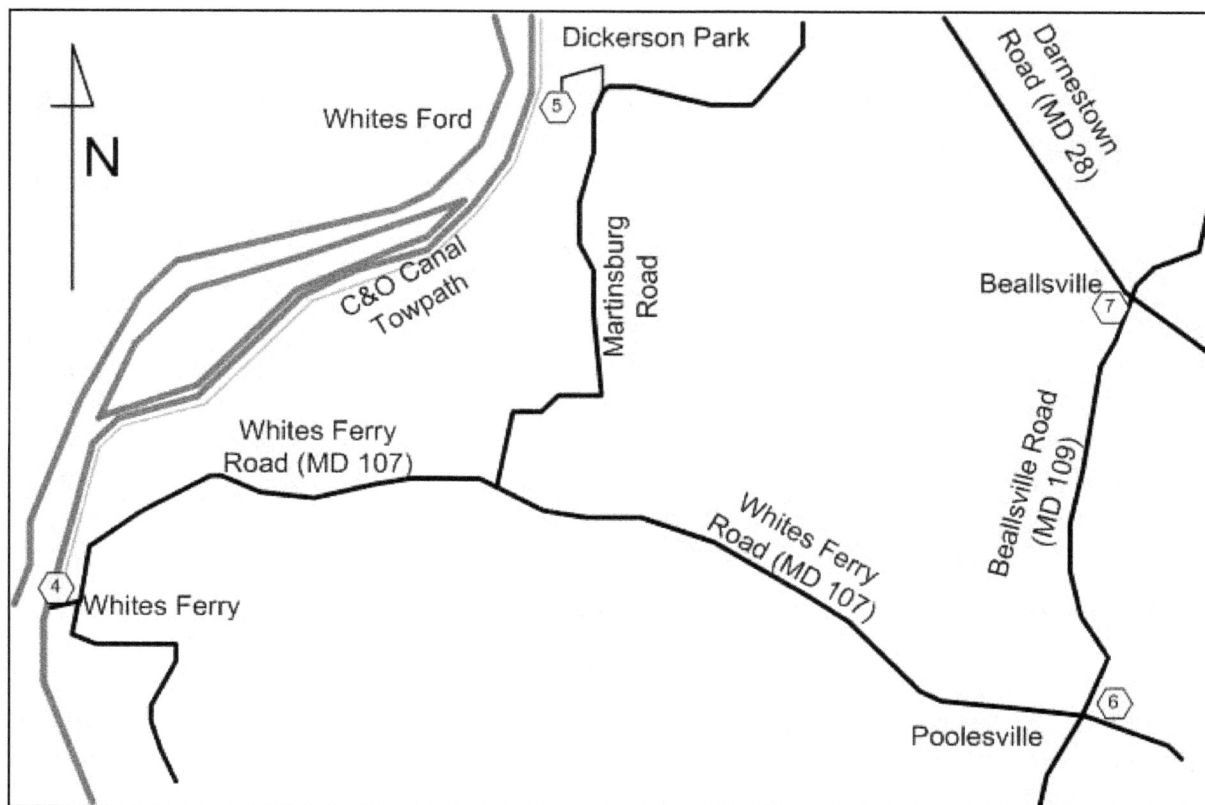

Map 2: White's Ferry to Poolesville and Beallsville

5. White's Ford, MD (39° 11' 41" N, 77° 28' 10" W)

From the White's Ferry parking lot, turn left (east) onto White's Ferry Road (Maryland Rt. 107). After 2.6 miles, turn left (north) onto Martinsburg Road. Follow Martinsburg Road for 2.7 miles. Along the way, the road will make several sharp turns, generally to the north and east. The road enters the heavily wooded Dickerson Conservation Park. Watch for signs for the conservation park and the Chesapeake & Ohio Canal Trailhead for White's Ford. The road is unnamed, but there is a Civil War Trails trailblaze sign. Follow the road about a half mile to the canal parking area. A Civil War Trails marker in the parking lot describes White's Ford. If time permits, cross over the canal to the towpath, take a left (south), and follow the trail a half mile to a National Park Service marker close to the actual ford location (which was located another two tenths of a mile further south at the head of Mason Island).

White's Ford is named after the farmer who owned the land on the Potomac River, on which the ford is located on the Virginia side. Capt. Elijah White was the owner at the time and a well-known Confederate cavalry leader and partisan ranger. When he was attached to Jackson's command after Second Bull Run, he advised that his farm ford could be used to cross the Potomac. Its high banks did need some work to allow the passage of wagons, however. The Union army rarely used the ford as it was deemed too rocky for heavy wagons. White's Ford was also used by Stuart to return after his famous Second Ride Around McClellan, in October 1862, and by Jubal Early during his return from his expedition to Washington, D.C., in 1864. The ford is about three miles downstream of the mouth of the Monocacy River.

6. Poolesville, MD (39° 8' 46" N, 77° 24' 60" W)

Return to White's Ferry Road via Martinsburg Road, turning left (east) onto White's Ferry Road. Proceed 3.4 miles into Poolesville, to the intersection with Elgin Road (Maryland 109). Pull into the parking lot beside the red brick building on the northeast corner of the intersection. A Civil War Trails marker stands between the road and parking lot.

A detachment of 100 troopers from the 1st Massachusetts Cavalry rode out of Washington. D.C., and ran into trouble upon encountering Brig. Gen. Fitzhugh Lee's Brigade of cavalry, led by the 5th Virginia Cavalry, at Poolesville, Maryland, on 5 September. Earlier that day, Lee's Brigade, after breakfasting on roasted corn and apples, had crossed at Edward's Ferry "gaily singing 'My Maryland' – 'My Maryland." White's Ford is about three river miles upstream from today's White's Ferry, but about six road miles from it.

About dusk, the 1st Massachusetts Cavalry rode through the streets of Poolesville toward the Potomac, looking for any signs of Confederate activity, but not knowing that many in the town harbored strong southern sympathies due to close association with Loudoun County to the south across the Potomac. After the Bay State troopers passed through the tiny town, some Rebel sympathizers placed obstacles such as stones, furniture and other debris, in the road behind the Unionists. Down the road, the Massachusetts men were routed by superior numbers from Fitzhugh Lee's 3rd and 5th Virginia Cavalry. When the retreating Union troopers raced back through town, their horses fell over the obstacles. Thanks to the help of "secesh" townsfolk, the Confederates captured forty Federals including Capt. Samuel E. Chamberlain and nine wounded. The Confederates lost three killed and four wounded in this first cavalry fight of the Maryland Campaign—a clear Confederate victory. After this affray, Fitzhugh Lee's Brigade, followed by Hampton's, bivouacked about two miles east of Poolesville for the night.

Side Trip A: Edward's Ferry

A1: Edward's Ferry. (39° 6' 12.5" N, 77° 28' 23" W)

From the intersection in the center of Poolesville, proceed south on Elgin Road for one block, then turn right onto Wootton Avenue. After one block, turn left onto West Willard Road. Follow West Willard for half a mile and turn left onto Westerly Road. Continue for 1.4 miles and then turn left onto Edward's Ferry Road. Continue for 2.5 miles to the parking area for Edward's Ferry along the Chesapeake and Ohio Canal.

Fitzhugh Lee's Brigade crossed from Loudoun County at Edward's Ferry to avoid the crowds at White's Ford and Conrad's Ferry and provided flanking cover for Gen. Lee's infantry crossing at White's Ford.

Return to the main tour route, backtracking to Poolesville.

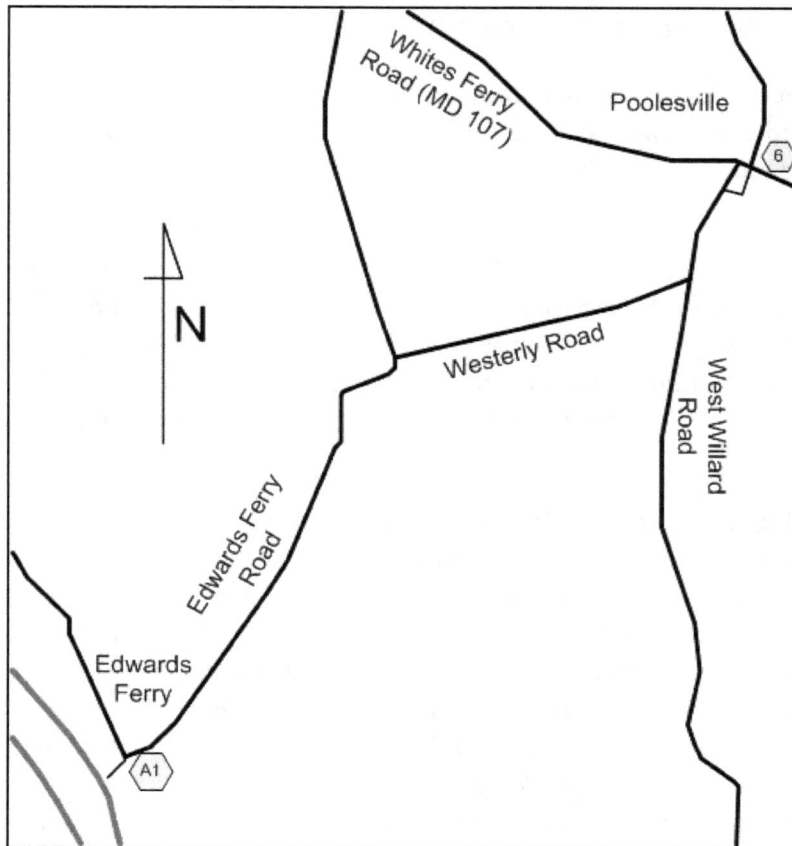

Map 3: Edward's Ferry

7. Beallsville (39° 10' 44" N, 77° 24' 48" W). (Beallsville was also known as Monocacy Church.)

From the parking lot, turn right onto Elgin Road (Maryland 109) and proceed north. About a half-mile at the north end of Poolesville veer to the left, as Maryland 109 becomes Beallsville Road. Continue north for two miles. Turn into the parking lot just before the intersection with Darnestown Road (Maryland 28). A Civil War Trails marker stands at the back edge of the parking lot. During the Civil War, Beallsville was known as Monocacy Church. The locality received its name from 1748 Anglican "Chapel of Ease," which still stands nearby. Union soldiers camped nearby in the fall of 1861 and virtually destroyed the church by using the pews for firewood, and stabling their horses inside. The crossroads here made Beallsville a strategic location.

A squadron of the 9th Virginia Cavalry, commanded by Col. William H. Fitzhugh Lee, in Brig. Gen. Fitzhugh Lee's Brigade, was left at Beallsville on picket duty. On the morning of 9 September, Col. John F. Farnsworth rode toward Barnesville and spotted a squadron of Rebel cavalry near Monocacy Church. He ordered Capt. Elon Farnsworth's squadron from the 8th Illinois Cavalry, to flank the Rebels. Farnsworth continued to Barnesville (Stop 8) chasing Confederate cavalry.

Side Trip B: The Confederate Advance into Maryland. This optional side trip follows the route of the main body of Confederate infantry as it entered Maryland. Although the detailed examination of the route used is outside the scope of this tour, this side trip provides some perspective of the infantry movements with respect to the cavalry. The side trip follows the main body of infantry as it moved toward Frederick.

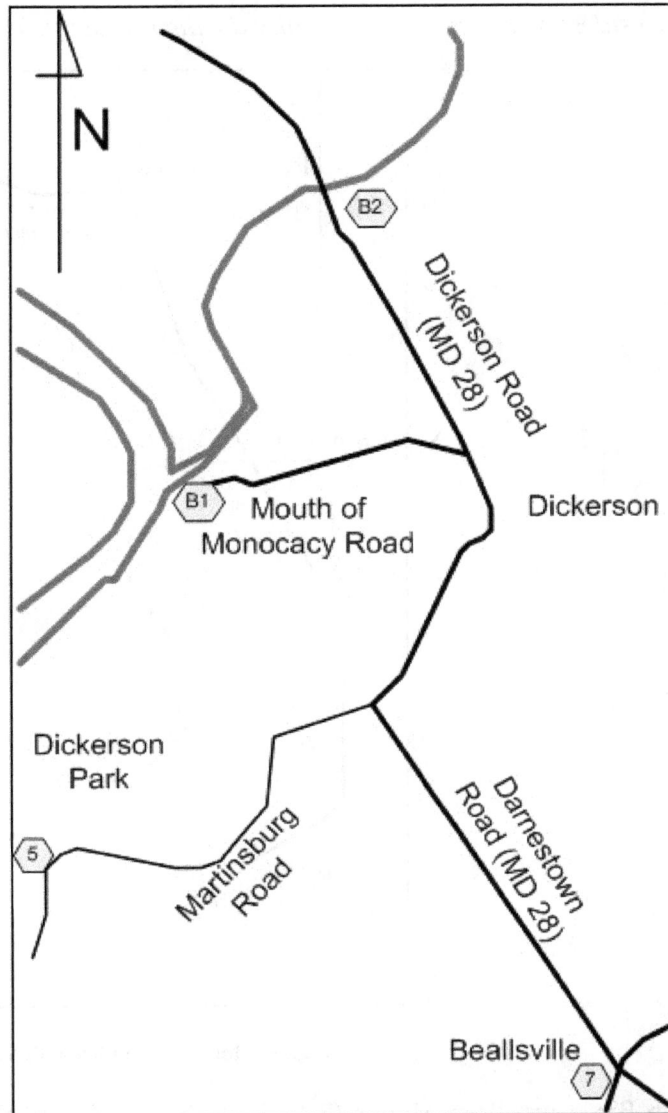

Map 4: Side Trip from Beallsville to Monocacy

Stop B1: The Monocacy Aqueduct (39° 13' 21" N, 77° 26' 60" W) – From Beallsville, turn left onto Darnestown Road (Maryland 28) and continue for 2.2 miles. Make a sharp right as Darnestown Road becomes Dickerson Road. Continue for another 1.5 miles, taking care at the overpass of the B&O Railroad in Dickerson. Make a left onto Mouth of Monocacy Road and follow that road for 1.2 miles to the Chesapeake and Ohio Canal. National Parks and Civil War Trails markers interpret the site.

On September 9, Gen. John G. Walker's division tried but failed to destroy the aqueduct.

Stop B2: Monocacy River Bridge (39° 14' 35" N, 77° 26' 20" W) – Follow the Mouth of Monocacy Road back to Dickerson Road (Maryland 28) and turn left. Follow Dickerson Road for 1.5 miles. Just before crossing the Monocacy River Bridge, pull into the parking area beside the river. Civil War Trails markers at the parking lot are overviews of the Antietam and Gettysburg campaigns.

Both sides used fords in this vicinity during the campaign and throughout the war.

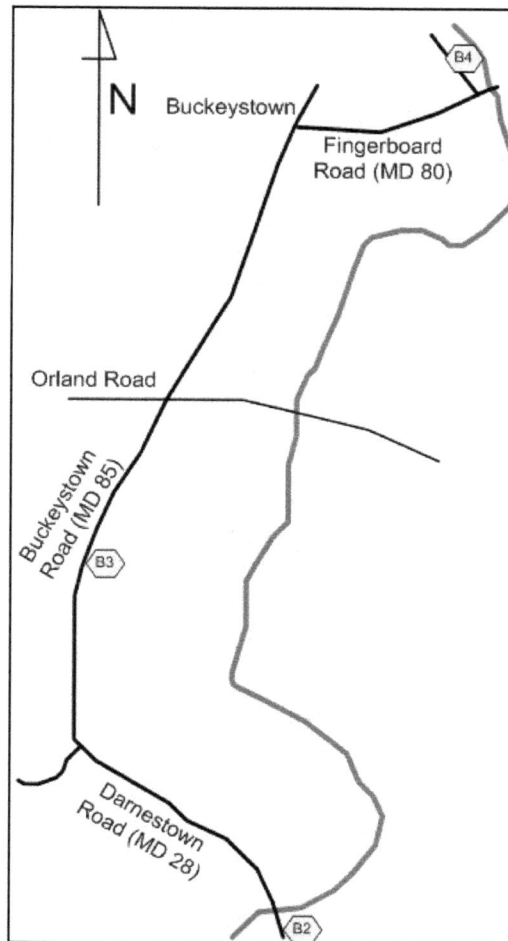

Map 5: Monocacy to Michael's Mill

Stop B3: Carrollton Manor (39° 16′ 48″ N, 77° 27′ 49″ W) – Return to Dickerson Road and continue west for 1.9 miles. Make a slight right as the road becomes Buckeystown Pike (Maryland 85). Continue north for 1.4 miles. Turn into the farm market parking area on the right side of the road.

A Civil War Trails marker notes the Confederate encampments in the area on September 5-6. General Jackson suffered a fall from his horse near this stop.

Stop B4: Michael's Mill (39° 19′ 38″ N, 77° 24′ 57″ W) – Continuing north on Buckeystown Road, proceed for 3.2 miles. Turn right onto Fingerboard Road (Maryland 80) and follow that road for 1.3 miles. Turn left onto Michael's Mill Road, looking for the entrance to Buckeystown Park.

The mill stands along the river just north of the park. During the brief Confederate stay in the area, the mill provided flour which was made into shortcakes to feed the troops.

Return to the normal tour route by way of Buckeystown Pike, Dickerson Road, and Darnestown Road.

479 Driving Tour Appendix D

8. Barnesville (39° 13' 16" N, 77° 22' 53" W)

From Beallsville, continue through the intersection with the Darnestown Road and proceed north on Beallsville Road for 3.5 miles. In Barnesville, turn left at the intersection with Barnesville Road and proceed 0.2 miles to the parking lot for the St. Mary's Catholic Church. Two Civil War Trails markers stand at the west edge of the parking lot.

The 8th Illinois' running fight, of 9 September, with the 12th Virginia Cavalry ended in Barnesville. The Virginians put up a brief stand here but were pushed beyond the village. The 8th Illinois killed four, wounded five, and captured twenty-seven Confederate cavalrymen along with the regimental flag.

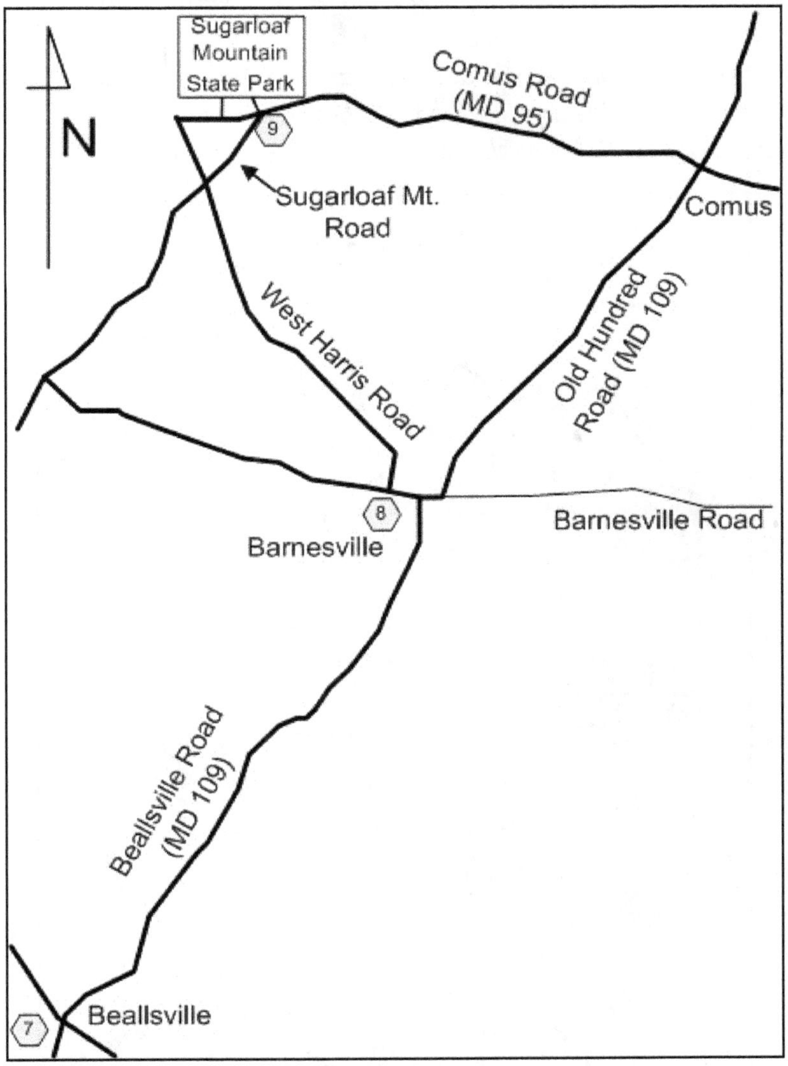

Map 6: Beallsville to Sugarloaf Mountain

9. Sugarloaf Mountain (39° 15' 6" N, 77° 23' 36" W)

From the church parking lot, turn right onto Barnesville Road and then make an **immediate** left onto West Harris Road running north out of town. Proceed on West Harris Road, running generally northwest, for two miles, to the intersection with Sugarloaf Mountain Road. Make a right onto Sugarloaf Mountain Road and drive a half mile to a five-way intersection at the entrance to Sugarloaf Mountain

Park, privately owned by Stronghold, Incorporated. Admission is free. It was designated a National Natural Landmark in 1969. A Civil War Trails marker stands beside the entrance. (http://www.sugarloafmd.com/)

From the summit of Sugarloaf Mountain, an observer can see the outskirts of Washington, 30 miles southeast, and Point of Rocks, where the Potomac crosses through Catoctin Ridge. Its summit is 1,282 feet above sea level and is about 800 feet higher than surrounding terrain, easily the most important key terrain feature east of the South Mountain range during the Maryland Campaign.

The Union Signal Corps occupied Sugarloaf Mountain on 3 September, transmitting messages by flag to Poolesville. Union flagmen on Sugarloaf are credited with sending the first official notice of the Confederate advance to Washington. However, the signal activity soon attracted the attention of Confederate cavalry who then captured the detachment. Sugarloaf Mountain offers excellent views of Maryland and Virginia. A three-mile driving loop reaches the crest of the mountain where networks of trails provide access to overlooks. Drive to the top and appreciate the views.

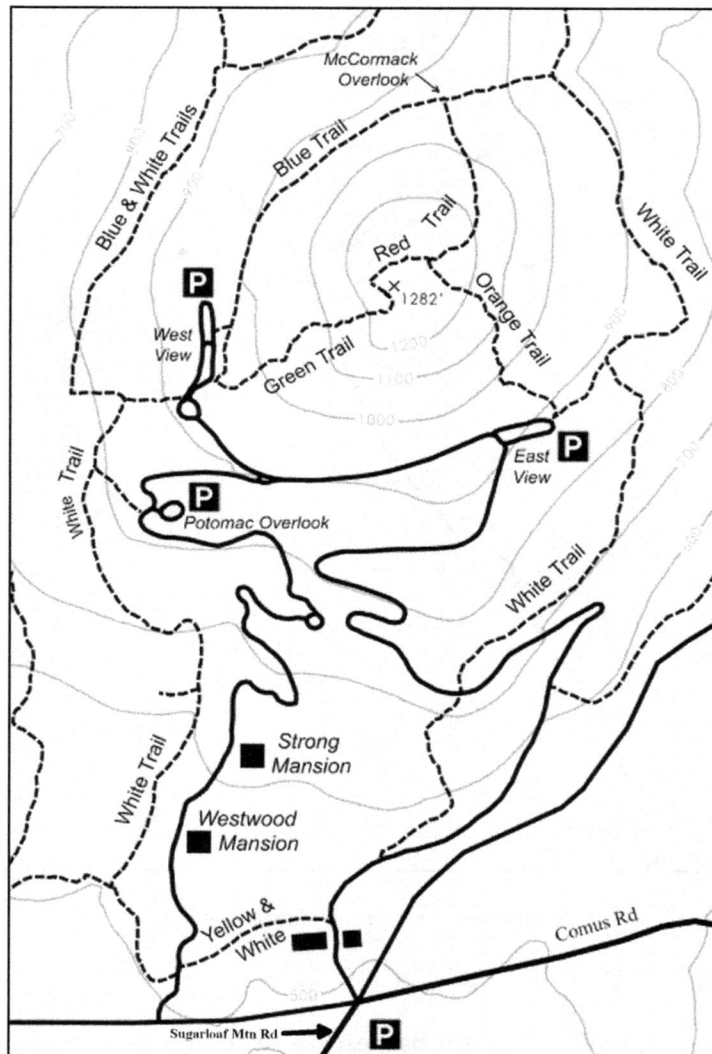

Map 7: Sugarloaf Mountain (courtesy of Stronghold, Inc.)

10. Hyattstown (39° 16' 47" N, 77° 18' 52" W)

From the exit of the Sugarloaf Mountain driving loop, turn left onto Comus Road for 300 yards and return to the entrance to the park. Continue on Comus Road to the east for 2.3 miles. At the intersection with Old Hundred Road (Maryland 109), turn left (north) and continue for 3.3 miles passing under Interstate 270. A Civil War Trails marker, discussing actions in the Maryland Campaign, stands at the back of the Comus Inn parking lot, at the intersection. The location affords a good view of Sugarloaf Mountain. Entering Hyattstown, turn right at the intersection with North Frederick Road (Maryland 355). After 300 feet, turn left onto Hyattstown Mill Road beside the Volunteer Fire Department. A Civil War Trails marker stands about fifty yards down the road in a section of Little Bennett State Park.

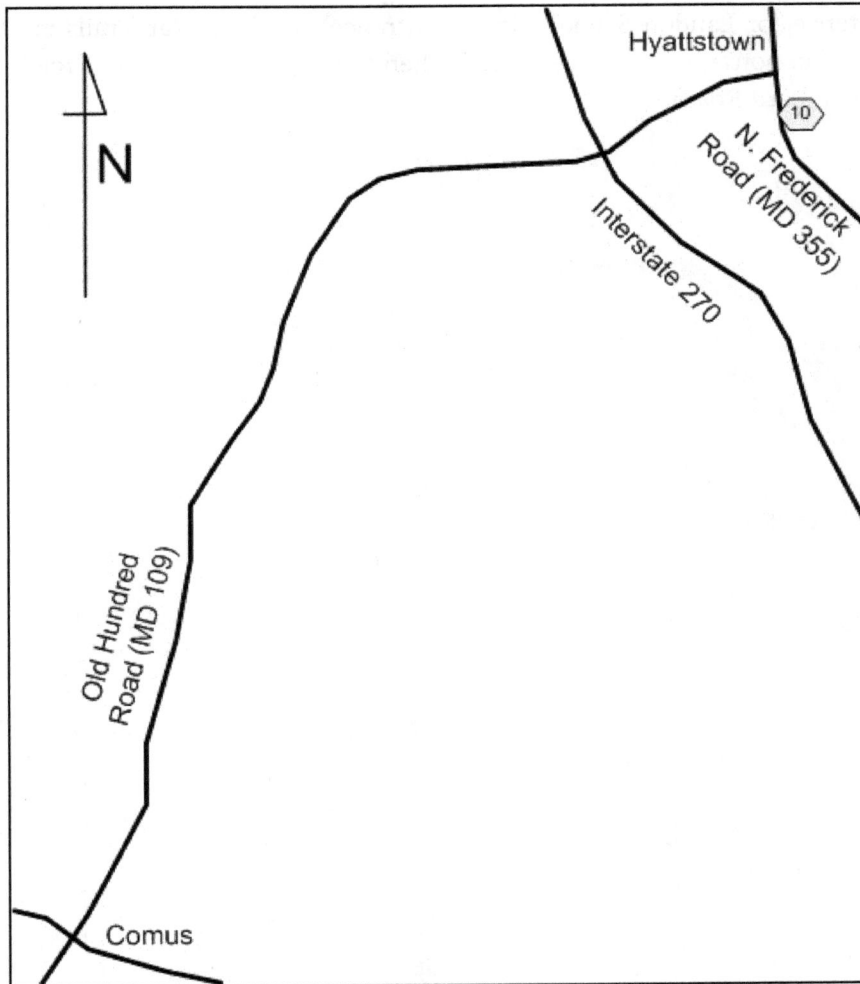

Map 8: Comus to Hyattstown

Stuart's first line - the Parr's Ridge/Sugarloaf Line - included the roads through Parr's Ridge and the Sugarloaf Mountain signal post. Parr's Ridge extends from just south of Poolesville north then northeast through Hyattstown to New Market on the National Pike and the B&O Railroad – the main links to Baltimore. Sugarloaf Mountain was just in the rear of the Parr's Ridge. Confederate pickets from Hampton's cavalry in Hyattstown were at the center of that line.

On 9 September, a battalion of the 1st New York Cavalry, under led by Maj. Alonzo W. Adams, charged into Hyattstown driving out pickets of Hampton's cavalry. Hampton's troopers returned the next day, with artillery. A spirited fight ensued. After reinforced by a squadron from the 1ˢᵗ U.S. Cavalry, under Capt. Marcus A. Reno, the Federal horsemen prevailed. Hampton's troopers retreated and the Union cavalry returned to Clarksburg.

11. Urbana Dance--Landon School; Stuart's HQ on grounds of the Cockey family (39° 19' 38" N, 77° 20' 53" W) and Cockey House.

Return to North Frederick Road (Maryland 355) and turn right. As the road continues north, it turns into Urbana Pike. Follow the pike for 3.7 miles. Upon entering Urbana, the original Urbana Pike **bears left** away from the continuation of Maryland 355—the Worthington Pike—so watch the intersection and bear left, remaining on the Urbana Pike. Pass Fingerboard Road (Rt. 80), and after 15 yards turn right into the entrance for Landon School (sign at entrance). A Civil War Trails marker stands in the school parking lot. The house on the left—passed when turning into the school road—was the Cockey House (3904A Fingerboard Road).

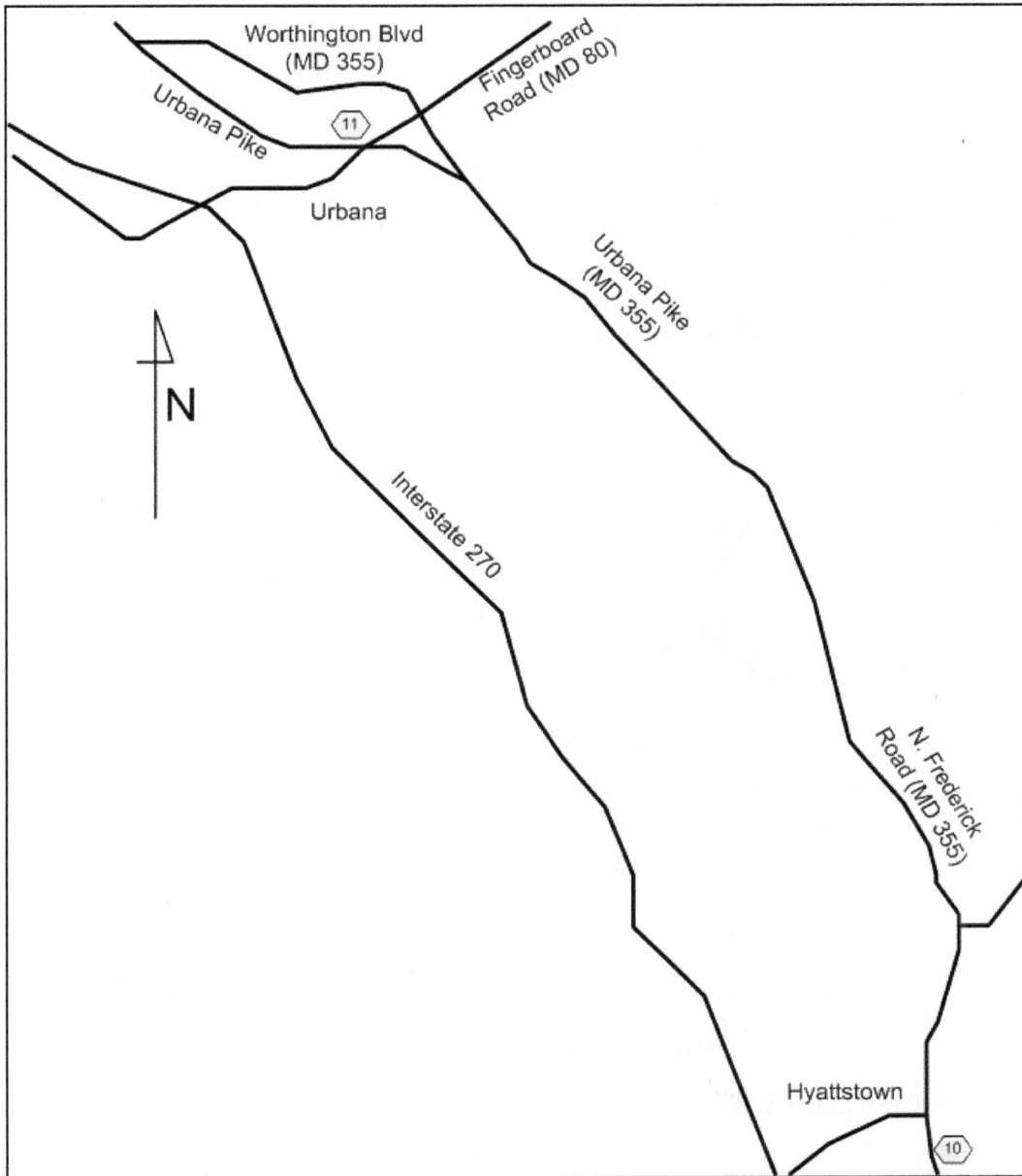

Map 9: Hyattstown to Urbana

On the evening of 8 September, Stuart made his headquarters on the Cockey House grounds. To thank the family for their hospitality, he organized the "Sabers and Roses Ball" at the Landon School. During the festivities, word came of sharp skirmishing in the direction of Hyattstown, temporarily breaking up the ball. After midnight, the Confederates returned to resume the dance, although some of their ladies went upstairs to treat wounded men. The party continued until dawn.

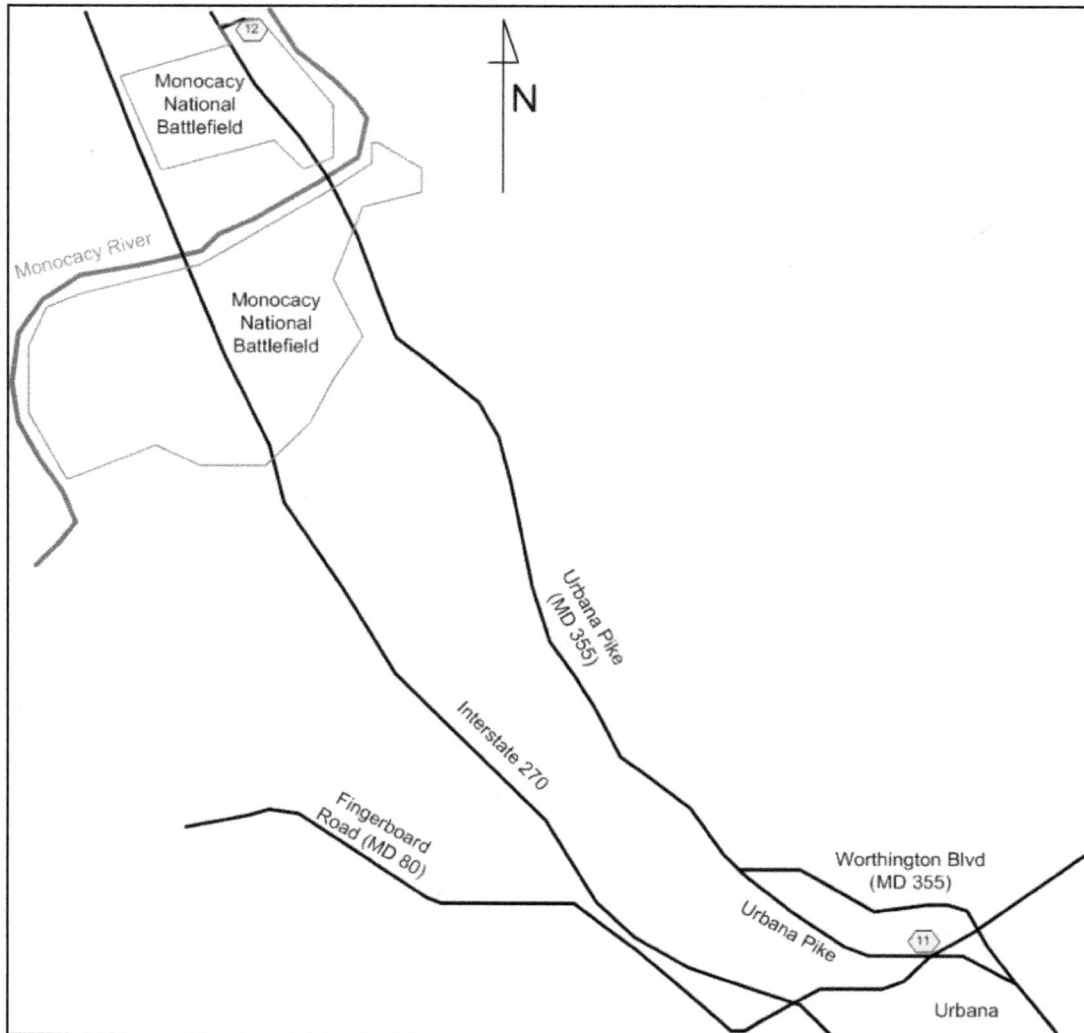

Map 10: Urbana to Monocacy Battlefield

12. Monocacy Battlefield and Site of the Lost Orders (39° 22' 38" N, 77° 23' 43" W)

Return to the Urbana Pike and turn right, continuing north toward Frederick (the pike will resume Maryland 355 at the edge of Urbana). After 4.5 miles, after crossing the Monocacy River, turn right into the entrance of Monocacy National Battlefield (http://www.nps.gov/mono/index.htm) and park at the visitor center. The location where the lost order was found is not known exactly. The park is working on interpretation for the incident, but the focus within the park is the July 1864 battle.

Here, on the same field as the 1864 battle, General Lee made his headquarters during the first phase of the Maryland Campaign. It is also here that one of the most controversial incidents of the Maryland Campaign, if not the entire war, took place--the Union's discovery of Lee's Lost Order, S.O. 191. On the afternoon of 9 September, after meeting with Longstreet and Jackson, Gen. Lee had his chief of staff write seven copies on single sheets of the order detailing the division of his army into four parts to deal with the Union garrisons remaining at Martinsburg and Harpers Ferry. In haste, and due to poor staff work, the copy addressed to Maj. Gen. Daniel H. Hill was lost. Soldiers of the 27th Indiana found the order on 13 September near the Myer's Farm.

13. Frederick (39° 24' 40" N, 77° 24' 24" W)

Exiting the visitor center, turn right (north) again on Urbana Pike (Maryland 355) for 1.5 miles. Turn right onto Buckeystown Pike (Maryland 85) and proceed over Interstate 70 and continue north for a total of one mile, as the road changes to South East Street (Maryland 475). The Frederick Visitor Center (http://www.fredericktourism.org/) is located at the intersection with Commerce Street. The city allows out-of-county visitors three hours free parking in an adjacent lot to the north side of Commerce Street.

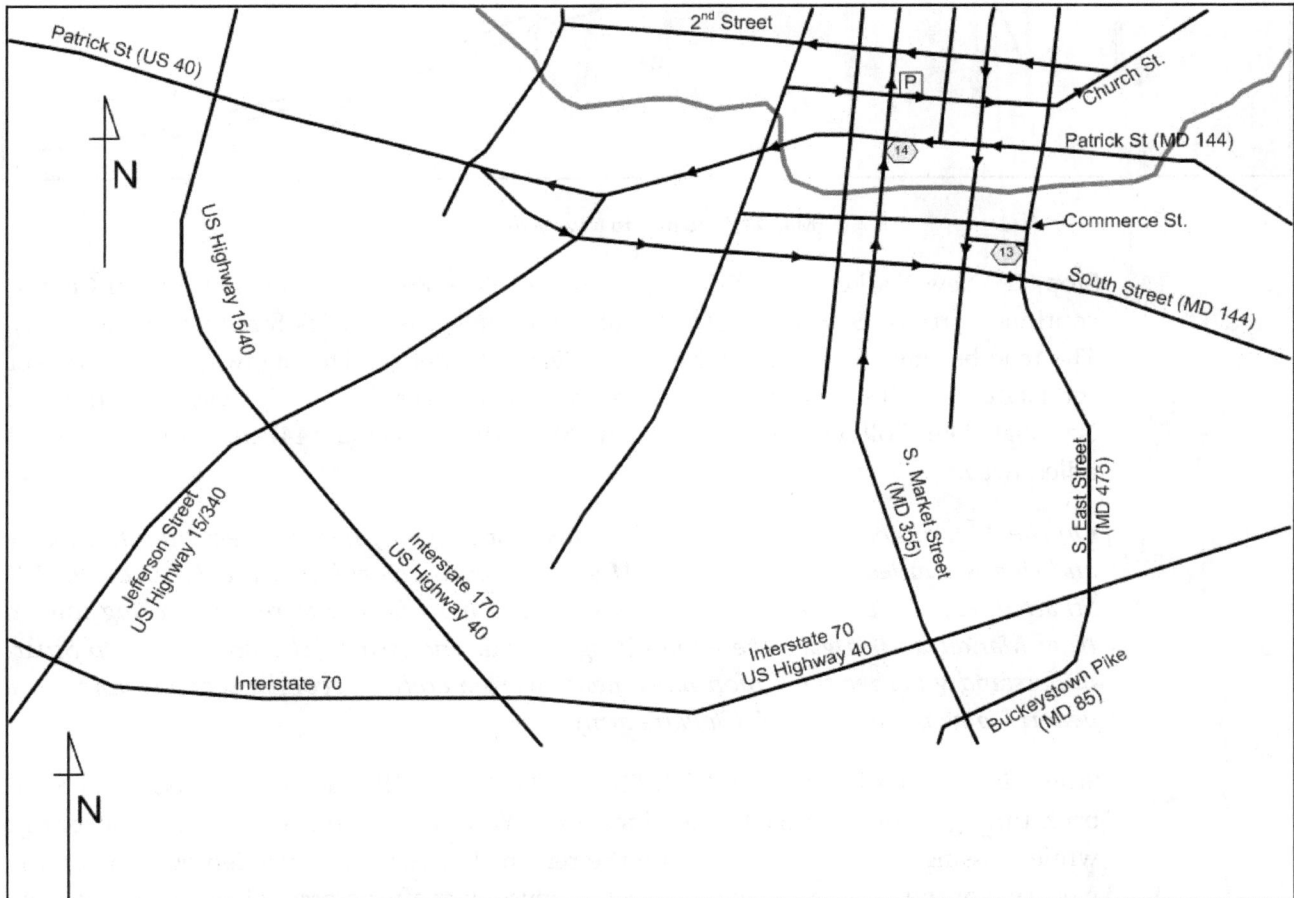

Map 11: Frederick

Frederick is truly a crossroads of history, with important historical sites covering colonial and Revolutionary War periods. Civil War-oriented visitors may wish to allocate time for the National Museum of Civil War Medicine, at 48 Patrick Street, or any of a number of other sites. Maps of the downtown area and information are available at the visitor center.

Side Trip C: Advance into Frederick on the Old National Road.

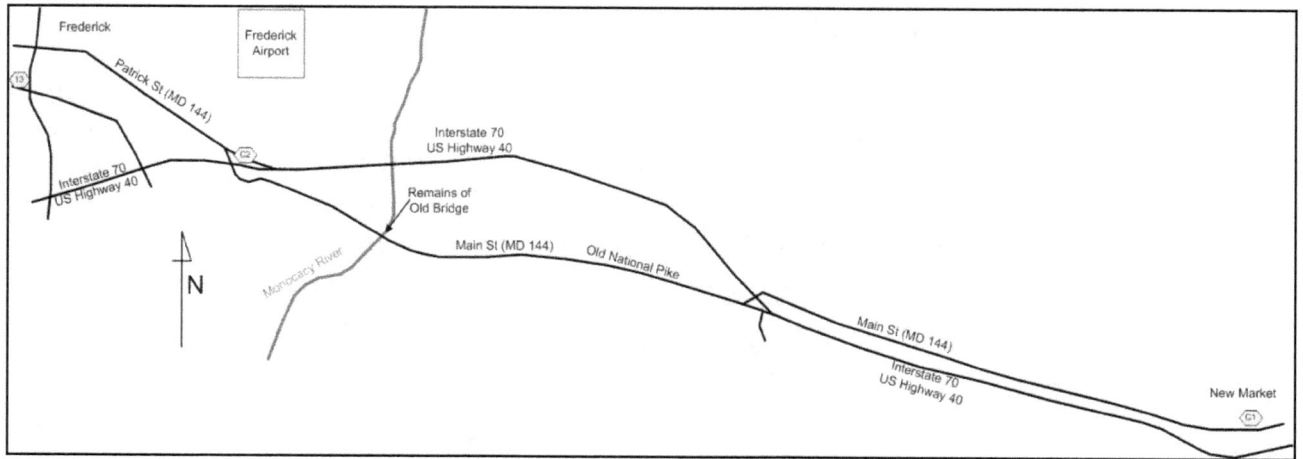

Map 12: Frederick to New Market

Stop C1: New Market (39° 22' 58" N, 77° 16' 14" W) – From the Frederick Visitor Center, continue north on South East Street. Turn right onto East Patrick Street (Maryland 144). The road becomes a divided highway as it leaves Frederick. The highway will cross over Interstate 70. After 4.6 miles carefully make a left across the highway onto the Old National Pike. Follow the Old National Pike (still Maryland 144) into New Market, 3 miles away.

On the 11th, Fitzhugh Lee fell back from his post at New Market seven miles to Liberty and then six miles west to cross the Monocacy on the morning of the 12th. On the 12th Stuart directed Fitzhugh to retrace his steps and head back east reconnoitering toward New Market and to gain the enemy's right flank and rear to the north to help Stuart understand whether the Union movements were merely a reconnaissance in force or a general movement of the McClellan's army.

Stop C2: The Jug Bridge (39° 24' 18" N, 77° 23' 1" W) – Retrace the Old National Road back through New Market toward Frederick. You may catch a view of the old bridge while crossing over the Monocacy on the return. The two story wooden building on the west side of the river is the old toll keeper house. Just after crossing back over Interstate 70, turn right onto East Patrick Street toward Bowmans Farm Road. You will see a small parking area on the right side of the road. The original bridge no longer stands, and the location is best visited by canoe on the Monocacy River. But the monument which gave the old bridge its name stands today in this small city park. The original bridge was used in the Antietam and Gettysburg campaigns. Both sides skirmished around the bridge during the Battle of Monocacy in 1864.

Hampton and his troopers had the assignment to hold the center of Stuart's line around Frederick, which included the National and Urbana pikes. Here, where the National Pike crosses the Monocacy, the 2nd South Carolina Cavalry fought a brief, but spirited, action against the advancing Federal cavalry supported by artillery.

Return to the main tour by proceeding west down Patrick Street into Frederick.

14. Frederick—downtown (39° 24' 51" N, 77° 24' 39" W)

From the town visitor center, continue north on South East Street for two blocks (0.2 mile) and turn left onto Patrick Street (Maryland 144). Patrick Street is the Old National Pike. Proceed for three blocks west (0.3 mile) on Patrick Street to the intersection with Market Street (Maryland 355 again). This intersection is truly a "crossroads of history." One very rare photo taken at this intersection captured Confederate soldiers under arms marching along the National Pike, in September 1862. Turn right onto Market Street and continue one block to Church Street. Making a right, look for parking on the street or in the parking garage on the left. Two blocks west along Church Street is the city hall and a marker discussing the Civil War related sites in the town center.

Pursuing Federals clashed in Frederick with the Confederate rear guard--Hampton's Brigade. The Confederates captured Colonel Augustus Moor, commander of the Second Brigade, Kanawha Division, after he was pressured into an unprepared attack, also gobbling up his escort, staff, and a cannon from Capt. Seth J. Simmond's Kentucky Battery. The likely location of the action is where Patrick Street (the Old National Pike) crosses Carroll Creek on the east side of town (the side tour above passes through the site, but there is no safe place to stop at the site).

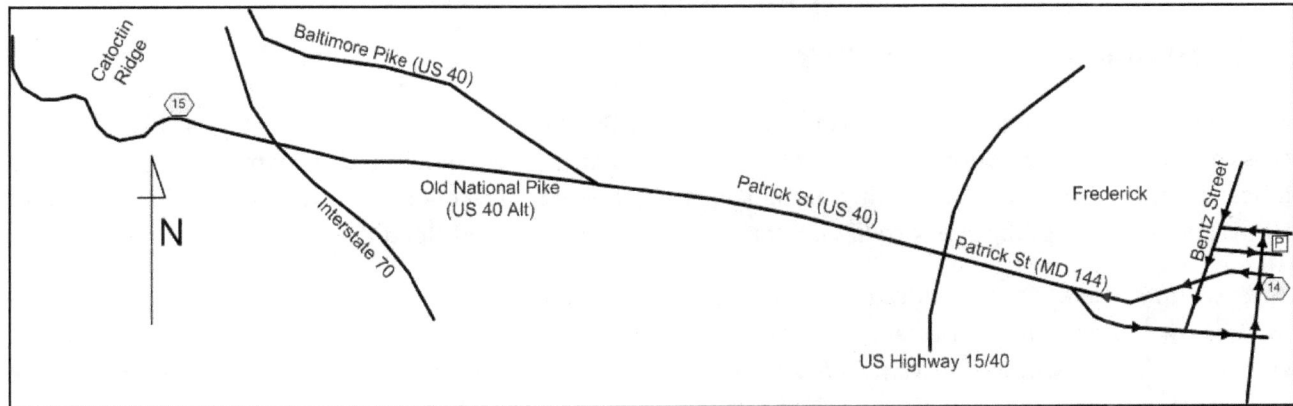

Map 13: To Catoctin Ridge

15. Hagan's Tavern (39° 25' 25" N, 77° 29' 37" W)

Leaving the parking garage on Church Street, continue east one block to the intersection with Maxwell Avenue. Turn right (south), and travel one block returning to Patrick Street. Continue three miles west on West Patrick Street, which picks up US Highway 40 after crossing over US Highway 15. After passing the Frederick Towne Mall Shopping Center, pay attention to the signs and make a slight left onto US Highway 40 Alternate/Old National Pike. Continue west for 1.5 miles, climbing Catoctin Ridge. Near the summit, turn right into the parking lot for Hagen's Tavern.

Hagen opened the tavern in the 1830's, using a structure dating to the late 1700's. Here on the eastern side of Catoctin Ridge, a section from Captain James F. Hart's South Carolina Artillery, supported by the Jeff Davis Legion, sparred with sections of two Federal horse batteries in the valley toward Frederick. Hampton soon arrived with reinforcements and barred Pleasonton's pursuing cavalry from the gap in the ridge. After a mostly ineffective artillery duel (due to the steep grade), Union infantry pushed the Confederates back toward Middletown in the mid-afternoon.

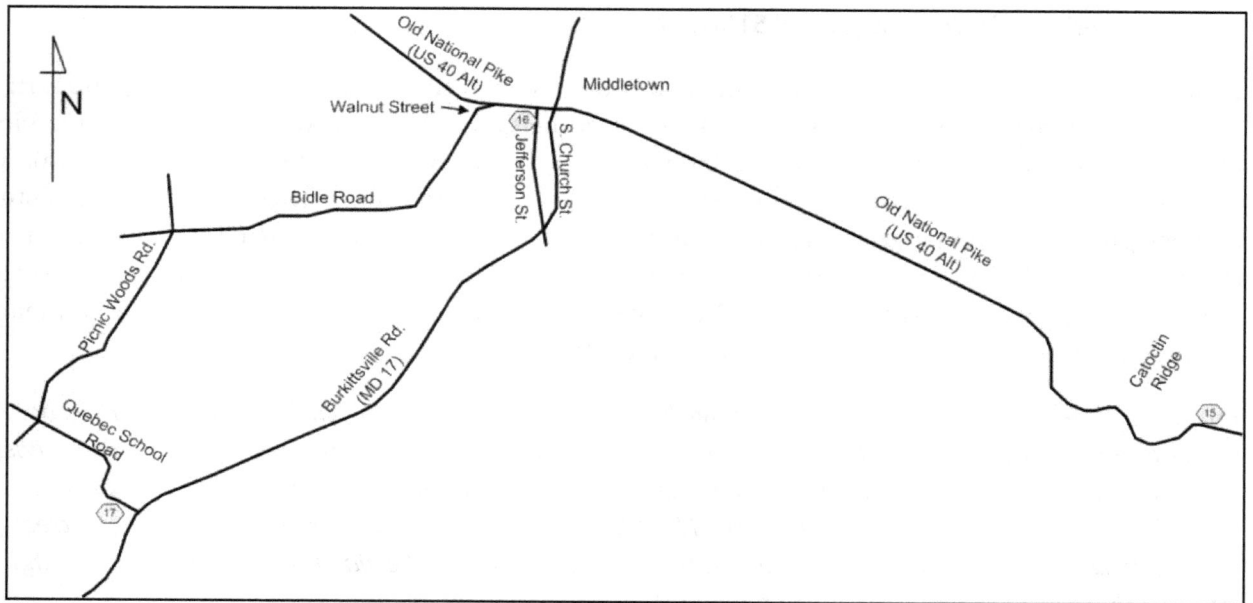

Map 14: Middletown and Quebec School House

16. Middletown (39° 26' 37" N, 77° 32' 52" W)

Exit the tavern parking lot and continue west (right) on the Old National Pike. Entering Middletown, pass through the intersection with Church Street and continue two blocks to Elm Street, for a total of 3.2 miles. Turn left and look for parking along the street. Several markers in front of the Central Maryland Heritage League building speak to Civil War events and the National Road.

After falling back from Catoctin Ridge, the Confederate rear guard made another stand east of Middletown along the National Pike. North Carolina cavalry under Col. Lawrence S. Baker, and a section of Hart's Battery, slowed Federal cavalry. But when numbers forced the grey-clad troopers to retreat, they faced not only Federal fire, but also that of townspeople shooting from houses along the town's main street.

Middletown hosts many other Civil War sites. Two blocks east, at the intersection of Church and Washington Streets, is the Christ Reformed Church. A Civil War Trails marker in the parking lot notes that the church's steeple served as a Union observation post during the Battle of South Mountain.

17. Quebec School House (39° 25' 2" N, 77° 34' 43"W)

From the parking lot along Elm Street, return to the Old National Pike and turn left (west). After 0.1 miles turn left onto Walnut Street, which becomes Bidle Road. You are now on the route Hampton took and on which Union cavalry followed. Continue on Bidle Road for 1.8 miles then take a left onto Picnic Woods Road. At the intersection of Quebec School Road, turn left. At the next intersection with Rt. 17, Burkittsville Road, turn right. You are in the area of the Quebec School House fight.

The cavalrymen sparred again southwest of Middletown in the vicinity of Quebec School House. The schoolhouse was at the intersection of Quebec School Road and Burkittsville Road—the southwest corner. However this area was extensively re-graded when Rt. 17 was constructed, extensively changing the physical site of the schoolhouse. There is no safe place to park near this site.

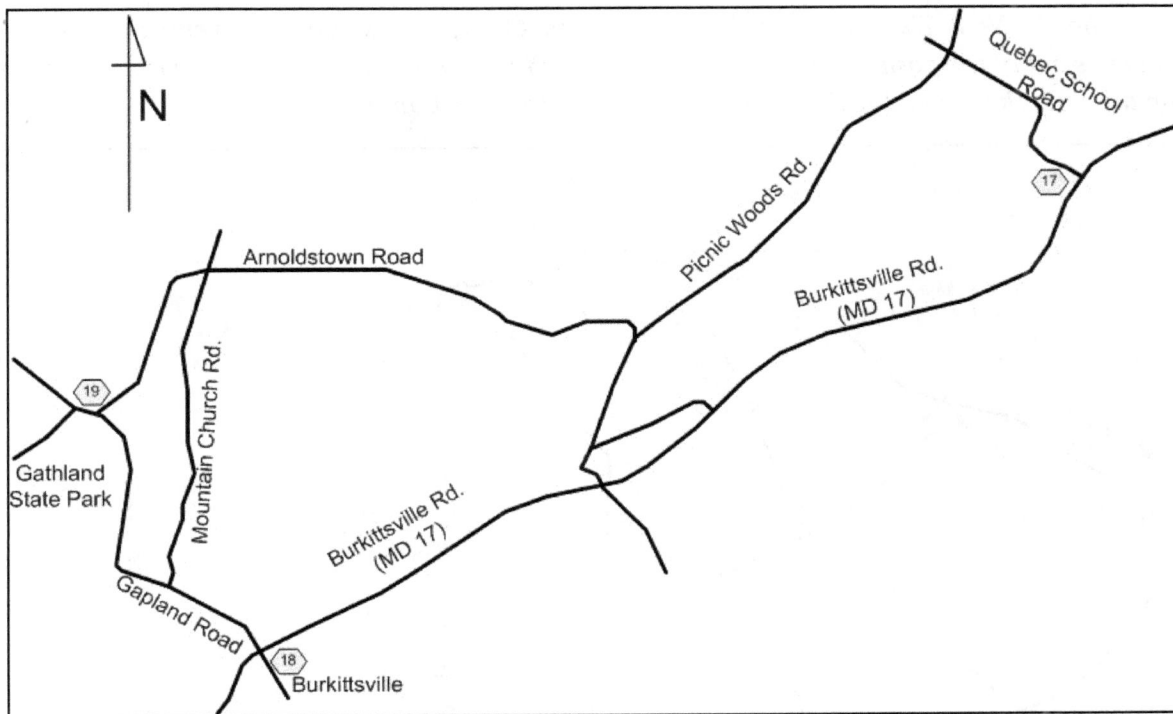

Map 15: Burkittsville and Crampton's Gap

Side Trip D: Federal Advance toward Crampton's Gap. This short side trip covers the other side of the Federal pursuit over Catoctin Mountain to South Mountain. Using Jefferson Pike (modern Maryland Highway 180), which leads southwest out of Frederick, Brig. Gen. Alfred Pleasonton placed Rush's Lancers in the lead of this advance. Munford's 2nd and 12th Virginia Cavalry, supported by Chew's Battery, defended Jefferson Gap, where the pike crossed Catoctin Mountain, just east of the town of Jefferson.

Stop D1: Jefferson (39° 21' 37.5" N, 77° 31' 54" W) – From the site of Quebec School House (Stop 17), turn left onto Burkittsville Road (Maryland 17) and proceed for 0.7 mile. Watch for the third left after turning onto Maryland 17 and turn onto Broad Run Road (Maryland 383). Pay attention to the road signs, as Broad Run Road makes several turns at intersections. Look for the Maryland 383 highway sign at each intersection. After 1.3 miles at the intersection with Picnic Woods Road and Catholic Church Road, turn left to stay on Broad Run Road. Continue on Broad Run Road for 1.8 miles to the intersection with Gapland Road. Turn left again to remain on Broad Run Road. After another 2.4 miles, Broad Run Road ends at the intersection with Jefferson Pike (Maryland 180). Turn left to proceed through Jefferson. Turn right after 0.8 mile onto Lander Road, then take the first left, just past the gas station (and do not cross the overpass of Route 180) to enter the parking lot of the Jefferson Volunteer Fire Department. Please park in the commuter lot on the south side (to the right) of the entrance. The Civil War Trails marker here discusses events pertaining to the Gettysburg Campaign. The modern highway parallels the old Jefferson Pike passing through Jefferson Gap to the east of this stop.

The Lancers encountered Munford's troopers as they moved up the east side of Catoctin Mountain through Jefferson Gap. Facing artillery and dismounted Confederates, the Lancers were unable to proceed. The 9ᵗʰ New York Infantry, from the Ninth Corps, moved up and eventually pressed the Confederates out of the position. The townspeople of Jefferson received the Federals with an outpouring of hospitality (as they would again a year later in the Gettysburg Campaign).

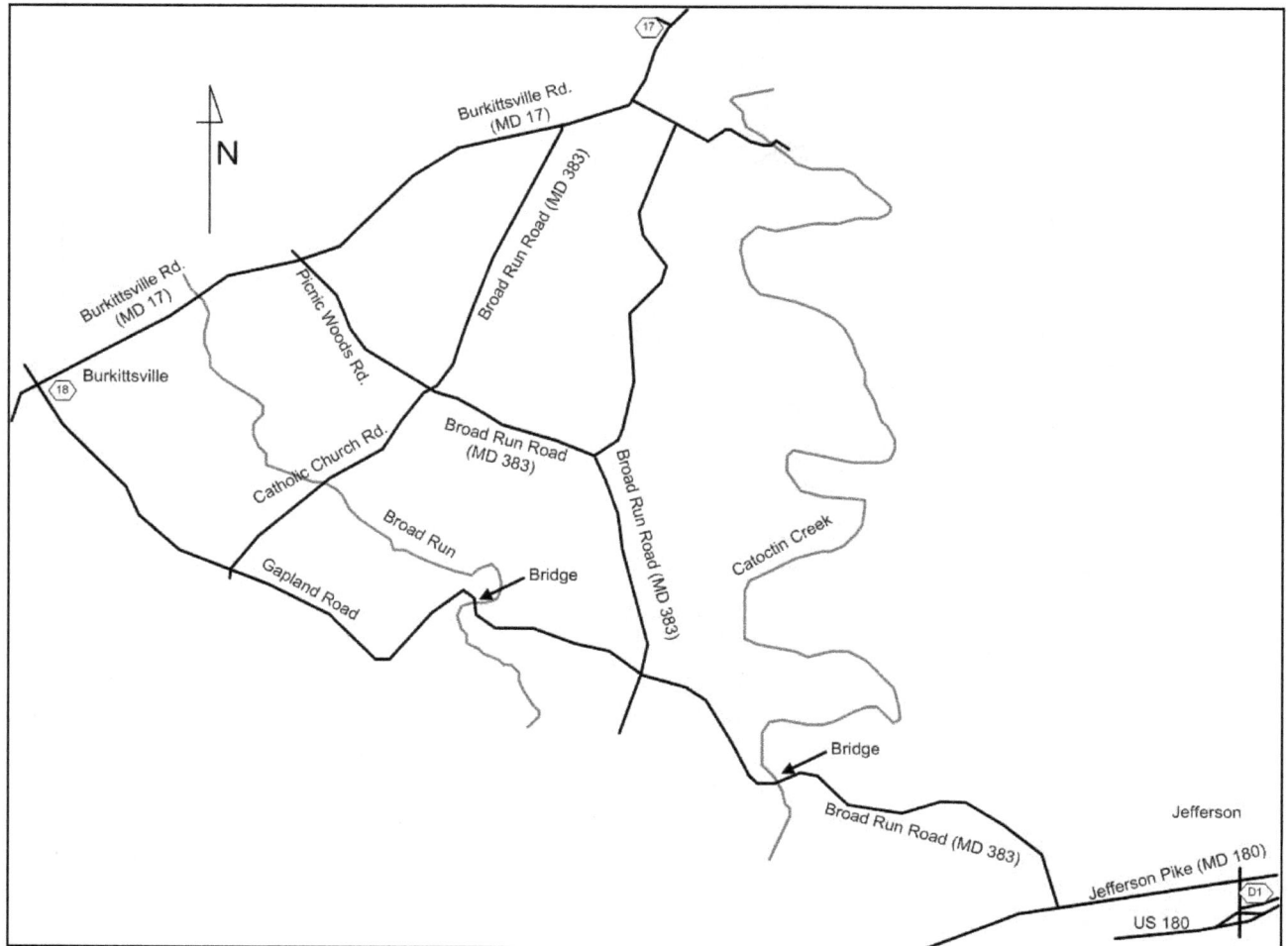

Map 16: Advance to Burkittsville

Return to Lander Road and turn left onto Jefferson Pike, retracing the path into Jefferson. Turn right back onto Broad Run Road (Maryland 383). After about 1.5 miles, the road crosses Catoctin Creek over a modern concrete bridge. Federal Cavalry pursued the Confederates across the creek in this vicinity. The Lancers later posted one company along Catoctin Creek after returning from their pursuit of Munford. If you chose to stop here, please do so east of the bridge where the shoulder is wider.

Continue for a mile further on Broad Run Road to the intersection with Gapland Road. This time, continue straight at the intersection (leaving Maryland 383) and proceed on Gapland Road toward Burkittsville. About 0.8 mile beyond the intersection, the road crosses Broad Run. Federals continued the pursuit of Munford's cavalry across Broad Run in this vicinity. Due to the sharp turns in the road, do not stop at this bridge, but continue on for 2.6 miles into Burkittsville and Stop 18 below.

18. Burkittsville (39° 23' 37" N, 77° 37' 44" W)

Continue south on Maryland 17 for 3.2 miles, into the town of Burkittsville. At the intersection with Main Street, turn left. Turn into the parking lot between the Resurrection Reformed Church and St. Paul Lutheran Church. A Civil War Trails marker in front of the Reformed Church discusses the many buildings in town which served as hospitals during the campaign. The parking lot between the church and cemetery is a good location for orientation to South Mountain and Crampton's Gap. The gap opens on the west side of town.

19. Crampton's Gap (39° 24' 23" N, 77° 38' 20" W)

Leaving the church parking lot, turn right onto Main Street and continue through the intersection with Maryland 17. Gapland Road ascends South Mountain into Crampton's Gap. You may wish to stop along the way to read some of the historical markers related to this portion of the Battle of South Mountain. Otherwise, continue 1.2 miles to the crest of the ridge, then turn right for a short distance on Arnoldstown Road, and then left into the parking lot for Gapland State Park.

On 14 September, Confederates delayed the Federal passage of South Mountain at Crampton's Gap in a series of stands. The forward-most included cavalry pickets along Arnoldstown Road near the intersection with Mountain Church Road. Although reinforced, the defenders numbered just over 2,000. They faced over 12,000 men of Maj. Gen. William B. Franklin's Sixth Corps. Due to the naturally good defensive position, narrow maneuver space, and delays deploying the infantry formations, the Federals were not able to push through the gap until 6 P.M. Franklin then vacillated instead of moving to relieve Harpers Ferry to the south in Pleasant Valley.

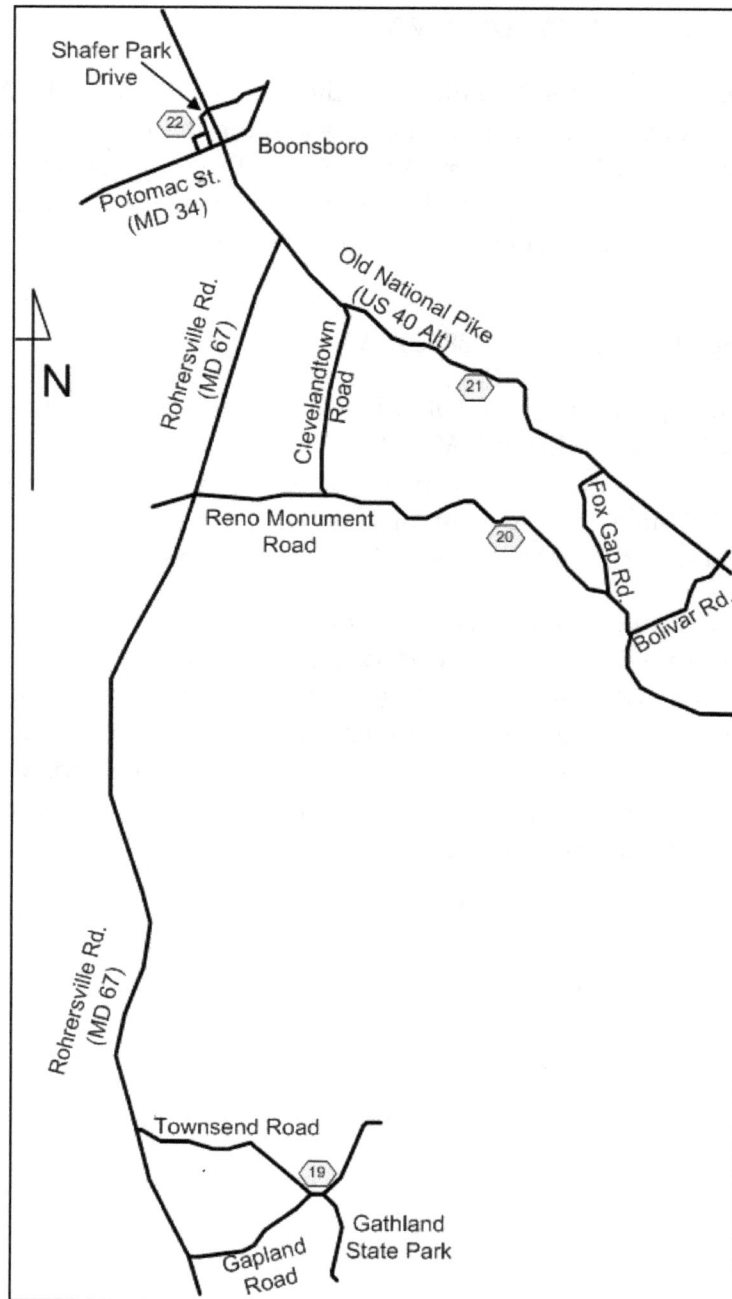

Map 17: South Mountain Gaps and Boonsboro

20. Fox's Gap (39° 28' 14" N, 77° 37' 4" W)

Leaving Gapland State Park, continue west for a short distance on Gapland Road, then make sure to follow to the right as the road becomes Townsend Road. Drive 1.3 miles to the intersection with Rohrersville Road (Maryland 67) and turn right (north). After 4.4 miles turn right onto Reno Monument Road, which will ascend the west side of South Mountain into Fox's Gap. After 2.2 miles pull off to the right into the parking area. Memorials and several historical markers around the small park interpret this portion of the Battle of South Mountain.

Initially on September 14, Col. Thomas L. Rosser's cavalry picketed Fox's Gap along the Old Sharpsburg Road (today the Reno Monument Road), supported by two guns from Capt. John Pelham's artillery. Rosser's troopers were among the last Confederates to fall back that day, not giving up the gap until 10 P.M.

21. Turner's Gap (39° 29' 4" N, 77° 37' 12" W)

Continue east on Reno Monument Road, descending the east side of South Mountain, for 0.8 mile. At the intersection with Fox Gap Road, make a sharp left turn and continue for one mile to the Old National Pike (US 40 Alternate). Turn left onto the Old National Pike and continue up South Mountain for one mile into Turner's Gap. At the crest of the ridge, park near the Old South Mountain Inn (Mountain House during the war) on the left of the highway. Civil War Trails markers discuss this portion of the Battle of South Mountain. You may wish to carefully cross the road to read the War Department Tablets. The Appalachian Trail (AT) crosses here and connects north to the Washington Monument and south to Fox's Gap, Crampton's Gap, Brownsville Gap, and Weverton, overlooking the Potomac. Check the AT website for Maryland; note that hiking the area along the South Mountain ridge, the one mile south to Fox's Gap is relatively easy, but other hikes on the AT are moderately difficult and must not be undertaken without proper preparation.

On Sunday, 14 September, Stuart rose early and rode seven miles from his camp on the western side of South Mountain near Boonsboro, down to Crampton's Gap. He probably had with him the Jeff Davis Legion and the two guns of Hart's Battery, but he left no cavalry at Turner's Gap. He apparently did not stop to confer with Rosser at Fox's Gap, a mile south of Turner's Gap, not even replying to a message from Rosser telling Stuart of the Union Ninth Corps approaching Turner's Gap.

About a mile further north along Washington Monument Road, is a stone tower built in 1827, as a monument to the nation's first president. Federals used the tower as a signal station during the Battle of Antietam (and also during the Gettysburg Campaign). It was in ruins at the time of the Civil War.

22. Boonsboro (39° 30' 32" N, 77° 39' 18" W)

Leaving the South Mountain Inn, carefully make a left turn and continue west on the Old National Pike. Continue through Boonsboro for a total of 2.6 miles. Turn left onto Shafer Park Drive and stop in the parking lot for the park. You may use the sidewalk back to the Old National Pike to visit the Civil War Trails markers.

As General Stonewall Jackson set up his headquarters east of Boonsboro on 10 September, he was nearly captured by a Federal cavalry patrol from the 1st Maryland Cavalry. Five days later, Federals from Gen. Israel Richardson's Division marched down South Mountain, toward Boonsboro, encountering Confederate cavalry skirmishers, but Federal numbers pushed the Rebels back. After fighting that included a series of mounted charges by Union cavalry along the National Pike, the Confederates withdrew toward Keedysville. Pleasonton would later recall this as his only personal hand-to-hand combat of the war.

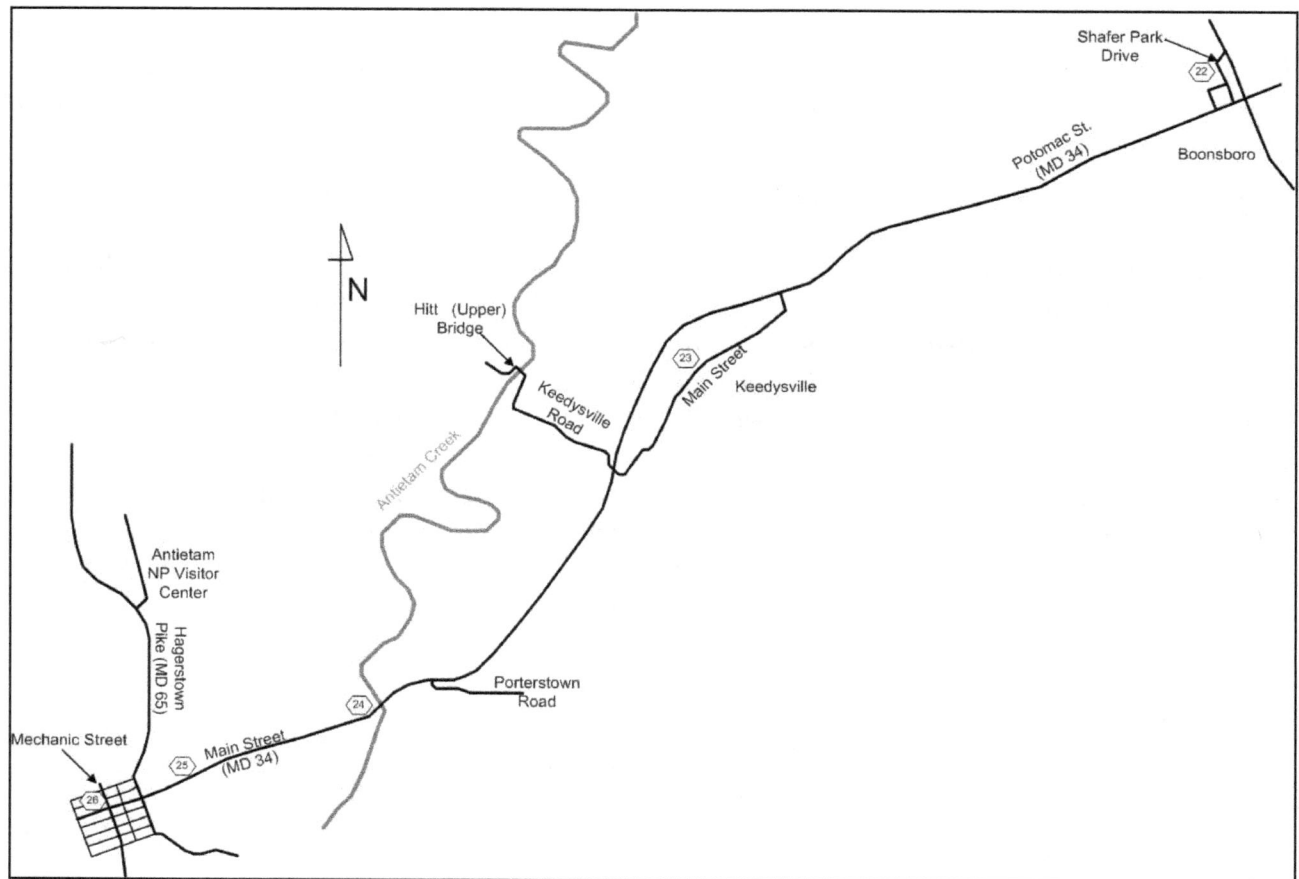

Map 18: Boonsboro to Sharpsburg

23. Keedysville (39° 29' 17" N, 77° 41' 56" W)

Turn back onto Shafer Park Drive. Continue as it turns into Park Lane, to the intersection with Potomac Street (Maryland Rt. 34). Turn right and continue toward Keedysville for 2.1 miles. At the north entrance to Keedysville, turn left onto Keedy Drive, and then turn immediately right onto North Main Street. After a half mile stop in the parking lot for Taylor Park, where a Civil War Trails marker stands. The Old Boonsboro Pike travelled from Boonsboro through Keedysville to Sharpsburg.

After the Battle of South Mountain ended late on September 14, 1862, much of the Confederate army marched through here from Boonsboro or from the east from Pleasant Valley. Much of the Rebel cavalry also rode by. On 15 September, Gen. McClellan's Army of the Potomac arrived, and he established his headquarters here in the German Reformed Church. His army bivouacked in and around Keedysville before it attacked Lee over Antietam Creek on 17 September. After the battle, the Federals established several temporary hospitals in Keedysville.

24. Middle Bridge and hills (39° 27' 53" N, 77° 43' 39" W)

Return to Main Street and continue south through town for about 0.3 mile on South Main Street, returning to Maryland Rt. 34.

If time permits (but buses should avoid this due to one-lane bridges), you may wish to take a short side trip, proceeding straight across Maryland Rt. 34 onto Keedysville Road. A short, one-mile drive crosses over the Pry Mill Bridge on Little Antietam Creek, and Hitt Bridge (also known as the Upper Bridge) on Antietam Creek.

Otherwise, continue 1.6 miles south, crossing over Antietam Creek at the Middle Bridge. Just after the bridge, turn right into the parking lot for the Newcomer House, on the Antietam Battlefield (http://www.nps.gov/ancm/index.htm). Please check the park's website regarding entrance fees for the battlefield (there are none collected at the Newcomer House, only at the park's visitor center). Walk the park's 3/10 mile Tidball Trail and if time permits, at least part of the Three-Farms Trail which heads south from the Middle Bridge downstream along Antietam Creek to Burnside Bridge. As you walk under the bridge, note the remains of buildings as well as the Newcomer Barn. Obtain trail brochures before beginning your hikes.

Skirmishing took place here on the 16 September. Around noon the next day, Pleasonton's Cavalry moved toward and then over the Middle Bridge. Here the troopers supported the horse artillery, under considerable but relatively inconsequential fire. Among the few killed in this sector of the battlefield was Colonel James H. Childs, commanding the 4ᵗʰ Pennsylvania Cavalry. A monument to Childs stands along Rt. 34.

25. National Cemetery Parking Lot (39°27' 40.5" N, 77° 44' 24" W)

Leave the Newcomer House and turn right onto Rt. 34 for .75 miles and then right again into the National Cemetery parking lot. Carefully cross Rt. 34 and walk to entrance of National Cemetery. Tour the cemetery and be sure to look to the east to understand the views which Gen. Robert E. Lee had from this point. He spent much time in that location because of the excellent vista which allowed him to see most of the battlefield. Note the observation tower at Bloody Lane to the north.

26. Grove House (39°27' 29.5" N, 77° 44' 57" W)

Exit the parking lot, taking a right onto Rt. 34, and follow the pike into Sharpsburg. As you enter Sharpsburg Square downtown, notice the Grove House on the southwest corner. The intersection is at South Mechanic Street and the Boonsboro Pike, Maryland Rt. 34. At the square, park and walk the area noticing the light-colored stone building to the northwest, just past the square, with a cannon shell still seen on its east-facing wall.

The Grove House was where General Stuart had his headquarters when he was not in the field, and where General Lee and his wing commanders, Longstreet and Jackson, met. You are on the route of retreat for parts of the Army of Northern Virginia, on the night of 18/19 September. On 19 September pursuing Union forces passed through here heading for Shepherdstown.

27. Ferry Hill (39° 26' 20" N, 77° 47' 52" W)

Proceed east on Boonsboro Pike (Rt. 34) for 3.0 miles, taking a right turn after a brown C&O Canal Park sign. Drive along the park road past Ferry Hill house to a parking lot on the left. (http://www.nps.gov/choh/historyculture/ferryhillplantation.htm)

On September 19, Pleasonton's cavalry advanced through Sharpsburg to the Potomac. Despite the retreat of the Confederates the night before, Pleasonton captured 167 stragglers and one cannon. Nearing the river, the cavalry came under fire from artillery of Jackson's division positioned on the Virginia side. The Federal horse artillery engaged the Confederate batteries in an inconclusive two hour artillery duel through mid-day. Ferry Hill mansion was owned by the father of Major Henry Kyd Douglas, one of Stonewall Jackson's aides.

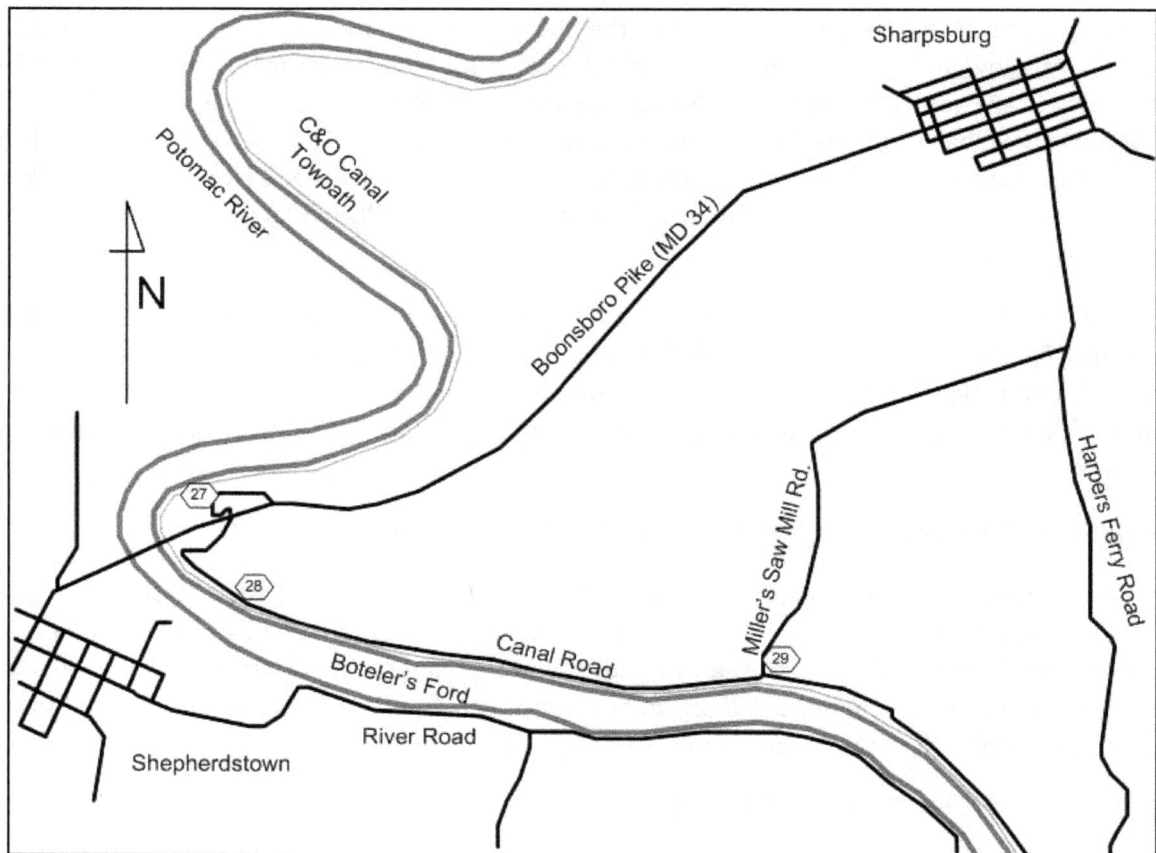

Map 19: Ferry Hill and Boteler's Ford

28. Boteler's Ford (39° 26' 2" N, 77° 47' 44" W)

Return to the entrance and continue straight across Rt. 34 to Canal Road, to the right of the barn. Note the grouping of wayside signs at the intersection of Rt. 34 and Canal Road. Continue on Canal Road, bypassing the canal lock parking area where the road turns sharply at the base of the highway bridge. At about 0.5 miles from Rt. 34, park in the trail parking lot to the left. Cross over to the canal towpath and find a wayside for Boteler's Ford. The site of the ford is roughly one mile east along the canal towpath (**39° 25' 50.60" N, 77° 46' 40.60" W**).

Boteler's Mill, also known as Potomac Mill, is seen on the West Virginia shore of the Potomac. Boteler's Mill dam was made of wooden cribs filled with rubble stones and covered with planks, providing water to the mill. The mill was burned by Federal troops in 1861. Munford picketed the area near the mouth of Antietam Creek with the 2nd, 7th and 12th Virginia Cavalry, along with the 17th Battalion, which had rejoined Munford after its detached duty south of Harpers Ferry. A.P. Hill's Division also crossed the Potomac at this ford, marching toward the battle on 17 September.

29. Miller's Saw Mill Road (39° 25' 50" N, 77° 45' 53" W)

Continue on Canal Road for .8 mile, and then turn left on Miller's Saw Mill Road. Continue for 1.7 miles to the intersection of Harpers Ferry Road.

This is the route that A.P. Hill took on the afternoon of 17 September to fall on Burnside's left flank, stopping the Union assault. You may now continue on the Harpers Ferry cavalry escape tour by turning left onto Harpers Ferry Road.

To get to the Antietam National Battlefield Park Visitor Center, go to direction number 8 below in Part 2. The tablet cluster mentioned there is to your left on Harpers Ferry Road, about 150 yards away at the intersection of Branch Avenue.

Part 2

Harpers Ferry and Cavalry Breakout Tour

1. Harpers Ferry Visitor Center (39° 19' 02" N, 77° 45' 26" W)

This tour begins at the Harpers Ferry National Historic Site (http://www.nps.gov/hafe/index.htm). The route includes a walking tour of sites in Harpers Ferry and a driving tour of sites related to the Federal cavalry breakout. Start this tour at the Harpers Ferry visitor center located off U.S. Highway 340 (Jefferson Pike). There is ample parking there and visitor center to orient you to the park (note that the park has an entrance fee). Maps and restrooms are available. Be sure to take advantage of the excellent bookstore in downtown Harpers Ferry.

Take the park shuttle bus (or hike) to downtown Harpers Ferry. From the bus parking area, walk toward the Shenandoah River under the railroad bridge. You are now on what was known as Bridge Street during the Civil War, as it led to the covered road bridge over the river to Virginia. It was burned by Gen. Joseph E. Johnston's troops in June 1861. Cavalry camped in this area, which is much changed from its 1862 appearance. Return to Shenandoah Street and walk east toward the Potomac River.

At about 8:30 P.M. on the evening of 14 September, the Federal cavalry commands assembled along Shenandoah Street, perhaps with some units which were bivouacked in the burned armory buildings, lining up on Potomac Street. After forage was distributed, the 1,500 troopers slowly rode down to the pontoon bridge past Col. Dixon S. Miles and Brig. Gen. Julius White standing near Miles's headquarters (Miles's HQ 39°19' 21.67 N, 77°43' 49.52"W). Maj. Henry A. Cole's Cavalry lead the procession. The column crossed the towpath and canal, then quietly turned left and picked up speed as best it could in the inky darkness, as it rode along the base of Maryland Heights.

2. Boat Ramp/Armory Grounds and Waysides (39°19' 23" N, 77°43' 43" W)

Walk down to the boat ramp in the river wall and look across the Potomac River to the Maryland shore. Note the rings in the boat ramp wall which reportedly held ropes for the pontoon bridge. Use caution when approaching the Potomac River.

Some cavalry camped on the Armory grounds. Walk the foundations on the grounds noting the waysides and the raceways which powered the mill wheels. The area is considerably changed due to the rerouting of the current railroad tracks. Note the current and original positions of the Armory fire house (John Brown Fort).

3. Bridge to Maryland (39°19' 26.87" N, 77°43' 34.48" W)

Walk across the foot bridge from Harpers Ferry into Maryland. Note that the pontoon bridge was upstream on the Potomac to your left; look for the opening in the river wall where you stood earlier near the Armory.

Within the first minutes of the escape, there was a fright as Capt. George H. Shears of Company D, 12th Illinois, turned right on the towpath rather than left after crossing the pontoon bridge, and ran into Confederate pickets, less than a half mile east of the end of the pontoon bridge, just outside Sandy Hook. The company quickly returned as the Rebels opened fire, suffering no losses.

You may wish to walk down the stairs to the C&O Towpath and walk downstream (to your right), about three-quarters of a mile, to view Sandy Hook across the railroad tracks (do not cross the tracks under any circumstance as this is an active line). You may also wish to walk upstream on the towpath, about a mile from the railroad bridge, to the point where the Harpers Ferry Road turns sharply uphill from the towpath area. Before leaving downtown, you may wish to visit the Appalachian Trail Conservancy Visitor Center, on 799 Washington Street, Harpers Ferry, WV 25425 (304) 535-6331 (appalachiantrail.org). It is located about 0.25 miles off the Appalachian Trail, in the same building as the Appalachian Trail Headquarters. This visitor center is a great place to learn about the Appalachian Trail and is a good starting point for day hikes. Return to downtown Harpers Ferry to catch the shuttle bus or hike back to the Harpers Ferry Visitor Center's parking lot.

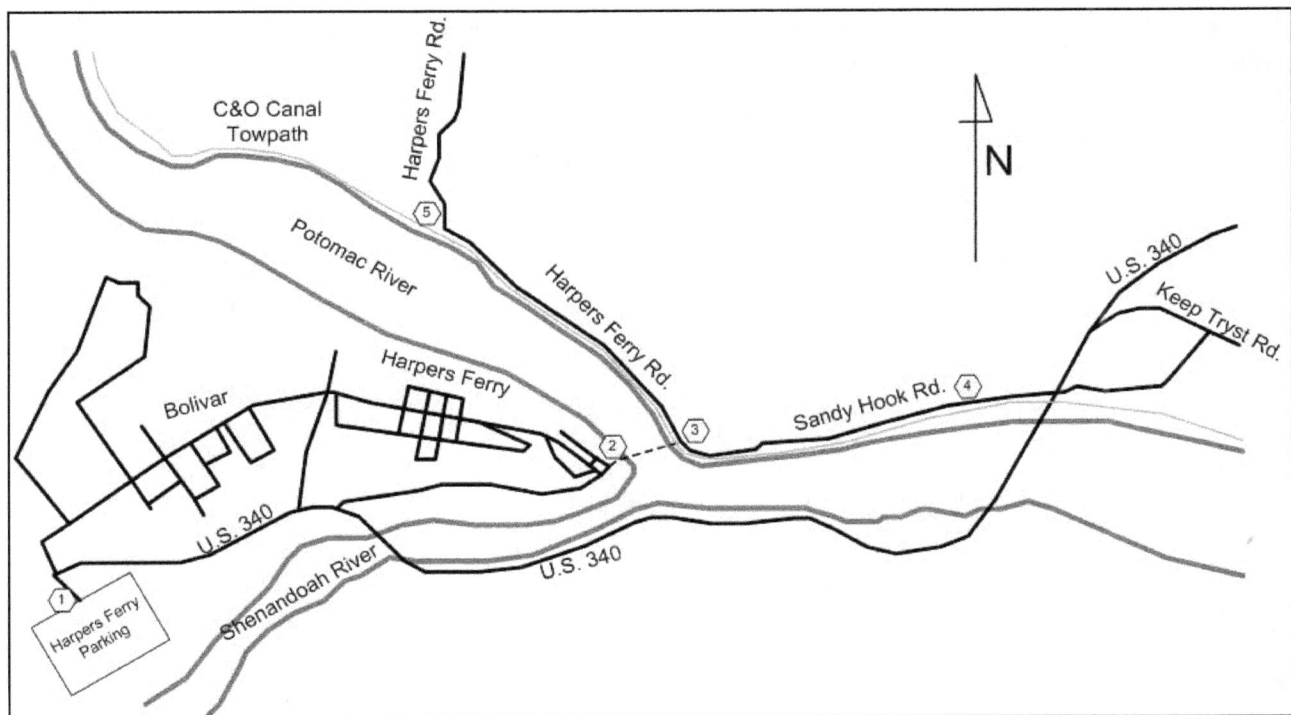

Map 20: Harpers Ferry and Vicinity

4. Sandy Hook (39° 19' 33" N, 77° 42' 40" W)

From the Visitors Center parking lot, turn right onto Shoreline Drive. Continue .1 mile to traffic light on U.S. 340 North (Jefferson Pike); turn right. Continue on Rt. 340, across the bridge over the Shenandoah River; Loudoun Heights will be on your right. (Notice before the bridge on the left, at .8 mile, is Shenandoah Street which continues to downtown Harpers Ferry). Stay on Rt. 340 into Virginia, through the traffic light at the intersection of Rt. 340 and Harpers Ferry Road (Rt. 671), and continue on the bridge over the Potomac River. Bear right onto Rt. 180, Keep Tryst Rd. (3.5 miles from the Visitor

Center), then at 0.4 mile, turn right onto Sandy Hook Rd. The road becomes very narrow, so use extreme caution as in some places it is only one lane wide with sharp turns. The railroad is close on your left. You will pass through the small village of Sandy Hook after 0.8 mile where the skirmish took place with the Illinoisans on the night of the cavalry escape.

5. C&O Canal Stop One (39° 20' 00" N, 77° 44' 19" W)

Continue along Sandy Hook Road, which becomes Harpers Ferry Road as it passes Harpers Ferry at the bridges across the Potomac, which you visited earlier. There are pulloffs to the right along this road which may be used to stop and view the town of Harpers Ferry, as well as the canal and river. The road turns sharply uphill to the north about 1.8 miles from Sandy Hook. Harpers Ferry Road is the road the escape column used after crossing the pontoon bridge.

Less than a mile after crossing the river, the road makes a sharp turn north around Maryland Heights. Moving in a column of twos, Cole's Cavalry likely encountered the first Confederate pickets here. Using a ruse, claiming to be Stuart's Cavalry, the column rushed passed the pickets before anyone could react. Also near this point, two sutlers wagons which had joined the column, slipped off the road and crashed as the column climbed the steep grade.

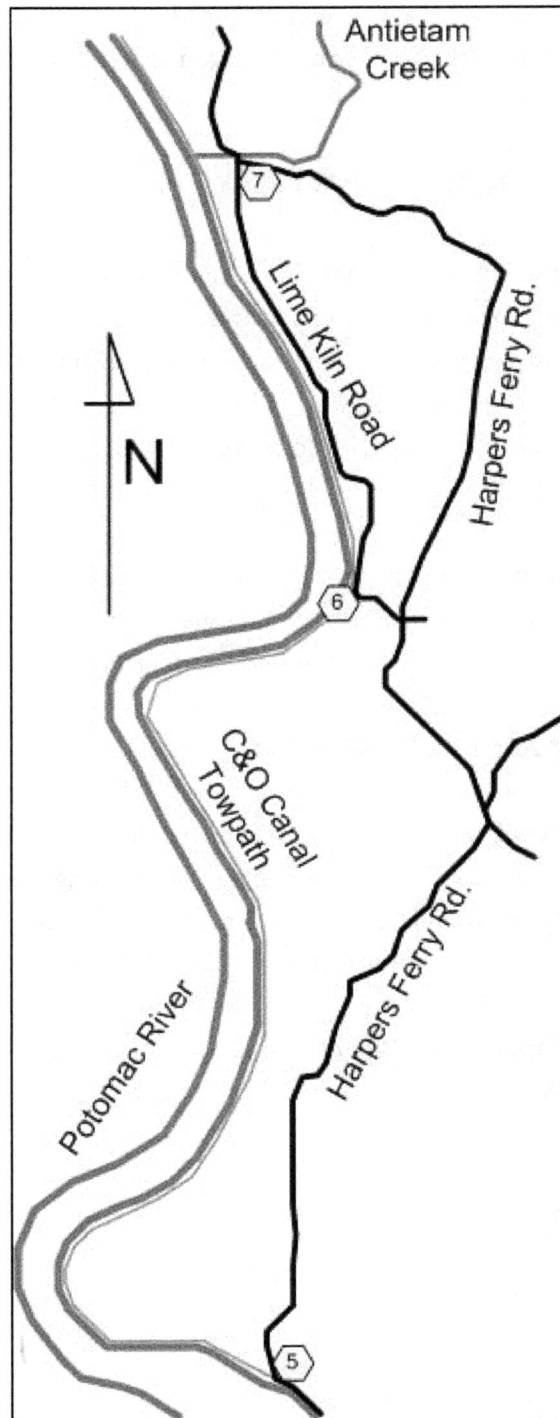

Map 21: To Antietam Creek

6. C&O Canal Stop Two (39° 23′ 16″ N, 77° 43′ 57″ W)

Harpers Ferry Road leaves the C&O Canal as it climbs to the right. Continue to use caution on this narrow and twisty road. At about three miles from the last stop, keep to the left as Harpers Ferry Road passes Bethel Cemetery. After 3.8 miles, turn left onto Limekiln Road, which was the wartime Harpers

Ferry Road. This road is even narrower, with steep drop-offs. Be wary of deer. There is a C&O Canal parking area on the left at 0.3 miles from the turn. Here you may walk to the canal and view the river, considering the movements of the cavalry.

7. Antietam Creek (39° 24' 59" N, 77° 44' 32" W)

Continue on Limekiln Road for 2.2 miles. Look for a safe location to park near the intersection of Limekiln Road and the modern Harpers Ferry Road at the stop sign. There are few places to safely park on the other side of the bridge over Antietam Creek, so you may wish to step out of the car and examine this bridge, built in 1832. A small historical marker on the north (far side) landing of the bridge discusses its history. It is the largest on the Antietam, with four arches. Nearby to the east (right) are the remains of the Antietam Iron Works.

Well after the Federal cavalry breakout, Munford's cavalry guarded the bridge during and after the battle on the 17th, as the extreme southern flank of the Confederate lines. Later in the day, elements of A.P. Hill's Light Division were sent to the area to provide further protection to Lee's southern flank.

8. Antietam Battlefield (39° 26' 51" N, 77° 44' 46" W).

Carefully cross the bridge and continue to Sharpsburg on the Harpers Ferry Road. This is the southern end of the Antietam National Battlefield tour road (http://www.nps.gov/ancm/index.htm). Note again there is an entrance fee for the battlefield payable at the visitors' center. Stop 8A is the Confederate tablet cluster at the intersection of Harpers Ferry Road and Branch Avenue. One of these tablets discusses the operations of Munford's Cavalry during the battle. Notice Millers Sawmill Road on left, from which A.P. Hill's troops approached during the afternoon of the 17th. Note also the view of the north end of the battlefield.

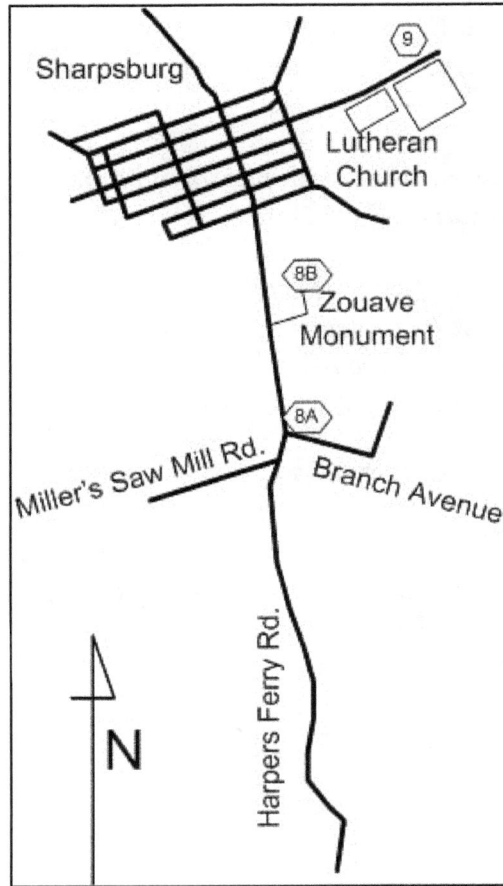

Map 22: Antietam Battlefield

Continue .3 mile and carefully pull off to the right shoulder; use caution as this one-car size area on the shoulder is next to the road. This is Stop 8B (**39° 27' 5" N, 77° 44' 49" W**). There is a paved, short walking path to 8th Connecticut Volunteer Infantry and Hawkins Zouaves monuments. There are also two wayside signs at this location on Harpers Ferry Road. From the location of the monuments, you will get a good view of much of the north end of the battlefield.

9. Lutheran Church and National Cemetery (39°27' 40.5" N, 77° 44' 24" W).

At the Sharpsburg Square—the intersection of Harpers Ferry Road and Main Street, Rt. 34—turn right onto Rt. 34, the Boonsboro Pike, and park at the National Cemetery parking lot, .4 mile on your left. Carefully cross the Pike and walk down to the area of the site of the Lutheran Church. After viewing the site of the missing church and its extant graveyard, return to the National Cemetery. Be sure to look to the east toward the Middle and Rohrbach (Burnside) Bridges, to appreciate the view Gen. Lee had from this hill, known as Cemetery Hill, although neither bridge can been seen from the cemetery. The ridge to the north across the pike is Cemetery Ridge, sometimes called Sharpsburg Ridge. The only cemetery at this time was the one next to the Lutheran Church. The National Cemetery and county cemetery to the north of the pike are post-war.

The cavalry escape column entered town along Harpers Ferry Road and attempted to move northeast toward Boonsboro, but was turned back here, under Rebel skirmish fire, from a point near the Lutheran Church.

Here the tour must consider the two different interpretations of the escape route as discussed in Chapter 8. Veteran of Antietam and historian Ezra Carman wrote that the column turned north out of Sharpsburg using Mondell Road. On the other hand, another veteran and historian, Isaac W. Heysinger, believed that the escape route followed the Hagerstown Pike north from Sharpsburg. This tour will first follow the "Carman" route, then later consider the "Heysinger" route. Both routes eventually meet at Lappans Road (Williamsport Road during the road). They both then end up at the Williamsport Pike but at different points, Heysinger's being closer to Williamsport.

10. Dovenberger's Mill (39° 29' 40" N, 77° 45' 48" W).

After touring the cemetery and appreciating the vistas, return to the parking lot. Reset your trip odometer to zero. Turn right out of the lot, toward Sharpsburg on Main Street (Rt. 34). In 0.5 mile, turn right onto North Mechanic Street at Sharpsburg Square; North Mechanic Street becomes Mondell Road after crossing West Chapline Street, 0.1 mile.

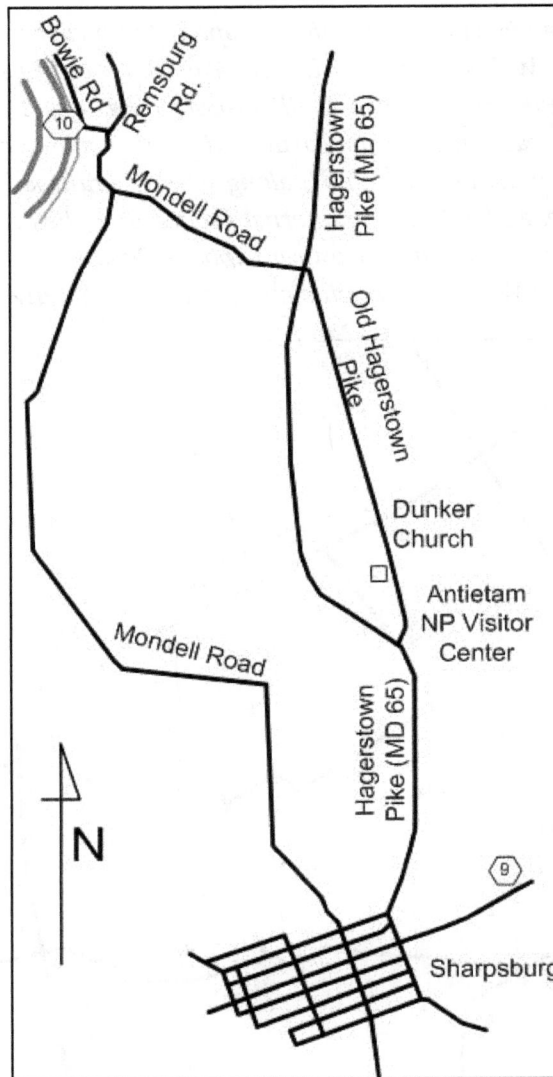

Map 23: Dovenberger's Mill

Continue on Mondell Road. After 2.8 miles, you will arrive at a "Y" intersection with Bowie Road to your left. Dovenberger's Mill was likely located near the stream which feeds the canal at this point. Note that the railroad track to the west did not exist at the time of the Civil War, but its construction altered the terrain and roads in the area. Pause here if traffic permits, to view the area from your vehicle.

11. Lappans Road Intersection (39° 34' 34" N, 77° 46' 52" W)

Turn right onto Remsburg Road. Carefully follow this narrow, sometimes dirt road to the intersection of Taylor's Landing Road, about .5 mile. Bear right on Taylor's Landing Road and follow the road to the left of the "Y" onto Fairplay Road. Proceed .8 mile to a stop sign at Bakersville, and turn left onto Bakersville Road. Continue on Bakersville Road at the next stop sign after 2.2 miles. Continue straight for 1.3 miles to Bakersville. Turn left onto Bakersville Road traveling 1.3 miles to Downsville.

At Downsville, turn right (north) onto Downsville Pike, Rt. 632. Continue north on Downsville Pike to the intersection of Lappans Road, Rt. 68 (Williamsport Road in 1862) 2.2 mile.

Near this point on Lappans Road is where the Union escape column captured Longstreet's wagon train if the capture took place on the Williamsport Road. The Yankees would then have diverted the wagon train north onto Downsville Pike then to the Williamsport Pike, which connected Williamsport and Hagerstown; this route today can only be approximated due to many changes to roads in the area impacted by construction of Interstates 70 and 81, along with the railroad. (Today Williamsport Pike is also known as Virginia Avenue, and Rt. 11). An alternate route after the capture on Lappans Road would have had the cavalry with the train continue west on Lappans Road and then northwest on roads which no longer exist to connect to the Williamsport Pike just north of Tammany Lane.

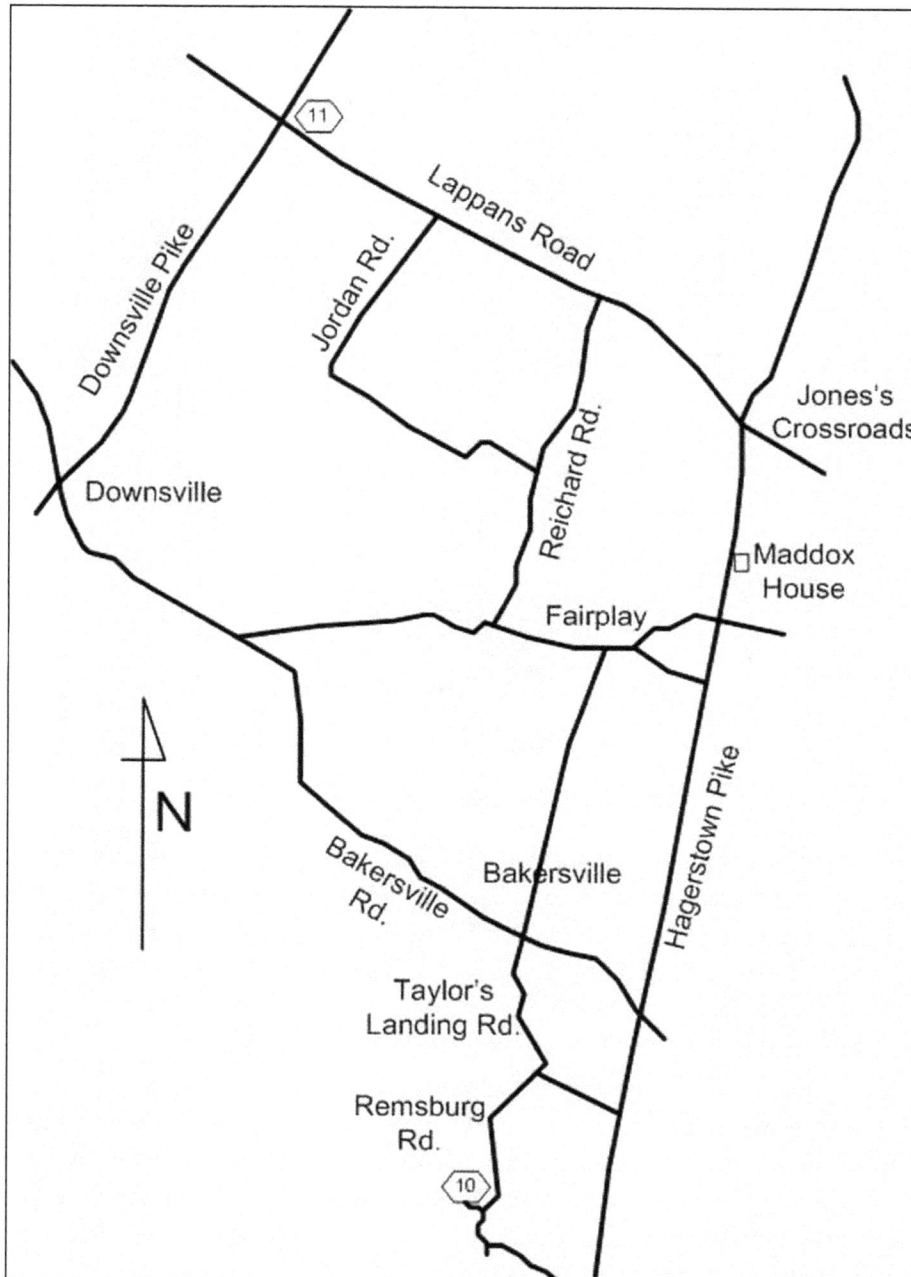

Map 24: To Lappans Road Intersection

Side Trip – Heysinger Version:

From the Antietam National Cemetery (Stop 9 above), leave the cemetery parking lot and turn right on Rt. 34 leading back toward Sharpsburg. In .3 mile, turn right onto Rt. 65, Hagerstown Pike. Continue .9 mile and turn right onto Dunker Church Road at the sign for Antietam National Battlefield. Note that the Dunker Church Road is the "old" Hagerstown Pike and was the roadbed in 1862. Continue .9 mile on Dunker Church Road and bear left to pick up the Hagerstown Pike, north on MD Rt. 65. Continue 3.9 miles to Dr. Maddox's house's driveway (privately owned) on the right; his house is set back about 500 yards from the pike **(39° 32' 37" N, 77° 44' 18" W)**. Continue north on the pike .5 mile to the traffic light at Jones's Cross Roads and turn left onto Lappans Road (Williamsport Road during the Civil War).

After being fired on by Confederate pickets near the Lutheran Church in Sharpsburg, the column turned north on the Hagerstown Pike and continued riding north until reaching Dr. Maddox's house (driveway at **39° 32' 35.67" N, 77° 44' 17.73" W** *) just south of Jones's Cross Roads. Heysinger's paraphrased account: "Just above Tilghmantown a doctor lived on the right side of the pike, Dr. Maddox. The column halted and I was told that the doctor who lived there knew what was ahead—three divisions of Rebels in Hagerstown with trains and artillery. The guides decided to take down the fence across the pike to the west and head cross country. There were several old mills on Marsh creek, across those fields and I knew some who were employed in one [Cross's Mill]. It was a difficult crossing—I lost the column but recognized the area; I heard the noise of our column into which I rode. The road on which I rejoined the column enters the Boonsborough-Williamsport pike [Lappans Road] nearly opposite the College of St. James, which is about a half-mile to the north. We then followed the Williamsport road about a mile to the west, and turned off into a road running north and northwest for about two miles, where it enters the Hagerstown and Williamsport pike, a little more than a mile and a half from Williamsport, which town we thus cleared by this cross-road." After reaching the Williamsport Pike, the column captured Longstreet's wagon train.*

Continue west on Lappans Road from Jones's Cross Roads one mile, then turn left onto Reichard Road. Continue on Reichard Road one mile and turn right onto Jordan Road. You are now back on the escape route. Cross's Mill was on Marsh Creek (today named Marsh Run south of Rt. 63, and St. James Run north of there) which you will cross after you go over the railroad tracks which did not exist in 1862. The mill would have been on the east bank of the creek between Jordan Road and the creek. You may wish to stop along this lightly-used road to view the area. Continue on Jordan Road until you return to the Lappans Road, Rt. 68, intersection. Turn left on Lappans Road then continue to the intersection of the Downsville Pike at the flashing red light. Turn right onto Downsville Pike and continue at 12 below. The route of both versions of the escape now rejoin at the Lappans Road intersection. The Heysinger version would have continued west on Lappans Road through the Downsville Pike crossroads then connected northwest to the Williamsport Pike. The escape column would have captured the wagon train just after entering the Williamsport Pike. This route cannot be followed today so it will be consolidated with the alternate version from the Lappans Road-Downsville Pike intersection next.

12. Escape Route Directions from Lappans Road Intersection.

To follow a second version of the rest of the escape route as closely as possible, follow Downsville Pike north from the Lappans Road intersection to a left turn on Sterling Road in 2.0 miles. Follow Sterling Road .6 miles to a right turn onto Bower Avenue. Follow Bower Avenue .9 miles to the intersection of Virginia Avenue, Rt. 11 (Williamsport Pike during the Civil War).

The marker for the capture is on Rt. 11, directly across the intersection of Bower Avenue and Virginia Avenue (39° 36' 58" N, 77° 46' 19" W), on the west side of Virginia Avenue just north of the railroad crossing; inscription: *"One of Lee's ammunition trains was captured here Sept. 15, 1862 by 1200 Federal cavalry under Col. B. F. Davis, escaping from Stonewall Jackson's capture of Harpers Ferry. This loss was felt by the Confederate army at the Battle of Antietam."*

The escape column continued south on Rt. 11/Virginia Avenue/Williamsport Pike for a short distance, and then captured the wagon train.

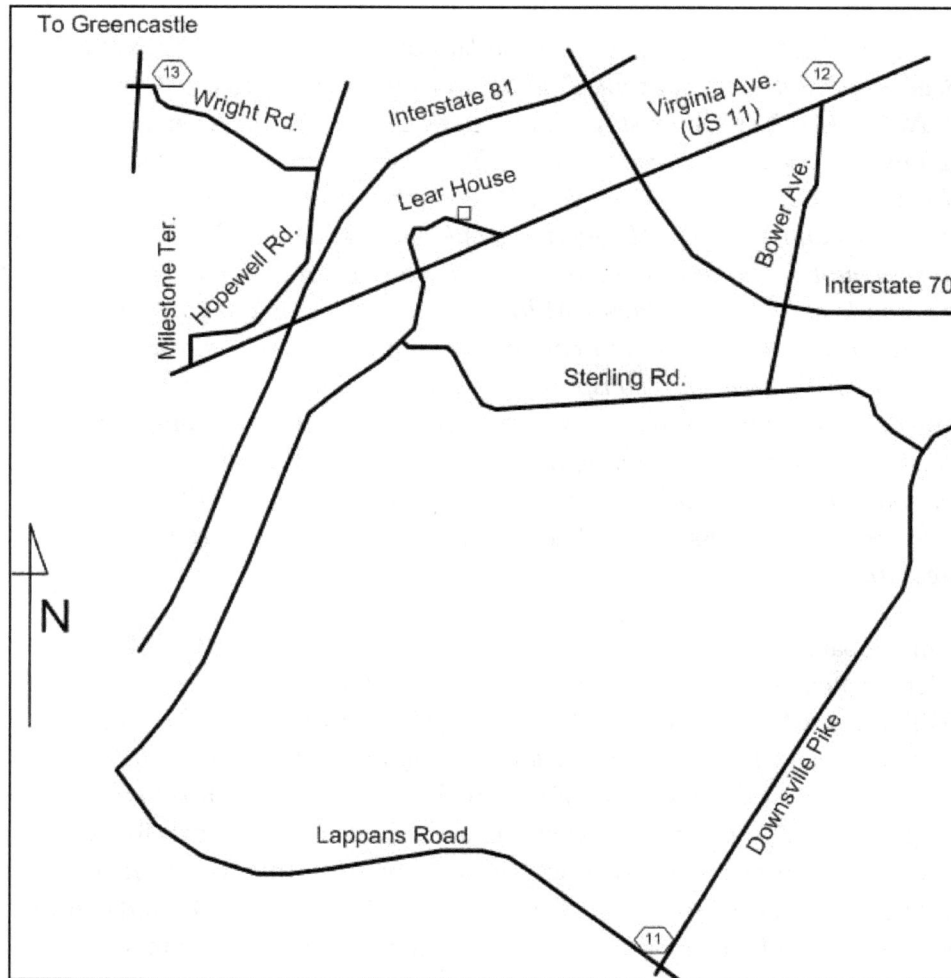

Map 25: Escape Route Past Williamsport

Carefully turn left (south) on Virginia Ave. from the Bower Road intersection and take a right turn in 1.1 miles onto Tammany Lane. As the road turns left on the lane, there is a period home, Tammany Hall. The manor house is .1 miles from the turn onto Tammany Lane. (39° 36' 38.76" N, 77° 47' 38.27" W). There is room for a car to stop and view the home, but note that you should not block driveways. At this point, the 1862 shortcut from the Williamsport Pike to the Greencastle Pike would have continued about .3 mile from there across the modern-day interstate to connect to Wright Road.

Tammany Lane was the entrance to John Van Lear's estate, dating from the mid 1780's. A wagon road was used to shorten the distance from the Williamsport Pike to the Greencastle Pike across the estate. It is also known today as Wright's Lane, which is on the north side of the interstate. The home is on the National Register of Historic Places and is a two-part brick home, facing south. Legend has it that a spring on the property was used by Gen. Edward Braddock in his famous 1755 march. The old shortcut to the Greencastle Pike can still be seen today as a depression near a barn on the property.

13. Continue to Wright Road and Greencastle Pike. To get to Wright Road, the continuation of the Tammany Lane shortcut, turn around and return to Virginia Avenue on Tammany Lane. Turn right and continue on Virginia Avenue (Williamsport Pike, turns into East Potomac Street) over Interstate 81. Then turn right on Milestone Terrace at 1.1 miles, and right on Hopewell Road, in 0.1 miles. Turn left on unmarked Wright Road **(39° 36' 47" N, 77° 48' 5" W)** in 0.8 miles, which is back on the escape route. Follow Wright Road .6 mile, crossing a railroad track to a stop sign at an intersection; turn left continuing on Wright Road a short distance to a stop sign on the Greencastle Pike, Rt. 63. **Rt. 63 here is not the roadbed of the 1862 Greencastle Pike; if you do not wish to follow the 1862 route, turn right here onto Rt. 63 to Greencastle.** To find the route of the old pike which the cavalry used, continue across Rt. 63 onto Kemps Mill Road **(39° 36' 59" N, 77° 48' 51" W)** and stay on it for .6 miles, then turn right on Rock Hill Road **(39° 37' 21" N, 77° 48' 56" W)**. Rock Hill Road today does not join with the Greencastle Pike, so you must turn right on Everly Road at .2 miles instead of following Rock Hill Road which dead ends. Everly Road joins the Greencastle Pike to Greencastle, Pennsylvania in 140 yards. Turn left—north—on Rt. 63 if you wish to drive to Greencastle some 13 miles distant.

Select Bibliography

Adams, Charles Francis, Jr. *A Cycle of Adams Letters 1861-1865*, Vols. 1-2. Ed. by Worthington Chauncey Ford. Houghton Mifflin Co., Boston, MA, 1920.

Adams, Michael C.C. *Our Masters the Rebels: A Speculation on Union Military Failure in the East, 1861-1865*, Cambridge, MA: Harvard University Press, 1978. Reprint, *Fighting for Defeat: Union Military Failure in the East, 1861-1865*, Bison Books, 1992.

Adkin, Mark. *The Gettysburg Companion: The Complete Guide to America's Most Famous Battle.* Mechanicsburg, PA: Stackpole Books, 2008.

Aldrich, Thomas M. *The History of Battery A, First Regiment Rhode Island Light Artillery, In the War to Preserve the Union 1861-1865.* Providence, RI: Snow & Farnham, Printers, 1904.

Alexander, Edward Porter. *Fighting for the Confederacy: The Personal Recollections of General Edward Porter Alexander.* Edited by Gary W. Gallagher. Chapel Hill, NC: The University of North Carolina Press, 1989.

———. *Military Memoirs of a Confederate: A Critical Narrative.* New York, NY: Charles Scribner's Sons, 1907.

———. "Sketch of Longstreet's Division—Yorktown and Williamsburg," in *Southern Historical Society Papers*, vol. 10, January to December 1882. Richmond: Southern Historical Society, n.d. Reprint, Millwood, NJ: Kraus Reprint Co, 1977.

Alexander, Ted. "Battle of Antietam: Two Great American Armies Engage in Combat." *Civil War Times*, September 2006.

Alexander, Ted and Conrad, William P. *When War Passed This Way.* Shippensburg, PA: White Mane Publishing Co., 1987.

Allan, William. "Memoranda of Conversations with General Robert E. Lee," in *Lee the Soldier.* Edited by Gary W. Gallagher. Lincoln, NB: University of Nebraska Press, 1996.

———. "Strategy of the Campaign of Sharpsburg or Antietam," in Papers *of the Military Historical Society of Massachusetts.* From vol. III, *Campaigns in Virginia, Maryland and Pennsylvania 1862-1863.* Boston, MA: Griffith-Stillings Press, 1903. Reprint, Wilmington, NC: Broadfoot Publishing Company, 1989.

Allardice, Bruce S. *More Generals in Gray.* Baton Rouge, LA: Louisiana State University Press, 1995.

Allen, John Owen. "The Strength of the Union and Confederate Forces at Second Manassas." Master's thesis. George Mason University, 1993.

Andrew, Rod, Jr. *Wade Hampton: Confederate Warrior to Southern Redeemer.* Chapel Hill, NC: University of North Carolina Press, 2008.

Andrews, George Leonard. "The Battle of Cedar Mountain, August 9, 1862." From *Papers of the Military Historical Society of Massachusetts*, vol. II, The Virginia Campaigns of 1862 Under General Pope. N.p.: Military Historical Society of Massachusetts, 1895. Reprint Wilmington, NC: Broadfoot Publishing Company, 1989.

Armstrong, Marion V., Jr. *Unfurl Those Colors! McClellan, Sumner, and the Second Army Corps in the Antietam Campaign*. Tuscaloosa, AL: The University of Alabama Press, 2008.

Armstrong, Richard L. *7ᵗʰ Virginia Cavalry*. Lynchburg, VA: H. E. Howard, Inc., 1992.

Averell, William W. "With the Cavalry on the Peninsula." *Battles and Leaders of the Civil War: Being for the Most Part Contributions by Union and Confederate Officers Based upon "The Century War Series."* Johnson, Robert U. and Buel, Clarence C. eds. 4 vols. New York: Thomas Yoseloff, 1956. 2:429-433

Axelrod, Alan. *The War Between the Spies: A History of Espionage During the Civil War*. New York: The Atlantic Monthly Press, 1992.

———. *The Army of Northern Virginia in 1862*. Cambridge, MA: The Riverside Press, 1892. Reprint, Dayton, OH: Morningside House, Inc., 1984.

Ayling, Augustus D. *Revised Register of the Soldiers and Sailors of New Hampshire in the War of the Rebellion 1981-1865*. Concord, NH: Ira C. Evans, Public Printer, 1895.

Bakeless, John. *Spies of the Confederacy*. Philadelphia: J. B. Lippincott Company, 1970. Reprint, Mineola, NY: Dover Publications, Inc. 1997.

Baker, Lafayette C. *History of the United States Secret Service*. Philadelphia, PA: King & Baird Printers, 1867.

Barron, Lee D. *The Chesapeake & Ohio Canal: "As It Is and As It Was."* Sharpsburg, MD: Graphics Design Press, 1973.

Barry, Joseph. *The Strange Story of Harper's Ferry, With Legends of the Surrounding Country*. Martinsburg, WV: Thompson Brothers, 1903.

Bartholomees, J. Boone, Jr. *Buff Facings and Gilt Buttons: Staff and Headquarters Operations in the Army of Northern Virginia, 1861-1865*. Columbia, SC: University of South Carolina University Press, 1998.

Barton, John V. "The Procurement of Horses," *Civil War Times Illustrated*, Vol. VI, no. 8, December 1967.

Bates, Samuel P. *History of Pennsylvania Volunteers, 1861-1865*, vol. 3. Harrisburg, PA: B. Singerly, State Printer, 1870.

———. *Martial Deeds of Pennsylvania*. Philadelphia, PA. T.H. Davis & Co., 1875.

Baylor, George. *Bull Run to Bull Run or Four Years in the Army of Northern Virginia*. Richmond, VA: B.F. Johnson Publishing Company, 1900.

Beach, William H. *The First New York (Lincoln) Cavalry from April 19, 1861 to July 7, 1865*. New York: The Lincoln Cavalry Association, 1902. Reprint, Annandale, VA: Bacon Race Books, 1988.

Beale, George William, *A Lieutenant Of Cavalry in Lee's Army*, Boston, MA: The Gorham Press, 1918.

Beale, R. L. T. *History of the Ninth Virginia Cavalry in the War Between the States*. Richmond, VA: B.F. Johnson Publishing Company, 1899. Reprint, Salem, MA: Higginson Book Company, 1998.

Bearss, Edwin C. "'Into the Very Jaws of the Enemy': Jeb Stuart's Ride Around McClellan." In *The Peninsula Campaign: Yorktown to the Seven Days*, vol. 1, ed. by William J. Miller. Campbell, CA: Savas Publishing Company, 1995.

Beatie, Russel H. *Army of the Potomac: McClellan's First Campaign, March-May 1862*. New York: Savas Beatie, 2007.

Bell, Thomas. *At Harper's Ferry, VA., September 14, 1862. How the Cavalry Escaped Out of the Toils*. Brooklyn, NY: n.p., 1900.

Beringer, Robert E., Herman Hattaway, Archer Jones, William N. Still, Jr., *Why the South Lost the Civil War*. Athens, GA: The University of Georgia Press, 1986.

Bigelow, John, Jr. *The Campaign of Chancellorsville: A Strategic and Tactical Study*. New Haven, CT: Yale University Press, 1910.

Bilby, Joseph G. *Civil War Firearms: Their Historical Background, Tactical Use and Modern Collecting and Shooting*. Conshohocken, PA: Combined Books, Inc., 1996.

Blackford, William W. *War Years with Jeb Stuart*. New York: Charles Scribner's Sons, 1945; Louisiana State University Press, 1993.

Blackwell, Samuel M., Jr. *In the First Line of Battle: The 12th Illinois Cavalry in the Civil War*. DeKalb, IL: Northern Illinois University Press, 2002.

Blair, William A. "Maryland, Our Maryland." In *The Antietam Campaign*, ed. Gary W. Gallagher. Chapel Hill, NC: The University of North Carolina Press, 1999.

Boatner, Mark M. III. *The Civil War Dictionary*. New York: David McKay Company, Inc. 1987.

Bonner, Robert L. "Roundheaded Cavaliers? The Context and Limits of a Confederate Racial Project." *Civil War History*. Vol. 48, no. 1, March 2002.

Brackett, Albert G. *History of the United States Cavalry, from the Formation of the Federal Government to the 1st of June, 1863*. N.p., 1865. Reprint, Freeport, NY: Books for Libraries Press, 1970.

Brennan, Patrick. "The Best Cavalry in the World." *North & South*, 2, no. 2, January 1999. 10-27.

Brereton, J. M. *The Horse in War*. New York: Arco Publishing Company, Inc., 1976.

Bridges, Hal. *Lee's Maverick General: Daniel Harvey Hill*. Lincoln: The University of Nebraska Press, 1991.

Brooks, Ulysses R. *Butler and His Cavalry in the War of Secession 1861-1865*. N.P., n.d. Reprint, Camden, SC: Gray Fox Books, n.d.

Brown, J. Willard. *The Signal Corps in the War of the Rebellion*. Boston: U.S. Signal Corps Association, 1896. Reprint, Baltimore: Butternut and Blue, 1996.

Brown, Kent Masterson. *Retreat from Gettysburg: Lee, Logistics, and the Pennsylvania Campaign*. Chapel Hill, NC: The University of North Carolina Press, 2005.

Brown, R. Shepard. *Stringfellow of the Fourth*. New York, NY: Crown Publishers, Inc., 1960.

Burlingame, Michael. "Abraham Lincoln: A Life." Unedited Manuscript from Knox College website, chap. 28.

Burns, James R. *Battle of Williamsburgh, with Reminiscences of the Campaign, Hospital Experiences, Debates, Etc.* New York, n.p., 1865.

Burton, Brian K. *Extraordinary Circumstances: The Seven Days Battles*. Bloomington, IN: Indiana University Press, 2001.

Busey, John W. and Martin, David G. *Regimental Strengths and Losses at Gettysburg*. Hightstown, NJ: Longstreet House, 2005.

Caldwell, James. *The History of a Brigade of South Carolinians*. Philadelphia, PA: King & Baird, Printers, 1866.

Carman, Ezra A. *The Maryland Campaign of September 1862: Ezra A. Carman's Definitive Study of the Union and Confederate Armies at Antietam*, ed. Joseph Pierro. New York: Routledge Taylor & Francis Group, 2008.

————. *The Maryland Campaign of September 1862. Vol. 1: South Mountain; Vol. 2: Antietam*, ed. Thomas G. Clemens. New York, NY; Woodland Hills, CA: Savas Beatie LLC, 2010, 2012.

Carter, Robert G. *Four Brothers in Blue*. Austin, TX: University of Texas Press, 1978.

Carter, William H. *From Yorktown to Santiago with the Sixth U.S. Cavalry*. Baltimore, MD: The Lord Baltimore Press, The Friedenwald Company, 1900.

Carter, William R. *Sabres, Saddles, and Spurs*. Ed. by Walbrook D. Swank. Shippensburg, PA: Burd Street Press, 1998.

Caughey, Donald. "Crossed Sabers: The Cavalry Escape from Harper's Ferry." Crossed Sabers blog.

————. "Crossed Sabers: Fiddler's Green: William J. Palmer."

Chamberlin, Taylor M. and Souders, John M. *Between Reb and Yank: A Civil War History of Northern Loudoun County, Virginia*. Jefferson, NC: McFarland & Company, Inc., 2011.

Cheney, Newel. *History of the Ninth Regiment, New York Volunteer Cavalry, War of 1861 to 1865*. Jamestown, NY: Martin Merz & Son, 1901.

Chiles, Paul. "Artillery Hell!—The Guns of Antietam." *Blue & Gray Magazine*, Vol. XVI, issue 2, 6.

Choukas-Bradley, Melanie. *Sugarloaf: The Mountain's History, Geology and Natural Lore*. Charlottesville, VA: University of Virginia Press, 2003.

Clausewitz, Carl von. *On War*. Edited and translated by Michael Howard and Peter Paret. Princeton, N.J.: Princeton University Press, 1989.

Clemens, Thomas G. "Ezra Ayers Carman and the Maryland Campaign of September 1862." D.A. diss., George Mason University, 2002.

Colgrove, Silas. "The Finding of Lee's Lost Order," *Battles and Leaders of the Civil War*. 2:603

Colston, Frederick M. "Last Months in the Army of Northern Virginia, *SHSP*, vol. 38.

Conrad, Holmes. "The Cavalry Corps of the Army of Northern Virginia." In *Photographic History of the Civil War*, vol. 4. Ed. by Theo. F. Rodenbough. New York, NY: The Review of Reviews Co. 1911.

Cooke, John Esten. *Wearing of the Gray: Being Personal Portraits, Scenes, and Adventures of the War*. New York: E. B. Treat & Co., 1867. Reprint, Baton Rough, LA: Louisiana University Press, 1959.

Cooke, Philip St. George. "The Charge of Cooke's Cavalry at Gaines's Mill." *Battles and Leaders of the Civil War*. 2:344-346.

Corliss, Augustus W. *History of the Seventh Squadron Rhode Island Cavalry*. Yarmouth, ME: "Old Times" Office, 1879.

Cox, Jacob D. "Forcing Fox's Gap and Turner's Gap." *Battles and Leaders of the Civil War*. 2:583-590

———. "The Battle of Antietam." *Battles and Leaders of the Civil War*. 2:630-660.

———. *Military Reminiscences of the Civil War*. New York, Charles Scribner's Sons, 1900.

Craighill, William P. *The 1862 Army Officer's Pocket Companion*. New York: D Van Nostrand, 1862. Reprint Mechanicsburg, PA: Stackpole Books, 2002.

Crosbie, Allison A. and Lee, Andrew S. *Cultural Landscape Report for the United States Armory at Harpers Ferry and Potomac Riverfront, Harpers Ferry National Historical Park*. Boston, MA: Olmsted Center for Landscape Preservation Boston National Historical Park Charlestown Navy Yard, n.d.

Cross, Edward E. *Stand Firm and Fire Low: The Civil War Writings of Colonel Edward E. Cross*. Lebanon, NH: University Press of New England, 2003.

Crouch, Richard C. "The Loudoun Rangers." Loudoun History Website.

Crowninshield, Benjamin W. *A History of the First Regiment of Massachusetts Cavalry Volunteers*. Boston, MA: Houghton, Mifflin and Company, 1891. Reprint, Baltimore, MD: Butternut and Blue, 1995.

Cullum, George W. *Biographical Register of the Officers and Graduates of the U.S. Military Academy at West Point, N.Y. from Its Establishment, in 1802, to 1890.* Boston and New York: Houghton, Mifflin and Company, 1891.

Cunliffe, Marcus. *Soldiers and Civilians: Martial Spirit in America, 1775-1865.* New York, NY: Free Press, 1973.

Currey, J. Seymour. *Abraham Lincoln's Visit to Evanston in 1860.* Evanston, IL: City National Bank, 1915.

Curry, William L. *Four Years in the Saddle: History of the First Regiment Ohio Volunteer Cavalry, War of the Rebellion, 1861-1865.* Columbus, OH: Champlin Printing Col., 1898.

Daughtry, Mary Bandy. *Gray Cavalier: The Life and Wars of General W. H. F. "Rooney" Lee.* Cambridge, MA: Da Capo Press, 2002.

Dawson, Francis W. *Reminiscences of Confederate Service, 1861-1865.* Charleston, SC: The News and Courier Book Presses, 1882. Reprint: Baton Rouge, LA: Louisiana State University Press, 1980, Edited by Bell I. Wiley.

Davis, Burke. *Jeb Stuart: The Last Cavalier.* New York: Rinehart, 1957; New York: Wings Books, 1992.

Davis, George B. "The Antietam Campaign," in *Campaigns in Virginia, Maryland, and Pennsylvania, 1862-1863,* vol. 3 of *Papers of the Military Historical Society of Massachusetts.* Boston, MA: Griffith-Stilling Press, 1903. Reprint, Wilmington, NC: Broadfoot Publishing Company, 1989.

Davis, Sidney M. *Common Soldier Uncommon War: Life as a Cavalryman in the Civil War.* Edited by John H. Davis, Jr. Baltimore, MD: Port City Press, 1993.

de Joinville, The Prince. *The Army of the Potomac: Its Organization, Its Commander, and Its Campaign.* New York: Anson D.F. Randolph, 1863.

de Paris, Comte. *History of the Civil War in America,* vol. 2. Trans. by Louis F. Tasistro, ed. by Henry Coppee. Philadelphia, PA: Jos. H. Coates and Co., 1876.

de Trobriand, Régis. *Four Years with the Army of the Potomac.* Boston, MA: Ticknor and Company, 1889.

Dean, Rob. "Commanders, Correspondents, and the Constitution: The Birth of Conflict between the Military and the Free Press during the Civil War" from MilitaryHistoryOnline.com.

Denison, Frederic. *Sabres and Spurs: The First Regiment Rhode Island Cavalry in the Civil War, 1861-1865,* Central Falls, RI: The First Rhode Island Cavalry Veteran Association, The Press of E. L. Freeman, and Co., 1876.

Derby, E.H. "Resources of the South," *Atlantic Monthly,* vol. 10, October 1862.

Divine, John, et al. *Loudoun County and the Civil War.* Leesburg, VA: Willow Bend Books, 1998.

Donaldson, Francis Adams. *Inside the Army of the Potomac: The Civil War Experience of Captain Francis Adams Donaldson.* Mechanicsburg, PA: Stackpole Books, 1998.

Douglas, Henry Kyd. *I Rode with Stonewall: Being Chiefly the War Experiences of the Youngest Member of Jackson's Staff from the John Brown Raid to the Hanging of Mrs. Surratt.* Chapel Hill: The University of North Carolina Press, 1940; Marietta, Ga.: Mockingbird Books, 1995.

Downey, Fairfax. *Clash of Cavalry: The Battle of Brandy Station, June 9, 1863.* New York: n.p., 1959.

———. *Famous Horses of the Civil War.* New York: Thomas Nelson & Sons, 1959.

Driver, Robert J. *1st Virginia Cavalry.* Lynchburg, VA: H.E. Howard, 1991.

———. *5th Virginia Cavalry.* Lynchburg, VA: H.E. Howard, 1997.

———. *10th Virginia Cavalry.* Lynchburg, VA: H.E. Howard, 1992.

Duncan, Richard R. "Invasion of Maryland," *Civil War History*, vol. 11, no. 4, December 1965.

Durham, Roger S. "'The Biggest Yankee in the World.'" *Civil War Times Illustrated*, May 1974, Vol. XIII, no. 2.

Dyer, Frederick H. *A Compendium of the War of the Rebellion.* 3 vols. Cedar Rapids, IA: 1909. Reprint, New York: Thomas Yoseloff, 1959.

Early, Jubal A. "Comments on Count of Paris' Civil War in America," *Southern Historical Society Papers*, vol. III, January to June 1877. Richmond, VA: Southern Historical Society, n.d. Reprint, Millwood, NJ: Kraus Reprint Co, 1977.

———. *Lieutenant General Jubal Anderson Early, C.S.A., Autobiographical Sketch and Narrative of the War Between the States.* Ed. by R.H. Early. Philadelphia, PA: J.B. Lippincott Company, 1912.

Eddy, T.M. *The Patriotism of Illinois.* 2 vols. Chicago, IL: Clarke & Co., 1865.

Eggleston, George C. *A Rebel's Recollections.* New York: G.P. Putnam's Sons, 1897.

Eicher, John H. and Eicher, David J. *Civil War High Commands.* Stanford, CA: Stanford University Press, 2001.

Ellis, William A., ed. *Norwich University 1819-1911: Her History, Her Graduates, Her Roll of Honor.* Montpelier, VT: The Capital City Press, 1911.

Emerson, Edward W. *Life and Letters of Charles Russell Lowell.* Boston, MA: Houghton Mifflin Company, 1907.

Engelbrecht, Jacob. *The Diary of Jacob Engelbrecht.* Ed. by William R. Quynn. Frederick, MD: Historical Society of Frederick County, 2001.

Engle, Stephen D. *Thunder in the Hills: Military Operations in Jefferson County, West Virginia, During the American Civil War.* Charleston, WV: Mountain State Press, 1989.

Ernst, Kathleen A. *Too Afraid to Cry: Maryland Civilians in the Antietam Campaign.* Mechanicsburg, PA: Stackpole Books, 1999.

Evans, Charles M. *The War of the Aeronauts: A History of Ballooning During the Civil War*. Mechanicsburg, PA: Stackpole Books, Inc., 2002.

Fishel, Edwin C. *The Secret War for the Union: The Untold Story of Military Intelligence in the Civil War*. Boston: Houghton Mifflin Company, 1996.

Fisher, John Stirling and Mellen, Chase. *A Builder of the West: The Life of General William Jackson Palmer*. Caldwell, ID: The Caxton Printers, Ltd., 1939.

Flaherty, Jane. "'The Exhausted Condition of the Treasury' on the Eve of the Civil War." *Civil War History*, vol. 55, no. 2, June 2009.

Fleagle, Amy L. "A History of Cole's Cavalry: The First Maryland Potomac Home Brigade Cavalry." Master's thesis, Shippensburg University, 2002.

Fox, William F. *Regimental Losses in the American Civil War 1861-1865*. Albany, NY: Brandow Printing Company, 1898. Reprint, Dayton, OH: Press of Morningside Bookshop, 1985.

Frassanito, William A. *Antietam: The Photographic Legacy of the America's Bloodiest Day*. New York: Charles Scribner's Sons, 1978.

Freeman, Douglas Southall. *R. E. Lee: A Biography*. 4 vols. New York: Charles Scribner's Sons, 1936.

———. *Lee's Lieutenants, Volume 2, Cedar Mountain to Chancellorsville*. New York: Charles Scribner's Sons, 1943.

Freiheit, Laurence. "Nutmeggers on Antietam Creek: Major Generals Joseph K. F. Mansfield, John Sedgwick, and Connecticut Regiments in the Maryland Campaign 2 September through 20 September 1862." Military History Online website.

French, S. Basset. *Centennial Tales: Memoirs of Colonel "Chester" S. Bassett French, Extra Aide-de-Camp to Generals Lee and Jackson, The Army of Northern Virginia, 1861-1865*. Comp. Glen Oldaker. New York: A Reflection Book, 1962.

Frye, Dennis E. *Civil War, the Magazine of the Civil War Society*, "Henry Kyd Douglas Challenged by His Peers," vol. IX, no. 5, Sept-October 1991, issue XXXI.

———. *Antietam Revealed*. Collingswood, NJ: C.W. Historicals, LLC, 2004.

———. "Stonewall Attacks!—The Siege of Harpers Ferry." *Blue & Gray Magazine*, Vol. V, issue 1, 8.

———. "The Cavalry Column from Harper's Ferry in the Antietam Campaign." *Morningside Notes*, no. 22, 1987.

Fuller, Claud E. and Steuart, Richard D. *Firearms of the Confederacy*. Fairfax, VA: Odysseus Editions, Inc., 1966.

Gardner, Charles. "Three Years Experience in the First Maine Cavalry." Photocopy of transcript in files of Harpers Ferry Research Library, extracted from originals in the U.S. Military History Research Collection, Carlisle, Pennsylvania.

Garnett, Theodore Stanford. *Riding with Stuart: Reminiscences of and Aide-de-Camp*. Ed. by Robert J. Trout. Shippensburg, PA: The White Mane Publishing Co., 1994.

Gary, Keith O. *Answering the Call: The Organization and Recruiting of the Potomac Home Brigade Maryland Volunteers Summer and Fall, 1861*. Bowie, MD, Heritage Books, Inc., 1996.

"Generals in the Saddle" in *Southern Historical Society Papers*, vol. 19, January 1891. Richmond: Southern Historical Society, n.d. Reprint, Millwood, NJ: Kraus Reprint Co, 1977.

Gerleman, David J. "War Horse! Union Cavalry Mounts, 1861-1865." *North & South*, 2, no. 2, January 1999.

Gibbon, John. *Artillerist's Manual*, Second Edition, n.p.: 1863: reprint, n.p., n.d.

Gilbert, David T. *A Walker's Guide to Harpers Ferry West Virginia*. Harpers Ferry, VA: Harpers Ferry Historical Association, 2008.

Gill, John. *Reminiscences of Four Years as a Private Soldier in the Confederate Army 1861-1865*. Baltimore, MD: Sun Printing Office, 1904.

Glatthaar, Joseph T. "Everyman's War: A Rich and Poor Man's Fight in Lee's Army." *Civil War History*, vol. 54, no. 3, September 2008.

———. *Soldiering in the Army of Northern Virginia: A Statistical Portrait of the Troops Who Served under Robert E. Lee*. Chapel Hill, NC: The University of North Carolina Press, 2011.

Goldsborough, W.W. *The Maryland Line in the Confederate Army 1861-1865*. Baltimore, MD: Press of Guggenheimer, Weil & Co., 1900.

Goodhart, Briscoe. *History of the Independent Loudoun Virginia Rangers, U.S. Vol. Cav. (Scouts), 1862-65*. Washington, DC: Press of McGill & Wallace, 1896.

Gordon, George Henry. *Brook Farm to Cedar Mountain in the War of the Great Rebellion, 1861-1862*. Boston, MA: Houghton, Mifflin and Co., 1885.

Gordon, Paul and Rita. *Never the Like Again*. Frederick, MD: M&B Printing Inc., 1995.

Gorgas, Josiah. "Notes on the Ordnance Department of the Confederate Government," *Southern Historical Society Papers*, vol. 12, January to December 1894. Richmond, VA: Southern Historical Society, n.d. Reprint, Millwood, NJ: Kraus Reprint Co, 1977.

Gracey, S. L. *Annals of the Sixth Pennsylvania Cavalry*. N.p.: E. H. Butler & Co., 1868.

Graham, Matthew J. *The Ninth Regiment New York Volunteers (Hawkins' Zouaves) Being a History of the Regiment and Veteran Association from 1860 to 1900*. New York: Coby and Co., Printers, 1900.

Grattan, George D. "The Battle of Boonsboro Gap or South Mountain," *SHSP*, vol. 39.

Gray, Alonzo. *Cavalry Tactics as Illustrated by the War of the Rebellion: Together with Many Interesting Facts Important for Cavalry to Know.* Leavenworth, KS: Press of Ketcheson Printing Co, 1910. Reprint, Whitefish, MT: Kessinger Publishing, n.d.

Griffith, Paddy. *Battle Tactics of the Civil War.* New Haven, CT: Yale University Press, 2001.

———. *Battle in the Civil War.* N.p.: Field Books, 1986.

Hagerman, Edward. *The American Civil War and the Origins of Modern Warfare: Ideas, Organization, and Field Command.* Bloomington, IN: Indiana University Press, 1992.

Hall, Hillman A. Chairman. *History of the Sixth New York Cavalry (Second Ira Harris Guard).* Worcester, MA: The Blanchard Press, 1908. Reprint, Salem, MA: Higginson Book Company, n.d.

Hanson, Victor. *A War Like No Other: How the Athenians and Spartans Fought the Peloponnesian War.* New York: Random House, 2006.

Hard, Abner. *History of the Eighth Cavalry Regiment Illinois Volunteers, During the Great Rebellion.* Aurora, IL: n.p., 1868. Reprint, Dayton, OH: Press of Morningside Bookshop, 1996.

Harris, Brayton. *Blue & Gray in Black & White: Newspapers in the Civil War.* Dulles, VA: Batsford Brassey, Inc., 1999.

Harsh, Joseph L. *Taken at the Flood: Robert E. Lee and Confederate Strategy and the Maryland Campaign of 1862.* Kent, OH: The Kent State University Press, 1999.

———. *Confederate Tide Rising: Robert E. Lee and the Making of Southern Strategy, 1861 – 1862.* Kent, OH: The Kent State University Press, 1998.

———. *Sounding the Shallows: A Confederate Companion for the Maryland Campaign of 1862.* Kent, OH: The Kent State University Press, 2000.

Hartley, Chris J. *Stuart's Tarheels: James B. Gordon and His North Carolina Cavalry.* Baltimore, MD: Butternut and Blue, 1996.

Hartwig, D. Scott. "Robert E. Lee and the Maryland Campaign" in *Lee the Soldier.* Edited by Gary W. Gallagher. Lincoln, NB: University of Nebraska Press, 1996.

———. *To Antietam Creek: The Maryland Campaign of September 1862.* Baltimore, MD: The Johns Hopkins University Press, 2012.

Harvey, Katherine A. "The Civil War and the Maryland Coal Trade." *Maryland Historical Magazine*, vol. 62, no. 4, December 1967.

Hassler, William Woods. *Colonel John Pelham: Lee's Boy Artillerist.* Chapel Hill, NC: The University of North Carolina Press, 1960.

Hastings, Earl C., Jr. and Hastings, David S. *A Pitiless Rain: The Battle of Williamsburg, 1862.* Shippensburg, PA: White Mane Publishing Co., Inc., 1997.

Hays, Helen Ashe. *The Antietam and Its Bridges: The Annals of an Historic Stream.* New York: G.P. Putnam's Sons, 1910.

Head, James W. *History and Comprehensive Description of Loudoun County Virginia.* N.p.: Park View Press, 1908.

Hearn, Chester G. *Six Years of Hell: Harpers Ferry during the Civil War.* Baton Rouge, LA: Louisiana State University Press, 1996.

Heidler, David S. and Jeanne T. *Encyclopedia of the American Civil War: A Political, Social, and Military History.* David S. and Jeanne T. Heidler, eds. New York: W.W. Norton, 2000.

Heitman, Francis B. *Historical Register and Dictionary of the United States Army, from Its Organization, September 29, 1789, to March 2, 1902.* 2 vols. Washington, D.C.: Government Printing Office 1903. Reprint, University of Illinois Press, Urbana, IL: 1965.

Helm, Lewis Marshall. *Black Horse Cavalry: Defend Our Beloved Country.* Falls Church, VA: Higher Education Publications, 2004.

Hennessy, John J. *Return to Bull Run: The Campaign and Battle of Second Manassas.* New York: Simon & Schuster, 1993.

Heysinger, Isaac W. *Antietam and the Maryland and Virginia Campaigns of 1862.* New York: The Neale Publishing Company, 1912.

———. "The Cavalry Column from Harper's Ferry in the Antietam Campaign." *The Journal of the U.S. Cavalry Association*, January 1914. Reprint, Leavenworth, KS: Press of Ketcheson Printing Co., n.d.

High, Mike. *The C&O Canal Companion.* Baltimore, MD: The Johns Hopkins University Press, 1997.

Hill, Daniel Harvey. "Reunion of Virginia Division A. N. V. Association." In *Southern Historical Society Papers*, vol. 13, January to December 1885. Richmond, VA: Southern Historical Society, n.d. Reprint, Millwood, NJ: Kraus Reprint Co, 1977.

———. "The Battle of South Mountain, or Boonsboro." *Battles and Leaders of the Civil War.* 2:559-582.

Hopkins, Donald A. *The Little Jeff: The Jeff Davis Legion, Cavalry Army of Northern Virginia.* Shippensburg, PA: White Mane Books, 1999.

Hotchkiss, Jedediah. *Make Me a Map of the Valley: The Civil War Journal of Stonewall Jackson's Topographer.* Edited by Archie P. McDonald. Dallas, TX: Southern Methodist University Press, 1973.

Howard, Wiley C. "Sketch of Cobb Legion Cavalry and Some Incidents and Scenes Remembered." Prepared and read under appointment of Atlanta Camp 159, U.C.V., August 19, 1901.

Hubard, Robert T., Jr. *The Civil War Memoirs of a Virginia Cavalryman*. Tuscaloosa, AL: The University of Alabama Press, 2007.

Hudgins, Robert S., II. *Recollections of an Old Dominion Dragoon: The Civil War Experiences of Sgt. Robert S. Hudgins II, Company B, 3rd Virginia Cavalry*. Ed. by Garland C. Hudgins and Richard B. Kleese. Orange, VA: Publisher's Press, Inc., 1993.

Humphreys, David. *Heroes and Spies of the Civil War*. New York: The Neale Publishing Company, 1903.

Hunt, Roger D. *Colonels in Blue: Union Army Colonels of the Civil War: The Mid-Atlantic States: Pennsylvania, New Jersey, Maryland, Delaware, and the District of Columbia*. Mechanicsburg, PA: Stackpole Books, 2007.

———. *Colonels in Blue: Union Army Colonels of the Civil War: New York*. Atglen, PA: Schiffer Publishing Ltd, 2003.

Hunter, Alexander. "A High Private's Account of the Battle of Sharpsburg" in *Southern Historical Society Papers*, vol. 10, January to June 1877. Richmond, VA: Southern Historical Society, n.d. Reprint, Millwood, NJ: Kraus Reprint Co, 1977.

Hyndman, William. *History of a Cavalry Company*. Philadelphia, PA: Jas. B. Rodgers Co., 1870.

Jacobs, Charles T. *Civil War Guide to Montgomery County, Maryland*. Rockville, MD: The Montgomery County Historical Society, 1996.

Jefferson, Thomas. Notes on the State of Virginia. N.p., 1787. Reprint, Richmond, VA: J. W. Randolph, 1853.

Johnson, Bradley T. "Reunion of Virginia Division A.N.V. Association." In *Southern Historical Society Papers*, vol. 12, January to December 1884. Richmond: Southern Historical Society, n.d. Reprint, Millwood, NJ: Kraus Reprint Co, 1977.

———. *Confederate Military History*. Vol. II. Atlanta, GA: Confederate Publishing Company, 1899. Reprint, Harrisburg, PA: The Archive Society, 1994.

Johnson, Charles F. *The Long Roll*. East Aurora, NY: The Roycrofters, 1911.

Johnson, Curt, and Anderson, Richard C., Jr. *Artillery Hell: The Employment of Artillery at Antietam*. College Station, TX: Texas A&M University Press, 1995.

Jomini, Baron de. *The Art of War*. Translated by G.H. Mendell and W.P. Craighill. Philadelphia, PA: J.B. Lippincott & Co., 1862. Reprint, Westport, CT: Westport Press, n.d.

Jones, Archer. *Civil War Command and Strategy: The Process of Victory and Defeat*. New York: The Free Press, 1992.

Jones, Howard. *Blue & Gray Diplomacy: A History of Union and Confederate Foreign Relations*. Chapel Hill, NC: The University of North Carolina Press, 2010.

John B. Jones. *A Rebel War Clerk's Diary at the Confederate States Capital*, Vol. 1. Philadelphia, PA: J.B. Lippincott & Co., 1866.

Jones, Wilbur D. *Giants in the Cornfield: The 27th Indiana Infantry*. Shippensburg, PA: White Mane Publishing Co., 1997.

———. "Who Lost the Lost Order?" *Civil War Regiments: A Journal of the American Civil War*. 5:3, 1997.

Katcher, Philip. *American Civil War Artillery 1861-1865, Field and Heavy Artillery*. Oxford, UK: Osprey Publishing Ltd, 2001.

Keegan, John. *A History of Warfare*. New York: Vintage Books, 1994.

Keller, Kenneth W. "The Best Thoroughfare in the South" in *The Great Valley Road of Virginia*, ed. by Warren R. Hofstra and Karl Raitz. Charlottesville, VA: University of Virginia Press, 2010.

Kelly, James E. *Generals in Bronze: Interviewing the Commanders of the Civil War*. Edited by William B. Styple. Kearney, NJ: Belle Grove Publishing Company, 2005.

Kenamond, A.D. "Potomac Crossings." In *Magazine of the Jefferson County Historical Society*, vol. XXIV, December 1958.

Kirk, Charles H. *History of the Fifteenth Pennsylvania Volunteer Cavalry Which Was Recruited and Known as the Anderson Cavalry in the Rebellion of 1861-1865*. Philadelphia, PA: Historical Committee of the Society of the Fifteenth Pennsylvania Cavalry, 1906.

Kirkland, Joseph. *The Story of Chicago*. Chicago, IL: The Dibble Publishing Co., 1892.

Krick, Robert E. L. "Defending Lee's Flank: J. E. B. Stuart, John Pelham, and Confederate Artillery on Nicodemus Heights." In *The Antietam Campaign*, ed. Gary W. Gallagher. Chapel Hill, NC: The University of North Carolina Press, 1999.

Krick, Robert K. *Stonewall Jackson at Cedar Mountain*. Chapel Hill, NC: The University of North Carolina Press, 1990.

———. *9th Virginia Cavalry*. Lynchburg, VA: H.E. Howard, Inc., 1982.

Lash, Jeffrey N. "Joseph E. Johnston and the Virginia Railways, 1861-62." *Civil War History*, vol. 35, no. 1, March 1989.

Lawford, James, ed., *The Cavalry*. Indianapolis, IN: Bobbs-Merrill, 1976.

Lee, Fitzhugh. *General Lee: A Biography of Robert E. Lee*. New York, NY: D. Appleton and Company, 1894. Reprint Cambridge, MA: Da Capo Press, 1994.

Lee, Robert E. *The Wartime Papers of R.E. Lee*. Edited by Dowdey, Clifford, and Manarin, Louis H. New York: Bramhall House, 1961.

———. *Lee the Soldier*, ed. Gary W. Gallagher. Lincoln: University of Nebraska Press, 1996.

————. *Lee's Dispatches: Unpublished Letters of General Robert E. Lee, C.S.A., to Jefferson Davis*. Edited by Douglas Southall Freeman. New York: G.P. Putnam's Sons, 1915.

Lee, Robert E., Jr. *Recollections and Letters of Robert E. Lee*. Old Saybrook, CT: Konecky & Konecky, 1998.

Leech, Margaret. *Reveille in Washington 1860-1865*. New York: Harper & Row, 1941. Reprint, Alexandria, VA: Time-Life Books, Inc., 1980.

Le Grand, Louis. *The Military Hand-Book and Soldier's Manual of Information*. New York, NY: Beadle and Company, 1862.

L'Estrange, W.D. *Under Fourteen Flags Being the Life and Adventures of Brigadier-General MacIver A Soldier of Fortune*, Vol. 1. London: Tinsley Brothers, 1884.

Lewis, Berkeley R. *Notes on Cavalry Weapons of the American Civil War 1861-1865*. Washington, D.C.: The American Ordnance Association, 1961.

Lincoln, Abraham. *The Collected Works of Abraham Lincoln*, ed. by Roy P. Basler. 9 vols. New Brunswick, NJ: Rutgers University Press, 1953.

————. *Political Debates Between Lincoln and Douglas*. Cleveland: Burrows Bros. Co., 1897.

Livermore, Thomas L. *Numbers and Losses in the Civil War in America 1861-65*. Boston, MA: n.p., 1900. Reprint, Carlisle, PA: John Kallmann, Publishers, 1996.

Lloyd, William P. *History of the First Regiment Pennsylvania Reserve Cavalry, from Its Organization, August, 1861, to September, 1864, with List of Names of All Officers and Enlisted Men Who Have Ever Belonged to the Regiment, and Remarks Attached to Each Name, Noting Change, etc.* Philadelphia: King & Baird, Printers, 1864.

Long, Armistead L. *Memoirs of Robert E. Lee: His Military and Personal History, Embracing a Large Amount of Information Hitherto Unpublished*. New York: J. M. Stoddard & Co., 1886.

Longacre, Edward G. *Fitz Lee: A Military Biography of Major General Fitzhugh Lee, C. S. A.* Cambridge, MA: Da Capo Press, 2005.

————. *General John Buford: A Military Biography*. Cambridge, MA: Da Capo Press, 2003.

————. *Gentleman and Soldier: A Biography of Wade Hampton III*. Nashville, TN: Rutledge Hill Press, 2003.

————. *Grant's Cavalryman: The Life and Wars of General James H. Wilson*. Mechanicsburg, PA: Stackpole Books, 1972.

————. *Lee's Cavalrymen: A History of the Mounted Forces of the Army of Northern Virginia*. Mechanicsburg, PA: Stackpole Books, 2002.

————. *Lincoln's Cavalrymen: A History of the Mounted Forces of the Army of the Potomac*. Mechanicsburg, PA: Stackpole Books, 2000.

———. *The Cavalry at Gettysburg: A Tactical Study of Mounted Operations during the Civil War's Pivotal Campaign, 9 June-14 June 1863*. Rutherford, NJ: Fairleigh Dickinson University Press, 1986. Reprint, Lincoln: University of Nebraska Press, 1993.

———. "Alfred Pleasonton: 'The Knight of Romance.'" *Civil War Times Illustrated*, vol. 13, no., 8, December 1974.

Longstreet, James. *From Manassas to Appomattox*. Philadelphia, PA: J. B. Lippincott Company, 1895. Reprint, Cambridge, MA: Da Capo Press, 1992.

Lowry, Thomas P. *Tarnished Eagles, The Courts-Martial of Fifty Colonels and Lieutenant Colonels*. Mechanicsburg, PA: Stackpole Books, 1997.

———. "The Forgotten General." *Civil War Times*, vol. 46, No. 7, September 2007.

Luff, William M. "March of the Cavalry from Harper's Ferry, September 14, 1862" in *Military Essays and Recollections: Papers read before the Commandery of the State of Illinois, Military Order of the Loyal Legion of the United States*. Vol. 2. Chicago, IL: A.C. McClurg and Co., 1894.

Luvaas, Jay. "Cavalry Lessons of the Civil War." *Civil War Times Illustrated*, vol. VI, no. 9, January 1968.

———. *The Military Legacy of the Civil War: The European Inheritance*. Lawrence, KS: University Press of Kansas, 1998.

Mahan, Dennis Hart. *An Elementary Treatise on Advanced-Guard, Out-Post, and Detachment Service of Troops, and the Manner of Posting and Handling Them in Presence of an Enemy*. New York, John Wiley, 1861.

Manakee, Harold R. *Maryland in the Civil War*. Baltimore, MD: Garamond/Pridemark Press, 1969.

Maier, Larry B. *Leather & Steel: The 12th Pennsylvania Cavalry in the Civil War*. Shippensburg, PA: Burd Street Press, 2001.

Mann, Thomas H. *Fighting with the Eighteenth Massachusetts: The Civil War Memoir of Thomas H. Mann*. Ed. by John J. Hennessy. Baton Rouge, LA: Louisiana State University Press, 2000.

Markell, Catherine S. *Frederick Maryland in Peace and War, 1856-1864: The Diary of Catherine Susannah Thomas Markell*. Edited by David H Wallace. Frederick, MD: Signature Book Printing, Inc., 2006.

Markle, Donald E. *Spies and Spymasters of the Civil War*. New York: Hippocrene Books, 2004.

Marquis, D. R., and Tevis, C. V. *The History of the Fighting Fourteenth, Published in Commemoration of the Fiftieth Anniversary of the Muster of the Regiment into the United States Service, May 23, 1881*. Brooklyn, NY: Brooklyn Eagle Press, 1911.

Mason, Jack C. *Until Antietam: The Life and Letters of Major General Israel B. Richardson, U.S. Army*. Carbondale, IL: Southern Illinois University Press, 2009.

McClellan, George B. *The Civil War Papers of George B. McClellan: Selected Correspondence, 1860-1865*. Edited by Stephen W. Sears. New York: Ticknor & Fields, 1989. Reprint, Cambridge, MA: Da Capo Press, 1992.

———. *McClellan's Own Story*. New York: Charles L. Webster & Company, 1887. Reprint, Scituate, MA: Digital Scanning, Inc., 1998.

———. *Report on the Organization and Campaigns of the Army of the Potomac*. New York: Sheldon & Company, 1864.

McClellan, Henry B. *I Rode With Jeb Stuart: The Life and Campaigns of Major General J. E. B. Stuart*. Bloomington, IN: Indiana University Press, 1958. Reprint, New York: Da Capo Press, 1994.

McClure, Alexander Kelly. *Abraham Lincoln and Men of War-Times: Some Personal Recollections of War and Politics During the Lincoln Administration*. Philadelphia, PA: The Times Publishing Company, 1892.

McDonald, William N. *A History of the Laurel Brigade Originally the Ashby Cavalry of the Army ofNorthern Virginia and Chew's Battery*. Edited by Bushrod C. Washington. Baltimore, MD: Sun Job Printing Office, 1907.

McGrath, Thomas A. *Shepherdstown: Last Clash of the Antietam Campaign, September 19-20, 1862*. Lynchburg, VA: Schroeder publications, 2007.

McMurry, Richard M. *Two Great Rebel Armies: An Essay in Confederate Military History*. Chapel Hill, NC: The University of North Carolina Press, 1989.

———. "Civil War Leaders" in *Leadership During the Civil War: The 1989 Deep Delta Civil War Symposium: Themes in Honor of T. Harry Williams*. Ed. Roman J. Heleniak and Lawrence L. Hewitt. Shippensburg, PA: White Mane Publishing Company, Inc., 1992.

McPherson, James M. *Crossroads of Freedom: Antietam*. New York: Oxford University Press, 2002.

———. *For Cause and Comrades: Why Men Fought in the Civil War*. New York: Oxford University Press, 1997.

———. *Ordeal by Fire: The Civil War and Reconstruction*. New York: McGraw-Hill, 2001.

McWhiney, Grady and Jamieson, Perry D. *Attack and Die: Civil War Military Tactics and the Southern Heritage*. Tuscaloosa, AL: The University of Alabama Press, 1982.

Meserve, Stevan F. *The Civil War in Loudoun County Virginia: A History of Hard Times*. Charleston, SC: The History Press, 2008.

Mesic, Harriet Bey. *Cobb's Legion Cavalry: A History and Roster of the Ninth Georgia Volunteers in the Civil War*. Jefferson, NC: McFarland & Company, Inc., 2009.

Meyer, Balthasar Henry. *History of Transportation in the United States before 1860*. Forge Village, MA: The Murray Printing Company, n.d. Reprint, n.p.: Peter Smith, 1948.

Mies, John W. "Breakout at Harper's Ferry." *Civil War History*, vol. II, no. 1, March 1956.

Milham, Charles G. *Gallant Pelham: American Extraordinary*. Washington, DC: Public Affairs Press, 1959.

Miller, Charles H. *History of the 16th Regiment Pennsylvania Cavalry, for the Year Ending October 31st, 1863, Commanded by Colonel John Irvin Gregg, of Centre County, Pa*. Philadelphia, PA: King & Baird, Printers, 1864.

Mindich, David. "Edwin M. Stanton, the Inverted Pyramid, and Information Control," in *The Civil War and the Press*. David B, Sachsman, S. Kittrell Rushing, and Debra Reddin van Tuyll, eds. New Brunswick, NJ: Transaction Publishers, 2000.

Monaghan, Jay. *Custer: The Life of George Armstrong Custer*. Lincoln, NE: University of Nebraska Press, 1959.

Moore, Edward A. The *Story of a Cannoneer Under Stonewall Jackson*. Lynchburg, VA: J.P. Bell Company, Inc., 1910.

Moore, Frank, Ed. *The Rebellion Record: A Diary of American Events, with Documents, Narratives, Illustrative Incidents, Poetry, Etc*. Vols. 3, 5 and 6. New York: G. P. Putnam, 1863. Reprint, New York: Arno Press, 1977.

Moore, Robert H., II. *The 1st and 2nd Stuart Horse Artillery*. Lynchburg, VA: H.E. Howard, Inc., 1985.

Mosby, John S. *The Memoirs of Colonel John S. Mosby*. N.p.: Little, Brown and Company, 1917. Reprint, Nashville, TN: J. S. Sanders & Company, 1995.

Mosby, John S. "The Ride Around General McClellan." *Southern Historical Society Papers*, vol. 26, January to December 1898. Richmond: Southern Historical Society, n.d. Reprint, Millwood, NJ: Kraus Reprint Co, 1977.

Munford, Thomas T. "Reminiscences of Cavalry Operations." *Southern Historical Society Papers*, vol. 12, January to December 1884. Richmond, VA: Southern Historical Society, n.d. Reprint, Millwood, NJ: Kraus Reprint Co, 1977.

Murfin, James V. *The Gleam of Bayonets: The Battle of Antietam and the Maryland Campaign of 1862*. Baton Rouge: Louisiana State University Press, 1965.

Murray, Elizabeth Dunbar. *My Mother Used to Say: A Natchez Belle of the Sixties*. Boston, MA: The Christopher Publishing House, 1959.

Myers, Franklin M. *The Comanches: A History of White's Battalion, Virginia Cavalry, Laurel Brig., Hampton Division., A.N.V., C.S.A*. Baltimore, MD: Kelly, Piet & Co., Publishers, 1871. Reprint, Alexandria, VA: Stonewall House, 1985.

Naisawald, L. VanLoan. *Grape and Canister: The Story of the Field Artillery of the Army of the Potomac*. New York: Oxford University Press, Inc., 1960. Reprint, Gaithersburg, MD: Olde Soldier Books, Inc., n.d.

———. "Stuart as a Cavalryman's Cavalryman." *Civil War Times Illustrated*. Vol. 1, no. 10, February 1963, 6.

———. "Why Confederates Crossed Potomac." *Civil War Times Illustrated*. Vol. 1, no. 5, August 1962, 19.

Neese, George M. *Three Years in the Confederate Horse Artillery*. New York: The Neale Publishing Company, 1911. Reprint, Clearwater, SC: Eastern Digital Resources, 2003.

Ness, George T., Jr. *The Regular Army on the Eve of the Civil War*. Baltimore, MD: Toomey Press, 1990.

Nevins, Allan. *The War for the Union*. Vol. 1. New York: Charles Scribner's Sons, 1959.

———. *The War for the Union*. Vol. II. New York: Charles Scribner's Sons, 1960.

Newcomer, Christopher A. *Cole's Cavalry or Three Years in the Saddle in the Shenandoah Valley*. Baltimore, MD: Cushing & Company, 1895.

Newell, Clayton R. and Shrader, Charles R. *Of Duty Well and Faithfully Done: A History of the Regular Army in the Civil War*. Lincoln, NB: University of Nebraska Press, 2011.

Newton, Steven H. *Joseph E. Johnston and the Defense of Richmond*. Lawrence, KS, University of Kansas Press, 1998.

Norton, Henry. *Deeds of Daring or History of the Eighth N. Y. Volunteer Cavalry*. Norwich, NY: Chenango Telegraph Printing House, 1889. Reprint, Salem, MA: Higginson Book Company, 1998.

O'Donoghue, Louis B. *Gazetteer of Old, Odd & Obscure Place Names of Frederick County, Maryland*. Frederick, MD: The Historical Society of Frederick County, 2008.

O'Ferrall, Charles T. *Forty Years of Active Service*. New York: The Neale Publishing Company, 1904.

Older, Curtis L. *The Braddock Expedition and Fox's Gap in Maryland*. Westminster, MD: Willow Bend Books, 2000.

———. *The Land Tracts of the Battlefield of South Mountain*. Westminster, MD: Heritage Books, 2008.

O'Neill, Robert. "'What Men We Have Got are Good Soldiers & Brave Ones Too'; Federal Cavalry Operations in the Peninsula Campaign." In *The Peninsula Campaign: Yorktown to the Seven Days*. Vol. 3, ed. by William J. Miller. Campbell, CA: Savas Publishing Company, 1997.

———. "Cavalry On the Peninsula: Fort Monroe to the Gates of Richmond, March to May, 1862." *Blue & Gray Magazine*, Vol. XIX, issue 5, 6.

Opie, John N. *A Rebel Cavalryman with Lee, Stuart, and Jackson*. Chicago: W. B. Conkey Company, 1899. Reprint, Dayton, OH: Morningside Press, 1997.

"The Opposing Forces at Cedar Mountain, VA." "The Opposing Forces at the Second Bull Run." *Battles and Leaders of the Civil War*. 2:495-500.

O'Toole, George J.A. *Honorable Treachery: A History of U.S Intelligence, Espionage, and Covert Action from the American Revolution to the CIA*. New York: The Atlantic Monthly Press, 1991.

Pettengill, S.B. *The College Cavaliers: A Sketch of the Service of A Company of College Students in the Union Army in 1862*. Chicago: H. McAllaster & Co., 1883. Reprint, Salem, MA: Higginson Book Company, n.d.

Pfanz, Harry. "Special History Report; Troop Movement Maps, September 12-14, 1862, Harpers Ferry, NHP." Denver: NPS Center, 1976.

Phillips, John T. II., Ed. *The Bulletin of the Historical Society of Loudoun County, Virginia, 1957-1976*. Goose Creek Productions: Leesburg, Virginia, 1997.

Phisterer, Frederick. *New York in the War of the Rebellion 1861-1865*. 6 vols. Albany, NY: J. R. Lyon Col, 1912.

———. *Statistical Record of the Armies of the United States*. N.p., 1883. Reprint, Edison, NJ: Castle Books, 2002.

Pickerill, William N. *History of the Third Indiana Cavalry*. Indianapolis, IN: Aetna Printing Co., 1906. Reprint, Salem, MA: Higginson Book Company, n.d.

———. "The Battle of Quebec School House." *Valley Register* (Middletown, MD), 8 April 1898.

Pinkerton, Allan *Spy of the Rebellion*. New York: G.W. Dillingham Co., 1900.

Plum, William R. *The Military Telegraph During the Civil War in the United States*, vol. 1. Chicago, IL: Jansen, McClurg & Company, 1882.

Poague, William Thomas. *Gunner with Stonewall*. Jackson, TN: McCowat-Mercer Press, 1957. Reprint, Lincoln, NB: University of Nebraska Press, 1998.

Pope, John. *The Campaign in Virginia, July and August 1862*. Milwaukee, WI: Jermain & Brightman, Book and Job Printers, 1863.

Price, George F. *Across the Continent with the Fifth Cavalry*. New York: D. Van Nostrand, 1883.

Priest, John Michael. *Before Antietam: The Battle for South Mountain*. New York: Oxford University Press, 1996.

———. *Antietam: The Soldiers' Battle*. Shippensburg, PA: White Mane Publishing Company, 1989.

Rafuse, Ethan S. *McClellan's War: The Failure of Moderation in the Struggle for the Union*. Bloomington and Indianapolis: Indiana University Press, 2005.

———. "Culture and Cavalry, Discourse and Reality: Some Observations on the War in the East." *North & South*, 10, no. 4, January 2008, 72-86; 74.

———. "McClellan, von Clausewitz, and the Politics of War." *The Ongoing Civil War: New Versions of Old Stories*. Ed. by Herman Hattaway and Ethan Rafuse. Columbia, MO: University of Missouri Press, 2004.

Randall, James G. "The Newspaper Problem in Its Bearing upon Military Secrecy During the Civil War." *The American Historical Review,* 23, no. 2, January 1918.

Rawle, William B. *History of the Third Pennsylvania Cavalry, Sixtieth Regiment Pennsylvania Volunteers in the American Civil War 1861-1865.* Philadelphia, PA: Franklin Printing Company, 1905. Reprint, Salem, MA: Higginson Book Company, n.d.

Rawley, James A. *Turning Points of the Civil War.* Lincoln, NE: University of Nebraska Press, 1966.

Rea, D.B. "Cavalry Incidents of the Maryland Campaign." *The Maine Bugle,* January 1895.

Redfield, H. V. "Characteristics of the Armies," *Annals of the War Written by Leading Participants North and South.* Philadelphia, PA: Philadelphia Weekly Times, 1879. Reprint, Edison, NJ: Blue & Grey Press, 1996.

Redwood, Allen C. "The Horseman in Gray." *Civil War Times Illustrated,* vol. IX, no.3, June 1970.

Reese, Timothy J. "The Cavalry Clash at Quebec Schoolhouse." *Blue & Gray Magazine,* Vol. X, issue 3.

———. *Sealed with Their Lives: The Battle for Crampton's Gap, Burkittsville, Maryland, September 14, 1862.* Baltimore, MD: Butternut and Blue, 1998.

Reilly, O.T. "Stories of Antietam" in *The Battlefield of Antietam.* Hagerstown, MD: Hagerstown Bookbinding & Printing Co., c. 1921.

Reynolds, Kirk and Oroszi, Dave. *Baltimore & Ohio Railroad.* St. Paul, MN: MBI Publishing Company, 2000.

Rhodes, Charles D. "The Mounting and Remounting of the Federal Cavalry," *The Photographic History of The Civil War: Volume 4, The Cavalry,* ed. by Francis Trevelyan Miller. New York: Thomas Yoseloff, 1957.

———. *History of the Cavalry of the Army of the Potomac, Including That of the Army of Virginia (Pope's), and also the History of the Operations of the Federal Cavalry in West Virginia During the War.* Kansas City, MO: Hudson-Kimberly Publishing Co., 1900

Robertson, James I., Jr. *Stonewall Jackson: The Man, The Soldier, The Legend.* New York: Macmillan Publishing, 1997.

Rowland, Thomas J. "George B. McClellan Revisited." *Civil War History,* vol. 40, no. 3, September 1994.

Ruffner, Kevin Conley. *Maryland's Blue and Gray: A Border State's Union and Confederate Junior Officer Corps.* Baton Rouge, LA: Louisiana State University Press, 1997.

Russell, Steve, Lieutenant Colonel, USA. "The 27th Indiana Volunteer Infantry Regiment" from http://www.geocities.com/Pentagon/Barracks/3627/facts.html, accessed 20 September 2007.

Russell, William Howard. *My Diary North and South.* Boston, MA: T. O. H. O. Burnham, 1863.

Sanderlin, Walter S. *The Great National Project: A History of the Chesapeake and Ohio Canal.* Baltimore, MD: The Johns Hopkins Press, 1946. Reprint, Ft. Washington, PA: Eastern National, 2005.

Sanford, George B. *Fighting Rebels and Redskins: Experiences in Army Life of Colonel George B. Sanford 1861-1892.* Edited by E. R. Hageman. Norman, OK: University of Oklahoma Press, 1969.

Sayers, Alethea D. "Introduction to Civil War Cavalry." Ohio State University Online.

Schaefer, James A. "The Tactical and Strategic Evolution of Cavalry During the American Civil War." PhD. diss. The University of Toledo, 1982.

Scharf, J. Thomas. *History of Western Maryland.* Vol. I. Philadelphia, PA: Louis H. Everts, 1882. Excerpt reprint *The Civil War in Western Maryland.* N.p.: A Plus Printing Company, n.d.

Scheips, Paul J. "Union Signal Communications: Innovations and Conflicts." *Civil War History.* Vol. 9, no. 4, December 1993.

Scott, John. "The Black Horse Cavalry." *Annals of the War Written by Leading Participants North and South.* Philadelphia, PA: Philadelphia Weekly Times, 1879. Reprint, Edison, NJ: Blue & Grey Press, 1996.

Sears, Stephen W. *Landscape Turned Red: The Battle of Antietam.* Boston: Houghton Mifflin Company, 1983.

———. *Controversies and Commanders: Dispatches from the Army of the Potomac.* Boston: Houghton Mifflin Company, 1999.

———. *To the Gates of Richmond: The Peninsula Campaign.* New York: Ticknor & Fields, 1992.

———. *George B. McClellan: The Young Napoleon.* New York: Da Capo Press, 1999.

———. "The Twisted Tale of the Lost Order." *North & South,* Vol. 5, No. 7, Oct., 2002.

Simpson, W. A. "History of the 2nd U. S. Artillery." Excerpt. U.S. Regulars Online.

Smalley, George W. *Anglo-American Memories.* New York: G.P. Putnam's Sons, 1911.

Smith, Merritt Roe. *Harpers Ferry Armory and the New Technology: The Challenge of Change.* Ithaca, NY: Cornell University Press, 1977.

Smith, Thomas W. *"We Have It Damn Hard Out Here": The Civil War Letters of Sergeant Thomas W. Smith, 6th Pennsylvania Cavalry.* Ed. by Eric J. Wittenberg. Kent, OH: The Kent State University Press, 1999.

Smith, Wm. Prescott. *B&O in the Civil War: From the Papers of Wm. Prescott Smith* Ed. by William E. Bain. Denver, CO: Sage Books, 1966.

Snyder, Timothy R. "Civil War Fords of the Potomac River." Unpublished Manuscript.

———. "'I Hope They Will Get Away Soon': The Chesapeake and Ohio Canal and the Federal Authorities during the U.S. Civil War." Master's thesis. Shippensburg University, 1999.

———. "Securing the Potomac: Colonel Charles P. Stone and the Rockville Expedition, June-July 1861." *Catoctin History,* issue no. 11, 2009.

―――. *Trembling in the Balance: The Chesapeake and Ohio Canal During the Civil War.* Boston, MA: Blue Mustang Press, 2011.

Snell, Mark A. *From First to Last: The Life of Major General William B. Franklin.* New York: Fordham University Press, 2002.

Society of the Army of the Cumberland, Twenty-First Reunion, 1890. Cincinnati, OH: Robert Clarke & Co. 1891.

Sorrel, G. Moxley. *Recollections of a Confederate Staff Officer.* New York: Neale Publishing Company, 1905.

Stackpole, Edward J. *From Cedar Mountain to Antietam.* Harrisburg, PA: Stackpole Books, 1993.

Starr, Louis M. *Bohemian Brigade: Civil War Newsmen in Action.* Madison, WI: The University of Wisconsin Press, 1987.

Starr, Stephen Z. *The Union Cavalry in the Civil War, Volume 1, From Fort Sumter to Gettysburg 1861-1863.* Baton Rouge, LA: Louisiana State University Press, 1979.

Steele, Matthew Forney. *American Campaigns*, vol. 1. Washington, D.C., United States Infantry Association, 1922.

Steiner, Lewis H. *Report of Lewis H. Steiner, M. D., Inspector of the Sanitary Commission, Containing a Diary Kept During the Rebel Occupation of Frederick, Maryland, and an Account of the Operations of the U. S. Sanitary Commission During the Campaign in Maryland, September, 1862.* New York: Anson D. F. Randolph, 1862.

Stevenson, James H. *Boots and Saddles. A History of the First Volunteer Cavalry of the War, Known as the First New York (Lincoln) Cavalry and also as The Saber Regiment. Its Organization, Campaigns and Battles.* Harrisburg, PA: Patriot Publishing Company, 1879. Reprint, Salem, MA: Higginson Book Company, n.d.

Stiles, Kenneth L. *4th Virginia Cavalry.* Lynchburg, VA: H.E. Howard, Inc., 1985.

Stine, James Henry. *A History of the Army of the Potomac.* Washington, D.C.: Gibson Brothers, 1893.

Stonesifer, Roy P., Jr. " The Union Cavalry Comes of Age." *Civil War History*, vol. 11, no. 3, September 1965.

Stovall, Pleasant A. *Robert Toombs: Statesman, Speaker, Soldier, Sage.* New York: Cassell Publishing Company, 1892.

Strain, Paula M. *The Blue Hills of Maryland: History Along the Appalachian Trail on South Mountain and the Catoctins.* Vienna, VA: Potomac Appalachian Trail Club, 1993.

Stricker, Mark R. "Dragoon or Cavalryman, Major General John Buford in the American Civil War." Master's Thesis, U.S. Army Command and General Staff College, 1994.

Strong, Philip D. *Horses and Americans.* Garden City, NY: Garden City Publishing Co., Inc., 1939.

Strother, David Hunter. "Personal Recollections of the War. By A Virginian, [First Paper]." *Harper's New Monthly Magazine*, Vol. 33, June 1866.

———. *A Virginia Yankee in the Civil War: The Diaries of David Hunter Strother*. Ed. by Cecil D. Eby, Jr. Chapel Hill, NC: The University of North Carolina Press, 1961.

Stuart, James Ewell Brown. "Report of General J.E.B. Stuart of Cavalry Operations on First Maryland Campaign, from August 30th to September 18th, 1862." *Southern Historical Society Papers*, vol. 3, January to June 1877. Richmond, VA: Southern Historical Society, n.d. Reprint, Millwood, NJ: Kraus Reprint Co, 1977.

Styple, William B. *Generals in Bronze: Interviewing the Commanders of the Civil War*. Kearny, NJ: Belle Grove Publishing Company, 2005.

Summers, Festus P. *The Baltimore and Ohio in the Civil War*. New York: G. P. Putnam's Sons, 1939. Reprint, Gettysburg, PA: Stan Clark Military Books, 1993.

Supplement to the Official Records of the Union and Confederate Armies: Record of Events. Hewett, Janet B. et al., eds. Wilmington, NC: Broadfoot Publishing Co., 1994.

Survivors' Association, The. *History of the 118th Pennsylvania Volunteers Corn Exchange Regiment*. Philadelphia, PA: J.L. Smith, 1905.

Symonds, Craig L. *Joseph E. Johnston: A Civil War Biography*. W.W. Norton & Company: New York, NY, 1992.

Taylor, Richard. *Destruction and Reconstruction: Personal Experiences of the Late War in the United States*. Edinburgh, Scotland: William Blackwood and Sons, 1879.

Tenney, Leon. "Seven Days in 1862: Numbers in Union and Confederate Armies before Richmond." Master's thesis. George Mason University, 1992.

"The Signal Corps in the Confederate States Army." *Southern Historical Society Papers*, vol. 16, January to December 1888. Richmond, VA: Southern Historical Society, n.d. Reprint, Millwood, NJ: Kraus Reprint Co, 1977

Thiele, Thomas F. "The Evolution of Cavalry in the American Civil War; 1861-1863." Ph.D. diss., University of Michigan, 1951.

Thomas, Emory M. *Bold Dragoon: The Life of J.E.B. Stuart*. New York: Random House, 1988.

Thomason, John W., Jr. *Jeb Stuart*. London: Charles Scribner's Sons, 1929. Reprint, Lincoln, NE: University of Nebraska Press, 1994.

Thompson, William Y. "Robert Toombs, Confederate General." *Civil War History*, vol. 7, no. 4, Dec. 1961.

Tidball, John C. *Artillery Service in the War of the Rebellion 1861-1865*. Ed. by Lawrence M. Kaplan. Yardley, PA: Westholme Publishing, LLC., 2011.

Tidwell, William A., Hall, James O., and Gaddy, David Winfred. *Come Retribution: The Confederate Secret Service and the Assassination of Lincoln.* Jackson: University Press of Mississippi, 1988.

Time-Life Books. *The Civil War: Spies, Scouts and Raider, Irregular Operations.* Alexandria, VA: Time-Life Books, 1985.

Tischler, Allan L. *The History of the Harpers Ferry Cavalry Expedition, September 14 & 15, 1862.* Winchester, VA: Five Cedars Press, 1993.

Tobie, Edward P. History of the First Maine Cavalry. Boston, MA: Press of Emery & Hughes, 1887. Reprint, Salem, MA: Higginson Book Company, n.d.

Todd, Frederick P. *American Military Equipage, 1851-1872,* Volume II, State Forces. Published privately by M. P. Todd/Damerel, 1983.

———. *American Military Equipage, 1851-1872, Part I: The United States Army.* New York: Charles Scribner's Sons, 1980.

Todd, William. *The Seventy-Ninth Highlanders, New York Volunteers in the War of Rebellion 1861-1865.* Albany, NY: Press of Brandow, Barton & Co., 1886.

Toomey, Daniel Carroll. *The Civil War in Maryland.* Baltimore, MD: Toomey Press, 1983.

Trail, Susan W. "Remembering Antietam: Commemoration and Preservation of a Civil War Battlefield." PhD diss., University of Maryland, 2005.

Trout, Robert J. *Galloping Thunder: The Story of the Stuart Horse Artillery Battalion.* Mechanicsburg, PA: Stackpole Books, 2002.

———. *They Followed the Plume: The Story of J. E. B. Stuart and His Staff.* Mechanicsburg, PA: Stackpole Books, 1993.

———. *With Pen & Saber: The Letters and Diaries of J. E. B. Stuart's Staff Officers.* Mechanicsburg, PA: Stackpole Books, 1995.

Trout, W.E., III. *Rediscovering the History of the Shenandoah and its Branches.* Front Royal, VA: Virginia Canals & Navigations Society, 1997.

Tucker, Spencer T. *Brigadier General John D. Imboden: Confederate Commander in the Shenandoah.* Lexington, KY: The University Press of Kentucky, 2003.

U.S. Adjutant General's Office. Prepared by Francis Lieber. *Instructions for the Government of he United States in the Field, Originally Issued as General Order no. 100, Adjutant General's Office, 1863.* Washington, DC: Government Printing Office, 1898.

U.S. Central Intelligence Agency. Library: Publications: "Intelligence in the Civil War." CIA Website.

U.S. Department of Defense. *Department of Defense Dictionary of Military and Associated Terms,* Joint Pub 1-02, 2010. DOD Website.

U.S. Congress, *Report of the Joint Committee on the Conduct of the War*. Washington: Government Printing Office, 1863. Reprint, Wilmington, NC: Broadfoot Publishing Company, 1998.

U.S. Department of the Interior. National Park Service. "Cultural Landscape Report: Lower Town, Harpers Ferry National Historical Park." 1993.

———. Snell, Charles W. "The Fortifications at Harpers Ferry, VA., in 1861 and Jackson's Attack, May 1862." National Park Service, Research Project No. HF-98A, 1960.

———. Unrau, Harlan D. Historic Resource Study, Chesapeake & Ohio Canal National Historic Park, "The C&O Canal During the Civil War: 1861-1865." 1976.

U.S. War Department. *The War of the Rebellion: A Compilation of the Official Records of the Union and Confederate Armies*. 128 vols. Washington, D.C.: GPO, 1880-1901. Reprint, Harrisburg: Broadfoot Publishing Company, 1985.

———. *The Official Military Atlas of the Civil War: Atlas to Accompany the Official Records of the Union and Confederate Armies*. Washington, DC: GPO, 1891-1895. Reprint, New York: Arno Press, Inc., 1978.

———. *Revised Regulations for the Army of the United States, 1861*. Philadelphia, PA: J.G.L. Brown, Publishers, 1861. Reprint, Harrisburg, PA: The National Historical Society, 1980.

Vandiver, Frank E. *Mighty Stonewall*. New York: McGraw-Hill Book Company, Inc. 1957.

Volck, Adabert John. "Confederate War Etchings." *The Magazine of History with Notes and Queries*, Extra Number 60. London, n.p., 1863-1864. Reprint, Tarrytown, NY: William Abbatt, 1917.

Von Borcke, Heros. *Memoirs of the Confederate War for Independence*. Edinburgh: W. Blackwood & Sons, 1866. Reprint, Nashville, TN: J. S. Sanders & Company, 1999.

Wainwright, Charles S. *A Diary of Battle: The Personal Journals of Colonel Charles S. Wainwright 1861–1865*. Ed. by Allan Nevins. New York: Harcourt, 1962. Reprint, New York: Da Capo Press, 1998.

Waldhauer, David. "The Affair at Frederick City." *Southern Historical Society Papers*, vol. 13, January to December 1885. Richmond: Southern Historical Society, n.d. Reprint, Millwood, NJ: Kraus Reprint Co, 1977.

Walker, Keven M. *Antietam Farmsteads*. Sharpsburg, MD: Western Maryland Interpretive Association, 2010.

Warner, Abraham Joseph. *The Private Journal of Abraham Joseph Warner*. Extracted by Herbert B. Enderton. San Diego, CA: n.p., 1973.

Watson, George William. *George William Watson The Last Survivor: The Memoirs of George William Watson, A Horse Soldier in the 12ᵗʰ Virginia Cavalry (Confederate States Army)*. Brian Stuart Kesterson, ed. Washington, WV: Night Hawk Press, 1993.

Weisberger, Bernard A. *Reporters for the Union*. Boston, MA: Little, Brown and Company, 1953.

Welcher, Frank J. *The Union Army 1861-1865, Organization and Operations, Volume I: The Eastern Theater.* Bloomington, IN: Indiana University Press, 1989.

Welker, David A. *Tempest at Ox Hill: The Battle of Chantilly.* Cambridge, MA: Da Capo Press, 2002.

Wert, Jeffrey D. *Cavalryman of the Lost Cause: A Biography of J.E.B. Stuart.* New York: Simon and Schuster, 2008.

———. *Mosby's Rangers.* New York: Simon and Schuster, 1990.

———. "Reconnaissance" and "Scout." In *Historical Times Illustrated Encyclopedia of the Civil War,* Patricia L. Faust, ed. New York: Harper & Row, 1986.

———. *General James Longstreet: The South's Most Controversial Soldier—A Biography.* New York: Simon and Schuster, 1993.

Wheeler, Richard. *Sword Over Richmond: An Eyewitness History of McClellan's Peninsula Campaign.* New York: Harper and Row, 1986.

White, Julius. "The Surrender of Harper's Ferry." *Battles and Leaders of the Civil War.* 2:612-615.

———. "The First Saber Charge of the War." *Military Essays and Recollections, Papers Read Before the Commandery of the State of Illinois, Military Order of the Loyal Legion of the United States,* Vol. III. Chicago, IL: The Dial Press, 1899.

Whitney, J.H.E. *The Hawkins Zouaves: Their Battles and Marches.* New York: Published by Author, 1866.

Whittaker, Frederick. *Cavalry Doctrine: the Lessons of the Decade by a Volunteer Cavalryman.* New York: Printed by Author, 1871.

Wilkins, Eugene. "'To Destroy What I Cannot Defend," *The Harpers Ferry Anthology: Civil War-era Stories by Park Rangers and Volunteers.* Ed. by Catherine Baldau. Virginia Beach, VA: The Donning Company Publishers, 2011.

Williams, Alpheus S. *From the Cannon's Mouth: The Civil War Letters of General Alpheus S. Williams.* Ed. Milo M. Quaife. Detroit, MI: Wayne State University Press, 1959. Reprint, Lincoln, NE: University of Nebraska Press, 1995.

Wilmer, L. Allison, Jarrett, J.H., Vernon, Geo. W.F. *History and Roster of Maryland Volunteers, War of 1861-5.* Vol. I. Baltimore, MD: Press of Guggenheimer, Weil & Co., 1989. Reprint, Salem, MA: Higginson Book Company, n.d.

Wilson, James Harrison. *Under the Old Flag: Recollections of Military Operations in the War for the Union, the Spanish American War, the Boxer Rebellion, Etc.* Vol. I. New York: D. Appleton and Company, 1912.

Wilson, Suzanne Colton. *Column South with the Fifteenth Pennsylvania Cavalry from Antietam to the Capture of Jefferson Davis.* J. Ferrell Colton and Antoinette G. Smith, eds. Flagstaff, AZ: J.F. Colton & Co., 1960.

Wise, Barton H. *The Life of Henry A. Wise of Virginia, 1806-1876*. New York: The Macmillan Company, 1899.

Wise, Jennings Cropper. *The Long Arm of Lee or The History of the Artillery of the Army of Northern Virginia*. Vol. I. Lynchburg, VA: J. P. Bell Company, 1915. Reprint, Lincoln, NB: University of Nebraska Press, 1991.

Wistar, Isaac J. *Autobiography of Isaac Jones Wistar, 1827-1905: Half a Century in War and Peace*. Vol.2. Philadelphia, PA: The Wistar Institute of Anatomy and Biology, 1914.

Wittenberg, Eric J. and Petruzzi, J. David. *Plenty of Blame to Go Around: Jeb Stuart's Controversial Ride to Gettysburg*. New York: Savas Beatie, 2006.

Wittenberg, Eric J. *The Union Cavalry Comes of Age: Hartwood Church to Brandy Station, 1863*. Washington, DC: Potomac Books, Inc., 2003.

———. *Rush's Lancers: The Sixth Pennsylvania Cavalry in the Civil War*. Yardley, PA: Westholme Publishing, LLC, 2006.

———. "An Analysis of the Buford Manuscripts." *Gettysburg Magazine*, No. 15.

Woodworth, Steven E. *Davis and Lee at War*. Lawrence, KS: The University of Kansas Press, 1995.

Worsham, John H. *One of Jackson's Foot Cavalry*. New York: The Neale Publishing Company, 1912, Reprint, New York: Bantam Books, 1992.

Wright, John D. *The Language of the Civil War*. Westport, CT: Oryx Press, 2001.

Index

Poolesville, Md., 4, 133n4, *137*, 142, 142n15-16, 143n17,
        143n20, 144n21, 146n30, 147n32, 148, 149,
        151, 151n49-50, 152, 152n51, *153, 156,* 156,
        157, 158, 158n61, 160, 161n65-66, 164, 165,
        165n78, 166n78, 166n80, *167, 173,* 417n23,
        421, 425n53, **474, 475, 476, 481**
    Confederate sympathizers, 433n73
    8th N.Y. Cavalry at, 276, 445
    fight near, 236
    1st Rhode Island Cavalry sent to, 206, 206n75, 455
    received signals from South Mountain, 175
    shown on map, *179*
    signal station, *181*, 182
        at town hall, 176n8
    Stoneman's headquarters, 239n46
    Stringfellow, 412
Pope, Capt. Edmund M., 276
Pope, Maj. Gen. John, 1, 8n18, 86, *88*, 261n31, 318, 416,
        442
    after Second Bull Run, 117, 133n4, 138, 149n43,
        409n2
        army morale, 416n20
    almost captured, 97, 98
    army in jeopardy between rivers, 99-100, 442
    cavalry exhausted, 13n30, 33-34, 105, 116, 116n62
    cavalry units, 33
        Maryland Campaign, 34, 143n17, 164n73
        remains south of Potomac, 142
    chases Jackson, 108, 109
    commends his cavalry, 124
    consolidated cavalry units, 33, 34n3
    defeated by Lee, 126
    defenses after Second Bull Run, 116n59
    dispatch book captured by Stuart, 105
    escort, 102
    Gen. Lee's perceptions of, 187
    Halleck banned reporters, 415n16
    instructions to cavalry, 88n5
    placed White in Winchester, 261n31
    plans to capture Lee's army, 90
    position across Rappahannock thwarts Lee, 103
    requests horses from Washington, 116
    replaces Gen. Hatch, 87, *88*
    reports organization of his army 129
    Signal Corps with, 176n8
    threat to Gen. Lee, 80, 81, 82
    trains after Second Bull Run, 111, 124
Poplar Ford (at Bull Run), 109
Porter, Maj. Gen. Fitz John, 325, 420n38, 445n18, 455
    Maryland, 164n73, 206n75
        Antietam, 354n44, 381, 447
    McClellan to, 165
    Peninsula, 33n2, 38, 60, 66, 70, 71, 73, 73n63, 73n65
    Peninsula through Second Bull Run, 105, 108, 109
    Shepherdstown, 399, 402, 404, 404n30, 405, 446

Porterstown, Md., *339*, 347
Porterstown ridge, 362
"Portici", *110*
Portillo, 395n11
Portsmouth Artillery. *See* Virginia units
Potomac Furnace, 120n73
Potomac Home Brigade. *See* Maryland units
Potomac Restaurant, Harpers Ferry, *264*
Potomac River, 4 317, 319, 320, 323n134, 347, *349*,
        371n85, 413, 417n23, 432, 442, 450, 459
    Antietam, 351, 352n39, 354n44, 356, 368, 369, 371,
        379, 381, 383, 383n101, 387, 390, 391,
        406n35, *407*, 433, 449
    Boteler's Ford, *408*
    Capt. Palmer scouting, 428
    Harpers Ferry, 247, 249, *249, 291, 293*
    crossings, 119, 120, 122, 148, 176, 416, 434n74, **473**
    Gen. Lee's line, *179*
    Gen. Lee moved north, 420
    Henry Kyd Douglas lives near, 190
    Jackson crosses at Williamsport, 206
    Gen. Johnston's forces near, 424
    mentioned, 34n3, 133, 138n10, 158, 323, 325, 327,
        343, 361
    newspaper reporter saw Confederates crossing,
        426n54
    picketed, 146n30, 336n10
    Point of Rocks, 418n29
    Sharpsburg/Shepherdstown, 345, 352, 391n2, 400,
        400, 402, 402, *403,* 404, 405, 431
    spies, 412n11
    Stuart's cavalry line, 196, 426, 443
    Union cavalry units scouting south of river after
        Second Bull Run, 13n30
    Williamsport, 382, 395, 397, 397n14, 398
Potomac Street, Harpers Ferry, 254, 289, 289n86, *291,* **498**
Potts, Capt. Benjamin F., 271
Powell, Capt. W. Angelo, 288n84
Powhatan Troop, 413n12
Prendergast, Capt. Richard G., *72*
Price, Lt. Richard Channing, 151n49, 353, 353n43, 368n73
Price, George F., 73n62, 379n94
Priest, John Michael, 27n83, 146n31, 152n50, 158n61,
        164n72, 165n78, 168n83-85, 169n86,
        171n92, 176n8, 183n19, 193n37, 196n47,
        197n48, 201n58-59, 205n74, 213n2, 214n4,
        215n5-6, 218n10, 224n19, 235n32, 236n33,
        236n36, 328n3, 333n6-7, 336n11-12,
        336n14, 344n28, 359n51, 362n58, 367n69,
        369n75, 370n80, 372n87, 390n1, 442n4,
        443n8, 455, 462, 463, 464
Providence Forge, Va., 65
Providence, R.I., 269, 270, 271, 321
Provost Guard, 13
Prussia, 277